Compendium of Tourism Statistics

Data 2005-2009

2011 Edition

Compendium of Tourism Statistics, Data 2005 – 2009, 2011 Edition
ISBN 13: 978-92-844-1389-8

Published and printed by the World Tourism Organization (UNWTO), Madrid, Spain
First printing: 2011
All rights reserved

The designations employed and the presentation of material in this publication do not imply the expression of any opinions whatsoever on the part of the Secretariat of the World Tourism Organization concerning the legal status of any country, territory, city or area, or of its authorities or concerning the delimitation of its frontiers or boundaries.

World Tourism Organization
Calle Capitán Haya, 42
28020 Madrid
Spain
Tel.: (+34) 915 678 100
Fax: (+34) 915 713 733
Website: www.unwto.org
E-mail: omt@unwto.org

Permission to photocopy UNWTO material in Spain must be obtained through:
CEDRO, Centro Español de Derechos Reprográficos
Calle Monte Esquinza, 14
28010 Madrid
Spain
Tel.: (+34) 913 08 63 30
Fax: (+34) 913 08 63 27
Website: www.cedro.org
E-mail: cedro@cedro.org

For authorization of the reproduction of UNWTO works outside of Spain, please contact one of CEDRO's partner organizations, with which bilateral agreements are in place
(see: http://www.cedro.org/ingles_funcion_internacional.asp).

For all remaining countries as well as for other permissions, requests should be addressed directly to the World Tourism Organization. For applications see: http://www.unwto.org/pub/rights.htm

TABLE OF CONTENTS

TABLE OF CONTENTS

Pages   Pages

TABLE OF CONTENTS

COUNTRY TABLES BY GEOGRAPHICAL ORDER

AFRICA – AFRIQUE – ÁFRICA

East Africa – Afrique orientale – África Oriental

Central Africa – Afrique centrale – África Central

North Africa – Afrique du Nord – África del Norte

Southern Africa – Afrique australe – África Austral

West Africa – Afrique occidentale – África Occidental

TABLE OF CONTENTS

Pages

Pages

TABLE OF CONTENTS

INTRODUCTION

This publication and the *Yearbook of Tourism Statistics* constitute the UNWTO's two publications on general statistics, both under the responsibility of the Statistics and Tourism Satellite Account (TSA) Programme.

This edition of the *Compendium* is the thirty-first of a series that began in 1975 as a biennial publication, and which has been produced annually since 1986. The content of the data tables provided by the countries was revised on one occasion (in the 2005 edition) in order to adapt the terminology following the publication of the *Tourism Satellite Account*, as well as to slightly enhance the completeness of the information collected (especially relative to domestic tourism and estimated tourism expenditure based on the Balance of Payments).

However, the approval of the new *International Recommendations on Tourism Statistics 2008* (IRTS 2008) along with the new conceptual framework on which they are based have made it necessary to revise the structure and content of the basic data and indicators considered necessary for the international comparability of tourism activity. Consequently, both the thematic areas and the information collected have been significantly expanded.

The following table shows the reference conceptual framework used to design this revision of the *Compendium* (see also **Conceptual references and technical notes**).

1. Conceptual framework

Concepts	Observation units	Main related characteristics
Visitor	Visitor	Classes: Overnight visitor (tourist), same-day visitor (excursionist) Country of residence / regions
	Travel party	Size
Trip	Tourism trip	Main purpose Duration Main destination Modes of transport Types of accommodation used Organization Expenditure

Tourism industries	Establishment	Monetary
		  Output
		  Intermediate consumption
		  Gross value added
		  Compensation of employees
		  Gross Fixed Capital Formation
		Non-monetary
		  Non-monetary characteristics specific for each tourism industries

Employment	Establishment (in the tourism industries)	Persons Size Status in employment Jobs Duration of work Full-time equivalent jobs

2. Classifications
Forms of tourism
Classification of products acquired by visitors
Classification of activities serving visitors
Other classifications

3.   Tables of results
   1. Inbound tourism
   2. Domestic tourism
   3. Outbound tourism
   4. Tourism industries
   5. Employment
   6. Complementary indicators

The approval of the new IRTS 2008 marks the coming of age of tourism statistics with the official recognition of a tourism sector composed of a set of productive activities whose activity depends, to a significant degree, on the acquisition by a set of travellers identified as visitors (both tourists and same-day visitors).

The UNWTO is aware that for a significant number of countries the information provided will necessarily be incomplete for the time being, and therefore users will find limited coverage when trying to compare certain thematic areas. Furthermore, IRTS 2008 includes new concepts and definitions that are unfamiliar to a good number of users of this publication (see Annex 2. **Understanding tourism: basic glossary**).

The published data come from official sources and have undergone various checks on the part of the Statistics and Tourism Satellite Account (TSA) Programme, which consults the reporting entity in the event that discrepancies are detected.

The figures included in this edition of the *Compendium* correspond to data entered in the UNWTO's statistical database as of 15 April 2011. Therefore, any corrections or changes received after this date will appear in the next edition of the *Compendium*.

The *Compendium* includes only annual information and is meant to serve as a reference guide for the macroeconomic analysis of tourism activity. Users seeking the latest available updates and who wish to obtain more detailed statistics for shorter reference periods or presented as regional aggregates, etc., are invited to consult other statistical publications of the UNWTO or visit its website: *www.unwto.org.* More specifically, the Market Intelligence and Promotion Programme is the principal internal user of the statistical database and its publications may be of particular interest.

The World Tourism Organization wishes to express its gratitude to all the national and international institutions that provide the information published (national tourism administrations, national statistical offices, central banks, the International Monetary Fund and the World Bank) for their valuable contribution.

Madrid, April 2011

INTRODUCTION

Le présent document, ainsi que l'*Annuaire des statistiques du tourisme*, sont les deux publications statistiques de type général de l'OMT ; elles sont réalisées sous la responsabilité du programme Statistiques et compte satellite du tourisme (CST).

Ce numéro du *Compendium* est le trente-et-unième d'une série qui a vu le jour en 1975. Publié une fois tous les deux ans initialement, sa fréquence est annuelle depuis 1986. Le contenu des tableaux de données transmis par les pays n'a été actualisé qu'une seule fois (dans l'édition de 2005) pour adapter la terminologie suite à la publication du *Compte satellite du tourisme* et compléter, dans l'essentiel, l'information recueillie habituellement (notamment sur le tourisme interne et les dépenses touristiques estimées par les balances des paiements).

Néanmoins, l'approbation des nouvelles *Recommandations internationales pour les statistiques du tourisme 2008* (RIST 2008) et l'élaboration du nouveau cadre conceptuel correspondant ont entraîné une révision de la structure et du contenu des données de base et des indicateurs nécessaires pour comparer l'activité touristique sur le plan international. Les domaines thématiques et l'information recueillie ont donc été étoffés de manière significative.

Le tableau suivant présente le cadre conceptuel de référence qui a été utilisé pour réviser le *Compendium* (voir aussi **Références conceptuelles et notes techniques**).

1. Cadre conceptuel

Concepts	Unités d'observation	Principales caractéristiques connexes
Visiteur	Visiteur	Classes : Visiteur qui passe la nuit (touriste), visiteur de la journée (excursionniste) Pays de résidence/régions
	Groupe de voyageurs	Taille
Voyage	Voyage touristique	Motif principal Durée Destination principale Modes de transport Types d'hébergement utilisés Organisation Dépenses
Industries touristiques	Établissement	<u>Monétaires</u> Production Consommation intermédiaire Valeur ajoutée brute Rémunération des employés Formation brute de capital fixe <u>Non monétaires</u> Caractéristiques non monétaires propres à chaque industrie touristique
Emploi	Établissement (dans les industries touristiques)	Personnes Taille Statut Postes de travail Durée du travail Postes de travail équivalents à temps plein

2.   Classifications
Formes de tourisme
Classification des produits achetés par les visiteurs
Classification des activités proposées aux visiteurs
Autres classifications

3.   Tableaux de résultats
1. Tourisme récepteur
2. Tourisme interne
3. Tourisme émetteur
4. Industries touristiques
5. Emploi
6. Indicateurs complémentaires

L'approbation des nouvelles RIST 2008 a fait entrer les statistiques du tourisme dans l'âge adulte. En effet, le tourisme est désormais reconnu comme un secteur à part entière, composé d'un ensemble d'activités productives qui sont tributaires, en grande mesure, de leur acquisition par un ensemble de voyageurs identifiés comme visiteurs (touristes et excursionnistes).

L'OMT sait que, à court terme, de nombreux pays se verront dans l'impossibilité de fournir des informations complètes et que la couverture des statistiques sera limitée pour les usagers souhaitant comparer certains domaines thématiques. Elle sait aussi que les nouvelles RIST 2008 comprennent des concepts et définitions avec lesquels un grand nombre de lecteurs de la présente publication ne sont pas familiers (voir l'annexe 2. **Comprendre le tourisme : glossaire de base**).

Les données publiées ont un caractère officiel. Elles sont soumises à divers contrôles par le programme Statistiques et compte satellite du tourisme (CST), qui consulte, en cas de désaccord, l'unité déclarante correspondante.

Les chiffres compris dans la présente édition du *Compendium* ont été saisis dans la base de données statistiques de l'OMT jusqu'au 15 avril 2011. Les corrections ou modifications reçues après cette date figureront donc dans la prochaine édition du *Compendium*.

Le *Compendium* ne contient que des informations annuelles. Il est conçu comme un guide de référence pour une analyse macroéconomique de l'activité touristique. Les usagers souhaitant obtenir des statistiques plus détaillées, à caractère conjoncturel, présentées par totaux régionaux, ou compulser les dernières mises à jour disponibles, peuvent consulter d'autres publications statistiques de l'OMT ou le site Web : *www.unwto.org.* Concrètement, le programme Tendances du tourisme et stratégies de marketing, qui est le principal usager interne de la base de données statistiques, produit des publications particulièrement intéressantes.

L'Organisation mondiale du tourisme tient à exprimer sa gratitude, pour leur précieuse collaboration, à toutes les institutions nationales et internationales (administrations nationales du tourisme, instituts nationaux de statistiques, banques centrales, Fonds monétaire international et Banque mondiale) qui ont envoyé les informations publiées dans le présent Compendium.

Madrid, avril 2011

INTRODUCCIÓN

Esta publicación, conjuntamente con el *Anuario de Estadísticas de Turismo*, conforman las dos publicaciones estadísticas generales de la OMT; ambas están bajo la responsabilidad del Programa de Estadísticas y Cuenta Satélite de Turismo (CST).

Este número del *Compendio* es el trigésimo primero de una serie que comenzó en 1975 como publicación bienal y siguió publicándose desde 1986 anualmente. El contenido de las tablas de datos que facilitan los países solamente se ha actualizado en una ocasión (en la edición de 2005) con el objetivo de adaptar la terminología tras la publicación de la *Cuenta Satélite de Turismo*, así como completar, mínimamente, la información que tradicionalmente se venía recabando (especialmente en relación con el turismo interno y el gasto turístico estimado por las Balanzas de Pagos).

Sin embargo, la aprobación de las nuevas *Recomendaciones internacionales para estadísticas de turismo 2008* (RIET 2008) y el nuevo marco conceptual que las soporta han obligado a revisar la estructura y el contenido de los datos básicos e indicadores que se consideran necesarios para la comparabilidad internacional de la actividad turística. En consecuencia, tanto los ámbitos temáticos como la información recabada se han ampliado significativamente.

El siguiente cuadro identifica el marco conceptual de referencia utilizado para el diseño de esta revisión del *Compendio* (véase también **Referencias conceptuales y notas técnicas**).

1.   Marco conceptual

Conceptos	Unidades de observación	Principales características relacionadas
Visitante	Visitante	Clases: visitante que pernocta (turista), visitante del día (excursionista) País de residencia / regiones
	Grupo de viaje	Tamaño
Viaje	Viaje por turismo	Motivo principal Duración Destino principal Medio de transporte Tipos de alojamiento utilizado Organización Gasto

Industrias turísticas	Establecimiento	Monetarios
		  Producción
		  Consumo intermedio
		  Valor añadido bruto
		  Remuneración de los trabajadores asalariados
		  Formación bruta de capital fijo
		No monetarios
		  Características específicas no monetarias para cada industria turística

Empleo	Establecimiento (en las industrias turísticas)	Personas Tamaño Situación en el empleo Puestos de trabajo Duración del trabajo Puestos de trabajo equivalentes a tiempo completo

2. Clasificaciones
Formas de turismo
Clasificación de los productos adquiridos por los visitantes
Clasificación de las actividades de servicio de los visitantes
Otras clasificaciones

3. Tablas de resultados
1. Turismo receptor
2. Turismo interno
3. Turismo emisor
4. Industrias turísticas
5. Empleo
6. Indicadores complementarios

La aprobación de las nuevas RIET 2008 supone la mayoría de edad de la estadística turística con el reconocimiento oficial de un sector turístico, integrado por un conjunto de actividades productivas cuya actividad depende, en una proporción significativa, de la adquisición por parte de un conjunto de viajeros que son identificados como visitantes (tanto turistas como excursionistas).

La OMT es consciente que para un número significativo de países, la remisión de información será, por el momento, necesariamente incompleta lo que hará que el usuario encuentre una cobertura limitada al querer comparar algunos ámbitos temáticos. También, que las nuevas RIET 2008 incluyen nuevos conceptos y definiciones que no son familiares para un buen número de usuarios de esta publicación (ver Anexo 2. **Comprender el turismo: glosario básico**).

Los datos publicados tienen carácter oficial y se someten a diversos controles por parte del Programa de Estadísticas y Cuenta Satélite de Turismo (CST), que consulta a la correspondiente unidad informante en el caso de detectar discrepancias.

Las cifras incluidas en esta edición del *Compendio* han sido introducidas en la base de datos estadísticos de la OMT hasta el 15 de abril de 2011. Por consiguiente, cualquier corrección o cambio recibido después de esta fecha aparecerá en la próxima edición del *Compendio*.

El *Compendio* sólo incluye información anual y está concebido como guía de referencia para el análisis macroeconómico de la actividad turística. Los usuarios que deseen obtener estadísticas más detalladas, de carácter coyuntural, presentadas por agregaciones regionales, disponer de las últimas actualizaciones disponibles, etc., pueden consultar otras publicaciones estadísticas de la OMT o visitar el sitio: *www.unwto.org*. Más concretamente, el Programa de Tendencias del Turismo y Estrategias de Marketing es el principal usuario interno de la base de datos estadísticos y sus publicaciones pueden serle de especial interés.

La Organización Mundial del Turismo quiere expresar su gratitud a todas las instituciones nacionales e internacionales que remiten la información publicada (administraciones nacionales de turismo, institutos nacionales de estadística, bancos centrales, Fondo Monetario Internacional y Banco Mundial) por su valiosa contribución.

Madrid, abril de 2011

Country tables
2005-2009

ALBANIA

Basic data and indicators	Notes	Units	2005	2006	2007	2008	2009
1. INBOUND TOURISM							
Data							
Arrivals	(1)						
1.1 Total		('000)	748	937	1,127	1,420	1,856
1.2 ♦ Overnight visitors (tourists)		('000)	..	..	1,062	1,337	1,792
1.3 ♦ Same-day visitors (excursionists)		('000)	..	..	65	83	64
1.4 * of which, cruise passengers		('000)			..	..	..
Arrivals by region	(1)						
1.5 Total		('000)	747.6	936.6	1,126.7	1,418.8	1,854.9
1.6 ♦ Africa		('000)	0.2	0.2	0.3	0.3	0.2
1.7 ♦ Americas		('000)	35	42	52	61	60
1.8 ♦ East Asia and the Pacific		('000)	5	8	10	15	28
1.9 ♦ Europe		('000)	703	857	1,061	1,335	1,513
1.10 ♦ Middle East		('000)	1	1	1	1	1
1.11 ♦ South Asia		('000)	0.4	0.4	0.4	0.5	0.7
1.12 ♦ Other not classified		('000)	3	28	2	6	252
1.13 * of which, nationals residing abroad		('000)	..	..	..	..	..
Arrivals by main purpose	(1)						
1.14 Total		('000)	748	937	1,126	1,419	1,856
1.15 ♦ Personal		('000)	680	889	1,060	1,340	1,804
1.16 * holidays, leisure and recreation		('000)	263	227	187	227	521
1.17 * other personal purposes		('000)	417	662	873	1,113	1,283
1.18 ♦ Business and professional		('000)	68	48	66	79	52
Arrivals by mode of transport	(1)						
1.19 Total		('000)	748	937	1,126	1,419	1,856
1.20 ♦ Air		('000)	128	151	182	206	227
1.21 ♦ Water		('000)	130	141	162	189	215
1.22 ♦ Land		('000)	490	645	782	1,024	1,414
1.23 * railway		('000)	..	..	..	..	..
1.24 * road		('000)	490	645	782	1,024	1,414
1.25 * others		('000)	..	..	..	..	..
Accommodation							
Total							
1.29 ♦ Guests		('000)	..	..	..	..	..
1.30 ♦ Overnights		('000)	..	..	..	..	..
Hotels and similar establishments							
1.31 ♦ Guests	(2)	('000)	57	63	67	57	65
1.32 ♦ Overnights	(2)	('000)	130	137	173	131	170
Expenditure							
1.33 Total		US$ Mn	880	1,057	1,479	1,849	2,012
1.34 ♦ Travel		US$ Mn	854	1,012	1,378	1,714	1,827
1.35 ♦ Passenger transport		US$ Mn	26	45	101	135	185
Expenditure by main purpose of the trip							
1.36 Total		US$ Mn	853	1,012	1,379	1,714	1,827
1.37 ♦ Personal		US$ Mn	642	778	1,127	1,393	1,410
1.38 ♦ Business and professional		US$ Mn	211	234	252	321	417
Indicators							
1.39 Average size of travel party		Persons	..	..	..	..	..
Average length of stay							
1.40 Total		Days	..	..	..	..	..
1.41 ♦ For all commercial accommodation services	(2)	Nights	2.30	2.20	2.60	2.30	2.60
1.42 * of which, "hotels and similar establishments"		Nights	..	..	..	..	..
1.43 ♦ For non commercial accommodation services		Days	..	..	..	..	..
1.44 Average expenditure per day		US$	..	..	..	..	..

ALBANIA

Basic data and indicators	Notes	Units	2005	2006	2007	2008	2009
2. DOMESTIC TOURISM							
Data							
Accommodation							
Total							
2.19 ♦ Guests		('000)	..	..	..	..	..
2.20 ♦ Overnights		('000)	..	..	..	..	..
Hotels and similar establishments							
2.21 ♦ Guests	(2)	('000)	56	67	104	156	171
2.22 ♦ Overnights	(2)	('000)	214	323	375	360	370
Indicators							
2.23 Average size of travel party		Persons	..	..	..	..	..
Average length of stay							
2.24 Total		Days	..	..	..	..	..
2.25 ♦ For all commercial accommodation services	(2)	Nights	3.80	4.80	3.60	2.30	2.20
2.26 * of which, "hotels and similar establishments"		Nights	..	..	..	..	..
2.27 ♦ For non commercial accommodation services		Days	..	..	..	..	..
2.28 Average expenditure per day		US$	..	..	..	..	..
3. OUTBOUND TOURISM							
Data							
Departures							
3.1 Total		('000)	..	..	..	..	..
3.2 ♦ Overnight visitors (tourists)		('000)	2,097	2,616	2,979	3,716	3,404
3.3 ♦ Same-day visitors (excursionists)		('000)	..	..	..	..	..
Expenditure							
3.4 Total		US$ Mn	808	989	1,331	1,644	1,692
3.5 ♦ Travel		US$ Mn	786	965	1,268	1,555	1,585
3.6 ♦ Passenger transport		US$ Mn	22	24	63	89	107
Expenditure by main purpose of the trip							
3.7 Total		US$ Mn	786	965	1,268	1,556	1,584
3.8 ♦ Personal		US$ Mn	618	773	943	1,277	1,172
3.9 ♦ Business and professional		US$ Mn	168	192	325	279	412
4. TOURISM INDUSTRIES	(3)						
Data							
Number of establishments							
4.1 Total		Units	..	..	..	..	..
4.2 ♦ Accommodation for visitors		Units	7,701	9,044	9,630	10,936	..
4.3 * of which, "hotels and similar establishments"		Units	..	..	..	..	..
4.4 ♦ Food and beverage serving activities		Units	..	..	..	..	..
4.5 ♦ Passenger transportation		Units	4,704	4,839	5,597	6,290	..
4.6 ♦ Travel agencies and other reservation services activities		Units	330	407	473	443	..
4.7 ♦ Other tourism industries		Units	..	..	..	..	..
Accommodation for visitors in hotels and similar establishments							
Monetary data							
4.8 ♦ Output		US$ Mn	212.1	268.1	295.6	313.1	..
4.9 ♦ Intermediate consumption		US$ Mn	124.8	166.6	176.6	181.4	..
4.10 ♦ Gross value added	(4)	US$ Mn	87.3	101.5	119.0	131.7	..
4.11 ♦ Compensation of employees		US$ Mn	23.9	30.6	42.1	43.5	..
4.12 ♦ Gross fixed capital formation	(5)	US$ Mn	22.7	17.4	17.1	23.7	..
Non-monetary data							
4.13 ♦ Number of establishments		Units	..	..	..	..	..
4.14 ♦ Number of rooms	(6)	Units	4,341	4,834	6,876	8,690	..
4.15 ♦ Number of bed-places	(6)	Units	7,583	9,204	14,700	17,879	..
Indicators							
4.16 Occupancy rate / rooms		Percent	..	..	..	..	..
4.17 Occupancy rate / bed-places		Percent	..	..	..	..	..
4.18 Average length of stay		Nights	..	..	..	..	..
4.19 Available capacity (bed-places per 1000 inhabitants)		Units	2.44	2.95	4.69	5.69	..
Travel agencies and other reservation service activities							
Monetary data							
4.20 ♦ Output		US$ Mn	121.0	139.8	173.3	152.5	..
4.21 ♦ Intermediate consumption		US$ Mn	45.0	54.1	77.7	68.8	..
4.22 ♦ Gross value added	(4)	US$ Mn	76.0	85.7	95.6	83.7	..
4.23 ♦ Compensation of employees		US$ Mn	15.3	19.9	26.5	29.2	..
4.24 ♦ Gross fixed capital formation	(5)	US$ Mn	45.3	25.8	38.1	20.6	..

ALBANIA

Basic data and indicators	Notes	Units	2005	2006	2007	2008	2009
5. EMPLOYMENT	(3)						
Data							
Number of employees by tourism industries							
5.1 Total		('000)	..	..	..	..	..
5.2 ♦ Accommodation services for visitors (hotels and similar establishments)		('000)	8.5	9.6	10.5	9.2	..
5.3 ♦ Other accommodation services		('000)	..	..	..	..	..
5.4 ♦ Food and beverage serving activities		('000)	..	..	..	..	..
5.5 ♦ Passenger transportation		('000)	4.4	4.3	8.2	5.3	..
5.6 ♦ Travel agencies and other reservation services activities		('000)	2.7	2.8	3.0	3.0	..
5.7 ♦ Other tourism industries		('000)	..	..	..	..	..
Number of jobs by status in employment							
5.8 Total		('000)	31.2	33.4	36.5	37.4	..
5.9 ♦ Employees		('000)	15.5	16.7	18.7	17.5	..
5.10 ♦ Self employed		('000)	15.7	16.7	17.8	19.9	..
6. COMPLEMENTARY INDICATORS							
Demand							
6.1 Gross travel propensity		Units	..	..	..	..	..
6.2 Carrying capacity (arrivals/population)		Units	0.24	0.30	0.34	0.43	0.57
Macroeconomic indicators related to international tourism							
6.3 Inbound tourism expenditure over GDP		Percent	10.8	11.8	13.8	14.3	17.0
6.4 Outbound tourism expenditure over GDP		Percent	9.9	11.0	12.4	12.7	14.3
6.5 Tourism balance (inbound minus outbound tourism expenditure) over GDP		Percent	0.9	0.8	1.4	1.6	2.7
6.6 Tourism openness (inbound plus outbound tourism expenditure) over GDP		Percent	20.7	22.7	26.3	26.9	31.3
6.7 Tourism coverage (inbound over outbound tourism expenditure)		Percent	109.0	106.9	111.2	112.4	119.0
6.8 Inbound tourism expenditure over exports of goods		Percent	134.1	133.3	137.1	136.4	192.0
6.9 Inbound tourism expenditure over exports of services		Percent	75.6	70.3	76.0	74.6	83.5
6.10 Inbound tourism expenditure over exports of goods and services		Percent	48.3	46.0	48.9	48.2	58.2
6.11 Inbound tourism expenditure over current account credits		Percent	24.7	26.1	29.1	31.1	37.5
6.12 Outbound tourism expenditure over imports of goods		Percent	32.6	33.9	33.4	33.5	39.7
6.13 Outbound tourism expenditure over imports of services		Percent	58.4	62.4	69.1	69.1	75.8
6.14 Outbound tourism expenditure over imports of goods and services		Percent	20.9	22.0	22.5	22.6	26.0
6.15 Outbound tourism expenditure over current account debits		Percent	19.5	20.9	21.4	20.7	23.4

ALGERIA

Basic data and indicators	Notes	Units	2005	2006	2007	2008	2009
1. INBOUND TOURISM							
Data							
Arrivals							
1.1 Total	(1)	('000)	1,443	1,638	1,743	1,772	1,912
1.2 ♦ Overnight visitors (tourists)		('000)	..	..	..	..	..
1.3 ♦ Same-day visitors (excursionists)		('000)	..	..	..	..	..
1.4 * of which, cruise passengers		('000)	..	..	..	..	..
Arrivals by region							
1.5 Total		('000)	1,443	1,638	1,743	1,772	1,912
1.6 ♦ Africa		('000)	161	160	158	194	258
1.7 ♦ Americas		('000)	8	10	10	11	13
1.8 ♦ East Asia and the Pacific		('000)	15	19	27	39	47
1.9 ♦ Europe		('000)	228	253	271	268	284
1.10 ♦ Middle East		('000)	29	37	45	45	54
1.11 ♦ South Asia		('000)	..	..	..	..	..
1.12 ♦ Other not classified		('000)	1,002	1,159	1,232	1,215	1,256
1.13 * of which, nationals residing abroad		('000)	1,002	1,159	1,232	1,215	1,256
Arrivals by main purpose	(2)						
1.14 Total		('000)	441	467	511	557	656
1.15 ♦ Personal		('000)	323	321	326	391	429
1.16 * holidays, leisure and recreation		('000)	323	321	326	359	429
1.17 * other personal purposes		('000)	..	..	..	32	..
1.18 ♦ Business and professional		('000)	118	146	185	166	227
Accommodation							
Total							
1.29 ♦ Guests		('000)	..	..	..	..	..
1.30 ♦ Overnights		('000)	..	..	..	..	..
Hotels and similar establishments							
1.31 ♦ Guests		('000)	..	..	..	..	..
1.32 ♦ Overnights		('000)	483	528	574	596	674
Expenditure							
1.33 Total		US$ Mn	477	393	332	474	382
1.34 ♦ Travel		US$ Mn	184	220	219	324	267
1.35 ♦ Passenger transport		US$ Mn	293	173	113	150	115
Expenditure by main purpose of the trip							
1.36 Total		US$ Mn	184	..	219	324	267
1.37 ♦ Personal		US$ Mn	183	220	218	323	264
1.38 ♦ Business and professional		US$ Mn	1	..	1	1	3
2. DOMESTIC TOURISM							
Data							
Accommodation							
Total							
2.19 ♦ Guests		('000)	..	..	..	..	..
2.20 ♦ Overnights		('000)	..	..	..	..	..
Hotels and similar establishments							
2.21 ♦ Guests		('000)	..	..	..	..	..
2.22 ♦ Overnights		('000)	4,222	4,376	4,546	4,751	4,971
3. OUTBOUND TOURISM							
Data							
Departures							
3.1 Total		('000)	..	..	..	..	..
3.2 ♦ Overnight visitors (tourists)		('000)	1,513	1,349	1,499	1,539	1,677
3.3 ♦ Same-day visitors (excursionists)		('000)	..	..	..	..	..
Expenditure							
3.4 Total		US$ Mn	660	414	504	617	575
3.5 ♦ Travel		US$ Mn	370	349	376	469	456
3.6 ♦ Passenger transport		US$ Mn	290	65	128	148	119
Expenditure by main purpose of the trip							
3.7 Total		US$ Mn	370	349	376	469	456
3.8 ♦ Personal		US$ Mn	320	291	334	420	417
3.9 ♦ Business and professional		US$ Mn	50	58	42	49	39

ALGERIA

Basic data and indicators	Notes	Units	2005	2006	2007	2008	2009
4. TOURISM INDUSTRIES							
Data							
Accommodation for visitors in hotels and similar establishments							
Non-monetary data							
4.13 ♦ Number of establishments		Units	..	..	..	..	..
4.14 ♦ Number of rooms		Units	..	..	..	..	..
4.15 ♦ Number of bed-places		Units	82,808	84,559	84,869	85,000	86,383
Indicators							
4.16 Occupancy rate / rooms		Percent	..	..	..	..	..
4.17 Occupancy rate / bed-places		Percent	..	..	..	..	..
4.18 Average length of stay		Nights	..	..	..	..	..
4.19 Available capacity (bed-places per 1000 inhabitants)		Units	2.52	2.54	2.51	2.47	2.48
6. COMPLEMENTARY INDICATORS							
Demand							
6.1 Gross travel propensity		Units	..	..	..	..	..
6.2 Carrying capacity (arrivals/population)		Units	0.04	0.05	0.05	0.05	0.05

AMERICAN SAMOA

Basic data and indicators	Notes	Units	2005	2006	2007	2008	2009
1. INBOUND TOURISM							
Data							
Arrivals							
1.1 Total		('000)	..	..			
1.2 ♦ Overnight visitors (tourists)	(1)	('000)	24.5	25.3	..	..	..
1.3 ♦ Same-day visitors (excursionists)		('000)	..	..	..	..	..
1.4 * of which, cruise passengers		('000)	6.1	..	..	..	..
Arrivals by region							
1.5 Total		('000)	24.4	25.3	..	..	..
1.6 ♦ Africa		('000)	..	..	..	..	..
1.7 ♦ Americas		('000)	6.9	7.2	..	..	..
1.8 ♦ East Asia and the Pacific	(1)	('000)	16.9	17.6	..	..	..
1.9 ♦ Europe		('000)	0.4	0.4	..	..	..
1.10 ♦ Middle East		('000)	..	..	..	..	..
1.11 ♦ South Asia		('000)	..	..	..	..	..
1.12 ♦ Other not classified		('000)	0.2	0.1	..	..	..
1.13 * of which, nationals residing abroad		('000)	..	..	..	..	..
Arrivals by main purpose	(1)						
1.14 Total		('000)	24.5	25.3	..	..	..
1.15 ♦ Personal		('000)	20.1	20.7	..	..	..
1.16 * holidays, leisure and recreation		('000)	7.0	7.8	..	..	..
1.17 * other personal purposes	(2)	('000)	13.1	12.9	..	..	..
1.18 ♦ Business and professional		('000)	4.4	4.6	..	..	..
3. OUTBOUND TOURISM							
Data							
Departures							
3.1 Total		('000)	..	..	..	..	..
3.2 ♦ Overnight visitors (tourists)		('000)	35	41	..	..	..
3.3 ♦ Same-day visitors (excursionists)		('000)	..	..	..	..	..
4. TOURISM INDUSTRIES							
Data							
Accommodation for visitors in hotels and similar establishments							
Non-monetary data							
4.13 ♦ Number of establishments		Units	..	..	..	..	..
4.14 ♦ Number of rooms		Units	257	..	..	..	..
4.15 ♦ Number of bed-places		Units	..	..	..	..	..
6. COMPLEMENTARY INDICATORS							
Demand							
6.1 Gross travel propensity		Units	..	..	..	..	..
6.2 Carrying capacity (arrivals/population)		Units	0.39	0.40	..	..	..

ANDORRA

Basic data and indicators	Notes	Units	2005	2006	2007	2008	2009
1. INBOUND TOURISM							
Data							
Arrivals	(1)						
1.1 Total		('000)	11,049	10,737	10,743	10,194	9,112
1.2 ♦ Overnight visitors (tourists)		('000)	2,418	2,227	2,189	2,059	1,830
1.3 ♦ Same-day visitors (excursionists)		('000)	8,631	8,510	8,554	8,135	7,282
1.4 * of which, cruise passengers		('000)	..	..	..	..	..
Arrivals by main purpose	(1)						
1.14 Total		('000)	11,050	10,737	10,744	10,194	9,112
1.15 ♦ Personal		('000)	10,405	10,244	10,288	9,798	8,616
1.16 * holidays, leisure and recreation		('000)	8,713	8,980	9,274	8,994	7,838
1.17 * other personal purposes		('000)	1,692	1,264	1,014	804	778
1.18 ♦ Business and professional		('000)	645	493	456	396	496
Arrivals by mode of transport	(1)						
1.19 Total		('000)	11,049	10,737	10,743	10,194	9,112
1.20 ♦ Air		('000)	..	..	..	..	..
1.21 ♦ Water		('000)	..	..	..	..	..
1.22 ♦ Land		('000)	11,049	10,737	10,743	10,194	9,112
1.23 * railway		('000)	..	..	..	..	..
1.24 * road		('000)	11,049	10,737	10,743	10,194	9,112
1.25 * others		('000)	..	..	..	..	..
Accommodation	(1)						
Total							
1.29 ♦ Guests		('000)	..	..	..	..	..
1.30 ♦ Overnights		('000)	6,762	6,284	6,512	5,900	4,778
Hotels and similar establishments							
1.31 ♦ Guests		('000)	..	..	..	..	..
1.32 ♦ Overnights		('000)	5,199	4,911	4,644	4,298	3,522
Indicators							
1.39 Average size of travel party		Persons	..	..	..	..	..
Average length of stay							
1.40 Total		Days	..	..	..	..	..
1.41 ♦ For all commercial accommodation services		Nights	2.80	2.82	2.97	2.86	2.61
1.42 * of which, "hotels and similar establishments"		Nights	..	..	..	..	..
1.43 ♦ For non commercial accommodation services		Days	..	..	..	..	..
1.44 Average expenditure per day		US$	..	..	..	..	..
4. TOURISM INDUSTRIES							
Data							
Number of establishments							
4.1 Total		Units	..	..	..	..	..
4.2 ♦ Accommodation for visitors		Units	..	..	..	..	..
4.3 * of which, "hotels and similar establishments"		Units	294	258	267	270	260
4.4 ♦ Food and beverage serving activities		Units	..	..	..	..	..
4.5 ♦ Passenger transportation		Units	..	..	..	..	..
4.6 ♦ Travel agencies and other reservation services activities		Units	..	..	..	..	..
4.7 ♦ Other tourism industries		Units	..	..	..	..	..
Accommodation for visitors in hotels and similar establishments							
Non-monetary data							
4.13 ♦ Number of establishments		Units	294	258	267	270	260
4.14 ♦ Number of rooms		Units	14,096	12,677	12,882	13,011	12,613
4.15 ♦ Number of bed-places		Units	38,957	31,515	32,586	34,514	33,700
Indicators							
4.16 Occupancy rate / rooms		Percent	..	..	..	..	..
4.17 Occupancy rate / bed-places		Percent	..	..	..	..	..
4.18 Average length of stay		Nights	2.69	2.70	2.87	2.74	2.51
4.19 Available capacity (bed-places per 1000 inhabitants)		Units	501.30	394.50	396.52	411.81	395.69
6. COMPLEMENTARY INDICATORS							
Demand							
6.1 Gross travel propensity		Units	..	..	..	..	..
6.2 Carrying capacity (arrivals/population)		Units	31.11	27.88	26.64	24.57	21.49

ANGOLA

Basic data and indicators	Notes	Units	2005	2006	2007	2008	2009
1. INBOUND TOURISM							
Data							
Arrivals							
1.1 Total		('000)	..	..	..	..	..
1.2 ♦ Overnight visitors (tourists)		('000)	210	121	195	294	366
1.3 ♦ Same-day visitors (excursionists)		('000)	..	..	..	..	..
1.4 * of which, cruise passengers		('000)	..	..	..	..	..
Arrivals by region							
1.5 Total		('000)	209	121	194	294	364
1.6 ♦ Africa		('000)	43	19	33	38	46
1.7 ♦ Americas		('000)	36	21	38	59	76
1.8 ♦ East Asia and the Pacific		('000)	15	15	28	59	66
1.9 ♦ Europe		('000)	110	63	89	130	161
1.10 ♦ Middle East		('000)	3	1	2	2	4
1.11 ♦ South Asia		('000)	2	2	4	6	11
1.12 ♦ Other not classified		('000)	..	..	..	..	..
1.13 * of which, nationals residing abroad		('000)	..	..	..	..	..
Arrivals by main purpose							
1.14 Total		('000)	210	122	194	294	365
1.15 ♦ Personal		('000)	182	98	166	235	289
1.16 * holidays, leisure and recreation		('000)	32	34	54	87	154
1.17 * other personal purposes		('000)	150	64	112	148	135
1.18 ♦ Business and professional		('000)	28	24	28	59	76
Arrivals by mode of transport							
1.19 Total		('000)	210	121	194	..	..
1.20 ♦ Air		('000)	153	120	172	..	..
1.21 ♦ Water		('000)	5	..	18	..	..
1.22 ♦ Land		('000)	52	1	4	..	..
1.23 * railway		('000)	..	..	..	..	..
1.24 * road		('000)	52	1	4	..	..
1.25 * others		('000)	..	..	..	..	..
Accommodation							
Total							
1.29 ♦ Guests		('000)	127	83	122	185	305
1.30 ♦ Overnights		('000)	182	231	340	386	490
Hotels and similar establishments							
1.31 ♦ Guests	(1)	('000)	120	64	91	126	213
1.32 ♦ Overnights	(1)	('000)	176	199	292	260	349
Expenditure							
1.33 Total		US$ Mn	103	91	236	293	554
1.34 ♦ Travel		US$ Mn	88	75	225	285	534
1.35 ♦ Passenger transport		US$ Mn	15	16	11	8	20
Expenditure by main purpose of the trip							
1.36 Total		US$ Mn	..	..	225	285	534
1.37 ♦ Personal		US$ Mn	..	..	64	78	212
1.38 ♦ Business and professional		US$ Mn	..	..	161	207	322
2. DOMESTIC TOURISM							
Data							
Accommodation							
Total							
2.19 ♦ Guests		('000)	86	53	..	124	257
2.20 ♦ Overnights		('000)	124	79	117	139	383
Hotels and similar establishments							
2.21 ♦ Guests	(1)	('000)	47	36	59	28	59
2.22 ♦ Overnights	(1)	('000)	72	54	73	41	98
3. OUTBOUND TOURISM							
Data							
Expenditure							
3.4 Total		US$ Mn	135	393	473	447	270
3.5 ♦ Travel		US$ Mn	74	148	212	254	133
3.6 ♦ Passenger transport		US$ Mn	61	245	261	193	137
Expenditure by main purpose of the trip							
3.7 Total		US$ Mn	74	147	212	254	132
3.8 ♦ Personal		US$ Mn	50	118	50	134	56
3.9 ♦ Business and professional		US$ Mn	24	29	162	120	76

ANGOLA

Basic data and indicators	Notes	Units	2005	2006	2007	2008	2009
4. TOURISM INDUSTRIES							
Data							
Accommodation for visitors in hotels and similar establishments							
Non-monetary data							
4.13 ♦ Number of establishments		Units	..	..	..	..	..
4.14 ♦ Number of rooms		Units	9,593	9,593	9,593	..	..
4.15 ♦ Number of bed-places		Units	10,723	10,723	10,723	..	..
Indicators							
4.16 Occupancy rate / rooms		Percent	..	..	..	..	..
4.17 Occupancy rate / bed-places		Percent	97.60	79.00	92.00	92.00	..
4.18 Average length of stay		Nights	..	..	..	..	..
4.19 Available capacity (bed-places per 1000 inhabitants)		Units	0.65	0.63	0.61	..	..
6. COMPLEMENTARY INDICATORS							
Demand							
6.1 Gross travel propensity		Units	..	..	..	..	..
6.2 Carrying capacity (arrivals/population)		Units	0.01	0.01	0.01	0.02	0.02
Macroeconomic indicators related to international tourism							
6.3 Inbound tourism expenditure over GDP		Percent	0.3	0.2	0.4	0.3	..
6.4 Outbound tourism expenditure over GDP		Percent	0.4	0.9	0.8	0.5	..
6.5 Tourism balance (inbound minus outbound tourism expenditure) over GDP		Percent	-0.1	-0.7	-0.4	-0.2	..
6.6 Tourism openness (inbound plus outbound tourism expenditure) over GDP		Percent	0.8	1.1	1.2	0.9	..
6.7 Tourism coverage (inbound over outbound tourism expenditure)		Percent	76.8	23.1	49.9	65.7	..
6.8 Inbound tourism expenditure over exports of goods		Percent	0.4	0.3	0.5	0.5	..
6.9 Inbound tourism expenditure over exports of services		Percent	58.6	6.1	76.0	89.0	..
6.10 Inbound tourism expenditure over exports of goods and services		Percent	0.4	0.3	0.5	0.5	..
6.11 Inbound tourism expenditure over current account credits		Percent	0.4	0.3	0.5	0.5	..
6.12 Outbound tourism expenditure over imports of goods		Percent	1.6	4.5	3.5	2.1	..
6.13 Outbound tourism expenditure over imports of services		Percent	2.0	5.2	3.6	2.0	..
6.14 Outbound tourism expenditure over imports of goods and services		Percent	0.9	2.4	1.8	1.0	..
6.15 Outbound tourism expenditure over current account debits		Percent	0.7	1.7	1.3	0.8	..

ANGUILLA

Basic data and indicators	Notes	Units	2005	2006	2007	2008	2009
1. INBOUND TOURISM							
Data							
Arrivals	(1)						
1.1 Total		('000)	143	167	164	128	112
1.2 ♦ Overnight visitors (tourists)		('000)	62	73	78	68	58
1.3 ♦ Same-day visitors (excursionists)		('000)	81	94	86	60	54
1.4 * of which, cruise passengers		('000)	5	6	4	1	2
Arrivals by region	(1)						
1.5 Total		('000)	62	73	78	68	58
1.6 ♦ Africa		('000)	..	..	..	..	..
1.7 ♦ Americas		('000)	52	62	64	57	49
1.8 ♦ East Asia and the Pacific		('000)	..	..	..	..	..
1.9 ♦ Europe		('000)	8	9	11	9	7
1.10 ♦ Middle East		('000)	..	..	..	..	..
1.11 ♦ South Asia		('000)	..	..	..	..	..
1.12 ♦ Other not classified		('000)	2	2	3	2	2
1.13 * of which, nationals residing abroad		('000)	..	..	..	..	..
Arrivals by main purpose							
1.14 Total		('000)	143	167	163	129	112
1.15 ♦ Personal		('000)	138	160	155	123	108
1.16 * holidays, leisure and recreation		('000)	57	66	69	63	54
1.17 * other personal purposes	(2)	('000)	81	94	86	60	54
1.18 ♦ Business and professional		('000)	5	7	8	6	4
Arrivals by mode of transport							
1.19 Total		('000)	143	167	164	128	112
1.20 ♦ Air		('000)	32	33	35	27	17
1.21 ♦ Water		('000)	111	134	129	101	95
1.22 ♦ Land		('000)	..	..	..	..	..
1.23 * railway		('000)	..	..	..	..	..
1.24 * road		('000)	..	..	..	..	..
1.25 * others		('000)	..	..	..	..	..
Accommodation							
Total							
1.29 ♦ Guests		('000)	..	..	..	..	..
1.30 ♦ Overnights		('000)	503	581	594	534	462
Hotels and similar establishments							
1.31 ♦ Guests		('000)	..	..	..	..	..
1.32 ♦ Overnights		('000)	..	..	..	..	..
Expenditure							
1.33 Total		US$ Mn	..	..	..	..	..
1.34 ♦ Travel		US$ Mn	86	107	115	102	83
1.35 ♦ Passenger transport		US$ Mn	..	..	..	..	..
Indicators							
1.39 Average size of travel party		Persons	..	..	..	..	..
Average length of stay							
1.40 Total		Days	..	..	..	..	..
1.41 ♦ For all commercial accommodation services		Nights	8.10	7.96	7.66	7.82	7.98
1.42 * of which, "hotels and similar establishments"		Nights	..	..	..	..	..
1.43 ♦ For non commercial accommodation services		Days	..	..	..	..	..
1.44 Average expenditure per day		US$	..	..	..	..	..
3. OUTBOUND TOURISM							
Data							
Expenditure							
3.4 Total		US$ Mn	..	..	..	..	..
3.5 ♦ Travel		US$ Mn	10	13	15	17	13
3.6 ♦ Passenger transport		US$ Mn	..	..	..	..	..

ANGUILLA

Basic data and indicators	Notes	Units	2005	2006	2007	2008	2009
4. TOURISM INDUSTRIES							
Data							
Number of establishments							
4.1 Total		Units	..	..	..	..	..
4.2 ♦ Accommodation for visitors		Units	..	..	..	..	..
4.3 * of which, "hotels and similar establishments"		Units	50	..	..	..	..
4.4 ♦ Food and beverage serving activities		Units	..	..	..	..	..
4.5 ♦ Passenger transportation		Units	..	..	..	..	..
4.6 ♦ Travel agencies and other reservation services activities		Units	..	..	..	..	..
4.7 ♦ Other tourism industries		Units	..	..	..	..	..
Accommodation for visitors in hotels and similar establishments							
Non-monetary data							
4.13 ♦ Number of establishments		Units	50	..	..	..	..
4.14 ♦ Number of rooms		Units	746	739	720	602	547
4.15 ♦ Number of bed-places		Units	..	..	..	..	..
Indicators							
4.16 Occupancy rate / rooms		Percent	..	..	..	..	..
4.17 Occupancy rate / bed-places		Percent	..	..	..	..	..
4.18 Average length of stay		Nights	8.10	7.96	7.66	7.82	7.98
4.19 Available capacity (bed-places per 1000 inhabitants)		Units	..	..	..	..	..
6. COMPLEMENTARY INDICATORS							
Macroeconomic indicators related to international tourism							
6.3 Inbound tourism expenditure over GDP		Percent	50.6	49.1	41.8	35.1	39.6
6.4 Outbound tourism expenditure over GDP		Percent	5.8	5.8	5.6	6.0	6.0
6.5 Tourism balance (inbound minus outbound tourism expenditure) over GDP		Percent	44.8	43.4	36.2	29.2	33.6
6.6 Tourism openness (inbound plus outbound tourism expenditure) over GDP		Percent	56.4	54.9	47.5	41.1	45.6
6.7 Tourism coverage (inbound over outbound tourism expenditure)		Percent	877.4	853.5	744.1	587.0	661.2
6.8 Inbound tourism expenditure over exports of goods		Percent	571.9	875.1	1,243.4	887.7	315.4
6.9 Inbound tourism expenditure over exports of services		Percent	87.2	86.7	85.5	86.9	87.0
6.10 Inbound tourism expenditure over exports of goods and services		Percent	75.6	78.9	80.0	79.2	68.2
6.11 Inbound tourism expenditure over current account credits		Percent	63.2	64.9	68.8	70.5	61.0
6.12 Outbound tourism expenditure over imports of goods		Percent	8.6	6.4	7.1	7.3	8.2
6.13 Outbound tourism expenditure over imports of services		Percent	17.4	13.7	15.0	20.1	20.8
6.14 Outbound tourism expenditure over imports of goods and services		Percent	5.7	4.4	4.8	5.3	5.9
6.15 Outbound tourism expenditure over current account debits		Percent	5.2	4.1	4.4	4.9	5.3

ANTIGUA AND BARBUDA

Basic data and indicators	Notes	Units	2005	2006	2007	2008	2009
1. INBOUND TOURISM							
Data							
Arrivals							
1.1 Total	(1)	('000)	712	726	935	921	..
1.2 ♦ Overnight visitors (tourists)	(2)	('000)	245	254	262	266	234
1.3 ♦ Same-day visitors (excursionists)		('000)	467	472	673	655	..
1.4 * of which, cruise passengers		('000)	467	472	673	581	713
Arrivals by region	(2)						
1.5 Total		('000)	245	254	262	266	234
1.6 ♦ Africa		('000)	..	..	..	..	..
1.7 ♦ Americas		('000)	128	139	141	152	138
1.8 ♦ East Asia and the Pacific		('000)	..	..	..	..	..
1.9 ♦ Europe		('000)	108	107	115	110	93
1.10 ♦ Middle East		('000)	..	..	..	..	..
1.11 ♦ South Asia		('000)	..	..	..	..	..
1.12 ♦ Other not classified		('000)	9	8	6	4	3
1.13 * of which, nationals residing abroad		('000)	..	..	..	..	..
Arrivals by main purpose	(2)						
1.14 Total		('000)	245	254	262	266	234
1.15 ♦ Personal		('000)	231	240	251	258	228
1.16 * holidays, leisure and recreation		('000)	190	198	204	221	182
1.17 * other personal purposes		('000)	41	42	47	37	46
1.18 ♦ Business and professional		('000)	14	14	11	8	6
Arrivals by mode of transport							
1.19 Total		('000)	712	726	935	847	947
1.20 ♦ Air		('000)	245	254	262	266	234
1.21 ♦ Water	(3)	('000)	467	472	673	581	713
1.22 ♦ Land		('000)	..	..	..	..	..
1.23 * railway		('000)	..	..	..	..	..
1.24 * road		('000)	..	..	..	..	..
1.25 * others		('000)	..	..	..	..	..
Accommodation							
Total							
1.29 ♦ Guests	(2)	('000)	245	254	262	266	234
1.30 ♦ Overnights		('000)	..	..	..	..	..
Hotels and similar establishments							
1.31 ♦ Guests	(2)	('000)	179	182	188	196	..
1.32 ♦ Overnights		('000)	..	..	..	..	..
Expenditure							
1.33 Total		US$ Mn	..	..	..	..	..
1.34 ♦ Travel		US$ Mn	309	327	338	334	304
1.35 ♦ Passenger transport		US$ Mn	..	..	..	..	..
Indicators							
1.39 Average size of travel party		Persons	..	..	..	..	..
Average length of stay							
1.40 Total		Days	..	..	..	..	..
1.41 ♦ For all commercial accommodation services		Nights	9.26	9.54	9.97	10.02	10.12
1.42 * of which, "hotels and similar establishments"		Nights	..	..	..	..	..
1.43 ♦ For non commercial accommodation services		Days	..	..	..	..	..
1.44 Average expenditure per day		US$	..	..	..	..	..
3. OUTBOUND TOURISM							
Data							
Departures							
3.1 Total		('000)	..	..	..	..	..
3.2 ♦ Overnight visitors (tourists)		('000)	..	..	..	434	..
3.3 ♦ Same-day visitors (excursionists)		('000)	..	..	..	..	..
Expenditure							
3.4 Total		US$ Mn	..	..	..	..	..
3.5 ♦ Travel		US$ Mn	40	45	52	58	54
3.6 ♦ Passenger transport		US$ Mn	..	..	..	..	..

ANTIGUA AND BARBUDA

Basic data and indicators	Notes	Units	2005	2006	2007	2008	2009
4. TOURISM INDUSTRIES							
Data							
Accommodation for visitors in hotels and similar establishments							
Non-monetary data							
4.13 ♦ Number of establishments		Units	..	..	..	..	..
4.14 ♦ Number of rooms		Units	..	..	4,157	4,673	..
4.15 ♦ Number of bed-places		Units	..	..	..	6,075	..
Indicators							
4.16 Occupancy rate / rooms		Percent	..	..	..	..	..
4.17 Occupancy rate / bed-places		Percent	..	..	..	65.97	..
4.18 Average length of stay		Nights	..	..	..	..	..
4.19 Available capacity (bed-places per 1000 inhabitants)		Units	..	..	..	70.12	..
6. COMPLEMENTARY INDICATORS							
Demand							
6.1 Gross travel propensity		Units	..	..	..	..	..
6.2 Carrying capacity (arrivals/population)		Units	2.93	3.00	3.06	3.07	2.67
Macroeconomic indicators related to international tourism							
6.3 Inbound tourism expenditure over GDP		Percent	35.7	32.3	29.2	27.8	27.7
6.4 Outbound tourism expenditure over GDP		Percent	4.6	4.5	4.5	4.8	4.9
6.5 Tourism balance (inbound minus outbound tourism expenditure) over GDP		Percent	31.1	27.8	24.8	23.0	22.7
6.6 Tourism openness (inbound plus outbound tourism expenditure) over GDP		Percent	40.3	36.8	33.7	32.5	32.6
6.7 Tourism coverage (inbound over outbound tourism expenditure)		Percent	772.7	720.7	652.2	579.5	560.4
6.8 Inbound tourism expenditure over exports of goods		Percent	374.0	441.4	447.0	426.9	424.6
6.9 Inbound tourism expenditure over exports of services		Percent	66.9	68.4	64.2	59.3	58.0
6.10 Inbound tourism expenditure over exports of goods and services		Percent	56.8	59.3	56.2	52.0	51.1
6.11 Inbound tourism expenditure over current account credits		Percent	52.5	52.8	50.3	47.5	46.3
6.12 Outbound tourism expenditure over imports of goods		Percent	8.8	8.1	8.0	8.6	9.2
6.13 Outbound tourism expenditure over imports of services		Percent	17.6	17.5	18.3	21.2	21.9
6.14 Outbound tourism expenditure over imports of goods and services		Percent	5.9	5.5	5.6	6.1	6.5
6.15 Outbound tourism expenditure over current account debits		Percent	5.1	4.9	4.9	5.5	5.9

ARGENTINA

Basic data and indicators	Notes	Units	2005	2006	2007	2008	2009
1. INBOUND TOURISM							
Data							
Arrivals							
1.1 Total		('000)	..	..	..	..	..
1.2 ♦ Overnight visitors (tourists)		('000)	3,823	4,173	4,562	4,700	4,329
1.3 ♦ Same-day visitors (excursionists)		('000)	..	..	..	..	..
1.4 * of which, cruise passengers		('000)	..	..	..	..	..
Arrivals by region							
1.5 Total		('000)	3,823	4,173	4,562	4,700	4,329
1.6 ♦ Africa		('000)	..	..	..	..	..
1.7 ♦ Americas		('000)	2,984	3,283	3,609	3,710	3,413
1.8 ♦ East Asia and the Pacific		('000)	..	..	..	..	..
1.9 ♦ Europe		('000)	631	662	738	766	722
1.10 ♦ Middle East		('000)	..	..	..	..	..
1.11 ♦ South Asia		('000)	..	..	..	..	..
1.12 ♦ Other not classified		('000)	208	228	215	224	194
1.13 * of which, nationals residing abroad		('000)	..	..	..	..	..
Arrivals by main purpose							
1.14 Total		('000)	3,823	4,172	4,562	4,701	4,329
1.15 ♦ Personal		('000)	3,204	3,573	3,855	4,057	3,692
1.16 * holidays, leisure and recreation		('000)	3,204	3,573	3,855	4,057	3,692
1.17 * other personal purposes		('000)	..	..	..	..	..
1.18 ♦ Business and professional		('000)	619	599	707	644	637
Arrivals by mode of transport							
1.19 Total		('000)	3,823	4,173	4,562	4,700	4,329
1.20 ♦ Air		('000)	2,069	2,279	2,566	2,586	2,221
1.21 ♦ Water		('000)	318	391	453	492	474
1.22 ♦ Land		('000)	1,436	1,503	1,543	1,622	1,634
1.23 * railway		('000)	..	..	..	..	..
1.24 * road		('000)	1,436	1,503	1,543	1,622	1,634
1.25 * others		('000)	..	..	..	..	..
Accommodation							
Total							
1.29 ♦ Guests		('000)	..	..	..	..	..
1.30 ♦ Overnights		('000)	40,097	46,171	53,805	55,936	53,072
Hotels and similar establishments							
1.31 ♦ Guests	(1)	('000)	4,065	..	4,712	4,523	3,876
1.32 ♦ Overnights	(1)	('000)	9,482	9,782	10,905	10,573	8,955
Expenditure							
1.33 Total		US$ Mn	3,209	3,899	4,984	5,296	4,478
1.34 ♦ Travel		US$ Mn	2,729	3,344	4,314	4,646	3,962
1.35 ♦ Passenger transport		US$ Mn	480	555	670	650	516
Expenditure by main purpose of the trip							
1.36 Total		US$ Mn	2,730	3,344	4,314	4,646	3,962
1.37 ♦ Personal		US$ Mn	2,226	2,824	3,630	3,953	3,342
1.38 ♦ Business and professional		US$ Mn	504	520	684	693	620
Indicators							
1.39 Average size of travel party		Persons	..	..	..	..	..
Average length of stay							
1.40 Total		Days	10.47	11.07	11.79	11.90	12.30
1.41 ♦ For all commercial accommodation services		Nights	..	..	..	..	..
1.42 * of which, "hotels and similar establishments"		Nights	..	..	..	..	..
1.43 ♦ For non commercial accommodation services		Days	..	..	..	..	..
1.44 Average expenditure per day		US$	65.9	70.4	78.4	81.0	72.4
2. DOMESTIC TOURISM							
Data							
Trips							
2.1 Total		('000)	..	38,850	..	..	..
2.2 ♦ Overnight visitors (tourists)		('000)	..	20,706	..	..	..
2.3 ♦ Same-day visitors (excursionists)		('000)	..	18,144	..	..	..
Trips by main purpose							
2.4 Total		('000)	..	20,706	..	..	..
2.5 ♦ Personal		('000)	..	19,624	..	..	..
2.6 * holidays, leisure and recreation		('000)	..	9,575	..	..	..
2.7 * other personal purposes		('000)	..	10,049	..	..	..
2.8 ♦ Business and professional		('000)	..	1,082	..	..	..

ARGENTINA

Basic data and indicators	Notes	Units	2005	2006	2007	2008	2009
Trips by mode of transport							
2.9 Total		('000)	..	20,707	..	..	..
2.10 ♦ Air		('000)	..	478	..	..	..
2.11 ♦ Water		('000)	..	2	..	..	..
2.12 ♦ Land		('000)	..	20,227	..	..	..
2.13 * railway		('000)	..	181	..	..	..
2.14 * road		('000)	..	20,022	..	..	..
2.15 * others		('000)	..	24	..	..	..
Trips by form of organization							
2.16 Total		('000)	..	20,706	..	..	..
2.17 ♦ Package tour		('000)	..	549	..	..	..
2.18 ♦ Other forms		('000)	..	20,157	..	..	..
Accommodation							
Total							
2.19 ♦ Guests		('000)	..	..	..	..	..
2.20 ♦ Overnights		('000)	..	..	..	..	..
Hotels and similar establishments							
2.21 ♦ Guests	(1)	('000)	11,813	..	15,088	14,674	13,588
2.22 ♦ Overnights	(1)	('000)	28,569	32,965	35,608	34,279	31,043
3. OUTBOUND TOURISM							
Data							
Departures							
3.1 Total		('000)	..	..	..	..	..
3.2 ♦ Overnight visitors (tourists)		('000)	3,894	3,892	4,167	4,614	4,975
3.3 ♦ Same-day visitors (excursionists)		('000)	..	..	..	..	..
Expenditure							
3.4 Total		US$ Mn	3,554	4,038	5,063	5,962	5,759
3.5 ♦ Travel		US$ Mn	2,790	3,099	3,921	4,561	4,482
3.6 ♦ Passenger transport		US$ Mn	764	939	1,142	1,401	1,277
Expenditure by main purpose of the trip							
3.7 Total		US$ Mn	2,790	3,099	3,920	4,561	4,482
3.8 ♦ Personal		US$ Mn	1,760	1,979	2,405	3,146	3,349
3.9 ♦ Business and professional		US$ Mn	1,030	1,120	1,515	1,415	1,133
Indicators							
3.10 Average length of stay		Days	11.44	11.08	11.84	11.59	11.21
3.11 Average expenditure per day		US$	60.8	69.7	77.6	83.4	78.0
4. TOURISM INDUSTRIES							
Data							
Number of establishments							
4.1 Total		Units	13,177	13,907	14,794	15,592	16,680
4.2 ♦ Accommodation for visitors		Units	9,466	10,152	10,751	11,474	12,227
4.3 * of which, "hotels and similar establishments"		Units	9,159	9,813	10,347	11,030	11,742
4.4 ♦ Food and beverage serving activities		Units	..	..	..	..	..
4.5 ♦ Passenger transportation		Units	..	..	..	..	..
4.6 ♦ Travel agencies and other reservation services activities		Units	3,711	3,755	4,043	4,118	4,453
4.7 ♦ Other tourism industries		Units	..	..	..	..	..
Accommodation for visitors in hotels and similar establishments							
Non-monetary data							
4.13 ♦ Number of establishments		Units	9,159	9,813	10,347	11,030	11,742
4.14 ♦ Number of rooms		Units	187,255	193,216	199,752	208,414	216,815
4.15 ♦ Number of bed-places		Units	469,345	484,085	504,128	527,145	549,236
Indicators							
4.16 Occupancy rate / rooms	(1)	Percent	41.92	44.94	45.86	43.27	36.90
4.17 Occupancy rate / bed-places	(1)	Percent	32.55	35.07	42.35	33.66	28.93
4.18 Average length of stay	(1)	Nights	2.40	..	2.35	2.34	2.29
4.19 Available capacity (bed-places per 1000 inhabitants)		Units	12.16	12.42	12.81	13.26	13.68

ARGENTINA

Basic data and indicators	Notes	Units	2005	2006	2007	2008	2009
5. EMPLOYMENT	(2)						
Data							
Number of employees by tourism industries							
5.1 Total		('000)	..	956.5	1,018.1	1,005.4	1,005.5
5.2 ♦ Accommodation services for visitors (hotels and similar establishments)		('000)	..	42.4	56.5	49.0	55.8
5.3 ♦ Other accommodation services		('000)	..	..	..	..	..
5.4 ♦ Food and beverage serving activities		('000)	..	316.5	321.2	325.2	307.1
5.5 ♦ Passenger transportation		('000)	..	313.4	339.9	336.1	349.4
5.6 ♦ Travel agencies and other reservation services activities		('000)	..	31.3	35.0	24.3	27.9
5.7 ♦ Other tourism industries		('000)	..	252.9	265.5	270.8	265.3
Number of jobs by status in employment	(3)						
5.8 Total		('000)	..	..	1,018.1	1,005.5	1,005.4
5.9 ♦ Employees		('000)	..	..	792.9	795.8	784.1
5.10 ♦ Self employed	(4)	('000)	..	..	225.2	209.7	221.3
6. COMPLEMENTARY INDICATORS							
Demand							
6.1 Gross travel propensity		Units	..	0.6	..	..	..
6.2 Carrying capacity (arrivals/population)		Units	0.10	0.64	0.12	0.12	0.11
Macroeconomic indicators related to international tourism							
6.3 Inbound tourism expenditure over GDP		Percent	1.8	1.8	1.9	1.6	1.5
6.4 Outbound tourism expenditure over GDP		Percent	1.9	1.9	1.9	1.8	1.9
6.5 Tourism balance (inbound minus outbound tourism expenditure) over GDP		Percent	-0.2	-0.1	0.0	-0.2	-0.4
6.6 Tourism openness (inbound plus outbound tourism expenditure) over GDP		Percent	3.7	3.7	3.8	3.4	3.3
6.7 Tourism coverage (inbound over outbound tourism expenditure)		Percent	90.3	96.6	98.5	88.8	77.8
6.8 Inbound tourism expenditure over exports of goods		Percent	7.9	8.4	8.9	7.6	8.0
6.9 Inbound tourism expenditure over exports of services		Percent	48.4	48.6	48.1	44.1	41.1
6.10 Inbound tourism expenditure over exports of goods and services		Percent	6.8	7.1	7.5	6.5	6.7
6.11 Inbound tourism expenditure over current account credits		Percent	6.1	6.3	6.7	5.9	6.2
6.12 Outbound tourism expenditure over imports of goods		Percent	13.0	12.4	11.9	10.9	15.5
6.13 Outbound tourism expenditure over imports of services		Percent	46.6	47.4	46.5	45.3	49.6
6.14 Outbound tourism expenditure over imports of goods and services		Percent	10.2	9.8	9.5	8.8	11.8
6.15 Outbound tourism expenditure over current account debits		Percent	7.5	7.5	7.5	7.2	9.1

ARMENIA

Basic data and indicators	Notes	Units	2005	2006	2007	2008	2009
1. INBOUND TOURISM							
Data							
Arrivals							
1.1 Total		('000)	..	..	..	..	..
1.2 ♦ Overnight visitors (tourists)		('000)	319	382	511	558	575
1.3 ♦ Same-day visitors (excursionists)		('000)	..	..	..	..	..
1.4 * of which, cruise passengers		('000)	..	..	..	..	..
Arrivals by region							
1.5 Total		('000)	318	382	510	558	575
1.6 ♦ Africa		('000)	..	..	..	1	..
1.7 ♦ Americas		('000)	86	98	127	135	135
1.8 ♦ East Asia and the Pacific		('000)	14	16	23	24	25
1.9 ♦ Europe		('000)	160	203	278	308	311
1.10 ♦ Middle East		('000)	28	33	41	44	45
1.11 ♦ South Asia		('000)	30	32	41	46	59
1.12 ♦ Other not classified		('000)	..	..	..	..	..
1.13 * of which, nationals residing abroad		('000)	..	..	..	..	..
Arrivals by main purpose							
1.14 Total		('000)	318	382	511	558	575
1.15 ♦ Personal		('000)	251	268	336	369	378
1.16 * holidays, leisure and recreation		('000)	235	246	294	321	325
1.17 * other personal purposes		('000)	16	22	42	48	53
1.18 ♦ Business and professional		('000)	67	114	175	189	197
Arrivals by mode of transport							
1.19 Total		('000)	318	381	511	558	575
1.20 ♦ Air		('000)	225	270	344	371	382
1.21 ♦ Water		('000)	..	..	..	..	..
1.22 ♦ Land		('000)	93	111	167	187	193
1.23 * railway		('000)	19	19	43	58	62
1.24 * road		('000)	74	92	124	129	131
1.25 * others		('000)	..	..	..	..	..
Accommodation							
Total							
1.29 ♦ Guests		('000)	..	..	..	..	..
1.30 ♦ Overnights		('000)	420	840	1,780	2,500	4,025
Hotels and similar establishments							
1.31 ♦ Guests		('000)	..	..	..	..	..
1.32 ♦ Overnights		('000)	..	..	..	..	..
Expenditure							
1.33 Total		US$ Mn	240	307	343	377	374
1.34 ♦ Travel		US$ Mn	220	271	305	331	334
1.35 ♦ Passenger transport		US$ Mn	20	36	38	46	40
Expenditure by main purpose of the trip							
1.36 Total		US$ Mn	220	271	305	331	334
1.37 ♦ Personal		US$ Mn	121	160	196	215	217
1.38 ♦ Business and professional		US$ Mn	99	111	109	116	117
Indicators							
1.39 Average size of travel party		Persons	..	..	..	..	..
Average length of stay							
1.40 Total		Days	..	..	..	..	..
1.41 ♦ For all commercial accommodation services		Nights	10.00	10.00	10.00	10.00	7.00
1.42 * of which, "hotels and similar establishments"		Nights	..	..	..	..	..
1.43 ♦ For non commercial accommodation services		Days	..	..	..	..	..
1.44 Average expenditure per day		US$	..	..	..	..	..

ARMENIA

Basic data and indicators	Notes	Units	2005	2006	2007	2008	2009
2. DOMESTIC TOURISM							
Data							
Trips							
2.1 Total		('000)	..	..	..	..	..
2.2 ♦ Overnight visitors (tourists)		('000)	..	..	..	447	436
2.3 ♦ Same-day visitors (excursionists)		('000)	..	..	..	..	..
Trips by main purpose							
2.4 Total		('000)	..	..	..	..	436
2.5 ♦ Personal		('000)	..	..	..	..	251
2.6 * holidays, leisure and recreation		('000)	..	..	..	..	165
2.7 * other personal purposes		('000)	..	..	..	..	86
2.8 ♦ Business and professional		('000)	..	..	..	..	185
Trips by mode of transport							
2.9 Total		('000)	..	..	..	..	436
2.10 ♦ Air		('000)	..	..	..	..	..
2.11 ♦ Water		('000)	..	..	..	..	..
2.12 ♦ Land		('000)	..	..	..	..	436
2.13 * railway		('000)	..	..	..	..	261
2.14 * road		('000)	..	..	..	..	111
2.15 * others		('000)	..	..	..	..	64
Accommodation							
Total							
2.19 ♦ Guests		('000)	..	..	..	..	..
2.20 ♦ Overnights		('000)	1,350	1,540	2,583	3,129	3,924
Hotels and similar establishments							
2.21 ♦ Guests		('000)	..	..	..	..	..
2.22 ♦ Overnights		('000)	..	308	..	..	..
Indicators							
2.23 Average size of travel party		Persons	..	..	..	..	..
Average length of stay							
2.24 Total		Days	..	..	..	..	..
2.25 ♦ For all commercial accommodation services		Nights	..	5.00	7.00	7.00	9.00
2.26 * of which, "hotels and similar establishments"		Nights	..	..	..	..	..
2.27 ♦ For non commercial accommodation services		Days	..	..	..	..	..
2.28 Average expenditure per day		US$	..	..	..	..	..
3. OUTBOUND TOURISM							
Data							
Departures							
3.1 Total		('000)	..	..	..	..	..
3.2 ♦ Overnight visitors (tourists)		('000)	269	329	468	516	526
3.3 ♦ Same-day visitors (excursionists)		('000)	..	..	..	..	..
Expenditure							
3.4 Total		US$ Mn	284	321	345	383	379
3.5 ♦ Travel		US$ Mn	236	286	294	324	326
3.6 ♦ Passenger transport		US$ Mn	48	35	51	59	53
Expenditure by main purpose of the trip							
3.7 Total		US$ Mn	236	286	294	324	326
3.8 ♦ Personal		US$ Mn	110	151	198	203	246
3.9 ♦ Business and professional		US$ Mn	126	135	96	121	80
4. TOURISM INDUSTRIES							
Data							
Number of establishments							
4.1 Total		Units	588	672	889	1,110	1,166
4.2 ♦ Accommodation for visitors		Units	588	672	889	1,110	1,166
4.3 * of which, "hotels and similar establishments"		Units	522	595	792	994	1,039
4.4 ♦ Food and beverage serving activities		Units	..	..	..	..	..
4.5 ♦ Passenger transportation		Units	..	..	..	..	..
4.6 ♦ Travel agencies and other reservation services activities		Units	..	..	..	..	..
4.7 ♦ Other tourism industries		Units	..	..	..	..	..

ARMENIA

Basic data and indicators		Notes	Units	2005	2006	2007	2008	2009
	Accommodation for visitors in hotels and similar establishments							
	Non-monetary data							
4.13	♦ Number of establishments		Units	522	595	792	994	1,039
4.14	♦ Number of rooms		Units	..	3,109	..	..	..
4.15	♦ Number of bed-places		Units	14,442	15,745	18,709	21,040	23,290
	Indicators							
4.16	Occupancy rate / rooms		Percent	..	..	..	..	..
4.17	Occupancy rate / bed-places		Percent	59.00	61.00	64.00	69.00	66.00
4.18	Average length of stay		Nights	10.00	10.00	10.00	10.00	10.00
4.19	Available capacity (bed-places per 1000 inhabitants)		Units	4.71	5.13	6.09	6.84	7.55
6.	**COMPLEMENTARY INDICATORS**							
	Demand							
6.1	Gross travel propensity		Units	..	..	..	..	..
6.2	Carrying capacity (arrivals/population)		Units	0.10	0.12	0.17	0.33	0.33
	Macroeconomic indicators related to international tourism							
6.3	Inbound tourism expenditure over GDP		Percent	4.9	4.8	3.7	3.2	4.4
6.4	Outbound tourism expenditure over GDP		Percent	5.8	5.0	3.8	3.3	4.5
6.5	Tourism balance (inbound minus outbound tourism expenditure) over GDP		Percent	-0.9	-0.2	0.0	-0.1	-0.1
6.6	Tourism openness (inbound plus outbound tourism expenditure) over GDP		Percent	10.7	9.8	7.5	6.5	8.8
6.7	Tourism coverage (inbound over outbound tourism expenditure)		Percent	84.2	95.5	99.3	98.2	98.1
6.8	Inbound tourism expenditure over exports of goods		Percent	23.8	29.9	28.7	33.8	51.8
6.9	Inbound tourism expenditure over exports of services		Percent	58.3	63.2	59.2	58.3	63.8
6.10	Inbound tourism expenditure over exports of goods and services		Percent	16.9	20.3	19.3	21.4	28.6
6.11	Inbound tourism expenditure over current account credits		Percent	9.7	10.5	9.5	9.4	12.7
6.12	Outbound tourism expenditure over imports of goods		Percent	17.9	16.7	12.4	10.2	13.5
6.13	Outbound tourism expenditure over imports of services		Percent	53.6	52.1	43.6	39.4	44.7
6.14	Outbound tourism expenditure over imports of goods and services		Percent	13.4	12.6	9.6	8.1	10.4
6.15	Outbound tourism expenditure over current account debits		Percent	11.2	10.5	8.2	7.1	8.9

ARUBA

Basic data and indicators	Notes	Units	2005	2006	2007	2008	2009
1. INBOUND TOURISM							
Data							
Arrivals							
1.1 Total		('000)	1,286	1,285	1,254	1,383	1,420
1.2 ♦ Overnight visitors (tourists)	(1)	('000)	733	694	772	827	813
1.3 ♦ Same-day visitors (excursionists)		('000)	553	591	482	556	607
1.4 * of which, cruise passengers		('000)	553	591	482	556	607
Arrivals by region	(1)						
1.5 Total		('000)	732	694	771	827	813
1.6 ♦ Africa		('000)	..	..	..	..	..
1.7 ♦ Americas		('000)	666	630	703	749	735
1.8 ♦ East Asia and the Pacific		('000)	..	..	..	..	..
1.9 ♦ Europe		('000)	63	62	67	74	75
1.10 ♦ Middle East		('000)	..	..	..	..	..
1.11 ♦ South Asia		('000)	..	..	..	..	..
1.12 ♦ Other not classified		('000)	3	2	1	4	3
1.13 * of which, nationals residing abroad		('000)	..	..	..	..	..
Arrivals by main purpose	(1)						
1.14 Total		('000)	733	694	772	827	..
1.15 ♦ Personal		('000)	699	660	737	799	..
1.16 * holidays, leisure and recreation		('000)	681	644	718	781	..
1.17 * other personal purposes		('000)	18	16	19	18	..
1.18 ♦ Business and professional		('000)	34	34	35	28	..
Arrivals by mode of transport							
1.19 Total		('000)	1,286	1,285	1,254	1,383	1,420
1.20 ♦ Air		('000)	733	694	772	827	813
1.21 ♦ Water	(2)	('000)	553	591	482	556	607
1.22 ♦ Land		('000)	..	..	..	..	..
1.23 * railway		('000)	..	..	..	..	..
1.24 * road		('000)	..	..	..	..	..
1.25 * others		('000)	..	..	..	..	..
Accommodation							
Total							
1.29 ♦ Guests	(1)	('000)	733	694	772	827	813
1.30 ♦ Overnights		('000)	5,695	5,471	5,879	6,268	6,173
Hotels and similar establishments							
1.31 ♦ Guests	(1)	('000)	653	619	688	728	719
1.32 ♦ Overnights		('000)	4,735	4,515	4,904	5,170	5,139
Expenditure							
1.33 Total		US$ Mn	..	1,080	1,256	1,412	1,296
1.34 ♦ Travel		US$ Mn	1,094	1,080	1,256	1,411	1,295
1.35 ♦ Passenger transport		US$ Mn	..	0.1	0.3	0.8	0.7
Indicators							
1.39 Average size of travel party		Persons	..	..	..	..	..
Average length of stay							
1.40 Total		Days	..	..	..	..	..
1.41 ♦ For all commercial accommodation services		Nights	..	..	..	..	..
1.42 * of which, "hotels and similar establishments"		Nights	7.77	7.90	7.60	7.60	7.60
1.43 ♦ For non commercial accommodation services		Days	..	..	..	..	..
1.44 Average expenditure per day		US$	119.6	110.1	97.8	96.7	102.7
3. OUTBOUND TOURISM							
Data							
Expenditure							
3.4 Total		US$ Mn	240	255	300	344	326
3.5 ♦ Travel		US$ Mn	216	232	281	322	305
3.6 ♦ Passenger transport		US$ Mn	24	23	19	22	21

ARUBA

Basic data and indicators	Notes	Units	2005	2006	2007	2008	2009
4. TOURISM INDUSTRIES							
Data							
Accommodation for visitors in hotels and similar establishments							
Non-monetary data							
4.13 ♦ Number of establishments		Units	..	..	..	..	..
4.14 ♦ Number of rooms		Units	7,966	9,062	9,062	9,856	9,856
4.15 ♦ Number of bed-places		Units	15,932	18,124	18,124	19,712	19,712
Indicators							
4.16 Occupancy rate / rooms		Percent	81.70	76.80	77.80	76.60	74.70
4.17 Occupancy rate / bed-places		Percent	..	..	..	..	..
4.18 Average length of stay		Nights	..	..	..	..	..
4.19 Available capacity (bed-places per 1000 inhabitants)		Units	157.69	176.48	173.97	186.92	185.05
6. COMPLEMENTARY INDICATORS							
Demand							
6.1 Gross travel propensity		Units	..	..	..	..	..
6.2 Carrying capacity (arrivals/population)		Units	7.25	6.76	7.41	7.84	7.63
Macroeconomic indicators related to international tourism							
6.3 Inbound tourism expenditure over GDP		Percent	47.1	44.6	48.3	50.6	49.4
6.4 Outbound tourism expenditure over GDP		Percent	10.3	10.5	11.5	12.3	12.4
6.5 Tourism balance (inbound minus outbound tourism expenditure) over GDP		Percent	36.7	34.1	36.7	38.2	37.0
6.6 Tourism openness (inbound plus outbound tourism expenditure) over GDP		Percent	57.4	55.1	59.8	62.9	61.8
6.7 Tourism coverage (inbound over outbound tourism expenditure)		Percent	455.6	424.1	419.0	410.0	397.5
6.8 Inbound tourism expenditure over exports of goods		Percent	31.4	29.4	46.7	38.1	89.6
6.9 Inbound tourism expenditure over exports of services		Percent	83.9	81.5	83.0	83.5	80.9
6.10 Inbound tourism expenditure over exports of goods and services		Percent	22.8	21.6	29.9	26.2	42.5
6.11 Inbound tourism expenditure over current account credits		Percent	22.4	21.1	28.9	25.5	40.9
6.12 Outbound tourism expenditure over imports of goods		Percent	6.9	6.7	10.5	8.2	17.0
6.13 Outbound tourism expenditure over imports of services		Percent	26.3	25.4	31.7	30.5	39.5
6.14 Outbound tourism expenditure over imports of goods and services		Percent	5.5	5.3	7.9	6.5	11.9
6.15 Outbound tourism expenditure over current account debits		Percent	4.7	5.0	6.7	6.1	10.8

AUSTRALIA

Basic data and indicators	Notes	Units	2005	2006	2007	2008	2009
1. INBOUND TOURISM							
Data							
Arrivals							
1.1 Total	(1)	('000)	5,499	5,532	5,644	5,586	5,584
1.2 ♦ Overnight visitors (tourists)	(2)	('000)	5,020	5,064	..	..	..
1.3 ♦ Same-day visitors (excursionists)	(2)	('000)	26	35	..	..	..
1.4 * of which, cruise passengers		('000)	..	..	..	..	..
Arrivals by region	(1)						
1.5 Total		('000)	5,498	5,532	5,644	5,585	5,584
1.6 ♦ Africa		('000)	71	78	85	93	84
1.7 ♦ Americas		('000)	584	611	629	644	670
1.8 ♦ East Asia and the Pacific		('000)	3,375	3,315	3,387	3,244	3,226
1.9 ♦ Europe		('000)	1,330	1,368	1,355	1,381	1,362
1.10 ♦ Middle East		('000)	49	52	63	75	80
1.11 ♦ South Asia		('000)	89	108	125	148	162
1.12 ♦ Other not classified		('000)	..	..	..	..	..
1.13 * of which, nationals residing abroad		('000)	..	..	..	..	..
Arrivals by main purpose	(1)						
1.14 Total		('000)	5,499	5,533	5,645	5,586	5,584
1.15 ♦ Personal		('000)	4,395	4,315	4,336	4,247	4,330
1.16 * holidays, leisure and recreation		('000)	2,952	2,887	2,827	2,655	2,596
1.17 * other personal purposes		('000)	1,443	1,428	1,509	1,592	1,734
1.18 ♦ Business and professional		('000)	1,104	1,218	1,309	1,339	1,254
Arrivals by mode of transport	(1)						
1.19 Total		('000)	5,499	5,533	5,645	5,585	5,584
1.20 ♦ Air		('000)	5,486	5,514	5,619	5,558	5,558
1.21 ♦ Water		('000)	13	19	26	27	26
1.22 ♦ Land		('000)	..	..	..	..	..
1.23 * railway		('000)	..	..	..	..	..
1.24 * road		('000)	..	..	..	..	..
1.25 * others		('000)	..	..	..	..	..
Expenditure							
1.33 Total		US$ Mn	20,023	20,924	25,803	27,997	27,864
1.34 ♦ Travel		US$ Mn	16,848	17,840	22,308	24,756	25,594
1.35 ♦ Passenger transport		US$ Mn	3,175	3,084	3,495	3,241	2,270
Expenditure by main purpose of the trip							
1.36 Total		US$ Mn	16,848	17,840	22,308	24,756	25,594
1.37 ♦ Personal		US$ Mn	15,402	16,121	20,111	22,461	23,482
1.38 ♦ Business and professional		US$ Mn	1,446	1,719	2,197	2,295	2,112
3. OUTBOUND TOURISM							
Data							
Departures							
3.1 Total		('000)	..	..	..	..	..
3.2 ♦ Overnight visitors (tourists)		('000)	4,756	4,941	5,462	5,808	6,285
3.3 ♦ Same-day visitors (excursionists)		('000)	..	..	..	..	..
Expenditure							
3.4 Total		US$ Mn	15,869	16,644	20,543	24,348	21,459
3.5 ♦ Travel		US$ Mn	11,255	11,679	14,732	18,448	17,575
3.6 ♦ Passenger transport		US$ Mn	4,614	4,965	5,811	5,900	3,884
Expenditure by main purpose of the trip							
3.7 Total		US$ Mn	11,255	11,680	14,733	18,448	17,575
3.8 ♦ Personal		US$ Mn	9,392	9,728	12,454	15,704	15,288
3.9 ♦ Business and professional		US$ Mn	1,863	1,952	2,279	2,744	2,287
4. TOURISM INDUSTRIES							
Data							
Accommodation for visitors in hotels and similar establishments							
Non-monetary data							
4.13 ♦ Number of establishments		Units	..	..	..	..	..
4.14 ♦ Number of rooms	(3)	Units	232,077	233,803	236,787	241,486	244,020
4.15 ♦ Number of bed-places	(3)	Units	659,731	673,792	679,095	690,555	692,327
Indicators							
4.16 Occupancy rate / rooms		Percent	64.50	66.90	65.20	63.80	63.40
4.17 Occupancy rate / bed-places		Percent	..	..	..	..	..
4.18 Average length of stay		Nights	2.30	2.30	2.20	2.20	2.30
4.19 Available capacity (bed-places per 1000 inhabitants)		Units	32.35	32.55	32.23	32.22	31.65

AUSTRALIA

Basic data and indicators	Notes	Units	2005	2006	2007	2008	2009
5. EMPLOYMENT							
Data							
Number of employees by tourism industries							
5.1 Total		('000)	691.8	667.3	707.3	716.0	737.8
5.2 ♦ Accommodation services for visitors (hotels and similar establishments)		('000)	111.5	108.3	117.3	111.5	107.5
5.3 ♦ Other accommodation services		('000)	..	..	..	..	..
5.4 ♦ Food and beverage serving activities		('000)	580.3	559.0	590.0	604.5	630.3
5.5 ♦ Passenger transportation		('000)	..	..	..	..	..
5.6 ♦ Travel agencies and other reservation services activities		('000)	..	..	..	..	..
5.7 ♦ Other tourism industries		('000)	..	..	..	..	..
6. COMPLEMENTARY INDICATORS							
Demand							
6.1 Gross travel propensity		Units	..	..	..	..	..
6.2 Carrying capacity (arrivals/population)		Units	0.25	0.24	0.27	0.26	0.26
Macroeconomic indicators related to international tourism							
6.3 Inbound tourism expenditure over GDP		Percent	3.1	3.0	2.8	2.7	..
6.4 Outbound tourism expenditure over GDP		Percent	2.1	2.1	2.2	2.4	..
6.5 Tourism balance (inbound minus outbound tourism expenditure) over GDP		Percent	0.9	0.9	0.6	0.3	..
6.6 Tourism openness (inbound plus outbound tourism expenditure) over GDP		Percent	5.2	5.1	5.0	5.1	..
6.7 Tourism coverage (inbound over outbound tourism expenditure)		Percent	144.7	144.8	129.2	114.3	..
6.8 Inbound tourism expenditure over exports of goods		Percent	21.1	19.0	18.7	15.1	..
6.9 Inbound tourism expenditure over exports of services		Percent	72.7	71.7	65.8	62.9	..
6.10 Inbound tourism expenditure over exports of goods and services		Percent	16.3	15.0	14.6	12.2	..
6.11 Inbound tourism expenditure over current account credits		Percent	14.3	12.9	12.1	10.3	..
6.12 Outbound tourism expenditure over imports of goods		Percent	13.0	12.2	12.9	12.8	..
6.13 Outbound tourism expenditure over imports of services		Percent	51.1	50.9	51.6	51.5	..
6.14 Outbound tourism expenditure over imports of goods and services		Percent	10.3	9.8	10.3	10.3	..
6.15 Outbound tourism expenditure over current account debits		Percent	7.8	7.3	7.4	7.7	..

25

AUSTRIA

Basic data and indicators	Notes	Units	2005	2006	2007	2008	2009
1. INBOUND TOURISM							
Data							
Arrivals							
1.1　Total		('000)	..	..	..	..	..
1.2　♦ Overnight visitors (tourists)	(1) (2)	('000)	19,952	20,269	20,773	21,935	21,355
1.3　♦ Same-day visitors (excursionists)		('000)	..	..	..	..	..
1.4　　* of which, cruise passengers		('000)	..	..	..	..	..
Arrivals by region	(1) (2)						
1.5　Total		('000)	19,952	20,269	20,772	21,935	21,355
1.6　♦ Africa		('000)	42	43	40	40	39
1.7　♦ Americas		('000)	692	780	756	673	617
1.8　♦ East Asia and the Pacific		('000)	792	797	747	706	645
1.9　♦ Europe		('000)	18,031	18,265	18,795	19,993	19,613
1.10　♦ Middle East		('000)	68	75	91	102	97
1.11　♦ South Asia		('000)	39	50	46	47	48
1.12　♦ Other not classified		('000)	288	259	297	374	296
1.13　　* of which, nationals residing abroad		('000)	..	..	..	..	..
Accommodation							
Total							
1.29　♦ Guests	(2)	('000)	19,952	20,269	20,773	21,935	21,355
1.30　♦ Overnights	(2)	('000)	87,741	87,274	88,443	92,840	89,864
Hotels and similar establishments							
1.31　♦ Guests	(3)	('000)	14,542	14,951	15,348	16,091	15,520
1.32　♦ Overnights	(3)	('000)	56,690	57,133	57,882	60,469	57,798
Expenditure							
1.33　Total		US$ Mn	18,471	18,886	21,088	24,346	21,239
1.34　♦ Travel		US$ Mn	16,243	16,510	18,559	21,630	19,176
1.35　♦ Passenger transport		US$ Mn	2,228	2,376	2,529	2,716	2,063
Expenditure by main purpose of the trip							
1.36　Total		US$ Mn	16,243	16,511	18,559	21,631	19,176
1.37　♦ Personal		US$ Mn	13,362	13,458	14,917	17,926	16,034
1.38　♦ Business and professional		US$ Mn	2,881	3,053	3,642	3,705	3,142
Indicators							
1.39　Average size of travel party		Persons	..	..	..	..	..
Average length of stay							
1.40　Total		Days	..	..	..	..	..
1.41　♦ For all commercial accommodation services		Nights	4.40	4.30	4.26	4.23	4.20
1.42　　* of which, "hotels and similar establishments"		Nights	..	..	..	..	..
1.43　♦ For non commercial accommodation services		Days	..	..	..	..	..
1.44　Average expenditure per day		US$	..	..	..	..	..
2. DOMESTIC TOURISM							
Data							
Accommodation							
Total							
2.19　♦ Guests	(2)	('000)	9,385	9,874	10,367	10,681	10,961
2.20　♦ Overnights	(2)	('000)	31,501	32,130	33,008	33,879	34,443
Hotels and similar establishments							
2.21　♦ Guests	(3)	('000)	6,896	7,400	7,875	8,119	8,323
2.22　♦ Overnights	(3)	('000)	19,383	20,278	21,285	21,902	22,273
Indicators							
2.23　Average size of travel party		Persons	..	..	..	..	..
Average length of stay							
2.24　Total		Days	..	..	..	..	..
2.25　♦ For all commercial accommodation services		Nights	3.36	3.25	3.18	3.17	3.10
2.26　　* of which, "hotels and similar establishments"		Nights	..	..	..	..	..
2.27　♦ For non commercial accommodation services		Days	..	..	..	..	..
2.28　Average expenditure per day		US$	..	..	..	..	..

AUSTRIA

Basic data and indicators	Notes	Units	2005	2006	2007	2008	2009
3. OUTBOUND TOURISM							
Data							
Departures							
3.1 Total	(4)	('000)	..	..	..	..	..
3.2 ♦ Overnight visitors (tourists)		('000)	8,206	10,042	9,876	9,677	10,121
3.3 ♦ Same-day visitors (excursionists)		('000)	..	..	..	..	..
Expenditure							
3.4 Total		US$ Mn	11,077	11,719	12,825	13,993	12,771
3.5 ♦ Travel		US$ Mn	9,316	9,626	10,561	11,432	10,817
3.6 ♦ Passenger transport		US$ Mn	1,761	2,093	2,264	2,561	1,954
Expenditure by main purpose of the trip							
3.7 Total		US$ Mn	9,316	9,627	10,561	11,431	10,817
3.8 ♦ Personal		US$ Mn	7,359	7,669	8,312	9,087	9,042
3.9 ♦ Business and professional		US$ Mn	1,957	1,958	2,249	2,344	1,775
4. TOURISM INDUSTRIES							
Data							
Number of establishments							
4.1 Total		Units	..	..	..	..	..
4.2 ♦ Accommodation for visitors		Units	55,208	55,118	55,291	55,033	54,909
4.3 * of which, "hotels and similar establishments"	(3)	Units	14,267	14,051	14,204	13,756	13,645
4.4 ♦ Food and beverage serving activities		Units	..	..	..	..	..
4.5 ♦ Passenger transportation		Units	..	..	..	..	..
4.6 ♦ Travel agencies and other reservation services activities		Units	..	..	..	..	..
4.7 ♦ Other tourism industries		Units	..	..	..	..	..
Accommodation for visitors in hotels and similar establishments							
Non-monetary data	(3)						
4.13 ♦ Number of establishments		Units	14,267	14,051	14,204	13,756	13,645
4.14 ♦ Number of rooms		Units	289,879	282,002	285,558	286,571	288,934
4.15 ♦ Number of bed-places		Units	571,377	572,514	573,726	579,750	587,899
Indicators							
4.16 Occupancy rate / rooms		Percent	..	..	..	..	..
4.17 Occupancy rate / bed-places	(5)	Percent	37.48	37.61	39.17	39.74	37.31
4.18 Average length of stay		Nights	3.55	3.46	3.41	3.40	3.40
4.19 Available capacity (bed-places per 1000 inhabitants)		Units	69.40	69.12	69.12	69.70	70.40
5. EMPLOYMENT	(6)						
Data							
Number of employees by tourism industries	(7)						
5.1 Total		('000)	207.7	..	213.9	221.4	..
5.2 ♦ Accommodation services for visitors (hotels and similar establishments)		('000)	59.1	..	60.3	55.3	..
5.3 ♦ Other accommodation services		('000)	..	..	..	..	..
5.4 ♦ Food and beverage serving activities		('000)	76.7	..	79.3	75.5	..
5.5 ♦ Passenger transportation		('000)	29.0	..	31.3	43.7	..
5.6 ♦ Travel agencies and other reservation services activities		('000)	29.4	..	30.3	31.9	..
5.7 ♦ Other tourism industries		('000)	13.5	..	12.7	15.0	..
Indicators							
Number of full-time equivalent jobs by status in employment							
5.11 Total		('000)	246.8	..	257.5	262.1	..
5.12 ♦ Employees		('000)	207.9	..	213.9	221.4	..
5.13 * male		('000)	99.0	..	102.9	111.0	..
5.14 * female		('000)	108.9	..	111.0	110.4	..
5.15 ♦ Self employed		('000)	38.9	..	43.6	40.7	..
5.16 * male		('000)	20.8	..	23.4	22.2	..
5.17 * female		('000)	18.1	..	20.2	18.5	..

AUSTRIA

Basic data and indicators	Notes	Units	2005	2006	2007	2008	2009
6. COMPLEMENTARY INDICATORS							
Demand							
6.1 Gross travel propensity		Units	2.5	3.0	3.0	2.9	3.0
6.2 Carrying capacity (arrivals/population)		Units	2.42	2.45	2.50	2.63	2.55
Macroeconomic indicators related to international tourism							
6.3 Inbound tourism expenditure over GDP		Percent	6.1	5.9	5.7	5.9	5.5
6.4 Outbound tourism expenditure over GDP		Percent	3.7	3.6	3.5	3.4	3.4
6.5 Tourism balance (inbound minus outbound tourism expenditure) over GDP		Percent	2.4	2.2	2.2	2.5	2.2
6.6 Tourism openness (inbound plus outbound tourism expenditure) over GDP		Percent	9.8	9.5	9.2	9.3	8.9
6.7 Tourism coverage (inbound over outbound tourism expenditure)		Percent	166.7	161.2	164.4	174.0	164.6
6.8 Inbound tourism expenditure over exports of goods		Percent	15.5	14.1	12.9	13.6	15.6
6.9 Inbound tourism expenditure over exports of services		Percent	43.4	41.0	38.8	39.2	39.9
6.10 Inbound tourism expenditure over exports of goods and services		Percent	11.4	10.5	9.7	10.1	11.2
6.11 Inbound tourism expenditure over current account credits		Percent	9.6	8.9	8.0	8.3	9.3
6.12 Outbound tourism expenditure over imports of goods		Percent	9.2	8.8	8.0	7.8	9.3
6.13 Outbound tourism expenditure over imports of services		Percent	36.0	35.0	32.8	32.6	34.7
6.14 Outbound tourism expenditure over imports of goods and services		Percent	7.3	7.0	6.4	6.3	7.3
6.15 Outbound tourism expenditure over current account debits		Percent	6.0	5.7	5.1	5.0	5.9

AZERBAIJAN

Basic data and indicators	Notes	Units	2005	2006	2007	2008	2009
1. INBOUND TOURISM							
Data							
Arrivals							
1.1 Total		('000)	1,177	1,194	1,333	1,899	1,830
1.2 ♦ Overnight visitors (tourists)		('000)	693	682	732	1,043	1,005
1.3 ♦ Same-day visitors (excursionists)		('000)	484	512	601	856	825
1.4 * of which, cruise passengers		('000)	..	..	..	..	..
Arrivals by region							
1.5 Total		('000)	1,177	1,194	1,332	1,899	1,830
1.6 ♦ Africa		('000)	1	1	1	2	2
1.7 ♦ Americas		('000)	11	10	11	17	15
1.8 ♦ East Asia and the Pacific		('000)	7	7	8	16	14
1.9 ♦ Europe		('000)	945	1,008	1,104	1,541	1,454
1.10 ♦ Middle East		('000)	2	2	2	4	3
1.11 ♦ South Asia		('000)	211	165	205	317	340
1.12 ♦ Other not classified		('000)	..	1	1	2	2
1.13 * of which, nationals residing abroad		('000)	..	..	..	..	..
Arrivals by main purpose							
1.14 Total		('000)	1,177	1,194	1,333	1,899	1,830
1.15 ♦ Personal		('000)	890	910	1,028	1,465	1,412
1.16 * holidays, leisure and recreation		('000)	405	398	427	609	587
1.17 * other personal purposes		('000)	485	512	601	856	825
1.18 ♦ Business and professional		('000)	287	284	305	434	418
Arrivals by mode of transport							
1.19 Total		('000)	1,177	1,193	1,332	1,899	1,830
1.20 ♦ Air		('000)	276	281	297	572	624
1.21 ♦ Water		('000)	10	9	9	15	13
1.22 ♦ Land		('000)	891	903	1,026	1,312	1,193
1.23 * railway		('000)	204	204	212	323	287
1.24 * road		('000)	687	699	814	989	906
1.25 * others		('000)	..	..	..	..	..
Accommodation							
Total							
1.29 ♦ Guests		('000)	..	..	..	..	..
1.30 ♦ Overnights		('000)	..	..	..	..	..
Hotels and similar establishments							
1.31 ♦ Guests		('000)	130	151	153	224	209
1.32 ♦ Overnights		('000)	540	557	573	637	561
Expenditure							
1.33 Total		US$ Mn	100	201	317	381	516
1.34 ♦ Travel		US$ Mn	78	117	178	190	350
1.35 ♦ Passenger transport		US$ Mn	22	84	139	191	166
Expenditure by main purpose of the trip							
1.36 Total		US$ Mn	77	117	178	190	350
1.37 ♦ Personal		US$ Mn	61	87	119	116	194
1.38 ♦ Business and professional		US$ Mn	16	30	59	74	156
Indicators							
1.39 Average size of travel party		Persons	..	..	..	..	..
Average length of stay							
1.40 Total		Days	..	..	..	..	..
1.41 ♦ For all commercial accommodation services		Nights	4.10	3.70	3.70	2.80	2.70
1.42 * of which, "hotels and similar establishments"		Nights	..	..	..	..	..
1.43 ♦ For non commercial accommodation services		Days	..	..	..	..	..
1.44 Average expenditure per day		US$	..	..	..	..	..

AZERBAIJAN

Basic data and indicators	Notes	Units	2005	2006	2007	2008	2009
2. DOMESTIC TOURISM							
Data							
Accommodation							
Total							
2.19 ♦ Guests		('000)	..	..	..	..	..
2.20 ♦ Overnights		('000)	..	..	..	..	..
Hotels and similar establishments							
2.21 ♦ Guests		('000)	134	141	152	207	215
2.22 ♦ Overnights		('000)	525	558	558	724	754
Indicators							
2.23 Average size of travel party		Persons	..	..	..	..	..
Average length of stay							
2.24 Total		Days	..	..	..	..	..
2.25 ♦ For all commercial accommodation services		Nights	3.90	3.90	3.70	3.50	3.50
2.26 * of which, "hotels and similar establishments"		Nights	..	..	..	..	..
2.27 ♦ For non commercial accommodation services		Days	..	..	..	..	..
2.28 Average expenditure per day		US$	..	..	..	..	..
3. OUTBOUND TOURISM							
Data							
Departures							
3.1 Total		('000)	1,830	1,836	1,631	2,162	2,363
3.2 ♦ Overnight visitors (tourists)		('000)	887	890	791	1,048	1,145
3.3 ♦ Same-day visitors (excursionists)		('000)	943	946	840	1,114	1,217
Expenditure							
3.4 Total		US$ Mn	188	256	381	454	456
3.5 ♦ Travel		US$ Mn	164	201	264	341	374
3.6 ♦ Passenger transport		US$ Mn	24	55	117	113	82
Expenditure by main purpose of the trip							
3.7 Total		US$ Mn	164	201	263	341	374
3.8 ♦ Personal		US$ Mn	146	179	245	314	313
3.9 ♦ Business and professional		US$ Mn	18	22	18	27	61
4. TOURISM INDUSTRIES							
Data							
Number of establishments							
4.1 Total		Units	..	..	..	..	..
4.2 ♦ Accommodation for visitors		Units	346	365	395	445	527
4.3 * of which, "hotels and similar establishments"		Units	262	285	320	370	452
4.4 ♦ Food and beverage serving activities		Units	..	..	..	..	..
4.5 ♦ Passenger transportation		Units	..	..	..	..	..
4.6 ♦ Travel agencies and other reservation services activities		Units	..	..	..	..	..
4.7 ♦ Other tourism industries		Units	..	..	..	..	..
Accommodation for visitors in hotels and similar establishments							
Monetary data							
4.8 ♦ Output		US$ Mn	66.5	74.3	89.8	98.6	97.0
4.9 ♦ Intermediate consumption		US$ Mn	14.7	11.9	8.4	10.1	8.5
4.10 ♦ Gross value added		US$ Mn	47.4	52.3	62.0	66.7	63.6
4.11 ♦ Compensation of employees		US$ Mn	9.0	9.6	10.8	12.9	15.0
4.12 ♦ Gross fixed capital formation		US$ Mn	7.9	6.3	28.6	28.6	18.8
Non-monetary data							
4.13 ♦ Number of establishments		Units	262	285	320	370	452
4.14 ♦ Number of rooms		Units	10,661	11,403	11,829	12,789	13,964
4.15 ♦ Number of bed-places		Units	22,492	24,706	25,483	28,286	30,571
Indicators							
4.16 Occupancy rate / rooms		Percent	61.20	51.20	56.20	61.80	58.40
4.17 Occupancy rate / bed-places		Percent	53.50	51.50	53.20	61.60	55.10
4.18 Average length of stay		Nights	4.00	3.80	3.70	3.10	3.10
4.19 Available capacity (bed-places per 1000 inhabitants)		Units	2.68	2.91	2.97	3.26	3.48
Travel agencies and other reservation service activities							
Monetary data							
4.20 ♦ Output		US$ Mn	6.0	8.5	15.9	17.1	17.8
4.21 ♦ Intermediate consumption		US$ Mn	0.5	0.3	0.8	1.2	1.4
4.22 ♦ Gross value added		US$ Mn	4.0	4.8	11.6	13.0	14.0
4.23 ♦ Compensation of employees		US$ Mn	0.4	0.6	1.5	2.2	4.1
4.24 ♦ Gross fixed capital formation		US$ Mn	0.2	0.3	0.5	0.6	0.8

AZERBAIJAN

Basic data and indicators	Notes	Units	2005	2006	2007	2008	2009
5. EMPLOYMENT							
Data							
Number of employees by tourism industries							
5.1 Total		('000)	4.7	5.1	5.9	6.8	7.3
5.2 ♦ Accommodation services for visitors (hotels and similar establishments)		('000)	4.1	4.3	4.7	5.6	5.9
5.3 ♦ Other accommodation services		('000)	..	..	..	..	..
5.4 ♦ Food and beverage serving activities		('000)	..	..	..	..	..
5.5 ♦ Passenger transportation		('000)	..	..	..	..	..
5.6 ♦ Travel agencies and other reservation services activities		('000)	0.6	0.8	1.1	1.2	1.4
5.7 ♦ Other tourism industries		('000)	..	..	..	..	..
6. COMPLEMENTARY INDICATORS							
Demand							
6.1 Gross travel propensity		Units	..	..	..	..	..
6.2 Carrying capacity (arrivals/population)		Units	0.08	0.08	0.09	0.12	0.11
Macroeconomic indicators related to international tourism							
6.3 Inbound tourism expenditure over GDP		Percent	0.8	1.0	1.0	0.8	1.2
6.4 Outbound tourism expenditure over GDP		Percent	1.4	1.2	1.2	0.9	1.1
6.5 Tourism balance (inbound minus outbound tourism expenditure) over GDP		Percent	-0.7	-0.3	-0.2	-0.1	0.1
6.6 Tourism openness (inbound plus outbound tourism expenditure) over GDP		Percent	2.2	2.2	2.1	1.7	2.3
6.7 Tourism coverage (inbound over outbound tourism expenditure)		Percent	52.9	78.4	83.4	84.0	113.1
6.8 Inbound tourism expenditure over exports of goods		Percent	1.3	1.5	1.5	1.2	2.4
6.9 Inbound tourism expenditure over exports of services		Percent	14.6	21.4	25.4	24.7	29.5
6.10 Inbound tourism expenditure over exports of goods and services		Percent	1.2	1.4	1.4	1.2	2.3
6.11 Inbound tourism expenditure over current account credits		Percent	1.1	1.3	1.3	1.1	2.1
6.12 Outbound tourism expenditure over imports of goods		Percent	4.3	4.9	6.3	6.0	7.0
6.13 Outbound tourism expenditure over imports of services		Percent	7.1	9.0	11.3	11.7	13.6
6.14 Outbound tourism expenditure over imports of goods and services		Percent	2.7	3.2	4.0	4.0	4.6
6.15 Outbound tourism expenditure over current account debits		Percent	2.1	2.3	2.5	2.6	3.1

BAHAMAS

Basic data and indicators	Notes	Units	2005	2006	2007	2008	2009
1. INBOUND TOURISM							
Data							
Arrivals							
1.1 Total		('000)	4,779	4,731	4,601	4,394	4,645
1.2 ♦ Overnight visitors (tourists)		('000)	1,608	1,601	1,528	1,463	1,327
1.3 ♦ Same-day visitors (excursionists)		('000)	3,171	3,130	3,073	2,931	3,318
1.4 * of which, cruise passengers		('000)	3,079	3,079	2,971	2,861	3,256
Arrivals by region							
1.5 Total		('000)	1,608	1,601	1,528	1,463	1,328
1.6 ♦ Africa		('000)	2	2	2	2	2
1.7 ♦ Americas		('000)	1,485	1,485	1,404	1,331	1,213
1.8 ♦ East Asia and the Pacific		('000)	7	7	7	7	6
1.9 ♦ Europe		('000)	86	83	88	94	80
1.10 ♦ Middle East		('000)	1	1	1	1	1
1.11 ♦ South Asia		('000)	..	1	1	1	1
1.12 ♦ Other not classified		('000)	27	22	25	27	25
1.13 * of which, nationals residing abroad		('000)	..	..	..	..	..
Arrivals by main purpose							
1.14 Total		('000)	1,608	1,600	1,528	1,463	1,327
1.15 ♦ Personal		('000)	1,456	1,473	1,385	1,336	1,235
1.16 * holidays, leisure and recreation		('000)	1,337	1,322	1,248	1,185	1,079
1.17 * other personal purposes		('000)	119	151	137	151	156
1.18 ♦ Business and professional		('000)	152	127	143	127	92
Arrivals by mode of transport							
1.19 Total		('000)	4,780	4,731	4,601	4,394	4,645
1.20 ♦ Air		('000)	1,515	1,492	1,487	1,393	1,252
1.21 ♦ Water		('000)	3,265	3,239	3,114	3,001	3,393
1.22 ♦ Land		('000)	..	..	..	..	..
1.23 * railway		('000)	..	..	..	..	..
1.24 * road		('000)	..	..	..	..	..
1.25 * others		('000)	..	..	..	..	..
Accommodation							
Total							
1.29 ♦ Guests		('000)	1,608	1,601	1,528	1,463	1,327
1.30 ♦ Overnights		('000)	10,297	10,272	10,054	9,679	9,039
Hotels and similar establishments							
1.31 ♦ Guests	(1)	('000)	1,219	1,186	1,110	1,061	940
1.32 ♦ Overnights		('000)	6,125	5,993	5,646	5,423	4,868
Expenditure							
1.33 Total		US$ Mn	2,081	2,066	2,198	2,164	1,948
1.34 ♦ Travel		US$ Mn	2,071	2,056	2,187	2,153	1,938
1.35 ♦ Passenger transport		US$ Mn	10	10	11	11	10
Indicators							
1.39 Average size of travel party		Persons	..	..	..	..	..
Average length of stay							
1.40 Total		Days	..	..	..	..	..
1.41 ♦ For all commercial accommodation services		Nights	6.40	6.40	6.60	6.60	6.80
1.42 * of which, "hotels and similar establishments"		Nights	..	..	..	..	..
1.43 ♦ For non commercial accommodation services		Days	..	..	..	..	..
1.44 Average expenditure per day		US$	..	..	..	..	..
3. OUTBOUND TOURISM							
Data							
Expenditure							
3.4 Total		US$ Mn	528	541	538	460	386
3.5 ♦ Travel		US$ Mn	344	385	377	305	240
3.6 ♦ Passenger transport		US$ Mn	184	156	161	155	146
Expenditure by main purpose of the trip							
3.7 Total		US$ Mn	344	385	377	305	240
3.8 ♦ Personal		US$ Mn	305	332	338	268	214
3.9 ♦ Business and professional		US$ Mn	39	53	39	37	26

BAHAMAS

Basic data and indicators	Notes	Units	2005	2006	2007	2008	2009
4. TOURISM INDUSTRIES							
Data							
Number of establishments							
4.1 Total		Units	..	..	..	..	..
4.2 ♦ Accommodation for visitors		Units	..	..	..	..	..
4.3 * of which, "hotels and similar establishments"	(2)	Units	291	283	284	281	280
4.4 ♦ Food and beverage serving activities		Units	..	..	..	..	..
4.5 ♦ Passenger transportation		Units	..	..	..	..	..
4.6 ♦ Travel agencies and other reservation services activities		Units	..	..	..	..	..
4.7 ♦ Other tourism industries		Units	..	..	..	..	..
Accommodation for visitors in hotels and similar establishments							
Non-monetary data							
4.13 ♦ Number of establishments	(2)	Units	291	283	284	281	280
4.14 ♦ Number of rooms	(2)	Units	14,800	14,929	15,111	16,297	15,276
4.15 ♦ Number of bed-places	(2)	Units	29,600	29,858	30,222	32,594	30,552
Indicators							
4.16 Occupancy rate / rooms		Percent	70.40	68.40	60.90	54.10	49.40
4.17 Occupancy rate / bed-places		Percent	..	..	..	..	..
4.18 Average length of stay		Nights	..	..	..	..	..
4.19 Available capacity (bed-places per 1000 inhabitants)		Units	90.94	90.60	90.59	96.53	89.41
6. COMPLEMENTARY INDICATORS							
Demand							
6.1 Gross travel propensity		Units	..	..	..	..	..
6.2 Carrying capacity (arrivals/population)		Units	4.94	4.86	4.58	4.33	3.88
Macroeconomic indicators related to international tourism							
6.3 Inbound tourism expenditure over GDP		Percent	30.6	28.4	29.3	28.6	..
6.4 Outbound tourism expenditure over GDP		Percent	7.8	7.4	7.2	6.1	..
6.5 Tourism balance (inbound minus outbound tourism expenditure) over GDP		Percent	22.8	20.9	22.1	22.5	..
6.6 Tourism openness (inbound plus outbound tourism expenditure) over GDP		Percent	38.4	35.8	36.5	34.7	..
6.7 Tourism coverage (inbound over outbound tourism expenditure)		Percent	394.0	381.7	408.0	471.3	503.6
6.8 Inbound tourism expenditure over exports of goods		Percent	378.8	293.7	274.1	226.4	274.1
6.9 Inbound tourism expenditure over exports of services		Percent	82.8	84.8	84.6	85.1	85.7
6.10 Inbound tourism expenditure over exports of goods and services		Percent	68.0	65.8	64.6	61.9	65.3
6.11 Inbound tourism expenditure over current account credits		Percent	63.8	62.1	61.2	58.7	62.0
6.12 Outbound tourism expenditure over imports of goods		Percent	22.2	19.6	18.2	14.4	15.2
6.13 Outbound tourism expenditure over imports of services		Percent	41.0	33.6	34.1	32.7	32.3
6.14 Outbound tourism expenditure over imports of goods and services		Percent	14.4	12.4	11.9	10.0	10.4
6.15 Outbound tourism expenditure over current account debits		Percent	13.3	11.4	11.0	9.5	9.7

BAHRAIN

Basic data and indicators	Notes	Units	2005	2006	2007	2008	2009
1. INBOUND TOURISM							
Data							
Arrivals	(1)						
1.1 Total		('000)	6,313	7,289	7,833	..	..
1.2 ♦ Overnight visitors (tourists)		('000)	3,914	4,519	4,935	..	..
1.3 ♦ Same-day visitors (excursionists)		('000)	2,399	2,770	2,898	..	..
1.4 * of which, cruise passengers		('000)	..	..	..	..	..
Arrivals by region	(1)						
1.5 Total		('000)	6,313	7,289	7,833	..	..
1.6 ♦ Africa		('000)	82	99	109	..	..
1.7 ♦ Americas		('000)	190	234	267	..	..
1.8 ♦ East Asia and the Pacific		('000)	287	374	390	..	..
1.9 ♦ Europe		('000)	358	430	507	..	..
1.10 ♦ Middle East		('000)	4,676	5,210	5,451	..	..
1.11 ♦ South Asia		('000)	720	942	1,109	..	..
1.12 ♦ Other not classified		('000)	..	..	..	..	..
1.13 * of which, nationals residing abroad		('000)	..	..	..	..	..
Arrivals by main purpose	(1)						
1.14 Total		('000)	6,314	7,289	7,833	..	..
1.15 ♦ Personal		('000)	5,687	6,421	6,788	..	..
1.16 * holidays, leisure and recreation		('000)	4,187	5,087	5,274	..	..
1.17 * other personal purposes		('000)	1,500	1,334	1,514	..	..
1.18 ♦ Business and professional		('000)	627	868	1,045	..	..
Arrivals by mode of transport	(1)						
1.19 Total		('000)	6,313	7,289	7,834	..	..
1.20 ♦ Air	(2)	('000)	1,301	1,544	1,642	..	..
1.21 ♦ Water	(3)	('000)	5	12	53	..	..
1.22 ♦ Land	(4)	('000)	5,007	5,733	6,139	..	..
1.23 * railway		('000)	..	..	..	..	..
1.24 * road		('000)	5,007	5,733	6,139	..	..
1.25 * others		('000)	..	..	..	..	..
Accommodation							
Total							
1.29 ♦ Guests		('000)	..	..	..	..	..
1.30 ♦ Overnights		('000)	..	..	..	..	..
Hotels and similar establishments							
1.31 ♦ Guests		('000)	1,237	1,285	1,320	1,154	1,069
1.32 ♦ Overnights	(5)	('000)	2,224	2,477	2,494	2,368	2,069
Expenditure							
1.33 Total		US$ Mn	1,603	1,786	1,854	1,927	1,873
1.34 ♦ Travel		US$ Mn	920	1,048	1,105	1,166	1,118
1.35 ♦ Passenger transport		US$ Mn	683	738	749	761	755
Indicators							
1.39 Average size of travel party		Persons	..	..	..	..	..
Average length of stay							
1.40 Total		Days	..	..	..	..	..
1.41 ♦ For all commercial accommodation services		Nights	1.80	1.93	1.88	2.05	1.90
1.42 * of which, "hotels and similar establishments"		Nights	..	..	..	..	..
1.43 ♦ For non commercial accommodation services		Days	..	..	..	..	..
1.44 Average expenditure per day		US$	..	..	..	..	..
3. OUTBOUND TOURISM							
Data							
Expenditure							
3.4 Total		US$ Mn	574	639	671	704	597
3.5 ♦ Travel		US$ Mn	414	455	479	503	408
3.6 ♦ Passenger transport		US$ Mn	160	184	192	201	189

BAHRAIN

Basic data and indicators	Notes	Units	2005	2006	2007	2008	2009
4. TOURISM INDUSTRIES							
Data							
Number of establishments							
4.1 Total		Units	..	..	..	..	..
4.2 ♦ Accommodation for visitors		Units	..	..	..	..	..
4.3 * of which, "hotels and similar establishments"		Units	99	95	100	101	96
4.4 ♦ Food and beverage serving activities		Units	..	..	..	..	..
4.5 ♦ Passenger transportation		Units	..	..	..	..	..
4.6 ♦ Travel agencies and other reservation services activities		Units	..	..	..	..	..
4.7 ♦ Other tourism industries		Units	..	..	..	..	..
Accommodation for visitors in hotels and similar establishments							
Non-monetary data							
4.13 ♦ Number of establishments		Units	99	95	100	101	96
4.14 ♦ Number of rooms	(5)	Units	..	7,426	..	..	8,057
4.15 ♦ Number of bed-places		Units	..	..	..	..	..
Indicators							
4.16 Occupancy rate / rooms		Percent	..	..	..	..	..
4.17 Occupancy rate / bed-places		Percent	56.30	57.40	57.80	..	..
4.18 Average length of stay		Nights	..	..	..	..	..
4.19 Available capacity (bed-places per 1000 inhabitants)		Units	..	..	..	..	..
6. COMPLEMENTARY INDICATORS							
Demand							
6.1 Gross travel propensity		Units	..	..	..	..	..
6.2 Carrying capacity (arrivals/population)		Units	5.38	6.08	6.50	..	..
Macroeconomic indicators related to international tourism							
6.3 Inbound tourism expenditure over GDP		Percent	11.9	11.3	10.0	8.8	..
6.4 Outbound tourism expenditure over GDP		Percent	4.3	4.0	3.6	3.2	..
6.5 Tourism balance (inbound minus outbound tourism expenditure) over GDP		Percent	7.6	7.2	6.4	5.6	..
6.6 Tourism openness (inbound plus outbound tourism expenditure) over GDP		Percent	16.2	15.3	13.7	12.0	..
6.7 Tourism coverage (inbound over outbound tourism expenditure)		Percent	279.3	279.2	276.3	273.6	..
6.8 Inbound tourism expenditure over exports of goods		Percent	15.5	14.5	13.4	11.0	..
6.9 Inbound tourism expenditure over exports of services		Percent	52.6	53.7	52.6	51.5	..
6.10 Inbound tourism expenditure over exports of goods and services		Percent	12.0	11.4	10.7	9.1	..
6.11 Inbound tourism expenditure over current account credits		Percent	8.7	7.7	6.7	6.8	..
6.12 Outbound tourism expenditure over imports of goods		Percent	6.5	6.4	6.1	4.9	..
6.13 Outbound tourism expenditure over imports of services		Percent	40.5	39.8	39.4	34.7	..
6.14 Outbound tourism expenditure over imports of goods and services		Percent	5.6	5.5	5.3	4.3	..
6.15 Outbound tourism expenditure over current account debits		Percent	3.4	3.0	2.7	2.7	..

BANGLADESH

Basic data and indicators	Notes	Units	2005	2006	2007	2008	2009
1. INBOUND TOURISM							
Data							
Arrivals							
1.1 Total		('000)	..	..	..	..	..
1.2 ♦ Overnight visitors (tourists)		('000)	208	200	289	467	267
1.3 ♦ Same-day visitors (excursionists)		('000)	..	..	..	..	..
1.4 * of which, cruise passengers		('000)	..	..	..	..	..
Arrivals by region							
1.5 Total		('000)	208	200	289	..	..
1.6 ♦ Africa		('000)	2	2	2	..	..
1.7 ♦ Americas		('000)	19	25	46	..	..
1.8 ♦ East Asia and the Pacific		('000)	36	37	57	..	..
1.9 ♦ Europe		('000)	49	57	77	..	..
1.10 ♦ Middle East		('000)	3	4	5	..	..
1.11 ♦ South Asia		('000)	99	75	102	..	..
1.12 ♦ Other not classified		('000)	..	..	..	..	..
1.13 * of which, nationals residing abroad		('000)	..	..	..	..	..
Arrivals by main purpose							
1.14 Total		('000)	208	200	289	467	267
1.15 ♦ Personal		('000)	105	109	156	340	145
1.16 * holidays, leisure and recreation		('000)	68	85	142	128	123
1.17 * other personal purposes		('000)	37	24	14	212	22
1.18 ♦ Business and professional		('000)	103	91	133	127	122
Arrivals by mode of transport							
1.19 Total		('000)	208	200	289	..	..
1.20 ♦ Air		('000)	140	151	227	..	..
1.21 ♦ Water		('000)	..	..	..	..	..
1.22 ♦ Land		('000)	68	49	62	..	..
1.23 * railway		('000)	..	..	..	..	..
1.24 * road		('000)	68	49	62	..	..
1.25 * others		('000)	..	..	..	..	..
Expenditure							
1.33 Total		US$ Mn	79	80	..	..	76
1.34 ♦ Travel		US$ Mn	70	80	76	75	69
1.35 ♦ Passenger transport		US$ Mn	9	0.2	..	..	7
Expenditure by main purpose of the trip							
1.36 Total		US$ Mn	70.0	80.4	76.4	74.5	69.3
1.37 ♦ Personal		US$ Mn	67.9	78.6	74.6	73.9	68.5
1.38 ♦ Business and professional		US$ Mn	2.1	1.8	1.8	0.6	0.8
Indicators							
1.39 Average size of travel party		Persons	..	..	..	..	..
Average length of stay							
1.40 Total		Days	..	..	..	..	..
1.41 ♦ For all commercial accommodation services		Nights	4.50	4.50	4.50	..	..
1.42 * of which, "hotels and similar establishments"		Nights	..	..	..	..	..
1.43 ♦ For non commercial accommodation services		Days	..	..	..	..	..
1.44 Average expenditure per day		US$	..	..	..	..	..
3. OUTBOUND TOURISM							
Data							
Departures							
3.1 Total		('000)	..	..	..	..	..
3.2 ♦ Overnight visitors (tourists)		('000)	1,767	1,819	2,327	875	2,254
3.3 ♦ Same-day visitors (excursionists)		('000)	..	..	..	..	..
Expenditure							
3.4 Total		US$ Mn	375	444	530	735	651
3.5 ♦ Travel		US$ Mn	136	140	156	184	249
3.6 ♦ Passenger transport		US$ Mn	239	304	374	551	402
Expenditure by main purpose of the trip							
3.7 Total		US$ Mn	136	140	155	184	249
3.8 ♦ Personal		US$ Mn	112	114	131	160	227
3.9 ♦ Business and professional		US$ Mn	24	26	24	24	22

BANGLADESH

Basic data and indicators	Notes	Units	2005	2006	2007	2008	2009
4. TOURISM INDUSTRIES							
Data							
Accommodation for visitors in hotels and similar establishments							
Non-monetary data							
4.13 ♦ Number of establishments		Units	..	..	..	..	..
4.14 ♦ Number of rooms		Units	4,590	4,590	4,830	4,890	3,026
4.15 ♦ Number of bed-places		Units	10,557	10,557	11,037	11,173	..
Indicators							
4.16 Occupancy rate / rooms		Percent	..	..	..	..	..
4.17 Occupancy rate / bed-places		Percent	38.63	43.76	42.31	40.92	51.87
4.18 Average length of stay		Nights	..	..	..	..	..
4.19 Available capacity (bed-places per 1000 inhabitants)		Units	0.07	0.07	0.07	0.07	..
6. COMPLEMENTARY INDICATORS							
Demand							
6.1 Gross travel propensity		Units	..	..	..	..	..
6.2 Carrying capacity (arrivals/population)		Units	0.001	0.001	0.002	0.003	0.002
Macroeconomic indicators related to international tourism							
6.3 Inbound tourism expenditure over GDP		Percent	0.1	0.1	0.1	0.1	0.1
6.4 Outbound tourism expenditure over GDP		Percent	0.7	0.7	0.8	0.9	0.7
6.5 Tourism balance (inbound minus outbound tourism expenditure) over GDP		Percent	-0.5	-0.6	-0.7	-0.8	-0.6
6.6 Tourism openness (inbound plus outbound tourism expenditure) over GDP		Percent	0.8	0.9	0.9	1.0	0.8
6.7 Tourism coverage (inbound over outbound tourism expenditure)		Percent	20.9	18.2	14.4	10.1	11.7
6.8 Inbound tourism expenditure over exports of goods		Percent	0.8	0.7	0.6	0.5	0.5
6.9 Inbound tourism expenditure over exports of services		Percent	6.3	6.0	4.7	3.7	3.9
6.10 Inbound tourism expenditure over exports of goods and services		Percent	0.7	0.6	0.5	0.4	0.4
6.11 Inbound tourism expenditure over current account credits		Percent	0.5	0.4	0.4	0.3	0.3
6.12 Outbound tourism expenditure over imports of goods		Percent	3.0	3.1	3.2	3.4	3.3
6.13 Outbound tourism expenditure over imports of services		Percent	17.0	18.9	18.4	20.1	19.1
6.14 Outbound tourism expenditure over imports of goods and services		Percent	2.6	2.6	2.7	2.9	2.8
6.15 Outbound tourism expenditure over current account debits		Percent	2.4	2.5	2.6	2.8	2.6

BARBADOS

Basic data and indicators	Notes	Units	2005	2006	2007	2008	2009
1. INBOUND TOURISM							
Data							
Arrivals							
1.1 Total		('000)	1,111	1,102	1,191	1,165	1,154
1.2 ♦ Overnight visitors (tourists)		('000)	548	563	575	568	519
1.3 ♦ Same-day visitors (excursionists)		('000)	563	539	616	597	635
1.4　* of which, cruise passengers		('000)	563	539	616	597	635
Arrivals by region							
1.5 Total		('000)	547	562	574	567	518
1.6 ♦ Africa		('000)	1	1	3	1	1
1.7 ♦ Americas		('000)	311	312	303	309	292
1.8 ♦ East Asia and the Pacific		('000)	3	3	10	4	3
1.9 ♦ Europe		('000)	230	241	251	250	219
1.10 ♦ Middle East		('000)	..	..	..	..	..
1.11 ♦ South Asia		('000)	1	1	4	1	1
1.12 ♦ Other not classified		('000)	1	4	3	2	2
1.13　* of which, nationals residing abroad		('000)	..	..	..	..	..
Arrivals by main purpose							
1.14 Total		('000)	548	563	574	568	518
1.15 ♦ Personal		('000)	476	503	516	508	463
1.16　* holidays, leisure and recreation		('000)	432	470	493	469	430
1.17　* other personal purposes		('000)	44	33	23	39	33
1.18 ♦ Business and professional		('000)	72	60	58	60	55
Arrivals by mode of transport							
1.19 Total		('000)	1,111	1,101	1,191	1,165	1,154
1.20 ♦ Air		('000)	544	557	575	568	519
1.21 ♦ Water		('000)	567	544	616	597	635
1.22 ♦ Land		('000)	..	..	..	..	..
1.23　* railway		('000)	..	..	..	..	..
1.24　* road		('000)	..	..	..	..	..
1.25　* others		('000)	..	..	..	..	..
Expenditure							
1.33 Total		US$ Mn	905	1,064	1,206	1,201	1,078
1.34 ♦ Travel		US$ Mn	897	1,057	1,199	1,194	1,068
1.35 ♦ Passenger transport		US$ Mn	8	7	7	7	10
Expenditure by main purpose of the trip							
1.36 Total		US$ Mn	897	1,057	1,199	1,194	1,068
1.37 ♦ Personal		US$ Mn	894	1,054	1,197	1,194	1,067
1.38 ♦ Business and professional		US$ Mn	3	3	2	0.4	0.7
Indicators							
1.39 Average size of travel party		Persons	..	..	..	..	..
Average length of stay							
1.40 Total		Days	..	..	..	..	..
1.41 ♦ For all commercial accommodation services		Nights	9.80	..	..	..	..
1.42　* of which, "hotels and similar establishments"		Nights	..	..	..	..	..
1.43 ♦ For non commercial accommodation services		Days	..	..	..	..	..
1.44 Average expenditure per day		US$	..	..	..	..	..
3. OUTBOUND TOURISM							
Data							
Expenditure							
3.4 Total		US$ Mn	153	166	177	154	148
3.5 ♦ Travel		US$ Mn	96	104	99	80	71
3.6 ♦ Passenger transport		US$ Mn	57	62	78	74	77
Expenditure by main purpose of the trip							
3.7 Total		US$ Mn	95	105	99	80	71
3.8 ♦ Personal		US$ Mn	68	74	69	62	55
3.9 ♦ Business and professional		US$ Mn	27	31	30	18	16

BARBADOS

Basic data and indicators	Notes	Units	2005	2006	2007	2008	2009
4. TOURISM INDUSTRIES							
Data							
Accommodation for visitors in hotels and similar establishments							
Non-monetary data							
4.13 ◆ Number of establishments		Units	..	..	..	..	..
4.14 ◆ Number of rooms	(1)	Units	6,353	6,403	6,324	6,984	6,570
4.15 ◆ Number of bed-places	(1)	Units	12,417	..	..	..	..
Indicators							
4.16 Occupancy rate / rooms		Percent	54.00	52.80	56.10	..	..
4.17 Occupancy rate / bed-places		Percent	55.50	53.00	57.20	..	..
4.18 Average length of stay		Nights	7.40	7.20	7.40	..	..
4.19 Available capacity (bed-places per 1000 inhabitants)		Units	49.03	..	..	..	..
6. COMPLEMENTARY INDICATORS							
Demand							
6.1 Gross travel propensity		Units	..	..	..	..	..
6.2 Carrying capacity (arrivals/population)		Units	2.16	2.22	2.26	2.23	2.03
Macroeconomic indicators related to international tourism							
6.3 Inbound tourism expenditure over GDP		Percent	30.1	32.7	..	..	..
6.4 Outbound tourism expenditure over GDP		Percent	5.1	5.1	..	..	..
6.5 Tourism balance (inbound minus outbound tourism expenditure) over GDP		Percent	25.0	27.6	..	..	..
6.6 Tourism openness (inbound plus outbound tourism expenditure) over GDP		Percent	35.2	37.8	..	..	..
6.7 Tourism coverage (inbound over outbound tourism expenditure)		Percent	594.4	640.5	681.4	..	..
6.8 Inbound tourism expenditure over exports of goods		Percent	250.3	240.9	246.1	..	..
6.9 Inbound tourism expenditure over exports of services		Percent	68.7	73.2	73.5	..	..
6.10 Inbound tourism expenditure over exports of goods and services		Percent	53.9	56.2	56.6	..	..
6.11 Inbound tourism expenditure over current account credits		Percent	47.0	49.9	49.3	..	..
6.12 Outbound tourism expenditure over imports of goods		Percent	10.6	11.4	11.6	..	..
6.13 Outbound tourism expenditure over imports of services		Percent	22.5	22.8	21.7	..	..
6.14 Outbound tourism expenditure over imports of goods and services		Percent	7.2	7.6	7.5	..	..
6.15 Outbound tourism expenditure over current account debits		Percent	6.3	6.5	6.4	..	..

BELARUS

Basic data and indicators	Notes	Units	2005	2006	2007	2008	2009
1. INBOUND TOURISM							
Data							
Arrivals							
1.1 Total		('000)	4,738	5,276	5,283	5,262	4,872
1.2 ♦ Overnight visitors (tourists)	(1)	('000)	91	90	105	92	95
1.3 ♦ Same-day visitors (excursionists)		('000)	..	..	..	..	..
1.4 * of which, cruise passengers		('000)	..	..	..	..	..
Arrivals by region	(1)						
1.5 Total		('000)	91	89	105	90	94
1.6 ♦ Africa		('000)	..	..	..	..	..
1.7 ♦ Americas		('000)	5	4	6	1	1
1.8 ♦ East Asia and the Pacific		('000)	2	2	2	1	1
1.9 ♦ Europe		('000)	82	81	95	88	92
1.10 ♦ Middle East		('000)	1	1	1	..	..
1.11 ♦ South Asia		('000)	1	1	1	..	..
1.12 ♦ Other not classified		('000)	..	..	..	..	..
1.13 * of which, nationals residing abroad		('000)	..	..	..	..	..
Arrivals by main purpose							
1.14 Total		('000)	4,738	5,276	5,283	5,262	4,872
1.15 ♦ Personal		('000)	4,324	4,751	4,837	4,837	4,505
1.16 * holidays, leisure and recreation		('000)	2,609	2,930	2,947	3,179	3,325
1.17 * other personal purposes		('000)	1,715	1,821	1,890	1,658	1,180
1.18 ♦ Business and professional		('000)	414	525	446	425	367
Arrivals by mode of transport							
1.19 Total		('000)	..	5,168	5,177	5,181	4,725
1.20 ♦ Air		('000)	..	122	162	194	200
1.21 ♦ Water		('000)	..	..	..	..	..
1.22 ♦ Land		('000)	..	5,046	5,015	4,987	4,525
1.23 * railway		('000)	..	1,760	1,772	1,629	1,418
1.24 * road		('000)	..	3,286	3,243	3,358	3,107
1.25 * others		('000)	..	..	..	..	..
Arrivals by form of organization of the trip							
1.26 Total		('000)	4,738	5,276	5,283	5,262	4,872
1.27 ♦ Package tour		('000)	91	90	105	92	95
1.28 ♦ Other forms		('000)	4,647	5,186	5,178	5,170	4,777
Accommodation							
Total							
1.29 ♦ Guests		('000)	253	292	368	477	512
1.30 ♦ Overnights		('000)	..	..	..	..	..
Hotels and similar establishments							
1.31 ♦ Guests		('000)	246	272	304	372	384
1.32 ♦ Overnights		('000)	597	688	791	1,001	1,042
Expenditure							
1.33 Total		US$ Mn	346	401	479	582	562
1.34 ♦ Travel		US$ Mn	253	286	324	363	369
1.35 ♦ Passenger transport		US$ Mn	93	115	155	219	193
Expenditure by main purpose of the trip							
1.36 Total		US$ Mn	253	286	323	363	369
1.37 ♦ Personal		US$ Mn	148	175	204	227	235
1.38 ♦ Business and professional		US$ Mn	105	111	119	136	134
2. DOMESTIC TOURISM							
Data							
Trips							
2.1 Total		('000)	..	..	..	..	..
2.2 ♦ Overnight visitors (tourists)		('000)	50	55	49	59	51
2.3 ♦ Same-day visitors (excursionists)		('000)	..	..	..	..	..
Trips by form of organization							
2.16 Total		('000)	50	55	49	59	51
2.17 ♦ Package tour		('000)	50	55	49	59	51
2.18 ♦ Other forms		('000)	..	..	..	..	..
Accommodation							
Total							
2.19 ♦ Guests		('000)	1,702	1,722	1,751	1,734	1,636
2.20 ♦ Overnights		('000)	..	..	..	..	..
Hotels and similar establishments							
2.21 ♦ Guests		('000)	1,084	1,171	1,184	1,174	1,098
2.22 ♦ Overnights		('000)	3,306	3,649	3,739	3,624	3,275

BELARUS

Basic data and indicators	Notes	Units	2005	2006	2007	2008	2009
3. OUTBOUND TOURISM							
Data							
Departures							
3.1 Total		('000)	6,596	6,811	7,512	6,323	6,440
3.2 ♦ Overnight visitors (tourists)		('000)	572	525	517	380	316
3.3 ♦ Same-day visitors (excursionists)		('000)	6,024	6,286	6,995	5,943	6,124
Expenditure							
3.4 Total		US$ Mn	516	675	724	810	702
3.5 ♦ Travel		US$ Mn	448	586	606	668	588
3.6 ♦ Passenger transport		US$ Mn	68	89	118	142	114
Expenditure by main purpose of the trip							
3.7 Total		US$ Mn	448	586	606	668	588
3.8 ♦ Personal		US$ Mn	350	459	472	518	462
3.9 ♦ Business and professional		US$ Mn	98	127	134	150	126
4. TOURISM INDUSTRIES							
Data							
Number of establishments							
4.1 Total		Units	1,002	1,021	1,077	1,204	1,375
4.2 ♦ Accommodation for visitors		Units	600	587	614	627	655
4.3 * of which, "hotels and similar establishments"		Units	279	284	303	312	331
4.4 ♦ Food and beverage serving activities		Units	..	..	..	..	..
4.5 ♦ Passenger transportation		Units	..	..	..	..	..
4.6 ♦ Travel agencies and other reservation services activities		Units	402	434	463	577	720
4.7 ♦ Other tourism industries		Units	..	..	..	..	..
Accommodation for visitors in hotels and similar establishments							
Non-monetary data							
4.13 ♦ Number of establishments		Units	286	291	307	315	335
4.14 ♦ Number of rooms		Units	12,946	13,292	13,743	13,876	14,591
4.15 ♦ Number of bed-places		Units	23,504	24,095	24,616	24,437	25,609
Indicators							
4.16 Occupancy rate / rooms		Percent	82.61	89.40	90.31	91.07	81.07
4.17 Occupancy rate / bed-places		Percent	45.50	49.32	50.42	51.71	46.05
4.18 Average length of stay		Nights	2.93	3.00	3.04	2.99	2.91
4.19 Available capacity (bed-places per 1000 inhabitants)		Units	2.41	2.48	2.54	2.53	2.66
Travel agencies and other reservation service activities							
Non-monetary data							
♦ Domestic trips							
4.25 * with package tour		Percent	..	..	..	..	..
4.26 * without package tour		Percent	..	..	..	..	..
♦ Inbound trips							
4.27 * with package tour		Percent	1.9	1.7	2.0	1.7	2.0
4.28 * without package tour		Percent	98.1	98.3	98.0	98.2	98.0
♦ Outbound trips							
4.29 * with package tour		Percent	8.7	7.7	6.9	6.0	4.9
4.30 * without package tour		Percent	91.3	92.3	93.1	94.0	95.1

BELARUS

Basic data and indicators	Notes	Units	2005	2006	2007	2008	2009
6. COMPLEMENTARY INDICATORS							
Demand							
6.1 Gross travel propensity		Units	..	..	..	..	..
6.2 Carrying capacity (arrivals/population)		Units	0.01	0.01	0.02	0.02	0.02
Macroeconomic indicators related to international tourism							
6.3 Inbound tourism expenditure over GDP		Percent	1.1	1.1	1.1	1.0	1.1
6.4 Outbound tourism expenditure over GDP		Percent	1.7	1.8	1.6	1.3	1.4
6.5 Tourism balance (inbound minus outbound tourism expenditure) over GDP		Percent	-0.6	-0.7	-0.5	-0.4	-0.3
6.6 Tourism openness (inbound plus outbound tourism expenditure) over GDP		Percent	2.9	2.9	2.7	2.3	2.6
6.7 Tourism coverage (inbound over outbound tourism expenditure)		Percent	67.0	59.5	66.2	71.9	80.6
6.8 Inbound tourism expenditure over exports of goods		Percent	2.1	2.0	2.0	1.8	2.6
6.9 Inbound tourism expenditure over exports of services		Percent	16.7	16.7	14.7	13.9	16.1
6.10 Inbound tourism expenditure over exports of goods and services		Percent	1.9	1.8	1.7	1.6	2.3
6.11 Inbound tourism expenditure over current account credits		Percent	1.9	1.8	1.7	1.5	2.2
6.12 Outbound tourism expenditure over imports of goods		Percent	3.1	3.1	2.5	2.1	2.5
6.13 Outbound tourism expenditure over imports of services		Percent	47.2	40.6	35.6	30.9	33.8
6.14 Outbound tourism expenditure over imports of goods and services		Percent	2.9	2.8	2.4	1.9	2.3
6.15 Outbound tourism expenditure over current account debits		Percent	2.8	2.8	2.3	1.9	2.2

BELGIUM

Basic data and indicators	Notes	Units	2005	2006	2007	2008	2009
1. INBOUND TOURISM							
Data							
Arrivals							
1.1 Total		('000)	..	..	..	..	..
1.2 ♦ Overnight visitors (tourists)	(1)	('000)	6,747	6,995	7,045	7,165	6,815
1.3 ♦ Same-day visitors (excursionists)		('000)	..	..	..	..	..
1.4 * of which, cruise passengers		('000)	..	..	..	..	..
Arrivals by region	(1)						
1.5 Total		('000)	6,747	6,995	7,044	7,164	6,815
1.6 ♦ Africa		('000)	62	65	62	63	63
1.7 ♦ Americas		('000)	390	407	421	399	375
1.8 ♦ East Asia and the Pacific		('000)	298	305	302	268	238
1.9 ♦ Europe		('000)	5,836	6,036	6,061	6,187	5,956
1.10 ♦ Middle East		('000)	20	21	20	22	20
1.11 ♦ South Asia		('000)	35	33	44	64	47
1.12 ♦ Other not classified		('000)	106	128	134	161	116
1.13 * of which, nationals residing abroad		('000)	..	..	..	..	..
Arrivals by main purpose	(1)						
1.14 Total		('000)	6,747	6,995	7,045	7,164	6,815
1.15 ♦ Personal		('000)	4,381	4,503	4,605	4,588	4,532
1.16 * holidays, leisure and recreation		('000)	4,381	4,503	4,605	4,588	4,532
1.17 * other personal purposes		('000)	..	..	..	..	..
1.18 ♦ Business and professional		('000)	2,366	2,492	2,440	2,576	2,283
Accommodation							
Total							
1.29 ♦ Guests		('000)	6,747	6,995	7,045	7,165	6,815
1.30 ♦ Overnights		('000)	15,553	16,040	16,271	16,361	15,453
Hotels and similar establishments	(2)						
1.31 ♦ Guests		('000)	5,409	5,665	5,713	5,820	5,452
1.32 ♦ Overnights		('000)	10,297	10,634	10,976	11,120	10,337
Expenditure							
1.33 Total		US$ Mn	10,881	11,625	12,371	13,053	11,144
1.34 ♦ Travel		US$ Mn	9,845	10,311	11,017	11,801	9,967
1.35 ♦ Passenger transport		US$ Mn	1,036	1,314	1,354	1,252	1,177
Expenditure by main purpose of the trip							
1.36 Total		US$ Mn	9,844	10,311	11,017	11,802	9,967
1.37 ♦ Personal		US$ Mn	8,071	8,375	8,714	9,036	7,612
1.38 ♦ Business and professional		US$ Mn	1,773	1,936	2,303	2,766	2,355
Indicators							
1.39 Average size of travel party		Persons	..	..	..	..	..
Average length of stay							
1.40 Total		Days	..	..	..	..	..
1.41 ♦ For all commercial accommodation services		Nights	2.31	2.29	2.31	2.28	2.27
1.42 * of which, "hotels and similar establishments"		Nights	..	..	..	..	1.90
1.43 ♦ For non commercial accommodation services		Days	..	..	..	..	..
1.44 Average expenditure per day		US$	..	..	..	..	..
2. DOMESTIC TOURISM							
Data							
Trips							
2.1 Total		('000)	..	..	..	..	..
2.2 ♦ Overnight visitors (tourists)		('000)	..	..	..	..	5,431
2.3 ♦ Same-day visitors (excursionists)		('000)	..	..	..	..	..
Trips by main purpose							
2.4 Total		('000)	..	..	..	..	5,431
2.5 ♦ Personal		('000)	..	..	..	..	4,322
2.6 * holidays, leisure and recreation		('000)	..	..	..	..	4,322
2.7 * other personal purposes		('000)	..	..	..	..	..
2.8 ♦ Business and professional		('000)	..	..	..	..	1,109
Accommodation							
Total							
2.19 ♦ Guests		('000)	4,572	4,806	5,068	5,265	5,431
2.20 ♦ Overnights		('000)	12,827	13,332	13,578	13,611	13,803
Hotels and similar establishments	(2)						
2.21 ♦ Guests		('000)	2,364	2,596	2,877	3,081	3,218
2.22 ♦ Overnights		('000)	4,313	4,737	5,220	5,422	5,606

BELGIUM

Basic data and indicators		Notes	Units	2005	2006	2007	2008	2009
	Indicators							
2.23	Average size of travel party		Persons	..	..	..	..	..
	Average length of stay							
2.24	Total		Days	..	..	..	..	..
2.25	♦ For all commercial accommodation services		Nights	2.80	2.77	2.68	2.58	2.54
2.26	* of which, "hotels and similar establishments"		Nights	..	..	..	..	1.74
2.27	♦ For non commercial accommodation services		Days	..	..	..	..	..
2.28	Average expenditure per day		US$	..	..	..	..	..

3. OUTBOUND TOURISM

	Data							
	Departures							
3.1	Total		('000)	..	..	..	..	..
3.2	♦ Overnight visitors (tourists)		('000)	9,327	7,852	8,371	8,887	11,123
3.3	♦ Same-day visitors (excursionists)		('000)	..	..	..	..	..
	Expenditure							
3.4	Total		US$ Mn	16,771	17,891	19,215	21,393	19,673
3.5	♦ Travel		US$ Mn	14,948	15,574	17,506	19,822	17,923
3.6	♦ Passenger transport		US$ Mn	1,823	2,317	1,709	1,571	1,750
	Expenditure by main purpose of the trip							
3.7	Total		US$ Mn	14,948	15,573	17,506	19,822	17,923
3.8	♦ Personal		US$ Mn	12,819	13,281	14,671	16,763	14,999
3.9	♦ Business and professional		US$ Mn	2,129	2,292	2,835	3,059	2,924

4. TOURISM INDUSTRIES

	Data							
	Number of establishments							
4.1	Total		Units	..	..	..	..	..
4.2	♦ Accommodation for visitors		Units	3,449	3,485	3,521	3,536	3,527
4.3	* of which, "hotels and similar establishments"		Units	1,974	2,028	2,077	2,069	2,095
4.4	♦ Food and beverage serving activities		Units	..	..	..	..	..
4.5	♦ Passenger transportation		Units	..	..	..	..	..
4.6	♦ Travel agencies and other reservation services activities		Units	..	..	..	..	..
4.7	♦ Other tourism industries		Units	..	..	..	..	..
	Accommodation for visitors in hotels and similar establishments							
	Non-monetary data	(3)						
4.13	♦ Number of establishments		Units	1,974	2,028	2,077	2,069	2,095
4.14	♦ Number of rooms		Units	66,568	67,811	67,719	67,910	68,708
4.15	♦ Number of bed-places		Units	168,443	172,883	172,035	170,914	170,904
	Indicators							
4.16	Occupancy rate / rooms		Percent	..	..	..	..	..
4.17	Occupancy rate / bed-places		Percent	..	..	..	..	..
4.18	Average length of stay		Nights	..	..	..	..	..
4.19	Available capacity (bed-places per 1000 inhabitants)		Units	16.07	16.39	16.19	15.96	15.84

6. COMPLEMENTARY INDICATORS

			Units	2005	2006	2007	2008	2009
	Demand							
6.1	Gross travel propensity		Units	..	..	..	..	..
6.2	Carrying capacity (arrivals/population)		Units	0.64	0.66	0.66	0.67	1.14
	Macroeconomic indicators related to international tourism							
6.3	Inbound tourism expenditure over GDP		Percent	2.9	2.9	2.7	2.6	2.3
6.4	Outbound tourism expenditure over GDP		Percent	4.4	4.5	4.2	4.2	4.2
6.5	Tourism balance (inbound minus outbound tourism expenditure) over GDP		Percent	-1.6	-1.6	-1.5	-1.7	-1.8
6.6	Tourism openness (inbound plus outbound tourism expenditure) over GDP		Percent	7.3	7.4	6.9	6.8	6.5
6.7	Tourism coverage (inbound over outbound tourism expenditure)		Percent	64.9	65.0	64.0	61.0	56.1
6.8	Inbound tourism expenditure over exports of goods		Percent	4.1	4.1	3.8	3.9	4.4
6.9	Inbound tourism expenditure over exports of services		Percent	19.4	19.5	16.6	14.9	13.5
6.10	Inbound tourism expenditure over exports of goods and services		Percent	3.4	3.4	3.1	3.1	3.3
6.11	Inbound tourism expenditure over current account credits		Percent	2.8	2.7	2.4	2.4	2.6
6.12	Outbound tourism expenditure over imports of goods		Percent	6.5	6.4	6.0	6.1	7.7
6.13	Outbound tourism expenditure over imports of services		Percent	32.8	33.6	28.0	25.7	26.5
6.14	Outbound tourism expenditure over imports of goods and services		Percent	5.4	5.4	4.9	5.0	5.9
6.15	Outbound tourism expenditure over current account debits		Percent	4.4	4.3	3.9	3.8	4.6

BELIZE

Basic data and indicators	Notes	Units	2005	2006	2007	2008	2009
1. INBOUND TOURISM							
Data							
Arrivals							
1.1 Total		('000)	1,037	903	875	842	937
1.2 ◆ Overnight visitors (tourists)		('000)	237	247	251	245	232
1.3 ◆ Same-day visitors (excursionists)		('000)	800	656	624	597	705
1.4 * of which, cruise passengers		('000)	800	656	624	597	705
Arrivals by region							
1.5 Total		('000)	235	246	250	246	..
1.6 ◆ Africa		('000)	..	..	..	1	..
1.7 ◆ Americas		('000)	190	199	202	196	..
1.8 ◆ East Asia and the Pacific		('000)	4	5	5	5	..
1.9 ◆ Europe		('000)	33	34	34	34	..
1.10 ◆ Middle East		('000)	..	..	..	1	..
1.11 ◆ South Asia		('000)	..	..	..	..	..
1.12 ◆ Other not classified		('000)	8	8	9	9	..
1.13 * of which, nationals residing abroad		('000)	8	8	9	9	..
Arrivals by main purpose							
1.14 Total		('000)	237	247	251	245	..
1.15 ◆ Personal		('000)	225	235	238	235	..
1.16 * holidays, leisure and recreation		('000)	225	235	238	235	..
1.17 * other personal purposes		('000)	..	..	..	..	..
1.18 ◆ Business and professional		('000)	12	12	13	10	..
Arrivals by mode of transport							
1.19 Total		('000)	237	247	252	245	..
1.20 ◆ Air		('000)	175	179	183	178	..
1.21 ◆ Water		('000)	8	8	10	10	..
1.22 ◆ Land		('000)	54	60	59	57	..
1.23 * railway		('000)	..	..	..	..	..
1.24 * road		('000)	54	60	59	57	..
1.25 * others		('000)	..	..	..	..	..
Expenditure							
1.33 Total		US$ Mn	..	..	..	..	..
1.34 ◆ Travel		US$ Mn	214	260	289	278	256
1.35 ◆ Passenger transport		US$ Mn	..	..	..	..	..
Expenditure by main purpose of the trip							
1.36 Total		US$ Mn	213	260	288	279	256
1.37 ◆ Personal		US$ Mn	203	242	271	262	241
1.38 ◆ Business and professional		US$ Mn	10	18	17	17	15
Indicators							
1.39 Average size of travel party		Persons	..	..	..	..	..
Average length of stay							
1.40 Total		Days	..	..	..	..	..
1.41 ◆ For all commercial accommodation services		Nights	..	..	8.56	..	..
1.42 * of which, "hotels and similar establishments"		Nights	..	..	..	..	..
1.43 ◆ For non commercial accommodation services		Days	..	..	..	..	..
1.44 Average expenditure per day		US$	..	..	..	..	..
3. OUTBOUND TOURISM							
Data							
Expenditure							
3.4 Total		US$ Mn	45	43	46	44	43
3.5 ◆ Travel		US$ Mn	42	41	43	41	41
3.6 ◆ Passenger transport		US$ Mn	3	2	3	3	2
Expenditure by main purpose of the trip							
3.7 Total		US$ Mn	41	41	43	41	41
3.8 ◆ Personal		US$ Mn	39	39	41	39	39
3.9 ◆ Business and professional		US$ Mn	2	2	2	2	2

BELIZE

Basic data and indicators	Notes	Units	2005	2006	2007	2008	2009
4. TOURISM INDUSTRIES							
Data							
Number of establishments							
4.1 Total		Units	..	..	..	..	..
4.2 ♦ Accommodation for visitors		Units	..	..	..	..	..
4.3 * of which, "hotels and similar establishments"		Units	557	561	591	611	..
4.4 ♦ Food and beverage serving activities		Units	..	..	..	..	..
4.5 ♦ Passenger transportation		Units	..	..	..	..	..
4.6 ♦ Travel agencies and other reservation services activities		Units	..	..	..	..	..
4.7 ♦ Other tourism industries		Units	..	..	..	..	..
Accommodation for visitors in hotels and similar establishments							
Non-monetary data							
4.13 ♦ Number of establishments		Units	557	561	591	611	..
4.14 ♦ Number of rooms		Units	5,593	5,789	6,200	6,471	..
4.15 ♦ Number of bed-places		Units	9,327	9,651	10,502	11,133	..
Indicators							
4.16 Occupancy rate / rooms		Percent	..	..	..	..	..
4.17 Occupancy rate / bed-places		Percent	42.10	42.90	44.31	41.10	..
4.18 Average length of stay		Nights	..	..	8.56	..	..
4.19 Available capacity (bed-places per 1000 inhabitants)		Units	31.96	32.02	33.71	34.56	..
6. COMPLEMENTARY INDICATORS							
Demand							
6.1 Gross travel propensity		Units	..	..	..	..	..
6.2 Carrying capacity (arrivals/population)		Units	0.81	0.82	0.81	0.76	0.70
Macroeconomic indicators related to international tourism							
6.3 Inbound tourism expenditure over GDP		Percent	19.2	21.4	22.6	20.5	18.9
6.4 Outbound tourism expenditure over GDP		Percent	4.0	3.6	3.6	3.2	3.2
6.5 Tourism balance (inbound minus outbound tourism expenditure) over GDP		Percent	15.1	17.9	19.1	17.3	15.8
6.6 Tourism openness (inbound plus outbound tourism expenditure) over GDP		Percent	23.2	25.0	26.2	23.7	22.1
6.7 Tourism coverage (inbound over outbound tourism expenditure)		Percent	477.7	599.4	636.3	633.5	595.5
6.8 Inbound tourism expenditure over exports of goods		Percent	65.7	60.9	67.8	58.0	67.1
6.9 Inbound tourism expenditure over exports of services		Percent	70.8	71.7	72.5	72.1	74.3
6.10 Inbound tourism expenditure over exports of goods and services		Percent	34.1	32.9	35.0	32.1	35.3
6.11 Inbound tourism expenditure over current account credits		Percent	30.4	29.1	29.8	27.5	30.7
6.12 Outbound tourism expenditure over imports of goods		Percent	8.0	7.1	7.1	5.6	6.9
6.13 Outbound tourism expenditure over imports of services		Percent	28.2	28.5	27.0	25.9	26.6
6.14 Outbound tourism expenditure over imports of goods and services		Percent	6.3	5.7	5.6	4.6	5.5
6.15 Outbound tourism expenditure over current account debits		Percent	5.2	4.7	4.5	3.8	4.6

BENIN

Basic data and indicators	Notes	Units	2005	2006	2007	2008	2009
1. INBOUND TOURISM							
Data							
Arrivals							
1.1 Total		('000)	960	975	1,010	1,027	..
1.2 ♦ Overnight visitors (tourists)		('000)	176	180	186	188	190
1.3 ♦ Same-day visitors (excursionists)		('000)	..	..	..	..	..
1.4 * of which, cruise passengers		('000)	..	..	..	..	..
Arrivals by region							
1.5 Total		('000)	176.0	180.0	186.4	187.9	190.1
1.6 ♦ Africa		('000)	140.2	152.0	153.0	117.9	90.8
1.7 ♦ Americas		('000)	0.5	1.0	2.3	3.9	5.1
1.8 ♦ East Asia and the Pacific		('000)	0.3	0.6	0.8	1.6	0.9
1.9 ♦ Europe		('000)	31.5	22.3	26.3	50.7	35.4
1.10 ♦ Middle East		('000)	0.5	0.6	1.8	0.3	0.4
1.11 ♦ South Asia		('000)	3.0	3.5	2.2	0.7	0.5
1.12 ♦ Other not classified		('000)	..	..	..	12.8	57.0
1.13 * of which, nationals residing abroad		('000)	..	..	..	..	..
Arrivals by main purpose							
1.14 Total		('000)	..	..	185	188	190
1.15 ♦ Personal		('000)	..	..	88	103	82
1.16 * holidays, leisure and recreation		('000)	..	..	38	48	35
1.17 * other personal purposes		('000)	..	..	50	55	47
1.18 ♦ Business and professional		('000)	..	..	97	85	108
Arrivals by mode of transport							
1.19 Total		('000)	..	..	185	188	190
1.20 ♦ Air		('000)	..	..	81	71	81
1.21 ♦ Water		('000)	..	..	7	27	8
1.22 ♦ Land		('000)	..	..	97	90	101
1.23 * railway		('000)	..	..	..	..	..
1.24 * road		('000)	..	..	97	90	101
1.25 * others		('000)	..	..	..	..	..
Accommodation							
Total							
1.29 ♦ Guests		('000)	..	..	..	..	..
1.30 ♦ Overnights		('000)	348	321	412	547	..
Hotels and similar establishments							
1.31 ♦ Guests		('000)	..	..	..	..	..
1.32 ♦ Overnights		('000)	..	..	..	..	..
Expenditure							
1.33 Total		US$ Mn	107.7	121.6	206.3	236.4	..
1.34 ♦ Travel		US$ Mn	103	116	206	236	..
1.35 ♦ Passenger transport		US$ Mn	4.7	5.6	0.3	0.4	..
Expenditure by main purpose of the trip							
1.36 Total		US$ Mn	103	116	206	236	..
1.37 ♦ Personal		US$ Mn	65	72	139	137	..
1.38 ♦ Business and professional		US$ Mn	38	44	67	99	..
Indicators							
1.39 Average size of travel party		Persons	..	..	..	..	..
Average length of stay							
1.40 Total		Days	..	..	..	..	..
1.41 ♦ For all commercial accommodation services		Nights	..	..	3.00	4.40	..
1.42 * of which, "hotels and similar establishments"		Nights	..	..	..	..	..
1.43 ♦ For non commercial accommodation services		Days	..	..	..	..	..
1.44 Average expenditure per day		US$	..	..	..	..	..

BENIN

Basic data and indicators	Notes	Units	2005	2006	2007	2008	2009
2. DOMESTIC TOURISM							
Data							
Accommodation							
Total							
2.19 ♦ Guests		('000)	..	..	..	..	..
2.20 ♦ Overnights		('000)	..	138	150	158	..
Hotels and similar establishments							
2.21 ♦ Guests		('000)	..	..	..	..	..
2.22 ♦ Overnights		('000)	..	..	..	..	..
Indicators							
2.23 Average size of travel party		Persons	..	..	..	..	..
Average length of stay							
2.24 Total		Days	..	..	..	..	..
2.25 ♦ For all commercial accommodation services		Nights	..	..	1.00	..	..
2.26 * of which, "hotels and similar establishments"		Nights					
2.27 ♦ For non commercial accommodation services		Days	..	..	..	..	..
2.28 Average expenditure per day		US$	..	..	..	..	..
3. OUTBOUND TOURISM							
Data							
Expenditure							
3.4 Total		US$ Mn	58	71	107	102	..
3.5 ♦ Travel		US$ Mn	27	34	72	64	..
3.6 ♦ Passenger transport		US$ Mn	31	37	35	38	..
Expenditure by main purpose of the trip							
3.7 Total		US$ Mn	27	34	72	64	..
3.8 ♦ Personal		US$ Mn	17	17	43	36	..
3.9 ♦ Business and professional		US$ Mn	10	17	29	28	..
4. TOURISM INDUSTRIES							
Data							
Accommodation for visitors in hotels and similar establishments							
Non-monetary data							
4.13 ♦ Number of establishments		Units	..	..	..	..	..
4.14 ♦ Number of rooms		Units	..	6,942	10,160	11,200	11,980
4.15 ♦ Number of bed-places		Units	..	13,884	20,320	22,900	23,960
Indicators							
4.16 Occupancy rate / rooms		Percent	..	..	..	..	..
4.17 Occupancy rate / bed-places		Percent	..	33.00	12.19	9.63	..
4.18 Average length of stay		Nights	..	2.55	2.93	3.00	..
4.19 Available capacity (bed-places per 1000 inhabitants)		Units	..	1.71	2.42	2.64	2.68
6. COMPLEMENTARY INDICATORS							
Demand							
6.1 Gross travel propensity		Units	..	..	..	..	..
6.2 Carrying capacity (arrivals/population)		Units	0.02	0.02	0.02	0.02	0.02
Macroeconomic indicators related to international tourism							
6.3 Inbound tourism expenditure over GDP		Percent	2.3	2.4	3.5	..	..
6.4 Outbound tourism expenditure over GDP		Percent	1.2	1.4	1.8	..	..
6.5 Tourism balance (inbound minus outbound tourism expenditure) over GDP		Percent	1.1	1.0	1.7	..	..
6.6 Tourism openness (inbound plus outbound tourism expenditure) over GDP		Percent	3.5	3.8	5.3	..	..
6.7 Tourism coverage (inbound over outbound tourism expenditure)		Percent	188.4	171.3	194.2	..	..
6.8 Inbound tourism expenditure over exports of goods		Percent	18.7	16.6	19.8	..	..
6.9 Inbound tourism expenditure over exports of services		Percent	55.8	56.1	68.6	..	..
6.10 Inbound tourism expenditure over exports of goods and services		Percent	14.0	12.8	15.3	..	..
6.11 Inbound tourism expenditure over current account credits		Percent	10.9	9.4	11.7	..	..
6.12 Outbound tourism expenditure over imports of goods		Percent	6.6	6.8	6.6	..	..
6.13 Outbound tourism expenditure over imports of services		Percent	20.6	20.2	21.3	..	..
6.14 Outbound tourism expenditure over imports of goods and services		Percent	5.0	5.1	5.1	..	..
6.15 Outbound tourism expenditure over current account debits		Percent	4.7	4.7	4.6	..	..

BERMUDA

Basic data and indicators	Notes	Units	2005	2006	2007	2008	2009
1. INBOUND TOURISM							
Data							
Arrivals	(1)						
1.1 Total		('000)	517	635	660	550	559
1.2 ♦ Overnight visitors (tourists)		('000)	270	299	306	264	236
1.3 ♦ Same-day visitors (excursionists)		('000)	247	336	354	286	323
1.4 * of which, cruise passengers		('000)	247	336	354	286	323
Arrivals by region							
1.5 Total	(2)	('000)	271	299	306	264	236
1.6 ♦ Africa		('000)	..	..	..	..	..
1.7 ♦ Americas		('000)	233	255	257	217	198
1.8 ♦ East Asia and the Pacific		('000)	1	1	1	1	1
1.9 ♦ Europe		('000)	27	32	36	35	29
1.10 ♦ Middle East		('000)	..	..	..	..	..
1.11 ♦ South Asia		('000)	..	..	..	..	..
1.12 ♦ Other not classified		('000)	10	11	12	11	8
1.13 * of which, nationals residing abroad		('000)	..	..	..	..	..
Arrivals by main purpose							
1.14 Total	(2)	('000)	270	299	306	264	235
1.15 ♦ Personal		('000)	211	242	238	203	185
1.16 * holidays, leisure and recreation		('000)	170	202	191	158	144
1.17 * other personal purposes		('000)	41	40	47	45	41
1.18 ♦ Business and professional		('000)	59	57	68	61	50
Arrivals by mode of transport							
1.19 Total		('000)	517	635	660	550	559
1.20 ♦ Air		('000)	270	299	306	264	236
1.21 ♦ Water	(3)	('000)	247	336	354	286	323
1.22 ♦ Land		('000)	..	..	..	..	..
1.23 * railway		('000)	..	..	..	..	..
1.24 * road		('000)	..	..	..	..	..
1.25 * others		('000)	..	..	..	..	..
Accommodation							
Total							
1.29 ♦ Guests		('000)	270	299	306	264	236
1.30 ♦ Overnights	(4)	('000)	1,729	1,931	1,898	1,679	1,437
Hotels and similar establishments							
1.31 ♦ Guests		('000)	207	227	230	189	171
1.32 ♦ Overnights		('000)	1,047	1,159	1,120	948	827
Expenditure							
1.33 Total		US$ Mn	..	..	..	..	..
1.34 ♦ Travel		US$ Mn	429	495	569	431	363
1.35 ♦ Passenger transport		US$ Mn	..	..	..	..	..
Expenditure by main purpose of the trip							
1.36 Total		US$ Mn	..	495	569	431	363
1.37 ♦ Personal		US$ Mn	..	396	446	322	283
1.38 ♦ Business and professional		US$ Mn	..	99	123	109	80
Indicators							
1.39 Average size of travel party		Persons	..	..	..	..	..
Average length of stay							
1.40 Total		Days	..	..	..	..	..
1.41 ♦ For all commercial accommodation services		Nights	6.40	6.50	6.21	6.37	6.09
1.42 * of which, "hotels and similar establishments"		Nights	..	..	..	..	..
1.43 ♦ For non commercial accommodation services		Days	..	..	..	..	..
1.44 Average expenditure per day		US$	..	..	..	..	..

BERMUDA

Basic data and indicators	Notes	Units	2005	2006	2007	2008	2009
3. OUTBOUND TOURISM							
Data							
Departures							
3.1 Total		('000)	..	..	..	..	..
3.2 ♦ Overnight visitors (tourists)		('000)	161	170	181	192	..
3.3 ♦ Same-day visitors (excursionists)		('000)	..	..	..	..	..
Expenditure							
3.4 Total		US$ Mn	..	395	453	459	407
3.5 ♦ Travel		US$ Mn	239	269	288	307	295
3.6 ♦ Passenger transport		US$ Mn	..	126	165	152	112
Expenditure by main purpose of the trip							
3.7 Total		US$ Mn	..	268	288	306	295
3.8 ♦ Personal		US$ Mn	..	258	276	291	284
3.9 ♦ Business and professional		US$ Mn	..	10	12	15	11
4. TOURISM INDUSTRIES							
Data							
Accommodation for visitors in hotels and similar establishments							
Non-monetary data							
4.13 ♦ Number of establishments		Units	..	..	..	..	..
4.14 ♦ Number of rooms		Units	3,067	3,011	2,766	2,736	2,782
4.15 ♦ Number of bed-places		Units	6,167	6,065	5,590	5,538	5,820
Indicators							
4.16 Occupancy rate / rooms		Percent	56.90	63.80	67.10	59.10	51.10
4.17 Occupancy rate / bed-places		Percent	..	..	..	..	..
4.18 Average length of stay		Nights	6.40	6.50	4.88	5.00	4.84
4.19 Available capacity (bed-places per 1000 inhabitants)		Units	97.01	95.06	87.34	86.26	90.37
6. COMPLEMENTARY INDICATORS							
Demand							
6.1 Gross travel propensity		Units	..	..	..	..	..
6.2 Carrying capacity (arrivals/population)		Units	4.25	4.69	4.78	4.11	3.66

BHUTAN

Basic data and indicators	Notes	Units	2005	2006	2007	2008	2009
1. INBOUND TOURISM							
Data							
Arrivals							
1.1 Total		('000)	..	..	..	..	..
1.2 ♦ Overnight visitors (tourists)		('000)	13.6	17.3	21.1	27.6	23.5
1.3 ♦ Same-day visitors (excursionists)		('000)	..	..	..	..	..
1.4 * of which, cruise passengers		('000)	..	..	..	..	..
Arrivals by region							
1.5 Total		('000)	13.6	17.3	21.1	27.6	23.5
1.6 ♦ Africa		('000)	..	..	..	..	..
1.7 ♦ Americas		('000)	5.2	5.6	6.7	8.2	5.7
1.8 ♦ East Asia and the Pacific		('000)	2.8	4.3	5.4	7.4	7.7
1.9 ♦ Europe		('000)	5.6	7.3	8.9	11.8	9.9
1.10 ♦ Middle East		('000)	..	..	..	..	..
1.11 ♦ South Asia		('000)	..	..	..	0.1	0.1
1.12 ♦ Other not classified		('000)	..	0.1	0.1	0.1	0.1
1.13 * of which, nationals residing abroad		('000)	..	..	..	..	..
Arrivals by main purpose							
1.14 Total		('000)	13.6	17.3	21.1	27.6	23.5
1.15 ♦ Personal		('000)	13.6	17.3	21.1	26.0	21.5
1.16 * holidays, leisure and recreation		('000)	13.6	17.3	21.1	24.0	18.8
1.17 * other personal purposes		('000)	..	..	..	2.0	2.7
1.18 ♦ Business and professional		('000)	..	..	..	1.6	2.0
Arrivals by mode of transport							
1.19 Total		('000)	13.6	17.3	21.1	27.6	23.5
1.20 ♦ Air		('000)	11.7	14.0	16.1	22.6	19.6
1.21 ♦ Water		('000)	..	..	..	..	..
1.22 ♦ Land		('000)	1.9	3.3	5.0	5.0	3.9
1.23 * railway		('000)	..	..	..	..	..
1.24 * road		('000)	1.9	3.3	5.0	5.0	3.9
1.25 * others		('000)	..	..	..	..	..
Accommodation							
Total							
1.29 ♦ Guests		('000)	..	..	..	..	..
1.30 ♦ Overnights		('000)	..	..	..	..	..
Hotels and similar establishments							
1.31 ♦ Guests		('000)	..	..	..	..	..
1.32 ♦ Overnights		('000)	74	..	170	220	..
Expenditure							
1.33 Total		US$ Mn	19	36	47	46	51
1.34 ♦ Travel		US$ Mn	..	23	28	36	42
1.35 ♦ Passenger transport		US$ Mn	..	13	19	10	9
Expenditure by main purpose of the trip							
1.36 Total		US$ Mn	..	..	..	..	42
1.37 ♦ Personal		US$ Mn	..	..	..	..	41
1.38 ♦ Business and professional		US$ Mn	..	..	..	..	1
Indicators							
1.39 Average size of travel party		Persons	..	..	..	..	..
Average length of stay							
1.40 Total		Days	..	..	..	..	..
1.41 ♦ For all commercial accommodation services		Nights	8.00	8.00	7.90	7.80	7.60
1.42 * of which, "hotels and similar establishments"		Nights	..	..	..	..	..
1.43 ♦ For non commercial accommodation services		Days	..	..	..	..	..
1.44 Average expenditure per day		US$	..	..	..	..	..
3. OUTBOUND TOURISM							
Data							
Expenditure							
3.4 Total		US$ Mn	..	..	..	66	40
3.5 ♦ Travel		US$ Mn	..	22	26	65	39
3.6 ♦ Passenger transport		US$ Mn	..	..	..	1	1
Expenditure by main purpose of the trip							
3.7 Total		US$ Mn	..	23	26	65	38
3.8 ♦ Personal		US$ Mn	..	19	21	30	28
3.9 ♦ Business and professional		US$ Mn	..	4	5	35	10

BHUTAN

Basic data and indicators	Notes	Units	2005	2006	2007	2008	2009
4. **TOURISM INDUSTRIES**							
Data							
Accommodation for visitors in hotels and similar establishments							
Non-monetary data							
4.13 ♦ Number of establishments		Units	..	..	..	..	..
4.14 ♦ Number of rooms		Units	1,436	1,532	1,860	2,004	..
4.15 ♦ Number of bed-places		Units	2,636	2,746	3,320	3,531	..
Indicators							
4.16 Occupancy rate / rooms		Percent	..	..	..	..	..
4.17 Occupancy rate / bed-places		Percent	25.00	26.50	12.40	..	..
4.18 Average length of stay		Nights	8.50	8.00	7.90	7.80	..
4.19 Available capacity (bed-places per 1000 inhabitants)		Units	4.06	4.14	4.91	5.14	..
6. **COMPLEMENTARY INDICATORS**							
Demand							
6.1 Gross travel propensity		Units	..	..	..	..	..
6.2 Carrying capacity (arrivals/population)		Units	0.02	0.03	0.03	0.04	0.03

BOLIVIA

Basic data and indicators	Notes	Units	2005	2006	2007	2008	2009
1. INBOUND TOURISM							
Data							
Arrivals							
1.1 Total		('000)	..	..	..	..	..
1.2 ♦ Overnight visitors (tourists)		('000)	524	521	573	594	671
1.3 ♦ Same-day visitors (excursionists)		('000)	..	..	..	..	..
1.4 * of which, cruise passengers		('000)	..	..	..	..	..
Arrivals by region							
1.5 Total		('000)	524	521	573	594	..
1.6 ♦ Africa		('000)	2	1	2	3	..
1.7 ♦ Americas		('000)	314	308	341	353	..
1.8 ♦ East Asia and the Pacific		('000)	25	31	35	39	..
1.9 ♦ Europe		('000)	174	169	182	187	..
1.10 ♦ Middle East		('000)	..	..	..	..	..
1.11 ♦ South Asia		('000)	..	..	..	..	..
1.12 ♦ Other not classified		('000)	9	12	13	12	..
1.13 * of which, nationals residing abroad		('000)	..	..	..	..	..
Arrivals by main purpose	(1)						
1.14 Total		('000)	524	522	573	594	..
1.15 ♦ Personal		('000)	479	484	531	547	..
1.16 * holidays, leisure and recreation		('000)	322	319	339	341	..
1.17 * other personal purposes		('000)	157	165	192	206	..
1.18 ♦ Business and professional		('000)	45	38	42	47	..
Arrivals by mode of transport							
1.19 Total		('000)	524	521	572	593	671
1.20 ♦ Air		('000)	267	242	247	223	247
1.21 ♦ Water	(2)	('000)	1	1	1	1	1
1.22 ♦ Land		('000)	256	278	324	369	423
1.23 * railway		('000)	6	6	3	4	5
1.24 * road		('000)	250	272	321	365	418
1.25 * others		('000)	..	..	..	..	..
Accommodation							
Total							
1.29 ♦ Guests		('000)	..	..	..	..	..
1.30 ♦ Overnights		('000)	..	..	..	..	..
Hotels and similar establishments	(3)						
1.31 ♦ Guests		('000)	413	515	489	510	601
1.32 ♦ Overnights		('000)	1,099	871	807	819	1,018
Expenditure							
1.33 Total		US$ Mn	345	330	326	302	306
1.34 ♦ Travel		US$ Mn	239	244	292	275	279
1.35 ♦ Passenger transport		US$ Mn	106	86	34	27	27
Expenditure by main purpose of the trip							
1.36 Total		US$ Mn	238	244	292	275	279
1.37 ♦ Personal		US$ Mn	170	179	217	196	189
1.38 ♦ Business and professional		US$ Mn	68	65	75	79	90
Indicators							
1.39 Average size of travel party		Persons	..	..	..	..	..
Average length of stay							
1.40 Total		Days	..	..	..	..	..
1.41 ♦ For all commercial accommodation services	(3)	Nights	2.66	1.69	1.65	1.61	..
1.42 * of which, "hotels and similar establishments"		Nights	..	..	..	..	..
1.43 ♦ For non commercial accommodation services		Days	..	..	..	..	..
1.44 Average expenditure per day		US$	..	..	..	..	..
2. DOMESTIC TOURISM							
Data							
Accommodation							
Total							
2.19 ♦ Guests		('000)	..	..	..	..	..
2.20 ♦ Overnights		('000)	..	..	..	..	..
Hotels and similar establishments	(3)						
2.21 ♦ Guests		('000)	933	1,107	1,120	1,103	1,321
2.22 ♦ Overnights		('000)	1,644	..	..	..	1,627
Indicators							
2.23 Average size of travel party		Persons	..	..	..	..	..
Average length of stay							
2.24 Total		Days	..	..	..	..	..
2.25 ♦ For all commercial accommodation services	(3)	Nights	1.76	0.83	0.80	0.83	..
2.26 * of which, "hotels and similar establishments"		Nights	..	..	..	..	..
2.27 ♦ For non commercial accommodation services		Days	..	..	..	..	..
2.28 Average expenditure per day		US$	..	..	..	..	..

BOLIVIA

Basic data and indicators	Notes	Units	2005	2006	2007	2008	2009
3. OUTBOUND TOURISM							
Data							
Departures							
3.1 Total		('000)	..	..	..	..	..
3.2 ♦ Overnight visitors (tourists)		('000)	386	472	526	589	628
3.3 ♦ Same-day visitors (excursionists)		('000)	..	..	..	..	..
Expenditure							
3.4 Total		US$ Mn	257	360	385	381	388
3.5 ♦ Travel		US$ Mn	186	273	304	281	290
3.6 ♦ Passenger transport		US$ Mn	71	87	81	100	98
Expenditure by main purpose of the trip							
3.7 Total		US$ Mn	187	273	304	281	290
3.8 ♦ Personal		US$ Mn	140	190	202	161	176
3.9 ♦ Business and professional		US$ Mn	47	83	102	120	114
4. TOURISM INDUSTRIES							
Data							
Number of establishments							
4.1 Total		Units	..	..	..	..	..
4.2 ♦ Accommodation for visitors		Units	..	..	..	..	..
4.3 * of which, "hotels and similar establishments"	(3)	Units	1,049	1,013	1,082	1,172	1,248
4.4 ♦ Food and beverage serving activities		Units	..	..	..	..	..
4.5 ♦ Passenger transportation		Units	..	..	..	..	..
4.6 ♦ Travel agencies and other reservation services activities		Units	..	..	..	..	..
4.7 ♦ Other tourism industries		Units	..	..	..	..	..
Accommodation for visitors in hotels and similar establishments							
Non-monetary data	(3)						
4.13 ♦ Number of establishments		Units	1,049	1,013	1,082	1,172	1,248
4.14 ♦ Number of rooms		Units	21,999	21,791	22,923	22,954	22,982
4.15 ♦ Number of bed-places		Units	36,242	35,641	37,254	37,314	37,360
Indicators							
4.16 Occupancy rate / rooms		Percent	..	..	..	..	..
4.17 Occupancy rate / bed-places		Percent	21.04	..	27.92	..	..
4.18 Average length of stay	(4)	Nights	2.04	..	..	..	..
4.19 Available capacity (bed-places per 1000 inhabitants)		Units	3.95	3.81	3.91	3.85	3.79
6. COMPLEMENTARY INDICATORS							
Demand							
6.1 Gross travel propensity		Units	..	..	..	..	..
6.2 Carrying capacity (arrivals/population)		Units	0.06	0.06	0.06	0.06	0.07
Macroeconomic indicators related to international tourism							
6.3 Inbound tourism expenditure over GDP		Percent	3.6	2.9	2.5	1.8	..
6.4 Outbound tourism expenditure over GDP		Percent	2.7	3.1	2.9	2.3	..
6.5 Tourism balance (inbound minus outbound tourism expenditure) over GDP		Percent	0.9	-0.3	-0.4	-0.5	..
6.6 Tourism openness (inbound plus outbound tourism expenditure) over GDP		Percent	6.3	6.0	5.4	4.1	..
6.7 Tourism coverage (inbound over outbound tourism expenditure)		Percent	134.0	91.8	84.8	79.2	..
6.8 Inbound tourism expenditure over exports of goods		Percent	12.3	8.5	7.3	4.7	..
6.9 Inbound tourism expenditure over exports of services		Percent	70.5	69.3	65.3	60.4	..
6.10 Inbound tourism expenditure over exports of goods and services		Percent	10.5	7.6	6.6	4.3	..
6.11 Inbound tourism expenditure over current account credits		Percent	8.5	6.0	4.9	3.5	..
6.12 Outbound tourism expenditure over imports of goods		Percent	11.8	13.7	11.9	8.2	..
6.13 Outbound tourism expenditure over imports of services		Percent	37.7	43.5	42.8	36.7	..
6.14 Outbound tourism expenditure over imports of goods and services		Percent	9.0	10.4	9.3	6.7	..
6.15 Outbound tourism expenditure over current account debits		Percent	7.5	8.6	7.6	5.7	..

BONAIRE

Basic data and indicators	Notes	Units	2005	2006	2007	2008	2009
1. INBOUND TOURISM							
Data							
Arrivals							
1.1 Total		('000)	103	126	172	250	280
1.2 ♦ Overnight visitors (tourists)		('000)	63	64	74	74	67
1.3 ♦ Same-day visitors (excursionists)		('000)	40	62	98	176	213
1.4 * of which, cruise passengers		('000)	40	62	98	176	213
Arrivals by region							
1.5 Total		('000)	62	63	73	74	67
1.6 ♦ Africa		('000)	..	..	..	..	..
1.7 ♦ Americas		('000)	32	35	42	43	36
1.8 ♦ East Asia and the Pacific		('000)	..	..	..	..	..
1.9 ♦ Europe		('000)	30	28	31	31	30
1.10 ♦ Middle East		('000)	..	..	..	..	..
1.11 ♦ South Asia		('000)	..	..	..	..	..
1.12 ♦ Other not classified		('000)	..	..	..	..	1
1.13 * of which, nationals residing abroad		('000)	..	..	..	..	..
Arrivals by mode of transport							
1.19 Total		('000)	103	126	172	250	280
1.20 ♦ Air		('000)	63	64	74	74	67
1.21 ♦ Water		('000)	40	62	98	176	213
1.22 ♦ Land		('000)	..	..	..	..	..
1.23 * railway		('000)	..	..	..	..	..
1.24 * road		('000)	..	..	..	..	..
1.25 * others		('000)	..	..	..	..	..
Accommodation							
Total							
1.29 ♦ Guests		('000)	..	..	..	..	..
1.30 ♦ Overnights		('000)	566	621	732	694	670
Hotels and similar establishments							
1.31 ♦ Guests		('000)	..	..	..	..	..
1.32 ♦ Overnights		('000)	428	435	496	501	461
Expenditure							
1.33 Total		US$ Mn	..	..	..	..	..
1.34 ♦ Travel	(1)	US$ Mn	87	91	110	121	107
1.35 ♦ Passenger transport		US$ Mn	..	..	..	..	..
Indicators							
1.39 Average size of travel party		Persons	..	..	..	..	..
Average length of stay							
1.40 Total		Days	..	..	..	..	..
1.41 ♦ For all commercial accommodation services		Nights	9.66	9.77	9.87	9.31	10.10
1.42 * of which, "hotels and similar establishments"		Nights	..	..	..	..	..
1.43 ♦ For non commercial accommodation services		Days	..	..	..	..	..
1.44 Average expenditure per day		US$	..	..	..	..	..
3. OUTBOUND TOURISM							
Data							
Expenditure							
3.4 Total		US$ Mn	..	..	..	..	..
3.5 ♦ Travel	(1)	US$ Mn	5	5	6	7	7
3.6 ♦ Passenger transport		US$ Mn	..	..	..	..	..

BONAIRE

Basic data and indicators	Notes	Units	2005	2006	2007	2008	2009
4. TOURISM INDUSTRIES							
Data							
Number of establishments							
4.1 Total		Units	..	..	..	..	..
4.2 ♦ Accommodation for visitors		Units	..	..	..	..	..
4.3 * of which, "hotels and similar establishments"		Units	55	63	83	83	82
4.4 ♦ Food and beverage serving activities		Units	..	..	..	..	..
4.5 ♦ Passenger transportation		Units	..	..	..	..	..
4.6 ♦ Travel agencies and other reservation services activities		Units	..	..	..	..	..
4.7 ♦ Other tourism industries		Units	..	..	..	..	..
Accommodation for visitors in hotels and similar establishments							
Non-monetary data							
4.13 ♦ Number of establishments		Units	55	63	83	83	82
4.14 ♦ Number of rooms		Units	1,172	1,157	1,258	1,256	1,246
4.15 ♦ Number of bed-places		Units	3,256	3,758	3,837	3,836	3,972
Indicators							
4.16 Occupancy rate / rooms		Percent	..	..	..	..	..
4.17 Occupancy rate / bed-places		Percent	64.00	66.00	78.00	69.00	67.00
4.18 Average length of stay		Nights	..	..	..	..	..
4.19 Available capacity (bed-places per 1000 inhabitants)		Units	..	..	..	..	..

BOSNIA AND HERZEGOVINA

Basic data and indicators	Notes	Units	2005	2006	2007	2008	2009
1. INBOUND TOURISM							
Data							
Arrivals							
1.1 Total		('000)	..	..	..	..	..
1.2 ♦ Overnight visitors (tourists)	(1)	('000)	217	256	306	322	311
1.3 ♦ Same-day visitors (excursionists)		('000)	..	..	..	..	..
1.4 * of which, cruise passengers		('000)	..	..	..	..	..
Arrivals by region	(1)						
1.5 Total		('000)	217	255	305	321	310
1.6 ♦ Africa	(2)	('000)	..	..	..	..	..
1.7 ♦ Americas		('000)	8	10	10	9	8
1.8 ♦ East Asia and the Pacific		('000)	2	3	4	5	4
1.9 ♦ Europe		('000)	204	239	286	301	292
1.10 ♦ Middle East	(2)	('000)	..	..	..	..	..
1.11 ♦ South Asia	(2)	('000)	..	..	..	..	..
1.12 ♦ Other not classified		('000)	3	3	5	6	6
1.13 * of which, nationals residing abroad		('000)	..	..	..	..	..
Accommodation							
Total							
1.29 ♦ Guests		('000)	217	256	306	322	311
1.30 ♦ Overnights		('000)	485	594	695	719	671
Hotels and similar establishments							
1.31 ♦ Guests		('000)	..	..	295	311	299
1.32 ♦ Overnights		('000)	..	..	672	697	646
Expenditure							
1.33 Total		US$ Mn	557	658	809	920	761
1.34 ♦ Travel		US$ Mn	519	607	729	826	681
1.35 ♦ Passenger transport		US$ Mn	38	51	80	94	80
Expenditure by main purpose of the trip							
1.36 Total		US$ Mn	519	607	729	826	681
1.37 ♦ Personal		US$ Mn	474	562	680	774	636
1.38 ♦ Business and professional		US$ Mn	45	45	49	52	45
Indicators							
1.39 Average size of travel party		Persons	..	..	..	..	..
Average length of stay							
1.40 Total		Days	..	..	..	..	..
1.41 ♦ For all commercial accommodation services		Nights	..	..	2.30	2.20	2.20
1.42 * of which, "hotels and similar establishments"		Nights	..	..	..	..	..
1.43 ♦ For non commercial accommodation services		Days	..	..	..	..	..
1.44 Average expenditure per day		US$	..	..	..	..	..
2. DOMESTIC TOURISM							
Data							
Accommodation							
Total							
2.19 ♦ Guests		('000)	..	..	277	289	262
2.20 ♦ Overnights		('000)	533	583	642	678	597
Hotels and similar establishments							
2.21 ♦ Guests		('000)	..	..	265	275	246
2.22 ♦ Overnights		('000)	..	..	598	625	539
Indicators							
2.23 Average size of travel party		Persons	..	..	..	..	..
Average length of stay							
2.24 Total		Days	..	..	..	..	..
2.25 ♦ For all commercial accommodation services		Nights	..	..	2.30	2.30	2.30
2.26 * of which, "hotels and similar establishments"		Nights	..	..	..	..	..
2.27 ♦ For non commercial accommodation services		Days	..	..	..	..	..
2.28 Average expenditure per day		US$	..	..	..	..	..

BOSNIA AND HERZEGOVINA

Basic data and indicators	Notes	Units	2005	2006	2007	2008	2009
3. OUTBOUND TOURISM							
Data							
Expenditure							
3.4 Total		US$ Mn	158	210	257	360	284
3.5 ♦ Travel		US$ Mn	122	170	203	304	236
3.6 ♦ Passenger transport		US$ Mn	36	40	54	56	48
Expenditure by main purpose of the trip							
3.7 Total		US$ Mn	122	170	203	304	236
3.8 ♦ Personal		US$ Mn	90	136	162	263	201
3.9 ♦ Business and professional		US$ Mn	32	34	41	41	35
4. TOURISM INDUSTRIES							
Data							
Accommodation for visitors in hotels and similar establishments							
Non-monetary data							
4.13 ♦ Number of establishments		Units	..	..	..	..	..
4.14 ♦ Number of rooms	(3)	Units	8,687	9,030	10,789	11,064	11,757
4.15 ♦ Number of bed-places	(3)	Units	18,164	20,036	22,442	23,015	24,471
Indicators							
4.16 Occupancy rate / rooms		Percent	..	..	..	..	..
4.17 Occupancy rate / bed-places		Percent	..	..	..	..	..
4.18 Average length of stay		Nights	..	..	..	..	..
4.19 Available capacity (bed-places per 1000 inhabitants)		Units	4.80	5.30	5.94	6.10	6.50
6. COMPLEMENTARY INDICATORS							
Demand							
6.1 Gross travel propensity		Units	..	..	..	..	..
6.2 Carrying capacity (arrivals/population)		Units	0.06	0.07	0.08	0.09	0.08
Macroeconomic indicators related to international tourism							
6.3 Inbound tourism expenditure over GDP		Percent	4.8	4.8	4.7	4.4	..
6.4 Outbound tourism expenditure over GDP		Percent	1.4	1.6	1.5	1.7	..
6.5 Tourism balance (inbound minus outbound tourism expenditure) over GDP		Percent	3.4	3.2	3.2	2.7	..
6.6 Tourism openness (inbound plus outbound tourism expenditure) over GDP		Percent	6.2	6.4	6.2	6.1	..
6.7 Tourism coverage (inbound over outbound tourism expenditure)		Percent	350.4	309.2	313.9	255.5	268.8
6.8 Inbound tourism expenditure over exports of goods		Percent	21.8	19.5	19.1	17.7	18.7
6.9 Inbound tourism expenditure over exports of services		Percent	56.3	57.8	55.5	55.3	55.2
6.10 Inbound tourism expenditure over exports of goods and services		Percent	15.7	14.6	14.2	13.4	14.0
6.11 Inbound tourism expenditure over current account credits		Percent	8.7	8.6	8.4	8.3	8.6
6.12 Outbound tourism expenditure over imports of goods		Percent	2.1	2.8	2.6	2.9	3.2
6.13 Outbound tourism expenditure over imports of services		Percent	36.5	45.0	44.6	50.1	44.6
6.14 Outbound tourism expenditure over imports of goods and services		Percent	2.0	2.6	2.4	2.8	3.0
6.15 Outbound tourism expenditure over current account debits		Percent	1.9	2.5	2.3	2.6	2.8

BOTSWANA

Basic data and indicators	Notes	Units	2005	2006	2007	2008	2009
1. INBOUND TOURISM							
Data							
Arrivals							
1.1 Total		('000)	1,684	1,642	1,760	1,814	1,877
1.2 ♦ Overnight visitors (tourists)		('000)	1,474	1,426	1,455	1,500	1,553
1.3 ♦ Same-day visitors (excursionists)		('000)	210	216	305	314	324
1.4 * of which, cruise passengers		('000)	..	..	..	..	..
Arrivals by region							
1.5 Total		('000)	..	1,426	1,455	..	..
1.6 ♦ Africa		('000)	..	1,240	1,297	..	..
1.7 ♦ Americas		('000)	..	25	29	..	..
1.8 ♦ East Asia and the Pacific		('000)	..	15	15	..	..
1.9 ♦ Europe		('000)	..	67	68	..	..
1.10 ♦ Middle East		('000)	..	..	..	..	..
1.11 ♦ South Asia		('000)	..	4	2	..	..
1.12 ♦ Other not classified		('000)	..	75	44	..	..
1.13 * of which, nationals residing abroad		('000)	..	..	..	..	..
Arrivals by main purpose							
1.14 Total		('000)	1,474	1,426	1,455	1,500	1,553
1.15 ♦ Personal		('000)	1,396	1,349	1,370	1,414	1,465
1.16 * holidays, leisure and recreation		('000)	254	260	257	264	273
1.17 * other personal purposes		('000)	1,142	1,089	1,113	1,150	1,192
1.18 ♦ Business and professional		('000)	78	77	85	86	88
Arrivals by mode of transport							
1.19 Total		('000)	..	1,426	1,455	..	..
1.20 ♦ Air		('000)	..	68	69	..	..
1.21 ♦ Water		('000)	..	..	..	..	..
1.22 ♦ Land		('000)	..	1,358	1,386	..	..
1.23 * railway		('000)	..	37	76	..	..
1.24 * road		('000)	..	1,320	1,310	..	..
1.25 * others		('000)	..	1	..	..	..
Accommodation							
Total							
1.29 ♦ Guests		('000)	..	..	..	..	..
1.30 ♦ Overnights		('000)	..	..	..	..	..
Hotels and similar establishments							
1.31 ♦ Guests		('000)	271	..	..	..	..
1.32 ♦ Overnights		('000)	..	..	..	..	..
Expenditure							
1.33 Total		US$ Mn	563	539	549	555	454
1.34 ♦ Travel		US$ Mn	562	537	546	553	452
1.35 ♦ Passenger transport		US$ Mn	1	2	3	2	2
Expenditure by main purpose of the trip							
1.36 Total		US$ Mn	562	537	546	553	451
1.37 ♦ Personal		US$ Mn	365	349	349	360	309
1.38 ♦ Business and professional		US$ Mn	197	188	197	193	142
2. DOMESTIC TOURISM							
Data							
Accommodation							
Total							
2.19 ♦ Guests		('000)	..	..	..	..	..
2.20 ♦ Overnights		('000)	..	..	..	..	..
Hotels and similar establishments							
2.21 ♦ Guests		('000)	145	..	..	..	..
2.22 ♦ Overnights		('000)	..	..	..	..	..
3. OUTBOUND TOURISM							
Data							
Expenditure							
3.4 Total		US$ Mn	301	285	284	286	231
3.5 ♦ Travel		US$ Mn	282	277	281	284	230
3.6 ♦ Passenger transport		US$ Mn	19	8	3	2	1
Expenditure by main purpose of the trip							
3.7 Total		US$ Mn	283	276	281	284	230
3.8 ♦ Personal		US$ Mn	215	210	211	216	168
3.9 ♦ Business and professional		US$ Mn	68	66	70	68	62

BOTSWANA

Basic data and indicators	Notes	Units	2005	2006	2007	2008	2009
4. TOURISM INDUSTRIES							
Data							
Accommodation for visitors in hotels and similar establishments							
Non-monetary data							
4.13 ♦ Number of establishments		Units	..	..	..	..	..
4.14 ♦ Number of rooms		Units	4,795	4,801	4,832	4,942	..
4.15 ♦ Number of bed-places		Units	8,040	8,468	8,509	8,681	..
Indicators							
4.16 Occupancy rate / rooms		Percent	41.50	54.40	35.60	40.30	..
4.17 Occupancy rate / bed-places		Percent	36.00	43.90	27.20	36.10	..
4.18 Average length of stay		Nights	2.50	2.10	2.00	2.70	..
4.19 Available capacity (bed-places per 1000 inhabitants)		Units	4.37	4.54	4.50	4.52	..
6. COMPLEMENTARY INDICATORS							
Demand							
6.1 Gross travel propensity		Units	..	..	..	..	..
6.2 Carrying capacity (arrivals/population)		Units	0.80	0.76	0.77	0.78	0.80
Macroeconomic indicators related to international tourism							
6.3 Inbound tourism expenditure over GDP		Percent	5.5	4.8	2.1	3.8	..
6.4 Outbound tourism expenditure over GDP		Percent	2.9	2.5	3.6	3.6	..
6.5 Tourism balance (inbound minus outbound tourism expenditure) over GDP		Percent	2.5	2.3	-1.5	0.2	..
6.6 Tourism openness (inbound plus outbound tourism expenditure) over GDP		Percent	8.4	7.3	5.8	7.5	..
6.7 Tourism coverage (inbound over outbound tourism expenditure)		Percent	186.4	189.9	59.2	105.2	..
6.8 Inbound tourism expenditure over exports of goods		Percent	12.7	11.9	5.3	10.9	..
6.9 Inbound tourism expenditure over exports of services		Percent	65.7	70.0	46.6	58.6	..
6.10 Inbound tourism expenditure over exports of goods and services		Percent	10.6	10.2	4.7	9.2	..
6.11 Inbound tourism expenditure over current account credits		Percent	8.5	7.8	3.6	6.9	..
6.12 Outbound tourism expenditure over imports of goods		Percent	11.2	10.9	13.0	10.9	..
6.13 Outbound tourism expenditure over imports of services		Percent	35.2	34.0	37.6	36.3	..
6.14 Outbound tourism expenditure over imports of goods and services		Percent	8.5	8.2	9.7	8.4	..
6.15 Outbound tourism expenditure over current account debits		Percent	6.0	5.7	7.4	7.1	..

BRAZIL

Basic data and indicators	Notes	Units	2005	2006	2007	2008	2009
1. INBOUND TOURISM							
Data							
Arrivals							
1.1 Total		('000)	..	..	..	..	..
1.2 ♦ Overnight visitors (tourists)	(1)	('000)	5,358	5,017	5,026	5,050	4,802
1.3 ♦ Same-day visitors (excursionists)		('000)	..	..	..	..	..
1.4 * of which, cruise passengers		('000)	..	..	..	..	..
Arrivals by region	(1)						
1.5 Total		('000)	5,358	5,017	5,026	5,050	4,802
1.6 ♦ Africa		('000)	76	84	75	76	78
1.7 ♦ Americas		('000)	2,998	2,717	2,779	2,884	2,862
1.8 ♦ East Asia and the Pacific		('000)	177	217	206	256	208
1.9 ♦ Europe		('000)	2,097	1,980	1,938	1,814	1,642
1.10 ♦ Middle East		('000)	7	18	26	..	..
1.11 ♦ South Asia		('000)	..	..	..	19	11
1.12 ♦ Other not classified		('000)	3	1	2	1	1
1.13 * of which, nationals residing abroad		('000)	..	..	..	..	..
Arrivals by main purpose	(1)						
1.14 Total		('000)	5,358	5,017	5,026	5,050	4,802
1.15 ♦ Personal		('000)	3,799	3,607	3,649	3,676	3,702
1.16 * holidays, leisure and recreation		('000)	2,588	2,383	2,428	2,312	2,353
1.17 * other personal purposes		('000)	1,211	1,224	1,221	1,364	1,349
1.18 ♦ Business and professional		('000)	1,559	1,410	1,377	1,374	1,100
Arrivals by mode of transport	(1)						
1.19 Total		('000)	5,358	5,017	5,026	5,050	4,802
1.20 ♦ Air		('000)	3,938	3,713	3,747	3,691	3,349
1.21 ♦ Water	(2)	('000)	106	123	129	110	154
1.22 ♦ Land		('000)	1,314	1,181	1,150	1,249	1,299
1.23 * railway		('000)	..	..	..	..	..
1.24 * road		('000)	1,314	1,181	1,150	1,249	1,299
1.25 * others		('000)	..	..	..	..	..
Expenditure							
1.33 Total		US$ Mn	4,168	4,577	5,284	6,109	5,635
1.34 ♦ Travel		US$ Mn	3,861	4,316	4,953	5,785	5,305
1.35 ♦ Passenger transport		US$ Mn	307	261	331	324	330
Expenditure by main purpose of the trip							
1.36 Total		US$ Mn	3,862	4,316	4,953	5,785	5,305
1.37 ♦ Personal		US$ Mn	3,794	4,253	4,883	5,701	5,235
1.38 ♦ Business and professional		US$ Mn	68	63	70	84	70
3. OUTBOUND TOURISM							
Data							
Departures							
3.1 Total		('000)	..	..	..	..	..
3.2 ♦ Overnight visitors (tourists)		('000)	3,466	3,930	4,683	5,181	4,952
3.3 ♦ Same-day visitors (excursionists)		('000)	..	..	..	..	..
Expenditure							
3.4 Total		US$ Mn	5,905	7,501	10,434	13,269	12,897
3.5 ♦ Travel		US$ Mn	4,720	5,764	8,211	10,962	10,898
3.6 ♦ Passenger transport		US$ Mn	1,185	1,737	2,223	2,307	1,999
Expenditure by main purpose of the trip							
3.7 Total		US$ Mn	4,720	5,763	8,211	10,961	10,898
3.8 ♦ Personal		US$ Mn	4,429	5,444	7,841	10,455	10,524
3.9 ♦ Business and professional		US$ Mn	291	319	370	506	374
4. TOURISM INDUSTRIES	(3)						
Data							
Number of establishments							
4.1 Total		Units	..	..	..	..	..
4.2 ♦ Accommodation for visitors		Units	..	..	..	..	..
4.3 * of which, "hotels and similar establishments"		Units	..	..	..	..	17,189
4.4 ♦ Food and beverage serving activities		Units	..	..	..	..	..
4.5 ♦ Passenger transportation		Units	..	..	..	..	..
4.6 ♦ Travel agencies and other reservation services activities		Units	..	..	..	..	..
4.7 ♦ Other tourism industries		Units	..	..	..	..	..

BRAZIL

Basic data and indicators	Notes	Units	2005	2006	2007	2008	2009
Accommodation for visitors in hotels and similar establishments							
Non-monetary data							
4.13 ♦ Number of establishments		Units	..	..	..	..	17,189
4.14 ♦ Number of rooms		Units	..	..	..	..	963,576
4.15 ♦ Number of bed-places		Units	..	..	..	..	2,160,568
Indicators							
4.16 Occupancy rate / rooms		Percent	..	..	..	..	..
4.17 Occupancy rate / bed-places		Percent	..	..	..	..	..
4.18 Average length of stay		Nights	..	..	..	..	..
4.19 Available capacity (bed-places per 1000 inhabitants)		Units	..	..	..	..	11.15
5. EMPLOYMENT							
Data							
Number of employees by tourism industries	**(4)**						
5.1 Total		('000)	746.3	784.5	830.0	878.7	..
5.2 ♦ Accommodation services for visitors (hotels and similar establishments)		('000)	164.1	177.9	186.0	192.7	..
5.3 ♦ Other accommodation services		('000)	..	..	..	..	..
5.4 ♦ Food and beverage serving activities		('000)	140.0	152.6	168.6	184.6	..
5.5 ♦ Passenger transportation		('000)	345.1	345.7	359.6	374.8	..
5.6 ♦ Travel agencies and other reservation services activities		('000)	37.1	40.3	41.8	46.6	..
5.7 ♦ Other tourism industries		('000)	60.0	68.0	74.0	80.0	..
Number of jobs by status in employment							
5.8 Total		('000)	1,796.5	1,837.0	1,910.1	1,995.7	..
5.9 ♦ Employees	(4)	('000)	746.3	784.5	830.0	878.7	..
5.10 ♦ Self employed	(5)	('000)	1050.2	1052.5	1080.1	1117.0	..
Indicators							
Number of full-time equivalent jobs by status in employment							
5.11 Total		('000)	..	..	..	1,858.7	..
5.12 ♦ Employees	(4)	('000)	746.3	784.5	860.0	878.9	..
5.13 * male		('000)	..	..	..	573.1	..
5.14 * female		('000)	..	..	..	305.8	..
5.15 ♦ Self employed	(6)	('000)	..	..	..	979.8	..
5.16 * male		('000)	..	..	..	679.0	..
5.17 * female		('000)	..	..	..	300.8	..
6. COMPLEMENTARY INDICATORS							
Demand							
6.1 Gross travel propensity		Units	..	..	..	..	..
6.2 Carrying capacity (arrivals/population)		Units	0.03	0.03	0.03	0.03	0.02
Macroeconomic indicators related to international tourism							
6.3 Inbound tourism expenditure over GDP		Percent	0.5	0.4	0.4	0.4	0.4
6.4 Outbound tourism expenditure over GDP		Percent	0.7	0.7	0.8	0.8	0.8
6.5 Tourism balance (inbound minus outbound tourism expenditure) over GDP		Percent	-0.2	-0.3	-0.4	-0.4	-0.5
6.6 Tourism openness (inbound plus outbound tourism expenditure) over GDP		Percent	1.1	1.1	1.1	1.2	1.2
6.7 Tourism coverage (inbound over outbound tourism expenditure)		Percent	70.6	61.0	50.6	46.0	43.7
6.8 Inbound tourism expenditure over exports of goods		Percent	3.5	3.3	3.3	3.1	3.7
6.9 Inbound tourism expenditure over exports of services		Percent	26.0	23.5	22.1	20.1	20.3
6.10 Inbound tourism expenditure over exports of goods and services		Percent	3.1	2.9	2.9	2.7	3.1
6.11 Inbound tourism expenditure over current account credits		Percent	2.9	2.7	2.6	2.5	2.9
6.12 Outbound tourism expenditure over imports of goods		Percent	8.0	8.2	8.7	7.7	10.1
6.13 Outbound tourism expenditure over imports of services		Percent	24.2	25.8	28.1	28.1	27.5
6.14 Outbound tourism expenditure over imports of goods and services		Percent	6.0	6.2	6.6	6.0	7.4
6.15 Outbound tourism expenditure over current account debits		Percent	4.6	4.8	5.2	4.8	5.9

BRITISH VIRGIN ISLANDS

Basic data and indicators	Notes	Units	2005	2006	2007	2008	2009
1. INBOUND TOURISM							
Data							
Arrivals							
1.1 Total		('000)	821	825	948	934	857
1.2 ♦ Overnight visitors (tourists)		('000)	337	356	358	346	309
1.3 ♦ Same-day visitors (excursionists)		('000)	483	469	590	588	548
1.4 * of which, cruise passengers		('000)	449	444	575	572	530
Arrivals by mode of transport							
1.19 Total		('000)	821	..	..	..	..
1.20 ♦ Air		('000)	205	..	..	..	..
1.21 ♦ Water		('000)	616	..	..	..	..
1.22 ♦ Land		('000)	..	..	..	..	..
1.23 * railway		('000)	..	..	..	..	..
1.24 * road		('000)	..	..	..	..	..
1.25 * others		('000)	..	..	..	..	..
Accommodation							
Total							
1.29 ♦ Guests		('000)	337	..	..	..	..
1.30 ♦ Overnights		('000)	..	..	..	..	..
Hotels and similar establishments							
1.31 ♦ Guests		('000)	94	..	..	..	..
1.32 ♦ Overnights		('000)	..	..	..	..	..
Expenditure							
1.33 Total	(1)	US$ Mn	437	..	..	446	369
1.34 ♦ Travel		US$ Mn	..	..	..	..	..
1.35 ♦ Passenger transport		US$ Mn	..	..	..	..	..
4. TOURISM INDUSTRIES							
Data							
Accommodation for visitors in hotels and similar establishments							
Non-monetary data							
4.13 ♦ Number of establishments		Units	..	..	..	..	..
4.14 ♦ Number of rooms		Units	2,722	..	..	..	..
4.15 ♦ Number of bed-places		Units	..	..	..	..	..
Indicators							
4.16 Occupancy rate / rooms		Percent	68.60	..	..	..	..
4.17 Occupancy rate / bed-places		Percent	..	..	..	..	..
4.18 Average length of stay		Nights	9.00	..	..	..	..
4.19 Available capacity (bed-places per 1000 inhabitants)		Units	..	..	..	..	..

BRUNEI DARUSSALAM

Basic data and indicators	Notes	Units	2005	2006	2007	2008	2009
1. INBOUND TOURISM							
Data							
Arrivals							
1.1 Total		('000)	815	836	877	..	..
1.2 ♦ Overnight visitors (tourists)	(1)	('000)	126	158	179	226	157
1.3 ♦ Same-day visitors (excursionists)		('000)	689	678	..	..	..
1.4 * of which, cruise passengers		('000)	4	1	..	..	..
Arrivals by region							
1.5 Total		('000)	125	158	178	226	157
1.6 ♦ Africa		('000)	..	..	..		
1.7 ♦ Americas		('000)	3	4	5	6	5
1.8 ♦ East Asia and the Pacific		('000)	76	100	144	186	122
1.9 ♦ Europe		('000)	14	21	21	23	21
1.10 ♦ Middle East		('000)	..	1	1	..	1
1.11 ♦ South Asia		('000)	..	..	5	5	4
1.12 ♦ Other not classified		('000)	32	32	2	6	4
1.13 * of which, nationals residing abroad		('000)	..	..	..	..	..
Arrivals by main purpose	(2)						
1.14 Total		('000)	815	..	178	..	157
1.15 ♦ Personal		('000)	811	..	142	..	118
1.16 * holidays, leisure and recreation		('000)	27	..	75	..	62
1.17 * other personal purposes		('000)	784	..	67	..	56
1.18 ♦ Business and professional		('000)	4	..	36	..	39
Arrivals by mode of transport							
1.19 Total		('000)	126	158	179	226	157
1.20 ♦ Air		('000)	126	158	179	226	157
1.21 ♦ Water		('000)	..	..	..	..	..
1.22 ♦ Land		('000)	..	..	..	..	..
1.23 * railway		('000)	..	..	..	..	..
1.24 * road		('000)	..	..	..	..	..
1.25 * others		('000)	..	..	..	..	..
Accommodation							
Total							
1.29 ♦ Guests		('000)	..	..	..	..	..
1.30 ♦ Overnights		('000)	..	..	..	..	..
Hotels and similar establishments							
1.31 ♦ Guests	(2)	('000)	300	..	109	..	..
1.32 ♦ Overnights		('000)	..	..	..	..	..
Expenditure							
1.33 Total		US$ Mn	..	..	..	..	..
1.34 ♦ Travel		US$ Mn	191	224	233	242	254
1.35 ♦ Passenger transport		US$ Mn	..	..	..	..	..
3. OUTBOUND TOURISM							
Data							
Expenditure							
3.4 Total		US$ Mn	..	..	..	..	..
3.5 ♦ Travel		US$ Mn	374	408	430	459	477
3.6 ♦ Passenger transport		US$ Mn	..	..	..	..	..
4. TOURISM INDUSTRIES							
Data							
Accommodation for visitors in hotels and similar establishments							
Non-monetary data							
4.13 ♦ Number of establishments		Units	..	..	..	..	..
4.14 ♦ Number of rooms		Units	2,371	2,548	..	..	2,952
4.15 ♦ Number of bed-places		Units	3,501	..	..	..	..
Indicators							
4.16 Occupancy rate / rooms		Percent	..	..	..	..	..
4.17 Occupancy rate / bed-places		Percent	39.30	..	..	..	..
4.18 Average length of stay		Nights	..	..	..	..	..
4.19 Available capacity (bed-places per 1000 inhabitants)		Units	9.46	..	..	..	..

BRUNEI DARUSSALAM

Basic data and indicators	Notes	Units	2005	2006	2007	2008	2009
6. COMPLEMENTARY INDICATORS							
Demand							
6.1 Gross travel propensity		Units	..	..	..	..	..
6.2 Carrying capacity (arrivals/population)		Units	0.34	0.42	0.47	0.58	0.39
Macroeconomic indicators related to international tourism							
6.3 Inbound tourism expenditure over GDP		Percent	2.0	1.9	1.9	1.7	..
6.4 Outbound tourism expenditure over GDP		Percent	3.9	3.5	3.5	3.2	..
6.5 Tourism balance (inbound minus outbound tourism expenditure) over GDP		Percent	-1.9	-1.6	-1.6	-1.5	..
6.6 Tourism openness (inbound plus outbound tourism expenditure) over GDP		Percent	5.9	5.5	5.4	4.9	..
6.7 Tourism coverage (inbound over outbound tourism expenditure)		Percent	51.2	54.8	54.1	52.8	..
6.8 Inbound tourism expenditure over exports of goods		Percent	3.1	2.9	3.0	2.3	..
6.9 Inbound tourism expenditure over exports of services		Percent	31.1	30.1	28.6	27.9	..
6.10 Inbound tourism expenditure over exports of goods and services		Percent	2.8	2.7	2.7	2.1	..
6.11 Inbound tourism expenditure over current account credits		Percent	2.7	2.6	2.7	2.0	..
6.12 Outbound tourism expenditure over imports of goods		Percent	26.5	25.7	21.6	16.1	..
6.13 Outbound tourism expenditure over imports of services		Percent	33.7	33.7	32.7	32.7	..
6.14 Outbound tourism expenditure over imports of goods and services		Percent	14.8	14.6	13.0	10.8	..
6.15 Outbound tourism expenditure over current account debits		Percent	12.1	12.0	10.9	9.3	..

BULGARIA

Basic data and indicators	Notes	Units	2005	2006	2007	2008	2009
1. INBOUND TOURISM							
Data							
Arrivals							
1.1 Total		('000)	7,282	7,499	7,726	8,533	7,873
1.2 ♦ Overnight visitors (tourists)		('000)	4,837	5,158	5,151	5,780	5,739
1.3 ♦ Same-day visitors (excursionists)	(1)	('000)	2,445	2,341	2,574	2,753	2,134
1.4 * of which, cruise passengers		('000)	..	..	..	..	..
Arrivals by region							
1.5 Total		('000)	7,282	7,499	7,726	8,533	7,872
1.6 ♦ Africa		('000)	3	3	2	2	2
1.7 ♦ Americas		('000)	77	85	90	92	82
1.8 ♦ East Asia and the Pacific		('000)	35	38	44	48	42
1.9 ♦ Europe		('000)	7,088	7,287	7,372	8,261	7,602
1.10 ♦ Middle East		('000)	18	14	19	22	21
1.11 ♦ South Asia		('000)	11	13	15	21	23
1.12 ♦ Other not classified		('000)	50	59	184	87	100
1.13 * of which, nationals residing abroad		('000)	..	..	..	..	..
Arrivals by main purpose							
1.14 Total		('000)	7,282	7,499	7,726	8,533	7,873
1.15 ♦ Personal		('000)	6,942	7,167	7,350	8,115	6,798
1.16 * holidays, leisure and recreation		('000)	4,090	4,365	4,219	4,766	3,810
1.17 * other personal purposes		('000)	2,852	2,802	3,131	3,349	2,988
1.18 ♦ Business and professional		('000)	340	332	376	418	1,075
Arrivals by mode of transport							
1.19 Total		('000)	7,282	7,499	7,726	..	..
1.20 ♦ Air		('000)	2,007	2,203	2,318	..	..
1.21 ♦ Water	(2)	('000)	178	169	211	..	..
1.22 ♦ Land		('000)	5,097	5,127	5,197	..	..
1.23 * railway		('000)	157	173	178	..	..
1.24 * road		('000)	4,940	4,954	5,019	..	..
1.25 * others		('000)	..	..	..	..	..
Accommodation							
Total							
1.29 ♦ Guests		('000)	1,936	2,054	2,232	2,226	1,948
1.30 ♦ Overnights		('000)	11,624	11,960	12,022	11,802	9,472
Hotels and similar establishments							
1.31 ♦ Guests		('000)	1,909	2,023	2,206	2,205	1,931
1.32 ♦ Overnights		('000)	11,471	11,776	11,868	11,641	9,378
Expenditure							
1.33 Total		US$ Mn	3,063	3,317	4,181	4,852	4,273
1.34 ♦ Travel		US$ Mn	2,412	2,612	3,713	4,306	3,776
1.35 ♦ Passenger transport		US$ Mn	651	705	468	546	497
Expenditure by main purpose of the trip							
1.36 Total		US$ Mn	2,412	2,611	3,713	4,306	3,776
1.37 ♦ Personal		US$ Mn	2,138	2,320	2,820	3,292	2,877
1.38 ♦ Business and professional		US$ Mn	274	291	893	1,014	899
Indicators							
1.39 Average size of travel party		Persons	..	..	..	..	..
Average length of stay							
1.40 Total		Days	..	..	..	..	..
1.41 ♦ For all commercial accommodation services		Nights	6.01	5.82	5.39	..	..
1.42 * of which, "hotels and similar establishments"		Nights	..	..	..	..	..
1.43 ♦ For non commercial accommodation services		Days	..	..	..	..	..
1.44 Average expenditure per day		US$	..	..	..	..	..
2. DOMESTIC TOURISM							
Data							
Accommodation							
Total							
2.19 ♦ Guests		('000)	1,894	2,232	2,582	2,799	2,443
2.20 ♦ Overnights		('000)	4,447	5,467	6,059	6,493	5,900
Hotels and similar establishments							
2.21 ♦ Guests		('000)	1,721	1,921	2,228	2,442	2,100
2.22 ♦ Overnights		('000)	3,957	4,342	4,867	5,370	4,676
Indicators							
2.23 Average size of travel party		Persons	..	..	..	..	..
Average length of stay							
2.24 Total		Days	..	..	..	..	..
2.25 ♦ For all commercial accommodation services		Nights	2.35	2.45	2.35	2.32	2.42
2.26 * of which, "hotels and similar establishments"		Nights	2.30	2.26	2.18	2.20	2.23
2.27 ♦ For non commercial accommodation services		Days	..	..	..	..	..
2.28 Average expenditure per day		US$	..	..	..	..	..

BULGARIA

Basic data and indicators	Notes	Units	2005	2006	2007	2008	2009
3. OUTBOUND TOURISM							
Data							
Departures							
3.1 Total		('000)	..	..	..	..	..
3.2 ♦ Overnight visitors (tourists)		('000)	4,235	4,180	4,515	5,727	4,993
3.3 ♦ Same-day visitors (excursionists)		('000)	..	..	..	..	..
Expenditure							
3.4 Total		US$ Mn	1,858	2,099	2,142	2,602	1,955
3.5 ♦ Travel		US$ Mn	1,309	1,478	1,880	2,311	1,755
3.6 ♦ Passenger transport		US$ Mn	549	621	262	291	200
Expenditure by main purpose of the trip							
3.7 Total		US$ Mn	1,308	1,477	1,880	2,311	1,755
3.8 ♦ Personal		US$ Mn	365	408	1,194	1,485	1,191
3.9 ♦ Business and professional		US$ Mn	943	1,069	686	826	564
4. TOURISM INDUSTRIES							
Data							
Number of establishments							
4.1 Total		Units	..	..	..	..	..
4.2 ♦ Accommodation for visitors		Units	1,555	2,887	3,300	3,217	3,533
4.3 * of which, "hotels and similar establishments"		Units	1,230	1,348	1,526	1,646	1,784
4.4 ♦ Food and beverage serving activities		Units	..	..	..	..	..
4.5 ♦ Passenger transportation		Units	..	..	..	..	..
4.6 ♦ Travel agencies and other reservation services activities		Units	..	180	360	246	180
4.7 ♦ Other tourism industries		Units	..	..	..	..	..
Accommodation for visitors in hotels and similar establishments							
Non-monetary data							
4.13 ♦ Number of establishments		Units	1,230	1,348	1,526	1,646	1,784
4.14 ♦ Number of rooms		Units	..	..	..	..	..
4.15 ♦ Number of bed-places	(3)	Units	200,940	211,565	231,303	239,706	249,193
Indicators							
4.16 Occupancy rate / rooms		Percent	..	..	..	..	..
4.17 Occupancy rate / bed-places	(3)	Percent	37.60	35.80	33.20	32.10	26.30
4.18 Average length of stay		Nights	4.20	4.07	3.80	3.60	3.50
4.19 Available capacity (bed-places per 1000 inhabitants)		Units	25.96	27.48	30.20	31.44	32.85
6. COMPLEMENTARY INDICATORS							
Demand							
6.1 Gross travel propensity		Units	..	..	..	..	..
6.2 Carrying capacity (arrivals/population)		Units	0.62	0.67	0.67	0.76	0.76
Macroeconomic indicators related to international tourism							
6.3 Inbound tourism expenditure over GDP		Percent	11.3	10.5	10.6	9.7	9.1
6.4 Outbound tourism expenditure over GDP		Percent	6.8	6.6	5.4	5.2	4.2
6.5 Tourism balance (inbound minus outbound tourism expenditure) over GDP		Percent	4.4	3.9	5.2	4.5	4.9
6.6 Tourism openness (inbound plus outbound tourism expenditure) over GDP		Percent	18.1	17.1	16.0	14.9	13.2
6.7 Tourism coverage (inbound over outbound tourism expenditure)		Percent	164.8	158.1	195.2	186.5	218.5
6.8 Inbound tourism expenditure over exports of goods		Percent	26.1	22.0	21.5	21.6	25.9
6.9 Inbound tourism expenditure over exports of services		Percent	69.5	62.7	61.2	60.7	62.5
6.10 Inbound tourism expenditure over exports of goods and services		Percent	19.0	16.3	15.9	15.9	18.3
6.11 Inbound tourism expenditure over current account credits		Percent	16.2	14.4	14.3	14.1	16.1
6.12 Outbound tourism expenditure over imports of goods		Percent	10.8	9.5	7.1	7.4	8.8
6.13 Outbound tourism expenditure over imports of services		Percent	54.6	51.1	41.2	43.7	42.3
6.14 Outbound tourism expenditure over imports of goods and services		Percent	9.0	8.0	6.1	6.3	7.3
6.15 Outbound tourism expenditure over current account debits		Percent	8.3	7.3	5.3	5.6	6.3

BURKINA FASO

Basic data and indicators	Notes	Units	2005	2006	2007	2008	2009
1. INBOUND TOURISM							
Data							
Arrivals							
1.1 Total		('000)	..	..	..	..	..
1.2 ♦ Overnight visitors (tourists)	(1)	('000)	245	264	289	272	269
1.3 ♦ Same-day visitors (excursionists)		('000)	..	..	..	..	..
1.4 * of which, cruise passengers		('000)	..	..	..	..	..
Arrivals by region	(1)						
1.5 Total		('000)	245	263	289	272	269
1.6 ♦ Africa		('000)	101	108	121	113	119
1.7 ♦ Americas		('000)	15	16	20	18	18
1.8 ♦ East Asia and the Pacific		('000)	7	6	12	6	7
1.9 ♦ Europe		('000)	113	123	127	124	116
1.10 ♦ Middle East		('000)	2	2	2	2	2
1.11 ♦ South Asia		('000)	..	..	..	..	..
1.12 ♦ Other not classified		('000)	7	8	7	9	7
1.13 * of which, nationals residing abroad		('000)	..	..	..	..	..
Arrivals by main purpose	(2)						
1.14 Total		('000)	324	358	374	376	400
1.15 ♦ Personal		('000)	99	125	163	155	154
1.16 * holidays, leisure and recreation		('000)	50	65	83	82	78
1.17 * other personal purposes		('000)	49	60	80	73	76
1.18 ♦ Business and professional		('000)	225	233	211	221	246
Accommodation							
Total							
1.29 ♦ Guests		('000)	..	..	..	..	..
1.30 ♦ Overnights		('000)	..	..	..	..	..
Hotels and similar establishments							
1.31 ♦ Guests		('000)	245	264	289	272	269
1.32 ♦ Overnights		('000)	789	794	926	814	793
Expenditure							
1.33 Total		US$ Mn	46	55	61	82	..
1.34 ♦ Travel		US$ Mn	45	53	56	62	..
1.35 ♦ Passenger transport		US$ Mn	1	2	5	20	..
Expenditure by main purpose of the trip							
1.36 Total		US$ Mn	45	52	56	62	..
1.37 ♦ Personal		US$ Mn	20	22	24	27	..
1.38 ♦ Business and professional		US$ Mn	25	30	32	35	..
Indicators							
1.39 Average size of travel party		Persons	..	..	..	..	..
Average length of stay							
1.40 Total		Days	..	..	..	..	..
1.41 ♦ For all commercial accommodation services		Nights	2.90	3.00	3.20	2.99	2.95
1.42 * of which, "hotels and similar establishments"		Nights					
1.43 ♦ For non commercial accommodation services		Days	..	..	..	..	..
1.44 Average expenditure per day		US$	..	..	82.5	106.4	..
2. DOMESTIC TOURISM							
Data							
Accommodation							
Total							
2.19 ♦ Guests		('000)	..	..	..	..	..
2.20 ♦ Overnights		('000)	..	..	..	..	..
Hotels and similar establishments							
2.21 ♦ Guests		('000)	80	95	85	104	132
2.22 ♦ Overnights		('000)	173	204	185	193	224
Indicators							
2.23 Average size of travel party		Persons	..	..	..	..	..
Average length of stay							
2.24 Total		Days	..	..	..	..	..
2.25 ♦ For all commercial accommodation services		Nights	..	..	..	1.86	1.70
2.26 * of which, "hotels and similar establishments"		Nights					
2.27 ♦ For non commercial accommodation services		Days	..	..	..	..	..
2.28 Average expenditure per day		US$	..	..	..	..	..

BURKINA FASO

Basic data and indicators	Notes	Units	2005	2006	2007	2008	2009
3. OUTBOUND TOURISM							
Data							
Expenditure							
3.4 Total		US$ Mn	74	84	93	110	..
3.5 ♦ Travel		US$ Mn	46	55	58	63	..
3.6 ♦ Passenger transport		US$ Mn	28	29	35	47	..
Expenditure by main purpose of the trip							
3.7 Total		US$ Mn	45	55	57	62	..
3.8 ♦ Personal		US$ Mn	18	25	21	24	..
3.9 ♦ Business and professional		US$ Mn	27	30	36	38	..
4. TOURISM INDUSTRIES							
Data							
Number of establishments							
4.1 Total		Units	..	..	..	..	..
4.2 ♦ Accommodation for visitors		Units	..	..	..	..	..
4.3 * of which, "hotels and similar establishments"		Units	..	..	293	..	..
4.4 ♦ Food and beverage serving activities		Units	..	..	..	..	..
4.5 ♦ Passenger transportation		Units	..	..	..	..	..
4.6 ♦ Travel agencies and other reservation services activities		Units	..	..	..	..	48
4.7 ♦ Other tourism industries		Units	..	..	..	..	..
Accommodation for visitors in hotels and similar establishments							
Non-monetary data							
4.13 ♦ Number of establishments		Units	..	..	293	..	..
4.14 ♦ Number of rooms		Units	..	..	5,771	..	..
4.15 ♦ Number of bed-places		Units	..	..	10,113	..	..
Indicators							
4.16 Occupancy rate / rooms		Percent	69.00	64.79	54.75	47.70	45.00
4.17 Occupancy rate / bed-places		Percent	..	..	..	27.70	28.00
4.18 Average length of stay		Nights	..	..	3.20	2.70	2.50
4.19 Available capacity (bed-places per 1000 inhabitants)		Units	..	..	0.69	..	..
5. EMPLOYMENT							
Data							
Number of employees by tourism industries							
5.1 Total		('000)	..	..	..	..	..
5.2 ♦ Accommodation services for visitors (hotels and similar establishments)		('000)	..	..	2.9	..	..
5.3 ♦ Other accommodation services		('000)	..	..	..	..	..
5.4 ♦ Food and beverage serving activities		('000)	..	..	..	..	..
5.5 ♦ Passenger transportation		('000)	..	..	..	..	..
5.6 ♦ Travel agencies and other reservation services activities		('000)	..	..	..	..	..
5.7 ♦ Other tourism industries		('000)	..	..	..	..	..
6. COMPLEMENTARY INDICATORS							
Demand							
6.1 Gross travel propensity		Units	..	..	..	..	..
6.2 Carrying capacity (arrivals/population)		Units	0.02	0.02	0.02	0.02	0.02

BURUNDI

Basic data and indicators	Notes	Units	2005	2006	2007	2008	2009
1. INBOUND TOURISM							
Data							
Arrivals							
1.1　Total		('000)	..	..	..	..	..
1.2　♦ Overnight visitors (tourists)	(1)	('000)	148	201	..	..	..
1.3　♦ Same-day visitors (excursionists)		('000)	..	..	..	..	..
1.4　　* of which, cruise passengers		('000)	..	..	..	..	..
Arrivals by region	(1)						
1.5　Total		('000)	148	201	..	..	..
1.6　♦ Africa		('000)	49	141	..	..	..
1.7　♦ Americas		('000)	10	4	..	..	..
1.8　♦ East Asia and the Pacific		('000)	4	10	..	..	..
1.9　♦ Europe		('000)	29	32	..	..	..
1.10　♦ Middle East		('000)	..	..	..	..	..
1.11　♦ South Asia		('000)	..	..	..	..	..
1.12　♦ Other not classified		('000)	56	14	..	..	..
1.13　　* of which, nationals residing abroad		('000)	..	..	..	..	..
Arrivals by main purpose	(1)						
1.14　Total		('000)	149	201	..	..	..
1.15　♦ Personal		('000)	100	137	..	..	..
1.16　　* holidays, leisure and recreation		('000)	49	66	..	..	..
1.17　　* other personal purposes		('000)	51	71	..	..	..
1.18　♦ Business and professional		('000)	49	64	..	..	..
Arrivals by mode of transport	(1)						
1.19　Total		('000)	148	201	..	..	..
1.20　♦ Air		('000)	49	50	..	..	..
1.21　♦ Water	(2)	('000)	49	40	..	..	..
1.22　♦ Land		('000)	50	111	..	..	..
1.23　　* railway		('000)	..	..	..	..	..
1.24　　* road		('000)	50	111	..	..	..
1.25　　* others		('000)	..	..	..	..	..
Expenditure							
1.33　Total		US$ Mn	1.9	1.6	2.3	1.6	1.7
1.34　♦ Travel		US$ Mn	1.5	1.3	1.3	1.3	1.5
1.35　♦ Passenger transport		US$ Mn	0.4	0.3	1.0	0.3	0.2
3. OUTBOUND TOURISM							
Data							
Expenditure							
3.4　Total		US$ Mn	62	126	106	151	71
3.5　♦ Travel		US$ Mn	60	125	104	144	62
3.6　♦ Passenger transport		US$ Mn	2	1	2	7	9
Expenditure by main purpose of the trip							
3.7　Total		US$ Mn	60	126	104	144	62
3.8　♦ Personal		US$ Mn	6	5	5	10	9
3.9　♦ Business and professional		US$ Mn	54	121	99	134	53
4. TOURISM INDUSTRIES							
Data							
Accommodation for visitors in hotels and similar establishments							
Non-monetary data							
4.13　♦ Number of establishments		Units	..	..	..	..	..
4.14　♦ Number of rooms		Units	130	130	..	..	..
4.15　♦ Number of bed-places		Units	1,420	1,420	..	..	..
Indicators							
4.16　Occupancy rate / rooms		Percent	..	..	..	..	..
4.17　Occupancy rate / bed-places		Percent	..	..	..	..	..
4.18　Average length of stay		Nights	..	2.00	..	..	..
4.19　Available capacity (bed-places per 1000 inhabitants)		Units	0.19	0.19	..	..	..

BURUNDI

Basic data and indicators	Notes	Units	2005	2006	2007	2008	2009
6. **COMPLEMENTARY INDICATORS**							
Demand							
6.1 Gross travel propensity		Units	..	..	..	..	..
6.2 Carrying capacity (arrivals/population)		Units	0.02	0.03	..	..	..
Macroeconomic indicators related to international tourism							
6.3 Inbound tourism expenditure over GDP		Percent	0.2	0.2	0.2	0.1	..
6.4 Outbound tourism expenditure over GDP		Percent	7.9	13.9	10.8	8.4	..
6.5 Tourism balance (inbound minus outbound tourism expenditure) over GDP		Percent	-7.6	-13.7	-10.6	-8.2	..
6.6 Tourism openness (inbound plus outbound tourism expenditure) over GDP		Percent	8.1	14.1	11.1	8.5	..
6.7 Tourism coverage (inbound over outbound tourism expenditure)		Percent	3.0	1.3	2.2	1.6	..
6.8 Inbound tourism expenditure over exports of goods		Percent	3.1	2.7	3.9	2.3	..
6.9 Inbound tourism expenditure over exports of services		Percent	5.3	4.6	7.5	2.4	..
6.10 Inbound tourism expenditure over exports of goods and services		Percent	1.9	1.7	2.6	1.2	..
6.11 Inbound tourism expenditure over current account credits		Percent	0.5	0.5	0.7	0.5	..
6.12 Outbound tourism expenditure over imports of goods		Percent	33.2	51.7	41.2	28.8	..
6.13 Outbound tourism expenditure over imports of services		Percent	46.8	62.5	59.9	51.0	..
6.14 Outbound tourism expenditure over imports of goods and services		Percent	19.4	28.3	24.4	18.4	..
6.15 Outbound tourism expenditure over current account debits		Percent	18.1	27.3	23.6	17.8	..

CAMBODIA

Basic data and indicators	Notes	Units	2005	2006	2007	2008	2009
1. INBOUND TOURISM							
Data							
Arrivals							
1.1 Total	(1)	('000)	1,422	1,700	2,015	2,125	2,162
1.2 ◆ Overnight visitors (tourists)		('000)	1,333	1,591	1,873	2,001	2,046
1.3 ◆ Same-day visitors (excursionists)		('000)	89	109	142	124	116
1.4 * of which, cruise passengers		('000)	..	..	..	..	..
Arrivals by region							
1.5 Total		('000)	1,333	1,590	1,873	2,002	2,045
1.6 ◆ Africa		('000)	..	..	3	4	5
1.7 ◆ Americas		('000)	152	159	195	205	201
1.8 ◆ East Asia and the Pacific		('000)	787	1,022	1,242	1,312	1,352
1.9 ◆ Europe		('000)	310	314	417	464	470
1.10 ◆ Middle East		('000)	..	..	1	1	1
1.11 ◆ South Asia		('000)	8	9	15	16	16
1.12 ◆ Other not classified		('000)	76	86	..	..	..
1.13 * of which, nationals residing abroad		('000)	..	..	..	..	..
Arrivals by main purpose							
1.14 Total		('000)	1,333	1,591	1,873	2,001	2,046
1.15 ◆ Personal		('000)	1,246	1,482	1,727	1,842	1,913
1.16 * holidays, leisure and recreation		('000)	1,197	1,446	1,690	1,808	1,876
1.17 * other personal purposes		('000)	49	36	37	34	37
1.18 ◆ Business and professional		('000)	87	109	146	159	133
Arrivals by mode of transport							
1.19 Total		('000)	1,334	1,592	1,873	2,001	2,046
1.20 ◆ Air		('000)	857	1,027	1,297	1,239	1,112
1.21 ◆ Water	(2)	('000)	32	40	44	72	78
1.22 ◆ Land		('000)	445	525	532	690	856
1.23 * railway		('000)	..	..	..	..	..
1.24 * road		('000)	445	525	532	690	856
1.25 * others		('000)	..	..	..	..	..
Expenditure							
1.33 Total		US$ Mn	929	1,080	1,284	1,398	1,312
1.34 ◆ Travel		US$ Mn	840	963	1,135	1,219	1,185
1.35 ◆ Passenger transport		US$ Mn	89	117	149	179	127
Expenditure by main purpose of the trip							
1.36 Total		US$ Mn	839	963	1,134	1,219	1,184
1.37 ◆ Personal		US$ Mn	775	882	1,038	1,110	1,092
1.38 ◆ Business and professional		US$ Mn	64	81	96	109	92
Indicators							
1.39 Average size of travel party		Persons	..	..	..	..	..
Average length of stay							
1.40 Total		Days	..	..	..	..	..
1.41 ◆ For all commercial accommodation services	(3)	Nights	6.30	6.50	6.50	6.65	6.45
1.42 * of which, "hotels and similar establishments"		Nights	..	..	..	..	..
1.43 ◆ For non commercial accommodation services		Days	..	..	..	..	..
1.44 Average expenditure per day		US$	..	..	..	..	..
3. OUTBOUND TOURISM							
Data							
Departures							
3.1 Total		('000)	..	..	..	..	..
3.2 ◆ Overnight visitors (tourists)		('000)	568	787	996	786	340
3.3 ◆ Same-day visitors (excursionists)		('000)	..	..	..	..	..
Expenditure							
3.4 Total		US$ Mn	138	176	194	180	162
3.5 ◆ Travel		US$ Mn	97	122	123	97	103
3.6 ◆ Passenger transport		US$ Mn	41	54	71	83	59
Expenditure by main purpose of the trip							
3.7 Total		US$ Mn	97	122	123	97	103
3.8 ◆ Personal		US$ Mn	8	8	9	10	8
3.9 ◆ Business and professional		US$ Mn	89	114	114	87	95

CAMBODIA

Basic data and indicators	Notes	Units	2005	2006	2007	2008	2009
4. TOURISM INDUSTRIES							
Data							
Number of establishments							
4.1 Total		Units	..	..	..	..	..
4.2 ♦ Accommodation for visitors		Units	..	..	..	..	..
4.3 * of which, "hotels and similar establishments"		Units	1,001	1,093	1,286	1,323	1,469
4.4 ♦ Food and beverage serving activities		Units	..	..	..	..	..
4.5 ♦ Passenger transportation		Units	..	..	..	..	..
4.6 ♦ Travel agencies and other reservation services activities		Units	..	..	..	..	..
4.7 ♦ Other tourism industries		Units	..	..	..	..	..
Accommodation for visitors in hotels and similar establishments							
Non-monetary data							
4.13 ♦ Number of establishments		Units	1,001	1,093	1,286	1,323	1,469
4.14 ♦ Number of rooms		Units	24,465	27,080	32,033	32,858	37,522
4.15 ♦ Number of bed-places		Units	41,600	46,036	54,456	55,859	63,787
Indicators							
4.16 Occupancy rate / rooms		Percent	..	..	..	..	..
4.17 Occupancy rate / bed-places		Percent	52.00	54.79	54.79	62.68	63.57
4.18 Average length of stay		Nights	..	..	..	..	..
4.19 Available capacity (bed-places per 1000 inhabitants)		Units	3.00	3.27	3.80	3.84	4.31
6. COMPLEMENTARY INDICATORS							
Demand							
6.1 Gross travel propensity		Units	..	..	..	..	..
6.2 Carrying capacity (arrivals/population)		Units	0.10	0.11	0.13	0.14	0.14
Macroeconomic indicators related to international tourism							
6.3 Inbound tourism expenditure over GDP		Percent	14.7	14.8	14.9	..	..
6.4 Outbound tourism expenditure over GDP		Percent	2.2	2.4	2.2	..	..
6.5 Tourism balance (inbound minus outbound tourism expenditure) over GDP		Percent	12.6	12.4	12.6	..	..
6.6 Tourism openness (inbound plus outbound tourism expenditure) over GDP		Percent	16.9	17.3	17.1	..	..
6.7 Tourism coverage (inbound over outbound tourism expenditure)		Percent	673.8	613.7	664.4	778.6	809.1
6.8 Inbound tourism expenditure over exports of goods		Percent	31.9	29.2	31.4	29.7	30.5
6.9 Inbound tourism expenditure over exports of services		Percent	83.0	83.3	83.0	85.0	80.7
6.10 Inbound tourism expenditure over exports of goods and services		Percent	23.0	21.6	22.8	22.0	22.1
6.11 Inbound tourism expenditure over current account credits		Percent	20.0	18.8	20.2	19.7	19.9
6.12 Outbound tourism expenditure over imports of goods		Percent	3.5	3.7	3.6	2.8	2.8
6.13 Outbound tourism expenditure over imports of services		Percent	21.4	21.9	21.1	17.3	15.9
6.14 Outbound tourism expenditure over imports of goods and services		Percent	3.0	3.2	3.0	2.4	2.3
6.15 Outbound tourism expenditure over current account debits		Percent	2.8	2.9	2.8	2.2	2.2

CAMEROON

Basic data and indicators	Notes	Units	2005	2006	2007	2008	2009
1. INBOUND TOURISM							
Data							
Arrivals							
1.1 Total		('000)	..	..	..	..	..
1.2 ♦ Overnight visitors (tourists)	(1)	('000)	176	185	..	..	..
1.3 ♦ Same-day visitors (excursionists)		('000)	..	..	..	..	..
1.4 * of which, cruise passengers		('000)	..	..	..	..	..
Arrivals by region	(1)						
1.5 Total		('000)	176	185	..	..	..
1.6 ♦ Africa		('000)	89	97	..	..	..
1.7 ♦ Americas		('000)	10	9	..	..	..
1.8 ♦ East Asia and the Pacific		('000)	4	5	..	..	..
1.9 ♦ Europe		('000)	68	63	..	..	..
1.10 ♦ Middle East		('000)	2	4	..	..	..
1.11 ♦ South Asia		('000)	..	..	..	..	..
1.12 ♦ Other not classified		('000)	3	7	..	..	..
1.13 * of which, nationals residing abroad		('000)	..	..	..	..	..
Accommodation							
Total							
1.29 ♦ Guests		('000)	..	..	..	..	..
1.30 ♦ Overnights		('000)	..	..	..	..	..
Hotels and similar establishments							
1.31 ♦ Guests		('000)	176	185	..	..	..
1.32 ♦ Overnights		('000)	355	370	..	..	..
Expenditure							
1.33 Total		US$ Mn	229	231	254	167	..
1.34 ♦ Travel		US$ Mn	175	181	226	156	222
1.35 ♦ Passenger transport		US$ Mn	54	50	28	11	..
Expenditure by main purpose of the trip							
1.36 Total		US$ Mn	175	181	226	155	222
1.37 ♦ Personal		US$ Mn	159	158	170	127	85
1.38 ♦ Business and professional		US$ Mn	16	23	56	28	137
Indicators							
1.39 Average size of travel party		Persons	..	..	..	..	..
Average length of stay							
1.40 Total		Days	..	..	..	..	..
1.41 ♦ For all commercial accommodation services		Nights	..	1.81	..	..	..
1.42 * of which, "hotels and similar establishments"		Nights	..	..	..	..	..
1.43 ♦ For non commercial accommodation services		Days	..	..	..	..	..
1.44 Average expenditure per day		US$	..	..	..	..	..
2. DOMESTIC TOURISM							
Data							
Accommodation							
Total							
2.19 ♦ Guests		('000)	..	..	..	..	..
2.20 ♦ Overnights		('000)	..	..	..	..	..
Hotels and similar establishments							
2.21 ♦ Guests		('000)	977	876	..	..	..
2.22 ♦ Overnights		('000)	1,399	1,221	..	..	..
Indicators							
2.23 Average size of travel party		Persons	..	..	..	..	..
Average length of stay							
2.24 Total		Days	..	..	..	..	..
2.25 ♦ For all commercial accommodation services		Nights	..	1.36	..	..	..
2.26 * of which, "hotels and similar establishments"		Nights	..	..	..	..	..
2.27 ♦ For non commercial accommodation services		Days	..	..	..	..	..
2.28 Average expenditure per day		US$	..	..	..	..	..

CAMEROON

Basic data and indicators	Notes	Units	2005	2006	2007	2008	2009
3. OUTBOUND TOURISM							
Data							
Expenditure							
3.4 Total		US$ Mn	480	521	466	563	549
3.5 ♦ Travel		US$ Mn	355	412	368	410	361
3.6 ♦ Passenger transport		US$ Mn	125	109	98	153	188
Expenditure by main purpose of the trip							
3.7 Total		US$ Mn	355	412	368	410	361
3.8 ♦ Personal		US$ Mn	202	236	169	213	138
3.9 ♦ Business and professional		US$ Mn	153	176	199	197	223
4. TOURISM INDUSTRIES							
Data							
Number of establishments							
4.1 Total		Units	..	..	..	..	..
4.2 ♦ Accommodation for visitors		Units	..	..	..	..	..
4.3 * of which, "hotels and similar establishments"		Units	1,591	1,719	1,845	..	..
4.4 ♦ Food and beverage serving activities		Units	..	..	..	..	..
4.5 ♦ Passenger transportation		Units	..	..	..	..	..
4.6 ♦ Travel agencies and other reservation services activities		Units	..	..	..	..	..
4.7 ♦ Other tourism industries		Units	..	..	..	..	..
Accommodation for visitors in hotels and similar establishments							
Non-monetary data							
4.13 ♦ Number of establishments		Units	1,591	1,719	1,845	..	..
4.14 ♦ Number of rooms		Units	22,112	23,458	24,803	..	..
4.15 ♦ Number of bed places		Units	24,598	25,586	26,573	..	..
Indicators							
4.16 Occupancy rate / rooms		Percent	..	..	..	..	..
4.17 Occupancy rate / bed-places		Percent	..	17.18	..	..	..
4.18 Average length of stay		Nights	..	1.39	..	..	..
4.19 Available capacity (bed-places per 1000 inhabitants)		Units	1.38	1.40	1.42	..	..
6. COMPLEMENTARY INDICATORS							
Demand							
6.1 Gross travel propensity		Units	..	..	..	..	..
6.2 Carrying capacity (arrivals/population)		Units	0.01	0.01	..	..	..
Macroeconomic indicators related to international tourism							
6.3 Inbound tourism expenditure over GDP		Percent	1.4	1.3	..	..	..
6.4 Outbound tourism expenditure over GDP		Percent	2.9	2.9	..	..	..
6.5 Tourism balance (inbound minus outbound tourism expenditure) over GDP		Percent	-1.5	-1.6	..	..	..
6.6 Tourism openness (inbound plus outbound tourism expenditure) over GDP		Percent	4.3	4.2	..	..	..
6.7 Tourism coverage (inbound over outbound tourism expenditure)		Percent	47.7	44.4	54.5	29.6	40.5
6.8 Inbound tourism expenditure over exports of goods		Percent	7.0	6.0	5.1	2.8	5.5
6.9 Inbound tourism expenditure over exports of services		Percent	23.6	22.8	18.5	11.2	18.0
6.10 Inbound tourism expenditure over exports of goods and services		Percent	5.4	4.8	4.0	2.3	4.2
6.11 Inbound tourism expenditure over current account credits		Percent	5.0	4.3	3.6	2.0	3.8
6.12 Outbound tourism expenditure over imports of goods		Percent	16.6	16.4	11.0	10.4	12.5
6.13 Outbound tourism expenditure over imports of services		Percent	33.0	35.4	26.4	21.2	25.7
6.14 Outbound tourism expenditure over imports of goods and services		Percent	11.0	11.2	7.8	7.0	8.4
6.15 Outbound tourism expenditure over current account debits		Percent	9.4	9.9	6.9	6.5	7.9

CANADA

Basic data and indicators	Notes	Units	2005	2006	2007	2008	2009
1. INBOUND TOURISM							
Data							
Arrivals							
1.1 Total	(1)	('000)	36,160	33,390	30,373	27,370	24,706
1.2 ♦ Overnight visitors (tourists)		('000)	18,771	18,265	17,935	17,142	15,737
1.3 ♦ Same-day visitors (excursionists)	(1)	('000)	17,389	15,125	12,438	10,228	8,969
1.4 * of which, cruise passengers		('000)	..	..	..	..	..
Arrivals by region							
1.5 Total		('000)	18,770	18,264	17,936	17,143	15,738
1.6 ♦ Africa		('000)	62	72	76	80	76
1.7 ♦ Americas		('000)	14,867	14,372	13,946	13,112	12,150
1.8 ♦ East Asia and the Pacific		('000)	1,282	1,282	1,267	1,231	1,026
1.9 ♦ Europe		('000)	2,397	2,360	2,443	2,498	2,262
1.10 ♦ Middle East		('000)	52	59	68	77	78
1.11 ♦ South Asia		('000)	110	119	136	145	146
1.12 ♦ Other not classified		('000)	..	..	..	..	..
1.13 * of which, nationals residing abroad		('000)	..	..	..	..	..
Arrivals by main purpose							
1.14 Total		('000)	18,611	18,128	17,776	16,998	15,586
1.15 ♦ Personal		('000)	15,989	15,477	15,189	14,332	13,240
1.16 * holidays, leisure and recreation		('000)	9,951	9,744	9,617	8,681	7,766
1.17 * other personal purposes		('000)	6,038	5,733	5,572	5,651	5,474
1.18 ♦ Business and professional		('000)	2,622	2,651	2,587	2,666	2,346
Arrivals by mode of transport							
1.19 Total		('000)	18,770	18,265	17,935	17,142	15,737
1.20 ♦ Air		('000)	7,746	7,785	7,818	7,651	6,781
1.21 ♦ Water		('000)	706	754	833	845	812
1.22 ♦ Land		('000)	10,318	9,726	9,284	8,646	8,144
1.23 * railway		('000)	97	109	106	105	92
1.24 * road		('000)	10,221	9,617	9,178	8,541	8,052
1.25 * others		('000)	..	..	..	..	..
Accommodation							
Total							
1.29 ♦ Guests		('000)	..	..	..	..	..
1.30 ♦ Overnights		('000)	125,656	123,265	123,862	126,067	114,889
Hotels and similar establishments							
1.31 ♦ Guests		('000)	..	..	..	..	..
1.32 ♦ Overnights		('000)	..	..	..	..	..
Expenditure							
1.33 Total		US$ Mn	16,006	16,844	17,949	18,228	15,555
1.34 ♦ Travel		US$ Mn	13,768	14,555	15,568	15,668	13,707
1.35 ♦ Passenger transport		US$ Mn	2,238	2,289	2,381	2,560	1,848
Expenditure by main purpose of the trip							
1.36 Total		US$ Mn	13,768	14,555	15,568	15,668	13,707
1.37 ♦ Personal		US$ Mn	11,467	12,003	12,864	12,802	11,486
1.38 ♦ Business and professional		US$ Mn	2,301	2,552	2,704	2,866	2,221
2. DOMESTIC TOURISM							
Data							
Accommodation							
Total							
2.19 ♦ Guests		('000)	..	..	..	..	..
2.20 ♦ Overnights		('000)	..	260,286	264,488	263,256	266,555
Hotels and similar establishments							
2.21 ♦ Guests		('000)	..	..	..	..	..
2.22 ♦ Overnights		('000)	..	44,033	43,418	43,561	42,809

CANADA

Basic data and indicators	Notes	Units	2005	2006	2007	2008	2009
3. OUTBOUND TOURISM							
Data							
Departures							
3.1 Total		('000)	..	..	..	..	..
3.2 ♦ Overnight visitors (tourists)	(2)	('000)	21,099	22,732	25,163	27,037	26,204
3.3 ♦ Same-day visitors (excursionists)		('000)	..	..	..	..	..
Expenditure							
3.4 Total		US$ Mn	22,734	25,997	31,199	33,908	30,232
3.5 ♦ Travel		US$ Mn	18,017	20,542	24,716	27,210	24,169
3.6 ♦ Passenger transport		US$ Mn	4,717	5,455	6,483	6,698	6,063
Expenditure by main purpose of the trip							
3.7 Total		US$ Mn	18,017	20,542	24,716	27,210	24,169
3.8 ♦ Personal		US$ Mn	15,076	17,240	20,742	23,366	21,076
3.9 ♦ Business and professional		US$ Mn	2,941	3,302	3,974	3,844	3,093
4. TOURISM INDUSTRIES							
Indicators							
4.16 Occupancy rate / rooms		Percent	..	..	..	..	..
4.17 Occupancy rate / bed-places		Percent	59.90	..	..	..	..
4.18 Average length of stay		Nights	..	..	..	..	..
4.19 Available capacity (bed-places per 1000 inhabitants)		Units	..	..	..	..	..
6. COMPLEMENTARY INDICATORS							
Demand							
6.1 Gross travel propensity		Units	..	..	..	..	..
6.2 Carrying capacity (arrivals/population)		Units	0.58	0.56	0.54	0.51	0.47
Macroeconomic indicators related to international tourism							
6.3 Inbound tourism expenditure over GDP		Percent	1.4	1.3	1.3	1.2	1.2
6.4 Outbound tourism expenditure over GDP		Percent	2.0	2.0	2.2	2.3	2.3
6.5 Tourism balance (inbound minus outbound tourism expenditure) over GDP		Percent	-0.6	-0.7	-0.9	-1.0	-1.1
6.6 Tourism openness (inbound plus outbound tourism expenditure) over GDP		Percent	3.4	3.4	3.4	3.5	3.4
6.7 Tourism coverage (inbound over outbound tourism expenditure)		Percent	70.4	64.8	57.5	53.8	51.5
6.8 Inbound tourism expenditure over exports of goods		Percent	4.3	4.2	4.2	3.9	4.8
6.9 Inbound tourism expenditure over exports of services		Percent	28.7	27.9	27.5	26.8	26.3
6.10 Inbound tourism expenditure over exports of goods and services		Percent	3.7	3.7	3.6	3.4	4.1
6.11 Inbound tourism expenditure over current account credits		Percent	3.4	3.2	3.1	3.0	3.5
6.12 Outbound tourism expenditure over imports of goods		Percent	7.4	7.6	8.4	8.5	9.7
6.13 Outbound tourism expenditure over imports of services		Percent	34.6	35.7	37.7	38.0	38.4
6.14 Outbound tourism expenditure over imports of goods and services		Percent	6.1	6.2	6.8	6.9	7.7
6.15 Outbound tourism expenditure over current account debits		Percent	5.1	5.2	5.7	5.8	6.5

CAPE VERDE

Basic data and indicators	Notes	Units	2005	2006	2007	2008	2009
1. INBOUND TOURISM							
Data							
Arrivals							
1.1　Total		('000)	..	..	..	..	..
1.2　♦ Overnight visitors (tourists)	(1)	('000)	198	242	267	285	287
1.3　♦ Same-day visitors (excursionists)		('000)	..	..	..	..	..
1.4　　* of which, cruise passengers		('000)	..	..	..	..	..
Arrivals by region	(1)						
1.5　Total		('000)	197	242	267	285	287
1.6　♦ Africa		('000)	9	5	0.3	0.2	0.2
1.7　♦ Americas		('000)	2	6	5	4	4
1.8　♦ East Asia and the Pacific		('000)	..	..	..	..	..
1.9　♦ Europe		('000)	173	208	228	234	244
1.10　♦ Middle East		('000)	..	..	..	..	..
1.11　♦ South Asia		('000)	..	..	..	..	..
1.12　♦ Other not classified		('000)	13	23	34	47	39
1.13　　* of which, nationals residing abroad		('000)	..	..	..	..	..
Accommodation							
Total							
1.29　♦ Guests		('000)	..	..	..	..	..
1.30　♦ Overnights		('000)	..	..	..	..	..
Hotels and similar establishments							
1.31　♦ Guests		('000)	198	242	267	285	287
1.32　♦ Overnights		('000)	850	1,261	1,308	1,712	1,898
Expenditure							
1.33　Total		US$ Mn	177	280	375	432	355
1.34　♦ Travel		US$ Mn	122	209	304	352	292
1.35　♦ Passenger transport		US$ Mn	55	71	71	80	63
Expenditure by main purpose of the trip							
1.36　Total		US$ Mn	122	209	304	352	292
1.37　♦ Personal		US$ Mn	116	200	293	338	268
1.38　♦ Business and professional		US$ Mn	6	9	11	14	24
2. DOMESTIC TOURISM							
Data							
Accommodation							
Total							
2.19　♦ Guests		('000)	..	..	..	..	..
2.20　♦ Overnights		('000)	..	..	..	..	..
Hotels and similar establishments							
2.21　♦ Guests		('000)	36	39	46	48	43
2.22　♦ Overnights		('000)	85	107	125	115	124
3. OUTBOUND TOURISM							
Data							
Expenditure							
3.4　Total		US$ Mn	82	106	123	143	145
3.5　♦ Travel		US$ Mn	67	82	107	133	136
3.6　♦ Passenger transport		US$ Mn	15	24	16	10	9
Expenditure by main purpose of the trip							
3.7　Total		US$ Mn	67	82	107	133	136
3.8　♦ Personal		US$ Mn	55	63	78	98	83
3.9　♦ Business and professional		US$ Mn	12	19	29	35	53

CAPE VERDE

Basic data and indicators	Notes	Units	2005	2006	2007	2008	2009
4. TOURISM INDUSTRIES							
Data							
Number of establishments							
4.1 Total		Units	..	..	..	..	..
4.2 ♦ Accommodation for visitors		Units	..	..	..	..	..
4.3 * of which, "hotels and similar establishments"		Units	132	142	150	158	173
4.4 ♦ Food and beverage serving activities		Units	..	..	..	..	..
4.5 ♦ Passenger transportation		Units	..	..	..	..	..
4.6 ♦ Travel agencies and other reservation							
services activities		Units	..	..	..	..	..
4.7 ♦ Other tourism industries		Units	..	..	..	..	..
Accommodation for visitors in hotels and similar establishments							
Non-monetary data							
4.13 ♦ Number of establishments		Units	132	142	150	158	173
4.14 ♦ Number of rooms		Units	4,406	4,836	5,368	6,172	6,367
4.15 ♦ Number of bed-places		Units	8,278	8,828	9,767	11,420	11,720
Indicators							
4.16 Occupancy rate / rooms		Percent	..	..	..	..	..
4.17 Occupancy rate / bed-places		Percent	39.85	44.34	40.13	48.33	44.90
4.18 Average length of stay		Nights	3.89	4.61	4.30	5.21	5.89
4.19 Available capacity (bed-places per 1000 inhabitants)		Units	17.34	18.21	19.86	22.90	23.18
6. COMPLEMENTARY INDICATORS							
Demand							
6.1 Gross travel propensity		Units	..	..	..	..	..
6.2 Carrying capacity (arrivals/population)		Units	0.41	0.50	0.54	0.57	0.57
Macroeconomic indicators related to international tourism							
6.3 Inbound tourism expenditure over GDP		Percent	17.1	..	..	..	..
6.4 Outbound tourism expenditure over GDP		Percent	8.0	..	..	..	..
6.5 Tourism balance (inbound minus outbound tourism expenditure) over GDP		Percent	9.1	..	..	..	..
6.6 Tourism openness (inbound plus outbound tourism expenditure) over GDP		Percent	25.1	..	..	..	..
6.7 Tourism coverage (inbound over outbound tourism expenditure)		Percent	214.5	263.1	304.9	301.5	..
6.8 Inbound tourism expenditure over exports of goods		Percent	199.5	292.5	458.4	373.0	..
6.9 Inbound tourism expenditure over exports of services		Percent	65.8	73.2	76.4	71.8	..
6.10 Inbound tourism expenditure over exports of goods and services		Percent	49.5	58.6	65.5	60.2	..
6.11 Inbound tourism expenditure over current account credits		Percent	25.7	33.7	37.3	37.0	..
6.12 Outbound tourism expenditure over imports of goods		Percent	18.9	19.0	16.5	17.2	..
6.13 Outbound tourism expenditure over imports of services		Percent	39.6	42.6	41.8	39.9	..
6.14 Outbound tourism expenditure over imports of goods and services		Percent	12.8	13.1	11.8	12.0	..
6.15 Outbound tourism expenditure over current account debits		Percent	11.3	11.6	10.2	10.4	..

CAYMAN ISLANDS

Basic data and indicators	Notes	Units	2005	2006	2007	2008	2009
1. INBOUND TOURISM							
Data							
Arrivals							
1.1 Total		('000)	1,967	2,197	2,008	1,856	1,792
1.2 ♦ Overnight visitors (tourists)	(1)	('000)	168	267	292	303	272
1.3 ♦ Same-day visitors (excursionists)		('000)	1,799	1,930	1,716	1,553	1,520
1.4 * of which, cruise passengers		('000)	1,799	1,930	1,716	1,553	1,520
Arrivals by region	(1)						
1.5 Total		('000)	168	267	292	303	272
1.6 ♦ Africa		('000)	..	..	1	1	1
1.7 ♦ Americas		('000)	153	247	268	279	250
1.8 ♦ East Asia and the Pacific		('000)	1	1	2	2	2
1.9 ♦ Europe		('000)	13	18	20	21	19
1.10 ♦ Middle East		('000)	..	..	..	..	..
1.11 ♦ South Asia		('000)	..	..	..	..	..
1.12 ♦ Other not classified		('000)	1	1	1	..	..
1.13 * of which, nationals residing abroad		('000)	..	..	..	..	..
Arrivals by main purpose	(1)						
1.14 Total		('000)	168	267	292	303	272
1.15 ♦ Personal		('000)	156	248	271	284	256
1.16 * holidays, leisure and recreation		('000)	100	194	219	231	207
1.17 * other personal purposes		('000)	56	54	52	53	49
1.18 ♦ Business and professional		('000)	12	19	21	19	16
Arrivals by mode of transport							
1.19 Total		('000)	1,967	2,197	2,008	1,856	1,792
1.20 ♦ Air		('000)	168	267	292	303	272
1.21 ♦ Water	(2)	('000)	1,799	1,930	1,716	1,553	1,520
1.22 ♦ Land		('000)	..	..	..	..	..
1.23 * railway		('000)	..	..	..	..	..
1.24 * road		('000)	..	..	..	..	..
1.25 * others		('000)	..	..	..	..	..
Accommodation							
Total							
1.29 ♦ Guests	(1)	('000)	168	267	292	303	272
1.30 ♦ Overnights		('000)	..	..	..	..	..
Hotels and similar establishments							
1.31 ♦ Guests	(3)	('000)	96	157	167	171	201
1.32 ♦ Overnights		('000)	..	..	..	..	..
Expenditure							
1.33 Total	(4)(5)	US$ Mn	356	534	501	539	486
1.34 ♦ Travel		US$ Mn	..	..	..	..	..
1.35 ♦ Passenger transport		US$ Mn	..	..	..	..	..
Indicators							
1.39 Average size of travel party		Persons	..	..	..	..	..
Average length of stay							
1.40 Total		Days	..	..	..	..	..
1.41 ♦ For all commercial accommodation services		Nights	..	..	..	..	..
1.42 * of which, "hotels and similar establishments"	(6)	Nights	4.90	4.50	4.70	4.50	4.40
1.43 ♦ For non commercial accommodation services		Days	..	..	..	..	..
1.44 Average expenditure per day		US$	..	..	..	..	..
3. OUTBOUND TOURISM							
Data							
Expenditure							
3.4 Total	(4)	US$ Mn	..	103	120	121	102
3.5 ♦ Travel		US$ Mn	..	..	..	..	..
3.6 ♦ Passenger transport		US$ Mn	..	..	..	..	..

CAYMAN ISLANDS

Basic data and indicators	Notes	Units	2005	2006	2007	2008	2009
4. TOURISM INDUSTRIES							
Data							
Accommodation for visitors in hotels and similar establishments							
Non-monetary data							
4.13 ♦ Number of establishments		Units	..	..	..	..	..
4.14 ♦ Number of rooms	(3)	Units	2,954	3,907	4,484	4,605	4,332
4.15 ♦ Number of bed-places		Units	..	..	..	..	..
Indicators							
4.16 Occupancy rate / rooms		Percent	55.80	59.40	61.70	62.20	59.00
4.17 Occupancy rate / bed-places		Percent	..	..	..	..	..
4.18 Average length of stay	(6)	Nights	4.90	4.50	4.70	4.50	4.40
4.19 Available capacity (bed-places per 1000 inhabitants)		Units	..	..	..	..	..
6. COMPLEMENTARY INDICATORS							
Demand							
6.1 Gross travel propensity		Units	..	..	..	..	..
6.2 Carrying capacity (arrivals/population)		Units	3.78	5.06	5.46	5.59	4.95

CENTRAL AFRICAN REPUBLIC

Basic data and indicators	Notes	Units	2005	2006	2007	2008	2009
1. INBOUND TOURISM							
Data							
Arrivals							
1.1 Total		('000)	..	..	..	..	..
1.2 ♦ Overnight visitors (tourists)	(1)	('000)	12.0	13.8	17.1	30.6	52.4
1.3 ♦ Same-day visitors (excursionists)		('000)	..	..	..	..	..
1.4 * of which, cruise passengers		('000)	..	..	..	..	..
Arrivals by region	(1)						
1.5 Total		('000)	12.0	13.8	17.1	30.6	52.4
1.6 ♦ Africa		('000)	6.2	7.1	8.3	16.0	27.0
1.7 ♦ Americas		('000)	0.6	0.7	0.9	1.3	3.2
1.8 ♦ East Asia and the Pacific		('000)	0.4	0.4	0.5	2.2	3.9
1.9 ♦ Europe		('000)	4.3	5.0	6.7	10.6	16.6
1.10 ♦ Middle East		('000)	0.4	0.5	0.6	0.4	1.2
1.11 ♦ South Asia		('000)	..	..	..	..	..
1.12 ♦ Other not classified		('000)	0.1	0.1	0.1	0.1	0.5
1.13 * of which, nationals residing abroad		('000)	..	..	..	..	..
Arrivals by main purpose	(1)						
1.14 Total		('000)	12.0	13.7	17.1	30.6	52.4
1.15 ♦ Personal		('000)	7.8	8.1	11.2	16.7	26.9
1.16 * holidays, leisure and recreation		('000)	1.3	1.9	2.0	4.4	8.7
1.17 * other personal purposes		('000)	6.5	6.2	9.2	12.3	18.2
1.18 ♦ Business and professional		('000)	4.2	5.6	5.9	13.9	25.5
Arrivals by mode of transport							
1.19 Total		('000)	12.0	13.7	17.1	30.6	52.4
1.20 ♦ Air		('000)	12.0	13.7	17.1	30.6	52.4
1.21 ♦ Water		('000)	..	..	..	..	..
1.22 ♦ Land		('000)	..	..	..	..	..
1.23 * railway		('000)	..	..	..	..	..
1.24 * road		('000)	..	..	..	..	..
1.25 * others		('000)	..	..	..	..	..
Accommodation							
Total							
1.29 ♦ Guests		('000)	..	..	..	..	..
1.30 ♦ Overnights		('000)	..	..	..	..	..
Hotels and similar establishments							
1.31 ♦ Guests		('000)	8	11	19	28	17
1.32 ♦ Overnights		('000)	33	42	46	90	52
Expenditure							
1.33 Total		US$ Mn	7.2	10.2	10.8	11.8	6.0
1.34 ♦ Travel		US$ Mn	5.0	8.0	8.4	9.0	4.5
1.35 ♦ Passenger transport		US$ Mn	2.2	2.2	2.4	2.8	1.5
Indicators							
1.39 Average size of travel party		Persons	..	..	..	..	..
Average length of stay							
1.40 Total		Days	..	..	..	..	..
1.41 ♦ For all commercial accommodation services		Nights	..	..	..	..	..
1.42 * of which, "hotels and similar establishments"		Nights	4.16	3.84	2.87	3.18	2.99
1.43 ♦ For non commercial accommodation services		Days	..	..	..	..	..
1.44 Average expenditure per day		US$	..	..	..	..	..
2. DOMESTIC TOURISM							
Data							
Accommodation							
Total							
2.19 ♦ Guests		('000)	..	..	..	..	..
2.20 ♦ Overnights		('000)	..	..	..	..	..
Hotels and similar establishments							
2.21 ♦ Guests		('000)	..	..	1	3	2
2.22 ♦ Overnights		('000)	..	..	3	9	3
Indicators							
2.23 Average size of travel party		Persons	..	..	..	..	..
Average length of stay							
2.24 Total		Days	..	..	..	..	..
2.25 ♦ For all commercial accommodation services		Nights	..	..	2.17	3.00	1.25
2.26 * of which, "hotels and similar establishments"		Nights	..	..	..	..	..
2.27 ♦ For non commercial accommodation services		Days	..	..	..	..	..
2.28 Average expenditure per day		US$	..	..	..	..	..

CENTRAL AFRICAN REPUBLIC

Basic data and indicators	Notes	Units	2005	2006	2007	2008	2009
3. OUTBOUND TOURISM							
Data							
Departures							
3.1 Total		('000)	..	..	..	..	..
3.2 ♦ Overnight visitors (tourists)		('000)	8	11	..	..	..
3.3 ♦ Same-day visitors (excursionists)		('000)	..	..	..	..	..
Expenditure							
3.4 Total		US$ Mn	46	47	54	56	61
3.5 ♦ Travel		US$ Mn	44	44	48	49	52
3.6 ♦ Passenger transport		US$ Mn	2	3	6	7	9
4. TOURISM INDUSTRIES							
Data							
Number of establishments							
4.1 Total		Units	..	..	..	..	..
4.2 ♦ Accommodation for visitors		Units	..	..	..	..	..
4.3 * of which, "hotels and similar establishments"		Units	..	..	..	..	56
4.4 ♦ Food and beverage serving activities		Units	..	..	..	..	..
4.5 ♦ Passenger transportation		Units	..	..	..	..	..
4.6 ♦ Travel agencies and other reservation services activities		Units	..	..	..	..	..
4.7 ♦ Other tourism industries		Units	..	..	..	..	..
Accommodation for visitors in hotels and similar establishments							
Non-monetary data							
4.13 ♦ Number of establishments		Units	..	..	..	..	56
4.14 ♦ Number of rooms		Units	241	241	319	507	722
4.15 ♦ Number of bed-places		Units	355	355	423	665	880
Indicators							
4.16 Occupancy rate / rooms		Percent	41.00	49.00	51.72	60.42	60.01
4.17 Occupancy rate / bed-places		Percent	..	..	..	..	..
4.18 Average length of stay		Nights	4.22	3.82	2.45	2.99	2.99
4.19 Available capacity (bed-places per 1000 inhabitants)		Units	0.09	0.08	0.10	0.15	0.88
6. COMPLEMENTARY INDICATORS							
Demand							
6.1 Gross travel propensity		Units	..	..	..	..	..
6.2 Carrying capacity (arrivals/population)		Units	0.003	0.003	0.004	0.01	0.01
Macroeconomic indicators related to international tourism	(2)						
6.3 Inbound tourism expenditure over GDP		Percent	..	..	..	..	0.6
6.4 Outbound tourism expenditure over GDP		Percent	..	..	..	..	3.0
6.5 Tourism balance (inbound minus outbound tourism expenditure) over GDP		Percent	..	..	..	..	-2.4
6.6 Tourism openness (inbound plus outbound tourism expenditure) over GDP		Percent	..	..	..	..	3.6
6.7 Tourism coverage (inbound over outbound tourism expenditure)		Percent	..	..	..	..	501.7
6.8 Inbound tourism expenditure over exports of goods		Percent	..	..	..	..	10.8
6.9 Inbound tourism expenditure over exports of services		Percent	..	..	..	..	19.6
6.10 Inbound tourism expenditure over exports of goods and services		Percent	..	..	..	..	6.9
6.11 Inbound tourism expenditure over current account credits		Percent	..	..	..	..	..
6.12 Outbound tourism expenditure over imports of goods		Percent	..	..	..	..	22.7
6.13 Outbound tourism expenditure over imports of services		Percent	..	..	..	..	40.0
6.14 Outbound tourism expenditure over imports of goods and services		Percent	..	..	..	..	14.5
6.15 Outbound tourism expenditure over current account debits		Percent	..	..	..	..	..

CHAD

Basic data and indicators	Notes	Units	2005	2006	2007	2008	2009
1. INBOUND TOURISM							
Data							
Arrivals							
1.1 Total		('000)	59	..	..	..	..
1.2 ♦ Overnight visitors (tourists)	(1)	('000)	29	16	25	22	31
1.3 ♦ Same-day visitors (excursionists)		('000)	..	..	..	..	..
1.4 * of which, cruise passengers		('000)	..	..	..	..	..
Arrivals by region	(1)						
1.5 Total		('000)	30	15	24	22	31
1.6 ♦ Africa		('000)	7	4	6	6	8
1.7 ♦ Americas		('000)	6	2	5	2	4
1.8 ♦ East Asia and the Pacific		('000)	1	..	1	1	1
1.9 ♦ Europe		('000)	15	9	11	12	16
1.10 ♦ Middle East		('000)	1	..	1	1	2
1.11 ♦ South Asia		('000)	..	..	..	..	..
1.12 ♦ Other not classified		('000)	..	..	..	..	..
1.13 * of which, nationals residing abroad		('000)	..	..	..	..	..
Arrivals by mode of transport	(1)						
1.19 Total		('000)	30	..	..	..	..
1.20 ♦ Air		('000)	21	..	..	..	..
1.21 ♦ Water		('000)	..	..	..	..	..
1.22 ♦ Land		('000)	9	..	..	..	..
1.23 * railway		('000)	..	..	..	..	..
1.24 * road		('000)	9	..	..	..	..
1.25 * others		('000)	..	..	..	..	..
Accommodation							
Total							
1.29 ♦ Guests		('000)	..	..	..	..	..
1.30 ♦ Overnights		('000)	..	..	..	..	..
Hotels and similar establishments							
1.31 ♦ Guests		('000)	29	16	25	22	31
1.32 ♦ Overnights		('000)	64	42	65	..	..
Indicators							
1.39 Average size of travel party		Persons	..	..	..	..	..
Average length of stay							
1.40 Total		Days	..	..	..	..	..
1.41 ♦ For all commercial accommodation services		Nights	3.00	..	..	..	..
1.42 * of which, "hotels and similar establishments"		Nights	..	..	..	..	..
1.43 ♦ For non commercial accommodation services		Days	..	..	..	..	..
1.44 Average expenditure per day		US$	..	..	..	..	..
2. DOMESTIC TOURISM							
Data							
Accommodation							
Total							
2.19 ♦ Guests		('000)	..	..	..	..	..
2.20 ♦ Overnights		('000)	..	..	..	..	..
Hotels and similar establishments							
2.21 ♦ Guests		('000)	..	..	..	..	..
2.22 ♦ Overnights		('000)	4	..	..	..	..
4. TOURISM INDUSTRIES							
Data							
Accommodation for visitors in hotels and similar establishments							
Non-monetary data							
4.13 ♦ Number of establishments		Units	..	..	..	..	..
4.14 ♦ Number of rooms		Units	922	..	..	..	..
4.15 ♦ Number of bed-places		Units	1,434	..	..	..	..
Indicators							
4.16 Occupancy rate / rooms		Percent	..	..	..	..	..
4.17 Occupancy rate / bed-places		Percent	..	..	..	..	..
4.18 Average length of stay		Nights	3.00	..	..	..	..
4.19 Available capacity (bed-places per 1000 inhabitants)		Units	0.14	..	..	..	..
6. COMPLEMENTARY INDICATORS							
Demand							
6.1 Gross travel propensity		Units	..	..	..	..	..
6.2 Carrying capacity (arrivals/population)		Units	0.003	0.002	0.002	0.002	0.003

CHILE

Basic data and indicators	Notes	Units	2005	2006	2007	2008	2009
1. INBOUND TOURISM							
Data							
Arrivals							
1.1 Total		('000)	..	..	..	..	..
1.2 ♦ Overnight visitors (tourists)		('000)	2,027	2,253	2,507	2,699	2,750
1.3 ♦ Same-day visitors (excursionists)		('000)	959	957	741	990	897
1.4 * of which, cruise passengers		('000)	..	..	..	..	..
Arrivals by region							
1.5 Total		('000)	2,027	2,253	2,507	2,699	2,750
1.6 ♦ Africa		('000)	4	4	4	5	4
1.7 ♦ Americas		('000)	1,553	1,755	1,968	2,154	2,252
1.8 ♦ East Asia and the Pacific		('000)	75	84	91	88	79
1.9 ♦ Europe		('000)	385	402	437	447	411
1.10 ♦ Middle East		('000)	1	2	1	1	1
1.11 ♦ South Asia		('000)	4	4	4	4	3
1.12 ♦ Other not classified		('000)	5	2	2	..	..
1.13 * of which, nationals residing abroad		('000)	..	..	..	..	..
Arrivals by main purpose							
1.14 Total	(1)	('000)	2,069	2,273	2,534	2,710	2,758
1.15 ♦ Personal		('000)	1,719	1,795	2,075	2,142	2,044
1.16 * holidays, leisure and recreation		('000)	1,185	1,312	1,344	1,316	1,199
1.17 * other personal purposes		('000)	534	483	731	826	845
1.18 ♦ Business and professional		('000)	350	478	459	568	714
Arrivals by mode of transport							
1.19 Total		('000)	2,027	2,253	2,507	2,699	2,750
1.20 ♦ Air		('000)	855	912	1,055	1,039	979
1.21 ♦ Water		('000)	75	95	104	122	113
1.22 ♦ Land		('000)	1,097	1,246	1,348	1,538	1,658
1.23 * railway		('000)	3	2	2	3	2
1.24 * road		('000)	1,094	1,244	1,346	1,535	1,656
1.25 * others		('000)	..	..	..	..	..
Accommodation							
Total							
1.29 ♦ Guests		('000)	..	..	..	..	..
1.30 ♦ Overnights		('000)	..	..	..	..	..
Hotels and similar establishments	(2)						
1.31 ♦ Guests		('000)	1,397	1,460	1,563	1,564	1,424
1.32 ♦ Overnights		('000)	2,877	3,203	3,605	3,709	3,221
Expenditure							
1.33 Total		US$ Mn	1,682	1,891	2,226	2,537	2,270
1.34 ♦ Travel		US$ Mn	1,109	1,213	1,477	1,674	1,568
1.35 ♦ Passenger transport		US$ Mn	573	678	749	863	702
Expenditure by main purpose of the trip							
1.36 Total		US$ Mn	1,109	1,214	1,478	1,674	1,568
1.37 ♦ Personal		US$ Mn	958	1,042	1,217	1,123	1,062
1.38 ♦ Business and professional		US$ Mn	151	172	261	551	506
Indicators							
1.39 Average size of travel party		Persons	..	..	..	..	..
Average length of stay							
1.40 Total		Days	..	..	..	..	..
1.41 ♦ For all commercial accommodation services		Nights	12.50	10.40	10.90	9.80	9.20
1.42 * of which, "hotels and similar establishments"		Nights	..	..	..	..	..
1.43 ♦ For non commercial accommodation services		Days	..	..	..	..	..
1.44 Average expenditure per day		US$	..	..	..	..	..
2. DOMESTIC TOURISM							
Data							
Accommodation							
Total							
2.19 ♦ Guests		('000)	..	..	..	..	..
2.20 ♦ Overnights		('000)	..	..	..	..	..
Hotels and similar establishments	(2)						
2.21 ♦ Guests		('000)	2,888	3,082	3,371	3,531	3,328
2.22 ♦ Overnights		('000)	5,799	6,170	6,578	6,900	6,607

85

CHILE

Basic data and indicators	Notes	Units	2005	2006	2007	2008	2009
3. OUTBOUND TOURISM							
Data							
Departures							
3.1 Total		('000)	..	..	..	..	..
3.2 ♦ Overnight visitors (tourists)		('000)	2,651	3,005	3,234	3,061	2,895
3.3 ♦ Same-day visitors (excursionists)		('000)	..	..	..	..	..
Expenditure							
3.4 Total		US$ Mn	1,355	1,573	2,042	1,789	1,956
3.5 ♦ Travel		US$ Mn	1,051	1,239	1,660	1,397	1,625
3.6 ♦ Passenger transport		US$ Mn	304	334	382	392	331
Expenditure by main purpose of the trip							
3.7 Total		US$ Mn	1,050	1,240	1,661	1,398	1,624
3.8 ♦ Personal		US$ Mn	671	795	1,167	801	1,163
3.9 ♦ Business and professional		US$ Mn	379	445	494	597	461
Indicators							
3.10 Average length of stay		Days	10.00	10.00	9.00	7.00	8.40
3.11 Average expenditure per day		US$	45.0	47.0	54.0	70.0	71.0
4. TOURISM INDUSTRIES							
Data							
Number of establishments							
4.1 Total		Units	..	..	..	..	..
4.2 ♦ Accommodation for visitors		Units	..	..	..	..	..
4.3 * of which, "hotels and similar establishments"		Units	3,433	3,484	3,528	3,657	4,005
4.4 ♦ Food and beverage serving activities		Units	..	..	..	..	..
4.5 ♦ Passenger transportation		Units	..	..	..	..	..
4.6 ♦ Travel agencies and other reservation services activities		Units	..	..	..	..	..
4.7 ♦ Other tourism industries		Units	..	..	..	..	..
Accommodation for visitors in hotels and similar establishments							
Non-monetary data							
4.13 ♦ Number of establishments		Units	3,433	3,484	3,528	3,657	4,005
4.14 ♦ Number of rooms		Units	53,079	62,212	63,146	66,144	70,883
4.15 ♦ Number of bed-places		Units	130,295	136,550	138,126	143,528	151,738
Indicators							
4.16 Occupancy rate / rooms		Percent	34.10	35.90	36.40	38.60	37.90
4.17 Occupancy rate / bed-places		Percent	31.70	34.60	36.90	28.50	27.10
4.18 Average length of stay		Nights	2.00	2.10	2.10	2.10	2.10
4.19 Available capacity (bed-places per 1000 inhabitants)		Units	7.99	8.29	8.30	8.54	8.94
6. COMPLEMENTARY INDICATORS							
Demand							
6.1 Gross travel propensity		Units	..	..	..	..	..
6.2 Carrying capacity (arrivals/population)		Units	0.12	0.14	0.15	0.16	0.16
Macroeconomic indicators related to international tourism							
6.3 Inbound tourism expenditure over GDP		Percent	1.4	1.3	1.4	1.5	1.4
6.4 Outbound tourism expenditure over GDP		Percent	1.1	1.1	1.2	1.0	1.2
6.5 Tourism balance (inbound minus outbound tourism expenditure) over GDP		Percent	0.3	0.2	0.1	0.4	0.2
6.6 Tourism openness (inbound plus outbound tourism expenditure) over GDP		Percent	2.6	2.4	2.6	2.5	2.6
6.7 Tourism coverage (inbound over outbound tourism expenditure)		Percent	124.2	120.3	109.0	141.8	116.1
6.8 Inbound tourism expenditure over exports of goods		Percent	4.1	3.2	3.3	3.8	4.2
6.9 Inbound tourism expenditure over exports of services		Percent	23.6	24.2	24.8	23.5	26.7
6.10 Inbound tourism expenditure over exports of goods and services		Percent	3.5	2.8	2.9	3.3	3.6
6.11 Inbound tourism expenditure over current account credits		Percent	3.2	2.6	2.6	2.9	3.2
6.12 Outbound tourism expenditure over imports of goods		Percent	4.4	4.4	4.6	3.1	4.9
6.13 Outbound tourism expenditure over imports of services		Percent	17.5	18.6	20.5	15.3	20.4
6.14 Outbound tourism expenditure over imports of goods and services		Percent	3.5	3.5	3.8	2.6	4.0
6.15 Outbound tourism expenditure over current account debits		Percent	2.6	2.4	2.6	2.0	3.0

CHINA

Basic data and indicators	Notes	Units	2005	2006	2007	2008	2009
1. INBOUND TOURISM							
Data							
Arrivals							
1.1 Total	(1)	('000)	120,292	124,942	131,873	130,027	126,476
1.2 ♦ Overnight visitors (tourists)		('000)	46,809	49,913	54,720	53,049	50,875
1.3 ♦ Same-day visitors (excursionists)		('000)	..	..	..	..	..
1.4 * of which, cruise passengers		('000)	..	..	..	..	..
Arrivals by region	(1)						
1.5 Total		('000)	120,292	124,941	131,873	130,027	126,474
1.6 ♦ Africa		('000)	211	255	327	324	340
1.7 ♦ Americas		('000)	2,146	2,406	2,721	2,582	2,491
1.8 ♦ East Asia and the Pacific		('000)	112,053	115,700	120,956	119,584	117,589
1.9 ♦ Europe		('000)	5,166	5,769	6,937	6,688	5,131
1.10 ♦ Middle East		('000)	111	136	180	178	207
1.11 ♦ South Asia		('000)	599	671	749	669	714
1.12 ♦ Other not classified		('000)	6	4	3	2	2
1.13 * of which, nationals residing abroad		('000)	..	..	..	..	..
Arrivals by main purpose	(2)						
1.14 Total		('000)	20,255	22,210	26,110	24,326	21,938
1.15 ♦ Personal		('000)	15,657	16,662	19,149	18,648	16,701
1.16 * holidays, leisure and recreation		('000)	9,345	11,332	13,141	12,040	10,133
1.17 * other personal purposes		('000)	6,312	5,330	6,008	6,608	6,568
1.18 ♦ Business and professional		('000)	4,598	5,548	6,961	5,678	5,237
Arrivals by mode of transport	(1)						
1.19 Total		('000)	120,293	124,942	131,872	130,027	126,476
1.20 ♦ Air		('000)	14,736	16,500	18,815	16,813	16,301
1.21 ♦ Water		('000)	5,212	5,484	5,920	5,480	4,672
1.22 ♦ Land		('000)	100,345	102,958	107,137	107,734	105,503
1.23 * railway		('000)	1,610	1,661	1,664	1,613	1,229
1.24 * road		('000)	31,938	33,540	34,773	32,681	30,484
1.25 * others		('000)	66,797	67,757	70,700	73,440	73,790
Accommodation							
Total							
1.29 ♦ Guests		('000)	..	..	..	..	..
1.30 ♦ Overnights		('000)	..	..	..	..	..
Hotels and similar establishments							
1.31 ♦ Guests		('000)	53,258	61,396	73,114	75,007	80,392
1.32 ♦ Overnights		('000)	138,411	163,680	195,080	197,912	215,661
Expenditure							
1.33 Total		US$ Mn	31,842	37,132	41,126	44,130	42,632
1.34 ♦ Travel		US$ Mn	29,296	33,949	37,233	40,843	39,675
1.35 ♦ Passenger transport		US$ Mn	2,546	3,183	3,893	3,287	2,957
Indicators							
1.39 Average size of travel party		Persons	..	..	..	..	..
Average length of stay							
1.40 Total		Days	..	..	..	..	..
1.41 ♦ For all commercial accommodation services		Nights	2.60	2.67	2.67	2.64	2.68
1.42 * of which, "hotels and similar establishments"		Nights	..	..	..	..	..
1.43 ♦ For non commercial accommodation services		Days	..	..	..	..	..
1.44 Average expenditure per day		US$	..	..	..	..	..
2. DOMESTIC TOURISM							
Data							
Accommodation							
Total							
2.19 ♦ Guests		('000)	..	..	..	..	..
2.20 ♦ Overnights		('000)	..	..	..	..	..
Hotels and similar establishments							
2.21 ♦ Guests		('000)	..	..	..	..	..
2.22 ♦ Overnights	(3)	('000)	369,000	413,645	435,849	437,213	439,717

CHINA

Basic data and indicators	Notes	Units	2005	2006	2007	2008	2009
3. OUTBOUND TOURISM							
Data							
Departures							
3.1 Total		('000)	..	..	..	..	..
3.2 ♦ Overnight visitors (tourists)	(4)	('000)	31,026	34,524	40,954	45,844	47,656
3.3 ♦ Same-day visitors (excursionists)		('000)	..	..	..	..	..
Expenditure							
3.4 Total		US$ Mn	24,715	28,242	33,264	40,987	47,108
3.5 ♦ Travel		US$ Mn	21,759	24,322	29,786	36,157	43,702
3.6 ♦ Passenger transport		US$ Mn	2,956	3,920	3,478	4,830	3,406
4. TOURISM INDUSTRIES							
Data							
Number of establishments							
4.1 Total		Units	..	..	..	..	..
4.2 ♦ Accommodation for visitors		Units	..	..	..	..	..
4.3 * of which, "hotels and similar establishments"	(3)	Units	11,828	12,751	13,583	14,099	14,237
4.4 ♦ Food and beverage serving activities		Units	..	..	..	..	..
4.5 ♦ Passenger transportation		Units	..	..	..	..	..
4.6 ♦ Travel agencies and other reservation services activities		Units	..	..	..	..	..
4.7 ♦ Other tourism industries		Units	..	..	..	..	..
Accommodation for visitors in hotels and similar establishments							
Non-monetary data	(3)						
4.13 ♦ Number of establishments		Units	11,828	12,751	13,583	14,099	14,237
4.14 ♦ Number of rooms		Units	1,332,083	1,459,836	1,573,784	1,591,379	1,673,475
4.15 ♦ Number of bed-places		Units	2,571,664	2,785,481	2,969,434	2,934,758	3,064,684
Indicators							
4.16 Occupancy rate / rooms		Percent	60.96	61.03	60.96	58.30	57.88
4.17 Occupancy rate / bed-places		Percent	..	..	..	..	..
4.18 Average length of stay	(5)	Nights	2.60	2.67	2.67	2.64	2.68
4.19 Available capacity (bed-places per 1000 inhabitants)		Units	1.97	2.12	2.25	2.22	2.30
6. COMPLEMENTARY INDICATORS							
Demand							
6.1 Gross travel propensity		Units	..	..	..	..	..
6.2 Carrying capacity (arrivals/population)		Units	0.04	0.04	0.04	0.04	0.04
Macroeconomic indicators related to international tourism							
6.3 Inbound tourism expenditure over GDP		Percent	1.4	1.4	1.2	1.0	0.9
6.4 Outbound tourism expenditure over GDP		Percent	1.1	1.1	1.0	0.9	1.0
6.5 Tourism balance (inbound minus outbound tourism expenditure) over GDP		Percent	0.3	0.3	0.2	0.1	-0.1
6.6 Tourism openness (inbound plus outbound tourism expenditure) over GDP		Percent	2.5	2.5	2.2	2.0	1.8
6.7 Tourism coverage (inbound over outbound tourism expenditure)		Percent	128.8	131.5	123.6	107.7	90.5
6.8 Inbound tourism expenditure over exports of goods		Percent	4.2	3.8	3.4	3.1	3.5
6.9 Inbound tourism expenditure over exports of services		Percent	42.8	40.4	33.7	30.0	32.9
6.10 Inbound tourism expenditure over exports of goods and services		Percent	3.8	3.5	3.1	2.8	3.2
6.11 Inbound tourism expenditure over current account credits		Percent	3.5	3.2	2.8	2.5	2.9
6.12 Outbound tourism expenditure over imports of goods		Percent	3.9	3.8	3.7	3.8	4.9
6.13 Outbound tourism expenditure over imports of services		Percent	29.5	28.0	25.6	25.8	29.6
6.14 Outbound tourism expenditure over imports of goods and services		Percent	3.5	3.3	3.2	3.3	4.2
6.15 Outbound tourism expenditure over current account debits		Percent	3.3	3.2	3.0	3.2	4.0

COLOMBIA

Basic data and indicators	Notes	Units	2005	2006	2007	2008	2009
1. INBOUND TOURISM							
Data							
Arrivals							
1.1 Total	(1)(2)(3)	('000)	981	1,104	2,242	2,396	2,494
1.2 ♦ Overnight visitors (tourists)		('000)	933	1,053	2,115	2,168	2,147
1.3 ♦ Same-day visitors (excursionists)		('000)	48	51	127	228	347
1.4 * of which, cruise passengers		('000)	48	51	127	228	347
Arrivals by region	(1)(4)(5)						
1.5 Total		('000)	933	1,054	1,195	1,223	1,354
1.6 ♦ Africa		('000)	1	2	4	2	2
1.7 ♦ Americas		('000)	730	827	944	969	1,064
1.8 ♦ East Asia and the Pacific		('000)	15	17	24	21	26
1.9 ♦ Europe		('000)	183	205	220	227	258
1.10 ♦ Middle East		('000)	1	1	1	1	1
1.11 ♦ South Asia		('000)	2	2	2	2	3
1.12 ♦ Other not classified		('000)	1	..	..	1	..
1.13 * of which, nationals residing abroad		('000)	..	..	..	..	..
Arrivals by main purpose	(1)(5)						
1.14 Total		('000)	933	..	..	..	..
1.15 ♦ Personal		('000)	667	..	..	..	..
1.16 * holidays, leisure and recreation		('000)	581	..	..	..	..
1.17 * other personal purposes		('000)	86	..	..	..	..
1.18 ♦ Business and professional		('000)	266	..	..	..	..
Arrivals by mode of transport	(1)						
1.19 Total		('000)	981	1,104	1,322	1,451	2,494
1.20 ♦ Air		('000)	834	936	1,055	1,068	1,192
1.21 ♦ Water	(3)	('000)	50	52	128	231	353
1.22 ♦ Land		('000)	97	116	139	152	949
1.23 * railway		('000)	..	..	..	..	..
1.24 * road	(6)	('000)	97	116	139	152	949
1.25 * others		('000)	..	..	..	..	..
Expenditure							
1.33 Total		US$ Mn	1,574	2,009	2,262	2,499	2,671
1.34 ♦ Travel		US$ Mn	1,222	1,554	1,669	1,844	1,999
1.35 ♦ Passenger transport		US$ Mn	352	455	593	655	672
3. OUTBOUND TOURISM							
Data							
Departures							
3.1 Total		('000)	..	..	..	..	..
3.2 ♦ Overnight visitors (tourists)		('000)	1,553	1,768	2,041	2,042	2,122
3.3 ♦ Same-day visitors (excursionists)		('000)	..	..	..	..	..
Expenditure							
3.4 Total		US$ Mn	1,565	1,799	2,093	2,337	2,302
3.5 ♦ Travel		US$ Mn	1,130	1,332	1,537	1,739	1,752
3.6 ♦ Passenger transport		US$ Mn	435	467	556	598	550
4. TOURISM INDUSTRIES							
Data							
Number of establishments							
4.1 Total		Units	..	..	..	..	13,181
4.2 ♦ Accommodation for visitors		Units	..	..	..	..	5,845
4.3 * of which, "hotels and similar establishments"		Units	2,930	..	..	..	..
4.4 ♦ Food and beverage serving activities		Units	..	..	..	..	..
4.5 ♦ Passenger transportation		Units	..	..	..	..	..
4.6 ♦ Travel agencies and other reservation services activities		Units	..	..	..	..	4,133
4.7 ♦ Other tourism industries		Units	..	..	..	..	3,203
Accommodation for visitors in hotels and similar establishments							
Non-monetary data							
4.13 ♦ Number of establishments		Units	2,930	..	..	..	5,845
4.14 ♦ Number of rooms		Units	71,247	..	..	..	136,581
4.15 ♦ Number of bed-places		Units	141,151	..	..	..	259,478
Indicators							
4.16 Occupancy rate / rooms	(7)	Percent	51.00	53.90	55.05	54.10	49.70
4.17 Occupancy rate / bed-places		Percent	..	..	..	..	..
4.18 Average length of stay		Nights	..	..	..	..	..
4.19 Available capacity (bed-places per 1000 inhabitants)		Units	3.28	..	..	..	5.68

COLOMBIA

Basic data and indicators	Notes	Units	2005	2006	2007	2008	2009
6. **COMPLEMENTARY INDICATORS**							
Demand							
6.1 Gross travel propensity		Units	..	..	..	..	..
6.2 Carrying capacity (arrivals/population)		Units	0.02	0.02	0.05	0.05	0.05
Macroeconomic indicators related to international tourism							
6.3 Inbound tourism expenditure over GDP		Percent	1.1	1.2	1.1	1.0	1.2
6.4 Outbound tourism expenditure over GDP		Percent	1.1	1.1	1.0	1.0	1.0
6.5 Tourism balance (inbound minus outbound tourism expenditure) over GDP		Percent	0.0	0.1	0.1	0.1	0.2
6.6 Tourism openness (inbound plus outbound tourism expenditure) over GDP		Percent	2.2	2.3	2.1	2.0	2.2
6.7 Tourism coverage (inbound over outbound tourism expenditure)		Percent	100.5	111.7	108.1	106.9	116.0
6.8 Inbound tourism expenditure over exports of goods		Percent	7.2	8.0	7.4	6.5	7.8
6.9 Inbound tourism expenditure over exports of services		Percent	59.0	59.5	62.2	60.4	63.7
6.10 Inbound tourism expenditure over exports of goods and services		Percent	6.5	7.0	6.6	5.9	7.0
6.11 Inbound tourism expenditure over current account credits		Percent	5.3	5.7	5.4	5.0	6.0
6.12 Outbound tourism expenditure over imports of goods		Percent	7.8	7.2	6.7	6.2	7.3
6.13 Outbound tourism expenditure over imports of services		Percent	32.8	32.7	33.5	32.5	33.4
6.14 Outbound tourism expenditure over imports of goods and services		Percent	6.3	5.9	5.6	5.2	6.0
6.15 Outbound tourism expenditure over current account debits		Percent	4.9	4.7	4.4	4.1	4.6

COMOROS

Basic data and indicators	Notes	Units	2005	2006	2007	2008	2009
1. INBOUND TOURISM							
Data							
Arrivals							
1.1 Total		('000)	..	..	..	..	..
1.2 ♦ Overnight visitors (tourists)	(1)	('000)	25.9	28.5	14.6	..	..
1.3 ♦ Same-day visitors (excursionists)		('000)	..	..	..	..	..
1.4 * of which, cruise passengers		('000)	..	..	..	..	..
Arrivals by region	(2)						
1.5 Total		('000)	19.5	17.1	14.6	..	..
1.6 ♦ Africa		('000)	8.8	6.1	4.2	..	..
1.7 ♦ Americas		('000)	0.1	0.4	0.4	..	..
1.8 ♦ East Asia and the Pacific		('000)	0.5	0.6	0.4	..	..
1.9 ♦ Europe		('000)	9.6	9.5	9.5	..	..
1.10 ♦ Middle East		('000)	..	..	..	..	..
1.11 ♦ South Asia		('000)	..	..	..	..	..
1.12 ♦ Other not classified		('000)	0.5	0.5	0.1	..	..
1.13 * of which, nationals residing abroad		('000)	..	..	..	..	..
Arrivals by main purpose	(1)						
1.14 Total		('000)	25.9	28.5	14.6	..	..
1.15 ♦ Personal		('000)	21.0	23.1	10.2	..	..
1.16 * holidays, leisure and recreation		('000)	4.7	5.1	2.9	..	..
1.17 * other personal purposes		('000)	16.3	18.0	7.3	..	..
1.18 ♦ Business and professional		('000)	4.9	5.4	4.4	..	..
Arrivals by mode of transport							
1.19 Total		('000)	19.6	17.1	14.6	..	..
1.20 ♦ Air		('000)	19.6	17.1	14.6	..	..
1.21 ♦ Water		('000)	..	..	..	..	..
1.22 ♦ Land		('000)	..	..	..	..	..
1.23 * railway		('000)	..	..	..	..	..
1.24 * road		('000)	..	..	..	..	..
1.25 * others		('000)	..	..	..	..	..
Accommodation							
Total							
1.29 ♦ Guests		('000)	..	..	..	..	..
1.30 ♦ Overnights		('000)	137	136	119	..	..
Hotels and similar establishments							
1.31 ♦ Guests		('000)	..	..	..	..	..
1.32 ♦ Overnights		('000)	..	..	..	..	..
Expenditure							
1.33 Total	(3)	US$ Mn	23.6	26.8	..	..	..
1.34 ♦ Travel		US$ Mn	..	..	..	..	..
1.35 ♦ Passenger transport		US$ Mn	..	..	..	..	..
Indicators							
1.39 Average size of travel party		Persons	..	..	..	..	..
Average length of stay							
1.40 Total		Days	..	..	..	..	..
1.41 ♦ For all commercial accommodation services		Nights	7.00	7.00	7.00	..	..
1.42 * of which, "hotels and similar establishments"		Nights	..	..	..	..	..
1.43 ♦ For non commercial accommodation services		Days	..	..	..	..	..
1.44 Average expenditure per day		US$	..	..	..	..	..
3. OUTBOUND TOURISM							
Data							
Expenditure							
3.4 Total	(3)	US$ Mn	9.6	10.8	..	..	..
3.5 ♦ Travel		US$ Mn	..	..	..	..	..
3.6 ♦ Passenger transport		US$ Mn	..	..	..	..	..

COMOROS

Basic data and indicators	Notes	Units	2005	2006	2007	2008	2009
4. TOURISM INDUSTRIES							
Data							
Number of establishments							
4.1 Total		Units	..	..	..	..	..
4.2 ♦ Accommodation for visitors		Units	..	..	..	..	..
4.3 * of which, "hotels and similar establishments"		Units	33	33	38	..	..
4.4 ♦ Food and beverage serving activities		Units	..	..	..	..	..
4.5 ♦ Passenger transportation		Units	..	..	..	..	..
4.6 ♦ Travel agencies and other reservation services activities		Units	..	..	..	..	..
4.7 ♦ Other tourism industries		Units	..	..	..	..	..
Accommodation for visitors in hotels and similar establishments							
Non-monetary data							
4.13 ♦ Number of establishments		Units	33	33	38	..	..
4.14 ♦ Number of rooms		Units	328	328	235	..	..
4.15 ♦ Number of bed-places		Units	656	656	441	..	..
Indicators							
4.16 Occupancy rate / rooms		Percent	..	..	..	..	..
4.17 Occupancy rate / bed-places		Percent	..	..	..	..	..
4.18 Average length of stay		Nights	7.00	7.00	7.00	..	..
4.19 Available capacity (bed-places per 1000 inhabitants)		Units	1.09	1.07	0.70	..	..
6. COMPLEMENTARY INDICATORS							
Demand							
6.1 Gross travel propensity		Units	..	..	..	..	..
6.2 Carrying capacity (arrivals/population)		Units	0.04	0.05	0.02	..	..

CONGO

Basic data and indicators	Notes	Units	2005	2006	2007	2008	2009
1. INBOUND TOURISM							
Data							
Arrivals							
1.1 Total		('000)	..	..	..	..	..
1.2 ♦ Overnight visitors (tourists)		('000)	35	43	54	63	85
1.3 ♦ Same-day visitors (excursionists)		('000)	..	..	..	..	..
1.4 * of which, cruise passengers		('000)	..	..	..	..	..
Arrivals by region							
1.5 Total		('000)	35	43	54	63	85
1.6 ♦ Africa		('000)	13	20	28	25	30
1.7 ♦ Americas		('000)	2	1	3	4	11
1.8 ♦ East Asia and the Pacific		('000)	..	..	..	..	..
1.9 ♦ Europe		('000)	13	14	19	30	40
1.10 ♦ Middle East		('000)	..	..	..	..	..
1.11 ♦ South Asia		('000)	..	..	..	..	..
1.12 ♦ Other not classified		('000)	7	8	4	4	4
1.13 * of which, nationals residing abroad		('000)	..	..	..	..	..
Accommodation							
Total							
1.29 ♦ Guests		('000)	..	..	..	..	..
1.30 ♦ Overnights		('000)	..	..	..	..	..
Hotels and similar establishments							
1.31 ♦ Guests		('000)	35	43	54	63	85
1.32 ♦ Overnights		('000)	106	124	169	180	240
Expenditure							
1.33 Total		US$ Mn	..	..	..	..	..
1.34 ♦ Travel		US$ Mn	40	45	54	..	..
1.35 ♦ Passenger transport		US$ Mn	..	..	..	..	..
Indicators							
1.39 Average size of travel party		Persons	..	..	..	..	..
Average length of stay							
1.40 Total		Days	4.80	5.60	6.20	7.30	7.00
1.41 ♦ For all commercial accommodation services		Nights	..	..		..	..
1.42 * of which, "hotels and similar establishments"		Nights	..	..	..	..	..
1.43 ♦ For non commercial accommodation services		Days	..	..		..	..
1.44 Average expenditure per day		US$	..	..	..	..	..
2. DOMESTIC TOURISM							
Data							
Accommodation							
Total							
2.19 ♦ Guests		('000)	..	..	..	..	..
2.20 ♦ Overnights		('000)	..	..	..	..	..
Hotels and similar establishments							
2.21 ♦ Guests		('000)	15	17	20	25	36
2.22 ♦ Overnights		('000)	39	46	50	63	92
Indicators							
2.23 Average size of travel party		Persons	..	..	..	..	..
Average length of stay							
2.24 Total		Days	5.20	5.30	5.20	7.70	7.00
2.25 ♦ For all commercial accommodation services		Nights	..	..	..	..	..
2.26 * of which, "hotels and similar establishments"		Nights	..	..	..	..	..
2.27 ♦ For non commercial accommodation services		Days	..	..	..	..	..
2.28 Average expenditure per day		US$	..	..	..	..	..
3. OUTBOUND TOURISM							
Data							
Expenditure							
3.4 Total		US$ Mn	..	..	..	..	..
3.5 ♦ Travel		US$ Mn	112	132	168	..	..
3.6 ♦ Passenger transport		US$ Mn	..	..	..	..	..

CONGO

Basic data and indicators	Notes	Units	2005	2006	2007	2008	2009
4. TOURISM INDUSTRIES							
Data							
Number of establishments							
4.1 Total		Units	..	..	..	..	..
4.2 ♦ Accommodation for visitors		Units	..	..	..	..	..
4.3 * of which, "hotels and similar establishments"		Units	506	668	717	..	..
4.4 ♦ Food and beverage serving activities		Units	..	..	..	..	..
4.5 ♦ Passenger transportation		Units	..	..	..	..	..
4.6 ♦ Travel agencies and other reservation services activities		Units	..	..	..	..	..
4.7 ♦ Other tourism industries		Units	..	..	..	..	..
Accommodation for visitors in hotels and similar establishments							
Non-monetary data							
4.13 ♦ Number of establishments		Units	506	668	717	..	..
4.14 ♦ Number of rooms		Units	4,628	6,739	7,272	..	..
4.15 ♦ Number of bed-places		Units	..	..	..	..	..
6. COMPLEMENTARY INDICATORS							
Demand							
6.1 Gross travel propensity		Units	..	..	..	..	..
6.2 Carrying capacity (arrivals/population)		Units	0.01	0.01	0.02	0.02	0.02
Macroeconomic indicators related to international tourism							
6.3 Inbound tourism expenditure over GDP		Percent	0.7	0.6	0.7	..	..
6.4 Outbound tourism expenditure over GDP		Percent	1.9	1.8	2.2	..	..
6.5 Tourism balance (inbound minus outbound tourism expenditure) over GDP		Percent	-1.2	-1.2	-1.5	..	..
6.6 Tourism openness (inbound plus outbound tourism expenditure) over GDP		Percent	2.5	2.4	2.9	..	..
6.7 Tourism coverage (inbound over outbound tourism expenditure)		Percent	36.1	34.3	32.5	..	..
6.8 Inbound tourism expenditure over exports of goods		Percent	0.9	0.7	0.9	..	..
6.9 Inbound tourism expenditure over exports of services		Percent	18.3	17.0	17.0	..	..
6.10 Inbound tourism expenditure over exports of goods and services		Percent	0.8	0.7	0.9	..	..
6.11 Inbound tourism expenditure over current account credits		Percent	0.8	0.7	0.9	..	..
6.12 Outbound tourism expenditure over imports of goods		Percent	8.6	6.6	5.9	..	..
6.13 Outbound tourism expenditure over imports of services		Percent	7.9	5.5	4.7	..	..
6.14 Outbound tourism expenditure over imports of goods and services		Percent	4.1	3.0	2.6	..	..
6.15 Outbound tourism expenditure over current account debits		Percent	2.6	2.1	2.0	..	..

COOK ISLANDS

Basic data and indicators	Notes	Units	2005	2006	2007	2008	2009
1. INBOUND TOURISM							
Data							
Arrivals							
1.1 Total		('000)	..	..	..	..	..
1.2 ♦ Overnight visitors (tourists)	(1)	('000)	88	92	97	95	101
1.3 ♦ Same-day visitors (excursionists)		('000)	..	..	..	..	..
1.4 * of which, cruise passengers		('000)	..	..	..	..	..
Arrivals by region	(1)						
1.5 Total		('000)	88	92	97	95	101
1.6 ♦ Africa		('000)	..	..	..	..	..
1.7 ♦ Americas		('000)	6	8	7	6	6
1.8 ♦ East Asia and the Pacific		('000)	63	66	75	75	81
1.9 ♦ Europe		('000)	18	18	15	13	12
1.10 ♦ Middle East		('000)	..	..	..	..	..
1.11 ♦ South Asia		('000)	..	..	..	..	..
1.12 ♦ Other not classified		('000)	1	..	..	1	2
1.13 * of which, nationals residing abroad		('000)	..	..	..	..	..
Arrivals by main purpose	(1)						
1.14 Total		('000)	88	92	97	95	101
1.15 ♦ Personal		('000)	85	89	93	91	97
1.16 * holidays, leisure and recreation		('000)	73	76	79	78	80
1.17 * other personal purposes		('000)	12	13	14	13	17
1.18 ♦ Business and professional		('000)	3	3	4	4	4
Accommodation							
Total							
1.29 ♦ Guests		('000)	..	..	..	..	..
1.30 ♦ Overnights		('000)	..	..	..	..	..
Hotels and similar establishments							
1.31 ♦ Guests		('000)	..	..	..	..	..
1.32 ♦ Overnights		('000)	230	241	226	224	242
Expenditure							
1.33 Total	(2)	US$ Mn	91	90	107	105	..
1.34 ♦ Travel		US$ Mn	..	..	..	..	..
1.35 ♦ Passenger transport		US$ Mn	..	..	..	..	..
Indicators							
1.39 Average size of travel party		Persons	..	..	..	..	..
Average length of stay							
1.40 Total		Days	..	..	..	..	..
1.41 ♦ For all commercial accommodation services		Nights	10.27	10.43	10.18	10.28	10.28
1.42 * of which, "hotels and similar establishments"		Nights	..	..	..	..	..
1.43 ♦ For non commercial accommodation services		Days	..	..	..	..	..
1.44 Average expenditure per day		US$	..	..	..	..	..
3. OUTBOUND TOURISM							
Data							
Departures							
3.1 Total		('000)	..	..	..	..	..
3.2 ♦ Overnight visitors (tourists)		('000)	13	13	13	13	12
3.3 ♦ Same-day visitors (excursionists)		('000)	..	..	..	..	..
4. TOURISM INDUSTRIES							
Data							
Accommodation for visitors in hotels and similar establishments							
Non-monetary data							
4.13 ♦ Number of establishments		Units	..	..	..	..	..
4.14 ♦ Number of rooms	(3)	Units	997	1,069	1,191	1,173	1,328
4.15 ♦ Number of bed-places	(3)	Units	2,772	2,698	3,143	3,138	3,510
Indicators							
4.16 Occupancy rate / rooms		Percent	48.40	61.50	52.67	52.70	50.10
4.17 Occupancy rate / bed-places		Percent	44.20	54.10	46.50	46.10	46.30
4.18 Average length of stay		Nights	..	..	..	..	..
4.19 Available capacity (bed-places per 1000 inhabitants)		Units	..	..	..	..	..

COSTA RICA

Basic data and indicators	Notes	Units	2005	2006	2007	2008	2009
1. INBOUND TOURISM							
Data							
Arrivals							
1.1 Total		('000)	1,959	2,071	2,302	2,409	2,289
1.2 ♦ Overnight visitors (tourists)		('000)	1,679	1,725	1,980	2,089	1,923
1.3 ♦ Same-day visitors (excursionists)		('000)	280	346	322	320	366
1.4 * of which, cruise passengers		('000)	280	346	322	320	366
Arrivals by region							
1.5 Total		('000)	1,680	1,725	1,980	2,089	1,923
1.6 ♦ Africa		('000)	1	1	2	2	2
1.7 ♦ Americas		('000)	1,412	1,457	1,670	1,755	1,635
1.8 ♦ East Asia and the Pacific		('000)	24	23	26	28	27
1.9 ♦ Europe		('000)	242	243	282	300	259
1.10 ♦ Middle East		('000)	..	..	..	..	..
1.11 ♦ South Asia		('000)	..	..	..	..	..
1.12 ♦ Other not classified		('000)	1	1	..	4	..
1.13 * of which, nationals residing abroad		('000)	..	..	..	..	..
Arrivals by main purpose							
1.14 Total		('000)	1,679	1,725	1,980	2,089	1,923
1.15 ♦ Personal		('000)	1,407	1,432	1,702	1,688	1,729
1.16 * holidays, leisure and recreation	(1)	('000)	1,357	1,311	1,597	1,574	1,652
1.17 * other personal purposes		('000)	50	121	105	114	77
1.18 ♦ Business and professional		('000)	272	293	278	401	194
Arrivals by mode of transport							
1.19 Total		('000)	1,680	1,725	1,980	2,089	1,923
1.20 ♦ Air		('000)	1,244	1,232	1,357	1,424	1,320
1.21 ♦ Water		('000)	9	6	5	4	2
1.22 ♦ Land		('000)	427	487	618	661	601
1.23 * railway		('000)	..	..	..	..	..
1.24 * road		('000)	427	487	618	661	601
1.25 * others		('000)	..	..	..	..	..
Expenditure							
1.33 Total		US$ Mn	1,810	1,865	2,221	2,533	1,985
1.34 ♦ Travel		US$ Mn	1,671	1,707	2,026	2,283	1,799
1.35 ♦ Passenger transport		US$ Mn	139	158	195	250	186
Expenditure by main purpose of the trip							
1.36 Total		US$ Mn	1,671	1,707	2,026	2,283	1,799
1.37 ♦ Personal		US$ Mn	1,669	1,706	2,025	2,281	1,797
1.38 ♦ Business and professional		US$ Mn	2	1	1	2	2
Indicators							
1.39 Average size of travel party		Persons	..	..	..	..	..
Average length of stay							
1.40 Total		Days	..	..	..	..	..
1.41 ♦ For all commercial accommodation services	(2)	Nights	10.50	12.50	12.00	11.00	11.90
1.42 * of which, "hotels and similar establishments"		Nights	..	..	..	..	..
1.43 ♦ For non commercial accommodation services		Days	..	..	..	..	..
1.44 Average expenditure per day		US$	..	..	..	..	..
3. OUTBOUND TOURISM							
Data							
Departures							
3.1 Total		('000)	..	..	..	..	..
3.2 ♦ Overnight visitors (tourists)		('000)	487	485	577	519	579
3.3 ♦ Same-day visitors (excursionists)		('000)	..	..	..	..	..
Expenditure							
3.4 Total		US$ Mn	556	577	751	718	463
3.5 ♦ Travel		US$ Mn	470	485	634	593	368
3.6 ♦ Passenger transport		US$ Mn	86	92	117	125	95
Expenditure by main purpose of the trip							
3.7 Total		US$ Mn	469	485	633	593	368
3.8 ♦ Personal		US$ Mn	468	484	632	592	367
3.9 ♦ Business and professional		US$ Mn	1	1	1	1	1

COSTA RICA

Basic data and indicators	Notes	Units	2005	2006	2007	2008	2009
4. TOURISM INDUSTRIES							
Data							
Number of establishments							
4.1 Total		Units	..	..	..	..	..
4.2 ♦ Accommodation for visitors		Units	..	..	..	..	..
4.3 * of which, "hotels and similar establishments"		Units	2,376	2,576	2,595	2,599	2,508
4.4 ♦ Food and beverage serving activities		Units	..	..	..	..	..
4.5 ♦ Passenger transportation		Units	..	..	..	..	..
4.6 ♦ Travel agencies and other reservation services activities		Units	..	..	..	..	..
4.7 ♦ Other tourism industries		Units	..	..	..	..	..
Accommodation for visitors in hotels and similar establishments							
Monetary data							
4.8 ♦ Output		US$ Mn	927.8	1,004.1	1,138.8	1,230.1	1,082.5
4.9 ♦ Intermediate consumption		US$ Mn	376.4	407.3	461.9	499.0	439.1
4.10 ♦ Gross value added		US$ Mn	551.5	596.8	676.8	731.1	643.4
4.11 ♦ Compensation of employees		US$ Mn	188.0	198.5	235.2	267.7	242.9
4.12 ♦ Gross fixed capital formation		US$ Mn	..	..	..	..	..
Non-monetary data							
4.13 ♦ Number of establishments		Units	2,376	2,576	2,595	2,599	2,508
4.14 ♦ Number of rooms		Units	38,737	40,811	41,340	41,759	42,058
4.15 ♦ Number of bed-places		Units	..	..	..	..	..
Indicators							
4.16 Occupancy rate / rooms		Percent	..	..	..	..	..
4.17 Occupancy rate / bed-places	(3)	Percent	58.90	58.30	59.70	58.00	..
4.18 Average length of stay		Nights	..	..	..	..	..
4.19 Available capacity (bed-places per 1000 inhabitants)		Units	..	..	..	..	..
Travel agencies and other reservation service activities							
Monetary data							
4.20 ♦ Output		US$ Mn	138.5	142.6	185.5	194.7	167.1
4.21 ♦ Intermediate consumption		US$ Mn	61.3	63.8	83.7	86.1	74.1
4.22 ♦ Gross value added		US$ Mn	77.3	78.8	101.8	108.7	93.0
4.23 ♦ Compensation of employees		US$ Mn	18.9	19.6	25.7	23.9	23.0
4.24 ♦ Gross fixed capital formation		US$ Mn	..	..	..	..	..
5. EMPLOYMENT							
Data							
Number of employees by tourism industries							
5.1 Total	(4)	('000)	98.0	97.8	108.3	100.3	105.7
5.2 ♦ Accommodation services for visitors (hotels and similar establishments)		('000)	..	..	..	..	..
5.3 ♦ Other accommodation services		('000)	..	..	..	..	..
5.4 ♦ Food and beverage serving activities		('000)	..	..	..	..	..
5.5 ♦ Passenger transportation		('000)	..	..	..	..	..
5.6 ♦ Travel agencies and other reservation services activities		('000)	..	..	..	..	..
5.7 ♦ Other tourism industries		('000)	..	..	..	..	..
Number of jobs by status in employment	(5)						
5.8 Total		('000)	1,309.6	1,789.0	1,890.6	1,927.3	1,924.0
5.9 ♦ Employees		('000)	1268.9	1293.7	1406.6	1426.6	1421.3
5.10 ♦ Self employed		('000)	40.7	495.3	484.0	500.7	502.7
Indicators							
Number of full-time equivalent jobs by status in employment	(6)						
5.11 Total		('000)	102.7	97.6	89.2	76.8	100.9
5.12 ♦ Employees		('000)	51.5	46.3	48.0	37.2	54.2
5.13 * male		('000)	26.7	19.6	20.6	16.2	25.5
5.14 * female		('000)	24.8	26.6	27.4	21.0	28.7
5.15 ♦ Self employed		('000)	51.2	51.3	41.2	39.7	46.7
5.16 * male		('000)	25.6	26.5	21.1	19.5	23.2
5.17 * female		('000)	25.6	24.9	20.1	20.2	23.6

COSTA RICA

Basic data and indicators	Notes	Units	2005	2006	2007	2008	2009
6. COMPLEMENTARY INDICATORS							
Demand							
6.1 Gross travel propensity		Units	..	..	..	..	..
6.2 Carrying capacity (arrivals/population)		Units	0.39	0.39	0.44	0.46	0.42
Macroeconomic indicators related to international tourism							
6.3 Inbound tourism expenditure over GDP		Percent	9.1	8.3	8.5	8.5	..
6.4 Outbound tourism expenditure over GDP		Percent	2.8	2.6	2.9	2.4	..
6.5 Tourism balance (inbound minus outbound tourism expenditure) over GDP		Percent	6.3	5.7	5.6	6.1	..
6.6 Tourism openness (inbound plus outbound tourism expenditure) over GDP		Percent	11.8	10.8	11.3	10.9	..
6.7 Tourism coverage (inbound over outbound tourism expenditure)		Percent	325.5	323.2	296.1	351.9	..
6.8 Inbound tourism expenditure over exports of goods		Percent	25.5	23.0	23.9	26.4	..
6.9 Inbound tourism expenditure over exports of services		Percent	69.0	62.8	62.5	61.9	..
6.10 Inbound tourism expenditure over exports of goods and services		Percent	18.6	16.8	17.3	18.5	..
6.11 Inbound tourism expenditure over current account credits		Percent	16.5	14.6	15.5	16.8	..
6.12 Outbound tourism expenditure over imports of goods		Percent	6.0	5.3	6.1	4.9	..
6.13 Outbound tourism expenditure over imports of services		Percent	36.9	35.6	41.3	38.1	..
6.14 Outbound tourism expenditure over imports of goods and services		Percent	5.2	4.6	5.3	4.4	..
6.15 Outbound tourism expenditure over current account debits		Percent	4.6	4.2	4.7	4.0	..

CROATIA

Basic data and indicators	Notes	Units	2005	2006	2007	2008	2009
1. INBOUND TOURISM							
Data							
Arrivals							
1.1 Total		('000)	45,762	47,733	52,271	51,336	47,573
1.2 ♦ Overnight visitors (tourists)	(1)(2)	('000)	8,467	8,659	9,307	9,415	9,335
1.3 ♦ Same-day visitors (excursionists)		('000)	..	..	..	..	..
1.4 * of which, cruise passengers		('000)	..	..	..	..	..
Arrivals by region	(1)(2)						
1.5 Total		('000)	8,467	8,659	9,306	9,414	9,334
1.6 ♦ Africa		('000)	..	..	12	12	11
1.7 ♦ Americas		('000)	140	183	242	223	187
1.8 ♦ East Asia and the Pacific		('000)	83	133	212	280	275
1.9 ♦ Europe		('000)	8,192	8,282	8,840	8,899	8,861
1.10 ♦ Middle East		('000)	..	..	..	..	..
1.11 ♦ South Asia		('000)	..	..	..	..	..
1.12 ♦ Other not classified		('000)	52	61	..	..	..
1.13 * of which, nationals residing abroad		('000)	..	..	..	..	..
Arrivals by mode of transport							
1.19 Total		('000)	45,762	47,733	52,271	51,336	47,573
1.20 ♦ Air	(3)	('000)	1,566	1,825	2,033	2,055	1,947
1.21 ♦ Water	(4)	('000)	984	1,036	1,200	1,367	1,405
1.22 ♦ Land		('000)	43,212	44,872	49,038	47,914	44,221
1.23 * railway		('000)	302	312	306	316	286
1.24 * road		('000)	42,910	44,560	48,732	47,598	43,935
1.25 * others		('000)	..	..	..	..	..
Accommodation							
Total							
1.29 ♦ Guests	(2)	('000)	8,467	8,659	9,307	9,415	9,335
1.30 ♦ Overnights	(5)	('000)	45,987	47,022	49,575	50,626	50,501
Hotels and similar establishments							
1.31 ♦ Guests		('000)	3,744	3,742	3,910	3,920	3,684
1.32 ♦ Overnights		('000)	18,415	17,807	17,988	17,675	16,085
Expenditure							
1.33 Total		US$ Mn	7,625	8,296	9,601	11,681	9,224
1.34 ♦ Travel		US$ Mn	7,370	7,990	9,233	11,280	9,000
1.35 ♦ Passenger transport		US$ Mn	255	306	368	401	224
Expenditure by main purpose of the trip							
1.36 Total		US$ Mn	7,370	7,990	9,233	11,280	9,000
1.37 ♦ Personal		US$ Mn	6,747	7,501	8,700	10,708	8,644
1.38 ♦ Business and professional		US$ Mn	623	489	533	572	356
Indicators							
1.39 Average size of travel party		Persons	..	..	..	..	..
Average length of stay							
1.40 Total		Days	..	..	..	..	..
1.41 ♦ For all commercial accommodation services		Nights	5.43	5.43	5.33	5.38	5.41
1.42 * of which, "hotels and similar establishments"		Nights	..	..	..	..	..
1.43 ♦ For non commercial accommodation services		Days	..	..	..	..	..
1.44 Average expenditure per day		US$	..	..	..	..	..

CROATIA

Basic data and indicators	Notes	Units	2005	2006	2007	2008	2009
2. DOMESTIC TOURISM							
Data							
Trips							
2.1 Total		('000)	..	..	..	13,637	13,105
2.2 ♦ Overnight visitors (tourists)		('000)	..	..	..	6,023	5,738
2.3 ♦ Same-day visitors (excursionists)		('000)	..	..	..	7,614	7,367
Trips by main purpose							
2.4 Total		('000)	..	..	..	13,637	13,105
2.5 ♦ Personal		('000)	..	..	..	10,824	10,827
2.6 * holidays, leisure and recreation		('000)	..	..	..	10,824	10,827
2.7 * other personal purposes		('000)	..	..	..	..	..
2.8 ♦ Business and professional		('000)	..	..	..	2,813	2,278
Trips by mode of transport							
2.9 Total		('000)	..	..	..	..	13,105
2.10 ♦ Air		('000)	..	..	..	..	127
2.11 ♦ Water		('000)	..	..	..	..	309
2.12 ♦ Land		('000)	..	..	..	..	12,669
2.13 * railway		('000)	..	..	..	..	447
2.14 * road		('000)	..	..	..	..	12,112
2.15 * others		('000)	..	..	..	..	110
Trips by form of organization							
2.16 Total		('000)	..	..	..	..	13,105
2.17 ♦ Package tour		('000)	..	..	..	..	279
2.18 ♦ Other forms		('000)	..	..	..	..	12,826
Accommodation							
Total							
2.19 ♦ Guests	(2)	('000)	1,528	1,726	1,856	1,846	1,600
2.20 ♦ Overnights	(5)	('000)	5,434	5,985	6,431	6,478	5,799
Hotels and similar establishments							
2.21 ♦ Guests		('000)	1,002	1,071	1,153	1,168	1,003
2.22 ♦ Overnights		('000)	2,862	2,961	3,038	3,028	2,605
Indicators							
2.23 Average size of travel party		Persons	..	..	..	..	..
Average length of stay							
2.24 Total		Days	..	..	..	..	..
2.25 ♦ For all commercial accommodation services		Nights	3.56	3.47	3.47	3.51	3.62
2.26 * of which, "hotels and similar establishments"		Nights	..	..	..	2.59	2.60
2.27 ♦ For non commercial accommodation services		Days	..	..	..	..	..
2.28 Average expenditure per day		US$	..	..	..	..	..
3. OUTBOUND TOURISM							
Data							
Departures							
3.1 Total		('000)	..	..	..	4,393	4,823
3.2 ♦ Overnight visitors (tourists)		('000)	..	..	..	2,357	2,497
3.3 ♦ Same-day visitors (excursionists)		('000)	..	..	..	2,036	2,326
Expenditure							
3.4 Total		US$ Mn	786	770	1,025	1,156	1,034
3.5 ♦ Travel		US$ Mn	754	737	985	1,113	1,013
3.6 ♦ Passenger transport		US$ Mn	32	33	40	43	21
Expenditure by main purpose of the trip							
3.7 Total		US$ Mn	754	737	985	1,112	1,013
3.8 ♦ Personal		US$ Mn	420	448	616	731	676
3.9 ♦ Business and professional		US$ Mn	334	289	369	381	337

CROATIA

Basic data and indicators	Notes	Units	2005	2006	2007	2008	2009
4. TOURISM INDUSTRIES							
Data							
Number of establishments							
4.1 Total		Units	..	..	..	..	..
4.2 ♦ Accommodation for visitors		Units	1,530	1,643	1,811	1,985	2,088
4.3 * of which, "hotels and similar establishments"		Units	1,015	830	873	905	883
4.4 ♦ Food and beverage serving activities		Units	..	..	..	..	..
4.5 ♦ Passenger transportation		Units	..	..	..	..	..
4.6 ♦ Travel agencies and other reservation services activities		Units	..	..	..	..	..
4.7 ♦ Other tourism industries		Units	..	..	..	..	..
Accommodation for visitors in hotels and similar establishments							
Non-monetary data							
4.13 ♦ Number of establishments		Units	1,015	830	873	905	883
4.14 ♦ Number of rooms		Units	80,743	77,321	77,472	77,157	73,787
4.15 ♦ Number of bed-places		Units	203,464	165,936	165,970	165,956	152,260
Indicators							
4.16 Occupancy rate / rooms		Percent	..	..	..	..	..
4.17 Occupancy rate / bed-places		Percent	28.65	34.75	35.20	34.17	34.00
4.18 Average length of stay		Nights	4.48	4.33	4.17	4.07	4.00
4.19 Available capacity (bed-places per 1000 inhabitants)		Units	45.80	37.37	37.41	37.43	34.35
6. COMPLEMENTARY INDICATORS							
Demand							
6.1 Gross travel propensity		Units	..	..	..	..	..
6.2 Carrying capacity (arrivals/population)		Units	1.91	1.95	2.10	3.48	3.40
Macroeconomic indicators related to international tourism							
6.3 Inbound tourism expenditure over GDP		Percent	17.2	16.9	16.4	16.8	14.6
6.4 Outbound tourism expenditure over GDP		Percent	1.8	1.6	1.7	1.7	1.6
6.5 Tourism balance (inbound minus outbound tourism expenditure) over GDP		Percent	15.4	15.3	14.6	15.2	13.0
6.6 Tourism openness (inbound plus outbound tourism expenditure) over GDP		Percent	18.9	18.5	18.1	18.5	16.2
6.7 Tourism coverage (inbound over outbound tourism expenditure)		Percent	970.3	1,077.5	936.8	1,010.6	897.6
6.8 Inbound tourism expenditure over exports of goods		Percent	85.1	77.9	76.1	80.8	85.9
6.9 Inbound tourism expenditure over exports of services		Percent	76.9	76.8	77.0	77.0	77.7
6.10 Inbound tourism expenditure over exports of goods and services		Percent	40.4	38.7	38.3	39.4	40.8
6.11 Inbound tourism expenditure over current account credits		Percent	35.0	33.7	33.1	34.3	35.6
6.12 Outbound tourism expenditure over imports of goods		Percent	4.3	3.6	4.0	3.8	4.9
6.13 Outbound tourism expenditure over imports of services		Percent	23.1	21.7	26.2	25.2	26.5
6.14 Outbound tourism expenditure over imports of goods and services		Percent	3.6	3.1	3.5	3.3	4.1
6.15 Outbound tourism expenditure over current account debits		Percent	3.2	2.8	3.1	2.9	3.5

CUBA

Basic data and indicators	Notes	Units	2005	2006	2007	2008	2009
1. INBOUND TOURISM							
Data							
Arrivals							
1.1 Total		('000)	2,319	2,221	2,152	2,348	2,430
1.2 ♦ Overnight visitors (tourists)	(1)	('000)	2,261	2,150	2,119	2,316	2,405
1.3 ♦ Same-day visitors (excursionists)		('000)	58	71	33	32	25
1.4 * of which, cruise passengers		('000)	17	30	7	5	4
Arrivals by region							
1.5 Total		('000)	2,319	2,221	2,152	2,347	2,430
1.6 ♦ Africa		('000)	6	7	7	7	9
1.7 ♦ Americas		('000)	1,216	1,149	1,173	1,380	1,536
1.8 ♦ East Asia and the Pacific		('000)	42	44	42	44	41
1.9 ♦ Europe		('000)	1,048	1,014	924	909	838
1.10 ♦ Middle East		('000)	2	2	2	2	2
1.11 ♦ South Asia		('000)	5	5	4	5	4
1.12 ♦ Other not classified		('000)	..	..	..	..	..
1.13 * of which, nationals residing abroad		('000)	..	..	..	..	..
Arrivals by main purpose	(1)						
1.14 Total		('000)	2,261	2,150	2,119	2,316	2,405
1.15 ♦ Personal		('000)	2,249	2,137	2,107	2,304	2,393
1.16 * holidays, leisure and recreation		('000)	1,982	1,931	1,989	2,190	2,289
1.17 * other personal purposes		('000)	267	206	118	114	104
1.18 ♦ Business and professional		('000)	12	13	12	12	12
Arrivals by mode of transport							
1.19 Total		('000)	2,261	2,150	2,119	2,316	2,405
1.20 ♦ Air		('000)	2,261	2,150	2,119	2,316	2,405
1.21 ♦ Water		('000)	..	..	..	..	..
1.22 ♦ Land		('000)	..	..	..	..	..
1.23 * railway		('000)	..	..	..	..	..
1.24 * road		('000)	..	..	..	..	..
1.25 * others		('000)	..	..	..	..	..
Accommodation							
Total							
1.29 ♦ Guests	(2)	('000)	3,088	2,928	3,006	3,244	3,215
1.30 ♦ Overnights	(2)	('000)	15,401	15,235	15,038	16,321	16,277
Hotels and similar establishments							
1.31 ♦ Guests	(3)	('000)	2,911	2,808	2,872	3,108	3,074
1.32 ♦ Overnights	(3)	('000)	14,572	14,634	14,544	15,799	15,751
Expenditure	(4)						
1.33 Total		US$ Mn	2,399	2,235	2,236	2,347	2,106
1.34 ♦ Travel		US$ Mn	2,150	1,969	1,982	2,090	1,926
1.35 ♦ Passenger transport		US$ Mn	249	266	254	257	180
Indicators							
1.39 Average size of travel party		Persons	..	..	..	..	..
Average length of stay							
1.40 Total		Days	..	..	..	..	..
1.41 ♦ For all commercial accommodation services		Nights	10.50	11.00	11.70	11.13	11.10
1.42 * of which, "hotels and similar establishments"		Nights	..	..	..	..	..
1.43 ♦ For non commercial accommodation services		Days	..	..	..	..	..
1.44 Average expenditure per day		US$	..	..	..	..	..
2. DOMESTIC TOURISM							
Data							
Accommodation							
Total							
2.19 ♦ Guests		('000)	..	..	..	..	..
2.20 ♦ Overnights	(2)	('000)	7,125	7,592	7,912	8,297	8,175
Hotels and similar establishments							
2.21 ♦ Guests		('000)	..	..	..	..	..
2.22 ♦ Overnights	(3)	('000)	2,548	3,033	3,052	3,338	2,404
3. OUTBOUND TOURISM							
Data							
Departures							
3.1 Total		('000)	..	..	..	..	..
3.2 ♦ Overnight visitors (tourists)	(5)	('000)	162	199	194	202	206
3.3 ♦ Same-day visitors (excursionists)		('000)	..	..	..	..	..

CUBA

Basic data and indicators	Notes	Units	2005	2006	2007	2008	2009
4. TOURISM INDUSTRIES							
Data							
Number of establishments							
4.1 Total		Units	..	..	..	..	..
4.2 ♦ Accommodation for visitors		Units	..	..	..	..	..
4.3 * of which, "hotels and similar establishments"	(3)	Units	464	451	449	427	438
4.4 ♦ Food and beverage serving activities		Units	..	..	..	..	..
4.5 ♦ Passenger transportation		Units	..	..	..	..	..
4.6 ♦ Travel agencies and other reservation services activities		Units	..	..	..	..	..
4.7 ♦ Other tourism industries		Units	..	..	..	..	..
Accommodation for visitors in hotels and similar establishments							
Non-monetary data							
4.13 ♦ Number of establishments	(3)	Units	464	451	449	427	438
4.14 ♦ Number of rooms	(3)	Units	46,626	46,811	47,370	49,094	52,774
4.15 ♦ Number of bed-places	(3)	Units	87,252	89,302	89,838	92,672	99,132
Indicators							
4.16 Occupancy rate / rooms		Percent	63.60	61.30	60.90	60.10	59.80
4.17 Occupancy rate / bed-places		Percent	..	..	..	..	..
4.18 Average length of stay		Nights	..	..	..	..	..
4.19 Available capacity (bed-places per 1000 inhabitants)		Units	7.80	7.97	8.02	8.27	8.85
6. COMPLEMENTARY INDICATORS							
Demand							
6.1 Gross travel propensity		Units	..	..	..	..	..
6.2 Carrying capacity (arrivals/population)		Units	0.20	0.19	0.19	0.21	0.21

CURAÇAO

Basic data and indicators	Notes	Units	2005	2006	2007	2008	2009
1. INBOUND TOURISM							
Data							
Arrivals							
1.1 Total		('000)	510	572	664	773	808
1.2 ♦ Overnight visitors (tourists)	(1)	('000)	222	234	300	409	367
1.3 ♦ Same-day visitors (excursionists)		('000)	288	338	364	364	441
1.4 * of which, cruise passengers		('000)	276	322	341	353	423
Arrivals by region	(1)						
1.5 Total		('000)	222	234	299	409	367
1.6 ♦ Africa		('000)	..	..	..	..	..
1.7 ♦ Americas		('000)	123	127	174	265	211
1.8 ♦ East Asia and the Pacific		('000)	..	..	..	..	..
1.9 ♦ Europe		('000)	95	104	121	137	150
1.10 ♦ Middle East		('000)	..	..	..	..	..
1.11 ♦ South Asia		('000)	..	..	..	..	..
1.12 ♦ Other not classified		('000)	4	3	4	7	6
1.13 * of which, nationals residing abroad		('000)	..	..	..	..	..
Arrivals by main purpose	(1)(2)						
1.14 Total		('000)	222	233	299	407	367
1.15 ♦ Personal		('000)	207	218	287	384	333
1.16 * holidays, leisure and recreation		('000)	198	213	283	373	306
1.17 * other personal purposes		('000)	9	5	4	11	27
1.18 ♦ Business and professional		('000)	15	15	12	23	34
Arrivals by mode of transport							
1.19 Total		('000)	510	572	664	773	808
1.20 ♦ Air		('000)	234	250	323	420	385
1.21 ♦ Water	(3)	('000)	276	322	341	353	423
1.22 ♦ Land		('000)	..	..	..	..	..
1.23 * railway		('000)	..	..	..	..	..
1.24 * road		('000)	..	..	..	..	..
1.25 * others		('000)	..	..	..	..	..
Accommodation							
Total							
1.29 ♦ Guests		('000)	221	233	299	323	327
1.30 ♦ Overnights		('000)	1,958	2,156	2,560	2,978	2,697
Hotels and similar establishments							
1.31 ♦ Guests	(4)	('000)	158	165	214	224	234
1.32 ♦ Overnights		('000)	842	919	1,089	1,313	995
Expenditure							
1.33 Total	(5)	US$ Mn	244	277	327	378	361
1.34 ♦ Travel		US$ Mn	..	..	..	..	..
1.35 ♦ Passenger transport		US$ Mn	..	..	..	..	..
Indicators							
1.39 Average size of travel party		Persons	..	..	..	..	..
Average length of stay							
1.40 Total		Days	..	..	..	..	..
1.41 ♦ For all commercial accommodation services		Nights	8.82	9.20	8.54	7.28	7.18
1.42 * of which, "hotels and similar establishments"		Nights	..	..	..	..	..
1.43 ♦ For non commercial accommodation services		Days	..	..	..	..	..
1.44 Average expenditure per day		US$	..	..	..	..	..
3. OUTBOUND TOURISM							
Data							
Expenditure							
3.4 Total	(5)	US$ Mn	164	191	204	203	209
3.5 ♦ Travel		US$ Mn	..	..	..	..	..
3.6 ♦ Passenger transport		US$ Mn	..	..	..	..	..
4. TOURISM INDUSTRIES							
Data							
Accommodation for visitors in hotels and similar establishments							
Non-monetary data							
4.13 ♦ Number of establishments		Units	..	..	..	..	..
4.14 ♦ Number of rooms	(6)	Units	3,647	4,366	4,599	4,841	5,212
4.15 ♦ Number of bed-places		Units	..	..	..	..	..
Indicators							
4.16 Occupancy rate / rooms		Percent	81.74	..	83.39	84.99	74.80
4.17 Occupancy rate / bed-places		Percent	..	..	..	..	..
4.18 Average length of stay		Nights	8.82	9.20	8.54	7.28	7.18
4.19 Available capacity (bed-places per 1000 inhabitants)		Units	..	..	..	..	..

CYPRUS

Basic data and indicators	Notes	Units	2005	2006	2007	2008	2009
1. INBOUND TOURISM							
Data							
Arrivals							
1.1 Total		('000)	2,657	2,629	2,671	2,631	2,370
1.2 ♦ Overnight visitors (tourists)		('000)	2,470	2,401	2,416	2,404	2,141
1.3 ♦ Same-day visitors (excursionists)	(1)	('000)	187	228	255	227	229
1.4 * of which, cruise passengers		('000)	176	220	246	221	225
Arrivals by region							
1.5 Total		('000)	2,470	2,401	2,416	2,404	2,141
1.6 ♦ Africa		('000)	7	7	7	7	7
1.7 ♦ Americas		('000)	29	26	30	28	24
1.8 ♦ East Asia and the Pacific		('000)	15	16	17	17	15
1.9 ♦ Europe		('000)	2,375	2,308	2,304	2,300	2,040
1.10 ♦ Middle East		('000)	40	39	51	48	50
1.11 ♦ South Asia		('000)	3	4	7	4	5
1.12 ♦ Other not classified		('000)	1	1	..	..	..
1.13 * of which, nationals residing abroad		('000)	..	..	..	..	..
Arrivals by main purpose							
1.14 Total		('000)	2,470	2,401	2,416	2,404	2,141
1.15 ♦ Personal		('000)	2,327	2,250	2,241	2,239	1,984
1.16 * holidays, leisure and recreation		('000)	2,194	2,091	1,973	1,961	1,690
1.17 * other personal purposes		('000)	133	159	268	278	294
1.18 ♦ Business and professional		('000)	143	151	175	165	157
Arrivals by mode of transport							
1.19 Total		('000)	2,657	2,629	2,671	2,631	2,370
1.20 ♦ Air		('000)	2,479	2,408	2,425	2,410	2,145
1.21 ♦ Water	(2)	('000)	178	221	246	221	225
1.22 ♦ Land		('000)	..	..	..	..	..
1.23 * railway		('000)	..	..	..	..	..
1.24 * road		('000)	..	..	..	..	..
1.25 * others		('000)	..	..	..	..	..
Arrivals by form of organization of the trip							
1.26 Total		('000)	2,470	2,401	2,416	2,404	2,141
1.27 ♦ Package tour		('000)	1,623	1,508	1,488	1,471	1,248
1.28 ♦ Other forms		('000)	847	893	928	933	893
Accommodation	(3)						
Total							
1.29 ♦ Guests		('000)	1,763	1,771	1,785	1,762	1,672
1.30 ♦ Overnights		('000)	14,006	13,310	13,197	13,209	11,667
Hotels and similar establishments							
1.31 ♦ Guests		('000)	1,750	1,761	1,775	1,754	1,647
1.32 ♦ Overnights		('000)	13,899	13,227	13,129	13,151	11,488
Expenditure							
1.33 Total		US$ Mn	2,644	2,691	3,108	3,222	2,467
1.34 ♦ Travel		US$ Mn	2,318	2,381	2,686	2,770	2,188
1.35 ♦ Passenger transport		US$ Mn	326	310	422	452	279
Expenditure by main purpose of the trip							
1.36 Total		US$ Mn	2,318	2,381	2,686	2,770	2,188
1.37 ♦ Personal		US$ Mn	2,198	2,247	2,487	2,596	2,041
1.38 ♦ Business and professional		US$ Mn	120	134	199	174	147
Indicators							
1.39 Average size of travel party		Persons	2.1	2.0	2.0	1.9	1.9
Average length of stay							
1.40 Total		Days	10.40	10.40	10.00	10.10	9.90
1.41 ♦ For all commercial accommodation services		Nights	9.73	9.60	9.20	9.20	8.89
1.42 * of which, "hotels and similar establishments"		Nights	9.43	9.23	8.80	8.81	8.54
1.43 ♦ For non commercial accommodation services		Days	16.57	16.37	15.10	15.48	15.68
1.44 Average expenditure per day	(4)	US$	102.2	106.8	127.3	131.5	115.2
2. DOMESTIC TOURISM							
Data							
Trips	(5)						
2.1 Total		('000)	7,846	8,168	8,359	..	..
2.2 ♦ Overnight visitors (tourists)		('000)	1,140	1,291	1,352	..	..
2.3 ♦ Same-day visitors (excursionists)		('000)	6,706	6,877	7,007	..	..
Trips by main purpose	(5)						
2.4 Total		('000)	..	..	..	..	..
2.5 ♦ Personal		('000)	7,846	8,168	8,359	..	..
2.6 * holidays, leisure and recreation		('000)	..	..	..	..	..
2.7 * other personal purposes		('000)	..	..	..	..	..
2.8 ♦ Business and professional		('000)	..	..	..	..	..

CYPRUS

Basic data and indicators	Notes	Units	2005	2006	2007	2008	2009
Trips by mode of transport	(5)						
2.9 Total		('000)	7,846	8,168	8,359	..	..
2.10 ♦ Air		('000)	..	..	..	..	..
2.11 ♦ Water		('000)	..	..	..	..	..
2.12 ♦ Land		('000)	7,846	8,168	8,359	..	..
2.13 * railway		('000)	..	..	..	..	..
2.14 * road		('000)	..	..	..	..	..
2.15 * others		('000)	..	..	..	..	..
Accommodation							
Total							
2.19 ♦ Guests		('000)	456	517	541	535	597
2.20 ♦ Overnights		('000)	1,052	1,128	1,181	1,171	1,337
Hotels and similar establishments							
2.21 ♦ Guests		('000)	449	509	535	528	593
2.22 ♦ Overnights		('000)	1,040	1,114	1,169	1,159	1,320
Indicators							
2.23 Average size of travel party		Persons	..	..	..	..	..
Average length of stay							
2.24 Total		Days	..	..	..	..	..
2.25 ♦ For all commercial accommodation services	(6)	Nights	2.31	2.18	2.18	2.22	2.24
2.26 * of which, "hotels and similar establishments"	(6)	Nights	2.32	2.19	2.19	2.20	2.23
2.27 ♦ For non commercial accommodation services		Days	..	..	..	..	..
2.28 Average expenditure per day		US$	..	..	..	..	..
3. OUTBOUND TOURISM							
Data							
Departures							
3.1 Total		('000)	789	796	947	1,062	1,051
3.2 ♦ Overnight visitors (tourists)		('000)	766	772	919	1,030	1,019
3.3 ♦ Same-day visitors (excursionists)		('000)	24	24	28	32	32
Expenditure							
3.4 Total		US$ Mn	1,001	1,031	1,554	1,874	1,613
3.5 ♦ Travel		US$ Mn	932	967	1,479	1,571	1,275
3.6 ♦ Passenger transport	(7)	US$ Mn	69	64	75	303	338
Expenditure by main purpose of the trip	(8)						
3.7 Total		US$ Mn	932	967	1,480	1,571	1,275
3.8 ♦ Personal		US$ Mn	914	945	1,448	1,243	1,000
3.9 ♦ Business and professional		US$ Mn	18	22	32	328	275
Indicators							
3.10 Average length of stay		Days	9.20	9.30	10.10	9.60	9.80
3.11 Average expenditure per day	(9)	US$	141.6	143.2	167.0	188.8	161.0
4. TOURISM INDUSTRIES							
Data							
Number of establishments	(5)						
4.1 Total		Units	12,874	13,182	14,206	..	..
4.2 ♦ Accommodation for visitors		Units	773	781	806	..	..
4.3 * of which, "hotels and similar establishments"		Units	..	..	..	..	..
4.4 ♦ Food and beverage serving activities		Units	6,140	6,351	6,926	..	..
4.5 ♦ Passenger transportation		Units	3,354	3,360	3,310	..	..
4.6 ♦ Travel agencies and other reservation services activities		Units	652	660	768	..	..
4.7 ♦ Other tourism industries		Units	1,955	2,030	2,396	..	..
Accommodation for visitors in hotels and similar establishments							
Monetary data	(5)(10)						
4.8 ♦ Output		US$ Mn	838.0	878.4	1,040.4	..	..
4.9 ♦ Intermediate consumption		US$ Mn	485.4	497.7	610.0	..	..
4.10 ♦ Gross value added		US$ Mn	352.6	380.6	430.4	..	..
4.11 ♦ Compensation of employees		US$ Mn	..	..	..	..	..
4.12 ♦ Gross fixed capital formation		US$ Mn	70.8	75.1	60.6	..	..
Non-monetary data	(11)						
4.13 ♦ Number of establishments		Units	784	753	735	708	699
4.14 ♦ Number of rooms		Units	45,209	44,404	43,799	42,898	41,988
4.15 ♦ Number of bed-places		Units	91,208	89,490	87,804	85,681	84,327
Indicators							
4.16 Occupancy rate / rooms	(11)	Percent	59.58	58.71	60.35	60.97	56.39
4.17 Occupancy rate / bed-places	(11)	Percent	61.55	59.91	61.79	63.52	56.13
4.18 Average length of stay	(11)(12)	Nights	6.79	6.32	6.19	6.27	5.72
4.19 Available capacity (bed-places per 1000 inhabitants)		Units	0.12	0.12	0.11	0.11	96.81

CYPRUS

Basic data and indicators		Notes	Units	2005	2006	2007	2008	2009
	Travel agencies and other reservation service activities							
	Monetary data	(5)						
4.20	♦ Output		US$ Mn	169.3	174.8	217.7	..	..
4.21	♦ Intermediate consumption		US$ Mn	57.3	59.8	79.9	..	..
4.22	♦ Gross value added		US$ Mn	112.0	115.0	137.8	..	..
4.23	♦ Compensation of employees		US$ Mn	..	..	..	..	..
4.24	♦ Gross fixed capital formation		US$ Mn	3.8	3.0	2.5	..	..
	Non-monetary data							
	♦ Domestic trips							
4.25	* with package tour		Percent	..	..	..	..	..
4.26	* without package tour		Percent	..	..	..	..	..
	♦ Inbound trips							
4.27	* with package tour		Percent	65.7	62.8	61.6	61.2	58.3
4.28	* without package tour		Percent	34.3	37.2	38.4	38.8	41.7
	♦ Outbound trips							
4.29	* with package tour		Percent	..	..	18.0	19.0	15.0
4.30	* without package tour		Percent	..	..	82.0	81.0	85.0
5.	**EMPLOYMENT**	(5)						
	Data							
	Number of employees by tourism industries							
5.1	Total		('000)	48.4	49.1	50.3	..	..
5.2	♦ Accommodation services for visitors (hotels and similar establishments)		('000)	13.7	13.9	14.2	..	..
5.3	♦ Other accommodation services		('000)	..	..	..	..	..
5.4	♦ Food and beverage serving activities		('000)	16.1	17.1	18.1	..	..
5.5	♦ Passenger transportation		('000)	10.3	10.2	10.1	..	..
5.6	♦ Travel agencies and other reservation services activities		('000)	2.7	2.6	2.6	..	..
5.7	♦ Other tourism industries		('000)	5.5	5.2	5.3	..	..
	Number of jobs by status in employment							
5.8	Total		('000)	61.7	62.9	63.3	..	..
5.9	♦ Employees		('000)	48.3	49.1	50.3	..	..
5.10	♦ Self employed		('000)	13.3	13.8	13.0	..	..
	Indicators							
	Number of full-time equivalent jobs by status in employment							
5.11	Total		('000)	56.1	57.2	58.2	..	..
5.12	♦ Employees		('000)	39.4	41.0	42.1	..	..
5.13	* male		('000)	19.5	19.8	18.9	..	..
5.14	* female		('000)	19.9	21.2	23.2	..	..
5.15	♦ Self employed		('000)	16.7	16.1	16.2	..	..
5.16	* male		('000)	11.4	11.7	12.0	..	..
5.17	* female		('000)	5.3	4.4	4.2	..	..
6.	**COMPLEMENTARY INDICATORS**							
	Demand							
6.1	Gross travel propensity		Units	11.4	11.6	11.8	..	..
6.2	Carrying capacity (arrivals/population)		Units	13.90	14.00	14.00	..	..
	Macroeconomic indicators related to international tourism							
6.3	Inbound tourism expenditure over GDP		Percent	15.6	14.6	14.5	12.8	10.5
6.4	Outbound tourism expenditure over GDP		Percent	5.9	5.6	7.3	7.4	6.9
6.5	Tourism balance (inbound minus outbound tourism expenditure) over GDP		Percent	9.7	9.0	7.3	5.3	3.6
6.6	Tourism openness (inbound plus outbound tourism expenditure) over GDP		Percent	21.5	20.2	21.8	20.2	17.3
6.7	Tourism coverage (inbound over outbound tourism expenditure)		Percent	264.1	261.0	200.0	171.9	152.9
6.8	Inbound tourism expenditure over exports of goods		Percent	171.1	193.1	209.6	151.3	119.5
6.9	Inbound tourism expenditure over exports of services		Percent	40.7	37.6	35.3	26.8	25.0
6.10	Inbound tourism expenditure over exports of goods and services		Percent	32.9	31.5	30.2	22.8	20.6
6.11	Inbound tourism expenditure over current account credits		Percent	25.6	23.4	20.4	16.8	15.5
6.12	Outbound tourism expenditure over imports of goods		Percent	17.3	16.3	19.5	16.9	20.2
6.13	Outbound tourism expenditure over imports of services		Percent	37.0	35.1	41.3	37.6	39.6
6.14	Outbound tourism expenditure over imports of goods and services		Percent	11.8	11.1	13.3	11.7	13.4
6.15	Outbound tourism expenditure over current account debits		Percent	8.9	8.1	9.1	8.0	9.0

CZECH REPUBLIC

Basic data and indicators	Notes	Units	2005	2006	2007	2008	2009
1. INBOUND TOURISM							
Data							
Arrivals							
1.1 Total		('000)	..	..	..	..	..
1.2 ♦ Overnight visitors (tourists)	(1)	('000)	6,336	6,435	6,680	6,649	6,032
1.3 ♦ Same-day visitors (excursionists)		('000)	..	..	..	..	..
1.4 * of which, cruise passengers		('000)	..	..	..	..	..
Arrivals by region	(1)						
1.5 Total		('000)	6,336	6,435	6,680	6,650	6,033
1.6 ♦ Africa		('000)	18	19	20	23	20
1.7 ♦ Americas		('000)	401	435	441	434	398
1.8 ♦ East Asia and the Pacific		('000)	421	493	504	502	485
1.9 ♦ Europe		('000)	5,496	5,488	5,715	5,691	5,130
1.10 ♦ Middle East		('000)	..	..	..	..	..
1.11 ♦ South Asia		('000)	..	..	..	..	..
1.12 ♦ Other not classified		('000)	..	..	..	..	..
1.13 * of which, nationals residing abroad		('000)	..	..	..	..	..
Accommodation							
Total							
1.29 ♦ Guests		('000)	6,336	6,435	6,680	6,649	6,032
1.30 ♦ Overnights		('000)	19,595	20,090	20,610	19,987	17,747
Hotels and similar establishments							
1.31 ♦ Guests		('000)	5,686	5,781	6,098	6,135	5,609
1.32 ♦ Overnights		('000)	16,607	17,035	17,838	17,741	16,013
Expenditure							
1.33 Total		US$ Mn	5,635	6,359	7,247	8,213	7,396
1.34 ♦ Travel		US$ Mn	4,676	5,541	6,388	7,204	6,477
1.35 ♦ Passenger transport		US$ Mn	959	818	859	1,009	919
Expenditure by main purpose of the trip							
1.36 Total		US$ Mn	4,676	5,541	6,387	7,204	6,477
1.37 ♦ Personal		US$ Mn	3,588	4,362	5,055	5,237	4,785
1.38 ♦ Business and professional		US$ Mn	1,088	1,179	1,332	1,967	1,692
Indicators							
1.39 Average size of travel party		Persons	..	..	..	..	..
Average length of stay							
1.40 Total		Days	..	..	..	..	..
1.41 ♦ For all commercial accommodation services		Nights	3.09	3.12	3.09	3.01	3.33
1.42 * of which, "hotels and similar establishments"		Nights	2.68	2.71	2.71	2.75	2.75
1.43 ♦ For non commercial accommodation services		Days	..	..	..	..	..
1.44 Average expenditure per day		US$	..	..	..	..	..
2. DOMESTIC TOURISM							
Data							
Trips							
2.1 Total		('000)	..	..	..	..	..
2.2 ♦ Overnight visitors (tourists)		('000)	25,113	24,154	22,121	20,448	22,088
2.3 ♦ Same-day visitors (excursionists)		('000)	..	..	..	..	..
Trips by main purpose							
2.4 Total		('000)	25,113	24,153	22,121	20,448	22,088
2.5 ♦ Personal		('000)	22,940	21,767	19,586	18,074	20,514
2.6 * holidays, leisure and recreation		('000)	22,940	21,767	19,586	18,074	20,514
2.7 * other personal purposes		('000)	..	..	..	..	..
2.8 ♦ Business and professional		('000)	2,173	2,386	2,535	2,374	1,574
Accommodation							
Total							
2.19 ♦ Guests		('000)	6,026	6,289	6,281	6,186	5,954
2.20 ♦ Overnights		('000)	20,725	21,357	20,221	19,296	18,915
Hotels and similar establishments							
2.21 ♦ Guests		('000)	3,388	3,595	3,795	3,954	3,726
2.22 ♦ Overnights		('000)	8,601	8,854	9,206	9,686	9,328
Indicators							
2.23 Average size of travel party		Persons	..	..	..	..	..
Average length of stay							
2.24 Total		Days	..	..	..	..	..
2.25 ♦ For all commercial accommodation services		Nights	3.44	3.40	3.22	3.12	3.18
2.26 * of which, "hotels and similar establishments"		Nights	1.75	1.73	1.70	1.78	1.87
2.27 ♦ For non commercial accommodation services		Days	..	..	..	..	..
2.28 Average expenditure per day		US$	..	..	..	..	..

CZECH REPUBLIC

Basic data and indicators	Notes	Units	2005	2006	2007	2008	2009
3. OUTBOUND TOURISM							
Data							
Departures							
3.1 Total		('000)	..	..	..	..	..
3.2 ♦ Overnight visitors (tourists)		('000)	6,963	6,393	7,247	7,685	6,618
3.3 ♦ Same-day visitors (excursionists)		('000)	..	..	..	..	..
Expenditure							
3.4 Total		US$ Mn	2,603	2,874	3,772	4,729	4,157
3.5 ♦ Travel		US$ Mn	2,405	2,765	3,648	4,585	4,077
3.6 ♦ Passenger transport		US$ Mn	198	109	124	144	80
Expenditure by main purpose of the trip							
3.7 Total		US$ Mn	2,404	2,765	3,648	4,585	4,077
3.8 ♦ Personal		US$ Mn	1,939	2,276	3,057	3,801	3,400
3.9 ♦ Business and professional		US$ Mn	465	489	591	784	677
4. TOURISM INDUSTRIES							
Data							
Number of establishments							
4.1 Total		Units	143,270	144,730	142,519	141,697	146,920
4.2 ♦ Accommodation for visitors		Units	7,605	7,616	7,845	7,705	7,557
4.3 * of which, "hotels and similar establishments"		Units	4,278	4,314	4,559	4,482	4,469
4.4 ♦ Food and beverage serving activities		Units	105,952	107,089	105,007	113,044	119,976
4.5 ♦ Passenger transportation		Units	16,603	16,749	16,425	8,230	7,078
4.6 ♦ Travel agencies and other reservation services activities		Units	13,110	13,276	13,242	12,718	12,309
4.7 ♦ Other tourism industries		Units	..	..	..	..	..
Accommodation for visitors in hotels and similar establishments							
Monetary data	(2)						
4.8 ♦ Output		US$ Mn	8,857.7	10,375.8	13,627.8	16,828.4	13,634.3
4.9 ♦ Intermediate consumption		US$ Mn	5,514.3	6,736.1	9,134.8	10,873.3	8,155.1
4.10 ♦ Gross value added		US$ Mn	3,343.4	3,639.7	4,493.0	5,955.1	5,479.2
4.11 ♦ Compensation of employees		US$ Mn	1,143.0	1,319.6	1,469.1	1,751.4	1,565.6
4.12 ♦ Gross fixed capital formation		US$ Mn	..	..	..	..	..
Non-monetary data							
4.13 ♦ Number of establishments		Units	4,278	4,314	4,559	4,482	4,469
4.14 ♦ Number of rooms		Units	99,916	101,563	106,907	111,775	114,452
4.15 ♦ Number of bed-places		Units	232,211	236,104	248,077	257,849	260,736
Indicators							
4.16 Occupancy rate / rooms		Percent	42.37	42.98	42.80	42.39	38.65
4.17 Occupancy rate / bed-places	(3)	Percent	35.75	35.80	35.81	35.73	32.82
4.18 Average length of stay		Nights	2.68	2.71	2.71	2.75	2.75
4.19 Available capacity (bed-places per 1000 inhabitants)		Units	22.69	23.00	24.03	24.72	24.85
Travel agencies and other reservation service activities							
Monetary data	(4)						
4.20 ♦ Output		US$ Mn	4,981.1	5,641.3	6,685.0	8,561.0	7,247.1
4.21 ♦ Intermediate consumption		US$ Mn	2,774.6	3,314.6	3,977.2	5,022.2	4,028.7
4.22 ♦ Gross value added		US$ Mn	2,206.5	2,326.7	2,707.8	3,538.8	3,218.4
4.23 ♦ Compensation of employees		US$ Mn	660.8	807.2	898.7	1,071.4	957.7
4.24 ♦ Gross fixed capital formation		US$ Mn	..	..	..	..	..
Non-monetary data							
♦ Domestic trips							
4.25 * with package tour		Percent	..	..	..	1.7	1.1
4.26 * without package tour		Percent	..	..	..	98.3	98.9
♦ Inbound trips							
4.27 * with package tour		Percent	..	..	..	..	..
4.28 * without package tour		Percent	..	..	..	..	..
♦ Outbound trips							
4.29 * with package tour		Percent	..	..	..	50.2	42.6
4.30 * without package tour		Percent	..	..	..	49.8	57.4

CZECH REPUBLIC

Basic data and indicators	Notes	Units	2005	2006	2007	2008	2009
5. EMPLOYMENT							
Data							
Number of employees by tourism industries							
5.1 Total		('000)	233.7	231.5	233.5	236.4	..
5.2 ♦ Accommodation services for visitors (hotels and similar establishments)		('000)	39.6	40.5	41.8	44.4	..
5.3 ♦ Other accommodation services		('000)	..	..	..	..	..
5.4 ♦ Food and beverage serving activities		('000)	67.1	63.8	64.5	62.8	..
5.5 ♦ Passenger transportation		('000)	37.8	36.9	36.0	37.0	..
5.6 ♦ Travel agencies and other reservation services activities		('000)	14.3	15.1	14.2	14.7	..
5.7 ♦ Other tourism industries		('000)	74.9	75.2	77.0	77.5	..
Number of jobs by status in employment							
5.8 Total		('000)	233.7	231.5	233.5	236.5	..
5.9 ♦ Employees		('000)	180.1	180.9	180.9	185.4	..
5.10 ♦ Self employed		('000)	53.6	50.6	52.5	51.2	..
Indicators							
Number of full-time equivalent jobs by status in employment							
5.11 Total		('000)	236.7	235.9	236.0	241.2	..
5.12 ♦ Employees		('000)	182.8	185.1	184.7	189.6	..
5.13 * male		('000)	85.7	85.3	85.4	87.4	..
5.14 * female		('000)	97.1	99.8	99.3	102.2	..
5.15 ♦ Self employed		('000)	53.9	50.9	51.3	51.6	..
5.16 * male		('000)	28.7	26.2	25.4	28.3	..
5.17 * female		('000)	25.2	24.6	26.0	23.3	..
6. COMPLEMENTARY INDICATORS							
Demand							
6.1 Gross travel propensity		Units	..	..	..	..	..
6.2 Carrying capacity (arrivals/population)		Units	3.07	2.98	2.79	2.60	2.68
Macroeconomic indicators related to international tourism							
6.3 Inbound tourism expenditure over GDP		Percent	4.5	4.5	4.2	3.8	3.9
6.4 Outbound tourism expenditure over GDP		Percent	2.1	2.0	2.2	2.2	2.2
6.5 Tourism balance (inbound minus outbound tourism expenditure) over GDP		Percent	2.4	2.4	2.0	1.6	1.7
6.6 Tourism openness (inbound plus outbound tourism expenditure) over GDP		Percent	6.6	6.5	6.3	6.0	6.1
6.7 Tourism coverage (inbound over outbound tourism expenditure)		Percent	216.5	221.3	192.1	173.7	177.9
6.8 Inbound tourism expenditure over exports of goods		Percent	7.2	6.7	5.9	5.6	6.6
6.9 Inbound tourism expenditure over exports of services		Percent	47.9	45.6	42.8	37.7	36.4
6.10 Inbound tourism expenditure over exports of goods and services		Percent	6.3	5.8	5.2	4.9	5.6
6.11 Inbound tourism expenditure over current account credits		Percent	5.8	5.4	4.8	4.5	5.2
6.12 Outbound tourism expenditure over imports of goods		Percent	3.5	3.1	3.2	3.4	4.0
6.13 Outbound tourism expenditure over imports of services		Percent	25.5	24.1	26.0	26.4	21.9
6.14 Outbound tourism expenditure over imports of goods and services		Percent	3.0	2.8	2.9	3.0	3.4
6.15 Outbound tourism expenditure over current account debits		Percent	2.6	2.4	2.4	2.6	2.9

DEMOCRATIC REPUBLIC OF THE CONGO

Basic data and indicators	Notes	Units	2005	2006	2007	2008	2009
1. INBOUND TOURISM							
Data							
Arrivals							
1.1 Total		('000)	..	..	..	..	..
1.2 ♦ Overnight visitors (tourists)	(1)	('000)	61	55	47	50	53
1.3 ♦ Same-day visitors (excursionists)		('000)	..	..	..	..	..
1.4 * of which, cruise passengers		('000)	..	..	..	..	..
Arrivals by region	(1)						
1.5 Total		('000)	61	55	47	50	53
1.6 ♦ Africa		('000)	36	33	28	28	31
1.7 ♦ Americas		('000)	4	3	3	4	3
1.8 ♦ East Asia and the Pacific		('000)	6	6	5	5	6
1.9 ♦ Europe		('000)	15	13	11	13	13
1.10 ♦ Middle East		('000)	..	..	..	..	..
1.11 ♦ South Asia		('000)	..	..	..	..	..
1.12 ♦ Other not classified		('000)	..	..	..	..	..
1.13 * of which, nationals residing abroad		('000)	..	..	..	..	..
Arrivals by main purpose	(1)						
1.14 Total		('000)	61	55	47	50	53
1.15 ♦ Personal		('000)	19	20	21	18	19
1.16 * holidays, leisure and recreation		('000)	8	10	8	8	8
1.17 * other personal purposes		('000)	11	10	13	10	11
1.18 ♦ Business and professional		('000)	42	35	26	32	34
Arrivals by mode of transport							
1.19 Total		('000)	61	55	47	50	53
1.20 ♦ Air		('000)	39	41	47	50	53
1.21 ♦ Water		('000)	..	..	..	..	..
1.22 ♦ Land		('000)	22	14	..	..	..
1.23 * railway		('000)	..	..	..	..	..
1.24 * road		('000)	22	14	..	..	..
1.25 * others		('000)	..	..	..	..	..
Accommodation							
Total							
1.29 ♦ Guests		('000)	..	..	..	..	..
1.30 ♦ Overnights		('000)	165	189	126	144	156
Hotels and similar establishments							
1.31 ♦ Guests		('000)	48	54	27	39	42
1.32 ♦ Overnights		('000)	..	..	..	..	..
Indicators							
1.39 Average size of travel party		Persons	..	..	..	..	..
Average length of stay							
1.40 Total		Days	..	..	..	..	..
1.41 ♦ For all commercial accommodation services		Nights	5.00	5.00	4.00	4.00	4.00
1.42 * of which, "hotels and similar establishments"		Nights	..	..	..	..	..
1.43 ♦ For non commercial accommodation services		Days	..	..	..	..	..
1.44 Average expenditure per day		US$	..	..	..	..	..
2. DOMESTIC TOURISM							
Data							
Accommodation							
Total							
2.19 ♦ Guests		('000)	..	..	..	..	..
2.20 ♦ Overnights		('000)	156	113	69	105	110
Hotels and similar establishments							
2.21 ♦ Guests		('000)	13	11	9	12	11
2.22 ♦ Overnights		('000)	..	..	..	..	..
Indicators							
2.23 Average size of travel party		Persons	..	..	..	..	..
Average length of stay							
2.24 Total		Days	..	..	..	..	..
2.25 ♦ For all commercial accommodation services		Nights	7.00	6.00	4.00	4.00	5.00
2.26 * of which, "hotels and similar establishments"		Nights	..	..	..	..	..
2.27 ♦ For non commercial accommodation services		Days	..	..	..	..	..
2.28 Average expenditure per day		US$	..	..	..	..	..

DEMOCRATIC REPUBLIC OF THE CONGO

Basic data and indicators	Notes	Units	2005	2006	2007	2008	2009
4. **TOURISM INDUSTRIES**							
Indicators							
4.16 Occupancy rate / rooms		Percent	..	..	..	..	..
4.17 Occupancy rate / bed-places		Percent	..	..	76.00	76.00	76.00
4.18 Average length of stay		Nights	..	..	4.00	4.00	5.00
4.19 Available capacity (bed-places per 1000 inhabitants)		Units	..	..	..	..	..
6. **COMPLEMENTARY INDICATORS**							
Demand							
6.1 Gross travel propensity		Units	..	..	..	..	..
6.2 Carrying capacity (arrivals/population)		Units	0.001	0.001	0.001	0.001	0.001

DENMARK

Basic data and indicators	Notes	Units	2005	2006	2007	2008	2009
1. INBOUND TOURISM							
Data							
Arrivals							
1.1 Total		('000)	26,927	26,936	27,138	26,870	26,571
1.2 ♦ Overnight visitors (tourists)		('000)	9,178	9,256	9,284	9,016	8,547
1.3 ♦ Same-day visitors (excursionists)		('000)	17,749	17,680	17,854	17,854	18,024
1.4 * of which, cruise passengers		('000)	409	374	548	548	718
Arrivals by region	(1)(2)						
1.5 Total		('000)	9,586	9,630	9,833	9,564	9,265
1.6 ♦ Africa		('000)	..	..	..	..	..
1.7 ♦ Americas		('000)	698	711	625	627	648
1.8 ♦ East Asia and the Pacific		('000)	223	193	198	191	182
1.9 ♦ Europe		('000)	8,290	8,277	8,558	8,330	7,989
1.10 ♦ Middle East		('000)	..	..	..	..	..
1.11 ♦ South Asia		('000)	..	..	..	..	..
1.12 ♦ Other not classified		('000)	375	449	452	416	446
1.13 * of which, nationals residing abroad		('000)	..	..	..	..	..
Arrivals by main purpose							
1.14 Total		('000)	26,927	26,936	27,138	26,870	26,571
1.15 ♦ Personal		('000)	25,692	25,718	25,963	25,713	25,536
1.16 * holidays, leisure and recreation		('000)	25,692	25,718	25,963	25,713	25,536
1.17 * other personal purposes		('000)	..	..	..	..	..
1.18 ♦ Business and professional		('000)	1,235	1,218	1,175	1,157	1,035
Accommodation							
Total	(2)						
1.29 ♦ Guests		('000)	9,587	9,630	9,832	9,564	9,265
1.30 ♦ Overnights		('000)	45,916	46,658	47,332	45,852	43,984
Hotels and similar establishments	(3)(4)						
1.31 ♦ Guests		('000)	2,230	2,164	2,100	2,057	1,892
1.32 ♦ Overnights		('000)	5,015	5,021	4,846	4,752	4,435
Expenditure							
1.33 Total		US$ Mn	..	..	..	..	..
1.34 ♦ Travel	(5)	US$ Mn	5,293	5,587	5,976	6,242	5,679
1.35 ♦ Passenger transport		US$ Mn	..	..	..	..	..
Indicators							
1.39 Average size of travel party		Persons	..	..	..	..	..
Average length of stay							
1.40 Total		Days	..	..	..	..	..
1.41 ♦ For all commercial accommodation services		Nights	4.90	5.01	5.08	5.06	5.14
1.42 * of which, "hotels and similar establishments"		Nights	..	..	..	..	..
1.43 ♦ For non commercial accommodation services		Days	..	..	..	..	..
1.44 Average expenditure per day		US$	..	..	..	..	..
2. DOMESTIC TOURISM							
Data							
Accommodation							
Total	(2)						
2.19 ♦ Guests		('000)	11,358	10,941	11,442	11,346	14,531
2.20 ♦ Overnights		('000)	38,394	39,962	41,283	41,533	61,559
Hotels and similar establishments	(3)(4)						
2.21 ♦ Guests		('000)	3,348	3,799	4,186	4,082	3,706
2.22 ♦ Overnights		('000)	5,806	6,352	6,999	6,825	6,198
Indicators							
2.23 Average size of travel party		Persons	..	..	..	..	..
Average length of stay							
2.24 Total		Days	..	..	..	..	..
2.25 ♦ For all commercial accommodation services		Nights	3.38	3.49	3.43	3.51	3.57
2.26 * of which, "hotels and similar establishments"		Nights	..	..	..	..	..
2.27 ♦ For non commercial accommodation services		Days	..	..	..	..	..
2.28 Average expenditure per day		US$	..	..	..	..	..

DENMARK

Basic data and indicators	Notes	Units	2005	2006	2007	2008	2009
3. OUTBOUND TOURISM							
Data							
Departures							
3.1 Total		('000)	..	..	..	..	..
3.2 ♦ Overnight visitors (tourists)	(3)	('000)	5,469	6,129	6,564	6,347	..
3.3 ♦ Same-day visitors (excursionists)		('000)	..	..	..	..	..
Expenditure							
3.4 Total		US$ Mn	..	..	..	..	..
3.5 ♦ Travel	(5)	US$ Mn	6,850	7,428	8,791	9,678	..
3.6 ♦ Passenger transport		US$ Mn	..	..	..	..	..
4. TOURISM INDUSTRIES							
Data							
Number of establishments							
4.1 Total		Units	..	..	..	..	..
4.2 ♦ Accommodation for visitors		Units	..	..	..	..	..
4.3 * of which, "hotels and similar establishments"	(6)	Units	479	472	473	469	467
4.4 ♦ Food and beverage serving activities		Units	..	..	..	..	..
4.5 ♦ Passenger transportation		Units	..	..	..	..	..
4.6 ♦ Travel agencies and other reservation services activities		Units	..	..	..	..	..
4.7 ♦ Other tourism industries		Units	..	..	..	..	..
Accommodation for visitors in hotels and similar establishments							
Non-monetary data	(6)						
4.13 ♦ Number of establishments		Units	479	472	473	469	467
4.14 ♦ Number of rooms		Units	35,286	35,657	36,059	36,923	37,911
4.15 ♦ Number of bed-places		Units	69,364	70,044	71,329	72,775	74,733
Indicators							
4.16 Occupancy rate / rooms		Percent	54.00	56.00	57.00	56.00	51.00
4.17 Occupancy rate / bed-places	(6)	Percent	41.00	43.00	44.00	42.00	38.00
4.18 Average length of stay		Nights	..	..	..	..	..
4.19 Available capacity (bed-places per 1000 inhabitants)		Units	12.81	12.88	13.06	13.25	13.52
6. COMPLEMENTARY INDICATORS							
Demand							
6.1 Gross travel propensity		Units	..	..	..	..	..
6.2 Carrying capacity (arrivals/population)		Units	1.69	1.70	1.70	1.64	1.55

DJIBOUTI

Basic data and indicators	Notes	Units	2005	2006	2007	2008	2009
1. INBOUND TOURISM							
Data							
Arrivals							
1.1 Total		('000)	..	..	..	..	..
1.2 ♦ Overnight visitors (tourists)	(1)	('000)	30.2	39.5	40.0	52.8	..
1.3 ♦ Same-day visitors (excursionists)		('000)	..	..	..	..	..
1.4 * of which, cruise passengers		('000)	..	..	..	..	..
Accommodation							
Total							
1.29 ♦ Guests		('000)	..	..	..	..	..
1.30 ♦ Overnights		('000)	..	..	..	..	..
Hotels and similar establishments							
1.31 ♦ Guests		('000)	30.2	39.5	40.0	52.8	..
1.32 ♦ Overnights		('000)	66.9	59.3	74.8	81.6	..
Expenditure							
1.33 Total		US$ Mn	..	..	..	..	..
1.34 ♦ Travel		US$ Mn	7.1	9.8	6.8	7.8	16.0
1.35 ♦ Passenger transport		US$ Mn	..	..	..	..	..
3. OUTBOUND TOURISM							
Data							
Expenditure							
3.4 Total		US$ Mn	14.4	15.0	14.2	15.5	17.5
3.5 ♦ Travel		US$ Mn	2.9	3.5	2.6	3.7	5.8
3.6 ♦ Passenger transport		US$ Mn	11.5	11.5	11.6	11.8	11.7
4. TOURISM INDUSTRIES							
Data							
Accommodation for visitors in hotels and similar establishments							
Non-monetary data							
4.13 ♦ Number of establishments		Units	..	..	..	..	..
4.14 ♦ Number of rooms		Units	416	416	643	861	..
4.15 ♦ Number of bed-places		Units	602	602	1,019	1,292	..
Indicators							
4.16 Occupancy rate / rooms		Percent	..	..	..	..	..
4.17 Occupancy rate / bed-places		Percent	30.40	23.80	20.10	28.30	..
4.18 Average length of stay		Nights	..	..	..	..	..
4.19 Available capacity (bed-places per 1000 inhabitants)		Units	0.75	0.73	1.22	1.52	..
6. COMPLEMENTARY INDICATORS							
Demand							
6.1 Gross travel propensity		Units	..	..	..	..	..
6.2 Carrying capacity (arrivals/population)		Units	0.04	0.05	0.05	0.06	..
Macroeconomic indicators related to international tourism							
6.3 Inbound tourism expenditure over GDP		Percent	1.0	1.3	0.8	0.8	..
6.4 Outbound tourism expenditure over GDP		Percent	2.0	1.9	1.7	1.6	..
6.5 Tourism balance (inbound minus outbound tourism expenditure) over GDP		Percent	-1.0	-0.7	-0.9	-0.8	..
6.6 Tourism openness (inbound plus outbound tourism expenditure) over GDP		Percent	3.0	3.2	2.5	2.4	..
6.7 Tourism coverage (inbound over outbound tourism expenditure)		Percent	49.5	65.7	48.1	49.4	..
6.8 Inbound tourism expenditure over exports of goods		Percent	17.9	17.8	11.7	11.4	..
6.9 Inbound tourism expenditure over exports of services		Percent	2.9	3.9	2.7	2.6	..
6.10 Inbound tourism expenditure over exports of goods and services		Percent	2.5	3.2	2.2	2.1	..
6.11 Inbound tourism expenditure over current account credits		Percent	1.8	2.3	1.6	1.6	..
6.12 Outbound tourism expenditure over imports of goods		Percent	5.2	4.5	3.0	2.8	..
6.13 Outbound tourism expenditure over imports of services		Percent	17.1	16.7	13.1	12.4	..
6.14 Outbound tourism expenditure over imports of goods and services		Percent	4.0	3.5	2.4	2.3	..
6.15 Outbound tourism expenditure over current account debits		Percent	3.8	3.4	2.4	2.2	..

DOMINICA

Basic data and indicators	Notes	Units	2005	2006	2007	2008	2009
1. INBOUND TOURISM							
Data							
Arrivals							
1.1 Total		('000)	381	465	437	468	608
1.2 ♦ Overnight visitors (tourists)		('000)	79	84	81	81	75
1.3 ♦ Same-day visitors (excursionists)		('000)	303	381	356	387	533
1.4 * of which, cruise passengers		('000)	302	380	355	386	532
Arrivals by region							
1.5 Total		('000)	79.3	84.0	81.1	81.1	75.0
1.6 ♦ Africa		('000)	..	..	..	..	..
1.7 ♦ Americas		('000)	68.2	71.8	69.4	66.6	62.9
1.8 ♦ East Asia and the Pacific		('000)	0.5	0.5	0.5	0.4	0.4
1.9 ♦ Europe		('000)	10.3	11.3	10.8	13.8	11.6
1.10 ♦ Middle East		('000)	..	..	..	..	..
1.11 ♦ South Asia		('000)	..	..	..	..	..
1.12 ♦ Other not classified		('000)	0.3	0.4	0.4	0.3	0.1
1.13 * of which, nationals residing abroad		('000)	..	..	..	..	..
Arrivals by main purpose							
1.14 Total		('000)	79.5	84.5	81.5	80.9	74.5
1.15 ♦ Personal		('000)	66.5	70.5	71.5	65.9	60.5
1.16 * holidays, leisure and recreation		('000)	66	70	71	65	60
1.17 * other personal purposes		('000)	0.5	0.5	0.5	0.9	0.5
1.18 ♦ Business and professional		('000)	13	14	10	15	14
Arrivals by mode of transport							
1.19 Total		('000)	79	85	80	81	75
1.20 ♦ Air		('000)	58	62	56	55	48
1.21 ♦ Water		('000)	21	23	24	26	27
1.22 ♦ Land		('000)	..	..	..	..	..
1.23 * railway		('000)	..	..	..	..	..
1.24 * road		('000)	..	..	..	..	..
1.25 * others		('000)	..	..	..	..	..
Accommodation							
Total							
1.29 ♦ Guests		('000)	79	84	81	81	75
1.30 ♦ Overnights		('000)	..	..	..	..	..
Hotels and similar establishments							
1.31 ♦ Guests		('000)	27	35	30	31	29
1.32 ♦ Overnights		('000)	..	..	..	..	..
Expenditure							
1.33 Total		US$ Mn	..	..	..	..	..
1.34 ♦ Travel		US$ Mn	57	72	74	72	68
1.35 ♦ Passenger transport		US$ Mn	..	..	..	..	..
Indicators							
1.39 Average size of travel party		Persons	..	..	..	..	..
Average length of stay							
1.40 Total		Days	..	..	..	..	..
1.41 ♦ For all commercial accommodation services	(1)	Nights	8.70	9.20	9.10	9.61	10.92
1.42 * of which, "hotels and similar establishments"		Nights	..	..	..	7.52	8.75
1.43 ♦ For non commercial accommodation services		Days	..	..	..	14.90	14.46
1.44 Average expenditure per day		US$	..	..	..	..	..
3. OUTBOUND TOURISM							
Data							
Expenditure							
3.4 Total		US$ Mn	..	..	..	..	..
3.5 ♦ Travel		US$ Mn	10	10	11	11	10
3.6 ♦ Passenger transport		US$ Mn	..	..	..	..	..

DOMINICA

Basic data and indicators	Notes	Units	2005	2006	2007	2008	2009
4. TOURISM INDUSTRIES							
Data							
Accommodation for visitors in hotels and similar establishments							
Non-monetary data							
4.13 ♦ Number of establishments		Units	..	..	..	..	..
4.14 ♦ Number of rooms		Units	787	818	901	920	963
4.15 ♦ Number of bed-places		Units	..	..	..	1,386	1,451
Indicators							
4.16 Occupancy rate / rooms		Percent	..	..	..	..	..
4.17 Occupancy rate / bed-places		Percent	..	..	..	..	..
4.18 Average length of stay		Nights	..	..	..	..	..
4.19 Available capacity (bed-places per 1000 inhabitants)		Units	..	..	..	18.94	19.72
6. COMPLEMENTARY INDICATORS							
Demand							
6.1 Gross travel propensity		Units	..	..	..	..	..
6.2 Carrying capacity (arrivals/population)		Units	1.10	1.16	1.11	1.11	1.02
Macroeconomic indicators related to international tourism							
6.3 Inbound tourism expenditure over GDP		Percent	19.1	22.7	21.6	19.1	18.0
6.4 Outbound tourism expenditure over GDP		Percent	3.3	3.1	3.1	3.0	2.6
6.5 Tourism balance (inbound minus outbound tourism expenditure) over GDP		Percent	15.8	19.6	18.6	16.1	15.4
6.6 Tourism openness (inbound plus outbound tourism expenditure) over GDP		Percent	22.3	25.8	24.7	22.1	20.5
6.7 Tourism coverage (inbound over outbound tourism expenditure)		Percent	585.5	732.3	704.5	642.5	702.7
6.8 Inbound tourism expenditure over exports of goods		Percent	132.9	162.0	190.9	163.1	179.6
6.9 Inbound tourism expenditure over exports of services		Percent	66.0	71.6	68.4	66.1	65.1
6.10 Inbound tourism expenditure over exports of goods and services		Percent	44.1	49.6	50.4	47.0	47.8
6.11 Inbound tourism expenditure over current account credits		Percent	34.8	40.7	40.3	38.3	39.5
6.12 Outbound tourism expenditure over imports of goods		Percent	6.7	6.7	6.1	5.1	4.7
6.13 Outbound tourism expenditure over imports of services		Percent	19.4	18.8	16.5	15.9	15.2
6.14 Outbound tourism expenditure over imports of goods and services		Percent	5.0	4.9	4.5	3.9	3.6
6.15 Outbound tourism expenditure over current account debits		Percent	4.1	4.3	3.9	3.4	3.3

DOMINICAN REPUBLIC

Basic data and indicators	Notes	Units	2005	2006	2007	2008	2009
1. INBOUND TOURISM							
Data							
Arrivals	(1)						
1.1 Total		('000)	3,981	4,268	4,365	4,455	4,489
1.2 ♦ Overnight visitors (tourists)	(2)	('000)	3,691	3,965	3,980	3,980	3,992
1.3 ♦ Same-day visitors (excursionists)		('000)	290	303	385	475	497
1.4 * of which, cruise passengers	(3)	('000)	290	303	385	475	497
Arrivals by region	(2)						
1.5 Total		('000)	3,690	3,966	3,980	3,981	3,993
1.6 ♦ Africa		('000)	..	..	..	..	..
1.7 ♦ Americas		('000)	1,711	1,948	2,046	2,128	2,203
1.8 ♦ East Asia and the Pacific		('000)	4	5	8	8	7
1.9 ♦ Europe		('000)	1,372	1,389	1,343	1,311	1,205
1.10 ♦ Middle East		('000)	..	..	..	..	..
1.11 ♦ South Asia		('000)	..	..	1	1	1
1.12 ♦ Other not classified		('000)	603	624	582	533	577
1.13 * of which, nationals residing abroad		('000)	602	623	581	532	576
Arrivals by main purpose	(2)						
1.14 Total		('000)	3,691	3,965	3,980	3,980	3,992
1.15 ♦ Personal		('000)	3,563	3,822	3,821	3,839	3,851
1.16 * holidays, leisure and recreation		('000)	3,475	3,674	3,681	3,698	3,688
1.17 * other personal purposes		('000)	88	148	140	141	163
1.18 ♦ Business and professional		('000)	128	143	159	141	141
Arrivals by mode of transport							
1.19 Total		('000)	3,981	4,268	4,365	4,455	4,489
1.20 ♦ Air		('000)	3,691	3,965	3,980	3,980	3,992
1.21 ♦ Water		('000)	290	303	385	475	497
1.22 ♦ Land		('000)	..	..	..	..	..
1.23 * railway		('000)	..	..	..	..	..
1.24 * road		('000)	..	..	..	..	..
1.25 * others		('000)	..	..	..	..	..
Accommodation							
Total							
1.29 ♦ Guests		('000)	..	..	..	..	..
1.30 ♦ Overnights		('000)	..	..	..	..	..
Hotels and similar establishments							
1.31 ♦ Guests		('000)	..	..	..	..	..
1.32 ♦ Overnights		('000)	28,411	31,082	31,469	28,166	27,656
Expenditure							
1.33 Total		US$ Mn	..	..	..	..	..
1.34 ♦ Travel		US$ Mn	3,518	3,917	4,064	4,166	4,051
1.35 ♦ Passenger transport		US$ Mn	..	..	..	..	..
Expenditure by main purpose of the trip							
1.36 Total		US$ Mn	3,518	3,916	4,064	4,166	4,051
1.37 ♦ Personal		US$ Mn	3,497	3,894	4,041	4,149	4,037
1.38 ♦ Business and professional		US$ Mn	21	22	23	17	14
Indicators							
1.39 Average size of travel party		Persons	..	..	..	..	..
Average length of stay							
1.40 Total		Days	..	..	..	..	..
1.41 ♦ For all commercial accommodation services		Nights	9.20	9.30	9.26	9.23	9.19
1.42 * of which, "hotels and similar establishments"		Nights	..	..	..	..	..
1.43 ♦ For non commercial accommodation services		Days	..	..	..	..	..
1.44 Average expenditure per day		US$	103.3	101.3	105.1	110.4	107.0
3. OUTBOUND TOURISM							
Data							
Departures							
3.1 Total		('000)	..	..	..	..	..
3.2 ♦ Overnight visitors (tourists)		('000)	419	420	443	413	415
3.3 ♦ Same-day visitors (excursionists)		('000)	..	..	..	..	..
Expenditure							
3.4 Total		US$ Mn	511	495	531	532	514
3.5 ♦ Travel		US$ Mn	352	333	326	327	350
3.6 ♦ Passenger transport		US$ Mn	159	162	205	205	164
Indicators							
3.10 Average length of stay		Days	14.38	13.45	14.24	13.17	13.40
3.11 Average expenditure per day		US$	58.3	58.6	51.4	57.4	59.9

DOMINICAN REPUBLIC

Basic data and indicators	Notes	Units	2005	2006	2007	2008	2009
4. TOURISM INDUSTRIES							
Data							
Number of establishments							
4.1 Total		Units	..	..	..	..	..
4.2 ♦ Accommodation for visitors		Units	..	..	..	..	..
4.3 * of which, "hotels and similar establishments"		Units	656	670	676	679	676
4.4 ♦ Food and beverage serving activities		Units	..	..	..	..	..
4.5 ♦ Passenger transportation		Units	..	..	..	..	..
4.6 ♦ Travel agencies and other reservation services activities		Units	..	..	..	..	..
4.7 ♦ Other tourism industries		Units	..	..	..	..	..
Accommodation for visitors in hotels and similar establishments							
Monetary data							
4.8 ♦ Output		US$ Mn	..	..	..	..	..
4.9 ♦ Intermediate consumption		US$ Mn	..	..	..	..	..
4.10 ♦ Gross value added		US$ Mn	658.3	629.2	653.5	648.7	600.7
4.11 ♦ Compensation of employees		US$ Mn	..	..	..	..	..
4.12 ♦ Gross fixed capital formation		US$ Mn	..	..	..	..	..
Non-monetary data							
4.13 ♦ Number of establishments		Units	656	670	676	679	676
4.14 ♦ Number of rooms	(4)	Units	60,088	63,549	65,072	66,192	67,197
4.15 ♦ Number of bed-places	(4)	Units	149,675	158,430	162,245	165,290	167,321
Indicators							
4.16 Occupancy rate / rooms		Percent	73.90	73.00	72.20	70.40	66.00
4.17 Occupancy rate / bed-places		Percent	..	..	..	..	..
4.18 Average length of stay		Nights	9.20	9.30	9.26	9.23	9.19
4.19 Available capacity (bed-places per 1000 inhabitants)		Units	16.57	17.23	17.33	17.35	17.25
5. EMPLOYMENT							
Data							
Number of employees by tourism industries							
5.1 Total		('000)	172.1	188.3	190.3	195.5	196.2
5.2 ♦ Accommodation services for visitors (hotels and similar establishments)		('000)	49.2	53.8	54.4	55.9	56.1
5.3 ♦ Other accommodation services		('000)	..	..	..	..	..
5.4 ♦ Food and beverage serving activities		('000)	..	..	..	..	..
5.5 ♦ Passenger transportation		('000)	..	..	..	..	..
5.6 ♦ Travel agencies and other reservation services activities		('000)	..	..	..	..	..
5.7 ♦ Other tourism industries		('000)	122.9	134.5	135.9	139.6	140.1
Indicators							
Number of full-time equivalent jobs by status in employment							
5.11 Total		('000)	..	..	..	..	..
5.12 ♦ Employees		('000)	172.1	188.3	190.3	195.5	196.2
5.13 * male		('000)	..	..	..	..	..
5.14 * female		('000)	..	..	..	..	..
5.15 ♦ Self employed		('000)	..	..	..	..	..
5.16 * male		('000)	..	..	..	..	..
5.17 * female		('000)	..	..	..	..	..

DOMINICAN REPUBLIC

Basic data and indicators	Notes	Units	2005	2006	2007	2008	2009
6. COMPLEMENTARY INDICATORS							
Demand							
6.1 Gross travel propensity		Units	5.0	5.0	5.0	4.0	4.0
6.2 Carrying capacity (arrivals/population)		Units	34.20	36.30	36.30	36.20	35.20
Macroeconomic indicators related to international tourism	(5)						
6.3 Inbound tourism expenditure over GDP		Percent	10.5	11.0	9.9	9.2	8.7
6.4 Outbound tourism expenditure over GDP		Percent	1.5	1.4	1.3	1.1	1.0
6.5 Tourism balance (inbound minus outbound tourism expenditure) over GDP		Percent	9.0	9.6	8.6	8.0	8.0
6.6 Tourism openness (inbound plus outbound tourism expenditure) over GDP		Percent	12.0	12.4	11.2	10.3	9.4
6.7 Tourism coverage (inbound over outbound tourism expenditure)		Percent	688.1	791.8	765.1	800.8	820.0
6.8 Inbound tourism expenditure over exports of goods		Percent	57.3	59.3	56.8	60.1	73.4
6.9 Inbound tourism expenditure over exports of services		Percent	89.4	85.8	84.8	84.6	82.4
6.10 Inbound tourism expenditure over exports of goods and services		Percent	34.9	35.0	34.0	35.1	38.8
6.11 Inbound tourism expenditure over current account credits		Percent	26.2	25.7	24.8	25.7	29.4
6.12 Outbound tourism expenditure over imports of goods		Percent	5.2	4.1	3.9	3.2	2.9
6.13 Outbound tourism expenditure over imports of services		Percent	34.6	31.3	30.0	28.3	21.1
6.14 Outbound tourism expenditure over imports of goods and services		Percent	4.5	3.6	3.5	2.9	2.4
6.15 Outbound tourism expenditure over current account debits		Percent	3.7	3.0	2.9	2.5	2.0

ECUADOR

Basic data and indicators	Notes	Units	2005	2006	2007	2008	2009
1. INBOUND TOURISM							
Data							
Arrivals							
1.1 Total	(1)	('000)	860	841	937	1,005	968
1.2 ♦ Overnight visitors (tourists)		('000)	..	..	..	..	..
1.3 ♦ Same-day visitors (excursionists)		('000)	..	..	..	..	..
1.4 * of which, cruise passengers		('000)	..	..	..	..	..
Arrivals by region	(1)						
1.5 Total		('000)	860	841	937	1,005	969
1.6 ♦ Africa		('000)	2	1	1	2	3
1.7 ♦ Americas		('000)	691	642	730	753	735
1.8 ♦ East Asia and the Pacific		('000)	18	18	24	34	30
1.9 ♦ Europe		('000)	147	145	180	198	197
1.10 ♦ Middle East		('000)	..	..	..	..	1
1.11 ♦ South Asia		('000)	2	1	1	2	3
1.12 ♦ Other not classified		('000)	..	34	1	16	..
1.13 * of which, nationals residing abroad		('000)	..	..	..	..	..
Arrivals by mode of transport	(1)						
1.19 Total		('000)	860	840	937	1,006	968
1.20 ♦ Air		('000)	540	557	639	714	699
1.21 ♦ Water		('000)	5	4	7	10	8
1.22 ♦ Land		('000)	315	279	291	282	261
1.23 * railway		('000)	..	..	..	..	..
1.24 * road		('000)	315	279	291	282	261
1.25 * others		('000)	..	..	..	..	..
Expenditure							
1.33 Total		US$ Mn	488	492	626	745	674
1.34 ♦ Travel		US$ Mn	486	490	623	742	670
1.35 ♦ Passenger transport		US$ Mn	2	2	3	3	4
Expenditure by main purpose of the trip							
1.36 Total		US$ Mn	486	490	623	742	670
1.37 ♦ Personal		US$ Mn	363	364	462	550	497
1.38 ♦ Business and professional		US$ Mn	123	126	161	192	173
3. OUTBOUND TOURISM							
Data							
Departures							
3.1 Total		('000)	..	..	..	..	..
3.2 ♦ Overnight visitors (tourists)		('000)	664	733	801	815	814
3.3 ♦ Same-day visitors (excursionists)		('000)	..	..	..	..	..
Expenditure							
3.4 Total		US$ Mn	644	706	733	790	806
3.5 ♦ Travel		US$ Mn	429	466	504	542	549
3.6 ♦ Passenger transport		US$ Mn	215	240	229	248	257
Expenditure by main purpose of the trip							
3.7 Total		US$ Mn	428	466	504	542	549
3.8 ♦ Personal		US$ Mn	312	340	367	395	400
3.9 ♦ Business and professional		US$ Mn	116	126	137	147	149

ECUADOR

Basic data and indicators	Notes	Units	2005	2006	2007	2008	2009
4. TOURISM INDUSTRIES							
Data							
Number of establishments							
4.1 Total		Units	13,506	13,503	14,467	15,700	16,660
4.2 ♦ Accommodation for visitors		Units	3,077	3,058	3,213	3,399	3,615
4.3 * of which, "hotels and similar establishments"		Units	1,992	2,134	2,291	2,446	2,582
4.4 ♦ Food and beverage serving activities		Units	8,109	8,120	8,898	10,299	11,089
4.5 ♦ Passenger transportation		Units	395	396	416	377	363
4.6 ♦ Travel agencies and other reservation services activities		Units	1,217	1,218	1,264	1,443	1,404
4.7 ♦ Other tourism industries		Units	708	711	676	182	189
Accommodation for visitors in hotels and similar establishments							
Non-monetary data							
4.13 ♦ Number of establishments		Units	1,992	2,134	2,291	2,446	2,582
4.14 ♦ Number of rooms		Units	41,342	44,046	52,127	62,204	55,490
4.15 ♦ Number of bed-places		Units	93,215	101,371	112,535	132,391	120,456
Indicators							
4.16 Occupancy rate / rooms		Percent	..	..	..	..	..
4.17 Occupancy rate / bed-places		Percent	..	..	..	..	..
4.18 Average length of stay		Nights	..	..	..	..	..
4.19 Available capacity (bed-places per 1000 inhabitants)		Units	7.14	7.68	8.43	9.82	8.84
5. EMPLOYMENT							
Data							
Number of employees by tourism industries							
5.1 Total		('000)	72.1	78.5	77.0	84.7	90.1
5.2 ♦ Accommodation services for visitors (hotels and similar establishments)		('000)	21.7	22.6	21.7	23.9	24.9
5.3 ♦ Other accommodation services		('000)	..	..	..	..	..
5.4 ♦ Food and beverage serving activities		('000)	37.2	41.7	43.0	49.0	53.9
5.5 ♦ Passenger transportation		('000)	..	..	2.7	2.8	2.5
5.6 ♦ Travel agencies and other reservation services activities		('000)	5.5	5.9	5.8	6.3	6.2
5.7 ♦ Other tourism industries		('000)	7.7	8.3	3.9	2.7	2.7
6. COMPLEMENTARY INDICATORS							
Demand							
6.1 Gross travel propensity		Units	..	..	..	..	..
6.2 Carrying capacity (arrivals/population)		Units	0.07	0.06	0.07	0.07	0.07
Macroeconomic indicators related to international tourism							
6.3 Inbound tourism expenditure over GDP		Percent	1.3	1.2	1.4	1.4	..
6.4 Outbound tourism expenditure over GDP		Percent	1.7	1.7	1.6	1.4	..
6.5 Tourism balance (inbound minus outbound tourism expenditure) over GDP		Percent	-0.4	-0.5	-0.2	-0.1	..
6.6 Tourism openness (inbound plus outbound tourism expenditure) over GDP		Percent	3.0	2.9	3.0	2.8	..
6.7 Tourism coverage (inbound over outbound tourism expenditure)		Percent	75.7	69.7	85.4	94.4	83.4
6.8 Inbound tourism expenditure over exports of goods		Percent	4.7	3.7	4.2	3.9	4.7
6.9 Inbound tourism expenditure over exports of services		Percent	48.2	47.5	52.2	56.7	55.0
6.10 Inbound tourism expenditure over exports of goods and services		Percent	4.2	3.5	3.9	3.6	4.3
6.11 Inbound tourism expenditure over current account credits		Percent	3.4	2.8	3.2	3.1	3.6
6.12 Outbound tourism expenditure over imports of goods		Percent	6.6	6.2	5.6	4.4	5.6
6.13 Outbound tourism expenditure over imports of services		Percent	30.1	30.2	28.5	26.7	30.7
6.14 Outbound tourism expenditure over imports of goods and services		Percent	5.4	5.1	4.7	3.8	4.7
6.15 Outbound tourism expenditure over current account debits		Percent	4.6	4.4	4.1	3.5	4.3

EGYPT

Basic data and indicators	Notes	Units	2005	2006	2007	2008	2009
1. INBOUND TOURISM							
Data							
Arrivals							
1.1 Total		('000)	8,608	9,083	11,091	12,835	12,536
1.2 ♦ Overnight visitors (tourists)		('000)	8,244	8,646	10,610	12,296	11,914
1.3 ♦ Same-day visitors (excursionists)		('000)	363	437	481	540	622
1.4 * of which, cruise passengers		('000)	..	..	..	..	..
Arrivals by region							
1.5 Total		('000)	8,608	9,083	11,091	12,835	12,535
1.6 ♦ Africa		('000)	264	302	387	401	455
1.7 ♦ Americas		('000)	298	341	430	486	489
1.8 ♦ East Asia and the Pacific		('000)	411	389	526	495	448
1.9 ♦ Europe		('000)	6,047	6,260	7,937	9,622	9,416
1.10 ♦ Middle East		('000)	1,511	1,706	1,687	1,676	1,571
1.11 ♦ South Asia		('000)	73	81	106	116	118
1.12 ♦ Other not classified		('000)	4	4	18	39	38
1.13 * of which, nationals residing abroad		('000)	..	..	..	..	..
Arrivals by main purpose							
1.14 Total		('000)	8,244	8,646	10,610	12,296	11,914
1.15 ♦ Personal		('000)	8,062	8,504	10,515	12,185	11,783
1.16 * holidays, leisure and recreation		('000)	7,993	8,436	10,366	12,013	11,640
1.17 * other personal purposes		('000)	69	68	149	172	143
1.18 ♦ Business and professional		('000)	182	142	95	111	131
Arrivals by mode of transport							
1.19 Total		('000)	8,607	9,082	11,091	12,836	12,536
1.20 ♦ Air		('000)	6,713	7,610	9,917	11,500	11,396
1.21 ♦ Water		('000)	1,094	660	268	287	242
1.22 ♦ Land		('000)	800	812	906	1,049	898
1.23 * railway		('000)	..	..	..	..	..
1.24 * road		('000)	800	812	906	1,049	898
1.25 * others		('000)	..	..	..	..	..
Accommodation							
Total							
1.29 ♦ Guests		('000)	..	..	..	..	..
1.30 ♦ Overnights		('000)	..	..	..	..	..
Hotels and similar establishments							
1.31 ♦ Guests		('000)	..	8,449	..	..	..
1.32 ♦ Overnights		('000)	85,172	89,304	111,466	129,234	126,534
Expenditure							
1.33 Total		US$ Mn	7,206	8,133	10,327	12,104	11,757
1.34 ♦ Travel		US$ Mn	6,851	7,591	9,303	10,985	10,755
1.35 ♦ Passenger transport		US$ Mn	355	542	1,024	1,119	1,002
Indicators							
1.39 Average size of travel party		Persons	..	..	..	..	..
Average length of stay							
1.40 Total		Days	..	..	..	..	..
1.41 ♦ For all commercial accommodation services		Nights	9.90	10.20	10.00	10.00	10.09
1.42 * of which, "hotels and similar establishments"		Nights	..	..	..	..	..
1.43 ♦ For non commercial accommodation services		Days	..	..	..	..	..
1.44 Average expenditure per day		US$	..	..	..	..	..
3. OUTBOUND TOURISM							
Data							
Departures							
3.1 Total		('000)	..	..	..	..	..
3.2 ♦ Overnight visitors (tourists)	(1)	('000)	5,307	4,531	..	..	..
3.3 ♦ Same-day visitors (excursionists)		('000)	..	..	..	..	..
Expenditure							
3.4 Total		US$ Mn	1,932	2,156	2,886	3,390	2,941
3.5 ♦ Travel		US$ Mn	1,629	1,784	2,446	2,915	2,538
3.6 ♦ Passenger transport		US$ Mn	303	372	440	475	403
Expenditure by main purpose of the trip							
3.7 Total		US$ Mn	1,629	1,784	2,446	2,915	2,538
3.8 ♦ Personal		US$ Mn	1,549	1,705	2,344	2,835	2,418
3.9 ♦ Business and professional		US$ Mn	80	79	102	80	120

EGYPT

Basic data and indicators	Notes	Units	2005	2006	2007	2008	2009
4. TOURISM INDUSTRIES							
Data							
Number of establishments							
4.1　Total		Units	..	..	..	..	..
4.2　◆ Accommodation for visitors		Units	..	..	..	..	..
4.3　　* of which, "hotels and similar establishments"		Units	1,321	1,309	1,370	1,490	1,458
4.4　◆ Food and beverage serving activities		Units	..	..	..	..	..
4.5　◆ Passenger transportation		Units	..	..	..	..	..
4.6　◆ Travel agencies and other reservation services activities		Units	..	..	..	..	..
4.7　◆ Other tourism industries		Units	..	..	..	..	..
Accommodation for visitors in hotels and similar establishments							
Non-monetary data							
4.13　◆ Number of establishments		Units	1,321	1,309	1,370	1,490	1,458
4.14　◆ Number of rooms		Units	170,776	177,613	190,191	210,847	214,533
4.15　◆ Number of bed-places		Units	341,552	355,226	380,382	421,694	429,066
Indicators							
4.16　Occupancy rate / rooms		Percent	64.00	61.00	63.00	76.00	68.70
4.17　Occupancy rate / bed-places		Percent	..	..	..	..	..
4.18　Average length of stay		Nights	10.40	10.20	10.00	10.00	10.09
4.19　Available capacity (bed-places per 1000 inhabitants)		Units	4.43	4.52	4.75	5.17	5.17
6. COMPLEMENTARY INDICATORS							
Demand							
6.1　Gross travel propensity		Units	..	..	..	..	..
6.2　Carrying capacity (arrivals/population)		Units	0.11	0.11	0.13	0.15	0.14
Macroeconomic indicators related to international tourism							
6.3　Inbound tourism expenditure over GDP		Percent	7.7	7.5	7.8	7.3	6.3
6.4　Outbound tourism expenditure over GDP		Percent	2.1	2.0	2.2	2.1	1.6
6.5　Tourism balance (inbound minus outbound tourism expenditure) over GDP		Percent	5.7	5.5	5.6	5.3	4.7
6.6　Tourism openness (inbound plus outbound tourism expenditure) over GDP		Percent	9.8	9.6	10.0	9.4	7.8
6.7　Tourism coverage (inbound over outbound tourism expenditure)		Percent	373.1	377.2	357.8	357.1	399.8
6.8　Inbound tourism expenditure over exports of goods		Percent	44.8	39.6	42.2	40.6	50.9
6.9　Inbound tourism expenditure over exports of services		Percent	49.2	50.4	51.8	48.6	54.6
6.10　Inbound tourism expenditure over exports of goods and services		Percent	23.5	22.2	23.3	22.1	26.4
6.11　Inbound tourism expenditure over current account credits		Percent	19.0	18.0	18.4	17.8	21.8
6.12　Outbound tourism expenditure over imports of goods		Percent	8.1	7.4	7.3	6.8	7.4
6.13　Outbound tourism expenditure over imports of services		Percent	18.4	18.6	20.1	19.2	21.1
6.14　Outbound tourism expenditure over imports of goods and services		Percent	5.6	5.3	5.4	5.0	5.5
6.15　Outbound tourism expenditure over current account debits		Percent	5.4	5.1	5.2	4.9	5.1

EL SALVADOR

Basic data and indicators	Notes	Units	2005	2006	2007	2008	2009
1. INBOUND TOURISM							
Data							
Arrivals	(1)						
1.1 Total		('000)	1,306	1,501	1,720	1,875	1,482
1.2 ♦ Overnight visitors (tourists)		('000)	1,127	1,279	1,339	1,385	1,091
1.3 ♦ Same-day visitors (excursionists)		('000)	179	222	381	490	391
1.4 * of which, cruise passengers		('000)	..	..	..	..	..
Arrivals by region							
1.5 Total		('000)	1,128	1,280	1,339	1,385	1,091
1.6 ♦ Africa		('000)	1	1	1	..	..
1.7 ♦ Americas		('000)	1,086	1,240	1,285	1,343	1,067
1.8 ♦ East Asia and the Pacific		('000)	10	10	12	9	5
1.9 ♦ Europe		('000)	31	29	41	33	19
1.10 ♦ Middle East		('000)	..	..	..	..	..
1.11 ♦ South Asia		('000)	..	..	..	..	..
1.12 ♦ Other not classified		('000)	..	..	..	..	..
1.13 * of which, nationals residing abroad		('000)	..	..	..	..	..
Arrivals by main purpose							
1.14 Total		('000)	1,127	1,278	1,339	1,385	1,091
1.15 ♦ Personal		('000)	863	937	996	968	923
1.16 * holidays, leisure and recreation		('000)	331	357	379	317	409
1.17 * other personal purposes		('000)	532	580	617	651	514
1.18 ♦ Business and professional		('000)	264	341	343	417	168
Arrivals by mode of transport							
1.19 Total		('000)	1,127	1,279	1,339	1,385	1,091
1.20 ♦ Air		('000)	499	483	527	490	430
1.21 ♦ Water		('000)	1	1	1	3	..
1.22 ♦ Land		('000)	627	795	811	892	661
1.23 * railway		('000)	..	..	..	..	..
1.24 * road		('000)	627	795	811	892	661
1.25 * others		('000)	..	..	..	..	..
Accommodation							
Total							
1.29 ♦ Guests		('000)	..	..	..	..	..
1.30 ♦ Overnights	(2)	('000)	7,303	7,793	9,383	9,642	..
Hotels and similar establishments							
1.31 ♦ Guests		('000)	329	374	375	376	..
1.32 ♦ Overnights		('000)	..	..	..	..	..
Expenditure							
1.33 Total		US$ Mn	838	1,097	1,158	1,180	549
1.34 ♦ Travel		US$ Mn	543	793	847	894	319
1.35 ♦ Passenger transport		US$ Mn	295	304	311	286	230
Expenditure by main purpose of the trip							
1.36 Total		US$ Mn	542	793	846	894	319
1.37 ♦ Personal		US$ Mn	497	647	663	700	263
1.38 ♦ Business and professional		US$ Mn	45	146	183	194	56
Indicators							
1.39 Average size of travel party		Persons	..	..	..	..	..
Average length of stay							
1.40 Total		Days	..	..	..	..	..
1.41 ♦ For all commercial accommodation services		Nights	6.00	7.30	7.30	7.10	6.20
1.42 * of which, "hotels and similar establishments"		Nights	..	..	..	..	..
1.43 ♦ For non commercial accommodation services		Days	..	..	..	..	..
1.44 Average expenditure per day		US$	77.6	75.6	84.1	71.8	77.1
3. OUTBOUND TOURISM							
Data							
Departures							
3.1 Total		('000)	..	..	..	..	..
3.2 ♦ Overnight visitors (tourists)	(1)	('000)	1,239	1,242	1,012	..	..
3.3 ♦ Same-day visitors (excursionists)		('000)	..	..	..	..	..
Expenditure							
3.4 Total		US$ Mn	430	606	690	709	253
3.5 ♦ Travel		US$ Mn	347	523	605	624	187
3.6 ♦ Passenger transport		US$ Mn	83	83	85	85	66
Expenditure by main purpose of the trip							
3.7 Total		US$ Mn	347	523	605	624	187
3.8 ♦ Personal		US$ Mn	276	391	456	470	157
3.9 ♦ Business and professional		US$ Mn	71	132	149	154	30

EL SALVADOR

Basic data and indicators	Notes	Units	2005	2006	2007	2008	2009
4. **TOURISM INDUSTRIES**							
Data							
Number of establishments							
4.1 Total		Units	..	..	..	..	..
4.2 ♦ Accommodation for visitors		Units	..	..	..	..	..
4.3 * of which, "hotels and similar establishments"		Units	270	286	315	352	394
4.4 ♦ Food and beverage serving activities		Units	..	..	..	..	..
4.5 ♦ Passenger transportation		Units	..	..	..	..	..
4.6 ♦ Travel agencies and other reservation services activities		Units	..	..	..	..	..
4.7 ♦ Other tourism industries		Units	..	..	..	..	..
Accommodation for visitors in hotels and similar establishments							
Non-monetary data							
4.13 ♦ Number of establishments		Units	270	286	315	352	394
4.14 ♦ Number of rooms		Units	5,757	6,518	7,264	7,967	8,298
4.15 ♦ Number of bed-places		Units	10,113	12,089	12,872	14,061	14,061
Indicators							
4.16 Occupancy rate / rooms		Percent	..	..	..	..	..
4.17 Occupancy rate / bed-places		Percent	59.50	61.40	56.70	59.00	59.00
4.18 Average length of stay		Nights	6.20	6.00	5.80	7.10	6.20
4.19 Available capacity (bed-places per 1000 inhabitants)		Units	1.67	1.99	2.11	2.29	2.28
5. **EMPLOYMENT**							
Data							
Number of employees by tourism industries							
5.1 Total		('000)	..	..	42.1	42.3	40.8
5.2 ♦ Accommodation services for visitors (hotels and similar establishments)		('000)	..	..	4.3	4.9	5.0
5.3 ♦ Other accommodation services		('000)	..	..			
5.4 ♦ Food and beverage serving activities		('000)	..	..	16.1	15.4	18.1
5.5 ♦ Passenger transportation		('000)	..	..	13.1	13.4	11.2
5.6 ♦ Travel agencies and other reservation services activities		('000)	..	..	..	..	..
5.7 ♦ Other tourism industries		('000)	..	..	8.6	8.6	6.5
6. **COMPLEMENTARY INDICATORS**							
Demand							
6.1 Gross travel propensity		Units	..	..	..	..	..
6.2 Carrying capacity (arrivals/population)		Units	0.19	0.21	0.22	0.23	0.18
Macroeconomic indicators related to international tourism							
6.3 Inbound tourism expenditure over GDP		Percent	4.9	5.9	5.7	5.3	..
6.4 Outbound tourism expenditure over GDP		Percent	2.5	3.2	3.4	3.2	..
6.5 Tourism balance (inbound minus outbound tourism expenditure) over GDP		Percent	2.4	2.6	2.3	2.1	..
6.6 Tourism openness (inbound plus outbound tourism expenditure) over GDP		Percent	7.4	9.1	9.1	8.5	..
6.7 Tourism coverage (inbound over outbound tourism expenditure)		Percent	195.1	181.0	167.9	166.4	..
6.8 Inbound tourism expenditure over exports of goods		Percent	24.3	29.2	28.7	25.6	..
6.9 Inbound tourism expenditure over exports of services		Percent	74.3	76.9	77.5	78.1	..
6.10 Inbound tourism expenditure over exports of goods and services		Percent	18.3	21.2	20.9	19.3	..
6.11 Inbound tourism expenditure over current account credits		Percent	10.7	12.2	12.0	11.5	..
6.12 Outbound tourism expenditure over imports of goods		Percent	6.7	8.3	8.5	7.9	..
6.13 Outbound tourism expenditure over imports of services		Percent	35.4	40.3	39.5	35.3	..
6.14 Outbound tourism expenditure over imports of goods and services		Percent	5.6	6.9	7.0	6.4	..
6.15 Outbound tourism expenditure over current account debits		Percent	5.1	6.3	6.4	6.0	..

ERITREA

Basic data and indicators	Notes	Units	2005	2006	2007	2008	2009
1. INBOUND TOURISM							
Data							
Arrivals							
1.1 Total	(1)	('000)	83	78	81	70	79
1.2 ♦ Overnight visitors (tourists)		('000)	..	..	..	..	..
1.3 ♦ Same-day visitors (excursionists)		('000)	..	..	..	..	..
1.4 * of which, cruise passengers		('000)	..	..	..	..	..
Arrivals by region	(1)						
1.5 Total		('000)	82	78	80	69	78
1.6 ♦ Africa		('000)	3	4	5	5	7
1.7 ♦ Americas		('000)	2	1	1	1	1
1.8 ♦ East Asia and the Pacific		('000)	2	2	2	2	1
1.9 ♦ Europe		('000)	8	6	5	5	5
1.10 ♦ Middle East		('000)	4	3	2	1	1
1.11 ♦ South Asia		('000)	3	3	3	..	..
1.12 ♦ Other not classified		('000)	60	59	62	55	63
1.13 * of which, nationals residing abroad		('000)	60	59	62	55	63
Arrivals by main purpose	(1)						
1.14 Total		('000)	84	78	81	70	79
1.15 ♦ Personal		('000)	71	66	71	62	72
1.16 * holidays, leisure and recreation		('000)	6	6	6	..	..
1.17 * other personal purposes		('000)	65	60	65	62	72
1.18 ♦ Business and professional		('000)	13	12	10	8	7
Arrivals by mode of transport	(1)						
1.19 Total		('000)	83	78	81	70	79
1.20 ♦ Air		('000)	45	35	38	38	35
1.21 ♦ Water		('000)	1	2	2	1	..
1.22 ♦ Land		('000)	37	41	41	31	44
1.23 * railway		('000)	..	..	..	..	..
1.24 * road		('000)	37	41	41	31	44
1.25 * others		('000)	..	..	..	..	..
Accommodation							
Total							
1.29 ♦ Guests		('000)	..	..	..	..	..
1.30 ♦ Overnights		('000)	..	..	..	..	..
Hotels and similar establishments							
1.31 ♦ Guests		('000)	..	..	..	..	..
1.32 ♦ Overnights	(2)	('000)	176	137	154	133	134
Expenditure							
1.33 Total	(3)	US$ Mn	66	60	61	46	26
1.34 ♦ Travel		US$ Mn	..	..	..	..	..
1.35 ♦ Passenger transport		US$ Mn	..	..	..	..	..
Indicators							
1.39 Average size of travel party		Persons	..	..	..	..	..
Average length of stay							
1.40 Total		Days	..	..	..	..	..
1.41 ♦ For all commercial accommodation services		Nights	3.10	3.30	3.10	3.40	2.30
1.42 * of which, "hotels and similar establishments"		Nights	..	..	..	..	..
1.43 ♦ For non commercial accommodation services		Days	..	..	..	..	..
1.44 Average expenditure per day		US$	..	..	..	..	..
2. DOMESTIC TOURISM							
Data							
Accommodation							
Total							
2.19 ♦ Guests		('000)	..	..	..	..	..
2.20 ♦ Overnights		('000)	..	..	..	..	..
Hotels and similar establishments							
2.21 ♦ Guests		('000)	..	..	..	..	..
2.22 ♦ Overnights	(4)(5)	('000)	669	672	1,012	853	1,122
Indicators							
2.23 Average size of travel party		Persons	..	..	..	..	..
Average length of stay							
2.24 Total		Days	..	..	..	..	..
2.25 ♦ For all commercial accommodation services		Nights	1.40	1.30	1.20	1.20	1.20
2.26 * of which, "hotels and similar establishments"		Nights	..	..	..	..	..
2.27 ♦ For non commercial accommodation services		Days	..	..	..	..	..
2.28 Average expenditure per day		US$	..	..	..	..	..

ERITREA

Basic data and indicators	Notes	Units	2005	2006	2007	2008	2009
4. TOURISM INDUSTRIES							
Data							
Number of establishments							
4.1 Total		Units	..	..	..	..	..
4.2 ♦ Accommodation for visitors		Units	..	..	..	..	..
4.3 * of which, "hotels and similar establishments"	(6)	Units	449	529	601	620	637
4.4 ♦ Food and beverage serving activities		Units	..	..	..	..	..
4.5 ♦ Passenger transportation		Units	..	..	..	..	..
4.6 ♦ Travel agencies and other reservation services activities		Units	..	..	..	..	..
4.7 ♦ Other tourism industries		Units	..	..	..	..	..
Accommodation for visitors in hotels and similar establishments							
Non-monetary data							
4.13 ♦ Number of establishments	(6)	Units	449	529	601	620	637
4.14 ♦ Number of rooms	(6)	Units	5,447	5,447	4,711	4,761	5,147
4.15 ♦ Number of bed-places	(6)	Units	10,720	10,720	9,921	9,912	13,509
Indicators							
4.16 Occupancy rate / rooms		Percent	..	..	..	..	..
4.17 Occupancy rate / bed-places		Percent	43.00	43.00	34.20	34.36	30.46
4.18 Average length of stay		Nights	3.00	3.00	3.10	3.40	2.30
4.19 Available capacity (bed-places per 1000 inhabitants)		Units	2.40	2.31	2.08	2.01	2.66
6. COMPLEMENTARY INDICATORS							
Demand							
6.1 Gross travel propensity		Units	..	..	..	..	..
6.2 Carrying capacity (arrivals/population)		Units	0.02	0.02	0.02	0.01	0.02

ESTONIA

Basic data and indicators	Notes	Units	2005	2006	2007	2008	2009
1. INBOUND TOURISM							
Data							
Arrivals							
1.1 Total		('000)	..	..	..	..	..
1.2 ♦ Overnight visitors (tourists)	(1)	('000)	1,917	1,940	1,900	1,970	1,900
1.3 ♦ Same-day visitors (excursionists)		('000)	307	313	295	378	417
1.4 * of which, cruise passengers		('000)	307	313	295	378	417
Arrivals by region	(2)						
1.5 Total		('000)	1,453	1,428	1,380	1,433	1,380
1.6 ♦ Africa		('000)	1	1	1	1	1
1.7 ♦ Americas		('000)	24	24	28	25	23
1.8 ♦ East Asia and the Pacific		('000)	15	18	17	18	20
1.9 ♦ Europe		('000)	1,411	1,382	1,333	1,388	1,332
1.10 ♦ Middle East		('000)	..	..	..	..	..
1.11 ♦ South Asia		('000)	..	..	..	..	..
1.12 ♦ Other not classified		('000)	2	3	1	1	4
1.13 * of which, nationals residing abroad		('000)	..	..	..	..	..
Accommodation							
Total							
1.29 ♦ Guests		('000)	1,453	1,428	1,380	1,433	1,381
1.30 ♦ Overnights		('000)	2,982	3,020	2,915	2,933	2,741
Hotels and similar establishments							
1.31 ♦ Guests		('000)	1,358	1,330	1,286	1,353	1,308
1.32 ♦ Overnights		('000)	2,791	2,772	2,668	2,727	2,555
Expenditure							
1.33 Total		US$ Mn	1,229	1,361	1,416	1,639	1,444
1.34 ♦ Travel		US$ Mn	971	1,024	1,036	1,189	1,090
1.35 ♦ Passenger transport		US$ Mn	258	337	380	450	354
Expenditure by main purpose of the trip							
1.36 Total		US$ Mn	971	1,024	1,036	1,189	1,090
1.37 ♦ Personal		US$ Mn	741	796	786	942	863
1.38 ♦ Business and professional		US$ Mn	230	228	250	247	227
Indicators							
1.39 Average size of travel party		Persons	..	..	..	..	..
Average length of stay							
1.40 Total		Days	..	..	..	..	..
1.41 ♦ For all commercial accommodation services		Nights	2.05	2.12	2.11	2.05	1.99
1.42 * of which, "hotels and similar establishments"		Nights	..	..	..	..	1.95
1.43 ♦ For non commercial accommodation services		Days	..	..	..	..	..
1.44 Average expenditure per day		US$	..	..	..	..	..
2. DOMESTIC TOURISM							
Data							
Accommodation							
Total							
2.19 ♦ Guests		('000)	619	832	963	944	767
2.20 ♦ Overnights		('000)	1,129	1,523	1,759	1,670	1,382
Hotels and similar establishments							
2.21 ♦ Guests		('000)	428	571	676	658	560
2.22 ♦ Overnights		('000)	751	989	1,175	1,120	944
Indicators							
2.23 Average size of travel party		Persons	..	..	..	..	..
Average length of stay							
2.24 Total		Days	..	..	..	..	..
2.25 ♦ For all commercial accommodation services		Nights	1.82	1.83	1.83	1.77	1.80
2.26 * of which, "hotels and similar establishments"		Nights	1.76	1.73	1.74	1.70	1.69
2.27 ♦ For non commercial accommodation services		Days	..	..	..	..	..
2.28 Average expenditure per day		US$	..	..	..	..	..
3. OUTBOUND TOURISM							
Data							
Departures							
3.1 Total		('000)	..	..	..	..	..
3.2 ♦ Overnight visitors (tourists)	(3)	('000)	..	438	677	692	752
3.3 ♦ Same-day visitors (excursionists)		('000)	..	..	..	..	..

ESTONIA

Basic data and indicators	Notes	Units	2005	2006	2007	2008	2009
Expenditure							
3.4 Total		US$ Mn	530	706	804	938	697
3.5 ♦ Travel		US$ Mn	439	586	670	808	606
3.6 ♦ Passenger transport		US$ Mn	91	120	134	130	91
Expenditure by main purpose of the trip							
3.7 Total		US$ Mn	439	585	670	808	605
3.8 ♦ Personal		US$ Mn	265	362	424	559	444
3.9 ♦ Business and professional		US$ Mn	174	223	246	249	161

4. TOURISM INDUSTRIES

Data

Number of establishments

Basic data and indicators	Notes	Units	2005	2006	2007	2008	2009
4.1 Total		Units	2,187	2,378	2,512	2,640	2,702
4.2 ♦ Accommodation for visitors		Units	784	951	984	1,048	1,091
4.3 * of which, "hotels and similar establishments"		Units	317	341	346	368	387
4.4 ♦ Food and beverage serving activities		Units	1,127	1,196	1,241	1,270	1,330
4.5 ♦ Passenger transportation		Units	..	..	..	..	..
4.6 ♦ Travel agencies and other reservation services activities		Units	276	231	287	322	281
4.7 ♦ Other tourism industries		Units	..	..	..	..	..

Accommodation for visitors in hotels and similar establishments

Non-monetary data

	Notes	Units	2005	2006	2007	2008	2009
4.13 ♦ Number of establishments		Units	317	341	346	368	387
4.14 ♦ Number of rooms		Units	12,312	12,826	13,875	14,565	14,923
4.15 ♦ Number of bed-places		Units	25,228	26,058	28,634	29,760	30,826

Indicators

	Notes	Units	2005	2006	2007	2008	2009
4.16 Occupancy rate / rooms	(4)	Percent	48.00	47.00	44.00	42.81	37.61
4.17 Occupancy rate / bed-places		Percent	..	..	..	35.41	31.10
4.18 Average length of stay	(4)	Nights	1.98	2.01	2.00	1.91	1.87
4.19 Available capacity (bed-places per 1000 inhabitants)		Units	18.72	19.38	21.33	22.20	23.00

5. EMPLOYMENT

Data

Number of employees by tourism industries

	Notes	Units	2005	2006	2007	2008	2009
5.1 Total		('000)	17.5	19.9	21.8	22.1	19.3
5.2 ♦ Accommodation services for visitors (hotels and similar establishments)		('000)	4.8	5.2	5.8	6.3	5.0
5.3 ♦ Other accommodation services		('000)	..	0.6	0.7	..	0.6
5.4 ♦ Food and beverage serving activities		('000)	11.0	12.3	13.6	14.1	12.2
5.5 ♦ Passenger transportation		('000)	..	..	..	..	..
5.6 ♦ Travel agencies and other reservation services activities		('000)	1.7	1.8	1.7	1.7	1.5
5.7 ♦ Other tourism industries		('000)	..	..	..	..	..

6. COMPLEMENTARY INDICATORS

Demand

	Notes	Units	2005	2006	2007	2008	2009
6.1 Gross travel propensity		Units	..	..	..	..	..
6.2 Carrying capacity (arrivals/population)		Units	1.42	1.44	1.42	1.47	1.42

Macroeconomic indicators related to international tourism

	Notes	Units	2005	2006	2007	2008	2009
6.3 Inbound tourism expenditure over GDP		Percent	8.8	8.2	6.6	7.0	7.6
6.4 Outbound tourism expenditure over GDP		Percent	3.8	4.3	3.8	4.0	3.6
6.5 Tourism balance (inbound minus outbound tourism expenditure) over GDP		Percent	5.0	3.9	2.9	3.0	3.9
6.6 Tourism openness (inbound plus outbound tourism expenditure) over GDP		Percent	12.7	12.4	10.4	11.0	11.2
6.7 Tourism coverage (inbound over outbound tourism expenditure)		Percent	232.1	192.8	176.0	174.7	207.5
6.8 Inbound tourism expenditure over exports of goods		Percent	15.6	13.9	12.7	13.0	15.8
6.9 Inbound tourism expenditure over exports of services		Percent	37.9	37.6	32.3	31.8	32.7
6.10 Inbound tourism expenditure over exports of goods and services		Percent	11.1	10.2	9.1	9.2	10.7
6.11 Inbound tourism expenditure over current account credits		Percent	10.0	9.1	7.9	8.1	9.5
6.12 Outbound tourism expenditure over imports of goods		Percent	5.4	5.6	5.4	6.0	7.0
6.13 Outbound tourism expenditure over imports of services		Percent	24.1	28.3	26.1	27.9	27.5
6.14 Outbound tourism expenditure over imports of goods and services		Percent	4.4	4.7	4.5	4.9	5.6
6.15 Outbound tourism expenditure over current account debits		Percent	3.9	4.0	3.7	4.2	4.9

ETHIOPIA

Basic data and indicators	Notes	Units	2005	2006	2007	2008	2009
1. INBOUND TOURISM							
Data							
Arrivals							
1.1 Total		('000)	..	..	..	..	..
1.2 ♦ Overnight visitors (tourists)	(1)	('000)	227	290	312	330	..
1.3 ♦ Same-day visitors (excursionists)		('000)	..	..	..	..	..
1.4 * of which, cruise passengers		('000)	..	..	..	..	..
Arrivals by region	(1)						
1.5 Total		('000)	226	290	311	329	..
1.6 ♦ Africa		('000)	82	90	92	116	..
1.7 ♦ Americas		('000)	41	61	68	59	..
1.8 ♦ East Asia and the Pacific		('000)	13	20	26	23	..
1.9 ♦ Europe		('000)	62	76	89	95	..
1.10 ♦ Middle East		('000)	20	31	27	25	..
1.11 ♦ South Asia		('000)	8	8	9	11	..
1.12 ♦ Other not classified		('000)	..	4	..	..	..
1.13 * of which, nationals residing abroad		('000)	..	..	..	..	..
Arrivals by main purpose	(1)						
1.14 Total		('000)	227	290	312	330	..
1.15 ♦ Personal		('000)	165	192	251	265	..
1.16 * holidays, leisure and recreation		('000)	63	86	129	99	..
1.17 * other personal purposes		('000)	102	106	122	166	..
1.18 ♦ Business and professional		('000)	62	98	61	65	..
Arrivals by mode of transport	(1)						
1.19 Total		('000)	227	..	..	..	..
1.20 ♦ Air		('000)	193	..	..	..	..
1.21 ♦ Water		('000)	..	..	..	..	..
1.22 ♦ Land		('000)	34	..	..	..	..
1.23 * railway		('000)	..	..	..	..	..
1.24 * road		('000)	34	..	..	..	..
1.25 * others		('000)	..	..	..	..	..
Expenditure							
1.33 Total		US$ Mn	533	639	790	1,184	1,119
1.34 ♦ Travel		US$ Mn	168	162	176	377	329
1.35 ♦ Passenger transport		US$ Mn	365	477	614	807	790
Expenditure by main purpose of the trip							
1.36 Total		US$ Mn	168	162	176	376	329
1.37 ♦ Personal		US$ Mn	133	132	167	369	325
1.38 ♦ Business and professional		US$ Mn	35	30	9	7	4
3. OUTBOUND TOURISM							
Data							
Expenditure							
3.4 Total		US$ Mn	..	..	..	..	139
3.5 ♦ Travel		US$ Mn	77	97	107	156	138
3.6 ♦ Passenger transport		US$ Mn	..	..	..	..	1
Expenditure by main purpose of the trip							
3.7 Total		US$ Mn	77	97	107	156	139
3.8 ♦ Personal		US$ Mn	28	32	32	70	58
3.9 ♦ Business and professional		US$ Mn	49	65	75	86	81
4. TOURISM INDUSTRIES							
Data							
Accommodation for visitors in hotels and similar establishments							
Non-monetary data							
4.13 ♦ Number of establishments		Units	..	..	..	..	..
4.14 ♦ Number of rooms	(2)	Units	3,387	9,836	12,791	13,683	..
4.15 ♦ Number of bed-places	(2)	Units	5,170	12,605	16,619	17,217	..
Indicators							
4.16 Occupancy rate / rooms		Percent	..	..	..	..	..
4.17 Occupancy rate / bed-places		Percent	..	..	..	..	..
4.18 Average length of stay		Nights	..	..	..	..	..
4.19 Available capacity (bed-places per 1000 inhabitants)		Units	0.07	0.16	0.21	0.21	..

ETHIOPIA

Basic data and indicators	Notes	Units	2005	2006	2007	2008	2009
6. COMPLEMENTARY INDICATORS							
Demand							
6.1 Gross travel propensity		Units	..	..	..	..	..
6.2 Carrying capacity (arrivals/population)		Units	0.003	0.004	0.004	0.004	..
Macroeconomic indicators related to international tourism							
6.3 Inbound tourism expenditure over GDP		Percent	4.3	4.2	4.1	4.6	..
6.4 Outbound tourism expenditure over GDP		Percent	0.6	0.6	0.6	0.6	..
6.5 Tourism balance (inbound minus outbound tourism expenditure) over GDP		Percent	3.7	3.6	3.6	4.0	..
6.6 Tourism openness (inbound plus outbound tourism expenditure) over GDP		Percent	5.0	4.9	4.7	5.2	..
6.7 Tourism coverage (inbound over outbound tourism expenditure)		Percent	695.8	660.4	739.6	759.7	..
6.8 Inbound tourism expenditure over exports of goods		Percent	58.2	62.4	61.5	76.1	..
6.9 Inbound tourism expenditure over exports of services		Percent	52.7	54.4	57.8	60.4	..
6.10 Inbound tourism expenditure over exports of goods and services		Percent	27.7	29.1	29.8	33.7	..
6.11 Inbound tourism expenditure over current account credits		Percent	15.7	18.0	12.9	15.0	..
6.12 Outbound tourism expenditure over imports of goods		Percent	2.1	2.4	2.1	2.2	..
6.13 Outbound tourism expenditure over imports of services		Percent	6.4	8.3	6.1	6.5	..
6.14 Outbound tourism expenditure over imports of goods and services		Percent	1.6	1.8	1.5	1.6	..
6.15 Outbound tourism expenditure over current account debits		Percent	1.5	1.8	1.5	1.6	..

FIJI

Basic data and indicators	Notes	Units	2005	2006	2007	2008	2009
1. INBOUND TOURISM							
Data							
Arrivals	(1)						
1.1 Total		('000)	547	..	542	627	605
1.2 ♦ Overnight visitors (tourists)		('000)	545	549	540	585	542
1.3 ♦ Same-day visitors (excursionists)		('000)	2	..	2	42	63
1.4 * of which, cruise passengers		('000)	2	..	2	42	63
Arrivals by region	(1)						
1.5 Total		('000)	545	549	540	585	542
1.6 ♦ Africa		('000)	..	..	..	..	..
1.7 ♦ Americas		('000)	75	81	82	82	65
1.8 ♦ East Asia and the Pacific		('000)	389	394	388	431	415
1.9 ♦ Europe		('000)	70	65	61	63	55
1.10 ♦ Middle East		('000)	..	..	..	..	..
1.11 ♦ South Asia		('000)	..	..	..	..	..
1.12 ♦ Other not classified		('000)	11	9	9	9	7
1.13 * of which, nationals residing abroad		('000)	..	..	..	..	..
Arrivals by main purpose	(1)						
1.14 Total		('000)	545	549	540	585	542
1.15 ♦ Personal		('000)	502	503	504	540	500
1.16 * holidays, leisure and recreation		('000)	408	400	399	440	402
1.17 * other personal purposes		('000)	94	103	105	100	98
1.18 ♦ Business and professional		('000)	43	46	36	45	42
Arrivals by mode of transport	(1)						
1.19 Total		('000)	545	549	540	585	542
1.20 ♦ Air		('000)	537	538	527	570	528
1.21 ♦ Water		('000)	8	11	13	15	14
1.22 ♦ Land		('000)	..	..	..	..	..
1.23 * railway		('000)	..	..	..	..	..
1.24 * road		('000)	..	..	..	..	..
1.25 * others		('000)	..	..	..	..	..
Accommodation							
Total							
1.29 ♦ Guests		('000)	..		..	..	..
1.30 ♦ Overnights		('000)	..	..	..	..	..
Hotels and similar establishments							
1.31 ♦ Guests		('000)	..		..	..	..
1.32 ♦ Overnights		('000)	2,760	2,643	2,390	2,489	2,357
Expenditure							
1.33 Total		US$ Mn	722	684	725	841	606
1.34 ♦ Travel		US$ Mn	485	480	499	547	422
1.35 ♦ Passenger transport		US$ Mn	237	204	226	294	184
Expenditure by main purpose of the trip							
1.36 Total		US$ Mn	485	480	499	547	422
1.37 ♦ Personal		US$ Mn	457	449	471	513	393
1.38 ♦ Business and professional		US$ Mn	28	31	28	34	29
Indicators							
1.39 Average size of travel party		Persons	..	..	..	..	..
Average length of stay							
1.40 Total		Days	..	..	..	..	..
1.41 ♦ For all commercial accommodation services	(2)	Nights	9.60	9.80	9.50	9.60	9.80
1.42 * of which, "hotels and similar establishments"		Nights	..	..	..	..	..
1.43 ♦ For non commercial accommodation services		Days	..	..	..	..	..
1.44 Average expenditure per day		US$	..	..	..	..	..
2. DOMESTIC TOURISM							
Data							
Accommodation							
Total							
2.19 ♦ Guests		('000)	..	..	..	..	..
2.20 ♦ Overnights		('000)	..	..	..	..	..
Hotels and similar establishments							
2.21 ♦ Guests		('000)	..	..	..	..	..
2.22 ♦ Overnights		('000)	479	499	554	579	582

FIJI

Basic data and indicators	Notes	Units	2005	2006	2007	2008	2009
3. OUTBOUND TOURISM							
Data							
Departures							
3.1 Total		('000)	..	..	..	..	..
3.2 ♦ Overnight visitors (tourists)		('000)	109	121	120	124	125
3.3 ♦ Same-day visitors (excursionists)		('000)	..	..	..	..	..
Expenditure							
3.4 Total		US$ Mn	132	123	130	139	128
3.5 ♦ Travel		US$ Mn	106	101	92	96	94
3.6 ♦ Passenger transport		US$ Mn	26	22	38	43	34
Expenditure by main purpose of the trip							
3.7 Total		US$ Mn	106	101	92	96	94
3.8 ♦ Personal		US$ Mn	100	95	86	90	89
3.9 ♦ Business and professional		US$ Mn	6	6	6	6	5
4. TOURISM INDUSTRIES							
Data							
Accommodation for visitors in hotels and similar establishments							
Non-monetary data							
4.13 ♦ Number of establishments		Units	..	..	..	..	..
4.14 ♦ Number of rooms		Units	6,713	8,091	8,244	9,525	9,826
4.15 ♦ Number of bed-places		Units	16,536	17,091	18,765	22,352	22,823
Indicators							
4.16 Occupancy rate / rooms		Percent	64.40	56.20	49.70	45.20	40.20
4.17 Occupancy rate / bed-places		Percent	..	..	..	..	..
4.18 Average length of stay		Nights	..	..	..	..	..
4.19 Available capacity (bed-places per 1000 inhabitants)		Units	19.97	20.51	22.37	26.48	26.88
6. COMPLEMENTARY INDICATORS							
Demand							
6.1 Gross travel propensity		Units	..	..	..	..	..
6.2 Carrying capacity (arrivals/population)		Units	0.66	0.66	0.64	0.69	0.64
Macroeconomic indicators related to international tourism							
6.3 Inbound tourism expenditure over GDP		Percent	24.1	..	..	..	..
6.4 Outbound tourism expenditure over GDP		Percent	4.4	..	..	..	..
6.5 Tourism balance (inbound minus outbound tourism expenditure) over GDP		Percent	19.7	..	..	..	..
6.6 Tourism openness (inbound plus outbound tourism expenditure) over GDP		Percent	28.5	..	..	..	..
6.7 Tourism coverage (inbound over outbound tourism expenditure)		Percent	546.4	552.3	557.3	604.8	..
6.8 Inbound tourism expenditure over exports of goods		Percent	105.8	102.6	99.1	96.3	..
6.9 Inbound tourism expenditure over exports of services		Percent	84.4	83.3	84.3	84.7	..
6.10 Inbound tourism expenditure over exports of goods and services		Percent	46.9	46.0	45.5	45.1	..
6.11 Inbound tourism expenditure over current account credits		Percent	38.3	37.0	38.1	38.3	..
6.12 Outbound tourism expenditure over imports of goods		Percent	9.1	7.6	7.9	6.8	..
6.13 Outbound tourism expenditure over imports of services		Percent	26.1	23.7	25.0	23.3	..
6.14 Outbound tourism expenditure over imports of goods and services		Percent	6.7	5.7	6.0	5.2	..
6.15 Outbound tourism expenditure over current account debits		Percent	6.1	5.1	5.5	4.9	..

FINLAND

Basic data and indicators	Notes	Units	2005	2006	2007	2008	2009
1. INBOUND TOURISM							
Data							
Arrivals							
1.1 Total	(1)	('000)	5,038	5,345	5,736	6,072	5,695
1.2 ♦ Overnight visitors (tourists)		('000)	3,140	3,375	3,519	3,583	3,423
1.3 ♦ Same-day visitors (excursionists)		('000)	1,898	1,970	2,217	2,489	2,272
1.4 * of which, cruise passengers		('000)	..	..	..	..	..
Arrivals by region	(1)						
1.5 Total		('000)	5,038	5,345	5,736	6,072	5,695
1.6 ♦ Africa		('000)	12	13	11	11	7
1.7 ♦ Americas		('000)	160	167	174	163	151
1.8 ♦ East Asia and the Pacific		('000)	273	262	312	314	310
1.9 ♦ Europe		('000)	4,581	4,891	5,205	5,540	5,182
1.10 ♦ Middle East		('000)	4	4	12	12	9
1.11 ♦ South Asia		('000)	8	8	22	32	23
1.12 ♦ Other not classified		('000)	..	..	..	..	13
1.13 * of which, nationals residing abroad		('000)	..	..	..	..	..
Arrivals by main purpose	(1)						
1.14 Total		('000)	5,038	5,345	5,736	6,072	5,695
1.15 ♦ Personal		('000)	3,558	3,738	4,040	4,284	4,244
1.16 * holidays, leisure and recreation		('000)	2,107	2,189	2,308	2,591	2,821
1.17 * other personal purposes		('000)	1,451	1,549	1,732	1,693	1,423
1.18 ♦ Business and professional		('000)	1,480	1,607	1,696	1,788	1,451
Arrivals by mode of transport	(1)						
1.19 Total		('000)	5,038	5,345	5,736	6,072	5,695
1.20 ♦ Air		('000)	1,734	1,999	2,049	2,265	2,036
1.21 ♦ Water		('000)	1,538	1,593	1,694	1,637	1,606
1.22 ♦ Land		('000)	1,766	1,753	1,993	2,170	2,053
1.23 * railway		('000)	80	79	110	140	..
1.24 * road		('000)	1,686	1,674	1,883	2,030	2,053
1.25 * others		('000)	..	..	..	..	..
Arrivals by form of organization of the trip	(1)						
1.26 Total		('000)	5,038	5,345	5,736	6,072	5,695
1.27 ♦ Package tour		('000)	806	909	975	1,154	854
1.28 ♦ Other forms		('000)	4,232	4,436	4,761	4,918	4,841
Accommodation	(2)						
Total							
1.29 ♦ Guests		('000)	2,080	2,317	2,472	2,494	2,220
1.30 ♦ Overnights		('000)	4,499	5,004	5,328	5,503	4,890
Hotels and similar establishments							
1.31 ♦ Guests		('000)	1,828	2,045	2,188	2,045	1,957
1.32 ♦ Overnights		('000)	3,887	4,339	4,635	4,768	4,216
Expenditure	(3)						
1.33 Total		US$ Mn	3,070	3,509	4,287	4,861	4,141
1.34 ♦ Travel		US$ Mn	2,180	2,380	2,837	3,220	2,814
1.35 ♦ Passenger transport		US$ Mn	890	1,129	1,450	1,641	1,327
Expenditure by main purpose of the trip	(3)						
1.36 Total		US$ Mn	2,181	2,380	2,837	3,220	2,814
1.37 ♦ Personal		US$ Mn	1,299	1,351	1,689	2,049	1,794
1.38 ♦ Business and professional		US$ Mn	882	1,029	1,148	1,171	1,020
Indicators							
1.39 Average size of travel party		Persons	..	..	..	..	..
Average length of stay							
1.40 Total		Days	..	..	..	..	..
1.41 ♦ For all commercial accommodation services	(2)	Nights	2.21	2.21	2.16	2.16	2.16
1.42 * of which, "hotels and similar establishments"	(2)	Nights	2.15	2.15	2.12	2.12	2.13
1.43 ♦ For non commercial accommodation services	(1)	Days	10.45	11.31	11.86	11.76	10.51
1.44 Average expenditure per day	(1)	US$	65.0	67.0	73.0	81.0	80.0
2. DOMESTIC TOURISM							
Data							
Trips	(4)						
2.1 Total		('000)	..	..	..	..	..
2.2 ♦ Overnight visitors (tourists)		('000)	30,931	28,245	30,633	31,091	31,015
2.3 ♦ Same-day visitors (excursionists)		('000)	..	..	..	..	..
Trips by main purpose	(4)						
2.4 Total		('000)	30,931	28,245	30,633	31,091	31,015
2.5 ♦ Personal		('000)	27,360	25,043	26,974	27,138	27,523
2.6 * holidays, leisure and recreation		('000)	9,968	9,701	10,024	10,151	10,669
2.7 * other personal purposes		('000)	17,392	15,342	16,950	16,987	16,854
2.8 ♦ Business and professional		('000)	3,571	3,202	3,659	3,953	3,492

FINLAND

Basic data and indicators	Notes	Units	2005	2006	2007	2008	2009
Trips by mode of transport	**(4)**						
2.9 Total		('000)	30,931	28,245	30,633	31,091	31,015
2.10 ♦ Air		('000)	832	720	879	636	641
2.11 ♦ Water		('000)	244	307	227	277	332
2.12 ♦ Land		('000)	29,855	27,218	29,527	30,178	30,042
2.13 * railway		('000)	2,918	2,686	3,035	3,306	3,135
2.14 * road		('000)	26,619	24,110	26,218	26,574	26,620
2.15 * others		('000)	318	422	274	298	287
Trips by form of organization	**(4)**						
2.16 Total	(5)	('000)	4,637	4,873	4,869	5,080	5,228
2.17 ♦ Package tour	(5)	('000)	232	146	243	152	157
2.18 ♦ Other forms	(5)	('000)	4,405	4,727	4,626	4,928	5,071
Accommodation	**(2)**						
Total							
2.19 ♦ Guests		('000)	7,009	7,318	7,627	7,746	7,545
2.20 ♦ Overnights		('000)	12,760	13,165	13,708	13,963	13,677
Hotels and similar establishments							
2.21 ♦ Guests		('000)	5,948	6,203	6,520	6,671	6,429
2.22 ♦ Overnights		('000)	10,388	10,676	11,182	11,339	10,930
Indicators							
2.23 Average size of travel party		Persons	..	..	..	..	..
Average length of stay							
2.24 Total		Days	..	..	..	..	..
2.25 ♦ For all commercial accommodation services	(2)	Nights	1.82	1.80	1.80	1.80	1.81
2.26 * of which, "hotels and similar establishments"	(2)	Nights	1.75	1.72	1.71	1.70	1.70
2.27 ♦ For non commercial accommodation services	(4)	Days	2.63	2.76	2.66	2.65	2.67
2.28 Average expenditure per day		US$	..	..	..	..	..

3. OUTBOUND TOURISM

Data

Basic data and indicators	Notes	Units	2005	2006	2007	2008	2009
Departures	**(4)**						
3.1 Total		('000)	6,668	6,428	6,413	6,564	6,680
3.2 ♦ Overnight visitors (tourists)	(6)	('000)	5,902	5,756	5,749	5,854	5,832
3.3 ♦ Same-day visitors (excursionists)		('000)	766	672	664	710	848
Expenditure	**(3)**						
3.4 Total		US$ Mn	3,622	4,094	4,812	5,534	5,205
3.5 ♦ Travel		US$ Mn	3,057	3,424	3,983	4,501	4,373
3.6 ♦ Passenger transport		US$ Mn	565	670	829	1,033	832
Expenditure by main purpose of the trip	**(3)**						
3.7 Total		US$ Mn	3,056	3,424	3,983	4,501	4,373
3.8 ♦ Personal		US$ Mn	2,047	2,220	2,822	3,180	3,370
3.9 ♦ Business and professional		US$ Mn	1,009	1,204	1,161	1,321	1,003
Indicators							
3.10 Average length of stay	(4)	Days	4.61	4.77	4.91	4.90	5.17
3.11 Average expenditure per day	(4)	US$	115.2	111.2	138.9	122.3	122.6

4. TOURISM INDUSTRIES

Data

Basic data and indicators	Notes	Units	2005	2006	2007	2008	2009
Number of establishments	**(7)**						
4.1 Total	(8)	Units	27,820	28,504	29,305	28,961	29,419
4.2 ♦ Accommodation for visitors		Units	1,820	1,867	1,928	1,950	1,940
4.3 * of which, "hotels and similar establishments"		Units	922	916	937	916	892
4.4 ♦ Food and beverage serving activities		Units	11,974	12,110	12,298	12,425	12,615
4.5 ♦ Passenger transportation		Units	9,354	9,490	9,694	9,768	9,815
4.6 ♦ Travel agencies and other reservation services activities		Units	1,271	1,370	1,431	1,557	1,566
4.7 ♦ Other tourism industries		Units	3,401	3,667	3,954	3,261	3,483
Accommodation for visitors in hotels and similar establishments							
Monetary data	(9)						
4.8 ♦ Output		US$ Mn	1,690.7	1,783.0	2,053.0	..	..
4.9 ♦ Intermediate consumption		US$ Mn	1,026.4	1,068.5	1,207.4	..	..
4.10 ♦ Gross value added		US$ Mn	664.3	714.4	845.6	..	..
4.11 ♦ Compensation of employees		US$ Mn	513.8	536.1	..	..	..
4.12 ♦ Gross fixed capital formation		US$ Mn	..	..	..	..	..
Non-monetary data	(2)						
4.13 ♦ Number of establishments		Units	922	916	937	916	892
4.14 ♦ Number of rooms		Units	54,354	54,936	54,731	54,844	55,146
4.15 ♦ Number of bed-places		Units	117,605	119,045	118,888	119,182	120,175

FINLAND

Basic data and indicators	Notes	Units	2005	2006	2007	2008	2009
Indicators	(2)						
4.16 Occupancy rate / rooms		Percent	47.80	49.90	51.60	51.90	47.60
4.17 Occupancy rate / bed-places		Percent	36.70	38.30	39.70	40.00	37.20
4.18 Average length of stay		Nights	1.84	1.82	1.82	1.81	1.80
4.19 Available capacity (bed-places per 1000 inhabitants)		Units	22.38	22.55	22.43	22.38	22.46
Travel agencies and other reservation service activities							
Monetary data	(9)						
4.20 ♦ Output		US$ Mn	459.1	428.2	512.6	..	..
4.21 ♦ Intermediate consumption		US$ Mn	156.8	145.6	175.4	..	..
4.22 ♦ Gross value added		US$ Mn	302.3	282.5	337.1	..	..
4.23 ♦ Compensation of employees		US$ Mn	154.3	151.9	..	..	..
4.24 ♦ Gross fixed capital formation		US$ Mn	..	..	..	..	..
Non-monetary data							
♦ Domestic trips	(4)						
4.25 * with package tour	(5)	Percent	5.0	3.0	5.0	3.0	3.0
4.26 * without package tour		Percent	95.0	97.0	95.0	97.0	97.0
♦ Inbound trips	(1)						
4.27 * with package tour		Percent	16.0	17.0	17.0	19.0	15.0
4.28 * without package tour		Percent	84.0	83.0	83.0	81.0	85.0
♦ Outbound trips	(4)						
4.29 * with package tour		Percent	50.8	46.1	43.3	43.4	41.7
4.30 * without package tour		Percent	49.2	53.9	56.7	56.6	58.3

5. EMPLOYMENT

Data							
Number of employees by tourism industries	(7)						
5.1 Total	(8)	('000)	109.4	114.0	116.9	109.6	108.5
5.2 ♦ Accommodation services for visitors (hotels and similar establishments)		('000)	10.8	10.8	10.9	10.7	10.2
5.3 ♦ Other accommodation services		('000)	0.8	1.1	1.2	1.2	1.2
5.4 ♦ Food and beverage serving activities		('000)	43.2	46.2	47.2	47.2	48.2
5.5 ♦ Passenger transportation		('000)	38.0	38.2	38.9	31.5	31.0
5.6 ♦ Travel agencies and other reservation services activities		('000)	4.6	4.7	4.7	5.0	4.6
5.7 ♦ Other tourism industries		('000)	12.0	13.0	14.0	14.0	13.3
Number of jobs by status in employment	(10)						
5.8 Total	(11)	('000)	78.0	78.0	84.0	88.0	85.0
5.9 ♦ Employees		('000)	11.0	10.0	11.0	10.0	11.0
5.10 ♦ Self employed		('000)	67.0	68.0	73.0	78.0	74.0

6. COMPLEMENTARY INDICATORS

Demand							
6.1 Gross travel propensity		Units	6.5	6.0	6.4	6.5	6.5
6.2 Carrying capacity (arrivals/population)		Units	6.80	6.40	6.90	6.90	6.90
Macroeconomic indicators related to international tourism							
6.3 Inbound tourism expenditure over GDP		Percent	1.6	1.7	1.7	1.8	1.8
6.4 Outbound tourism expenditure over GDP		Percent	1.9	2.0	2.0	2.1	2.2
6.5 Tourism balance (inbound minus outbound tourism expenditure) over GDP		Percent	-0.3	-0.3	-0.2	-0.2	-0.4
6.6 Tourism openness (inbound plus outbound tourism expenditure) over GDP		Percent	3.4	3.7	3.7	3.9	4.0
6.7 Tourism coverage (inbound over outbound tourism expenditure)		Percent	84.8	85.7	89.1	87.8	80.8
6.8 Inbound tourism expenditure over exports of goods		Percent	4.7	4.5	4.8	5.0	6.8
6.9 Inbound tourism expenditure over exports of services		Percent	18.0	20.0	18.3	15.2	16.6
6.10 Inbound tourism expenditure over exports of goods and services		Percent	3.7	3.7	3.8	3.8	4.8
6.11 Inbound tourism expenditure over current account credits		Percent	3.1	3.0	3.1	3.1	4.1
6.12 Outbound tourism expenditure over imports of goods		Percent	6.5	6.2	6.2	6.4	9.2
6.13 Outbound tourism expenditure over imports of services		Percent	20.4	22.0	21.2	18.2	22.5
6.14 Outbound tourism expenditure over imports of goods and services		Percent	4.9	4.8	4.8	4.7	6.5
6.15 Outbound tourism expenditure over current account debits		Percent	3.9	3.9	3.7	3.8	5.2

FRANCE

Basic data and indicators	Notes	Units	2005	2006	2007	2008	2009
1. INBOUND TOURISM							
Data							
Arrivals	(1)						
1.1 Total		('000)	185,829	193,882	193,319	193,571	192,574
1.2 ♦ Overnight visitors (tourists)		('000)	74,988	77,916	80,853	79,218	76,824
1.3 ♦ Same-day visitors (excursionists)		('000)	110,841	115,966	112,466	114,353	115,750
1.4 * of which, cruise passengers		('000)	..	..	..	..	..
Arrivals by region	(1)						
1.5 Total		('000)	74,988	77,915	80,853	79,219	76,824
1.6 ♦ Africa		('000)	1,421	1,434	1,576	1,765	1,821
1.7 ♦ Americas		('000)	4,950	5,406	6,024	5,963	5,492
1.8 ♦ East Asia and the Pacific		('000)	2,827	3,139	3,206	3,483	3,366
1.9 ♦ Europe		('000)	65,217	67,392	69,272	67,305	65,312
1.10 ♦ Middle East		('000)	573	544	775	703	833
1.11 ♦ South Asia		('000)	..	..	..	..	..
1.12 ♦ Other not classified		('000)	..	..	..	..	..
1.13 * of which, nationals residing abroad		('000)	..	..	..	..	..
Arrivals by main purpose	(1)						
1.14 Total		('000)	74,988	77,916	80,853	79,218	76,824
1.15 ♦ Personal		('000)	66,627	69,876	72,570	68,107	66,599
1.16 * holidays, leisure and recreation	(2)	('000)	50,845	53,473	56,394	56,536	55,839
1.17 * other personal purposes	(3)	('000)	15,782	16,403	16,176	11,571	10,760
1.18 ♦ Business and professional		('000)	8,361	8,040	8,283	11,111	10,225
Arrivals by mode of transport	(1)						
1.19 Total		('000)	74,988	77,916	80,852	79,218	76,824
1.20 ♦ Air		('000)	16,325	17,825	20,710	21,895	19,540
1.21 ♦ Water		('000)	7,488	7,793	7,675	7,309	6,971
1.22 ♦ Land		('000)	51,175	52,298	52,467	50,014	50,313
1.23 * railway		('000)	4,361	4,899	5,037	5,035	4,866
1.24 * road		('000)	46,814	47,399	47,430	44,979	45,447
1.25 * others		('000)	..	..	..	..	..
Accommodation							
Total							
1.29 ♦ Guests		('000)	..	..	..	..	..
1.30 ♦ Overnights	(1)(4)	('000)	502,700	513,732	536,348	526,160	517,648
Hotels and similar establishments							
1.31 ♦ Guests	(5)	('000)	34,806	32,304	33,252	32,137	28,766
1.32 ♦ Overnights	(5)	('000)	72,054	68,821	72,391	71,065	63,203
Expenditure							
1.33 Total		US$ Mn	51,691	54,728	62,916	67,383	59,391
1.34 ♦ Travel		US$ Mn	43,954	46,512	54,209	57,236	49,450
1.35 ♦ Passenger transport	(6)	US$ Mn	7,737	8,216	8,707	10,147	9,941
Indicators							
1.39 Average size of travel party		Persons	..	..	..	..	..
Average length of stay							
1.40 Total		Days	..	..	..	..	..
1.41 ♦ For all commercial accommodation services	(7)	Nights	6.70	6.59	6.63	6.64	..
1.42 * of which, "hotels and similar establishments"		Nights	..	..	..	..	2.20
1.43 ♦ For non commercial accommodation services		Days	..	..	..	..	..
1.44 Average expenditure per day		US$	..	..	..	..	..

FRANCE

Basic data and indicators	Notes	Units	2005	2006	2007	2008	2009
2. DOMESTIC TOURISM							
Data							
Trips	(8)						
2.1 Total		('000)	..	..	..	..	318,463
2.2 ♦ Overnight visitors (tourists)		('000)	210,755	210,518	211,883	200,675	202,064
2.3 ♦ Same-day visitors (excursionists)		('000)	..	..	..	..	116,399
Trips by main purpose	(8)						
2.4 Total		('000)	210,755	210,518	211,882	200,675	202,063
2.5 ♦ Personal		('000)	191,692	190,348	192,326	181,351	181,002
2.6 * holidays, leisure and recreation		('000)	..	..	..	..	55,404
2.7 * other personal purposes		('000)	..	..	..	..	125,598
2.8 ♦ Business and professional		('000)	19,063	20,170	19,556	19,324	21,061
Trips by mode of transport	(8)(9)						
2.9 Total		('000)	191,692	190,348	192,327	181,352	181,003
2.10 ♦ Air		('000)	2,318	2,222	2,248	2,344	2,254
2.11 ♦ Water		('000)	583	551	595	572	597
2.12 ♦ Land		('000)	188,791	187,575	189,484	178,436	178,152
2.13 * railway		('000)	24,606	25,206	25,447	24,557	24,364
2.14 * road		('000)	163,235	161,460	163,273	152,890	152,924
2.15 * others		('000)	950	909	764	989	864
Accommodation	(8)						
Total							
2.19 ♦ Guests		('000)	..	..	..	..	..
2.20 ♦ Overnights	(4)(8)(9)(10)	('000)	1,051,527	1,048,237	1,045,220	991,980	961,874
Hotels and similar establishments							
2.21 ♦ Guests	(5)	('000)	72,587	72,230	74,892	75,144	74,904
2.22 ♦ Overnights	(5)	('000)	122,222	123,105	126,536	126,550	124,769
Indicators							
2.23 Average size of travel party		Persons	..	..	..	..	..
Average length of stay							
2.24 Total		Days	..	..	..	..	..
2.25 ♦ For all commercial accommodation services	(8)(9)	Nights	5.49	5.51	5.43	5.47	5.31
2.26 * of which, "hotels and similar establishments"		Nights	..	..	..	..	1.67
2.27 ♦ For non commercial accommodation services		Days	..	..	..	..	..
2.28 Average expenditure per day		US$	..	..	..	..	..
3. OUTBOUND TOURISM							
Data							
Departures							
3.1 Total		('000)	..	..	..	..	27,034
3.2 ♦ Overnight visitors (tourists)	(8)(10)	('000)	22,480	22,240	22,226	21,080	21,281
3.3 ♦ Same-day visitors (excursionists)		('000)	..	..	..	..	5,752
Expenditure							
3.4 Total		US$ Mn	38,813	39,331	46,029	50,334	46,009
3.5 ♦ Travel		US$ Mn	31,727	32,693	38,261	41,570	38,575
3.6 ♦ Passenger transport	(6)	US$ Mn	7,086	6,638	7,768	8,764	7,434
4. TOURISM INDUSTRIES							
Data							
Number of establishments							
4.1 Total		Units	..	..	..	..	..
4.2 ♦ Accommodation for visitors		Units	..	..	..	..	..
4.3 * of which, "hotels and similar establishments"	(11)	Units	18,085	17,877	17,721	17,487	17,283
4.4 ♦ Food and beverage serving activities		Units	..	..	..	..	..
4.5 ♦ Passenger transportation		Units	..	..	..	..	..
4.6 ♦ Travel agencies and other reservation services activities		Units	..	..	..	..	..
4.7 ♦ Other tourism industries		Units	..	..	..	..	..
Accommodation for visitors in hotels and similar establishments							
Non-monetary data	(11)						
4.13 ♦ Number of establishments		Units	18,085	17,877	17,721	17,487	17,283
4.14 ♦ Number of rooms		Units	613,798	612,424	614,532	612,082	612,475
4.15 ♦ Number of bed-places		Units	1,227,596	1,224,848	1,229,064	1,224,164	1,224,950
Indicators							
4.16 Occupancy rate / rooms	(5)(12)	Percent	59.10	60.40	61.87	61.38	58.06
4.17 Occupancy rate / bed-places		Percent	..	..	..	..	..
4.18 Average length of stay	(5)	Nights	1.81	1.82	1.84	1.84	1.81
4.19 Available capacity (bed-places per 1000 inhabitants)		Units	20.17	19.96	19.84	19.66	19.56

FRANCE

Basic data and indicators		Notes	Units	2005	2006	2007	2008	2009
6.	**COMPLEMENTARY INDICATORS**							
	Demand							
6.1	Gross travel propensity		Units	..	..	..	..	..
6.2	Carrying capacity (arrivals/population)		Units	4.69	4.70	4.73	4.49	4.45
	Macroeconomic indicators related to international tourism							
6.3	Inbound tourism expenditure over GDP		Percent	2.0	2.1	2.1	2.0	1.9
6.4	Outbound tourism expenditure over GDP		Percent	1.5	1.4	1.5	1.5	1.4
6.5	Tourism balance (inbound minus outbound tourism expenditure) over GDP		Percent	0.6	0.6	0.6	0.5	0.4
6.6	Tourism openness (inbound plus outbound tourism expenditure) over GDP		Percent	3.5	3.5	3.6	3.5	3.3
6.7	Tourism coverage (inbound over outbound tourism expenditure)		Percent	138.5	142.3	141.7	137.7	128.2
6.8	Inbound tourism expenditure over exports of goods		Percent	10.0	9.6	9.9	9.5	10.4
6.9	Inbound tourism expenditure over exports of services		Percent	36.0	36.1	36.2	34.1	34.5
6.10	Inbound tourism expenditure over exports of goods and services		Percent	7.8	7.6	7.8	7.4	8.0
6.11	Inbound tourism expenditure over current account credits		Percent	5.9	5.5	5.5	5.4	5.9
6.12	Outbound tourism expenditure over imports of goods		Percent	6.8	6.3	6.3	6.0	7.2
6.13	Outbound tourism expenditure over imports of services		Percent	29.7	28.8	29.5	29.3	30.3
6.14	Outbound tourism expenditure over imports of goods and services		Percent	5.5	5.1	5.2	5.0	5.8
6.15	Outbound tourism expenditure over current account debits		Percent	4.2	3.8	3.8	3.7	4.3

FRENCH GUIANA

Basic data and indicators	Notes	Units	2005	2006	2007	2008	2009
1. INBOUND TOURISM							
Data							
Arrivals							
1.1 Total		('000)	..	..	..	..	..
1.2 ♦ Overnight visitors (tourists)	(1)	('000)	95	..	109	..	..
1.3 ♦ Same-day visitors (excursionists)		('000)	1.7	..	..	..	..
1.4 * of which, cruise passengers		('000)	..	..	..	..	..
Arrivals by region							
1.5 Total		('000)	95	..	109	..	..
1.6 ♦ Africa		('000)	..	..	..	..	..
1.7 ♦ Americas		('000)	25	..	37	..	..
1.8 ♦ East Asia and the Pacific		('000)	..	..	..	..	..
1.9 ♦ Europe		('000)	64	..	67	..	..
1.10 ♦ Middle East		('000)	..	..	..	..	..
1.11 ♦ South Asia		('000)	..	..	..	..	..
1.12 ♦ Other not classified		('000)	6	..	5	..	..
1.13 * of which, nationals residing abroad		('000)	..	..	..	..	..
Arrivals by main purpose							
1.14 Total		('000)	95	..	109	..	..
1.15 ♦ Personal		('000)	47	..	42	..	..
1.16 * holidays, leisure and recreation		('000)	21	..	25	..	..
1.17 * other personal purposes		('000)	26	..	17	..	..
1.18 ♦ Business and professional		('000)	48	..	67	..	..
Accommodation							
Total							
1.29 ♦ Guests		('000)	..	..	..	..	..
1.30 ♦ Overnights	(2)	('000)	391	..	996	..	..
Hotels and similar establishments							
1.31 ♦ Guests		('000)	..	..	..	..	..
1.32 ♦ Overnights	(3)	('000)	..	..	280	..	..
Expenditure							
1.33 Total	(1)	US$ Mn	44	..	49	..	..
1.34 ♦ Travel		US$ Mn	..	..	..	..	..
1.35 ♦ Passenger transport		US$ Mn	..	..	..	..	..
Indicators							
1.39 Average size of travel party		Persons	..	..	..	..	..
Average length of stay							
1.40 Total		Days	..	..	..	..	..
1.41 ♦ For all commercial accommodation services		Nights	2.70	..	..	..	..
1.42 * of which, "hotels and similar establishments"		Nights	..	..	..	..	..
1.43 ♦ For non commercial accommodation services		Days	..	..	..	..	..
1.44 Average expenditure per day		US$	..	..	..	..	..
4. TOURISM INDUSTRIES							
Data							
Accommodation for visitors in hotels and similar establishments							
Non-monetary data							
4.13 ♦ Number of establishments		Units	..	..	..	..	..
4.14 ♦ Number of rooms		Units	1,184	..	..	..	..
4.15 ♦ Number of bed-places		Units	..	..	..	..	..
Indicators							
4.16 Occupancy rate / rooms		Percent	50.90	51.70	53.70	..	..
4.17 Occupancy rate / bed-places		Percent	..	..	..	..	..
4.18 Average length of stay		Nights	..	..	..	..	..
4.19 Available capacity (bed-places per 1000 inhabitants)		Units	..	..	..	..	..

FRENCH POLYNESIA

Basic data and indicators	Notes	Units	2005	2006	2007	2008	2009
1. INBOUND TOURISM							
Data							
Arrivals							
1.1 Total		('000)	..	..	..	..	..
1.2 ♦ Overnight visitors (tourists)	(1)	('000)	208	222	218	196	160
1.3 ♦ Same-day visitors (excursionists)		('000)	..	..	..	..	..
1.4 * of which, cruise passengers		('000)	..	..	..	..	..
Arrivals by region	(1)						
1.5 Total		('000)	208	221	217	196	160
1.6 ♦ Africa		('000)	..	..	1	..	..
1.7 ♦ Americas		('000)	80	89	81	71	52
1.8 ♦ East Asia and the Pacific		('000)	46	48	50	42	35
1.9 ♦ Europe		('000)	82	83	85	83	73
1.10 ♦ Middle East		('000)	..	..	..	..	..
1.11 ♦ South Asia		('000)	..	..	..	..	..
1.12 ♦ Other not classified		('000)	..	1	..	..	..
1.13 * of which, nationals residing abroad		('000)	..	..	..	..	..
Arrivals by main purpose	(1)						
1.14 Total		('000)	208	222	218	196	160
1.15 ♦ Personal		('000)	195	208	206	181	147
1.16 * holidays, leisure and recreation		('000)	190	203	200	160	128
1.17 * other personal purposes		('000)	5	5	6	21	19
1.18 ♦ Business and professional		('000)	13	14	12	15	13
Arrivals by mode of transport							
1.19 Total		('000)	208	222	218	196	160
1.20 ♦ Air		('000)	208	222	218	196	160
1.21 ♦ Water		('000)	..	..	..	..	..
1.22 ♦ Land		('000)	..	..	..	..	..
1.23 * railway		('000)	..	..	..	..	..
1.24 * road		('000)	..	..	..	..	..
1.25 * others		('000)	..	..	..	..	..
Arrivals by form of organization of the trip							
1.26 Total		('000)	..	..	..	..	160
1.27 ♦ Package tour		('000)	..	..	..	..	101
1.28 ♦ Other forms		('000)	..	..	..	..	59
Accommodation							
Total							
1.29 ♦ Guests		('000)	208	222	218	196	160
1.30 ♦ Overnights		('000)	2,787	2,926	2,897	2,603	2,205
Hotels and similar establishments							
1.31 ♦ Guests		('000)	176	193	190	173	138
1.32 ♦ Overnights		('000)	1,897	2,093	2,133	1,968	1,601
Expenditure							
1.33 Total		US$ Mn	759	691	807	745	736
1.34 ♦ Travel		US$ Mn	530	463	539	522	438
1.35 ♦ Passenger transport		US$ Mn	229	228	268	223	298
Expenditure by main purpose of the trip							
1.36 Total		US$ Mn	..	..	..	..	438
1.37 ♦ Personal		US$ Mn	..	..	..	..	414
1.38 ♦ Business and professional		US$ Mn	..	..	..	..	24
Indicators							
1.39 Average size of travel party		Persons	..	..	..	..	..
Average length of stay							
1.40 Total		Days	..	..	..	..	..
1.41 ♦ For all commercial accommodation services	(2)	Nights	13.49	13.21	13.30	13.20	13.70
1.42 * of which, "hotels and similar establishments"		Nights	..	..	11.20	11.40	11.60
1.43 ♦ For non commercial accommodation services		Days	..	..	..	26.80	27.10
1.44 Average expenditure per day		US$	..	..	..	..	..
3. OUTBOUND TOURISM							
Data							
Departures							
3.1 Total		('000)	..	..	..	..	..
3.2 ♦ Overnight visitors (tourists)		('000)	..	..	..	..	88
3.3 ♦ Same-day visitors (excursionists)		('000)	..	..	..	..	..
Expenditure							
3.4 Total		US$ Mn	430	256	408	412	..
3.5 ♦ Travel		US$ Mn	312	122	159	159	164
3.6 ♦ Passenger transport		US$ Mn	118	134	249	253	..
Expenditure by main purpose of the trip							
3.7 Total		US$ Mn	..	..	..	..	164
3.8 ♦ Personal		US$ Mn	..	..	..	..	134
3.9 ♦ Business and professional		US$ Mn	..	..	..	..	30

FRENCH POLYNESIA

Basic data and indicators	Notes	Units	2005	2006	2007	2008	2009
4. TOURISM INDUSTRIES							
Data							
Number of establishments							
4.1 Total		Units	..	..	..	..	..
4.2 ♦ Accommodation for visitors		Units	..	..	..	..	..
4.3 * of which, "hotels and similar establishments"	(3)	Units	306	310	309	321	335
4.4 ♦ Food and beverage serving activities		Units	..	..	..	..	..
4.5 ♦ Passenger transportation		Units	..	..	..	..	..
4.6 ♦ Travel agencies and other reservation services activities		Units	..	..	..	..	..
4.7 ♦ Other tourism industries		Units	..	..	..	..	..
Accommodation for visitors in hotels and similar establishments							
Non-monetary data							
4.13 ♦ Number of establishments	(3)	Units	306	310	309	321	335
4.14 ♦ Number of rooms	(3)	Units	4,484	4,733	4,649	4,696	4,828
4.15 ♦ Number of bed-places	(3)	Units	11,464	12,192	11,382	11,681	12,081
Indicators							
4.16 Occupancy rate / rooms	(4)	Percent	65.60	62.00	57.40	53.30	46.50
4.17 Occupancy rate / bed-places		Percent	..	..	..	..	..
4.18 Average length of stay	(2)	Nights	10.80	11.11	11.20	11.40	11.60
4.19 Available capacity (bed-places per 1000 inhabitants)		Units	44.90	47.09	43.39	43.96	44.90
5. EMPLOYMENT							
Data							
Number of employees by tourism industries							
5.1 Total		('000)	..	..	..	..	11.0
5.2 ♦ Accommodation services for visitors (hotels and similar establishments)		('000)	..	..	..	..	4.4
5.3 ♦ Other accommodation services		('000)	..	..	..	..	..
5.4 ♦ Food and beverage serving activities		('000)	..	..	..	..	2.5
5.5 ♦ Passenger transportation		('000)	..	..	..	..	3.5
5.6 ♦ Travel agencies and other reservation services activities		('000)	..	..	..	..	0.4
5.7 ♦ Other tourism industries		('000)	..	..	..	..	0.3
6. COMPLEMENTARY INDICATORS							
Demand							
6.1 Gross travel propensity		Units	..	..			..
6.2 Carrying capacity (arrivals/population)		Units	0.81	0.86	0.83	0.74	0.59
Macroeconomic indicators related to international tourism							
6.3 Inbound tourism expenditure over GDP		Percent	..	..	..	..	..
6.4 Outbound tourism expenditure over GDP		Percent	..	..	..	..	..
6.5 Tourism balance (inbound minus outbound tourism expenditure) over GDP		Percent	..	..	..	..	..
6.6 Tourism openness (inbound plus outbound tourism expenditure) over GDP		Percent	..	..	..	..	..
6.7 Tourism coverage (inbound over outbound tourism expenditure)		Percent	177.0	270.1	197.7	181.0	..
6.8 Inbound tourism expenditure over exports of goods		Percent	358.8	350.8	418.8	369.9	..
6.9 Inbound tourism expenditure over exports of services		Percent	70.3	66.9	67.1	58.8	..
6.10 Inbound tourism expenditure over exports of goods and services		Percent	58.8	56.2	57.8	50.8	..
6.11 Inbound tourism expenditure over current account credits		Percent	28.9	25.8	25.2	22.1	..
6.12 Outbound tourism expenditure over imports of goods		Percent	27.0	15.9	22.3	19.1	..
6.13 Outbound tourism expenditure over imports of services		Percent	58.3	46.8	65.5	52.0	..
6.14 Outbound tourism expenditure over imports of goods and services		Percent	18.4	11.8	16.6	14.0	..
6.15 Outbound tourism expenditure over current account debits		Percent	16.4	10.1	14.0	12.0	..

GABON

Basic data and indicators	Notes	Units	2005	2006	2007	2008	2009
1. INBOUND TOURISM							
Data							
Arrivals							
1.1 Total		('000)	526	789	781	822	..
1.2 ♦ Overnight visitors (tourists)		('000)	269	296	325	358	..
1.3 ♦ Same-day visitors (excursionists)		('000)	257	493	456	464	..
1.4 * of which, cruise passengers		('000)	..	..	..	..	..
Expenditure							
1.33 Total		US$ Mn	13	..	..	..	..
1.34 ♦ Travel		US$ Mn	9	..	..	..	..
1.35 ♦ Passenger transport		US$ Mn	4	..	..	..	..
Expenditure by main purpose of the trip							
1.36 Total		US$ Mn	9.2	..	..	..	..
1.37 ♦ Personal		US$ Mn	7.4	..	..	..	..
1.38 ♦ Business and professional		US$ Mn	1.8	..	..	..	..
3. OUTBOUND TOURISM							
Data							
Expenditure							
3.4 Total		US$ Mn	346	..	..	..	..
3.5 ♦ Travel		US$ Mn	274	..	..	..	..
3.6 ♦ Passenger transport		US$ Mn	72	..	..	..	..
Expenditure by main purpose of the trip							
3.7 Total		US$ Mn	274	..	..	..	..
3.8 ♦ Personal		US$ Mn	177	..	..	..	..
3.9 ♦ Business and professional		US$ Mn	97	..	..	..	..
6. COMPLEMENTARY INDICATORS							
Demand							
6.1 Gross travel propensity		Units	..	..	..	..	..
6.2 Carrying capacity (arrivals/population)		Units	0.20	0.21	0.23	0.25	..
Macroeconomic indicators related to international tourism							
6.3 Inbound tourism expenditure over GDP		Percent	0.2	..	..	..	..
6.4 Outbound tourism expenditure over GDP		Percent	4.1	..	..	..	..
6.5 Tourism balance (inbound minus outbound tourism expenditure) over GDP		Percent	-3.9	..	..	..	..
6.6 Tourism openness (inbound plus outbound tourism expenditure) over GDP		Percent	4.2	..	..	..	..
6.7 Tourism coverage (inbound over outbound tourism expenditure)		Percent	3.8	..	..	..	..
6.8 Inbound tourism expenditure over exports of goods		Percent	0.2	..	..	..	..
6.9 Inbound tourism expenditure over exports of services		Percent	9.0	..	..	..	..
6.10 Inbound tourism expenditure over exports of goods and services		Percent	0.2	..	..	..	..
6.11 Inbound tourism expenditure over current account credits		Percent	0.2	..	..	..	..
6.12 Outbound tourism expenditure over imports of goods		Percent	25.5	..	..	..	..
6.13 Outbound tourism expenditure over imports of services		Percent	33.2	..	..	..	..
6.14 Outbound tourism expenditure over imports of goods and services		Percent	14.4	..	..	..	..
6.15 Outbound tourism expenditure over current account debits		Percent	9.4	..	..	..	..

GAMBIA

Basic data and indicators	Notes	Units	2005	2006	2007	2008	2009
1. INBOUND TOURISM							
Data							
Arrivals	(1)						
1.1 Total		('000)	460	613	487	643	..
1.2 ♦ Overnight visitors (tourists)	(2)	('000)	108	125	143	147	142
1.3 ♦ Same-day visitors (excursionists)		('000)	..	..	..	..	..
1.4 * of which, cruise passengers		('000)	..	..	..	..	..
Arrivals by region	(1)(2)						
1.5 Total		('000)	108	124	143	147	141
1.6 ♦ Africa		('000)	3	4	3	3	3
1.7 ♦ Americas		('000)	1	2	2	2	2
1.8 ♦ East Asia and the Pacific		('000)	..	..	..	..	..
1.9 ♦ Europe		('000)	93	101	121	123	115
1.10 ♦ Middle East		('000)	..	..	..	..	..
1.11 ♦ South Asia		('000)	..	..	..	..	..
1.12 ♦ Other not classified		('000)	11	17	17	19	21
1.13 * of which, nationals residing abroad		('000)	9	14	14	16	17
Arrivals by main purpose	(1)(2)						
1.14 Total		('000)	108	125	142	147	142
1.15 ♦ Personal		('000)	103	122	140	139	101
1.16 * holidays, leisure and recreation		('000)	93	111	126	122	81
1.17 * other personal purposes		('000)	10	11	14	17	20
1.18 ♦ Business and professional		('000)	5	3	2	8	41
Arrivals by mode of transport	(1)						
1.19 Total		('000)	460	614	488	643	..
1.20 ♦ Air	(2)	('000)	108	125	143	147	142
1.21 ♦ Water		('000)	5	3	..	..	..
1.22 ♦ Land		('000)	347	486	345	496	..
1.23 * railway		('000)	..	..	..	..	..
1.24 * road		('000)	347	486	345	496	..
1.25 * others		('000)	..	..	..	..	..
Expenditure							
1.33 Total		US$ Mn	59	69	100	81	64
1.34 ♦ Travel		US$ Mn	58	66	97	81	63
1.35 ♦ Passenger transport		US$ Mn	1	3	3	0.3	1
3. OUTBOUND TOURISM							
Data							
Departures							
3.1 Total		('000)	..	..	..	..	..
3.2 ♦ Overnight visitors (tourists)		('000)	387	307	..	..	..
3.3 ♦ Same-day visitors (excursionists)		('000)	..	..	..	..	..
Expenditure							
3.4 Total		US$ Mn	7	8	10	..	..
3.5 ♦ Travel		US$ Mn	5	6	8	8	9
3.6 ♦ Passenger transport		US$ Mn	2	2	2	..	..
Expenditure by main purpose of the trip							
3.7 Total		US$ Mn	5.5	6.5	7.8	7.8	8.9
3.8 ♦ Personal		US$ Mn	1.8	2.9	4.3	3.7	2.9
3.9 ♦ Business and professional		US$ Mn	3.7	3.6	3.5	4.1	6.0

GAMBIA

Basic data and indicators	Notes	Units	2005	2006	2007	2008	2009
4. TOURISM INDUSTRIES							
Data							
Number of establishments							
4.1 Total		Units	..	..	..	..	..
4.2 ♦ Accommodation for visitors		Units	..	..	..	..	..
4.3 * of which, "hotels and similar establishments"		Units	35	..	..	..	33
4.4 ♦ Food and beverage serving activities		Units	..	..	..	..	..
4.5 ♦ Passenger transportation		Units	..	..	..	..	..
4.6 ♦ Travel agencies and other reservation services activities		Units	..	..	..	..	..
4.7 ♦ Other tourism industries		Units	..	..	..	..	..
Accommodation for visitors in hotels and similar establishments							
Non-monetary data							
4.13 ♦ Number of establishments		Units	35	..	..	..	33
4.14 ♦ Number of rooms		Units	3,066	3,992	5,004	..	4,793
4.15 ♦ Number of bed-places		Units	..	7,984	8,719	..	6,743
Indicators							
4.16 Occupancy rate / rooms		Percent	..	..	..	..	..
4.17 Occupancy rate / bed-places		Percent	..	..	..	..	..
4.18 Average length of stay		Nights	..	14.00	7.00	7.00	7.00
4.19 Available capacity (bed-places per 1000 inhabitants)		Units	..	5.08	5.40	..	3.95
6. COMPLEMENTARY INDICATORS							
Demand							
6.1 Gross travel propensity		Units	..	..	..		
6.2 Carrying capacity (arrivals/population)		Units	0.07	0.08	0.09	0.09	0.08
Macroeconomic indicators related to international tourism							
6.3 Inbound tourism expenditure over GDP		Percent	9.9	10.5	10.9	8.2	..
6.4 Outbound tourism expenditure over GDP		Percent	1.2	1.2	1.1	0.8	..
6.5 Tourism balance (inbound minus outbound tourism expenditure) over GDP		Percent	8.7	9.3	9.8	7.4	..
6.6 Tourism openness (inbound plus outbound tourism expenditure) over GDP		Percent	11.2	11.7	12.1	9.0	..
6.7 Tourism coverage (inbound over outbound tourism expenditure)		Percent	796.6	874.9	971.7	1,042.7	..
6.8 Inbound tourism expenditure over exports of goods		Percent	56.4	63.9	69.4	56.6	..
6.9 Inbound tourism expenditure over exports of services		Percent	71.6	75.6	75.6	67.8	..
6.10 Inbound tourism expenditure over exports of goods and services		Percent	31.5	34.6	36.2	30.9	..
6.11 Inbound tourism expenditure over current account credits		Percent	20.4	21.8	22.7	21.4	..
6.12 Outbound tourism expenditure over imports of goods		Percent	3.3	3.6	3.4	2.8	..
6.13 Outbound tourism expenditure over imports of services		Percent	15.8	8.5	11.6	9.1	..
6.14 Outbound tourism expenditure over imports of goods and services		Percent	2.7	2.5	2.6	2.2	..
6.15 Outbound tourism expenditure over current account debits		Percent	2.2	2.1	2.2	1.8	..

GEORGIA

Basic data and indicators	Notes	Units	2005	2006	2007	2008	2009
1. INBOUND TOURISM							
Data							
Arrivals							
1.1 Total		('000)	560	983	1,052	1,290	1,500
1.2 ♦ Overnight visitors (tourists)		('000)	..	..	..	..	..
1.3 ♦ Same-day visitors (excursionists)		('000)	..	2	1	2	5
1.4 * of which, cruise passengers		('000)	..	2	1	2	5
Arrivals by region							
1.5 Total		('000)	560	983	1,052	1,289	1,500
1.6 ♦ Africa		('000)	..	1	1	1	1
1.7 ♦ Americas		('000)	15	19	17	17	20
1.8 ♦ East Asia and the Pacific		('000)	3	14	9	9	11
1.9 ♦ Europe		('000)	533	936	1,010	1,244	1,448
1.10 ♦ Middle East		('000)	1	2	2	3	3
1.11 ♦ South Asia		('000)	7	10	11	13	14
1.12 ♦ Other not classified		('000)	1	1	2	2	3
1.13 * of which, nationals residing abroad		('000)	..	..	..	..	..
Arrivals by main purpose	(1)						
1.14 Total		('000)	63	82	104	104	150
1.15 ♦ Personal		('000)	12	25	33	34	52
1.16 * holidays, leisure and recreation		('000)	7	13	19	24	30
1.17 * other personal purposes		('000)	5	12	14	10	22
1.18 ♦ Business and professional		('000)	51	57	71	70	98
Arrivals by mode of transport							
1.19 Total		('000)	560	983	1,051	1,290	1,500
1.20 ♦ Air		('000)	131	179	161	192	199
1.21 ♦ Water		('000)	..	50	41	48	54
1.22 ♦ Land		('000)	429	754	849	1,050	1,247
1.23 * railway		('000)	7	63	31	29	39
1.24 * road		('000)	422	691	818	1,021	1,208
1.25 * others		('000)	..	..	..	..	..
Accommodation							
Total							
1.29 ♦ Guests		('000)	..	..	..	..	..
1.30 ♦ Overnights		('000)	..	..	..	..	..
Hotels and similar establishments							
1.31 ♦ Guests		('000)	63	82	104	104	151
1.32 ♦ Overnights		('000)	..	..	..	..	..
Expenditure							
1.33 Total		US$ Mn	287	361	440	505	531
1.34 ♦ Travel		US$ Mn	241	313	384	447	470
1.35 ♦ Passenger transport		US$ Mn	46	48	56	58	61
Expenditure by main purpose of the trip							
1.36 Total		US$ Mn	241	313	384	447	470
1.37 ♦ Personal		US$ Mn	98	145	174	189	209
1.38 ♦ Business and professional		US$ Mn	143	168	210	258	261
2. DOMESTIC TOURISM							
Data							
Accommodation							
Total							
2.19 ♦ Guests		('000)	..	..	..	..	..
2.20 ♦ Overnights		('000)	..	..	..	..	..
Hotels and similar establishments							
2.21 ♦ Guests		('000)	89	134	179	163	199
2.22 ♦ Overnights		('000)	..	..	..	..	..
3. OUTBOUND TOURISM							
Data							
Departures							
3.1 Total		('000)	..	..	..	..	..
3.2 ♦ Overnight visitors (tourists)		('000)	857	1,346	1,473	1,872	1,980
3.3 ♦ Same-day visitors (excursionists)		('000)	..	..	..	..	..
Expenditure							
3.4 Total		US$ Mn	237	257	277	337	311
3.5 ♦ Travel		US$ Mn	169	167	176	203	181
3.6 ♦ Passenger transport		US$ Mn	68	90	101	134	130
Expenditure by main purpose of the trip							
3.7 Total		US$ Mn	169	167	176	203	181
3.8 ♦ Personal		US$ Mn	58	54	60	56	52
3.9 ♦ Business and professional		US$ Mn	111	113	116	147	129

GEORGIA

Basic data and indicators	Notes	Units	2005	2006	2007	2008	2009
4. TOURISM INDUSTRIES							
Data							
Number of establishments							
4.1 Total		Units	2,590	2,447	2,036	1,883	1,897
4.2 ♦ Accommodation for visitors		Units	250	374	339	353	386
4.3 * of which, "hotels and similar establishments"	(2)	Units	250	374	339	353	386
4.4 ♦ Food and beverage serving activities		Units	1,580	1,371	1,074	959	966
4.5 ♦ Passenger transportation		Units	679	609	510	465	397
4.6 ♦ Travel agencies and other reservation services activities		Units	81	93	113	106	148
4.7 ♦ Other tourism industries		Units	..	..	..	..	..
Accommodation for visitors in hotels and similar establishments							
Monetary data							
4.8 ♦ Output		US$ Mn	39.6	45.7	56.1	70.3	62.5
4.9 ♦ Intermediate consumption		US$ Mn	17.8	20.0	26.3	35.5	28.3
4.10 ♦ Gross value added		US$ Mn	21.8	25.7	29.8	34.9	34.2
4.11 ♦ Compensation of employees		US$ Mn	7.1	8.9	12.6	14.3	15.7
4.12 ♦ Gross fixed capital formation	(3)	US$ Mn	4.8	6.2	44.9	29.2	81.2
Non-monetary data							
4.13 ♦ Number of establishments	(2)	Units	250	374	339	353	386
4.14 ♦ Number of rooms	(2)	Units	6,757	10,022	8,311	8,582	9,393
4.15 ♦ Number of bed-places	(2)	Units	18,162	20,488	16,704	17,573	18,741
Indicators							
4.16 Occupancy rate / rooms		Percent	..	..	..	..	..
4.17 Occupancy rate / bed-places		Percent	..	..	..	..	..
4.18 Average length of stay	(2)	Nights	7.00	..	8.00	6.00	4.00
4.19 Available capacity (bed-places per 1000 inhabitants)	(2)	Units	4.00	5.00	4.00	4.00	4.00
Travel agencies and other reservation service activities							
Monetary data							
4.20 ♦ Output		US$ Mn	3.5	16.5	24.2	12.8	8.6
4.21 ♦ Intermediate consumption		US$ Mn	2.1	12.5	11.4	6.8	3.9
4.22 ♦ Gross value added		US$ Mn	1.4	3.9	12.7	6.0	4.6
4.23 ♦ Compensation of employees		US$ Mn	0.6	1.5	2.5	3.0	2.6
4.24 ♦ Gross fixed capital formation	(3)	US$ Mn	0.1	1.1	0.7	0.5	0.2
5. EMPLOYMENT							
Data							
Number of employees by tourism industries							
5.1 Total		('000)	37.6	34.7	33.7	34.6	34.7
5.2 ♦ Accommodation services for visitors (hotels and similar establishments)		('000)	3.0	3.0	4.0	4.0	4.0
5.3 ♦ Other accommodation services		('000)	..	..	..	..	..
5.4 ♦ Food and beverage serving activities		('000)	7.0	8.0	7.0	7.0	9.0
5.5 ♦ Passenger transportation		('000)	27.0	23.0	22.0	23.0	21.0
5.6 ♦ Travel agencies and other reservation services activities		('000)	0.6	0.7	0.7	0.6	0.7
5.7 ♦ Other tourism industries		('000)	..	..	..	..	..
Number of jobs by status in employment							
5.8 Total		('000)	..	..	..	..	..
5.9 ♦ Employees		('000)	37.6	34.7	33.7	34.6	34.7
5.10 ♦ Self employed		('000)	..	..	..	..	..
Indicators							
Number of full-time equivalent jobs by status in employment							
5.11 Total		('000)	..	..	..	..	..
5.12 ♦ Employees		('000)	..	35.0	34.0	35.0	35.0
5.13 * male		('000)	..	24.0	23.0	25.0	23.0
5.14 * female		('000)	..	11.0	11.0	10.0	12.0
5.15 ♦ Self employed		('000)	..	..	..	..	..
5.16 * male		('000)	..	..	..	..	..
5.17 * female		('000)	..	..	..	..	..

GEORGIA

Basic data and indicators	Notes	Units	2005	2006	2007	2008	2009
6. **COMPLEMENTARY INDICATORS**							
Demand							
6.1 Gross travel propensity		Units	..	..	..	..	..
6.2 Carrying capacity (arrivals/population)		Units	0.13	0.22	0.24	0.30	0.35
Macroeconomic indicators related to international tourism							
6.3 Inbound tourism expenditure over GDP		Percent	4.5	4.7	4.3	3.9	4.9
6.4 Outbound tourism expenditure over GDP		Percent	3.7	3.3	2.7	2.6	2.9
6.5 Tourism balance (inbound minus outbound tourism expenditure) over GDP		Percent	0.8	1.3	1.6	1.3	2.0
6.6 Tourism openness (inbound plus outbound tourism expenditure) over GDP		Percent	8.2	8.0	7.0	6.6	7.8
6.7 Tourism coverage (inbound over outbound tourism expenditure)		Percent	120.9	140.4	158.8	149.4	170.6
6.8 Inbound tourism expenditure over exports of goods		Percent	19.5	21.6	21.1	20.8	28.1
6.9 Inbound tourism expenditure over exports of services		Percent	40.1	40.7	40.2	40.0	40.7
6.10 Inbound tourism expenditure over exports of goods and services		Percent	13.1	14.1	13.8	13.7	16.6
6.11 Inbound tourism expenditure over current account credits		Percent	10.0	10.4	9.9	9.5	11.4
6.12 Outbound tourism expenditure over imports of goods		Percent	8.8	7.0	5.6	5.4	7.3
6.13 Outbound tourism expenditure over imports of services		Percent	37.6	35.3	29.7	27.3	32.1
6.14 Outbound tourism expenditure over imports of goods and services		Percent	7.2	5.8	4.7	4.5	5.9
6.15 Outbound tourism expenditure over current account debits		Percent	6.6	5.5	4.3	4.1	5.3

GERMANY

Basic data and indicators	Notes	Units	2005	2006	2007	2008	2009
1. INBOUND TOURISM							
Data							
Arrivals							
1.1 Total		('000)	..	..	..	..	..
1.2 ♦ Overnight visitors (tourists)	(1)	('000)	21,500	23,569	24,421	24,884	24,220
1.3 ♦ Same-day visitors (excursionists)		('000)	..	..	..	..	..
1.4 * of which, cruise passengers		('000)	..	..	..	..	..
Arrivals by region	(1)						
1.5 Total		('000)	21,500	23,569	24,421	24,884	24,219
1.6 ♦ Africa		('000)	144	167	164	160	158
1.7 ♦ Americas		('000)	2,398	2,783	2,706	2,572	2,476
1.8 ♦ East Asia and the Pacific		('000)	2,001	2,176	2,105	1,991	1,790
1.9 ♦ Europe		('000)	16,100	17,504	18,423	19,096	18,782
1.10 ♦ Middle East		('000)	185	202	223	242	259
1.11 ♦ South Asia		('000)	..	..	..	..	..
1.12 ♦ Other not classified		('000)	672	737	800	823	754
1.13 * of which, nationals residing abroad		('000)	..	..	..	..	..
Arrivals by mode of transport							
1.19 Total		('000)	62,079	65,655	69,808	70,529	67,215
1.20 ♦ Air		('000)	62,079	65,655	69,808	70,529	67,215
1.21 ♦ Water		('000)	..	..	..	..	..
1.22 ♦ Land		('000)	..	..	..	..	..
1.23 * railway		('000)	..	..	..	..	..
1.24 * road		('000)	..	..	..	..	..
1.25 * others		('000)	..	..	..	..	..
Accommodation							
Total							
1.29 ♦ Guests		('000)	21,500	23,569	24,421	24,884	24,220
1.30 ♦ Overnights		('000)	48,246	52,947	54,779	56,537	54,824
Hotels and similar establishments							
1.31 ♦ Guests		('000)	19,171	21,057	21,870	22,131	21,467
1.32 ♦ Overnights		('000)	40,839	44,921	46,508	47,562	45,843
Expenditure							
1.33 Total		US$ Mn	40,531	45,538	49,332	53,495	47,505
1.34 ♦ Travel		US$ Mn	29,121	32,888	36,101	40,021	34,781
1.35 ♦ Passenger transport		US$ Mn	11,410	12,650	13,231	13,474	12,724
Indicators							
1.39 Average size of travel party		Persons	..	..	..	..	..
Average length of stay							
1.40 Total		Days	..	..	..	..	..
1.41 ♦ For all commercial accommodation services		Nights	2.20	2.20	2.20	2.30	2.30
1.42 * of which, "hotels and similar establishments"		Nights	..	..	..	..	..
1.43 ♦ For non commercial accommodation services		Days	..	..	..	..	..
1.44 Average expenditure per day		US$	..	..	..	..	..
2. DOMESTIC TOURISM							
Data							
Accommodation							
Total							
2.19 ♦ Guests		('000)	99,074	101,667	105,443	108,075	108,618
2.20 ♦ Overnights		('000)	295,735	298,277	307,060	313,043	313,914
Hotels and similar establishments							
2.21 ♦ Guests		('000)	75,363	78,037	80,988	82,654	82,847
2.22 ♦ Overnights		('000)	168,843	172,428	177,586	180,259	180,122
Indicators							
2.23 Average size of travel party		Persons	..	..	..	..	..
Average length of stay							
2.24 Total		Days	..	..	..	..	..
2.25 ♦ For all commercial accommodation services		Nights	3.00	2.90	2.90	2.90	2.90
2.26 * of which, "hotels and similar establishments"		Nights	..	..	..	..	..
2.27 ♦ For non commercial accommodation services		Days	..	..	..	..	..
2.28 Average expenditure per day		US$	..	..	..	..	..

GERMANY

Basic data and indicators	Notes	Units	2005	2006	2007	2008	2009
3. OUTBOUND TOURISM							
Data							
Departures							
3.1 Total		('000)	..	..	..	..	..
3.2 ♦ Overnight visitors (tourists)		('000)	77,400	71,200	70,400	73,000	72,300
3.3 ♦ Same-day visitors (excursionists)		('000)	..	..	..	..	..
Expenditure							
3.4 Total		US$ Mn	84,838	85,974	96,549	106,020	92,738
3.5 ♦ Travel		US$ Mn	74,189	74,123	83,156	91,598	81,044
3.6 ♦ Passenger transport		US$ Mn	10,649	11,851	13,393	14,422	11,694
Expenditure by main purpose of the trip							
3.7 Total		US$ Mn	74,190	74,123	83,155	91,598	81,044
3.8 ♦ Personal		US$ Mn	62,500	62,941	70,196	79,592	67,126
3.9 ♦ Business and professional		US$ Mn	11,690	11,182	12,959	12,006	13,918
4. TOURISM INDUSTRIES							
Data							
Number of establishments							
4.1 Total		Units	..	..	..	..	..
4.2 ♦ Accommodation for visitors		Units	55,287	54,797	54,699	54,861	54,912
4.3 * of which, "hotels and similar establishments"		Units	36,678	36,289	36,028	35,984	35,982
4.4 ♦ Food and beverage serving activities		Units	..	..	..	..	..
4.5 ♦ Passenger transportation		Units	..	..	..	..	..
4.6 ♦ Travel agencies and other reservation services activities		Units	..	..	..	..	..
4.7 ♦ Other tourism industries		Units	..	..	..	..	..
Accommodation for visitors in hotels and similar establishments							
Non-monetary data							
4.13 ♦ Number of establishments		Units	36,678	36,289	36,028	35,984	35,982
4.14 ♦ Number of rooms		Units	890,153	896,980	899,068	915,577	926,610
4.15 ♦ Number of bed-places		Units	1,678,284	1,690,932	1,703,286	1,737,890	1,812,964
Indicators							
4.16 Occupancy rate / rooms		Percent	..	..	..	..	..
4.17 Occupancy rate / bed-places		Percent	35.00	35.90	36.70	36.50	35.70
4.18 Average length of stay	(2)	Nights	2.22	2.19	2.18	2.17	2.17
4.19 Available capacity (bed-places per 1000 inhabitants)		Units	20.35	20.53	20.70	21.17	22.14
6. COMPLEMENTARY INDICATORS							
Demand							
6.1 Gross travel propensity		Units	..	..	..	..	..
6.2 Carrying capacity (arrivals/population)		Units	0.26	0.29	0.30	0.30	0.30
Macroeconomic indicators related to international tourism							
6.3 Inbound tourism expenditure over GDP		Percent	1.5	1.6	1.5	1.5	1.4
6.4 Outbound tourism expenditure over GDP		Percent	3.0	2.9	2.9	2.9	2.8
6.5 Tourism balance (inbound minus outbound tourism expenditure) over GDP		Percent	-1.6	-1.4	-1.4	-1.4	-1.4
6.6 Tourism openness (inbound plus outbound tourism expenditure) over GDP		Percent	4.5	4.5	4.4	4.4	4.2
6.7 Tourism coverage (inbound over outbound tourism expenditure)		Percent	47.8	53.0	51.1	50.5	51.2
6.8 Inbound tourism expenditure over exports of goods		Percent	4.1	4.0	3.7	3.6	4.1
6.9 Inbound tourism expenditure over exports of services		Percent	24.3	23.4	21.5	20.5	20.5
6.10 Inbound tourism expenditure over exports of goods and services		Percent	3.5	3.4	3.1	3.1	3.5
6.11 Inbound tourism expenditure over current account credits		Percent	3.0	2.8	2.6	2.5	2.9
6.12 Outbound tourism expenditure over imports of goods		Percent	10.7	9.2	8.9	8.7	9.7
6.13 Outbound tourism expenditure over imports of services		Percent	40.1	38.0	36.9	36.4	36.4
6.14 Outbound tourism expenditure over imports of goods and services		Percent	8.5	7.4	7.2	7.0	7.7
6.15 Outbound tourism expenditure over current account debits		Percent	6.9	6.1	5.8	5.7	6.3

GHANA

Basic data and indicators	Notes	Units	2005	2006	2007	2008	2009
1. INBOUND TOURISM							
Data							
Arrivals							
1.1 Total		('000)	..	..	..	..	..
1.2 ♦ Overnight visitors (tourists)	(1)	('000)	429	497	587	698	803
1.3 ♦ Same-day visitors (excursionists)		('000)	..	..	..	..	..
1.4 * of which, cruise passengers		('000)	..	..	..	..	..
Arrivals by region	(1)						
1.5 Total		('000)	429	..	..	..	..
1.6 ♦ Africa		('000)	173	..	..	..	..
1.7 ♦ Americas		('000)	63	..	..	..	..
1.8 ♦ East Asia and the Pacific		('000)	11	..	..	..	..
1.9 ♦ Europe		('000)	100	..	..	..	..
1.10 ♦ Middle East		('000)	11	..	..	..	..
1.11 ♦ South Asia		('000)	11	..	..	..	..
1.12 ♦ Other not classified		('000)	60	..	..	..	..
1.13 * of which, nationals residing abroad		('000)	60	..	..	..	..
Arrivals by main purpose	(1)						
1.14 Total		('000)	428	497	587	698	..
1.15 ♦ Personal		('000)	270	308	329	419	..
1.16 * holidays, leisure and recreation		('000)	83	99	106	133	..
1.17 * other personal purposes		('000)	187	209	223	286	..
1.18 ♦ Business and professional		('000)	158	189	258	279	..
Expenditure							
1.33 Total		US$ Mn	867	910	990	970	1,049
1.34 ♦ Travel		US$ Mn	836	861	908	919	968
1.35 ♦ Passenger transport		US$ Mn	31	49	82	51	81
Expenditure by main purpose of the trip							
1.36 Total		US$ Mn	836	861	908	919	968
1.37 ♦ Personal		US$ Mn	251	258	272	276	290
1.38 ♦ Business and professional		US$ Mn	585	603	636	643	678
Indicators							
1.39 Average size of travel party		Persons	..	..	..	..	..
Average length of stay							
1.40 Total		Days	..	..	..	..	..
1.41 ♦ For all commercial accommodation services		Nights	10.67	..	..	..	..
1.42 * of which, "hotels and similar establishments"		Nights	..	..	..	..	..
1.43 ♦ For non commercial accommodation services		Days	..	..	..	..	..
1.44 Average expenditure per day		US$	..	..	..	..	..
3. OUTBOUND TOURISM							
Data							
Expenditure							
3.4 Total		US$ Mn	472	575	816	870	848
3.5 ♦ Travel		US$ Mn	303	345	558	542	584
3.6 ♦ Passenger transport		US$ Mn	169	230	258	328	264
Expenditure by main purpose of the trip							
3.7 Total		US$ Mn	303	344	558	542	584
3.8 ♦ Personal		US$ Mn	91	103	167	163	175
3.9 ♦ Business and professional		US$ Mn	212	241	391	379	409
4. TOURISM INDUSTRIES							
Data							
Accommodation for visitors in hotels and similar establishments							
Non-monetary data							
4.13 ♦ Number of establishments		Units	1,345	1,428	1,432	1,595	..
4.14 ♦ Number of rooms		Units	18,752	22,835	20,788	24,410	..
4.15 ♦ Number of bed-places		Units	23,924	27,839	26,057	29,645	..
Indicators							
4.16 Occupancy rate / rooms		Percent	..	..	..	..	..
4.17 Occupancy rate / bed-places		Percent	75.00	..	..	..	..
4.18 Average length of stay		Nights	..	..	..	..	..
4.19 Available capacity (bed-places per 1000 inhabitants)		Units	1.09	1.24	1.14	1.27	..

GHANA

Basic data and indicators	Notes	Units	2005	2006	2007	2008	2009
6. COMPLEMENTARY INDICATORS							
Demand							
6.1 Gross travel propensity		Units	..	..	..	..	..
6.2 Carrying capacity (arrivals/population)		Units	0.02	0.02	0.03	0.03	0.03
Macroeconomic indicators related to international tourism							
6.3 Inbound tourism expenditure over GDP		Percent	..	..	..	..	..
6.4 Outbound tourism expenditure over GDP		Percent	..	..	..	..	..
6.5 Tourism balance (inbound minus outbound tourism expenditure) over GDP		Percent	..	..	..	..	..
6.6 Tourism openness (inbound plus outbound tourism expenditure) over GDP		Percent	..	..	..	..	..
6.7 Tourism coverage (inbound over outbound tourism expenditure)		Percent	183.9	158.6	121.4	111.4	123.7
6.8 Inbound tourism expenditure over exports of goods		Percent	31.0	24.4	23.7	18.4	18.0
6.9 Inbound tourism expenditure over exports of services		Percent	78.4	65.8	54.1	53.9	53.3
6.10 Inbound tourism expenditure over exports of goods and services		Percent	22.2	17.8	16.5	13.7	13.4
6.11 Inbound tourism expenditure over current account credits		Percent	15.1	12.3	12.2	10.4	10.5
6.12 Outbound tourism expenditure over imports of goods		Percent	8.8	8.5	10.1	8.5	10.5
6.13 Outbound tourism expenditure over imports of services		Percent	37.1	37.8	40.9	37.9	30.9
6.14 Outbound tourism expenditure over imports of goods and services		Percent	7.1	6.9	8.1	6.9	7.9
6.15 Outbound tourism expenditure over current account debits		Percent	6.9	6.8	7.9	6.7	7.6

GREECE

Basic data and indicators	Notes	Units	2005	2006	2007	2008	2009
1. INBOUND TOURISM							
Data							
Arrivals							
1.1 Total		('000)	15,938	17,284	..	..	..
1.2 ♦ Overnight visitors (tourists)	(1)	('000)	14,765	16,039	16,165	15,939	14,915
1.3 ♦ Same-day visitors (excursionists)		('000)	1,173	1,245	..	..	..
1.4 * of which, cruise passengers		('000)	1,173	1,245	..	..	..
Arrivals by region	(1)						
1.5 Total		('000)	14,766	16,039	16,165	15,939	14,915
1.6 ♦ Africa		('000)	23	30	46	44	26
1.7 ♦ Americas		('000)	417	513	843	849	729
1.8 ♦ East Asia and the Pacific		('000)	254	316	230	218	206
1.9 ♦ Europe		('000)	13,996	15,104	14,988	14,767	13,884
1.10 ♦ Middle East		('000)	72	71	46	48	56
1.11 ♦ South Asia		('000)	4	5	1	1	2
1.12 ♦ Other not classified		('000)	..	..	11	12	12
1.13 * of which, nationals residing abroad		('000)	..	..	..	..	..
Arrivals by mode of transport							
1.19 Total		('000)	15,937	17,284	16,164	15,939	14,915
1.20 ♦ Air		('000)	10,915	11,509	11,920	11,692	10,748
1.21 ♦ Water	(2)	('000)	1,932	2,255	1,081	1,080	1,008
1.22 ♦ Land		('000)	3,090	3,520	3,163	3,167	3,159
1.23 * railway		('000)	104	79	66	66	55
1.24 * road		('000)	2,986	3,441	3,097	3,101	3,104
1.25 * others		('000)	..	..	..	..	..
Accommodation							
Total							
1.29 ♦ Guests		('000)	7,349	7,748	8,954	8,886	8,781
1.30 ♦ Overnights		('000)	40,734	43,055	48,081	47,974	46,677
Hotels and similar establishments							
1.31 ♦ Guests		('000)	7,143	7,548	8,746	8,658	8,542
1.32 ♦ Overnights		('000)	40,075	42,459	47,410	47,234	45,926
Expenditure							
1.33 Total		US$ Mn	13,453	14,495	15,687	17,586	14,796
1.34 ♦ Travel		US$ Mn	13,334	14,402	15,550	17,416	14,681
1.35 ♦ Passenger transport		US$ Mn	119	93	137	170	115
Expenditure by main purpose of the trip							
1.36 Total		US$ Mn	13,333	14,402	15,550	17,416	14,681
1.37 ♦ Personal		US$ Mn	12,157	13,246	14,204	16,080	13,705
1.38 ♦ Business and professional		US$ Mn	1,176	1,156	1,346	1,336	976
Indicators							
1.39 Average size of travel party		Persons	..	..	..	..	..
Average length of stay							
1.40 Total		Days	..	..	..	..	..
1.41 ♦ For all commercial accommodation services		Nights	5.54	5.56	5.37	5.40	5.32
1.42 * of which, "hotels and similar establishments"		Nights	5.61	5.63	5.42	5.46	5.38
1.43 ♦ For non commercial accommodation services		Days	..	..	..	..	..
1.44 Average expenditure per day		US$	..	..	..	..	..
2. DOMESTIC TOURISM							
Data							
Trips							
2.1 Total		('000)	..	..	..	..	..
2.2 ♦ Overnight visitors (tourists)		('000)	13,315	15,884	14,568	12,905	..
2.3 ♦ Same-day visitors (excursionists)		('000)	..	..	..	..	..
Trips by main purpose							
2.4 Total		('000)	13,315	15,884	14,568	12,905	..
2.5 ♦ Personal		('000)	12,227	14,846	13,563	12,295	..
2.6 * holidays, leisure and recreation		('000)	12,227	14,846	13,563	12,295	..
2.7 * other personal purposes		('000)	..	..	..	..	..
2.8 ♦ Business and professional		('000)	1,088	1,038	1,005	610	..
Trips by mode of transport							
2.9 Total		('000)	..	15,884	14,568	12,905	..
2.10 ♦ Air		('000)	..	590	539	401	..
2.11 ♦ Water		('000)	..	2,855	2,427	1,850	..
2.12 ♦ Land		('000)	..	12,439	11,602	10,654	..
2.13 * railway		('000)	..	287	235	227	..
2.14 * road		('000)	..	12,052	11,324	10,362	..
2.15 * others		('000)	..	100	43	65	..

GREECE

Basic data and indicators	Notes	Units	2005	2006	2007	2008	2009
Trips by form of organization							
2.16 Total		('000)	..	15,884	14,568	12,905	..
2.17 ◆ Package tour		('000)	..	289	347	351	..
2.18 ◆ Other forms		('000)	..	15,595	14,221	12,554	..
Accommodation							
Total							
2.19 ◆ Guests		('000)	6,064	6,234	7,084	7,127	7,524
2.20 ◆ Overnights		('000)	14,530	14,741	17,339	17,651	19,345
Hotels and similar establishments							
2.21 ◆ Guests		('000)	5,933	6,128	6,950	6,968	7,352
2.22 ◆ Overnights		('000)	13,942	14,249	16,675	16,840	18,367
Indicators							
2.23 Average size of travel party		Persons	..	..	..	..	..
Average length of stay							
2.24 Total		Days	..	..	..	..	..
2.25 ◆ For all commercial accommodation services		Nights	2.40	2.37	2.45	2.48	2.57
2.26 * of which, "hotels and similar establishments"		Nights	2.35	2.33	2.40	2.42	2.50
2.27 ◆ For non commercial accommodation services		Days	..	..	..	..	..
2.28 Average expenditure per day		US$	..	..	..	..	..

3. OUTBOUND TOURISM

Data

	Notes	Units	2005	2006	2007	2008	2009
Expenditure							
3.4 Total		US$ Mn	3,045	3,004	3,430	3,946	3,401
3.5 ◆ Travel		US$ Mn	3,039	2,997	3,423	3,930	3,381
3.6 ◆ Passenger transport		US$ Mn	6	7	7	16	20
Expenditure by main purpose of the trip							
3.7 Total		US$ Mn	3,039	2,997	3,423	3,930	3,380
3.8 ◆ Personal		US$ Mn	1,779	1,643	1,964	2,338	2,101
3.9 ◆ Business and professional		US$ Mn	1,260	1,354	1,459	1,592	1,279

4. TOURISM INDUSTRIES

Data

	Notes	Units	2005	2006	2007	2008	2009
Number of establishments							
4.1 Total		Units	..	..	..	..	..
4.2 ◆ Accommodation for visitors		Units	..	..	..	..	..
4.3 * of which, "hotels and similar establishments"	(3)	Units	9,036	9,111	9,207	9,385	9,559
4.4 ◆ Food and beverage serving activities		Units	..	..	..	..	..
4.5 ◆ Passenger transportation		Units	..	..	..	..	..
4.6 ◆ Travel agencies and other reservation services activities		Units	..	..	..	..	..
4.7 ◆ Other tourism industries		Units	..	..	..	..	..
Accommodation for visitors in hotels and similar establishments							
Non-monetary data							
4.13 ◆ Number of establishments	(3)	Units	9,036	9,111	9,207	9,385	9,559
4.14 ◆ Number of rooms	(3)	Units	358,721	364,179	367,992	375,067	383,008
4.15 ◆ Number of bed-places	(3)	Units	682,050	693,252	700,933	715,857	732,279
Indicators							
4.16 Occupancy rate / rooms		Percent	..	..	..	..	..
4.17 Occupancy rate / bed-places		Percent	58.60	59.80	57.00	56.70	51.10
4.18 Average length of stay		Nights	4.13	4.15	4.08	4.10	4.05
4.19 Available capacity (bed-places per 1000 inhabitants)		Units	61.42	62.18	62.62	63.70	64.90

5. EMPLOYMENT

Data

	Notes	Units	2005	2006	2007	2008	2009
Number of employees by tourism industries	(4)						
5.1 Total		('000)	280.2	303.7	298.1	..	..
5.2 ◆ Accommodation services for visitors (hotels and similar establishments)		('000)	64.3	73.8	71.3	..	..
5.3 ◆ Other accommodation services		('000)	..	..	..	..	..
5.4 ◆ Food and beverage serving activities		('000)	215.9	229.9	226.8	..	..
5.5 ◆ Passenger transportation		('000)	..	..	..	..	..
5.6 ◆ Travel agencies and other reservation services activities		('000)	..	..	..	..	..
5.7 ◆ Other tourism industries		('000)	..	..	..	..	..

GREECE

Basic data and indicators		Notes	Units	2005	2006	2007	2008	2009
6.	**COMPLEMENTARY INDICATORS**							
	Demand							
6.1	Gross travel propensity		Units	..	..	..	..	..
6.2	Carrying capacity (arrivals/population)		Units	2.53	2.86	2.75	2.57	1.32
	Macroeconomic indicators related to international tourism							
6.3	Inbound tourism expenditure over GDP		Percent	5.5	5.5	5.1	5.0	4.5
6.4	Outbound tourism expenditure over GDP		Percent	1.3	1.1	1.1	1.1	1.0
6.5	Tourism balance (inbound minus outbound tourism expenditure) over GDP		Percent	4.3	4.4	4.0	3.9	3.5
6.6	Tourism openness (inbound plus outbound tourism expenditure) over GDP		Percent	6.8	6.6	6.2	6.1	5.5
6.7	Tourism coverage (inbound over outbound tourism expenditure)		Percent	441.7	482.5	457.2	445.6	435.2
6.8	Inbound tourism expenditure over exports of goods		Percent	76.3	71.4	65.4	60.3	69.3
6.9	Inbound tourism expenditure over exports of services		Percent	39.7	40.5	36.4	34.8	39.2
6.10	Inbound tourism expenditure over exports of goods and services		Percent	26.1	25.9	23.4	22.1	25.0
6.11	Inbound tourism expenditure over current account credits		Percent	20.9	20.9	19.0	17.9	20.5
6.12	Outbound tourism expenditure over imports of goods		Percent	5.9	4.7	4.2	4.2	5.3
6.13	Outbound tourism expenditure over imports of services		Percent	20.7	18.4	16.9	15.8	17.0
6.14	Outbound tourism expenditure over imports of goods and services		Percent	4.6	3.7	3.4	3.3	4.0
6.15	Outbound tourism expenditure over current account debits		Percent	3.7	3.0	2.7	2.6	3.1

GRENADA

Basic data and indicators	Notes	Units	2005	2006	2007	2008	2009
1. INBOUND TOURISM							
Data							
Arrivals							
1.1 Total		('000)	380	342	406	428	460
1.2 ♦ Overnight visitors (tourists)		('000)	99	119	130	130	114
1.3 ♦ Same-day visitors (excursionists)		('000)	281	224	275	298	346
1.4 * of which, cruise passengers		('000)	275	219	270	293	343
Arrivals by region							
1.5 Total		('000)	98	119	130	131	114
1.6 ♦ Africa		('000)	..	..	1	1	1
1.7 ♦ Americas		('000)	59	65	64	66	62
1.8 ♦ East Asia and the Pacific		('000)	1	2	3	1	1
1.9 ♦ Europe		('000)	22	33	42	45	36
1.10 ♦ Middle East		('000)	..	..	..	..	..
1.11 ♦ South Asia		('000)	..	..	..	..	..
1.12 ♦ Other not classified		('000)	16	19	20	18	14
1.13 * of which, nationals residing abroad		('000)	16	18	20	17	14
Arrivals by main purpose							
1.14 Total		('000)	98	119	130	130	114
1.15 ♦ Personal		('000)	79	100	104	104	95
1.16 * holidays, leisure and recreation		('000)	49	59	68	73	73
1.17 * other personal purposes		('000)	30	41	36	31	22
1.18 ♦ Business and professional		('000)	19	19	26	26	19
Arrivals by mode of transport							
1.19 Total		('000)	99	119	130	130	113
1.20 ♦ Air		('000)	94	114	125	125	109
1.21 ♦ Water		('000)	5	5	5	5	4
1.22 ♦ Land		('000)	..	..	..	..	..
1.23 * railway		('000)	..	..	..	..	..
1.24 * road		('000)	..	..	..	..	..
1.25 * others		('000)	..	..	..	..	..
Accommodation							
Total							
1.29 ♦ Guests		('000)	99	119	130	130	114
1.30 ♦ Overnights		('000)	..	..	..	..	..
Hotels and similar establishments							
1.31 ♦ Guests		('000)	36	54	66	62	51
1.32 ♦ Overnights		('000)	..	..	..	..	..
Expenditure							
1.33 Total		US$ Mn	..	..	..	..	..
1.34 ♦ Travel		US$ Mn	71	94	109	109	99
1.35 ♦ Passenger transport		US$ Mn	..	..	..	..	..
Indicators							
1.39 Average size of travel party		Persons	..	..	..	..	..
Average length of stay							
1.40 Total		Days	..	..	..	..	..
1.41 ♦ For all commercial accommodation services		Nights	7.42	7.63	8.70	8.44	8.35
1.42 * of which, "hotels and similar establishments"		Nights	..	..	..	..	..
1.43 ♦ For non commercial accommodation services		Days	..	..	..	..	..
1.44 Average expenditure per day		US$	..	..	..	..	..
3. OUTBOUND TOURISM							
Data							
Expenditure							
3.4 Total		US$ Mn	..	..	..	..	..
3.5 ♦ Travel		US$ Mn	10	16	16	11	10
3.6 ♦ Passenger transport		US$ Mn	..	..	..	..	..

GRENADA

Basic data and indicators	Notes	Units	2005	2006	2007	2008	2009
4. TOURISM INDUSTRIES							
Data							
Number of establishments							
4.1 Total		Units					
4.2 ♦ Accommodation for visitors		Units	..	..	..	..	..
4.3 * of which, "hotels and similar establishments"		Units	75	78	70	74	80
4.4 ♦ Food and beverage serving activities		Units	..	..	..	..	..
4.5 ♦ Passenger transportation		Units	..	..	..	..	..
4.6 ♦ Travel agencies and other reservation services activities		Units	..	..	..	..	..
4.7 ♦ Other tourism industries		Units	..	..	..	..	..
Accommodation for visitors in hotels and similar establishments							
Non-monetary data							
4.13 ♦ Number of establishments		Units	75	78	70	74	80
4.14 ♦ Number of rooms	(1)	Units	1,470	1,584	1,628	1,782	1,884
4.15 ♦ Number of bed-places	(1)	Units	2,326	3,139	2,548	2,617	2,676
Indicators							
4.16 Occupancy rate / rooms		Percent					
4.17 Occupancy rate / bed-places		Percent	..	..	..	..	..
4.18 Average length of stay		Nights	7.42	7.63	8.70	8.44	8.52
4.19 Available capacity (bed-places per 1000 inhabitants)		Units	22.69	30.53	24.70	25.28	25.75
6. COMPLEMENTARY INDICATORS							
Demand							
6.1 Gross travel propensity		Units					
6.2 Carrying capacity (arrivals/population)		Units	0.97	1.16	1.26	1.26	1.10
Macroeconomic indicators related to international tourism							
6.3 Inbound tourism expenditure over GDP		Percent	12.9	16.6	17.8	16.0	15.8
6.4 Outbound tourism expenditure over GDP		Percent	1.8	2.7	2.6	1.6	1.6
6.5 Tourism balance (inbound minus outbound tourism expenditure) over GDP		Percent	11.1	13.9	15.2	14.4	14.2
6.6 Tourism openness (inbound plus outbound tourism expenditure) over GDP		Percent	14.7	19.4	20.4	17.6	17.4
6.7 Tourism coverage (inbound over outbound tourism expenditure)		Percent	711.3	604.4	688.6	981.7	992.9
6.8 Inbound tourism expenditure over exports of goods		Percent	217.2	290.4	267.0	268.3	255.3
6.9 Inbound tourism expenditure over exports of services		Percent	61.6	72.1	72.0	71.1	70.4
6.10 Inbound tourism expenditure over exports of goods and services		Percent	48.0	57.8	56.7	56.2	55.2
6.11 Inbound tourism expenditure over current account credits		Percent	28.8	41.8	44.2	42.9	41.8
6.12 Outbound tourism expenditure over imports of goods		Percent	3.3	5.2	4.8	3.3	3.9
6.13 Outbound tourism expenditure over imports of services		Percent	10.4	14.7	14.6	9.8	10.7
6.14 Outbound tourism expenditure over imports of goods and services		Percent	2.5	3.9	3.6	2.4	2.9
6.15 Outbound tourism expenditure over current account debits		Percent	2.3	3.4	3.1	2.1	2.4

GUADELOUPE

Basic data and indicators	Notes	Units	2005	2006	2007	2008	2009
1. INBOUND TOURISM							
Data							
Arrivals							
1.1 Total		('000)	445	465	499	554	458
1.2 ♦ Overnight visitors (tourists)	(1)(2)	('000)	372	393	408	439	347
1.3 ♦ Same-day visitors (excursionists)		('000)	73	72	91	115	111
1.4 * of which, cruise passengers		('000)	73	72	91	115	111
Arrivals by region	(1)(2)						
1.5 Total		('000)	372	..	..	..	346
1.6 ♦ Africa		('000)	..	..	..	..	..
1.7 ♦ Americas		('000)	..	..	..	..	2
1.8 ♦ East Asia and the Pacific		('000)	..		..	..	
1.9 ♦ Europe		('000)	370	..	..	..	343
1.10 ♦ Middle East		('000)	..		..	..	..
1.11 ♦ South Asia		('000)	..				..
1.12 ♦ Other not classified		('000)	2	..	..	..	1
1.13 * of which, nationals residing abroad		('000)	..	..	..	..	..
Arrivals by mode of transport	(2)						
1.19 Total		('000)	445	465	499	554	458
1.20 ♦ Air		('000)	372	393	408	439	347
1.21 ♦ Water		('000)	73	72	91	115	111
1.22 ♦ Land		('000)	..	..	..	..	..
1.23 * railway		('000)	..	..	..	..	..
1.24 * road		('000)	..	..	..	..	..
1.25 * others		('000)	..	..	..	..	..
Expenditure							
1.33 Total		US$ Mn	306	299	344	384	..
1.34 ♦ Travel		US$ Mn	..	..	..	..	..
1.35 ♦ Passenger transport		US$ Mn	..	..	..	..	..
4. TOURISM INDUSTRIES							
Data							
Number of establishments							
4.1 Total		Units	..	..	..	..	..
4.2 ♦ Accommodation for visitors		Units	..	..	..	..	..
4.3 * of which, "hotels and similar establishments"	(3)	Units	67	..	..	75	..
4.4 ♦ Food and beverage serving activities		Units	..	..	..	..	..
4.5 ♦ Passenger transportation		Units	..	..	..	..	..
4.6 ♦ Travel agencies and other reservation services activities		Units	..	..	..	..	..
4.7 ♦ Other tourism industries		Units	..	..	..	..	..
Accommodation for visitors in hotels and similar establishments							
Non-monetary data							
4.13 ♦ Number of establishments	(3)	Units	67	..	..	75	..
4.14 ♦ Number of rooms	(3)	Units	3,506	..	..	4,542	..
4.15 ♦ Number of bed-places	(3)	Units	7,012	..	..	..	..
Indicators							
4.16 Occupancy rate / rooms		Percent	..	52.00	58.60	56.70	49.70
4.17 Occupancy rate / bed-places		Percent	..	..	..	..	..
4.18 Average length of stay		Nights	3.50	3.90	3.40	3.40	3.50
4.19 Available capacity (bed-places per 1000 inhabitants)		Units	..	..	..	..	..

GUAM

Basic data and indicators	Notes	Units	2005	2006	2007	2008	2009
1. INBOUND TOURISM							
Data							
Arrivals							
1.1 Total		('000)	..	..	..	..	..
1.2 ♦ Overnight visitors (tourists)	(1)	('000)	1,228	1,212	1,225	1,142	1,053
1.3 ♦ Same-day visitors (excursionists)		('000)	..	..	..	..	..
1.4 * of which, cruise passengers		('000)	..	..	..	..	..
Arrivals by region							
1.5 Total		('000)	1,228	1,211	1,225	1,142	1,053
1.6 ♦ Africa		('000)	..	..	..	..	..
1.7 ♦ Americas		('000)	46	45	50	54	56
1.8 ♦ East Asia and the Pacific		('000)	1,134	1,134	1,125	1,034	983
1.9 ♦ Europe		('000)	2	1	2	2	2
1.10 ♦ Middle East		('000)	..	..	..	..	..
1.11 ♦ South Asia		('000)	..	..	..	..	..
1.12 ♦ Other not classified		('000)	46	31	48	52	12
1.13 * of which, nationals residing abroad		('000)	..	..	..	..	..
Arrivals by main purpose	(2)						
1.14 Total		('000)	1,185	1,184	1,181	1,092	..
1.15 ♦ Personal		('000)	1,148	1,149	1,145	1,061	..
1.16 * holidays, leisure and recreation		('000)	938	937	917	814	..
1.17 * other personal purposes		('000)	210	212	228	247	..
1.18 ♦ Business and professional		('000)	37	35	36	31	..
Arrivals by mode of transport							
1.19 Total		('000)	1,228	1,212	1,225	1,142	1,052
1.20 ♦ Air		('000)	1,185	1,184	1,181	1,093	1,044
1.21 ♦ Water		('000)	43	28	44	49	8
1.22 ♦ Land		('000)	..	..	..	..	..
1.23 * railway		('000)	..	..	..	..	..
1.24 * road		('000)	..	..	..	..	..
1.25 * others		('000)	..	..	..	..	..
Accommodation							
Total							
1.29 ♦ Guests		('000)	..	..	..	..	..
1.30 ♦ Overnights		('000)	..	..	..	..	..
Hotels and similar establishments							
1.31 ♦ Guests		('000)	..	953	934	859	..
1.32 ♦ Overnights		('000)	..	..	..	..	..
Indicators							
1.39 Average size of travel party		Persons	..	..	..	..	..
Average length of stay							
1.40 Total		Days	..	..	..	..	..
1.41 ♦ For all commercial accommodation services		Nights	..	3.34	3.37	3.40	..
1.42 * of which, "hotels and similar establishments"		Nights	..	..	..	..	..
1.43 ♦ For non commercial accommodation services		Days	..	..	..	..	..
1.44 Average expenditure per day		US$	..	..	..	..	..
4. TOURISM INDUSTRIES							
Data							
Accommodation for visitors in hotels and similar establishments							
Non-monetary data							
4.13 ♦ Number of establishments		Units	..	..	..	..	..
4.14 ♦ Number of rooms		Units	9,236	9,113	9,429	9,000	..
4.15 ♦ Number of bed-places		Units	..	..	..	..	..
Indicators							
4.16 Occupancy rate / rooms	(3)	Percent	63.00	60.00	68.00	64.00	..
4.17 Occupancy rate / bed-places		Percent	..	..	..	..	..
4.18 Average length of stay		Nights	..	..	..	..	..
4.19 Available capacity (bed-places per 1000 inhabitants)		Units	..	..	..	..	..
6. COMPLEMENTARY INDICATORS							
Demand							
6.1 Gross travel propensity		Units	..	..	..	..	..
6.2 Carrying capacity (arrivals/population)		Units	7.28	7.09	7.07	6.51	5.93

GUATEMALA

Basic data and indicators	Notes	Units	2005	2006	2007	2008	2009
1. INBOUND TOURISM							
Data							
Arrivals							
1.1 Total		('000)	1,316	1,502	1,628	1,715	1,777
1.2 ♦ Overnight visitors (tourists)		('000)	..	..	1,448	1,527	1,392
1.3 ♦ Same-day visitors (excursionists)		('000)	18	35	179	189	385
1.4 * of which, cruise passengers		('000)	18	35	42	63	81
Arrivals by region							
1.5 Total		('000)	1,315	1,501	1,627	1,715	1,776
1.6 ♦ Africa		('000)	..	..	..	..	..
1.7 ♦ Americas		('000)	1,148	1,325	1,444	1,518	1,564
1.8 ♦ East Asia and the Pacific		('000)	25	28	30	30	30
1.9 ♦ Europe		('000)	140	147	152	165	180
1.10 ♦ Middle East		('000)	1	..	..	..	..
1.11 ♦ South Asia		('000)	..	..	..	..	..
1.12 ♦ Other not classified		('000)	1	1	1	2	2
1.13 * of which, nationals residing abroad		('000)	..	..	..	..	..
Arrivals by main purpose							
1.14 Total		('000)	..	1,502	1,627	1,715	..
1.15 ♦ Personal		('000)	..	1,187	1,285	1,320	..
1.16 * holidays, leisure and recreation		('000)	..	661	732	703	..
1.17 * other personal purposes		('000)	..	526	553	617	..
1.18 ♦ Business and professional		('000)	..	315	342	395	..
Arrivals by mode of transport							
1.19 Total		('000)	1,316	1,502	1,627	1,715	1,777
1.20 ♦ Air		('000)	480	497	558	556	517
1.21 ♦ Water		('000)	31	63	52	71	92
1.22 ♦ Land		('000)	805	942	1,017	1,088	1,168
1.23 * railway		('000)	..	..	..	..	..
1.24 * road		('000)	805	942	1,017	1,088	1,168
1.25 * others		('000)	..	..	..	..	..
Expenditure							
1.33 Total		US$ Mn	..	..	..	..	..
1.34 ♦ Travel		US$ Mn	791	919	1,055	1,068	1,179
1.35 ♦ Passenger transport		US$ Mn	..	..	..	..	..
Expenditure by main purpose of the trip							
1.36 Total		US$ Mn	791	919	1,054	1,069	1,178
1.37 ♦ Personal		US$ Mn	656	763	875	887	978
1.38 ♦ Business and professional		US$ Mn	135	156	179	182	200
3. OUTBOUND TOURISM							
Data							
Departures							
3.1 Total		('000)	..	..	..	..	..
3.2 ♦ Overnight visitors (tourists)		('000)	982	1,055	1,168	1,277	1,326
3.3 ♦ Same-day visitors (excursionists)		('000)	..	..	..	..	..
Expenditure	(1)						
3.4 Total		US$ Mn	532	655	737	740	862
3.5 ♦ Travel		US$ Mn	421	529	597	606	715
3.6 ♦ Passenger transport		US$ Mn	111	126	140	134	147
Expenditure by main purpose of the trip							
3.7 Total		US$ Mn	421	529	597	606	715
3.8 ♦ Personal		US$ Mn	303	382	431	438	514
3.9 ♦ Business and professional		US$ Mn	118	147	166	168	201

GUATEMALA

Basic data and indicators	Notes	Units	2005	2006	2007	2008	2009
4. TOURISM INDUSTRIES							
Data							
Number of establishments							
4.1 Total		Units	..	..	..	..	..
4.2 ♦ Accommodation for visitors		Units	..	..	..	..	..
4.3 * of which, "hotels and similar establishments"		Units	..	..	..	2,640	2,611
4.4 ♦ Food and beverage serving activities		Units	..	..	..	..	..
4.5 ♦ Passenger transportation		Units	..	..	..	..	..
4.6 ♦ Travel agencies and other reservation services activities		Units	..	..	..	..	..
4.7 ♦ Other tourism industries		Units	..	..	..	..	..
Accommodation for visitors in hotels and similar establishments							
Non-monetary data							
4.13 ♦ Number of establishments		Units	..	..	..	2,640	2,611
4.14 ♦ Number of rooms	(2)	Units	19,357	39,832	42,726	43,708	44,451
4.15 ♦ Number of bed-places	(2)	Units	51,955	97,301	105,242	109,067	110,795
Indicators							
4.16 Occupancy rate / rooms		Percent	..	..	..	..	..
4.17 Occupancy rate / bed-places		Percent	44.39	46.18	47.63	48.01	43.27
4.18 Average length of stay		Nights	..	7.10	7.60	..	..
4.19 Available capacity (bed-places per 1000 inhabitants)		Units	4.09	7.47	7.88	7.97	7.90
6. COMPLEMENTARY INDICATORS							
Demand							
6.1 Gross travel propensity		Units	..	..	..	..	..
6.2 Carrying capacity (arrivals/population)		Units	0.10	0.12	0.11	0.11	0.10
Macroeconomic indicators related to international tourism							
6.3 Inbound tourism expenditure over GDP		Percent	2.9	3.0	3.1	2.7	2.2
6.4 Outbound tourism expenditure over GDP		Percent	2.0	2.2	2.2	1.9	1.8
6.5 Tourism balance (inbound minus outbound tourism expenditure) over GDP		Percent	1.0	0.9	0.9	0.8	0.4
6.6 Tourism openness (inbound plus outbound tourism expenditure) over GDP		Percent	4.9	5.2	5.3	4.6	4.0
6.7 Tourism coverage (inbound over outbound tourism expenditure)		Percent	148.8	140.5	143.2	144.2	120.5
6.8 Inbound tourism expenditure over exports of goods		Percent	14.5	15.1	15.1	13.6	11.2
6.9 Inbound tourism expenditure over exports of services		Percent	60.5	60.5	60.9	57.1	54.2
6.10 Inbound tourism expenditure over exports of goods and services		Percent	11.7	12.1	12.1	11.0	9.3
6.11 Inbound tourism expenditure over current account credits		Percent	7.4	7.4	7.5	7.0	6.0
6.12 Outbound tourism expenditure over imports of goods		Percent	5.5	6.0	5.9	5.5	6.4
6.13 Outbound tourism expenditure over imports of services		Percent	36.7	36.8	36.1	34.5	36.1
6.14 Outbound tourism expenditure over imports of goods and services		Percent	4.8	5.1	5.1	4.8	5.4
6.15 Outbound tourism expenditure over current account debits		Percent	4.5	4.7	4.6	4.3	4.9

GUINEA

Basic data and indicators	Notes	Units	2005	2006	2007	2008	2009
1. INBOUND TOURISM							
Data							
Arrivals							
1.1 Total		('000)	..	46.6	..	..	..
1.2 ♦ Overnight visitors (tourists)	(1)	('000)	45	46.1	30	..	..
1.3 ♦ Same-day visitors (excursionists)		('000)	..	..	..	..	..
1.4 * of which, cruise passengers		('000)	..	0.5	..	..	..
Arrivals by region	(1)						
1.5 Total		('000)	45	46	30	..	..
1.6 ♦ Africa		('000)	15	18	10	..	..
1.7 ♦ Americas		('000)	5	2	2	..	..
1.8 ♦ East Asia and the Pacific		('000)	3	3	3	..	..
1.9 ♦ Europe		('000)	15	15	9	..	..
1.10 ♦ Middle East		('000)	1	1	1	..	..
1.11 ♦ South Asia		('000)	1	1	0.4	..	..
1.12 ♦ Other not classified		('000)	5	6	5	..	..
1.13 * of which, nationals residing abroad		('000)	5	4	5	..	..
Arrivals by main purpose	(1)						
1.14 Total		('000)	45	46	30	..	..
1.15 ♦ Personal		('000)	25	26	18	..	..
1.16 * holidays, leisure and recreation		('000)	5	8	4	..	..
1.17 * other personal purposes		('000)	20	18	14	..	..
1.18 ♦ Business and professional		('000)	20	20	12	..	..
Arrivals by mode of transport							
1.19 Total		('000)	45	46.6	30	..	..
1.20 ♦ Air	(1)	('000)	45	46.1	30	..	..
1.21 ♦ Water		('000)	..	0.5	..	..	..
1.22 ♦ Land		('000)	..	..	..	..	..
1.23 * railway		('000)	..	..	..	..	..
1.24 * road		('000)	..	..	..	..	..
1.25 * others		('000)	..	..	..	..	..
Accommodation							
Total							
1.29 ♦ Guests	(1)	('000)	45	46	30	..	..
1.30 ♦ Overnights		('000)	1,318	959	704	..	..
Hotels and similar establishments							
1.31 ♦ Guests	(1)(2)	('000)	15	19	11	..	..
1.32 ♦ Overnights		('000)	195	188	249	..	..
Expenditure							
1.33 Total		US$ Mn	..	..	1.1	4.0	4.9
1.34 ♦ Travel		US$ Mn	..	..	0.2	3.0	2.8
1.35 ♦ Passenger transport		US$ Mn	..	..	0.9	1.0	2.1
Expenditure by main purpose of the trip							
1.36 Total		US$ Mn	..	..	0.2	3.0	2.8
1.37 ♦ Personal		US$ Mn	..	..	0.1	2.9	2.6
1.38 ♦ Business and professional		US$ Mn	..	..	0.1	0.1	0.2
Indicators							
1.39 Average size of travel party		Persons	..	..	..	..	..
Average length of stay							
1.40 Total		Days	..	..	..	..	..
1.41 ♦ For all commercial accommodation services		Nights	4.85	4.80	8.10	..	..
1.42 * of which, "hotels and similar establishments"		Nights	..	..	..	..	..
1.43 ♦ For non commercial accommodation services		Days	..	..	..	..	..
1.44 Average expenditure per day		US$	..	..	..	..	..
3. OUTBOUND TOURISM							
Data							
Expenditure							
3.4 Total		US$ Mn	..	..	96	59	28
3.5 ♦ Travel		US$ Mn	..	..	29	36	13
3.6 ♦ Passenger transport		US$ Mn	..	..	67	23	15
Expenditure by main purpose of the trip							
3.7 Total		US$ Mn	..	..	29	35	13
3.8 ♦ Personal		US$ Mn	..	..	28	34	12
3.9 ♦ Business and professional		US$ Mn	..	..	1	1	1

GUINEA

Basic data and indicators	Notes	Units	2005	2006	2007	2008	2009
4. TOURISM INDUSTRIES							
Data							
Number of establishments							
4.1 Total		Units	..	..	..	..	..
4.2 ♦ Accommodation for visitors		Units	..	..	..	..	..
4.3 * of which, "hotels and similar establishments"		Units	..	370	..	..	..
4.4 ♦ Food and beverage serving activities		Units	..	..	..	..	..
4.5 ♦ Passenger transportation		Units	..	..	..	..	..
4.6 ♦ Travel agencies and other reservation services activities		Units	..	..	..	..	..
4.7 ♦ Other tourism industries		Units	..	..	..	..	..
Accommodation for visitors in hotels and similar establishments							
Non-monetary data							
4.13 ♦ Number of establishments		Units	..	370	..	..	..
4.14 ♦ Number of rooms		Units	..	4,495	..	..	..
4.15 ♦ Number of bed-places		Units	..	5,394	..	..	..
Indicators							
4.16 Occupancy rate / rooms		Percent	..	..	..	..	..
4.17 Occupancy rate / bed-places		Percent	..	..	..	..	..
4.18 Average length of stay		Nights	..	3.80	8.06	..	..
4.19 Available capacity (bed-places per 1000 inhabitants)		Units	..	0.57	..	..	..
6. COMPLEMENTARY INDICATORS							
Demand							
6.1 Gross travel propensity		Units	..	..	..	..	..
6.2 Carrying capacity (arrivals/population)		Units	0.005	0.005	0.003	..	..
Macroeconomic indicators related to international tourism							
6.3 Inbound tourism expenditure over GDP		Percent	..	..	..	..	..
6.4 Outbound tourism expenditure over GDP		Percent	..	..	..	..	..
6.5 Tourism balance (inbound minus outbound tourism expenditure) over GDP		Percent	..	..	..	..	..
6.6 Tourism openness (inbound plus outbound tourism expenditure) over GDP		Percent	..	..	..	..	..
6.7 Tourism coverage (inbound over outbound tourism expenditure)		Percent	..	..	1.2	7.8	..
6.8 Inbound tourism expenditure over exports of goods		Percent	..	..	0.1	0.2	..
6.9 Inbound tourism expenditure over exports of services		Percent	..	..	2.3	2.2	..
6.10 Inbound tourism expenditure over exports of goods and services		Percent	..	..	0.1	0.2	..
6.11 Inbound tourism expenditure over current account credits		Percent	..	..	0.1	0.2	..
6.12 Outbound tourism expenditure over imports of goods		Percent	..	..	7.8	2.2	..
6.13 Outbound tourism expenditure over imports of services		Percent	..	..	32.2	6.9	..
6.14 Outbound tourism expenditure over imports of goods and services		Percent	..	..	6.3	1.7	..
6.15 Outbound tourism expenditure over current account debits		Percent	..	..	5.5	1.5	..

GUINEA-BISSAU

Basic data and indicators	Notes	Units	2005	2006	2007	2008	2009
1. INBOUND TOURISM							
Data							
Arrivals							
1.1 Total		('000)	..	..	..	..	..
1.2 ♦ Overnight visitors (tourists)	(1)	('000)	5.0	11.6	30.1	..	..
1.3 ♦ Same-day visitors (excursionists)		('000)	..	..	..	..	..
1.4 * of which, cruise passengers		('000)	..	..	..	..	..
Arrivals by region	(1)						
1.5 Total		('000)	5.0	11.7	30.2	..	..
1.6 ♦ Africa		('000)	1.2	2.7	13.4	..	..
1.7 ♦ Americas		('000)	0.5	2.0	2.4	..	..
1.8 ♦ East Asia and the Pacific		('000)	0.1	1.6	2.9	..	..
1.9 ♦ Europe		('000)	3.1	5.1	10.3	..	..
1.10 ♦ Middle East		('000)	..	0.1	0.4	..	..
1.11 ♦ South Asia		('000)	0.1	0.2	0.8	..	..
1.12 ♦ Other not classified		('000)	..	..	..	..	..
1.13 * of which, nationals residing abroad		('000)	..	..	..	..	..
Arrivals by main purpose	(1)						
1.14 Total		('000)	5.0	11.6	30.1	..	..
1.15 ♦ Personal		('000)	3.2	7.2	20.8	..	..
1.16 * holidays, leisure and recreation		('000)	1.2	3.0	11.7	..	..
1.17 * other personal purposes		('000)	2.0	4.2	9.1	..	..
1.18 ♦ Business and professional		('000)	1.8	4.4	9.3	..	..
Arrivals by mode of transport	(1)						
1.19 Total		('000)	5.0	11.6	30.1	..	..
1.20 ♦ Air		('000)	5.0	11.6	30.1	..	..
1.21 ♦ Water		('000)	..	..	..	..	..
1.22 ♦ Land		('000)	..	..	..	..	..
1.23 * railway		('000)	..	..	..	..	..
1.24 * road		('000)	..	..	..	..	..
1.25 * others		('000)	..	..	..	..	..
Expenditure							
1.33 Total		US$ Mn	..	..	..	..	..
1.34 ♦ Travel		US$ Mn	1.6	2.8	28.4	38.2	..
1.35 ♦ Passenger transport		US$ Mn	..	..	..	..	..
Expenditure by main purpose of the trip							
1.36 Total		US$ Mn	1.6	..	28.4	38.2	..
1.37 ♦ Personal		US$ Mn	1.5	..	27.2	30.2	..
1.38 ♦ Business and professional		US$ Mn	0.1	..	1.2	8.0	..
3. OUTBOUND TOURISM							
Data							
Expenditure							
3.4 Total		US$ Mn	18.9	17.8	40.7	46.1	..
3.5 ♦ Travel		US$ Mn	9.8	15.5	40.2	45.6	..
3.6 ♦ Passenger transport		US$ Mn	9.1	2.3	0.5	0.5	..
Expenditure by main purpose of the trip							
3.7 Total		US$ Mn	9.8	15.5	40.2	45.6	..
3.8 ♦ Personal		US$ Mn	8.8	6.2	27.5	34.7	..
3.9 ♦ Business and professional		US$ Mn	1.0	9.3	12.7	10.9	..
6. COMPLEMENTARY INDICATORS							
Demand							
6.1 Gross travel propensity		Units	..	..	..	..	..
6.2 Carrying capacity (arrivals/population)		Units	0.003	0.01	0.02	..	..

GUYANA

Basic data and indicators	Notes	Units	2005	2006	2007	2008	2009
1. INBOUND TOURISM							
Data							
Arrivals							
1.1 Total		('000)	..	..	..	..	..
1.2 ♦ Overnight visitors (tourists)	(1)	('000)	117	113	134	130	141
1.3 ♦ Same-day visitors (excursionists)		('000)	..	..	..	..	..
1.4 * of which, cruise passengers		('000)	..	..	..	..	..
Arrivals by region	(1)						
1.5 Total		('000)	117	113	134	129	141
1.6 ♦ Africa		('000)	..	..	..	..	..
1.7 ♦ Americas		('000)	105	102	118	118	131
1.8 ♦ East Asia and the Pacific		('000)	..	..	..	..	..
1.9 ♦ Europe		('000)	9	8	10	9	8
1.10 ♦ Middle East		('000)	..	..	..	..	..
1.11 ♦ South Asia		('000)	..	..	..	..	..
1.12 ♦ Other not classified		('000)	3	3	6	2	2
1.13 * of which, nationals residing abroad		('000)	..	..	..	..	..
Arrivals by mode of transport	(1)						
1.19 Total		('000)	117	113	134	130	141
1.20 ♦ Air		('000)	117	113	134	130	141
1.21 ♦ Water		('000)	..	..	..	..	..
1.22 ♦ Land		('000)	..	..	..	..	..
1.23 * railway		('000)	..	..	..	..	..
1.24 * road		('000)	..	..	..	..	..
1.25 * others		('000)	..	..	..	..	..
Expenditure							
1.33 Total		US$ Mn	..	..	..	..	..
1.34 ♦ Travel		US$ Mn	35	37	50	59	..
1.35 ♦ Passenger transport		US$ Mn	..	..	..	..	..
3. OUTBOUND TOURISM							
Data							
Expenditure							
3.4 Total		US$ Mn	..	..	..	..	..
3.5 ♦ Travel		US$ Mn	40	49	58	52	..
3.6 ♦ Passenger transport		US$ Mn	..	..	..	..	..
6. COMPLEMENTARY INDICATORS							
Demand							
6.1 Gross travel propensity		Units	..	..	..	..	..
6.2 Carrying capacity (arrivals/population)		Units	0.15	0.15	0.17	0.17	..
Macroeconomic indicators related to international tourism							
6.3 Inbound tourism expenditure over GDP		Percent	4.3	4.1	4.7	5.1	..
6.4 Outbound tourism expenditure over GDP		Percent	4.8	5.4	5.4	4.5	..
6.5 Tourism balance (inbound minus outbound tourism expenditure) over GDP		Percent	-0.5	-1.3	-0.7	0.6	..
6.6 Tourism openness (inbound plus outbound tourism expenditure) over GDP		Percent	9.0	9.4	10.0	9.6	..
6.7 Tourism coverage (inbound over outbound tourism expenditure)		Percent	88.7	75.7	87.7	112.9	..
6.8 Inbound tourism expenditure over exports of goods		Percent	6.4	6.4	7.3	7.5	..
6.9 Inbound tourism expenditure over exports of services		Percent	23.7	25.1	29.2	27.9	..
6.10 Inbound tourism expenditure over exports of goods and services		Percent	5.1	5.1	5.9	5.9	..
6.11 Inbound tourism expenditure over current account credits		Percent	3.7	3.6	3.8	3.9	..
6.12 Outbound tourism expenditure over imports of goods		Percent	5.5	6.1	5.9	4.4	..
6.13 Outbound tourism expenditure over imports of services		Percent	19.7	20.0	21.1	16.2	..
6.14 Outbound tourism expenditure over imports of goods and services		Percent	4.3	4.6	4.6	3.5	..
6.15 Outbound tourism expenditure over current account debits		Percent	3.7	4.0	4.0	3.1	..

HAITI

Basic data and indicators	Notes	Units	2005	2006	2007	2008	2009
1. INBOUND TOURISM							
Data							
Arrivals							
1.1 Total		('000)	480	558	868	804	961
1.2 ♦ Overnight visitors (tourists)	(1)(2)	('000)	112	108	386	304	423
1.3 ♦ Same-day visitors (excursionists)		('000)	368	450	482	500	538
1.4 * of which, cruise passengers		('000)	368	450	482	500	538
Arrivals by region	(1)(2)						
1.5 Total		('000)	113	108	386	303	..
1.6 ♦ Africa		('000)	..	..	..	..	..
1.7 ♦ Americas		('000)	104	99	332	261	..
1.8 ♦ East Asia and the Pacific		('000)	..	..	..	..	..
1.9 ♦ Europe		('000)	7	7	23	18	..
1.10 ♦ Middle East		('000)	..	..	..	..	..
1.11 ♦ South Asia		('000)	..	..	..	..	..
1.12 ♦ Other not classified		('000)	2	2	31	24	..
1.13 * of which, nationals residing abroad		('000)	..	..	..	..	..
Arrivals by main purpose	(1)(2)						
1.14 Total		('000)	112	109	386	304	..
1.15 ♦ Personal		('000)	90	87	369	283	..
1.16 * holidays, leisure and recreation		('000)	39	38	135	119	..
1.17 * other personal purposes		('000)	51	49	234	164	..
1.18 ♦ Business and professional		('000)	22	22	17	21	..
Arrivals by mode of transport							
1.19 Total		('000)	480	558	868	804	961
1.20 ♦ Air	(2)	('000)	112	108	386	304	423
1.21 ♦ Water		('000)	368	450	482	500	538
1.22 ♦ Land		('000)	..	..	..	..	..
1.23 * railway		('000)	..	..	..	..	..
1.24 * road		('000)	..	..	..	..	..
1.25 * others		('000)	..	..	..	..	..
Accommodation							
Total							
1.29 ♦ Guests		('000)	..	..	..	..	..
1.30 ♦ Overnights		('000)	337	323	1,158	912	..
Hotels and similar establishments							
1.31 ♦ Guests		('000)	..	..	..	..	..
1.32 ♦ Overnights		('000)	..	..	..	..	..
Expenditure							
1.33 Total		US$ Mn	..	..	..	..	..
1.34 ♦ Travel		US$ Mn	80	126	190	276	315
1.35 ♦ Passenger transport		US$ Mn	..	..	..	..	..
Indicators							
1.39 Average size of travel party		Persons	..	..	..	..	..
Average length of stay							
1.40 Total		Days	..	..	..	..	..
1.41 ♦ For all commercial accommodation services		Nights	3.00	3.00	3.00	3.00	..
1.42 * of which, "hotels and similar establishments"		Nights	..	..	..	..	..
1.43 ♦ For non commercial accommodation services		Days	..	..	..	..	..
1.44 Average expenditure per day		US$	..	..	..	..	..
3. OUTBOUND TOURISM							
Data							
Expenditure							
3.4 Total		US$ Mn	174	239	331	383	442
3.5 ♦ Travel		US$ Mn	55	56	56	64	63
3.6 ♦ Passenger transport		US$ Mn	119	183	275	319	379

HAITI

Basic data and indicators	Notes	Units	2005	2006	2007	2008	2009
6. COMPLEMENTARY INDICATORS							
Demand							
6.1 Gross travel propensity		Units	..	..	..	..	..
6.2 Carrying capacity (arrivals/population)		Units	0.01	0.01	0.04	0.03	0.04
Macroeconomic indicators related to international tourism							
6.3 Inbound tourism expenditure over GDP		Percent	1.9	2.5	..	..	..
6.4 Outbound tourism expenditure over GDP		Percent	4.2	4.8	..	..	..
6.5 Tourism balance (inbound minus outbound tourism expenditure) over GDP		Percent	-2.3	-2.3	..	..	..
6.6 Tourism openness (inbound plus outbound tourism expenditure) over GDP		Percent	6.1	7.4	..	..	..
6.7 Tourism coverage (inbound over outbound tourism expenditure)		Percent	45.7	52.8	57.3	72.0	71.2
6.8 Inbound tourism expenditure over exports of goods		Percent	17.3	25.4	36.4	56.2	57.1
6.9 Inbound tourism expenditure over exports of services		Percent	54.7	64.9	73.9	80.4	82.5
6.10 Inbound tourism expenditure over exports of goods and services		Percent	13.1	18.3	24.4	33.1	33.8
6.11 Inbound tourism expenditure over current account credits		Percent	4.1	5.9	7.9	10.2	11.5
6.12 Outbound tourism expenditure over imports of goods		Percent	13.3	15.4	19.4	18.2	21.8
6.13 Outbound tourism expenditure over imports of services		Percent	32.0	40.2	48.7	51.3	56.6
6.14 Outbound tourism expenditure over imports of goods and services		Percent	9.4	11.1	13.9	13.4	15.7
6.15 Outbound tourism expenditure over current account debits		Percent	8.9	10.7	13.2	12.8	14.9

HONDURAS

Basic data and indicators	Notes	Units	2005	2006	2007	2008	2009
1. INBOUND TOURISM							
Data							
Arrivals							
1.1 Total		('000)	1,118	1,136	1,337	1,592	1,624
1.2 ♦ Overnight visitors (tourists)		('000)	673	739	831	899	870
1.3 ♦ Same-day visitors (excursionists)		('000)	445	398	505	692	754
1.4 * of which, cruise passengers		('000)	277	205	297	434	430
Arrivals by region							
1.5 Total		('000)	671.9	738.2	831.0	900.1	869.4
1.6 ♦ Africa		('000)	0.2	0.3	0.2	0.2	0.3
1.7 ♦ Americas		('000)	610	666	785	810	770
1.8 ♦ East Asia and the Pacific		('000)	8	11	7	8	10
1.9 ♦ Europe		('000)	53	60	38	81	88
1.10 ♦ Middle East		('000)	0.1	0.1	0.1	0.1	0.1
1.11 ♦ South Asia		('000)	0.3	0.4	0.3	0.3	0.4
1.12 ♦ Other not classified		('000)	0.3	0.4	0.4	0.5	0.6
1.13 * of which, nationals residing abroad		('000)	..	..	..	..	..
Arrivals by main purpose							
1.14 Total		('000)	673	739	831	899	869
1.15 ♦ Personal		('000)	571	603	581	607	572
1.16 * holidays, leisure and recreation		('000)	309	398	268	261	289
1.17 * other personal purposes		('000)	262	205	313	346	283
1.18 ♦ Business and professional		('000)	102	136	250	292	297
Arrivals by mode of transport							
1.19 Total		('000)	672	739	832	899	870
1.20 ♦ Air		('000)	301	352	383	398	391
1.21 ♦ Water		('000)	23	26	28	31	34
1.22 ♦ Land		('000)	348	361	421	470	445
1.23 * railway		('000)	..	..	..	..	..
1.24 * road		('000)	348	361	421	470	445
1.25 * others		('000)	..	..	..	..	..
Arrivals by form of organization of the trip							
1.26 Total		('000)	..	..	831	899	870
1.27 ♦ Package tour		('000)	..	..	44	39	43
1.28 ♦ Other forms		('000)	..	..	787	860	827
Expenditure							
1.33 Total		US$ Mn	465	516	547	620	611
1.34 ♦ Travel		US$ Mn	463	515	546	619	611
1.35 ♦ Passenger transport		US$ Mn	2	1	1	1	0.1
Expenditure by main purpose of the trip							
1.36 Total		US$ Mn	463	515	545	619	611
1.37 ♦ Personal		US$ Mn	278	309	327	371	367
1.38 ♦ Business and professional		US$ Mn	185	206	218	248	244
2. DOMESTIC TOURISM							
Indicators							
2.23 Average size of travel party		Persons	..	..	..	..	..
Average length of stay							
2.24 Total		Days	..	..	..	..	..
2.25 ♦ For all commercial accommodation services		Nights	..	..	5.60	4.60	..
2.26 * of which, "hotels and similar establishments"		Nights	..	..	..	..	..
2.27 ♦ For non commercial accommodation services		Days	..	..	..	..	..
2.28 Average expenditure per day		US$	..	..	..	..	..
3. OUTBOUND TOURISM							
Data							
Departures							
3.1 Total		('000)	..	..	..	..	..
3.2 ♦ Overnight visitors (tourists)		('000)	284	295	315	387	395
3.3 ♦ Same-day visitors (excursionists)		('000)	..	..	..	..	..
Expenditure							
3.4 Total		US$ Mn	321	425	309	374	355
3.5 ♦ Travel		US$ Mn	262	355	212	291	296
3.6 ♦ Passenger transport		US$ Mn	59	70	97	83	59
Expenditure by main purpose of the trip							
3.7 Total		US$ Mn	262	355	212	290	296
3.8 ♦ Personal		US$ Mn	157	213	127	174	178
3.9 ♦ Business and professional		US$ Mn	105	142	85	116	118

HONDURAS

Basic data and indicators	Notes	Units	2005	2006	2007	2008	2009
4. TOURISM INDUSTRIES							
Data							
Number of establishments							
4.1 Total		Units	..	..	7,753	..	..
4.2 ♦ Accommodation for visitors		Units	..	..	949	..	..
4.3 * of which, "hotels and similar establishments"		Units	..	..	949	..	..
4.4 ♦ Food and beverage serving activities		Units	..	..	5,381	..	..
4.5 ♦ Passenger transportation		Units	..	..	261	..	..
4.6 ♦ Travel agencies and other reservation services activities		Units	..	..	114	..	..
4.7 ♦ Other tourism industries		Units	..	..	1,048	..	..
Accommodation for visitors in hotels and similar establishments							
Monetary data							
4.8 ♦ Output		US$ Mn	94.2	103.7	110.7	127.6	139.5
4.9 ♦ Intermediate consumption		US$ Mn	41.4	44.8	48.5	55.9	61.1
4.10 ♦ Gross value added		US$ Mn	52.9	58.9	62.2	71.7	78.4
4.11 ♦ Compensation of employees		US$ Mn	..	..	..	..	..
4.12 ♦ Gross fixed capital formation		US$ Mn	..	..	..	..	..
Non-monetary data							
4.13 ♦ Number of establishments		Units	908	928	949	..	..
4.14 ♦ Number of rooms		Units	20,453	21,015	19,583	..	..
4.15 ♦ Number of bed-places		Units	29,032	29,976	32,917	..	..
Indicators							
4.16 Occupancy rate / rooms		Percent	..	..	..	..	..
4.17 Occupancy rate / bed-places	(1)	Percent	..	..	57.00	64.00	43.00
4.18 Average length of stay		Nights	..	..	4.19	6.00	..
4.19 Available capacity (bed-places per 1000 inhabitants)		Units	4.21	4.26	4.59	..	..
Travel agencies and other reservation service activities							
Monetary data							
4.20 ♦ Output		US$ Mn	14.9	19.3	22.9	25.9	26.5
4.21 ♦ Intermediate consumption		US$ Mn	5.3	6.8	8.2	6.6	6.7
4.22 ♦ Gross value added		US$ Mn	9.6	12.5	14.7	19.3	19.8
4.23 ♦ Compensation of employees		US$ Mn	..	..	..	..	..
4.24 ♦ Gross fixed capital formation		US$ Mn	..	..	..	..	..
6. COMPLEMENTARY INDICATORS							
Demand							
6.1 Gross travel propensity		Units	..	..	..	..	..
6.2 Carrying capacity (arrivals/population)		Units	0.10	0.11	0.12	0.12	0.12
Macroeconomic indicators related to international tourism							
6.3 Inbound tourism expenditure over GDP		Percent	4.8	4.7	4.4	4.4	..
6.4 Outbound tourism expenditure over GDP		Percent	3.3	3.9	3.8	3.0	..
6.5 Tourism balance (inbound minus outbound tourism expenditure) over GDP		Percent	1.5	0.8	0.6	1.4	..
6.6 Tourism openness (inbound plus outbound tourism expenditure) over GDP		Percent	8.1	8.6	8.2	7.5	..
6.7 Tourism coverage (inbound over outbound tourism expenditure)		Percent	145.0	121.4	116.9	147.4	..
6.8 Inbound tourism expenditure over exports of goods		Percent	9.2	9.8	9.7	10.3	..
6.9 Inbound tourism expenditure over exports of services		Percent	66.6	69.3	69.3	68.3	..
6.10 Inbound tourism expenditure over exports of goods and services		Percent	8.1	8.6	8.5	8.9	..
6.11 Inbound tourism expenditure over current account credits		Percent	5.9	5.8	5.7	6.0	..
6.12 Outbound tourism expenditure over imports of goods		Percent	4.9	5.8	5.3	4.1	..
6.13 Outbound tourism expenditure over imports of services		Percent	34.6	41.0	41.1	34.7	..
6.14 Outbound tourism expenditure over imports of goods and services		Percent	4.3	5.1	4.7	3.6	..
6.15 Outbound tourism expenditure over current account debits		Percent	3.9	4.6	4.3	3.4	..

HONG KONG, CHINA

Basic data and indicators	Notes	Units	2005	2006	2007	2008	2009
1. INBOUND TOURISM							
Data							
Arrivals							
1.1 Total		('000)	23,359	25,251	28,169	29,507	29,591
1.2 ♦ Overnight visitors (tourists)		('000)	14,773	15,821	17,154	17,319	16,926
1.3 ♦ Same-day visitors (excursionists)		('000)	8,586	9,430	11,015	12,187	12,665
1.4 * of which, cruise passengers		('000)	19	20	27	27	44
Arrivals by region							
1.5 Total		('000)	23,359	25,251	28,169	29,506	29,590
1.6 ♦ Africa		('000)	206	218	231	210	182
1.7 ♦ Americas		('000)	1,565	1,631	1,784	1,685	1,568
1.8 ♦ East Asia and the Pacific		('000)	19,707	21,330	23,848	25,348	25,659
1.9 ♦ Europe		('000)	1,472	1,635	1,877	1,810	1,709
1.10 ♦ Middle East		('000)	46	62	79	71	75
1.11 ♦ South Asia		('000)	363	375	350	382	397
1.12 ♦ Other not classified		('000)	..	..	..	..	..
1.13 * of which, nationals residing abroad		('000)	..	..	..	..	..
Arrivals by main purpose							
1.14 Total		('000)	14,773	15,821	17,154	17,319	16,926
1.15 ♦ Personal		('000)	11,201	11,959	13,638	13,689	13,855
1.16 * holidays, leisure and recreation		('000)	7,450	8,211	9,416	9,505	9,458
1.17 * other personal purposes		('000)	3,751	3,748	4,222	4,184	4,397
1.18 ♦ Business and professional		('000)	3,572	3,862	3,516	3,630	3,071
Arrivals by mode of transport							
1.19 Total		('000)	23,359	25,251	28,169	29,507	29,591
1.20 ♦ Air		('000)	7,803	8,625	9,223	9,114	8,624
1.21 ♦ Water		('000)	2,788	3,076	3,793	3,975	3,343
1.22 ♦ Land		('000)	12,768	13,550	15,153	16,418	17,624
1.23 * railway		('000)	..	..	..	..	..
1.24 * road		('000)	12,768	13,550	15,153	16,418	17,624
1.25 * others		('000)	..	..	..	..	..
Expenditure	(1)						
1.33 Total		US$ Mn	13,588	15,476	18,237	20,236	20,884
1.34 ♦ Travel		US$ Mn	10,179	11,461	13,566	15,018	16,020
1.35 ♦ Passenger transport		US$ Mn	3,409	4,015	4,671	5,218	4,864
Indicators							
1.39 Average size of travel party		Persons	..	..	..	..	..
Average length of stay							
1.40 Total		Days	..	..	..	..	..
1.41 ♦ For all commercial accommodation services		Nights	3.66	3.46	3.28	3.26	3.20
1.42 * of which, "hotels and similar establishments"		Nights	..	..	..	..	..
1.43 ♦ For non commercial accommodation services		Days	..	..	..	..	..
1.44 Average expenditure per day		US$	..	..	..	..	..
3. OUTBOUND TOURISM							
Data							
Departures							
3.1 Total		('000)	..	..	..	..	..
3.2 ♦ Overnight visitors (tourists)	(2)	('000)	72,300	75,812	80,682	81,911	81,958
3.3 ♦ Same-day visitors (excursionists)		('000)	..	..	..	..	..
Expenditure							
3.4 Total		US$ Mn	..	..	..	..	..
3.5 ♦ Travel	(3)	US$ Mn	13,305	14,044	15,042	16,095	15,960
3.6 ♦ Passenger transport		US$ Mn	..	..	..	..	..

HONG KONG, CHINA

Basic data and indicators	Notes	Units	2005	2006	2007	2008	2009
4. TOURISM INDUSTRIES							
Data							
Number of establishments							
4.1 Total		Units	..	..	..	..	..
4.2 ♦ Accommodation for visitors		Units	..	..	..	..	..
4.3 * of which, "hotels and similar establishments"	(4)	Units	585	612	651	695	758
4.4 ♦ Food and beverage serving activities		Units	..	..	..	..	..
4.5 ♦ Passenger transportation		Units	..	..	..	..	..
4.6 ♦ Travel agencies and other reservation services activities		Units	..	..	..	..	..
4.7 ♦ Other tourism industries		Units	..	..	..	..	..
Accommodation for visitors in hotels and similar establishments							
Non-monetary data							
4.13 ♦ Number of establishments	(4)	Units	585	612	651	695	758
4.14 ♦ Number of rooms	(4)	Units	48,891	52,512	56,649	60,273	65,386
4.15 ♦ Number of bed-places		Units	..	..	..	..	..
Indicators							
4.16 Occupancy rate / rooms		Percent	86.00	87.00	86.00	85.00	78.00
4.17 Occupancy rate / bed-places		Percent	..	..	..	..	..
4.18 Average length of stay		Nights	..	..	..	..	..
4.19 Available capacity (bed-places per 1000 inhabitants)		Units	..	..	..	..	..
6. COMPLEMENTARY INDICATORS							
Demand							
6.1 Gross travel propensity		Units	..	..	..	..	..
6.2 Carrying capacity (arrivals/population)		Units	2.17	2.31	2.48	2.48	2.42
Macroeconomic indicators related to international tourism							
6.3 Inbound tourism expenditure over GDP		Percent	5.8	6.1	6.6	7.1	..
6.4 Outbound tourism expenditure over GDP		Percent	7.5	7.4	7.3	7.5	..
6.5 Tourism balance (inbound minus outbound tourism expenditure) over GDP		Percent	-1.7	-1.3	-0.6	-0.4	..
6.6 Tourism openness (inbound plus outbound tourism expenditure) over GDP		Percent	13.3	13.5	13.9	14.6	..
6.7 Tourism coverage (inbound over outbound tourism expenditure)		Percent	77.4	82.9	91.5	95.1	..
6.8 Inbound tourism expenditure over exports of goods		Percent	3.6	3.7	4.0	4.2	..
6.9 Inbound tourism expenditure over exports of services		Percent	16.2	16.0	16.2	16.6	..
6.10 Inbound tourism expenditure over exports of goods and services		Percent	2.9	3.0	3.2	3.3	..
6.11 Inbound tourism expenditure over current account credits		Percent	2.5	2.4	2.5	2.7	..
6.12 Outbound tourism expenditure over imports of goods		Percent	4.5	4.2	4.1	4.1	..
6.13 Outbound tourism expenditure over imports of services		Percent	39.2	37.9	35.3	34.2	..
6.14 Outbound tourism expenditure over imports of goods and services		Percent	4.0	3.8	3.7	3.7	..
6.15 Outbound tourism expenditure over current account debits		Percent	3.3	3.1	2.9	2.9	..

HUNGARY

Basic data and indicators	Notes	Units	2005	2006	2007	2008	2009
1. INBOUND TOURISM							
Data							
Arrivals	(1)						
1.1 Total		('000)	36,173	38,318	39,379	39,554	40,624
1.2 ♦ Overnight visitors (tourists)		('000)	9,979	9,259	8,638	8,814	9,058
1.3 ♦ Same-day visitors (excursionists)		('000)	26,194	29,059	30,741	30,740	31,565
1.4 * of which, cruise passengers		('000)	428	232	179	..	..
Arrivals by region	(1)(2)						
1.5 Total		('000)	36,172	38,319	39,380	39,554	40,624
1.6 ♦ Africa		('000)	17	20	22	21	22
1.7 ♦ Americas		('000)	490	521	533	548	557
1.8 ♦ East Asia and the Pacific		('000)	396	416	440	433	439
1.9 ♦ Europe		('000)	35,269	37,362	38,385	38,552	39,606
1.10 ♦ Middle East		('000)	..	..	..	..	..
1.11 ♦ South Asia		('000)	..	..	..	..	..
1.12 ♦ Other not classified		('000)	..	..	..	..	..
1.13 * of which, nationals residing abroad		('000)	..	..	..	..	..
Arrivals by main purpose	(1)						
1.14 Total		('000)	36,173	38,318	39,379	39,554	40,624
1.15 ♦ Personal		('000)	34,433	36,608	37,755	37,704	39,030
1.16 * holidays, leisure and recreation		('000)	10,982	10,709	10,468	10,803	11,076
1.17 * other personal purposes		('000)	23,451	25,899	27,287	26,901	27,954
1.18 ♦ Business and professional		('000)	1,740	1,710	1,624	1,850	1,594
Arrivals by mode of transport	(3)(4)						
1.19 Total		('000)	38,555	40,963	42,466	39,554	40,624
1.20 ♦ Air		('000)	2,084	2,110	2,230	2,923	3,258
1.21 ♦ Water	(5)	('000)	290	249	294	..	..
1.22 ♦ Land		('000)	36,181	38,604	39,942	36,631	37,366
1.23 * railway		('000)	1,516	1,653	1,508	..	..
1.24 * road	(6)	('000)	34,665	36,951	38,434	36,631	37,366
1.25 * others		('000)	..	..	..	..	..
Accommodation							
Total							
1.29 ♦ Guests		('000)	3,446	3,310	3,451	3,516	3,228
1.30 ♦ Overnights		('000)	10,779	10,046	10,171	10,010	9,220
Hotels and similar establishments							
1.31 ♦ Guests		('000)	3,140	3,009	3,131	3,197	2,914
1.32 ♦ Overnights		('000)	9,127	8,524	8,635	8,489	7,773
Expenditure							
1.33 Total		US$ Mn	4,761	4,998	5,628	7,113	6,740
1.34 ♦ Travel		US$ Mn	4,120	4,254	4,739	6,033	5,712
1.35 ♦ Passenger transport		US$ Mn	641	744	889	1,080	1,028
Expenditure by main purpose of the trip							
1.36 Total		US$ Mn	4,120	4,254	4,739	6,033	5,711
1.37 ♦ Personal		US$ Mn	3,357	3,466	3,836	5,046	4,881
1.38 ♦ Business and professional		US$ Mn	763	788	903	987	830
Indicators							
1.39 Average size of travel party		Persons	..	..	..	..	..
Average length of stay							
1.40 Total		Days	2.60	2.60	2.50	2.50	2.40
1.41 ♦ For all commercial accommodation services		Nights	3.13	3.04	2.95	2.85	2.86
1.42 * of which, "hotels and similar establishments"		Nights	2.91	2.83	2.76	2.66	2.67
1.43 ♦ For non commercial accommodation services	(7)	Days	7.07	7.73	7.10	6.77	6.50
1.44 Average expenditure per day		US$	119.7	120.2	128.4	160.1	146.3
2. DOMESTIC TOURISM							
Data							
Trips							
2.1 Total		('000)	..	..	..	..	..
2.2 ♦ Overnight visitors (tourists)		('000)	..	..	..	21,753	17,920
2.3 ♦ Same-day visitors (excursionists)		('000)	..	..	..	..	..
Trips by main purpose							
2.4 Total		('000)	..	..	..	21,754	17,920
2.5 ♦ Personal		('000)	..	..	..	21,172	17,475
2.6 * holidays, leisure and recreation		('000)	..	..	..	10,062	18,927
2.7 * other personal purposes		('000)	..	..	..	11,110	8,548
2.8 ♦ Business and professional		('000)	..	..	..	582	445

HUNGARY

Basic data and indicators	Notes	Units	2005	2006	2007	2008	2009
Trips by mode of transport							
2.9 Total		('000)	..	..	..	21,754	17,921
2.10 ♦ Air		('000)	..	..	..	5	7
2.11 ♦ Water		('000)	..	..	..	3	8
2.12 ♦ Land		('000)	..	..	..	21,746	17,906
2.13 * railway		('000)	..	..	..	2,432	2,443
2.14 * road		('000)	..	..	..	19,277	15,395
2.15 * others		('000)	..	..	..	37	68
Trips by form of organization							
2.16 Total		('000)	..	..	..	21,753	17,920
2.17 ♦ Package tour		('000)	..	..	..	291	298
2.18 ♦ Other forms		('000)	..	..	..	21,462	17,622
Accommodation							
Total							
2.19 ♦ Guests		('000)	3,618	3,873	4,023	4,135	3,923
2.20 ♦ Overnights		('000)	8,958	9,606	9,958	9,965	9,490
Hotels and similar establishments							
2.21 ♦ Guests		('000)	2,778	3,007	3,188	3,313	3,066
2.22 ♦ Overnights		('000)	6,622	7,284	7,662	7,794	7,201
Indicators							
2.23 Average size of travel party		Persons	..	..	..	..	..
Average length of stay							
2.24 Total		Days	..	..	..	4.03	4.09
2.25 ♦ For all commercial accommodation services		Nights	2.48	2.48	2.48	2.41	2.42
2.26 * of which, "hotels and similar establishments"		Nights	2.38	2.42	2.40	2.35	2.35
2.27 ♦ For non commercial accommodation services		Days	..	..	..	3.81	3.82
2.28 Average expenditure per day		US$	..	..	..	19.4	16.0
3. OUTBOUND TOURISM							
Data							
Departures							
3.1 Total		('000)	17,759	16,597	17,269	17,428	16,905
3.2 ♦ Overnight visitors (tourists)		('000)	6,994	6,007	5,949	6,421	5,924
3.3 ♦ Same-day visitors (excursionists)		('000)	10,765	10,590	11,322	11,006	10,981
Expenditure							
3.4 Total		US$ Mn	2,826	2,566	3,491	4,645	4,117
3.5 ♦ Travel		US$ Mn	2,382	2,126	2,949	4,037	3,638
3.6 ♦ Passenger transport		US$ Mn	444	440	542	608	479
Expenditure by main purpose of the trip							
3.7 Total		US$ Mn	2,382	2,126	2,949	4,037	3,638
3.8 ♦ Personal		US$ Mn	2,029	1,614	2,190	2,622	2,068
3.9 ♦ Business and professional		US$ Mn	353	512	759	1,415	1,570
Indicators							
3.10 Average length of stay		Days	3.40	3.70	4.10	4.80	4.90
3.11 Average expenditure per day		US$	41.7	37.5	44.4	50.3	46.2
4. TOURISM INDUSTRIES							
Data							
Number of establishments							
4.1 Total		Units	60,540	60,737	61,311	60,726	72,097
4.2 ♦ Accommodation for visitors	(8)	Units	3,117	3,056	2,956	2,924	2,993
4.3 * of which, "hotels and similar establishments"		Units	2,061	2,032	1,999	2,001	2,042
4.4 ♦ Food and beverage serving activities		Units	56,294	56,494	57,171	56,612	56,991
4.5 ♦ Passenger transportation		Units	..	..	..	..	10,901
4.6 ♦ Travel agencies and other reservation services activities		Units	1,129	1,187	1,184	1,190	1,212
4.7 ♦ Other tourism industries		Units	..	..	..	..	..
Accommodation for visitors in hotels and similar establishments							
Monetary data							
4.8 ♦ Output		US$ Mn	802.0	851.0	989.0	1,098.0	..
4.9 ♦ Intermediate consumption		US$ Mn	430.0	460.0	547.0	651.0	..
4.10 ♦ Gross value added		US$ Mn	371.0	391.0	443.0	446.0	..
4.11 ♦ Compensation of employees		US$ Mn	..	..	..	..	..
4.12 ♦ Gross fixed capital formation		US$ Mn	..	..	..	..	..
Non-monetary data							
4.13 ♦ Number of establishments		Units	2,061	2,032	1,999	2,001	2,042
4.14 ♦ Number of rooms		Units	66,066	66,873	65,638	65,815	67,310
4.15 ♦ Number of bed-places		Units	162,235	158,762	154,088	154,521	157,464

HUNGARY

Basic data and indicators		Notes	Units	2005	2006	2007	2008	2009
	Indicators							
4.16	Occupancy rate / rooms	(9)	Percent	42.10	42.40	45.00	43.80	39.10
4.17	Occupancy rate / bed-places		Percent	34.60	32.10	33.70	33.10	29.80
4.18	Average length of stay		Nights	2.66	2.63	2.58	2.50	2.50
4.19	Available capacity (bed-places per 1000 inhabitants)		Units	16.10	15.80	15.30	15.40	15.70
	Travel agencies and other reservation service activities							
	Monetary data							
4.20	♦ Output		US$ Mn	249.0	297.0	291.0	320.0	..
4.21	♦ Intermediate consumption		US$ Mn	145.0	198.0	165.0	179.0	..
4.22	♦ Gross value added		US$ Mn	104.0	99.0	126.0	141.0	..
4.23	♦ Compensation of employees		US$ Mn	..	..	..	..	..
4.24	♦ Gross fixed capital formation		US$ Mn	..	..	..	..	..
	Non-monetary data							
	♦ Domestic trips							
4.25	* with package tour		Percent	..	74.1	69.7	64.6	62.3
4.26	* without package tour		Percent	..	25.9	30.3	35.4	37.7
	♦ Inbound trips							
4.27	* with package tour		Percent	..	79.4	84.5	85.9	79.4
4.28	* without package tour		Percent	..	20.6	15.5	14.1	20.6
	♦ Outbound trips							
4.29	* with package tour		Percent	..	87.1	88.0	88.1	84.8
4.30	* without package tour		Percent	..	12.9	12.0	11.9	15.2
5.	**EMPLOYMENT**							
	Data							
	Number of employees by tourism industries	(10)(11)	('000)					
5.1	Total		('000)	249.2	264.6	272.8	177.9	178.1
5.2	♦ Accommodation services for visitors (hotels and similar establishments)		('000)	24.7	25.9	26.1	25.4	21.2
5.3	♦ Other accommodation services		('000)	5.5	4.9	4.8	4.9	6.1
5.4	♦ Food and beverage serving activities		('000)	69.2	74.6	79.0	83.2	79.8
5.5	♦ Passenger transportation		('000)	144.0	152.0	157.2	59.2	65.5
5.6	♦ Travel agencies and other reservation services activities		('000)	5.8	7.1	5.5	5.3	5.5
5.7	♦ Other tourism industries		('000)	..	..	..	..	..
	Number of jobs by status in employment	(12)						
5.8	Total		('000)	3,901.5	3,930.1	3,926.2	3,879.4	3,781.9
5.9	♦ Employees		('000)	3367.2	3431.4	3439.8	3405.0	3309.9
5.10	♦ Self employed		('000)	534.3	498.7	486.4	474.4	472.0
	Indicators							
	Number of full-time equivalent jobs by status in employment	(12)						
5.11	Total		('000)	3,628.4	3,660.6	3,671.4	3,629.3	3,528.2
5.12	♦ Employees		('000)	3,094.0	3,160.1	3,183.6	3,156.6	3,059.6
5.13	* male		('000)	1678.9	1726.0	1747.2	1714.8	1646.3
5.14	* female		('000)	1415.0	1434.1	1436.4	1441.8	1413.4
5.15	♦ Self employed		('000)	534.5	500.5	487.8	472.7	468.5
5.16	* male		('000)	371.1	348.6	336.2	332.2	321.7
5.17	* female		('000)	163.4	151.9	151.6	140.5	146.8
6.	**COMPLEMENTARY INDICATORS**							
	Demand							
6.1	Gross travel propensity		Units	..	..	..	..	..
6.2	Carrying capacity (arrivals/population)		Units	0.99	0.92	0.86	3.05	2.69
	Macroeconomic indicators related to international tourism							
6.3	Inbound tourism expenditure over GDP		Percent	4.3	4.4	4.1	4.6	5.2
6.4	Outbound tourism expenditure over GDP		Percent	2.6	2.3	2.5	3.0	3.2
6.5	Tourism balance (inbound minus outbound tourism expenditure) over GDP		Percent	1.8	2.2	1.5	1.6	2.0
6.6	Tourism openness (inbound plus outbound tourism expenditure) over GDP		Percent	6.9	6.7	6.6	7.6	8.4
6.7	Tourism coverage (inbound over outbound tourism expenditure)		Percent	168.5	194.8	161.2	153.1	163.7
6.8	Inbound tourism expenditure over exports of goods		Percent	7.7	6.8	6.0	6.6	8.2
6.9	Inbound tourism expenditure over exports of services		Percent	37.0	36.5	32.6	35.1	37.0
6.10	Inbound tourism expenditure over exports of goods and services		Percent	6.4	5.7	5.1	5.6	6.7
6.11	Inbound tourism expenditure over current account credits		Percent	5.9	5.1	4.4	4.9	5.9
6.12	Outbound tourism expenditure over imports of goods		Percent	4.4	3.4	3.7	4.3	5.4
6.13	Outbound tourism expenditure over imports of services		Percent	24.7	21.1	22.0	24.7	25.5
6.14	Outbound tourism expenditure over imports of goods and services		Percent	3.7	2.9	3.2	3.7	4.4
6.15	Outbound tourism expenditure over current account debits		Percent	3.2	2.4	2.6	3.0	3.6

ICELAND

Basic data and indicators	Notes	Units	2005	2006	2007	2008	2009
1. INBOUND TOURISM							
Data							
Arrivals							
1.1 Total		('000)	..	..	..	..	..
1.2 ♦ Overnight visitors (tourists)	(1)	('000)	871	971	1,058	1,106	1,235
1.3 ♦ Same-day visitors (excursionists)		('000)	55	55	54	59	69
1.4 * of which, cruise passengers		('000)	55	55	54	59	69
Arrivals by region	(1)						
1.5 Total		('000)	872	972	1,057	1,106	1,234
1.6 ♦ Africa		('000)	1	2	1	2	2
1.7 ♦ Americas		('000)	85	87	86	87	94
1.8 ♦ East Asia and the Pacific		('000)	30	33	29	30	37
1.9 ♦ Europe		('000)	715	785	853	918	1,027
1.10 ♦ Middle East		('000)	..	..	..	..	..
1.11 ♦ South Asia		('000)	..	..	..	..	..
1.12 ♦ Other not classified		('000)	41	65	88	69	74
1.13 * of which, nationals residing abroad		('000)	..	..	..	..	..
Arrivals by mode of transport	(2)						
1.19 Total		('000)	427	471	530	548	547
1.20 ♦ Air		('000)	361	399	459	473	465
1.21 ♦ Water		('000)	66	72	71	75	82
1.22 ♦ Land		('000)	..	..	..	..	..
1.23 * railway		('000)	..	..	..	..	..
1.24 * road		('000)	..	..	..	..	..
1.25 * others		('000)	..	..	..	..	..
Accommodation							
Total							
1.29 ♦ Guests		('000)	871	971	1,058	1,106	1,235
1.30 ♦ Overnights		('000)	1,550	1,719	1,885	1,943	2,066
Hotels and similar establishments							
1.31 ♦ Guests		('000)	643	714	782	806	843
1.32 ♦ Overnights		('000)	1,208	1,341	1,480	1,517	1,554
Expenditure							
1.33 Total		US$ Mn	635	702	848	881	..
1.34 ♦ Travel		US$ Mn	413	478	601	624	555
1.35 ♦ Passenger transport		US$ Mn	222	224	247	257	..
Indicators							
1.39 Average size of travel party		Persons	..	..	..	..	..
Average length of stay							
1.40 Total		Days	..	..	..	..	..
1.41 ♦ For all commercial accommodation services		Nights	1.80	1.80	1.80	1.70	1.70
1.42 * of which, "hotels and similar establishments"		Nights	1.90	1.90	1.90	1.90	1.80
1.43 ♦ For non commercial accommodation services		Days	..	..	..	..	..
1.44 Average expenditure per day		US$	..	..	..	..	..
2. DOMESTIC TOURISM							
Data							
Accommodation							
Total							
2.19 ♦ Guests		('000)	432	466	490	503	547
2.20 ♦ Overnights		('000)	683	738	777	793	851
Hotels and similar establishments							
2.21 ♦ Guests		('000)	229	245	274	270	243
2.22 ♦ Overnights		('000)	361	387	437	429	386
Indicators							
2.23 Average size of travel party		Persons	..	..	..	..	..
Average length of stay							
2.24 Total		Days	..	..	..	..	..
2.25 ♦ For all commercial accommodation services		Nights	1.60	1.60	1.60	1.60	1.60
2.26 * of which, "hotels and similar establishments"		Nights	1.60	1.60	1.60	1.60	1.60
2.27 ♦ For non commercial accommodation services		Days	..	..	..	..	..
2.28 Average expenditure per day		US$	..	..	..	..	..

ICELAND

Basic data and indicators	Notes	Units	2005	2006	2007	2008	2009
3. OUTBOUND TOURISM							
Data							
Departures							
3.1 Total		('000)	..	..	..	..	..
3.2 ♦ Overnight visitors (tourists)		('000)	364	440	460	414	259
3.3 ♦ Same-day visitors (excursionists)		('000)	..	..	..	..	..
Expenditure							
3.4 Total		US$ Mn	991	1,084	1,336	1,107	..
3.5 ♦ Travel		US$ Mn	980	1,076	1,326	1,103	533
3.6 ♦ Passenger transport		US$ Mn	11	8	10	4	..
4. TOURISM INDUSTRIES							
Data							
Number of establishments							
4.1 Total		Units	..	..	..	..	..
4.2 ♦ Accommodation for visitors		Units	613	595	588	586	600
4.3 * of which, "hotels and similar establishments"		Units	319	308	298	301	296
4.4 ♦ Food and beverage serving activities		Units	..	..	..	..	..
4.5 ♦ Passenger transportation		Units	..	..	..	..	..
4.6 ♦ Travel agencies and other reservation services activities		Units	..	..	..	..	..
4.7 ♦ Other tourism industries		Units	..	..	..	..	..
Accommodation for visitors in hotels and similar establishments							
Non-monetary data							
4.13 ♦ Number of establishments		Units	319	308	298	301	296
4.14 ♦ Number of rooms		Units	8,005	8,025	8,498	9,074	8,993
4.15 ♦ Number of bed-places		Units	16,639	16,849	17,876	19,255	18,937
Indicators							
4.16 Occupancy rate / rooms		Percent	45.00	47.00	46.70	47.40	46.00
4.17 Occupancy rate / bed-places		Percent	..	..	..	37.40	37.70
4.18 Average length of stay		Nights	1.80	1.80	1.80	1.80	1.80
4.19 Available capacity (bed-places per 1000 inhabitants)		Units	56.07	55.46	57.37	60.66	59.35
5. EMPLOYMENT							
Data							
Number of employees by tourism industries							
5.1 Total		('000)	8.5	8.9	9.1	9.2	8.4
5.2 ♦ Accommodation services for visitors (hotels and similar establishments)		('000)	0.7	0.7	0.7	1.0	0.9
5.3 ♦ Other accommodation services		('000)	0.3	0.3	0.3	0.3	0.3
5.4 ♦ Food and beverage serving activities		('000)	1.5	1.6	1.6	1.8	1.7
5.5 ♦ Passenger transportation		('000)	2.4	2.4	2.5	2.2	1.8
5.6 ♦ Travel agencies and other reservation services activities		('000)	0.7	0.8	0.7	0.6	0.6
5.7 ♦ Other tourism industries		('000)	2.9	3.1	3.3	3.3	3.1
Indicators							
Number of full-time equivalent jobs by status in employment							
5.11 Total		('000)	164.7	173.4	175.0	179.5	164.2
5.12 ♦ Employees		('000)	..	..	..	..	..
5.13 * male		('000)	..	..	..	..	..
5.14 * female		('000)	..	..	..	..	..
5.15 ♦ Self employed		('000)	..	..	..	..	..
5.16 * male		('000)	..	..	..	..	..
5.17 * female		('000)	..	..	..	..	..

ICELAND

Basic data and indicators	Notes	Units	2005	2006	2007	2008	2009
6. COMPLEMENTARY INDICATORS							
Demand							
6.1 Gross travel propensity		Units	..	..	..	..	..
6.2 Carrying capacity (arrivals/population)		Units	2.94	3.20	3.40	3.48	3.87
Macroeconomic indicators related to international tourism							
6.3 Inbound tourism expenditure over GDP		Percent	3.9	4.2	4.2	5.2	4.6
6.4 Outbound tourism expenditure over GDP		Percent	6.1	6.5	6.5	6.6	5.2
6.5 Tourism balance (inbound minus outbound tourism expenditure) over GDP		Percent	-2.2	-2.3	-2.4	-1.3	-0.5
6.6 Tourism openness (inbound plus outbound tourism expenditure) over GDP		Percent	10.0	10.7	10.7	11.8	9.8
6.7 Tourism coverage (inbound over outbound tourism expenditure)		Percent	64.1	64.7	63.4	79.6	89.6
6.8 Inbound tourism expenditure over exports of goods		Percent	20.4	20.2	17.7	16.3	14.0
6.9 Inbound tourism expenditure over exports of services		Percent	31.2	37.5	37.2	40.2	25.0
6.10 Inbound tourism expenditure over exports of goods and services		Percent	12.3	13.1	12.0	11.6	9.0
6.11 Inbound tourism expenditure over current account credits		Percent	9.6	8.9	7.4	8.8	7.3
6.12 Outbound tourism expenditure over imports of goods		Percent	21.6	19.0	21.6	19.4	19.0
6.13 Outbound tourism expenditure over imports of services		Percent	38.8	42.3	45.0	43.7	32.3
6.14 Outbound tourism expenditure over imports of goods and services		Percent	13.9	13.1	14.6	13.4	12.0
6.15 Outbound tourism expenditure over current account debits		Percent	10.7	9.1	9.1	8.2	7.8

INDIA

Basic data and indicators	Notes	Units	2005	2006	2007	2008	2009
1. INBOUND TOURISM							
Data							
Arrivals	(1)						
1.1 Total		('000)	4,038	4,626	5,244	5,373	5,295
1.2 ♦ Overnight visitors (tourists)		('000)	3,919	4,447	5,082	5,283	5,168
1.3 ♦ Same-day visitors (excursionists)		('000)	119	179	162	90	127
1.4 * of which, cruise passengers		('000)	119	179	162	90	127
Arrivals by region	(1)						
1.5 Total		('000)	3,918	4,446	5,081	5,282	5,167
1.6 ♦ Africa		('000)	131	137	151	136	159
1.7 ♦ Americas		('000)	804	912	1,050	1,071	1,098
1.8 ♦ East Asia and the Pacific		('000)	585	702	823	866	865
1.9 ♦ Europe		('000)	1,435	1,662	1,900	1,956	1,869
1.10 ♦ Middle East		('000)	86	98	118	166	159
1.11 ♦ South Asia		('000)	842	909	982	1,052	1,001
1.12 ♦ Other not classified		('000)	35	26	57	35	16
1.13 * of which, nationals residing abroad		('000)	..	..	..	..	..
Arrivals by main purpose	(1)						
1.14 Total		('000)	3,918	4,448	5,082	5,282	5,168
1.15 ♦ Personal		('000)	3,785	4,360	4,807	3,724	4,267
1.16 * holidays, leisure and recreation	(2)	('000)	3,785	4,360	4,807	3,724	4,267
1.17 * other personal purposes		('000)	..	..	..	..	..
1.18 ♦ Business and professional		('000)	133	88	275	1,558	901
Arrivals by mode of transport	(1)						
1.19 Total		('000)	3,919	4,447	5,082	5,283	5,168
1.20 ♦ Air		('000)	3,390	3,873	4,542	4,707	4,642
1.21 ♦ Water		('000)	16	27	31	37	53
1.22 ♦ Land		('000)	513	547	509	539	473
1.23 * railway		('000)	..	..	..	..	..
1.24 * road		('000)	513	547	509	539	473
1.25 * others		('000)	..	..	..	..	..
Expenditure							
1.33 Total		US$ Mn	7,659	8,915	11,234	12,462	11,509
1.34 ♦ Travel		US$ Mn	7,493	8,634	10,730	11,832	11,136
1.35 ♦ Passenger transport		US$ Mn	166	281	504	630	373
3. OUTBOUND TOURISM							
Data							
Departures							
3.1 Total		('000)	..	..	..	..	..
3.2 ♦ Overnight visitors (tourists)	(3)	('000)	7,185	8,340	9,783	10,868	11,067
3.3 ♦ Same-day visitors (excursionists)		('000)	..	..	..	..	..
Expenditure							
3.4 Total		US$ Mn	8,277	8,738	10,690	12,083	11,507
3.5 ♦ Travel		US$ Mn	6,187	6,845	8,219	9,606	9,310
3.6 ♦ Passenger transport		US$ Mn	2,090	1,893	2,471	2,477	2,197
Expenditure by main purpose of the trip							
3.7 Total		US$ Mn	6,187	6,845	8,219	9,606	9,310
3.8 ♦ Personal		US$ Mn	4,586	5,849	7,325	8,646	6,349
3.9 ♦ Business and professional		US$ Mn	1,601	996	894	960	2,961

INDIA

Basic data and indicators	Notes	Units	2005	2006	2007	2008	2009
4. TOURISM INDUSTRIES							
Data							
Number of establishments							
4.1 Total		Units	..	..	..	..	..
4.2 ♦ Accommodation for visitors		Units	..	..	..	..	..
4.3 * of which, "hotels and similar establishments"	(4)	Units	1,190	1,208	1,425	1,593	2,468
4.4 ♦ Food and beverage serving activities		Units	..	..	..	..	..
4.5 ♦ Passenger transportation		Units	..	..	..	..	..
4.6 ♦ Travel agencies and other reservation services activities		Units	..	..	..	..	..
4.7 ♦ Other tourism industries		Units	..	..	..	..	..
Accommodation for visitors in hotels and similar establishments							
Non-monetary data							
4.13 ♦ Number of establishments	(4)	Units	1,190	1,208	1,425	1,593	2,468
4.14 ♦ Number of rooms	(4)	Units	67,613	75,502	83,781	95,087	121,092
4.15 ♦ Number of bed-places	(4)	Units	135,226	151,672	167,562	190,174	242,184
Indicators							
4.16 Occupancy rate / rooms		Percent	67.70	60.40	59.60	55.30	..
4.17 Occupancy rate / bed-places		Percent	..	..	..	..	..
4.18 Average length of stay		Nights	..	..	..	..	..
4.19 Available capacity (bed-places per 1000 inhabitants)		Units	0.12	0.14	0.15	0.17	0.21
6. COMPLEMENTARY INDICATORS							
Demand							
6.1 Gross travel propensity		Units	..	..	..	..	..
6.2 Carrying capacity (arrivals/population)		Units	0.004	0.004	0.005	0.005	0.004
Macroeconomic indicators related to international tourism							
6.3 Inbound tourism expenditure over GDP		Percent	0.9	0.9	0.9	1.0	..
6.4 Outbound tourism expenditure over GDP		Percent	1.0	0.9	0.9	0.9	..
6.5 Tourism balance (inbound minus outbound tourism expenditure) over GDP		Percent	-0.1	0.0	0.0	0.0	..
6.6 Tourism openness (inbound plus outbound tourism expenditure) over GDP		Percent	1.9	1.9	1.8	1.9	..
6.7 Tourism coverage (inbound over outbound tourism expenditure)		Percent	92.5	102.0	105.1	103.1	..
6.8 Inbound tourism expenditure over exports of goods		Percent	7.5	7.2	7.5	6.6	..
6.9 Inbound tourism expenditure over exports of services		Percent	14.6	12.8	12.9	12.1	..
6.10 Inbound tourism expenditure over exports of goods and services		Percent	5.0	4.6	4.8	4.3	..
6.11 Inbound tourism expenditure over current account credits		Percent	4.1	3.8	3.9	3.5	..
6.12 Outbound tourism expenditure over imports of goods		Percent	6.1	5.2	5.1	4.3	..
6.13 Outbound tourism expenditure over imports of services		Percent	17.5	14.9	15.2	13.7	..
6.14 Outbound tourism expenditure over imports of goods and services		Percent	4.5	3.9	3.8	3.3	..
6.15 Outbound tourism expenditure over current account debits		Percent	4.2	3.6	3.6	3.1	..

INDONESIA

Basic data and indicators	Notes	Units	2005	2006	2007	2008	2009
1. INBOUND TOURISM							
Data							
Arrivals							
1.1 Total		('000)	..	..	..	..	..
1.2 ♦ Overnight visitors (tourists)		('000)	5,002	4,871	5,506	6,234	6,324
1.3 ♦ Same-day visitors (excursionists)		('000)	..	..	..	..	..
1.4 * of which, cruise passengers		('000)	..	..	..	..	..
Arrivals by region							
1.5 Total		('000)	5,002	4,871	5,506	6,235	6,323
1.6 ♦ Africa		('000)	27	23	28	30	28
1.7 ♦ Americas		('000)	210	185	220	240	230
1.8 ♦ East Asia and the Pacific		('000)	3,837	3,795	4,316	4,849	4,835
1.9 ♦ Europe		('000)	798	730	797	925	978
1.10 ♦ Middle East		('000)	61	55	55	67	122
1.11 ♦ South Asia		('000)	69	83	90	124	130
1.12 ♦ Other not classified		('000)	..	..	..	..	..
1.13 * of which, nationals residing abroad		('000)	..	..	..	..	..
Arrivals by main purpose							
1.14 Total		('000)	5,002	4,872	5,505	6,234	6,323
1.15 ♦ Personal		('000)	2,939	2,861	3,344	3,801	4,006
1.16 * holidays, leisure and recreation		('000)	2,835	2,754	3,195	3,628	3,788
1.17 * other personal purposes		('000)	104	107	149	173	218
1.18 ♦ Business and professional		('000)	2,063	2,011	2,161	2,433	2,317
Arrivals by mode of transport							
1.19 Total		('000)	5,002	4,871	5,506	6,234	6,324
1.20 ♦ Air		('000)	2,889	2,822	3,304	4,091	4,396
1.21 ♦ Water		('000)	2,082	2,019	2,163	2,095	1,874
1.22 ♦ Land		('000)	31	30	39	48	54
1.23 * railway		('000)	..	..	..	..	..
1.24 * road		('000)	31	30	39	48	54
1.25 * others		('000)	..	..	..	..	..
Accommodation							
Total							
1.29 ♦ Guests		('000)	4,821	4,576	5,273	5,912	6,009
1.30 ♦ Overnights		('000)	..	..	..	..	..
Hotels and similar establishments							
1.31 ♦ Guests	(1)	('000)	3,883	3,653	4,298	4,805	5,359
1.32 ♦ Overnights		('000)	..	..	..	..	..
Expenditure							
1.33 Total		US$ Mn	5,094	4,890	5,831	8,150	6,773
1.34 ♦ Travel		US$ Mn	4,522	4,448	5,346	7,377	6,318
1.35 ♦ Passenger transport		US$ Mn	572	442	485	773	455
Expenditure by main purpose of the trip							
1.36 Total		US$ Mn	4,522	4,448	5,346	7,377	6,317
1.37 ♦ Personal		US$ Mn	3,165	3,114	3,742	5,164	4,422
1.38 ♦ Business and professional		US$ Mn	1,357	1,334	1,604	2,213	1,895
Indicators							
1.39 Average size of travel party		Persons	..	..	..	..	..
Average length of stay							
1.40 Total		Days	9.05	9.09	9.02	8.58	7.69
1.41 ♦ For all commercial accommodation services		Nights	..	..	..	..	..
1.42 * of which, "hotels and similar establishments"	(1)	Nights	2.90	3.20	2.80	2.95	2.70
1.43 ♦ For non commercial accommodation services		Days	..	..	..	..	..
1.44 Average expenditure per day		US$	99.9	100.5	107.7	137.4	129.6

INDONESIA

Basic data and indicators	Notes	Units	2005	2006	2007	2008	2009
2. DOMESTIC TOURISM							
Data							
Trips							
2.1 Total		('000)	..	..	..	..	..
2.2 ♦ Overnight visitors (tourists)		('000)	..	..	222,389	225,041	229,730
2.3 ♦ Same-day visitors (excursionists)		('000)	..	..			..
Accommodation							
Total							
2.19 ♦ Guests		('000)	31,266	32,808	37,672	38,544	42,980
2.20 ♦ Overnights		('000)	..	..	..	..	..
Hotels and similar establishments							
2.21 ♦ Guests	(1)	('000)	11,610	11,659	13,113	14,351	17,213
2.22 ♦ Overnights		('000)	..	..	..	..	..
Indicators							
2.23 Average size of travel party		Persons	..	..	..	..	..
Average length of stay							
2.24 Total		Days	..	..	..	..	..
2.25 ♦ For all commercial accommodation services		Nights	..	..	..	..	..
2.26 * of which, "hotels and similar establishments"	(1)	Nights	1.70	1.86	1.86	1.77	1.74
2.27 ♦ For non commercial accommodation services		Days	..	..	..	..	..
2.28 Average expenditure per day		US$	..	..	..	..	..
3. OUTBOUND TOURISM							
Data							
Departures							
3.1 Total		('000)	..	..	..	..	..
3.2 ♦ Overnight visitors (tourists)		('000)	4,106	4,967	5,158	5,486	5,053
3.3 ♦ Same-day visitors (excursionists)		('000)	..	..	..	..	..
Expenditure							
3.4 Total		US$ Mn	4,740	5,458	6,578	8,801	9,579
3.5 ♦ Travel		US$ Mn	3,584	4,030	4,904	5,554	5,165
3.6 ♦ Passenger transport		US$ Mn	1,156	1,428	1,674	3,247	4,414
Expenditure by main purpose of the trip							
3.7 Total		US$ Mn	3,584	4,030	4,904	5,554	5,165
3.8 ♦ Personal		US$ Mn	2,508	2,783	3,368	3,791	3,534
3.9 ♦ Business and professional		US$ Mn	1,076	1,247	1,536	1,763	1,631
Indicators							
3.10 Average length of stay		Days	8.15	7.71	9.50	10.62	8.27
3.11 Average expenditure per day		US$	83.9	100.9	88.8	96.7	109.8
4. TOURISM INDUSTRIES							
Data							
Number of establishments							
4.1 Total		Units	..	..	..	..	..
4.2 ♦ Accommodation for visitors		Units	..	..	..	..	..
4.3 * of which, "hotels and similar establishments"	(2)	Units	11,350	11,461	13,584	13,751	13,932
4.4 ♦ Food and beverage serving activities		Units	..	..	..	..	..
4.5 ♦ Passenger transportation		Units	..	..	..	..	..
4.6 ♦ Travel agencies and other reservation services activities		Units	..	..	..	..	..
4.7 ♦ Other tourism industries		Units	..	..	..	..	..
Accommodation for visitors in hotels and similar establishments							
Non-monetary data							
4.13 ♦ Number of establishments	(2)	Units	11,350	11,461	13,584	13,751	13,932
4.14 ♦ Number of rooms	(2)	Units	280,433	285,530	317,824	325,218	334,817
4.15 ♦ Number of bed-places	(2)	Units	449,622	456,021	516,919	523,940	519,205
Indicators							
4.16 Occupancy rate / rooms	(1)	Percent	45.03	46.18	46.89	48.06	46.12
4.17 Occupancy rate / bed-places		Percent	..	..	..	..	..
4.18 Average length of stay	(1)	Nights	1.99	2.17	2.08	2.03	2.02
4.19 Available capacity (bed-places per 1000 inhabitants)		Units	2.05	2.05	2.30	2.30	2.26

INDONESIA

Basic data and indicators	Notes	Units	2005	2006	2007	2008	2009
6. COMPLEMENTARY INDICATORS							
Demand							
6.1 Gross travel propensity		Units	..	..	..	..	..
6.2 Carrying capacity (arrivals/population)		Units	0.02	0.02	1.01	1.02	1.03
Macroeconomic indicators related to international tourism							
6.3 Inbound tourism expenditure over GDP		Percent	1.8	1.3	1.3	1.6	1.3
6.4 Outbound tourism expenditure over GDP		Percent	1.7	1.5	1.5	1.7	1.8
6.5 Tourism balance (inbound minus outbound tourism expenditure) over GDP		Percent	0.1	-0.2	-0.2	-0.1	-0.5
6.6 Tourism openness (inbound plus outbound tourism expenditure) over GDP		Percent	3.4	2.8	2.9	3.3	3.0
6.7 Tourism coverage (inbound over outbound tourism expenditure)		Percent	107.4	89.6	88.6	92.6	70.7
6.8 Inbound tourism expenditure over exports of goods		Percent	5.9	4.7	4.9	5.8	5.7
6.9 Inbound tourism expenditure over exports of services		Percent	39.4	42.4	46.7	53.5	49.2
6.10 Inbound tourism expenditure over exports of goods and services		Percent	5.1	4.3	4.5	5.3	5.1
6.11 Inbound tourism expenditure over current account credits		Percent	4.7	4.0	4.1	4.9	4.8
6.12 Outbound tourism expenditure over imports of goods		Percent	6.8	7.4	7.7	7.5	11.4
6.13 Outbound tourism expenditure over imports of services		Percent	21.5	25.5	27.0	31.2	34.3
6.14 Outbound tourism expenditure over imports of goods and services		Percent	5.2	5.7	6.0	6.1	8.5
6.15 Outbound tourism expenditure over current account debits		Percent	4.4	4.8	5.0	5.3	7.3

IRAN, ISLAMIC REPUBLIC OF

Basic data and indicators	Notes	Units	2005	2006	2007	2008	2009
1. INBOUND TOURISM							
Data							
Arrivals							
1.1 Total		('000)	..	..	..	..	..
1.2 ♦ Overnight visitors (tourists)		('000)	1,889	2,735	2,219	2,034	..
1.3 ♦ Same-day visitors (excursionists)		('000)	..	..	..	..	..
1.4 * of which, cruise passengers		('000)	..	..	..	..	..
Arrivals by mode of transport							
1.19 Total		('000)	..	..	..	2,034	..
1.20 ♦ Air		('000)	..	..	..	730	..
1.21 ♦ Water		('000)	..	..	..	22	..
1.22 ♦ Land		('000)	..	..	..	1,282	..
1.23 * railway		('000)	..	..	..	..	..
1.24 * road	(1)	('000)	..	..	..	1,282	..
1.25 * others		('000)	..	..	..	..	..
Expenditure	(2)						
1.33 Total		US$ Mn	1,025	1,464	1,950	2,202	2,310
1.34 ♦ Travel		US$ Mn	791	1,216	1,677	1,914	2,012
1.35 ♦ Passenger transport		US$ Mn	234	248	273	288	298
Expenditure by main purpose of the trip	(2)						
1.36 Total		US$ Mn	791	1,216	1,677	1,914	2,012
1.37 ♦ Personal		US$ Mn	554	943	1,332	1,517	1,593
1.38 ♦ Business and professional		US$ Mn	237	273	345	397	419
3. OUTBOUND TOURISM							
Data							
Expenditure	(2)						
3.4 Total		US$ Mn	4,112	5,066	7,335	8,418	10,133
3.5 ♦ Travel		US$ Mn	3,724	4,684	6,809	7,643	9,108
3.6 ♦ Passenger transport		US$ Mn	388	382	526	775	1,025
Expenditure by main purpose of the trip	(2)						
3.7 Total		US$ Mn	3,724	4,684	6,810	7,642	9,108
3.8 ♦ Personal		US$ Mn	2,984	3,777	5,550	6,259	7,572
3.9 ♦ Business and professional		US$ Mn	740	907	1,260	1,383	1,536
4. TOURISM INDUSTRIES							
Data							
Accommodation for visitors in hotels and similar establishments							
Non-monetary data							
4.13 ♦ Number of establishments		Units	..	..	..	..	..
4.14 ♦ Number of rooms	(3)	Units	29,159	..	..	67,616	..
4.15 ♦ Number of bed-places	(3)	Units	60,310	..	..	164,083	..
Indicators							
4.16 Occupancy rate / rooms		Percent	..	..	..	..	..
4.17 Occupancy rate / bed-places		Percent	..	..	..	..	..
4.18 Average length of stay		Nights	..	..	..	..	..
4.19 Available capacity (bed-places per 1000 inhabitants)		Units	0.87	..	..	2.28	..
6. COMPLEMENTARY INDICATORS							
Demand							
6.1 Gross travel propensity		Units	..	..	..	..	..
6.2 Carrying capacity (arrivals/population)		Units	0.03	0.04	0.03	0.03	..

IRAQ

Basic data and indicators	Notes	Units	2005	2006	2007	2008	2009
1. INBOUND TOURISM							
Data							
Arrivals							
1.1 Total		('000)	..	..	..	864	1,262
1.2 ♦ Overnight visitors (tourists)		('000)	..	..	..	..	..
1.3 ♦ Same-day visitors (excursionists)		('000)	..	..	..	..	..
1.4 * of which, cruise passengers		('000)	..	..	..	..	..
Arrivals by region							
1.5 Total		('000)	..	..	..	863	1,262
1.6 ♦ Africa		('000)	..	..	..	..	..
1.7 ♦ Americas		('000)	..	..	..	..	..
1.8 ♦ East Asia and the Pacific		('000)	..	..	..	..	..
1.9 ♦ Europe		('000)	..	..	..	1	9
1.10 ♦ Middle East		('000)	..	..	..	4	11
1.11 ♦ South Asia		('000)	..	..	..	852	1,194
1.12 ♦ Other not classified		('000)	..	..	..	6	48
1.13 * of which, nationals residing abroad		('000)	..	..	..	..	..
Expenditure							
1.33 Total		US$ Mn	186	170	555	..	..
1.34 ♦ Travel		US$ Mn	168	144	516	..	..
1.35 ♦ Passenger transport		US$ Mn	18	26	39	..	..
3. OUTBOUND TOURISM							
Data							
Expenditure							
3.4 Total		US$ Mn	627	526	705	813	..
3.5 ♦ Travel		US$ Mn	439	395	639	794	..
3.6 ♦ Passenger transport		US$ Mn	188	131	66	19	..
Expenditure by main purpose of the trip							
3.7 Total		US$ Mn	439	395	639	793	..
3.8 ♦ Personal		US$ Mn	101	177	516	757	..
3.9 ♦ Business and professional		US$ Mn	330	218	123	36	..
4. TOURISM INDUSTRIES							
Data							
Accommodation for visitors in hotels and similar establishments							
Non-monetary data							
4.13 ♦ Number of establishments		Units	..	..	..	..	..
4.14 ♦ Number of rooms		Units	..	..	834	786	794
4.15 ♦ Number of bed-places		Units	..	..	..	..	..

IRELAND

Basic data and indicators	Notes	Units	2005	2006	2007	2008	2009
1. INBOUND TOURISM							
Data							
Arrivals							
1.1 Total		('000)	..	..	..	..	..
1.2 ♦ Overnight visitors (tourists)	(1)	('000)	7,333	8,001	8,332	8,026	7,189
1.3 ♦ Same-day visitors (excursionists)		('000)	367	424	422	551	479
1.4 * of which, cruise passengers		('000)	..	..	..	..	..
Arrivals by region	(1)						
1.5 Total		('000)	7,334	8,001	8,333	8,026	7,189
1.6 ♦ Africa		('000)	39	48	39	54	43
1.7 ♦ Americas		('000)	956	1,058	1,099	985	921
1.8 ♦ East Asia and the Pacific		('000)	226	237	249	256	233
1.9 ♦ Europe		('000)	6,113	6,658	6,946	6,731	5,992
1.10 ♦ Middle East		('000)	..	..	..	..	..
1.11 ♦ South Asia		('000)	..	..	..	..	..
1.12 ♦ Other not classified		('000)	..	..	..	..	..
1.13 * of which, nationals residing abroad		('000)	..	..	..	..	..
Arrivals by main purpose	(1)						
1.14 Total		('000)	7,333	8,002	8,332	8,026	7,189
1.15 ♦ Personal		('000)	6,423	6,976	7,224	6,819	6,225
1.16 * holidays, leisure and recreation		('000)	3,832	4,177	4,420	4,045	3,396
1.17 * other personal purposes		('000)	2,591	2,799	2,804	2,774	2,829
1.18 ♦ Business and professional		('000)	910	1,026	1,108	1,207	964
Arrivals by mode of transport							
1.19 Total		('000)	7,333	8,001	8,332	8,025	7,190
1.20 ♦ Air		('000)	5,546	6,304	6,578	6,468	5,703
1.21 ♦ Water		('000)	1,082	964	1,006	892	787
1.22 ♦ Land		('000)	705	733	748	665	700
1.23 * railway		('000)	..	..	..	..	..
1.24 * road	(1)(2)	('000)	705	733	748	665	700
1.25 * others		('000)	..	..	..	..	..
Accommodation							
Total							
1.29 ♦ Guests		('000)	..	..	..	..	..
1.30 ♦ Overnights		('000)	50,678	56,342	56,330	60,059	52,917
Hotels and similar establishments							
1.31 ♦ Guests		('000)	..	..	..	..	..
1.32 ♦ Overnights		('000)	17,446	19,080	19,737	19,285	15,393
Expenditure							
1.33 Total		US$ Mn	6,780	7,664	9,263	9,967	8,187
1.34 ♦ Travel		US$ Mn	4,782	5,369	6,074	6,356	4,894
1.35 ♦ Passenger transport		US$ Mn	1,998	2,295	3,189	3,611	3,293
Expenditure by main purpose of the trip							
1.36 Total		US$ Mn	4,782	5,369	6,074	6,356	4,894
1.37 ♦ Personal		US$ Mn	4,723	5,266	5,919	5,333	4,180
1.38 ♦ Business and professional		US$ Mn	59	103	155	1,023	714
Indicators							
1.39 Average size of travel party		Persons	..	..	..	..	..
Average length of stay							
1.40 Total		Days	..	..	..	..	..
1.41 ♦ For all commercial accommodation services	(1)	Nights	7.49	7.60	7.30	8.10	8.10
1.42 * of which, "hotels and similar establishments"		Nights	..	..	..	..	..
1.43 ♦ For non commercial accommodation services		Days	..	..	..	..	..
1.44 Average expenditure per day		US$	..	..	..	..	..
2. DOMESTIC TOURISM							
Data							
Accommodation							
Total							
2.19 ♦ Guests		('000)	..	..	..	..	..
2.20 ♦ Overnights		('000)	24,607	24,203	26,328	26,195	26,027
Hotels and similar establishments							
2.21 ♦ Guests		('000)	..	..	..	..	..
2.22 ♦ Overnights		('000)	8,174	7,978	8,791	8,794	8,451
Indicators							
2.23 Average size of travel party		Persons	..	..	..	..	..
Average length of stay							
2.24 Total		Days	..	..	..	..	..
2.25 ♦ For all commercial accommodation services		Nights	3.40	3.30	3.30	3.10	3.10
2.26 * of which, "hotels and similar establishments"		Nights	..	..	..	..	..
2.27 ♦ For non commercial accommodation services		Days	..	..	..	..	..
2.28 Average expenditure per day		US$	..	..	..	..	..

IRELAND

Basic data and indicators	Notes	Units	2005	2006	2007	2008	2009
3. OUTBOUND TOURISM							
Data							
Departures							
3.1 Total		('000)	6,113	6,848	7,713	7,877	7,047
3.2 ♦ Overnight visitors (tourists)		('000)	..	..	..	..	..
3.3 ♦ Same-day visitors (excursionists)		('000)	..	..	..	..	..
Expenditure							
3.4 Total		US$ Mn	6,186	6,978	8,785	10,539	8,887
3.5 ♦ Travel		US$ Mn	6,074	6,862	8,656	10,413	8,773
3.6 ♦ Passenger transport		US$ Mn	112	116	129	126	114
Expenditure by main purpose of the trip							
3.7 Total		US$ Mn	6,074	6,862	8,656	10,413	8,773
3.8 ♦ Personal		US$ Mn	5,992	6,773	8,563	8,856	7,611
3.9 ♦ Business and professional		US$ Mn	82	89	93	1,557	1,162
4. TOURISM INDUSTRIES							
Data							
Accommodation for visitors in hotels and similar establishments							
Non-monetary data							
4.13 ♦ Number of establishments		Units	..	..	..	..	..
4.14 ♦ Number of rooms	(3)	Units	64,163	63,413	67,622	72,946	74,497
4.15 ♦ Number of bed-places		Units	149,617	148,819	157,355	168,660	163,637
Indicators							
4.16 Occupancy rate / rooms	(4)	Percent	62.00	64.00	64.00	58.00	55.00
4.17 Occupancy rate / bed-places		Percent	..	..	..	..	..
4.18 Average length of stay		Nights	..	..	..	..	..
4.19 Available capacity (bed-places per 1000 inhabitants)		Units	35.97	34.93	36.12	38.11	36.77
6. COMPLEMENTARY INDICATORS							
Demand							
6.1 Gross travel propensity		Units	..	..	..	..	..
6.2 Carrying capacity (arrivals/population)		Units	1.76	1.88	1.91	1.81	1.62
Macroeconomic indicators related to international tourism							
6.3 Inbound tourism expenditure over GDP		Percent	3.4	3.5	3.6	3.7	3.6
6.4 Outbound tourism expenditure over GDP		Percent	3.1	3.1	3.4	4.0	3.9
6.5 Tourism balance (inbound minus outbound tourism expenditure) over GDP		Percent	0.3	0.3	0.2	-0.2	-0.3
6.6 Tourism openness (inbound plus outbound tourism expenditure) over GDP		Percent	6.4	6.6	6.9	7.7	7.5
6.7 Tourism coverage (inbound over outbound tourism expenditure)		Percent	109.6	109.8	105.4	94.3	92.5
6.8 Inbound tourism expenditure over exports of goods		Percent	6.6	7.3	8.0	8.3	7.6
6.9 Inbound tourism expenditure over exports of services		Percent	11.3	11.1	9.9	9.8	8.5
6.10 Inbound tourism expenditure over exports of goods and services		Percent	4.2	4.4	4.4	4.5	4.0
6.11 Inbound tourism expenditure over current account credits		Percent	3.0	3.0	2.8	2.8	2.9
6.12 Outbound tourism expenditure over imports of goods		Percent	9.1	9.6	10.0	12.4	14.1
6.13 Outbound tourism expenditure over imports of services		Percent	8.7	8.9	9.3	9.7	8.6
6.14 Outbound tourism expenditure over imports of goods and services		Percent	4.4	4.6	4.8	5.4	5.3
6.15 Outbound tourism expenditure over current account debits		Percent	2.7	2.6	2.5	2.9	3.0

ISRAEL

Basic data and indicators	Notes	Units	2005	2006	2007	2008	2009
1. INBOUND TOURISM							
Data							
Arrivals	(1)						
1.1 Total		('000)	1,916	1,834	2,294	3,034	2,740
1.2 ♦ Overnight visitors (tourists)		('000)	1,903	1,825	2,067	2,572	2,321
1.3 ♦ Same-day visitors (excursionists)		('000)	13	9	227	462	418
1.4 * of which, cruise passengers		('000)	13	9	26	46	68
Arrivals by region	(1)						
1.5 Total		('000)	1,903	1,825	2,067	2,572	2,321
1.6 ♦ Africa		('000)	41	54	66	74	76
1.7 ♦ Americas		('000)	603	607	673	783	687
1.8 ♦ East Asia and the Pacific		('000)	88	94	110	130	95
1.9 ♦ Europe		('000)	1,114	1,018	1,171	1,521	1,407
1.10 ♦ Middle East		('000)	30	21	13	18	18
1.11 ♦ South Asia		('000)	23	23	28	33	26
1.12 ♦ Other not classified		('000)	4	8	6	13	12
1.13 * of which, nationals residing abroad		('000)	..	..	..	..	..
Arrivals by main purpose	(1)						
1.14 Total		('000)	1,903	1,825	2,067	2,572	2,321
1.15 ♦ Personal		('000)	1,591	1,588	1,840	2,238	1,973
1.16 * holidays, leisure and recreation		('000)	478	347	537	720	696
1.17 * other personal purposes	(2)	('000)	1,113	1,241	1,303	1,518	1,277
1.18 ♦ Business and professional		('000)	312	237	227	334	348
Arrivals by mode of transport	(1)						
1.19 Total		('000)	1,903.0	1,825.0	2,066.0	2,572.5	2,321.0
1.20 ♦ Air		('000)	1,653	1,568	1,747	2,114	1,963
1.21 ♦ Water	(3)	('000)	5.0	2.0	1.0	0.5	..
1.22 ♦ Land		('000)	245	255	318	458	358
1.23 * railway		('000)	..	..	..	..	..
1.24 * road	(4)	('000)	245	255	318	458	358
1.25 * others		('000)	..	..	..	..	..
Arrivals by form of organization of the trip							
1.26 Total		('000)	1,903	1,825	2,066	2,572	2,321
1.27 ♦ Package tour		('000)	171	128	145	772	650
1.28 ♦ Other forms		('000)	1,732	1,697	1,921	1,800	1,671
Accommodation							
Total							
1.29 ♦ Guests		('000)	..	..	..	..	..
1.30 ♦ Overnights		('000)	7,149	7,309	8,878	10,752	10,123
Hotels and similar establishments							
1.31 ♦ Guests		('000)	2,005	2,131	2,748	3,373	2,621
1.32 ♦ Overnights	(5)	('000)	6,783	6,854	8,406	10,187	8,109
Expenditure							
1.33 Total		US$ Mn	3,427	3,334	3,789	5,030	4,332
1.34 ♦ Travel	(6)	US$ Mn	2,866	2,794	3,136	4,279	3,741
1.35 ♦ Passenger transport		US$ Mn	561	540	653	751	591
Expenditure by main purpose of the trip							
1.36 Total		US$ Mn	1,677	1,787	1,934	3,014	2,594
1.37 ♦ Personal		US$ Mn	1,470	1,634	1,746	2,719	2,245
1.38 ♦ Business and professional		US$ Mn	207	153	188	295	349
Indicators							
1.39 Average size of travel party		Persons	1.8	1.6	1.8	2.0	1.9
Average length of stay							
1.40 Total		Days	..	..	..	..	..
1.41 ♦ For all commercial accommodation services		Nights	17.80	16.60	14.40	12.60	12.70
1.42 * of which, "hotels and similar establishments"		Nights	..	..	..	..	..
1.43 ♦ For non commercial accommodation services		Days	..	..	..	..	..
1.44 Average expenditure per day		US$	48.0	62.0	67.0	107.0	107.0

ISRAEL

Basic data and indicators	Notes	Units	2005	2006	2007	2008	2009
2. DOMESTIC TOURISM							
Data							
Accommodation							
Total							
2.19 ♦ Guests		('000)	..	..	..	..	..
2.20 ♦ Overnights		('000)	15,238	15,344	15,522	15,021	16,202
Hotels and similar establishments							
2.21 ♦ Guests		('000)	5,154	5,178	5,101	4,800	4,915
2.22 ♦ Overnights		('000)	12,304	12,454	12,073	11,409	11,796
Indicators							
2.23 Average size of travel party		Persons	..	..	..	..	..
Average length of stay							
2.24 Total		Days	..	..	..	..	..
2.25 ♦ For all commercial accommodation services		Nights	3.00	3.00	3.00	3.13	3.30
2.26 * of which, "hotels and similar establishments"		Nights	..	..	..	..	..
2.27 ♦ For non commercial accommodation services		Days	..	..	..	..	..
2.28 Average expenditure per day		US$	..	..	..	..	..
3. OUTBOUND TOURISM							
Data							
Departures							
3.1 Total		('000)	..	..	..	..	..
3.2 ♦ Overnight visitors (tourists)		('000)	3,687	3,713	4,147	4,207	4,007
3.3 ♦ Same-day visitors (excursionists)		('000)	..	..	..	..	..
Expenditure							
3.4 Total		US$ Mn	3,780	3,870	4,251	4,445	3,869
3.5 ♦ Travel		US$ Mn	2,895	2,983	3,260	3,439	2,909
3.6 ♦ Passenger transport		US$ Mn	885	887	991	1,006	960
4. TOURISM INDUSTRIES							
Data							
Number of establishments							
4.1 Total		Units	..	..	..	..	..
4.2 ♦ Accommodation for visitors		Units	..	..	..	..	..
4.3 * of which, "hotels and similar establishments"		Units	334	331	331	335	336
4.4 ♦ Food and beverage serving activities		Units	..	..	..	..	..
4.5 ♦ Passenger transportation		Units	..	..	..	..	..
4.6 ♦ Travel agencies and other reservation services activities		Units	..	..	..	..	..
4.7 ♦ Other tourism industries		Units	..	..	..	..	..
Accommodation for visitors in hotels and similar establishments							
Non-monetary data							
4.13 ♦ Number of establishments		Units	334	331	331	335	336
4.14 ♦ Number of rooms		Units	50,314	50,318	50,582	50,910	51,468
4.15 ♦ Number of bed-places		Units	126,831	127,305	128,356	128,350	125,455
Indicators							
4.16 Occupancy rate / rooms		Percent	..	..	..	..	..
4.17 Occupancy rate / bed-places	(7)	Percent	47.70	47.40	49.30	52.40	49.60
4.18 Average length of stay	(8)	Nights	3.50	3.22	2.61	3.13	3.30
4.19 Available capacity (bed-places per 1000 inhabitants)		Units	18.30	18.05	17.88	17.56	16.86
5. EMPLOYMENT							
Data							
Number of employees by tourism industries							
5.1 Total		('000)	24.8	30.7	31.9	33.4	33.1
5.2 ♦ Accommodation services for visitors (hotels and similar establishments)		('000)	..	..	..	..	..
5.3 ♦ Other accommodation services		('000)	..	..	..	..	..
5.4 ♦ Food and beverage serving activities		('000)	..	..	..	..	..
5.5 ♦ Passenger transportation		('000)	..	..	..	..	..
5.6 ♦ Travel agencies and other reservation services activities		('000)	..	..	..	..	..
5.7 ♦ Other tourism industries		('000)	..	..	..	..	..

ISRAEL

Basic data and indicators	Notes	Units	2005	2006	2007	2008	2009
6. COMPLEMENTARY INDICATORS							
Demand							
6.1 Gross travel propensity		Units	..	..	..	..	..
6.2 Carrying capacity (arrivals/population)		Units	0.27	0.26	0.29	0.35	0.31
Macroeconomic indicators related to international tourism							
6.3 Inbound tourism expenditure over GDP		Percent	2.5	2.3	2.2	2.4	2.2
6.4 Outbound tourism expenditure over GDP		Percent	2.8	2.7	2.5	2.2	2.0
6.5 Tourism balance (inbound minus outbound tourism expenditure) over GDP		Percent	-0.3	-0.4	-0.3	0.2	0.2
6.6 Tourism openness (inbound plus outbound tourism expenditure) over GDP		Percent	5.3	4.9	4.8	4.6	4.2
6.7 Tourism coverage (inbound over outbound tourism expenditure)		Percent	88.5	85.1	88.2	110.1	109.2
6.8 Inbound tourism expenditure over exports of goods		Percent	8.4	7.6	7.5	8.6	9.2
6.9 Inbound tourism expenditure over exports of services		Percent	19.2	17.2	17.8	20.3	19.3
6.10 Inbound tourism expenditure over exports of goods and services		Percent	5.8	5.3	5.2	6.0	6.2
6.11 Inbound tourism expenditure over current account credits		Percent	4.8	4.1	4.1	5.0	5.2
6.12 Outbound tourism expenditure over imports of goods		Percent	8.6	8.2	7.6	6.9	8.4
6.13 Outbound tourism expenditure over imports of services		Percent	27.6	26.4	24.2	22.3	22.6
6.14 Outbound tourism expenditure over imports of goods and services		Percent	6.6	6.3	5.8	5.3	6.1
6.15 Outbound tourism expenditure over current account debits		Percent	5.8	5.4	4.9	4.6	5.2

ITALY

Basic data and indicators	Notes	Units	2005	2006	2007	2008	2009
1. INBOUND TOURISM							
Data							
Arrivals	(1)(2)						
1.1 Total		('000)	59,230	66,353	70,271	70,719	71,692
1.2 ♦ Overnight visitors (tourists)		('000)	36,513	41,058	43,654	42,734	43,239
1.3 ♦ Same-day visitors (excursionists)	(3)	('000)	22,717	25,295	26,617	27,985	28,453
1.4 * of which, cruise passengers		('000)	..	..	..	..	..
Arrivals by region	(1)(2)						
1.5 Total		('000)	36,513	41,058	43,655	42,733	43,238
1.6 ♦ Africa		('000)	251	254	265	300	248
1.7 ♦ Americas		('000)	3,250	3,579	3,440	3,395	3,390
1.8 ♦ East Asia and the Pacific		('000)	1,112	1,189	1,327	1,253	1,300
1.9 ♦ Europe		('000)	31,571	35,598	38,208	37,342	37,854
1.10 ♦ Middle East		('000)	213	247	242	236	222
1.11 ♦ South Asia		('000)	115	190	173	207	224
1.12 ♦ Other not classified		('000)	1	1	..	..	..
1.13 * of which, nationals residing abroad		('000)	..	..	..	..	..
Arrivals by main purpose	(1)(2)						
1.14 Total		('000)	59,229	66,353	70,270	70,719	71,692
1.15 ♦ Personal		('000)	50,039	55,520	58,278	58,327	58,247
1.16 * holidays, leisure and recreation		('000)	25,991	29,146	31,677	28,596	27,998
1.17 * other personal purposes		('000)	24,048	26,374	26,601	29,731	30,249
1.18 ♦ Business and professional		('000)	9,190	10,833	11,992	12,392	13,445
Arrivals by mode of transport	(1)(2)						
1.19 Total		('000)	59,230	66,353	70,270	70,718	71,692
1.20 ♦ Air		('000)	18,592	21,520	23,226	21,368	19,930
1.21 ♦ Water		('000)	2,126	1,901	1,650	2,118	2,365
1.22 ♦ Land		('000)	38,512	42,932	45,394	47,232	49,397
1.23 * railway		('000)	1,935	1,900	1,899	1,776	1,565
1.24 * road		('000)	36,577	41,032	43,495	45,456	47,832
1.25 * others		('000)	..	..	..	..	..
Accommodation							
Total							
1.29 ♦ Guests		('000)	38,127	41,194	42,873	41,797	41,125
1.30 ♦ Overnights		('000)	148,501	156,861	163,466	161,797	159,494
Hotels and similar establishments	(4)						
1.31 ♦ Guests		('000)	30,943	33,513	34,769	33,667	32,633
1.32 ♦ Overnights		('000)	102,312	107,859	113,017	110,492	106,829
Expenditure							
1.33 Total		US$ Mn	38,374	41,644	46,144	48,757	41,872
1.34 ♦ Travel		US$ Mn	35,319	38,257	42,660	46,192	40,311
1.35 ♦ Passenger transport		US$ Mn	3,055	3,387	3,484	2,565	1,561
Expenditure by main purpose of the trip							
1.36 Total		US$ Mn	35,319	38,257	42,660	46,192	40,311
1.37 ♦ Personal		US$ Mn	28,170	30,062	33,304	36,072	31,651
1.38 ♦ Business and professional		US$ Mn	7,149	8,195	9,356	10,120	8,660
Indicators							
1.39 Average size of travel party		Persons	..	..	..	..	..
Average length of stay							
1.40 Total		Days	..	..	..	..	..
1.41 ♦ For all commercial accommodation services		Nights	3.89	3.81	3.81	3.87	3.88
1.42 * of which, "hotels and similar establishments"		Nights	..	..	..	..	..
1.43 ♦ For non commercial accommodation services		Days	..	..	..	..	..
1.44 Average expenditure per day		US$	..	..	..	..	..
2. DOMESTIC TOURISM							
Data							
Accommodation							
Total							
2.19 ♦ Guests		('000)	50,212	51,851	53,277	53,749	54,375
2.20 ♦ Overnights		('000)	206,754	209,903	213,176	211,869	211,268
Hotels and similar establishments							
2.21 ♦ Guests		('000)	41,276	42,521	43,282	43,498	43,698
2.22 ♦ Overnights		('000)	138,123	140,397	141,311	141,187	139,789
Indicators							
2.23 Average size of travel party		Persons	..	..	..	..	..
Average length of stay							
2.24 Total		Days	..	..	..	..	..
2.25 ♦ For all commercial accommodation services		Nights	4.12	4.05	4.00	3.94	3.89
2.26 * of which, "hotels and similar establishments"		Nights	..	..	..	..	..
2.27 ♦ For non commercial accommodation services		Days	..	..	..	..	..
2.28 Average expenditure per day		US$	..	..	..	..	..

ITALY

Basic data and indicators	Notes	Units	2005	2006	2007	2008	2009
3. OUTBOUND TOURISM							
Data							
Departures							
3.1 Total		('000)	..	..	..	..	..
3.2 ♦ Overnight visitors (tourists)	(2)(5)	('000)	24,796	25,697	27,734	28,284	29,060
3.3 ♦ Same-day visitors (excursionists)		('000)	..	..	..	..	..
Expenditure							
3.4 Total		US$ Mn	26,774	27,437	32,754	37,803	34,329
3.5 ♦ Travel		US$ Mn	22,370	23,152	27,329	30,927	27,864
3.6 ♦ Passenger transport		US$ Mn	4,404	4,285	5,425	6,876	6,465
Expenditure by main purpose of the trip							
3.7 Total		US$ Mn	22,370	23,152	27,329	30,928	27,864
3.8 ♦ Personal		US$ Mn	14,482	15,003	17,453	20,696	19,229
3.9 ♦ Business and professional		US$ Mn	7,888	8,149	9,876	10,232	8,635
4. TOURISM INDUSTRIES							
Data							
Number of establishments							
4.1 Total		Units	..	..	..	..	..
4.2 ♦ Accommodation for visitors	(6)	Units	61,551	66,331	69,239	74,263	91,778
4.3 * of which, "hotels and similar establishments"		Units	33,527	33,768	34,058	34,155	33,967
4.4 ♦ Food and beverage serving activities		Units	..	..	..	..	..
4.5 ♦ Passenger transportation		Units	..	..	..	..	..
4.6 ♦ Travel agencies and other reservation services activities		Units	..	..	..	..	..
4.7 ♦ Other tourism industries		Units	..	..	..	..	..
Accommodation for visitors in hotels and similar establishments							
Non-monetary data							
4.13 ♦ Number of establishments		Units	33,527	33,768	34,058	34,155	33,967
4.14 ♦ Number of rooms		Units	1,020,478	1,034,710	1,058,910	1,079,465	1,088,088
4.15 ♦ Number of bed-places		Units	2,028,452	2,087,010	2,142,786	2,201,838	2,227,832
Indicators							
4.16 Occupancy rate / rooms		Percent	..	..	..	..	..
4.17 Occupancy rate / bed-places		Percent	40.10	40.80	41.80	40.20	38.80
4.18 Average length of stay		Nights	3.33	3.27	3.26	3.26	3.26
4.19 Available capacity (bed-places per 1000 inhabitants)		Units	34.61	35.41	36.09	36.80	36.99
6. COMPLEMENTARY INDICATORS							
Demand							
6.1 Gross travel propensity		Units	..	..	..	..	..
6.2 Carrying capacity (arrivals/population)		Units	0.62	0.70	0.74	0.71	0.72
Macroeconomic indicators related to international tourism							
6.3 Inbound tourism expenditure over GDP		Percent	2.2	2.2	2.2	2.1	2.0
6.4 Outbound tourism expenditure over GDP		Percent	1.5	1.5	1.5	1.6	1.6
6.5 Tourism balance (inbound minus outbound tourism expenditure) over GDP		Percent	0.7	0.8	0.6	0.5	0.4
6.6 Tourism openness (inbound plus outbound tourism expenditure) over GDP		Percent	3.7	3.7	3.7	3.8	3.6
6.7 Tourism coverage (inbound over outbound tourism expenditure)		Percent	143.3	151.8	140.9	129.0	122.0
6.8 Inbound tourism expenditure over exports of goods		Percent	10.3	10.0	9.2	8.9	10.3
6.9 Inbound tourism expenditure over exports of services		Percent	43.0	42.1	41.1	40.6	40.8
6.10 Inbound tourism expenditure over exports of goods and services		Percent	8.3	8.1	7.5	7.3	8.2
6.11 Inbound tourism expenditure over current account credits		Percent	7.0	6.8	6.3	6.1	7.0
6.12 Outbound tourism expenditure over imports of goods		Percent	7.2	6.4	6.6	6.9	8.5
6.13 Outbound tourism expenditure over imports of services		Percent	29.7	27.3	26.9	29.0	29.4
6.14 Outbound tourism expenditure over imports of goods and services		Percent	5.8	5.2	5.3	5.6	6.6
6.15 Outbound tourism expenditure over current account debits		Percent	4.6	4.2	4.2	4.3	5.1

JAMAICA

Basic data and indicators	Notes	Units	2005	2006	2007	2008	2009
1. INBOUND TOURISM							
Data							
Arrivals							
1.1 Total		('000)	2,615	3,016	2,880	2,859	2,753
1.2 ♦ Overnight visitors (tourists)	(1)	('000)	1,479	1,679	1,701	1,767	1,831
1.3 ♦ Same-day visitors (excursionists)		('000)	1,136	1,337	1,180	1,092	922
1.4 * of which, cruise passengers		('000)	1,136	1,337	1,180	1,092	922
Arrivals by region	(1)						
1.5 Total		('000)	1,478	1,678	1,700	1,767	1,831
1.6 ♦ Africa		('000)	1	1	1	1	1
1.7 ♦ Americas		('000)	1,234	1,411	1,398	1,470	1,543
1.8 ♦ East Asia and the Pacific		('000)	8	8	9	8	7
1.9 ♦ Europe		('000)	235	257	290	286	278
1.10 ♦ Middle East		('000)	..	..	..	1	1
1.11 ♦ South Asia		('000)	..	1	2	1	1
1.12 ♦ Other not classified		('000)	..	..	..	..	..
1.13 * of which, nationals residing abroad		('000)	..	..	..	..	..
Arrivals by main purpose	(1)						
1.14 Total		('000)	1,478	1,679	1,701	1,767	1,831
1.15 ♦ Personal		('000)	1,394	1,578	1,597	1,658	1,730
1.16 * holidays, leisure and recreation		('000)	1,166	1,347	1,296	1,333	1,404
1.17 * other personal purposes		('000)	228	231	301	325	326
1.18 ♦ Business and professional		('000)	84	101	104	109	101
Arrivals by mode of transport							
1.19 Total		('000)	2,615	3,016	2,881	2,859	2,753
1.20 ♦ Air	(1)	('000)	1,479	1,679	1,701	1,767	1,831
1.21 ♦ Water	(2)	('000)	1,136	1,337	1,180	1,092	922
1.22 ♦ Land		('000)	..	..	..	..	..
1.23 * railway		('000)	..	..	..	..	..
1.24 * road		('000)	..	..	..	..	..
1.25 * others		('000)	..	..	..	..	..
Accommodation							
Total							
1.29 ♦ Guests		('000)	1,479	1,679	1,701	1,767	1,831
1.30 ♦ Overnights	(3)	('000)	15,410	17,142	17,308	17,488	17,964
Hotels and similar establishments							
1.31 ♦ Guests		('000)	995	1,125	1,119	1,190	1,242
1.32 ♦ Overnights		('000)	6,967	7,812	7,984	8,400	8,792
Expenditure							
1.33 Total		US$ Mn	1,783	2,094	2,142	2,222	2,070
1.34 ♦ Travel		US$ Mn	1,545	1,870	1,910	1,976	1,925
1.35 ♦ Passenger transport		US$ Mn	238	224	232	246	145
Indicators							
1.39 Average size of travel party		Persons	..	..	..	..	..
Average length of stay							
1.40 Total		Days	..	..	..	..	..
1.41 ♦ For all commercial accommodation services	(4)	Nights	10.42	10.21	10.18	9.90	9.81
1.42 * of which, "hotels and similar establishments"		Nights	7.00	6.90	7.10	7.10	7.10
1.43 ♦ For non commercial accommodation services		Days	18.24	17.51	16.52	16.37	16.22
1.44 Average expenditure per day	(5)	US$	103.5	110.6	114.5	119.5	114.0
3. OUTBOUND TOURISM							
Data							
Expenditure							
3.4 Total		US$ Mn	290	315	340	312	259
3.5 ♦ Travel		US$ Mn	249	273	298	268	216
3.6 ♦ Passenger transport		US$ Mn	41	42	42	44	43

JAMAICA

Basic data and indicators	Notes	Units	2005	2006	2007	2008	2009
4. TOURISM INDUSTRIES							
Data							
Number of establishments							
4.1 Total		Units	..	..	..	..	..
4.2 ♦ Accommodation for visitors		Units	..	..	..	..	..
4.3 * of which, "hotels and similar establishments"		Units	1,000	983	1,008	1,004	965
4.4 ♦ Food and beverage serving activities		Units	..	..	..	..	..
4.5 ♦ Passenger transportation		Units	..	..	..	..	..
4.6 ♦ Travel agencies and other reservation services activities		Units	..	..	..	..	..
4.7 ♦ Other tourism industries		Units	..	..	..	..	..
Accommodation for visitors in hotels and similar establishments							
Non-monetary data							
4.13 ♦ Number of establishments		Units	1,000	983	1,008	1,004	965
4.14 ♦ Number of rooms		Units	22,528	23,104	24,122	26,155	26,725
4.15 ♦ Number of bed-places		Units	46,905	48,040	49,802	53,600	55,400
Indicators							
4.16 Occupancy rate / rooms		Percent	61.90	62.80	63.20	60.40	59.00
4.17 Occupancy rate / bed-places		Percent	58.90	60.30	60.30	58.50	57.80
4.18 Average length of stay	(6)	Nights	6.90	6.90	7.00	7.00	7.00
4.19 Available capacity (bed-places per 1000 inhabitants)		Units	17.70	18.04	18.61	19.95	20.52
6. COMPLEMENTARY INDICATORS							
Demand							
6.1 Gross travel propensity		Units	..	..	..	..	..
6.2 Carrying capacity (arrivals/population)		Units	0.56	0.63	0.64	0.66	0.68
Macroeconomic indicators related to international tourism							
6.3 Inbound tourism expenditure over GDP		Percent	16.0	17.5	16.6	15.9	..
6.4 Outbound tourism expenditure over GDP		Percent	2.6	2.6	2.6	2.2	..
6.5 Tourism balance (inbound minus outbound tourism expenditure) over GDP		Percent	13.4	14.9	14.0	13.6	..
6.6 Tourism openness (inbound plus outbound tourism expenditure) over GDP		Percent	18.6	20.1	19.2	18.1	..
6.7 Tourism coverage (inbound over outbound tourism expenditure)		Percent	614.2	664.9	630.2	711.7	..
6.8 Inbound tourism expenditure over exports of goods		Percent	107.1	98.2	90.6	88.9	..
6.9 Inbound tourism expenditure over exports of services		Percent	76.5	79.1	79.1	79.5	..
6.10 Inbound tourism expenditure over exports of goods and services		Percent	44.6	43.8	42.2	42.0	..
6.11 Inbound tourism expenditure over current account credits		Percent	28.5	28.9	26.9	26.9	..
6.12 Outbound tourism expenditure over imports of goods		Percent	6.8	6.2	5.5	4.1	..
6.13 Outbound tourism expenditure over imports of services		Percent	16.9	15.6	14.9	13.2	..
6.14 Outbound tourism expenditure over imports of goods and services		Percent	4.9	4.4	4.0	3.1	..
6.15 Outbound tourism expenditure over current account debits		Percent	4.0	3.7	3.4	2.8	..

JAPAN

Basic data and indicators	Notes	Units	2005	2006	2007	2008	2009
1. INBOUND TOURISM							
Data							
Arrivals							
1.1 Total	(1)	('000)	6,728	7,334	8,347	8,351	6,790
1.2 ♦ Overnight visitors (tourists)		('000)	..	..	..	..	..
1.3 ♦ Same-day visitors (excursionists)		('000)	..	..	..	..	..
1.4 * of which, cruise passengers		('000)	..	..	..	..	..
Arrivals by region	(1)						
1.5 Total		('000)	6,728	7,334	8,347	8,352	6,789
1.6 ♦ Africa		('000)	21	19	20	21	17
1.7 ♦ Americas		('000)	1,032	1,035	1,054	1,006	908
1.8 ♦ East Asia and the Pacific		('000)	4,761	5,362	6,268	6,307	4,941
1.9 ♦ Europe		('000)	817	818	898	910	820
1.10 ♦ Middle East		('000)	3	3	3	4	7
1.11 ♦ South Asia		('000)	93	96	103	103	95
1.12 ♦ Other not classified		('000)	1	1	1	1	1
1.13 * of which, nationals residing abroad		('000)	..	..	..	..	..
Arrivals by main purpose	(1)						
1.14 Total		('000)	6,728	7,334	8,347	8,351	6,790
1.15 ♦ Personal		('000)	5,251	5,811	6,771	6,896	5,597
1.16 * holidays, leisure and recreation		('000)	4,369	4,981	5,954	6,049	4,760
1.17 * other personal purposes		('000)	882	830	817	847	837
1.18 ♦ Business and professional		('000)	1,477	1,523	1,576	1,455	1,193
Arrivals by mode of transport	(2)						
1.19 Total		('000)	7,450	8,108	9,152	9,146	7,582
1.20 ♦ Air		('000)	7,022	7,607	8,486	8,448	7,147
1.21 ♦ Water		('000)	428	501	666	698	435
1.22 ♦ Land		('000)	..	..	..	..	..
1.23 * railway		('000)	..	..	..	..	..
1.24 * road		('000)	..	..	..	..	..
1.25 * others		('000)	..	..	..	..	..
Accommodation							
Total							
1.29 ♦ Guests		('000)	..	..	..	..	..
1.30 ♦ Overnights		('000)	..	..	22,654	22,248	18,298
Hotels and similar establishments							
1.31 ♦ Guests		('000)	..	..	..	..	..
1.32 ♦ Overnights		('000)	..	..	..	..	..
Expenditure							
1.33 Total		US$ Mn	15,555	11,490	12,422	13,781	12,537
1.34 ♦ Travel	(3)	US$ Mn	12,430	8,470	9,345	10,820	10,329
1.35 ♦ Passenger transport		US$ Mn	3,125	3,020	3,077	2,961	2,208
Expenditure by main purpose of the trip							
1.36 Total		US$ Mn	12,431	8,470	9,345	10,820	10,329
1.37 ♦ Personal		US$ Mn	8,364	6,042	6,839	8,070	8,452
1.38 ♦ Business and professional		US$ Mn	4,067	2,428	2,506	2,750	1,877
Indicators							
1.39 Average size of travel party		Persons	..	..	..	..	..
Average length of stay							
1.40 Total		Days	8.00	7.20	6.50	6.40	6.90
1.41 ♦ For all commercial accommodation services		Nights	..	..	..	..	..
1.42 * of which, "hotels and similar establishments"		Nights	..	..	..	..	..
1.43 ♦ For non commercial accommodation services		Days	..	..	..	..	..
1.44 Average expenditure per day		US$	230.9	160.4	172.2	202.5	220.5
2. DOMESTIC TOURISM							
Data							
Accommodation							
Total							
2.19 ♦ Guests		('000)	..	..	..	..	..
2.20 ♦ Overnights		('000)	..	..	28,673	28,745	27,519
Hotels and similar establishments							
2.21 ♦ Guests		('000)	..	..	..	..	..
2.22 ♦ Overnights		('000)	..	..	..	..	..

JAPAN

Basic data and indicators	Notes	Units	2005	2006	2007	2008	2009
3. OUTBOUND TOURISM							
Data							
Departures							
3.1 Total		('000)	17,404	17,535	17,295	15,987	15,446
3.2 ♦ Overnight visitors (tourists)		('000)	..	..	..	..	..
3.3 ♦ Same-day visitors (excursionists)		('000)	..	..	..	..	..
Expenditure							
3.4 Total		US$ Mn	48,102	37,659	37,261	38,976	34,788
3.5 ♦ Travel	(3)	US$ Mn	37,565	26,876	26,511	27,901	25,199
3.6 ♦ Passenger transport		US$ Mn	10,537	10,783	10,750	11,075	9,589
Expenditure by main purpose of the trip							
3.7 Total		US$ Mn	37,565	26,876	26,511	27,900	25,199
3.8 ♦ Personal		US$ Mn	30,163	21,493	21,575	22,366	19,876
3.9 ♦ Business and professional		US$ Mn	7,402	5,383	4,936	5,534	5,323
Indicators							
3.10 Average length of stay		Days	8.80	8.80	8.80	9.20	9.10
3.11 Average expenditure per day		US$	245.3	174.2	174.2	189.7	179.3
4. TOURISM INDUSTRIES							
Data							
Number of establishments							
4.1 Total		Units	..	..	..	..	..
4.2 ♦ Accommodation for visitors		Units	..	..	..	..	..
4.3 * of which, "hotels and similar establishments"	(4)	Units	64,557	63,287	61,737	60,449	58,654
4.4 ♦ Food and beverage serving activities		Units	..	..	..	..	..
4.5 ♦ Passenger transportation		Units	..	..	..	..	..
4.6 ♦ Travel agencies and other reservation services activities		Units	10,702	10,621	10,684	10,606	10,436
4.7 ♦ Other tourism industries		Units	..	..	..	..	..
Accommodation for visitors in hotels and similar establishments							
Non-monetary data							
4.13 ♦ Number of establishments	(4)	Units	64,557	63,287	61,737	60,449	58,654
4.14 ♦ Number of rooms	(4)	Units	1,548,449	1,565,100	1,578,511	1,588,202	1,589,963
4.15 ♦ Number of bed-places		Units	..	..	..	..	..
Indicators							
4.16 Occupancy rate / rooms	(5)	Percent	73.10	76.30	74.30	71.90	67.90
4.17 Occupancy rate / bed-places		Percent	..	..	..	..	..
4.18 Average length of stay		Nights	..	..	..	..	..
4.19 Available capacity (bed-places per 1000 inhabitants)		Units	..	..	..	..	..
5. EMPLOYMENT							
Data							
Number of employees by tourism industries							
5.1 Total		('000)	..	..	..	..	..
5.2 ♦ Accommodation services for visitors (hotels and similar establishments)		('000)	..	..	..	..	..
5.3 ♦ Other accommodation services		('000)	..	..	..	..	..
5.4 ♦ Food and beverage serving activities		('000)	..	..	..	..	..
5.5 ♦ Passenger transportation		('000)	..	..	..	..	..
5.6 ♦ Travel agencies and other reservation services activities		('000)	110.6	116.1	108.7	105.7	..
5.7 ♦ Other tourism industries		('000)	..	..	..	..	..

JAPAN

Basic data and indicators	Notes	Units	2005	2006	2007	2008	2009
6. COMPLEMENTARY INDICATORS							
Demand							
6.1 Gross travel propensity		Units	..	..	..	..	..
6.2 Carrying capacity (arrivals/population)		Units	0.05	0.06	0.07	0.07	0.05
Macroeconomic indicators related to international tourism							
6.3 Inbound tourism expenditure over GDP		Percent	0.3	0.3	0.3	0.3	0.2
6.4 Outbound tourism expenditure over GDP		Percent	1.1	0.9	0.9	0.8	0.7
6.5 Tourism balance (inbound minus outbound tourism expenditure) over GDP		Percent	-0.7	-0.6	-0.6	-0.5	-0.4
6.6 Tourism openness (inbound plus outbound tourism expenditure) over GDP		Percent	1.4	1.1	1.1	1.1	0.9
6.7 Tourism coverage (inbound over outbound tourism expenditure)		Percent	32.3	30.5	33.4	35.4	36.0
6.8 Inbound tourism expenditure over exports of goods		Percent	2.7	1.9	1.8	1.8	2.3
6.9 Inbound tourism expenditure over exports of services		Percent	14.1	9.8	9.6	9.3	9.8
6.10 Inbound tourism expenditure over exports of goods and services		Percent	2.3	1.6	1.5	1.5	1.9
6.11 Inbound tourism expenditure over current account credits		Percent	1.9	1.3	1.2	1.2	1.5
6.12 Outbound tourism expenditure over imports of goods		Percent	10.2	7.0	6.5	5.5	6.9
6.13 Outbound tourism expenditure over imports of services		Percent	35.8	27.8	24.8	23.0	23.4
6.14 Outbound tourism expenditure over imports of goods and services		Percent	7.9	5.6	5.1	4.4	5.3
6.15 Outbound tourism expenditure over current account debits		Percent	7.3	5.1	4.6	4.1	4.9

JORDAN

Basic data and indicators	Notes	Units	2005	2006	2007	2008	2009
1. INBOUND TOURISM							
Data							
Arrivals	(1)						
1.1 Total		('000)	5,817	6,573	6,529	7,100	7,085
1.2 ♦ Overnight visitors (tourists)		('000)	2,987	3,225	3,431	3,729	3,789
1.3 ♦ Same-day visitors (excursionists)		('000)	2,831	3,348	3,098	3,372	3,295
1.4 * of which, cruise passengers		('000)	26	41	45	32	41
Arrivals by region	(1)						
1.5 Total		('000)	2,987	3,225	3,432	3,729	3,788
1.6 ♦ Africa		('000)	30	50	55	50	46
1.7 ♦ Americas		('000)	112	164	178	200	190
1.8 ♦ East Asia and the Pacific		('000)	64	83	126	146	138
1.9 ♦ Europe		('000)	392	424	571	658	602
1.10 ♦ Middle East		('000)	1,829	1,880	1,690	1,777	1,867
1.11 ♦ South Asia		('000)	43	42	65	74	72
1.12 ♦ Other not classified		('000)	517	582	747	824	873
1.13 * of which, nationals residing abroad		('000)	512	577	744	819	861
Arrivals by main purpose							
1.14 Total		('000)	2,987	3,225	3,431	3,729	3,789
1.15 ♦ Personal		('000)	2,636	2,863	3,063	3,332	3,389
1.16 * holidays, leisure and recreation		('000)	734	920	937	1,036	1,058
1.17 * other personal purposes		('000)	1,902	1,943	2,126	2,296	2,331
1.18 ♦ Business and professional		('000)	351	362	368	397	400
Arrivals by mode of transport	(2)						
1.19 Total		('000)	8,378	8,993	8,476	9,232	9,260
1.20 ♦ Air		('000)	1,449	1,885	1,705	1,735	1,883
1.21 ♦ Water		('000)	356	425	592	608	507
1.22 ♦ Land		('000)	6,573	6,683	6,179	6,889	6,870
1.23 * railway		('000)	1	1	..	..	..
1.24 * road		('000)	6,572	6,682	6,179	6,889	6,870
1.25 * others		('000)	..	..	..	..	..
Arrivals by form of organization of the trip							
1.26 Total		('000)	5,816.8	6,573.5	6,528.6	7,100.2	7,084.9
1.27 ♦ Package tour		('000)	397.8	365.5	494.6	673.2	615.9
1.28 ♦ Other forms		('000)	5,419	6,208	6,034	6,427	6,469
Accommodation							
Total							
1.29 ♦ Guests		('000)	1,795	1,590	1,758	2,081	1,933
1.30 ♦ Overnights		('000)	4,488	3,822	4,239	4,726	4,104
Hotels and similar establishments							
1.31 ♦ Guests		('000)	2,300	2,189	2,011	2,693	2,424
1.32 ♦ Overnights		('000)	4,460	3,796	4,206	4,692	4,073
Expenditure							
1.33 Total		US$ Mn	1,759	2,426	2,754	3,539	3,468
1.34 ♦ Travel		US$ Mn	1,441	2,060	2,311	2,943	2,911
1.35 ♦ Passenger transport		US$ Mn	318	366	443	596	557
Indicators							
1.39 Average size of travel party		Persons	..	..	..	..	..
Average length of stay							
1.40 Total		Days	..	..	..	..	..
1.41 ♦ For all commercial accommodation services	(3)	Nights	5.00	4.20	4.37	4.40	4.80
1.42 * of which, "hotels and similar establishments"		Nights	..	..	..	..	..
1.43 ♦ For non commercial accommodation services		Days	..	..	..	..	..
1.44 Average expenditure per day		US$	..	..	..	..	..
2. DOMESTIC TOURISM							
Data							
Trips							
2.1 Total		('000)	..	..	..	..	1,208
2.2 ♦ Overnight visitors (tourists)		('000)	..	..	..	..	258
2.3 ♦ Same-day visitors (excursionists)		('000)	..	..	..	..	950
Trips by main purpose							
2.4 Total		('000)	..	..	..	..	1,208
2.5 ♦ Personal		('000)	..	..	..	..	1,204
2.6 * holidays, leisure and recreation		('000)	..	..	..	..	641
2.7 * other personal purposes		('000)	..	..	..	..	563
2.8 ♦ Business and professional		('000)	..	..	..	..	4

JORDAN

Basic data and indicators	Notes	Units	2005	2006	2007	2008	2009
Trips by mode of transport							
2.9 Total		('000)	..	..	..	..	1,208
2.10 ♦ Air		('000)	..	..	..	..	..
2.11 ♦ Water		('000)	..	..	..	..	..
2.12 ♦ Land		('000)	..	..	..	..	1,208
2.13 * railway		('000)	..	..	..	..	..
2.14 * road		('000)	..	..	..	..	1,208
2.15 * others		('000)	..	..	..	..	..
Accommodation							
Total							
2.19 ♦ Guests		('000)	..	..	..	..	258
2.20 ♦ Overnights		('000)	1,064	1,201	1,221	1,293	999
Hotels and similar establishments							
2.21 ♦ Guests		('000)	505	559	595	633	515
2.22 ♦ Overnights		('000)	1,061	1,199	1,220	1,292	997
Indicators							
2.23 Average size of travel party		Persons	..	..	..	..	..
Average length of stay							
2.24 Total		Days	..	..	..	..	..
2.25 ♦ For all commercial accommodation services		Nights	2.11	2.14	2.05	2.03	2.00
2.26 * of which, "hotels and similar establishments"		Nights	..	..	..	..	..
2.27 ♦ For non commercial accommodation services		Days	..	..	..	..	..
2.28 Average expenditure per day		US$	..	..	..	..	..
3. OUTBOUND TOURISM							
Data							
Departures							
3.1 Total		('000)	..	..	..	..	..
3.2 ♦ Overnight visitors (tourists)		('000)	1,523	2,139	2,094	2,288	2,368
3.3 ♦ Same-day visitors (excursionists)		('000)	..	..	..	..	..
Expenditure							
3.4 Total		US$ Mn	653	956	1,024	1,140	1,202
3.5 ♦ Travel		US$ Mn	585	837	883	1,004	1,064
3.6 ♦ Passenger transport		US$ Mn	68	119	141	136	138
4. TOURISM INDUSTRIES							
Data							
Number of establishments							
4.1 Total		Units	1,663	1,797	1,978	2,115	2,199
4.2 ♦ Accommodation for visitors		Units	468	476	478	481	485
4.3 * of which, "hotels and similar establishments"		Units	460	467	469	468	469
4.4 ♦ Food and beverage serving activities		Units	525	602	675	776	773
4.5 ♦ Passenger transportation		Units	3	4	6	..	..
4.6 ♦ Travel agencies and other reservation services activities		Units	431	441	536	585	653
4.7 ♦ Other tourism industries		Units	236	274	283	273	288
Accommodation for visitors in hotels and similar establishments							
Non-monetary data							
4.13 ♦ Number of establishments		Units	460	467	469	468	469
4.14 ♦ Number of rooms		Units	20,465	21,180	21,353	21,890	22,416
4.15 ♦ Number of bed-places		Units	39,674	41,007	41,359	42,542	42,842
Indicators							
4.16 Occupancy rate / rooms		Percent	48.00	40.70	45.20	53.50	45.80
4.17 Occupancy rate / bed-places		Percent	39.40	33.70	37.30	42.80	36.10
4.18 Average length of stay		Nights	2.40	2.30	2.34	2.20	2.09
4.19 Available capacity (bed-places per 1000 inhabitants)		Units	7.33	7.40	7.29	7.32	7.20
Travel agencies and other reservation service activities							
Non-monetary data							
♦ Domestic trips							
4.25 * with package tour		Percent	..	..	..	..	..
4.26 * without package tour		Percent	..	..	..	..	..
♦ Inbound trips							
4.27 * with package tour		Percent	12.0	8.0	11.0	14.0	13.0
4.28 * without package tour		Percent	88.0	92.0	89.0	86.0	87.0
♦ Outbound trips							
4.29 * with package tour		Percent	10.0	10.0	10.0	10.0	10.0
4.30 * without package tour		Percent	90.0	90.0	90.0	90.0	90.0

JORDAN

Basic data and indicators	Notes	Units	2005	2006	2007	2008	2009
5. EMPLOYMENT							
Data							
Number of employees by tourism industries							
5.1 Total		('000)	29.4	31.1	34.4	38.0	40.1
5.2 ♦ Accommodation services for visitors (hotels and similar establishments)		('000)	12.9	13.5	13.2	14.0	14.7
5.3 ♦ Other accommodation services		('000)	..	..	..	..	..
5.4 ♦ Food and beverage serving activities		('000)	10.0	10.7	13.5	15.5	16.5
5.5 ♦ Passenger transportation		('000)	0.6	0.8	0.8	0.9	0.9
5.6 ♦ Travel agencies and other reservation services activities		('000)	2.8	2.9	3.4	3.7	4.0
5.7 ♦ Other tourism industries		('000)	3.2	3.2	3.5	3.9	4.0
Indicators							
Number of full-time equivalent jobs by status in employment							
5.11 Total		('000)	29.4	31.1	34.4	38.0	40.1
5.12 ♦ Employees		('000)	29.4	31.1	34.4	38.0	40.1
5.13 * male		('000)	26.7	28.3	31.0	34.0	36.1
5.14 * female		('000)	2.7	2.8	3.4	3.9	4.0
5.15 ♦ Self employed		('000)	..	..	..	..	..
5.16 * male		('000)	..	..	..	..	..
5.17 * female		('000)	..	..	..	..	..
6. COMPLEMENTARY INDICATORS							
Demand							
6.1 Gross travel propensity		Units	..	..	..	..	..
6.2 Carrying capacity (arrivals/population)		Units	0.55	0.58	0.60	0.64	0.68
Macroeconomic indicators related to international tourism							
6.3 Inbound tourism expenditure over GDP		Percent	14.0	16.6	16.2	16.7	15.1
6.4 Outbound tourism expenditure over GDP		Percent	5.2	6.5	6.0	5.4	5.2
6.5 Tourism balance (inbound minus outbound tourism expenditure) over GDP		Percent	8.8	10.0	10.2	11.3	9.9
6.6 Tourism openness (inbound plus outbound tourism expenditure) over GDP		Percent	19.2	23.1	22.2	22.1	20.4
6.7 Tourism coverage (inbound over outbound tourism expenditure)		Percent	269.2	253.8	269.0	310.4	288.4
6.8 Inbound tourism expenditure over exports of goods		Percent	40.9	46.6	48.1	44.6	54.5
6.9 Inbound tourism expenditure over exports of services		Percent	75.4	83.5	77.6	79.0	76.2
6.10 Inbound tourism expenditure over exports of goods and services		Percent	26.5	29.9	29.7	28.5	31.8
6.11 Inbound tourism expenditure over current account credits		Percent	16.8	19.4	19.3	19.3	21.3
6.12 Outbound tourism expenditure over imports of goods		Percent	7.0	9.3	8.4	7.5	9.6
6.13 Outbound tourism expenditure over imports of services		Percent	25.7	32.2	29.1	27.6	31.6
6.14 Outbound tourism expenditure over imports of goods and services		Percent	5.5	7.2	6.5	5.9	7.4
6.15 Outbound tourism expenditure over current account debits		Percent	5.1	6.7	6.0	5.6	6.9

KAZAKHSTAN

Basic data and indicators	Notes	Units	2005	2006	2007	2008	2009
1. INBOUND TOURISM							
Data							
Arrivals							
1.1 Total		('000)	4,365	4,707	5,311	4,722	4,330
1.2 ♦ Overnight visitors (tourists)		('000)	3,143	3,468	3,876	3,447	3,118
1.3 ♦ Same-day visitors (excursionists)		('000)	1,222	1,239	1,435	1,275	1,212
1.4 * of which, cruise passengers		('000)	..	..	..	..	..
Arrivals by region							
1.5 Total		('000)	4,365	4,707	5,311	4,722	..
1.6 ♦ Africa		('000)	2	5	2	2	..
1.7 ♦ Americas		('000)	31	32	33	29	..
1.8 ♦ East Asia and the Pacific		('000)	114	153	220	212	..
1.9 ♦ Europe		('000)	4,194	4,487	5,019	4,448	..
1.10 ♦ Middle East		('000)	2	3	5	4	..
1.11 ♦ South Asia		('000)	19	22	26	23	..
1.12 ♦ Other not classified		('000)	3	5	6	4	..
1.13 * of which, nationals residing abroad		('000)	..	..	..	..	..
Arrivals by main purpose							
1.14 Total		('000)	4,365	4,707	5,310	4,722	..
1.15 ♦ Personal		('000)	3,472	3,684	4,050	3,422	..
1.16 * holidays, leisure and recreation		('000)	80	110	116	90	..
1.17 * other personal purposes		('000)	3,392	3,574	3,934	3,332	..
1.18 ♦ Business and professional		('000)	893	1,023	1,260	1,300	..
Arrivals by mode of transport							
1.19 Total		('000)	4,365	4,707	5,310	4,722	..
1.20 ♦ Air		('000)	298	504	584	519	..
1.21 ♦ Water		('000)	12	14	15	14	..
1.22 ♦ Land		('000)	4,055	4,189	4,711	4,189	..
1.23 * railway		('000)	1,242	1,298	1,466	1,307	..
1.24 * road		('000)	2,813	2,891	3,245	2,882	..
1.25 * others		('000)	..	..	..	..	..
Accommodation							
Total							
1.29 ♦ Guests		('000)	..	..	..	..	..
1.30 ♦ Overnights		('000)	..	..	..	..	..
Hotels and similar establishments							
1.31 ♦ Guests		('000)	..	..	..	..	..
1.32 ♦ Overnights		('000)	261	331	548	543	514
Expenditure							
1.33 Total		US$ Mn	801	973	1,213	1,255	1,184
1.34 ♦ Travel		US$ Mn	701	838	1,013	1,012	963
1.35 ♦ Passenger transport		US$ Mn	100	135	200	243	221
Expenditure by main purpose of the trip							
1.36 Total		US$ Mn	701	838	1,013	1,011	963
1.37 ♦ Personal		US$ Mn	568	685	846	855	822
1.38 ♦ Business and professional		US$ Mn	133	153	167	156	141
Indicators							
1.39 Average size of travel party		Persons	..	..	..	..	..
Average length of stay							
1.40 Total		Days	..	..	..	..	..
1.41 ♦ For all commercial accommodation services		Nights	3.00	3.00	3.00	3.00	..
1.42 * of which, "hotels and similar establishments"		Nights	..	..	..	..	..
1.43 ♦ For non commercial accommodation services		Days	..	..	..	..	..
1.44 Average expenditure per day		US$	..	..	..	..	..
2. DOMESTIC TOURISM							
Data							
Accommodation							
Total							
2.19 ♦ Guests		('000)	..	..	..	..	..
2.20 ♦ Overnights		('000)	..	..	..	..	..
Hotels and similar establishments							
2.21 ♦ Guests		('000)	..	..	..	..	..
2.22 ♦ Overnights		('000)	963	1,140	1,416	1,258	1,793

KAZAKHSTAN

Basic data and indicators	Notes	Units	2005	2006	2007	2008	2009
3. OUTBOUND TOURISM							
Data							
Departures							
3.1 Total		('000)	..	..	..	..	..
3.2 ♦ Overnight visitors (tourists)		('000)	2,975	3,688	4,544	5,243	6,414
3.3 ♦ Same-day visitors (excursionists)		('000)	..	..	..	..	..
Expenditure							
3.4 Total		US$ Mn	940	1,060	1,396	1,361	1,320
3.5 ♦ Travel		US$ Mn	753	821	1,082	1,078	1,131
3.6 ♦ Passenger transport		US$ Mn	187	239	314	283	189
Expenditure by main purpose of the trip							
3.7 Total		US$ Mn	753	821	1,081	1,078	1,131
3.8 ♦ Personal		US$ Mn	593	696	930	961	954
3.9 ♦ Business and professional		US$ Mn	160	125	151	117	177
4. TOURISM INDUSTRIES							
Data							
Number of establishments							
4.1 Total		Units	..	..	..	..	..
4.2 ♦ Accommodation for visitors		Units	..	..	..	..	..
4.3 * of which, "hotels and similar establishments"		Units	385	465	469	528	562
4.4 ♦ Food and beverage serving activities		Units	..	..	..	..	..
4.5 ♦ Passenger transportation		Units	..	..	..	..	..
4.6 ♦ Travel agencies and other reservation services activities		Units	..	..	..	..	..
4.7 ♦ Other tourism industries		Units	..	..	..	..	..
Accommodation for visitors in hotels and similar establishments							
Non-monetary data							
4.13 ♦ Number of establishments		Units	385	465	469	528	562
4.14 ♦ Number of rooms		Units	15,515	18,838	19,552	21,214	22,441
4.15 ♦ Number of bed-places		Units	33,399	43,045	43,801	46,226	49,849
Indicators							
4.16 Occupancy rate / rooms		Percent	..	..	..	..	..
4.17 Occupancy rate / bed-places		Percent	24.90	24.30	28.70	23.50	20.40
4.18 Average length of stay		Nights	..	..	..	..	..
4.19 Available capacity (bed-places per 1000 inhabitants)		Units	2.20	2.81	2.83	2.95	3.14
6. COMPLEMENTARY INDICATORS							
Demand							
6.1 Gross travel propensity		Units	..	..	..	..	..
6.2 Carrying capacity (arrivals/population)		Units	0.21	0.23	0.25	0.22	0.20
Macroeconomic indicators related to international tourism							
6.3 Inbound tourism expenditure over GDP		Percent	1.4	1.2	1.2	0.9	1.1
6.4 Outbound tourism expenditure over GDP		Percent	1.6	1.3	1.4	1.0	1.3
6.5 Tourism balance (inbound minus outbound tourism expenditure) over GDP		Percent	-0.2	-0.1	-0.2	-0.1	-0.1
6.6 Tourism openness (inbound plus outbound tourism expenditure) over GDP		Percent	3.0	2.5	2.5	1.9	2.4
6.7 Tourism coverage (inbound over outbound tourism expenditure)		Percent	85.3	91.8	86.9	92.2	89.7
6.8 Inbound tourism expenditure over exports of goods		Percent	2.8	2.5	2.5	1.7	2.7
6.9 Inbound tourism expenditure over exports of services		Percent	35.9	34.5	34.0	28.3	27.8
6.10 Inbound tourism expenditure over exports of goods and services		Percent	2.6	2.3	2.3	1.6	2.5
6.11 Inbound tourism expenditure over current account credits		Percent	2.5	2.2	2.2	1.6	2.3
6.12 Outbound tourism expenditure over imports of goods		Percent	5.2	4.4	4.2	3.5	4.6
6.13 Outbound tourism expenditure over imports of services		Percent	12.5	12.1	11.9	12.2	13.1
6.14 Outbound tourism expenditure over imports of goods and services		Percent	3.7	3.2	3.1	2.7	3.4
6.15 Outbound tourism expenditure over current account debits		Percent	2.8	2.3	2.2	1.8	2.4

KENYA

Basic data and indicators	Notes	Units	2005	2006	2007	2008	2009
1. INBOUND TOURISM							
Data							
Arrivals	(1)						
1.1 Total		('000)	1,479	1,601	1,817	1,203	1,490
1.2 ♦ Overnight visitors (tourists)		('000)	1,399	1,464	1,686	1,141	1,392
1.3 ♦ Same-day visitors (excursionists)		('000)	80	137	131	62	98
1.4 * of which, cruise passengers		('000)	..	..	..	..	..
Arrivals by region	(1)						
1.5 Total		('000)	1,480	1,601	1,817	..	..
1.6 ♦ Africa		('000)	113	181	205	..	..
1.7 ♦ Americas		('000)	94	114	134	..	..
1.8 ♦ East Asia and the Pacific		('000)	92	153	168	..	..
1.9 ♦ Europe		('000)	1,123	1,084	1,237	..	..
1.10 ♦ Middle East		('000)	..	..	..	..	..
1.11 ♦ South Asia		('000)	..	..	..	..	..
1.12 ♦ Other not classified		('000)	58	69	73	..	..
1.13 * of which, nationals residing abroad		('000)	..	..	..	..	..
Arrivals by main purpose	(1)						
1.14 Total		('000)	1,479	1,601	1,817	1,203	1,490
1.15 ♦ Personal		('000)	1,273	1,375	1,575	1,094	1,310
1.16 * holidays, leisure and recreation		('000)	1,063	1,088	1,279	936	1,061
1.17 * other personal purposes		('000)	210	287	296	158	249
1.18 ♦ Business and professional		('000)	206	226	242	109	180
Arrivals by mode of transport	(1)						
1.19 Total		('000)	1,479	1,601	1,817	..	..
1.20 ♦ Air		('000)	842	964	1,118	..	..
1.21 ♦ Water		('000)	5	12	16	..	..
1.22 ♦ Land		('000)	632	625	683	..	..
1.23 * railway		('000)	..	..	..	..	..
1.24 * road		('000)	632	625	683	..	..
1.25 * others		('000)	..	..	..	..	..
Accommodation							
Total							
1.29 ♦ Guests		('000)	..	..	..	..	..
1.30 ♦ Overnights		('000)	..	..	..	..	..
Hotels and similar establishments							
1.31 ♦ Guests		('000)	..	..	..	..	..
1.32 ♦ Overnights		('000)	3,302	4,501	5,044	2,080	4,062
Expenditure							
1.33 Total		US$ Mn	969	1,181	1,514	1,398	1,095
1.34 ♦ Travel		US$ Mn	579	687	917	752	690
1.35 ♦ Passenger transport		US$ Mn	390	494	597	646	405
Expenditure by main purpose of the trip							
1.36 Total		US$ Mn	579	688	916	752	690
1.37 ♦ Personal		US$ Mn	515	590	809	668	634
1.38 ♦ Business and professional		US$ Mn	64	98	107	84	56
Indicators							
1.39 Average size of travel party		Persons	..	..	..	..	..
Average length of stay							
1.40 Total		Days	..	..	..	..	..
1.41 ♦ For all commercial accommodation services		Nights	14.00	11.00	11.90	..	..
1.42 * of which, "hotels and similar establishments"		Nights	..	..	..	..	..
1.43 ♦ For non commercial accommodation services		Days	..	..	..	..	..
1.44 Average expenditure per day		US$	..	..	..	..	..
2. DOMESTIC TOURISM							
Data							
Accommodation							
Total							
2.19 ♦ Guests		('000)	..	..	..	..	..
2.20 ♦ Overnights		('000)	..	..	..	..	..
Hotels and similar establishments							
2.21 ♦ Guests		('000)	..	..	..	..	..
2.22 ♦ Overnights		('000)	1,130	1,375	1,870	1,567	2,151
Indicators							
2.23 Average size of travel party		Persons	..	..	..	..	..
Average length of stay							
2.24 Total		Days	..	..	..	..	..
2.25 ♦ For all commercial accommodation services		Nights	5.00	5.00	10.00	..	..
2.26 * of which, "hotels and similar establishments"		Nights	..	..	..	..	..
2.27 ♦ For non commercial accommodation services		Days	..	..	..	..	..
2.28 Average expenditure per day		US$	..	..	..	..	..

KENYA

Basic data and indicators	Notes	Units	2005	2006	2007	2008	2009
3. OUTBOUND TOURISM							
Data							
Expenditure							
3.4 Total		US$ Mn	..	..	..	..	..
3.5 ♦ Travel		US$ Mn	124	178	265	266	234
3.6 ♦ Passenger transport		US$ Mn	..	..	..	..	..
Expenditure by main purpose of the trip							
3.7 Total		US$ Mn	124	178	265	266	234
3.8 ♦ Personal		US$ Mn	70	111	168	147	120
3.9 ♦ Business and professional		US$ Mn	54	67	97	119	114
4. TOURISM INDUSTRIES							
Data							
Accommodation for visitors in hotels and similar establishments							
Non-monetary data							
4.13 ♦ Number of establishments		Units	..	..	..	..	..
4.14 ♦ Number of rooms		Units	20,037	22,140	24,354	..	..
4.15 ♦ Number of bed-places		Units	40,074	44,280	48,708	..	..
Indicators							
4.16 Occupancy rate / rooms		Percent	..	..	..	..	..
4.17 Occupancy rate / bed-places		Percent	85.00	87.00	92.00	..	..
4.18 Average length of stay	(2)	Nights	14.00	11.00	12.10	..	..
4.19 Available capacity (bed-places per 1000 inhabitants)		Units	1.12	1.20	1.29	..	..
6. COMPLEMENTARY INDICATORS							
Demand							
6.1 Gross travel propensity		Units	..	..	..	..	..
6.2 Carrying capacity (arrivals/population)		Units	0.04	0.04	0.04	0.03	0.03
Macroeconomic indicators related to international tourism							
6.3 Inbound tourism expenditure over GDP		Percent	5.1	5.2	5.6	4.6	..
6.4 Outbound tourism expenditure over GDP		Percent	0.6	0.8	1.0	0.9	..
6.5 Tourism balance (inbound minus outbound tourism expenditure) over GDP		Percent	4.4	4.4	4.6	3.7	..
6.6 Tourism openness (inbound plus outbound tourism expenditure) over GDP		Percent	5.7	6.0	6.6	5.5	..
6.7 Tourism coverage (inbound over outbound tourism expenditure)		Percent	782.4	664.2	572.0	526.5	..
6.8 Inbound tourism expenditure over exports of goods		Percent	28.0	33.6	36.6	27.7	..
6.9 Inbound tourism expenditure over exports of services		Percent	51.5	48.6	51.6	43.0	..
6.10 Inbound tourism expenditure over exports of goods and services		Percent	18.1	19.9	21.4	16.9	..
6.11 Inbound tourism expenditure over current account credits		Percent	14.4	15.0	16.1	12.8	..
6.12 Outbound tourism expenditure over imports of goods		Percent	2.2	2.6	3.2	2.5	..
6.13 Outbound tourism expenditure over imports of services		Percent	10.9	12.7	15.8	14.2	..
6.14 Outbound tourism expenditure over imports of goods and services		Percent	1.8	2.2	2.6	2.1	..
6.15 Outbound tourism expenditure over current account debits		Percent	1.8	2.1	2.5	2.1	..

KIRIBATI

Basic data and indicators	Notes	Units	2005	2006	2007	2008	2009
1. INBOUND TOURISM							
Data							
Arrivals							
1.1 Total		('000)	50.2	10.8	32.3	..	..
1.2 ♦ Overnight visitors (tourists)	(1)	('000)	4.1	4.4	4.7	3.9	3.9
1.3 ♦ Same-day visitors (excursionists)		('000)	46.1	6.4	27.6	..	..
1.4 * of which, cruise passengers		('000)	46.1	6.4	27.6	..	..
Arrivals by region	(1)						
1.5 Total		('000)	4.1	4.4	4.7	3.9	3.9
1.6 ♦ Africa		('000)	..	..	..	..	..
1.7 ♦ Americas		('000)	1.0	0.8	1.1	0.9	0.7
1.8 ♦ East Asia and the Pacific		('000)	2.4	2.7	3.1	2.5	2.7
1.9 ♦ Europe		('000)	0.2	0.2	0.3	0.3	0.4
1.10 ♦ Middle East		('000)	..	..	..	..	..
1.11 ♦ South Asia		('000)	..	..	..	..	..
1.12 ♦ Other not classified		('000)	0.5	0.7	0.2	0.2	0.1
1.13 * of which, nationals residing abroad		('000)	..	..	..	..	..
Arrivals by main purpose	(1)(2)						
1.14 Total		('000)	4.1	2.7	4.8	3.9	3.9
1.15 ♦ Personal		('000)	2.1	1.8	3.4	2.7	2.2
1.16 * holidays, leisure and recreation		('000)	0.8	0.2	1.1	0.9	0.6
1.17 * other personal purposes		('000)	1.3	1.6	2.3	1.8	1.6
1.18 ♦ Business and professional		('000)	2.0	0.9	1.4	1.2	1.7
Arrivals by mode of transport							
1.19 Total		('000)	50.2	10.8	32.3	3.9	3.9
1.20 ♦ Air	(1)	('000)	4.1	4.4	4.7	3.9	3.9
1.21 ♦ Water		('000)	46.1	6.4	27.6	..	..
1.22 ♦ Land		('000)	..	..	..	..	..
1.23 * railway		('000)	..	..	..	..	..
1.24 * road		('000)	..	..	..	..	..
1.25 * others		('000)	..	..	..	..	..
6. COMPLEMENTARY INDICATORS							
Demand							
6.1 Gross travel propensity		Units	..	..	..	..	..
6.2 Carrying capacity (arrivals/population)		Units	0.04	0.05	0.05	0.04	0.04

KOREA, REPUBLIC OF

Basic data and indicators	Notes	Units	2005	2006	2007	2008	2009
1. INBOUND TOURISM							
Data							
Arrivals							
1.1 Total	(1)	('000)	6,023	6,155	6,448	6,891	7,818
1.2 ♦ Overnight visitors (tourists)		('000)	..	..	..	..	..
1.3 ♦ Same-day visitors (excursionists)		('000)	..	..	..	..	..
1.4 * of which, cruise passengers		('000)	..	..	..	..	..
Arrivals by region	(1)						
1.5 Total		('000)	6,023	6,155	6,448	6,891	7,817
1.6 ♦ Africa		('000)	14	16	19	21	22
1.7 ♦ Americas		('000)	640	673	716	745	752
1.8 ♦ East Asia and the Pacific		('000)	4,442	4,554	4,697	5,035	6,029
1.9 ♦ Europe		('000)	541	572	605	646	645
1.10 ♦ Middle East		('000)	13	15	16	18	20
1.11 ♦ South Asia		('000)	92	95	101	118	114
1.12 ♦ Other not classified		('000)	281	230	294	308	235
1.13 * of which, nationals residing abroad		('000)	280	227	294	308	234
Arrivals by main purpose	(1)						
1.14 Total		('000)	6,022	6,155	6,448	6,891	7,818
1.15 ♦ Personal		('000)	5,718	5,807	6,089	6,529	7,506
1.16 * holidays, leisure and recreation		('000)	4,347	4,365	4,388	4,642	5,685
1.17 * other personal purposes		('000)	1,371	1,442	1,701	1,887	1,821
1.18 ♦ Business and professional		('000)	304	348	359	362	312
Arrivals by mode of transport	(2)						
1.19 Total		('000)	5,180	6,155	6,448	6,891	7,818
1.20 ♦ Air		('000)	4,776	5,116	5,447	5,822	6,725
1.21 ♦ Water		('000)	404	1,039	1,001	1,069	1,093
1.22 ♦ Land		('000)	..	..	..	..	..
1.23 * railway		('000)	..	..	..	..	..
1.24 * road		('000)	..	..	..	..	..
1.25 * others		('000)	..	..	..	..	..
Expenditure							
1.33 Total		US$ Mn	8,290	8,508	9,288	13,479	12,927
1.34 ♦ Travel		US$ Mn	5,806	5,788	6,138	9,774	9,442
1.35 ♦ Passenger transport		US$ Mn	2,484	2,720	3,150	3,705	3,485
Expenditure by main purpose of the trip							
1.36 Total		US$ Mn	..	5,788	6,138	9,774	9,442
1.37 ♦ Personal		US$ Mn	..	3,334	3,683	5,692	5,659
1.38 ♦ Business and professional		US$ Mn	..	2,454	2,455	4,082	3,783
Indicators							
1.39 Average size of travel party		Persons	..	..	..	..	..
Average length of stay							
1.40 Total		Days	..	..	..	..	..
1.41 ♦ For all commercial accommodation services		Nights	6.80	10.90	8.10	..	..
1.42 * of which, "hotels and similar establishments"		Nights	..	..	..	..	..
1.43 ♦ For non commercial accommodation services		Days	..	..	..	..	..
1.44 Average expenditure per day		US$	..	..	..	..	..
3. OUTBOUND TOURISM							
Data							
Departures							
3.1 Total		('000)	..	..	..	..	..
3.2 ♦ Overnight visitors (tourists)		('000)	10,080	11,610	13,325	11,996	9,494
3.3 ♦ Same-day visitors (excursionists)		('000)	..	..	..	..	..
Expenditure							
3.4 Total		US$ Mn	16,924	20,989	24,449	21,456	14,648
3.5 ♦ Travel	(3)	US$ Mn	15,406	18,851	21,975	19,065	13,330
3.6 ♦ Passenger transport		US$ Mn	1,518	2,138	2,474	2,391	1,318
Expenditure by main purpose of the trip							
3.7 Total		US$ Mn	..	18,850	21,975	19,065	13,330
3.8 ♦ Personal		US$ Mn	..	14,922	17,500	14,633	10,866
3.9 ♦ Business and professional		US$ Mn	..	3,928	4,475	4,432	2,464

KOREA, REPUBLIC OF

Basic data and indicators	Notes	Units	2005	2006	2007	2008	2009
4. **TOURISM INDUSTRIES**							
Data							
Number of establishments							
4.1 Total		Units	..	..	..	..	..
4.2 ♦ Accommodation for visitors		Units	..	..	..	..	..
4.3 * of which, "hotels and similar establishments"	(4)	Units	554	580	593	610	621
4.4 ♦ Food and beverage serving activities		Units	..	..	..	..	..
4.5 ♦ Passenger transportation		Units	..	..	..	..	..
4.6 ♦ Travel agencies and other reservation services activities		Units	..	..	..	..	..
4.7 ♦ Other tourism industries		Units	..	..	..	..	..
Accommodation for visitors in hotels and similar establishments							
Non-monetary data							
4.13 ♦ Number of establishments	(4)	Units	554	580	593	610	621
4.14 ♦ Number of rooms	(4)	Units	58,950	60,596	61,540	64,154	67,171
4.15 ♦ Number of bed-places		Units	..	..	..	..	..
Indicators							
4.16 Occupancy rate / rooms		Percent	57.10	52.00	57.00	57.60	60.10
4.17 Occupancy rate / bed-places		Percent	..	..	..	..	..
4.18 Average length of stay		Nights	..	..	..	..	..
4.19 Available capacity (bed-places per 1000 inhabitants)		Units	..	..	..	..	..
6. **COMPLEMENTARY INDICATORS**							
Demand							
6.1 Gross travel propensity		Units	..	..	..	..	..
6.2 Carrying capacity (arrivals/population)		Units	0.13	0.13	0.13	0.14	0.16
Macroeconomic indicators related to international tourism							
6.3 Inbound tourism expenditure over GDP		Percent	1.0	0.9	0.9	1.4	1.6
6.4 Outbound tourism expenditure over GDP		Percent	2.0	2.2	2.3	2.3	1.8
6.5 Tourism balance (Inbound minus outbound tourism expenditure) over GDP		Percent	-1.0	-1.3	-1.4	-0.9	-0.2
6.6 Tourism openness (inbound plus outbound tourism expenditure) over GDP		Percent	3.0	3.1	3.2	3.8	3.3
6.7 Tourism coverage (inbound over outbound tourism expenditure)		Percent	49.0	40.5	38.0	62.8	88.3
6.8 Inbound tourism expenditure over exports of goods		Percent	2.9	2.6	2.5	3.1	3.5
6.9 Inbound tourism expenditure over exports of services		Percent	18.4	17.1	14.7	17.5	22.1
6.10 Inbound tourism expenditure over exports of goods and services		Percent	2.5	2.2	2.1	2.6	3.0
6.11 Inbound tourism expenditure over current account credits		Percent	2.3	2.1	2.0	2.5	2.8
6.12 Outbound tourism expenditure over imports of goods		Percent	6.6	6.9	7.0	5.0	4.6
6.13 Outbound tourism expenditure over imports of services		Percent	28.8	30.5	29.4	22.9	19.3
6.14 Outbound tourism expenditure over imports of goods and services		Percent	5.4	5.6	5.6	4.1	3.7
6.15 Outbound tourism expenditure over current account debits		Percent	5.0	5.2	5.2	3.9	3.5

KUWAIT

Basic data and indicators	Notes	Units	2005	2006	2007	2008	2009
1. INBOUND TOURISM							
Data							
Arrivals							
1.1 Total		('000)	3,474	3,899	4,482	4,736	5,088
1.2 ♦ Overnight visitors (tourists)	(1)	('000)	104	185	293	259	297
1.3 ♦ Same-day visitors (excursionists)		('000)	..	..	..	..	..
1.4 * of which, cruise passengers		('000)	..	..	..	..	..
Arrivals by region							
1.5 Total		('000)	3,475	3,899	4,482	4,736	5,088
1.6 ♦ Africa		('000)	35	43	55	65	73
1.7 ♦ Americas		('000)	132	155	190	219	229
1.8 ♦ East Asia and the Pacific		('000)	185	227	235	244	250
1.9 ♦ Europe		('000)	137	155	177	181	184
1.10 ♦ Middle East		('000)	2,005	2,223	2,619	2,778	2,997
1.11 ♦ South Asia		('000)	978	1,093	1,192	1,225	1,316
1.12 ♦ Other not classified		('000)	3	3	14	24	39
1.13 * of which, nationals residing abroad		('000)	..	..	..	..	..
Arrivals by main purpose	(1)						
1.14 Total		('000)	105	185	292	260	297
1.15 ♦ Personal		('000)	95	169	271	245	283
1.16 * holidays, leisure and recreation		('000)	9	20	27	26	16
1.17 * other personal purposes		('000)	86	149	244	219	267
1.18 ♦ Business and professional		('000)	10	16	21	15	14
Arrivals by mode of transport							
1.19 Total		('000)	3,474	3,899	4,482	4,735	5,088
1.20 ♦ Air		('000)	1,657	1,857	2,126	2,248	2,425
1.21 ♦ Water		('000)	41	39	31	33	35
1.22 ♦ Land		('000)	1,776	2,003	2,325	2,454	2,628
1.23 * railway		('000)	..	..	..	..	..
1.24 * road		('000)	1,776	2,003	2,325	2,454	2,628
1.25 * others		('000)	..	..	..	..	..
Accommodation							
Total							
1.29 ♦ Guests		('000)					
1.30 ♦ Overnights		('000)	..	..	..	..	..
Hotels and similar establishments							
1.31 ♦ Guests		('000)	104	185	293	259	297
1.32 ♦ Overnights		('000)	272	291	413	341	314
Expenditure							
1.33 Total		US$ Mn	413	508	530	610	553
1.34 ♦ Travel		US$ Mn	165	205	223	257	248
1.35 ♦ Passenger transport		US$ Mn	248	303	307	353	305
Indicators							
1.39 Average size of travel party		Persons	..	..	..	..	..
Average length of stay							
1.40 Total		Days	..	..	..	..	..
1.41 ♦ For all commercial accommodation services		Nights	2.60	1.60	..	..	..
1.42 * of which, "hotels and similar establishments"		Nights	..	..	..	..	..
1.43 ♦ For non commercial accommodation services		Days	..	..	..	..	..
1.44 Average expenditure per day		US$	..	..	..	..	..
3. OUTBOUND TOURISM							
Data							
Departures							
3.1 Total		('000)	..	..	..	..	..
3.2 ♦ Overnight visitors (tourists)		('000)	2,173	2,529	2,649	..	..
3.3 ♦ Same-day visitors (excursionists)		('000)	..	..	..	..	..
Expenditure							
3.4 Total		US$ Mn	4,997	6,074	7,267	8,584	8,244
3.5 ♦ Travel		US$ Mn	4,532	5,573	6,636	7,570	7,441
3.6 ♦ Passenger transport		US$ Mn	465	501	631	1,014	803

KUWAIT

Basic data and indicators	Notes	Units	2005	2006	2007	2008	2009
4. TOURISM INDUSTRIES							
Data							
Number of establishments							
4.1 Total		Units	..	..	..	..	..
4.2 ♦ Accommodation for visitors		Units	..	..	..	..	..
4.3 * of which, "hotels and similar establishments"		Units	59	66	66	84	86
4.4 ♦ Food and beverage serving activities		Units	..	..	..	..	..
4.5 ♦ Passenger transportation		Units	..	..	..	..	..
4.6 ♦ Travel agencies and other reservation services activities		Units	..	..	..	..	..
4.7 ♦ Other tourism industries		Units	..	..	..	..	..
Accommodation for visitors in hotels and similar establishments							
Non-monetary data							
4.13 ♦ Number of establishments		Units	59	66	66	84	86
4.14 ♦ Number of rooms		Units	5,919	6,572	6,572	7,405	7,636
4.15 ♦ Number of bed-places		Units	9,847	11,387	11,387	13,086	13,612
Indicators							
4.16 Occupancy rate / rooms		Percent	..	..	..	..	..
4.17 Occupancy rate / bed-places		Percent	..	..	..	..	..
4.18 Average length of stay		Nights	..	..	..	..	..
4.19 Available capacity (bed-places per 1000 inhabitants)		Units	3.88	4.38	4.28	4.80	4.87
6. COMPLEMENTARY INDICATORS							
Demand							
6.1 Gross travel propensity		Units	..	..		..	..
6.2 Carrying capacity (arrivals/population)		Units	0.04	0.07	0.11	0.09	0.11
Macroeconomic indicators related to international tourism							
6.3 Inbound tourism expenditure over GDP		Percent	0.5	0.5	0.5	0.4	..
6.4 Outbound tourism expenditure over GDP		Percent	6.2	6.0	6.3	5.8	..
6.5 Tourism balance (inbound minus outbound tourism expenditure) over GDP		Percent	-5.7	-5.5	-5.9	-5.4	..
6.6 Tourism openness (inbound plus outbound tourism expenditure) over GDP		Percent	6.7	6.5	6.8	6.2	..
6.7 Tourism coverage (inbound over outbound tourism expenditure)		Percent	8.3	8.4	7.3	7.1	6.7
6.8 Inbound tourism expenditure over exports of goods		Percent	0.9	0.9	0.8	0.7	1.1
6.9 Inbound tourism expenditure over exports of services		Percent	8.7	6.0	5.2	5.3	4.9
6.10 Inbound tourism expenditure over exports of goods and services		Percent	0.8	0.8	0.7	0.6	0.9
6.11 Inbound tourism expenditure over current account credits		Percent	0.7	0.7	0.6	0.5	0.8
6.12 Outbound tourism expenditure over imports of goods		Percent	33.2	37.4	38.0	37.4	48.3
6.13 Outbound tourism expenditure over imports of services		Percent	57.3	57.1	54.5	56.2	60.6
6.14 Outbound tourism expenditure over imports of goods and services		Percent	21.0	22.6	22.4	22.5	26.9
6.15 Outbound tourism expenditure over current account debits		Percent	17.8	18.9	15.5	16.5	19.0

KYRGYZSTAN

Basic data and indicators	Notes	Units	2005	2006	2007	2008	2009
1. INBOUND TOURISM							
Data							
Arrivals							
1.1 Total		('000)	..	..	..	..	..
1.2 ♦ Overnight visitors (tourists)	(1)	('000)	319	766	1,656	2,435	2,147
1.3 ♦ Same-day visitors (excursionists)		('000)	..	..	..	..	..
1.4 * of which, cruise passengers		('000)	..	..	..	..	..
Arrivals by region	(1)						
1.5 Total		('000)	319	765	1,655	2,436	..
1.6 ♦ Africa		('000)	..	..	..	..	..
1.7 ♦ Americas		('000)	13	14	15	10	..
1.8 ♦ East Asia and the Pacific		('000)	22	26	31	30	..
1.9 ♦ Europe		('000)	274	715	1,595	2,384	..
1.10 ♦ Middle East		('000)	..	..	..	..	..
1.11 ♦ South Asia		('000)	6	5	7	7	..
1.12 ♦ Other not classified		('000)	4	5	7	5	..
1.13 * of which, nationals residing abroad		('000)	..	..	..	..	..
Accommodation							
Total							
1.29 ♦ Guests		('000)	..	..	..	..	..
1.30 ♦ Overnights		('000)	..	457	508	439	..
Hotels and similar establishments							
1.31 ♦ Guests		('000)	34	38	47	37	..
1.32 ♦ Overnights		('000)	94	116	107	103	..
Expenditure							
1.33 Total		US$ Mn	94	189	392	569	506
1.34 ♦ Travel		US$ Mn	73	167	346	514	459
1.35 ♦ Passenger transport		US$ Mn	21	22	46	55	47
Expenditure by main purpose of the trip							
1.36 Total		US$ Mn	72	167	346	514	459
1.37 ♦ Personal		US$ Mn	33	81	169	253	255
1.38 ♦ Business and professional		US$ Mn	39	86	177	261	204
2. DOMESTIC TOURISM							
Data							
Accommodation							
Total							
2.19 ♦ Guests		('000)	..	..	..	..	..
2.20 ♦ Overnights		('000)	..	1,120	1,172	1,207	..
Hotels and similar establishments							
2.21 ♦ Guests		('000)	92	95	117	129	..
2.22 ♦ Overnights		('000)	128	141	159	162	..
3. OUTBOUND TOURISM							
Data							
Departures							
3.1 Total		('000)	..	..	..	..	..
3.2 ♦ Overnight visitors (tourists)	(1)	('000)	201	454	559	1,521	..
3.3 ♦ Same-day visitors (excursionists)		('000)	..	..	..	..	..
Expenditure							
3.4 Total		US$ Mn	94	142	215	451	391
3.5 ♦ Travel		US$ Mn	58	92	112	304	265
3.6 ♦ Passenger transport		US$ Mn	36	50	103	147	126
Expenditure by main purpose of the trip							
3.7 Total		US$ Mn	58	91	112	304	265
3.8 ♦ Personal		US$ Mn	17	27	34	91	115
3.9 ♦ Business and professional		US$ Mn	41	64	78	213	150

KYRGYZSTAN

Basic data and indicators	Notes	Units	2005	2006	2007	2008	2009
4. **TOURISM INDUSTRIES**							
Data							
Number of establishments							
4.1 Total		Units	..	..	..	..	..
4.2 ♦ Accommodation for visitors		Units	..	..	..	..	..
4.3 * of which, "hotels and similar establishments"		Units	120	123	119	152	154
4.4 ♦ Food and beverage serving activities		Units	..	..	..	..	..
4.5 ♦ Passenger transportation		Units	..	..	..	..	..
4.6 ♦ Travel agencies and other reservation services activities		Units	..	..	..	..	..
4.7 ♦ Other tourism industries		Units	..	..	..	..	..
Accommodation for visitors in hotels and similar establishments							
Non-monetary data							
4.13 ♦ Number of establishments		Units	120	123	119	152	154
4.14 ♦ Number of rooms		Units	2,244	2,357	2,352	2,481	2,787
4.15 ♦ Number of bed-places		Units	4,472	4,733	4,783	4,532	4,990
Indicators							
4.16 Occupancy rate / rooms		Percent	..	..	..	..	..
4.17 Occupancy rate / bed-places		Percent	..	..	..	..	..
4.18 Average length of stay		Nights	..	..	..	..	..
4.19 Available capacity (bed-places per 1000 inhabitants)		Units	0.87	0.91	0.91	0.86	..
6. **COMPLEMENTARY INDICATORS**							
Demand							
6.1 Gross travel propensity		Units	..	..	..	..	..
6.2 Carrying capacity (arrivals/population)		Units	0.06	0.15	0.32	0.46	..
Macroeconomic indicators related to international tourism							
6.3 Inbound tourism expenditure over GDP		Percent	3.8	6.7	10.3	11.1	..
6.4 Outbound tourism expenditure over GDP		Percent	3.8	5.0	5.1	8.8	
6.5 Tourism balance (inbound minus outbound tourism expenditure) over GDP		Percent	0.0	1.7	5.2	2.3	..
6.6 Tourism openness (inbound plus outbound tourism expenditure) over GDP		Percent	7.7	11.7	15.4	19.9	..
6.7 Tourism coverage (inbound over outbound tourism expenditure)		Percent	99.3	133.3	202.8	126.1	
6.8 Inbound tourism expenditure over exports of goods		Percent	13.7	20.9	29.3	30.8	..
6.9 Inbound tourism expenditure over exports of services		Percent	36.2	49.9	57.2	63.5	..
6.10 Inbound tourism expenditure over exports of goods and services		Percent	9.9	14.7	19.4	20.8	..
6.11 Inbound tourism expenditure over current account credits		Percent	6.3	9.0	12.4	13.1	..
6.12 Outbound tourism expenditure over imports of goods		Percent	8.5	7.9	7.3	12.0	..
6.13 Outbound tourism expenditure over imports of services		Percent	32.4	30.8	33.2	45.4	
6.14 Outbound tourism expenditure over imports of goods and services		Percent	6.8	6.3	6.0	9.5	..
6.15 Outbound tourism expenditure over current account debits		Percent	6.2	5.9	5.7	9.1	..

LAO PEOPLE´S DEMOCRATIC REPUBLIC

Basic data and indicators	Notes	Units	2005	2006	2007	2008	2009
1. INBOUND TOURISM							
Data							
Arrivals							
1.1 Total		('000)	1,095	1,215	1,624	1,737	2,008
1.2 ♦ Overnight visitors (tourists)		('000)	672	842	1,142	1,295	1,239
1.3 ♦ Same-day visitors (excursionists)		('000)	423	373	482	442	769
1.4 * of which, cruise passengers		('000)	..	..	..	..	..
Arrivals by region							
1.5 Total		('000)	1,095	1,216	1,623	1,737	2,008
1.6 ♦ Africa		('000)	..	..	..	..	..
1.7 ♦ Americas		('000)	60	61	61	75	53
1.8 ♦ East Asia and the Pacific		('000)	897	1,007	1,404	1,480	1,818
1.9 ♦ Europe		('000)	134	144	152	173	133
1.10 ♦ Middle East		('000)	..	..	..	..	..
1.11 ♦ South Asia		('000)	2	2	2	3	2
1.12 ♦ Other not classified		('000)	2	2	4	6	2
1.13 * of which, nationals residing abroad		('000)	..	..	..	..	..
Arrivals by main purpose							
1.14 Total		('000)	1,095	1,215	1,624	1,737	2,008
1.15 ♦ Personal		('000)	1,029	996	1,445	1,459	1,707
1.16 * holidays, leisure and recreation		('000)	964	911	1,299	1,355	1,627
1.17 * other personal purposes		('000)	65	85	146	104	80
1.18 ♦ Business and professional		('000)	66	219	179	278	301
Arrivals by mode of transport							
1.19 Total		('000)	1,095	1,215	1,624	1,737	2,008
1.20 ♦ Air		('000)	438	389	650	556	582
1.21 ♦ Water		('000)	..	..	..	..	..
1.22 ♦ Land		('000)	657	826	974	1,181	1,426
1.23 * railway		('000)	..	..	..	..	..
1.24 * road		('000)	657	826	974	1,181	1,426
1.25 * others		('000)	..	..	..	..	..
Expenditure							
1.33 Total		US$ Mn	143	160	190	280	271
1.34 ♦ Travel		US$ Mn	139	158	189	276	268
1.35 ♦ Passenger transport		US$ Mn	4	2	1	4	3
Indicators							
1.39 Average size of travel party		Persons	..	..	..	..	..
Average length of stay							
1.40 Total		Days	..	..	..	..	..
1.41 ♦ For all commercial accommodation services	(1)	Nights	4.50	4.50	4.50	4.25	4.50
1.42 * of which, "hotels and similar establishments"		Nights	..	..	..	..	..
1.43 ♦ For non commercial accommodation services		Days	..	..	..	..	..
1.44 Average expenditure per day		US$	..	..	..	..	..
3. OUTBOUND TOURISM							
Data							
Expenditure							
3.4 Total		US$ Mn	10	15	14	51	91
3.5 ♦ Travel		US$ Mn	5	9	8	41	83
3.6 ♦ Passenger transport		US$ Mn	5	6	6	10	8

LAO PEOPLE´S DEMOCRATIC REPUBLIC

Basic data and indicators	Notes	Units	2005	2006	2007	2008	2009
4. **TOURISM INDUSTRIES**							
Data							
Number of establishments							
4.1 Total		Units	..	..	..	..	..
4.2 ♦ Accommodation for visitors		Units	..	..	..	..	..
4.3 * of which, "hotels and similar establishments"		Units	1,088	1,193	1,331	1,385	1,701
4.4 ♦ Food and beverage serving activities		Units	..	..	..	..	..
4.5 ♦ Passenger transportation		Units	..	..	..	..	..
4.6 ♦ Travel agencies and other reservation services activities		Units	..	..	..	..	..
4.7 ♦ Other tourism industries		Units	..	..	..	..	..
Accommodation for visitors in hotels and similar establishments							
Non-monetary data							
4.13 ♦ Number of establishments		Units	1,088	1,193	1,331	1,385	1,701
4.14 ♦ Number of rooms		Units	15,828	17,633	19,142	22,173	26,558
4.15 ♦ Number of bed-places		Units	22,142	26,846	27,544	31,519	37,492
Indicators							
4.16 Occupancy rate / rooms		Percent	..	..	..	..	..
4.17 Occupancy rate / bed-places		Percent	50.00	51.00	54.00	57.00	54.00
4.18 Average length of stay		Nights	..	..	..	..	..
4.19 Available capacity (bed-places per 1000 inhabitants)		Units	3.77	4.49	4.52	5.08	5.93
6. **COMPLEMENTARY INDICATORS**							
Demand							
6.1 Gross travel propensity		Units	..	..	..	..	..
6.2 Carrying capacity (arrivals/population)		Units	0.11	0.14	0.19	0.21	0.20

LATVIA

Basic data and indicators	Notes	Units	2005	2006	2007	2008	2009
1. INBOUND TOURISM							
Data							
Arrivals							
1.1 Total	(1)	('000)	3,791	4,649	5,209	5,496	4,727
1.2 ♦ Overnight visitors (tourists)	(2)	('000)	1,116	1,535	1,653	1,684	1,323
1.3 ♦ Same-day visitors (excursionists)	(2)	('000)	2,658	3,109	3,583	3,812	3,404
1.4 * of which, cruise passengers	(2)	('000)	92	89	120	177	181
Arrivals by region	(2)						
1.5 Total		('000)	3,771	4,643	5,207	5,474	4,726
1.6 ♦ Africa		('000)	..	1	3	..	5
1.7 ♦ Americas		('000)	22	20	32	38	60
1.8 ♦ East Asia and the Pacific		('000)	8	19	18	22	35
1.9 ♦ Europe		('000)	3,739	4,601	5,150	5,410	4,611
1.10 ♦ Middle East		('000)	..	1	2	..	2
1.11 ♦ South Asia		('000)	2	1	2	4	8
1.12 ♦ Other not classified		('000)	..	..	..	..	5
1.13 * of which, nationals residing abroad		('000)	..	..	..	..	..
Arrivals by main purpose	(2)						
1.14 Total		('000)	3,774	4,644	5,209	5,496	4,726
1.15 ♦ Personal		('000)	3,333	4,048	4,485	4,618	4,075
1.16 * holidays, leisure and recreation		('000)	1,227	1,738	1,737	2,236	1,513
1.17 * other personal purposes	(3)	('000)	2,106	2,310	2,748	2,382	2,562
1.18 ♦ Business and professional		('000)	441	596	724	878	651
Arrivals by mode of transport	(1)						
1.19 Total		('000)	3,790	4,649	5,209	5,496	4,726
1.20 ♦ Air		('000)	494	641	857	982	1,277
1.21 ♦ Water		('000)	210	231	318	328	319
1.22 ♦ Land		('000)	3,086	3,777	4,034	4,186	3,130
1.23 * railway		('000)	147	155	176	146	123
1.24 * road		('000)	2,939	3,622	3,858	4,040	3,007
1.25 * others		('000)	..	..	..	..	..
Accommodation							
Total							
1.29 ♦ Guests		('000)	730	816	845	945	754
1.30 ♦ Overnights	(4)	('000)	1,613	1,872	1,936	2,116	1,700
Hotels and similar establishments							
1.31 ♦ Guests		('000)	680	746	765	846	697
1.32 ♦ Overnights		('000)	1,507	1,745	1,780	1,913	1,587
Expenditure							
1.33 Total		US$ Mn	446	622	880	1,134	1,013
1.34 ♦ Travel		US$ Mn	341	480	671	803	723
1.35 ♦ Passenger transport		US$ Mn	105	142	209	331	290
Expenditure by main purpose of the trip							
1.36 Total		US$ Mn	341	479	671	803	723
1.37 ♦ Personal		US$ Mn	232	337	471	567	522
1.38 ♦ Business and professional		US$ Mn	109	142	200	236	201
Indicators							
1.39 Average size of travel party		Persons	..	..	..	..	..
Average length of stay							
1.40 Total		Days	..	..	..	..	..
1.41 ♦ For all commercial accommodation services	(5)	Nights	2.21	2.29	2.29	2.24	2.90
1.42 * of which, "hotels and similar establishments"	(5)	Nights	..	..	..	..	2.90
1.43 ♦ For non commercial accommodation services	(5)	Days	..	..	..	..	5.70
1.44 Average expenditure per day	(5)	US$	..	..	..	..	101.5

LATVIA

Basic data and indicators	Notes	Units	2005	2006	2007	2008	2009
2. DOMESTIC TOURISM							
Data							
Trips	(6)						
2.1 Total		('000)	..	..	..	..	15,908
2.2 ♦ Overnight visitors (tourists)		('000)	..	..	..	..	3,598
2.3 ♦ Same-day visitors (excursionists)		('000)	..	..	..	..	12,310
Trips by main purpose	(6)						
2.4 Total		('000)	..	..	..	..	15,909
2.5 ♦ Personal		('000)	..	..	..	..	15,653
2.6 * holidays, leisure and recreation		('000)	..	..	..	..	15,653
2.7 * other personal purposes		('000)	..	..	..	..	..
2.8 ♦ Business and professional		('000)	..	..	..	..	256
Trips by mode of transport	(6)						
2.9 Total		('000)	..	..	..	..	3,598
2.10 ♦ Air		('000)	..	..	..	..	6
2.11 ♦ Water		('000)	..	..	..	..	..
2.12 ♦ Land		('000)	..	..	..	..	3,592
2.13 * railway		('000)	..	..	..	..	251
2.14 * road		('000)	..	..	..	..	3,322
2.15 * others		('000)	..	..	..	..	19
Accommodation							
Total							
2.19 ♦ Guests		('000)	..	..	..	..	360
2.20 ♦ Overnights	(4)	('000)	1,022	1,241	1,389	1,385	843
Hotels and similar establishments							
2.21 ♦ Guests		('000)	354	418	541	483	302
2.22 ♦ Overnights		('000)	796	855	979	941	599
Indicators							
2.23 Average size of travel party		Persons	..	..	..	..	..
Average length of stay							
2.24 Total		Days	..	..	..	..	..
2.25 ♦ For all commercial accommodation services		Nights	2.41	2.42	2.16	2.27	2.30
2.26 * of which, "hotels and similar establishments"		Nights	..	..	..	..	2.60
2.27 ♦ For non commercial accommodation services		Days	..	..	..	..	2.30
2.28 Average expenditure per day		US$	..	..	..	..	18.0
3. OUTBOUND TOURISM							
Data							
Departures	(7)						
3.1 Total		('000)	2,959	3,151	3,398	3,782	3,268
3.2 ♦ Overnight visitors (tourists)		('000)	..	..	..	..	1,573
3.3 ♦ Same-day visitors (excursionists)		('000)	..	..	..	..	1,695
Expenditure							
3.4 Total		US$ Mn	655	788	1,021	1,250	906
3.5 ♦ Travel		US$ Mn	584	704	927	1,142	799
3.6 ♦ Passenger transport		US$ Mn	71	84	94	108	107
Expenditure by main purpose of the trip							
3.7 Total		US$ Mn	583	704	927	1,142	799
3.8 ♦ Personal		US$ Mn	423	564	772	926	627
3.9 ♦ Business and professional		US$ Mn	160	140	155	216	172
Indicators							
3.10 Average length of stay		Days	..	..	..	..	10.10
3.11 Average expenditure per day		US$	..	..	..	..	45.5

LATVIA

Basic data and indicators	Notes	Units	2005	2006	2007	2008	2009
4. TOURISM INDUSTRIES							
Data							
Number of establishments							
4.1 Total		Units	..	..	..	..	..
4.2 ♦ Accommodation for visitors		Units	..	..	..	..	
4.3 * of which, "hotels and similar establishments"		Units	337	321	318	387	451
4.4 ♦ Food and beverage serving activities		Units	..	..	..	..	..
4.5 ♦ Passenger transportation		Units	..	..	..	..	..
4.6 ♦ Travel agencies and other reservation services activities		Units	..	..	..	..	..
4.7 ♦ Other tourism industries		Units	..	..	..	..	..
Accommodation for visitors in hotels and similar establishments							
Non-monetary data							
4.13 ♦ Number of establishments		Units	337	321	318	387	451
4.14 ♦ Number of rooms		Units	9,219	9,706	10,017	11,646	..
4.15 ♦ Number of bed-places		Units	19,229	19,650	20,685	23,541	25,392
Indicators							
4.16 Occupancy rate / rooms		Percent	..	..	..	..	..
4.17 Occupancy rate / bed-places		Percent	36.38	35.60	36.54	33.20	22.30
4.18 Average length of stay		Nights	2.23	2.23	2.11	2.15	2.19
4.19 Available capacity (bed-places per 1000 inhabitants)		Units	8.36	8.59	9.09	10.39	11.26
6. COMPLEMENTARY INDICATORS							
Demand							
6.1 Gross travel propensity		Units	..	..	..	..	..
6.2 Carrying capacity (arrivals/population)		Units	0.49	0.67	0.73	0.74	2.18
Macroeconomic indicators related to international tourism							
6.3 Inbound tourism expenditure over GDP		Percent	2.8	3.1	3.1	3.4	3.9
6.4 Outbound tourism expenditure over GDP		Percent	4.1	4.0	3.5	3.7	3.3
6.5 Tourism balance (inbound minus outbound tourism expenditure) over GDP		Percent	-1.3	-0.8	-0.5	-0.3	0.6
6.6 Tourism openness (inbound plus outbound tourism expenditure) over GDP		Percent	6.9	7.1	6.6	7.1	7.2
6.7 Tourism coverage (inbound over outbound tourism expenditure)		Percent	68.2	78.9	86.2	90.7	117.4
6.8 Inbound tourism expenditure over exports of goods		Percent	8.3	10.1	10.7	11.8	14.0
6.9 Inbound tourism expenditure over exports of services		Percent	20.7	23.5	23.8	25.0	26.5
6.10 Inbound tourism expenditure over exports of goods and services		Percent	5.9	7.1	7.4	8.0	9.2
6.11 Inbound tourism expenditure over current account credits		Percent	4.6	5.3	5.7	6.2	7.0
6.12 Outbound tourism expenditure over imports of goods		Percent	7.8	7.0	6.7	8.0	9.7
6.13 Outbound tourism expenditure over imports of services		Percent	42.0	39.8	37.8	39.2	39.3
6.14 Outbound tourism expenditure over imports of goods and services		Percent	6.6	5.9	5.7	6.6	7.8
6.15 Outbound tourism expenditure over current account debits		Percent	5.6	4.9	4.7	5.5	7.3

LEBANON

Basic data and indicators	Notes	Units	2005	2006	2007	2008	2009
1. INBOUND TOURISM							
Data							
Arrivals							
1.1 Total		('000)	..	..	..	..	..
1.2 ♦ Overnight visitors (tourists)	(1)	('000)	1,140	1,063	1,017	1,333	1,844
1.3 ♦ Same-day visitors (excursionists)		('000)	..	..		..	..
1.4 * of which, cruise passengers		('000)	..	..		..	..
Arrivals by region	(1)						
1.5 Total		('000)	1,140	1,061	1,018	1,333	1,844
1.6 ♦ Africa		('000)	31	39	60	51	66
1.7 ♦ Americas		('000)	137	130	122	177	233
1.8 ♦ East Asia and the Pacific		('000)	88	74	64	89	129
1.9 ♦ Europe		('000)	317	269	278	348	455
1.10 ♦ Middle East		('000)	437	433	388	533	762
1.11 ♦ South Asia		('000)	129	115	105	133	198
1.12 ♦ Other not classified		('000)	1	1	1	2	1
1.13 * of which, nationals residing abroad		('000)	..	..	..	..	..
Accommodation							
Total							
1.29 ♦ Guests		('000)	..	..	..	..	..
1.30 ♦ Overnights		('000)	..	..	..	..	..
Hotels and similar establishments							
1.31 ♦ Guests		('000)	..	..	..	..	598
1.32 ♦ Overnights		('000)	1,133	1,150	984	1,452	1,628
Expenditure							
1.33 Total		US$ Mn	5,969	5,457	5,796	6,317	7,157
1.34 ♦ Travel		US$ Mn	5,532	4,981	5,216	5,819	6,774
1.35 ♦ Passenger transport		US$ Mn	437	476	580	498	383
Expenditure by main purpose of the trip							
1.36 Total		US$ Mn	5,531	4,981	5,216	5,819	6,774
1.37 ♦ Personal		US$ Mn	5,002	4,909	5,116	5,641	6,541
1.38 ♦ Business and professional		US$ Mn	529	72	100	178	233
Indicators							
1.39 Average size of travel party		Persons	..	..	..	..	..
Average length of stay							
1.40 Total		Days	..	..	..	..	..
1.41 ♦ For all commercial accommodation services		Nights	2.49	2.46	2.23	2.29	2.54
1.42 * of which, "hotels and similar establishments"		Nights	..	..		..	..
1.43 ♦ For non commercial accommodation services		Days	..	..	..	..	..
1.44 Average expenditure per day		US$	..	..	..	..	..
2. DOMESTIC TOURISM							
Data							
Accommodation							
Total							
2.19 ♦ Guests		('000)	..	..	..	..	..
2.20 ♦ Overnights		('000)	..	..	..	..	..
Hotels and similar establishments							
2.21 ♦ Guests		('000)	..	..	..	..	172
2.22 ♦ Overnights		('000)	..	..	..	..	327
Indicators							
2.23 Average size of travel party		Persons	..	..	..	..	..
Average length of stay							
2.24 Total		Days	..	..	..	..	..
2.25 ♦ For all commercial accommodation services		Nights	..	..	..	..	..
2.26 * of which, "hotels and similar establishments"		Nights	..	..	..	..	1.90
2.27 ♦ For non commercial accommodation services		Days	..	..	..	..	..
2.28 Average expenditure per day		US$	..	..	..	..	..

LEBANON

Basic data and indicators	Notes	Units	2005	2006	2007	2008	2009
3. OUTBOUND TOURISM							
Data							
Expenditure							
3.4 Total		US$ Mn	3,565	3,783	3,914	4,297	4,928
3.5 ♦ Travel		US$ Mn	2,908	3,006	3,114	3,564	4,012
3.6 ♦ Passenger transport		US$ Mn	657	777	800	733	916
Expenditure by main purpose of the trip							
3.7 Total		US$ Mn	2,908	3,006	3,114	3,564	4,012
3.8 ♦ Personal		US$ Mn	2,729	2,924	3,020	3,296	3,815
3.9 ♦ Business and professional		US$ Mn	179	82	94	268	197
4. TOURISM INDUSTRIES							
Data							
Accommodation for visitors in hotels and similar establishments							
Non-monetary data							
4.13 ♦ Number of establishments		Units	..	..	..	..	..
4.14 ♦ Number of rooms		Units	16,735	16,680	17,760	18,362	21,343
4.15 ♦ Number of bed-places		Units	28,953	27,544	29,071	30,062	32,217
Indicators							
4.16 Occupancy rate / rooms		Percent	..	..	..	..	..
4.17 Occupancy rate / bed-places		Percent	..	..	..	..	..
4.18 Average length of stay		Nights	..	..	..	..	..
4.19 Available capacity (bed-places per 1000 inhabitants)		Units	7.09	6.68	6.98	7.17	7.63
6. COMPLEMENTARY INDICATORS							
Demand							
6.1 Gross travel propensity		Units	..	..	..	..	..
6.2 Carrying capacity (arrivals/population)		Units	0.28	0.26	0.24	0.32	0.44
Macroeconomic indicators related to international tourism							
6.3 Inbound tourism expenditure over GDP		Percent	27.3	24.3	23.1	21.1	..
6.4 Outbound tourism expenditure over GDP		Percent	16.3	16.9	15.6	14.4	..
6.5 Tourism balance (inbound minus outbound tourism expenditure) over GDP		Percent	11.0	7.5	7.5	6.7	..
6.6 Tourism openness (inbound plus outbound tourism expenditure) over GDP		Percent	43.6	41.2	38.8	35.5	..
6.7 Tourism coverage (inbound over outbound tourism expenditure)		Percent	167.4	144.3	148.1	147.0	145.2
6.8 Inbound tourism expenditure over exports of goods		Percent	225.1	169.0	143.2	120.3	151.8
6.9 Inbound tourism expenditure over exports of services		Percent	55.0	47.1	45.4	35.9	42.4
6.10 Inbound tourism expenditure over exports of goods and services		Percent	44.2	36.9	34.5	27.7	33.1
6.11 Inbound tourism expenditure over current account credits		Percent	30.4	24.4	23.1	20.0	23.7
6.12 Outbound tourism expenditure over imports of goods		Percent	38.6	40.5	32.8	26.4	31.0
6.13 Outbound tourism expenditure over imports of services		Percent	45.2	43.3	39.2	31.9	34.4
6.14 Outbound tourism expenditure over imports of goods and services		Percent	20.8	20.9	17.9	14.5	16.3
6.15 Outbound tourism expenditure over current account debits		Percent	15.9	16.1	14.6	12.0	13.0

LESOTHO

Basic data and indicators	Notes	Units	2005	2006	2007	2008	2009
1. INBOUND TOURISM							
Data							
Arrivals							
1.1 Total		('000)	304	357	300	293	344
1.2 ♦ Overnight visitors (tourists)		('000)	..	347	292	285	320
1.3 ♦ Same-day visitors (excursionists)		('000)	..	10	8	8	24
1.4 * of which, cruise passengers		('000)	..	..	..	..	..
Arrivals by region							
1.5 Total		('000)	304	357	300	293	344
1.6 ♦ Africa		('000)	289	330	271	259	314
1.7 ♦ Americas		('000)	1	3	3	5	4
1.8 ♦ East Asia and the Pacific		('000)	3	3	5	6	5
1.9 ♦ Europe		('000)	8	20	20	23	20
1.10 ♦ Middle East		('000)	..	..	..	..	..
1.11 ♦ South Asia		('000)	..	..	..	..	..
1.12 ♦ Other not classified		('000)	3	1	1	..	1
1.13 * of which, nationals residing abroad		('000)	..	..	..	..	..
Arrivals by main purpose							
1.14 Total		('000)	304	..	300	293	344
1.15 ♦ Personal		('000)	244	..	254	254	304
1.16 * holidays, leisure and recreation		('000)	67	..	109	111	126
1.17 * other personal purposes		('000)	177	..	145	143	178
1.18 ♦ Business and professional		('000)	60	..	46	39	40
Arrivals by mode of transport							
1.19 Total		('000)	304	357	300	293	344
1.20 ♦ Air		('000)	11	13	15	15	14
1.21 ♦ Water		('000)	..	..	..	..	..
1.22 ♦ Land		('000)	293	344	285	278	330
1.23 * railway		('000)	..	..	..	..	..
1.24 * road		('000)	293	344	285	278	330
1.25 * others		('000)	..	..	..	..	..
Expenditure							
1.33 Total		US$ Mn	..	..	..	..	..
1.34 ♦ Travel		US$ Mn	26	27	43	24	40
1.35 ♦ Passenger transport		US$ Mn	..	..	..	..	..
Expenditure by main purpose of the trip							
1.36 Total		US$ Mn	25	27	43	24	40
1.37 ♦ Personal		US$ Mn	22	24	35	21	20
1.38 ♦ Business and professional		US$ Mn	3	3	8	3	20
3. OUTBOUND TOURISM							
Data							
Expenditure							
3.4 Total		US$ Mn	36	22	24	19	22
3.5 ♦ Travel		US$ Mn	27	19	16	14	14
3.6 ♦ Passenger transport		US$ Mn	9	3	8	5	8
Expenditure by main purpose of the trip							
3.7 Total		US$ Mn	27	19	16	13	14
3.8 ♦ Personal		US$ Mn	25	17	14	12	13
3.9 ♦ Business and professional		US$ Mn	2	2	2	1	1

LESOTHO

Basic data and indicators	Notes	Units	2005	2006	2007	2008	2009
4. TOURISM INDUSTRIES							
Data							
Number of establishments							
4.1 Total		Units	..	..	..	..	..
4.2 ♦ Accommodation for visitors		Units	..	..	..	..	..
4.3 * of which, "hotels and similar establishments"		Units	..	..	103	108	121
4.4 ♦ Food and beverage serving activities		Units	..	..	..	..	..
4.5 ♦ Passenger transportation		Units	..	..	..	..	..
4.6 ♦ Travel agencies and other reservation services activities		Units	..	..	..	..	..
4.7 ♦ Other tourism industries		Units	..	..	..	..	..
Accommodation for visitors in hotels and similar establishments							
Non-monetary data							
4.13 ♦ Number of establishments		Units	..	..	103	108	121
4.14 ♦ Number of rooms		Units	1,209	1,770	2,105	2,254	2,429
4.15 ♦ Number of bed-places		Units	2,498	3,574	4,350	4,532	4,791
Indicators							
4.16 Occupancy rate / rooms		Percent	..	..	..	..	..
4.17 Occupancy rate / bed-places		Percent	14.60	17.30	17.00	18.20	17.90
4.18 Average length of stay		Nights	..	7.20	7.96	9.10	9.00
4.19 Available capacity (bed-places per 1000 inhabitants)		Units	1.25	1.77	2.14	2.21	2.32
5. EMPLOYMENT							
Data							
Number of employees by tourism industries							
5.1 Total		('000)	..	..	..	..	..
5.2 ♦ Accommodation services for visitors (hotels and similar establishments)		('000)	..	..	1.8	2.2	2.6
5.3 ♦ Other accommodation services		('000)	..	..	..	..	..
5.4 ♦ Food and beverage serving activities		('000)	..	..	..	..	..
5.5 ♦ Passenger transportation		('000)	..	..	..	..	..
5.6 ♦ Travel agencies and other reservation services activities		('000)	..	..	..	..	..
5.7 ♦ Other tourism industries		('000)	..	..	..	..	..
6. COMPLEMENTARY INDICATORS							
Demand							
6.1 Gross travel propensity		Units	..	..	..	..	..
6.2 Carrying capacity (arrivals/population)		Units	0.15	0.17	0.14	0.14	0.15
Macroeconomic indicators related to international tourism							
6.3 Inbound tourism expenditure over GDP		Percent	1.9	1.8	2.6	..	..
6.4 Outbound tourism expenditure over GDP		Percent	2.6	1.4	1.4	..	..
6.5 Tourism balance (inbound minus outbound tourism expenditure) over GDP		Percent	-0.7	0.3	1.1	..	..
6.6 Tourism openness (inbound plus outbound tourism expenditure) over GDP		Percent	4.5	3.2	4.0	..	..
6.7 Tourism coverage (inbound over outbound tourism expenditure)		Percent	72.2	122.9	177.5	178.3	..
6.8 Inbound tourism expenditure over exports of goods		Percent	4.0	3.9	5.3	3.8	..
6.9 Inbound tourism expenditure over exports of services		Percent	49.7	45.4	55.9	50.1	..
6.10 Inbound tourism expenditure over exports of goods and services		Percent	3.7	3.6	4.8	3.5	..
6.11 Inbound tourism expenditure over current account credits		Percent	1.9	1.7	2.1	1.7	..
6.12 Outbound tourism expenditure over imports of goods		Percent	2.8	1.6	1.5	1.2	..
6.13 Outbound tourism expenditure over imports of services		Percent	34.8	22.9	21.8	17.2	..
6.14 Outbound tourism expenditure over imports of goods and services		Percent	2.6	1.5	1.4	1.1	..
6.15 Outbound tourism expenditure over current account debits		Percent	2.4	1.5	1.3	1.1	..

LIBYAN ARAB JAMAHIRIYA

Basic data and indicators	Notes	Units	2005	2006	2007	2008	2009
1. INBOUND TOURISM							
Data							
Arrivals							
1.1 Total		('000)	..	125	106	760	..
1.2 ♦ Overnight visitors (tourists)	(1)	('000)	81	42	38	34	..
1.3 ♦ Same-day visitors (excursionists)		('000)	..	84	68	8	..
1.4 * of which, cruise passengers		('000)	..	84	68	8	..
Arrivals by region							
1.5 Total		('000)	..	125	106	..	..
1.6 ♦ Africa		('000)	..	..	0.2	..	..
1.7 ♦ Americas		('000)	..	3	0.8	..	..
1.8 ♦ East Asia and the Pacific		('000)	..	5	3.7	..	..
1.9 ♦ Europe		('000)	..	117	101.3	..	..
1.10 ♦ Middle East		('000)	..	..	..	..	..
1.11 ♦ South Asia		('000)	..	..	..	..	..
1.12 ♦ Other not classified		('000)	..	..	..	..	..
1.13 * of which, nationals residing abroad		('000)	..	..	..	..	..
Accommodation							
Total							
1.29 ♦ Guests		('000)	..	..	..	..	..
1.30 ♦ Overnights		('000)	..	..	..	..	..
Hotels and similar establishments							
1.31 ♦ Guests		('000)	81	42	38	34	..
1.32 ♦ Overnights		('000)	569	291	266	237	..
Expenditure							
1.33 Total		US$ Mn	301	244	99	99	159
1.34 ♦ Travel		US$ Mn	250	190	74	74	50
1.35 ♦ Passenger transport		US$ Mn	51	54	25	25	109
Expenditure by main purpose of the trip							
1.36 Total		US$ Mn	250	190	..	..	..
1.37 ♦ Personal		US$ Mn	9	10	..	..	..
1.38 ♦ Business and professional		US$ Mn	241	180	..	..	..
Indicators							
1.39 Average size of travel party		Persons	..	..	..	..	..
Average length of stay							
1.40 Total		Days	..	..	..	..	..
1.41 ♦ For all commercial accommodation services		Nights	7.00	7.00	7.00	7.00	..
1.42 * of which, "hotels and similar establishments"		Nights	..	..	..	..	..
1.43 ♦ For non commercial accommodation services		Days	..	..	..	..	..
1.44 Average expenditure per day		US$	..	..	..	..	..
3. OUTBOUND TOURISM							
Data							
Expenditure							
3.4 Total		US$ Mn	920	915	1,010	1,339	1,683
3.5 ♦ Travel		US$ Mn	680	668	889	1,277	1,587
3.6 ♦ Passenger transport		US$ Mn	240	247	121	62	96
Expenditure by main purpose of the trip							
3.7 Total		US$ Mn	680	668	889	1,277	1,587
3.8 ♦ Personal		US$ Mn	655	638	759	1,064	1,299
3.9 ♦ Business and professional		US$ Mn	25	30	130	213	288
4. TOURISM INDUSTRIES							
Data							
Accommodation for visitors in hotels and similar establishments							
Non-monetary data							
4.13 ♦ Number of establishments		Units	..	256	268	277	..
4.14 ♦ Number of rooms		Units	..	13,162	13,638	13,916	..
4.15 ♦ Number of bed-places		Units	..	24,393	26,423	27,334	..
Indicators							
4.16 Occupancy rate / rooms		Percent	..	..	..	..	..
4.17 Occupancy rate / bed-places		Percent	..	..	..	..	..
4.18 Average length of stay		Nights	..	..	..	..	..
4.19 Available capacity (bed-places per 1000 inhabitants)		Units	..	4.04	4.28	4.34	..

LIBYAN ARAB JAMAHIRIYA

Basic data and indicators	Notes	Units	2005	2006	2007	2008	2009
6. COMPLEMENTARY INDICATORS							
Demand							
6.1 Gross travel propensity		Units	..	..	..	..	..
6.2 Carrying capacity (arrivals/population)		Units	0.01	0.01	0.01	0.01	..
Macroeconomic indicators related to international tourism							
6.3 Inbound tourism expenditure over GDP		Percent	0.6	0.4	0.1	0.1	..
6.4 Outbound tourism expenditure over GDP		Percent	1.8	1.5	1.4	1.4	..
6.5 Tourism balance (inbound minus outbound tourism expenditure) over GDP		Percent	-1.2	-1.1	-1.2	-1.3	..
6.6 Tourism openness (inbound plus outbound tourism expenditure) over GDP		Percent	2.4	1.9	1.5	1.5	..
6.7 Tourism coverage (inbound over outbound tourism expenditure)		Percent	32.7	26.7	9.8	7.4	..
6.8 Inbound tourism expenditure over exports of goods		Percent	1.0	0.7	0.2	0.2	..
6.9 Inbound tourism expenditure over exports of services		Percent	56.4	49.9	91.6	47.9	..
6.10 Inbound tourism expenditure over exports of goods and services		Percent	1.0	0.6	0.2	0.2	..
6.11 Inbound tourism expenditure over current account credits		Percent	1.0	0.6	0.2	0.1	..
6.12 Outbound tourism expenditure over imports of goods		Percent	8.2	6.9	5.7	6.2	..
6.13 Outbound tourism expenditure over imports of services		Percent	39.2	35.7	37.9	30.8	..
6.14 Outbound tourism expenditure over imports of goods and services		Percent	6.8	5.8	5.0	5.2	..
6.15 Outbound tourism expenditure over current account debits		Percent	5.5	4.7	4.3	4.3	..

LIECHTENSTEIN

Basic data and indicators	Notes	Units	2005	2006	2007	2008	2009
1. INBOUND TOURISM							
Data							
Arrivals							
1.1 Total		('000)	..	..	..	..	..
1.2 ♦ Overnight visitors (tourists)	(1)	('000)	49.8	54.9	58.3	58.5	52.3
1.3 ♦ Same-day visitors (excursionists)		('000)	..	..	..	..	..
1.4 * of which, cruise passengers		('000)	..	..	..	..	..
Arrivals by region	(1)						
1.5 Total		('000)	49.7	54.8	58.3	58.4	52.3
1.6 ♦ Africa		('000)	0	0	0	0	0
1.7 ♦ Americas		('000)	2.9	3.0	3.2	2.4	2.3
1.8 ♦ East Asia and the Pacific		('000)	1.6	1.7	1.7	1.7	1.3
1.9 ♦ Europe		('000)	44.9	49.8	53.1	54.1	48.2
1.10 ♦ Middle East		('000)	..	..	..	..	..
1.11 ♦ South Asia		('000)	..	..	..	..	..
1.12 ♦ Other not classified		('000)	0.1	0.1	0.1	..	0.3
1.13 * of which, nationals residing abroad		('000)	..	..	..	..	..
Accommodation							
Total							
1.29 ♦ Guests		('000)	..	..	..	..	..
1.30 ♦ Overnights		('000)	..	..	..	..	..
Hotels and similar establishments							
1.31 ♦ Guests		('000)	49.8	54.9	58.3	58.5	52.3
1.32 ♦ Overnights		('000)	108.4	115.4	126.1	131.1	117.8
Indicators							
1.39 Average size of travel party		Persons	..	..	..	..	..
Average length of stay							
1.40 Total		Days	..	..	..	..	..
1.41 ♦ For all commercial accommodation services		Nights	2.20	2.10	2.20	2.20	2.30
1.42 * of which, "hotels and similar establishments"		Nights	..	..	..	..	..
1.43 ♦ For non commercial accommodation services		Days	..	..	..	..	..
1.44 Average expenditure per day		US$	..	..	..	..	..
2. DOMESTIC TOURISM							
Data							
Accommodation							
Total							
2.19 ♦ Guests		('000)	..	..	..	..	..
2.20 ♦ Overnights		('000)	..	..	..	..	..
Hotels and similar establishments							
2.21 ♦ Guests		('000)	1.3	1.3	1.3	1.8	2.1
2.22 ♦ Overnights		('000)	2.9	2.7	2.5	3.4	3.8
4. TOURISM INDUSTRIES							
Data							
Accommodation for visitors in hotels and similar establishments							
Non-monetary data							
4.13 ♦ Number of establishments		Units	..	..	..	..	..
4.14 ♦ Number of rooms		Units	608	646	646	624	590
4.15 ♦ Number of bed-places		Units	1,188	1,263	1,265	1,195	1,127
Indicators							
4.16 Occupancy rate / rooms		Percent	..	..	..	..	..
4.17 Occupancy rate / bed-places		Percent	25.60	25.60	27.90	30.90	30.00
4.18 Average length of stay		Nights	2.20	2.10	2.20	2.20	2.20
4.19 Available capacity (bed-places per 1000 inhabitants)		Units	34.22	36.05	35.79	33.54	31.38
6. COMPLEMENTARY INDICATORS							
Demand							
6.1 Gross travel propensity		Units	..	..	..	..	..
6.2 Carrying capacity (arrivals/population)		Units	1.43	1.57	1.65	1.64	1.46

223

LITHUANIA

Basic data and indicators	Notes	Units	2005	2006	2007	2008	2009
1. INBOUND TOURISM							
Data							
Arrivals							
1.1 Total	(1)	('000)	..	..	4,251	4,491	4,001
1.2 ♦ Overnight visitors (tourists)	(2)	('000)	2,000	2,180	1,486	1,611	1,341
1.3 ♦ Same-day visitors (excursionists)		('000)	..	..	2,765	2,880	2,660
1.4 * of which, cruise passengers		('000)	24	25	37	32	34
Arrivals by region	(3)						
1.5 Total		('000)	682	758	849	909	752
1.6 ♦ Africa		('000)	1	1	1	1	1
1.7 ♦ Americas		('000)	24	26	27	26	20
1.8 ♦ East Asia and the Pacific		('000)	15	16	16	19	18
1.9 ♦ Europe		('000)	623	694	791	849	698
1.10 ♦ Middle East		('000)	..	..	..	..	..
1.11 ♦ South Asia		('000)	..	..	..	..	..
1.12 ♦ Other not classified		('000)	19	21	14	14	15
1.13 * of which, nationals residing abroad		('000)	..	..	..	..	..
Arrivals by main purpose							
1.14 Total		('000)	2,000	2,180	1,486	1,611	1,341
1.15 ♦ Personal		('000)	1,500	1,640	1,062	1,051	856
1.16 * holidays, leisure and recreation		('000)	555	750	448	498	404
1.17 * other personal purposes		('000)	945	890	614	553	452
1.18 ♦ Business and professional		('000)	500	540	424	560	485
Arrivals by mode of transport							
1.19 Total		('000)	2,000	2,180	1,486	1,611	1,341
1.20 ♦ Air		('000)	320	400	517	579	422
1.21 ♦ Water		('000)	95	170	41	39	38
1.22 ♦ Land		('000)	1,585	1,610	928	993	881
1.23 * railway		('000)	625	450	112	94	76
1.24 * road		('000)	960	1,160	816	899	805
1.25 * others		('000)	..	..	..	..	..
Arrivals by form of organization of the trip							
1.26 Total		('000)	..	..	1,486	1,611	1,341
1.27 ♦ Package tour		('000)	136	124	110	102	77
1.28 ♦ Other forms		('000)	..	..	1,376	1,509	1,264
Accommodation							
Total							
1.29 ♦ Guests		('000)	681	759	849	910	752
1.30 ♦ Overnights		('000)	1,762	1,913	2,049	2,056	1,758
Hotels and similar establishments							
1.31 ♦ Guests	(4)	('000)	623	692	767	825	684
1.32 ♦ Overnights	(4)	('000)	1,334	1,451	1,509	1,544	1,323
Expenditure							
1.33 Total		US$ Mn	975	1,077	1,192	1,410	1,183
1.34 ♦ Travel		US$ Mn	921	1,038	1,153	1,343	1,092
1.35 ♦ Passenger transport		US$ Mn	54	39	39	67	91
Expenditure by main purpose of the trip							
1.36 Total		US$ Mn	921	1,038	1,153	1,343	1,092
1.37 ♦ Personal		US$ Mn	750	761	795	884	776
1.38 ♦ Business and professional		US$ Mn	171	277	358	459	316
Indicators							
1.39 Average size of travel party		Persons	..	..	..	..	..
Average length of stay							
1.40 Total		Days	..	..	5.42	4.89	4.52
1.41 ♦ For all commercial accommodation services		Nights	2.59	2.52	2.41	2.26	2.34
1.42 * of which, "hotels and similar establishments"		Nights	2.14	2.10	1.97	1.87	1.93
1.43 ♦ For non commercial accommodation services		Days	..	..	9.93	7.18	5.97
1.44 Average expenditure per day		US$	..	..	80.7	86.7	82.3
2. DOMESTIC TOURISM							
Data							
Trips							
2.1 Total		('000)	26,205	20,644	19,950	19,951	16,825
2.2 ♦ Overnight visitors (tourists)		('000)	2,297	2,485	2,806	2,819	2,431
2.3 ♦ Same-day visitors (excursionists)		('000)	23,908	18,159	17,144	17,132	14,395
Trips by main purpose							
2.4 Total		('000)	2,298	2,485	2,806	2,819	2,431
2.5 ♦ Personal		('000)	2,109	2,233	2,414	2,418	2,164
2.6 * holidays, leisure and recreation		('000)	560	727	865	826	666
2.7 * other personal purposes		('000)	1,549	1,506	1,549	1,592	1,498
2.8 ♦ Business and professional		('000)	189	252	392	401	267

LITHUANIA

Basic data and indicators	Notes	Units	2005	2006	2007	2008	2009
Trips by mode of transport							
2.9 Total		('000)	2,297	2,485	2,806	2,819	2,431
2.10 ♦ Air		('000)	..	..	..	..	..
2.11 ♦ Water		('000)	..	..	..	..	..
2.12 ♦ Land		('000)	2,297	2,485	2,806	2,819	2,431
2.13 * railway		('000)	69	67	58	44	45
2.14 * road		('000)	2,228	2,418	2,748	2,775	2,386
2.15 * others		('000)	..	..	..	..	..
Accommodation							
Total							
2.19 ♦ Guests		('000)	644	781	931	916	675
2.20 ♦ Overnights		('000)	2,489	2,809	3,142	3,021	2,272
Hotels and similar establishments							
2.21 ♦ Guests	(4)	('000)	347	463	567	565	414
2.22 ♦ Overnights	(4)	('000)	728	934	1,082	1,057	755
Indicators							
2.23 Average size of travel party		Persons	..	..	..	..	..
Average length of stay							
2.24 Total		Days	..	..	..	..	..
2.25 ♦ For all commercial accommodation services		Nights	3.86	3.60	3.37	3.30	3.37
2.26 * of which, "hotels and similar establishments"		Nights	2.10	2.02	1.91	1.87	1.82
2.27 ♦ For non commercial accommodation services		Days	1.93	2.08	2.57	2.55	2.32
2.28 Average expenditure per day		US$	15.1	15.6	17.5	19.1	18.5

3. OUTBOUND TOURISM

Data

	Notes	Units	2005	2006	2007	2008	2009
Departures							
3.1 Total		('000)	..	..	..	..	..
3.2 ♦ Overnight visitors (tourists)		('000)	1,633	1,789	1,661	1,757	1,288
3.3 ♦ Same-day visitors (excursionists)		('000)	..	..	..	..	..
Expenditure							
3.4 Total		US$ Mn	757	931	1,168	1,533	1,140
3.5 ♦ Travel		US$ Mn	744	909	1,144	1,497	1,131
3.6 ♦ Passenger transport		US$ Mn	13	22	24	36	9
Expenditure by main purpose of the trip							
3.7 Total		US$ Mn	744	909	1,144	1,497	1,131
3.8 ♦ Personal		US$ Mn	537	642	983	1,289	991
3.9 ♦ Business and professional		US$ Mn	207	267	161	208	140
Indicators							
3.10 Average length of stay		Days	9.63	7.17	6.86	7.14	6.98
3.11 Average expenditure per day		US$	51.9	74.3	94.6	92.7	75.4

4. TOURISM INDUSTRIES

Data

	Notes	Units	2005	2006	2007	2008	2009
Number of establishments							
4.1 Total		Units	3,565	3,684	4,018	4,159	1,108
4.2 ♦ Accommodation for visitors		Units	663	715	748	810	807
4.3 * of which, "hotels and similar establishments"	(4)	Units	331	338	348	365	380
4.4 ♦ Food and beverage serving activities		Units	2,648	2,706	2,994	3,067	..
4.5 ♦ Passenger transportation		Units	..	..	..	..	..
4.6 ♦ Travel agencies and other reservation services activities		Units	254	263	276	282	301
4.7 ♦ Other tourism industries		Units	..	..	..	..	..
Accommodation for visitors in hotels and similar establishments							
Monetary data	(5)						
4.8 ♦ Output		US$ Mn	485.6	614.4	765.5	947.4	..
4.9 ♦ Intermediate consumption		US$ Mn	206.6	240.4	292.8	344.1	..
4.10 ♦ Gross value added		US$ Mn	279.1	374.1	472.6	603.2	..
4.11 ♦ Compensation of employees		US$ Mn	182.6	245.5	316.3	384.1	281.5
4.12 ♦ Gross fixed capital formation		US$ Mn	78.6	130.3	108.8	115.6	50.6
Non-monetary data	(4)						
4.13 ♦ Number of establishments		Units	331	338	348	365	380
4.14 ♦ Number of rooms		Units	10,134	10,843	10,973	11,141	11,962
4.15 ♦ Number of bed-places		Units	19,940	21,504	21,871	22,024	23,839
Indicators							
4.16 Occupancy rate / rooms		Percent	40.49	42.10	46.29	44.90	34.03
4.17 Occupancy rate / bed-places		Percent	31.56	32.94	36.04	34.18	25.46
4.18 Average length of stay		Nights	2.14	2.10	1.97	1.87	1.93
4.19 Available capacity (bed-places per 1000 inhabitants)		Units	5.82	6.32	6.46	6.54	7.12

LITHUANIA

Basic data and indicators	Notes	Units	2005	2006	2007	2008	2009
Travel agencies and other reservation service activities							
Monetary data							
4.20 ♦ Output		US$ Mn	170.0	208.5	333.0	399.5	..
4.21 ♦ Intermediate consumption		US$ Mn	81.1	129.2	200.9	237.9	..
4.22 ♦ Gross value added		US$ Mn	88.9	79.4	131.9	161.4	..
4.23 ♦ Compensation of employees		US$ Mn	14.7	18.9	25.9	36.3	..
4.24 ♦ Gross fixed capital formation		US$ Mn	..	..	..	..	..
Non-monetary data							
♦ Domestic trips							
4.25 * with package tour		Percent	..	..	..	..	..
4.26 * without package tour		Percent	..	..	..	..	..
♦ Inbound trips							
4.27 * with package tour		Percent	..	..	7.4	6.3	5.7
4.28 * without package tour		Percent	..	..	92.6	93.7	94.3
♦ Outbound trips							
4.29 * with package tour		Percent	..	..	15.2	18.1	17.4
4.30 * without package tour		Percent	..	..	84.8	81.9	82.6
5. EMPLOYMENT							
Data							
Number of employees by tourism industries							
5.1 Total		('000)	36.5	41.3	43.7	46.6	42.6
5.2 ♦ Accommodation services for visitors (hotels and similar establishments)		('000)	5.8	6.4	7.0	7.5	6.5
5.3 ♦ Other accommodation services		('000)	4.3	4.3	4.5	4.7	4.1
5.4 ♦ Food and beverage serving activities		('000)	8.0	12.4	10.9	12.8	12.5
5.5 ♦ Passenger transportation		('000)	9.5	8.1	9.2	11.3	10.0
5.6 ♦ Travel agencies and other reservation services activities		('000)	2.0	2.2	2.4	2.6	2.3
5.7 ♦ Other tourism industries		('000)	6.9	7.9	9.7	7.7	7.2
6. COMPLEMENTARY INDICATORS							
Demand							
6.1 Gross travel propensity		Units	0.5	0.5	0.5	0.5	0.4
6.2 Carrying capacity (arrivals/population)		Units	1.26	1.37	0.44	0.48	0.40
Macroeconomic indicators related to international tourism							
6.3 Inbound tourism expenditure over GDP		Percent	3.8	3.6	3.0	3.0	3.2
6.4 Outbound tourism expenditure over GDP		Percent	2.9	3.1	3.0	3.3	3.1
6.5 Tourism balance (inbound minus outbound tourism expenditure) over GDP		Percent	0.8	0.5	0.1	-0.3	0.1
6.6 Tourism openness (inbound plus outbound tourism expenditure) over GDP		Percent	6.7	6.7	6.0	6.2	6.3
6.7 Tourism coverage (inbound over outbound tourism expenditure)		Percent	128.9	115.6	102.1	91.9	103.8
6.8 Inbound tourism expenditure over exports of goods		Percent	8.3	7.6	6.9	5.9	7.2
6.9 Inbound tourism expenditure over exports of services		Percent	31.4	29.7	29.6	29.2	31.2
6.10 Inbound tourism expenditure over exports of goods and services		Percent	6.6	6.1	5.6	4.9	5.8
6.11 Inbound tourism expenditure over current account credits		Percent	6.0	5.4	5.0	4.4	5.0
6.12 Outbound tourism expenditure over imports of goods		Percent	5.2	5.1	5.1	5.2	6.5
6.13 Outbound tourism expenditure over imports of services		Percent	36.8	36.7	34.4	36.1	38.6
6.14 Outbound tourism expenditure over imports of goods and services		Percent	4.5	4.5	4.4	4.5	5.6
6.15 Outbound tourism expenditure over current account debits		Percent	4.2	4.0	3.9	4.1	5.1

LUXEMBOURG

Basic data and indicators	Notes	Units	2005	2006	2007	2008	2009
1. INBOUND TOURISM							
Data							
Arrivals							
1.1 Total		('000)	..	..	..	..	..
1.2 ♦ Overnight visitors (tourists)	(1)	('000)	913	908	917	879	849
1.3 ♦ Same-day visitors (excursionists)		('000)	..	..	..	..	..
1.4 * of which, cruise passengers		('000)	..	..	..	..	..
Arrivals by region	(1)						
1.5 Total		('000)	912	908	917	879	849
1.6 ♦ Africa		('000)	..	..	..	..	..
1.7 ♦ Americas		('000)	32	35	33	32	29
1.8 ♦ East Asia and the Pacific		('000)	..	..	..	..	..
1.9 ♦ Europe		('000)	840	831	841	808	781
1.10 ♦ Middle East		('000)	..	..	..	..	..
1.11 ♦ South Asia		('000)	..	..	..	..	..
1.12 ♦ Other not classified		('000)	40	42	43	39	39
1.13 * of which, nationals residing abroad		('000)	..	..	..	..	..
Accommodation							
Total							
1.29 ♦ Guests	(2)	('000)	913	908	917	879	849
1.30 ♦ Overnights	(2)	('000)	2,465	2,414	2,341	2,259	2,076
Hotels and similar establishments							
1.31 ♦ Guests	(3)	('000)	667	673	706	675	650
1.32 ♦ Overnights	(3)	('000)	1,275	1,284	1,360	1,297	1,185
Expenditure							
1.33 Total		US$ Mn	..	..	..	..	..
1.34 ♦ Travel		US$ Mn	3,612	3,636	4,032	4,491	4,180
1.35 ♦ Passenger transport		US$ Mn	..	..	..	..	..
Indicators							
1.39 Average size of travel party		Persons	..	..	..	..	..
Average length of stay							
1.40 Total		Days	..	..	..	..	..
1.41 ♦ For all commercial accommodation services		Nights	2.70	2.70	2.60	2.60	2.40
1.42 * of which, "hotels and similar establishments"		Nights	..	..	1.90	1.90	1.80
1.43 ♦ For non commercial accommodation services		Days	..	..	..	..	..
1.44 Average expenditure per day		US$	..	..	..	..	..
2. DOMESTIC TOURISM							
Data							
Accommodation							
Total							
2.19 ♦ Guests	(2)	('000)	..	..	64	59	59
2.20 ♦ Overnights	(2)	('000)	246	223	207	192	180
Hotels and similar establishments							
2.21 ♦ Guests	(3)	('000)	29	29	31	30	30
2.22 ♦ Overnights	(3)	('000)	85	77	78	78	80
Indicators							
2.23 Average size of travel party		Persons	..	..	..	..	..
Average length of stay							
2.24 Total		Days	..	..	..	..	..
2.25 ♦ For all commercial accommodation services		Nights	3.80	3.60	3.20	3.20	3.10
2.26 * of which, "hotels and similar establishments"		Nights	..	..	2.50	2.60	2.70
2.27 ♦ For non commercial accommodation services		Days	..	..	..	..	..
2.28 Average expenditure per day		US$	..	..	..	..	..
3. OUTBOUND TOURISM							
Data							
Expenditure							
3.4 Total		US$ Mn	..	..	..	..	..
3.5 ♦ Travel		US$ Mn	2,977	3,138	3,476	3,837	3,650
3.6 ♦ Passenger transport		US$ Mn	..	..	..	..	..

LUXEMBOURG

Basic data and indicators	Notes	Units	2005	2006	2007	2008	2009
4. TOURISM INDUSTRIES							
Data							
Number of establishments							
4.1 Total		Units	..	..	..	..	..
4.2 ♦ Accommodation for visitors		Units	..	..	..	..	..
4.3 * of which, "hotels and similar establishments"		Units	293	277	273	267	261
4.4 ♦ Food and beverage serving activities		Units	..	..	..	..	..
4.5 ♦ Passenger transportation		Units	..	..	..	..	..
4.6 ♦ Travel agencies and other reservation services activities		Units	..	..	..	..	..
4.7 ♦ Other tourism industries		Units	..	..	..	..	..
Accommodation for visitors in hotels and similar establishments							
Non-monetary data							
4.13 ♦ Number of establishments		Units	293	277	273	267	261
4.14 ♦ Number of rooms		Units	7,516	7,414	7,639	7,591	7,751
4.15 ♦ Number of bed-places		Units	..	..	14,559	14,445	14,709
Indicators							
4.16 Occupancy rate / rooms		Percent	..	..	59.90	54.20	48.80
4.17 Occupancy rate / bed-places		Percent	29.50	29.90	31.60	28.50	25.70
4.18 Average length of stay		Nights	2.00	1.90	1.90	2.00	1.90
4.19 Available capacity (bed-places per 1000 inhabitants)		Units	..	..	30.33	29.56	29.54
6. COMPLEMENTARY INDICATORS							
Demand							
6.1 Gross travel propensity		Units	..	..	..	..	..
6.2 Carrying capacity (arrivals/population)		Units	1.96	1.92	1.91	1.80	1.71
Macroeconomic indicators related to international tourism							
6.3 Inbound tourism expenditure over GDP		Percent	9.6	8.5	7.9	7.8	7.8
6.4 Outbound tourism expenditure over GDP		Percent	7.9	7.3	6.8	6.7	6.9
6.5 Tourism balance (inbound minus outbound tourism expenditure) over GDP		Percent	1.7	1.2	1.1	1.1	0.9
6.6 Tourism openness (inbound plus outbound tourism expenditure) over GDP		Percent	17.5	15.8	14.6	14.5	14.7
6.7 Tourism coverage (inbound over outbound tourism expenditure)		Percent	121.3	115.9	115.8	116.9	113.5
6.8 Inbound tourism expenditure over exports of goods		Percent	24.7	22.0	22.1	20.9	26.5
6.9 Inbound tourism expenditure over exports of services		Percent	8.8	7.2	6.1	6.3	6.7
6.10 Inbound tourism expenditure over exports of goods and services		Percent	6.5	5.4	4.8	4.8	5.4
6.11 Inbound tourism expenditure over current account credits		Percent	2.3	1.8	1.6	1.5	1.8
6.12 Outbound tourism expenditure over imports of goods		Percent	15.8	15.1	15.1	13.9	18.3
6.13 Outbound tourism expenditure over imports of services		Percent	12.1	10.5	9.2	9.3	10.0
6.14 Outbound tourism expenditure over imports of goods and services		Percent	6.9	6.2	5.7	5.6	6.5
6.15 Outbound tourism expenditure over current account debits		Percent	1.9	1.6	1.4	1.3	1.6

MACAO, CHINA

Basic data and indicators	Notes	Units	2005	2006	2007	2008	2009
1. INBOUND TOURISM							
Data							
Arrivals	(1)(2)						
1.1 Total		('000)	18,711	21,998	26,993	22,933	21,753
1.2 ♦ Overnight visitors (tourists)		('000)	9,014	10,683	12,942	10,610	10,402
1.3 ♦ Same-day visitors (excursionists)		('000)	9,697	11,315	14,051	12,323	11,351
1.4 * of which, cruise passengers		('000)	..	..	..	..	..
Arrivals by region	(1)						
1.5 Total		('000)	18,711	21,998	26,993	22,933	21,753
1.6 ♦ Africa		('000)	8	13	31	22	17
1.7 ♦ Americas		('000)	183	219	306	313	279
1.8 ♦ East Asia and the Pacific	(2)	('000)	18,321	21,526	26,325	22,223	21,078
1.9 ♦ Europe		('000)	161	188	252	266	248
1.10 ♦ Middle East		('000)	3	4	7	8	8
1.11 ♦ South Asia		('000)	32	43	64	95	118
1.12 ♦ Other not classified		('000)	3	5	8	6	5
1.13 * of which, nationals residing abroad		('000)	..	..	..	..	..
Arrivals by main purpose	(1)(2)						
1.14 Total		('000)	18,711	21,999	26,992	22,933	21,753
1.15 ♦ Personal		('000)	15,717	19,139	24,023	20,410	19,578
1.16 * holidays, leisure and recreation		('000)	13,098	16,059	21,324	17,200	16,750
1.17 * other personal purposes		('000)	2,619	3,080	2,699	3,210	2,828
1.18 ♦ Business and professional		('000)	2,994	2,860	2,969	2,523	2,175
Arrivals by mode of transport	(1)(2)						
1.19 Total		('000)	18,711	21,998	26,993	22,933	21,753
1.20 ♦ Air	(3)	('000)	1,040	1,236	1,474	1,665	1,619
1.21 ♦ Water		('000)	6,720	7,656	8,980	9,173	8,685
1.22 ♦ Land		('000)	10,951	13,106	16,539	12,095	11,449
1.23 * railway		('000)	..	..	..	..	..
1.24 * road		('000)	10,951	13,106	16,539	12,095	11,449
1.25 * others		('000)	..	..	..	..	..
Arrivals by form of organization of the trip							
1.26 Total		('000)	18,711	21,998	26,993	22,933	21,753
1.27 ♦ Package tour		('000)	2,676	2,926	4,234	4,902	4,648
1.28 ♦ Other forms		('000)	16,035	19,072	22,759	18,031	17,105
Accommodation							
Total							
1.29 ♦ Guests		('000)	..	..	..	..	..
1.30 ♦ Overnights		('000)	..	..	..	..	..
Hotels and similar establishments							
1.31 ♦ Guests		('000)	3,903	4,429	5,442	6,194	6,398
1.32 ♦ Overnights		('000)	4,563	5,129	6,942	8,605	9,134
Expenditure							
1.33 Total		US$ Mn	8,016	9,755	13,404	17,096	..
1.34 ♦ Travel		US$ Mn	7,759	9,449	13,076	16,761	17,886
1.35 ♦ Passenger transport		US$ Mn	257	306	328	335	..
Expenditure by main purpose of the trip							
1.36 Total		US$ Mn	7,759	9,449	13,076	16,761	17,886
1.37 ♦ Personal		US$ Mn	6,523	8,227	11,644	14,925	16,102
1.38 ♦ Business and professional		US$ Mn	1,236	1,222	1,432	1,836	1,784
Indicators							
1.39 Average size of travel party		Persons	..	..	..	..	..
Average length of stay							
1.40 Total		Days	1.10	1.10	1.10	1.10	1.10
1.41 ♦ For all commercial accommodation services		Nights	1.21	1.20	1.33	1.45	1.49
1.42 * of which, "hotels and similar establishments"		Nights	1.21	1.20	1.33	1.45	1.49
1.43 ♦ For non commercial accommodation services		Days	..	..	..	..	..
1.44 Average expenditure per day		US$	166.4	185.6	181.2	187.8	188.7
2. DOMESTIC TOURISM							
Data							
Accommodation							
Total							
2.19 ♦ Guests		('000)	..	..	..	..	..
2.20 ♦ Overnights		('000)	..	..	..	..	..
Hotels and similar establishments							
2.21 ♦ Guests		('000)	218	252	298	344	316
2.22 ♦ Overnights		('000)	281	338	450	443	503

MACAO, CHINA

Basic data and indicators	Notes	Units	2005	2006	2007	2008	2009
Indicators							
2.23 Average size of travel party		Persons	..	..	..	..	..
Average length of stay							
2.24 Total		Days	..	..	..	..	..
2.25 ♦ For all commercial accommodation services		Nights	1.30	1.40	1.25	1.35	1.68
2.26 * of which, "hotels and similar establishments"		Nights	..	..	..	..	..
2.27 ♦ For non commercial accommodation services		Days	..	..	..	..	..
2.28 Average expenditure per day		US$	..	..	..	..	..

3. OUTBOUND TOURISM

Data

Departures

	Notes	Units	2005	2006	2007	2008	2009
3.1 Total		('000)	629	645	599	606	671
3.2 ♦ Overnight visitors (tourists)	(4)	('000)	295	272	212	229	206
3.3 ♦ Same-day visitors (excursionists)		('000)	..	..	..	..	..
Expenditure							
3.4 Total		US$ Mn	428	452	537	621	..
3.5 ♦ Travel		US$ Mn	358	378	463	554	510
3.6 ♦ Passenger transport		US$ Mn	70	74	74	67	..
Expenditure by main purpose of the trip							
3.7 Total		US$ Mn	358	378	463	554	510
3.8 ♦ Personal		US$ Mn	351	366	446	534	492
3.9 ♦ Business and professional		US$ Mn	7	12	17	20	18

4. TOURISM INDUSTRIES

Data

Number of establishments

	Notes	Units	2005	2006	2007	2008	2009
4.1 Total		Units	..	..	3,780	3,968	..
4.2 ♦ Accommodation for visitors		Units	..	..	..	..	..
4.3 * of which, "hotels and similar establishments"	(5)	Units	75	80	82	86	91
4.4 ♦ Food and beverage serving activities		Units	..	..	1,529	1,568	..
4.5 ♦ Passenger transportation		Units	..	1,886	2,012	2,159	..
4.6 ♦ Travel agencies and other reservation services activities		Units	..	145	157	155	169
4.7 ♦ Other tourism industries		Units	..	..	..	..	..

Accommodation for visitors in hotels and similar establishments

Monetary data

	Notes	Units	2005	2006	2007	2008	2009
4.8 ♦ Output		US$ Mn	..	452.2	834.8	1,274.4	1,358.3
4.9 ♦ Intermediate consumption		US$ Mn	..	279.5	546.6	751.9	728.8
4.10 ♦ Gross value added		US$ Mn	..	198.2	296.3	545.7	649.9
4.11 ♦ Compensation of employees		US$ Mn	..	185.4	345.7	478.3	467.5
4.12 ♦ Gross fixed capital formation		US$ Mn	..	1,200.2	1,770.7	919.4	321.1

Non-monetary data (5)

	Notes	Units	2005	2006	2007	2008	2009
4.13 ♦ Number of establishments		Units	75	80	82	86	91
4.14 ♦ Number of rooms		Units	10,832	12,978	16,148	17,533	19,259
4.15 ♦ Number of bed-places		Units	21,460	26,851	36,467	48,565	52,799

Indicators

	Notes	Units	2005	2006	2007	2008	2009
4.16 Occupancy rate / rooms		Percent	70.93	72.23	77.18	74.27	71.40
4.17 Occupancy rate / bed-places		Percent	..	63.86	68.59	59.50	52.73
4.18 Average length of stay		Nights	1.22	1.21	1.34	1.44	1.50
4.19 Available capacity (bed-places per 1000 inhabitants)		Units	44.01	52.30	67.77	88.43	97.38

Travel agencies and other reservation service activities

Monetary data

	Notes	Units	2005	2006	2007	2008	2009
4.20 ♦ Output		US$ Mn	..	300.9	418.0	450.1	447.8
4.21 ♦ Intermediate consumption		US$ Mn	..	270.9	355.8	390.7	383.5
4.22 ♦ Gross value added		US$ Mn	..	29.9	62.3	59.0	63.7
4.23 ♦ Compensation of employees		US$ Mn	..	17.5	27.4	40.0	41.9
4.24 ♦ Gross fixed capital formation		US$ Mn	..	12.1	7.3	8.8	4.8

Non-monetary data

	Notes	Units	2005	2006	2007	2008	2009
♦ Domestic trips							
4.25 * with package tour		Percent	..	..	..	..	..
4.26 * without package tour		Percent	..	..	..	..	..
♦ Inbound trips							
4.27 * with package tour		Percent	..	13.3	15.7	21.4	21.4
4.28 * without package tour		Percent	..	86.7	84.3	78.6	78.6
♦ Outbound trips							
4.29 * with package tour		Percent	..	42.3	35.4	37.8	30.8
4.30 * without package tour		Percent	..	57.7	64.6	62.2	69.2

MACAO, CHINA

Basic data and indicators	Notes	Units	2005	2006	2007	2008	2009
5. EMPLOYMENT							
Data							
Number of employees by tourism industries							
5.1 Total		('000)	25.6	26.0	54.0	61.2	29.2
5.2 ♦ Accommodation services for visitors (hotels and similar establishments)		('000)	..	14.2	23.4	26.5	26.3
5.3 ♦ Other accommodation services		('000)	..	..	..	..	..
5.4 ♦ Food and beverage serving activities		('000)	14.6	..	16.9	19.0	..
5.5 ♦ Passenger transportation		('000)	9.4	10.1	11.4	12.9	..
5.6 ♦ Travel agencies and other reservation services activities		('000)	1.6	1.7	2.3	2.8	2.9
5.7 ♦ Other tourism industries		('000)	..	..	..	..	..
6. COMPLEMENTARY INDICATORS							
Demand							
6.1 Gross travel propensity		Units	..	..	..	..	..
6.2 Carrying capacity (arrivals/population)		Units	18.49	21.37	25.22	20.16	19.34
Macroeconomic indicators related to international tourism							
6.3 Inbound tourism expenditure over GDP		Percent	69.7	68.6	71.7	79.0	..
6.4 Outbound tourism expenditure over GDP		Percent	3.7	3.2	2.9	2.9	..
6.5 Tourism balance (inbound minus outbound tourism expenditure) over GDP		Percent	65.9	65.5	68.8	76.1	..
6.6 Tourism openness (inbound plus outbound tourism expenditure) over GDP		Percent	73.4	71.8	74.6	81.9	..
6.7 Tourism coverage (inbound over outbound tourism expenditure)		Percent	1,874.2	2,157.7	2,494.8	2,753.3	..
6.8 Inbound tourism expenditure over exports of goods		Percent	323.5	381.2	526.8	853.1	..
6.9 Inbound tourism expenditure over exports of services		Percent	95.5	96.0	96.6	97.6	..
6.10 Inbound tourism expenditure over exports of goods and services		Percent	73.7	76.7	81.6	87.6	..
6.11 Inbound tourism expenditure over current account credits		Percent	68.2	68.4	72.6	80.4	..
6.12 Outbound tourism expenditure over imports of goods		Percent	8.3	7.2	7.3	8.6	..
6.13 Outbound tourism expenditure over imports of services		Percent	26.8	23.4	19.7	17.5	..
6.14 Outbound tourism expenditure over imports of goods and services		Percent	6.4	5.5	5.3	5.8	..
6.15 Outbound tourism expenditure over current account debits		Percent	5.0	3.9	4.2	4.0	..

MADAGASCAR

Basic data and indicators	Notes	Units	2005	2006	2007	2008	2009
1. INBOUND TOURISM							
Data							
Arrivals							
1.1 Total		('000)	..	..	..	..	..
1.2 ♦ Overnight visitors (tourists)	(1)	('000)	277	312	344	375	163
1.3 ♦ Same-day visitors (excursionists)		('000)	..	..	..	..	..
1.4 * of which, cruise passengers		('000)	..	..	..	..	..
Arrivals by region	(1)						
1.5 Total		('000)	277	312	344	375	163
1.6 ♦ Africa		('000)	52	59	64	84	37
1.7 ♦ Americas		('000)	14	16	14	11	5
1.8 ♦ East Asia and the Pacific		('000)	6	7	14	16	6
1.9 ♦ Europe		('000)	203	228	247	262	111
1.10 ♦ Middle East		('000)	..	..	..	..	..
1.11 ♦ South Asia		('000)	..	..	..	..	..
1.12 ♦ Other not classified		('000)	2	2	5	2	4
1.13 * of which, nationals residing abroad		('000)	..	..	..	..	..
Arrivals by main purpose	(1)						
1.14 Total		('000)	277	312	344	375	163
1.15 ♦ Personal		('000)	197	222	245	267	130
1.16 * holidays, leisure and recreation		('000)	172	194	213	232	106
1.17 * other personal purposes		('000)	25	28	32	35	24
1.18 ♦ Business and professional		('000)	80	90	99	108	33
Arrivals by mode of transport							
1.19 Total		('000)	277	312	344	375	163
1.20 ♦ Air		('000)	277	312	344	375	163
1.21 ♦ Water		('000)	..	..	..	..	..
1.22 ♦ Land		('000)	..	..	..	..	..
1.23 * railway		('000)	..	..	..	..	..
1.24 * road		('000)	..	..	..	..	..
1.25 * others		('000)	..	..	..	..	..
Accommodation							
Total							
1.29 ♦ Guests		('000)	..	..	..	..	..
1.30 ♦ Overnights		('000)	..	..	..	..	..
Hotels and similar establishments							
1.31 ♦ Guests		('000)	..	..	..	..	..
1.32 ♦ Overnights		('000)	5,221	5,299	5,608	5,815	2,413
Expenditure							
1.33 Total		US$ Mn	290	386	506	620	518
1.34 ♦ Travel		US$ Mn	183	237	262	351	308
1.35 ♦ Passenger transport		US$ Mn	107	149	244	269	210
Expenditure by main purpose of the trip							
1.36 Total		US$ Mn	183.4	..	..	..	..
1.37 ♦ Personal		US$ Mn	183	..	..	..	..
1.38 ♦ Business and professional		US$ Mn	0.4	..	..	..	..
Indicators							
1.39 Average size of travel party		Persons	..	..	..	..	..
Average length of stay							
1.40 Total		Days	..	..	..	..	..
1.41 ♦ For all commercial accommodation services		Nights	20.00	17.00	17.00	17.00	20.00
1.42 * of which, "hotels and similar establishments"		Nights	..	..	..	..	..
1.43 ♦ For non commercial accommodation services		Days	..	..	..	..	..
1.44 Average expenditure per day		US$	..	..	..	..	..
3. OUTBOUND TOURISM							
Data							
Expenditure							
3.4 Total		US$ Mn	80	..	..	..	..
3.5 ♦ Travel		US$ Mn	74	86	94	143	123
3.6 ♦ Passenger transport		US$ Mn	6	..	..	..	..
Expenditure by main purpose of the trip							
3.7 Total		US$ Mn	73.3	..	..	..	..
3.8 ♦ Personal		US$ Mn	73	..	..	..	..
3.9 ♦ Business and professional		US$ Mn	0.3	..	..	..	..

MADAGASCAR

Basic data and indicators	Notes	Units	2005	2006	2007	2008	2009
4. TOURISM INDUSTRIES							
Data							
Number of establishments							
4.1 Total		Units	..	..	..	..	..
4.2 ♦ Accommodation for visitors		Units	..	..	..	..	..
4.3 * of which, "hotels and similar establishments"		Units	937	1,015	1,181	1,292	1,396
4.4 ♦ Food and beverage serving activities		Units	..	..	..	..	..
4.5 ♦ Passenger transportation		Units	..	..	..	..	..
4.6 ♦ Travel agencies and other reservation services activities		Units	709	755	825	861	902
4.7 ♦ Other tourism industries		Units	..	..	..	..	..
Accommodation for visitors in hotels and similar establishments							
Non-monetary data							
4.13 ♦ Number of establishments		Units	937	1,015	1,181	1,292	1,396
4.14 ♦ Number of rooms		Units	10,879	11,872	13,340	14,443	16,055
4.15 ♦ Number of bed-places		Units	18,494	20,182	22,678	23,534	25,688
Indicators							
4.16 Occupancy rate / rooms		Percent	57.00	57.00	63.00	64.00	39.00
4.17 Occupancy rate / bed-places		Percent	..	..	..	..	..
4.18 Average length of stay		Nights	4.00	4.00	4.00	4.00	4.00
4.19 Available capacity (bed-places per 1000 inhabitants)		Units	1.05	1.11	1.22	1.23	1.31
5. EMPLOYMENT							
Data							
Number of employees by tourism industries							
5.1 Total		('000)	21.2	22.3	24.2	25.7	27.3
5.2 ♦ Accommodation services for visitors (hotels and similar establishments)		('000)	16.9	17.8	19.4	20.6	22.0
5.3 ♦ Other accommodation services		('000)	..	..	..	..	..
5.4 ♦ Food and beverage serving activities		('000)	..	..	..	..	..
5.5 ♦ Passenger transportation		('000)	..	..	..	..	..
5.6 ♦ Travel agencies and other reservation services activities		('000)	4.3	4.5	4.9	5.0	5.3
5.7 ♦ Other tourism industries		('000)	..	..	..	..	..
6. COMPLEMENTARY INDICATORS							
Demand							
6.1 Gross travel propensity		Units	..	..	..	..	..
6.2 Carrying capacity (arrivals/population)		Units	0.02	0.02	0.02	0.02	0.01
Macroeconomic indicators related to international tourism							
6.3 Inbound tourism expenditure over GDP		Percent	5.8	..	..	..	..
6.4 Outbound tourism expenditure over GDP		Percent	1.6	..	..	..	..
6.5 Tourism balance (inbound minus outbound tourism expenditure) over GDP		Percent	4.2	..	..	..	..
6.6 Tourism openness (inbound plus outbound tourism expenditure) over GDP		Percent	7.3	..	..	..	..
6.7 Tourism coverage (inbound over outbound tourism expenditure)		Percent	365.7	..	..	..	..
6.8 Inbound tourism expenditure over exports of goods		Percent	34.7	..	..	..	..
6.9 Inbound tourism expenditure over exports of services		Percent	58.2	..	..	..	..
6.10 Inbound tourism expenditure over exports of goods and services		Percent	21.8	..	..	..	..
6.11 Inbound tourism expenditure over current account credits		Percent	17.7	..	..	..	..
6.12 Outbound tourism expenditure over imports of goods		Percent	5.6	..	..	..	..
6.13 Outbound tourism expenditure over imports of services		Percent	12.9	..	..	..	..
6.14 Outbound tourism expenditure over imports of goods and services		Percent	3.9	..	..	..	..
6.15 Outbound tourism expenditure over current account debits		Percent	3.6	..	..	..	..

MALAWI

Basic data and indicators	Notes	Units	2005	2006	2007	2008	2009
1. INBOUND TOURISM							
Data							
Arrivals							
1.1 Total		('000)	..	..	..	..	..
1.2 ♦ Overnight visitors (tourists)	(1)	('000)	438	638	735	742	755
1.3 ♦ Same-day visitors (excursionists)		('000)	..	..	..	..	..
1.4 * of which, cruise passengers		('000)	..	..	..	..	..
Arrivals by region	(1)						
1.5 Total		('000)	438	638	734	742	755
1.6 ♦ Africa		('000)	337	484	559	574	574
1.7 ♦ Americas		('000)	19	36	47	45	46
1.8 ♦ East Asia and the Pacific		('000)	9	10	13	12	12
1.9 ♦ Europe		('000)	60	94	99	98	105
1.10 ♦ Middle East		('000)	..	6	2	2	2
1.11 ♦ South Asia		('000)	10	..	13	10	14
1.12 ♦ Other not classified		('000)	3	8	1	1	2
1.13 * of which, nationals residing abroad		('000)	..	..	..	..	..
Arrivals by main purpose	(1)						
1.14 Total		('000)	437	638	734	742	755
1.15 ♦ Personal		('000)	210	326	429	370	373
1.16 * holidays, leisure and recreation		('000)	114	168	212	179	245
1.17 * other personal purposes		('000)	96	158	217	191	128
1.18 ♦ Business and professional		('000)	227	312	305	372	382
Arrivals by mode of transport	(1)						
1.19 Total		('000)	438	638	735	742	755
1.20 ♦ Air		('000)	106	201	232	227	251
1.21 ♦ Water		('000)	7	5	9	15	21
1.22 ♦ Land		('000)	325	432	494	500	483
1.23 * railway		('000)	8	6	10	13	15
1.24 * road		('000)	317	426	484	487	468
1.25 * others		('000)	..	..	..	..	..
Accommodation							
Total							
1.29 ♦ Guests		('000)	..	..	..	..	..
1.30 ♦ Overnights		('000)	3,372	5,570	5,460	5,864	5,167
Hotels and similar establishments							
1.31 ♦ Guests		('000)	..	..	..	..	..
1.32 ♦ Overnights		('000)	..	..	..	..	..
Expenditure	(2)						
1.33 Total		US$ Mn	43	43	48	..	..
1.34 ♦ Travel		US$ Mn	24	24	27	..	..
1.35 ♦ Passenger transport		US$ Mn	19	19	21	..	..
Indicators							
1.39 Average size of travel party		Persons	..	..	..	..	..
Average length of stay							
1.40 Total		Days	..	..	..	..	..
1.41 ♦ For all commercial accommodation services		Nights	8.00	9.80	7.70	8.40	8.00
1.42 * of which, "hotels and similar establishments"		Nights	..	..	..	..	..
1.43 ♦ For non commercial accommodation services		Days	..	..	..	..	..
1.44 Average expenditure per day		US$	..	..	..	..	..
3. OUTBOUND TOURISM							
Data							
Expenditure	(2)						
3.4 Total		US$ Mn	75	75	84	..	..
3.5 ♦ Travel		US$ Mn	65	65	73	..	..
3.6 ♦ Passenger transport		US$ Mn	10	10	11	..	..
4. TOURISM INDUSTRIES							
Indicators							
4.16 Occupancy rate / rooms		Percent	..	..	..	..	..
4.17 Occupancy rate / bed-places		Percent	54.00	60.48	55.00	58.00	..
4.18 Average length of stay		Nights	8.00	9.80	7.70	8.40	8.00
4.19 Available capacity (bed-places per 1000 inhabitants)		Units	..	..	..	..	..
6. COMPLEMENTARY INDICATORS							
Demand							
6.1 Gross travel propensity		Units	..	..	..	..	..
6.2 Carrying capacity (arrivals/population)		Units	0.03	0.05	0.05	0.05	0.05

MALAYSIA

Basic data and indicators	Notes	Units	2005	2006	2007	2008	2009
1. INBOUND TOURISM							
Data							
Arrivals							
1.1 Total		('000)	24,209	25,298	28,325	25,321	31,509
1.2 ♦ Overnight visitors (tourists)	(1)	('000)	16,431	17,547	20,973	22,052	23,646
1.3 ♦ Same-day visitors (excursionists)		('000)	7,778	7,751	7,352	3,269	7,863
1.4 * of which, cruise passengers		('000)	..	..	..	..	..
Arrivals by region	(1)						
1.5 Total		('000)	16,430	17,546	20,974	22,052	23,646
1.6 ♦ Africa		('000)	128	157	308	127	85
1.7 ♦ Americas		('000)	275	312	472	345	346
1.8 ♦ East Asia and the Pacific		('000)	14,686	15,478	17,657	18,973	20,830
1.9 ♦ Europe		('000)	618	673	830	1,026	1,166
1.10 ♦ Middle East		('000)	145	174	225	216	197
1.11 ♦ South Asia		('000)	321	390	687	826	930
1.12 ♦ Other not classified		('000)	257	362	795	539	92
1.13 * of which, nationals residing abroad		('000)	..	..	..	..	..
Arrivals by main purpose	(2)(3)						
1.14 Total		('000)	14,644	16,236	20,973	22,052	..
1.15 ♦ Personal		('000)	12,361	13,932	17,986	18,921	..
1.16 * holidays, leisure and recreation		('000)	5,026	5,337	6,884	7,211	..
1.17 * other personal purposes		('000)	7,335	8,595	11,102	11,710	..
1.18 ♦ Business and professional		('000)	2,283	2,304	2,987	3,131	..
Arrivals by mode of transport	(4)						
1.19 Total		('000)	15,420	16,236	19,217	19,762	..
1.20 ♦ Air		('000)	2,846	3,348	4,032	4,883	..
1.21 ♦ Water		('000)	449	523	1,005	832	..
1.22 ♦ Land		('000)	12,125	12,365	14,180	14,047	..
1.23 * railway		('000)	247	196	136	133	..
1.24 * road		('000)	11,878	12,169	14,044	13,914	..
1.25 * others		('000)	..	..	..	..	..
Accommodation							
Total							
1.29 ♦ Guests		('000)	..	..	..	..	..
1.30 ♦ Overnights		('000)	..	..	..	..	..
Hotels and similar establishments							
1.31 ♦ Guests		('000)	21,448	22,457	25,395	28,276	28,443
1.32 ♦ Overnights		('000)	..	..	..	..	..
Expenditure							
1.33 Total		US$ Mn	10,389	12,280	17,948	18,553	17,231
1.34 ♦ Travel		US$ Mn	8,846	10,427	14,050	15,293	15,798
1.35 ♦ Passenger transport		US$ Mn	1,543	1,853	3,898	3,260	1,433
Expenditure by main purpose of the trip							
1.36 Total		US$ Mn	8,846	10,427	14,049	15,293	15,797
1.37 ♦ Personal		US$ Mn	108	180	241	237	215
1.38 ♦ Business and professional		US$ Mn	8,738	10,247	13,808	15,056	15,582
Indicators							
1.39 Average size of travel party		Persons	..	..	..	..	..
Average length of stay							
1.40 Total		Days	..	..	..	..	..
1.41 ♦ For all commercial accommodation services		Nights	6.10	6.20	6.30	6.40	6.70
1.42 * of which, "hotels and similar establishments"		Nights	..	..	..	..	..
1.43 ♦ For non commercial accommodation services		Days	..	..	..	..	..
1.44 Average expenditure per day		US$	..	..	..	..	..
2. DOMESTIC TOURISM							
Data							
Trips	(5)						
2.1 Total		('000)	..	..	..	63,283	90,505
2.2 ♦ Overnight visitors (tourists)		('000)	..	..	..	29,380	35,524
2.3 ♦ Same-day visitors (excursionists)		('000)	..	..	..	33,903	54,981
Trips by main purpose	(5)						
2.4 Total		('000)	..	..	..	63,283	90,505
2.5 ♦ Personal		('000)	..	..	..	60,751	86,885
2.6 * holidays, leisure and recreation		('000)	..	..	..	10,125	10,861
2.7 * other personal purposes		('000)	..	..	..	50,626	76,024
2.8 ♦ Business and professional		('000)	..	..	..	2,532	3,620

MALAYSIA

Basic data and indicators		Notes	Units	2005	2006	2007	2008	2009
	Trips by mode of transport	(5)						
2.9	Total		('000)	..	..	..	63,283	90,505
2.10	♦ Air		('000)	..	..	..	1,013	1,176
2.11	♦ Water		('000)	..	..	..	1,835	1,991
2.12	♦ Land		('000)	..	..	..	60,435	87,338
2.13	* railway		('000)	..	..	..	696	724
2.14	* road		('000)	..	..	..	58,220	80,822
2.15	* others		('000)	..	..	..	1,519	5,792
	Accommodation							
	Total							
2.19	♦ Guests		('000)	..	..	..	..	..
2.20	♦ Overnights		('000)	..	..	..	..	..
	Hotels and similar establishments							
2.21	♦ Guests		('000)	29,926	31,900	36,254	40,610	32,920
2.22	♦ Overnights		('000)	..	..	..	..	..

3. OUTBOUND TOURISM

Data

	Expenditure							
3.4	Total		US$ Mn	4,339	5,085	6,600	7,724	7,196
3.5	♦ Travel		US$ Mn	3,711	4,257	5,601	6,709	6,508
3.6	♦ Passenger transport		US$ Mn	628	828	999	1,015	688
	Expenditure by main purpose of the trip							
3.7	Total		US$ Mn	3,711	4,257	5,601	6,709	6,508
3.8	♦ Personal		US$ Mn	940	1,123	1,376	1,703	1,674
3.9	♦ Business and professional		US$ Mn	2,771	3,134	4,225	5,006	4,834

4. TOURISM INDUSTRIES

Data

	Number of establishments							
4.1	Total		Units	..	..	..	..	..
4.2	♦ Accommodation for visitors		Units	..	..	..	..	..
4.3	* of which, "hotels and similar establishments"	(6)(7)	Units	2,269	2,336	2,360	2,373	2,373
4.4	♦ Food and beverage serving activities		Units	..	..	..	..	..
4.5	♦ Passenger transportation		Units	..	..	..	..	..
4.6	♦ Travel agencies and other reservation services activities	(8)(9)	Units	1,079	1,135	..	1,146	..
4.7	♦ Other tourism industries		Units	..	..	..	..	..
	Accommodation for visitors in hotels and similar establishments							
	Monetary data	(8)						
4.8	♦ Output		US$ Mn	1,860.8	2,017.8	2,456.6	2,657.1	..
4.9	♦ Intermediate consumption		US$ Mn	798.8	859.9	1,045.9	1,131.3	..
4.10	♦ Gross value added		US$ Mn	1,062.0	1,157.9	1,410.6	1,525.8	..
4.11	♦ Compensation of employees		US$ Mn	522.9	549.1	630.3	674.9	..
4.12	♦ Gross fixed capital formation		US$ Mn	..	..	..	..	..
	Non-monetary data							
4.13	♦ Number of establishments	(6)(7)	Units	2,269	2,336	2,360	2,373	2,373
4.14	♦ Number of rooms	(6)(7)	Units	155,356	157,251	160,327	165,739	168,844
4.15	♦ Number of bed-places		Units	..	..	..	..	..
	Indicators							
4.16	Occupancy rate / rooms	(7)	Percent	63.60	65.50	70.00	66.30	60.90
4.17	Occupancy rate / bed-places		Percent	..	..	..	..	..
4.18	Average length of stay		Nights	..	..	..	..	..
4.19	Available capacity (bed-places per 1000 inhabitants)		Units	..	..	..	..	..
	Travel agencies and other reservation service activities	(9)						
	Monetary data	(8)						
4.20	♦ Output		US$ Mn	1,311.0	1,474.8	..	2,045.4	..
4.21	♦ Intermediate consumption		US$ Mn	1,057.3	1,230.5	..	1,675.0	..
4.22	♦ Gross value added		US$ Mn	253.6	244.2	..	370.4	..
4.23	♦ Compensation of employees		US$ Mn	..	..	..	..	..
4.24	♦ Gross fixed capital formation		US$ Mn	..	..	..	..	..

MALAYSIA

Basic data and indicators	Notes	Units	2005	2006	2007	2008	2009
5. EMPLOYMENT							
Data							
Number of employees by tourism industries							
5.1 Total		('000)	..	..	..	..	..
5.2 ◆ Accommodation services for visitors (hotels and similar establishments)		('000)	99.0	99.7	103.4	101.0	..
5.3 ◆ Other accommodation services		('000)	..	..	..	..	..
5.4 ◆ Food and beverage serving activities		('000)	..	..	..	..	..
5.5 ◆ Passenger transportation		('000)	..	..	..	..	..
5.6 ◆ Travel agencies and other reservation services activities		('000)	14.9	15.0	..	18.2	..
5.7 ◆ Other tourism industries		('000)	..	..	..	..	..
6. COMPLEMENTARY INDICATORS							
Demand							
6.1 Gross travel propensity		Units	..	..	..	..	..
6.2 Carrying capacity (arrivals/population)		Units	0.64	0.67	0.79	1.90	2.15
Macroeconomic indicators related to international tourism							
6.3 Inbound tourism expenditure over GDP		Percent	7.5	7.8	9.6	8.4	..
6.4 Outbound tourism expenditure over GDP		Percent	3.1	3.2	3.5	3.5	..
6.5 Tourism balance (inbound minus outbound tourism expenditure) over GDP		Percent	4.4	4.6	6.1	4.9	..
6.6 Tourism openness (inbound plus outbound tourism expenditure) over GDP		Percent	10.7	11.1	13.2	11.9	..
6.7 Tourism coverage (inbound over outbound tourism expenditure)		Percent	239.4	241.5	272.6	240.2	..
6.8 Inbound tourism expenditure over exports of goods		Percent	7.3	7.6	10.2	9.3	..
6.9 Inbound tourism expenditure over exports of services		Percent	53.1	56.6	60.9	61.2	..
6.10 Inbound tourism expenditure over exports of goods and services		Percent	6.4	6.7	8.7	8.1	..
6.11 Inbound tourism expenditure over current account credits		Percent	6.2	6.4	8.2	7.6	..
6.12 Outbound tourism expenditure over imports of goods		Percent	4.0	4.1	4.7	5.2	..
6.13 Outbound tourism expenditure over imports of services		Percent	19.8	21.5	22.9	25.5	..
6.14 Outbound tourism expenditure over imports of goods and services		Percent	3.3	3.5	3.9	4.3	..
6.15 Outbound tourism expenditure over current account debits		Percent	3.0	3.1	3.5	3.8	..

MALDIVES

Basic data and indicators	Notes	Units	2005	2006	2007	2008	2009
1. INBOUND TOURISM							
Data							
Arrivals							
1.1 Total		('000)	..	..	..	..	..
1.2 ♦ Overnight visitors (tourists)	(1)	('000)	395	602	676	683	656
1.3 ♦ Same-day visitors (excursionists)		('000)	4	3	6	2	3
1.4 * of which, cruise passengers		('000)	4	3	6	2	3
Arrivals by region	(1)						
1.5 Total		('000)	394	602	675	683	656
1.6 ♦ Africa		('000)	3	4	5	6	5
1.7 ♦ Americas		('000)	7	11	14	14	15
1.8 ♦ East Asia and the Pacific		('000)	56	102	125	127	138
1.9 ♦ Europe		('000)	307	458	495	498	462
1.10 ♦ Middle East		('000)	2	4	6	9	10
1.11 ♦ South Asia		('000)	19	23	30	29	26
1.12 ♦ Other not classified		('000)	..	..	..	..	..
1.13 * of which, nationals residing abroad		('000)	..	..	..	..	..
Arrivals by main purpose	(1)						
1.14 Total		('000)	..	..	..	..	..
1.15 ♦ Personal		('000)	395	602	676	683	656
1.16 * holidays, leisure and recreation		('000)	395	602	676	683	656
1.17 * other personal purposes		('000)	..	..	..	..	..
1.18 ♦ Business and professional		('000)	..	..	..	..	..
Arrivals by mode of transport							
1.19 Total		('000)	395	602	676	683	656
1.20 ♦ Air		('000)	395	602	676	683	656
1.21 ♦ Water		('000)	..	..	..	..	..
1.22 ♦ Land		('000)	..	..	..	..	..
1.23 * railway		('000)	..	..	..	..	..
1.24 * road		('000)	..	..	..	..	..
1.25 * others		('000)	..	..	..	..	..
Accommodation							
Total							
1.29 ♦ Guests		('000)	..	..	..	..	..
1.30 ♦ Overnights		('000)	..	..	..	..	..
Hotels and similar establishments							
1.31 ♦ Guests		('000)	..	..	..	..	..
1.32 ♦ Overnights		('000)	3,300	4,822	5,293	5,447	5,152
Expenditure							
1.33 Total		US$ Mn	..	..	..	..	..
1.34 ♦ Travel		US$ Mn	287	512	602	636	608
1.35 ♦ Passenger transport		US$ Mn	..	..	..	..	..
3. OUTBOUND TOURISM							
Data							
Departures							
3.1 Total		('000)	..	..	..	..	..
3.2 ♦ Overnight visitors (tourists)		('000)	77	74	102	123	..
3.3 ♦ Same-day visitors (excursionists)		('000)	..	..	..	..	..
Expenditure							
3.4 Total		US$ Mn	94	106	127	148	133
3.5 ♦ Travel		US$ Mn	70	78	93	109	97
3.6 ♦ Passenger transport		US$ Mn	24	28	34	39	36
Expenditure by main purpose of the trip							
3.7 Total		US$ Mn	70	78	93	109	97
3.8 ♦ Personal		US$ Mn	67	76	91	106	95
3.9 ♦ Business and professional		US$ Mn	3	2	2	3	2

MALDIVES

Basic data and indicators	Notes	Units	2005	2006	2007	2008	2009
4. TOURISM INDUSTRIES							
Data							
Number of establishments							
4.1 Total		Units	..	..	..	..	..
4.2 ♦ Accommodation for visitors		Units	..	..	..	..	..
4.3 * of which, "hotels and similar establishments"		Units	245	235	260	274	279
4.4 ♦ Food and beverage serving activities		Units	..	..	..	..	..
4.5 ♦ Passenger transportation		Units	..	..	..	..	..
4.6 ♦ Travel agencies and other reservation services activities		Units	..	..	..	..	..
4.7 ♦ Other tourism industries		Units	..	..	..	..	..
Accommodation for visitors in hotels and similar establishments							
Non-monetary data							
4.13 ♦ Number of establishments		Units	245	235	260	274	279
4.14 ♦ Number of rooms		Units	10,100	10,254	11,094	11,732	12,325
4.15 ♦ Number of bed-places		Units	20,198	20,505	22,187	23,464	24,650
Indicators							
4.16 Occupancy rate / rooms		Percent	..	..	..	..	..
4.17 Occupancy rate / bed-places		Percent	64.39	81.40	82.76	77.83	70.22
4.18 Average length of stay	(2)	Nights	8.35	8.02	8.51	7.97	8.56
4.19 Available capacity (bed-places per 1000 inhabitants)		Units	69.08	69.15	73.78	76.92	79.66
6. COMPLEMENTARY INDICATORS							
Demand							
6.1 Gross travel propensity		Units	..	..	..	..	..
6.2 Carrying capacity (arrivals/population)		Units	1.35	2.03	2.25	2.24	2.12
Macroeconomic indicators related to international tourism							
6.3 Inbound tourism expenditure over GDP		Percent	38.2	56.0	57.1	50.5	..
6.4 Outbound tourism expenditure over GDP		Percent	12.6	11.6	12.1	11.8	..
6.5 Tourism balance (inbound minus outbound tourism expenditure) over GDP		Percent	25.7	44.3	45.1	38.7	..
6.6 Tourism openness (inbound plus outbound tourism expenditure) over GDP		Percent	50.8	67.6	69.2	62.2	..
6.7 Tourism coverage (inbound over outbound tourism expenditure)		Percent	304.1	481.0	473.0	428.8	..
6.8 Inbound tourism expenditure over exports of goods		Percent	177.3	227.5	264.2	192.4	..
6.9 Inbound tourism expenditure over exports of services		Percent	88.8	92.9	92.8	90.3	..
6.10 Inbound tourism expenditure over exports of goods and services		Percent	59.2	65.9	68.7	61.5	..
6.11 Inbound tourism expenditure over current account credits		Percent	40.6	58.0	60.8	56.4	..
6.12 Outbound tourism expenditure over imports of goods		Percent	14.4	13.1	13.2	12.1	..
6.13 Outbound tourism expenditure over imports of services		Percent	44.2	46.1	47.3	42.6	..
6.14 Outbound tourism expenditure over imports of goods and services		Percent	10.9	10.2	10.3	9.4	..
6.15 Outbound tourism expenditure over current account debits		Percent	9.6	9.0	8.9	8.3	..

MALI

Basic data and indicators	Notes	Units	2005	2006	2007	2008	2009
1. INBOUND TOURISM							
Data							
Arrivals							
1.1 Total		('000)	..	..	..	..	..
1.2 ♦ Overnight visitors (tourists)	(1)	('000)	143	153	164	190	160
1.3 ♦ Same-day visitors (excursionists)		('000)	..	..	..	..	..
1.4 * of which, cruise passengers		('000)	..	..	..	..	..
Arrivals by region	(1)						
1.5 Total		('000)	142	153	163	190	160
1.6 ♦ Africa		('000)	36	39	29	47	45
1.7 ♦ Americas		('000)	13	19	18	20	27
1.8 ♦ East Asia and the Pacific		('000)	2	2	1	5	1
1.9 ♦ Europe		('000)	81	86	104	101	73
1.10 ♦ Middle East		('000)	1	1	1	4	3
1.11 ♦ South Asia		('000)	..	..	..	..	..
1.12 ♦ Other not classified		('000)	9	6	10	13	11
1.13 * of which, nationals residing abroad		('000)	..	..	..	..	..
Arrivals by main purpose							
1.14 Total		('000)	..	..	..	189	160
1.15 ♦ Personal		('000)	..	..	..	115	64
1.16 * holidays, leisure and recreation		('000)	..	..	..	50	30
1.17 * other personal purposes		('000)	..	..	..	65	34
1.18 ♦ Business and professional		('000)	..	..	..	74	96
Arrivals by mode of transport	(1)						
1.19 Total		('000)	143	153	164	190	160
1.20 ♦ Air		('000)	143	153	164	190	144
1.21 ♦ Water		('000)	..	..	..	..	..
1.22 ♦ Land		('000)	..	..	..	..	16
1.23 * railway		('000)	..	..	..	..	..
1.24 * road		('000)	..	..	..	..	16
1.25 * others		('000)	..	..	..	..	..
Accommodation							
Total							
1.29 ♦ Guests		('000)	..	..	..	..	..
1.30 ♦ Overnights		('000)	..	..	..	..	..
Hotels and similar establishments							
1.31 ♦ Guests		('000)	143	153	164	190	160
1.32 ♦ Overnights		('000)	310	322	384	465	353
Expenditure							
1.33 Total		US$ Mn	149	175	227	286	..
1.34 ♦ Travel		US$ Mn	148	175	221	275	..
1.35 ♦ Passenger transport		US$ Mn	1	0.4	6	11	..
Expenditure by main purpose of the trip							
1.36 Total		US$ Mn	148	175	221	274	..
1.37 ♦ Personal		US$ Mn	81	83	88	158	..
1.38 ♦ Business and professional		US$ Mn	67	92	133	116	..
Indicators							
1.39 Average size of travel party		Persons	..	..	..	..	..
Average length of stay							
1.40 Total		Days	..	..	..	..	..
1.41 ♦ For all commercial accommodation services		Nights	2.20	2.20	2.40	2.45	2.50
1.42 * of which, "hotels and similar establishments"		Nights	..	..	..	..	..
1.43 ♦ For non commercial accommodation services		Days	..	..	..	..	..
1.44 Average expenditure per day		US$	..	..	..	..	..

MALI

Basic data and indicators	Notes	Units	2005	2006	2007	2008	2009
2. DOMESTIC TOURISM							
Data							
Trips							
2.1 Total		('000)	..	..	..	..	..
2.2 ♦ Overnight visitors (tourists)		('000)	..	..	..	45	44
2.3 ♦ Same-day visitors (excursionists)		('000)	..	..	..	..	..
Trips by mode of transport							
2.9 Total		('000)	..	..	..	45	44
2.10 ♦ Air		('000)	..	..	..	1	1
2.11 ♦ Water		('000)	..	..	..	..	..
2.12 ♦ Land		('000)	..	..	..	44	43
2.13 * railway		('000)	..	..	..	4	2
2.14 * road		('000)	..	..	..	40	41
2.15 * others		('000)	..	..	..	..	..
Accommodation							
Total							
2.19 ♦ Guests		('000)	..	..	..	..	..
2.20 ♦ Overnights		('000)	..	..	..	..	..
Hotels and similar establishments							
2.21 ♦ Guests		('000)	44	47	57	45	44
2.22 ♦ Overnights		('000)	71	112	124	88	92
Indicators							
2.23 Average size of travel party		Persons	..	..	..	..	..
Average length of stay							
2.24 Total		Days	..	..	..	..	..
2.25 ♦ For all commercial accommodation services		Nights	2.00	2.38	2.18	2.00	2.50
2.26 * of which, "hotels and similar establishments"		Nights	..	..	..	..	..
2.27 ♦ For non commercial accommodation services		Days	..	..	..	..	..
2.28 Average expenditure per day		US$	..	..	..	..	..
3. OUTBOUND TOURISM							
Data							
Expenditure							
3.4 Total		US$ Mn	133	196	201	228	..
3.5 ♦ Travel		US$ Mn	77	120	137	147	..
3.6 ♦ Passenger transport		US$ Mn	56	76	64	81	..
Expenditure by main purpose of the trip							
3.7 Total		US$ Mn	77	120	137	147	..
3.8 ♦ Personal		US$ Mn	23	47	54	58	..
3.9 ♦ Business and professional		US$ Mn	54	73	83	89	..
4. TOURISM INDUSTRIES							
Data							
Number of establishments							
4.1 Total		Units	..	..	..	..	..
4.2 ♦ Accommodation for visitors		Units	..	..	..	..	..
4.3 * of which, "hotels and similar establishments"		Units	251	358	439	514	551
4.4 ♦ Food and beverage serving activities		Units	..	..	..	..	..
4.5 ♦ Passenger transportation		Units	..	..	..	..	..
4.6 ♦ Travel agencies and other reservation services activities		Units	..	..	..	..	..
4.7 ♦ Other tourism industries		Units	..	..	..	..	..
Accommodation for visitors in hotels and similar establishments							
Non-monetary data							
4.13 ♦ Number of establishments		Units	251	358	439	514	551
4.14 ♦ Number of rooms		Units	5,311	6,011	6,842	7,896	8,361
4.15 ♦ Number of bed-places		Units	7,521	9,016	9,400	9,768	10,498
Indicators							
4.16 Occupancy rate / rooms		Percent	40.00	40.00	40.00	40.00	40.00
4.17 Occupancy rate / bed-places		Percent	..	..	..	..	..
4.18 Average length of stay		Nights	2.20	2.30	2.40	2.45	2.50
4.19 Available capacity (bed-places per 1000 inhabitants)		Units	0.64	0.74	0.76	0.77	0.81

MALI

Basic data and indicators	Notes	Units	2005	2006	2007	2008	2009
6. COMPLEMENTARY INDICATORS							
Demand							
6.1 Gross travel propensity		Units	..	..	..	..	..
6.2 Carrying capacity (arrivals/population)		Units	0.01	0.01	0.01	0.02	0.02
Macroeconomic indicators related to international tourism							
6.3 Inbound tourism expenditure over GDP		Percent	2.5	2.7	3.1	..	..
6.4 Outbound tourism expenditure over GDP		Percent	2.2	3.1	2.7	..	..
6.5 Tourism balance (inbound minus outbound tourism expenditure) over GDP		Percent	0.3	-0.3	0.4	..	..
6.6 Tourism openness (inbound plus outbound tourism expenditure) over GDP		Percent	4.7	5.8	5.7	..	..
6.7 Tourism coverage (inbound over outbound tourism expenditure)		Percent	112.2	89.6	113.2	125.2	..
6.8 Inbound tourism expenditure over exports of goods		Percent	13.6	11.3	14.6	13.6	..
6.9 Inbound tourism expenditure over exports of services		Percent	54.5	56.0	60.3	62.8	..
6.10 Inbound tourism expenditure over exports of goods and services		Percent	10.9	9.4	11.8	11.2	..
6.11 Inbound tourism expenditure over current account credits		Percent	8.7	7.6	9.1	8.9	..
6.12 Outbound tourism expenditure over imports of goods		Percent	10.7	13.3	10.9	8.3	..
6.13 Outbound tourism expenditure over imports of services		Percent	22.7	29.0	25.8	22.3	..
6.14 Outbound tourism expenditure over imports of goods and services		Percent	7.3	9.1	7.7	6.1	..
6.15 Outbound tourism expenditure over current account debits		Percent	6.2	7.7	6.5	5.3	..

MALTA

Basic data and indicators	Notes	Units	2005	2006	2007	2008	2009
1. INBOUND TOURISM							
Data							
Arrivals							
1.1 Total		('000)	1,491	1,532	1,732	1,847	1,623
1.2 ♦ Overnight visitors (tourists)	(1)	('000)	1,171	1,124	1,244	1,291	1,183
1.3 ♦ Same-day visitors (excursionists)		('000)	320	408	488	556	440
1.4 * of which, cruise passengers		('000)	320	408	488	556	440
Arrivals by region	(1)						
1.5 Total		('000)	1,171	1,124	1,243	1,290	1,183
1.6 ♦ Africa		('000)	..	..	..	..	..
1.7 ♦ Americas		('000)	18	17	20	18	14
1.8 ♦ East Asia and the Pacific		('000)	..	..	..	..	..
1.9 ♦ Europe		('000)	1,078	1,032	1,143	1,195	1,095
1.10 ♦ Middle East		('000)	11	9	9	9	12
1.11 ♦ South Asia		('000)	..	..	..	..	..
1.12 ♦ Other not classified		('000)	64	66	71	68	62
1.13 * of which, nationals residing abroad		('000)	..	..	..	..	..
Arrivals by main purpose							
1.14 Total	(2)(3)	('000)	1,152	1,104	1,244	1,290	1,183
1.15 ♦ Personal		('000)	1,057	1,002	1,145	1,178	1,075
1.16 * holidays, leisure and recreation		('000)	955	883	993	1,014	921
1.17 * other personal purposes		('000)	102	119	152	164	154
1.18 ♦ Business and professional		('000)	95	102	99	112	108
Arrivals by mode of transport	(1)						
1.19 Total		('000)	1,171	1,124	1,244	1,291	1,183
1.20 ♦ Air		('000)	1,151	1,104	1,224	1,270	1,167
1.21 ♦ Water		('000)	20	20	20	21	16
1.22 ♦ Land		('000)	..	..	..	..	..
1.23 * railway		('000)	..	..	..	..	..
1.24 * road		('000)	..	..	..	..	..
1.25 * others		('000)	..	..	..	..	..
Accommodation							
Total							
1.29 ♦ Guests		('000)	1,151	1,104	1,244	1,291	1,183
1.30 ♦ Overnights	(4)	('000)	10,933	10,503	11,017	10,962	9,997
Hotels and similar establishments							
1.31 ♦ Guests	(4)	('000)	906	868	982	1,008	910
1.32 ♦ Overnights	(4)	('000)	7,603	7,377	7,976	7,813	6,859
Expenditure							
1.33 Total		US$ Mn	924	966	1,142	1,215	1,026
1.34 ♦ Travel		US$ Mn	755	767	913	959	827
1.35 ♦ Passenger transport		US$ Mn	169	199	229	256	199
Indicators							
1.39 Average size of travel party		Persons	..	..	..	..	..
Average length of stay							
1.40 Total		Days	..	..	..	..	..
1.41 ♦ For all commercial accommodation services		Nights	9.50	9.50	8.90	8.50	8.50
1.42 * of which, "hotels and similar establishments"		Nights	..	..	..	..	..
1.43 ♦ For non commercial accommodation services		Days	..	..	..	..	..
1.44 Average expenditure per day		US$	..	..	..	..	..
3. OUTBOUND TOURISM							
Data							
Departures							
3.1 Total		('000)	..	..	..	..	..
3.2 ♦ Overnight visitors (tourists)		('000)	225	257	280	301	302
3.3 ♦ Same-day visitors (excursionists)		('000)	..	..	..	..	..
Expenditure							
3.4 Total		US$ Mn	311	362	420	482	503
3.5 ♦ Travel		US$ Mn	268	320	376	431	440
3.6 ♦ Passenger transport		US$ Mn	43	42	44	51	63

MALTA

Basic data and indicators	Notes	Units	2005	2006	2007	2008	2009
4. TOURISM INDUSTRIES							
Data							
Number of establishments							
4.1 Total		Units	..	..	..	..	..
4.2 ♦ Accommodation for visitors		Units	..	..	..	..	..
4.3 * of which, "hotels and similar establishments"		Units	..	..	..	163	164
4.4 ♦ Food and beverage serving activities		Units	..	..	..	..	..
4.5 ♦ Passenger transportation		Units	..	..	..	..	..
4.6 ♦ Travel agencies and other reservation services activities		Units	..	..	..	..	..
4.7 ♦ Other tourism industries		Units	..	..	..	..	..
Accommodation for visitors in hotels and similar establishments							
Non-monetary data							
4.13 ♦ Number of establishments		Units	..	..	..	163	164
4.14 ♦ Number of rooms		Units	..	..	17,528	18,318	18,363
4.15 ♦ Number of bed-places		Units	39,431	39,388	38,050	38,929	39,138
Indicators							
4.16 Occupancy rate / rooms		Percent	..	..	..	..	..
4.17 Occupancy rate / bed-places		Percent	52.82	51.18	59.90	57.70	50.60
4.18 Average length of stay		Nights	8.40	8.40	8.12	7.75	7.53
4.19 Available capacity (bed-places per 1000 inhabitants)		Units	97.72	96.92	93.02	94.50	94.32
6. COMPLEMENTARY INDICATORS							
Demand							
6.1 Gross travel propensity		Units	..	..	..	..	..
6.2 Carrying capacity (arrivals/population)		Units	2.90	2.77	3.04	3.13	2.85
Macroeconomic indicators related to international tourism							
6.3 Inbound tourism expenditure over GDP		Percent	15.5	15.1	15.3	14.6	12.9
6.4 Outbound tourism expenditure over GDP		Percent	5.2	5.6	5.6	5.8	6.3
6.5 Tourism balance (inbound minus outbound tourism expenditure) over GDP		Percent	10.3	9.4	9.7	8.8	6.6
6.6 Tourism openness (inbound plus outbound tourism expenditure) over GDP		Percent	20.7	20.7	20.9	20.3	19.3
6.7 Tourism coverage (inbound over outbound tourism expenditure)		Percent	297.1	266.8	272.5	252.0	203.7
6.8 Inbound tourism expenditure over exports of goods		Percent	35.7	32.9	34.6	38.2	43.0
6.9 Inbound tourism expenditure over exports of services		Percent	46.0	36.2	33.4	32.4	30.1
6.10 Inbound tourism expenditure over exports of goods and services		Percent	20.1	17.2	17.0	17.5	17.7
6.11 Inbound tourism expenditure over current account credits		Percent	15.0	12.1	11.2	10.7	10.8
6.12 Outbound tourism expenditure over imports of goods		Percent	8.4	8.7	9.0	10.0	14.0
6.13 Outbound tourism expenditure over imports of services		Percent	25.8	20.5	18.9	20.8	23.5
6.14 Outbound tourism expenditure over imports of goods and services		Percent	6.3	6.1	6.1	6.7	8.8
6.15 Outbound tourism expenditure over current account debits		Percent	4.7	4.2	3.9	4.1	5.0

MARSHALL ISLANDS

Basic data and indicators	Notes	Units	2005	2006	2007	2008	2009
1. INBOUND TOURISM							
Data							
Arrivals							
1.1 Total		('000)	..	..	..	..	..
1.2 ♦ Overnight visitors (tourists)	(1)(2)	('000)	9.2	5.8	7.2	6.0	5.4
1.3 ♦ Same-day visitors (excursionists)		('000)	..	..	..	..	..
1.4 * of which, cruise passengers		('000)	..	..	..	..	..
Arrivals by region	(1)(2)						
1.5 Total		('000)	9.2	5.8	7.2	6.1	5.4
1.6 ♦ Africa		('000)	..	..	..	..	..
1.7 ♦ Americas		('000)	1.7	1.5	1.7	1.5	1.3
1.8 ♦ East Asia and the Pacific		('000)	5.6	3.9	4.4	3.7	3.3
1.9 ♦ Europe		('000)	0.2	0.2	0.3	0.2	0.2
1.10 ♦ Middle East		('000)	..	..	..	..	..
1.11 ♦ South Asia		('000)	..	..	..	..	..
1.12 ♦ Other not classified		('000)	1.7	0.2	0.8	0.7	0.6
1.13 * of which, nationals residing abroad		('000)	..	..	..	..	..
Arrivals by main purpose	(1)(2)						
1.14 Total		('000)	9.2	5.8	7.2	6.0	5.3
1.15 ♦ Personal		('000)	6.1	3.8	4.9	3.9	3.2
1.16 * holidays, leisure and recreation		('000)	2.7	1.3	2.2	1.4	1.4
1.17 * other personal purposes		('000)	3.4	2.5	2.7	2.5	1.8
1.18 ♦ Business and professional		('000)	3.1	2.0	2.3	2.1	2.1
Arrivals by mode of transport	(1)(2)						
1.19 Total		('000)	9.2	5.8	7.2	6.0	5.4
1.20 ♦ Air		('000)	7.5	5.8	7.2	6.0	4.9
1.21 ♦ Water		('000)	1.7	..	..	..	0.5
1.22 ♦ Land		('000)	..	..	..	..	..
1.23 * railway		('000)	..	..	..	..	..
1.24 * road		('000)	..	..	..	..	..
1.25 * others		('000)	..	..	..	..	..
Accommodation							
Total							
1.29 ♦ Guests		('000)	..	..	..	..	..
1.30 ♦ Overnights		('000)	41	37	34	24	28
Hotels and similar establishments							
1.31 ♦ Guests		('000)	..	..	..	..	..
1.32 ♦ Overnights		('000)	..	..	..	..	..
Expenditure by main purpose of the trip							
1.36 Total	(3)	US$ Mn	5.7	6.6	4.5	3.0	2.7
1.37 ♦ Personal		US$ Mn	..	..	..	..	..
1.38 ♦ Business and professional		US$ Mn	..	..	..	..	..
Indicators							
1.39 Average size of travel party		Persons	..	..	..	..	..
Average length of stay							
1.40 Total		Days	..	..	..	..	..
1.41 ♦ For all commercial accommodation services		Nights	4.50	6.33	4.66	4.01	5.15
1.42 * of which, "hotels and similar establishments"		Nights	..	..	..	..	..
1.43 ♦ For non commercial accommodation services		Days	..	..	..	..	..
1.44 Average expenditure per day		US$	..	..	..	..	..
3. OUTBOUND TOURISM							
Data							
Expenditure							
3.4 Total	(3)	US$ Mn	0.4	0.4	..	..	..
3.5 ♦ Travel		US$ Mn	..	..	..	..	..
3.6 ♦ Passenger transport		US$ Mn	..	..	..	..	..
6. COMPLEMENTARY INDICATORS							
Demand							
6.1 Gross travel propensity		Units	..	..	..	..	..
6.2 Carrying capacity (arrivals/population)		Units	0.16	0.10	0.12	0.10	0.09

MARTINIQUE

Basic data and indicators	Notes	Units	2005	2006	2007	2008	2009
1. INBOUND TOURISM							
Data							
Arrivals							
1.1 Total		('000)	577	599	573	568	511
1.2 ♦ Overnight visitors (tourists)		('000)	484	503	501	481	442
1.3 ♦ Same-day visitors (excursionists)		('000)	93	96	72	87	70
1.4 * of which, cruise passengers		('000)	93	96	72	87	70
Arrivals by region							
1.5 Total		('000)	484	503	501	481	442
1.6 ♦ Africa		('000)	..	..	..	..	..
1.7 ♦ Americas		('000)	81	79	93	86	63
1.8 ♦ East Asia and the Pacific		('000)	..	..	..	..	..
1.9 ♦ Europe		('000)	399	422	405	391	367
1.10 ♦ Middle East		('000)	..	..	..	..	..
1.11 ♦ South Asia		('000)	..	..	..	..	..
1.12 ♦ Other not classified		('000)	4	2	3	4	12
1.13 * of which, nationals residing abroad		('000)	..	..	..	..	..
Arrivals by main purpose							
1.14 Total		('000)	484	503	501	481	442
1.15 ♦ Personal		('000)	405	445	421	409	377
1.16 * holidays, leisure and recreation		('000)	374	424	399	383	357
1.17 * other personal purposes		('000)	31	21	22	26	20
1.18 ♦ Business and professional		('000)	79	58	80	72	65
Arrivals by mode of transport							
1.19 Total		('000)	484	503	501	481	442
1.20 ♦ Air		('000)	439	465	469	457	418
1.21 ♦ Water		('000)	45	38	32	24	24
1.22 ♦ Land		('000)	..	..	..	..	..
1.23 * railway		('000)	..	..	..	..	..
1.24 * road		('000)	..	..	..	..	..
1.25 * others		('000)	..	..	..	..	..
Arrivals by form of organization of the trip							
1.26 Total		('000)	484	503	502	482	442
1.27 ♦ Package tour		('000)	163	178	166	131	118
1.28 ♦ Other forms		('000)	321	325	336	351	324
Accommodation							
Total							
1.29 ♦ Guests		('000)	484	503	501	481	442
1.30 ♦ Overnights		('000)	6,496	6,965	6,475	6,312	5,793
Hotels and similar establishments							
1.31 ♦ Guests		('000)	216	204	209	166	174
1.32 ♦ Overnights		('000)	1,924	1,707	1,761	1,341	1,389
Expenditure by main purpose of the trip							
1.36 Total	(1)	US$ Mn	280	306	299	316	302
1.37 ♦ Personal		US$ Mn	..	..	..	..	..
1.38 ♦ Business and professional		US$ Mn	..	..	..	..	..
Indicators							
1.39 Average size of travel party		Persons	..	..	..	..	..
Average length of stay							
1.40 Total		Days	13.40	13.80	12.90	13.00	13.10
1.41 ♦ For all commercial accommodation services		Nights	..	..	..	..	..
1.42 * of which, "hotels and similar establishments"		Nights	8.90	8.40	8.40	8.07	7.96
1.43 ♦ For non commercial accommodation services		Days	..	..	..	..	..
1.44 Average expenditure per day		US$	40.3	42.4	50.5	57.7	56.3

MARTINIQUE

Basic data and indicators	Notes	Units	2005	2006	2007	2008	2009
4. TOURISM INDUSTRIES							
Data							
Number of establishments							
4.1 Total		Units	..	..	2,207	..	..
4.2 ♦ Accommodation for visitors		Units	..	..	919	..	..
4.3 * of which, "hotels and similar establishments"		Units	162	162	151	..	141
4.4 ♦ Food and beverage serving activities		Units	..	..	528	..	..
4.5 ♦ Passenger transportation		Units	..	..	346	..	..
4.6 ♦ Travel agencies and other reservation services activities		Units	..	..	19	..	..
4.7 ♦ Other tourism industries		Units	..	..	395	..	..
Accommodation for visitors in hotels and similar establishments							
Non-monetary data							
4.13 ♦ Number of establishments	(2)	Units	162	162	151	..	141
4.14 ♦ Number of rooms		Units	6,153	6,153	6,228	..	6,163
4.15 ♦ Number of bed-places		Units	13,548	13,548	11,680	..	11,359
Indicators							
4.16 Occupancy rate / rooms		Percent	57.30	59.40	59.60	54.92	52.33
4.17 Occupancy rate / bed-places		Percent	..	..	..	..	..
4.18 Average length of stay		Nights	8.50	8.40	8.60	8.07	7.96
4.19 Available capacity (bed-places per 1000 inhabitants)		Units	..	..	..	..	..
5. EMPLOYMENT							
Data							
Number of employees by tourism industries							
5.1 Total		('000)	..	10.2	..	..	..
5.2 ♦ Accommodation services for visitors (hotels and similar establishments)		('000)	..	2.2	..	..	..
5.3 ♦ Other accommodation services		('000)	..	0.9	..	..	..
5.4 ♦ Food and beverage serving activities		('000)	..	3.0	..	..	..
5.5 ♦ Passenger transportation		('000)	..	1.3	..	..	..
5.6 ♦ Travel agencies and other reservation services activities		('000)	..	0.2	..	..	..
5.7 ♦ Other tourism industries		('000)	..	2.6	..	..	..
Number of jobs by status in employment							
5.8 Total		('000)	..	10.2	..	..	..
5.9 ♦ Employees		('000)	..	8.6	..	..	..
5.10 ♦ Self employed		('000)	..	1.6	..	..	..

MAURITIUS

Basic data and indicators	Notes	Units	2005	2006	2007	2008	2009
1. INBOUND TOURISM							
Data							
Arrivals							
1.1 Total		('000)	782	807	933	970	904
1.2 ♦ Overnight visitors (tourists)		('000)	761	788	907	930	871
1.3 ♦ Same-day visitors (excursionists)		('000)	20	19	26	40	33
1.4 * of which, cruise passengers		('000)	9	8	9	13	14
Arrivals by region							
1.5 Total		('000)	761	788	907	930	871
1.6 ♦ Africa		('000)	185	189	211	213	204
1.7 ♦ Americas		('000)	9	10	10	14	13
1.8 ♦ East Asia and the Pacific		('000)	29	34	40	40	26
1.9 ♦ Europe		('000)	503	511	596	609	580
1.10 ♦ Middle East		('000)	4	5	5	7	6
1.11 ♦ South Asia		('000)	31	39	45	46	41
1.12 ♦ Other not classified		('000)	..	..	..	1	1
1.13 * of which, nationals residing abroad		('000)	..	..	..	..	..
Arrivals by main purpose							
1.14 Total		('000)	781	807	933	970	904
1.15 ♦ Personal		('000)	751	775	898	933	875
1.16 * holidays, leisure and recreation		('000)	692	713	819	821	820
1.17 * other personal purposes		('000)	59	62	79	112	55
1.18 ♦ Business and professional		('000)	30	32	35	37	29
Arrivals by mode of transport							
1.19 Total		('000)	761	788	907	930	871
1.20 ♦ Air		('000)	748	775	895	914	848
1.21 ♦ Water		('000)	13	13	12	16	23
1.22 ♦ Land		('000)	..	..	..	..	..
1.23 * railway		('000)	..	..	..	..	..
1.24 * road		('000)	..	..	..	..	..
1.25 * others		('000)	..	..	..	..	..
Accommodation							
Total							
1.29 ♦ Guests		('000)	..	..	..	..	..
1.30 ♦ Overnights		('000)	..	..	..	..	..
Hotels and similar establishments							
1.31 ♦ Guests		('000)	..	..	..	..	..
1.32 ♦ Overnights		('000)	7,498	7,761	8,987	9,090	8,639
Expenditure							
1.33 Total		US$ Mn	1,189	1,302	1,663	1,823	1,390
1.34 ♦ Travel		US$ Mn	871	1,005	1,304	1,454	1,120
1.35 ♦ Passenger transport		US$ Mn	318	297	359	369	270
Expenditure by main purpose of the trip							
1.36 Total		US$ Mn	871	1,005	1,303	1,454	1,120
1.37 ♦ Personal		US$ Mn	503	638	853	937	731
1.38 ♦ Business and professional		US$ Mn	368	367	450	517	389
Indicators							
1.39 Average size of travel party		Persons	..	..	..	..	..
Average length of stay							
1.40 Total		Days	..	..	..	..	..
1.41 ♦ For all commercial accommodation services	(1)	Nights	10.70	10.10	10.30	10.10	10.30
1.42 * of which, "hotels and similar establishments"		Nights	..	..	..	..	..
1.43 ♦ For non commercial accommodation services		Days	..	..	..	..	..
1.44 Average expenditure per day		US$	..	..	..	..	..
3. OUTBOUND TOURISM							
Data							
Departures							
3.1 Total		('000)	..	..	..	..	..
3.2 ♦ Overnight visitors (tourists)		('000)	183	186	213	226	196
3.3 ♦ Same-day visitors (excursionists)		('000)	..	..	..	..	..
Expenditure							
3.4 Total		US$ Mn	295	347	384	489	384
3.5 ♦ Travel		US$ Mn	275	327	357	452	354
3.6 ♦ Passenger transport		US$ Mn	20	20	27	37	30
Expenditure by main purpose of the trip							
3.7 Total		US$ Mn	275	326	357	452	354
3.8 ♦ Personal		US$ Mn	250	312	332	407	308
3.9 ♦ Business and professional		US$ Mn	25	14	25	45	46

MAURITIUS

Basic data and indicators	Notes	Units	2005	2006	2007	2008	2009
4. TOURISM INDUSTRIES							
Data							
Number of establishments							
4.1 Total		Units	..	..	..	..	..
4.2 ♦ Accommodation for visitors		Units	..	..	..	..	..
4.3 * of which, "hotels and similar establishments"		Units	99	98	97	102	102
4.4 ♦ Food and beverage serving activities		Units	..	..	..	..	..
4.5 ♦ Passenger transportation		Units	..	..	..	..	..
4.6 ♦ Travel agencies and other reservation services activities		Units	..	..	..	..	..
4.7 ♦ Other tourism industries		Units	..	..	..	..	..
Accommodation for visitors in hotels and similar establishments							
Non-monetary data							
4.13 ♦ Number of establishments		Units	99	98	97	102	102
4.14 ♦ Number of rooms		Units	10,497	10,666	10,857	11,488	11,456
4.15 ♦ Number of bed-places		Units	21,072	21,403	21,788	23,095	23,235
Indicators							
4.16 Occupancy rate / rooms		Percent	63.00	66.00	76.00	68.00	61.00
4.17 Occupancy rate / bed-places		Percent	..	..	68.00	61.00	54.00
4.18 Average length of stay		Nights	..	..	..	..	..
4.19 Available capacity (bed-places per 1000 inhabitants)		Units	16.95	17.08	17.28	18.20	18.22
6. COMPLEMENTARY INDICATORS							
Demand							
6.1 Gross travel propensity		Units	..	..	..	..	..
6.2 Carrying capacity (arrivals/population)		Units	0.61	0.63	0.72	0.73	0.68
Macroeconomic indicators related to international tourism							
6.3 Inbound tourism expenditure over GDP		Percent	18.9	20.0	22.1	19.5	16.0
6.4 Outbound tourism expenditure over GDP		Percent	4.7	5.3	5.1	5.2	4.4
6.5 Tourism balance (inbound minus outbound tourism expenditure) over GDP		Percent	14.2	14.7	17.0	14.3	11.6
6.6 Tourism openness (inbound plus outbound tourism expenditure) over GDP		Percent	23.6	25.4	27.2	24.8	20.5
6.7 Tourism coverage (inbound over outbound tourism expenditure)		Percent	402.4	375.1	432.9	373.2	362.0
6.8 Inbound tourism expenditure over exports of goods		Percent	55.6	55.9	74.3	76.5	71.6
6.9 Inbound tourism expenditure over exports of services		Percent	73.5	77.9	75.4	71.7	62.1
6.10 Inbound tourism expenditure over exports of goods and services		Percent	31.6	32.6	37.4	37.0	33.2
6.11 Inbound tourism expenditure over current account credits		Percent	29.3	28.6	30.2	29.6	27.7
6.12 Outbound tourism expenditure over imports of goods		Percent	10.1	10.2	10.5	11.1	11.0
6.13 Outbound tourism expenditure over imports of services		Percent	24.7	26.4	24.5	25.4	23.9
6.14 Outbound tourism expenditure over imports of goods and services		Percent	7.1	7.3	7.4	7.7	7.5
6.15 Outbound tourism expenditure over current account debits		Percent	6.7	6.7	6.5	6.8	6.7

MEXICO

Basic data and indicators	Notes	Units	2005	2006	2007	2008	2009
1. INBOUND TOURISM							
Data							
Arrivals							
1.1 Total		('000)	103,146	97,701	92,179	91,462	86,189
1.2 ♦ Overnight visitors (tourists)	(1)	('000)	21,915	21,353	21,370	22,637	21,454
1.3 ♦ Same-day visitors (excursionists)	(2)	('000)	81,231	76,348	70,810	68,825	64,735
1.4 * of which, cruise passengers		('000)	6,707	6,516	6,815	6,431	5,690
Arrivals by region	(1)						
1.5 Total		('000)	21,914	21,352	21,369	22,637	21,454
1.6 ♦ Africa		('000)	..	..	..	..	..
1.7 ♦ Americas		('000)	19,012	18,713	18,788	19,875	19,494
1.8 ♦ East Asia and the Pacific	(3)	('000)	92	100	109	106	78
1.9 ♦ Europe		('000)	1,134	1,295	1,423	1,509	1,189
1.10 ♦ Middle East		('000)	..	..	..	..	..
1.11 ♦ South Asia		('000)	..	..	..	..	..
1.12 ♦ Other not classified		('000)	1,676	1,244	1,049	1,147	693
1.13 * of which, nationals residing abroad		('000)	..	..	..	..	..
Arrivals by main purpose	(1)						
1.14 Total		('000)	21,915	21,353	21,370	22,637	21,454
1.15 ♦ Personal		('000)	21,129	20,578	20,530	21,858	20,777
1.16 * holidays, leisure and recreation		('000)	7,697	7,743	8,302	8,063	7,231
1.17 * other personal purposes		('000)	13,432	12,835	12,228	13,795	13,546
1.18 ♦ Business and professional		('000)	786	775	840	779	677
Arrivals by mode of transport	(1)						
1.19 Total		('000)	21,915	21,352	21,369	22,638	21,454
1.20 ♦ Air		('000)	9,936	10,153	10,611	10,969	9,672
1.21 ♦ Water		('000)	..	..	..	..	..
1.22 ♦ Land		('000)	11,979	11,199	10,758	11,669	11,782
1.23 * railway		('000)	..	..	..	..	..
1.24 * road	(4)	('000)	11,979	11,199	10,758	11,669	11,782
1.25 * others		('000)	..	..	..	..	..
Accommodation							
Total							
1.29 ♦ Guests		('000)	..	..	..	..	..
1.30 ♦ Overnights		('000)	..	..	..	..	..
Hotels and similar establishments							
1.31 ♦ Guests	(5)	('000)	10,691	9,689	13,250	14,731	12,043
1.32 ♦ Overnights	(6)	('000)	33,623	30,236	48,780	52,746	42,904
Expenditure							
1.33 Total		US$ Mn	12,801	13,329	13,988	14,647	12,309
1.34 ♦ Travel		US$ Mn	11,803	12,177	12,852	13,289	11,275
1.35 ♦ Passenger transport		US$ Mn	998	1,152	1,136	1,358	1,034
Expenditure by main purpose of the trip							
1.36 Total		US$ Mn	11,803	12,177	12,852	13,289	11,275
1.37 ♦ Personal		US$ Mn	11,087	11,445	12,107	12,538	10,658
1.38 ♦ Business and professional		US$ Mn	716	732	745	751	617
Indicators							
1.39 Average size of travel party		Persons	..	..	..	..	..
Average length of stay							
1.40 Total		Days	..	..	..	..	..
1.41 ♦ For all commercial accommodation services		Nights	9.93	9.93	9.94	10.00	9.65
1.42 * of which, "hotels and similar establishments"		Nights	..	..	..	..	..
1.43 ♦ For non commercial accommodation services		Days	..	..	..	..	..
1.44 Average expenditure per day		US$	..	..	..	..	..
2. DOMESTIC TOURISM							
Data							
Accommodation							
Total							
2.19 ♦ Guests		('000)	..	..	..	..	..
2.20 ♦ Overnights		('000)	..	..	..	..	..
Hotels and similar establishments							
2.21 ♦ Guests	(5)	('000)	34,547	35,192	41,961	45,420	43,088
2.22 ♦ Overnights		('000)	64,607	64,124	74,600	78,498	73,514

MEXICO

Basic data and indicators	Notes	Units	2005	2006	2007	2008	2009
3. OUTBOUND TOURISM							
Data							
Departures							
3.1 Total		('000)	..	..	..	..	..
3.2 ♦ Overnight visitors (tourists)		('000)	13,305	14,002	15,083	14,450	13,942
3.3 ♦ Same-day visitors (excursionists)		('000)	..	..	..	..	..
Expenditure							
3.4 Total		US$ Mn	8,951	9,387	9,831	10,185	8,626
3.5 ♦ Travel		US$ Mn	7,600	8,108	8,375	8,526	7,132
3.6 ♦ Passenger transport		US$ Mn	1,351	1,279	1,456	1,659	1,494
Expenditure by main purpose of the trip							
3.7 Total		US$ Mn	7,600	8,108	8,375	8,526	7,131
3.8 ♦ Personal		US$ Mn	6,773	7,303	7,405	7,485	6,161
3.9 ♦ Business and professional		US$ Mn	827	805	970	1,041	970
4. TOURISM INDUSTRIES							
Data							
Number of establishments							
4.1 Total		Units	48,996	50,636	52,983	55,532	56,046
4.2 ♦ Accommodation for visitors		Units	..	..	..	..	..
4.3 * of which, "hotels and similar establishments"		Units	13,751	14,410	14,970	15,754	16,231
4.4 ♦ Food and beverage serving activities		Units	30,503	30,884	32,885	34,205	34,532
4.5 ♦ Passenger transportation		Units	..	..	..	..	..
4.6 ♦ Travel agencies and other reservation services activities		Units	4,742	5,342	5,128	5,573	5,283
4.7 ♦ Other tourism industries		Units	..	..	..	..	..
Accommodation for visitors in hotels and similar establishments							
Monetary data							
4.8 ♦ Output		US$ Mn	1,406.5	1,487.5	1,611.9	1,707.5	..
4.9 ♦ Intermediate consumption		US$ Mn	413.7	440.6	475.5	509.2	..
4.10 ♦ Gross value added		US$ Mn	992.8	1,046.9	1,136.4	1,198.2	..
4.11 ♦ Compensation of employees		US$ Mn	105.8	110.4	117.1	123.0	..
4.12 ♦ Gross fixed capital formation		US$ Mn	..	..	..	..	..
Non-monetary data							
4.13 ♦ Number of establishments		Units	13,751	14,410	14,970	15,754	16,231
4.14 ♦ Number of rooms		Units	535,639	562,039	584,331	603,781	623,555
4.15 ♦ Number of bed-places		Units	1,071,278	1,124,078	1,168,662	1,207,562	1,247,110
Indicators							
4.16 Occupancy rate / rooms		Percent	52.88	52.78	54.83	53.96	46.31
4.17 Occupancy rate / bed-places		Percent	..	..	..	..	..
4.18 Average length of stay	(7)	Nights	3.15	3.12	3.68	3.58	3.56
4.19 Available capacity (bed-places per 1000 inhabitants)		Units	10.39	10.79	11.10	11.35	11.61
Travel agencies and other reservation service activities							
Monetary data							
4.20 ♦ Output		US$ Mn	136.8	147.9	158.6	174.6	..
4.21 ♦ Intermediate consumption		US$ Mn	60.5	64.8	70.0	77.3	..
4.22 ♦ Gross value added		US$ Mn	76.3	83.1	88.6	97.3	..
4.23 ♦ Compensation of employees		US$ Mn	16.8	17.8	19.6	21.3	..
4.24 ♦ Gross fixed capital formation		US$ Mn	..	..	..	..	..
5. EMPLOYMENT							
Data							
Number of employees by tourism industries	(8)						
5.1 Total		('000)	2,428.6	2,431.6	2,471.1	2,523.8	..
5.2 ♦ Accommodation services for visitors (hotels and similar establishments)		('000)	188.6	186.0	188.2	186.0	..
5.3 ♦ Other accommodation services		('000)	..	..	..	..	..
5.4 ♦ Food and beverage serving activities		('000)	887.3	876.4	880.5	890.4	..
5.5 ♦ Passenger transportation		('000)	441.4	441.3	453.5	452.5	..
5.6 ♦ Travel agencies and other reservation services activities		('000)	15.6	15.9	16.6	16.8	..
5.7 ♦ Other tourism industries		('000)	895.7	912.0	932.3	978.1	..

MEXICO

Basic data and indicators	Notes	Units	2005	2006	2007	2008	2009
6. COMPLEMENTARY INDICATORS							
Demand							
6.1 Gross travel propensity		Units	..	..	..	..	..
6.2 Carrying capacity (arrivals/population)		Units	0.21	0.20	0.20	0.21	0.20
Macroeconomic indicators related to international tourism							
6.3 Inbound tourism expenditure over GDP		Percent	1.5	1.4	1.4	1.3	1.4
6.4 Outbound tourism expenditure over GDP		Percent	1.1	1.0	1.0	0.9	1.0
6.5 Tourism balance (inbound minus outbound tourism expenditure) over GDP		Percent	0.5	0.4	0.4	0.4	0.4
6.6 Tourism openness (inbound plus outbound tourism expenditure) over GDP		Percent	2.6	2.4	2.3	2.3	2.4
6.7 Tourism coverage (inbound over outbound tourism expenditure)		Percent	143.0	142.0	142.3	143.8	142.7
6.8 Inbound tourism expenditure over exports of goods		Percent	6.0	5.3	5.1	5.0	5.4
6.9 Inbound tourism expenditure over exports of services		Percent	79.3	81.3	79.4	79.3	79.8
6.10 Inbound tourism expenditure over exports of goods and services		Percent	5.6	5.0	4.8	4.7	5.0
6.11 Inbound tourism expenditure over current account credits		Percent	5.0	4.5	4.3	4.3	4.5
6.12 Outbound tourism expenditure over imports of goods		Percent	4.0	3.7	3.5	3.3	3.7
6.13 Outbound tourism expenditure over imports of services		Percent	41.8	41.1	40.9	40.4	37.2
6.14 Outbound tourism expenditure over imports of goods and services		Percent	3.7	3.4	3.2	3.1	3.3
6.15 Outbound tourism expenditure over current account debits		Percent	3.4	3.1	3.0	2.8	3.1

MICRONESIA, FEDERATED STATES OF

Basic data and indicators	Notes	Units	2005	2006	2007	2008	2009
1. INBOUND TOURISM							
Data							
Arrivals							
1.1 Total		('000)	..	..	..	..	..
1.2 ♦ Overnight visitors (tourists)	(1)	('000)	19.0	19.1	21.1	25.6	..
1.3 ♦ Same-day visitors (excursionists)		('000)	..	..	..	..	..
1.4 * of which, cruise passengers		('000)	..	..	..	..	..
Arrivals by region	(1)						
1.5 Total		('000)	19.0	19.2	21.2	25.6	..
1.6 ♦ Africa		('000)	..	..	..	..	..
1.7 ♦ Americas		('000)	8.0	8.3	8.5	9.2	..
1.8 ♦ East Asia and the Pacific		('000)	8.9	8.4	10.1	13.4	..
1.9 ♦ Europe		('000)	2.0	2.4	2.5	2.8	..
1.10 ♦ Middle East		('000)	..	..	..	..	..
1.11 ♦ South Asia		('000)	..	..	..	..	..
1.12 ♦ Other not classified		('000)	0.1	0.1	0.1	0.2	..
1.13 * of which, nationals residing abroad		('000)	..	..	..	..	..
Arrivals by main purpose	(1)						
1.14 Total		('000)	18.9	19.1	21.1	25.6	..
1.15 ♦ Personal		('000)	14.6	14.6	15.6	20.5	..
1.16 * holidays, leisure and recreation		('000)	13.4	13.3	14.2	15.9	..
1.17 * other personal purposes		('000)	1.2	1.3	1.4	4.6	..
1.18 ♦ Business and professional		('000)	4.3	4.5	5.5	5.1	..
Expenditure by main purpose of the trip							
1.36 Total	(2)	US$ Mn	17.1	18.3	..	..	..
1.37 ♦ Personal		US$ Mn	..	..	..	..	..
1.38 ♦ Business and professional		US$ Mn	..	..	..	..	..
3. OUTBOUND TOURISM							
Data							
Expenditure							
3.4 Total	(2)	US$ Mn	5.5	5.7	..	..	..
3.5 ♦ Travel		US$ Mn	..	..	..	..	..
3.6 ♦ Passenger transport		US$ Mn	..	..	..	..	..
6. COMPLEMENTARY INDICATORS							
Demand							
6.1 Gross travel propensity		Units	..	..	..	..	..
6.2 Carrying capacity (arrivals/population)		Units	0.17	0.17	0.19	0.23	..

MONACO

Basic data and indicators	Notes	Units	2005	2006	2007	2008	2009
1. INBOUND TOURISM							
Data							
Arrivals							
1.1 Total		('000)	..	..	..		
1.2 ♦ Overnight visitors (tourists)	(1)	('000)	286	313	328	324	265
1.3 ♦ Same-day visitors (excursionists)		('000)	133	180	182	232	..
1.4 * of which, cruise passengers		('000)	133	180	182	232	
Arrivals by region	(1)						
1.5 Total		('000)	286	314	327	324	265
1.6 ♦ Africa		('000)	3	3	3	3	2
1.7 ♦ Americas		('000)	29	34	41	35	27
1.8 ♦ East Asia and the Pacific		('000)	12	11	12	13	10
1.9 ♦ Europe		('000)	214	240	244	261	216
1.10 ♦ Middle East		('000)	3	4	4	7	4
1.11 ♦ South Asia		('000)	..	..	..	..	..
1.12 ♦ Other not classified		('000)	25	22	23	5	6
1.13 * of which, nationals residing abroad		('000)	..	..	..	..	..
Arrivals by main purpose	(1)						
1.14 Total		('000)	286	313	328	324	265
1.15 ♦ Personal		('000)	219	244	251	251	213
1.16 * holidays, leisure and recreation		('000)	219	244	251	251	213
1.17 * other personal purposes		('000)	..	..	..	..	..
1.18 ♦ Business and professional		('000)	67	69	77	73	52
Arrivals by mode of transport	(1)						
1.19 Total		('000)	286	313	328	..	..
1.20 ♦ Air		('000)	196	222	230	..	..
1.21 ♦ Water		('000)	90	91	98	..	..
1.22 ♦ Land		('000)	..	..	..	..	..
1.23 * railway		('000)	..	..	..	..	..
1.24 * road		('000)	..	..	..	..	..
1.25 * others		('000)	..	..	..	..	..
Accommodation							
Total							
1.29 ♦ Guests		('000)	..	..	..	..	..
1.30 ♦ Overnights		('000)	..	..	..	..	..
Hotels and similar establishments							
1.31 ♦ Guests		('000)	286	313	328	324	265
1.32 ♦ Overnights		('000)	803	916	944	944	778
4. TOURISM INDUSTRIES							
Data							
Number of establishments							
4.1 Total		Units	..	..	..	..	..
4.2 ♦ Accommodation for visitors		Units	..	..	..	..	..
4.3 * of which, "hotels and similar establishments"		Units	18	16	17	15	16
4.4 ♦ Food and beverage serving activities		Units	..	..	..	..	..
4.5 ♦ Passenger transportation		Units	..	..	..	..	..
4.6 ♦ Travel agencies and other reservation services activities		Units	..	..	..	..	..
4.7 ♦ Other tourism industries		Units	..	..	..	..	..
Accommodation for visitors in hotels and similar establishments							
Non-monetary data							
4.13 ♦ Number of establishments		Units	18	16	17	15	16
4.14 ♦ Number of rooms		Units	2,649	2,555	2,773	2,623	2,591
4.15 ♦ Number of bed-places		Units	5,312	5,288	4,248	5,940	5,665
Indicators							
4.16 Occupancy rate / rooms		Percent	..	..	..	..	..
4.17 Occupancy rate / bed-places		Percent	58.39	58.77	63.58	61.09	..
4.18 Average length of stay		Nights	2.81	2.92	2.88	3.00	..
4.19 Available capacity (bed-places per 1000 inhabitants)		Units	163.68	162.54	130.23	181.57	172.65
6. COMPLEMENTARY INDICATORS							
Demand							
6.1 Gross travel propensity		Units	..	..	..	..	..
6.2 Carrying capacity (arrivals/population)		Units	8.81	9.62	10.06	9.90	8.08

MONGOLIA

Basic data and indicators	Notes	Units	2005	2006	2007	2008	2009
1. INBOUND TOURISM							
Data							
Arrivals							
1.1 Total	(1)	('000)	345	390	456	469	468
1.2 ◆ Overnight visitors (tourists)	(1)	('000)	338	386	452	446	411
1.3 ◆ Same-day visitors (excursionists)		('000)	..	..	..	..	..
1.4 * of which, cruise passengers		('000)	..	..	..	..	..
Arrivals by region	(1)						
1.5 Total		('000)	337	386	451	446	411
1.6 ◆ Africa		('000)	..	1	1	1	..
1.7 ◆ Americas		('000)	13	14	15	16	14
1.8 ◆ East Asia and the Pacific		('000)	223	246	283	267	241
1.9 ◆ Europe		('000)	100	124	149	160	154
1.10 ◆ Middle East		('000)	..	..	..	1	1
1.11 ◆ South Asia		('000)	1	1	1	1	1
1.12 ◆ Other not classified		('000)	..	..	2	..	..
1.13 * of which, nationals residing abroad		('000)	..	..	..	..	..
Arrivals by main purpose	(1)						
1.14 Total		('000)	338	386	451	446	411
1.15 ◆ Personal		('000)	252	306	348	361	323
1.16 * holidays, leisure and recreation		('000)	65	128	127	104	101
1.17 * other personal purposes		('000)	187	178	221	257	222
1.18 ◆ Business and professional		('000)	86	80	103	85	88
Expenditure							
1.33 Total		US$ Mn	203	261	354	272	253
1.34 ◆ Travel		US$ Mn	177	225	312	247	235
1.35 ◆ Passenger transport		US$ Mn	26	36	42	25	18
Expenditure by main purpose of the trip							
1.36 Total		US$ Mn	176.7	225.0	311.0	247.0	235.0
1.37 ◆ Personal		US$ Mn	176	223	306	233	201
1.38 ◆ Business and professional		US$ Mn	0.7	2.0	5.0	14.0	34.0
3. OUTBOUND TOURISM							
Data							
Expenditure							
3.4 Total		US$ Mn	173	212	227	249	242
3.5 ◆ Travel		US$ Mn	157	188	205	217	210
3.6 ◆ Passenger transport		US$ Mn	16	24	22	32	32
Expenditure by main purpose of the trip							
3.7 Total		US$ Mn	157	188	205	217	210
3.8 ◆ Personal		US$ Mn	152	182	200	213	208
3.9 ◆ Business and professional		US$ Mn	5	6	5	4	2
4. TOURISM INDUSTRIES							
Data							
Number of establishments							
4.1 Total		Units	..	..	..	..	..
4.2 ◆ Accommodation for visitors		Units	..	..	..	..	..
4.3 * of which, "hotels and similar establishments"		Units	..	..	318	336	347
4.4 ◆ Food and beverage serving activities		Units	..	..	..	..	..
4.5 ◆ Passenger transportation		Units	..	..	..	..	..
4.6 ◆ Travel agencies and other reservation services activities		Units	..	..	..	..	..
4.7 ◆ Other tourism industries		Units	..	..	..	..	..
Accommodation for visitors in hotels and similar establishments							
Non-monetary data							
4.13 ◆ Number of establishments		Units	..	..	318	336	347
4.14 ◆ Number of rooms		Units	..	..	5,153	5,282	..
4.15 ◆ Number of bed-places		Units	..	..	..	..	..

MONGOLIA

Basic data and indicators	Notes	Units	2005	2006	2007	2008	2009
6. **COMPLEMENTARY INDICATORS**							
Demand							
6.1 Gross travel propensity		Units	..	..	..	..	..
6.2 Carrying capacity (arrivals/population)		Units	0.13	0.15	0.17	0.17	0.15
Macroeconomic indicators related to international tourism							
6.3 Inbound tourism expenditure over GDP		Percent	8.7	8.2	..	..	..
6.4 Outbound tourism expenditure over GDP		Percent	7.4	6.6	..	..	..
6.5 Tourism balance (inbound minus outbound tourism expenditure) over GDP		Percent	1.3	1.5	..	..	..
6.6 Tourism openness (inbound plus outbound tourism expenditure) over GDP		Percent	16.1	14.8	..	..	..
6.7 Tourism coverage (inbound over outbound tourism expenditure)		Percent	117.5	123.2	..	..	..
6.8 Inbound tourism expenditure over exports of goods		Percent	19.0	16.9	..	..	..
6.9 Inbound tourism expenditure over exports of services		Percent	49.0	53.8	..	..	..
6.10 Inbound tourism expenditure over exports of goods and services		Percent	13.7	12.9	..	..	..
6.11 Inbound tourism expenditure over current account credits		Percent	11.5	11.2	..	..	..
6.12 Outbound tourism expenditure over imports of goods		Percent	15.8	15.6	..	..	..
6.13 Outbound tourism expenditure over imports of services		Percent	36.3	40.5	..	..	..
6.14 Outbound tourism expenditure over imports of goods and services		Percent	11.0	11.3	..	..	..
6.15 Outbound tourism expenditure over current account debits		Percent	10.3	10.0	..	..	..

MONTENEGRO

Basic data and indicators	Notes	Units	2005	2006	2007	2008	2009
1. INBOUND TOURISM							
Data							
Arrivals							
1.1 Total		('000)	..	..	..	..	..
1.2 ♦ Overnight visitors (tourists)	(1)	('000)	272	378	984	1,031	1,044
1.3 ♦ Same-day visitors (excursionists)		('000)	..	..	..	..	..
1.4 * of which, cruise passengers		('000)	..	..	..	..	..
Arrivals by region	(1)						
1.5 Total		('000)	272	378	984	1,031	1,043
1.6 ♦ Africa		('000)	..	..	..	..	..
1.7 ♦ Americas		('000)	4	7	9	9	8
1.8 ♦ East Asia and the Pacific		('000)	1	2	2	3	2
1.9 ♦ Europe		('000)	264	366	968	1,013	1,028
1.10 ♦ Middle East		('000)	..	..	..	..	..
1.11 ♦ South Asia		('000)	..	..	..	..	..
1.12 ♦ Other not classified		('000)	3	3	5	6	5
1.13 * of which, nationals residing abroad		('000)	..	..	..	..	..
Accommodation							
Total							
1.29 ♦ Guests		('000)	272	378	984	1,031	1,044
1.30 ♦ Overnights		('000)	1,584	2,196	6,443	6,966	6,696
Hotels and similar establishments							
1.31 ♦ Guests		('000)	191	269	545	566	468
1.32 ♦ Overnights		('000)	1,033	1,453	3,062	3,234	2,388
Expenditure							
1.33 Total		US$ Mn	..	..	659	801	705
1.34 ♦ Travel		US$ Mn	..	..	629	755	659
1.35 ♦ Passenger transport		US$ Mn	..	..	30	46	46
Indicators							
1.39 Average size of travel party		Persons	..	..	..	..	..
Average length of stay							
1.40 Total		Days	..	..	..	..	..
1.41 ♦ For all commercial accommodation services		Nights	..	..	6.55	6.76	6.41
1.42 * of which, "hotels and similar establishments"		Nights	..	..	..	..	..
1.43 ♦ For non commercial accommodation services		Days	..	..	..	..	..
1.44 Average expenditure per day		US$	..	..	..	..	..
2. DOMESTIC TOURISM							
Data							
Accommodation							
Total							
2.19 ♦ Guests		('000)	548	576	149	157	164
2.20 ♦ Overnights		('000)	3,628	3,740	851	828	856
Hotels and similar establishments							
2.21 ♦ Guests		('000)	197	169	84	96	88
2.22 ♦ Overnights		('000)	1,505	1,200	331	348	326
Indicators							
2.23 Average size of travel party		Persons	..	..	..	..	..
Average length of stay							
2.24 Total		Days	..	..	..	..	..
2.25 ♦ For all commercial accommodation services		Nights	..	..	5.70	5.29	3.63
2.26 * of which, "hotels and similar establishments"		Nights	..	..	..	..	..
2.27 ♦ For non commercial accommodation services		Days	..	..	..	..	..
2.28 Average expenditure per day		US$	..	..	..	..	..
3. OUTBOUND TOURISM							
Data							
Expenditure							
3.4 Total		US$ Mn	..	..	58	80	76
3.5 ♦ Travel		US$ Mn	..	..	37	43	49
3.6 ♦ Passenger transport		US$ Mn	..	..	21	37	27
Expenditure by main purpose of the trip							
3.7 Total		US$ Mn	..	..	37	43	49
3.8 ♦ Personal		US$ Mn	..	..	34	41	48
3.9 ♦ Business and professional		US$ Mn	..	..	3	2	1

MONTENEGRO

Basic data and indicators	Notes	Units	2005	2006	2007	2008	2009
4. TOURISM INDUSTRIES							
Data							
Number of establishments							
4.1 Total		Units	..	..	..	..	..
4.2 ♦ Accommodation for visitors		Units	..	..	369	397	427
4.3 * of which, "hotels and similar establishments"		Units	..	..	257	278	303
4.4 ♦ Food and beverage serving activities		Units	..	..	..	..	..
4.5 ♦ Passenger transportation		Units	..	..	..	..	..
4.6 ♦ Travel agencies and other reservation services activities		Units	..	..	..	..	..
4.7 ♦ Other tourism industries		Units	..	..	..	..	..
Accommodation for visitors in hotels and similar establishments							
Non-monetary data							
4.13 ♦ Number of establishments		Units	..	..	257	278	303
4.14 ♦ Number of rooms		Units	17,494	17,898	18,004	18,083	18,808
4.15 ♦ Number of bed-places		Units	41,674	42,321	43,069	43,198	43,786
Indicators							
4.16 Occupancy rate / rooms		Percent	..	..	..	..	..
4.17 Occupancy rate / bed-places		Percent	..	..	..	19.33	17.07
4.18 Average length of stay		Nights	..	..	..	..	..
4.19 Available capacity (bed-places per 1000 inhabitants)		Units	66.72	68.10	69.36	69.41	70.15
5. EMPLOYMENT							
Data							
Number of employees by tourism industries							
5.1 Total		('000)	11.0	11.0	11.0	15.0	17.0
5.2 ♦ Accommodation services for visitors (hotels and similar establishments)		('000)	..	..	..	..	..
5.3 ♦ Other accommodation services		('000)	..	..	..	..	..
5.4 ♦ Food and beverage serving activities		('000)	..	..	..	..	..
5.5 ♦ Passenger transportation		('000)	..	..	..	..	..
5.6 ♦ Travel agencies and other reservation services activities		('000)	..	..	..	..	..
5.7 ♦ Other tourism industries		('000)	..	..	..	..	..
6. COMPLEMENTARY INDICATORS							
Demand							
6.1 Gross travel propensity		Units	..	..	..	..	..
6.2 Carrying capacity (arrivals/population)		Units	0.44	0.61	1.58	1.66	1.67

MONTSERRAT

Basic data and indicators	Notes	Units	2005	2006	2007	2008	2009
1. INBOUND TOURISM							
Data							
Arrivals							
1.1 Total		('000)	13.1	9.5	8.7	8.4	7.3
1.2 ♦ Overnight visitors (tourists)		('000)	9.7	8.0	7.7	7.4	6.3
1.3 ♦ Same-day visitors (excursionists)		('000)	3.4	1.5	1.0	1.0	1.0
1.4 * of which, cruise passengers		('000)	0.3	0.1	0.3	0.3	..
Arrivals by region							
1.5 Total		('000)	9.7	8.0	7.8	7.4	6.3
1.6 ♦ Africa		('000)	..	..	..	..	..
1.7 ♦ Americas		('000)	6.4	5.4	5.3	5.0	4.2
1.8 ♦ East Asia and the Pacific		('000)	..	..	..	..	..
1.9 ♦ Europe		('000)	3.2	2.5	2.4	2.3	2.0
1.10 ♦ Middle East		('000)	..	..	..	..	..
1.11 ♦ South Asia		('000)	..	..	..	..	..
1.12 ♦ Other not classified		('000)	0.1	0.1	0.1	0.1	0.1
1.13 * of which, nationals residing abroad		('000)	..	..	..	..	..
Arrivals by main purpose							
1.14 Total		('000)	9.7	8.0	7.8	7.4	..
1.15 ♦ Personal		('000)	7.8	6.7	6.3	5.5	..
1.16 * holidays, leisure and recreation		('000)	3.6	4.3	4.4	4.0	..
1.17 * other personal purposes		('000)	4.2	2.4	1.9	1.5	..
1.18 ♦ Business and professional		('000)	1.9	1.3	1.5	1.9	..
Arrivals by mode of transport							
1.19 Total		('000)	9.7	8.0	7.8	7.4	..
1.20 ♦ Air		('000)	5.6	7.9	7.7	6.8	..
1.21 ♦ Water		('000)	4.1	0.1	0.1	0.6	..
1.22 ♦ Land		('000)	..	..	..	..	..
1.23 * railway		('000)	..	..	..	..	..
1.24 * road		('000)	..	..	..	..	..
1.25 * others		('000)	..	..	..	..	..
Accommodation							
Total							
1.29 ♦ Guests		('000)	..	..	..	..	..
1.30 ♦ Overnights		('000)	..	..	..	..	..
Hotels and similar establishments							
1.31 ♦ Guests		('000)	2.5	2.3	2.6	2.8	..
1.32 ♦ Overnights		('000)	..	..	..	..	..
Expenditure							
1.33 Total		US$ Mn	..	..	..	..	..
1.34 ♦ Travel		US$ Mn	9	8	7	7	5
1.35 ♦ Passenger transport		US$ Mn	..	..	..	..	..
3. OUTBOUND TOURISM							
Data							
Expenditure							
3.4 Total		US$ Mn	..	..	..	..	..
3.5 ♦ Travel		US$ Mn	3	3	3	3	3
3.6 ♦ Passenger transport		US$ Mn	..	..	..	..	..
6. COMPLEMENTARY INDICATORS							
Macroeconomic indicators related to international tourism							
6.3 Inbound tourism expenditure over GDP		Percent	20.8	17.2	16.1	14.1	9.8
6.4 Outbound tourism expenditure over GDP		Percent	6.1	6.3	6.2	6.4	6.4
6.5 Tourism balance (inbound minus outbound tourism expenditure) over GDP		Percent	14.8	10.9	9.8	7.6	3.4
6.6 Tourism openness (inbound plus outbound tourism expenditure) over GDP		Percent	26.9	23.5	22.3	20.5	16.2
6.7 Tourism coverage (inbound over outbound tourism expenditure)		Percent	344.1	272.9	258.3	218.6	152.4
6.8 Inbound tourism expenditure over exports of goods		Percent	477.7	433.0	241.6	173.0	163.0
6.9 Inbound tourism expenditure over exports of services		Percent	60.7	52.5	50.5	50.8	42.2
6.10 Inbound tourism expenditure over exports of goods and services		Percent	53.8	46.9	41.8	39.2	33.5
6.11 Inbound tourism expenditure over current account credits		Percent	19.2	17.4	16.5	15.0	11.9
6.12 Outbound tourism expenditure over imports of goods		Percent	10.0	10.7	11.0	9.6	13.0
6.13 Outbound tourism expenditure over imports of services		Percent	10.1	16.4	15.1	13.8	17.2
6.14 Outbound tourism expenditure over imports of goods and services		Percent	5.0	6.5	6.4	5.7	7.4
6.15 Outbound tourism expenditure over current account debits		Percent	4.2	5.5	5.2	4.8	6.0

MOROCCO

Basic data and indicators	Notes	Units	2005	2006	2007	2008	2009
1. INBOUND TOURISM							
Data							
Arrivals	**(1)**						
1.1 Total		('000)	6,077	6,777	7,701	8,209	8,661
1.2 ♦ Overnight visitors (tourists)		('000)	5,843	6,558	7,408	7,879	8,341
1.3 ♦ Same-day visitors (excursionists)		('000)	233	218	293	330	319
1.4 * of which, cruise passengers		('000)	233	218	293	330	319
Arrivals by region	**(1)**						
1.5 Total		('000)	5,844	6,558	7,408	7,879	8,341
1.6 ♦ Africa		('000)	144	165	193	214	223
1.7 ♦ Americas		('000)	140	173	196	202	215
1.8 ♦ East Asia and the Pacific		('000)	52	65	74	76	77
1.9 ♦ Europe		('000)	2,608	3,025	3,406	3,564	3,623
1.10 ♦ Middle East		('000)	91	106	116	127	135
1.11 ♦ South Asia		('000)	8	9	12	12	12
1.12 ♦ Other not classified		('000)	2,801	3,015	3,411	3,684	4,056
1.13 * of which, nationals residing abroad		('000)	2,788	2,986	3,377	3,667	4,048
Arrivals by main purpose	**(1)**						
1.14 Total		('000)	5,843	6,558	..	..	8,341
1.15 ♦ Personal		('000)	5,700	6,393	..	..	7,882
1.16 * holidays, leisure and recreation		('000)	3,145	3,620	..	..	3,703
1.17 * other personal purposes		('000)	2,555	2,773	..	..	4,179
1.18 ♦ Business and professional		('000)	143	165	..	..	459
Arrivals by mode of transport	**(1)**						
1.19 Total		('000)	5,844	6,558	7,408	7,879	8,341
1.20 ♦ Air		('000)	2,986	3,549	4,395	4,792	5,108
1.21 ♦ Water		('000)	2,040	1,937	1,745	1,756	1,913
1.22 ♦ Land		('000)	818	1,072	1,268	1,331	1,320
1.23 * railway		('000)	..	..	..	..	..
1.24 * road		('000)	818	1,072	1,268	1,331	1,320
1.25 * others		('000)	..	..	..	..	..
Accommodation							
Total							
1.29 ♦ Guests		('000)	..	..	..	..	..
1.30 ♦ Overnights		('000)	..	..	..	..	..
Hotels and similar establishments							
1.31 ♦ Guests	(2)	('000)	3,470	3,815	3,910	3,824	3,669
1.32 ♦ Overnights	(2)	('000)	12,259	13,346	13,703	13,068	12,521
Expenditure							
1.33 Total		US$ Mn	5,426	6,900	8,307	8,885	7,978
1.34 ♦ Travel		US$ Mn	4,610	5,984	7,181	7,221	6,625
1.35 ♦ Passenger transport		US$ Mn	816	916	1,126	1,664	1,353
Indicators							
1.39 Average size of travel party		Persons	..	..	..	..	1.6
Average length of stay							
1.40 Total		Days	..	..	..	..	16.20
1.41 ♦ For all commercial accommodation services		Nights	..	..	..	..	4.58
1.42 * of which, "hotels and similar establishments"		Nights	..	..	..	..	4.24
1.43 ♦ For non commercial accommodation services		Days	..	..	..	..	8.36
1.44 Average expenditure per day		US$	..	..	..	..	..
2. DOMESTIC TOURISM							
Data							
Accommodation							
Total							
2.19 ♦ Guests		('000)	..	..	..	..	..
2.20 ♦ Overnights		('000)	..	..	..	..	..
Hotels and similar establishments							
2.21 ♦ Guests	(2)	('000)	1,400	1,403	1,502	1,587	1,702
2.22 ♦ Overnights	(2)	('000)	2,956	2,981	3,191	3,394	3,718

MOROCCO

Basic data and indicators	Notes	Units	2005	2006	2007	2008	2009
3. OUTBOUND TOURISM							
Data							
Departures							
3.1 Total		('000)	..	..	..	..	..
3.2 ♦ Overnight visitors (tourists)		('000)	2,247	2,135	2,669	3,058	2,293
3.3 ♦ Same-day visitors (excursionists)		('000)	..	..	..	..	..
Expenditure							
3.4 Total		US$ Mn	999	1,113	1,418	1,910	1,712
3.5 ♦ Travel		US$ Mn	612	693	880	1,090	1,106
3.6 ♦ Passenger transport		US$ Mn	387	420	538	820	606
Expenditure by main purpose of the trip							
3.7 Total		US$ Mn	612	692	880	1,090	1,106
3.8 ♦ Personal		US$ Mn	515	593	731	867	923
3.9 ♦ Business and professional		US$ Mn	97	99	149	223	183
4. TOURISM INDUSTRIES							
Data							
Number of establishments							
4.1 Total		Units	..	..	..	..	..
4.2 ♦ Accommodation for visitors		Units	..	..	..	..	..
4.3 * of which, "hotels and similar establishments"	(2)	Units	1,148	1,354	1,544	1,720	1,806
4.4 ♦ Food and beverage serving activities		Units	..	..	..	..	..
4.5 ♦ Passenger transportation		Units	..	..	..	..	..
4.6 ♦ Travel agencies and other reservation services activities		Units	..	..	..	..	..
4.7 ♦ Other tourism industries		Units	..	..	..	..	..
Accommodation for visitors in hotels and similar establishments							
Non-monetary data							
4.13 ♦ Number of establishments	(2)	Units	1,148	1,354	1,544	1,720	1,806
4.14 ♦ Number of rooms	(2)	Units	59,864	63,900	68,454	73,061	78,217
4.15 ♦ Number of bed-places	(2)	Units	124,270	133,230	143,221	152,936	164,612
Indicators							
4.16 Occupancy rate / rooms	(2)	Percent	47.00	49.00	48.00	45.00	41.00
4.17 Occupancy rate / bed-places		Percent	38.00	41.00	40.00	36.00	33.00
4.18 Average length of stay	(3)	Nights	6.30	6.50	7.00	7.20	7.00
4.19 Available capacity (bed-places per 1000 inhabitants)		Units	4.08	4.32	4.59	4.84	5.15
6. COMPLEMENTARY INDICATORS							
Demand							
6.1 Gross travel propensity		Units	..	..	..	..	..
6.2 Carrying capacity (arrivals/population)		Units	0.19	0.21	0.24	0.25	0.26
Macroeconomic indicators related to international tourism							
6.3 Inbound tourism expenditure over GDP		Percent	9.1	10.5	11.0	10.0	8.8
6.4 Outbound tourism expenditure over GDP		Percent	1.7	1.7	1.9	2.1	1.9
6.5 Tourism balance (inbound minus outbound tourism expenditure) over GDP		Percent	7.4	8.8	9.2	7.8	6.9
6.6 Tourism openness (inbound plus outbound tourism expenditure) over GDP		Percent	10.8	12.2	12.9	12.1	10.7
6.7 Tourism coverage (inbound over outbound tourism expenditure)		Percent	543.4	620.0	585.7	465.1	466.0
6.8 Inbound tourism expenditure over exports of goods		Percent	50.8	57.9	54.8	43.7	57.3
6.9 Inbound tourism expenditure over exports of services		Percent	67.0	70.5	68.3	66.2	63.8
6.10 Inbound tourism expenditure over exports of goods and services		Percent	28.9	31.8	30.4	26.3	30.2
6.11 Inbound tourism expenditure over current account credits		Percent	21.7	23.8	23.0	20.3	22.9
6.12 Outbound tourism expenditure over imports of goods		Percent	5.3	5.1	4.8	4.8	5.6
6.13 Outbound tourism expenditure over imports of services		Percent	26.0	24.9	26.2	28.5	25.1
6.14 Outbound tourism expenditure over imports of goods and services		Percent	4.4	4.3	4.1	4.1	4.6
6.15 Outbound tourism expenditure over current account debits		Percent	4.2	4.0	3.9	4.0	4.3

MOZAMBIQUE

Basic data and indicators	Notes	Units	2005	2006	2007	2008	2009
1. INBOUND TOURISM							
Data							
Arrivals	(1)						
1.1 Total		('000)	954	1,095	1,259	2,617	3,110
1.2 ♦ Overnight visitors (tourists)		('000)	578	664	771	1,815	2,224
1.3 ♦ Same-day visitors (excursionists)		('000)	376	431	488	802	886
1.4 * of which, cruise passengers		('000)	..	..	..	..	..
Arrivals by region	(1)						
1.5 Total		('000)	954	1,094	1,259	2,617	3,110
1.6 ♦ Africa		('000)	852	977	1,043	2,143	2,647
1.7 ♦ Americas		('000)	12	14	19	32	72
1.8 ♦ East Asia and the Pacific		('000)	8	9	13	..	51
1.9 ♦ Europe		('000)	48	55	66	158	300
1.10 ♦ Middle East		('000)	..	..	..	..	..
1.11 ♦ South Asia		('000)	..	..	..	..	..
1.12 ♦ Other not classified		('000)	34	39	118	284	40
1.13 * of which, nationals residing abroad		('000)	..	..	..	..	..
Arrivals by main purpose	(1)						
1.14 Total		('000)	578	664	771	1,815	2,224
1.15 ♦ Personal		('000)	303	354	420	1,638	1,599
1.16 * holidays, leisure and recreation		('000)	175	214	261	1,252	1,095
1.17 * other personal purposes		('000)	128	140	159	386	504
1.18 ♦ Business and professional		('000)	275	310	351	177	625
Arrivals by mode of transport	(1)						
1.19 Total		('000)	954	1,095	1,259	2,617	3,110
1.20 ♦ Air		('000)	156	175	88	917	532
1.21 ♦ Water		('000)	..	..	..	..	..
1.22 ♦ Land		('000)	798	920	1,171	1,700	2,578
1.23 * railway		('000)	..	..	..	..	..
1.24 * road		('000)	798	920	1,171	1,700	2,578
1.25 * others		('000)	..	..	..	..	..
Accommodation							
Total							
1.29 ♦ Guests		('000)	..	..	..	..	..
1.30 ♦ Overnights		('000)	..	..	..	..	..
Hotels and similar establishments							
1.31 ♦ Guests		('000)	250	238	257	257	237
1.32 ♦ Overnights		('000)	389	518	479	456	424
Expenditure							
1.33 Total		US$ Mn	138	145	182	213	217
1.34 ♦ Travel		US$ Mn	130	140	163	190	196
1.35 ♦ Passenger transport		US$ Mn	8	5	19	23	21
Expenditure by main purpose of the trip							
1.36 Total		US$ Mn	130	140	163	190	196
1.37 ♦ Personal		US$ Mn	124	136	152	188	195
1.38 ♦ Business and professional		US$ Mn	6	4	11	2	0.5
Indicators							
1.39 Average size of travel party		Persons	..	..	..	..	..
Average length of stay							
1.40 Total		Days	..	..	..	..	..
1.41 ♦ For all commercial accommodation services		Nights	2.10	2.00	1.70	1.80	1.90
1.42 * of which, "hotels and similar establishments"		Nights	..	..	..	..	..
1.43 ♦ For non commercial accommodation services		Days	..	..	..	..	..
1.44 Average expenditure per day		US$	..	..	..	..	..
2. DOMESTIC TOURISM							
Data							
Accommodation							
Total							
2.19 ♦ Guests		('000)	..	..	..	..	..
2.20 ♦ Overnights		('000)	..	..	..	..	..
Hotels and similar establishments							
2.21 ♦ Guests		('000)	248	181	217	245	246
2.22 ♦ Overnights		('000)	467	363	393	437	433
Indicators							
2.23 Average size of travel party		Persons	..	..	..	..	..
Average length of stay							
2.24 Total		Days	..	..	..	..	..
2.25 ♦ For all commercial accommodation services		Nights	..	..	1.80	2.00	1.90
2.26 * of which, "hotels and similar establishments"		Nights	..	..	..	..	..
2.27 ♦ For non commercial accommodation services		Days	..	..	..	..	..
2.28 Average expenditure per day		US$	..	..	..	..	..

MOZAMBIQUE

Basic data and indicators	Notes	Units	2005	2006	2007	2008	2009
3. OUTBOUND TOURISM							
Data							
Expenditure							
3.4 Total		US$ Mn	187	205	209	241	249
3.5 ♦ Travel		US$ Mn	176	179	180	208	212
3.6 ♦ Passenger transport		US$ Mn	11	26	29	33	37
Expenditure by main purpose of the trip							
3.7 Total		US$ Mn	176	179	180	208	212
3.8 ♦ Personal		US$ Mn	171	162	145	154	170
3.9 ♦ Business and professional		US$ Mn	5	17	35	54	42
4. TOURISM INDUSTRIES							
Data							
Number of establishments							
4.1 Total		Units	..	..	..	..	..
4.2 ♦ Accommodation for visitors		Units	..	521	521	536	542
4.3 * of which, "hotels and similar establishments"		Units	..	519	519	524	531
4.4 ♦ Food and beverage serving activities		Units	..	..	..	..	..
4.5 ♦ Passenger transportation		Units	..	..	..	..	..
4.6 ♦ Travel agencies and other reservation services activities		Units	..	..	..	..	..
4.7 ♦ Other tourism industries		Units	..	..	..	..	..
Accommodation for visitors in hotels and similar establishments							
Non-monetary data							
4.13 ♦ Number of establishments		Units	..	519	519	524	531
4.14 ♦ Number of rooms		Units	..	9,780	11,583	..	..
4.15 ♦ Number of bed-places		Units	14,827	15,740	17,035	17,505	18,412
Indicators							
4.16 Occupancy rate / rooms		Percent	..	..	..	..	..
4.17 Occupancy rate / bed-places		Percent	..	..	27.20	27.40	26.90
4.18 Average length of stay		Nights	2.10	2.10	1.70	1.80	1.90
4.19 Available capacity (bed-places per 1000 inhabitants)		Units	0.71	0.74	0.78	0.78	0.80
6. COMPLEMENTARY INDICATORS							
Demand							
6.1 Gross travel propensity		Units	..	..	..	..	..
6.2 Carrying capacity (arrivals/population)		Units	0.03	0.03	0.04	0.08	0.10
Macroeconomic indicators related to international tourism							
6.3 Inbound tourism expenditure over GDP		Percent	2.1	2.0	2.3	..	..
6.4 Outbound tourism expenditure over GDP		Percent	2.8	2.9	2.6	..	..
6.5 Tourism balance (inbound minus outbound tourism expenditure) over GDP		Percent	-0.8	-0.8	-0.3	..	..
6.6 Tourism openness (inbound plus outbound tourism expenditure) over GDP		Percent	4.9	4.9	4.8	..	..
6.7 Tourism coverage (inbound over outbound tourism expenditure)		Percent	73.3	70.6	87.2	88.1	86.9
6.8 Inbound tourism expenditure over exports of goods		Percent	7.9	6.1	7.6	8.0	11.7
6.9 Inbound tourism expenditure over exports of services		Percent	40.2	37.5	39.8	38.4	35.3
6.10 Inbound tourism expenditure over exports of goods and services		Percent	6.6	5.2	6.4	6.6	8.8
6.11 Inbound tourism expenditure over current account credits		Percent	5.2	4.1	4.9	4.9	6.1
6.12 Outbound tourism expenditure over imports of goods		Percent	8.4	7.7	7.4	6.6	7.7
6.13 Outbound tourism expenditure over imports of services		Percent	28.9	27.0	24.5	25.0	23.4
6.14 Outbound tourism expenditure over imports of goods and services		Percent	6.5	6.0	5.7	5.2	5.8
6.15 Outbound tourism expenditure over current account debits		Percent	5.5	4.8	4.6	4.4	5.3

MYANMAR

Basic data and indicators	Notes	Units	2005	2006	2007	2008	2009
1. INBOUND TOURISM							
Data							
Arrivals							
1.1 Total		('000)	660	630	716	731	763
1.2 ♦ Overnight visitors (tourists)	(1)	('000)	232	264	248	193	243
1.3 ♦ Same-day visitors (excursionists)		('000)	428	369	468	538	520
1.4 * of which, cruise passengers		('000)	2	3	2	3	2
Arrivals by region	(1)						
1.5 Total		('000)	232	264	247	193	243
1.6 ♦ Africa		('000)	..	1	..	1	1
1.7 ♦ Americas		('000)	21	23	19	16	19
1.8 ♦ East Asia and the Pacific		('000)	130	148	143	124	157
1.9 ♦ Europe		('000)	68	81	73	41	53
1.10 ♦ Middle East		('000)	2	2	2	1	1
1.11 ♦ South Asia		('000)	11	9	10	10	12
1.12 ♦ Other not classified		('000)	..	..	..	..	..
1.13 * of which, nationals residing abroad		('000)	..	..	..	..	..
Arrivals by main purpose							
1.14 Total		('000)	660	630	716	731	763
1.15 ♦ Personal		('000)	624	594	681	695	720
1.16 * holidays, leisure and recreation		('000)	151	180	168	111	146
1.17 * other personal purposes		('000)	473	414	513	584	574
1.18 ♦ Business and professional		('000)	36	36	35	36	43
Arrivals by mode of transport							
1.19 Total		('000)	660	630	716	732	763
1.20 ♦ Air		('000)	230	261	246	191	236
1.21 ♦ Water		('000)	2	3	2	3	2
1.22 ♦ Land		('000)	428	366	468	538	525
1.23 * railway		('000)	..	..	..	..	..
1.24 * road		('000)	428	366	468	538	525
1.25 * others		('000)	..	..	..	..	..
Accommodation							
Total							
1.29 ♦ Guests		('000)	..	..	..	..	..
1.30 ♦ Overnights		('000)	..	..	..	..	..
Hotels and similar establishments							
1.31 ♦ Guests		('000)	..	..	..	..	..
1.32 ♦ Overnights	(2)	('000)	1,626	1,845	1,641	1,737	2,068
Expenditure							
1.33 Total		US$ Mn	85	59	..	..	..
1.34 ♦ Travel		US$ Mn	68	46	..	..	..
1.35 ♦ Passenger transport		US$ Mn	17	13	..	..	..
Indicators							
1.39 Average size of travel party		Persons	..	..	..	..	..
Average length of stay							
1.40 Total		Days	..	..	..	..	..
1.41 ♦ For all commercial accommodation services		Nights	7.00	7.00	7.50	9.00	..
1.42 * of which, "hotels and similar establishments"		Nights	..	..	..	..	..
1.43 ♦ For non commercial accommodation services		Days	..	..	..	..	..
1.44 Average expenditure per day		US$	..	..	..	..	..
2. DOMESTIC TOURISM							
Data							
Accommodation							
Total							
2.19 ♦ Guests		('000)	..	..	..	..	..
2.20 ♦ Overnights		('000)	..	822	..	..	..
Hotels and similar establishments							
2.21 ♦ Guests		('000)	..	..	..	..	..
2.22 ♦ Overnights		('000)	..	601	..	..	..
Indicators							
2.23 Average size of travel party		Persons	..	..	..	..	..
Average length of stay							
2.24 Total		Days	..	..	..	..	..
2.25 ♦ For all commercial accommodation services		Nights	..	2.00	..	..	..
2.26 * of which, "hotels and similar establishments"		Nights	..	..	..	..	..
2.27 ♦ For non commercial accommodation services		Days	..	..	..	..	..
2.28 Average expenditure per day		US$	..	..	..	..	..

MYANMAR

Basic data and indicators	Notes	Units	2005	2006	2007	2008	2009
3. OUTBOUND TOURISM							
Data							
Expenditure							
3.4 Total		US$ Mn	34	40	..	..	..
3.5 ♦ Travel		US$ Mn	31	37	..	..	..
3.6 ♦ Passenger transport		US$ Mn	3	3	..	..	..
4. TOURISM INDUSTRIES							
Data							
Number of establishments							
4.1 Total		Units	..	..	..	..	..
4.2 ♦ Accommodation for visitors		Units	..	..	..	..	..
4.3 * of which, "hotels and similar establishments"	(3)	Units	222	220	223	230	228
4.4 ♦ Food and beverage serving activities		Units	..	..	..	..	..
4.5 ♦ Passenger transportation		Units	..	..	..	..	..
4.6 ♦ Travel agencies and other reservation services activities		Units	..	..	..	..	..
4.7 ♦ Other tourism industries		Units	..	..	..	..	..
Accommodation for visitors in hotels and similar establishments							
Non-monetary data							
4.13 ♦ Number of establishments	(3)	Units	222	220	223	230	228
4.14 ♦ Number of rooms	(3)	Units	19,040	19,506	18,527	20,357	20,942
4.15 ♦ Number of bed-places	(3)	Units	38,080	39,012	37,054	40,714	41,884
Indicators							
4.16 Occupancy rate / rooms		Percent	20.00	26.00	27.00	30.00	..
4.17 Occupancy rate / bed-places		Percent	..	..	..	..	..
4.18 Average length of stay	(2)	Nights	4.00	4.00	4.00	4.00	..
4.19 Available capacity (bed-places per 1000 inhabitants)		Units	0.79	0.80	0.75	0.82	0.84
6. COMPLEMENTARY INDICATORS							
Demand							
6.1 Gross travel propensity		Units	..	..	..	..	..
6.2 Carrying capacity (arrivals/population)		Units	0.005	0.01	0.01	0.004	0.005
Macroeconomic indicators related to international tourism							
6.3 Inbound tourism expenditure over GDP		Percent	..	..	..	..	..
6.4 Outbound tourism expenditure over GDP		Percent	..	..	..	..	..
6.5 Tourism balance (inbound minus outbound tourism expenditure) over GDP		Percent	..	..	..	..	..
6.6 Tourism openness (inbound plus outbound tourism expenditure) over GDP		Percent	..	..	..	..	..
6.7 Tourism coverage (inbound over outbound tourism expenditure)		Percent	249.5	149.3	..	..	..
6.8 Inbound tourism expenditure over exports of goods		Percent	2.2	1.3	..	..	..
6.9 Inbound tourism expenditure over exports of services		Percent	32.5	21.3	..	..	..
6.10 Inbound tourism expenditure over exports of goods and services		Percent	2.1	1.2	..	..	..
6.11 Inbound tourism expenditure over current account credits		Percent	2.0	1.2	..	..	..
6.12 Outbound tourism expenditure over imports of goods		Percent	1.9	1.7	..	..	..
6.13 Outbound tourism expenditure over imports of services		Percent	6.7	7.1	..	..	..
6.14 Outbound tourism expenditure over imports of goods and services		Percent	1.5	1.4	..	..	..
6.15 Outbound tourism expenditure over current account debits		Percent	0.9	0.9	..	..	..

NAMIBIA

Basic data and indicators	Notes	Units	2005	2006	2007	2008	2009
1. INBOUND TOURISM							
Data							
Arrivals							
1.1 Total		('000)	856	961	1,048	1,079	..
1.2 ♦ Overnight visitors (tourists)		('000)	778	833	929	931	..
1.3 ♦ Same-day visitors (excursionists)		('000)	78	127	119	148	..
1.4 * of which, cruise passengers		('000)	..	..	..	..	..
Arrivals by region							
1.5 Total		('000)	778	834	929	931	..
1.6 ♦ Africa		('000)	602	629	690	676	..
1.7 ♦ Americas		('000)	12	16	19	24	..
1.8 ♦ East Asia and the Pacific		('000)	4	5	6	10	..
1.9 ♦ Europe		('000)	146	167	195	204	..
1.10 ♦ Middle East		('000)	..	..	..	..	..
1.11 ♦ South Asia		('000)	..	..	..	..	..
1.12 ♦ Other not classified		('000)	14	17	19	17	..
1.13 * of which, nationals residing abroad		('000)	..	..	..	..	..
Arrivals by main purpose							
1.14 Total		('000)	778	833	928	..	..
1.15 ♦ Personal		('000)	677	731	839	..	..
1.16 * holidays, leisure and recreation		('000)	322	406	474	..	..
1.17 * other personal purposes		('000)	355	325	365	..	..
1.18 ♦ Business and professional		('000)	101	102	89	..	..
Arrivals by mode of transport							
1.19 Total		('000)	777	833	929	931	..
1.20 ♦ Air		('000)	185	217	246	273	..
1.21 ♦ Water		('000)	3	3	6	9	..
1.22 ♦ Land		('000)	589	613	677	649	..
1.23 * railway		('000)	2	2	..	..	..
1.24 * road		('000)	587	611	677	649	..
1.25 * others		('000)	..	..	..	..	..
Accommodation							
Total							
1.29 ♦ Guests		('000)	706	..	..	1,254	769
1.30 ♦ Overnights		('000)	1,409	1,372	..	..	..
Hotels and similar establishments							
1.31 ♦ Guests		('000)	426	698	..	..	..
1.32 ♦ Overnights		('000)	606	722	..	..	..
Expenditure							
1.33 Total		US$ Mn	363	473	542	484	469
1.34 ♦ Travel		US$ Mn	349	381	434	382	363
1.35 ♦ Passenger transport		US$ Mn	14	92	108	102	106
Expenditure by main purpose of the trip							
1.36 Total		US$ Mn	349	381	434	382	363
1.37 ♦ Personal		US$ Mn	260	320	385	333	314
1.38 ♦ Business and professional		US$ Mn	89	61	49	49	49
Indicators							
1.39 Average size of travel party		Persons	..	..	..	..	..
Average length of stay							
1.40 Total		Days	..	..	..	..	..
1.41 ♦ For all commercial accommodation services		Nights	19.10	19.00	19.00	17.00	..
1.42 * of which, "hotels and similar establishments"		Nights	..	..	..	..	..
1.43 ♦ For non commercial accommodation services		Days	..	..	..	..	..
1.44 Average expenditure per day		US$	..	..	..	..	..
2. DOMESTIC TOURISM							
Data							
Accommodation							
Total							
2.19 ♦ Guests		('000)	..	..	..	548	287
2.20 ♦ Overnights		('000)	..	..	..	..	..
Hotels and similar establishments							
2.21 ♦ Guests		('000)	..	..	..	..	..
2.22 ♦ Overnights		('000)	..	..	..	..	..
Indicators							
2.23 Average size of travel party		Persons	..	..	..	..	..
Average length of stay							
2.24 Total		Days	..	..	..	..	..
2.25 ♦ For all commercial accommodation services		Nights	..	1.94	..	..	..
2.26 * of which, "hotels and similar establishments"		Nights	..	..	..	..	..
2.27 ♦ For non commercial accommodation services		Days	..	..	..	..	..
2.28 Average expenditure per day		US$	..	..	..	..	..

NAMIBIA

Basic data and indicators	Notes	Units	2005	2006	2007	2008	2009
3. OUTBOUND TOURISM							
Data							
Expenditure							
3.4 Total		US$ Mn	..	..	..	..	..
3.5 ♦ Travel		US$ Mn	108	118	132	114	109
3.6 ♦ Passenger transport		US$ Mn	..	..	..	..	..
Expenditure by main purpose of the trip							
3.7 Total		US$ Mn	108	118	132	114	109
3.8 ♦ Personal		US$ Mn	95	109	125	108	103
3.9 ♦ Business and professional		US$ Mn	13	9	7	6	6
4. TOURISM INDUSTRIES							
Data							
Number of establishments							
4.1 Total		Units	..	..	..	..	..
4.2 ♦ Accommodation for visitors		Units	..	..	..	..	..
4.3 * of which, "hotels and similar establishments"		Units	61	..	..	394	266
4.4 ♦ Food and beverage serving activities		Units	..	..	..	..	..
4.5 ♦ Passenger transportation		Units	..	..	..	..	..
4.6 ♦ Travel agencies and other reservation services activities		Units	..	..	..	..	..
4.7 ♦ Other tourism industries		Units	..	..	..	..	..
Accommodation for visitors in hotels and similar establishments							
Non-monetary data							
4.13 ♦ Number of establishments		Units	61	..	..	394	266
4.14 ♦ Number of rooms		Units	2,900	..	..	5,704	4,035
4.15 ♦ Number of bed-places		Units	7,240	..	..	11,557	8,239
Indicators							
4.16 Occupancy rate / rooms		Percent	..	..	..	..	..
4.17 Occupancy rate / bed-places		Percent	39.00	59.60	..	..	..
4.18 Average length of stay		Nights	1.90	1.94	..	..	..
4.19 Available capacity (bed-places per 1000 inhabitants)		Units	3.60	..	..	5.43	3.79
6. COMPLEMENTARY INDICATORS							
Demand							
6.1 Gross travel propensity		Units	..	..	..	..	..
6.2 Carrying capacity (arrivals/population)		Units	0.39	0.41	0.44	0.44	..
Macroeconomic indicators related to international tourism							
6.3 Inbound tourism expenditure over GDP		Percent	..	..	..	..	..
6.4 Outbound tourism expenditure over GDP		Percent	..	..	..	..	..
6.5 Tourism balance (inbound minus outbound tourism expenditure) over GDP		Percent	..	..	..	..	..
6.6 Tourism openness (inbound plus outbound tourism expenditure) over GDP		Percent	..	..	..	..	..
6.7 Tourism coverage (inbound over outbound tourism expenditure)		Percent	335.6	400.6	410.3	423.5	431.4
6.8 Inbound tourism expenditure over exports of goods		Percent	17.5	17.9	18.6	15.5	13.3
6.9 Inbound tourism expenditure over exports of services		Percent	88.0	90.1	90.6	87.3	90.0
6.10 Inbound tourism expenditure over exports of goods and services		Percent	14.6	14.9	15.4	13.2	11.6
6.11 Inbound tourism expenditure over current account credits		Percent	10.6	10.7	11.2	9.4	8.2
6.12 Outbound tourism expenditure over imports of goods		Percent	4.7	4.6	4.3	3.0	2.4
6.13 Outbound tourism expenditure over imports of services		Percent	29.3	27.5	25.7	19.4	17.9
6.14 Outbound tourism expenditure over imports of goods and services		Percent	4.0	4.0	3.7	2.6	2.1
6.15 Outbound tourism expenditure over current account debits		Percent	3.5	3.5	3.2	2.3	1.9

NEPAL

Basic data and indicators	Notes	Units	2005	2006	2007	2008	2009
1. INBOUND TOURISM							
Data							
Arrivals							
1.1 Total		('000)	..	..	..	..	..
1.2 ♦ Overnight visitors (tourists)	(1)	('000)	375	384	527	500	510
1.3 ♦ Same-day visitors (excursionists)		('000)	..	..	..	..	..
1.4 * of which, cruise passengers		('000)	..	..	..	..	..
Arrivals by region							
1.5 Total		('000)	374	383	527	500	510
1.6 ♦ Africa		('000)	1	2	1	1	1
1.7 ♦ Americas		('000)	26	28	41	42	42
1.8 ♦ East Asia and the Pacific		('000)	93	95	140	129	135
1.9 ♦ Europe		('000)	112	107	158	147	144
1.10 ♦ Middle East		('000)	..	..	..	6	5
1.11 ♦ South Asia		('000)	139	137	168	150	151
1.12 ♦ Other not classified		('000)	3	14	19	25	32
1.13 * of which, nationals residing abroad		('000)	..	..	..	..	..
Arrivals by main purpose							
1.14 Total		('000)	376	384	526	500	510
1.15 ♦ Personal		('000)	337	345	472	427	453
1.16 * holidays, leisure and recreation		('000)	222	213	319	253	174
1.17 * other personal purposes		('000)	115	132	153	174	279
1.18 ♦ Business and professional		('000)	39	39	54	73	57
Arrivals by mode of transport							
1.19 Total		('000)	375	384	527	500	510
1.20 ♦ Air		('000)	277	284	361	375	379
1.21 ♦ Water		('000)	..	..	..	..	..
1.22 ♦ Land		('000)	98	100	166	125	131
1.23 * railway		('000)	..	..	..	..	..
1.24 * road		('000)	98	100	166	125	131
1.25 * others		('000)	..	..	..	..	..
Expenditure							
1.33 Total		US$ Mn	160	157	234	353	397
1.34 ♦ Travel		US$ Mn	131	128	200	335	371
1.35 ♦ Passenger transport		US$ Mn	29	29	34	18	26
Indicators							
1.39 Average size of travel party		Persons	..	..	..	..	..
Average length of stay							
1.40 Total		Days	..	..	..	..	..
1.41 ♦ For all commercial accommodation services	(2)	Nights	9.09	10.20	11.96	11.78	11.32
1.42 * of which, "hotels and similar establishments"		Nights	..	..	..	..	..
1.43 ♦ For non commercial accommodation services		Days	..	..	..	..	..
1.44 Average expenditure per day		US$	..	..	..	..	..
3. OUTBOUND TOURISM							
Data							
Departures							
3.1 Total		('000)	..	..	..	..	..
3.2 ♦ Overnight visitors (tourists)		('000)	373	415	469	561	589
3.3 ♦ Same-day visitors (excursionists)		('000)	..	..	..	..	..
Expenditure							
3.4 Total		US$ Mn	221	261	402	545	511
3.5 ♦ Travel		US$ Mn	163	185	274	381	434
3.6 ♦ Passenger transport		US$ Mn	58	76	128	164	77

NEPAL

Basic data and indicators	Notes	Units	2005	2006	2007	2008	2009
4. TOURISM INDUSTRIES							
Data							
Number of establishments							
4.1 Total		Units	..	..	..	..	..
4.2 ♦ Accommodation for visitors		Units	..	..	..	..	..
4.3 * of which, "hotels and similar establishments"	(3)	Units	..	..	..	669	736
4.4 ♦ Food and beverage serving activities		Units	..	..	..	..	..
4.5 ♦ Passenger transportation		Units	..	..	..	..	..
4.6 ♦ Travel agencies and other reservation services activities		Units	..	..	..	..	..
4.7 ♦ Other tourism industries		Units	..	..	..	..	..
Accommodation for visitors in hotels and similar establishments							
Non-monetary data							
4.13 ♦ Number of establishments	(3)	Units	..	..	..	669	736
4.14 ♦ Number of rooms	(3)	Units	20,801	12,253	12,482	13,088	14,272
4.15 ♦ Number of bed-places	(3)	Units	39,384	24,260	24,681	26,063	28,485
Indicators							
4.16 Occupancy rate / rooms		Percent	..	..	..	..	..
4.17 Occupancy rate / bed-places		Percent	..	..	..	..	..
4.18 Average length of stay		Nights	..	..	..	..	..
4.19 Available capacity (bed-places per 1000 inhabitants)		Units	1.45	0.87	0.87	0.90	0.97
6. COMPLEMENTARY INDICATORS							
Demand							
6.1 Gross travel propensity		Units	..	..	..	..	..
6.2 Carrying capacity (arrivals/population)		Units	0.01	0.01	0.02	0.02	0.02
Macroeconomic indicators related to international tourism							
6.3 Inbound tourism expenditure over GDP		Percent	2.3	2.2	3.0	..	..
6.4 Outbound tourism expenditure over GDP		Percent	3.2	3.7	5.1	..	..
6.5 Tourism balance (inbound minus outbound tourism expenditure) over GDP		Percent	-0.9	-1.5	-2.1	..	..
6.6 Tourism openness (inbound plus outbound tourism expenditure) over GDP		Percent	5.5	6.0	8.1	..	..
6.7 Tourism coverage (inbound over outbound tourism expenditure)		Percent	72.7	60.0	58.4	64.9	77.6
6.8 Inbound tourism expenditure over exports of goods		Percent	17.8	18.5	25.3	35.8	47.2
6.9 Inbound tourism expenditure over exports of services		Percent	42.2	40.7	45.8	48.8	60.8
6.10 Inbound tourism expenditure over exports of goods and services		Percent	12.5	12.7	16.3	20.6	26.6
6.11 Inbound tourism expenditure over current account credits		Percent	5.3	4.8	6.2	6.7	7.6
6.12 Outbound tourism expenditure over imports of goods		Percent	9.7	10.7	13.7	15.5	11.9
6.13 Outbound tourism expenditure over imports of services		Percent	50.8	53.1	55.5	63.9	65.2
6.14 Outbound tourism expenditure over imports of goods and services		Percent	8.1	8.9	11.0	12.5	10.1
6.15 Outbound tourism expenditure over current account debits		Percent	7.7	8.4	10.6	12.1	9.7

NETHERLANDS

Basic data and indicators	Notes	Units	2005	2006	2007	2008	2009
1. INBOUND TOURISM							
Data							
Arrivals							
1.1 Total		('000)	..	..		..	..
1.2 ♦ Overnight visitors (tourists)	(1)	('000)	10,012	10,739	11,008	10,104	9,921
1.3 ♦ Same-day visitors (excursionists)		('000)	..	..		..	..
1.4 * of which, cruise passengers		('000)	..	..	..	..	..
Arrivals by region	(1)						
1.5 Total		('000)	10,012	10,739	11,008	10,105	9,921
1.6 ♦ Africa		('000)	101	93	92	84	84
1.7 ♦ Americas		('000)	1,222	1,325	1,274	1,068	1,018
1.8 ♦ East Asia and the Pacific		('000)	749	723	738	668	673
1.9 ♦ Europe		('000)	7,940	8,598	8,904	8,285	8,146
1.10 ♦ Middle East		('000)	..	..	..	..	..
1.11 ♦ South Asia		('000)	..	..	..	..	..
1.12 ♦ Other not classified		('000)	..	..	..	..	..
1.13 * of which, nationals residing abroad		('000)	..	..	..	..	..
Accommodation							
Total							
1.29 ♦ Guests		('000)	10,012	10,739	11,008	10,104	9,921
1.30 ♦ Overnights		('000)	25,210	26,887	27,952	25,268	25,014
Hotels and similar establishments							
1.31 ♦ Guests	(2)	('000)	8,081	8,567	8,713	8,035	7,754
1.32 ♦ Overnights	(2)	('000)	15,143	15,976	16,328	14,961	14,429
Expenditure							
1.33 Total		US$ Mn	16,528	17,529	19,922	20,526	17,876
1.34 ♦ Travel		US$ Mn	10,450	11,382	13,339	13,346	12,408
1.35 ♦ Passenger transport		US$ Mn	6,078	6,147	6,583	7,180	5,468
Expenditure by main purpose of the trip							
1.36 Total		US$ Mn	10,450	11,382	13,339	13,346	12,408
1.37 ♦ Personal		US$ Mn	6,986	7,755	9,011	8,955	8,543
1.38 ♦ Business and professional		US$ Mn	3,464	3,627	4,328	4,391	3,865
Indicators							
1.39 Average size of travel party		Persons	..	..	..	..	..
Average length of stay							
1.40 Total		Days	..	..	..	..	..
1.41 ♦ For all commercial accommodation services		Nights	2.50	2.50	2.54	2.50	2.52
1.42 * of which, "hotels and similar establishments"		Nights	..	..	..	..	..
1.43 ♦ For non commercial accommodation services		Days	..	..	..	..	..
1.44 Average expenditure per day		US$	..	..	..	..	..
2. DOMESTIC TOURISM							
Data							
Accommodation							
Total							
2.19 ♦ Guests		('000)	16,182	17,765	19,252	18,998	19,039
2.20 ♦ Overnights		('000)	54,951	57,057	60,315	59,185	59,502
Hotels and similar establishments							
2.21 ♦ Guests	(2)	('000)	8,301	9,463	10,516	10,461	10,092
2.22 ♦ Overnights	(2)	('000)	14,375	15,783	17,831	17,657	17,052
Indicators							
2.23 Average size of travel party		Persons	..	..	..	..	..
Average length of stay							
2.24 Total		Days	..	..	..	..	..
2.25 ♦ For all commercial accommodation services		Nights	3.40	3.21	3.13	3.12	3.13
2.26 * of which, "hotels and similar establishments"		Nights	..	..	..	..	..
2.27 ♦ For non commercial accommodation services		Days	..	..	..	..	..
2.28 Average expenditure per day		US$	..	..	..	..	..

NETHERLANDS

Basic data and indicators	Notes	Units	2005	2006	2007	2008	2009
3. OUTBOUND TOURISM							
Data							
Departures							
3.1　Total		('000)	..	..	..	..	..
3.2　♦ Overnight visitors (tourists)	(3)	('000)	17,039	16,695	17,556	18,458	18,408
3.3　♦ Same-day visitors (excursionists)		('000)	..	..	..	..	..
Expenditure							
3.4　Total		US$ Mn	16,621	17,453	19,477	22,212	21,076
3.5　♦ Travel		US$ Mn	16,140	17,087	19,110	21,825	20,757
3.6　♦ Passenger transport		US$ Mn	481	366	367	387	319
Expenditure by main purpose of the trip							
3.7　Total		US$ Mn	16,140	17,087	19,109	21,825	20,757
3.8　♦ Personal		US$ Mn	12,219	12,931	14,427	16,620	15,764
3.9　♦ Business and professional		US$ Mn	3,921	4,156	4,682	5,205	4,993
4. TOURISM INDUSTRIES							
Data							
Number of establishments							
4.1　Total		Units	..	..	..	..	..
4.2　♦ Accommodation for visitors		Units	..	..	..	..	..
4.3　　* of which, "hotels and similar establishments"		Units	3,135	3,099	3,196	3,180	3,151
4.4　♦ Food and beverage serving activities		Units	..	..	..	..	..
4.5　♦ Passenger transportation		Units	..	..	..	..	..
4.6　♦ Travel agencies and other reservation services activities		Units	..	..	..	..	..
4.7　♦ Other tourism industries		Units	..	..	..	..	..
Accommodation for visitors in hotels and similar establishments							
Non-monetary data							
4.13　♦ Number of establishments		Units	3,135	3,099	3,196	3,180	3,151
4.14　♦ Number of rooms	(4)	Units	94,364	94,509	98,966	98,155	100,493
4.15　♦ Number of bed-places	(4)	Units	192,215	192,067	200,254	198,647	203,852
Indicators							
4.16　Occupancy rate / rooms		Percent	..	..	..	..	..
4.17　Occupancy rate / bed-places		Percent	42.10	45.30	46.73	44.99	42.31
4.18　Average length of stay	(5)	Nights	1.80	1.80	1.78	1.76	1.76
4.19　Available capacity (bed-places per 1000 inhabitants)		Units	11.78	11.75	12.22	12.08	12.33
6. COMPLEMENTARY INDICATORS							
Demand							
6.1　Gross travel propensity		Units	..	..	..	..	..
6.2　Carrying capacity (arrivals/population)		Units	0.61	0.66	0.67	0.61	0.60
Macroeconomic indicators related to international tourism							
6.3　Inbound tourism expenditure over GDP		Percent	2.6	2.6	2.6	2.4	2.3
6.4　Outbound tourism expenditure over GDP		Percent	2.6	2.6	2.5	2.5	2.7
6.5　Tourism balance (inbound minus outbound tourism expenditure) over GDP		Percent	0.0	0.0	0.1	-0.2	-0.4
6.6　Tourism openness (inbound plus outbound tourism expenditure) over GDP		Percent	5.2	5.2	5.1	4.9	4.9
6.7　Tourism coverage (inbound over outbound tourism expenditure)		Percent	99.4	100.4	102.3	92.4	84.8
6.8　Inbound tourism expenditure over exports of goods		Percent	4.8	4.5	4.3	3.9	4.3
6.9　Inbound tourism expenditure over exports of services		Percent	20.6	20.7	20.6	19.4	19.1
6.10　Inbound tourism expenditure over exports of goods and services		Percent	3.9	3.7	3.6	3.2	3.5
6.11　Inbound tourism expenditure over current account credits		Percent	3.1	2.8	2.7	2.6	2.8
6.12　Outbound tourism expenditure over imports of goods		Percent	5.6	5.1	4.8	4.7	5.7
6.13　Outbound tourism expenditure over imports of services		Percent	22.7	23.1	23.0	24.0	24.6
6.14　Outbound tourism expenditure over imports of goods and services		Percent	4.5	4.2	4.0	3.9	4.6
6.15　Outbound tourism expenditure over current account debits		Percent	3.4	3.1	2.9	3.0	3.6

NEW CALEDONIA

Basic data and indicators	Notes	Units	2005	2006	2007	2008	2009
1. INBOUND TOURISM							
Data							
Arrivals							
1.1 Total		('000)	182	219	227	256	230
1.2 ♦ Overnight visitors (tourists)	(1)	('000)	101	100	103	104	99
1.3 ♦ Same-day visitors (excursionists)		('000)	81	119	124	152	131
1.4 * of which, cruise passengers		('000)	81	119	124	152	131
Arrivals by region	(1)						
1.5 Total		('000)	101	101	103	104	99
1.6 ♦ Africa		('000)	1	1	1	1	2
1.7 ♦ Americas		('000)	2	2	2	3	2
1.8 ♦ East Asia and the Pacific		('000)	68	66	68	64	63
1.9 ♦ Europe		('000)	30	32	32	36	32
1.10 ♦ Middle East		('000)	..	..	..	..	..
1.11 ♦ South Asia		('000)	..	..	..	..	..
1.12 ♦ Other not classified		('000)	..	..	..	..	..
1.13 * of which, nationals residing abroad		('000)	..	..	..	..	..
Arrivals by main purpose	(1)						
1.14 Total		('000)	101	100	103	104	99
1.15 ♦ Personal		('000)	89	86	86	84	81
1.16 * holidays, leisure and recreation		('000)	56	56	56	54	51
1.17 * other personal purposes		('000)	33	30	30	30	30
1.18 ♦ Business and professional		('000)	12	14	17	20	18
Arrivals by mode of transport	(1)						
1.19 Total		('000)	101	100	103	104	99
1.20 ♦ Air		('000)	101	100	103	104	99
1.21 ♦ Water		('000)	..	..	..	..	..
1.22 ♦ Land		('000)	..	..	..	..	..
1.23 * railway		('000)	..	..	..	..	..
1.24 * road		('000)	..	..	..	..	..
1.25 * others		('000)	..	..	..	..	..
Accommodation							
Total							
1.29 ♦ Guests		('000)	..	..	..	..	..
1.30 ♦ Overnights		('000)	..	..	..	..	..
Hotels and similar establishments							
1.31 ♦ Guests	(2)	('000)	77	85	129	102	115
1.32 ♦ Overnights	(2)	('000)	350	379	347	360	304
Expenditure							
1.33 Total		US$ Mn	..	..	..	..	..
1.34 ♦ Travel		US$ Mn	149	122	142	152	141
1.35 ♦ Passenger transport		US$ Mn	..	..	..	..	..
Indicators							
1.39 Average size of travel party		Persons	..	..	..	..	..
Average length of stay							
1.40 Total		Days	..	..	..	..	..
1.41 ♦ For all commercial accommodation services		Nights	16.80	19.10	19.60	19.70	21.10
1.42 * of which, "hotels and similar establishments"		Nights	..	..	..	..	..
1.43 ♦ For non commercial accommodation services		Days	..	..	..	..	..
1.44 Average expenditure per day		US$	..	..	..	..	..
2. DOMESTIC TOURISM							
Data							
Accommodation							
Total							
2.19 ♦ Guests		('000)	..	..	..	..	..
2.20 ♦ Overnights		('000)	..	..	..	..	..
Hotels and similar establishments							
2.21 ♦ Guests	(2)	('000)	69	82	100	112	117
2.22 ♦ Overnights	(2)	('000)	193	233	207	255	265

NEW CALEDONIA

Basic data and indicators	Notes	Units	2005	2006	2007	2008	2009
3. OUTBOUND TOURISM							
Data							
Departures							
3.1 Total	(3)	('000)	..	..	..	..	..
3.2 ♦ Overnight visitors (tourists)		('000)	96	100	106	112	119
3.3 ♦ Same-day visitors (excursionists)		('000)	..	..	..	..	..
Expenditure							
3.4 Total		US$ Mn	..	..	..	..	..
3.5 ♦ Travel		US$ Mn	122	129	149	168	170
3.6 ♦ Passenger transport		US$ Mn	..	..	..	..	..
4. TOURISM INDUSTRIES							
Data							
Number of establishments							
4.1 Total		Units	..	..	..	..	..
4.2 ♦ Accommodation for visitors		Units	..	..	..	..	..
4.3 * of which, "hotels and similar establishments"		Units	106	110	..	53	..
4.4 ♦ Food and beverage serving activities		Units	..	..	..	..	..
4.5 ♦ Passenger transportation		Units	..	..	..	..	..
4.6 ♦ Travel agencies and other reservation services activities		Units	..	..	..	..	..
4.7 ♦ Other tourism industries		Units	..	..	..	..	..
Accommodation for visitors in hotels and similar establishments							
Non-monetary data							
4.13 ♦ Number of establishments		Units	106	110	..	53	..
4.14 ♦ Number of rooms		Units	2,245	..	..	2,214	..
4.15 ♦ Number of bed-places		Units	..	..	..	..	..
Indicators							
4.16 Occupancy rate / rooms	(4)	Percent	61.30	61.90	60.90	62.30	58.80
4.17 Occupancy rate / bed-places		Percent	..	..	..	..	..
4.18 Average length of stay	(5)	Nights	4.40	3.70	2.40	2.90	2.50
4.19 Available capacity (bed-places per 1000 inhabitants)		Units	..	..	..	..	..
6. COMPLEMENTARY INDICATORS							
Demand							
6.1 Gross travel propensity		Units	..	..	..	..	..
6.2 Carrying capacity (arrivals/population)		Units	0.43	0.42	0.42	0.42	0.40
Macroeconomic indicators related to international tourism							
6.3 Inbound tourism expenditure over GDP		Percent	..	..	..	..	..
6.4 Outbound tourism expenditure over GDP		Percent	..	..	..	..	..
6.5 Tourism balance (inbound minus outbound tourism expenditure) over GDP		Percent	..	..	..	..	..
6.6 Tourism openness (inbound plus outbound tourism expenditure) over GDP		Percent	..	..	..	..	..
6.7 Tourism coverage (inbound over outbound tourism expenditure)		Percent	121.7	94.9	95.2	90.4	..
6.8 Inbound tourism expenditure over exports of goods		Percent	13.6	9.1	6.6	11.2	..
6.9 Inbound tourism expenditure over exports of services		Percent	39.1	27.0	26.1	25.0	..
6.10 Inbound tourism expenditure over exports of goods and services		Percent	10.1	6.8	5.3	7.7	..
6.11 Inbound tourism expenditure over current account credits		Percent	5.5	4.0	3.4	4.1	..
6.12 Outbound tourism expenditure over imports of goods		Percent	7.4	6.7	5.8	5.6	..
6.13 Outbound tourism expenditure over imports of services		Percent	14.5	11.4	11.3	12.0	..
6.14 Outbound tourism expenditure over imports of goods and services		Percent	4.9	4.2	3.8	3.8	..
6.15 Outbound tourism expenditure over current account debits		Percent	4.4	3.7	3.4	3.3	..

NEW ZEALAND

Basic data and indicators	Notes	Units	2005	2006	2007	2008	2009
1. INBOUND TOURISM							
Data							
Arrivals							
1.1 Total	(1)	('000)	2,366	2,409	2,455	2,447	2,448
1.2 ♦ Overnight visitors (tourists)		('000)	2,353	2,390	2,434	2,411	2,422
1.3 ♦ Same-day visitors (excursionists)		('000)	13	19	21	36	26
1.4 * of which, cruise passengers		('000)	13	19	21	36	26
Arrivals by region	(1)						
1.5 Total		('000)	2,364	2,409	2,455	2,448	2,447
1.6 ♦ Africa		('000)	20	21	25	29	22
1.7 ♦ Americas		('000)	276	295	290	296	276
1.8 ♦ East Asia and the Pacific		('000)	1,469	1,494	1,530	1,509	1,562
1.9 ♦ Europe		('000)	521	516	517	519	491
1.10 ♦ Middle East		('000)	9	10	11	13	15
1.11 ♦ South Asia		('000)	20	23	25	27	28
1.12 ♦ Other not classified		('000)	49	50	57	55	53
1.13 * of which, nationals residing abroad		('000)	16	18	21	24	23
Arrivals by main purpose	(1)						
1.14 Total		('000)	2,366	2,409	2,455	2,447	2,448
1.15 ♦ Personal		('000)	2,047	2,081	2,125	2,135	2,170
1.16 * holidays, leisure and recreation		('000)	1,192	1,195	1,211	1,184	1,185
1.17 * other personal purposes		('000)	855	886	914	951	985
1.18 ♦ Business and professional		('000)	319	328	330	312	278
Arrivals by mode of transport	(1)						
1.19 Total		('000)	2,366	2,409	2,456	2,447	2,448
1.20 ♦ Air		('000)	2,349	2,387	2,431	2,408	2,420
1.21 ♦ Water		('000)	17	22	25	39	28
1.22 ♦ Land		('000)	..	..	..	..	..
1.23 * railway		('000)	..	..	..	..	..
1.24 * road		('000)	..	..	..	..	..
1.25 * others		('000)	..	..	..	..	..
Accommodation							
Total							
1.29 ♦ Guests		('000)	..	..	..	..	..
1.30 ♦ Overnights	(2)	('000)	..	..	..	13,657	13,279
Hotels and similar establishments							
1.31 ♦ Guests		('000)	..	..	..	..	..
1.32 ♦ Overnights	(2)	('000)	..	..	..	8,090	7,601
Expenditure							
1.33 Total		US$ Mn	..	..	..	..	..
1.34 ♦ Travel		US$ Mn	5,211	4,792	5,415	5,130	4,396
1.35 ♦ Passenger transport		US$ Mn	..	..	..	..	..
Expenditure by main purpose of the trip							
1.36 Total		US$ Mn	5,210	4,790	5,413	5,130	4,396
1.37 ♦ Personal		US$ Mn	4,693	4,328	4,821	4,524	3,991
1.38 ♦ Business and professional		US$ Mn	517	462	592	606	405
Indicators							
1.39 Average size of travel party		Persons	..	..	..	..	..
Average length of stay							
1.40 Total	(1)	Days	19.95	20.39	20.22	20.91	20.49
1.41 ♦ For all commercial accommodation services		Nights	..	..	..	..	..
1.42 * of which, "hotels and similar establishments"		Nights	..	..	..	..	..
1.43 ♦ For non commercial accommodation services		Days	..	..	..	..	..
1.44 Average expenditure per day	(3)	US$	89.2	85.5	92.4	93.4	77.6

NEW ZEALAND

Basic data and indicators	Notes	Units	2005	2006	2007	2008	2009
2. DOMESTIC TOURISM							
Data							
Trips	(4)						
2.1 Total		('000)	..	..	..	..	48,076
2.2 ♦ Overnight visitors (tourists)		('000)	..	..	..	..	31,395
2.3 ♦ Same-day visitors (excursionists)		('000)	..	..	..	..	16,681
Trips by main purpose	(4)						
2.4 Total		('000)	..	..	..	..	48,076
2.5 ♦ Personal		('000)	..	..	..	..	36,364
2.6 * holidays, leisure and recreation		('000)	..	..	..	..	34,215
2.7 * other personal purposes		('000)	..	..	..	..	2,149
2.8 ♦ Business and professional		('000)	..	..	..	..	11,712
Trips by mode of transport	(4)						
2.9 Total		('000)	..	..	..	..	48,076
2.10 ♦ Air		('000)	..	..	..	..	3,411
2.11 ♦ Water		('000)	..	..	..	..	1,433
2.12 ♦ Land		('000)	..	..	..	..	43,232
2.13 * railway		('000)	..	..	..	..	509
2.14 * road		('000)	..	..	..	..	42,655
2.15 * others		('000)	..	..	..	..	68
Trips by form of organization	(4)						
2.16 Total		('000)	..	..	..	..	48,076
2.17 ♦ Package tour		('000)	..	..	..	..	86
2.18 ♦ Other forms		('000)	..	..	..	..	47,990
Accommodation							
Total							
2.19 ♦ Guests		('000)	..	..	..	..	..
2.20 ♦ Overnights	(2)	('000)	..	..	..	18,823	18,735
Hotels and similar establishments							
2.21 ♦ Guests		('000)	..	..	..	..	..
2.22 ♦ Overnights	(2)	('000)	..	..	..	13,279	13,353
Indicators							
2.23 Average size of travel party		Persons	..	..	..	..	..
Average length of stay							
2.24 Total	(4)	Days	..	..	..	..	3.00
2.25 ♦ For all commercial accommodation services		Nights	..	..	..	..	..
2.26 * of which, "hotels and similar establishments"		Nights	..	..	..	..	..
2.27 ♦ For non commercial accommodation services		Days	..	..	..	..	..
2.28 Average expenditure per day	(4)	US$	..	..	..	..	75.0
3. OUTBOUND TOURISM							
Data							
Departures							
3.1 Total		('000)	..	..	..	..	..
3.2 ♦ Overnight visitors (tourists)	(1)	('000)	1,872	1,861	1,978	1,965	1,917
3.3 ♦ Same-day visitors (excursionists)		('000)	..	..	..	..	..
Expenditure							
3.4 Total		US$ Mn	..	..	..	..	..
3.5 ♦ Travel		US$ Mn	2,671	2,534	3,084	2,983	2,559
3.6 ♦ Passenger transport		US$ Mn	..	..	..	..	..
Expenditure by main purpose of the trip							
3.7 Total		US$ Mn	2,670	2,534	3,084	2,983	2,559
3.8 ♦ Personal		US$ Mn	2,124	2,017	2,478	2,381	2,078
3.9 ♦ Business and professional		US$ Mn	546	517	606	602	481
Indicators							
3.10 Average length of stay	(1)	Days	19.53	19.57	19.69	19.88	19.62
3.11 Average expenditure per day		US$	..	..	..	..	..

NEW ZEALAND

Basic data and indicators	Notes	Units	2005	2006	2007	2008	2009
4. TOURISM INDUSTRIES							
Data							
Number of establishments	(5)						
4.1 Total		Units	13,890	14,089	14,099	14,308	14,499
4.2 ♦ Accommodation for visitors		Units	5,009	5,042	5,024	5,018	5,002
4.3 * of which, "hotels and similar establishments"		Units	2,499	2,479	2,477	2,457	2,452
4.4 ♦ Food and beverage serving activities		Units	8,881	9,047	9,075	9,290	9,497
4.5 ♦ Passenger transportation		Units	..	..	..	..	..
4.6 ♦ Travel agencies and other reservation services activities		Units	..	..	..	..	..
4.7 ♦ Other tourism industries		Units	..	..	..	..	..
Accommodation for visitors in hotels and similar establishments							
Non-monetary data	(6)						
4.13 ♦ Number of establishments		Units	2,774	2,812	2,881	2,932	2,927
4.14 ♦ Number of rooms		Units	29,031	29,926	30,830	31,864	32,641
4.15 ♦ Number of bed-places		Units	..	..	..	..	..
Indicators	(6)						
4.16 Occupancy rate / rooms		Percent	52.00	52.00	52.00	50.00	48.00
4.17 Occupancy rate / bed-places		Percent	..	..	..	..	..
4.18 Average length of stay		Nights	2.00	2.00	2.00	2.00	2.00
4.19 Available capacity (bed-places per 1000 inhabitants)		Units	..	..	..	..	..
5. EMPLOYMENT							
Data							
Number of employees by tourism industries	(5)						
5.1 Total		('000)	107.7	111.8	115.5	117.1	110.4
5.2 ♦ Accommodation services for visitors (hotels and similar establishments)		('000)	25.9	25.9	26.4	26.4	24.3
5.3 ♦ Other accommodation services		('000)	7.5	7.5	8.1	7.9	7.8
5.4 ♦ Food and beverage serving activities		('000)	74.3	78.5	81.1	82.8	78.3
5.5 ♦ Passenger transportation		('000)	..	..	..	..	..
5.6 ♦ Travel agencies and other reservation services activities		('000)	..	..	..	..	..
5.7 ♦ Other tourism industries		('000)	..	..	..	..	..
6. COMPLEMENTARY INDICATORS							
Demand							
6.1 Gross travel propensity		Units	..	..	..	..	..
6.2 Carrying capacity (arrivals/population)		Units	0.57	0.57	0.58	0.56	7.84
Macroeconomic indicators related to international tourism							
6.3 Inbound tourism expenditure over GDP		Percent	4.9	4.6	4.4	4.0	3.8
6.4 Outbound tourism expenditure over GDP		Percent	2.5	2.4	2.5	2.3	2.2
6.5 Tourism balance (inbound minus outbound tourism expenditure) over GDP		Percent	2.4	2.2	1.9	1.7	1.6
6.6 Tourism openness (inbound plus outbound tourism expenditure) over GDP		Percent	7.4	7.0	6.9	6.4	6.0
6.7 Tourism coverage (inbound over outbound tourism expenditure)		Percent	195.1	189.1	175.6	172.0	171.8
6.8 Inbound tourism expenditure over exports of goods		Percent	23.7	21.2	19.8	16.4	17.3
6.9 Inbound tourism expenditure over exports of services		Percent	60.0	58.7	57.8	56.2	58.0
6.10 Inbound tourism expenditure over exports of goods and services		Percent	17.0	15.6	14.8	12.7	13.3
6.11 Inbound tourism expenditure over current account credits		Percent	15.6	14.3	13.3	11.6	12.4
6.12 Outbound tourism expenditure over imports of goods		Percent	10.9	10.3	10.6	9.1	10.7
6.13 Outbound tourism expenditure over imports of services		Percent	32.4	32.1	33.5	30.8	32.7
6.14 Outbound tourism expenditure over imports of goods and services		Percent	8.1	7.8	8.1	7.0	8.1
6.15 Outbound tourism expenditure over current account debits		Percent	6.3	5.9	6.0	5.4	6.5

NICARAGUA

Basic data and indicators	Notes	Units	2005	2006	2007	2008	2009
1. INBOUND TOURISM							
Data							
Arrivals							
1.1 Total		('000)	804	891	978	1,118	1,132
1.2 ♦ Overnight visitors (tourists)	(1)	('000)	712	749	800	858	932
1.3 ♦ Same-day visitors (excursionists)		('000)	92	142	178	260	200
1.4 * of which, cruise passengers		('000)	13	15	21	54	56
Arrivals by region	(1)						
1.5 Total		('000)	713	749	800	858	932
1.6 ♦ Africa		('000)	1	1	..	1	1
1.7 ♦ Americas		('000)	619	623	672	714	770
1.8 ♦ East Asia and the Pacific		('000)	11	13	9	9	12
1.9 ♦ Europe		('000)	59	58	53	58	71
1.10 ♦ Middle East		('000)	..	..	..	..	..
1.11 ♦ South Asia		('000)	2	1	..	2	1
1.12 ♦ Other not classified		('000)	21	53	66	74	77
1.13 * of which, nationals residing abroad		('000)	21	53	65	74	77
Arrivals by main purpose	(1)						
1.14 Total		('000)	712	749	800	858	932
1.15 ♦ Personal		('000)	574	609	656	701	792
1.16 * holidays, leisure and recreation		('000)	504	551	607	644	755
1.17 * other personal purposes		('000)	70	58	49	57	37
1.18 ♦ Business and professional		('000)	138	140	144	157	140
Arrivals by mode of transport	(1)						
1.19 Total		('000)	712	749	800	858	932
1.20 ♦ Air		('000)	235	279	323	356	353
1.21 ♦ Water		('000)	26	28	15	26	26
1.22 ♦ Land		('000)	451	442	462	476	553
1.23 * railway		('000)	..	..	..	..	..
1.24 * road		('000)	451	442	462	476	553
1.25 * others		('000)	..	..	..	..	..
Accommodation							
Total							
1.29 ♦ Guests	(2)	('000)	221	230	277	309	266
1.30 ♦ Overnights	(2)	('000)	523	427	774	892	755
Hotels and similar establishments							
1.31 ♦ Guests	(3)	('000)	174	203	248	287	255
1.32 ♦ Overnights	(3)	('000)	422	366	707	844	728
Expenditure							
1.33 Total		US$ Mn	..	..	..	..	..
1.34 ♦ Travel		US$ Mn	206	231	255	276	346
1.35 ♦ Passenger transport		US$ Mn	..	..	..	..	..
Indicators							
1.39 Average size of travel party		Persons	..	..	..	..	..
Average length of stay							
1.40 Total		Days	9.20	7.60	6.70	5.60	7.50
1.41 ♦ For all commercial accommodation services		Nights	2.40	1.90	2.80	2.90	2.80
1.42 * of which, "hotels and similar establishments"		Nights	..	..	..	..	..
1.43 ♦ For non commercial accommodation services		Days	..	..	..	..	..
1.44 Average expenditure per day		US$	39.7	45.0	47.5	57.2	47.2
2. DOMESTIC TOURISM							
Data							
Accommodation							
Total							
2.19 ♦ Guests	(2)	('000)	118	142	128	150	144
2.20 ♦ Overnights	(2)	('000)	205	322	326	248	239
Hotels and similar establishments							
2.21 ♦ Guests	(3)	('000)	71	87	107	111	108
2.22 ♦ Overnights	(3)	('000)	130	245	285	189	182
Indicators							
2.23 Average size of travel party		Persons	..	..	..	..	..
Average length of stay							
2.24 Total		Days	..	..	..	..	..
2.25 ♦ For all commercial accommodation services		Nights	1.70	2.30	2.60	1.70	1.70
2.26 * of which, "hotels and similar establishments"		Nights	..	..	..	..	..
2.27 ♦ For non commercial accommodation services		Days	..	..	..	..	..
2.28 Average expenditure per day		US$	..	..	..	..	..

NICARAGUA

Basic data and indicators	Notes	Units	2005	2006	2007	2008	2009
3. OUTBOUND TOURISM							
Data							
Departures							
3.1 Total	(4)	('000)	..	..	..	..	..
3.2 ♦ Overnight visitors (tourists)		('000)	740	773	949	1,100	858
3.3 ♦ Same-day visitors (excursionists)		('000)	..	..	..	..	..
Expenditure							
3.4 Total		US$ Mn	162	171	195	218	224
3.5 ♦ Travel		US$ Mn	91	97	121	142	147
3.6 ♦ Passenger transport		US$ Mn	71	74	74	76	77
Indicators							
3.10 Average length of stay		Days	..	..	..	..	6.10
3.11 Average expenditure per day		US$	..	..	..	..	24.4
4. TOURISM INDUSTRIES							
Data							
Number of establishments							
4.1 Total		Units	..	..	..	..	..
4.2 ♦ Accommodation for visitors		Units	..	..	..	..	..
4.3 * of which, "hotels and similar establishments"	(5)	Units	345	380	406	503	529
4.4 ♦ Food and beverage serving activities		Units	..	..	..	..	..
4.5 ♦ Passenger transportation		Units	..	..	..	..	..
4.6 ♦ Travel agencies and other reservation services activities		Units	..	..	..	..	..
4.7 ♦ Other tourism industries		Units	..	..	..	..	..
Accommodation for visitors in hotels and similar establishments							
Non-monetary data							
4.13 ♦ Number of establishments	(5)	Units	345	380	406	503	529
4.14 ♦ Number of rooms	(5)	Units	5,335	5,889	6,233	7,408	7,817
4.15 ♦ Number of bed-places	(5)	Units	9,036	9,787	10,272	12,494	12,800
Indicators							
4.16 Occupancy rate / rooms		Percent	..	..	..	..	..
4.17 Occupancy rate / bed-places		Percent	..	..	..	..	..
4.18 Average length of stay	(6)	Nights	2.20	2.00	2.70	2.50	2.40
4.19 Available capacity (bed-places per 1000 inhabitants)		Units	1.66	1.77	1.84	2.20	2.23
6. COMPLEMENTARY INDICATORS							
Demand							
6.1 Gross travel propensity		Units	..	..	..	..	..
6.2 Carrying capacity (arrivals/population)		Units	0.13	0.14	0.14	0.15	0.16
Macroeconomic indicators related to international tourism							
6.3 Inbound tourism expenditure over GDP		Percent	4.2	4.4	4.6	4.4	5.6
6.4 Outbound tourism expenditure over GDP		Percent	3.3	3.3	3.5	3.5	3.6
6.5 Tourism balance (inbound minus outbound tourism expenditure) over GDP		Percent	0.9	1.1	1.1	0.9	2.0
6.6 Tourism openness (inbound plus outbound tourism expenditure) over GDP		Percent	7.6	7.7	8.0	7.9	9.3
6.7 Tourism coverage (inbound over outbound tourism expenditure)		Percent	127.6	134.9	131.1	126.9	154.4
6.8 Inbound tourism expenditure over exports of goods		Percent	12.5	11.3	10.9	10.9	14.5
6.9 Inbound tourism expenditure over exports of services		Percent	66.9	67.1	68.4	69.2	73.6
6.10 Inbound tourism expenditure over exports of goods and services		Percent	10.5	9.7	9.4	9.4	12.1
6.11 Inbound tourism expenditure over current account credits		Percent	7.3	6.7	6.7	6.9	8.9
6.12 Outbound tourism expenditure over imports of goods		Percent	5.5	4.9	4.8	4.6	5.7
6.13 Outbound tourism expenditure over imports of services		Percent	36.1	35.8	35.1	35.8	40.4
6.14 Outbound tourism expenditure over imports of goods and services		Percent	4.7	4.3	4.2	4.1	5.0
6.15 Outbound tourism expenditure over current account debits		Percent	4.5	4.1	4.0	3.9	4.7

NIGER

Basic data and indicators	Notes	Units	2005	2006	2007	2008	2009
1. INBOUND TOURISM							
Data							
Arrivals							
1.1 Total		('000)	..	..	..	..	..
1.2 ♦ Overnight visitors (tourists)		('000)	58	60	48	73	66
1.3 ♦ Same-day visitors (excursionists)		('000)	..	..	..	..	..
1.4 * of which, cruise passengers		('000)	..	..	..	..	..
Arrivals by region							
1.5 Total		('000)	58	60	46	72	65
1.6 ♦ Africa		('000)	35	36	25	47	42
1.7 ♦ Americas		('000)	4	4	3	4	4
1.8 ♦ East Asia and the Pacific		('000)	3	3	2	3	3
1.9 ♦ Europe		('000)	16	17	16	18	16
1.10 ♦ Middle East		('000)	..	..	..	..	..
1.11 ♦ South Asia		('000)	..	..	..	..	..
1.12 ♦ Other not classified		('000)	..	..	..	..	..
1.13 * of which, nationals residing abroad		('000)	..	..	..	..	..
Arrivals by main purpose							
1.14 Total		('000)	58	60	48	73	66
1.15 ♦ Personal		('000)	30	29	23	36	32
1.16 * holidays, leisure and recreation		('000)	14	14	11	9	8
1.17 * other personal purposes		('000)	16	15	12	27	24
1.18 ♦ Business and professional		('000)	28	31	25	37	34
Arrivals by mode of transport							
1.19 Total		('000)	58	60	48	73	66
1.20 ♦ Air		('000)	58	60	48	73	66
1.21 ♦ Water		('000)	..	..	..	..	..
1.22 ♦ Land		('000)	..	..	..	..	..
1.23 * railway		('000)	..	..	..	..	..
1.24 * road		('000)	..	..	..	..	..
1.25 * others		('000)	..	..	..	..	..
Accommodation							
Total							
1.29 ♦ Guests		('000)	..	..	..	..	..
1.30 ♦ Overnights		('000)	146	154	146	161	..
Hotels and similar establishments							
1.31 ♦ Guests		('000)	..	..	..	..	..
1.32 ♦ Overnights		('000)	140	147	146	161	..
Expenditure							
1.33 Total		US$ Mn	44	39	44	86	..
1.34 ♦ Travel		US$ Mn	43	36	41	79	..
1.35 ♦ Passenger transport		US$ Mn	0.9	3.1	3.3	6.8	..
Expenditure by main purpose of the trip							
1.36 Total		US$ Mn	43.2	36.1	41.2	78.6	..
1.37 ♦ Personal		US$ Mn	12.4	12.7	20.4	29.3	..
1.38 ♦ Business and professional		US$ Mn	30.8	23.4	20.8	49.3	..
Indicators							
1.39 Average size of travel party		Persons	..	..	..	..	..
Average length of stay							
1.40 Total		Days	..	..	..	..	..
1.41 ♦ For all commercial accommodation services	(1)	Nights	8.00	8.00	8.00	8.00	..
1.42 * of which, "hotels and similar establishments"		Nights	..	..	..	..	..
1.43 ♦ For non commercial accommodation services		Days	..	..	..	..	..
1.44 Average expenditure per day		US$	..	..	..	..	..
2. DOMESTIC TOURISM							
Data							
Accommodation							
Total							
2.19 ♦ Guests		('000)	..	..	..	..	..
2.20 ♦ Overnights		('000)	..	..	..	..	..
Hotels and similar establishments							
2.21 ♦ Guests		('000)	8	9	17	23	..
2.22 ♦ Overnights		('000)	18	19	39	35	..
Indicators							
2.23 Average size of travel party		Persons	..	..	..	..	..
Average length of stay							
2.24 Total		Days	..	..	..	..	..
2.25 ♦ For all commercial accommodation services	(1)	Nights	5.00	5.00	5.00	1.00	..
2.26 * of which, "hotels and similar establishments"		Nights	..	..	..	..	..
2.27 ♦ For non commercial accommodation services		Days	..	..	..	..	..
2.28 Average expenditure per day		US$	..	..	..	..	..

NIGER

Basic data and indicators	Notes	Units	2005	2006	2007	2008	2009
3. OUTBOUND TOURISM							
Data							
Expenditure							
3.4 Total		US$ Mn	42	42	48	98	..
3.5 ♦ Travel		US$ Mn	30	28	29	68	..
3.6 ♦ Passenger transport		US$ Mn	12	14	19	30	..
Expenditure by main purpose of the trip							
3.7 Total		US$ Mn	30	28	29	68	..
3.8 ♦ Personal		US$ Mn	10	9	14	30	..
3.9 ♦ Business and professional		US$ Mn	20	19	15	38	..
4. TOURISM INDUSTRIES							
Data							
Number of establishments							
4.1 Total		Units	..	..	..	..	..
4.2 ♦ Accommodation for visitors		Units	..	..	..	..	..
4.3 * of which, "hotels and similar establishments"		Units	76	80	87	88	90
4.4 ♦ Food and beverage serving activities		Units	..	..	..	..	..
4.5 ♦ Passenger transportation		Units	..	..	..	..	..
4.6 ♦ Travel agencies and other reservation services activities		Units	..	..	..	..	..
4.7 ♦ Other tourism industries		Units	..	..	..	..	..
Accommodation for visitors in hotels and similar establishments							
Non-monetary data							
4.13 ♦ Number of establishments		Units	76	80	87	88	90
4.14 ♦ Number of rooms		Units	1,873	1,919	1,973	1,990	2,010
4.15 ♦ Number of bed-places		Units	3,285	3,246	3,306	3,299	3,320
Indicators							
4.16 Occupancy rate / rooms		Percent	..	..	..	..	..
4.17 Occupancy rate / bed-places		Percent	46.00	48.00	48.00	49.00	..
4.18 Average length of stay	(1)	Nights	7.00	7.00	8.00	8.00	..
4.19 Available capacity (bed-places per 1000 inhabitants)		Units	0.25	0.24	0.23	0.22	0.22
6. COMPLEMENTARY INDICATORS							
Demand							
6.1 Gross travel propensity		Units	..	..	..	..	..
6.2 Carrying capacity (arrivals/population)		Units	0.004	0.004	0.003	0.005	0.004
Macroeconomic indicators related to international tourism							
6.3 Inbound tourism expenditure over GDP		Percent	1.3	1.0	1.0	..	..
6.4 Outbound tourism expenditure over GDP		Percent	1.2	1.1	1.1	..	..
6.5 Tourism balance (inbound minus outbound tourism expenditure) over GDP		Percent	0.1	-0.1	-0.1	..	..
6.6 Tourism openness (inbound plus outbound tourism expenditure) over GDP		Percent	2.4	2.1	2.1	..	..
6.7 Tourism coverage (inbound over outbound tourism expenditure)		Percent	104.8	95.3	91.9	..	..
6.8 Inbound tourism expenditure over exports of goods		Percent	9.2	7.7	6.7	..	..
6.9 Inbound tourism expenditure over exports of services		Percent	50.4	43.3	52.5	..	..
6.10 Inbound tourism expenditure over exports of goods and services		Percent	7.8	6.6	5.9	..	..
6.11 Inbound tourism expenditure over current account credits		Percent	5.4	4.7	4.4	..	..
6.12 Outbound tourism expenditure over imports of goods		Percent	5.5	5.5	5.3	..	..
6.13 Outbound tourism expenditure over imports of services		Percent	15.1	12.5	13.1	..	..
6.14 Outbound tourism expenditure over imports of goods and services		Percent	4.0	3.8	3.8	..	..
6.15 Outbound tourism expenditure over current account debits		Percent	3.7	3.6	3.5	..	..

NIGERIA

Basic data and indicators	Notes	Units	2005	2006	2007	2008	2009
1. INBOUND TOURISM							
Data							
Arrivals							
1.1 Total		('000)	2,778	3,056	5,239	5,820	6,053
1.2 ♦ Overnight visitors (tourists)		('000)	1,010	1,111	1,212	1,313	1,414
1.3 ♦ Same-day visitors (excursionists)		('000)	..	..	..	..	..
1.4 * of which, cruise passengers		('000)	..	..	..	..	..
Arrivals by region							
1.5 Total		('000)	2,779	3,056	5,239	5,820	6,053
1.6 ♦ Africa		('000)	1,916	2,108	3,614	4,015	4,175
1.7 ♦ Americas		('000)	117	129	222	244	256
1.8 ♦ East Asia and the Pacific		('000)	161	177	302	338	351
1.9 ♦ Europe		('000)	460	506	867	964	1,001
1.10 ♦ Middle East		('000)	50	55	95	105	110
1.11 ♦ South Asia		('000)	65	72	124	137	143
1.12 ♦ Other not classified		('000)	10	9	15	17	17
1.13 * of which, nationals residing abroad		('000)	..	..	..	..	..
Arrivals by main purpose							
1.14 Total		('000)	1,010	3,055	5,239	5,820	6,053
1.15 ♦ Personal		('000)	503	1,528	3,367	3,689	4,011
1.16 * holidays, leisure and recreation		('000)	331	1,222	1,567	1,780	1,993
1.17 * other personal purposes		('000)	172	306	1,800	1,909	2,018
1.18 ♦ Business and professional		('000)	507	1,527	1,872	2,131	2,042
Arrivals by mode of transport							
1.19 Total		('000)	2,778	3,055	5,239	5,603	6,053
1.20 ♦ Air		('000)	2,618	2,879	3,140	3,401	3,662
1.21 ♦ Water		('000)	29	32	560	407	520
1.22 ♦ Land		('000)	131	144	1,539	1,795	1,871
1.23 * railway		('000)	..	..	..	..	..
1.24 * road		('000)	131	144	1,539	1,795	1,871
1.25 * others		('000)	..	..	..	..	..
Arrivals by form of organization of the trip							
1.26 Total		('000)	2,778	3,056	5,239	5,820	6,053
1.27 ♦ Package tour		('000)	556	764	1,572	2,037	2,422
1.28 ♦ Other forms		('000)	2,222	2,292	3,667	3,783	3,631
Expenditure							
1.33 Total		US$ Mn	139	90	337	959	791
1.34 ♦ Travel		US$ Mn	54	65	213	569	602
1.35 ♦ Passenger transport		US$ Mn	85	25	124	390	189
Expenditure by main purpose of the trip							
1.36 Total		US$ Mn	139	90	337	959	791
1.37 ♦ Personal		US$ Mn	42	31	134	431	395
1.38 ♦ Business and professional		US$ Mn	97	59	203	528	396
3. OUTBOUND TOURISM							
Data							
Expenditure							
3.4 Total		US$ Mn	501	2,088	3,475	11,009	5,308
3.5 ♦ Travel		US$ Mn	240	1,831	2,400	9,779	4,084
3.6 ♦ Passenger transport		US$ Mn	261	257	1,075	1,230	1,224
Expenditure by main purpose of the trip							
3.7 Total		US$ Mn	240	1,831	2,400	9,779	4,083
3.8 ♦ Personal		US$ Mn	151	1,803	2,132	8,851	3,656
3.9 ♦ Business and professional		US$ Mn	89	28	268	928	427

NIGERIA

Basic data and indicators	Notes	Units	2005	2006	2007	2008	2009
4. TOURISM INDUSTRIES							
Data							
Number of establishments							
4.1 Total		Units	..	..	..	..	..
4.2 ♦ Accommodation for visitors		Units	..	..	..	..	..
4.3 * of which, "hotels and similar establishments"		Units	1,880	1,974	2,012	..	..
4.4 ♦ Food and beverage serving activities		Units	..	..	..	..	..
4.5 ♦ Passenger transportation		Units	..	..	..	..	..
4.6 ♦ Travel agencies and other reservation services activities		Units	..	..	..	..	..
4.7 ♦ Other tourism industries		Units	..	..	..	..	..
Accommodation for visitors in hotels and similar establishments							
Non-monetary data							
4.13 ♦ Number of establishments		Units	1,880	1,974	2,012	..	..
4.14 ♦ Number of rooms		Units	..	..	..	..	..
4.15 ♦ Number of bed-places		Units	38,870	40,814	42,723	43,875	..
Indicators							
4.16 Occupancy rate / rooms		Percent	..	..	..	..	..
4.17 Occupancy rate / bed-places		Percent	81.20	87.54	84.20	87.30	..
4.18 Average length of stay		Nights	..	..	..	..	..
4.19 Available capacity (bed-places per 1000 inhabitants)		Units	0.28	0.28	0.29	0.29	..
6. COMPLEMENTARY INDICATORS							
Demand							
6.1 Gross travel propensity		Units	..	..	..	..	..
6.2 Carrying capacity (arrivals/population)		Units	0.01	0.01	0.01	0.01	0.04
Macroeconomic indicators related to international tourism							
6.3 Inbound tourism expenditure over GDP		Percent	0.1	0.1	0.2	0.5	..
6.4 Outbound tourism expenditure over GDP		Percent	0.4	1.4	2.1	5.5	..
6.5 Tourism balance (inbound minus outbound tourism expenditure) over GDP		Percent	-0.3	-1.4	-1.9	-5.0	..
6.6 Tourism openness (inbound plus outbound tourism expenditure) over GDP		Percent	0.6	1.5	2.3	5.9	..
6.7 Tourism coverage (inbound over outbound tourism expenditure)		Percent	27.8	4.3	9.7	8.7	14.9
6.8 Inbound tourism expenditure over exports of goods		Percent	0.3	0.2	0.5	1.1	1.3
6.9 Inbound tourism expenditure over exports of services		Percent	7.8	4.1	23.4	42.3	35.5
6.10 Inbound tourism expenditure over exports of goods and services		Percent	0.2	0.2	0.5	1.1	1.3
6.11 Inbound tourism expenditure over current account credits		Percent	0.2	0.1	0.4	0.9	1.0
6.12 Outbound tourism expenditure over imports of goods		Percent	1.9	9.5	12.3	29.9	18.3
6.13 Outbound tourism expenditure over imports of services		Percent	7.6	18.0	24.0	46.3	30.2
6.14 Outbound tourism expenditure over imports of goods and services		Percent	1.5	6.2	8.1	18.2	11.4
6.15 Outbound tourism expenditure over current account debits		Percent	1.4	4.7	6.1	14.5	9.1

NIUE

Basic data and indicators	Notes	Units	2005	2006	2007	2008	2009
1. INBOUND TOURISM							
Data							
Arrivals							
1.1 Total		('000)	..	..	..	..	..
1.2 ♦ Overnight visitors (tourists)	(1)	('000)	2.8	3.0	3.5	4.7	4.7
1.3 ♦ Same-day visitors (excursionists)		('000)	..	..	..	..	..
1.4 * of which, cruise passengers		('000)	..	..	..	..	..
Arrivals by region							
1.5 Total		('000)	2.8	3.0	3.4	4.7	4.7
1.6 ♦ Africa		('000)	..	..	..	..	..
1.7 ♦ Americas		('000)	0.2	0.2	0.2	0.3	0.2
1.8 ♦ East Asia and the Pacific		('000)	2.3	2.6	3.0	3.9	3.6
1.9 ♦ Europe		('000)	0.3	0.2	0.2	0.5	0.9
1.10 ♦ Middle East		('000)	..	..	..	..	..
1.11 ♦ South Asia		('000)	..	..	..	..	..
1.12 ♦ Other not classified		('000)	..	..	..	..	..
1.13 * of which, nationals residing abroad		('000)	..	..	..	..	..
Arrivals by main purpose							
1.14 Total		('000)	2.8	3.0	3.4	4.7	4.7
1.15 ♦ Personal		('000)	2.1	2.6	3.0	3.6	3.7
1.16 * holidays, leisure and recreation		('000)	1.2	1.5	1.8	2.2	2.3
1.17 * other personal purposes		('000)	0.9	1.1	1.2	1.4	1.4
1.18 ♦ Business and professional		('000)	0.7	0.4	0.4	1.1	1.0
Arrivals by mode of transport							
1.19 Total		('000)	2.8	3.0	3.5	4.7	4.7
1.20 ♦ Air		('000)	2.8	3.0	3.3	4.7	4.7
1.21 ♦ Water		('000)	..	..	0.2	..	..
1.22 ♦ Land		('000)	..	..	..	..	..
1.23 * railway		('000)	..	..	..	..	..
1.24 * road		('000)	..	..	..	..	..
1.25 * others		('000)	..	..	..	..	..
Expenditure							
1.33 Total		US$ Mn	1.2	1.1	1.6	2.0	1.7
1.34 ♦ Travel		US$ Mn	..	..	..	..	..
1.35 ♦ Passenger transport		US$ Mn	..	..	..	..	..
3. OUTBOUND TOURISM							
Data							
Departures							
3.1 Total		('000)	..	..	..	..	..
3.2 ♦ Overnight visitors (tourists)		('000)	1.6	1.6	1.8	1.8	1.7
3.3 ♦ Same-day visitors (excursionists)		('000)	..	..	..	..	..
4. TOURISM INDUSTRIES							
Data							
Number of establishments							
4.1 Total		Units	..	..	..	..	26
4.2 ♦ Accommodation for visitors		Units	..	..	..	..	..
4.3 * of which, "hotels and similar establishments"		Units	6	7	9	10	12
4.4 ♦ Food and beverage serving activities		Units	..	..	..	..	8
4.5 ♦ Passenger transportation		Units	..	..	..	..	5
4.6 ♦ Travel agencies and other reservation services activities		Units	..	..	..	..	1
4.7 ♦ Other tourism industries		Units	..	..	..	..	..
Accommodation for visitors in hotels and similar establishments							
Non-monetary data							
4.13 ♦ Number of establishments		Units	6	7	9	10	12
4.14 ♦ Number of rooms		Units	58	54	54	55	59
4.15 ♦ Number of bed-places		Units	110	89	96	97	113
Indicators							
4.16 Occupancy rate / rooms		Percent	..	..	..	..	..
4.17 Occupancy rate / bed-places		Percent	..	..	..	..	..
4.18 Average length of stay		Nights	7.00	7.00	7.00	7.00	7.00
4.19 Available capacity (bed-places per 1000 inhabitants)		Units	..	..	..	..	..

NORTHERN MARIANA ISLANDS

Basic data and indicators	Notes	Units	2005	2006	2007	2008	2009
1. INBOUND TOURISM							
Data							
Arrivals							
1.1 Total		('000)	507	436	389	397	354
1.2 ♦ Overnight visitors (tourists)	(1)	('000)	498	429	385	388	345
1.3 ♦ Same-day visitors (excursionists)		('000)	9	7	4	9	9
1.4 * of which, cruise passengers		('000)	9	7	4	9	9
Arrivals by region							
1.5 Total		('000)	506	436	390	397	354
1.6 ♦ Africa		('000)	..	..	..	..	..
1.7 ♦ Americas		('000)	38	33	28	31	30
1.8 ♦ East Asia and the Pacific	(2)	('000)	465	399	356	357	316
1.9 ♦ Europe		('000)	1	2	5	8	7
1.10 ♦ Middle East		('000)	..	..	..	..	..
1.11 ♦ South Asia		('000)	..	..	..	..	..
1.12 ♦ Other not classified		('000)	2	2	1	1	1
1.13 * of which, nationals residing abroad		('000)	..	..	..	..	..
Arrivals by main purpose							
1.14 Total		('000)	..	..	..	..	..
1.15 ♦ Personal		('000)	507	436	389	397	354
1.16 * holidays, leisure and recreation		('000)	507	436	389	397	354
1.17 * other personal purposes		('000)	..	..	..	..	..
1.18 ♦ Business and professional		('000)	..	..	..	..	..
Arrivals by mode of transport							
1.19 Total		('000)	507	436	389	397	354
1.20 ♦ Air		('000)	498	429	385	388	345
1.21 ♦ Water		('000)	9	7	4	9	9
1.22 ♦ Land		('000)	..	..	..	..	..
1.23 * railway		('000)	..	..	..	..	..
1.24 * road		('000)	..	..	..	..	..
1.25 * others		('000)	..	..	..	..	..
4. TOURISM INDUSTRIES							
Data							
Number of establishments							
4.1 Total		Units	..	..	..	..	..
4.2 ♦ Accommodation for visitors		Units	..	..	..	..	..
4.3 * of which, "hotels and similar establishments"	(3)	Units	47	39	40	37	36
4.4 ♦ Food and beverage serving activities		Units	..	..	..	..	..
4.5 ♦ Passenger transportation		Units	..	..	..	..	..
4.6 ♦ Travel agencies and other reservation services activities		Units	..	..	..	..	..
4.7 ♦ Other tourism industries		Units	..	..	..	..	..
Accommodation for visitors in hotels and similar establishments							
Non-monetary data							
4.13 ♦ Number of establishments	(3)	Units	47	39	40	37	36
4.14 ♦ Number of rooms	(3)	Units	4,122	4,003	4,011	3,838	3,731
4.15 ♦ Number of bed-places		Units	..	..	..	..	..
Indicators							
4.16 Occupancy rate / rooms		Percent	70.16	63.57	58.89	61.89	58.28
4.17 Occupancy rate / bed-places		Percent	..	..	..	..	..
4.18 Average length of stay		Nights	..	..	..	..	..
4.19 Available capacity (bed-places per 1000 inhabitants)		Units	..	..	..	..	..
6. COMPLEMENTARY INDICATORS							
Demand							
6.1 Gross travel propensity		Units	..	..	..	..	..
6.2 Carrying capacity (arrivals/population)		Units	6.21	5.23	4.60	4.55	3.97

284

NORWAY

Basic data and indicators	Notes	Units	2005	2006	2007	2008	2009
1. INBOUND TOURISM							
Data							
Arrivals	(1)						
1.1 Total		('000)	5,418	5,738	6,017	6,054	6,056
1.2 ♦ Overnight visitors (tourists)		('000)	3,824	4,070	4,377	4,347	4,288
1.3 ♦ Same-day visitors (excursionists)		('000)	1,594	1,668	1,640	1,707	1,768
1.4 * of which, cruise passengers		('000)	324	355	332	381	430
Arrivals by region	(1)						
1.5 Total		('000)	3,824	4,070	4,377	4,347	4,288
1.6 ♦ Africa		('000)	..	..	..	..	..
1.7 ♦ Americas	(2)	('000)	146	163	177	136	125
1.8 ♦ East Asia and the Pacific	(3)	('000)	41	37	32	29	25
1.9 ♦ Europe		('000)	3,508	3,698	3,939	3,967	3,911
1.10 ♦ Middle East		('000)	..	..	..	..	..
1.11 ♦ South Asia		('000)	..	..	..	..	..
1.12 ♦ Other not classified		('000)	129	172	229	215	227
1.13 * of which, nationals residing abroad		('000)	..	..	..	..	..
Arrivals by main purpose	(1)						
1.14 Total		('000)	3,824	4,071	4,378	4,347	4,288
1.15 ♦ Personal		('000)	2,913	3,101	3,296	3,212	3,238
1.16 * holidays, leisure and recreation		('000)	2,913	3,101	3,296	3,212	3,238
1.17 * other personal purposes		('000)	..	..	..	..	..
1.18 ♦ Business and professional		('000)	911	970	1,082	1,135	1,050
Arrivals by mode of transport	(1)						
1.19 Total		('000)	3,824	4,071	4,378	4,348	4,288
1.20 ♦ Air		('000)	1,588	1,756	1,916	1,901	1,786
1.21 ♦ Water		('000)	709	750	808	731	748
1.22 ♦ Land		('000)	1,527	1,565	1,654	1,716	1,754
1.23 * railway		('000)	80	91	92	106	109
1.24 * road		('000)	1,447	1,474	1,562	1,610	1,645
1.25 * others		('000)	..	..	..	..	..
Accommodation							
Total							
1.29 ♦ Guests		('000)	..	..	..	..	..
1.30 ♦ Overnights		('000)	7,651	7,944	8,326	8,147	7,525
Hotels and similar establishments							
1.31 ♦ Guests		('000)	2,656	2,841	2,899	2,725	2,503
1.32 ♦ Overnights	(4)(5)	('000)	4,761	4,914	5,068	4,894	4,427
Expenditure							
1.33 Total		US$ Mn	4,030	4,251	5,037	5,857	4,444
1.34 ♦ Travel		US$ Mn	3,332	3,613	4,222	4,807	4,082
1.35 ♦ Passenger transport		US$ Mn	698	638	815	1,050	362
2. DOMESTIC TOURISM							
Data							
Accommodation							
Total							
2.19 ♦ Guests		('000)	..	..	..	..	..
2.20 ♦ Overnights		('000)	18,628	19,567	20,338	20,449	20,502
Hotels and similar establishments							
2.21 ♦ Guests		('000)	7,736	8,122	8,446	8,348	8,294
2.22 ♦ Overnights		('000)	12,349	12,859	13,458	13,328	13,227
3. OUTBOUND TOURISM							
Data							
Departures							
3.1 Total		('000)	..	..	..	..	..
3.2 ♦ Overnight visitors (tourists)	(6)	('000)	3,166	3,236	3,395	..	..
3.3 ♦ Same-day visitors (excursionists)		('000)	..	..	..	..	..
Expenditure							
3.4 Total		US$ Mn	10,591	12,072	..	..	..
3.5 ♦ Travel		US$ Mn	10,111	11,586	14,043	14,228	12,366
3.6 ♦ Passenger transport		US$ Mn	480	486	..	..	..
Expenditure by main purpose of the trip							
3.7 Total		US$ Mn	10,111	11,586	14,043	14,228	12,366
3.8 ♦ Personal		US$ Mn	6,907	9,062	11,163	10,993	9,554
3.9 ♦ Business and professional		US$ Mn	3,204	2,524	2,880	3,235	2,812

NORWAY

Basic data and indicators	Notes	Units	2005	2006	2007	2008	2009
4. TOURISM INDUSTRIES							
Data							
Number of establishments							
4.1 Total		Units	..	..	..	..	..
4.2 ♦ Accommodation for visitors		Units	2,257	2,282	2,265	2,296	2,295
4.3 * of which, "hotels and similar establishments"	(5)	Units	1,136	1,119	1,112	1,108	1,122
4.4 ♦ Food and beverage serving activities		Units	..	..	..	..	..
4.5 ♦ Passenger transportation		Units	..	..	..	..	..
4.6 ♦ Travel agencies and other reservation services activities		Units	..	..	..	..	..
4.7 ♦ Other tourism industries		Units	..	..	..	..	..
Accommodation for visitors in hotels and similar establishments							
Non-monetary data							
4.13 ♦ Number of establishments	(5)	Units	1,136	1,119	1,112	1,108	1,122
4.14 ♦ Number of rooms	(5)	Units	67,522	69,477	70,965	72,406	75,423
4.15 ♦ Number of bed-places	(5)	Units	143,568	151,252	154,311	157,266	169,245
Indicators							
4.16 Occupancy rate / rooms		Percent	..	..	..	..	..
4.17 Occupancy rate / bed-places		Percent	38.10	38.90	39.50	37.80	34.80
4.18 Average length of stay		Nights	1.65	1.62	1.63	1.65	1.64
4.19 Available capacity (bed-places per 1000 inhabitants)		Units	31.05	32.45	32.77	32.98	35.06
6. COMPLEMENTARY INDICATORS							
Demand							
6.1 Gross travel propensity		Units	..	..	..	..	..
6.2 Carrying capacity (arrivals/population)		Units	0.83	0.87	0.93	0.91	0.89
Macroeconomic indicators related to international tourism							
6.3 Inbound tourism expenditure over GDP		Percent	1.3	1.3	1.3	1.2	1.2
6.4 Outbound tourism expenditure over GDP		Percent	3.5	3.6	3.6	3.5	3.2
6.5 Tourism balance (inbound minus outbound tourism expenditure) over GDP		Percent	-2.2	-2.3	-2.3	-2.3	-2.0
6.6 Tourism openness (inbound plus outbound tourism expenditure) over GDP		Percent	4.8	4.8	4.9	4.8	4.4
6.7 Tourism coverage (inbound over outbound tourism expenditure)		Percent	38.0	35.2	35.9	34.9	37.8
6.8 Inbound tourism expenditure over exports of goods		Percent	3.9	3.5	3.7	3.2	3.8
6.9 Inbound tourism expenditure over exports of services		Percent	13.5	12.8	12.4	12.1	12.1
6.10 Inbound tourism expenditure over exports of goods and services		Percent	3.0	2.7	2.8	2.5	2.9
6.11 Inbound tourism expenditure over current account credits		Percent	2.5	2.2	2.3	2.1	2.4
6.12 Outbound tourism expenditure over imports of goods		Percent	19.2	19.2	18.2	18.5	18.4
6.13 Outbound tourism expenditure over imports of services		Percent	36.3	37.8	35.3	35.6	32.2
6.14 Outbound tourism expenditure over imports of goods and services		Percent	12.6	12.7	12.0	12.2	11.7
6.15 Outbound tourism expenditure over current account debits		Percent	9.4	9.1	8.8	8.7	8.8

OMAN

Basic data and indicators	Notes	Units	2005	2006	2007	2008	2009
1. INBOUND TOURISM							
Data							
Arrivals							
1.1 Total		('000)	1,101	1,385	1,360	1,615	1,587
1.2 ◆ Overnight visitors (tourists)		('000)	896	1,116	1,271	1,471	1,524
1.3 ◆ Same-day visitors (excursionists)		('000)	205	269	89	144	63
1.4 * of which, cruise passengers		('000)	..	..	..	..	..
Arrivals by region							
1.5 Total		('000)	1,102	1,385	1,360	1,615	1,587
1.6 ◆ Africa		('000)	..	..	..	..	..
1.7 ◆ Americas		('000)	..	..	..	..	..
1.8 ◆ East Asia and the Pacific		('000)	141	166	167	295	249
1.9 ◆ Europe		('000)	220	846	818	932	917
1.10 ◆ Middle East		('000)	646	259	261	248	270
1.11 ◆ South Asia		('000)	..	..	..	..	..
1.12 ◆ Other not classified		('000)	95	114	114	140	151
1.13 * of which, nationals residing abroad		('000)	..	..	..	..	..
Arrivals by main purpose							
1.14 Total		('000)	1,102	1,385	1,359	1,615	1,587
1.15 ◆ Personal		('000)	854	1,012	1,093	1,262	1,305
1.16 * holidays, leisure and recreation		('000)	451	556	777	703	726
1.17 * other personal purposes		('000)	403	456	316	559	579
1.18 ◆ Business and professional		('000)	248	373	266	353	282
Accommodation							
Total							
1.29 ◆ Guests		('000)	..	..	..	..	..
1.30 ◆ Overnights		('000)	..	..	..	..	..
Hotels and similar establishments							
1.31 ◆ Guests		('000)	1,114	1,336	1,182	1,378	1,276
1.32 ◆ Overnights		('000)	1,392	1,689	1,686	1,661	..
Expenditure							
1.33 Total		US$ Mn	627	749	908	1,113	1,108
1.34 ◆ Travel		US$ Mn	429	544	648	804	700
1.35 ◆ Passenger transport		US$ Mn	198	205	260	309	408
Expenditure by main purpose of the trip							
1.36 Total		US$ Mn	429	543	648	804	699
1.37 ◆ Personal		US$ Mn	299	379	452	561	488
1.38 ◆ Business and professional		US$ Mn	130	164	196	243	211
Indicators							
1.39 Average size of travel party		Persons	..	..	..	..	..
Average length of stay							
1.40 Total		Days	4.00	4.00	5.00	4.30	4.30
1.41 ◆ For all commercial accommodation services		Nights	..	..	..	..	..
1.42 * of which, "hotels and similar establishments"		Nights	..	..	..	..	..
1.43 ◆ For non commercial accommodation services		Days	..	..	..	..	..
1.44 Average expenditure per day		US$	..	..	..	..	..
2. DOMESTIC TOURISM							
Data							
Accommodation							
Total							
2.19 ◆ Guests		('000)	..	..	..	..	..
2.20 ◆ Overnights		('000)	..	..	..	..	..
Hotels and similar establishments							
2.21 ◆ Guests		('000)	293	350	392	465	520
2.22 ◆ Overnights		('000)	357	417	458	483	..

OMAN

Basic data and indicators	Notes	Units	2005	2006	2007	2008	2009
3. OUTBOUND TOURISM							
Data							
Departures							
3.1 Total		('000)	2,496	2,664	2,945	3,100	2,470
3.2 ♦ Overnight visitors (tourists)		('000)	2,018	2,248	2,285	2,074	1,672
3.3 ♦ Same-day visitors (excursionists)		('000)	478	416	660	1,026	798
Expenditure							
3.4 Total		US$ Mn	863	894	952	1,197	1,277
3.5 ♦ Travel		US$ Mn	668	712	752	856	871
3.6 ♦ Passenger transport		US$ Mn	195	182	200	341	406
Expenditure by main purpose of the trip							
3.7 Total		US$ Mn	668	712	751	856	871
3.8 ♦ Personal		US$ Mn	575	605	631	721	720
3.9 ♦ Business and professional		US$ Mn	93	107	120	135	151
4. TOURISM INDUSTRIES							
Data							
Number of establishments							
4.1 Total		Units	..	..	..	..	..
4.2 ♦ Accommodation for visitors		Units	..	..	..	..	..
4.3 * of which, "hotels and similar establishments"		Units	161	173	190	196	223
4.4 ♦ Food and beverage serving activities		Units	..	..	..	..	..
4.5 ♦ Passenger transportation		Units	..	..	..	..	..
4.6 ♦ Travel agencies and other reservation services activities		Units	..	..	..	..	..
4.7 ♦ Other tourism industries		Units	..	..	..	..	..
Accommodation for visitors in hotels and similar establishments							
Monetary data							
4.8 ♦ Output		US$ Mn	203.6	287.8	346.0	448.5	425.4
4.9 ♦ Intermediate consumption		US$ Mn	..	..	..	..	..
4.10 ♦ Gross value added		US$ Mn	..	..	..	..	..
4.11 ♦ Compensation of employees		US$ Mn	..	..	..	..	..
4.12 ♦ Gross fixed capital formation		US$ Mn	..	..	..	..	..
Non-monetary data							
4.13 ♦ Number of establishments		Units	161	173	190	196	223
4.14 ♦ Number of rooms		Units	8,132	8,563	9,298	9,318	10,491
4.15 ♦ Number of bed-places		Units	12,575	13,417	14,665	14,826	16,681
Indicators							
4.16 Occupancy rate / rooms		Percent	47.00	58.00	58.00	58.00	49.00
4.17 Occupancy rate / bed-places		Percent	..	..	..	..	..
4.18 Average length of stay		Nights	..	..	..	..	..
4.19 Available capacity (bed-places per 1000 inhabitants)		Units	4.80	5.02	5.38	5.32	5.86
5. EMPLOYMENT							
Data							
Number of employees by tourism industries							
5.1 Total		('000)	..	..	..	..	18.3
5.2 ♦ Accommodation services for visitors (hotels and similar establishments)		('000)	5.5	7.3	8.0	9.2	7.9
5.3 ♦ Other accommodation services		('000)	..	..	..	..	..
5.4 ♦ Food and beverage serving activities		('000)	..	..	..	..	0.6
5.5 ♦ Passenger transportation		('000)	..	..	..	..	6.7
5.6 ♦ Travel agencies and other reservation services activities		('000)	..	..	..	..	1.5
5.7 ♦ Other tourism industries		('000)	..	..	..	..	1.6

OMAN

Basic data and indicators	Notes	Units	2005	2006	2007	2008	2009
6. **COMPLEMENTARY INDICATORS**							
Demand							
6.1 Gross travel propensity		Units	..	..	..	..	..
6.2 Carrying capacity (arrivals/population)		Units	0.34	0.42	0.47	0.53	0.54
Macroeconomic indicators related to international tourism							
6.3 Inbound tourism expenditure over GDP		Percent	2.0	2.0	2.2	1.8	..
6.4 Outbound tourism expenditure over GDP		Percent	2.8	2.4	2.3	2.0	..
6.5 Tourism balance (inbound minus outbound tourism expenditure) over GDP		Percent	-0.8	-0.4	-0.1	-0.1	..
6.6 Tourism openness (inbound plus outbound tourism expenditure) over GDP		Percent	4.8	4.5	4.4	3.8	..
6.7 Tourism coverage (inbound over outbound tourism expenditure)		Percent	72.6	83.8	95.4	92.6	..
6.8 Inbound tourism expenditure over exports of goods		Percent	3.4	3.5	3.7	2.9	..
6.9 Inbound tourism expenditure over exports of services		Percent	66.8	57.4	55.7	56.3	..
6.10 Inbound tourism expenditure over exports of goods and services		Percent	3.2	3.3	3.4	2.8	..
6.11 Inbound tourism expenditure over current account credits		Percent	3.1	3.0	3.2	2.7	..
6.12 Outbound tourism expenditure over imports of goods		Percent	10.8	9.0	6.6	5.8	..
6.13 Outbound tourism expenditure over imports of services		Percent	27.5	22.9	19.5	19.6	..
6.14 Outbound tourism expenditure over imports of goods and services		Percent	7.7	6.5	5.0	4.5	..
6.15 Outbound tourism expenditure over current account debits		Percent	5.7	4.7	3.7	3.4	..

PAKISTAN

Basic data and indicators	Notes	Units	2005	2006	2007	2008	2009
1. INBOUND TOURISM							
Data							
Arrivals							
1.1 Total		('000)	..	..	..	..	..
1.2 ♦ Overnight visitors (tourists)		('000)	798	898	840	823	855
1.3 ♦ Same-day visitors (excursionists)		('000)	..	..	..	..	..
1.4 * of which, cruise passengers		('000)	..	..	..	..	..
Arrivals by region							
1.5 Total		('000)	798	898	840	823	855
1.6 ♦ Africa		('000)	15	19	16	16	15
1.7 ♦ Americas		('000)	146	161	161	156	162
1.8 ♦ East Asia and the Pacific		('000)	84	99	87	76	89
1.9 ♦ Europe		('000)	357	394	387	389	379
1.10 ♦ Middle East		('000)	32	38	36	29	28
1.11 ♦ South Asia		('000)	158	182	149	153	178
1.12 ♦ Other not classified		('000)	6	5	4	4	4
1.13 * of which, nationals residing abroad		('000)	..	..	..	..	..
Arrivals by main purpose							
1.14 Total		('000)	798	898	840	823	855
1.15 ♦ Personal		('000)	595	670	627	614	638
1.16 * holidays, leisure and recreation		('000)	122	138	128	126	131
1.17 * other personal purposes		('000)	473	532	499	488	507
1.18 ♦ Business and professional		('000)	203	228	213	209	217
Arrivals by mode of transport							
1.19 Total		('000)	798	898	840	823	855
1.20 ♦ Air		('000)	682	763	732	718	679
1.21 ♦ Water		('000)	..	..	..	..	37
1.22 ♦ Land		('000)	116	135	108	105	139
1.23 * railway		('000)	34	37	26	32	27
1.24 * road		('000)	82	98	82	73	112
1.25 * others		('000)	..	..	..	..	..
Accommodation							
Total							
1.29 ♦ Guests		('000)	..	..	..	..	..
1.30 ♦ Overnights		('000)	..	..	..	..	..
Hotels and similar establishments							
1.31 ♦ Guests		('000)	2,206	2,059	..	..	..
1.32 ♦ Overnights		('000)	2,213	..	..	..	..
Expenditure							
1.33 Total		US$ Mn	828	919	912	986	903
1.34 ♦ Travel		US$ Mn	182	255	276	316	269
1.35 ♦ Passenger transport		US$ Mn	646	664	636	670	634
Expenditure by main purpose of the trip							
1.36 Total		US$ Mn	182	255	276	316	269
1.37 ♦ Personal		US$ Mn	174	242	262	297	260
1.38 ♦ Business and professional		US$ Mn	8	13	14	19	9
Indicators							
1.39 Average size of travel party		Persons	..	..	..	..	..
Average length of stay							
1.40 Total		Days	..	..	..	..	..
1.41 ♦ For all commercial accommodation services	(1)	Nights	25.00	25.00	25.00	25.00	25.00
1.42 * of which, "hotels and similar establishments"		Nights	..	..	..	..	..
1.43 ♦ For non commercial accommodation services		Days	..	..	..	..	..
1.44 Average expenditure per day		US$	..	..	..	11.8	11.3
2. DOMESTIC TOURISM							
Data							
Accommodation							
Total							
2.19 ♦ Guests		('000)	..	..	..	..	..
2.20 ♦ Overnights		('000)	..	..	..	..	..
Hotels and similar establishments							
2.21 ♦ Guests		('000)	9,947	11,086	11,197	8,386	..
2.22 ♦ Overnights		('000)	13,173	..	..	..	..

PAKISTAN

Basic data and indicators	Notes	Units	2005	2006	2007	2008	2009
3. OUTBOUND TOURISM							
Data							
Expenditure							
3.4 Total		US$ Mn	1,753	2,029	2,083	2,163	1,098
3.5 ♦ Travel		US$ Mn	1,280	1,545	1,593	1,518	685
3.6 ♦ Passenger transport		US$ Mn	473	484	490	645	413
Expenditure by main purpose of the trip							
3.7 Total		US$ Mn	1,280	1,545	1,593	1,518	685
3.8 ♦ Personal		US$ Mn	1,159	1,474	1,547	1,489	662
3.9 ♦ Business and professional		US$ Mn	121	71	46	29	23
4. TOURISM INDUSTRIES							
Data							
Number of establishments							
4.1 Total		Units	..	..	..	..	..
4.2 ♦ Accommodation for visitors		Units	..	..	..	..	..
4.3 * of which, "hotels and similar establishments"		Units	1,633	1,761	1,886	1,729	..
4.4 ♦ Food and beverage serving activities		Units	..	..	..	..	..
4.5 ♦ Passenger transportation		Units	..	..	..	..	..
4.6 ♦ Travel agencies and other reservation services activities		Units	..	..	..	..	..
4.7 ♦ Other tourism industries		Units	..	..	..	..	..
Accommodation for visitors in hotels and similar establishments							
Non-monetary data							
4.13 ♦ Number of establishments		Units	1,633	1,761	1,886	1,729	..
4.14 ♦ Number of rooms		Units	38,183	41,146	43,499	41,171	..
4.15 ♦ Number of bed-places		Units	57,275	61,719	65,174	61,757	..
Indicators							
4.16 Occupancy rate / rooms		Percent	..	..	..	..	..
4.17 Occupancy rate / bed-places		Percent	61.00	64.00	63.00	51.00	..
4.18 Average length of stay		Nights	1.27	..	..	..	..
4.19 Available capacity (bed-places per 1000 inhabitants)		Units	0.37	0.39	0.40	0.37	..
6. COMPLEMENTARY INDICATORS							
Demand							
6.1 Gross travel propensity		Units	..	..	..	..	
6.2 Carrying capacity (arrivals/population)		Units	0.01	0.01	0.01	0.00	0.01
Macroeconomic indicators related to international tourism							
6.3 Inbound tourism expenditure over GDP		Percent	0.8	0.7	0.6	0.7	..
6.4 Outbound tourism expenditure over GDP		Percent	1.6	1.6	1.5	1.5	..
6.5 Tourism balance (inbound minus outbound tourism expenditure) over GDP		Percent	-0.8	-0.9	-0.8	-0.8	..
6.6 Tourism openness (inbound plus outbound tourism expenditure) over GDP		Percent	2.4	2.3	2.1	2.2	..
6.7 Tourism coverage (inbound over outbound tourism expenditure)		Percent	47.2	45.3	43.8	45.6	..
6.8 Inbound tourism expenditure over exports of goods		Percent	5.4	5.4	5.0	4.6	..
6.9 Inbound tourism expenditure over exports of services		Percent	22.5	26.2	24.2	23.1	..
6.10 Inbound tourism expenditure over exports of goods and services		Percent	4.3	4.5	4.2	3.9	..
6.11 Inbound tourism expenditure over current account credits		Percent	2.9	2.8	2.6	2.6	..
6.12 Outbound tourism expenditure over imports of goods		Percent	8.1	7.6	7.2	5.7	..
6.13 Outbound tourism expenditure over imports of services		Percent	23.3	24.1	23.6	22.3	..
6.14 Outbound tourism expenditure over imports of goods and services		Percent	6.0	5.8	5.5	4.5	..
6.15 Outbound tourism expenditure over current account debits		Percent	5.4	5.2	4.9	4.0	..

PALAU

Basic data and indicators	Notes	Units	2005	2006	2007	2008	2009
1. INBOUND TOURISM							
Data							
Arrivals							
1.1 Total		('000)	..	..	..	..	..
1.2 ♦ Overnight visitors (tourists)	(1)	('000)	86	87	93	83	84
1.3 ♦ Same-day visitors (excursionists)		('000)	..	..	..	..	..
1.4 * of which, cruise passengers		('000)	..	..	..	..	..
Arrivals by region	(1)						
1.5 Total		('000)	86	87	92	83	84
1.6 ♦ Africa		('000)	..	..	..	..	..
1.7 ♦ Americas		('000)	6	9	6	10	6
1.8 ♦ East Asia and the Pacific		('000)	76	74	82	67	67
1.9 ♦ Europe		('000)	2	2	2	3	3
1.10 ♦ Middle East		('000)	..	..	..	..	..
1.11 ♦ South Asia		('000)	..	..	..	..	..
1.12 ♦ Other not classified		('000)	2	2	2	3	8
1.13 * of which, nationals residing abroad		('000)	..	..	..	..	..
Arrivals by main purpose	(1)						
1.14 Total		('000)	86	87	93	83	83
1.15 ♦ Personal		('000)	82	83	89	80	80
1.16 * holidays, leisure and recreation		('000)	76	78	84	76	68
1.17 * other personal purposes		('000)	6	5	5	4	12
1.18 ♦ Business and professional		('000)	4	4	4	3	3
Arrivals by mode of transport							
1.19 Total		('000)	86	87	93	83	84
1.20 ♦ Air		('000)	86	87	93	83	84
1.21 ♦ Water		('000)	..	..	..	..	..
1.22 ♦ Land		('000)	..	..	..	..	..
1.23 * railway		('000)	..	..	..	..	..
1.24 * road		('000)	..	..	..	..	..
1.25 * others		('000)	..	..	..	..	..
Expenditure							
1.33 Total	(2)	US$ Mn	97	90	..	..	..
1.34 ♦ Travel		US$ Mn	..	..	..	..	..
1.35 ♦ Passenger transport		US$ Mn	..	..	..	..	..
3. OUTBOUND TOURISM							
Data							
Expenditure							
3.4 Total	(2)	US$ Mn	1.5	1.4	..	..	..
3.5 ♦ Travel		US$ Mn	..	..	..	..	..
3.6 ♦ Passenger transport		US$ Mn	..	..	..	..	..
6. COMPLEMENTARY INDICATORS							
Demand							
6.1 Gross travel propensity		Units	..	..	..	..	..
6.2 Carrying capacity (arrivals/population)		Units	4.31	4.34	4.61	4.09	4.12

PALESTINE

Basic data and indicators	Notes	Units	2005	2006	2007	2008	2009
1. INBOUND TOURISM							
Data							
Arrivals							
1.1 Total		('000)	..	..	..	..	..
1.2 ♦ Overnight visitors (tourists)	(1)	('000)	88	123	264	387	396
1.3 ♦ Same-day visitors (excursionists)		('000)	..	..	..	..	..
1.4 * of which, cruise passengers		('000)	..	..	..	..	..
Arrivals by region	(1)						
1.5 Total		('000)	88	123	263	387	396
1.6 ♦ Africa		('000)	1	2	5	10	12
1.7 ♦ Americas		('000)	14	19	32	39	63
1.8 ♦ East Asia and the Pacific		('000)	16	17	20	41	41
1.9 ♦ Europe		('000)	55	83	203	294	276
1.10 ♦ Middle East		('000)	2	2	3	3	4
1.11 ♦ South Asia		('000)	..	..	..	..	..
1.12 ♦ Other not classified		('000)	..	..	..	..	..
1.13 * of which, nationals residing abroad		('000)	..	..	..	..	..
Accommodation							
Total							
1.29 ♦ Guests		('000)	..	..	..	..	..
1.30 ♦ Overnights		('000)	..	..	..	..	..
Hotels and similar establishments							
1.31 ♦ Guests	(2)	('000)	88	123	264	387	396
1.32 ♦ Overnights	(2)	('000)	251	331	597	1,013	926
Expenditure							
1.33 Total		US$ Mn	..	..	..	..	..
1.34 ♦ Travel	(3)	US$ Mn	119	89	212	269	..
1.35 ♦ Passenger transport		US$ Mn					
Indicators							
1.39 Average size of travel party		Persons	..	..	..	..	..
Average length of stay							
1.40 Total		Days	..	..	..	..	..
1.41 ♦ For all commercial accommodation services		Nights	2.85	2.69	2.26	2.61	2.34
1.42 * of which, "hotels and similar establishments"		Nights	..	..	..	..	..
1.43 ♦ For non commercial accommodation services		Days	..	..	..	..	..
1.44 Average expenditure per day		US$	..	..	..	..	..
2. DOMESTIC TOURISM							
Data							
Accommodation							
Total							
2.19 ♦ Guests		('000)	..	..	..	..	..
2.20 ♦ Overnights		('000)	..	..	..	..	..
Hotels and similar establishments							
2.21 ♦ Guests	(2)	('000)	44	29	52	59	57
2.22 ♦ Overnights	(2)	('000)	99	52	77	114	116
Indicators							
2.23 Average size of travel party		Persons	..	..	..	..	..
Average length of stay							
2.24 Total		Days	..	..	..	..	..
2.25 ♦ For all commercial accommodation services		Nights	2.30	1.80	1.50	1.90	2.00
2.26 * of which, "hotels and similar establishments"		Nights	..	..	..	..	..
2.27 ♦ For non commercial accommodation services		Days	..	..	..	..	..
2.28 Average expenditure per day		US$	..	..	..	..	..
3. OUTBOUND TOURISM							
Data							
Expenditure	(3)						
3.4 Total		US$ Mn	263	306	447	544	..
3.5 ♦ Travel		US$ Mn	254	303	436	534	..
3.6 ♦ Passenger transport		US$ Mn	9	3	11	10	..
Expenditure by main purpose of the trip							
3.7 Total		US$ Mn	254	303	436	535	..
3.8 ♦ Personal		US$ Mn	167	170	301	356	..
3.9 ♦ Business and professional		US$ Mn	87	133	135	179	..

PALESTINE

Basic data and indicators	Notes	Units	2005	2006	2007	2008	2009
4. TOURISM INDUSTRIES							
Data							
Number of establishments							
4.1 Total		Units	..	..	..	..	..
4.2 ♦ Accommodation for visitors		Units	..	..	..	..	..
4.3 * of which, "hotels and similar establishments"		Units	77	79	82	87	100
4.4 ♦ Food and beverage serving activities		Units	..	..	..	..	..
4.5 ♦ Passenger transportation		Units	..	..	..	..	..
4.6 ♦ Travel agencies and other reservation services activities		Units	..	..	..	..	..
4.7 ♦ Other tourism industries		Units	..	..	..	..	..
Accommodation for visitors in hotels and similar establishments							
Non-monetary data							
4.13 ♦ Number of establishments		Units	77	79	82	87	100
4.14 ♦ Number of rooms		Units	3,691	4,140	4,094	4,270	5,126
4.15 ♦ Number of bed-places		Units	7,923	8,863	8,901	8,985	11,301
Indicators							
4.16 Occupancy rate / rooms		Percent	..	..	..	..	25.20
4.17 Occupancy rate / bed-places		Percent	15.50	15.80	25.10	35.90	22.70
4.18 Average length of stay		Nights	2.70	2.50	2.10	2.50	2.30
4.19 Available capacity (bed-places per 1000 inhabitants)		Units	2.22	2.39	2.32	2.28	2.80
6. COMPLEMENTARY INDICATORS							
Demand							
6.1 Gross travel propensity		Units	..	..	..	..	..
6.2 Carrying capacity (arrivals/population)		Units	0.02	0.03	0.07	0.10	0.10

PANAMA

Basic data and indicators	Notes	Units	2005	2006	2007	2008	2009
1. INBOUND TOURISM							
Data							
Arrivals							
1.1 Total	(1)	('000)	1,070	1,215	1,428	1,575	1,562
1.2 ♦ Overnight visitors (tourists)		('000)	702	843	1,103	1,247	1,200
1.3 ♦ Same-day visitors (excursionists)		('000)	368	372	325	328	362
1.4 * of which, cruise passengers		('000)	334	335	283	234	311
Arrivals by region	(2)						
1.5 Total		('000)	575	703	949	1,136	1,055
1.6 ♦ Africa		('000)	..	..	1	1	1
1.7 ♦ Americas		('000)	507	620	836	984	916
1.8 ♦ East Asia and the Pacific		('000)	16	20	27	33	23
1.9 ♦ Europe		('000)	52	63	85	118	115
1.10 ♦ Middle East		('000)	..	..	..	..	..
1.11 ♦ South Asia		('000)	..	..	..	..	..
1.12 ♦ Other not classified		('000)	..	..	..	..	..
1.13 * of which, nationals residing abroad		('000)	..	..	..	..	..
Arrivals by main purpose	(3)						
1.14 Total		('000)	546	671	912	1,044	1,008
1.15 ♦ Personal		('000)	347	426	579	643	620
1.16 * holidays, leisure and recreation		('000)	299	373	510	564	540
1.17 * other personal purposes		('000)	48	53	69	79	80
1.18 ♦ Business and professional		('000)	199	245	333	401	388
Arrivals by mode of transport							
1.19 Total		('000)	702	843	1,103	1,246	1,200
1.20 ♦ Air		('000)	546	671	912	1,044	1,007
1.21 ♦ Water		('000)	21	21	13	..	..
1.22 ♦ Land		('000)	135	151	178	202	193
1.23 * railway		('000)	..	..	..	..	..
1.24 * road		('000)	81	97	113	125	123
1.25 * others		('000)	54	54	65	77	70
Accommodation							
Total							
1.29 ♦ Guests		('000)	..	..	..	..	..
1.30 ♦ Overnights		('000)	..	..	..	..	..
Hotels and similar establishments							
1.31 ♦ Guests		('000)	656	721	898	897	808
1.32 ♦ Overnights	(4)	('000)	1,453	1,756	2,253	2,499	2,140
Expenditure							
1.33 Total		US$ Mn	1,108	1,425	1,806	2,208	2,279
1.34 ♦ Travel		US$ Mn	780	960	1,185	1,408	1,483
1.35 ♦ Passenger transport		US$ Mn	328	465	621	800	796
Expenditure by main purpose of the trip							
1.36 Total		US$ Mn	780	960	1,185	1,408	1,483
1.37 ♦ Personal		US$ Mn	656	808	988	1,179	1,260
1.38 ♦ Business and professional		US$ Mn	124	152	197	229	223
Indicators							
1.39 Average size of travel party		Persons	..	..	..	..	..
Average length of stay							
1.40 Total		Days	..	..	..	..	..
1.41 ♦ For all commercial accommodation services		Nights	8.60	8.80	9.00	8.90	8.00
1.42 * of which, "hotels and similar establishments"		Nights	..	..	..	..	..
1.43 ♦ For non commercial accommodation services		Days	..	..	..	..	..
1.44 Average expenditure per day		US$	..	..	..	..	..

PANAMA

Basic data and indicators	Notes	Units	2005	2006	2007	2008	2009
3. OUTBOUND TOURISM							
Data							
Departures							
3.1 Total		('000)	..	..	..	..	..
3.2 ♦ Overnight visitors (tourists)		('000)	285	284	314	369	336
3.3 ♦ Same-day visitors (excursionists)		('000)	..	..	..	..	..
Expenditure							
3.4 Total		US$ Mn	388	403	457	560	503
3.5 ♦ Travel		US$ Mn	271	271	307	366	338
3.6 ♦ Passenger transport		US$ Mn	117	132	150	194	165
Expenditure by main purpose of the trip							
3.7 Total		US$ Mn	271	271	307	366	338
3.8 ♦ Personal		US$ Mn	238	238	267	318	292
3.9 ♦ Business and professional		US$ Mn	33	33	40	48	46
4. TOURISM INDUSTRIES							
Data							
Accommodation for visitors in hotels and similar establishments							
Non-monetary data							
4.13 ♦ Number of establishments		Units	..	..	..	..	..
4.14 ♦ Number of rooms	(5)	Units	15,341	15,460	16,158	16,441	17,531
4.15 ♦ Number of bed-places	(5)	Units	30,682	30,920	32,035	32,601	35,062
Indicators							
4.16 Occupancy rate / rooms		Percent	48.63	54.92	66.03	67.26	57.35
4.17 Occupancy rate / bed-places		Percent	..	..	..	..	..
4.18 Average length of stay		Nights	2.22	2.43	2.51	2.79	2.65
4.19 Available capacity (bed-places per 1000 inhabitants)		Units	9.49	9.41	9.58	9.59	10.15
6. COMPLEMENTARY INDICATORS							
Demand							
6.1 Gross travel propensity		Units	..	..	..	..	..
6.2 Carrying capacity (arrivals/population)		Units	0.22	0.26	0.33	0.37	0.35
Macroeconomic indicators related to international tourism							
6.3 Inbound tourism expenditure over GDP		Percent	7.2	8.3	9.3	..	..
6.4 Outbound tourism expenditure over GDP		Percent	2.5	2.4	2.3	..	..
6.5 Tourism balance (inbound minus outbound tourism expenditure) over GDP		Percent	4.7	6.0	6.9	..	..
6.6 Tourism openness (inbound plus outbound tourism expenditure) over GDP		Percent	9.7	10.7	11.6	..	..
6.7 Tourism coverage (inbound over outbound tourism expenditure)		Percent	285.6	353.1	395.2	394.5	453.4
6.8 Inbound tourism expenditure over exports of goods		Percent	15.0	16.8	19.3	21.4	20.9
6.9 Inbound tourism expenditure over exports of services		Percent	34.3	35.6	36.4	37.9	41.9
6.10 Inbound tourism expenditure over exports of goods and services		Percent	10.4	11.4	12.6	13.7	13.9
6.11 Inbound tourism expenditure over current account credits		Percent	9.2	10.0	10.9	11.9	12.4
6.12 Outbound tourism expenditure over imports of goods		Percent	4.3	4.0	3.6	3.8	3.9
6.13 Outbound tourism expenditure over imports of services		Percent	21.4	23.3	21.5	21.4	23.2
6.14 Outbound tourism expenditure over imports of goods and services		Percent	3.6	3.4	3.1	3.2	3.3
6.15 Outbound tourism expenditure over current account debits		Percent	3.0	2.7	2.5	2.6	2.7

PAPUA NEW GUINEA

Basic data and indicators	Notes	Units	2005	2006	2007	2008	2009
1. INBOUND TOURISM							
Data							
Arrivals							
1.1 Total		('000)	..	..	..	120	..
1.2 ◆ Overnight visitors (tourists)		('000)	69	78	104	114	..
1.3 ◆ Same-day visitors (excursionists)		('000)	..	..	..	6	..
1.4 * of which, cruise passengers		('000)	..	..	..	6	..
Arrivals by region							
1.5 Total		('000)	69	77	105	114	..
1.6 ◆ Africa		('000)	..	1	1	1	..
1.7 ◆ Americas		('000)	6	7	8	8	..
1.8 ◆ East Asia and the Pacific		('000)	58	63	85	94	..
1.9 ◆ Europe		('000)	4	5	9	9	..
1.10 ◆ Middle East		('000)	..	..	..	..	..
1.11 ◆ South Asia		('000)	1	1	2	2	..
1.12 ◆ Other not classified		('000)	..	..	..	..	..
1.13 * of which, nationals residing abroad		('000)	..	..	..	..	..
Arrivals by main purpose							
1.14 Total		('000)	69	78	104	114	..
1.15 ◆ Personal		('000)	24	28	34	58	..
1.16 * holidays, leisure and recreation		('000)	18	23	28	29	..
1.17 * other personal purposes		('000)	6	5	6	29	..
1.18 ◆ Business and professional		('000)	45	50	70	56	..
Arrivals by mode of transport							
1.19 Total		('000)	69	78	104	120	..
1.20 ◆ Air		('000)	69	78	104	114	..
1.21 ◆ Water		('000)	..	..	..	6	..
1.22 ◆ Land		('000)	..	..	..	..	..
1.23 * railway		('000)	..	..	..	..	..
1.24 * road		('000)	..	..	..	..	..
1.25 * others		('000)	..	..	..	..	..
Expenditure							
1.33 Total		US$ Mn	9.4	3.9	4.5	3.8	..
1.34 ◆ Travel		US$ Mn	3.6	3.9	4.2	2.2	1.2
1.35 ◆ Passenger transport		US$ Mn	5.8	0.03	0.3	1.6	..
Expenditure by main purpose of the trip							
1.36 Total		US$ Mn	3.6	3.9	4.2	2.2	1.2
1.37 ◆ Personal		US$ Mn	1.2	1.2	1.3	0.7	0.4
1.38 ◆ Business and professional		US$ Mn	2.4	2.7	2.9	1.5	0.8
3. OUTBOUND TOURISM							
Data							
Expenditure							
3.4 Total		US$ Mn	56	43	81	75	48
3.5 ◆ Travel		US$ Mn	56	16	21	29	29
3.6 ◆ Passenger transport		US$ Mn	0.6	27	60	46	19
Expenditure by main purpose of the trip							
3.7 Total		US$ Mn	56	16	21	29	29
3.8 ◆ Personal		US$ Mn	38	5	6	9	9
3.9 ◆ Business and professional		US$ Mn	18	11	15	20	20

PAPUA NEW GUINEA

Basic data and indicators	Notes	Units	2005	2006	2007	2008	2009
6. COMPLEMENTARY INDICATORS							
Demand							
6.1 Gross travel propensity		Units	..	..	..	..	..
6.2 Carrying capacity (arrivals/population)		Units	0.01	0.01	0.02	0.02	..
Macroeconomic indicators related to international tourism							
6.3 Inbound tourism expenditure over GDP		Percent	..	..	..	..	..
6.4 Outbound tourism expenditure over GDP		Percent	..	..	..	..	..
6.5 Tourism balance (inbound minus outbound tourism expenditure) over GDP		Percent	..	..	..	..	..
6.6 Tourism openness (inbound plus outbound tourism expenditure) over GDP		Percent	..	..	..	..	..
6.7 Tourism coverage (inbound over outbound tourism expenditure)		Percent	6.6	..	..	..	..
6.8 Inbound tourism expenditure over exports of goods		Percent	0.1	..	..	..	..
6.9 Inbound tourism expenditure over exports of services		Percent	1.2	..	..	..	..
6.10 Inbound tourism expenditure over exports of goods and services		Percent	0.1	..	..	..	..
6.11 Inbound tourism expenditure over current account credits		Percent	0.1	..	..	..	..
6.12 Outbound tourism expenditure over imports of goods		Percent	3.7	..	..	..	..
6.13 Outbound tourism expenditure over imports of services		Percent	4.8	..	..	..	..
6.14 Outbound tourism expenditure over imports of goods and services		Percent	2.1	..	..	..	..
6.15 Outbound tourism expenditure over current account debits		Percent	1.7	..	..	..	..

PARAGUAY

Basic data and indicators	Notes	Units	2005	2006	2007	2008	2009
1. INBOUND TOURISM							
Data							
Arrivals							
1.1 Total	(1)	('000)	2,648	2,830	3,005	3,118	3,183
1.2 ♦ Overnight visitors (tourists)	(1)(2)	('000)	341	388	416	428	439
1.3 ♦ Same-day visitors (excursionists)	(1)	('000)	2,307	2,442	2,589	2,690	2,744
1.4 * of which, cruise passengers		('000)	..	..	..	..	..
Arrivals by region	(1)(2)						
1.5 Total		('000)	340	388	414	427	439
1.6 ♦ Africa		('000)	..	..	..		
1.7 ♦ Americas		('000)	312	349	370	384	395
1.8 ♦ East Asia and the Pacific		('000)	5	8	9	8	8
1.9 ♦ Europe		('000)	23	31	35	34	35
1.10 ♦ Middle East		('000)	..	..	..	1	1
1.11 ♦ South Asia		('000)	..	..	..	..	..
1.12 ♦ Other not classified		('000)	..	..	..	..	..
1.13 * of which, nationals residing abroad		('000)	..	..	..	..	..
Arrivals by main purpose	(1)(2)						
1.14 Total	(3)	('000)	341	388	416	428	439
1.15 ♦ Personal		('000)	304	345	370	381	347
1.16 * holidays, leisure and recreation		('000)	164	186	200	206	79
1.17 * other personal purposes		('000)	140	159	170	175	268
1.18 ♦ Business and professional		('000)	37	43	46	47	92
Arrivals by mode of transport	(1)(2)						
1.19 Total		('000)	341	388	416	429	439
1.20 ♦ Air		('000)	99	102	129	143	135
1.21 ♦ Water	(4)	('000)	10	10	22	25	21
1.22 ♦ Land		('000)	232	276	265	261	283
1.23 * railway		('000)	..	..	..	..	..
1.24 * road		('000)	232	276	265	261	283
1.25 * others		('000)	..	..	..	..	..
Expenditure							
1.33 Total		US$ Mn	96	112	121	128	247
1.34 ♦ Travel		US$ Mn	78	92	102	109	227
1.35 ♦ Passenger transport		US$ Mn	18	20	19	19	20
Indicators							
1.39 Average size of travel party		Persons	..	..	..	..	..
Average length of stay							
1.40 Total		Days	..	..	..	..	..
1.41 ♦ For all commercial accommodation services	(3)	Nights	2.50	2.50	2.50	2.50	3.00
1.42 * of which, "hotels and similar establishments"		Nights	..	..	..	..	..
1.43 ♦ For non commercial accommodation services		Days	..	..	..	..	..
1.44 Average expenditure per day		US$	..	..	..	..	..
2. DOMESTIC TOURISM	(5)						
Data							
Trips							
2.1 Total		('000)	..	..	1,079	..	..
2.2 ♦ Overnight visitors (tourists)		('000)	..	..	833	..	..
2.3 ♦ Same-day visitors (excursionists)		('000)	..	..	246	..	..
Trips by main purpose							
2.4 Total		('000)	..	..	1,083	..	..
2.5 ♦ Personal		('000)	..	..	1,065	..	..
2.6 * holidays, leisure and recreation		('000)	..	..	258	..	..
2.7 * other personal purposes		('000)	..	..	807	..	..
2.8 ♦ Business and professional		('000)	..	..	18	..	..
Indicators							
2.23 Average size of travel party		Persons	..	..	..	..	..
Average length of stay							
2.24 Total		Days	..	..	..	..	..
2.25 ♦ For all commercial accommodation services		Nights	..	..	3.00	..	..
2.26 * of which, "hotels and similar establishments"		Nights	..	..	5.00	..	..
2.27 ♦ For non commercial accommodation services		Days	..	..	..	..	..
2.28 Average expenditure per day		US$	..	..	10.0	..	..

PARAGUAY

Basic data and indicators	Notes	Units	2005	2006	2007	2008	2009
3. OUTBOUND TOURISM							
Data							
Departures							
3.1 Total	(1)	('000)	..	..	..	..	..
3.2 ◆ Overnight visitors (tourists)		('000)	188	210	242	269	280
3.3 ◆ Same-day visitors (excursionists)		('000)	..	..	..	..	..
Expenditure							
3.4 Total		US$ Mn	130	144	184	207	288
3.5 ◆ Travel		US$ Mn	79	92	109	121	188
3.6 ◆ Passenger transport		US$ Mn	51	52	75	86	100
4. TOURISM INDUSTRIES							
Data							
Number of establishments							
4.1 Total		Units	..	..	..	..	..
4.2 ◆ Accommodation for visitors		Units	..	..	..	..	..
4.3 * of which, "hotels and similar establishments"		Units	164	168	177	216	263
4.4 ◆ Food and beverage serving activities		Units	..	..	..	..	..
4.5 ◆ Passenger transportation		Units	..	..	..	..	..
4.6 ◆ Travel agencies and other reservation services activities		Units	..	..	..	..	..
4.7 ◆ Other tourism industries		Units	..	..	..	..	..
Accommodation for visitors in hotels and similar establishments							
Non-monetary data							
4.13 ◆ Number of establishments		Units	164	168	177	216	263
4.14 ◆ Number of rooms		Units	5,058	5,355	5,560	6,411	7,250
4.15 ◆ Number of bed-places		Units	10,939	11,532	11,943	13,656	15,197
Indicators							
4.16 Occupancy rate / rooms		Percent	..	..	..	..	..
4.17 Occupancy rate / bed-places		Percent	44.00	45.00	46.00	46.00	48.00
4.18 Average length of stay		Nights	2.50	2.50	2.50	2.50	3.00
4.19 Available capacity (bed-places per 1000 inhabitants)		Units	1.85	1.92	1.95	2.19	2.39
6. COMPLEMENTARY INDICATORS							
Demand							
6.1 Gross travel propensity		Units	..	..	..	..	..
6.2 Carrying capacity (arrivals/population)		Units	0.06	0.06	0.20	0.07	0.07
Macroeconomic indicators related to international tourism							
6.3 Inbound tourism expenditure over GDP		Percent	1.3	1.2	1.0	0.8	..
6.4 Outbound tourism expenditure over GDP		Percent	1.7	1.6	1.5	1.2	..
6.5 Tourism balance (inbound minus outbound tourism expenditure) over GDP		Percent	-0.5	-0.4	-0.5	-0.5	..
6.6 Tourism openness (inbound plus outbound tourism expenditure) over GDP		Percent	3.0	2.8	2.5	2.0	..
6.7 Tourism coverage (inbound over outbound tourism expenditure)		Percent	73.6	77.3	65.6	60.9	53.5
6.8 Inbound tourism expenditure over exports of goods		Percent	2.8	2.5	2.1	1.6	2.1
6.9 Inbound tourism expenditure over exports of services		Percent	14.6	14.0	12.5	11.2	9.7
6.10 Inbound tourism expenditure over exports of goods and services		Percent	2.4	2.1	1.8	1.4	1.7
6.11 Inbound tourism expenditure over current account credits		Percent	2.2	1.9	1.6	1.3	1.5
6.12 Outbound tourism expenditure over imports of goods		Percent	3.4	2.9	3.0	2.3	3.3
6.13 Outbound tourism expenditure over imports of services		Percent	37.8	37.6	39.6	35.3	42.0
6.14 Outbound tourism expenditure over imports of goods and services		Percent	3.1	2.7	2.8	2.2	3.0
6.15 Outbound tourism expenditure over current account debits		Percent	2.9	2.5	2.6	2.1	2.8

PERU

Basic data and indicators	Notes	Units	2005	2006	2007	2008	2009
1. INBOUND TOURISM							
Data							
Arrivals							
1.1　Total		('000)	1,938	2,227	2,451	2,581	2,681
1.2　♦ Overnight visitors (tourists)	(1)	('000)	1,571	1,721	1,916	2,058	2,140
1.3　♦ Same-day visitors (excursionists)		('000)	367	506	535	523	541
1.4　　* of which, cruise passengers	(2)	('000)	8	60	60	75	71
Arrivals by region	(1)						
1.5　Total		('000)	1,570	1,721	1,917	2,057	2,139
1.6　♦ Africa		('000)	3	3	4	3	3
1.7　♦ Americas		('000)	1,066	1,190	1,315	1,405	1,497
1.8　♦ East Asia and the Pacific		('000)	74	82	92	105	99
1.9　♦ Europe		('000)	340	354	397	430	419
1.10　♦ Middle East		('000)	..	..	..	..	..
1.11　♦ South Asia		('000)	2	2	3	4	4
1.12　♦ Other not classified		('000)	85	90	106	110	117
1.13　　* of which, nationals residing abroad		('000)	84	86	104	109	116
Arrivals by main purpose	(1)						
1.14　Total		('000)	1,571	1,721	1,916	2,058	2,140
1.15　♦ Personal		('000)	1,530	1,676	1,867	2,005	2,085
1.16　　* holidays, leisure and recreation		('000)	1,478	1,619	1,804	1,937	2,014
1.17　　* other personal purposes		('000)	52	57	63	68	71
1.18　♦ Business and professional		('000)	41	45	49	53	55
Arrivals by mode of transport	(1)						
1.19　Total		('000)	1,570	1,720	1,916	2,058	2,140
1.20　♦ Air		('000)	950	970	1,132	1,292	1,344
1.21　♦ Water	(3)	('000)	11	20	25	30	38
1.22　♦ Land		('000)	609	730	759	736	758
1.23　　* railway		('000)	7	9	9	7	7
1.24　　* road		('000)	602	721	750	729	751
1.25　　* others		('000)	..	..	..	..	..
Accommodation							
Total							
1.29　♦ Guests		('000)	..	..	..	..	..
1.30　♦ Overnights		('000)	..	..	..	..	..
Hotels and similar establishments							
1.31　♦ Guests		('000)	2,960	2,983	3,385	4,455	4,044
1.32　♦ Overnights		('000)	5,550	5,845	6,654	8,275	7,556
Expenditure							
1.33　Total		US$ Mn	1,438	1,775	2,007	2,395	2,471
1.34　♦ Travel		US$ Mn	1,308	1,570	1,723	1,991	2,046
1.35　♦ Passenger transport		US$ Mn	130	205	284	404	425
Indicators							
1.39　Average size of travel party		Persons	..	..	..	..	..
Average length of stay							
1.40　Total		Days	..	..	..	..	..
1.41　♦ For all commercial accommodation services		Nights	1.88	1.96	1.97	1.86	1.87
1.42　　* of which, "hotels and similar establishments"		Nights	..	..	..	..	..
1.43　♦ For non commercial accommodation services		Days	..	..	..	..	..
1.44　Average expenditure per day		US$	..	..	..	..	..
2. DOMESTIC TOURISM							
Data							
Trips							
2.1　Total	(4)	('000)	..	..	74,629	..	..
2.2　♦ Overnight visitors (tourists)	(4)	('000)	..	..	24,223	..	..
2.3　♦ Same-day visitors (excursionists)	(4)	('000)	..	..	50,406	..	..
Accommodation							
Total							
2.19　♦ Guests		('000)	..	..	..	..	..
2.20　♦ Overnights		('000)	..	..	..	..	..
Hotels and similar establishments							
2.21　♦ Guests		('000)	17,167	16,176	18,351	20,467	21,579
2.22　♦ Overnights		('000)	20,783	20,910	23,849	26,060	27,578
Indicators							
2.23　Average size of travel party		Persons	..	..	..	..	..
Average length of stay							
2.24　Total		Days	..	..	..	..	..
2.25　♦ For all commercial accommodation services		Nights	1.21	1.29	1.30	1.27	1.30
2.26　　* of which, "hotels and similar establishments"		Nights	..	..	..	..	..
2.27　♦ For non commercial accommodation services		Days	..	..	..	..	..
2.28　Average expenditure per day		US$	..	..	17.0	..	..

PERU

Basic data and indicators	Notes	Units	2005	2006	2007	2008	2009
3. OUTBOUND TOURISM							
Data							
Departures							
3.1 Total		('000)	..	..	..	..	..
3.2 ♦ Overnight visitors (tourists)		('000)	1,883	1,903	1,966	1,971	1,958
3.3 ♦ Same-day visitors (excursionists)		('000)	..	..	..	..	..
Expenditure							
3.4 Total		US$ Mn	970	1,047	1,248	1,353	1,379
3.5 ♦ Travel		US$ Mn	752	798	973	1,067	1,086
3.6 ♦ Passenger transport		US$ Mn	218	249	275	286	293
4. TOURISM INDUSTRIES							
Data							
Number of establishments							
4.1 Total		Units	..	..	..	..	..
4.2 ♦ Accommodation for visitors		Units	..	..	..	..	..
4.3 * of which, "hotels and similar establishments"		Units	9,659	10,082	10,666	11,437	12,245
4.4 ♦ Food and beverage serving activities		Units	..	..	..	..	..
4.5 ♦ Passenger transportation		Units	..	..	..	..	..
4.6 ♦ Travel agencies and other reservation services activities		Units	..	..	..	..	..
4.7 ♦ Other tourism industries		Units	..	..	..	..	..
Accommodation for visitors in hotels and similar establishments							
Non-monetary data							
4.13 ♦ Number of establishments		Units	9,659	10,082	10,666	11,437	12,245
4.14 ♦ Number of rooms		Units	150,901	158,120	166,048	176,173	185,728
4.15 ♦ Number of bed-places		Units	263,588	276,320	290,794	308,765	325,407
Indicators							
4.16 Occupancy rate / rooms		Percent	..	..	..	..	..
4.17 Occupancy rate / bed-places		Percent	..	..	..	..	..
4.18 Average length of stay		Nights	1.31	1.40	1.40	1.38	1.40
4.19 Available capacity (bed-places per 1000 inhabitants)		Units	9.47	9.81	10.20	10.71	11.16
6. COMPLEMENTARY INDICATORS							
Demand							
6.1 Gross travel propensity		Units	..	..	..	..	..
6.2 Carrying capacity (arrivals/population)		Units	0.06	0.06	0.92	0.07	0.07
Macroeconomic indicators related to international tourism							
6.3 Inbound tourism expenditure over GDP		Percent	1.8	1.9	1.9	1.9	1.9
6.4 Outbound tourism expenditure over GDP		Percent	1.2	1.1	1.2	1.1	1.1
6.5 Tourism balance (inbound minus outbound tourism expenditure) over GDP		Percent	0.6	0.8	0.7	0.8	0.9
6.6 Tourism openness (inbound plus outbound tourism expenditure) over GDP		Percent	3.0	3.1	3.0	2.9	3.0
6.7 Tourism coverage (inbound over outbound tourism expenditure)		Percent	148.4	169.6	160.8	177.0	179.3
6.8 Inbound tourism expenditure over exports of goods		Percent	8.3	7.4	7.2	7.6	9.2
6.9 Inbound tourism expenditure over exports of services		Percent	62.8	66.7	63.7	65.6	67.6
6.10 Inbound tourism expenditure over exports of goods and services		Percent	7.3	6.7	6.5	6.8	8.1
6.11 Inbound tourism expenditure over current account credits		Percent	6.5	6.0	5.7	6.0	7.1
6.12 Outbound tourism expenditure over imports of goods		Percent	8.0	7.1	6.4	4.8	6.6
6.13 Outbound tourism expenditure over imports of services		Percent	31.0	30.8	28.7	24.1	28.9
6.14 Outbound tourism expenditure over imports of goods and services		Percent	6.4	5.7	5.2	4.0	5.3
6.15 Outbound tourism expenditure over current account debits		Percent	4.6	3.9	3.7	3.0	4.0

PHILIPPINES

Basic data and indicators	Notes	Units	2005	2006	2007	2008	2009
1. INBOUND TOURISM							
Data							
Arrivals							
1.1 Total		('000)	..	..	..	..	..
1.2 ♦ Overnight visitors (tourists)	(1)	('000)	2,623	2,843	3,092	3,139	3,017
1.3 ♦ Same-day visitors (excursionists)		('000)	2	4	17	21	21
1.4 * of which, cruise passengers		('000)	2	4	17	21	21
Arrivals by region	(1)						
1.5 Total		('000)	2,622	2,843	3,092	3,140	3,017
1.6 ♦ Africa		('000)	2	2	3	3	3
1.7 ♦ Americas		('000)	605	652	675	685	686
1.8 ♦ East Asia and the Pacific		('000)	1,565	1,691	1,829	1,799	1,644
1.9 ♦ Europe		('000)	246	264	300	323	330
1.10 ♦ Middle East		('000)	25	28	32	37	47
1.11 ♦ South Asia		('000)	28	32	38	44	47
1.12 ♦ Other not classified		('000)	151	174	215	249	260
1.13 * of which, nationals residing abroad		('000)	125	146	181	195	198
Arrivals by main purpose	(1)(2)						
1.14 Total		('000)	2,587	2,807	3,042	3,085	2,960
1.15 ♦ Personal		('000)	2,221	2,398	2,591	2,620	2,552
1.16 * holidays, leisure and recreation		('000)	1,174	1,319	1,439	1,439	1,327
1.17 * other personal purposes		('000)	1,047	1,079	1,152	1,181	1,225
1.18 ♦ Business and professional		('000)	366	409	451	465	408
Arrivals by mode of transport	(1)						
1.19 Total		('000)	2,623	2,843	3,092	3,140	3,017
1.20 ♦ Air		('000)	2,586	2,807	3,042	3,085	2,960
1.21 ♦ Water		('000)	37	36	50	55	57
1.22 ♦ Land		('000)	..	..	..	..	..
1.23 * railway		('000)	..	..	..	..	..
1.24 * road		('000)	..	..	..	..	..
1.25 * others		('000)	..	..	..	..	..
Arrivals by form of organization of the trip							
1.26 Total	(2)	('000)	2,586	2,807	3,042	3,085	2,960
1.27 ♦ Package tour		('000)	454	521	556	502	400
1.28 ♦ Other forms		('000)	2,132	2,286	2,486	2,583	2,560
Accommodation							
Total							
1.29 ♦ Guests		('000)	..	..	..	..	..
1.30 ♦ Overnights		('000)	..	..	..	..	..
Hotels and similar establishments							
1.31 ♦ Guests		('000)	955	1,013	1,027	980	670
1.32 ♦ Overnights		('000)	12,842	14,200	14,149	14,048	..
Expenditure							
1.33 Total		US$ Mn	2,755	4,019	5,520	3,024	2,837
1.34 ♦ Travel		US$ Mn	2,265	3,501	4,933	2,499	2,329
1.35 ♦ Passenger transport		US$ Mn	490	518	587	525	508
Indicators							
1.39 Average size of travel party		Persons	..	..	..	..	..
Average length of stay							
1.40 Total	(3)	Days	8.59	9.35	10.03	9.40	8.83
1.41 ♦ For all commercial accommodation services		Nights	8.41	12.06	16.70	12.99	8.83
1.42 * of which, "hotels and similar establishments"		Nights	..	..	..	..	..
1.43 ♦ For non commercial accommodation services		Days	..	..	..	..	..
1.44 Average expenditure per day		US$	83.6	85.6	87.0	74.9	75.8

PHILIPPINES

Basic data and indicators	Notes	Units	2005	2006	2007	2008	2009
3. OUTBOUND TOURISM							
Data							
Departures							
3.1 Total		('000)	..	..	..	..	..
3.2 ♦ Overnight visitors (tourists)	(4)	('000)	2,144	2,745	3,066	..	..
3.3 ♦ Same-day visitors (excursionists)		('000)	..	..	..	..	..
Expenditure							
3.4 Total		US$ Mn	1,547	1,558	2,055	2,553	2,989
3.5 ♦ Travel		US$ Mn	1,279	1,232	1,663	2,057	2,444
3.6 ♦ Passenger transport		US$ Mn	268	326	392	496	545
Expenditure by main purpose of the trip							
3.7 Total		US$ Mn	..	1,232	1,663	2,057	2,444
3.8 ♦ Personal		US$ Mn	..	1,196	1,624	2,003	2,396
3.9 ♦ Business and professional		US$ Mn	..	36	39	54	48
4. TOURISM INDUSTRIES							
Data							
Number of establishments							
4.1 Total		Units	..	..	..	..	..
4.2 ♦ Accommodation for visitors		Units	..	..	..	..	..
4.3 * of which, "hotels and similar establishments"	(5)	Units	403	433	451	416	323
4.4 ♦ Food and beverage serving activities		Units	..	..	..	..	..
4.5 ♦ Passenger transportation		Units	..	..	..	..	..
4.6 ♦ Travel agencies and other reservation services activities		Units	..	..	..	..	..
4.7 ♦ Other tourism industries		Units	..	..	..	..	..
Accommodation for visitors in hotels and similar establishments							
Non-monetary data							
4.13 ♦ Number of establishments	(5)	Units	403	433	451	416	323
4.14 ♦ Number of rooms	(5)	Units	29,757	30,272	31,523	30,571	21,602
4.15 ♦ Number of bed-places	(5)	Units	59,514	60,544	63,046	61,142	43,204
Indicators							
4.16 Occupancy rate / rooms		Percent	..	..	..	..	..
4.17 Occupancy rate / bed-places	(6)	Percent	71.71	71.95	73.06	69.79	64.76
4.18 Average length of stay	(6)	Nights	2.58	2.56	2.45	2.42	2.39
4.19 Available capacity (bed-places per 1000 inhabitants)		Units	0.70	0.70	0.71	0.68	0.47
6. COMPLEMENTARY INDICATORS							
Demand							
6.1 Gross travel propensity		Units	..	..	..	..	..
6.2 Carrying capacity (arrivals/population)		Units	0.03	0.03	0.03	0.03	0.03
Macroeconomic indicators related to international tourism							
6.3 Inbound tourism expenditure over GDP		Percent	2.8	3.4	3.8	1.8	1.8
6.4 Outbound tourism expenditure over GDP		Percent	1.6	1.3	1.4	1.5	1.9
6.5 Tourism balance (inbound minus outbound tourism expenditure) over GDP		Percent	1.2	2.1	2.4	0.3	-0.1
6.6 Tourism openness (inbound plus outbound tourism expenditure) over GDP		Percent	4.4	4.7	5.3	3.3	3.6
6.7 Tourism coverage (inbound over outbound tourism expenditure)		Percent	178.1	258.0	268.6	118.4	94.9
6.8 Inbound tourism expenditure over exports of goods		Percent	6.8	8.6	11.1	6.3	7.6
6.9 Inbound tourism expenditure over exports of services		Percent	60.9	62.4	56.5	31.1	28.1
6.10 Inbound tourism expenditure over exports of goods and services		Percent	6.2	7.6	9.3	5.2	6.0
6.11 Inbound tourism expenditure over current account credits		Percent	4.6	5.7	7.0	3.8	4.1
6.12 Outbound tourism expenditure over imports of goods		Percent	3.2	2.9	3.5	4.2	6.4
6.13 Outbound tourism expenditure over imports of services		Percent	26.4	24.7	27.3	29.8	34.9
6.14 Outbound tourism expenditure over imports of goods and services		Percent	2.9	2.6	3.1	3.7	5.4
6.15 Outbound tourism expenditure over current account debits		Percent	2.6	2.4	2.9	3.4	4.9

POLAND

Basic data and indicators	Notes	Units	2005	2006	2007	2008	2009
1. INBOUND TOURISM							
Data							
Arrivals							
1.1 Total	(1)	('000)	64,606	65,115	66,208	59,935	53,840
1.2 ♦ Overnight visitors (tourists)	(2)	('000)	15,200	15,670	14,975	12,960	11,890
1.3 ♦ Same-day visitors (excursionists)		('000)	49,406	49,445	51,233	46,975	41,950
1.4 * of which, cruise passengers		('000)	..	..	..	..	..
Arrivals by region	(1)						
1.5 Total		('000)	64,605	65,115	66,208	59,935	53,840
1.6 ♦ Africa		('000)	13	15	17	15	20
1.7 ♦ Americas		('000)	439	466	453	380	338
1.8 ♦ East Asia and the Pacific		('000)	163	194	229	220	207
1.9 ♦ Europe		('000)	63,927	64,367	65,373	59,290	53,221
1.10 ♦ Middle East		('000)	8	8	10	10	15
1.11 ♦ South Asia		('000)	13	15	20	20	20
1.12 ♦ Other not classified		('000)	42	50	106	..	19
1.13 * of which, nationals residing abroad		('000)	..	..	..	..	..
Arrivals by main purpose	(2)						
1.14 Total		('000)	15,200	15,670	14,975	12,960	11,890
1.15 ♦ Personal		('000)	10,960	11,430	10,890	9,170	8,320
1.16 * holidays, leisure and recreation		('000)	3,680	3,210	2,660	4,000	3,840
1.17 * other personal purposes		('000)	7,280	8,220	8,230	5,170	4,480
1.18 ♦ Business and professional		('000)	4,240	4,240	4,085	3,790	3,570
Arrivals by mode of transport	(1)						
1.19 Total		('000)	64,605	65,115	66,208	59,935	53,840
1.20 ♦ Air		('000)	2,004	2,432	2,884	2,800	2,650
1.21 ♦ Water		('000)	404	368	371	350	320
1.22 ♦ Land		('000)	62,197	62,315	62,953	56,785	50,870
1.23 * railway		('000)	1,606	1,669	1,831	1,430	1,220
1.24 * road		('000)	60,591	60,646	61,122	55,355	49,650
1.25 * others		('000)	..	..	..	..	..
Arrivals by form of organization of the trip	(2)						
1.26 Total		('000)	15,200	15,670	14,975	12,960	11,890
1.27 ♦ Package tour		('000)	1,430	1,660	1,390	2,020	1,600
1.28 ♦ Other forms		('000)	13,770	14,010	13,585	10,940	10,290
Accommodation	(3)						
Total							
1.29 ♦ Guests		('000)	4,310	4,314	4,387	4,046	3,862
1.30 ♦ Overnights		('000)	10,542	10,555	10,918	10,173	9,609
Hotels and similar establishments							
1.31 ♦ Guests		('000)	3,723	3,738	3,833	3,566	3,394
1.32 ♦ Overnights		('000)	7,869	7,911	8,409	7,939	7,478
Expenditure							
1.33 Total		US$ Mn	7,128	8,122	11,686	12,837	9,853
1.34 ♦ Travel		US$ Mn	6,274	7,239	10,599	11,768	9,011
1.35 ♦ Passenger transport		US$ Mn	854	883	1,087	1,069	842
Expenditure by main purpose of the trip							
1.36 Total		US$ Mn	6,274	7,239	10,599	11,768	9,011
1.37 ♦ Personal		US$ Mn	4,974	5,809	8,499	8,928	7,361
1.38 ♦ Business and professional		US$ Mn	1,300	1,430	2,100	2,840	1,650
Indicators							
1.39 Average size of travel party		Persons	1.8	1.5	1.4	1.6	1.6
Average length of stay							
1.40 Total		Days	..	..	..	..	..
1.41 ♦ For all commercial accommodation services	(4)	Nights	4.40	3.40	2.90	4.00	4.20
1.42 * of which, "hotels and similar establishments"		Nights	..	..	..	..	..
1.43 ♦ For non commercial accommodation services		Days	..	..	..	..	..
1.44 Average expenditure per day		US$	..	..	..	..	..
2. DOMESTIC TOURISM							
Data							
Trips							
2.1 Total		('000)	..	..	..	..	..
2.2 ♦ Overnight visitors (tourists)	(2)	('000)	35,900	38,500	34,900	34,900	30,800
2.3 ♦ Same-day visitors (excursionists)		('000)	..	..	..	..	..
Trips by main purpose	(2)(5)						
2.4 Total		('000)	14,700	16,900	15,800	14,300	13,300
2.5 ♦ Personal		('000)	13,230	14,530	14,060	13,010	12,370
2.6 * holidays, leisure and recreation		('000)	6,170	7,940	7,580	7,290	7,450
2.7 * other personal purposes		('000)	7,060	6,590	6,480	5,720	4,920
2.8 ♦ Business and professional		('000)	1,470	2,370	1,740	1,290	930

POLAND

Basic data and indicators		Notes	Units	2005	2006	2007	2008	2009
	Trips by form of organization	(2)(5)						
2.16	Total		('000)	14,700	16,900	15,800	14,300	13,300
2.17	♦ Package tour		('000)	1,320	2,200	1,580	1,430	1,060
2.18	♦ Other forms		('000)	13,380	14,700	14,220	12,870	12,240
	Accommodation	(3)						
	Total							
2.19	♦ Guests		('000)	12,287	13,199	14,560	15,510	15,492
2.20	♦ Overnights		('000)	38,076	40,680	44,036	46,472	45,411
	Hotels and similar establishments							
2.21	♦ Guests		('000)	6,805	7,564	8,652	9,510	9,592
2.22	♦ Overnights		('000)	12,464	13,910	15,898	17,300	17,036
	Indicators							
2.23	Average size of travel party		Persons	..	..	..	..	..
	Average length of stay							
2.24	Total		Days	..	..	..	..	..
2.25	♦ For all commercial accommodation services		Nights	3.10	3.08	3.02	3.00	2.93
2.26	* of which, "hotels and similar establishments"		Nights	..	..	..	..	..
2.27	♦ For non commercial accommodation services		Days	..	..	..	..	..
2.28	Average expenditure per day		US$	..	..	..	..	..

3. OUTBOUND TOURISM

		Notes	Units	2005	2006	2007	2008	2009
	Data							
	Departures							
3.1	Total	(6)	('000)	40,841	44,696	47,561	50,243	39,270
3.2	♦ Overnight visitors (tourists)		('000)	6,200	7,300	6,900	7,600	6,300
3.3	♦ Same-day visitors (excursionists)		('000)	34,641	37,396	40,661	42,643	32,970
	Expenditure							
3.4	Total		US$ Mn	5,894	7,654	8,342	10,689	7,842
3.5	♦ Travel		US$ Mn	5,548	7,224	7,753	9,903	7,327
3.6	♦ Passenger transport		US$ Mn	346	430	589	786	515
	Expenditure by main purpose of the trip							
3.7	Total		US$ Mn	5,548	7,224	7,753	9,903	7,327
3.8	♦ Personal		US$ Mn	4,038	5,584	4,703	7,143	5,417
3.9	♦ Business and professional		US$ Mn	1,510	1,640	3,050	2,760	1,910
	Indicators							
3.10	Average length of stay		Days	13.00	15.60	16.20	15.10	10.50
3.11	Average expenditure per day		US$	..	..	..	..	..

4. TOURISM INDUSTRIES

		Notes	Units	2005	2006	2007	2008	2009
	Data							
	Number of establishments							
4.1	Total		Units	103,018	104,403	99,311	94,005	85,616
4.2	♦ Accommodation for visitors		Units	6,723	6,694	6,718	6,857	6,992
4.3	* of which, "hotels and similar establishments"		Units	2,200	2,301	2,443	2,642	2,836
4.4	♦ Food and beverage serving activities		Units	91,150	92,072	86,973	81,131	78,624
4.5	♦ Passenger transportation		Units	..	..	..	..	..
4.6	♦ Travel agencies and other reservation services activities		Units	5,145	5,637	5,620	6,017	..
4.7	♦ Other tourism industries		Units	..	..	..	..	..
	Accommodation for visitors in hotels and similar establishments							
	Monetary data							
4.8	♦ Output		US$ Mn	1,324.8	1,445.1	1,954.7	2,288.6	..
4.9	♦ Intermediate consumption		US$ Mn	..	..	..	..	..
4.10	♦ Gross value added		US$ Mn	..	..	..	..	..
4.11	♦ Compensation of employees		US$ Mn	..	..	..	..	..
4.12	♦ Gross fixed capital formation		US$ Mn	..	..	..	..	..
	Non-monetary data							
4.13	♦ Number of establishments		Units	2,200	2,301	2,443	2,642	2,836
4.14	♦ Number of rooms		Units	84,865	88,409	93,944	103,705	109,534
4.15	♦ Number of bed-places		Units	169,609	178,056	190,387	210,507	221,633
	Indicators							
4.16	Occupancy rate / rooms		Percent	40.50	42.20	46.10	45.10	40.60
4.17	Occupancy rate / bed-places		Percent	34.50	35.20	36.70	35.30	32.20
4.18	Average length of stay		Nights	1.93	1.93	1.95	1.93	1.89
4.19	Available capacity (bed-places per 1000 inhabitants)		Units	4.44	4.67	4.99	5.52	5.81

POLAND

Basic data and indicators	Notes	Units	2005	2006	2007	2008	2009
Travel agencies and other reservation service activities							
Monetary data							
4.20 ♦ Output		US$ Mn	1,607.5	1,998.4	2,998.2	3,950.2	..
4.21 ♦ Intermediate consumption		US$ Mn	..	..	..	..	..
4.22 ♦ Gross value added		US$ Mn	..	..	..	..	..
4.23 ♦ Compensation of employees		US$ Mn	..	..	..	..	..
4.24 ♦ Gross fixed capital formation		US$ Mn	..	..	..	..	..
5. EMPLOYMENT							
Data							
Number of employees by tourism industries							
5.1 Total		('000)	607.1	627.6	..	686.8	..
5.2 ♦ Accommodation services for visitors (hotels and similar establishments)		('000)	40.5	39.3	..	46.8	..
5.3 ♦ Other accommodation services		('000)	26.1	28.3	..	33.1	..
5.4 ♦ Food and beverage serving activities		('000)	152.0	161.2	..	196.1	..
5.5 ♦ Passenger transportation		('000)	236.1	239.7	..	239.3	..
5.6 ♦ Travel agencies and other reservation services activities		('000)	13.0	15.5	..	18.0	..
5.7 ♦ Other tourism industries		('000)	139.4	143.6	..	153.5	..
Number of jobs by status in employment							
5.8 Total		('000)	607.1	627.5	..	686.8	..
5.9 ♦ Employees		('000)	524.8	552.8	..	593.0	..
5.10 ♦ Self employed		('000)	82.3	74.7	..	93.8	..
Indicators							
Number of full-time equivalent jobs by status in employment							
5.11 Total		('000)	607.1	627.5	..	686.8	..
5.12 ♦ Employees		('000)	524.8	552.8	..	593.0	..
5.13 * male		('000)	243.8	252.8	..	307.3	..
5.14 * female		('000)	281.0	300.0	..	285.7	..
5.15 ♦ Self employed		('000)	82.3	74.7	..	93.8	..
5.16 * male		('000)	37.9	32.9	..	54.7	..
5.17 * female		('000)	44.4	41.8	..	39.1	..
6. COMPLEMENTARY INDICATORS							
Demand							
6.1 Gross travel propensity		Units	..	..	..	..	..
6.2 Carrying capacity (arrivals/population)		Units	1.34	1.42	1.31	1.26	1.12
Macroeconomic indicators related to international tourism							
6.3 Inbound tourism expenditure over GDP		Percent	2.3	2.4	2.7	2.4	2.3
6.4 Outbound tourism expenditure over GDP		Percent	1.9	2.2	2.0	2.0	1.8
6.5 Tourism balance (inbound minus outbound tourism expenditure) over GDP		Percent	0.4	0.1	0.8	0.4	0.5
6.6 Tourism openness (inbound plus outbound tourism expenditure) over GDP		Percent	4.3	4.6	4.7	4.5	4.1
6.7 Tourism coverage (inbound over outbound tourism expenditure)		Percent	120.9	106.1	140.1	120.1	125.6
6.8 Inbound tourism expenditure over exports of goods		Percent	7.4	6.9	8.0	7.2	7.0
6.9 Inbound tourism expenditure over exports of services		Percent	43.8	39.4	40.4	36.1	34.0
6.10 Inbound tourism expenditure over exports of goods and services		Percent	6.3	5.9	6.7	6.0	5.8
6.11 Inbound tourism expenditure over current account credits		Percent	5.5	5.1	5.9	5.3	5.1
6.12 Outbound tourism expenditure over imports of goods		Percent	5.9	6.1	5.1	5.2	5.4
6.13 Outbound tourism expenditure over imports of services		Percent	38.0	38.5	34.5	35.0	32.5
6.14 Outbound tourism expenditure over imports of goods and services		Percent	5.1	5.3	4.5	4.5	4.7
6.15 Outbound tourism expenditure over current account debits		Percent	4.4	4.5	3.8	4.0	3.9

PORTUGAL

Basic data and indicators	Notes	Units	2005	2006	2007	2008	2009
1. INBOUND TOURISM							
Data							
Arrivals	(1)						
1.1 Total		('000)	21,173	22,588	23,766	..	..
1.2 ♦ Overnight visitors (tourists)		('000)	10,612	11,282	12,321	..	..
1.3 ♦ Same-day visitors (excursionists)		('000)	10,561	11,306	11,446	..	..
1.4 * of which, cruise passengers		('000)	..	..	..	..	..
Arrivals by region	(1)						
1.5 Total		('000)	10,612	11,282	12,321	..	..
1.6 ♦ Africa		('000)	..	..	..	..	..
1.7 ♦ Americas		('000)	413	499	600	..	..
1.8 ♦ East Asia and the Pacific		('000)	37	32	40	..	..
1.9 ♦ Europe		('000)	9,271	9,831	10,693	..	..
1.10 ♦ Middle East		('000)	..	..	..	..	..
1.11 ♦ South Asia		('000)	..	..	..	..	..
1.12 ♦ Other not classified		('000)	891	920	988	..	..
1.13 * of which, nationals residing abroad		('000)	..	..	..	..	..
Arrivals by main purpose	(1)						
1.14 Total		('000)	21,172	22,588	23,731	..	..
1.15 ♦ Personal		('000)	17,864	19,033	19,607	..	..
1.16 * holidays, leisure and recreation		('000)	15,328	16,393	16,835	..	..
1.17 * other personal purposes		('000)	2,536	2,640	2,772	..	..
1.18 ♦ Business and professional		('000)	3,308	3,555	4,124	..	..
Arrivals by mode of transport	(1)						
1.19 Total		('000)	21,174	22,588	23,766	..	..
1.20 ♦ Air		('000)	6,137	6,734	7,459	..	..
1.21 ♦ Water		('000)	..	..	..	..	..
1.22 ♦ Land		('000)	15,037	15,854	16,307	..	..
1.23 * railway		('000)	..	..	..	..	..
1.24 * road		('000)	15,037	15,854	16,307	..	..
1.25 * others		('000)	..	..	..	..	..
Accommodation							
Total							
1.29 ♦ Guests		('000)	5,769	6,349	6,788	6,962	6,439
1.30 ♦ Overnights		('000)	25,388	26,842	28,670	28,127	25,025
Hotels and similar establishments							
1.31 ♦ Guests		('000)	5,355	5,883	6,291	6,422	5,911
1.32 ♦ Overnights		('000)	23,873	25,216	26,769	26,204	23,214
Expenditure							
1.33 Total		US$ Mn	9,008	10,438	12,917	14,047	12,329
1.34 ♦ Travel		US$ Mn	7,676	8,416	10,175	10,980	9,707
1.35 ♦ Passenger transport		US$ Mn	1,332	2,022	2,742	3,067	2,622
Expenditure by main purpose of the trip							
1.36 Total		US$ Mn	..	8,416	10,175	10,980	9,707
1.37 ♦ Personal		US$ Mn	..	7,567	9,147	9,871	8,707
1.38 ♦ Business and professional		US$ Mn	..	849	1,028	1,109	1,000
Indicators							
1.39 Average size of travel party		Persons	..	..	..	..	..
Average length of stay							
1.40 Total		Days	..	..	..	..	..
1.41 ♦ For all commercial accommodation services		Nights	4.40	3.85	4.20	4.00	3.89
1.42 * of which, "hotels and similar establishments"		Nights	..	..	..	..	3.93
1.43 ♦ For non commercial accommodation services		Days	..	..	..	..	..
1.44 Average expenditure per day		US$	..	..	..	..	..
2. DOMESTIC TOURISM							
Data							
Accommodation							
Total							
2.19 ♦ Guests		('000)	..	..	..	..	..
2.20 ♦ Overnights		('000)	17,877	18,680	19,295	19,190	19,340
Hotels and similar establishments							
2.21 ♦ Guests		('000)	5,274	5,866	6,058	6,050	6,189
2.22 ♦ Overnights		('000)	11,648	12,350	12,968	13,024	13,243
Indicators							
2.23 Average size of travel party		Persons	..	..	..	..	..
Average length of stay							
2.24 Total		Days	..	..	..	..	..
2.25 ♦ For all commercial accommodation services		Nights	2.10	2.10	2.62	2.58	2.53
2.26 * of which, "hotels and similar establishments"		Nights	..	..	..	..	2.14
2.27 ♦ For non commercial accommodation services		Days	..	..	..	..	..
2.28 Average expenditure per day		US$	..	..	..	..	..

PORTUGAL

Basic data and indicators	Notes	Units	2005	2006	2007	2008	2009
3. OUTBOUND TOURISM							
Data							
Departures							
3.1 Total		('000)	..	..	..	..	..
3.2 ♦ Overnight visitors (tourists)		('000)	18,110	18,378	20,989	..	..
3.3 ♦ Same-day visitors (excursionists)		('000)	..	..	..	..	..
Expenditure							
3.4 Total		US$ Mn	3,743	4,142	4,864	5,283	4,604
3.5 ♦ Travel		US$ Mn	3,050	3,340	3,937	4,328	3,776
3.6 ♦ Passenger transport		US$ Mn	693	802	927	955	828
Expenditure by main purpose of the trip							
3.7 Total		US$ Mn	..	3,340	3,937	4,328	3,776
3.8 ♦ Personal		US$ Mn	..	2,176	2,491	2,745	2,401
3.9 ♦ Business and professional		US$ Mn	..	1,164	1,446	1,583	1,375
4. TOURISM INDUSTRIES							
Data							
Number of establishments							
4.1 Total		Units	..	..	..	..	..
4.2 ♦ Accommodation for visitors		Units	2,300	2,324	2,339	2,354	2,299
4.3 * of which, "hotels and similar establishments"		Units	2,012	2,028	2,031	2,041	1,988
4.4 ♦ Food and beverage serving activities		Units	..	..	..	..	..
4.5 ♦ Passenger transportation		Units	..	..	..	..	..
4.6 ♦ Travel agencies and other reservation services activities		Units	..	..	..	..	..
4.7 ♦ Other tourism industries		Units	..	..	..	..	..
Accommodation for visitors in hotels and similar establishments							
Monetary data	(2)						
4.8 ♦ Output		US$ Mn	..	..	..	..	..
4.9 ♦ Intermediate consumption		US$ Mn	..	..	327.4	300.7	..
4.10 ♦ Gross value added		US$ Mn	..	..	1,295.6	1,251.4	..
4.11 ♦ Compensation of employees		US$ Mn	..	..	800.0	839.7	..
4.12 ♦ Gross fixed capital formation		US$ Mn	..	..	956.4	1,044.1	..
Non-monetary data							
4.13 ♦ Number of establishments		Units	2,012	2,028	2,031	2,041	1,988
4.14 ♦ Number of rooms		Units	116,123	117,565	117,976	121,013	120,737
4.15 ♦ Number of bed-places		Units	263,814	264,037	264,747	273,975	273,804
Indicators							
4.16 Occupancy rate / rooms	(3)	Percent	55.10	57.30	59.00	57.10	51.43
4.17 Occupancy rate / bed-places	(3)	Percent	46.60	48.30	50.30	47.30	42.16
4.18 Average length of stay	(4)	Nights	3.10	3.00	3.00	2.90	2.80
4.19 Available capacity (bed-places per 1000 inhabitants)		Units	25.01	24.95	24.96	25.79	25.75
Travel agencies and other reservation service activities							
Monetary data	(2)						
4.20 ♦ Output		US$ Mn	..	..	..	..	..
4.21 ♦ Intermediate consumption		US$ Mn	..	..	4.3	4.2	..
4.22 ♦ Gross value added		US$ Mn	..	..	262.2	254.3	..
4.23 ♦ Compensation of employees		US$ Mn	..	..	189.2	199.7	..
4.24 ♦ Gross fixed capital formation		US$ Mn	..	..	37.3	38.5	..
5. EMPLOYMENT	(5)						
Data							
Number of employees by tourism industries							
5.1 Total		('000)	391.9	401.9	406.5	..	..
5.2 ♦ Accommodation services for visitors (hotels and similar establishments)		('000)	55.9	58.3	59.4	..	..
5.3 ♦ Other accommodation services		('000)	..	..	..	..	..
5.4 ♦ Food and beverage serving activities		('000)	198.0	203.1	206.1	..	..
5.5 ♦ Passenger transportation		('000)	94.3	95.4	90.4	..	..
5.6 ♦ Travel agencies and other reservation services activities		('000)	3.8	3.9	9.4	..	..
5.7 ♦ Other tourism industries		('000)	39.9	41.2	41.2	..	..
Number of jobs by status in employment							
5.8 Total		('000)	392.0	402.0	406.6	..	..
5.9 ♦ Employees		('000)	357.9	370.5	372.2	..	..
5.10 ♦ Self employed		('000)	34.1	31.5	34.4	..	..

PORTUGAL

Basic data and indicators	Notes	Units	2005	2006	2007	2008	2009
Indicators							
Number of full-time equivalent jobs by status in employment							
5.11 Total		('000)	385.9	395.8	400.5	..	..
5.12 ♦ Employees		('000)	350.3	362.0	365.0	..	..
5.13 * male		('000)	..	..	..	..	..
5.14 * female		('000)	..	..	..	..	..
5.15 ♦ Self employed		('000)	35.6	33.8	35.5	..	..
5.16 * male		('000)	..	..	..	..	..
5.17 * female		('000)	..	..	..	..	..
6. COMPLEMENTARY INDICATORS							
Demand							
6.1 Gross travel propensity		Units	..	..	..	..	..
6.2 Carrying capacity (arrivals/population)		Units	1.01	1.07	1.16	..	..
Macroeconomic indicators related to international tourism							
6.3 Inbound tourism expenditure over GDP		Percent	4.9	5.4	5.8	5.8	5.4
6.4 Outbound tourism expenditure over GDP		Percent	2.0	2.1	2.2	2.2	2.0
6.5 Tourism balance (inbound minus outbound tourism expenditure) over GDP		Percent	2.8	3.2	3.6	3.6	3.4
6.6 Tourism openness (inbound plus outbound tourism expenditure) over GDP		Percent	6.9	7.5	8.0	7.9	7.4
6.7 Tourism coverage (inbound over outbound tourism expenditure)		Percent	240.6	252.0	265.6	265.9	267.8
6.8 Inbound tourism expenditure over exports of goods		Percent	23.2	23.2	24.5	24.3	27.7
6.9 Inbound tourism expenditure over exports of services		Percent	59.4	56.5	55.4	53.4	54.1
6.10 Inbound tourism expenditure over exports of goods and services		Percent	16.7	16.4	17.0	16.7	18.3
6.11 Inbound tourism expenditure over current account credits		Percent	12.8	12.3	12.7	12.5	14.1
6.12 Outbound tourism expenditure over imports of goods		Percent	6.1	6.1	6.1	5.8	6.7
6.13 Outbound tourism expenditure over imports of services		Percent	36.2	34.2	34.0	31.9	32.1
6.14 Outbound tourism expenditure over imports of goods and services		Percent	5.2	5.2	5.2	4.9	5.5
6.15 Outbound tourism expenditure over current account debits		Percent	4.1	3.9	3.9	3.7	4.1

PUERTO RICO

Basic data and indicators	Notes	Units	2005	2006	2007	2008	2009
1. INBOUND TOURISM							
Data							
Arrivals							
1.1 Total		('000)	5,073	5,022	5,062	5,213	4,783
1.2 ♦ Overnight visitors (tourists)	(1)	('000)	3,686	3,722	3,687	3,716	3,551
1.3 ♦ Same-day visitors (excursionists)		('000)	1,387	1,300	1,375	1,497	1,232
1.4 * of which, cruise passengers		('000)	1,387	1,300	1,375	1,497	1,232
Arrivals by region	(1)						
1.5 Total		('000)	3,686	3,722	3,687	3,716	3,551
1.6 ♦ Africa		('000)	..	..	..	..	..
1.7 ♦ Americas	(2)	('000)	2,847	2,930	2,887	2,912	3,017
1.8 ♦ East Asia and the Pacific		('000)	..	..	..	..	..
1.9 ♦ Europe		('000)	..	..	..	..	..
1.10 ♦ Middle East		('000)	..	..	..	..	..
1.11 ♦ South Asia		('000)	..	..	..	..	..
1.12 ♦ Other not classified		('000)	839	792	800	804	534
1.13 * of which, nationals residing abroad		('000)	..	..	..	..	..
Arrivals by mode of transport							
1.19 Total		('000)	5,073	5,022	5,062	5,213	4,783
1.20 ♦ Air		('000)	3,686	3,722	3,687	3,716	3,551
1.21 ♦ Water		('000)	1,387	1,300	1,375	1,497	1,232
1.22 ♦ Land		('000)	..	..	..	..	..
1.23 * railway		('000)	..	..	..	..	..
1.24 * road		('000)	..	..	..	..	..
1.25 * others		('000)	..	..	..	..	..
Accommodation							
Total							
1.29 ♦ Guests		('000)	..	..	..	..	..
1.30 ♦ Overnights		('000)	..	..	..	..	..
Hotels and similar establishments							
1.31 ♦ Guests		('000)	1,440	1,496	1,388	1,335	1,278
1.32 ♦ Overnights	(3)	('000)	2,928	3,021	2,880	2,878	2,737
Expenditure							
1.33 Total	(4)	US$ Mn	3,239	3,369	3,414	3,535	3,473
1.34 ♦ Travel		US$ Mn	..	..	..	..	..
1.35 ♦ Passenger transport		US$ Mn	..	..	..	..	..
Indicators							
1.39 Average size of travel party		Persons	..	..	..	..	..
Average length of stay							
1.40 Total		Days	..	..	..	..	..
1.41 ♦ For all commercial accommodation services	(3)	Nights	2.60	2.60	2.57	2.62	2.65
1.42 * of which, "hotels and similar establishments"		Nights					
1.43 ♦ For non commercial accommodation services		Days	..	..	..	..	..
1.44 Average expenditure per day		US$	..	..	..	..	..
2. DOMESTIC TOURISM							
Data							
Accommodation							
Total							
2.19 ♦ Guests		('000)	..	..	..	..	..
2.20 ♦ Overnights		('000)	..	..	..	..	..
Hotels and similar establishments							
2.21 ♦ Guests		('000)	658	664	656	662	658
2.22 ♦ Overnights		('000)	..	..	..	..	..
3. OUTBOUND TOURISM							
Data							
Departures							
3.1 Total		('000)	..	..	..	..	..
3.2 ♦ Overnight visitors (tourists)		('000)	1,410	1,468	1,441	1,438	1,319
3.3 ♦ Same-day visitors (excursionists)		('000)	..	..	..	..	..
Expenditure	(4)						
3.4 Total		US$ Mn	1,663	1,752	1,743	1,761	1,613
3.5 ♦ Travel		US$ Mn	1,143	1,205	1,192	1,213	1,106
3.6 ♦ Passenger transport		US$ Mn	520	547	551	548	507

PUERTO RICO

Basic data and indicators	Notes	Units	2005	2006	2007	2008	2009
4. TOURISM INDUSTRIES							
Data							
Accommodation for visitors in hotels and similar establishments							
Non-monetary data							
4.13 ◆ Number of establishments		Units	..	..	..	..	..
4.14 ◆ Number of rooms	(5)	Units	13,336	13,607	13,585	13,437	13,656
4.15 ◆ Number of bed-places		Units	..	..	..	..	..
Indicators							
4.16 Occupancy rate / rooms	(6)	Percent	67.70	67.90	68.70	67.60	63.40
4.17 Occupancy rate / bed-places		Percent	..	..	..	..	..
4.18 Average length of stay		Nights	2.63	2.60	2.57	2.62	2.65
4.19 Available capacity (bed-places per 1000 inhabitants)		Units	..	..	..	..	..
6. COMPLEMENTARY INDICATORS							
Demand							
6.1 Gross travel propensity		Units	..	..	..	..	..
6.2 Carrying capacity (arrivals/population)		Units	0.94	0.95	0.94	0.94	0.90

QATAR

Basic data and indicators	Notes	Units	2005	2006	2007	2008	2009
1. INBOUND TOURISM							
Data							
Arrivals							
1.1 Total		('000)	..	..	..	..	..
1.2 ♦ Overnight visitors (tourists)	(1)	('000)	913	946	964	1,405	1,659
1.3 ♦ Same-day visitors (excursionists)		('000)	..	..	..	..	..
1.4 * of which, cruise passengers		('000)	..	..	..	..	..
Arrivals by region	(1)						
1.5 Total		('000)	912	947	963	1,405	..
1.6 ♦ Africa		('000)	..	..	..	..	..
1.7 ♦ Americas		('000)	..	..	..	..	..
1.8 ♦ East Asia and the Pacific		('000)	159	181	203	217	..
1.9 ♦ Europe		('000)	233	201	266	329	..
1.10 ♦ Middle East		('000)	365	414	361	628	..
1.11 ♦ South Asia		('000)	..	..	..	..	..
1.12 ♦ Other not classified		('000)	155	151	133	231	..
1.13 * of which, nationals residing abroad		('000)	..	..	..	..	..
Arrivals by main purpose							
1.14 Total		('000)	..	962	..	..	..
1.15 ♦ Personal		('000)	..	240	..	..	..
1.16 * holidays, leisure and recreation		('000)	..	240	..	..	..
1.17 * other personal purposes		('000)	..	..	..	..	..
1.18 ♦ Business and professional		('000)	..	722	..	..	..
Accommodation							
Total							
1.29 ♦ Guests		('000)	..	..	..	..	..
1.30 ♦ Overnights		('000)	..	..	..	..	..
Hotels and similar establishments							
1.31 ♦ Guests	(1)	('000)	913	946	964	1,405	1,659
1.32 ♦ Overnights	(1)	('000)	1,024	1,147	1,245	1,993	..
Expenditure							
1.33 Total		US$ Mn	..	..	..	..	..
1.34 ♦ Travel	(2)	US$ Mn	760	874	..	..	..
1.35 ♦ Passenger transport		US$ Mn	..	..	..	..	..
Indicators							
1.39 Average size of travel party		Persons	..	..	..	..	..
Average length of stay							
1.40 Total		Days	..	..	..	..	..
1.41 ♦ For all commercial accommodation services	(1)	Nights	1.10	1.20	1.30	1.40	..
1.42 * of which, "hotels and similar establishments"		Nights	..	..	..	..	..
1.43 ♦ For non commercial accommodation services		Days	..	..	..	..	..
1.44 Average expenditure per day		US$	..	..	..	..	..
3. OUTBOUND TOURISM							
Data							
Expenditure							
3.4 Total		US$ Mn	..	..	..	..	..
3.5 ♦ Travel	(2)	US$ Mn	1,759	3,751	..	..	..
3.6 ♦ Passenger transport		US$ Mn	..	..	..	..	..

QATAR

Basic data and indicators	Notes	Units	2005	2006	2007	2008	2009
4. TOURISM INDUSTRIES							
Data							
Number of establishments							
4.1 Total		Units	..	..	..	..	..
4.2 ♦ Accommodation for visitors		Units	..	..	..	..	..
4.3 * of which, "hotels and similar establishments"	(1)	Units	35	39	43	48	58
4.4 ♦ Food and beverage serving activities		Units	..	..	..	..	..
4.5 ♦ Passenger transportation		Units	..	..	..	..	..
4.6 ♦ Travel agencies and other reservation services activities		Units	..	..	..	..	..
4.7 ♦ Other tourism industries		Units	..	..	..	..	..
Accommodation for visitors in hotels and similar establishments							
Non-monetary data							
4.13 ♦ Number of establishments	(1)	Units	35	39	43	48	58
4.14 ♦ Number of rooms	(1)	Units	4,180	6,871	5,422	6,679	8,277
4.15 ♦ Number of bed-places	(1)	Units	5,810	10,002	7,949	9,510	11,308
Indicators							
4.16 Occupancy rate / rooms		Percent	..	..	..	..	..
4.17 Occupancy rate / bed-places	(1)	Percent	74.90	74.50	43.00	58.00	50.00
4.18 Average length of stay		Nights	..	..	..	..	..
4.19 Available capacity (bed-places per 1000 inhabitants)		Units	6.56	10.00	6.99	7.42	8.02
6. COMPLEMENTARY INDICATORS							
Demand							
6.1 Gross travel propensity		Units	..	..	..	..	..
6.2 Carrying capacity (arrivals/population)		Units	1.03	0.95	0.85	1.10	1.18

314

REPUBLIC OF MOLDOVA

Basic data and indicators	Notes	Units	2005	2006	2007	2008	2009
1. INBOUND TOURISM							
Data							
Arrivals	(1)						
1.1 Total		('000)	25.1	14.2	14.7	8.7	9.2
1.2 ♦ Overnight visitors (tourists)		('000)	23	13	13	7	7
1.3 ♦ Same-day visitors (excursionists)		('000)	2	1	2	2	2
1.4 * of which, cruise passengers		('000)	..	..	..	..	..
Arrivals by region	(1)						
1.5 Total		('000)	25.1	14.1	14.7	8.7	9.1
1.6 ♦ Africa		('000)	..	..	..	..	..
1.7 ♦ Americas		('000)	3.2	1.1	0.6	0.3	0.2
1.8 ♦ East Asia and the Pacific		('000)	0.3	0.2	0.3	0.2	0.1
1.9 ♦ Europe		('000)	21.2	12.7	13.8	8.2	8.8
1.10 ♦ Middle East		('000)	0.4	0.1	..	..	..
1.11 ♦ South Asia		('000)	..	..	..	..	..
1.12 ♦ Other not classified		('000)	..	..	..	..	..
1.13 * of which, nationals residing abroad		('000)	..	..	..	..	..
Arrivals by main purpose	(1)						
1.14 Total		('000)	25.1	14.2	14.7	8.7	9.2
1.15 ♦ Personal		('000)	8.7	6.8	6.1	6.2	6.9
1.16 * holidays, leisure and recreation		('000)	7.8	6.2	5.8	5.7	6.5
1.17 * other personal purposes		('000)	0.9	0.6	0.3	0.5	0.4
1.18 ♦ Business and professional		('000)	16.4	7.4	8.6	2.5	2.3
Accommodation							
Total							
1.29 ♦ Guests		('000)	67	63	70	73	60
1.30 ♦ Overnights		('000)	187	214	201	202	148
Hotels and similar establishments							
1.31 ♦ Guests		('000)	66	62	69	72	57
1.32 ♦ Overnights		('000)	170	202	194	191	135
Expenditure							
1.33 Total		US$ Mn	138	148	225	289	235
1.34 ♦ Travel		US$ Mn	103	115	167	212	168
1.35 ♦ Passenger transport		US$ Mn	35	33	58	77	67
Expenditure by main purpose of the trip							
1.36 Total		US$ Mn	103	115	167	212	168
1.37 ♦ Personal		US$ Mn	79	85	124	153	113
1.38 ♦ Business and professional		US$ Mn	24	30	43	59	55
Indicators							
1.39 Average size of travel party		Persons	..	..	..	..	..
Average length of stay							
1.40 Total		Days	..	..	..	..	..
1.41 ♦ For all commercial accommodation services		Nights	2.80	3.40	2.90	2.80	2.50
1.42 * of which, "hotels and similar establishments"		Nights	..	..	..	..	..
1.43 ♦ For non commercial accommodation services		Days	..	..	..	..	..
1.44 Average expenditure per day		US$	..	..	..	..	..
2. DOMESTIC TOURISM							
Data							
Accommodation							
Total							
2.19 ♦ Guests		('000)	234	249	244	207	168
2.20 ♦ Overnights		('000)	1,432	1,539	1,544	1,525	1,252
Hotels and similar establishments							
2.21 ♦ Guests		('000)	104	107	90	74	56
2.22 ♦ Overnights		('000)	264	282	234	225	195
Indicators							
2.23 Average size of travel party		Persons	..	..	..	..	..
Average length of stay							
2.24 Total		Days	..	..	..	..	..
2.25 ♦ For all commercial accommodation services		Nights	6.10	6.20	6.32	7.36	7.44
2.26 * of which, "hotels and similar establishments"		Nights	..	..	..	..	..
2.27 ♦ For non commercial accommodation services		Days	..	..	..	..	..
2.28 Average expenditure per day		US$	..	..	..	..	..

REPUBLIC OF MOLDOVA

Basic data and indicators	Notes	Units	2005	2006	2007	2008	2009
3. OUTBOUND TOURISM							
Data							
Departures							
3.1 Total		('000)	..	..	..	..	..
3.2 ♦ Overnight visitors (tourists)	(1)	('000)	57	68	82	85	93
3.3 ♦ Same-day visitors (excursionists)		('000)	..	..	..	..	..
Expenditure							
3.4 Total		US$ Mn	170	224	290	359	307
3.5 ♦ Travel		US$ Mn	141	190	233	288	243
3.6 ♦ Passenger transport		US$ Mn	29	34	57	71	64
Expenditure by main purpose of the trip							
3.7 Total		US$ Mn	141	189	232	288	243
3.8 ♦ Personal		US$ Mn	58	89	125	153	131
3.9 ♦ Business and professional		US$ Mn	83	100	107	135	112
4. TOURISM INDUSTRIES							
Data							
Number of establishments							
4.1 Total		Units	..	..	..	..	..
4.2 ♦ Accommodation for visitors		Units	..	..	..	..	..
4.3 * of which, "hotels and similar establishments"		Units	71	76	78	79	93
4.4 ♦ Food and beverage serving activities		Units	..	..	..	..	..
4.5 ♦ Passenger transportation		Units	..	..	..	..	..
4.6 ♦ Travel agencies and other reservation services activities		Units	..	..	..	..	..
4.7 ♦ Other tourism industries		Units	..	..	..	..	..
Accommodation for visitors in hotels and similar establishments							
Non-monetary data							
4.13 ♦ Number of establishments		Units	71	76	78	79	93
4.14 ♦ Number of rooms		Units	2,475	2,457	2,297	2,350	2,517
4.15 ♦ Number of bed-places		Units	4,581	4,519	4,271	4,415	4,727
Indicators							
4.16 Occupancy rate / rooms		Percent	..	..	..	..	..
4.17 Occupancy rate / bed-places		Percent	26.60	30.90	28.30	28.60	20.60
4.18 Average length of stay		Nights	2.60	2.90	2.70	2.90	2.90
4.19 Available capacity (bed-places per 1000 inhabitants)		Units	1.22	1.22	1.16	1.22	1.31
6. COMPLEMENTARY INDICATORS							
Demand							
6.1 Gross travel propensity		Units	..	..	..	..	..
6.2 Carrying capacity (arrivals/population)		Units	0.01	0.00	0.00	0.00	0.00
Macroeconomic indicators related to international tourism							
6.3 Inbound tourism expenditure over GDP		Percent	4.6	4.3	5.1	4.8	4.3
6.4 Outbound tourism expenditure over GDP		Percent	5.7	6.6	6.2	5.7	5.4
6.5 Tourism balance (inbound minus outbound tourism expenditure) over GDP		Percent	-1.1	-2.2	-1.0	-0.9	-1.1
6.6 Tourism openness (inbound plus outbound tourism expenditure) over GDP		Percent	10.3	10.9	11.3	10.5	9.8
6.7 Tourism coverage (inbound over outbound tourism expenditure)		Percent	81.1	66.2	83.0	83.6	80.4
6.8 Inbound tourism expenditure over exports of goods		Percent	12.5	13.9	16.4	17.5	17.7
6.9 Inbound tourism expenditure over exports of services		Percent	34.6	31.8	36.0	34.5	34.8
6.10 Inbound tourism expenditure over exports of goods and services		Percent	9.2	9.7	11.3	11.6	11.7
6.11 Inbound tourism expenditure over current account credits		Percent	5.2	4.9	5.6	5.6	6.0
6.12 Outbound tourism expenditure over imports of goods		Percent	7.4	8.5	7.4	7.1	8.9
6.13 Outbound tourism expenditure over imports of services		Percent	40.5	45.8	42.9	41.8	41.5
6.14 Outbound tourism expenditure over imports of goods and services		Percent	6.3	7.1	6.3	6.1	7.3
6.15 Outbound tourism expenditure over current account debits		Percent	5.9	6.6	5.8	5.6	6.7

REUNION

Basic data and indicators	Notes	Units	2005	2006	2007	2008	2009
1. INBOUND TOURISM							
Data							
Arrivals							
1.1 Total		('000)	..	..	..	..	..
1.2 ♦ Overnight visitors (tourists)	(1)(2)	('000)	409	279	381	396	422
1.3 ♦ Same-day visitors (excursionists)		('000)	..	..	..	..	..
1.4 * of which, cruise passengers		('000)	..	..	..	..	..
Arrivals by region	(1)(2)						
1.5 Total		('000)	409	279	381	396	422
1.6 ♦ Africa		('000)	..	..	33	..	..
1.7 ♦ Americas		('000)	..	..	2	..	..
1.8 ♦ East Asia and the Pacific		('000)	..	..	2	..	..
1.9 ♦ Europe		('000)	344	224	303	328	360
1.10 ♦ Middle East		('000)	..	..	..	..	..
1.11 ♦ South Asia		('000)	..	..	..	..	..
1.12 ♦ Other not classified		('000)	65	55	41	68	62
1.13 * of which, nationals residing abroad		('000)	..	..	..	..	..
Arrivals by main purpose	(1)(2)						
1.14 Total		('000)	409	279	381	396	422
1.15 ♦ Personal		('000)	362	232	329	346	381
1.16 * holidays, leisure and recreation		('000)	162	80	125	136	143
1.17 * other personal purposes		('000)	200	152	204	210	238
1.18 ♦ Business and professional		('000)	47	47	52	50	41
Arrivals by mode of transport	(1)(2)						
1.19 Total		('000)	409	279	381	396	422
1.20 ♦ Air		('000)	409	279	381	396	422
1.21 ♦ Water		('000)	..	..	..	..	..
1.22 ♦ Land		('000)	..	..	..	..	..
1.23 * railway		('000)	..	..	..	..	..
1.24 * road		('000)	..	..	..	..	..
1.25 * others		('000)	..	..	..	..	..
Arrivals by form of organization of the trip	(1)(2)						
1.26 Total		('000)	..	..	..	..	422
1.27 ♦ Package tour		('000)	..	..	..	..	67
1.28 ♦ Other forms		('000)	..	..	..	..	355
Accommodation							
Total							
1.29 ♦ Guests		('000)	..	..	..	..	..
1.30 ♦ Overnights		('000)	..	..	..	..	..
Hotels and similar establishments	(3)						
1.31 ♦ Guests		('000)	180	98	142	156	149
1.32 ♦ Overnights	(4)	('000)	1,112	761	799	807	744
Expenditure							
1.33 Total	(5)	US$ Mn	384	282	401	448	425
1.34 ♦ Travel		US$ Mn	..	..	..	..	..
1.35 ♦ Passenger transport		US$ Mn	..	..	..	..	..
Indicators							
1.39 Average size of travel party		Persons	..	..	..	..	..
Average length of stay							
1.40 Total		Days	17.00	18.20	16.40	17.30	16.30
1.41 ♦ For all commercial accommodation services		Nights	..	..	..	..	..
1.42 * of which, "hotels and similar establishments"		Nights	6.90	7.00	6.70	6.50	6.60
1.43 ♦ For non commercial accommodation services		Days	..	..	..	..	..
1.44 Average expenditure per day		US$	..	..	..	..	..

REUNION

Basic data and indicators	Notes	Units	2005	2006	2007	2008	2009
4. **TOURISM INDUSTRIES**							
Data							
Number of establishments	(6)						
4.1 Total		Units	3,190	3,282	3,434	3,856	..
4.2 ♦ Accommodation for visitors		Units	527	514	497	548	..
4.3 * of which, "hotels and similar establishments"		Units	156	151	142	170	..
4.4 ♦ Food and beverage serving activities		Units	1,951	2,047	2,218	2,537	..
4.5 ♦ Passenger transportation		Units	593	602	598	629	..
4.6 ♦ Travel agencies and other reservation services activities		Units	119	119	121	142	
4.7 ♦ Other tourism industries		Units	..	..	..	..	..
Accommodation for visitors in hotels and similar establishments							
Non-monetary data	(3)						
4.13 ♦ Number of establishments	(7)	Units	63	56	50	50	49
4.14 ♦ Number of rooms	(7)	Units	2,930	2,982	2,259	2,143	2,074
4.15 ♦ Number of bed-places	(7)	Units	5,860	5,964	4,518	4,286	4,148
Indicators							
4.16 Occupancy rate / rooms		Percent	..	..	..	..	..
4.17 Occupancy rate / bed-places		Percent	60.20	51.80	58.40	59.10	..
4.18 Average length of stay		Nights	6.90	7.00	6.70	6.50	6.60
4.19 Available capacity (bed-places per 1000 inhabitants)		Units	..	..	..	..	..
5. **EMPLOYMENT**							
Data							
Number of employees by tourism industries	(8)						
5.1 Total		('000)	9.4	9.1	10.0	10.2	..
5.2 ♦ Accommodation services for visitors (hotels and similar establishments)		('000)	1.9	1.4	1.4	1.3	..
5.3 ♦ Other accommodation services		('000)	0.3	0.3	0.2	0.2	..
5.4 ♦ Food and beverage serving activities		('000)	3.7	3.8	4.6	4.7	..
5.5 ♦ Passenger transportation		('000)	2.9	2.9	3.2	3.3	..
5.6 ♦ Travel agencies and other reservation services activities		('000)	0.6	0.6	0.6	0.6	..
5.7 ♦ Other tourism industries		('000)	..	..	..	..	..
6. **COMPLEMENTARY INDICATORS**							
Demand							
6.1 Gross travel propensity		Units	..	..	..	..	..
6.2 Carrying capacity (arrivals/population)		Units	..	0.36	0.48	..	..

ROMANIA

Basic data and indicators	Notes	Units	2005	2006	2007	2008	2009
1. INBOUND TOURISM							
Data							
Arrivals							
1.1 Total		('000)	5,839	6,037	7,722	8,862	7,575
1.2 ♦ Overnight visitors (tourists)		('000)	..	..	..	..	..
1.3 ♦ Same-day visitors (excursionists)		('000)	..	..	..	..	..
1.4 * of which, cruise passengers		('000)	..	..	..	..	..
Arrivals by region							
1.5 Total		('000)	5,839	6,037	7,721	8,863	7,575
1.6 ♦ Africa		('000)	7	9	11	13	13
1.7 ♦ Americas		('000)	154	172	189	192	169
1.8 ♦ East Asia and the Pacific		('000)	57	62	80	97	70
1.9 ♦ Europe		('000)	5,580	5,752	7,394	8,506	7,279
1.10 ♦ Middle East		('000)	24	25	29	32	26
1.11 ♦ South Asia		('000)	16	16	17	21	17
1.12 ♦ Other not classified		('000)	1	1	1	2	1
1.13 * of which, nationals residing abroad		('000)	..	..	..	..	..
Arrivals by mode of transport							
1.19 Total		('000)	5,840	6,037	7,722	8,862	7,575
1.20 ♦ Air		('000)	919	1,122	1,460	1,462	1,277
1.21 ♦ Water		('000)	187	209	234	262	164
1.22 ♦ Land		('000)	4,734	4,706	6,028	7,138	6,134
1.23 * railway		('000)	305	316	275	253	208
1.24 * road		('000)	4,429	4,390	5,753	6,885	5,925
1.25 * others		('000)	..	..	..	..	1
Accommodation							
Total							
1.29 ♦ Guests		('000)	1,430	1,380	1,551	1,466	1,276
1.30 ♦ Overnights		('000)	3,464	3,242	3,586	3,359	2,668
Hotels and similar establishments							
1.31 ♦ Guests		('000)	1,407	1,363	1,531	1,439	1,256
1.32 ♦ Overnights		('000)	3,377	3,169	3,497	3,251	2,582
Expenditure							
1.33 Total		US$ Mn	1,325	1,676	2,073	2,625	1,669
1.34 ♦ Travel		US$ Mn	1,052	1,308	1,610	1,991	1,228
1.35 ♦ Passenger transport		US$ Mn	273	368	463	634	441
Expenditure by main purpose of the trip							
1.36 Total		US$ Mn	1,052	1,308	1,610	1,991	1,228
1.37 ♦ Personal		US$ Mn	538	480	453	414	334
1.38 ♦ Business and professional		US$ Mn	514	828	1,157	1,577	894
Indicators							
1.39 Average size of travel party		Persons	..	..	..	..	..
Average length of stay							
1.40 Total		Days	..	..	..	..	..
1.41 ♦ For all commercial accommodation services		Nights	2.40	2.30	2.30	2.30	2.09
1.42 * of which, "hotels and similar establishments"		Nights	2.40	2.33	2.28	2.26	2.06
1.43 ♦ For non commercial accommodation services		Days	..	..	..	..	..
1.44 Average expenditure per day		US$	..	..	..	..	..
2. DOMESTIC TOURISM							
Data							
Trips							
2.1 Total		('000)	..	..	..	..	..
2.2 ♦ Overnight visitors (tourists)	(1)	('000)	8,736	6,688	9,294	9,716	11,651
2.3 ♦ Same-day visitors (excursionists)		('000)	..	..	..	..	..
Trips by main purpose							
2.4 Total		('000)	..	..	..	9,716	11,650
2.5 ♦ Personal		('000)	..	..	..	9,429	11,361
2.6 * holidays, leisure and recreation		('000)	..	..	..	3,585	4,233
2.7 * other personal purposes	(2)	('000)	..	..	..	5,844	7,128
2.8 ♦ Business and professional		('000)	..	..	..	287	289
Trips by mode of transport							
2.9 Total		('000)	8,736	6,689	9,295	9,717	11,651
2.10 ♦ Air		('000)	..	..	..	..	..
2.11 ♦ Water		('000)	..	..	..	..	..
2.12 ♦ Land		('000)	8,736	6,689	9,295	9,717	11,651
2.13 * railway		('000)	1,835	1,456	2,432	2,172	1,989
2.14 * road		('000)	6,598	4,980	6,494	7,268	9,097
2.15 * others	(3)	('000)	303	253	369	277	565

ROMANIA

Basic data and indicators	Notes	Units	2005	2006	2007	2008	2009
Accommodation							
Total							
2.19 ♦ Guests		('000)	4,375	4,836	5,421	5,659	4,866
2.20 ♦ Overnights		('000)	14,909	15,750	17,007	17,367	14,658
Hotels and similar establishments							
2.21 ♦ Guests		('000)	4,139	4,604	5,186	5,420	4,663
2.22 ♦ Overnights		('000)	14,094	14,929	16,259	16,580	13,932
Indicators							
2.23 Average size of travel party		Persons	..	..	..	..	..
Average length of stay							
2.24 Total	(4)	Days	4.53	4.58	4.91	4.61	4.07
2.25 ♦ For all commercial accommodation services		Nights	3.40	3.20	3.10	3.07	3.01
2.26 * of which, "hotels and similar establishments"		Nights	3.41	3.24	3.14	3.06	2.99
2.27 ♦ For non commercial accommodation services		Days	..	..	..	..	..
2.28 Average expenditure per day	(5)	US$	..	..	28.9	32.7	28.9

3. OUTBOUND TOURISM

	Notes	Units	2005	2006	2007	2008	2009
Data							
Departures							
3.1 Total		('000)	..	..	..	..	..
3.2 ♦ Overnight visitors (tourists)		('000)	7,140	8,906	10,980	13,072	11,723
3.3 ♦ Same-day visitors (excursionists)		('000)	..	..	..	..	..
Expenditure							
3.4 Total		US$ Mn	1,073	1,459	1,725	2,409	1,769
3.5 ♦ Travel		US$ Mn	925	1,310	1,543	2,176	1,473
3.6 ♦ Passenger transport		US$ Mn	148	149	182	233	296
Expenditure by main purpose of the trip							
3.7 Total		US$ Mn	925	1,310	1,543	2,176	1,473
3.8 ♦ Personal		US$ Mn	285	373	747	1,071	543
3.9 ♦ Business and professional		US$ Mn	640	937	796	1,105	930
Indicators							
3.10 Average length of stay		Days	..	..	..	..	..
3.11 Average expenditure per day	(5)	US$	..	..	46.0	54.1	48.8

4. TOURISM INDUSTRIES

	Notes	Units	2005	2006	2007	2008	2009
Data							
Number of establishments							
4.1 Total		Units	..	..	..	..	..
4.2 ♦ Accommodation for visitors		Units	..	..	..	..	..
4.3 * of which, "hotels and similar establishments"		Units	3,608	4,125	4,163	4,362	4,566
4.4 ♦ Food and beverage serving activities		Units	..	..	..	..	..
4.5 ♦ Passenger transportation		Units	..	..	..	..	..
4.6 ♦ Travel agencies and other reservation services activities		Units	..	..	..	..	..
4.7 ♦ Other tourism industries		Units	..	..	..	..	..
Accommodation for visitors in hotels and similar establishments							
Monetary data	(6)						
4.8 ♦ Output		US$ Mn	1,766.6	2,263.5	2,959.2	..	..
4.9 ♦ Intermediate consumption		US$ Mn	608.9	789.7	986.8	..	..
4.10 ♦ Gross value added		US$ Mn	1,157.6	1,473.9	1,972.4	..	..
4.11 ♦ Compensation of employees		US$ Mn	294.2	335.6	461.7		..
4.12 ♦ Gross fixed capital formation		US$ Mn	..	..	..	..	..
Non-monetary data	(7)						
4.13 ♦ Number of establishments		Units	3,608	4,125	4,163	4,362	4,566
4.14 ♦ Number of rooms		Units	105,787	111,805	112,177	116,903	121,657
4.15 ♦ Number of bed-places		Units	216,499	228,126	228,123	237,917	248,424
Indicators							
4.16 Occupancy rate / rooms		Percent	..	..	..	..	..
4.17 Occupancy rate / bed-places		Percent	33.40	33.60	36.00	35.90	28.40
4.18 Average length of stay		Nights	3.20	3.18	2.94	2.89	2.82
4.19 Available capacity (bed-places per 1000 inhabitants)		Units	10.01	10.57	10.59	11.06	11.56

ROMANIA

Basic data and indicators	Notes	Units	2005	2006	2007	2008	2009
Travel agencies and other reservation service activities							
Monetary data							
4.20 ♦ Output		US$ Mn	489.6	637.1	982.3	..	..
4.21 ♦ Intermediate consumption		US$ Mn	167.5	220.6	337.2	..	..
4.22 ♦ Gross value added		US$ Mn	322.1	416.5	645.1	..	..
4.23 ♦ Compensation of employees		US$ Mn	31.5	37.4	56.7	..	..
4.24 ♦ Gross fixed capital formation		US$ Mn	..	..	..	..	..
Non-monetary data	(8)						
♦ Domestic trips							
4.25 * with package tour		Percent	..	..	..	..	61.9
4.26 * without package tour		Percent	..	..	..	..	38.1
♦ Inbound trips							
4.27 * with package tour		Percent	..	..	..	..	86.2
4.28 * without package tour		Percent	..	..	..	..	13.8
♦ Outbound trips							
4.29 * with package tour		Percent	..	..	..	..	67.9
4.30 * without package tour		Percent	..	..	..	..	32.1
5. EMPLOYMENT							
Data							
Number of employees by tourism industries	(9)						
5.1 Total		('000)	341.1	354.2	382.5	..	..
5.2 ♦ Accommodation services for visitors (hotels and similar establishments)		('000)	34.8	34.4	36.5	..	..
5.3 ♦ Other accommodation services		('000)	3.0	3.7	5.1	..	..
5.4 ♦ Food and beverage serving activities		('000)	71.5	79.8	88.6	..	..
5.5 ♦ Passenger transportation	(10)	('000)	205.9	207.0	219.6	..	..
5.6 ♦ Travel agencies and other reservation services activities		('000)	7.2	8.3	8.8	..	..
5.7 ♦ Other tourism industries	(11)	('000)	18.7	21.0	24.0	..	..
6. COMPLEMENTARY INDICATORS							
Demand							
6.1 Gross travel propensity		Units	..	..	..	..	..
6.2 Carrying capacity (arrivals/population)		Units	0.40	0.31	0.43	0.45	0.54
Macroeconomic indicators related to international tourism							
6.3 Inbound tourism expenditure over GDP		Percent	1.3	1.4	1.2	1.3	1.0
6.4 Outbound tourism expenditure over GDP		Percent	1.1	1.2	1.0	1.2	1.1
6.5 Tourism balance (inbound minus outbound tourism expenditure) over GDP		Percent	0.3	0.2	0.2	0.1	-0.1
6.6 Tourism openness (inbound plus outbound tourism expenditure) over GDP		Percent	2.4	2.6	2.2	2.5	2.1
6.7 Tourism coverage (inbound over outbound tourism expenditure)		Percent	123.4	114.9	120.2	109.0	94.6
6.8 Inbound tourism expenditure over exports of goods		Percent	4.8	5.2	5.1	5.3	4.1
6.9 Inbound tourism expenditure over exports of services		Percent	26.0	23.8	22.0	20.4	17.1
6.10 Inbound tourism expenditure over exports of goods and services		Percent	4.0	4.3	4.1	4.2	3.3
6.11 Inbound tourism expenditure over current account credits		Percent	3.4	3.5	3.3	3.3	2.7
6.12 Outbound tourism expenditure over imports of goods		Percent	2.9	3.1	2.6	3.1	3.5
6.13 Outbound tourism expenditure over imports of services		Percent	19.4	20.8	19.4	20.2	17.4
6.14 Outbound tourism expenditure over imports of goods and services		Percent	2.5	2.7	2.3	2.7	2.9
6.15 Outbound tourism expenditure over current account debits		Percent	2.2	2.4	2.0	2.3	2.6

RUSSIAN FEDERATION

Basic data and indicators	Notes	Units	2005	2006	2007	2008	2009
1. INBOUND TOURISM							
Data							
Arrivals							
1.1 Total		('000)	22,201	22,486	22,909	23,676	..
1.2 ♦ Overnight visitors (tourists)		('000)	19,940	..	..	..	..
1.3 ♦ Same-day visitors (excursionists)		('000)	831	573	1,149	1,252	..
1.4 * of which, cruise passengers		('000)	333	573	1,149	1,252	..
Arrivals by region							
1.5 Total		('000)	22,200	22,486	22,907	23,676	..
1.6 ♦ Africa		('000)	27	28	30	36	..
1.7 ♦ Americas		('000)	457	533	466	503	..
1.8 ♦ East Asia and the Pacific		('000)	1,315	1,346	1,381	1,478	..
1.9 ♦ Europe		('000)	19,691	19,873	20,395	21,187	..
1.10 ♦ Middle East		('000)	33	33	24	39	..
1.11 ♦ South Asia		('000)	68	72	100	96	..
1.12 ♦ Other not classified		('000)	609	601	511	337	..
1.13 * of which, nationals residing abroad		('000)	..	..	..	..	..
Arrivals by main purpose							
1.14 Total		('000)	22,201	22,486	22,909	23,676	..
1.15 ♦ Personal		('000)	18,975	19,252	19,639	19,564	..
1.16 * holidays, leisure and recreation		('000)	2,385	2,433	2,214	2,295	..
1.17 * other personal purposes		('000)	16,590	16,819	17,425	17,269	..
1.18 ♦ Business and professional		('000)	3,226	3,234	3,270	4,112	..
Arrivals by mode of transport							
1.19 Total		('000)	22,201	22,486	22,909	23,676	..
1.20 ♦ Air		('000)	4,135	4,426	5,097	5,532	..
1.21 ♦ Water		('000)	1,147	1,107	1,149	1,252	..
1.22 ♦ Land		('000)	16,919	16,953	16,663	16,892	..
1.23 * railway		('000)	6,899	7,188	7,292	7,372	..
1.24 * road		('000)	10,020	9,765	9,371	9,520	..
1.25 * others		('000)	..	..	..	..	..
Accommodation							
Total							
1.29 ♦ Guests		('000)	..	..	..	..	..
1.30 ♦ Overnights		('000)	11,643	12,637	11,673	11,259	..
Hotels and similar establishments							
1.31 ♦ Guests		('000)	3,438	3,680	3,940	3,696	..
1.32 ♦ Overnights		('000)	10,696	10,637	10,616	10,228	..
Expenditure							
1.33 Total		US$ Mn	7,806	9,720	12,427	15,774	12,300
1.34 ♦ Travel		US$ Mn	5,870	7,628	9,447	11,795	9,297
1.35 ♦ Passenger transport		US$ Mn	1,936	2,092	2,980	3,979	3,003
Expenditure by main purpose of the trip							
1.36 Total		US$ Mn	5,869	7,628	9,447	11,795	9,297
1.37 ♦ Personal		US$ Mn	3,490	3,819	4,518	4,850	4,011
1.38 ♦ Business and professional		US$ Mn	2,379	3,809	4,929	6,945	5,286
Indicators							
1.39 Average size of travel party		Persons	..	..	..	..	..
Average length of stay							
1.40 Total		Days	..	..	..	..	..
1.41 ♦ For all commercial accommodation services		Nights	4.63	5.20	..	7.00	..
1.42 * of which, "hotels and similar establishments"		Nights	..	..	..	..	..
1.43 ♦ For non commercial accommodation services		Days	..	..	..	..	..
1.44 Average expenditure per day		US$	..	..	..	..	..
2. DOMESTIC TOURISM							
Data							
Accommodation							
Total							
2.19 ♦ Guests		('000)	..	..	..	..	..
2.20 ♦ Overnights		('000)	155,635	157,207	156,980	178,422	..
Hotels and similar establishments							
2.21 ♦ Guests		('000)	15,047	16,451	18,304	18,975	..
2.22 ♦ Overnights		('000)	40,730	42,630	44,334	44,218	..
Indicators							
2.23 Average size of travel party		Persons	..	..	..	..	..
Average length of stay							
2.24 Total		Days	..	..	..	..	..
2.25 ♦ For all commercial accommodation services		Nights	9.00	11.52	..	9.00	..
2.26 * of which, "hotels and similar establishments"		Nights	..	..	..	..	..
2.27 ♦ For non commercial accommodation services		Days	..	..	..	..	..
2.28 Average expenditure per day		US$	..	..	..	..	..

RUSSIAN FEDERATION

Basic data and indicators	Notes	Units	2005	2006	2007	2008	2009
3. OUTBOUND TOURISM							
Data							
Departures							
3.1 Total		('000)	..	..	..	..	..
3.2 ♦ Overnight visitors (tourists)		('000)	28,416	29,107	34,285	36,538	..
3.3 ♦ Same-day visitors (excursionists)		('000)	..	..	..	..	..
Expenditure							
3.4 Total		US$ Mn	18,305	19,478	23,248	27,010	23,529
3.5 ♦ Travel		US$ Mn	17,314	18,112	21,217	23,778	20,763
3.6 ♦ Passenger transport		US$ Mn	991	1,366	2,031	3,232	2,766
Expenditure by main purpose of the trip							
3.7 Total		US$ Mn	17,314	18,112	21,217	23,778	20,763
3.8 ♦ Personal		US$ Mn	14,860	15,707	18,738	21,356	19,017
3.9 ♦ Business and professional		US$ Mn	2,454	2,405	2,479	2,422	1,746
4. TOURISM INDUSTRIES							
Data							
Accommodation for visitors in hotels and similar establishments							
Non-monetary data							
4.13 ♦ Number of establishments		Units	..	..	..	..	..
4.14 ♦ Number of rooms	(1)	Units	199,010	208,309	219,380	247,912	..
4.15 ♦ Number of bed-places	(1)	Units	414,086	430,970	447,126	499,956	..
Indicators							
4.16 Occupancy rate / rooms		Percent	..	..	..	..	..
4.17 Occupancy rate / bed-places		Percent	34.00	35.00	36.00	35.00	..
4.18 Average length of stay		Nights	4.81	5.30	..	..	..
4.19 Available capacity (bed-places per 1000 inhabitants)		Units	2.89	3.02	3.15	3.52	..
6. COMPLEMENTARY INDICATORS							
Demand							
6.1 Gross travel propensity		Units	..	..	..	..	..
6.2 Carrying capacity (arrivals/population)		Units	0.14	0.16	0.16	0.17	..
Macroeconomic indicators related to international tourism							
6.3 Inbound tourism expenditure over GDP		Percent	1.0	1.0	1.0	0.9	1.0
6.4 Outbound tourism expenditure over GDP		Percent	2.4	2.0	1.8	1.6	1.9
6.5 Tourism balance (inbound minus outbound tourism expenditure) over GDP		Percent	-1.4	-1.0	-0.8	-0.7	-0.9
6.6 Tourism openness (inbound plus outbound tourism expenditure) over GDP		Percent	3.4	3.0	2.8	2.5	2.9
6.7 Tourism coverage (inbound over outbound tourism expenditure)		Percent	42.6	49.9	53.5	58.4	52.3
6.8 Inbound tourism expenditure over exports of goods		Percent	3.2	3.2	3.5	3.3	4.1
6.9 Inbound tourism expenditure over exports of services		Percent	31.3	31.3	31.7	30.9	29.5
6.10 Inbound tourism expenditure over exports of goods and services		Percent	2.9	2.9	3.2	3.0	3.6
6.11 Inbound tourism expenditure over current account credits		Percent	2.7	2.6	2.8	2.6	3.2
6.12 Outbound tourism expenditure over imports of goods		Percent	14.6	11.9	10.4	9.3	12.3
6.13 Outbound tourism expenditure over imports of services		Percent	47.2	43.6	40.0	35.8	38.1
6.14 Outbound tourism expenditure over imports of goods and services		Percent	11.1	9.3	8.3	7.4	9.3
6.15 Outbound tourism expenditure over current account debits		Percent	8.9	7.1	6.3	5.5	6.9

RWANDA

Basic data and indicators	Notes	Units	2005	2006	2007	2008	2009
1. INBOUND TOURISM							
Data							
Arrivals							
1.1 Total		('000)	..	..	710	765	699
1.2 ♦ Overnight visitors (tourists)		('000)	..	..	..	..	..
1.3 ♦ Same-day visitors (excursionists)		('000)	..	..	..	..	..
1.4 * of which, cruise passengers		('000)	..	..	..	..	..
Arrivals by region							
1.5 Total		('000)	..	..	..	764	699
1.6 ♦ Africa		('000)	..	..	..	648	591
1.7 ♦ Americas		('000)	..	..	..	36	28
1.8 ♦ East Asia and the Pacific		('000)	..	..	..	7	9
1.9 ♦ Europe		('000)	..	..	..	50	52
1.10 ♦ Middle East		('000)	..	..	..	4	2
1.11 ♦ South Asia		('000)	..	..	..	19	17
1.12 ♦ Other not classified		('000)	..	..	..	..	..
1.13 * of which, nationals residing abroad		('000)	..	..	..	..	..
Arrivals by main purpose							
1.14 Total		('000)	..	..	710	765	699
1.15 ♦ Personal		('000)	..	..	434	420	357
1.16 * holidays, leisure and recreation		('000)	..	..	21	59	50
1.17 * other personal purposes		('000)	..	..	413	361	307
1.18 ♦ Business and professional		('000)	..	..	276	345	342
Arrivals by mode of transport							
1.19 Total		('000)	..	..	..	765	699
1.20 ♦ Air		('000)	..	..	..	95	99
1.21 ♦ Water		('000)	..	..	..	..	..
1.22 ♦ Land		('000)	..	..	..	670	600
1.23 * railway		('000)	..	..	..	..	..
1.24 * road		('000)	..	..	..	670	600
1.25 * others		('000)	..	..	..	..	..
Expenditure							
1.33 Total		US$ Mn	..	..	..	..	218
1.34 ♦ Travel		US$ Mn	49	31	65	202	174
1.35 ♦ Passenger transport		US$ Mn	..	..	..	..	44
3. OUTBOUND TOURISM							
Data							
Expenditure							
3.4 Total		US$ Mn	..	..	..	104	115
3.5 ♦ Travel		US$ Mn	37	35	69	70	72
3.6 ♦ Passenger transport		US$ Mn	..	..	..	34	43
Expenditure by main purpose of the trip							
3.7 Total		US$ Mn	..	35	69	70	72
3.8 ♦ Personal		US$ Mn	..	23	32	35	43
3.9 ♦ Business and professional		US$ Mn	..	12	37	35	29
6. COMPLEMENTARY INDICATORS							
Demand							
6.1 Gross travel propensity		Units	..	..	..	..	..
6.2 Carrying capacity (arrivals/population)		Units	..	..	0.08	0.08	0.07
Macroeconomic indicators related to international tourism							
6.3 Inbound tourism expenditure over GDP		Percent	1.9	1.0	1.8	4.3	..
6.4 Outbound tourism expenditure over GDP		Percent	1.4	1.1	1.8	2.2	..
6.5 Tourism balance (inbound minus outbound tourism expenditure) over GDP		Percent	0.5	-0.1	-0.1	2.1	..
6.6 Tourism openness (inbound plus outbound tourism expenditure) over GDP		Percent	3.3	2.1	3.6	6.5	..
6.7 Tourism coverage (inbound over outbound tourism expenditure)		Percent	132.7	89.2	94.8	194.3	189.8
6.8 Inbound tourism expenditure over exports of goods		Percent	38.2	21.6	35.6	78.8	113.6
6.9 Inbound tourism expenditure over exports of services		Percent	37.7	23.9	36.6	49.6	64.2
6.10 Inbound tourism expenditure over exports of goods and services		Percent	19.0	11.4	18.0	30.4	41.0
6.11 Inbound tourism expenditure over current account credits		Percent	7.3	5.0	7.7	16.2	18.2
6.12 Outbound tourism expenditure over imports of goods		Percent	10.3	7.2	10.9	11.8	12.0
6.13 Outbound tourism expenditure over imports of services		Percent	12.1	14.5	25.4	20.0	22.2
6.14 Outbound tourism expenditure over imports of goods and services		Percent	5.6	4.8	7.6	7.4	7.8
6.15 Outbound tourism expenditure over current account debits		Percent	5.1	4.4	7.0	6.9	7.3

SABA

Basic data and indicators	Notes	Units	2005	2006	2007	2008	2009
1. INBOUND TOURISM							
Data							
Arrivals							
1.1 Total		('000)	24.9	22.9	21.7	22.5	23.7
1.2 ♦ Overnight visitors (tourists)		('000)	11.5	11.0	11.7	12.0	12.0
1.3 ♦ Same-day visitors (excursionists)	(1)	('000)	13.4	11.9	10.0	10.5	11.7
1.4 * of which, cruise passengers		('000)	..	..	..	..	..
Arrivals by region							
1.5 Total		('000)	11.4	11.0	11.7	12.0	12.0
1.6 ♦ Africa		('000)	..	..	..	..	..
1.7 ♦ Americas		('000)	5.3	5.1	5.7	5.2	4.7
1.8 ♦ East Asia and the Pacific		('000)	..	..	..	..	..
1.9 ♦ Europe		('000)	5.5	5.2	5.2	5.6	6.2
1.10 ♦ Middle East		('000)	..	..	..	..	..
1.11 ♦ South Asia		('000)	..	..	..	..	..
1.12 ♦ Other not classified		('000)	0.6	0.7	0.8	1.2	1.1
1.13 * of which, nationals residing abroad		('000)	..	..	..	..	..
Arrivals by mode of transport							
1.19 Total		('000)	11.5	11.0	11.6	12.0	12.0
1.20 ♦ Air		('000)	7.4	6.9	7.0	7.1	7.7
1.21 ♦ Water		('000)	4	4	5	5	4
1.22 ♦ Land		('000)	..	..	..	..	..
1.23 * railway		('000)	..	..	..	..	..
1.24 * road		('000)	..	..	..	..	..
1.25 * others		('000)	..	..	..	..	..

SAINT EUSTATIUS

Basic data and indicators	Notes	Units	2005	2006	2007	2008	2009
1. INBOUND TOURISM							
Data							
Arrivals							
1.1 Total		('000)	..	..	..	..	..
1.2 ♦ Overnight visitors (tourists)	(1)	('000)	10.4	9.6	11.6	11.8	12.0
1.3 ♦ Same-day visitors (excursionists)		('000)	..	..	..	..	..
1.4 * of which, cruise passengers		('000)	..	..	..	..	..
Arrivals by region	(1)						
1.5 Total		('000)	10.4	9.6	11.5	11.8	12.0
1.6 ♦ Africa		('000)	..	..	..	..	..
1.7 ♦ Americas		('000)	3.5	3.2	3.9	3.8	3.6
1.8 ♦ East Asia and the Pacific		('000)	..	..	..	..	..
1.9 ♦ Europe		('000)	5.4	4.9	5.9	6.2	6.6
1.10 ♦ Middle East		('000)	..	..	..	..	..
1.11 ♦ South Asia		('000)	..	..	..	..	..
1.12 ♦ Other not classified		('000)	1.5	1.5	1.7	1.8	1.8
1.13 * of which, nationals residing abroad		('000)	..	..	..	..	..

SAINT KITTS AND NEVIS

Basic data and indicators	Notes	Units	2005	2006	2007	2008	2009
1. INBOUND TOURISM							
Data							
Arrivals							
1.1 Total		('000)	365	350	379	533	548
1.2 ♦ Overnight visitors (tourists)	(1)	('000)	141	139	123	128	93
1.3 ♦ Same-day visitors (excursionists)		('000)	224	211	256	405	455
1.4 * of which, cruise passengers	(2)	('000)	220	206	251	401	451
Arrivals by region	(1)						
1.5 Total		('000)	141	139	123	128	93
1.6 ♦ Africa		('000)	..	..	..	..	..
1.7 ♦ Americas		('000)	125	124	106	113	83
1.8 ♦ East Asia and the Pacific		('000)	..	..	..	..	..
1.9 ♦ Europe		('000)	11	11	12	10	6
1.10 ♦ Middle East		('000)	..	..	..	..	..
1.11 ♦ South Asia		('000)	..	..	..	..	..
1.12 ♦ Other not classified		('000)	5	4	5	5	4
1.13 * of which, nationals residing abroad		('000)	..	..	..	..	..
Arrivals by mode of transport							
1.19 Total		('000)	365	350	379	533	548
1.20 ♦ Air		('000)	145	144	128	131	97
1.21 ♦ Water	(2)	('000)	220	206	251	402	451
1.22 ♦ Land		('000)	..	..	..	..	..
1.23 * railway		('000)	..	..	..	..	..
1.24 * road		('000)	..	..	..	..	..
1.25 * others		('000)	..	..	..	..	..
Expenditure							
1.33 Total		US$ Mn	..	..	..	..	..
1.34 ♦ Travel		US$ Mn	121	132	125	110	83
1.35 ♦ Passenger transport		US$ Mn	..	..	..	..	..
3. OUTBOUND TOURISM							
Data							
Expenditure							
3.4 Total		US$ Mn	..	..	..	..	..
3.5 ♦ Travel		US$ Mn	11	14	12	15	13
3.6 ♦ Passenger transport		US$ Mn	..	..	..	..	..
4. TOURISM INDUSTRIES							
Data							
Accommodation for visitors in hotels and similar establishments							
Non-monetary data							
4.13 ♦ Number of establishments		Units	..	..	..	..	..
4.14 ♦ Number of rooms		Units	1,859	1,859	..	..	..
4.15 ♦ Number of bed-places		Units	..	..	..	..	..
6. COMPLEMENTARY INDICATORS							
Demand							
6.1 Gross travel propensity		Units	..	..	..	..	..
6.2 Carrying capacity (arrivals/population)		Units	2.94	2.87	2.52	2.60	1.88
Macroeconomic indicators related to international tourism							
6.3 Inbound tourism expenditure over GDP		Percent	27.6	27.0	24.3	19.3	15.3
6.4 Outbound tourism expenditure over GDP		Percent	2.5	2.8	2.4	2.5	2.5
6.5 Tourism balance (inbound minus outbound tourism expenditure) over GDP		Percent	25.1	24.2	21.9	16.8	12.9
6.6 Tourism openness (inbound plus outbound tourism expenditure) over GDP		Percent	30.1	29.8	26.7	21.8	17.8
6.7 Tourism coverage (inbound over outbound tourism expenditure)		Percent	1,105.4	973.0	999.1	758.5	623.5
6.8 Inbound tourism expenditure over exports of goods		Percent	190.8	225.9	216.3	159.6	145.0
6.9 Inbound tourism expenditure over exports of services		Percent	74.3	74.2	72.1	68.7	63.6
6.10 Inbound tourism expenditure over exports of goods and services		Percent	53.5	55.9	54.1	48.0	44.2
6.11 Inbound tourism expenditure over current account credits		Percent	44.2	44.8	43.1	37.9	32.8
6.12 Outbound tourism expenditure over imports of goods		Percent	5.9	6.2	5.2	5.1	5.0
6.13 Outbound tourism expenditure over imports of services		Percent	11.5	13.4	12.3	11.8	11.6
6.14 Outbound tourism expenditure over imports of goods and services		Percent	3.9	4.2	3.7	3.6	3.5
6.15 Outbound tourism expenditure over current account debits		Percent	3.2	3.6	3.1	3.1	3.0

SAINT LUCIA

Basic data and indicators	Notes	Units	2005	2006	2007	2008	2009
1. INBOUND TOURISM							
Data							
Arrivals	(1)						
1.1 Total	(2)	('000)	720	670	905	925	982
1.2 ♦ Overnight visitors (tourists)		('000)	318	303	287	296	278
1.3 ♦ Same-day visitors (excursionists)		('000)	402	367	618	629	704
1.4 * of which, cruise passengers		('000)	394	360	610	620	699
Arrivals by region	(1)						
1.5 Total		('000)	318	302	287	296	278
1.6 ♦ Africa		('000)	..	..	..	..	..
1.7 ♦ Americas		('000)	215	214	192	198	190
1.8 ♦ East Asia and the Pacific		('000)	..	..	..	..	..
1.9 ♦ Europe		('000)	102	86	90	94	84
1.10 ♦ Middle East		('000)	..	..	..	..	..
1.11 ♦ South Asia		('000)	..	..	..	..	..
1.12 ♦ Other not classified		('000)	1	2	5	4	4
1.13 * of which, nationals residing abroad		('000)	..	..	..	..	..
Arrivals by main purpose	(1)						
1.14 Total		('000)	318	302	288	296	278
1.15 ♦ Personal		('000)	302	290	277	283	263
1.16 * holidays, leisure and recreation		('000)	292	257	234	236	216
1.17 * other personal purposes		('000)	10	33	43	47	47
1.18 ♦ Business and professional		('000)	16	12	11	13	15
Arrivals by mode of transport	(1)						
1.19 Total		('000)	..	..	..	296	279
1.20 ♦ Air		('000)	..	..	..	280	261
1.21 ♦ Water		('000)	..	..	..	16	18
1.22 ♦ Land		('000)	..	..	..	..	..
1.23 * railway		('000)	..	..	..	..	..
1.24 * road		('000)	..	..	..	..	..
1.25 * others		('000)	..	..	..	..	..
Accommodation							
Total							
1.29 ♦ Guests		('000)	..	..	..	..	..
1.30 ♦ Overnights		('000)	..	..	..	..	..
Hotels and similar establishments							
1.31 ♦ Guests		('000)	285	..	208	237	209
1.32 ♦ Overnights		('000)	..	..	..	..	..
Expenditure							
1.33 Total		US$ Mn	..	..	..	..	..
1.34 ♦ Travel		US$ Mn	382	294	302	311	296
1.35 ♦ Passenger transport		US$ Mn	..	..	..	..	..
Indicators							
1.39 Average size of travel party		Persons	..	..	..	..	2.0
Average length of stay							
1.40 Total		Days	..	..	..	..	..
1.41 ♦ For all commercial accommodation services		Nights	..	..	..	9.00	11.00
1.42 * of which, "hotels and similar establishments"		Nights	..	..	..	..	..
1.43 ♦ For non commercial accommodation services		Days	..	..	..	..	..
1.44 Average expenditure per day		US$	..	..	..	..	149.0
3. OUTBOUND TOURISM							
Data							
Expenditure							
3.4 Total		US$ Mn	..	..	..	..	..
3.5 ♦ Travel		US$ Mn	39	39	42	45	41
3.6 ♦ Passenger transport		US$ Mn	..	..	..	..	..

SAINT LUCIA

Basic data and indicators	Notes	Units	2005	2006	2007	2008	2009
4. TOURISM INDUSTRIES							
Data							
Accommodation for visitors in hotels and similar establishments							
Non-monetary data							
4.13 ♦ Number of establishments		Units	..	..	..	..	..
4.14 ♦ Number of rooms		Units	4,511	3,093	4,889	5,396	4,685
4.15 ♦ Number of bed-places		Units	8,120	..	..	..	..
Indicators							
4.16 Occupancy rate / rooms		Percent	68.70	64.90	64.90	61.60	53.00
4.17 Occupancy rate / bed-places		Percent	..	..	..	..	..
4.18 Average length of stay		Nights	10.10	10.50	9.08	8.90	9.20
4.19 Available capacity (bed-places per 1000 inhabitants)		Units	49.27	..	..	..	..
6. COMPLEMENTARY INDICATORS							
Demand							
6.1 Gross travel propensity		Units	..	..	..	..	..
6.2 Carrying capacity (arrivals/population)		Units	1.93	1.82	1.70	1.74	1.62
Macroeconomic indicators related to international tourism							
6.3 Inbound tourism expenditure over GDP		Percent	44.5	31.6	31.5	31.5	31.3
6.4 Outbound tourism expenditure over GDP		Percent	4.5	4.2	4.4	4.6	4.3
6.5 Tourism balance (inbound minus outbound tourism expenditure) over GDP		Percent	39.9	27.3	27.1	26.9	27.0
6.6 Tourism openness (inbound plus outbound tourism expenditure) over GDP		Percent	49.0	35.8	35.9	36.1	35.6
6.7 Tourism coverage (inbound over outbound tourism expenditure)		Percent	980.6	747.2	713.7	686.7	726.7
6.8 Inbound tourism expenditure over exports of goods		Percent	429.9	304.1	298.0	187.7	161.8
6.9 Inbound tourism expenditure over exports of services		Percent	87.5	85.6	84.8	85.5	85.4
6.10 Inbound tourism expenditure over exports of goods and services		Percent	72.7	66.8	66.0	58.8	55.9
6.11 Inbound tourism expenditure over current account credits		Percent	67.8	60.8	59.8	54.1	51.9
6.12 Outbound tourism expenditure over imports of goods		Percent	9.3	7.6	7.8	7.5	8.6
6.13 Outbound tourism expenditure over imports of services		Percent	22.0	21.2	20.6	21.0	21.9
6.14 Outbound tourism expenditure over imports of goods and services		Percent	6.5	5.6	5.7	5.5	6.2
6.15 Outbound tourism expenditure over current account debits		Percent	5.6	5.0	5.0	4.9	5.4

SAINT MAARTEN

Basic data and indicators	Notes	Units	2005	2006	2007	2008	2009
1. INBOUND TOURISM							
Data							
Arrivals							
1.1 Total		('000)	1,956	1,890	1,891	1,821	1,655
1.2 ♦ Overnight visitors (tourists)	(1)	('000)	468	468	469	475	440
1.3 ♦ Same-day visitors (excursionists)		('000)	1,488	1,422	1,422	1,346	1,215
1.4 * of which, cruise passengers		('000)	1,488	1,422	1,422	1,346	1,215
Arrivals by region	(1)						
1.5 Total		('000)	468	467	469	476	440
1.6 ♦ Africa		('000)	..	..	..	..	..
1.7 ♦ Americas		('000)	332	328	335	336	310
1.8 ♦ East Asia and the Pacific		('000)	..	..	..	..	..
1.9 ♦ Europe		('000)	94	97	96	103	98
1.10 ♦ Middle East		('000)	..	..	..	..	..
1.11 ♦ South Asia		('000)	..	..	..	..	..
1.12 ♦ Other not classified		('000)	42	42	38	37	32
1.13 * of which, nationals residing abroad		('000)	17	16	16	..	..
Arrivals by mode of transport							
1.19 Total		('000)	1,956	1,890	1,891	1,821	1,655
1.20 ♦ Air	(2)	('000)	468	468	469	475	440
1.21 ♦ Water		('000)	1,488	1,422	1,422	1,346	1,215
1.22 ♦ Land		('000)	..	..	..	..	..
1.23 * railway		('000)	..	..	..	..	..
1.24 * road		('000)	..	..	..	..	..
1.25 * others		('000)	..	..	..	..	..
Expenditure							
1.33 Total		US$ Mn	..	..	..	..	..
1.34 ♦ Travel	(3)	US$ Mn	659	651	662	663	616
1.35 ♦ Passenger transport		US$ Mn	..	..	..	..	..
3. OUTBOUND TOURISM							
Data							
Expenditure							
3.4 Total		US$ Mn	..	..	..	..	..
3.5 ♦ Travel	(3)	US$ Mn	94	86	85	88	81
3.6 ♦ Passenger transport		US$ Mn	..	..	..	..	..
4. TOURISM INDUSTRIES							
Indicators							
4.16 Occupancy rate / rooms		Percent	..	..	..	..	..
4.17 Occupancy rate / bed-places		Percent	58.00	66.00	52.40	58.30	..
4.18 Average length of stay		Nights	..	..	..	..	..
4.19 Available capacity (bed-places per 1000 inhabitants)		Units	..	..	..	..	..

SAINT VINCENT AND THE GRENADINES

Basic data and indicators	Notes	Units	2005	2006	2007	2008	2009
1. INBOUND TOURISM							
Data							
Arrivals							
1.1 Total		('000)	256	306	328	250	271
1.2 ♦ Overnight visitors (tourists)	(1)	('000)	96	97	90	84	75
1.3 ♦ Same-day visitors (excursionists)		('000)	161	209	238	166	196
1.4 * of which, cruise passengers	(2)	('000)	152	200	231	160	190
Arrivals by region	(1)						
1.5 Total		('000)	95	97	90	84	75
1.6 ♦ Africa		('000)	..	..	..	..	..
1.7 ♦ Americas		('000)	74	74	65	61	55
1.8 ♦ East Asia and the Pacific		('000)	..	..	..	..	..
1.9 ♦ Europe		('000)	20	22	23	22	19
1.10 ♦ Middle East		('000)	..	..	..	..	..
1.11 ♦ South Asia		('000)	..	..	..	..	..
1.12 ♦ Other not classified		('000)	1	1	2	1	1
1.13 * of which, nationals residing abroad		('000)	..	..	..	..	..
Arrivals by main purpose	(1)						
1.14 Total		('000)	96	98	90	84	75
1.15 ♦ Personal		('000)	75	81	75	70	62
1.16 * holidays, leisure and recreation		('000)	68	80	74	69	36
1.17 * other personal purposes		('000)	7	1	1	1	26
1.18 ♦ Business and professional		('000)	21	17	15	14	13
Arrivals by mode of transport							
1.19 Total		('000)	256	306	327	250	271
1.20 ♦ Air		('000)	104	106	96	90	81
1.21 ♦ Water	(2)	('000)	152	200	231	160	190
1.22 ♦ Land		('000)	..	..	..	..	..
1.23 * railway		('000)	..	..	..	..	..
1.24 * road		('000)	..	..	..	..	..
1.25 * others		('000)	..	..	..	..	..
Accommodation							
Total							
1.29 ♦ Guests		('000)	..	..	..	..	..
1.30 ♦ Overnights		('000)	..	..	..	..	..
Hotels and similar establishments							
1.31 ♦ Guests		('000)	31	31	32	31	29
1.32 ♦ Overnights		('000)	..	..	..	..	..
Expenditure							
1.33 Total		US$ Mn	..	..	..	..	..
1.34 ♦ Travel		US$ Mn	104	113	110	96	90
1.35 ♦ Passenger transport		US$ Mn	..	..	..	..	..
Indicators							
1.39 Average size of travel party		Persons	..	..	..	..	..
Average length of stay							
1.40 Total		Days	..	..	..	..	..
1.41 ♦ For all commercial accommodation services		Nights	..	..	12.00	11.70	11.70
1.42 * of which, "hotels and similar establishments"		Nights	..	..	..	..	..
1.43 ♦ For non commercial accommodation services		Days	..	..	..	..	..
1.44 Average expenditure per day		US$	..	..	..	..	..
3. OUTBOUND TOURISM							
Data							
Expenditure							
3.4 Total		US$ Mn	..	..	..	..	..
3.5 ♦ Travel		US$ Mn	15	16	20	18	18
3.6 ♦ Passenger transport		US$ Mn	..	..	..	..	..

SAINT VINCENT AND THE GRENADINES

Basic data and indicators	Notes	Units	2005	2006	2007	2008	2009
4. TOURISM INDUSTRIES							
Data							
Accommodation for visitors in hotels and similar establishments							
Non-monetary data							
4.13 ♦ Number of establishments		Units	..	..	..	..	..
4.14 ♦ Number of rooms	(3)	Units	1,692	1,778	2,116	2,475	..
4.15 ♦ Number of bed-places	(3)	Units	3,384	3,556	4,232	4,950	..
Indicators							
4.16 Occupancy rate / rooms		Percent	..	..	..	..	..
4.17 Occupancy rate / bed-places		Percent	..	..	..	..	..
4.18 Average length of stay		Nights	..	..	..	..	..
4.19 Available capacity (bed-places per 1000 inhabitants)		Units	31.13	32.66	38.82	45.36	..
6. COMPLEMENTARY INDICATORS							
Demand							
6.1 Gross travel propensity		Units	..	..	..	..	..
6.2 Carrying capacity (arrivals/population)		Units	0.88	0.89	0.83	0.77	0.69
Macroeconomic indicators related to international tourism							
6.3 Inbound tourism expenditure over GDP		Percent	23.3	22.7	19.8	16.5	15.4
6.4 Outbound tourism expenditure over GDP		Percent	3.3	3.2	3.6	3.0	3.1
6.5 Tourism balance (inbound minus outbound tourism expenditure) over GDP		Percent	20.0	19.6	16.2	13.5	12.3
6.6 Tourism openness (inbound plus outbound tourism expenditure) over GDP		Percent	26.7	25.9	23.5	19.5	18.6
6.7 Tourism coverage (inbound over outbound tourism expenditure)		Percent	696.8	720.9	545.7	545.6	495.0
6.8 Inbound tourism expenditure over exports of goods		Percent	244.0	275.2	214.2	167.9	164.4
6.9 Inbound tourism expenditure over exports of services		Percent	65.8	66.3	68.5	63.0	61.5
6.10 Inbound tourism expenditure over exports of goods and services		Percent	51.8	53.4	51.9	45.8	44.7
6.11 Inbound tourism expenditure over current account credits		Percent	44.1	43.9	42.2	37.1	36.0
6.12 Outbound tourism expenditure over imports of goods		Percent	7.0	6.6	7.0	5.4	6.2
6.13 Outbound tourism expenditure over imports of services		Percent	18.9	17.8	17.7	15.9	17.1
6.14 Outbound tourism expenditure over imports of goods and services		Percent	5.1	4.8	5.0	4.0	4.5
6.15 Outbound tourism expenditure over current account debits		Percent	4.5	4.2	4.5	3.6	4.1

SAMOA

Basic data and indicators	Notes	Units	2005	2006	2007	2008	2009
1. INBOUND TOURISM							
Data							
Arrivals							
1.1 Total		('000)	..	..	..	..	..
1.2 ♦ Overnight visitors (tourists)		('000)	102	116	122	122	129
1.3 ♦ Same-day visitors (excursionists)		('000)	..	..	..	..	..
1.4 * of which, cruise passengers		('000)	..	..	..	..	..
Arrivals by region							
1.5 Total		('000)	102	115	121	122	129
1.6 ♦ Africa		('000)	..	..	..	..	..
1.7 ♦ Americas		('000)	10	9	8	9	10
1.8 ♦ East Asia and the Pacific		('000)	87	101	109	108	113
1.9 ♦ Europe		('000)	5	5	4	5	6
1.10 ♦ Middle East		('000)	..	..	..	..	..
1.11 ♦ South Asia		('000)	..	..	..	..	..
1.12 ♦ Other not classified		('000)	..	..	..	..	..
1.13 * of which, nationals residing abroad		('000)	..	..	..	..	..
Arrivals by main purpose							
1.14 Total		('000)	102	116	122	122	129
1.15 ♦ Personal		('000)	92	104	110	112	118
1.16 * holidays, leisure and recreation		('000)	34	43	44	53	51
1.17 * other personal purposes		('000)	58	61	66	59	67
1.18 ♦ Business and professional		('000)	10	12	12	10	11
Arrivals by mode of transport							
1.19 Total		('000)	102	115	123	122	129
1.20 ♦ Air		('000)	99	112	119	118	127
1.21 ♦ Water		('000)	3	3	4	4	2
1.22 ♦ Land		('000)	..	..	..	..	..
1.23 * railway		('000)	..	..	..	..	..
1.24 * road		('000)	..	..	..	..	..
1.25 * others		('000)	..	..	..	..	..
Accommodation							
Total							
1.29 ♦ Guests		('000)	..	110	111	105	122
1.30 ♦ Overnights		('000)	..	..	..	..	..
Hotels and similar establishments							
1.31 ♦ Guests		('000)	..	40	38	39	41
1.32 ♦ Overnights		('000)		..	..	..	..
Expenditure							
1.33 Total		US$ Mn	79.8	91.4	103.4	112.6	116.2
1.34 ♦ Travel		US$ Mn	79	90	103	112	116
1.35 ♦ Passenger transport		US$ Mn	0.8	1.4	0.4	0.6	0.2
3. OUTBOUND TOURISM							
Data							
Departures							
3.1 Total		('000)	..	..	..	..	..
3.2 ♦ Overnight visitors (tourists)		('000)	52	..	..	53	44
3.3 ♦ Same-day visitors (excursionists)		('000)	..	..	..	..	..
Expenditure							
3.4 Total		US$ Mn	16.6	15.1	19.8	21.6	20.0
3.5 ♦ Travel		US$ Mn	9.0	5.6	10.2	10.9	10.7
3.6 ♦ Passenger transport		US$ Mn	7.6	9.5	9.6	10.7	9.3
4. TOURISM INDUSTRIES							
Data							
Accommodation for visitors in hotels and similar establishments							
Non-monetary data							
4.13 ♦ Number of establishments		Units	..	..	..	..	..
4.14 ♦ Number of rooms		Units	1,099	1,092	..	..	..
4.15 ♦ Number of bed-places		Units	2,466	2,456	2,525	..	..
Indicators							
4.16 Occupancy rate / rooms		Percent	..	..	..	..	..
4.17 Occupancy rate / bed-places		Percent	..	..	..	..	..
4.18 Average length of stay		Nights	..	..	..	..	..
4.19 Available capacity (bed-places per 1000 inhabitants)		Units	13.78	13.72	14.11	..	..

SAMOA

Basic data and indicators	Notes	Units	2005	2006	2007	2008	2009
6. COMPLEMENTARY INDICATORS							
Demand							
6.1 Gross travel propensity		Units	..	..	..	..	..
6.2 Carrying capacity (arrivals/population)		Units	0.57	0.65	0.68	0.68	0.72
Macroeconomic indicators related to international tourism							
6.3 Inbound tourism expenditure over GDP		Percent	..	..	..	..	..
6.4 Outbound tourism expenditure over GDP		Percent	..	..	..	..	..
6.5 Tourism balance (inbound minus outbound tourism expenditure) over GDP		Percent	..	..	..	..	..
6.6 Tourism openness (inbound plus outbound tourism expenditure) over GDP		Percent	..	..	..	..	..
6.7 Tourism coverage (inbound over outbound tourism expenditure)		Percent	480.2	605.4	748.5	..	..
6.8 Inbound tourism expenditure over exports of goods		Percent	663.1	880.3	769.5	..	..
6.9 Inbound tourism expenditure over exports of services		Percent	70.1	68.3	77.1	..	..
6.10 Inbound tourism expenditure over exports of goods and services		Percent	63.4	63.4	70.1	..	..
6.11 Inbound tourism expenditure over current account credits		Percent	32.3	35.3	38.1	..	..
6.12 Outbound tourism expenditure over imports of goods		Percent	8.9	6.9	6.3	..	..
6.13 Outbound tourism expenditure over imports of services		Percent	29.5	26.5	25.7	..	..
6.14 Outbound tourism expenditure over imports of goods and services		Percent	6.8	5.5	5.1	..	..
6.15 Outbound tourism expenditure over current account debits		Percent	6.1	4.9	4.5	..	..

SAN MARINO

Basic data and indicators	Notes	Units	2005	2006	2007	2008	2009
1. INBOUND TOURISM							
Data							
Arrivals							
1.1 Total	(1)	('000)	2,107	2,136	2,164	2,112	2,056
1.2 ♦ Overnight visitors (tourists)	(2)	('000)	50	50	69	115	151
1.3 ♦ Same-day visitors (excursionists)		('000)	2,057	2,086	2,095	1,997	1,905
1.4 * of which, cruise passengers		('000)	..	..	..	..	..
Arrivals by region							
1.5 Total		('000)	2,107	2,136	2,164	2,112	..
1.6 ♦ Africa		('000)	..	..	..	..	..
1.7 ♦ Americas		('000)	17	22	37	19	..
1.8 ♦ East Asia and the Pacific		('000)	53	36	26	17	..
1.9 ♦ Europe		('000)	2,035	2,076	2,099	2,074	..
1.10 ♦ Middle East		('000)	..	..	..	..	..
1.11 ♦ South Asia		('000)	..	..	..	..	..
1.12 ♦ Other not classified		('000)	2	2	2	2	..
1.13 * of which, nationals residing abroad		('000)	..	..	..	..	..
Arrivals by main purpose							
1.14 Total		('000)	2,107	2,136	2,163	2,112	..
1.15 ♦ Personal		('000)	1,412	1,436	1,579	1,500	..
1.16 * holidays, leisure and recreation		('000)	738	880	930	866	..
1.17 * other personal purposes		('000)	674	556	649	634	..
1.18 ♦ Business and professional		('000)	695	700	584	612	..
Arrivals by mode of transport							
1.19 Total		('000)	2,107	2,136	2,164	2,112	2,056
1.20 ♦ Air		('000)	..	..	..	..	..
1.21 ♦ Water		('000)	..	..	..	..	..
1.22 ♦ Land		('000)	2,107	2,136	2,164	2,112	2,056
1.23 * railway		('000)	..	..	..	..	..
1.24 * road		('000)	2,107	2,136	2,164	2,112	2,056
1.25 * others		('000)	..	..	..	..	..
Accommodation							
Total							
1.29 ♦ Guests		('000)	..	..	..	..	..
1.30 ♦ Overnights		('000)	..	..	..	..	..
Hotels and similar establishments							
1.31 ♦ Guests		('000)	50	50	69	115	151
1.32 ♦ Overnights		('000)	80	80	116	179	193
Indicators							
1.39 Average size of travel party		Persons	..	..	..	..	..
Average length of stay							
1.40 Total		Days	..	..	..	..	..
1.41 ♦ For all commercial accommodation services		Nights	1.61	1.61	1.69	1.66	..
1.42 * of which, "hotels and similar establishments"		Nights	..	..	..	..	..
1.43 ♦ For non commercial accommodation services		Days	..	..	..	..	..
1.44 Average expenditure per day		US$	..	..	..	..	..
4. TOURISM INDUSTRIES							
Data							
Number of establishments							
4.1 Total		Units	..	..	..	..	..
4.2 ♦ Accommodation for visitors		Units	..	..	..	..	..
4.3 * of which, "hotels and similar establishments"	(3)	Units	28	29	30	28	..
4.4 ♦ Food and beverage serving activities		Units	..	..	..	..	..
4.5 ♦ Passenger transportation		Units	..	..	..	..	..
4.6 ♦ Travel agencies and other reservation services activities		Units	..	..	..	..	..
4.7 ♦ Other tourism industries		Units	..	..	..	..	..
Accommodation for visitors in hotels and similar establishments							
Non-monetary data							
4.13 ♦ Number of establishments	(3)	Units	28	29	30	28	..
4.14 ♦ Number of rooms	(3)	Units	718	718	767	746	..
4.15 ♦ Number of bed-places	(3)	Units	1,593	1,593	1,729	1,674	..
Indicators							
4.16 Occupancy rate / rooms		Percent	..	..	..	..	..
4.17 Occupancy rate / bed-places		Percent	54.10	55.00	56.50	54.00	..
4.18 Average length of stay		Nights	1.61	1.61	1.69	1.66	..
4.19 Available capacity (bed-places per 1000 inhabitants)		Units	53.39	52.78	56.54	53.95	..

SAN MARINO

Basic data and indicators	Notes	Units	2005	2006	2007	2008	2009
6. **COMPLEMENTARY INDICATORS**							
Demand							
6.1 Gross travel propensity		Units	..	..	..	..	..
6.2 Carrying capacity (arrivals/population)		Units	1.68	1.66	2.26	3.71	4.80

336

SAO TOME AND PRINCIPE

Basic data and indicators	Notes	Units	2005	2006	2007	2008	2009
1. INBOUND TOURISM							
Data							
Arrivals							
1.1 Total		('000)	..	..	..	..	..
1.2 ♦ Overnight visitors (tourists)		('000)	15.8	12.3	11.8	14.5	15.2
1.3 ♦ Same-day visitors (excursionists)		('000)	..	..	..	..	..
1.4 * of which, cruise passengers		('000)	..	..	..	..	..
Arrivals by region							
1.5 Total		('000)	15.8	12.3	11.8	14.5	..
1.6 ♦ Africa		('000)	4.4	2.8	2.2	2.5	..
1.7 ♦ Americas		('000)	0.6	0.5	0.3	0.4	..
1.8 ♦ East Asia and the Pacific		('000)	0.2	..	..	..	..
1.9 ♦ Europe		('000)	10.3	7.6	4.0	6.4	..
1.10 ♦ Middle East		('000)	..	..	..	..	..
1.11 ♦ South Asia		('000)	..	..	..	..	..
1.12 ♦ Other not classified		('000)	0.3	1.4	5.3	5.2	..
1.13 * of which, nationals residing abroad		('000)	..	..	..	..	..
Arrivals by main purpose							
1.14 Total		('000)	15.8	12.3	11.8	14.5	15.2
1.15 ♦ Personal		('000)	14.7	11.7	10.8	13.9	14.8
1.16 * holidays, leisure and recreation		('000)	9.3	6.7	5.3	7.9	9.2
1.17 * other personal purposes		('000)	5.4	5.0	5.5	6.0	5.6
1.18 ♦ Business and professional		('000)	1.1	0.6	1.0	0.6	0.4
Arrivals by mode of transport							
1.19 Total		('000)	15.8	12.3	11.8	14.5	15.2
1.20 ♦ Air		('000)	15.8	11.9	11.0	14.2	13.7
1.21 ♦ Water		('000)	..	0.4	0.8	0.3	1.5
1.22 ♦ Land		('000)	..	..	..	..	..
1.23 * railway		('000)	..	..	..	..	..
1.24 * road		('000)	..	..	..	..	..
1.25 * others		('000)	..	..	..	..	..
Expenditure							
1.33 Total		US$ Mn	..	..	..	..	..
1.34 ♦ Travel		US$ Mn	7.3	6.7	5.0	7.7	8.3
1.35 ♦ Passenger transport		US$ Mn	..	..	..	..	..
Expenditure by main purpose of the trip							
1.36 Total		US$ Mn	7.3	6.7	5.0	7.7	8.3
1.37 ♦ Personal		US$ Mn	4.4	4.0	3.0	4.6	5.0
1.38 ♦ Business and professional		US$ Mn	2.9	2.7	2.0	3.1	3.3
3. OUTBOUND TOURISM							
Data							
Departures							
3.1 Total		('000)	..	..	..	..	..
3.2 ♦ Overnight visitors (tourists)		('000)	..	..	8.6	10.3	..
3.3 ♦ Same-day visitors (excursionists)		('000)	..	..	..	..	..
Expenditure							
3.4 Total		US$ Mn	0.5	1.1	0.7	..	..
3.5 ♦ Travel		US$ Mn	0.1	0.2	0.1	..	..
3.6 ♦ Passenger transport		US$ Mn	0.4	0.9	0.6	0.3	0.4

SAO TOME AND PRINCIPE

Basic data and indicators	Notes	Units	2005	2006	2007	2008	2009
4. TOURISM INDUSTRIES							
Data							
Number of establishments							
4.1 Total		Units	..	..	..	..	..
4.2 ♦ Accommodation for visitors		Units	..	..	..	..	..
4.3 * of which, "hotels and similar establishments"		Units	..	..	..	..	23
4.4 ♦ Food and beverage serving activities		Units	..	..	..	..	..
4.5 ♦ Passenger transportation		Units	..	..	..	..	..
4.6 ♦ Travel agencies and other reservation services activities		Units	..	..	..	..	..
4.7 ♦ Other tourism industries		Units	..	..	..	..	..
Accommodation for visitors in hotels and similar establishments							
Non-monetary data							
4.13 ♦ Number of establishments		Units	..	..	..	..	23
4.14 ♦ Number of rooms		Units	..	..	..	..	479
4.15 ♦ Number of bed-places		Units	..	..	..	..	609
Indicators							
4.16 Occupancy rate / rooms		Percent	..	..	..	..	..
4.17 Occupancy rate / bed-places		Percent	..	..	..	..	..
4.18 Average length of stay	(1)	Nights	..	..	..	..	7.00
4.19 Available capacity (bed-places per 1000 inhabitants)		Units	..	..	..	..	3.74
6. COMPLEMENTARY INDICATORS							
Demand							
6.1 Gross travel propensity		Units	..	..	..	..	..
6.2 Carrying capacity (arrivals/population)		Units	0.10	0.08	0.07	0.09	0.09
Macroeconomic indicators related to international tourism							
6.3 Inbound tourism expenditure over GDP		Percent	..	..	..	..	..
6.4 Outbound tourism expenditure over GDP		Percent	..	..	..	..	..
6.5 Tourism balance (inbound minus outbound tourism expenditure) over GDP		Percent	..	..	..	..	..
6.6 Tourism openness (inbound plus outbound tourism expenditure) over GDP		Percent	..	..	..	..	..
6.7 Tourism coverage (inbound over outbound tourism expenditure)		Percent	1,626.7	605.4	675.7	2,211.4	997.8
6.8 Inbound tourism expenditure over exports of goods		Percent	107.8	87.2	73.4	98.9	98.6
6.9 Inbound tourism expenditure over exports of services		Percent	80.0	80.0	74.6	80.0	79.9
6.10 Inbound tourism expenditure over exports of goods and services		Percent	45.9	41.7	37.0	44.2	44.1
6.11 Inbound tourism expenditure over current account credits		Percent	28.8	24.4	18.7	27.4	27.1
6.12 Outbound tourism expenditure over imports of goods		Percent	1.1	1.9	1.1	0.4	1.1
6.13 Outbound tourism expenditure over imports of services		Percent	4.1	6.3	4.0	1.6	4.4
6.14 Outbound tourism expenditure over imports of goods and services		Percent	0.9	1.4	0.9	0.3	0.9
6.15 Outbound tourism expenditure over current account debits		Percent	0.7	1.3	0.8	0.3	0.8

SAUDI ARABIA

Basic data and indicators	Notes	Units	2005	2006	2007	2008	2009
1. INBOUND TOURISM							
Data							
Arrivals							
1.1 Total		('000)	10,417	10,962	13,479	17,717	13,319
1.2 ♦ Overnight visitors (tourists)		('000)	8,037	8,620	11,531	14,757	10,897
1.3 ♦ Same-day visitors (excursionists)		('000)	2,380	2,342	1,948	2,960	2,422
1.4 * of which, cruise passengers		('000)	..	..	..	..	..
Arrivals by region							
1.5 Total		('000)	8,035	8,620	11,531	14,757	10,897
1.6 ♦ Africa		('000)	436	489	601	1,033	261
1.7 ♦ Americas		('000)	70	66	236	297	57
1.8 ♦ East Asia and the Pacific		('000)	439	595	579	941	362
1.9 ♦ Europe		('000)	340	485	657	1,185	445
1.10 ♦ Middle East		('000)	5,607	5,516	7,444	9,334	8,678
1.11 ♦ South Asia		('000)	1,142	1,469	2,014	1,967	1,094
1.12 ♦ Other not classified		('000)	1	..	..	..	..
1.13 * of which, nationals residing abroad		('000)	..	..	..	..	..
Arrivals by main purpose							
1.14 Total		('000)	8,037	8,620	11,530	14,757	10,896
1.15 ♦ Personal		('000)	6,086	7,017	8,871	11,097	9,292
1.16 * holidays, leisure and recreation		('000)	397	566	591	1,154	1,570
1.17 * other personal purposes		('000)	5,689	6,451	8,280	9,943	7,722
1.18 ♦ Business and professional		('000)	1,951	1,603	2,659	3,660	1,604
Arrivals by mode of transport							
1.19 Total		('000)	8,076	8,620	11,530	14,758	10,897
1.20 ♦ Air		('000)	4,287	4,857	7,341	9,282	5,301
1.21 ♦ Water		('000)	488	270	581	1,020	289
1.22 ♦ Land		('000)	3,301	3,493	3,608	4,456	5,307
1.23 * railway		('000)	..	..	..	..	..
1.24 * road		('000)	3,301	3,493	3,608	4,456	5,307
1.25 * others		('000)	..	..	..	..	..
Accommodation							
Total							
1.29 ♦ Guests		('000)	8,037	8,620	11,531	14,757	10,896
1.30 ♦ Overnights		('000)	91,359	112,383	152,372	209,309	157,010
Hotels and similar establishments							
1.31 ♦ Guests		('000)	6,310	7,228	9,598	11,944	8,077
1.32 ♦ Overnights		('000)	69,341	98,979	121,974	170,267	133,876
Expenditure							
1.33 Total		US$ Mn	5,103	5,205	6,767	7,227	6,678
1.34 ♦ Travel		US$ Mn	4,626	4,769	5,971	5,910	5,964
1.35 ♦ Passenger transport	(1)	US$ Mn	477	436	796	1,317	714
Expenditure by main purpose of the trip	(1)						
1.36 Total		US$ Mn	4,626	4,768	5,972	..	5,964
1.37 ♦ Personal		US$ Mn	3,426	3,975	5,029	..	4,595
1.38 ♦ Business and professional		US$ Mn	1,200	793	943	..	1,369
Indicators							
1.39 Average size of travel party		Persons	..	..	..	..	..
Average length of stay							
1.40 Total	(2)	Days	10.70	13.00	13.20	14.20	14.40
1.41 ♦ For all commercial accommodation services		Nights	10.90	13.70	12.70	14.30	16.60
1.42 * of which, "hotels and similar establishments"		Nights	10.90	13.70	12.70	14.30	16.60
1.43 ♦ For non commercial accommodation services	(2)	Days	11.10	10.50	15.50	11.60	8.10
1.44 Average expenditure per day		US$	59.2	44.1	34.4	46.4	49.3
2. DOMESTIC TOURISM							
Data							
Trips							
2.1 Total		('000)	32,228	28,400	29,672	30,049	33,526
2.2 ♦ Overnight visitors (tourists)		('000)	30,236	27,080	28,549	28,775	32,014
2.3 ♦ Same-day visitors (excursionists)		('000)	1,992	1,320	1,123	1,274	1,512
Trips by main purpose							
2.4 Total		('000)	30,236	27,080	28,549	28,775	32,014
2.5 ♦ Personal		('000)	26,268	24,490	27,358	27,466	31,223
2.6 * holidays, leisure and recreation		('000)	10,942	11,350	13,165	13,255	15,625
2.7 * other personal purposes		('000)	15,326	13,140	14,193	14,211	15,598
2.8 ♦ Business and professional		('000)	3,968	2,590	1,191	1,309	791

SAUDI ARABIA

Basic data and indicators	Notes	Units	2005	2006	2007	2008	2009
Trips by mode of transport							
2.9 Total		('000)	30,235	27,080	28,549	28,774	32,015
2.10 ♦ Air		('000)	4,884	3,641	2,699	3,150	2,674
2.11 ♦ Water		('000)	..	..	..	..	..
2.12 ♦ Land		('000)	25,351	23,439	25,850	25,624	29,341
2.13 * railway		('000)	135	48	39	59	77
2.14 * road		('000)	25,216	23,260	25,719	25,553	29,169
2.15 * others		('000)	..	131	92	12	95
Accommodation							
Total							
2.19 ♦ Guests		('000)	30,236	27,080	28,549	28,775	32,014
2.20 ♦ Overnights		('000)	196,737	183,527	188,403	199,037	198,477
Hotels and similar establishments							
2.21 ♦ Guests		('000)	17,031	15,894	18,075	17,851	22,998
2.22 ♦ Overnights		('000)	108,236	99,858	117,811	121,884	136,998
Indicators							
2.23 Average size of travel party		Persons	..	..	..	..	..
Average length of stay							
2.24 Total	(2)	Days	6.50	6.50	6.60	6.90	6.20
2.25 ♦ For all commercial accommodation services		Nights	6.40	6.30	6.50	6.80	6.00
2.26 * of which, "hotels and similar establishments"		Nights	6.40	6.30	6.50	6.80	6.00
2.27 ♦ For non commercial accommodation services	(2)	Days	6.50	6.90	6.70	5.60	6.80
2.28 Average expenditure per day		US$	43.2	47.0	45.1	50.4	44.8
3. OUTBOUND TOURISM							
Data							
Departures							
3.1 Total		('000)	5,009	2,336	4,817	4,705	6,467
3.2 ♦ Overnight visitors (tourists)		('000)	4,403	2,000	4,126	4,087	6,032
3.3 ♦ Same-day visitors (excursionists)		('000)	606	335	691	618	435
Expenditure							
3.4 Total		US$ Mn	9,290	13,491	21,569	16,478	20,964
3.5 ♦ Travel		US$ Mn	9,087	12,979	20,170	15,129	18,814
3.6 ♦ Passenger transport	(3)	US$ Mn	203	512	1,399	1,349	2,150
Indicators							
3.10 Average length of stay		Days	13.00	13.00	11.00	10.00	9.10
3.11 Average expenditure per day		US$	67.3	69.7	107.5	124.3	138.7
4. TOURISM INDUSTRIES							
Data							
Number of establishments							
4.1 Total		Units	28,934	30,410	38,791	41,653	43,505
4.2 ♦ Accommodation for visitors		Units	..	..	..	..	..
4.3 * of which, "hotels and similar establishments"		Units	3,294	3,548	4,012	5,446	5,605
4.4 ♦ Food and beverage serving activities		Units	23,654	24,600	25,584	26,266	27,317
4.5 ♦ Passenger transportation		Units	741	771	1,167	1,469	1,528
4.6 ♦ Travel agencies and other reservation services activities		Units	816	1,045	1,320	1,488	1,792
4.7 ♦ Other tourism industries	(4)	Units	429	446	6,708	6,984	7,263
Accommodation for visitors in hotels and similar establishments							
Monetary data							
4.8 ♦ Output		US$ Mn	3,139.5	3,170.0	3,283.0	4,756.0	..
4.9 ♦ Intermediate consumption		US$ Mn	809.3	887.0	831.0	1,591.0	..
4.10 ♦ Gross value added		US$ Mn	2,330.1	2,283.0	2,452.0	3,165.0	..
4.11 ♦ Compensation of employees		US$ Mn	387.5	421.0	422.0	569.0	..
4.12 ♦ Gross fixed capital formation		US$ Mn	..	..	..	..	..
Non-monetary data							
4.13 ♦ Number of establishments		Units	3,294	3,548	4,012	5,446	5,605
4.14 ♦ Number of rooms		Units	156,931	167,736	193,720	201,631	204,911
4.15 ♦ Number of bed-places		Units	389,354	420,689	434,081	558,309	570,714
Indicators							
4.16 Occupancy rate / rooms		Percent	51.00	51.20	50.80	51.80	54.60
4.17 Occupancy rate / bed-places		Percent	46.00	43.80	43.70	50.20	50.40
4.18 Average length of stay		Nights	2.23	1.93	2.20	1.88	7.00
4.19 Available capacity (bed-places per 1000 inhabitants)		Units	16.80	17.80	17.90	22.50	22.70

SAUDI ARABIA

Basic data and indicators	Notes	Units	2005	2006	2007	2008	2009
Travel agencies and other reservation service activities							
Monetary data							
4.20 ♦ Output		US$ Mn	446.0	436.0	294.0	343.0	..
4.21 ♦ Intermediate consumption		US$ Mn	46.0	52.0	37.0	51.0	..
4.22 ♦ Gross value added		US$ Mn	400.0	384.0	257.0	293.0	..
4.23 ♦ Compensation of employees		US$ Mn	83.0	66.0	71.0	82.0	..
4.24 ♦ Gross fixed capital formation		US$ Mn	..	..	..	..	..
Non-monetary data							
♦ Domestic trips							
4.25 * with package tour		Percent	..	..	..	..	..
4.26 * without package tour		Percent	..	..	..	..	..
♦ Inbound trips							
4.27 * with package tour		Percent	34.4	46.3	40.6	47.0	31.0
4.28 * without package tour		Percent	65.6	53.7	59.4	53.0	69.0
♦ Outbound trips							
4.29 * with package tour		Percent	1.0	1.0	0.9	0.0	1.0
4.30 * without package tour		Percent	99.0	99.0	99.1	100.0	99.0

5. EMPLOYMENT

Data

	Notes	Units	2005	2006	2007	2008	2009
Number of employees by tourism industries	(5)						
5.1 Total		('000)	332.3	355.6	426.6	466.5	479.0
5.2 ♦ Accommodation services for visitors (hotels and similar establishments)		('000)	71.2	74.7	67.1	82.5	85.6
5.3 ♦ Other accommodation services		('000)	..	..	..	..	..
5.4 ♦ Food and beverage serving activities		('000)	200.5	215.6	222.0	245.2	243.4
5.5 ♦ Passenger transportation		('000)	40.8	41.1	96.2	90.9	100.1
5.6 ♦ Travel agencies and other reservation services activities		('000)	9.5	10.8	8.3	10.1	10.7
5.7 ♦ Other tourism industries		('000)	10.3	13.3	33.0	37.8	39.2
Number of jobs by status in employment	(5)						
5.8 Total		('000)	332.3	355.6	426.6	466.5	479.0
5.9 ♦ Employees		('000)	313.9	326.6	393.5	433.4	436.1
5.10 ♦ Self employed		('000)	18.4	28.9	33.1	33.1	42.9

6. COMPLEMENTARY INDICATORS

	Notes	Units	2005	2006	2007	2008	2009
Demand							
6.1 Gross travel propensity		Units	..	..	..	..	..
6.2 Carrying capacity (arrivals/population)		Units	1.66	1.51	1.65	1.75	1.69
Macroeconomic indicators related to international tourism							
6.3 Inbound tourism expenditure over GDP		Percent	1.5	1.3	1.6	1.2	1.6
6.4 Outbound tourism expenditure over GDP		Percent	2.9	3.6	5.3	3.2	5.1
6.5 Tourism balance (inbound minus outbound tourism expenditure) over GDP		Percent	-1.4	-2.3	-3.7	-1.9	-3.5
6.6 Tourism openness (inbound plus outbound tourism expenditure) over GDP		Percent	4.3	5.0	6.8	4.4	6.7
6.7 Tourism coverage (inbound over outbound tourism expenditure)		Percent	50.9	36.7	29.6	39.1	31.7
6.8 Inbound tourism expenditure over exports of goods		Percent	2.6	2.3	2.6	1.9	3.1
6.9 Inbound tourism expenditure over exports of services		Percent	40.5	33.6	37.4	63.0	61.8
6.10 Inbound tourism expenditure over exports of goods and services		Percent	2.4	2.1	2.4	1.8	3.0
6.11 Inbound tourism expenditure over current account credits		Percent	2.3	2.0	2.3	1.7	2.7
6.12 Outbound tourism expenditure over imports of goods		Percent	16.6	20.3	24.4	14.9	21.6
6.13 Outbound tourism expenditure over imports of services		Percent	27.4	26.2	32.2	20.1	25.6
6.14 Outbound tourism expenditure over imports of goods and services		Percent	10.4	11.4	13.9	8.6	11.7
6.15 Outbound tourism expenditure over current account debits		Percent	8.5	9.5	11.8	7.1	9.5

341

SENEGAL

Basic data and indicators	Notes	Units	2005	2006	2007	2008	2009
1. INBOUND TOURISM							
Data							
Arrivals							
1.1 Total		('000)	779	876	879	..	..
1.2 ♦ Overnight visitors (tourists)		('000)	769	866	875	..	..
1.3 ♦ Same-day visitors (excursionists)		('000)	9	10	4	..	..
1.4 * of which, cruise passengers		('000)	9	10	4	..	..
Arrivals by region							
1.5 Total		('000)	769	866	875	..	..
1.6 ♦ Africa		('000)	265	430	438	..	..
1.7 ♦ Americas		('000)	26	26	26	..	..
1.8 ♦ East Asia and the Pacific		('000)	..	..	..	..	..
1.9 ♦ Europe		('000)	393	324	324	..	..
1.10 ♦ Middle East		('000)	..	..	..	..	..
1.11 ♦ South Asia		('000)	..	..	..	..	..
1.12 ♦ Other not classified		('000)	85	86	87	..	..
1.13 * of which, nationals residing abroad		('000)	..	..	..	..	..
Arrivals by mode of transport							
1.19 Total		('000)	779	876	879	..	..
1.20 ♦ Air		('000)	564	522	487	..	..
1.21 ♦ Water		('000)	9	10	4	..	..
1.22 ♦ Land		('000)	206	344	388	..	..
1.23 * railway		('000)	..	..	..	..	..
1.24 * road		('000)	206	344	388	..	..
1.25 * others		('000)	..	..	..	..	..
Accommodation							
Total							
1.29 ♦ Guests		('000)	..	..	..	..	..
1.30 ♦ Overnights		('000)	..	..	..	..	..
Hotels and similar establishments							
1.31 ♦ Guests	(1)	('000)	387	406	387	..	..
1.32 ♦ Overnights	(1)	('000)	1,397	1,426	1,335	..	..
Expenditure							
1.33 Total		US$ Mn	334	329	622	637	..
1.34 ♦ Travel		US$ Mn	242	250	531	543	..
1.35 ♦ Passenger transport		US$ Mn	92	79	91	94	..
Expenditure by main purpose of the trip							
1.36 Total		US$ Mn	242	250	531	543	..
1.37 ♦ Personal		US$ Mn	144	152	392	436	..
1.38 ♦ Business and professional		US$ Mn	98	98	139	107	..
Indicators							
1.39 Average size of travel party		Persons	..	..	..	..	..
Average length of stay							
1.40 Total		Days	..	..	..	..	..
1.41 ♦ For all commercial accommodation services		Nights	3.40	3.50	3.50	..	..
1.42 * of which, "hotels and similar establishments"		Nights	..	..	..	..	..
1.43 ♦ For non commercial accommodation services		Days	..	..	..	..	..
1.44 Average expenditure per day		US$	..	..	..	..	..
2. DOMESTIC TOURISM							
Data							
Accommodation							
Total							
2.19 ♦ Guests		('000)	..	..	..	..	..
2.20 ♦ Overnights		('000)	..	..	..	..	..
Hotels and similar establishments							
2.21 ♦ Guests	(1)	('000)	81	72	93	..	..
2.22 ♦ Overnights	(1)	('000)	198	177	223	..	..
Indicators							
2.23 Average size of travel party		Persons	..	..	..	..	..
Average length of stay							
2.24 Total		Days	..	..	..	..	..
2.25 ♦ For all commercial accommodation services		Nights	..	..	2.39	..	..
2.26 * of which, "hotels and similar establishments"		Nights	..	..	..	..	..
2.27 ♦ For non commercial accommodation services		Days	..	..	..	..	..
2.28 Average expenditure per day		US$	..	..	..	..	..

SENEGAL

Basic data and indicators	Notes	Units	2005	2006	2007	2008	2009
3. OUTBOUND TOURISM							
Data							
Expenditure							
3.4 Total		US$ Mn	144	139	352	276	..
3.5 ♦ Travel		US$ Mn	65	54	253	175	..
3.6 ♦ Passenger transport		US$ Mn	79	85	99	101	..
Expenditure by main purpose of the trip							
3.7 Total		US$ Mn	65	53	253	175	..
3.8 ♦ Personal		US$ Mn	52	43	127	94	..
3.9 ♦ Business and professional		US$ Mn	13	10	126	81	..
4. TOURISM INDUSTRIES							
Data							
Number of establishments							
4.1 Total		Units	..	..	..	..	..
4.2 ♦ Accommodation for visitors		Units	..	..	..	..	..
4.3 * of which, "hotels and similar establishments"	(1)	Units	815	815	815	..	..
4.4 ♦ Food and beverage serving activities		Units	..	..	..	..	..
4.5 ♦ Passenger transportation		Units	..	..	..	..	..
4.6 ♦ Travel agencies and other reservation services activities		Units	..	..	..	..	..
4.7 ♦ Other tourism industries		Units	..	..	..	..	..
Accommodation for visitors in hotels and similar establishments							
Non-monetary data							
4.13 ♦ Number of establishments	(1)	Units	815	815	815	..	..
4.14 ♦ Number of rooms	(1)	Units	15,842	15,842	15,842	..	..
4.15 ♦ Number of bed-places	(1)	Units	31,229	31,229	31,229	..	..
Indicators							
4.16 Occupancy rate / rooms		Percent	..	..	..	..	..
4.17 Occupancy rate / bed-places		Percent	34.40	34.80	34.59	..	..
4.18 Average length of stay		Nights	3.40	3.50	3.50	..	..
4.19 Available capacity (bed-places per 1000 inhabitants)		Units	2.77	2.70	2.63	..	..
6. COMPLEMENTARY INDICATORS							
Demand							
6.1 Gross travel propensity		Units	..	..	..	..	..
6.2 Carrying capacity (arrivals/population)		Units	0.07	0.07	0.07	..	..
Macroeconomic indicators related to international tourism							
6.3 Inbound tourism expenditure over GDP		Percent	3.8	3.5	5.5	..	..
6.4 Outbound tourism expenditure over GDP		Percent	1.7	1.5	3.1	..	..
6.5 Tourism balance (inbound minus outbound tourism expenditure) over GDP		Percent	2.2	2.0	2.4	..	..
6.6 Tourism openness (inbound plus outbound tourism expenditure) over GDP		Percent	5.5	5.0	8.6	..	..
6.7 Tourism coverage (inbound over outbound tourism expenditure)		Percent	232.0	237.9	177.2	..	..
6.8 Inbound tourism expenditure over exports of goods		Percent	21.2	20.7	37.2	..	..
6.9 Inbound tourism expenditure over exports of services		Percent	43.0	40.8	51.8	..	..
6.10 Inbound tourism expenditure over exports of goods and services		Percent	14.2	13.7	21.7	..	..
6.11 Inbound tourism expenditure over current account credits		Percent	10.1	9.4	13.6	..	..
6.12 Outbound tourism expenditure over imports of goods		Percent	5.0	4.3	8.4	..	..
6.13 Outbound tourism expenditure over imports of services		Percent	17.9	16.4	28.4	..	..
6.14 Outbound tourism expenditure over imports of goods and services		Percent	3.9	3.4	6.5	..	..
6.15 Outbound tourism expenditure over current account debits		Percent	3.6	3.2	6.0	..	..

SERBIA

Basic data and indicators	Notes	Units	2005	2006	2007	2008	2009
1. INBOUND TOURISM							
Data							
Arrivals							
1.1 Total		('000)	..	..	..	..	..
1.2 ♦ Overnight visitors (tourists)	(1)	('000)	453	469	696	646	645
1.3 ♦ Same-day visitors (excursionists)		('000)	..	..	..	..	..
1.4 * of which, cruise passengers		('000)	..	..	..	..	..
Arrivals by region	(1)						
1.5 Total		('000)	453	468	696	646	645
1.6 ♦ Africa		('000)	..	..	..	..	..
1.7 ♦ Americas		('000)	16	17	19	15	16
1.8 ♦ East Asia and the Pacific		('000)	6	6	7	8	8
1.9 ♦ Europe		('000)	419	435	656	610	603
1.10 ♦ Middle East		('000)	..	..	..	..	..
1.11 ♦ South Asia		('000)	..	..	..	..	..
1.12 ♦ Other not classified		('000)	12	10	14	13	18
1.13 * of which, nationals residing abroad		('000)	..	..	..	..	..
Accommodation							
Total							
1.29 ♦ Guests		('000)	453	469	696	646	645
1.30 ♦ Overnights		('000)	992	1,015	1,476	1,399	1,469
Hotels and similar establishments							
1.31 ♦ Guests		('000)	434	448	586	564	570
1.32 ♦ Overnights		('000)	933	949	1,240	1,195	1,184
Expenditure							
1.33 Total		US$ Mn	308	398	1,011	1,116	986
1.34 ♦ Travel		US$ Mn	..	..	866	944	866
1.35 ♦ Passenger transport		US$ Mn	..	..	145	172	120
Expenditure by main purpose of the trip							
1.36 Total		US$ Mn	..	..	866	944	866
1.37 ♦ Personal		US$ Mn	..	..	861	935	857
1.38 ♦ Business and professional		US$ Mn	..	..	5	9	9
Indicators							
1.39 Average size of travel party		Persons	..	..	..	..	..
Average length of stay							
1.40 Total		Days	..	..	..	..	..
1.41 ♦ For all commercial accommodation services		Nights	2.19	2.16	2.12	2.16	2.28
1.42 * of which, "hotels and similar establishments"		Nights	2.15	2.12	2.12	2.12	2.08
1.43 ♦ For non commercial accommodation services		Days	..	..	..	..	..
1.44 Average expenditure per day		US$	..	..	..	..	..
2. DOMESTIC TOURISM							
Data							
Accommodation							
Total							
2.19 ♦ Guests		('000)	1,536	1,538	1,611	1,620	1,373
2.20 ♦ Overnights		('000)	5,508	5,577	5,853	5,935	5,293
Hotels and similar establishments							
2.21 ♦ Guests		('000)	1,079	1,058	1,097	1,090	906
2.22 ♦ Overnights		('000)	3,198	3,120	3,187	3,230	2,648
Indicators							
2.23 Average size of travel party		Persons	..	..	..	..	..
Average length of stay							
2.24 Total		Days	..	..	..	..	..
2.25 ♦ For all commercial accommodation services		Nights	3.59	3.63	3.63	3.66	3.86
2.26 * of which, "hotels and similar establishments"		Nights	2.96	2.95	2.91	2.96	2.92
2.27 ♦ For non commercial accommodation services		Days	..	..	..	..	..
2.28 Average expenditure per day		US$	..	..	..	..	..

SERBIA

Basic data and indicators	Notes	Units	2005	2006	2007	2008	2009
3. OUTBOUND TOURISM							
Data							
Expenditure							
3.4 Total		US$ Mn	260	322	1,194	1,449	1,076
3.5 ♦ Travel		US$ Mn	..	..	1,042	1,253	959
3.6 ♦ Passenger transport		US$ Mn	..	..	152	196	117
Expenditure by main purpose of the trip							
3.7 Total		US$ Mn	..	..	1,042	1,253	959
3.8 ♦ Personal		US$ Mn	..	..	908	1,033	778
3.9 ♦ Business and professional		US$ Mn	..	..	134	220	181
4. TOURISM INDUSTRIES							
Data							
Number of establishments							
4.1 Total		Units	..	..	..	..	..
4.2 ♦ Accommodation for visitors		Units	706	718	869	918	931
4.3 * of which, "hotels and similar establishments"		Units	495	505	634	670	687
4.4 ♦ Food and beverage serving activities		Units	..	..	..	..	..
4.5 ♦ Passenger transportation		Units	..	..	..	..	..
4.6 ♦ Travel agencies and other reservation services activities		Units	..	..	..	..	1,019
4.7 ♦ Other tourism industries		Units	..	..	..	..	..
Accommodation for visitors in hotels and similar establishments							
Non-monetary data							
4.13 ♦ Number of establishments		Units	495	505	634	670	687
4.14 ♦ Number of rooms		Units	22,236	22,631	24,023	25,142	25,370
4.15 ♦ Number of bed-places		Units	48,360	49,145	52,547	55,087	55,650
Indicators							
4.16 Occupancy rate / rooms		Percent	..	..	..	..	..
4.17 Occupancy rate / bed-places		Percent	23.40	22.69	23.08	21.94	18.87
4.18 Average length of stay		Nights	2.73	2.70	2.63	2.67	2.60
4.19 Available capacity (bed-places per 1000 inhabitants)		Units	6.50	6.63	7.12	7.49	7.60
5. EMPLOYMENT							
Data							
Number of employees by tourism industries							
5.1 Total		('000)	..	..	..	..	..
5.2 ♦ Accommodation services for visitors (hotels and similar establishments)	(2)	('000)	80.0	84.5	72.3	83.9	..
5.3 ♦ Other accommodation services		('000)	..	..	..	..	..
5.4 ♦ Food and beverage serving activities		('000)	..	..	..	..	..
5.5 ♦ Passenger transportation		('000)	..	..	..	..	..
5.6 ♦ Travel agencies and other reservation services activities		('000)	..	..	..	..	..
5.7 ♦ Other tourism industries		('000)	..	..	..	..	..
6. COMPLEMENTARY INDICATORS							
Demand							
6.1 Gross travel propensity		Units	..	..	..	..	..
6.2 Carrying capacity (arrivals/population)		Units	0.06	0.06	0.09	0.09	0.09

SEYCHELLES

Basic data and indicators	Notes	Units	2005	2006	2007	2008	2009
1. INBOUND TOURISM							
Data							
Arrivals							
1.1 Total		('000)	135	151	171	173	178
1.2 ♦ Overnight visitors (tourists)		('000)	129	141	161	159	158
1.3 ♦ Same-day visitors (excursionists)		('000)	6	10	10	14	20
1.4 * of which, cruise passengers		('000)	6	10	10	14	20
Arrivals by region							
1.5 Total		('000)	129	140	162	158	157
1.6 ♦ Africa		('000)	12	13	17	19	18
1.7 ♦ Americas		('000)	4	3	4	4	5
1.8 ♦ East Asia and the Pacific		('000)	3	3	4	3	4
1.9 ♦ Europe		('000)	104	114	130	125	122
1.10 ♦ Middle East		('000)	4	5	5	5	6
1.11 ♦ South Asia		('000)	2	2	2	2	2
1.12 ♦ Other not classified		('000)	..	..	..	..	..
1.13 * of which, nationals residing abroad		('000)	..	..	..	..	..
Arrivals by main purpose							
1.14 Total		('000)	129	141	161	159	157
1.15 ♦ Personal		('000)	122	134	153	149	147
1.16 * holidays, leisure and recreation		('000)	116	128	147	142	142
1.17 * other personal purposes		('000)	6	6	6	7	5
1.18 ♦ Business and professional		('000)	7	7	8	10	10
Arrivals by mode of transport							
1.19 Total		('000)	129	141	161	159	157
1.20 ♦ Air		('000)	125	137	159	156	155
1.21 ♦ Water		('000)	4	4	2	3	2
1.22 ♦ Land		('000)	..	..	..	..	..
1.23 * railway		('000)	..	..	..	..	..
1.24 * road		('000)	..	..	..	..	..
1.25 * others		('000)	..	..	..	..	..
Accommodation							
Total							
1.29 ♦ Guests		('000)	..	..	..	..	..
1.30 ♦ Overnights		('000)	1,248	1,378	1,597	1,605	1,607
Hotels and similar establishments							
1.31 ♦ Guests		('000)	104	114	135	129	130
1.32 ♦ Overnights		('000)	809	932	1,095	990	994
Expenditure							
1.33 Total		US$ Mn	269	323	366	360	302
1.34 ♦ Travel		US$ Mn	192	228	278	269	208
1.35 ♦ Passenger transport		US$ Mn	77	95	88	91	94
Indicators							
1.39 Average size of travel party		Persons	..	..	..	..	..
Average length of stay							
1.40 Total		Days	..	..	..	..	..
1.41 ♦ For all commercial accommodation services	(1)	Nights	9.69	9.82	9.90	10.10	10.20
1.42 * of which, "hotels and similar establishments"		Nights	..	..	..	..	..
1.43 ♦ For non commercial accommodation services		Days	..	..	..	..	..
1.44 Average expenditure per day		US$	..	..	..	..	..
2. DOMESTIC TOURISM							
Data							
Accommodation							
Total							
2.19 ♦ Guests		('000)	..	..	..	..	..
2.20 ♦ Overnights		('000)	..	..	..	..	..
Hotels and similar establishments							
2.21 ♦ Guests		('000)	..	..	..	..	..
2.22 ♦ Overnights		('000)	12	18	20	17	15

SEYCHELLES

Basic data and indicators	Notes	Units	2005	2006	2007	2008	2009
3. OUTBOUND TOURISM							
Data							
Departures							
3.1 Total		('000)	..	..	..	..	..
3.2 ♦ Overnight visitors (tourists)		('000)	52	55	58	54	49
3.3 ♦ Same-day visitors (excursionists)		('000)	..	..	..	..	..
Expenditure							
3.4 Total		US$ Mn	59	56	70	67	52
3.5 ♦ Travel		US$ Mn	39	36	40	37	32
3.6 ♦ Passenger transport		US$ Mn	20	20	30	30	20
4. TOURISM INDUSTRIES							
Data							
Accommodation for visitors in hotels and similar establishments							
Non-monetary data							
4.13 ♦ Number of establishments		Units	..	..	..	..	..
4.14 ♦ Number of rooms	(2)	Units	2,420	2,530	2,710	2,360	2,500
4.15 ♦ Number of bed-places	(2)	Units	4,920	5,140	5,460	4,840	5,080
Indicators							
4.16 Occupancy rate / rooms		Percent	48.00	54.00	58.00	60.00	56.00
4.17 Occupancy rate / bed-places		Percent	44.00	51.00	56.00	57.00	54.00
4.18 Average length of stay		Nights	..	..	..	..	..
4.19 Available capacity (bed-places per 1000 inhabitants)		Units	59.35	60.76	64.21	55.66	57.75
6. COMPLEMENTARY INDICATORS							
Demand							
6.1 Gross travel propensity		Units	..	..	..	..	..
6.2 Carrying capacity (arrivals/population)		Units	1.56	1.67	1.89	1.83	1.80
Macroeconomic indicators related to international tourism							
6.3 Inbound tourism expenditure over GDP		Percent	38.6	..	..	..	..
6.4 Outbound tourism expenditure over GDP		Percent	8.4	..	..	..	..
6.5 Tourism balance (inbound minus outbound tourism expenditure) over GDP		Percent	30.1	..	..	..	..
6.6 Tourism openness (inbound plus outbound tourism expenditure) over GDP		Percent	47.0	..	..	..	..
6.7 Tourism coverage (inbound over outbound tourism expenditure)		Percent	457.4	573.1	520.9	530.8	579.1
6.8 Inbound tourism expenditure over exports of goods		Percent	76.8	76.9	93.4	72.3	69.7
6.9 Inbound tourism expenditure over exports of services		Percent	73.0	75.0	77.5	76.0	74.6
6.10 Inbound tourism expenditure over exports of goods and services		Percent	37.4	38.0	42.4	37.0	36.0
6.11 Inbound tourism expenditure over current account credits		Percent	35.2	35.3	39.2	34.1	33.0
6.12 Outbound tourism expenditure over imports of goods		Percent	9.1	7.9	8.7	6.7	6.9
6.13 Outbound tourism expenditure over imports of services		Percent	25.1	20.5	23.2	20.4	16.9
6.14 Outbound tourism expenditure over imports of goods and services		Percent	6.7	5.7	6.3	5.1	4.9
6.15 Outbound tourism expenditure over current account debits		Percent	6.3	5.4	5.9	4.6	4.4

347

SIERRA LEONE

Basic data and indicators	Notes	Units	2005	2006	2007	2008	2009
1. INBOUND TOURISM							
Data							
Arrivals							
1.1 Total		('000)	..	..	..	..	..
1.2 ♦ Overnight visitors (tourists)	(1)	('000)	40	34	32	36	37
1.3 ♦ Same-day visitors (excursionists)		('000)	..	..	..	..	..
1.4 * of which, cruise passengers		('000)	..	..	..	..	..
Arrivals by region	(1)						
1.5 Total		('000)	40	34	32	36	37
1.6 ♦ Africa		('000)	22	10	11	12	13
1.7 ♦ Americas		('000)	5	7	6	7	7
1.8 ♦ East Asia and the Pacific		('000)	2	5	3	3	4
1.9 ♦ Europe		('000)	10	10	11	13	11
1.10 ♦ Middle East		('000)	1	2	1	1	2
1.11 ♦ South Asia		('000)	..	..	..	..	..
1.12 ♦ Other not classified		('000)	..	..	..	..	..
1.13 * of which, nationals residing abroad		('000)	..	..	..	..	..
Arrivals by main purpose	(1)						
1.14 Total		('000)	40	34	32	36	37
1.15 ♦ Personal		('000)	26	21	21	23	21
1.16 * holidays, leisure and recreation		('000)	5	3	4	4	9
1.17 * other personal purposes		('000)	21	18	17	19	12
1.18 ♦ Business and professional		('000)	14	13	11	13	16
Arrivals by mode of transport							
1.19 Total		('000)	40	34	32	36	37
1.20 ♦ Air		('000)	40	34	32	36	37
1.21 ♦ Water		('000)	..	..	..	..	..
1.22 ♦ Land		('000)	..	..	..	..	..
1.23 * railway		('000)	..	..	..	..	..
1.24 * road		('000)	..	..	..	..	..
1.25 * others		('000)	..	..	..	..	..
Accommodation							
Total							
1.29 ♦ Guests		('000)	..	..	..	..	..
1.30 ♦ Overnights		('000)	..	..	..	..	..
Hotels and similar establishments							
1.31 ♦ Guests		('000)	..	..	..	..	..
1.32 ♦ Overnights		('000)	280	236	226	250	257
Expenditure							
1.33 Total		US$ Mn	..	..	..	..	..
1.34 ♦ Travel		US$ Mn	64	23	22	34	25
1.35 ♦ Passenger transport		US$ Mn	..	..	..	..	..
Expenditure by main purpose of the trip							
1.36 Total		US$ Mn	64	23	22	34	25
1.37 ♦ Personal		US$ Mn	42	13	12	23	16
1.38 ♦ Business and professional		US$ Mn	22	10	10	11	9
Indicators							
1.39 Average size of travel party		Persons	..	..	..	..	..
Average length of stay							
1.40 Total		Days	..	..	..	..	..
1.41 ♦ For all commercial accommodation services		Nights	..	..	..	..	..
1.42 * of which, "hotels and similar establishments"		Nights	7.00	7.30	7.00	7.00	7.00
1.43 ♦ For non commercial accommodation services		Days	..	..	..	..	..
1.44 Average expenditure per day		US$	..	..	..	..	..

SIERRA LEONE

Basic data and indicators	Notes	Units	2005	2006	2007	2008	2009
3. OUTBOUND TOURISM							
Data							
Departures							
3.1 Total		('000)	..	..	..	..	..
3.2 ♦ Overnight visitors (tourists)		('000)	63	67	71	73	72
3.3 ♦ Same-day visitors (excursionists)		('000)	..	..	..	..	..
Expenditure							
3.4 Total		US$ Mn	33.6	15.0	17.3	24.4	15.8
3.5 ♦ Travel		US$ Mn	32	12	14	24	13
3.6 ♦ Passenger transport		US$ Mn	1.6	3.0	3.3	0.4	2.8
Expenditure by main purpose of the trip							
3.7 Total		US$ Mn	32	12	14	24	13
3.8 ♦ Personal		US$ Mn	21	4	7	14	6
3.9 ♦ Business and professional		US$ Mn	11	8	7	10	7
4. TOURISM INDUSTRIES							
Data							
Accommodation for visitors in hotels and similar establishments							
Non-monetary data							
4.13 ♦ Number of establishments		Units	..	..	..	..	..
4.14 ♦ Number of rooms	(2)	Units	2,012	2,156	2,654	1,123	2,653
4.15 ♦ Number of bed-places	(2)	Units	2,519	2,642	2,761	1,423	2,997
Indicators							
4.16 Occupancy rate / rooms		Percent	..	..	..	..	..
4.17 Occupancy rate / bed-places		Percent	11.00	23.00	24.00	35.00	36.00
4.18 Average length of stay		Nights	7.00	7.00	7.00	7,00	7.00
4.19 Available capacity (bed-places per 1000 inhabitants)		Units	0.49	0.50	0.51	0.26	0.53
6. COMPLEMENTARY INDICATORS							
Demand							
6.1 Gross travel propensity		Units	..	..	..	..	..
6.2 Carrying capacity (arrivals/population)		Units	0.01	0.01	0.01	0.01	0.01
Macroeconomic indicators related to international tourism							
6.3 Inbound tourism expenditure over GDP		Percent	5.5	..	..	..	..
6.4 Outbound tourism expenditure over GDP		Percent	2.9	..	..	..	..
6.5 Tourism balance (inbound minus outbound tourism expenditure) over GDP		Percent	2.6	..	..	..	..
6.6 Tourism openness (inbound plus outbound tourism expenditure) over GDP		Percent	8.4	..	..	..	..
6.7 Tourism coverage (inbound over outbound tourism expenditure)		Percent	189.5	149.0	126.7	136.6	158.5
6.8 Inbound tourism expenditure over exports of goods		Percent	34.9	8.8	7.7	12.3	9.4
6.9 Inbound tourism expenditure over exports of services		Percent	81.9	54.1	48.9	55.0	48.1
6.10 Inbound tourism expenditure over exports of goods and services		Percent	24.5	7.6	6.6	10.1	7.8
6.11 Inbound tourism expenditure over current account credits		Percent	15.8	5.8	4.6	7.2	5.2
6.12 Outbound tourism expenditure over imports of goods		Percent	9.3	4.4	4.4	5.2	3.1
6.13 Outbound tourism expenditure over imports of services		Percent	37.0	18.0	17.9	19.7	13.8
6.14 Outbound tourism expenditure over imports of goods and services		Percent	7.5	3.5	3.5	4.1	2.5
6.15 Outbound tourism expenditure over current account debits		Percent	6.6	3.1	2.7	3.5	2.4

SINGAPORE

Basic data and indicators	Notes	Units	2005	2006	2007	2008	2009
1. INBOUND TOURISM							
Data							
Arrivals							
1.1 Total	(1)	('000)	8,943	9,751	10,285	10,116	9,683
1.2 ♦ Overnight visitors (tourists)		('000)	7,079	7,588	7,957	7,778	7,489
1.3 ♦ Same-day visitors (excursionists)		('000)	1,864	2,163	2,328	2,338	2,194
1.4 * of which, cruise passengers		('000)	..	..	..	..	..
Arrivals by region	(1)						
1.5 Total		('000)	8,942	9,751	10,285	10,116	9,683
1.6 ♦ Africa		('000)	79	87	94	86	73
1.7 ♦ Americas		('000)	470	510	524	505	468
1.8 ♦ East Asia and the Pacific		('000)	6,445	7,012	7,323	7,070	6,785
1.9 ♦ Europe		('000)	1,136	1,220	1,277	1,334	1,318
1.10 ♦ Middle East		('000)	56	66	78	88	86
1.11 ♦ South Asia		('000)	751	850	968	1,027	953
1.12 ♦ Other not classified		('000)	5	6	21	6	..
1.13 * of which, nationals residing abroad		('000)	..	..	..	..	..
Arrivals by main purpose	(1)						
1.14 Total		('000)	8,943	9,751	10,285	10,116	9,683
1.15 ♦ Personal		('000)	6,394	6,865	7,117	6,950	6,972
1.16 * holidays, leisure and recreation		('000)	2,674	3,579	4,124	3,925	3,486
1.17 * other personal purposes		('000)	3,720	3,286	2,993	3,025	3,486
1.18 ♦ Business and professional		('000)	2,549	2,886	3,168	3,166	2,711
Arrivals by mode of transport	(1)						
1.19 Total		('000)	8,943	9,752	10,285	10,116	9,683
1.20 ♦ Air		('000)	6,267	6,758	7,172	7,234	7,228
1.21 ♦ Water		('000)	1,364	1,571	1,538	1,322	1,154
1.22 ♦ Land		('000)	1,312	1,423	1,575	1,560	1,301
1.23 * railway		('000)	..	..	..	..	..
1.24 * road		('000)	1,312	1,423	1,575	1,560	1,301
1.25 * others		('000)	..	..	..	..	..
Accommodation							
Total							
1.29 ♦ Guests		('000)	..	..	..	..	..
1.30 ♦ Overnights		('000)	..	..	..	..	..
Hotels and similar establishments							
1.31 ♦ Guests		('000)	5,321	5,968	6,304	5,817	5,906
1.32 ♦ Overnights		('000)	..	..	..	..	..
Expenditure							
1.33 Total		US$ Mn	..	..	..	..	..
1.34 ♦ Travel		US$ Mn	6,205	7,545	9,083	10,719	9,200
1.35 ♦ Passenger transport		US$ Mn	..	..	..	..	..
Indicators							
1.39 Average size of travel party		Persons	..	..	..	..	..
Average length of stay							
1.40 Total		Days	..	..	..	..	..
1.41 ♦ For all commercial accommodation services	(2)	Nights	3.38	3.38	3.63	3.96	3.96
1.42 * of which, "hotels and similar establishments"		Nights	..	..	..	..	..
1.43 ♦ For non commercial accommodation services		Days	..	..	..	..	..
1.44 Average expenditure per day		US$	..	..	..	..	..
3. OUTBOUND TOURISM							
Data							
Departures							
3.1 Total		('000)	..	..	..	..	..
3.2 ♦ Overnight visitors (tourists)		('000)	5,159	5,533	6,024	6,828	6,961
3.3 ♦ Same-day visitors (excursionists)		('000)	..	..	..	..	..
Expenditure							
3.4 Total		US$ Mn	..	..	..	..	..
3.5 ♦ Travel		US$ Mn	10,070	11,142	13,164	15,136	15,808
3.6 ♦ Passenger transport		US$ Mn	..	..	..	..	..

SINGAPORE

Basic data and indicators	Notes	Units	2005	2006	2007	2008	2009
4. TOURISM INDUSTRIES							
Data							
Number of establishments							
4.1 Total		Units	..	..	..	..	..
4.2 ♦ Accommodation for visitors		Units	..	..	..	..	..
4.3 * of which, "hotels and similar establishments"	(3)	Units	225	226	226	243	268
4.4 ♦ Food and beverage serving activities		Units	..	..	..	..	..
4.5 ♦ Passenger transportation		Units	..	..	..	..	..
4.6 ♦ Travel agencies and other reservation services activities		Units	..	..	..	..	..
4.7 ♦ Other tourism industries		Units	..	..	..	..	..
Accommodation for visitors in hotels and similar establishments							
Non-monetary data							
4.13 ♦ Number of establishments	(3)	Units	225	226	226	243	268
4.14 ♦ Number of rooms	(3)	Units	36,861	37,198	37,624	39,376	42,719
4.15 ♦ Number of bed-places		Units	..	..	..	..	..
Indicators							
4.16 Occupancy rate / rooms	(4)	Percent	83.80	85.20	87.00	81.00	75.80
4.17 Occupancy rate / bed-places		Percent	..	..	..	..	..
4.18 Average length of stay		Nights	..	..	..	..	..
4.19 Available capacity (bed-places per 1000 inhabitants)		Units	..	..	..	..	..
6. COMPLEMENTARY INDICATORS							
Demand							
6.1 Gross travel propensity		Units	..	..	..	..	..
6.2 Carrying capacity (arrivals/population)		Units	1.66	1.72	1.73	1.61	1.50
Macroeconomic indicators related to international tourism							
6.3 Inbound tourism expenditure over GDP		Percent	5.1	5.4	5.3	5.6	..
6.4 Outbound tourism expenditure over GDP		Percent	8.3	7.9	7.3	7.5	..
6.5 Tourism balance (inbound minus outbound tourism expenditure) over GDP		Percent	-3.2	-2.5	-1.9	-1.9	..
6.6 Tourism openness (inbound plus outbound tourism expenditure) over GDP		Percent	13.4	13.3	12.6	13.2	..
6.7 Tourism coverage (inbound over outbound tourism expenditure)		Percent	61.6	67.9	73.6	74.0	..
6.8 Inbound tourism expenditure over exports of goods		Percent	2.7	2.7	3.0	3.1	..
6.9 Inbound tourism expenditure over exports of services		Percent	11.7	11.8	11.4	12.7	..
6.10 Inbound tourism expenditure over exports of goods and services		Percent	2.2	2.2	2.4	2.5	..
6.11 Inbound tourism expenditure over current account credits		Percent	2.0	2.0	2.1	2.2	..
6.12 Outbound tourism expenditure over imports of goods		Percent	5.1	4.8	4.9	4.5	..
6.13 Outbound tourism expenditure over imports of services		Percent	18.3	17.1	16.6	17.9	..
6.14 Outbound tourism expenditure over imports of goods and services		Percent	4.0	3.7	3.8	3.6	..
6.15 Outbound tourism expenditure over current account debits		Percent	3.5	3.2	3.1	3.1	..

SLOVAKIA

Basic data and indicators	Notes	Units	2005	2006	2007	2008	2009
1. INBOUND TOURISM							
Data							
Arrivals	(1)						
1.1 Total		('000)	16,849	17,781	18,975	19,205	..
1.2 ♦ Overnight visitors (tourists)		('000)	6,184	6,579	7,269	6,643	..
1.3 ♦ Same-day visitors (excursionists)		('000)	10,665	11,202	11,706	12,562	..
1.4 * of which, cruise passengers		('000)	..	..	..	..	..
Arrivals by region	(2)						
1.5 Total		('000)	1,515	1,611	1,685	1,766	1,299
1.6 ♦ Africa		('000)	2	3	2	3	2
1.7 ♦ Americas		('000)	42	39	44	41	30
1.8 ♦ East Asia and the Pacific		('000)	56	69	74	71	54
1.9 ♦ Europe		('000)	1,413	1,499	1,559	1,648	1,210
1.10 ♦ Middle East		('000)	..	..	4	1	1
1.11 ♦ South Asia		('000)	1	..	1	1	1
1.12 ♦ Other not classified		('000)	1	1	1	1	1
1.13 * of which, nationals residing abroad		('000)	..	..	..	..	..
Accommodation							
Total							
1.29 ♦ Guests		('000)	1,515	1,612	1,685	1,767	1,298
1.30 ♦ Overnights		('000)	4,872	5,134	5,199	5,261	3,769
Hotels and similar establishments							
1.31 ♦ Guests		('000)	1,307	1,407	1,458	1,524	1,047
1.32 ♦ Overnights		('000)	4,055	4,362	4,406	4,443	2,908
Expenditure							
1.33 Total		US$ Mn	1,282	1,655	2,352	3,004	2,539
1.34 ♦ Travel		US$ Mn	1,210	1,521	2,026	2,589	2,341
1.35 ♦ Passenger transport		US$ Mn	72	134	326	415	198
Indicators							
1.39 Average size of travel party		Persons	..	..	..	..	..
Average length of stay							
1.40 Total		Days	..	..	..	..	..
1.41 ♦ For all commercial accommodation services		Nights	..	..	..	..	..
1.42 * of which, "hotels and similar establishments"		Nights	3.20	3.20	3.10	3.00	2.90
1.43 ♦ For non commercial accommodation services		Days	..	..	..	..	..
1.44 Average expenditure per day		US$	..	..	..	..	..
2. DOMESTIC TOURISM							
Data							
Trips							
2.1 Total		('000)	5,925	5,927	6,242	5,842	4,996
2.2 ♦ Overnight visitors (tourists)		('000)	..	..	..	..	..
2.3 ♦ Same-day visitors (excursionists)		('000)	..	..	..	..	..
Trips by main purpose							
2.4 Total		('000)	5,924	5,926	6,241	5,842	4,996
2.5 ♦ Personal		('000)	3,848	3,934	4,086	3,895	3,426
2.6 * holidays, leisure and recreation		('000)	1,922	1,829	2,107	1,959	1,764
2.7 * other personal purposes		('000)	1,926	2,105	1,979	1,936	1,662
2.8 ♦ Business and professional		('000)	2,076	1,992	2,155	1,947	1,570
Trips by mode of transport							
2.9 Total		('000)	5,924	5,926	6,241	5,842	4,995
2.10 ♦ Air		('000)	23	23	63	12	12
2.11 ♦ Water		('000)	..	3	8	..	..
2.12 ♦ Land		('000)	5,901	5,900	6,170	5,830	4,983
2.13 * railway		('000)	796	949	952	847	727
2.14 * road		('000)	5,018	4,851	5,187	4,956	4,216
2.15 * others		('000)	87	100	31	27	40
Trips by form of organization							
2.16 Total		('000)	5,925	5,927	6,242	5,842	4,996
2.17 ♦ Package tour		('000)	183	201	178	274	92
2.18 ♦ Other forms		('000)	5,742	5,726	6,064	5,568	4,904
Accommodation							
Total							
2.19 ♦ Guests		('000)	1,913	1,972	2,092	2,316	2,077
2.20 ♦ Overnights		('000)	5,861	6,004	6,368	7,203	6,612
Hotels and similar establishments							
2.21 ♦ Guests		('000)	1,495	1,521	1,585	1,769	1,570
2.22 ♦ Overnights		('000)	3,978	3,936	4,082	4,620	4,168

SLOVAKIA

Basic data and indicators		Notes	Units	2005	2006	2007	2008	2009
	Indicators							
2.23	Average size of travel party		Persons	..	..	..	..	..
	Average length of stay							
2.24	Total		Days	5.25	5.36	5.21	5.43	5.41
2.25	♦ For all commercial accommodation services		Nights	3.10	3.00	3.04	3.11	3.20
2.26	* of which, "hotels and similar establishments"		Nights	3.10	3.00	3.00	3.10	3.20
2.27	♦ For non commercial accommodation services		Days	5.37	5.40	5.27	5.54	5.49
2.28	Average expenditure per day		US$	32.0	32.0	35.0	38.0	41.0

3. OUTBOUND TOURISM

	Data							
	Departures							
3.1	Total		('000)	2,987	3,149	3,603	3,683	3,230
3.2	♦ Overnight visitors (tourists)		('000)	..	..	..	..	..
3.3	♦ Same-day visitors (excursionists)		('000)	..	..	..	..	..
	Expenditure							
3.4	Total		US$ Mn	1,122	1,230	1,825	2,596	2,249
3.5	♦ Travel		US$ Mn	844	1,060	1,533	2,165	2,098
3.6	♦ Passenger transport		US$ Mn	278	170	292	431	151
	Indicators							
3.10	Average length of stay		Days	9.50	8.80	9.00	8.20	8.90
3.11	Average expenditure per day		US$	69.0	73.0	75.0	80.0	73.0

4. TOURISM INDUSTRIES

	Data							
	Number of establishments							
4.1	Total		Units	23,852	23,578	24,733	24,843	25,327
4.2	♦ Accommodation for visitors		Units	2,016	2,043	2,672	2,767	2,677
4.3	* of which, "hotels and similar establishments"		Units	1,252	1,284	1,701	1,744	1,720
4.4	♦ Food and beverage serving activities	(3)	Units	15,155	15,716	16,164	16,098	16,370
4.5	♦ Passenger transportation	(4)	Units	5,805	4,929	5,057	5,150	5,456
4.6	♦ Travel agencies and other reservation services activities		Units	876	890	840	828	824
4.7	♦ Other tourism industries		Units	..	..	..	..	..
	Accommodation for visitors in hotels and similar establishments							
	Monetary data							
4.8	♦ Output		US$ Mn	560.0	628.0	575.0	637.0	..
4.9	♦ Intermediate consumption		US$ Mn	285.0	318.0	302.0	338.0	..
4.10	♦ Gross value added		US$ Mn	274.0	310.0	273.0	299.0	..
4.11	♦ Compensation of employees		US$ Mn	..	..	..	..	..
4.12	♦ Gross fixed capital formation		US$ Mn	..	..	..	..	..
	Non-monetary data							
4.13	♦ Number of establishments		Units	1,252	1,284	1,701	1,744	1,720
4.14	♦ Number of rooms		Units	35,688	35,948	41,569	42,537	43,635
4.15	♦ Number of bed-places		Units	90,093	91,036	105,697	108,792	109,555
	Indicators							
4.16	Occupancy rate / rooms		Percent	..	..	..	..	..
4.17	Occupancy rate / bed-places		Percent	35.00	35.70	33.70	31.90	22.40
4.18	Average length of stay		Nights	2.80	2.80	2.70	2.60	3.10
4.19	Available capacity (bed-places per 1000 inhabitants)		Units	16.72	16.89	19.58	20.12	20.22
	Travel agencies and other reservation service activities							
	Monetary data							
4.20	♦ Output		US$ Mn	521.0	570.0	638.0	733.0	..
4.21	♦ Intermediate consumption		US$ Mn	438.0	478.0	536.0	631.0	..
4.22	♦ Gross value added		US$ Mn	83.0	92.0	102.0	103.0	..
4.23	♦ Compensation of employees		US$ Mn	..	..	..	..	..
4.24	♦ Gross fixed capital formation		US$ Mn	..	..	..	..	..

SLOVAKIA

Basic data and indicators	Notes	Units	2005	2006	2007	2008	2009
5. EMPLOYMENT							
Data							
Number of employees by tourism industries	(5)						
5.1 Total		('000)	95.0	97.0	95.0	..	..
5.2 ♦ Accommodation services for visitors (hotels and similar establishments)		('000)	15.0	15.0	15.0	..	..
5.3 ♦ Other accommodation services		('000)	..	..	..	..	..
5.4 ♦ Food and beverage serving activities		('000)	28.0	31.0	31.0	..	..
5.5 ♦ Passenger transportation		('000)	28.0	28.0	26.0	..	..
5.6 ♦ Travel agencies and other reservation services activities		('000)	4.0	4.0	4.0	..	..
5.7 ♦ Other tourism industries		('000)	20.0	19.0	19.0	..	..
Indicators							
Number of full-time equivalent jobs by status in employment							
5.11 Total		('000)	113.0	114.0	113.0	..	..
5.12 ♦ Employees		('000)	92.0	93.0	93.0	..	..
5.13 * male		('000)	..	..	..	..	..
5.14 * female		('000)	..	..	..	..	..
5.15 ♦ Self employed		('000)	21.0	21.0	20.0	..	..
5.16 * male		('000)	..	..	..	..	..
5.17 * female		('000)	..	..	..	..	..
6. COMPLEMENTARY INDICATORS							
Demand							
6.1 Gross travel propensity	(6)	Units	198.9	201.3	217.0	208.7	179.4
6.2 Carrying capacity (arrivals/population)		Units	0.28	0.30	0.31	0.33	0.24
Macroeconomic indicators related to international tourism							
6.3 Inbound tourism expenditure over GDP		Percent	2.7	3.0	3.1	3.2	..
6.4 Outbound tourism expenditure over GDP		Percent	2.3	2.2	2.4	2.7	..
6.5 Tourism balance (inbound minus outbound tourism expenditure) over GDP		Percent	0.3	0.8	0.7	0.4	..
6.6 Tourism openness (inbound plus outbound tourism expenditure) over GDP		Percent	5.0	5.2	5.6	5.9	..
6.7 Tourism coverage (inbound over outbound tourism expenditure)		Percent	114.2	134.6	128.9	115.7	112.9
6.8 Inbound tourism expenditure over exports of goods		Percent	4.0	4.0	4.1	4.3	4.6
6.9 Inbound tourism expenditure over exports of services		Percent	29.1	30.4	33.3	35.4	40.4
6.10 Inbound tourism expenditure over exports of goods and services		Percent	3.5	3.5	3.6	3.8	4.1
6.11 Inbound tourism expenditure over current account credits		Percent	3.3	3.3	3.4	3.5	3.8
6.12 Outbound tourism expenditure over imports of goods		Percent	3.3	2.8	3.1	3.6	4.2
6.13 Outbound tourism expenditure over imports of services		Percent	27.5	26.3	28.0	28.3	28.1
6.14 Outbound tourism expenditure over imports of goods and services		Percent	2.9	2.5	2.8	3.2	3.6
6.15 Outbound tourism expenditure over current account debits		Percent	2.6	2.2	2.5	2.9	3.3

SLOVENIA

Basic data and indicators	Notes	Units	2005	2006	2007	2008	2009
1. INBOUND TOURISM							
Data							
Arrivals							
1.1 Total	(1)	('000)	60,230	58,274	61,293	..	..
1.2 ♦ Overnight visitors (tourists)	(2)	('000)	1,555	1,617	1,751	1,958	1,824
1.3 ♦ Same-day visitors (excursionists)		('000)	..	..	..	..	..
1.4 * of which, cruise passengers		('000)	..	..	..	..	..
Arrivals by region	(2)						
1.5 Total		('000)	1,555	1,616	1,751	1,959	1,824
1.6 ♦ Africa		('000)	2	1	2	4	3
1.7 ♦ Americas		('000)	59	67	67	66	55
1.8 ♦ East Asia and the Pacific		('000)	40	52	65	86	90
1.9 ♦ Europe		('000)	1,454	1,496	1,617	1,803	1,676
1.10 ♦ Middle East		('000)	..	..	..	..	..
1.11 ♦ South Asia		('000)	..	..	..	..	..
1.12 ♦ Other not classified		('000)	..	..	..	..	..
1.13 * of which, nationals residing abroad		('000)	..	..	..	..	..
Arrivals by main purpose	(3)						
1.14 Total		('000)	1,554	1,617	1,751	1,958	1,824
1.15 ♦ Personal		('000)	1,245	1,303	1,411	1,578	1,580
1.16 * holidays, leisure and recreation		('000)	1,012	940	1,018	1,139	1,295
1.17 * other personal purposes		('000)	233	363	393	439	285
1.18 ♦ Business and professional		('000)	309	314	340	380	244
Arrivals by mode of transport	(3)						
1.19 Total		('000)	1,555	1,617	1,751	1,958	1,824
1.20 ♦ Air		('000)	298	336	364	407	390
1.21 ♦ Water		('000)	2	2	2	2	..
1.22 ♦ Land		('000)	1,255	1,279	1,385	1,549	1,434
1.23 * railway		('000)	47	54	58	65	55
1.24 * road		('000)	1,208	1,225	1,327	1,484	1,379
1.25 * others		('000)	..	..	..	..	..
Arrivals by form of organization of the trip	(3)						
1.26 Total		('000)	1,555	1,617	1,751	1,958	1,824
1.27 ♦ Package tour		('000)	196	184	200	223	243
1.28 ♦ Other forms		('000)	1,359	1,433	1,551	1,735	1,581
Accommodation	(2)						
Total							
1.29 ♦ Guests		('000)	1,555	1,617	1,751	1,958	1,824
1.30 ♦ Overnights		('000)	4,399	4,489	4,868	5,351	4,936
Hotels and similar establishments							
1.31 ♦ Guests		('000)	1,192	1,247	1,354	1,532	1,411
1.32 ♦ Overnights		('000)	3,322	3,401	3,707	4,051	3,684
Expenditure							
1.33 Total		US$ Mn	1,894	1,911	2,465	3,095	2,733
1.34 ♦ Travel		US$ Mn	1,795	1,797	2,283	2,837	2,518
1.35 ♦ Passenger transport		US$ Mn	99	114	182	258	215
Expenditure by main purpose of the trip							
1.36 Total		US$ Mn	..	1,797	2,282	2,837	2,518
1.37 ♦ Personal		US$ Mn	..	1,718	2,184	2,722	2,412
1.38 ♦ Business and professional		US$ Mn	..	79	98	115	106
Indicators							
1.39 Average size of travel party	(4)	Persons	..	..	..	..	2.4
Average length of stay	(2)						
1.40 Total		Days	..	..	..	..	..
1.41 ♦ For all commercial accommodation services		Nights	2.80	2.78	2.78	2.73	2.71
1.42 * of which, "hotels and similar establishments"		Nights	2.79	2.73	2.74	2.64	2.61
1.43 ♦ For non commercial accommodation services		Days	..	..	..	..	..
1.44 Average expenditure per day	(4)	US$	..	..	..	..	148.4
2. DOMESTIC TOURISM							
Data							
Trips	(5)						
2.1 Total		('000)	..	..	..	..	..
2.2 ♦ Overnight visitors (tourists)		('000)	1,939	2,744	1,757	1,929	2,364
2.3 ♦ Same-day visitors (excursionists)		('000)	..	..	..	..	..
Trips by main purpose	(5)						
2.4 Total		('000)	1,940	2,744	1,756	1,928	2,364
2.5 ♦ Personal		('000)	1,780	2,569	1,632	1,795	2,230
2.6 * holidays, leisure and recreation		('000)	1,529	2,168	1,333	1,472	1,852
2.7 * other personal purposes		('000)	251	401	299	323	378
2.8 ♦ Business and professional		('000)	160	175	124	133	134

SLOVENIA

Basic data and indicators	Notes	Units	2005	2006	2007	2008	2009
Trips by mode of transport	(5)						
2.9 Total		('000)	1,937	2,739	1,752	1,929	2,364
2.10 ♦ Air		('000)	..	..	..	..	..
2.11 ♦ Water		('000)	..	..	..	..	..
2.12 ♦ Land		('000)	1,937	2,739	1,752	1,929	2,364
2.13 * railway		('000)	54	90	67	61	65
2.14 * road		('000)	1,883	2,649	1,685	1,868	2,299
2.15 * others		('000)	..	..	..	..	..
Trips by form of organization	(5)						
2.16 Total		('000)	1,939	2,743	1,756	1,929	2,364
2.17 ♦ Package tour		('000)	5	6	9	9	13
2.18 ♦ Other forms		('000)	1,934	2,737	1,747	1,920	2,351
Accommodation	(2)						
Total							
2.19 ♦ Guests		('000)	840	868	930	1,126	1,161
2.20 ♦ Overnights		('000)	3,171	3,233	3,393	3,963	4,077
Hotels and similar establishments							
2.21 ♦ Guests		('000)	459	484	523	643	648
2.22 ♦ Overnights		('000)	1,653	1,746	1,839	2,175	2,234
Indicators							
2.23 Average size of travel party	(6)	Persons	2.5	2.4	2.4	2.4	2.2
Average length of stay							
2.24 Total	(7)	Days	3.08	2.74	3.02	2.96	2.87
2.25 ♦ For all commercial accommodation services		Nights	3.71	3.69	3.78	3.64	3.51
2.26 * of which, "hotels and similar establishments"		Nights	3.48	3.59	3.78	3.42	3.45
2.27 ♦ For non commercial accommodation services	(7)	Days	2.53	2.16	2.27	2.44	2.43
2.28 Average expenditure per day		US$	30.9	34.0	48.8	51.9	53.8
3. OUTBOUND TOURISM							
Data							
Departures							
3.1 Total		('000)	6,736	6,814	5,569	5,490	5,575
3.2 ♦ Overnight visitors (tourists)		('000)	2,660	2,680	2,496	2,459	2,586
3.3 ♦ Same-day visitors (excursionists)		('000)	4,076	4,134	3,073	3,031	2,989
Expenditure							
3.4 Total		US$ Mn	1,019	1,058	1,260	1,648	1,533
3.5 ♦ Travel		US$ Mn	950	974	1,144	1,395	1,355
3.6 ♦ Passenger transport		US$ Mn	69	84	116	253	178
Expenditure by main purpose of the trip							
3.7 Total		US$ Mn	949	974	1,144	1,395	1,355
3.8 ♦ Personal		US$ Mn	838	752	849	1,010	1,045
3.9 ♦ Business and professional		US$ Mn	111	222	295	385	310
Indicators							
3.10 Average length of stay	(7)	Days	5.30	5.70	5.60	5.60	5.60
3.11 Average expenditure per day		US$	58.0	60.1	82.9	95.5	94.4
4. TOURISM INDUSTRIES							
Data							
Number of establishments	(8)						
4.1 Total		Units	7,088	7,703	7,985	9,386	..
4.2 ♦ Accommodation for visitors	(9)	Units	636	722	798	888	..
4.3 * of which, "hotels and similar establishments"		Units	248	296	310	335	..
4.4 ♦ Food and beverage serving activities		Units	6,021	6,517	6,672	6,725	..
4.5 ♦ Passenger transportation		Units	..	..	..	1,214	..
4.6 ♦ Travel agencies and other reservation services activities		Units	431	464	515	559	..
4.7 ♦ Other tourism industries		Units	..	..	..	..	..
Accommodation for visitors in hotels and similar establishments							
Monetary data	(8)						
4.8 ♦ Output		US$ Mn	438.5	501.9	602.1	725.5	..
4.9 ♦ Intermediate consumption		US$ Mn	207.8	277.1	289.1	365.8	..
4.10 ♦ Gross value added		US$ Mn	230.6	224.8	313.0	359.7	..
4.11 ♦ Compensation of employees		US$ Mn	159.9	175.9	202.4	248.3	..
4.12 ♦ Gross fixed capital formation		US$ Mn	120.1	170.3	271.6	339.3	..
Non-monetary data	(2)						
4.13 ♦ Number of establishments		Units	344	358	396	652	667
4.14 ♦ Number of rooms		Units	15,811	16,402	17,251	21,720	22,004
4.15 ♦ Number of bed-places		Units	33,151	34,415	36,247	48,282	48,627

SLOVENIA

Basic data and indicators	Notes	Units	2005	2006	2007	2008	2009
Indicators	(2)						
4.16 Occupancy rate / rooms		Percent	..	..	..	..	..
4.17 Occupancy rate / bed-places		Percent	47.56	47.58	47.42	43.90	39.76
4.18 Average length of stay		Nights	3.01	2.97	2.96	2.86	2.87
4.19 Available capacity (bed-places per 1000 inhabitants)		Units	16.60	17.18	18.03	23.83	23.93
Travel agencies and other reservation service activities							
Monetary data	(8)						
4.20 ♦ Output		US$ Mn	363.1	407.0	562.4	636.6	..
4.21 ♦ Intermediate consumption		US$ Mn	320.9	359.3	489.0	574.4	..
4.22 ♦ Gross value added		US$ Mn	42.2	47.7	73.4	62.2	..
4.23 ♦ Compensation of employees		US$ Mn	31.1	38.9	46.2	51.6	..
4.24 ♦ Gross fixed capital formation		US$ Mn	8.4	14.6	13.8	6.9	..
5. EMPLOYMENT							
Data							
Number of employees by tourism industries	(10)						
5.1 Total		('000)	50.8	52.0	54.2	57.1	52.6
5.2 ♦ Accommodation services for visitors (hotels and similar establishments)		('000)	8.5	8.7	9.4	9.7	9.4
5.3 ♦ Other accommodation services		('000)	1.2	1.2	1.2	1.2	1.2
5.4 ♦ Food and beverage serving activities		('000)	21.4	21.8	22.3	23.1	22.9
5.5 ♦ Passenger transportation		('000)	7.6	7.6	7.8	9.2	6.5
5.6 ♦ Travel agencies and other reservation services activities		('000)	1.8	1.8	2.0	2.1	1.8
5.7 ♦ Other tourism industries		('000)	10.3	10.9	11.4	11.9	10.8
Number of jobs by status in employment	(10)						
5.8 Total		('000)	50.8	52.0	54.2	57.1	52.6
5.9 ♦ Employees		('000)	43.0	44.0	46.0	48.4	44.2
5.10 ♦ Self employed		('000)	7.8	8.0	8.2	8.7	8.4
Indicators							
Number of full-time equivalent jobs by status in employment	(10)(11)						
5.11 Total		('000)	50.8	52.0	54.2	57.1	52.6
5.12 ♦ Employees		('000)	43.0	44.0	46.0	48.4	44.2
5.13 * male		('000)	20.4	20.8	21.6	23.1	20.5
5.14 * female		('000)	22.5	23.2	24.4	25.3	23.7
5.15 ♦ Self employed		('000)	7.8	8.0	8.2	8.7	8.4
5.16 * male		('000)	4.8	4.9	5.0	5.3	5.1
5.17 * female		('000)	3.1	3.2	3.2	3.3	3.3
6. COMPLEMENTARY INDICATORS							
Demand							
6.1 Gross travel propensity	(5)	Units	2.7	3.1	2.5	2.5	2.8
6.2 Carrying capacity (arrivals/population)	(2)	Units	1.20	1.24	1.33	1.52	1.47
Macroeconomic indicators related to international tourism							
6.3 Inbound tourism expenditure over GDP		Percent	5.3	4.9	5.2	5.7	5.6
6.4 Outbound tourism expenditure over GDP		Percent	2.9	2.7	2.7	3.0	3.2
6.5 Tourism balance (inbound minus outbound tourism expenditure) over GDP		Percent	2.5	2.2	2.5	2.7	2.5
6.6 Tourism openness (inbound plus outbound tourism expenditure) over GDP		Percent	8.2	7.7	7.9	8.7	8.8
6.7 Tourism coverage (inbound over outbound tourism expenditure)		Percent	186.0	180.5	195.6	187.8	178.3
6.8 Inbound tourism expenditure over exports of goods		Percent	10.4	8.9	9.1	10.5	12.1
6.9 Inbound tourism expenditure over exports of services		Percent	47.6	44.0	43.3	41.7	45.5
6.10 Inbound tourism expenditure over exports of goods and services		Percent	8.6	7.4	7.5	8.4	9.6
6.11 Inbound tourism expenditure over current account credits		Percent	8.0	6.9	6.9	7.7	8.9
6.12 Outbound tourism expenditure over imports of goods		Percent	5.2	4.6	4.3	4.9	6.5
6.13 Outbound tourism expenditure over imports of services		Percent	34.9	32.5	29.6	31.6	34.4
6.14 Outbound tourism expenditure over imports of goods and services		Percent	4.6	4.1	3.7	4.3	5.5
6.15 Outbound tourism expenditure over current account debits		Percent	4.2	3.7	3.3	3.8	4.9

SOLOMON ISLANDS

Basic data and indicators	Notes	Units	2005	2006	2007	2008	2009
1. INBOUND TOURISM							
Data							
Arrivals							
1.1 Total		('000)	..	..	..	..	..
1.2 ♦ Overnight visitors (tourists)	(1)	('000)	9.4	11.5	13.7	16.3	18.3
1.3 ♦ Same-day visitors (excursionists)		('000)	1.2	1.2	1.4	..	..
1.4 * of which, cruise passengers		('000)	..	..	..	..	..
Arrivals by region							
1.5 Total		('000)	9.3	11.5	13.7	16.3	18.3
1.6 ♦ Africa		('000)	..	..	..	..	..
1.7 ♦ Americas		('000)	0.6	0.9	1.0	1.2	1.2
1.8 ♦ East Asia and the Pacific		('000)	8.1	9.8	11.6	13.8	15.9
1.9 ♦ Europe		('000)	0.5	0.7	0.9	1.1	1.1
1.10 ♦ Middle East		('000)	..	..	..	..	..
1.11 ♦ South Asia		('000)	..	..	..	..	..
1.12 ♦ Other not classified		('000)	0.1	0.1	0.2	0.2	0.1
1.13 * of which, nationals residing abroad		('000)	..	..	..	..	..
Arrivals by main purpose							
1.14 Total		('000)	..	11.5	13.7	16.2	18.3
1.15 ♦ Personal		('000)	2.9	6.1	7.5	9.7	10.8
1.16 * holidays, leisure and recreation		('000)	2.9	3.1	3.8	5.1	5.3
1.17 * other personal purposes		('000)	..	3.0	3.7	4.6	5.5
1.18 ♦ Business and professional		('000)	..	5.4	6.2	6.5	7.5
Arrivals by mode of transport							
1.19 Total		('000)	9.4	11.5	13.7	16.3	18.3
1.20 ♦ Air		('000)	9.4	11.5	13.7	16.3	18.3
1.21 ♦ Water		('000)	..	..	..	..	..
1.22 ♦ Land		('000)	..	..	..	..	..
1.23 * railway		('000)	..	..	..	..	..
1.24 * road		('000)	..	..	..	..	..
1.25 * others		('000)	..	..	..	..	..
Expenditure							
1.33 Total		US$ Mn	6.4	35.3	37.8	40.6	52.4
1.34 ♦ Travel		US$ Mn	1.6	25.5	27.3	36.9	44.1
1.35 ♦ Passenger transport		US$ Mn	4.8	9.8	10.5	3.7	8.3
Expenditure by main purpose of the trip							
1.36 Total		US$ Mn	1.6	25.5	27.3	36.9	44.1
1.37 ♦ Personal		US$ Mn	1.3	11.1	12.5	18.8	23.0
1.38 ♦ Business and professional		US$ Mn	0.3	14.4	14.8	18.1	21.1
Indicators							
1.39 Average size of travel party		Persons	..	..	..	..	..
Average length of stay							
1.40 Total		Days	19.00	17.00	14.00	14.00	14.00
1.41 ♦ For all commercial accommodation services		Nights	..	..	..	..	..
1.42 * of which, "hotels and similar establishments"		Nights	..	..	..	..	..
1.43 ♦ For non commercial accommodation services		Days	..	..	..	..	..
1.44 Average expenditure per day		US$	..	..	174.3	172.2	165.7
3. OUTBOUND TOURISM							
Data							
Expenditure							
3.4 Total		US$ Mn	11.2	26.5	35.6	40.5	37.7
3.5 ♦ Travel		US$ Mn	4.7	22.2	29.0	34.0	31.7
3.6 ♦ Passenger transport		US$ Mn	6.5	4.3	6.6	6.5	6.0
Expenditure by main purpose of the trip							
3.7 Total		US$ Mn	4.7	22.2	29.0	34.0	31.7
3.8 ♦ Personal		US$ Mn	3	12	17	21	19
3.9 ♦ Business and professional		US$ Mn	1.5	10.0	11.8	12.6	12.7

SOLOMON ISLANDS

Basic data and indicators	Notes	Units	2005	2006	2007	2008	2009
4. TOURISM INDUSTRIES							
Data							
Accommodation for visitors in hotels and similar establishments							
Non-monetary data							
4.13 ♦ Number of establishments		Units	..	..	..	..	..
4.14 ♦ Number of rooms		Units	..	988	1,258	1,324	..
4.15 ♦ Number of bed-places		Units	..	2,306	2,574	2,544	..
Indicators							
4.16 Occupancy rate / rooms		Percent	..	..	..	..	..
4.17 Occupancy rate / bed-places		Percent	..	..	..	..	..
4.18 Average length of stay		Nights	19.00	17.00	14.00	14.00	..
4.19 Available capacity (bed-places per 1000 inhabitants)		Units	..	4.75	5.17	4.98	..
6. COMPLEMENTARY INDICATORS							
Demand							
6.1 Gross travel propensity		Units	..	..	..	..	..
6.2 Carrying capacity (arrivals/population)		Units	0.02	0.02	0.03	0.03	0.03
Macroeconomic indicators related to international tourism							
6.3 Inbound tourism expenditure over GDP		Percent	..	..	..	..	..
6.4 Outbound tourism expenditure over GDP		Percent	..	..	..	..	..
6.5 Tourism balance (inbound minus outbound tourism expenditure) over GDP		Percent				..	
6.6 Tourism openness (inbound plus outbound tourism expenditure) over GDP		Percent	..	..	..	..	..
6.7 Tourism coverage (inbound over outbound tourism expenditure)		Percent	56.5	133.4	106.4	100.2	138.8
6.8 Inbound tourism expenditure over exports of goods		Percent	6.0	31.0	23.0	19.3	32.0
6.9 Inbound tourism expenditure over exports of services		Percent	15.3	66.6	64.2	68.8	72.2
6.10 Inbound tourism expenditure over exports of goods and services		Percent	4.3	21.1	16.9	15.1	22.2
6.11 Inbound tourism expenditure over current account credits		Percent	3.2	13.4	11.2	9.8	14.2
6.12 Outbound tourism expenditure over imports of goods		Percent	6.0	13.5	13.6	13.8	15.8
6.13 Outbound tourism expenditure over imports of services		Percent	19.3	38.9	36.8	35.0	38.1
6.14 Outbound tourism expenditure over imports of goods and services		Percent	4.6	10.0	9.9	9.9	11.2
6.15 Outbound tourism expenditure over current account debits		Percent	3.9	8.7	8.5	7.5	7.7

SOUTH AFRICA

Basic data and indicators	Notes	Units	2005	2006	2007	2008	2009
1. INBOUND TOURISM							
Data							
Arrivals							
1.1 Total	(1)	('000)	7,518	8,509	9,208	9,729	10,098
1.2 ♦ Overnight visitors (tourists)	(2)	('000)	7,369	8,396	9,091	9,592	9,934
1.3 ♦ Same-day visitors (excursionists)		('000)	..	..	..	..	..
1.4 * of which, cruise passengers		('000)	..	..	..	..	..
Arrivals by region	(2)						
1.5 Total		('000)	7,369	8,396	9,091	9,592	9,934
1.6 ♦ Africa		('000)	5,370	6,281	6,862	7,344	7,758
1.7 ♦ Americas		('000)	322	358	387	407	380
1.8 ♦ East Asia and the Pacific		('000)	239	258	282	271	261
1.9 ♦ Europe		('000)	1,329	1,403	1,438	1,434	1,373
1.10 ♦ Middle East		('000)	17	20	21	23	25
1.11 ♦ South Asia		('000)	36	44	52	52	61
1.12 ♦ Other not classified		('000)	56	32	49	61	76
1.13 * of which, nationals residing abroad		('000)	..	..	..	..	..
Arrivals by main purpose	(2)						
1.14 Total		('000)	7,369	8,396	9,091	9,592	9,934
1.15 ♦ Personal		('000)	7,034	8,072	8,781	9,297	9,713
1.16 * holidays, leisure and recreation		('000)	6,812	7,859	8,572	9,081	9,484
1.17 * other personal purposes		('000)	222	213	209	216	229
1.18 ♦ Business and professional		('000)	335	324	310	295	221
Arrivals by mode of transport	(1)						
1.19 Total		('000)	7,518	8,509	9,208	9,729	10,099
1.20 ♦ Air		('000)	2,127	2,318	2,501	2,581	2,489
1.21 ♦ Water		('000)	3	7	5	2	2
1.22 ♦ Land		('000)	5,388	6,184	6,702	7,146	7,608
1.23 * railway		('000)	2	2	1	1	10
1.24 * road		('000)	5,209	5,961	6,320	6,960	7,394
1.25 * others		('000)	177	221	381	185	204
Expenditure							
1.33 Total		US$ Mn	8,629	9,211	10,226	9,178	8,683
1.34 ♦ Travel		US$ Mn	7,516	8,120	8,779	7,956	7,624
1.35 ♦ Passenger transport		US$ Mn	1,113	1,091	1,447	1,222	1,059
Expenditure by main purpose of the trip							
1.36 Total		US$ Mn	7,516	8,120	8,779	7,956	7,624
1.37 ♦ Personal		US$ Mn	6,251	6,749	7,231	6,565	6,211
1.38 ♦ Business and professional		US$ Mn	1,265	1,371	1,548	1,391	1,413
3. OUTBOUND TOURISM							
Data							
Departures							
3.1 Total		('000)	..	..	..	..	..
3.2 ♦ Overnight visitors (tourists)		('000)	..	4,339	4,433	4,429	4,424
3.3 ♦ Same-day visitors (excursionists)		('000)	..	..	..	..	..
Expenditure							
3.4 Total		US$ Mn	4,812	5,230	6,103	6,904	6,420
3.5 ♦ Travel		US$ Mn	3,374	3,384	3,927	4,404	4,151
3.6 ♦ Passenger transport		US$ Mn	1,438	1,846	2,176	2,500	2,269
Expenditure by main purpose of the trip							
3.7 Total		US$ Mn	3,374	3,384	3,927	4,404	4,151
3.8 ♦ Personal		US$ Mn	2,442	2,409	2,790	3,112	2,943
3.9 ♦ Business and professional		US$ Mn	932	975	1,137	1,292	1,208

SOUTH AFRICA

Basic data and indicators	Notes	Units	2005	2006	2007	2008	2009
4. TOURISM INDUSTRIES							
Data							
Number of establishments							
4.1 Total		Units	..	..	40,969	48,388	50,536
4.2 ♦ Accommodation for visitors		Units	..	..	9,256	9,387	10,175
4.3 * of which, "hotels and similar establishments"		Units	..	..	2,555	2,584	2,813
4.4 ♦ Food and beverage serving activities		Units	..	..	21,507	21,763	22,293
4.5 ♦ Passenger transportation		Units	..	..	1,880	6,924	7,178
4.6 ♦ Travel agencies and other reservation services activities		Units	..	..	2,158	1,834	2,023
4.7 ♦ Other tourism industries		Units	..	..	6,168	8,480	8,867
Accommodation for visitors in hotels and similar establishments							
Non-monetary data							
4.13 ♦ Number of establishments		Units	..	..	2,555	2,584	2,813
4.14 ♦ Number of rooms	(3)	Units	67,700	64,600	64,400	65,000	..
4.15 ♦ Number of bed-places		Units	..	..	..	..	..
Indicators							
4.16 Occupancy rate / rooms	(4)	Percent	56.00	59.29	57.70	..	..
4.17 Occupancy rate / bed-places		Percent	..	..	..	..	..
4.18 Average length of stay		Nights	8.40	8.20	7.90	8.20	7.50
4.19 Available capacity (bed-places per 1000 inhabitants)		Units	..	..	..	..	..
5. EMPLOYMENT							
Data							
Number of employees by tourism industries	(5)						
5.1 Total		('000)	507.4	553.7	569.7	599.4	..
5.2 ♦ Accommodation services for visitors (hotels and similar establishments)		('000)	101.6	100.0	108.6	109.8	..
5.3 ♦ Other accommodation services		('000)	..	..	..	..	..
5.4 ♦ Food and beverage serving activities		('000)	79.7	104.3	105.8	107.5	..
5.5 ♦ Passenger transportation		('000)	179.4	192.8	191.2	212.8	..
5.6 ♦ Travel agencies and other reservation services activities		('000)	22.9	15.6	16.6	19.8	..
5.7 ♦ Other tourism industries		('000)	123.8	141.0	147.4	149.6	..
6. COMPLEMENTARY INDICATORS							
Demand							
6.1 Gross travel propensity		Units	..	..	..	..	..
6.2 Carrying capacity (arrivals/population)		Units	0.16	0.18	0.19	0.20	0.20
Macroeconomic indicators related to international tourism							
6.3 Inbound tourism expenditure over GDP		Percent	3.5	3.5	3.6	3.3	3.0
6.4 Outbound tourism expenditure over GDP		Percent	1.9	2.0	2.1	2.5	2.2
6.5 Tourism balance (inbound minus outbound tourism expenditure) over GDP		Percent	1.5	1.5	1.4	0.8	0.8
6.6 Tourism openness (inbound plus outbound tourism expenditure) over GDP		Percent	5.4	5.5	5.7	5.8	5.3
6.7 Tourism coverage (inbound over outbound tourism expenditure)		Percent	179.3	176.1	167.6	132.9	135.2
6.8 Inbound tourism expenditure over exports of goods		Percent	15.3	14.0	13.5	10.7	13.0
6.9 Inbound tourism expenditure over exports of services		Percent	76.4	75.4	74.0	71.7	72.3
6.10 Inbound tourism expenditure over exports of goods and services		Percent	12.8	11.8	11.4	9.3	11.1
6.11 Inbound tourism expenditure over current account credits		Percent	11.8	10.8	10.5	8.6	10.4
6.12 Outbound tourism expenditure over imports of goods		Percent	8.5	7.5	7.5	7.6	9.7
6.13 Outbound tourism expenditure over imports of services		Percent	39.7	36.7	37.1	40.7	43.5
6.14 Outbound tourism expenditure over imports of goods and services		Percent	7.0	6.2	6.2	6.4	7.9
6.15 Outbound tourism expenditure over current account debits		Percent	5.9	5.3	5.2	5.5	6.8

SPAIN

Basic data and indicators	Notes	Units	2005	2006	2007	2008	2009
1. INBOUND TOURISM							
Data							
Arrivals	(1)						
1.1 Total		('000)	92,563	96,152	98,907	97,670	91,899
1.2 ♦ Overnight visitors (tourists)		('000)	55,914	58,004	58,666	57,192	52,178
1.3 ♦ Same-day visitors (excursionists)		('000)	36,649	38,148	40,241	40,478	39,721
1.4 * of which, cruise passengers		('000)	..	..	..	..	..
Arrivals by region	(1)						
1.5 Total		('000)	55,914	58,004	58,666	57,192	52,178
1.6 ♦ Africa		('000)	..	..	..	..	..
1.7 ♦ Americas		('000)	2,233	2,378	2,313	2,398	2,574
1.8 ♦ East Asia and the Pacific	(2)	('000)	181	255	346	237	230
1.9 ♦ Europe		('000)	52,190	54,313	54,927	53,512	47,668
1.10 ♦ Middle East		('000)	..	..	..	..	..
1.11 ♦ South Asia		('000)	..	..	..	..	..
1.12 ♦ Other not classified		('000)	1,310	1,058	1,080	1,045	1,706
1.13 * of which, nationals residing abroad		('000)	..	..	..	..	..
Arrivals by main purpose	(1)						
1.14 Total		('000)	55,913	58,005	58,666	57,192	52,178
1.15 ♦ Personal		('000)	49,973	53,090	53,391	51,921	47,842
1.16 * holidays, leisure and recreation		('000)	43,898	46,990	47,752	46,733	42,497
1.17 * other personal purposes		('000)	6,075	6,100	5,639	5,188	5,345
1.18 ♦ Business and professional		('000)	5,940	4,915	5,275	5,271	4,336
Arrivals by mode of transport	(1)						
1.19 Total		('000)	55,913	58,005	58,665	57,192	52,178
1.20 ♦ Air		('000)	40,730	42,445	44,324	44,397	40,233
1.21 ♦ Water		('000)	1,772	1,460	1,456	1,452	1,398
1.22 ♦ Land		('000)	13,411	14,100	12,885	11,343	10,547
1.23 * railway		('000)	290	281	146	143	139
1.24 * road		('000)	13,121	13,819	12,739	11,200	10,408
1.25 * others		('000)	..	..	..	..	..
Arrivals by form of organization of the trip							
1.26 Total		('000)	55,913	58,005	58,666	57,192	52,228
1.27 ♦ Package tour		('000)	20,391	19,651	17,871	17,071	15,524
1.28 ♦ Other forms		('000)	35,522	38,354	40,795	40,121	36,704
Accommodation							
Total							
1.29 ♦ Guests	(3)	('000)	37,407	43,114	44,036	43,728	39,204
1.30 ♦ Overnights	(3)	('000)	209,518	224,067	225,008	223,773	200,552
Hotels and similar establishments							
1.31 ♦ Guests	(4)	('000)	29,029	34,412	35,783	35,758	32,002
1.32 ♦ Overnights	(4)	('000)	138,762	151,940	155,093	155,364	141,228
Expenditure							
1.33 Total		US$ Mn	53,066	57,543	65,020	70,244	58,586
1.34 ♦ Travel		US$ Mn	47,789	51,297	57,734	61,978	53,337
1.35 ♦ Passenger transport		US$ Mn	5,277	6,246	7,286	8,266	5,249
Indicators							
1.39 Average size of travel party		Persons	..	..	..	..	..
Average length of stay							
1.40 Total		Days	9.70	9.50	9.30	9.50	9.70
1.41 ♦ For all commercial accommodation services		Nights	7.60	7.20	7.00	7.00	7.10
1.42 * of which, "hotels and similar establishments"	(4)	Nights	5.60	5.20	5.11	5.12	..
1.43 ♦ For non commercial accommodation services		Days	13.20	13.20	13.30	14.00	13.80
1.44 Average expenditure per day		US$	109.6	113.5	129.3	139.7	132.9
2. DOMESTIC TOURISM							
Data							
Trips							
2.1 Total		('000)	..	..	355,554.5	392,901.2	369,397.3
2.2 ♦ Overnight visitors (tourists)		('000)	157,005.4	154,968.4	146,781.7	157,614.5	158,876.1
2.3 ♦ Same-day visitors (excursionists)		('000)	..	..	208,772.8	235,286.7	210,521.2
Trips by main purpose							
2.4 Total		('000)	157,005.4	154,968.4	146,781.7	157,614.5	158,876.1
2.5 ♦ Personal		('000)	138,420.1	136,121.5	123,273.5	132,455.1	136,129.5
2.6 * holidays, leisure and recreation		('000)	77,047.5	80,669.5	76,602.8	82,023.2	85,935.0
2.7 * other personal purposes		('000)	61,372.6	55,452.0	46,670.7	50,431.9	50,194.5
2.8 ♦ Business and professional		('000)	18,585.2	18,846.9	23,508.2	25,159.4	22,746.6

SPAIN

Basic data and indicators	Notes	Units	2005	2006	2007	2008	2009
Trips by mode of transport							
2.9 Total		('000)	157,005.4	154,968.4	146,781.7	157,614.5	158,876.1
2.10 ♦ Air		('000)	6,866.7	7,053.9	8,376.4	8,203.8	8,175.5
2.11 ♦ Water		('000)	1,372.6	1,058.6	1,120.2	990.9	1,094.6
2.12 ♦ Land		('000)	148,766.1	146,855.9	137,285.2	148,419.9	149,605.9
2.13 * railway		('000)	6,096.2	6,496.4	5,839.2	6,544.5	6,770.0
2.14 * road		('000)	140,549.3	138,018.2	129,637.7	140,767.4	141,273.0
2.15 * others		('000)	2,120.6	2,341.3	1,808.3	1,108.1	1,562.9
Trips by form of organization							
2.16 Total		('000)	157,005.4	154,968.4	146,781.7	157,614.5	158,876.1
2.17 ♦ Package tour		('000)	3,195.3	3,731.2	3,227.9	3,207.9	2,825.7
2.18 ♦ Other forms		('000)	153,810.0	151,237.2	143,553.8	154,406.6	156,050.4
Accommodation							
Total							
2.19 ♦ Guests	(3)	('000)	50,152	56,727	58,117	56,429	54,470
2.20 ♦ Overnights	(3)	('000)	143,874	154,836	156,653	152,043	148,003
Hotels and similar establishments							
2.21 ♦ Guests	(4)	('000)	41,600	47,444	48,641	47,241	45,138
2.22 ♦ Overnights	(4)	('000)	106,875	115,088	116,597	113,188	109,757
Indicators							
2.23 Average size of travel party		Persons	..	..	..	..	..
Average length of stay							
2.24 Total		Days	..	..	..	..	..
2.25 ♦ For all commercial accommodation services		Nights	3.86	4.05	4.20	3.98	3.96
2.26 * of which, "hotels and similar establishments"	(4)	Nights	2.87	2.73	2.70	2.69	..
2.27 ♦ For non commercial accommodation services		Days	4.48	4.26	4.57	4.40	4.38
2.28 Average expenditure per day		US$	41.4	41.4	46.4	52.1	37.1
3. OUTBOUND TOURISM							
Data							
Departures							
3.1 Total		('000)	..	..	12,709	13,042	14,583
3.2 ♦ Overnight visitors (tourists)	(5)	('000)	10,464	10,678	11,276	11,229	12,844
3.3 ♦ Same-day visitors (excursionists)		('000)	..	..	1,433	1,813	1,739
Expenditure							
3.4 Total		US$ Mn	18,441	20,348	24,355	26,839	21,482
3.5 ♦ Travel		US$ Mn	15,046	16,697	19,724	20,363	16,911
3.6 ♦ Passenger transport		US$ Mn	3,395	3,651	4,631	6,476	4,571
Indicators							
3.10 Average length of stay		Days	8.92	8.91	9.37	8.84	8.36
3.11 Average expenditure per day		US$	106.9	103.2	113.6	130.5	96.1
4. TOURISM INDUSTRIES							
Data							
Number of establishments							
4.1 Total		Units	..	..	..	445,522	448,874
4.2 ♦ Accommodation for visitors		Units	..	..	..	22,603	23,079
4.3 * of which, "hotels and similar establishments"	(4)	Units	17,607	17,723	17,827	17,988	18,330
4.4 ♦ Food and beverage serving activities		Units	..	..	..	266,615	267,597
4.5 ♦ Passenger transportation		Units	..	..	..	86,231	85,731
4.6 ♦ Travel agencies and other reservation services activities		Units	..	..	..	10,970	11,028
4.7 ♦ Other tourism industries		Units	..	..	..	59,103	61,439
Accommodation for visitors in hotels and similar establishments							
Non-monetary data							
4.13 ♦ Number of establishments	(4)	Units	17,607	17,723	17,827	17,988	18,330
4.14 ♦ Number of rooms	(4)	Units	797,354	810,591	821,143	838,522	863,056
4.15 ♦ Number of bed-places	(4)	Units	1,578,629	1,615,284	1,642,417	1,682,559	1,733,383
Indicators							
4.16 Occupancy rate / rooms		Percent	..	..	..	..	..
4.17 Occupancy rate / bed-places	(4)	Percent	54.24	56.38	56.02	53.50	49.43
4.18 Average length of stay	(4)	Nights	3.48	3.26	3.22	3.24	3.25
4.19 Available capacity (bed-places per 1000 inhabitants)		Units	36.38	36.61	36.60	36.93	37.72

SPAIN

Basic data and indicators	Notes	Units	2005	2006	2007	2008	2009
Travel agencies and other reservation service activities							
Non-monetary data							
♦ Domestic trips							
4.25 * with package tour		Percent	2.0	2.4	2.2	2.0	1.8
4.26 * without package tour		Percent	98.0	97.6	97.8	98.0	98.2
♦ Inbound trips							
4.27 * with package tour		Percent	36.5	33.9	30.5	29.9	29.7
4.28 * without package tour		Percent	63.1	65.4	68.8	69.3	69.6
♦ Outbound trips							
4.29 * with package tour		Percent	19.3	19.7	18.0	17.8	13.4
4.30 * without package tour		Percent	80.7	80.3	82.1	82.3	86.6
5. EMPLOYMENT							
Data							
Number of employees by tourism industries							
5.1 Total		('000)	2,345.5	2,498.2	2,575.8	2,193.5	2,143.1
5.2 ♦ Accommodation services for visitors (hotels and similar establishments)		('000)	283.1	285.3	307.1	286.3	283.3
5.3 ♦ Other accommodation services		('000)	30.6	27.0	29.7	42.6	38.5
5.4 ♦ Food and beverage serving activities		('000)	977.5	1,090.4	1,113.6	1,123.7	1,099.3
5.5 ♦ Passenger transportation		('000)	630.8	660.7	672.5	269.6	274.4
5.6 ♦ Travel agencies and other reservation services activities		('000)	61.0	61.4	72.0	62.8	54.9
5.7 ♦ Other tourism industries		('000)	362.7	373.5	380.8	408.6	392.7
Number of jobs by status in employment							
5.8 Total		('000)	2,512.2	2,685.3	2,770.5	2,438.4	2,494.8
5.9 ♦ Employees		('000)	1925.4	2087.9	2155.9	1952.2	2024.3
5.10 ♦ Self employed		('000)	586.8	597.4	614.6	486.2	470.6
Indicators							
Number of full-time equivalent jobs by status in employment							
5.11 Total		('000)	1,967.6	2,105.1	2,180.8	1,819.2	1,749.2
5.12 ♦ Employees		('000)	1,457.8	1,582.2	1,642.1	1,394.3	1,341.1
5.13 * male		('000)	899.8	958.8	982.2	748.1	743.2
5.14 * female		('000)	558.0	623.4	659.9	646.2	598.0
5.15 ♦ Self employed		('000)	509.8	522.9	538.7	424.9	408.0
5.16 * male		('000)	378.6	384.1	392.1	277.7	260.9
5.17 * female		('000)	131.2	138.8	146.5	147.2	147.2
6. COMPLEMENTARY INDICATORS							
Demand							
6.1 Gross travel propensity		Units	..	..	..	..	..
6.2 Carrying capacity (arrivals/population)		Units	4.91	4.83	4.58	4.72	4.59
Macroeconomic indicators related to international tourism							
6.3 Inbound tourism expenditure over GDP		Percent	4.7	4.7	4.5	4.4	4.0
6.4 Outbound tourism expenditure over GDP		Percent	1.6	1.6	1.7	1.7	1.5
6.5 Tourism balance (inbound minus outbound tourism expenditure) over GDP		Percent	3.1	3.0	2.8	2.7	2.5
6.6 Tourism openness (inbound plus outbound tourism expenditure) over GDP		Percent	6.3	6.3	6.2	6.1	5.5
6.7 Tourism coverage (inbound over outbound tourism expenditure)		Percent	287.8	282.8	267.0	261.7	272.7
6.8 Inbound tourism expenditure over exports of goods		Percent	27.0	26.1	24.6	24.7	26.2
6.9 Inbound tourism expenditure over exports of services		Percent	56.1	53.9	50.7	49.0	47.7
6.10 Inbound tourism expenditure over exports of goods and services		Percent	18.2	17.6	16.6	16.4	16.9
6.11 Inbound tourism expenditure over current account credits		Percent	15.1	14.1	13.1	13.2	13.7
6.12 Outbound tourism expenditure over imports of goods		Percent	6.5	6.3	6.3	6.5	7.5
6.13 Outbound tourism expenditure over imports of services		Percent	27.5	25.9	25.2	25.6	24.6
6.14 Outbound tourism expenditure over imports of goods and services		Percent	5.3	5.0	5.0	5.2	5.7
6.15 Outbound tourism expenditure over current account debits		Percent	4.2	3.9	3.8	3.9	4.2

SRI LANKA

Basic data and indicators	Notes	Units	2005	2006	2007	2008	2009
1. INBOUND TOURISM							
Data							
Arrivals							
1.1 Total		('000)	669	689	592	526	538
1.2 ♦ Overnight visitors (tourists)	(1)	('000)	549	560	494	438	448
1.3 ♦ Same-day visitors (excursionists)		('000)	120	129	98	88	90
1.4 * of which, cruise passengers		('000)	..	..	..	..	..
Arrivals by region	(1)						
1.5 Total		('000)	548	559	495	438	448
1.6 ♦ Africa		('000)	2	3	3	2	2
1.7 ♦ Americas		('000)	47	36	32	28	26
1.8 ♦ East Asia and the Pacific		('000)	100	98	76	67	74
1.9 ♦ Europe		('000)	236	243	223	199	199
1.10 ♦ Middle East		('000)	10	10	11	12	20
1.11 ♦ South Asia		('000)	153	169	150	130	127
1.12 ♦ Other not classified		('000)	..	..	..	..	..
1.13 * of which, nationals residing abroad		('000)	..	..	..	..	..
Arrivals by main purpose	(1)						
1.14 Total		('000)	549	559	494	438	448
1.15 ♦ Personal		('000)	444	443	437	395	403
1.16 * holidays, leisure and recreation		('000)	382	377	343	321	358
1.17 * other personal purposes		('000)	62	66	94	74	45
1.18 ♦ Business and professional		('000)	105	116	57	43	45
Arrivals by mode of transport	(1)						
1.19 Total		('000)	549.3	559.4	494.3	438.1	447.4
1.20 ♦ Air		('000)	549	559	494	438	447
1.21 ♦ Water		('000)	0.3	0.4	0.3	0.1	0.4
1.22 ♦ Land		('000)	..	..	..	..	..
1.23 * railway		('000)	..	..	..	..	..
1.24 * road		('000)	..	..	..	..	..
1.25 * others		('000)	..	..	..	..	..
Accommodation							
Total							
1.29 ♦ Guests		('000)	..	..	..	..	..
1.30 ♦ Overnights		('000)	4,754	5,794	4,940	4,166	4,076
Hotels and similar establishments							
1.31 ♦ Guests		('000)	..	..	..	..	..
1.32 ♦ Overnights		('000)	3,249	3,815	3,377	3,464	3,598
Expenditure							
1.33 Total		US$ Mn	729	733	750	803	754
1.34 ♦ Travel		US$ Mn	429	410	385	342	350
1.35 ♦ Passenger transport		US$ Mn	300	323	365	461	404
Indicators							
1.39 Average size of travel party		Persons	..	..	..	..	..
Average length of stay							
1.40 Total		Days	..	..	..	..	..
1.41 ♦ For all commercial accommodation services		Nights	8.70	10.40	10.00	9.50	9.10
1.42 * of which, "hotels and similar establishments"		Nights	..	..	..	..	..
1.43 ♦ For non commercial accommodation services		Days	..	..	..	..	..
1.44 Average expenditure per day		US$	74.6	83.4	79.1	76.7	81.8
2. DOMESTIC TOURISM							
Data							
Accommodation							
Total							
2.19 ♦ Guests		('000)	..	..	..	..	..
2.20 ♦ Overnights		('000)	..	..	..	..	..
Hotels and similar establishments							
2.21 ♦ Guests		('000)	..	..	..	..	..
2.22 ♦ Overnights		('000)	1,292	1,302	1,534	1,401	1,635

SRI LANKA

Basic data and indicators	Notes	Units	2005	2006	2007	2008	2009
3. OUTBOUND TOURISM							
Data							
Departures							
3.1 Total		('000)	..	..	..	..	..
3.2 ♦ Overnight visitors (tourists)		('000)	727	757	862	966	963
3.3 ♦ Same-day visitors (excursionists)		('000)	..	..	..	..	..
Expenditure							
3.4 Total		US$ Mn	552	666	709	777	735
3.5 ♦ Travel		US$ Mn	314	373	393	428	411
3.6 ♦ Passenger transport		US$ Mn	238	293	316	349	324
4. TOURISM INDUSTRIES							
Data							
Number of establishments							
4.1 Total		Units	..	..	..	..	..
4.2 ♦ Accommodation for visitors		Units	..	..	..	..	..
4.3 * of which, "hotels and similar establishments"	(2)	Units	638	749	758	834	871
4.4 ♦ Food and beverage serving activities		Units	..	..	..	..	..
4.5 ♦ Passenger transportation		Units	..	..	..	..	..
4.6 ♦ Travel agencies and other reservation services activities		Units	..	..	..	..	..
4.7 ♦ Other tourism industries		Units	..	..	..	..	..
Accommodation for visitors in hotels and similar establishments							
Non-monetary data							
4.13 ♦ Number of establishments	(2)	Units	638	749	758	834	871
4.14 ♦ Number of rooms	(2)	Units	17,124	19,207	19,634	20,112	20,407
4.15 ♦ Number of bed-places	(2)	Units	31,277	35,349	35,799	38,411	39,998
Indicators							
4.16 Occupancy rate / rooms		Percent	45.40	47.80	46.20	43.90	48.40
4.17 Occupancy rate / bed-places		Percent	..	..	..	..	..
4.18 Average length of stay		Nights	..	..	..	..	..
4.19 Available capacity (bed-places per 1000 inhabitants)		Units	1.59	1.78	1.79	1.91	1.97
6. COMPLEMENTARY INDICATORS							
Demand							
6.1 Gross travel propensity		Units	..	..	..	..	..
6.2 Carrying capacity (arrivals/population)		Units	0.03	0.03	0.02	0.02	0.02
Macroeconomic indicators related to international tourism							
6.3 Inbound tourism expenditure over GDP		Percent	3.0	2.6	2.3	2.0	1.8
6.4 Outbound tourism expenditure over GDP		Percent	2.3	2.4	2.2	1.9	1.8
6.5 Tourism balance (inbound minus outbound tourism expenditure) over GDP		Percent	0.7	0.2	0.1	0.1	0.0
6.6 Tourism openness (inbound plus outbound tourism expenditure) over GDP		Percent	5.3	4.9	4.5	3.9	3.5
6.7 Tourism coverage (inbound over outbound tourism expenditure)		Percent	132.0	110.1	105.8	103.2	102.6
6.8 Inbound tourism expenditure over exports of goods		Percent	11.5	10.7	9.8	9.9	10.6
6.9 Inbound tourism expenditure over exports of services		Percent	47.4	45.1	42.2	40.1	39.8
6.10 Inbound tourism expenditure over exports of goods and services		Percent	9.2	8.6	8.0	7.9	8.4
6.11 Inbound tourism expenditure over current account credits		Percent	7.3	6.6	6.0	6.0	6.0
6.12 Outbound tourism expenditure over imports of goods		Percent	6.9	7.2	7.0	6.1	8.0
6.13 Outbound tourism expenditure over imports of services		Percent	26.5	27.8	27.2	25.8	29.1
6.14 Outbound tourism expenditure over imports of goods and services		Percent	5.5	5.7	5.5	5.0	6.3
6.15 Outbound tourism expenditure over current account debits		Percent	5.2	5.3	5.1	4.5	5.8

SUDAN

Basic data and indicators	Notes	Units	2005	2006	2007	2008	2009
1. INBOUND TOURISM							
Data							
Arrivals							
1.1 Total		('000)	..	..	..	..	..
1.2 ♦ Overnight visitors (tourists)	(1)	('000)	246	328	436	440	420
1.3 ♦ Same-day visitors (excursionists)		('000)	..	..	..	..	..
1.4 * of which, cruise passengers		('000)	..	..	..	..	..
Arrivals by region	(1)						
1.5 Total		('000)	246	329	436	439	421
1.6 ♦ Africa		('000)	59	51	65	66	100
1.7 ♦ Americas		('000)	21	12	16	15	60
1.8 ♦ East Asia and the Pacific		('000)	109	222	297	299	161
1.9 ♦ Europe		('000)	56	44	57	57	100
1.10 ♦ Middle East		('000)	..	..	..	..	..
1.11 ♦ South Asia		('000)	..	..	..	..	..
1.12 ♦ Other not classified		('000)	1	..	1	2	..
1.13 * of which, nationals residing abroad		('000)	..	..	..	..	..
Arrivals by main purpose	(1)						
1.14 Total		('000)	246	328	436	440	420
1.15 ♦ Personal		('000)	185	252	336	339	323
1.16 * holidays, leisure and recreation		('000)	172	215	279	291	277
1.17 * other personal purposes		('000)	13	37	57	48	46
1.18 ♦ Business and professional		('000)	61	76	100	101	97
Arrivals by mode of transport	(1)						
1.19 Total		('000)	246	328	436	440	420
1.20 ♦ Air		('000)	197	318	361	364	294
1.21 ♦ Water		('000)	37	7	59	58	84
1.22 ♦ Land		('000)	12	3	16	18	42
1.23 * railway		('000)	..	..	..	..	..
1.24 * road		('000)	12	3	16	18	42
1.25 * others		('000)	..	..	..	..	..
Expenditure							
1.33 Total		US$ Mn	..	..	..	..	..
1.34 ♦ Travel	(2)	US$ Mn	89	167	262	331	299
1.35 ♦ Passenger transport		US$ Mn	..	..	..	..	..
3. OUTBOUND TOURISM							
Data							
Expenditure							
3.4 Total		US$ Mn	..	..	..	..	..
3.5 ♦ Travel		US$ Mn	667	1,413	1,477	1,188	868
3.6 ♦ Passenger transport		US$ Mn	..	..	..	..	..
4. TOURISM INDUSTRIES							
Data							
Accommodation for visitors in hotels and similar establishments							
Non-monetary data							
4.13 ♦ Number of establishments		Units	245	281	284	..	..
4.14 ♦ Number of rooms		Units	4,200	4,746	5,854	4,450	..
4.15 ♦ Number of bed-places		Units	10,102	11,407	11,800	11,225	..
Indicators							
4.16 Occupancy rate / rooms		Percent	..	..	..	..	..
4.17 Occupancy rate / bed-places		Percent	..	..	..	..	..
4.18 Average length of stay		Nights	8.00	8.00	8.00	8.00	..
4.19 Available capacity (bed-places per 1000 inhabitants)		Units	0.26	0.29	0.29	0.27	..

SUDAN

Basic data and indicators	Notes	Units	2005	2006	2007	2008	2009
6. COMPLEMENTARY INDICATORS							
Demand							
6.1 Gross travel propensity		Units	..	..	..	..	..
6.2 Carrying capacity (arrivals/population)		Units	0.01	0.01	0.01	0.01	0.01
Macroeconomic indicators related to international tourism							
6.3 Inbound tourism expenditure over GDP		Percent	0.00	0.00	0.00	0.01	..
6.4 Outbound tourism expenditure over GDP		Percent	0.02	0.03	0.03	0.02	..
6.5 Tourism balance (inbound minus outbound tourism expenditure) over GDP		Percent	-0.02	-0.03	-0.02	-0.01	..
6.6 Tourism openness (inbound plus outbound tourism expenditure) over GDP		Percent	0.02	0.03	0.03	0.02	..
6.7 Tourism coverage (inbound over outbound tourism expenditure)		Percent	13.4	11.8	17.7	27.8	..
6.8 Inbound tourism expenditure over exports of goods		Percent	1.8	3.0	2.9	2.8	..
6.9 Inbound tourism expenditure over exports of services		Percent	78.3	67.7	68.1	67.1	..
6.10 Inbound tourism expenditure over exports of goods and services		Percent	1.8	2.8	2.8	2.7	..
6.11 Inbound tourism expenditure over current account credits		Percent	1.3	2.0	2.2	2.0	..
6.12 Outbound tourism expenditure over imports of goods		Percent	11.2	19.9	19.1	14.4	..
6.13 Outbound tourism expenditure over imports of services		Percent	36.2	50.5	50.3	45.4	..
6.14 Outbound tourism expenditure over imports of goods and services		Percent	8.6	14.3	13.9	11.0	..
6.15 Outbound tourism expenditure over current account debits		Percent	6.9	10.8	9.7	6.8	..

SURINAME

Basic data and indicators	Notes	Units	2005	2006	2007	2008	2009
1. INBOUND TOURISM							
Data							
Arrivals							
1.1 Total		('000)	..	..	..	..	..
1.2 ♦ Overnight visitors (tourists)		('000)	161	154	167	151	151
1.3 ♦ Same-day visitors (excursionists)		('000)	..	..	..	..	..
1.4 * of which, cruise passengers		('000)	..	..	..	..	..
Arrivals by region							
1.5 Total		('000)	161	154	167	151	151
1.6 ♦ Africa		('000)	0.3	0.3	0.2	0.2	0.2
1.7 ♦ Americas		('000)	56	51	52	52	59
1.8 ♦ East Asia and the Pacific		('000)	4	3	3	3	2
1.9 ♦ Europe		('000)	100	99	111	95	88
1.10 ♦ Middle East		('000)	..	..	..	..	..
1.11 ♦ South Asia		('000)	..	..	..	..	..
1.12 ♦ Other not classified		('000)	0.2	0.2	0.5	0.5	2.0
1.13 * of which, nationals residing abroad		('000)	..	..	..	..	..
Arrivals by main purpose							
1.14 Total		('000)	161	154	167	151	151
1.15 ♦ Personal		('000)	145	138	150	135	136
1.16 * holidays, leisure and recreation		('000)	44	40	43	44	46
1.17 * other personal purposes		('000)	101	98	107	91	90
1.18 ♦ Business and professional		('000)	16	16	17	16	15
Arrivals by mode of transport							
1.19 Total		('000)	160	..	..	..	..
1.20 ♦ Air	(1)	('000)	122	..	..	..	..
1.21 ♦ Water	(2)	('000)	38	..	..	..	..
1.22 ♦ Land		('000)	..	..	..	..	..
1.23 * railway		('000)	..	..	..	..	..
1.24 * road		('000)	..	..	..	..	..
1.25 * others		('000)	..	..	..	..	..
Expenditure							
1.33 Total		US$ Mn	96	109	73	83	70
1.34 ♦ Travel		US$ Mn	45	95	67	77	64
1.35 ♦ Passenger transport		US$ Mn	51	14	6	6	6
3. OUTBOUND TOURISM							
Data							
Expenditure							
3.4 Total		US$ Mn	94	33	28	35	35
3.5 ♦ Travel		US$ Mn	17	18	22	30	32
3.6 ♦ Passenger transport		US$ Mn	77	15	6	5	3
4. TOURISM INDUSTRIES							
Data							
Accommodation for visitors in hotels and similar establishments							
Non-monetary data							
4.13 ♦ Number of establishments		Units	..	..	..	..	..
4.14 ♦ Number of rooms		Units	4,575	..	..	..	..
4.15 ♦ Number of bed-places		Units	..	..	..	..	..

SURINAME

Basic data and indicators	Notes	Units	2005	2006	2007	2008	2009
6. COMPLEMENTARY INDICATORS							
Demand							
6.1 Gross travel propensity		Units	..	..	..	..	..
6.2 Carrying capacity (arrivals/population)		Units	0.32	0.30	0.32	0.29	0.29
Macroeconomic indicators related to international tourism							
6.3 Inbound tourism expenditure over GDP		Percent	..	..	..	..	..
6.4 Outbound tourism expenditure over GDP		Percent	..	..	..	..	..
6.5 Tourism balance (inbound minus outbound tourism expenditure) over GDP		Percent	..	..	..	..	..
6.6 Tourism openness (inbound plus outbound tourism expenditure) over GDP		Percent	..	..	..	..	..
6.7 Tourism coverage (inbound over outbound tourism expenditure)		Percent	101.1	329.8	262.2	239.5	..
6.8 Inbound tourism expenditure over exports of goods		Percent	7.9	9.2	5.4	4.9	..
6.9 Inbound tourism expenditure over exports of services		Percent	46.7	46.4	29.8	29.4	..
6.10 Inbound tourism expenditure over exports of goods and services		Percent	6.7	7.7	4.5	4.2	..
6.11 Inbound tourism expenditure over current account credits		Percent	6.4	7.2	4.1	3.8	..
6.12 Outbound tourism expenditure over imports of goods		Percent	7.9	3.2	2.3	2.6	..
6.13 Outbound tourism expenditure over imports of services		Percent	26.8	12.3	8.8	8.8	..
6.14 Outbound tourism expenditure over imports of goods and services		Percent	6.1	2.6	1.9	2.0	..
6.15 Outbound tourism expenditure over current account debits		Percent	5.8	2.4	1.7	1.9	..

SWAZILAND

Basic data and indicators	Notes	Units	2005	2006	2007	2008	2009
1. INBOUND TOURISM							
Data							
Arrivals							
1.1 Total		('000)	1,182	1,200	1,230	1,186	1,344
1.2 ♦ Overnight visitors (tourists)		('000)	837	873	870	754	908
1.3 ♦ Same-day visitors (excursionists)		('000)	129	173	205	171	138
1.4 * of which, cruise passengers		('000)	..	..	..	..	..
Arrivals by region							
1.5 Total		('000)	1,182	1,200	1,230	1,187	1,343
1.6 ♦ Africa		('000)	1,043	1,056	1,075	1,041	1,191
1.7 ♦ Americas		('000)	17	19	19	20	20
1.8 ♦ East Asia and the Pacific		('000)	10	10	12	12	11
1.9 ♦ Europe		('000)	108	110	119	108	114
1.10 ♦ Middle East		('000)	..	..	..	..	..
1.11 ♦ South Asia		('000)	4	5	5	6	7
1.12 ♦ Other not classified		('000)	..	..	..	..	..
1.13 * of which, nationals residing abroad		('000)	..	..	..	..	..
Arrivals by main purpose							
1.14 Total		('000)	1,182	1,200	1,230	1,186	1,344
1.15 ♦ Personal		('000)	1,014	1,026	1,065	1,035	1,193
1.16 * holidays, leisure and recreation		('000)	705	661	586	537	669
1.17 * other personal purposes		('000)	309	365	479	498	524
1.18 ♦ Business and professional		('000)	168	174	165	151	151
Arrivals by mode of transport							
1.19 Total		('000)	1,182	1,200	1,230	1,186	1,344
1.20 ♦ Air		('000)	22	22	27	27	59
1.21 ♦ Water		('000)	..	..	..	..	..
1.22 ♦ Land		('000)	1,160	1,178	1,203	1,159	1,285
1.23 * railway		('000)	..	..	..	..	..
1.24 * road		('000)	1,160	1,178	1,203	1,159	1,285
1.25 * others		('000)	..	..	..	..	..
Accommodation							
Total							
1.29 ♦ Guests		('000)	..	..	..	..	..
1.30 ♦ Overnights		('000)	..	..	..	..	..
Hotels and similar establishments							
1.31 ♦ Guests		('000)	312	316	299	324	334
1.32 ♦ Overnights		('000)	..	..	..	..	..
Expenditure							
1.33 Total		US$ Mn	77	75	32	26	40
1.34 ♦ Travel		US$ Mn	77	75	32	26	40
1.35 ♦ Passenger transport		US$ Mn	0.3	0.1	0.2	0.3	0.1
Expenditure by main purpose of the trip							
1.36 Total		US$ Mn	77	75	31	26	40
1.37 ♦ Personal		US$ Mn	33	34	4	9	12
1.38 ♦ Business and professional		US$ Mn	44	41	27	17	28
Indicators							
1.39 Average size of travel party		Persons	..	..	..	..	..
Average length of stay							
1.40 Total		Days	..	..	..	..	..
1.41 ♦ For all commercial accommodation services		Nights	1.25	1.00	1.00	1.23	1.29
1.42 * of which, "hotels and similar establishments"		Nights	..	..	..	..	..
1.43 ♦ For non commercial accommodation services		Days	..	..	..	..	..
1.44 Average expenditure per day		US$	..	..	..	..	..

SWAZILAND

Basic data and indicators	Notes	Units	2005	2006	2007	2008	2009
2. DOMESTIC TOURISM							
Data							
Accommodation							
Total							
2.19 ♦ Guests		('000)	..	..	..	..	..
2.20 ♦ Overnights		('000)	..	..	..	..	..
Hotels and similar establishments							
2.21 ♦ Guests		('000)	..	..	..	..	..
2.22 ♦ Overnights		('000)	39	54	86	93	121
Indicators							
2.23 Average size of travel party		Persons	..	..	..	..	..
Average length of stay							
2.24 Total		Days	..	..	..	..	..
2.25 ♦ For all commercial accommodation services		Nights	..	1.00	1.00	4.28	3.55
2.26 * of which, "hotels and similar establishments"		Nights	..	..	..	..	..
2.27 ♦ For non commercial accommodation services		Days	..	..	..	..	..
2.28 Average expenditure per day		US$	..	..	..	..	..
3. OUTBOUND TOURISM							
Data							
Departures							
3.1 Total		('000)	..	..	..	..	..
3.2 ♦ Overnight visitors (tourists)		('000)	1,082	1,072	1,130	1,177	1,245
3.3 ♦ Same-day visitors (excursionists)		('000)	..	..	..	..	..
Expenditure							
3.4 Total		US$ Mn	60	54	63	59	98
3.5 ♦ Travel		US$ Mn	49	49	51	46	72
3.6 ♦ Passenger transport		US$ Mn	11	5	12	13	26
Expenditure by main purpose of the trip							
3.7 Total		US$ Mn	49	49	51	46	72
3.8 ♦ Personal		US$ Mn	48	47	49	44	57
3.9 ♦ Business and professional		US$ Mn	1	2	2	2	15
4. TOURISM INDUSTRIES							
Data							
Accommodation for visitors in hotels and similar establishments							
Non-monetary data							
4.13 ♦ Number of establishments		Units	..	..	..	..	..
4.14 ♦ Number of rooms		Units	1,244	1,250	1,596	1,506	1,506
4.15 ♦ Number of bed-places		Units	2,377	2,520	3,296	2,947	2,947
Indicators							
4.16 Occupancy rate / rooms		Percent	..	..	..	..	..
4.17 Occupancy rate / bed-places		Percent	46.71	49.84	43.58	47.76	52.83
4.18 Average length of stay		Nights	1.08	0.97	0.77	1.23	1.29
4.19 Available capacity (bed-places per 1000 inhabitants)		Units	2.11	2.22	2.86	2.52	2.49
6. COMPLEMENTARY INDICATORS							
Demand							
6.1 Gross travel propensity		Units	..	..	..	..	..
6.2 Carrying capacity (arrivals/population)		Units	0.74	0.77	0.76	0.65	0.77
Macroeconomic indicators related to international tourism							
6.3 Inbound tourism expenditure over GDP		Percent	3.0	2.7	..	..	..
6.4 Outbound tourism expenditure over GDP		Percent	2.3	1.9	..	..	..
6.5 Tourism balance (inbound minus outbound tourism expenditure) over GDP		Percent	0.6	0.8	..	..	..
6.6 Tourism openness (inbound plus outbound tourism expenditure) over GDP		Percent	5.3	4.6	..	..	..
6.7 Tourism coverage (inbound over outbound tourism expenditure)		Percent	127.8	140.7	49.9	..	..
6.8 Inbound tourism expenditure over exports of goods		Percent	4.7	4.5	1.8	..	..
6.9 Inbound tourism expenditure over exports of services		Percent	27.3	26.6	7.0	..	..
6.10 Inbound tourism expenditure over exports of goods and services		Percent	4.0	3.9	1.4	..	..
6.11 Inbound tourism expenditure over current account credits		Percent	3.1	3.0	1.1	..	..
6.12 Outbound tourism expenditure over imports of goods		Percent	3.2	2.8	3.2	..	..
6.13 Outbound tourism expenditure over imports of services		Percent	15.0	14.4	12.6	..	..
6.14 Outbound tourism expenditure over imports of goods and services		Percent	2.6	2.3	2.5	..	..
6.15 Outbound tourism expenditure over current account debits		Percent	2.3	1.9	2.2	..	..

SWEDEN

Basic data and indicators	Notes	Units	2005	2006	2007	2008	2009
1. INBOUND TOURISM							
Data							
Arrivals							
1.1 Total		('000)	..	..	..	..	..
1.2 ♦ Overnight visitors (tourists)	(1)	('000)	4,883	4,729	5,224	4,555	4,678
1.3 ♦ Same-day visitors (excursionists)		('000)	..	..	..	..	..
1.4 * of which, cruise passengers		('000)	..	..	..	..	..
Arrivals by region	(1)						
1.5 Total		('000)	4,883	4,729	5,224	4,555	4,678
1.6 ♦ Africa		('000)	..	..	..	..	..
1.7 ♦ Americas		('000)	247	250	260	239	212
1.8 ♦ East Asia and the Pacific		('000)	183	191	199	216	183
1.9 ♦ Europe		('000)	4,176	3,982	4,425	3,848	4,005
1.10 ♦ Middle East		('000)	..	..	..	..	..
1.11 ♦ South Asia		('000)	..	..	..	..	..
1.12 ♦ Other not classified		('000)	277	306	340	252	278
1.13 * of which, nationals residing abroad		('000)	..	..	..	..	..
Accommodation							
Total							
1.29 ♦ Guests		('000)	4,883	4,729	5,224	4,555	4,678
1.30 ♦ Overnights		('000)	11,256	12,155	12,768	12,495	12,873
Hotels and similar establishments							
1.31 ♦ Guests	(2)	('000)	2,736	2,867	2,993	2,944	3,044
1.32 ♦ Overnights	(2)	('000)	5,382	5,606	5,842	5,830	6,087
Expenditure							
1.33 Total		US$ Mn	8,589	9,394	12,277	12,866	12,114
1.34 ♦ Travel		US$ Mn	7,394	8,170	10,642	11,026	10,275
1.35 ♦ Passenger transport		US$ Mn	1,195	1,224	1,635	1,840	1,839
Expenditure by main purpose of the trip							
1.36 Total		US$ Mn	..	8,170	10,642	11,026	10,275
1.37 ♦ Personal		US$ Mn	..	4,904	6,357	6,576	6,197
1.38 ♦ Business and professional		US$ Mn	..	3,266	4,285	4,450	4,078
Indicators							
1.39 Average size of travel party		Persons	..	..	..	..	..
Average length of stay							
1.40 Total		Days	..	..	..	..	..
1.41 ♦ For all commercial accommodation services		Nights	2.06	2.33	2.14	2.31	2.40
1.42 * of which, "hotels and similar establishments"		Nights	..	..	..	..	..
1.43 ♦ For non commercial accommodation services		Days	..	..	..	..	..
1.44 Average expenditure per day		US$	..	..	..	..	..
2. DOMESTIC TOURISM							
Data							
Trips							
2.1 Total		('000)	..	..	..	..	..
2.2 ♦ Overnight visitors (tourists)		('000)	..	..	..	..	39,068
2.3 ♦ Same-day visitors (excursionists)		('000)	..	..	..	..	..
Trips by main purpose							
2.4 Total		('000)	..	..	..	..	39,068
2.5 ♦ Personal		('000)	..	..	..	..	34,994
2.6 * holidays, leisure and recreation		('000)	..	..	..	..	34,994
2.7 * other personal purposes		('000)	..	..	..	..	..
2.8 ♦ Business and professional		('000)	..	..	..	..	4,074
Trips by mode of transport							
2.9 Total		('000)	..	..	..	..	39,068
2.10 ♦ Air		('000)	..	..	..	..	1,727
2.11 ♦ Water		('000)	..	..	..	..	623
2.12 ♦ Land		('000)	..	..	..	..	36,718
2.13 * railway		('000)	..	..	..	..	5,395
2.14 * road		('000)	..	..	..	..	31,266
2.15 * others		('000)	..	..	..	..	57
Accommodation							
Total							
2.19 ♦ Guests		('000)	17,682	16,918	17,957	17,733	17,936
2.20 ♦ Overnights		('000)	36,913	38,905	39,740	38,216	38,888
Hotels and similar establishments							
2.21 ♦ Guests	(2)	('000)	11,096	11,866	12,459	12,573	12,367
2.22 ♦ Overnights	(2)	('000)	17,518	18,606	19,574	20,042	19,871

SWEDEN

Basic data and indicators		Notes	Units	2005	2006	2007	2008	2009
	Indicators							
2.23	Average size of travel party		Persons	..	..	..	..	..
	Average length of stay							
2.24	Total		Days	..	..	..	..	..
2.25	♦ For all commercial accommodation services		Nights	1.97	2.17	2.08	2.01	2.02
2.26	* of which, "hotels and similar establishments"		Nights	..	..	..	..	..
2.27	♦ For non commercial accommodation services		Days	..	..	..	..	..
2.28	Average expenditure per day		US$	..	..	..	..	..

3. OUTBOUND TOURISM

Data

Departures

		Notes	Units	2005	2006	2007	2008	2009
3.1	Total		('000)	..	..	..	..	..
3.2	♦ Overnight visitors (tourists)		('000)	15,677	12,559	12,692	13,291	11,699
3.3	♦ Same-day visitors (excursionists)		('000)	..	..	..	..	..
	Expenditure							
3.4	Total		US$ Mn	11,844	12,237	15,273	16,458	13,432
3.5	♦ Travel		US$ Mn	10,771	11,151	13,496	14,618	11,856
3.6	♦ Passenger transport		US$ Mn	1,073	1,086	1,777	1,840	1,576
	Expenditure by main purpose of the trip							
3.7	Total		US$ Mn	10,771	11,151	13,496	14,618	11,856
3.8	♦ Personal		US$ Mn	7,238	7,480	9,343	10,167	8,161
3.9	♦ Business and professional		US$ Mn	3,533	3,671	4,153	4,451	3,695

4. TOURISM INDUSTRIES

Data

Number of establishments

		Notes	Units	2005	2006	2007	2008	2009
4.1	Total		Units	..	..	..	..	..
4.2	♦ Accommodation for visitors		Units	..	..	..	..	..
4.3	* of which, "hotels and similar establishments"	(2)	Units	1,857	1,888	1,893	1,940	1,982
4.4	♦ Food and beverage serving activities		Units	..	..	..	..	..
4.5	♦ Passenger transportation		Units	..	..	..	..	..
4.6	♦ Travel agencies and other reservation services activities		Units	..	..	..	..	..
4.7	♦ Other tourism industries		Units	..	..	..	..	..

Accommodation for visitors in hotels and similar establishments

Non-monetary data

		Notes	Units	2005	2006	2007	2008	2009
4.13	♦ Number of establishments	(2)	Units	1,857	1,888	1,893	1,940	1,982
4.14	♦ Number of rooms	(2)	Units	100,155	101,651	103,793	106,581	108,168
4.15	♦ Number of bed-places	(2)	Units	197,470	201,316	207,439	218,164	221,767
	Indicators							
4.16	Occupancy rate / rooms		Percent	..	..	..	..	..
4.17	Occupancy rate / bed-places		Percent	35.00	36.10	37.20	36.00	35.00
4.18	Average length of stay		Nights	..	..	..	..	..
4.19	Available capacity (bed-places per 1000 inhabitants)		Units	21.88	22.17	22.68	23.66	23.84

5. EMPLOYMENT

Data

Number of employees by tourism industries (3)

		Notes	Units	2005	2006	2007	2008	2009
5.1	Total		('000)	121.5	130.3	131.3	147.3	159.1
5.2	♦ Accommodation services for visitors (hotels and similar establishments)	(4)	('000)	48.9	54.4	54.6	56.8	62.0
5.3	♦ Other accommodation services		('000)	..	..	..	..	..
5.4	♦ Food and beverage serving activities		('000)	..	..	..	..	..
5.5	♦ Passenger transportation		('000)	16.3	16.9	18.2	17.9	19.1
5.6	♦ Travel agencies and other reservation services activities		('000)	10.0	9.8	9.8	9.9	8.3
5.7	♦ Other tourism industries		('000)	46.3	49.1	48.7	62.6	69.8

SWEDEN

Basic data and indicators	Notes	Units	2005	2006	2007	2008	2009
6. COMPLEMENTARY INDICATORS							
Demand							
6.1 Gross travel propensity		Units	..	..	..	..	..
6.2 Carrying capacity (arrivals/population)		Units	0.54	0.52	0.57	0.49	4.70
Macroeconomic indicators related to international tourism							
6.3 Inbound tourism expenditure over GDP		Percent	2.3	2.6	2.9	3.0	3.5
6.4 Outbound tourism expenditure over GDP		Percent	3.2	3.2	3.3	3.5	3.5
6.5 Tourism balance (inbound minus outbound tourism expenditure) over GDP		Percent	-0.9	-0.6	-0.5	-0.5	0.0
6.6 Tourism openness (inbound plus outbound tourism expenditure) over GDP		Percent	5.5	5.8	6.2	6.5	6.9
6.7 Tourism coverage (inbound over outbound tourism expenditure)		Percent	72.5	81.7	86.4	84.6	99.4
6.8 Inbound tourism expenditure over exports of goods		Percent	6.5	7.0	7.9	7.8	10.5
6.9 Inbound tourism expenditure over exports of services		Percent	20.0	21.1	21.0	20.1	22.9
6.10 Inbound tourism expenditure over exports of goods and services		Percent	4.9	5.3	5.7	5.6	7.2
6.11 Inbound tourism expenditure over current account credits		Percent	3.9	4.1	4.4	4.3	5.7
6.12 Outbound tourism expenditure over imports of goods		Percent	10.5	10.0	10.0	10.2	11.7
6.13 Outbound tourism expenditure over imports of services		Percent	33.6	32.4	33.4	32.3	30.6
6.14 Outbound tourism expenditure over imports of goods and services		Percent	8.0	7.6	7.7	7.7	8.5
6.15 Outbound tourism expenditure over current account debits		Percent	6.2	5.8	5.8	5.9	6.5

SWITZERLAND

Basic data and indicators	Notes	Units	2005	2006	2007	2008	2009
1. INBOUND TOURISM							
Data							
Arrivals							
1.1 Total		('000)	..	..	..	..	..
1.2 ♦ Overnight visitors (tourists)	(1)	('000)	7,229	7,863	8,448	8,608	8,294
1.3 ♦ Same-day visitors (excursionists)		('000)	..	..	..	..	..
1.4 * of which, cruise passengers		('000)	..	..	..	..	..
Arrivals by region	(1)						
1.5 Total		('000)	7,229	7,862	8,447	8,609	8,293
1.6 ♦ Africa		('000)	78	85	85	89	80
1.7 ♦ Americas		('000)	830	934	954	878	820
1.8 ♦ East Asia and the Pacific		('000)	847	896	941	861	893
1.9 ♦ Europe		('000)	5,305	5,747	6,226	6,521	6,250
1.10 ♦ Middle East		('000)	76	85	109	128	114
1.11 ♦ South Asia		('000)	93	115	132	132	136
1.12 ♦ Other not classified		('000)	..	..	..	..	..
1.13 * of which, nationals residing abroad		('000)	..	..	..	..	..
Accommodation							
Total							
1.29 ♦ Guests		('000)	..	..	..	..	..
1.30 ♦ Overnights		('000)	..	..	..	..	..
Hotels and similar establishments							
1.31 ♦ Guests	(1)	('000)	7,229	7,863	8,448	8,608	8,294
1.32 ♦ Overnights	(1)	('000)	18,321	19,644	20,918	21,508	20,164
Expenditure							
1.33 Total		US$ Mn	11,937	12,852	14,726	17,567	16,335
1.34 ♦ Travel		US$ Mn	10,041	10,808	12,183	14,458	13,816
1.35 ♦ Passenger transport		US$ Mn	1,896	2,044	2,543	3,109	2,519
Indicators							
1.39 Average size of travel party		Persons	..	..	..	..	..
Average length of stay							
1.40 Total		Days	..	..	..	..	..
1.41 ♦ For all commercial accommodation services		Nights	..	..	..	..	..
1.42 * of which, "hotels and similar establishments"	(1)	Nights	2.53	2.50	2.48	2.50	2.43
1.43 ♦ For non commercial accommodation services		Days	..	..	..	..	..
1.44 Average expenditure per day		US$	..	..	..	..	..
2. DOMESTIC TOURISM							
Data							
Trips							
2.1 Total		('000)	..	..	..	81,317	..
2.2 ♦ Overnight visitors (tourists)		('000)	..	..	..	8,922	..
2.3 ♦ Same-day visitors (excursionists)		('000)	..	..	..	72,394	..
Trips by main purpose							
2.4 Total		('000)	..	..	..	81,317	..
2.5 ♦ Personal		('000)	..	..	..	74,100	..
2.6 * holidays, leisure and recreation		('000)	..	..	..	37,007	..
2.7 * other personal purposes		('000)	..	..	..	37,093	..
2.8 ♦ Business and professional		('000)	..	..	..	7,217	..
Trips by mode of transport							
2.9 Total		('000)	..	..	..	80,334	..
2.10 ♦ Air		('000)	..	..	..	..	..
2.11 ♦ Water		('000)	..	..	..	..	..
2.12 ♦ Land		('000)	..	..	..	80,334	..
2.13 * railway		('000)	..	..	..	20,992	..
2.14 * road		('000)	..	..	..	57,080	..
2.15 * others		('000)	..	..	..	2,262	..
Accommodation							
Total							
2.19 ♦ Guests		('000)	..	..	..	..	..
2.20 ♦ Overnights		('000)	..	..	..	..	..
Hotels and similar establishments							
2.21 ♦ Guests	(1)	('000)	6,574	6,948	7,185	7,389	7,271
2.22 ♦ Overnights	(1)	('000)	14,622	15,204	15,447	15,825	15,424

SWITZERLAND

Basic data and indicators		Notes	Units	2005	2006	2007	2008	2009
	Indicators							
2.23	Average size of travel party		Persons	..	..	..	..	..
	Average length of stay							
2.24	Total		Days	..	..	..	..	..
2.25	♦ For all commercial accommodation services		Nights	..	..	..	..	..
2.26	* of which, "hotels and similar establishments"	(1)	Nights	2.20	2.20	2.15	2.14	2.12
2.27	♦ For non commercial accommodation services		Days	..	..	..	..	..
2.28	Average expenditure per day		US$	..	..	..	134.7	..

3. OUTBOUND TOURISM

Data

	Departures							
3.1	Total		('000)	..	..	..	17,407	..
3.2	♦ Overnight visitors (tourists)		('000)	..	..	..	11,147	..
3.3	♦ Same-day visitors (excursionists)		('000)	..	..	..	6,260	..
	Expenditure							
3.4	Total		US$ Mn	10,579	11,199	12,300	13,357	12,552
3.5	♦ Travel		US$ Mn	8,782	9,252	10,116	10,923	10,628
3.6	♦ Passenger transport		US$ Mn	1,797	1,947	2,184	2,434	1,924
	Indicators							
3.10	Average length of stay		Days	..	..	..	7.50	..
3.11	Average expenditure per day		US$	..	..	..	231.1	..

4. TOURISM INDUSTRIES

Data

	Number of establishments							
4.1	Total		Units	..	..	..	..	..
4.2	♦ Accommodation for visitors		Units	..	..	..	..	..
4.3	* of which, "hotels and similar establishments"	(1)(2)	Units	5,836	5,693	5,635	5,582	5,533
4.4	♦ Food and beverage serving activities		Units	20,648	..	..	21,241	..
4.5	♦ Passenger transportation		Units	3,398	..	..	3,601	..
4.6	♦ Travel agencies and other reservation services activities		Units	2,461	..	..	2,342	..
4.7	♦ Other tourism industries		Units	..	..	..	..	..

Accommodation for visitors in hotels and similar establishments

	Monetary data							
4.8	♦ Output		US$ Mn	2,866.0	..	..	..	..
4.9	♦ Intermediate consumption		US$ Mn	1,417.0	..	..	..	..
4.10	♦ Gross value added		US$ Mn	1,449.0	1,577.0	1,791.0	2,159.0	..
4.11	♦ Compensation of employees		US$ Mn	..	..	..	..	..
4.12	♦ Gross fixed capital formation		US$ Mn	..	..	..	..	..
	Non-monetary data							
4.13	♦ Number of establishments	(1)(2)	Units	5,836	5,693	5,635	5,582	5,533
4.14	♦ Number of rooms	(1)(3)	Units	143,796	142,514	141,596	141,680	142,551
4.15	♦ Number of bed-places	(1)(4)	Units	274,035	271,591	270,146	270,487	273,974
	Indicators							
4.16	Occupancy rate / rooms	(1)(5)	Percent	47.60	50.10	53.30	54.40	51.70
4.17	Occupancy rate / bed-places	(1)(5)	Percent	39.70	41.70	43.60	44.50	42.60
4.18	Average length of stay	(1)	Nights	2.40	2.40	2.33	2.33	2.29
4.19	Available capacity (bed-places per 1000 inhabitants)	(1)(4)	Units	36.74	36.17	35.58	35.12	35.19

Travel agencies and other reservation service activities

	Monetary data							
4.20	♦ Output		US$ Mn	1,631.0	..	..	..	..
4.21	♦ Intermediate consumption		US$ Mn	569.0	..	..	..	..
4.22	♦ Gross value added		US$ Mn	1,062.0	1,099.0	1,208.0	1,442.0	..
4.23	♦ Compensation of employees		US$ Mn	..	..	..	..	..
4.24	♦ Gross fixed capital formation		US$ Mn	..	..	..	..	..

SWITZERLAND

Basic data and indicators	Notes	Units	2005	2006	2007	2008	2009
5. EMPLOYMENT							
Data							
Number of employees by tourism industries	(6)						
5.1 Total		('000)	217.5	..	..	..	..
5.2 ♦ Accommodation services for visitors (hotels and similar establishments)		('000)	30.7	32.2	34.5	36.8	..
5.3 ♦ Other accommodation services		('000)	3.1	3.1	3.2	3.3	..
5.4 ♦ Food and beverage serving activities		('000)	129.9	..	..	..	..
5.5 ♦ Passenger transportation		('000)	41.3	..	..	..	..
5.6 ♦ Travel agencies and other reservation services activities		('000)	12.5	12.4	12.7	13.2	..
5.7 ♦ Other tourism industries		('000)	..	..	..	..	..
6. COMPLEMENTARY INDICATORS							
Demand							
6.1 Gross travel propensity		Units	..	..	..	..	..
6.2 Carrying capacity (arrivals/population)		Units	0.97	1.05	1.12	2.29	1.07
Macroeconomic indicators related to international tourism							
6.3 Inbound tourism expenditure over GDP		Percent	3.2	3.3	3.4	3.5	3.4
6.4 Outbound tourism expenditure over GDP		Percent	2.8	2.9	2.8	2.7	2.6
6.5 Tourism balance (inbound minus outbound tourism expenditure) over GDP		Percent	0.4	0.4	0.6	0.8	0.7
6.6 Tourism openness (inbound plus outbound tourism expenditure) over GDP		Percent	6.0	6.1	6.2	6.2	6.0
6.7 Tourism coverage (inbound over outbound tourism expenditure)		Percent	112.8	114.8	119.7	131.1	128.7
6.8 Inbound tourism expenditure over exports of goods		Percent	7.9	7.7	7.3	7.3	8.0
6.9 Inbound tourism expenditure over exports of services		Percent	24.0	23.4	22.4	22.5	23.4
6.10 Inbound tourism expenditure over exports of goods and services		Percent	5.9	5.8	5.5	5.5	6.0
6.11 Inbound tourism expenditure over current account credits		Percent	3.7	3.7	3.6	4.1	4.5
6.12 Outbound tourism expenditure over imports of goods		Percent	7.3	6.9	6.6	5.9	6.3
6.13 Outbound tourism expenditure over imports of services		Percent	41.1	41.9	38.7	36.8	35.9
6.14 Outbound tourism expenditure over imports of goods and services		Percent	6.2	5.9	5.6	5.1	5.3
6.15 Outbound tourism expenditure over current account debits		Percent	4.0	3.8	3.3	3.1	3.7

SYRIAN ARAB REPUBLIC

Basic data and indicators	Notes	Units	2005	2006	2007	2008	2009
1. INBOUND TOURISM							
Data							
Arrivals	(1)						
1.1 Total		('000)	5,859	5,682	5,434	6,951	7,721
1.2 ♦ Overnight visitors (tourists)	(2)	('000)	3,571	4,231	4,158	5,430	6,092
1.3 ♦ Same-day visitors (excursionists)		('000)	2,288	1,451	1,276	1,521	1,629
1.4 * of which, cruise passengers		('000)	..	..	..	..	..
Arrivals by region	(1)						
1.5 Total		('000)	5,859	5,682	5,434	6,951	7,720
1.6 ♦ Africa		('000)	93	81	78	85	76
1.7 ♦ Americas		('000)	58	59	59	75	84
1.8 ♦ East Asia and the Pacific		('000)	41	42	43	53	60
1.9 ♦ Europe		('000)	947	710	732	905	1,142
1.10 ♦ Middle East		('000)	3,456	3,445	3,124	4,391	4,712
1.11 ♦ South Asia		('000)	269	290	356	389	499
1.12 ♦ Other not classified		('000)	995	1,055	1,042	1,053	1,147
1.13 * of which, nationals residing abroad		('000)	934	962	961	959	1,065
Arrivals by main purpose	(1)(3)						
1.14 Total		('000)	5,859	5,682	5,435	6,950	6,656
1.15 ♦ Personal		('000)	5,390	5,227	5,000	6,394	6,117
1.16 * holidays, leisure and recreation		('000)	2,449	2,375	2,272	2,905	2,296
1.17 * other personal purposes		('000)	2,941	2,852	2,728	3,489	3,821
1.18 ♦ Business and professional		('000)	469	455	435	556	539
Arrivals by mode of transport	(1)(3)						
1.19 Total		('000)	5,858	5,681	5,434	6,951	6,656
1.20 ♦ Air		('000)	836	878	945	1,256	1,088
1.21 ♦ Water		('000)	33	27	24	29	9
1.22 ♦ Land		('000)	4,989	4,776	4,465	5,666	5,559
1.23 * railway		('000)	..	..	..	..	..
1.24 * road		('000)	4,989	4,776	4,465	5,666	5,559
1.25 * others		('000)	..	..	..	..	..
Accommodation							
Total							
1.29 ♦ Guests	(1)	('000)	3,571	4,231	4,158	5,430	6,092
1.30 ♦ Overnights	(1)	('000)	49,194	57,291	56,373	73,492	77,128
Hotels and similar establishments							
1.31 ♦ Guests	(1)	('000)	1,149	1,409	1,407	1,869	2,069
1.32 ♦ Overnights	(1)	('000)	7,184	7,713	7,894	10,686	11,530
Expenditure							
1.33 Total		US$ Mn	2,035	2,113	2,972	3,176	3,780
1.34 ♦ Travel		US$ Mn	1,944	2,025	2,884	3,150	3,757
1.35 ♦ Passenger transport		US$ Mn	91	88	88	26	23
Indicators							
1.39 Average size of travel party		Persons	..	..	..	..	..
Average length of stay							
1.40 Total		Days	..	..	..	..	..
1.41 ♦ For all commercial accommodation services		Nights	13.77	13.54	13.56	13.53	12.66
1.42 * of which, "hotels and similar establishments"		Nights	6.25	5.48	5.61	5.72	5.57
1.43 ♦ For non commercial accommodation services		Days	20.55	21.35	21.43	20.68	18.43
1.44 Average expenditure per day		US$	42.3	39.5	39.7	54.3	66.8
2. DOMESTIC TOURISM							
Data							
Accommodation							
Total							
2.19 ♦ Guests		('000)	..	..	..	..	..
2.20 ♦ Overnights		('000)	..	..	..	..	..
Hotels and similar establishments							
2.21 ♦ Guests		('000)	649	650	679	595	563
2.22 ♦ Overnights		('000)	964	1,013	1,116	977	934

SYRIAN ARAB REPUBLIC

Basic data and indicators	Notes	Units	2005	2006	2007	2008	2009
3. OUTBOUND TOURISM							
Data							
Departures							
3.1 Total		('000)	..	..	..	..	..
3.2 ♦ Overnight visitors (tourists)		('000)	4,564	4,042	4,196	5,253	5,215
3.3 ♦ Same-day visitors (excursionists)		('000)	..	..	..	..	..
Expenditure							
3.4 Total		US$ Mn	584	585	710	911	980
3.5 ♦ Travel		US$ Mn	550	540	645	800	882
3.6 ♦ Passenger transport		US$ Mn	34	45	65	111	98
4. TOURISM INDUSTRIES							
Data							
Number of establishments							
4.1 Total		Units	..	..	..	..	..
4.2 ♦ Accommodation for visitors		Units	..	..	..	..	..
4.3 * of which, "hotels and similar establishments"		Units	566	604	632	651	687
4.4 ♦ Food and beverage serving activities		Units	..	..	..	..	..
4.5 ♦ Passenger transportation		Units	..	..	..	..	..
4.6 ♦ Travel agencies and other reservation services activities		Units	..	..	..	..	..
4.7 ♦ Other tourism industries		Units	..	..	..	..	..
Accommodation for visitors in hotels and similar establishments							
Non-monetary data							
4.13 ♦ Number of establishments		Units	566	604	632	651	687
4.14 ♦ Number of rooms		Units	18,798	20,110	20,863	21,735	23,182
4.15 ♦ Number of bed-places		Units	43,262	45,523	47,077	48,585	50,903
Indicators							
4.16 Occupancy rate / rooms		Percent	64.00	65.00	67.00	66.00	67.00
4.17 Occupancy rate / bed-places		Percent	..	..	..	..	..
4.18 Average length of stay		Nights	..	..	..	..	..
4.19 Available capacity (bed-places per 1000 inhabitants)		Units	2.26	2.32	2.34	2.36	2.41
6. COMPLEMENTARY INDICATORS							
Demand							
6.1 Gross travel propensity		Units	..	..	..	..	..
6.2 Carrying capacity (arrivals/population)		Units	0.32	0.32	0.31	0.31	0.29
Macroeconomic indicators related to international tourism							
6.3 Inbound tourism expenditure over GDP		Percent	1.5	1.4	1.7	1.6	..
6.4 Outbound tourism expenditure over GDP		Percent	0.4	0.4	0.4	0.4	..
6.5 Tourism balance (inbound minus outbound tourism expenditure) over GDP		Percent	1.1	1.0	1.3	1.1	..
6.6 Tourism openness (inbound plus outbound tourism expenditure) over GDP		Percent	2.0	1.8	2.0	2.0	..
6.7 Tourism coverage (inbound over outbound tourism expenditure)		Percent	348.5	361.2	418.2	349.0	..
6.8 Inbound tourism expenditure over exports of goods		Percent	23.7	20.6	25.3	20.7	..
6.9 Inbound tourism expenditure over exports of services		Percent	69.9	72.3	76.9	78.6	..
6.10 Inbound tourism expenditure over exports of goods and services		Percent	17.7	16.0	19.0	16.4	..
6.11 Inbound tourism expenditure over current account credits		Percent	16.1	14.7	17.2	14.9	..
6.12 Outbound tourism expenditure over imports of goods		Percent	6.7	6.3	5.8	5.6	..
6.13 Outbound tourism expenditure over imports of services		Percent	24.8	23.2	23.6	28.4	..
6.14 Outbound tourism expenditure over imports of goods and services		Percent	5.3	4.9	4.6	4.7	..
6.15 Outbound tourism expenditure over current account debits		Percent	4.7	4.3	4.2	4.3	..

TAIWAN, PROVINCE OF CHINA

Basic data and indicators	Notes	Units	2005	2006	2007	2008	2009
1. INBOUND TOURISM							
Data							
Arrivals							
1.1 Total	(1)	('000)	3,378	3,520	3,716	3,845	4,395
1.2 ♦ Overnight visitors (tourists)		('000)	..	..	..	..	..
1.3 ♦ Same-day visitors (excursionists)		('000)	..	..	..	..	..
1.4 * of which, cruise passengers		('000)	..	..	..	..	..
Arrivals by region	(1)						
1.5 Total		('000)	3,377	3,520	3,716	3,845	4,396
1.6 ♦ Africa		('000)	9	9	8	8	8
1.7 ♦ Americas		('000)	453	457	465	456	437
1.8 ♦ East Asia and the Pacific		('000)	2,131	2,185	2,290	2,250	2,088
1.9 ♦ Europe		('000)	172	172	186	200	196
1.10 ♦ Middle East		('000)	13	13	13	12	12
1.11 ♦ South Asia		('000)	17	18	20	20	19
1.12 ♦ Other not classified		('000)	582	666	734	899	1,636
1.13 * of which, nationals residing abroad		('000)	580	664	727	883	1,625
Arrivals by main purpose	(1)						
1.14 Total		('000)	3,378	3,520	3,716	3,845	4,394
1.15 ♦ Personal		('000)	2,345	2,479	2,685	2,859	3,475
1.16 * holidays, leisure and recreation		('000)	1,382	1,510	1,648	1,775	2,298
1.17 * other personal purposes		('000)	963	969	1,037	1,084	1,177
1.18 ♦ Business and professional		('000)	1,033	1,041	1,031	986	919
Arrivals by mode of transport	(1)						
1.19 Total		('000)	3,378	3,520	3,716	3,846	4,395
1.20 ♦ Air		('000)	3,341	3,450	3,624	3,736	4,177
1.21 ♦ Water		('000)	37	70	92	110	218
1.22 ♦ Land		('000)	..	..	..	..	..
1.23 * railway		('000)	..	..	..	..	..
1.24 * road		('000)	..	..	..	..	..
1.25 * others		('000)	..	..	..	..	..
Accommodation							
Total							
1.29 ♦ Guests		('000)	2,902	3,056	3,241	3,369	3,900
1.30 ♦ Overnights		('000)	20,593	21,157	21,124	24,607	27,949
Hotels and similar establishments							
1.31 ♦ Guests		('000)	..	..	..	..	..
1.32 ♦ Overnights		('000)	..	..	..	..	..
Expenditure							
1.33 Total		US$ Mn	5,740	5,956	6,274	7,156	7,956
1.34 ♦ Travel		US$ Mn	4,977	5,136	5,213	5,937	6,816
1.35 ♦ Passenger transport		US$ Mn	763	820	1,061	1,219	1,140
Expenditure by main purpose of the trip							
1.36 Total		US$ Mn	4,977	5,136	5,213	5,937	6,816
1.37 ♦ Personal		US$ Mn	3,513	3,672	3,825	4,486	5,475
1.38 ♦ Business and professional		US$ Mn	1,464	1,464	1,388	1,451	1,341
Indicators							
1.39 Average size of travel party		Persons	..	..	..	..	..
Average length of stay							
1.40 Total		Days	..	..	..	..	..
1.41 ♦ For all commercial accommodation services		Nights	7.10	6.92	6.52	7.30	7.17
1.42 * of which, "hotels and similar establishments"		Nights	..	..	..	..	..
1.43 ♦ For non commercial accommodation services		Days	..	..	..	..	..
1.44 Average expenditure per day		US$	207.5	210.9	215.2	211.5	216.3

TAIWAN, PROVINCE OF CHINA

Basic data and indicators	Notes	Units	2005	2006	2007	2008	2009
2. DOMESTIC TOURISM							
Data							
Trips							
2.1 Total		('000)	..	..	..	..	4,394
2.2 ♦ Overnight visitors (tourists)		('000)	..	..	..	..	3,899
2.3 ♦ Same-day visitors (excursionists)		('000)	..	..	..	..	495
Trips by mode of transport							
2.9 Total		('000)	..	..	..	..	4,394
2.10 ♦ Air		('000)	..	..	..	..	4,176
2.11 ♦ Water		('000)	..	..	..	..	218
2.12 ♦ Land		('000)	..	..	..	..	..
2.13 * railway		('000)	..	..	..	..	..
2.14 * road		('000)	..	..	..	..	..
2.15 * others		('000)	..	..	..	..	..
3. OUTBOUND TOURISM							
Data							
Departures							
3.1 Total		('000)	..	..	..	..	..
3.2 ♦ Overnight visitors (tourists)		('000)	8,208	8,671	8,964	8,465	8,143
3.3 ♦ Same-day visitors (excursionists)		('000)	..	..	..	..	..
Expenditure							
3.4 Total		US$ Mn	10,047	10,406	10,729	10,710	8,668
3.5 ♦ Travel		US$ Mn	8,682	8,746	9,070	9,116	7,800
3.6 ♦ Passenger transport		US$ Mn	1,365	1,660	1,659	1,594	868
Expenditure by main purpose of the trip							
3.7 Total		US$ Mn	8,682	8,746	9,070	9,116	7,800
3.8 ♦ Personal		US$ Mn	6,431	6,358	6,578	6,679	5,943
3.9 ♦ Business and professional		US$ Mn	2,251	2,388	2,492	2,437	1,857
Indicators							
3.10 Average length of stay		Days	..	..	..	..	9.71
3.11 Average expenditure per day		US$	..	..	..	..	..
4. TOURISM INDUSTRIES							
Data							
Accommodation for visitors in hotels and similar establishments							
Non-monetary data							
4.13 ♦ Number of establishments		Units	..	..	..	..	..
4.14 ♦ Number of rooms		Units	116,565	120,287	123,497	126,950	129,258
4.15 ♦ Number of bed-places		Units	..	..	..	..	..
Indicators							
4.16 Occupancy rate / rooms		Percent	..	..	..	..	..
4.17 Occupancy rate / bed-places		Percent	72.00	69.20	67.16	64.70	62.55
4.18 Average length of stay		Nights	..	..	..	..	..
4.19 Available capacity (bed-places per 1000 inhabitants)		Units	..	..	..	..	..
6. COMPLEMENTARY INDICATORS							
Demand							
6.1 Gross travel propensity		Units	..	..	..	..	..
6.2 Carrying capacity (arrivals/population)		Units	0.15	0.15	0.16	0.17	0.19

TAJIKISTAN

Basic data and indicators	Notes	Units	2005	2006	2007	2008	2009
1. INBOUND TOURISM							
Data							
Arrivals							
1.1 Total		('000)	..	..	..	325	..
1.2 ♦ Overnight visitors (tourists)		('000)	..	..	..	..	..
1.3 ♦ Same-day visitors (excursionists)		('000)	..	..	..	..	..
1.4 * of which, cruise passengers		('000)	..	..	..	..	..
Arrivals by region							
1.5 Total		('000)	..	..	..	325	..
1.6 ♦ Africa		('000)	..	..	..	..	..
1.7 ♦ Americas		('000)	..	..	..	1	..
1.8 ♦ East Asia and the Pacific		('000)	..	..	..	3	..
1.9 ♦ Europe		('000)	..	..	..	310	..
1.10 ♦ Middle East		('000)	..	..	..	..	..
1.11 ♦ South Asia		('000)	..	..	..	11	..
1.12 ♦ Other not classified		('000)	..	..	..	..	..
1.13 * of which, nationals residing abroad		('000)	..	..	..	..	..
Expenditure							
1.33 Total		US$ Mn	9.1	11.2	16.5	23.7	19.5
1.34 ♦ Travel		US$ Mn	1.6	2.1	3.3	4.2	2.4
1.35 ♦ Passenger transport		US$ Mn	7.5	9.1	13.2	19.5	17.1
Expenditure by main purpose of the trip							
1.36 Total		US$ Mn	1.6	2.1	3.2	4.2	2.4
1.37 ♦ Personal		US$ Mn	0.3	0.5	1.6	2.8	1.0
1.38 ♦ Business and professional		US$ Mn	1.3	1.6	1.6	1.4	1.4
3. OUTBOUND TOURISM							
Data							
Expenditure							
3.4 Total		US$ Mn	..	..	..	..	..
3.5 ♦ Travel		US$ Mn	3.8	6.0	6.6	10.8	5.8
3.6 ♦ Passenger transport		US$ Mn	..	..	..	..	..
Expenditure by main purpose of the trip							
3.7 Total		US$ Mn	3.8	6.0	6.6	10.8	5.8
3.8 ♦ Personal		US$ Mn	2.1	3.4	5.0	9.1	5.7
3.9 ♦ Business and professional		US$ Mn	1.7	2.6	1.6	1.7	0.1
6. COMPLEMENTARY INDICATORS							
Demand							
6.1 Gross travel propensity		Units	..	..	..	..	..
6.2 Carrying capacity (arrivals/population)		Units	..	..	..	0.05	..
Macroeconomic indicators related to international tourism							
6.3 Inbound tourism expenditure over GDP		Percent	0.4	0.4	0.4	0.5	0.4
6.4 Outbound tourism expenditure over GDP		Percent	0.2	0.2	0.2	0.2	0.1
6.5 Tourism balance (inbound minus outbound tourism expenditure) over GDP		Percent	0.2	0.2	0.3	0.3	0.3
6.6 Tourism openness (inbound plus outbound tourism expenditure) over GDP		Percent	0.6	0.6	0.6	0.7	0.5
6.7 Tourism coverage (inbound over outbound tourism expenditure)		Percent	242.4	186.3	250.3	220.5	336.0
6.8 Inbound tourism expenditure over exports of goods		Percent	0.8	0.7	1.1	1.5	1.9
6.9 Inbound tourism expenditure over exports of services		Percent	6.2	8.3	11.1	13.1	10.9
6.10 Inbound tourism expenditure over exports of goods and services		Percent	0.7	0.7	1.0	1.4	1.6
6.11 Inbound tourism expenditure over current account credits		Percent	0.5	0.4	0.5	0.5	0.6
6.12 Outbound tourism expenditure over imports of goods		Percent	0.3	0.3	0.2	0.3	0.2
6.13 Outbound tourism expenditure over imports of services		Percent	1.5	1.5	1.1	2.4	2.0
6.14 Outbound tourism expenditure over imports of goods and services		Percent	0.2	0.3	0.2	0.3	0.2
6.15 Outbound tourism expenditure over current account debits		Percent	0.2	0.2	0.2	0.2	0.2

THAILAND

Basic data and indicators	Notes	Units	2005	2006	2007	2008	2009
1. INBOUND TOURISM							
Data							
Arrivals							
1.1 Total		('000)	..	..	..	..	..
1.2 ♦ Overnight visitors (tourists)	(1)	('000)	11,567	13,822	14,464	14,584	14,150
1.3 ♦ Same-day visitors (excursionists)		('000)	..	..	..	..	..
1.4 * of which, cruise passengers		('000)	..	..	..	..	..
Arrivals by region	(1)						
1.5 Total		('000)	11,568	13,822	14,465	14,584	14,149
1.6 ♦ Africa		('000)	73	96	105	109	108
1.7 ♦ Americas		('000)	740	825	818	853	795
1.8 ♦ East Asia and the Pacific		('000)	7,195	8,569	8,712	8,624	7,994
1.9 ♦ Europe		('000)	2,779	3,439	3,813	3,963	4,031
1.10 ♦ Middle East		('000)	179	239	331	283	298
1.11 ♦ South Asia		('000)	552	654	686	750	923
1.12 ♦ Other not classified		('000)	50	..	..	2	..
1.13 * of which, nationals residing abroad		('000)	50	..	..	..	..
Arrivals by main purpose	(2)						
1.14 Total		('000)	11,517	13,821	14,464	..	..
1.15 ♦ Personal		('000)	9,972	11,845	12,647	..	..
1.16 * holidays, leisure and recreation		('000)	9,458	11,387	12,016	..	..
1.17 * other personal purposes		('000)	514	458	631	..	..
1.18 ♦ Business and professional		('000)	1,545	1,976	1,817	..	..
Arrivals by mode of transport	(1)						
1.19 Total		('000)	11,567	13,822	14,464	14,584	14,150
1.20 ♦ Air		('000)	9,544	11,495	11,975	11,624	11,100
1.21 ♦ Water		('000)	242	303	280	213	254
1.22 ♦ Land		('000)	1,781	2,024	2,209	2,747	2,796
1.23 * railway		('000)	..	..	..	..	..
1.24 * road	(3)	('000)	1,781	2,024	2,209	2,747	2,796
1.25 * others		('000)	..	..	..	..	..
Accommodation							
Total							
1.29 ♦ Guests		('000)	..	..	..	..	..
1.30 ♦ Overnights		('000)	..	..	..	..	..
Hotels and similar establishments							
1.31 ♦ Guests		('000)	10,654	12,819	..	12,815	..
1.32 ♦ Overnights		('000)	..	..	..	..	..
Expenditure							
1.33 Total		US$ Mn	12,102	16,614	20,623	22,497	19,421
1.34 ♦ Travel		US$ Mn	9,577	13,393	16,667	18,163	15,665
1.35 ♦ Passenger transport		US$ Mn	2,525	3,221	3,956	4,334	3,756
Indicators							
1.39 Average size of travel party		Persons	..	..	..	..	..
Average length of stay							
1.40 Total		Days	..	..	..	..	..
1.41 ♦ For all commercial accommodation services	(4)	Nights	8.20	8.62	9.19	9.51	8.99
1.42 * of which, "hotels and similar establishments"		Nights	..	..	..	..	..
1.43 ♦ For non commercial accommodation services		Days	..	..	..	..	..
1.44 Average expenditure per day		US$	..	..	..	..	..
3. OUTBOUND TOURISM							
Data							
Departures							
3.1 Total		('000)	..	..	..	..	..
3.2 ♦ Overnight visitors (tourists)		('000)	3,047	3,382	4,018	3,908	4,535
3.3 ♦ Same-day visitors (excursionists)		('000)	..	..	..	..	..
Expenditure							
3.4 Total		US$ Mn	4,917	6,173	6,887	6,700	5,659
3.5 ♦ Travel		US$ Mn	3,800	4,598	5,143	5,003	4,343
3.6 ♦ Passenger transport		US$ Mn	1,117	1,575	1,744	1,697	1,316

THAILAND

Basic data and indicators	Notes	Units	2005	2006	2007	2008	2009
4.	**TOURISM INDUSTRIES**						
Data							
Number of establishments							
4.1 Total		Units	..	..	..	..	..
4.2 ♦ Accommodation for visitors		Units	..	..	..	..	..
4.3 * of which, "hotels and similar establishments"		Units	7,293	..	..	..	..
4.4 ♦ Food and beverage serving activities		Units	..	..	..	..	..
4.5 ♦ Passenger transportation		Units	..	..	..	..	..
4.6 ♦ Travel agencies and other reservation services activities		Units	..	..	..	..	..
4.7 ♦ Other tourism industries		Units	..	..	..	..	..
Accommodation for visitors in hotels and similar establishments							
Non-monetary data							
4.13 ♦ Number of establishments		Units	7,293	..	..	..	..
4.14 ♦ Number of rooms		Units	376,214	..	..	..	..
4.15 ♦ Number of bed-places		Units	..	..	..	..	..
6.	**COMPLEMENTARY INDICATORS**						
Demand							
6.1 Gross travel propensity		Units	..	..	..	..	..
6.2 Carrying capacity (arrivals/population)		Units	0.18	0.21	0.22	0.22	0.21
Macroeconomic indicators related to international tourism							
6.3 Inbound tourism expenditure over GDP		Percent	6.9	8.0	8.3	8.3	7.5
6.4 Outbound tourism expenditure over GDP		Percent	2.8	3.0	2.8	2.5	2.1
6.5 Tourism balance (inbound minus outbound tourism expenditure) over GDP		Percent	4.1	5.0	5.6	5.8	5.4
6.6 Tourism openness (inbound plus outbound tourism expenditure) over GDP		Percent	9.6	11.0	11.1	10.7	9.6
6.7 Tourism coverage (inbound over outbound tourism expenditure)		Percent	246.1	269.1	299.4	335.8	355.2
6.8 Inbound tourism expenditure over exports of goods		Percent	11.1	13.0	13.6	12.8	13.1
6.9 Inbound tourism expenditure over exports of services		Percent	60.0	66.9	67.9	67.4	65.5
6.10 Inbound tourism expenditure over exports of goods and services		Percent	9.3	10.9	11.4	10.8	10.9
6.11 Inbound tourism expenditure over current account credits		Percent	8.9	10.3	10.7	10.2	10.4
6.12 Outbound tourism expenditure over imports of goods		Percent	4.6	5.4	5.5	4.3	4.7
6.13 Outbound tourism expenditure over imports of services		Percent	18.2	18.7	17.9	14.5	14.6
6.14 Outbound tourism expenditure over imports of goods and services		Percent	3.7	4.2	4.2	3.3	3.6
6.15 Outbound tourism expenditure over current account debits		Percent	3.4	3.9	3.9	3.1	3.3

THE FORMER YUGOSLAV REP OF MACEDONIA

Basic data and indicators	Notes	Units	2005	2006	2007	2008	2009
1. INBOUND TOURISM							
Data							
Arrivals							
1.1 Total		('000)	3,246	3,369	3,903	4,058	4,553
1.2 ◆ Overnight visitors (tourists)	(1)	('000)	197	202	230	255	259
1.3 ◆ Same-day visitors (excursionists)		('000)	..	..	..	..	..
1.4 * of which, cruise passengers		('000)	..	..	..	..	..
Arrivals by region	(1)						
1.5 Total		('000)	197	202	230	255	259
1.6 ◆ Africa		('000)	..	..	..	..	..
1.7 ◆ Americas		('000)	8	9	9	10	9
1.8 ◆ East Asia and the Pacific		('000)	3	3	5	5	4
1.9 ◆ Europe		('000)	183	187	212	236	240
1.10 ◆ Middle East		('000)	..	..	..	..	..
1.11 ◆ South Asia		('000)	..	..	..	..	..
1.12 ◆ Other not classified		('000)	3	3	4	4	6
1.13 * of which, nationals residing abroad		('000)	..	..	..	..	..
Arrivals by mode of transport							
1.19 Total		('000)	3,246	3,369	3,903	4,058	4,553
1.20 ◆ Air		('000)	129	120	164	175	150
1.21 ◆ Water		('000)	..	..	..	..	..
1.22 ◆ Land		('000)	3,117	3,249	3,739	3,883	4,403
1.23 * railway		('000)	44	53	52	46	44
1.24 * road		('000)	3,073	3,196	3,687	3,837	4,359
1.25 * others		('000)	..	..	..	..	..
Accommodation							
Total							
1.29 ◆ Guests		('000)	197	202	230	255	259
1.30 ◆ Overnights		('000)	443	443	518	587	584
Hotels and similar establishments							
1.31 ◆ Guests		('000)	181	185	210	214	220
1.32 ◆ Overnights		('000)	391	392	457	475	469
Expenditure							
1.33 Total		US$ Mn	116	156	219	262	232
1.34 ◆ Travel		US$ Mn	89	129	186	228	218
1.35 ◆ Passenger transport		US$ Mn	27	27	33	34	14
Indicators							
1.39 Average size of travel party		Persons	..	..	..	..	..
Average length of stay							
1.40 Total		Days	..	..	..	..	..
1.41 ◆ For all commercial accommodation services		Nights	2.50	2.20	2.30	2.30	2.30
1.42 * of which, "hotels and similar establishments"		Nights	2.20	2.10	2.20	2.20	2.10
1.43 ◆ For non commercial accommodation services		Days	..	..	..	..	..
1.44 Average expenditure per day		US$	..	..	..	..	..
2. DOMESTIC TOURISM							
Data							
Accommodation							
Total							
2.19 ◆ Guests		('000)	312	297	306	350	329
2.20 ◆ Overnights		('000)	1,527	1,475	1,502	1,648	1,518
Hotels and similar establishments							
2.21 ◆ Guests		('000)	128	121	132	135	134
2.22 ◆ Overnights		('000)	275	267	283	277	267
Indicators							
2.23 Average size of travel party		Persons	..	..	..	..	..
Average length of stay							
2.24 Total		Days	..	..	..	..	..
2.25 ◆ For all commercial accommodation services		Nights	4.90	5.00	4.90	4.70	4.60
2.26 * of which, "hotels and similar establishments"		Nights	2.10	2.20	2.10	2.10	2.00
2.27 ◆ For non commercial accommodation services		Days	..	..	..	..	..
2.28 Average expenditure per day		US$	..	..	..	..	..

THE FORMER YUGOSLAV REP OF MACEDONIA

Basic data and indicators	Notes	Units	2005	2006	2007	2008	2009
3. OUTBOUND TOURISM							
Data							
Expenditure							
3.4 Total		US$ Mn	97	110	147	190	150
3.5 ♦ Travel		US$ Mn	62	71	102	136	100
3.6 ♦ Passenger transport		US$ Mn	35	39	45	54	50
Expenditure by main purpose of the trip							
3.7 Total		US$ Mn	62	71	101	136	100
3.8 ♦ Personal		US$ Mn	42	50	77	107	79
3.9 ♦ Business and professional		US$ Mn	20	21	24	29	21
4. TOURISM INDUSTRIES							
Data							
Number of establishments							
4.1 Total		Units	..	..	..	..	..
4.2 ♦ Accommodation for visitors		Units	347	359	364	378	402
4.3 * of which, "hotels and similar establishments"	(2)	Units	168	180	188	128	149
4.4 ♦ Food and beverage serving activities		Units	..	..	..	..	..
4.5 ♦ Passenger transportation		Units	..	..	..	..	..
4.6 ♦ Travel agencies and other reservation services activities		Units	..	..	..	..	..
4.7 ♦ Other tourism industries		Units	..	..	..	..	..
Accommodation for visitors in hotels and similar establishments							
Monetary data							
4.8 ♦ Output		US$ Mn	49.1	73.6	97.7	112.6	..
4.9 ♦ Intermediate consumption		US$ Mn	20.9	28.5	38.7	47.0	..
4.10 ♦ Gross value added		US$ Mn	28.2	45.1	59.1	65.6	..
4.11 ♦ Compensation of employees		US$ Mn	17.2	22.0	26.1	29.2	..
4.12 ♦ Gross fixed capital formation		US$ Mn	4.6	13.0	14.0	13..6	..
Non-monetary data							
4.13 ♦ Number of establishments	(2)	Units	168	180	188	128	149
4.14 ♦ Number of rooms	(2)	Units	6,883	7,043	7,214	4,970	5,380
4.15 ♦ Number of bed-places	(2)	Units	16,407	16,773	17,124	10,909	11,904
Indicators							
4.16 Occupancy rate / rooms		Percent	..	..	..	..	..
4.17 Occupancy rate / bed-places		Percent	11.10	10.80	11.80	18.90	16.90
4.18 Average length of stay	(3)	Nights	3.90	3.80	3.80	3.70	3.60
4.19 Available capacity (bed-places per 1000 inhabitants)		Units	8.06	8.23	8.39	5.34	5.83
Travel agencies and other reservation service activities							
Monetary data							
4.20 ♦ Output		US$ Mn	62.5	56.0	61.8	77.9	..
4.21 ♦ Intermediate consumption		US$ Mn	31.2	26.4	31.1	37.1	..
4.22 ♦ Gross value added		US$ Mn	31.3	29.5	30.8	40.8	..
4.23 ♦ Compensation of employees		US$ Mn	19.9	13.7	4.1	8.3	..
4.24 ♦ Gross fixed capital formation		US$ Mn	0.4	2.4	2.0	1.1	..
6. COMPLEMENTARY INDICATORS							
Demand							
6.1 Gross travel propensity		Units	..	..	..	..	..
6.2 Carrying capacity (arrivals/population)		Units	0.10	0.10	0.11	0.12	0.13
Macroeconomic indicators related to international tourism							
6.3 Inbound tourism expenditure over GDP		Percent	2.0	2.5	2.8	2.8	..
6.4 Outbound tourism expenditure over GDP		Percent	1.7	1.7	1.8	2.0	..
6.5 Tourism balance (inbound minus outbound tourism expenditure) over GDP		Percent	0.3	0.7	0.9	0.8	..
6.6 Tourism openness (inbound plus outbound tourism expenditure) over GDP		Percent	3.7	4.2	4.6	4.8	..
6.7 Tourism coverage (inbound over outbound tourism expenditure)		Percent	120.7	143.2	149.3	137.7	154.5
6.8 Inbound tourism expenditure over exports of goods		Percent	5.7	6.5	6.5	6.6	8.6
6.9 Inbound tourism expenditure over exports of services		Percent	22.6	26.0	26.7	26.0	26.8
6.10 Inbound tourism expenditure over exports of goods and services		Percent	4.6	5.2	5.2	5.3	6.5
6.11 Inbound tourism expenditure over current account credits		Percent	3.1	3.5	3.7	3.9	4.3
6.12 Outbound tourism expenditure over imports of goods		Percent	3.1	3.0	2.9	2.9	3.1
6.13 Outbound tourism expenditure over imports of services		Percent	17.6	19.1	18.7	18.9	18.2
6.14 Outbound tourism expenditure over imports of goods and services		Percent	2.6	2.6	2.5	2.5	2.6
6.15 Outbound tourism expenditure over current account debits		Percent	2.5	2.4	2.4	2.4	2.5

TIMOR-LESTE

Basic data and indicators	Notes	Units	2005	2006	2007	2008	2009
1. INBOUND TOURISM							
Data							
Arrivals							
1.1 Total		('000)	..	..	..	..	..
1.2 ♦ Overnight visitors (tourists)	(1)(2)	('000)	..	14	22	36	44
1.3 ♦ Same-day visitors (excursionists)		('000)					
1.4 * of which, cruise passengers		('000)	..	..	..	..	..
Arrivals by region	(1)(2)						
1.5 Total		('000)	..	13.7	22.3	36.0	44.2
1.6 ♦ Africa		('000)	..	..	..	..	..
1.7 ♦ Americas		('000)	..	1.2	2.0	2.9	3.4
1.8 ♦ East Asia and the Pacific		('000)		8.3	12.2	20.7	26.3
1.9 ♦ Europe		('000)		2.1	3.6	5.1	6.1
1.10 ♦ Middle East		('000)	..	..	..	..	..
1.11 ♦ South Asia		('000)	..	0.2	0.5	0.8	1.9
1.12 ♦ Other not classified		('000)	..	1.9	4.0	6.5	6.5
1.13 * of which, nationals residing abroad		('000)	..	..	..	..	..
Accommodation							
Total							
1.29 ♦ Guests		('000)	..	..	..	..	..
1.30 ♦ Overnights		('000)	..	..	..	..	..
Hotels and similar establishments	(3)						
1.31 ♦ Guests		('000)	..	..	..	..	14
1.32 ♦ Overnights		('000)	..	..	..	..	94
Expenditure							
1.33 Total		US$ Mn	..	..	..	..	..
1.34 ♦ Travel	(4)	US$ Mn	..	20.3	26.2	14.0	18.0
1.35 ♦ Passenger transport		US$ Mn	..	..	..	..	..
2. DOMESTIC TOURISM							
Data							
Accommodation							
Total							
2.19 ♦ Guests		('000)	..	..	..	..	..
2.20 ♦ Overnights		('000)	..	..	..	..	..
Hotels and similar establishments	(3)						
2.21 ♦ Guests		('000)	..	..	..	..	1.1
2.22 ♦ Overnights		('000)	..	..	..	..	2.5
3. OUTBOUND TOURISM							
Data							
Expenditure							
3.4 Total		US$ Mn	..	..	..	..	..
3.5 ♦ Travel	(4)	US$ Mn	..	1.6	2.6	36.2	39.8
3.6 ♦ Passenger transport		US$ Mn	..	..	..	..	..
4. TOURISM INDUSTRIES							
Data							
Number of establishments							
4.1 Total		Units	..	..	..	..	..
4.2 ♦ Accommodation for visitors		Units	..	..	..	..	..
4.3 * of which, "hotels and similar establishments"	(3)	Units	..	15	16	16	16
4.4 ♦ Food and beverage serving activities		Units	..	..	..	..	..
4.5 ♦ Passenger transportation		Units	..	..	..	..	..
4.6 ♦ Travel agencies and other reservation services activities		Units	..	..	..	..	..
4.7 ♦ Other tourism industries		Units	..	..	..	..	..
Accommodation for visitors in hotels and similar establishments							
Non-monetary data	(3)						
4.13 ♦ Number of establishments		Units	..	15	16	16	16
4.14 ♦ Number of rooms		Units	..	596	620	646	805
4.15 ♦ Number of bed-places		Units	..	740	764	796	995
Indicators							
4.16 Occupancy rate / rooms		Percent	..	..	..	..	..
4.17 Occupancy rate / bed-places		Percent	..	..	..	..	..
4.18 Average length of stay		Nights	..	..	..	..	..
4.19 Available capacity (bed-places per 1000 inhabitants)		Units	..	0.72	0.72	0.72	0.88

TIMOR-LESTE

Basic data and indicators	Notes	Units	2005	2006	2007	2008	2009
6. COMPLEMENTARY INDICATORS							
Demand							
6.1 Gross travel propensity		Units	..	..	..	..	..
6.2 Carrying capacity (arrivals/population)		Units	..	0.01	0.02	0.03	0.04

TOGO

Basic data and indicators	Notes	Units	2005	2006	2007	2008	2009
1. INBOUND TOURISM							
Data							
Arrivals							
1.1 Total		('000)	..	..	..	..	..
1.2 ♦ Overnight visitors (tourists)	(1)	('000)	81	94	86	74	150
1.3 ♦ Same-day visitors (excursionists)		('000)	..	..	..	..	..
1.4 * of which, cruise passengers		('000)	..	..	..	..	..
Arrivals by region	(1)						
1.5 Total		('000)	81	94	86	73	149
1.6 ♦ Africa		('000)	46	53	48	39	76
1.7 ♦ Americas		('000)	3	3	3	2	6
1.8 ♦ East Asia and the Pacific		('000)	3	3	3	3	6
1.9 ♦ Europe		('000)	27	33	31	29	61
1.10 ♦ Middle East		('000)	2	2	1	..	..
1.11 ♦ South Asia		('000)	..	..	..	..	..
1.12 ♦ Other not classified		('000)	..	..	..	..	..
1.13 * of which, nationals residing abroad		('000)	..	..	..	..	..
Accommodation							
Total							
1.29 ♦ Guests		('000)	..	..	..	..	..
1.30 ♦ Overnights		('000)	..	..	..	..	..
Hotels and similar establishments							
1.31 ♦ Guests		('000)	81	94	86	74	150
1.32 ♦ Overnights		('000)	157	209	192	209	318
Expenditure							
1.33 Total		US$ Mn	27	23	38	44	..
1.34 ♦ Travel		US$ Mn	20	21	34	40	..
1.35 ♦ Passenger transport		US$ Mn	7	2	4	4	..
Expenditure by main purpose of the trip							
1.36 Total		US$ Mn	20	21	34	40	..
1.37 ♦ Personal		US$ Mn	11	13	21	25	..
1.38 ♦ Business and professional		US$ Mn	9	8	13	15	..
Indicators							
1.39 Average size of travel party		Persons	..	..	..	..	..
Average length of stay							
1.40 Total		Days	..	..	..	..	..
1.41 ♦ For all commercial accommodation services		Nights	1.90	2.20	2.20	2.82	..
1.42 * of which, "hotels and similar establishments"		Nights	..	..	..	..	..
1.43 ♦ For non commercial accommodation services		Days	..	..	..	..	..
1.44 Average expenditure per day		US$	..	..	..	..	..
2. DOMESTIC TOURISM							
Data							
Accommodation							
Total							
2.19 ♦ Guests		('000)	..	..	..	..	..
2.20 ♦ Overnights		('000)	..	..	..	..	..
Hotels and similar establishments							
2.21 ♦ Guests		('000)	12	8	16	14	33
2.22 ♦ Overnights		('000)	25	15	28	30	95
Indicators							
2.23 Average size of travel party		Persons	..	..	..	..	..
Average length of stay							
2.24 Total		Days	..	..	..	..	..
2.25 ♦ For all commercial accommodation services		Nights	1.90	2.10	1.70	2.19	2.89
2.26 * of which, "hotels and similar establishments"		Nights	..	..	..	..	..
2.27 ♦ For non commercial accommodation services		Days	..	..	..	..	..
2.28 Average expenditure per day		US$	..	..	..	..	..

TOGO

Basic data and indicators	Notes	Units	2005	2006	2007	2008	2009
3. OUTBOUND TOURISM							
Data							
Expenditure							
3.4 Total		US$ Mn	42	42	59	68	..
3.5 ♦ Travel		US$ Mn	8	5	17	19	..
3.6 ♦ Passenger transport		US$ Mn	34	37	42	49	..
Expenditure by main purpose of the trip							
3.7 Total		US$ Mn	7.7	5.3	16.7	19.0	..
3.8 ♦ Personal		US$ Mn	1.0	0.5	4.4	5.8	..
3.9 ♦ Business and professional		US$ Mn	6.7	4.8	12.3	13.2	..
4. TOURISM INDUSTRIES							
Data							
Accommodation for visitors in hotels and similar establishments							
Non-monetary data							
4.13 ♦ Number of establishments		Units	..	..	..	..	..
4.14 ♦ Number of rooms	(2)	Units	4,944	5,201	5,404	5,557	30,260
4.15 ♦ Number of bed-places	(2)	Units	7,636	7,803	8,002	8,155	45,908
Indicators							
4.16 Occupancy rate / rooms		Percent	9.30	10.70	9.70	10.18	10.52
4.17 Occupancy rate / bed-places		Percent	..	..	..	..	..
4.18 Average length of stay		Nights	1.90	2.10	2.10	2.72	2.26
4.19 Available capacity (bed-places per 1000 inhabitants)		Units	1.27	1.27	1.27	1.26	6.94
5. EMPLOYMENT							
Data							
Number of employees by tourism industries							
5.1 Total		('000)	..	..	..	..	..
5.2 ♦ Accommodation services for visitors (hotels and similar establishments)	(2)	('000)	1.4	1.6	1.6	1.6	12.9
5.3 ♦ Other accommodation services		('000)	..	..	..	..	..
5.4 ♦ Food and beverage serving activities		('000)	..	..	..	..	..
5.5 ♦ Passenger transportation		('000)	..	..	..	..	..
5.6 ♦ Travel agencies and other reservation services activities		('000)	..	..	..	..	..
5.7 ♦ Other tourism industries		('000)	..	..	..	..	..
6. COMPLEMENTARY INDICATORS							
Demand							
6.1 Gross travel propensity		Units	..	..	..	..	..
6.2 Carrying capacity (arrivals/population)		Units	0.01	0.02	0.01	0.01	0.02
Macroeconomic indicators related to international tourism							
6.3 Inbound tourism expenditure over GDP		Percent	1.3	1.0	1.4	..	..
6.4 Outbound tourism expenditure over GDP		Percent	1.9	1.9	2.2	..	..
6.5 Tourism balance (inbound minus outbound tourism expenditure) over GDP		Percent	-0.7	-0.9	-0.8	..	..
6.6 Tourism openness (inbound plus outbound tourism expenditure) over GDP		Percent	3.2	2.9	3.7	..	..
6.7 Tourism coverage (inbound over outbound tourism expenditure)		Percent	65.3	53.4	64.3	64.2	..
6.8 Inbound tourism expenditure over exports of goods		Percent	4.3	3.6	5.6	5.2	..
6.9 Inbound tourism expenditure over exports of services		Percent	15.4	11.3	16.0	15.5	..
6.10 Inbound tourism expenditure over exports of goods and services		Percent	3.4	2.7	4.1	3.9	..
6.11 Inbound tourism expenditure over current account credits		Percent	2.5	1.9	2.9	2.7	..
6.12 Outbound tourism expenditure over imports of goods		Percent	4.6	4.5	5.5	5.2	..
6.13 Outbound tourism expenditure over imports of services		Percent	16.7	16.0	19.3	19.1	..
6.14 Outbound tourism expenditure over imports of goods and services		Percent	3.6	3.5	4.3	4.1	..
6.15 Outbound tourism expenditure over current account debits		Percent	3.2	3.2	3.9	3.8	..

TONGA

Basic data and indicators	Notes	Units	2005	2006	2007	2008	2009
1. INBOUND TOURISM							
Data							
Arrivals							
1.1 Total		('000)	60	54	..	73	72
1.2 ♦ Overnight visitors (tourists)	(1)	('000)	42	39	46	49	51
1.3 ♦ Same-day visitors (excursionists)		('000)	18	15	..	24	21
1.4 * of which, cruise passengers		('000)	18	15	..	24	21
Arrivals by region	(1)						
1.5 Total		('000)	41	39	46	49	51
1.6 ♦ Africa		('000)	..	..	..	..	..
1.7 ♦ Americas		('000)	8	6	6	6	7
1.8 ♦ East Asia and the Pacific		('000)	30	30	37	39	39
1.9 ♦ Europe		('000)	3	3	3	3	4
1.10 ♦ Middle East		('000)	..	..	..	..	..
1.11 ♦ South Asia		('000)	..	..	..	..	..
1.12 ♦ Other not classified		('000)	..	..	..	1	1
1.13 * of which, nationals residing abroad		('000)	..	..	..	..	..
Arrivals by mode of transport							
1.19 Total		('000)	60	54	46	73	72
1.20 ♦ Air		('000)	42	39	46	49	51
1.21 ♦ Water		('000)	18	15	..	24	21
1.22 ♦ Land		('000)	..	..	..	..	..
1.23 * railway		('000)	..	..	..	..	..
1.24 * road		('000)	..	..	..	..	..
1.25 * others		('000)	..	..	..	..	..
Expenditure							
1.33 Total		US$ Mn	15.0	..	15.2	19.5	..
1.34 ♦ Travel		US$ Mn	14.9	15.7	14.4	19.1	..
1.35 ♦ Passenger transport		US$ Mn	0.1	..	0.8	0.4	..
Expenditure by main purpose of the trip							
1.36 Total		US$ Mn	14.9	15.7	14.4	19.1	..
1.37 ♦ Personal		US$ Mn	8.8	1.1	6.0	4.1	..
1.38 ♦ Business and professional		US$ Mn	6.1	14.6	8.4	15.0	..
3. OUTBOUND TOURISM							
Data							
Expenditure							
3.4 Total		US$ Mn	16.0	16.4	19.2	25.1	..
3.5 ♦ Travel		US$ Mn	3.8	8.1	9.9	8.7	..
3.6 ♦ Passenger transport		US$ Mn	12.2	8.3	9.3	16.4	..
Expenditure by main purpose of the trip							
3.7 Total		US$ Mn	3.8	8.1	9.9	8.7	..
3.8 ♦ Personal		US$ Mn	2.1	3.3	4.6	3.2	..
3.9 ♦ Business and professional		US$ Mn	1.7	4.8	5.3	5.5	..
6. COMPLEMENTARY INDICATORS							
Demand							
6.1 Gross travel propensity		Units	..	..	..	..	..
6.2 Carrying capacity (arrivals/population)		Units	0.41	0.38	0.45	0.47	0.49
Macroeconomic indicators related to international tourism							
6.3 Inbound tourism expenditure over GDP		Percent	..	..	..	..	..
6.4 Outbound tourism expenditure over GDP		Percent	..	..	..	..	..
6.5 Tourism balance (inbound minus outbound tourism expenditure) over GDP		Percent	..	..	..	..	..
6.6 Tourism openness (inbound plus outbound tourism expenditure) over GDP		Percent	..	..	..	..	..
6.7 Tourism coverage (inbound over outbound tourism expenditure)		Percent	93.6	96.2	79.4	77.4	..
6.8 Inbound tourism expenditure over exports of goods		Percent	93.7	156.8	120.3	178.8	..
6.9 Inbound tourism expenditure over exports of services		Percent	42.3	60.3	58.0	50.5	..
6.10 Inbound tourism expenditure over exports of goods and services		Percent	29.2	43.6	39.1	39.4	..
6.11 Inbound tourism expenditure over current account credits		Percent	10.0	11.2	8.7	11.4	..
6.12 Outbound tourism expenditure over imports of goods		Percent	14.0	14.1	14.2	15.9	..
6.13 Outbound tourism expenditure over imports of services		Percent	39.5	41.7	45.0	45.6	..
6.14 Outbound tourism expenditure over imports of goods and services		Percent	10.3	10.5	10.8	11.8	..
6.15 Outbound tourism expenditure over current account debits		Percent	9.3	9.5	9.9	10.9	..

TRINIDAD AND TOBAGO

Basic data and indicators	Notes	Units	2005	2006	2007	2008	2009
1. INBOUND TOURISM							
Data							
Arrivals							
1.1 Total		('000)	530	543	526	482	533
1.2 ◆ Overnight visitors (tourists)	(1)	('000)	463	457	449	433	413
1.3 ◆ Same-day visitors (excursionists)		('000)	67	86	77	49	120
1.4 * of which, cruise passengers		('000)	67	86	77	49	120
Arrivals by region	(1)						
1.5 Total		('000)	462	456	449	432	413
1.6 ◆ Africa		('000)	1	1	2	2	1
1.7 ◆ Americas		('000)	365	365	356	360	345
1.8 ◆ East Asia and the Pacific		('000)	3	4	6	5	5
1.9 ◆ Europe		('000)	91	84	82	63	59
1.10 ◆ Middle East		('000)	..	..	..	..	..
1.11 ◆ South Asia		('000)	2	2	3	2	3
1.12 ◆ Other not classified		('000)	..	..	..	..	..
1.13 * of which, nationals residing abroad		('000)	..	..	..	..	..
Arrivals by main purpose	(1)						
1.14 Total		('000)	463	457	449	433	413
1.15 ◆ Personal		('000)	374	365	364	344	320
1.16 * holidays, leisure and recreation	(2)	('000)	313	293	303	301	283
1.17 * other personal purposes		('000)	61	72	61	43	37
1.18 ◆ Business and professional		('000)	89	92	85	89	93
Arrivals by mode of transport							
1.19 Total		('000)	530	543	526	482	533
1.20 ◆ Air		('000)	463	457	449	433	413
1.21 ◆ Water		('000)	67	86	77	49	120
1.22 ◆ Land		('000)	..	..	..	..	..
1.23 * railway		('000)	..	..	..	..	..
1.24 * road		('000)	..	..	..	..	..
1.25 * others		('000)	..	..	..	..	..
Expenditure							
1.33 Total		US$ Mn	593	517	621	557	..
1.34 ◆ Travel		US$ Mn	453	382	463	397	..
1.35 ◆ Passenger transport		US$ Mn	140	135	158	160	..
Expenditure by main purpose of the trip							
1.36 Total		US$ Mn	453	382	463	307	..
1.37 ◆ Personal		US$ Mn	364	287	356	189	..
1.38 ◆ Business and professional		US$ Mn	89	95	107	208	..
Indicators							
1.39 Average size of travel party		Persons	..	..	..	..	..
Average length of stay							
1.40 Total		Days	..	..	..	..	..
1.41 ◆ For all commercial accommodation services		Nights	14.30	14.80	15.70	15.70	15.66
1.42 * of which, "hotels and similar establishments"		Nights	..	..	..	..	..
1.43 ◆ For non commercial accommodation services		Days	..	..	..	..	..
1.44 Average expenditure per day		US$	..	..	..	..	..
3. OUTBOUND TOURISM							
Data							
Expenditure							
3.4 Total		US$ Mn	234	146	155	102	..
3.5 ◆ Travel		US$ Mn	180	93	94	75	..
3.6 ◆ Passenger transport		US$ Mn	54	53	61	27	..
4. TOURISM INDUSTRIES							
Data							
Accommodation for visitors in hotels and similar establishments							
Non-monetary data							
4.13 ◆ Number of establishments		Units	..	..	..	..	..
4.14 ◆ Number of rooms		Units	4,970	5,069	6,048	6,048	..
4.15 ◆ Number of bed-places		Units	..	..	..	..	..
Indicators							
4.16 Occupancy rate / rooms		Percent	..	..	..	..	..
4.17 Occupancy rate / bed-places		Percent	52.00	53.50	49.00	49.00	..
4.18 Average length of stay		Nights	..	..	..	..	..
4.19 Available capacity (bed-places per 1000 inhabitants)		Units	..	..	..	..	..

TRINIDAD AND TOBAGO

Basic data and indicators	Notes	Units	2005	2006	2007	2008	2009
6. COMPLEMENTARY INDICATORS							
Demand							
6.1 Gross travel propensity		Units	..	..	..	..	..
6.2 Carrying capacity (arrivals/population)		Units	0.35	0.35	0.34	0.32	0.31
Macroeconomic indicators related to international tourism							
6.3 Inbound tourism expenditure over GDP		Percent	3.7	2.7	2.9	..	..
6.4 Outbound tourism expenditure over GDP		Percent	1.5	0.8	0.7	..	..
6.5 Tourism balance (inbound minus outbound tourism expenditure) over GDP		Percent	2.3	1.9	2.1	..	..
6.6 Tourism openness (inbound plus outbound tourism expenditure) over GDP		Percent	5.2	3.4	3.6	..	..
6.7 Tourism coverage (inbound over outbound tourism expenditure)		Percent	253.2	354.6	401.6	..	..
6.8 Inbound tourism expenditure over exports of goods		Percent	6.1	3.6	4.6	..	..
6.9 Inbound tourism expenditure over exports of services		Percent	66.1	63.5	67.3	..	..
6.10 Inbound tourism expenditure over exports of goods and services		Percent	5.6	3.4	4.3	..	..
6.11 Inbound tourism expenditure over current account credits		Percent	5.5	3.4	4.2	..	..
6.12 Outbound tourism expenditure over imports of goods		Percent	4.1	2.2	2.0	..	..
6.13 Outbound tourism expenditure over imports of services		Percent	43.3	40.2	41.0	..	..
6.14 Outbound tourism expenditure over imports of goods and services		Percent	3.7	2.1	1.9	..	..
6.15 Outbound tourism expenditure over current account debits		Percent	3.3	1.8	1.7	..	..

TUNISIA

Basic data and indicators	Notes	Units	2005	2006	2007	2008	2009
1. INBOUND TOURISM							
Data							
Arrivals	(1)						
1.1 Total		('000)	6,975	7,176	7,512	7,750	7,611
1.2 ♦ Overnight visitors (tourists)		('000)	6,378	6,550	6,762	7,050	6,901
1.3 ♦ Same-day visitors (excursionists)		('000)	597	626	750	700	710
1.4 * of which, cruise passengers		('000)	597	626	750	700	710
Arrivals by region	(1)						
1.5 Total		('000)	6,378	6,549	6,762	7,050	6,901
1.6 ♦ Africa		('000)	993	1,010	1,046	1,043	1,036
1.7 ♦ Americas		('000)	35	34	36	39	39
1.8 ♦ East Asia and the Pacific		('000)	14	15	17	16	17
1.9 ♦ Europe		('000)	3,869	3,956	4,048	4,107	3,744
1.10 ♦ Middle East		('000)	1,440	1,507	1,582	1,809	2,034
1.11 ♦ South Asia		('000)	..	..	..	..	..
1.12 ♦ Other not classified		('000)	27	27	33	36	31
1.13 * of which, nationals residing abroad		('000)	..	..	..	..	..
Arrivals by mode of transport	(1)						
1.19 Total		('000)	6,379	6,550	6,762	7,050	6,902
1.20 ♦ Air		('000)	4,053	4,144	4,263	4,371	4,034
1.21 ♦ Water		('000)	94	101	105	103	109
1.22 ♦ Land		('000)	2,232	2,305	2,394	2,576	2,759
1.23 * railway		('000)	..	..	..	..	..
1.24 * road		('000)	2,232	2,305	2,394	2,576	2,759
1.25 * others		('000)	..	..	..	..	..
Accommodation							
Total							
1.29 ♦ Guests		('000)	..	..	..	..	..
1.30 ♦ Overnights		('000)	..	..	..	..	..
Hotels and similar establishments							
1.31 ♦ Guests		('000)	5,442	5,415	5,536	5,603	5,042
1.32 ♦ Overnights		('000)	33,587	34,086	34,546	35,049	31,557
Expenditure							
1.33 Total		US$ Mn	2,800	2,999	3,373	3,909	3,526
1.34 ♦ Travel		US$ Mn	2,143	2,275	2,575	2,953	2,773
1.35 ♦ Passenger transport		US$ Mn	657	724	798	956	753
Expenditure by main purpose of the trip							
1.36 Total		US$ Mn	2,143	2,275	2,575	2,953	2,773
1.37 ♦ Personal		US$ Mn	2,103	2,233	2,527	2,898	2,717
1.38 ♦ Business and professional		US$ Mn	40	42	48	55	56
Indicators							
1.39 Average size of travel party		Persons	..	..	..	..	..
Average length of stay							
1.40 Total		Days	..	..	..	..	..
1.41 ♦ For all commercial accommodation services		Nights	5.30	5.20	5.10	5.00	4.60
1.42 * of which, "hotels and similar establishments"		Nights	..	..	..	..	..
1.43 ♦ For non commercial accommodation services		Days	..	..	..	..	..
1.44 Average expenditure per day		US$	..	..	..	..	..
2. DOMESTIC TOURISM							
Data							
Accommodation							
Total							
2.19 ♦ Guests		('000)	..	..	..	..	..
2.20 ♦ Overnights		('000)	..	..	..	..	..
Hotels and similar establishments							
2.21 ♦ Guests		('000)	1,224	1,251	1,257	1,314	..
2.22 ♦ Overnights		('000)	2,723	2,754	2,815	3,064	3,067
Indicators							
2.23 Average size of travel party		Persons	..	..	..	..	..
Average length of stay							
2.24 Total		Days	..	..	..	..	..
2.25 ♦ For all commercial accommodation services		Nights	2.20	2.20	2.20	2.20	..
2.26 * of which, "hotels and similar establishments"		Nights	..	..	..	..	..
2.27 ♦ For non commercial accommodation services		Days	..	..	..	..	..
2.28 Average expenditure per day		US$	..	..	..	..	..

TUNISIA

Basic data and indicators	Notes	Units	2005	2006	2007	2008	2009
3. OUTBOUND TOURISM							
Data							
Departures							
3.1 Total		('000)	..	..	..	..	..
3.2 ♦ Overnight visitors (tourists)		('000)	2,241	2,302	2,743	3,118	2,623
3.3 ♦ Same-day visitors (excursionists)		('000)	..	..	..	..	..
Expenditure							
3.4 Total		US$ Mn	452	498	530	555	492
3.5 ♦ Travel		US$ Mn	374	410	437	458	415
3.6 ♦ Passenger transport		US$ Mn	78	88	93	97	77
Expenditure by main purpose of the trip							
3.7 Total		US$ Mn	374	410	437	458	415
3.8 ♦ Personal		US$ Mn	334	366	386	403	369
3.9 ♦ Business and professional		US$ Mn	40	44	51	55	46
4. TOURISM INDUSTRIES							
Data							
Number of establishments							
4.1 Total		Units	..	..	..	..	..
4.2 ♦ Accommodation for visitors		Units	..	..	..	..	..
4.3 * of which, "hotels and similar establishments"	(2)	Units	816	825	834	837	856
4.4 ♦ Food and beverage serving activities		Units	..	..	..	..	..
4.5 ♦ Passenger transportation		Units	..	..	..	..	..
4.6 ♦ Travel agencies and other reservation services activities		Units	..	..	..	..	..
4.7 ♦ Other tourism industries		Units	..	..	..	..	..
Accommodation for visitors in hotels and similar establishments							
Non-monetary data							
4.13 ♦ Number of establishments	(2)	Units	816	825	834	837	856
4.14 ♦ Number of rooms	(2)	Units	114,919	115,919	117,864	119,248	119,945
4.15 ♦ Number of bed-places	(2)	Units	229,837	231,838	235,727	238,495	239,890
Indicators							
4.16 Occupancy rate / rooms		Percent	..	..	..	..	..
4.17 Occupancy rate / bed-places		Percent	51.50	51.50	51.70	52.70	52.20
4.18 Average length of stay		Nights	6.20	6.30	6.20	6.30	6.30
4.19 Available capacity (bed-places per 1000 inhabitants)		Units	22.92	22.89	23.05	23.09	22.99
6. COMPLEMENTARY INDICATORS							
Demand							
6.1 Gross travel propensity		Units	..	..	..	..	..
6.2 Carrying capacity (arrivals/population)		Units	0.64	0.65	0.66	0.68	0.66
Macroeconomic indicators related to international tourism							
6.3 Inbound tourism expenditure over GDP		Percent	9.6	9.6	9.5	9.6	..
6.4 Outbound tourism expenditure over GDP		Percent	1.6	1.6	1.5	1.4	..
6.5 Tourism balance (inbound minus outbound tourism expenditure) over GDP		Percent	8.1	8.0	8.0	8.2	..
6.6 Tourism openness (inbound plus outbound tourism expenditure) over GDP		Percent	11.2	11.2	11.0	10.9	..
6.7 Tourism coverage (inbound over outbound tourism expenditure)		Percent	619.9	602.1	636.8	703.8	..
6.8 Inbound tourism expenditure over exports of goods		Percent	26.3	25.7	22.3	20.4	..
6.9 Inbound tourism expenditure over exports of services		Percent	69.6	69.8	68.7	65.0	..
6.10 Inbound tourism expenditure over exports of goods and services		Percent	19.1	18.8	16.8	15.5	..
6.11 Inbound tourism expenditure over current account credits		Percent	17.2	16.8	15.1	14.1	..
6.12 Outbound tourism expenditure over imports of goods		Percent	3.6	3.5	2.9	2.4	..
6.13 Outbound tourism expenditure over imports of services		Percent	20.6	20.3	18.9	16.5	..
6.14 Outbound tourism expenditure over imports of goods and services		Percent	3.1	3.0	2.5	2.1	..
6.15 Outbound tourism expenditure over current account debits		Percent	2.7	2.7	2.3	1.9	..

TURKEY

Basic data and indicators	Notes	Units	2005	2006	2007	2008	2009
1. INBOUND TOURISM							
Data							
Arrivals							
1.1 Total		('000)	21,125	19,820	23,341	26,337	27,077
1.2 ♦ Overnight visitors (tourists)		('000)	20,273	18,916	22,248	24,994	25,506
1.3 ♦ Same-day visitors (excursionists)	(1)	('000)	852	903	1,093	1,343	1,571
1.4 * of which, cruise passengers		('000)	..	..	..	..	..
Arrivals by region							
1.5 Total		('000)	20,273	18,916	22,249	24,994	25,506
1.6 ♦ Africa		('000)	154	153	167	203	286
1.7 ♦ Americas		('000)	391	459	523	558	556
1.8 ♦ East Asia and the Pacific		('000)	422	471	586	568	569
1.9 ♦ Europe		('000)	17,663	16,269	19,040	21,420	21,375
1.10 ♦ Middle East		('000)	626	630	788	1,010	1,228
1.11 ♦ South Asia		('000)	995	917	1,125	1,212	1,462
1.12 ♦ Other not classified		('000)	22	17	20	23	30
1.13 * of which, nationals residing abroad		('000)	..	..	..	..	..
Arrivals by main purpose	(2)						
1.14 Total		('000)	20,523	19,276	23,018	26,431	27,314
1.15 ♦ Personal		('000)	18,551	16,960	20,790	24,137	25,720
1.16 * holidays, leisure and recreation		('000)	15,769	13,698	17,219	20,167	21,045
1.17 * other personal purposes		('000)	2,782	3,262	3,571	3,970	4,675
1.18 ♦ Business and professional		('000)	1,972	2,316	2,228	2,294	1,594
Arrivals by mode of transport							
1.19 Total		('000)	21,125	19,820	23,341	26,336	27,077
1.20 ♦ Air		('000)	14,980	14,085	16,808	18,839	18,959
1.21 ♦ Water	(3)	('000)	1,320	1,457	1,743	2,037	2,019
1.22 ♦ Land		('000)	4,825	4,278	4,790	5,460	6,099
1.23 * railway		('000)	80	72	69	72	69
1.24 * road		('000)	4,745	4,206	4,721	5,388	6,030
1.25 * others		('000)	..	..	..	..	..
Accommodation							
Total							
1.29 ♦ Guests	(4)(5)	('000)	12,953	11,897	14,794	13,648	14,389
1.30 ♦ Overnights	(4)(5)	('000)	56,108	46,640	56,540	56,918	59,987
Hotels and similar establishments							
1.31 ♦ Guests		('000)	12,937	11,883	14,788	13,629	14,362
1.32 ♦ Overnights		('000)	55,996	46,588	56,491	56,873	59,874
Expenditure							
1.33 Total		US$ Mn	19,721	18,533	20,719	25,031	24,556
1.34 ♦ Travel	(6)	US$ Mn	18,152	16,853	18,487	21,951	21,250
1.35 ♦ Passenger transport		US$ Mn	1,569	1,680	2,232	3,080	3,306
Expenditure by main purpose of the trip							
1.36 Total		US$ Mn	18,152	16,853	18,487	21,951	21,250
1.37 ♦ Personal		US$ Mn	15,238	14,968	16,667	19,114	18,519
1.38 ♦ Business and professional		US$ Mn	2,914	1,885	1,820	2,837	2,731
Indicators							
1.39 Average size of travel party		Persons	..	..	..	..	..
Average length of stay							
1.40 Total		Days	..	..	..	..	..
1.41 ♦ For all commercial accommodation services		Nights	4.33	3.92	3.82	4.17	4.17
1.42 * of which, "hotels and similar establishments"		Nights	..	..	..	..	..
1.43 ♦ For non commercial accommodation services		Days	..	..	..	..	..
1.44 Average expenditure per day		US$	..	..	..	..	..
2. DOMESTIC TOURISM							
Data							
Accommodation							
Total							
2.19 ♦ Guests	(5)	('000)	10,458	11,570	12,039	11,286	12,138
2.20 ♦ Overnights	(5)	('000)	18,819	21,503	22,248	20,832	22,930
Hotels and similar establishments							
2.21 ♦ Guests		('000)	10,454	11,566	12,033	11,274	11,855
2.22 ♦ Overnights		('000)	18,807	21,476	22,223	20,809	22,340
Indicators							
2.23 Average size of travel party		Persons	..	..	..	..	..
Average length of stay							
2.24 Total		Days	..	..	..	..	..
2.25 ♦ For all commercial accommodation services		Nights	1.80	1.86	1.85	1.85	1.89
2.26 * of which, "hotels and similar establishments"		Nights	..	..	..	..	..
2.27 ♦ For non commercial accommodation services		Days	..	..	..	..	..
2.28 Average expenditure per day		US$	..	..	..	..	..

TURKEY

Basic data and indicators	Notes	Units	2005	2006	2007	2008	2009
3. OUTBOUND TOURISM							
Data							
Departures							
3.1 Total		('000)	..	..	..	..	..
3.2 ♦ Overnight visitors (tourists)		('000)	8,246	8,275	8,938	9,870	10,493
3.3 ♦ Same-day visitors (excursionists)		('000)	..	..	..	..	..
Expenditure							
3.4 Total		US$ Mn	3,275	3,217	3,811	4,127	4,627
3.5 ♦ Travel		US$ Mn	2,872	2,743	3,260	3,506	4,147
3.6 ♦ Passenger transport		US$ Mn	403	474	551	621	480
Expenditure by main purpose of the trip							
3.7 Total		US$ Mn	2,872	2,743	3,260	3,506	4,147
3.8 ♦ Personal		US$ Mn	1,809	1,723	2,053	2,206	2,608
3.9 ♦ Business and professional		US$ Mn	1,063	1,020	1,207	1,300	1,539
4. TOURISM INDUSTRIES							
Data							
Number of establishments							
4.1 Total		Units	..	..	..	..	..
4.2 ♦ Accommodation for visitors		Units	2,412	2,475	2,514	2,566	2,625
4.3 * of which, "hotels and similar establishments"		Units	2,405	2,467	2,505	2,547	2,597
4.4 ♦ Food and beverage serving activities		Units	..	..	..	..	..
4.5 ♦ Passenger transportation		Units	..	..	..	..	..
4.6 ♦ Travel agencies and other reservation services activities		Units	..	..	..	..	..
4.7 ♦ Other tourism industries		Units	..	..	..	..	..
Accommodation for visitors in hotels and similar establishments							
Non-monetary data							
4.13 ♦ Number of establishments		Units	2,405	2,467	2,505	2,547	2,597
4.14 ♦ Number of rooms		Units	230,605	241,257	251,470	266,881	286,114
4.15 ♦ Number of bed-places		Units	481,704	507,210	530,763	563,252	600,986
Indicators							
4.16 Occupancy rate / rooms		Percent	..	..	..	..	..
4.17 Occupancy rate / bed-places	(6)	Percent	52.38	47.26	51.12	51.51	48.90
4.18 Average length of stay	(6)	Nights	3.20	2.90	2.94	3.12	3.13
4.19 Available capacity (bed-places per 1000 inhabitants)		Units	6.77	7.04	7.27	7.62	8.03
6. COMPLEMENTARY INDICATORS							
Demand							
6.1 Gross travel propensity		Units	..	..	..	..	..
6.2 Carrying capacity (arrivals/population)		Units	0.28	0.26	0.30	0.34	0.34
Macroeconomic indicators related to international tourism							
6.3 Inbound tourism expenditure over GDP		Percent	4.1	3.5	3.2	3.4	4.0
6.4 Outbound tourism expenditure over GDP		Percent	0.7	0.6	0.6	0.6	0.8
6.5 Tourism balance (inbound minus outbound tourism expenditure) over GDP		Percent	3.4	2.9	2.6	2.9	3.2
6.6 Tourism openness (inbound plus outbound tourism expenditure) over GDP		Percent	4.8	4.1	3.8	4.0	4.7
6.7 Tourism coverage (inbound over outbound tourism expenditure)		Percent	602.2	576.1	543.7	606.5	530.3
6.8 Inbound tourism expenditure over exports of goods		Percent	25.2	19.8	18.0	17.8	22.4
6.9 Inbound tourism expenditure over exports of services		Percent	73.7	72.4	71.4	71.5	73.9
6.10 Inbound tourism expenditure over exports of goods and services		Percent	18.8	15.5	14.3	14.2	17.2
6.11 Inbound tourism expenditure over current account credits		Percent	17.9	14.7	13.5	13.5	16.3
6.12 Outbound tourism expenditure over imports of goods		Percent	2.9	2.4	2.4	2.1	3.4
6.13 Outbound tourism expenditure over imports of services		Percent	28.5	26.8	24.3	23.1	27.4
6.14 Outbound tourism expenditure over imports of goods and services		Percent	2.7	2.2	2.1	1.9	3.1
6.15 Outbound tourism expenditure over current account debits		Percent	2.5	2.0	2.0	1.8	2.8

TURKMENISTAN

Basic data and indicators	Notes	Units	2005	2006	2007	2008	2009
1. INBOUND TOURISM							
Data							
Arrivals							
1.1 Total		('000)	..	..	..	..	..
1.2 ♦ Overnight visitors (tourists)		('000)	11.6	5.6	8.2	..	..
1.3 ♦ Same-day visitors (excursionists)		('000)	..	..	..	..	..
1.4 * of which, cruise passengers		('000)	..	..	..	..	..
Arrivals by region							
1.5 Total		('000)	11.7	5.6	8.1	..	..
1.6 ♦ Africa		('000)	..	..	..	..	..
1.7 ♦ Americas		('000)	0.4	0.5	0.8	..	..
1.8 ♦ East Asia and the Pacific		('000)	0.8	0.9	0.9	..	..
1.9 ♦ Europe		('000)	3.3	2.7	4.3	..	..
1.10 ♦ Middle East		('000)	..	..	..	..	..
1.11 ♦ South Asia		('000)	7.2	1.5	2.1	..	..
1.12 ♦ Other not classified		('000)	..	..	..	..	..
1.13 * of which, nationals residing abroad		('000)	..	..	..	..	..
Arrivals by main purpose							
1.14 Total		('000)	11.6	5.6	8.2	..	..
1.15 ♦ Personal		('000)	10.3	5.2	5.2	..	..
1.16 * holidays, leisure and recreation		('000)	9.0	5.2	5.2	..	..
1.17 * other personal purposes		('000)	1.3	..	..	..	..
1.18 ♦ Business and professional		('000)	1.3	0.4	3.0	..	..
Arrivals by mode of transport							
1.19 Total		('000)	11.6	5.7	8.2	..	..
1.20 ♦ Air		('000)	2.7	4.0	4.8	..	..
1.21 ♦ Water		('000)	..	..	0.2	..	..
1.22 ♦ Land		('000)	8.9	1.7	3.2	..	..
1.23 * railway		('000)	..	0.2	..	..	..
1.24 * road		('000)	8.9	1.5	3.2	..	..
1.25 * others		('000)	..	..	..	..	..
Indicators							
1.39 Average size of travel party		Persons	..	..	..	..	..
Average length of stay							
1.40 Total		Days	..	..	..	..	..
1.41 ♦ For all commercial accommodation services		Nights	6.00	..	..	..	..
1.42 * of which, "hotels and similar establishments"		Nights	..	..	..	..	..
1.43 ♦ For non commercial accommodation services		Days	..	..	..	..	..
1.44 Average expenditure per day		US$	..	..	..	..	..
3. OUTBOUND TOURISM							
Data							
Departures							
3.1 Total		('000)	..	..	..	..	..
3.2 ♦ Overnight visitors (tourists)		('000)	33	33	38	..	..
3.3 ♦ Same-day visitors (excursionists)		('000)	..	..	..	..	..
4. TOURISM INDUSTRIES							
Data							
Accommodation for visitors in hotels and similar establishments							
Non-monetary data							
4.13 ♦ Number of establishments		Units	..	..	..	..	..
4.14 ♦ Number of rooms		Units	970	970	970	..	..
4.15 ♦ Number of bed-places		Units	1,675	1,675	1,675	..	..
Indicators							
4.16 Occupancy rate / rooms		Percent	..	..	..	..	..
4.17 Occupancy rate / bed-places		Percent	19.00	19.00	19.00	..	..
4.18 Average length of stay		Nights	8.00	8.00	8.00	..	..
4.19 Available capacity (bed-places per 1000 inhabitants)		Units	0.35	0.34	0.34	..	..
6. COMPLEMENTARY INDICATORS							
Demand							
6.1 Gross travel propensity		Units	..	..	..	..	..
6.2 Carrying capacity (arrivals/population)		Units	0.002	0.001	0.002	..	..

TURKS AND CAICOS ISLANDS

Basic data and indicators	Notes	Units	2005	2006	2007	2008	2009
1. INBOUND TOURISM							
Data							
Arrivals							
1.1 Total		('000)	..	..	..		..
1.2 ♦ Overnight visitors (tourists)		('000)	176	248	265	..	..
1.3 ♦ Same-day visitors (excursionists)		('000)	..	..	..	..	..
1.4 * of which, cruise passengers		('000)	..	..	..	..	..
Arrivals by region							
1.5 Total		('000)	177	248	..	..	..
1.6 ♦ Africa		('000)	..	..	..	..	..
1.7 ♦ Americas		('000)	157	221	..	..	..
1.8 ♦ East Asia and the Pacific		('000)	..	..	..	..	..
1.9 ♦ Europe		('000)	18	25	..	..	..
1.10 ♦ Middle East		('000)	..	..	..	..	..
1.11 ♦ South Asia		('000)	..	..	..	..	..
1.12 ♦ Other not classified		('000)	2	2	..	..	..
1.13 * of which, nationals residing abroad		('000)	..	..	..	..	..
Indicators							
1.39 Average size of travel party		Persons	..	..	..	..	..
Average length of stay							
1.40 Total		Days	..	..	..	..	..
1.41 ♦ For all commercial accommodation services		Nights	..	7.00	..	..	..
1.42 * of which, "hotels and similar establishments"		Nights	..	..	..	..	..
1.43 ♦ For non commercial accommodation services		Days	..	..	..	..	..
1.44 Average expenditure per day		US$	..	..	..	..	..
4. TOURISM INDUSTRIES							
Data							
Accommodation for visitors in hotels and similar establishments							
Non-monetary data							
4.13 ♦ Number of establishments		Units	..	..	..	..	..
4.14 ♦ Number of rooms		Units	2,227	2,297	2,632	..	..
4.15 ♦ Number of bed-places		Units	..	..	..	..	..
6. COMPLEMENTARY INDICATORS							
Demand							
6.1 Gross travel propensity		Units	..	..	..	..	..
6.2 Carrying capacity (arrivals/population)		Units	5.77	7.81	8.18	..	..

TUVALU

Basic data and indicators	Notes	Units	2005	2006	2007	2008	2009
1. INBOUND TOURISM							
Data							
Arrivals							
1.1 Total		('000)	..	..	..	..	..
1.2 ♦ Overnight visitors (tourists)		('000)	1.1	1.1	1.1	1.7	1.6
1.3 ♦ Same-day visitors (excursionists)		('000)	..	..	..	..	..
1.4 * of which, cruise passengers		('000)	..	..	..	..	..
Arrivals by region							
1.5 Total		('000)	1.0	1.1	1.1	1.7	1.6
1.6 ♦ Africa		('000)	..	..	..		
1.7 ♦ Americas		('000)	0.1	0.1	0.1	0.1	0.1
1.8 ♦ East Asia and the Pacific		('000)	0.8	0.9	0.9	1.3	1.3
1.9 ♦ Europe		('000)	0.1	0.1	0.1	0.2	0.1
1.10 ♦ Middle East		('000)	..	..	..	..	..
1.11 ♦ South Asia		('000)	..	..	..	..	..
1.12 ♦ Other not classified		('000)	..	..	..	0.1	0.1
1.13 * of which, nationals residing abroad		('000)	..	..	..	..	..
Arrivals by main purpose							
1.14 Total		('000)	1.1	1.2	1.1	..	..
1.15 ♦ Personal		('000)	0.5	1.0	1.0	..	..
1.16 * holidays, leisure and recreation		('000)	0.2	0.2	0.3	..	..
1.17 * other personal purposes		('000)	0.3	0.8	0.7	..	..
1.18 ♦ Business and professional		('000)	0.6	0.2	0.1	..	..
Arrivals by mode of transport							
1.19 Total		('000)	1.1	1.1	1.1	..	..
1.20 ♦ Air		('000)	0.9	0.9	1.0	..	..
1.21 ♦ Water		('000)	0.2	0.2	0.1	..	..
1.22 ♦ Land		('000)	..	..	..	..	..
1.23 * railway		('000)	..	..	..	..	..
1.24 * road		('000)	..	..	..	..	..
1.25 * others		('000)	..	..	..	..	..
3. OUTBOUND TOURISM							
Data							
Departures							
3.1 Total		('000)	..	..	..	..	..
3.2 ♦ Overnight visitors (tourists)		('000)	2.2	2.0	2.4	..	..
3.3 ♦ Same-day visitors (excursionists)		('000)	..	..	..	..	..
6. COMPLEMENTARY INDICATORS							
Demand							
6.1 Gross travel propensity		Units	..	..	..	..	..
6.2 Carrying capacity (arrivals/population)		Units	0.11	..	..	..	..

UGANDA

Basic data and indicators	Notes	Units	2005	2006	2007	2008	2009
1. INBOUND TOURISM							
Data							
Arrivals							
1.1 Total		('000)	..	..	..	..	..
1.2 ♦ Overnight visitors (tourists)		('000)	468	539	642	844	817
1.3 ♦ Same-day visitors (excursionists)		('000)	..	..	..	..	..
1.4 * of which, cruise passengers		('000)	..	..	..	..	..
Arrivals by region							
1.5 Total		('000)	468	538	641	844	817
1.6 ♦ Africa		('000)	337	397	480	624	641
1.7 ♦ Americas		('000)	29	36	42	54	47
1.8 ♦ East Asia and the Pacific		('000)	10	12	14	15	16
1.9 ♦ Europe		('000)	62	71	77	106	80
1.10 ♦ Middle East		('000)	4	4	5	10	12
1.11 ♦ South Asia		('000)	14	14	15	19	15
1.12 ♦ Other not classified		('000)	12	4	8	16	6
1.13 * of which, nationals residing abroad		('000)	..	..	..	..	..
Arrivals by main purpose							
1.14 Total		('000)	468	538	642	844	817
1.15 ♦ Personal		('000)	437	466	532	681	648
1.16 * holidays, leisure and recreation		('000)	9	30	140	144	128
1.17 * other personal purposes		('000)	428	436	392	537	520
1.18 ♦ Business and professional		('000)	31	72	110	163	169
Arrivals by mode of transport							
1.19 Total		('000)	468	539	642	844	817
1.20 ♦ Air		('000)	172	200	234	358	271
1.21 ♦ Water		('000)	..	..	..	..	..
1.22 ♦ Land		('000)	296	339	408	486	546
1.23 * railway		('000)	..	..	..	..	..
1.24 * road		('000)	296	339	408	486	546
1.25 * others		('000)	..	..	..	..	..
Expenditure							
1.33 Total		US$ Mn	382	347	402	531	683
1.34 ♦ Travel		US$ Mn	380	346	398	498	667
1.35 ♦ Passenger transport		US$ Mn	2	1	4	33	16
Expenditure by main purpose of the trip							
1.36 Total		US$ Mn	380	346	398	498	667
1.37 ♦ Personal		US$ Mn	274	249	287	359	262
1.38 ♦ Business and professional		US$ Mn	106	97	111	139	405
3. OUTBOUND TOURISM							
Data							
Departures							
3.1 Total		('000)	..	..	..	..	..
3.2 ♦ Overnight visitors (tourists)		('000)	189	254	272	337	..
3.3 ♦ Same-day visitors (excursionists)		('000)	..	..	..	..	..
Expenditure							
3.4 Total		US$ Mn	185	196	220	315	335
3.5 ♦ Travel		US$ Mn	124	123	132	156	179
3.6 ♦ Passenger transport		US$ Mn	61	73	88	159	156
Expenditure by main purpose of the trip							
3.7 Total		US$ Mn	124	123	132	155	179
3.8 ♦ Personal		US$ Mn	51	50	54	82	89
3.9 ♦ Business and professional		US$ Mn	73	73	78	73	90

UGANDA

Basic data and indicators	Notes	Units	2005	2006	2007	2008	2009
6. **COMPLEMENTARY INDICATORS**							
Demand							
6.1 Gross travel propensity		Units	..	..	..	..	..
6.2 Carrying capacity (arrivals/population)		Units	0.02	0.02	0.02	0.03	0.02
Macroeconomic indicators related to international tourism							
6.3 Inbound tourism expenditure over GDP		Percent	3.8	3.2	3.0	3.3	..
6.4 Outbound tourism expenditure over GDP		Percent	1.8	1.8	1.6	1.9	..
6.5 Tourism balance (inbound minus outbound tourism expenditure) over GDP		Percent	2.0	1.4	1.3	1.3	..
6.6 Tourism openness (inbound plus outbound tourism expenditure) over GDP		Percent	5.7	4.9	4.6	5.2	..
6.7 Tourism coverage (inbound over outbound tourism expenditure)		Percent	205.7	177.3	182.6	170.6	203.8
6.8 Inbound tourism expenditure over exports of goods		Percent	37.6	29.2	20.1	19.8	25.3
6.9 Inbound tourism expenditure over exports of services		Percent	76.1	71.8	74.6	73.2	75.7
6.10 Inbound tourism expenditure over exports of goods and services		Percent	25.2	20.8	15.8	15.6	19.0
6.11 Inbound tourism expenditure over current account credits		Percent	13.9	11.4	10.2	10.5	13.4
6.12 Outbound tourism expenditure over imports of goods		Percent	10.6	8.8	7.4	7.8	8.7
6.13 Outbound tourism expenditure over imports of services		Percent	30.5	25.4	22.5	25.0	23.3
6.14 Outbound tourism expenditure over imports of goods and services		Percent	7.9	6.6	5.6	5.9	6.3
6.15 Outbound tourism expenditure over current account debits		Percent	6.6	5.6	4.9	5.2	5.6

UKRAINE

Basic data and indicators	Notes	Units	2005	2006	2007	2008	2009
1. INBOUND TOURISM							
Data							
Arrivals							
1.1 Total		('000)	20,489	21,714	26,162	28,827	24,033
1.2 ♦ Overnight visitors (tourists)		('000)	17,631	18,936	23,122	25,449	20,798
1.3 ♦ Same-day visitors (excursionists)		('000)	2,858	2,778	3,040	3,378	3,235
1.4 * of which, cruise passengers		('000)	35	38	..	..	..
Arrivals by region							
1.5 Total		('000)	17,631	18,936	23,122	25,449	20,798
1.6 ♦ Africa		('000)	7	9	10	10	10
1.7 ♦ Americas		('000)	96	143	167	163	161
1.8 ♦ East Asia and the Pacific		('000)	35	45	49	46	44
1.9 ♦ Europe		('000)	17,442	18,680	22,826	25,164	20,514
1.10 ♦ Middle East		('000)	26	23	26	23	28
1.11 ♦ South Asia		('000)	15	16	18	17	20
1.12 ♦ Other not classified		('000)	10	20	26	26	21
1.13 * of which, nationals residing abroad		('000)	..	..	..	..	..
Arrivals by main purpose							
1.14 Total		('000)	17,631	18,935	23,122	25,449	20,798
1.15 ♦ Personal		('000)	16,591	17,879	22,164	24,335	19,953
1.16 * holidays, leisure and recreation		('000)	2,134	1,210	1,445	1,693	1,350
1.17 * other personal purposes		('000)	14,457	16,669	20,719	22,642	18,603
1.18 ♦ Business and professional		('000)	1,040	1,056	958	1,114	845
Arrivals by mode of transport							
1.19 Total		('000)	20,489	21,713	26,162	28,828	24,033
1.20 ♦ Air		('000)	1,069	1,217	1,478	1,662	1,457
1.21 ♦ Water		('000)	264	292	314	318	276
1.22 ♦ Land		('000)	19,156	20,204	24,370	26,848	22,300
1.23 * railway		('000)	7,898	7,701	..	..	..
1.24 * road		('000)	11,258	12,503	24,370	26,848	22,300
1.25 * others		('000)	..	..	..	..	..
Accommodation							
Total							
1.29 ♦ Guests		('000)	..	..	..	..	..
1.30 ♦ Overnights		('000)	3,895	..	..	..	..
Hotels and similar establishments							
1.31 ♦ Guests		('000)	..	..	..	..	..
1.32 ♦ Overnights		('000)	1,395	..	..	..	..
Expenditure							
1.33 Total		US$ Mn	3,542	4,018	5,320	6,722	4,349
1.34 ♦ Travel		US$ Mn	3,125	3,485	4,597	5,768	3,576
1.35 ♦ Passenger transport		US$ Mn	417	533	723	954	773
Expenditure by main purpose of the trip							
1.36 Total		US$ Mn	3,125	3,485	4,597	5,768	3,576
1.37 ♦ Personal		US$ Mn	2,837	3,161	4,291	5,371	3,349
1.38 ♦ Business and professional		US$ Mn	288	324	306	397	227
Indicators							
1.39 Average size of travel party		Persons	..	..	..	..	..
Average length of stay							
1.40 Total		Days	..	..	..	..	..
1.41 ♦ For all commercial accommodation services		Nights	3.80	..	..	..	..
1.42 * of which, "hotels and similar establishments"		Nights	..	..	..	..	..
1.43 ♦ For non commercial accommodation services		Days	..	..	..	..	..
1.44 Average expenditure per day		US$	..	..	..	..	..
2. DOMESTIC TOURISM							
Data							
Accommodation							
Total							
2.19 ♦ Guests		('000)	..	..	..	..	..
2.20 ♦ Overnights		('000)	37,336	..	..	..	..
Hotels and similar establishments							
2.21 ♦ Guests		('000)	..	..	..	..	..
2.22 ♦ Overnights		('000)	8,554	..	..	..	..

UKRAINE

Basic data and indicators	Notes	Units	2005	2006	2007	2008	2009
3. OUTBOUND TOURISM							
Data							
Departures							
3.1 Total		('000)	..	..	..	..	..
3.2 ♦ Overnight visitors (tourists)		('000)	16,454	16,875	17,335	15,499	15,334
3.3 ♦ Same-day visitors (excursionists)		('000)	..	..	..	..	..
Expenditure							
3.4 Total		US$ Mn	3,078	3,202	4,022	4,585	3,751
3.5 ♦ Travel		US$ Mn	2,805	2,834	3,569	4,023	3,330
3.6 ♦ Passenger transport		US$ Mn	273	368	453	562	421
Expenditure by main purpose of the trip							
3.7 Total		US$ Mn	2,805	2,834	3,569	4,023	3,330
3.8 ♦ Personal		US$ Mn	2,205	2,419	2,901	2,954	2,323
3.9 ♦ Business and professional		US$ Mn	600	415	668	1,069	1,007
4. TOURISM INDUSTRIES							
Data							
Accommodation for visitors in hotels and similar establishments							
Non-monetary data							
4.13 ♦ Number of establishments		Units	..	..	..	..	..
4.14 ♦ Number of rooms		Units	38,662	40,190	41,009	42,178	42,798
4.15 ♦ Number of bed-places		Units	69,785	72,548	73,792	75,659	77,610
Indicators							
4.16 Occupancy rate / rooms		Percent	..	..	..	..	..
4.17 Occupancy rate / bed-places		Percent	33.00	..	..	..	..
4.18 Average length of stay		Nights	2.60	..	..	..	..
4.19 Available capacity (bed-places per 1000 inhabitants)		Units	1.48	1.55	1.59	1.64	1.69
6. COMPLEMENTARY INDICATORS							
Demand							
6.1 Gross travel propensity		Units	..	..	..	..	..
6.2 Carrying capacity (arrivals/population)		Units	0.37	0.40	0.50	0.55	0.45
Macroeconomic indicators related to international tourism							
6.3 Inbound tourism expenditure over GDP		Percent	4.1	3.7	3.7	3.7	3.7
6.4 Outbound tourism expenditure over GDP		Percent	3.6	3.0	2.8	2.5	3.2
6.5 Tourism balance (inbound minus outbound tourism expenditure) over GDP		Percent	0.5	0.8	0.9	1.2	0.5
6.6 Tourism openness (inbound plus outbound tourism expenditure) over GDP		Percent	7.7	6.7	6.5	6.3	6.9
6.7 Tourism coverage (inbound over outbound tourism expenditure)		Percent	115.1	125.5	132.3	146.6	115.9
6.8 Inbound tourism expenditure over exports of goods		Percent	10.1	10.3	10.7	9.9	10.8
6.9 Inbound tourism expenditure over exports of services		Percent	37.9	35.6	37.6	37.6	31.4
6.10 Inbound tourism expenditure over exports of goods and services		Percent	8.0	8.0	8.3	7.9	8.0
6.11 Inbound tourism expenditure over current account credits		Percent	7.3	7.3	7.4	7.1	7.0
6.12 Outbound tourism expenditure over imports of goods		Percent	8.5	7.3	6.7	5.5	8.3
6.13 Outbound tourism expenditure over imports of services		Percent	40.8	34.9	34.3	28.4	33.4
6.14 Outbound tourism expenditure over imports of goods and services		Percent	7.0	6.0	5.6	4.6	6.7
6.15 Outbound tourism expenditure over current account debits		Percent	6.7	5.6	5.2	4.2	5.8

UNITED KINGDOM

Basic data and indicators	Notes	Units	2005	2006	2007	2008	2009
1. INBOUND TOURISM							
Data							
Arrivals							
1.1 Total		('000)	29,970	32,713	32,778	31,888	29,889
1.2 ♦ Overnight visitors (tourists)		('000)	28,039	30,654	30,870	30,142	28,199
1.3 ♦ Same-day visitors (excursionists)		('000)	1,931	2,059	1,908	1,746	1,690
1.4 * of which, cruise passengers		('000)	..	..	..	..	..
Arrivals by region							
1.5 Total		('000)	29,970	32,712	32,779	31,889	29,889
1.6 ♦ Africa		('000)	659	701	654	645	596
1.7 ♦ Americas		('000)	4,596	5,167	4,827	4,212	4,020
1.8 ♦ East Asia and the Pacific		('000)	2,231	2,310	2,316	2,147	2,066
1.9 ♦ Europe		('000)	21,706	23,541	24,020	23,826	22,241
1.10 ♦ Middle East		('000)	384	472	490	538	596
1.11 ♦ South Asia		('000)	394	521	472	521	370
1.12 ♦ Other not classified		('000)	..	..	..	..	..
1.13 * of which, nationals residing abroad		('000)	..	..	..	..	..
Arrivals by main purpose							
1.14 Total		('000)	29,970	32,713	32,778	31,888	29,889
1.15 ♦ Personal		('000)	21,197	22,996	23,282	23,205	22,807
1.16 * holidays, leisure and recreation		('000)	9,713	10,566	10,758	10,923	11,424
1.17 * other personal purposes		('000)	11,484	12,430	12,524	12,282	11,383
1.18 ♦ Business and professional		('000)	8,773	9,717	9,496	8,683	7,082
Arrivals by mode of transport							
1.19 Total		('000)	29,970	32,713	32,778	31,888	29,889
1.20 ♦ Air		('000)	22,043	24,588	25,089	24,024	22,080
1.21 ♦ Water		('000)	4,675	4,858	4,459	4,495	4,462
1.22 ♦ Land		('000)	3,252	3,267	3,230	3,369	3,347
1.23 * railway	(1)	('000)	3,252	3,267	3,230	3,369	3,347
1.24 * road		('000)	..	..	..	..	..
1.25 * others		('000)	..	..	..	..	..
Accommodation							
Total							
1.29 ♦ Guests		('000)	30,057	32,935	32,860	32,004	30,108
1.30 ♦ Overnights		('000)	249,181	273,417	251,520	245,775	229,387
Hotels and similar establishments							
1.31 ♦ Guests	(2)	('000)	13,746	15,225	15,397	14,649	14,143
1.32 ♦ Overnights	(2)	('000)	59,255	65,287	64,828	61,962	60,498
Expenditure							
1.33 Total		US$ Mn	39,411	43,803	48,193	46,285	38,545
1.34 ♦ Travel		US$ Mn	30,573	34,796	38,698	36,424	30,498
1.35 ♦ Passenger transport		US$ Mn	8,838	9,007	9,495	9,861	8,047
Expenditure by main purpose of the trip							
1.36 Total		US$ Mn	30,572	34,795	38,698	36,424	30,498
1.37 ♦ Personal		US$ Mn	22,693	25,520	28,902	27,486	24,339
1.38 ♦ Business and professional		US$ Mn	7,879	9,275	9,796	8,938	6,159
Indicators							
1.39 Average size of travel party		Persons	..	..	..	..	..
Average length of stay							
1.40 Total		Days	..	..	..	..	..
1.41 ♦ For all commercial accommodation services	(3)	Nights	8.30	8.40	7.70	7.70	7.70
1.42 * of which, "hotels and similar establishments"		Nights	..	..	..	..	..
1.43 ♦ For non commercial accommodation services		Days	..	..	..	..	..
1.44 Average expenditure per day		US$	..	..	..	..	..
2. DOMESTIC TOURISM							
Data							
Accommodation							
Total							
2.19 ♦ Guests		('000)	..	..	..	..	..
2.20 ♦ Overnights		('000)	442,300	400,100	394,413	378,388	398,749
Hotels and similar establishments							
2.21 ♦ Guests		('000)	52,611	46,783	47,010	46,256	48,279
2.22 ♦ Overnights		('000)	117,926	102,010	105,231	103,020	106,116

UNITED KINGDOM

Basic data and indicators	Notes	Units	2005	2006	2007	2008	2009
3. OUTBOUND TOURISM							
Data							
Departures							
3.1 Total		('000)	..	..	..	..	..
3.2 ♦ Overnight visitors (tourists)		('000)	66,494	69,536	69,450	69,011	58,614
3.3 ♦ Same-day visitors (excursionists)		('000)	..	..	..	..	..
Expenditure							
3.4 Total		US$ Mn	72,993	77,674	86,747	83,584	61,130
3.5 ♦ Travel		US$ Mn	59,532	63,319	71,519	69,792	50,559
3.6 ♦ Passenger transport		US$ Mn	13,461	14,355	15,228	13,792	10,571
Expenditure by main purpose of the trip							
3.7 Total		US$ Mn	59,532	63,319	71,519	69,792	50,559
3.8 ♦ Personal		US$ Mn	50,622	53,768	60,775	59,580	43,364
3.9 ♦ Business and professional		US$ Mn	8,910	9,551	10,744	10,212	7,195
4. TOURISM INDUSTRIES							
Data							
Accommodation for visitors in hotels and similar establishments							
Non-monetary data							
4.13 ♦ Number of establishments		Units	..	..	..	..	..
4.14 ♦ Number of rooms	(4)	Units	518,028	616,764	615,986	..	..
4.15 ♦ Number of bed-places	(4)	Units	1,062,342	1,255,693	1,250,536	..	..
Indicators							
4.16 Occupancy rate / rooms		Percent	..	..	..	..	..
4.17 Occupancy rate / bed-places	(5)	Percent	44.00	47.00	48.00	44.00	43.00
4.18 Average length of stay		Nights	..	..	..	..	..
4.19 Available capacity (bed-places per 1000 inhabitants)		Units	17.64	20.72	20.51	..	..
6. COMPLEMENTARY INDICATORS							
Demand							
6.1 Gross travel propensity		Units	..	..	..	..	..
6.2 Carrying capacity (arrivals/population)		Units	0.47	0.51	0.51	0.49	0.46
Macroeconomic indicators related to international tourism							
6.3 Inbound tourism expenditure over GDP		Percent	1.7	1.8	1.7	1.7	1.7
6.4 Outbound tourism expenditure over GDP		Percent	3.2	3.2	3.1	3.2	2.8
6.5 Tourism balance (inbound minus outbound tourism expenditure) over GDP		Percent	-1.5	-1.4	-1.4	-1.4	-1.0
6.6 Tourism openness (inbound plus outbound tourism expenditure) over GDP		Percent	4.9	5.0	4.8	4.9	4.5
6.7 Tourism coverage (inbound over outbound tourism expenditure)		Percent	54.0	56.4	55.1	55.0	63.2
6.8 Inbound tourism expenditure over exports of goods		Percent	10.3	9.8	10.9	9.9	10.7
6.9 Inbound tourism expenditure over exports of services		Percent	19.0	18.5	16.9	16.0	16.1
6.10 Inbound tourism expenditure over exports of goods and services		Percent	6.7	6.4	6.6	6.1	6.4
6.11 Inbound tourism expenditure over current account credits		Percent	4.1	3.8	3.6	3.6	4.3
6.12 Outbound tourism expenditure over imports of goods		Percent	14.3	13.2	14.1	13.1	12.4
6.13 Outbound tourism expenditure over imports of services		Percent	44.8	44.3	43.4	41.3	36.1
6.14 Outbound tourism expenditure over imports of goods and services		Percent	10.9	10.2	10.6	10.0	9.2
6.15 Outbound tourism expenditure over current account debits		Percent	7.1	6.3	6.2	6.4	6.5

UNITED REPUBLIC OF TANZANIA

Basic data and indicators	Notes	Units	2005	2006	2007	2008	2009
1. INBOUND TOURISM							
Data							
Arrivals							
1.1 Total		('000)	613	644	719	770	714
1.2 ♦ Overnight visitors (tourists)		('000)	590	622	692	750	714
1.3 ♦ Same-day visitors (excursionists)		('000)	23	22	27	20	..
1.4 * of which, cruise passengers		('000)	..	..	..	..	..
Arrivals by region							
1.5 Total		('000)	614	643	719	770	714
1.6 ♦ Africa		('000)	276	293	306	373	349
1.7 ♦ Americas		('000)	62	71	81	88	68
1.8 ♦ East Asia and the Pacific		('000)	25	28	30	32	31
1.9 ♦ Europe		('000)	220	229	274	246	233
1.10 ♦ Middle East		('000)	11	7	11	10	11
1.11 ♦ South Asia		('000)	20	15	17	21	22
1.12 ♦ Other not classified		('000)	..	..	..	..	..
1.13 * of which, nationals residing abroad		('000)	..	..	..	..	..
Arrivals by main purpose							
1.14 Total		('000)	613	644	718	770	715
1.15 ♦ Personal		('000)	528	573	661	733	686
1.16 * holidays, leisure and recreation		('000)	467	495	580	650	593
1.17 * other personal purposes		('000)	61	78	81	83	93
1.18 ♦ Business and professional		('000)	85	71	57	37	29
Arrivals by mode of transport							
1.19 Total		('000)	613	644	720	770	714
1.20 ♦ Air		('000)	331	359	389	439	380
1.21 ♦ Water		('000)	10	14	16	9	10
1.22 ♦ Land		('000)	272	271	315	322	324
1.23 * railway		('000)	6	5	5	5	3
1.24 * road		('000)	266	266	310	317	321
1.25 * others		('000)	..	..	..	..	..
Arrivals by form of organization of the trip							
1.26 Total		('000)	..	..	..	..	714
1.27 ♦ Package tour		('000)	..	..	..	..	480
1.28 ♦ Other forms		('000)	..	..	..	..	234
Accommodation							
Total							
1.29 ♦ Guests		('000)	..	..	..	..	..
1.30 ♦ Overnights		('000)	6,130	7,729	..	..	..
Hotels and similar establishments							
1.31 ♦ Guests		('000)	..	..	..	..	..
1.32 ♦ Overnights		('000)	..	..	..	..	..
Expenditure							
1.33 Total		US$ Mn	835	986	1,215	1,293	1,192
1.34 ♦ Travel		US$ Mn	824	950	1,199	1,289	1,160
1.35 ♦ Passenger transport		US$ Mn	11	36	16	4	32
2. DOMESTIC TOURISM							
Data							
Accommodation							
Total							
2.19 ♦ Guests		('000)	..	..	..	..	..
2.20 ♦ Overnights		('000)	4,500	..	..	..	..
Hotels and similar establishments							
2.21 ♦ Guests		('000)	..	..	..	..	..
2.22 ♦ Overnights		('000)	..	..	..	..	..
3. OUTBOUND TOURISM							
Data							
Expenditure							
3.4 Total		US$ Mn	577	571	616	746	806
3.5 ♦ Travel		US$ Mn	554	534	595	721	766
3.6 ♦ Passenger transport		US$ Mn	23	37	21	25	40

UNITED REPUBLIC OF TANZANIA

Basic data and indicators	Notes	Units	2005	2006	2007	2008	2009
4. TOURISM INDUSTRIES							
Data							
Accommodation for visitors in hotels and similar establishments							
Non-monetary data							
4.13 ♦ Number of establishments		Units	495	496	..	..	..
4.14 ♦ Number of rooms		Units	31,365	..	..	..	..
4.15 ♦ Number of bed-places		Units	56,562	..	..	..	..
Indicators							
4.16 Occupancy rate / rooms		Percent	..	..	..	..	..
4.17 Occupancy rate / bed-places		Percent	48.00	..	..	..	..
4.18 Average length of stay		Nights	12.00	12.00	12.00	..	..
4.19 Available capacity (bed-places per 1000 inhabitants)		Units	1.45	..	..	..	..
6. COMPLEMENTARY INDICATORS							
Demand							
6.1 Gross travel propensity		Units	..	..	..	..	..
6.2 Carrying capacity (arrivals/population)		Units	0.02	0.02	0.02	0.02	0.02
Macroeconomic indicators related to international tourism							
6.3 Inbound tourism expenditure over GDP		Percent	6.6	..	..	..	..
6.4 Outbound tourism expenditure over GDP		Percent	4.6	..	..	..	..
6.5 Tourism balance (inbound minus outbound tourism expenditure) over GDP		Percent	2.1	..	..	..	..
6.6 Tourism openness (inbound plus outbound tourism expenditure) over GDP		Percent	11.2	..	..	..	..
6.7 Tourism coverage (inbound over outbound tourism expenditure)		Percent	144.9	172.5	196.9	182.2	..
6.8 Inbound tourism expenditure over exports of goods		Percent	49.7	51.4	54.5	44.7	..
6.9 Inbound tourism expenditure over exports of services		Percent	65.8	64.5	64.7	62.6	..
6.10 Inbound tourism expenditure over exports of goods and services		Percent	28.3	28.6	29.6	26.1	..
6.11 Inbound tourism expenditure over current account credits		Percent	23.2	23.6	24.6	22.5	..
6.12 Outbound tourism expenditure over imports of goods		Percent	19.2	14.8	12.7	11.6	..
6.13 Outbound tourism expenditure over imports of services		Percent	47.7	45.7	43.6	46.6	..
6.14 Outbound tourism expenditure over imports of goods and services		Percent	13.7	11.2	9.8	9.3	..
6.15 Outbound tourism expenditure over current account debits		Percent	12.9	10.7	9.5	8.9	..

UNITED STATES OF AMERICA

Basic data and indicators	Notes	Units	2005	2006	2007	2008	2009
1. INBOUND TOURISM							
Data							
Arrivals							
1.1 Total		('000)	71,484	74,437	80,203	81,986	75,742
1.2 ♦ Overnight visitors (tourists)	(1)	('000)	49,206	50,977	55,979	57,937	54,884
1.3 ♦ Same-day visitors (excursionists)	(2)	('000)	22,278	23,460	24,224	24,049	20,858
1.4 * of which, cruise passengers		('000)	..	..	..	..	..
Arrivals by region							
1.5 Total		('000)	49,205	50,977	55,979	57,937	54,884
1.6 ♦ Africa		('000)	252	252	276	311	291
1.7 ♦ Americas	(1)	('000)	31,178	33,128	36,464	37,128	35,834
1.8 ♦ East Asia and the Pacific		('000)	6,518	6,428	6,563	6,343	5,906
1.9 ♦ Europe		('000)	10,702	10,531	11,839	13,250	11,978
1.10 ♦ Middle East		('000)	144	164	196	228	246
1.11 ♦ South Asia		('000)	411	474	641	677	629
1.12 ♦ Other not classified		('000)	..	..	..	..	..
1.13 * of which, nationals residing abroad		('000)	..	..	..	..	..
Arrivals by main purpose	(3)						
1.14 Total		('000)	21,679	21,669	23,892	25,341	23,756
1.15 ♦ Personal		('000)	16,042	16,100	17,107	18,448	17,953
1.16 * holidays, leisure and recreation		('000)	10,232	10,076	10,871	12,392	11,584
1.17 * other personal purposes		('000)	5,810	6,024	6,236	6,056	6,369
1.18 ♦ Business and professional		('000)	5,637	5,569	6,785	6,893	5,803
Arrivals by mode of transport	(4)						
1.19 Total		('000)	49,206	50,978	55,979	57,937	54,884
1.20 ♦ Air		('000)	27,678	27,807	30,325	32,045	30,007
1.21 ♦ Water		('000)	419	453	503	461	425
1.22 ♦ Land		('000)	21,109	22,718	25,151	25,431	24,452
1.23 * railway		('000)	23	25	31	31	27
1.24 * road	(5)	('000)	21,086	22,693	25,120	25,400	24,425
1.25 * others		('000)	..	..	..	..	..
Arrivals by form of organization of the trip	(3)						
1.26 Total		('000)	21,679	21,668	23,892	25,341	23,756
1.27 ♦ Package tour		('000)	4,076	3,857	3,871	4,055	3,706
1.28 ♦ Other forms		('000)	17,603	17,811	20,021	21,286	20,050
Accommodation							
Total							
1.29 ♦ Guests		('000)	..	..	..	..	..
1.30 ♦ Overnights		('000)	..	..	..	..	..
Hotels and similar establishments							
1.31 ♦ Guests	(3)	('000)	16,975	16,944	18,755	20,045	18,506
1.32 ♦ Overnights	(3)	('000)	132,402	127,083	148,166	166,371	151,749
Expenditure							
1.33 Total		US$ Mn	123,039	128,941	145,231	166,375	147,554
1.34 ♦ Travel	(6)	US$ Mn	102,070	106,906	119,586	134,972	121,131
1.35 ♦ Passenger transport		US$ Mn	20,969	22,035	25,645	31,403	26,423
Expenditure by main purpose of the trip							
1.36 Total		US$ Mn	102,070	106,906	119,586	134,972	121,131
1.37 ♦ Personal		US$ Mn	97,785	102,603	115,158	130,383	116,451
1.38 ♦ Business and professional		US$ Mn	4,285	4,303	4,428	4,589	4,680
Indicators							
1.39 Average size of travel party	(3)	Persons	1.6	1.6	1.5	1.6	1.6
Average length of stay							
1.40 Total	(3)	Days	16.20	15.80	16.00	16.40	17.70
1.41 ♦ For all commercial accommodation services		Nights	..	..	..	..	..
1.42 * of which, "hotels and similar establishments"	(3)	Nights	7.80	7.50	7.90	8.30	8.20
1.43 ♦ For non commercial accommodation services		Days	..	..	..	..	..
1.44 Average expenditure per day		US$	103.0	107.0	108.0	116.0	97.0

UNITED STATES OF AMERICA

Basic data and indicators	Notes	Units	2005	2006	2007	2008	2009
3. OUTBOUND TOURISM							
Data							
Departures							
3.1 Total		('000)	..	..	..	..	..
3.2 ♦ Overnight visitors (tourists)	(7)(8)	('000)	63,503	63,662	64,028	63,564	61,419
3.3 ♦ Same-day visitors (excursionists)	(9)	('000)	15,712	13,747	11,164	9,103	7,838
Expenditure							
3.4 Total		US$ Mn	99,469	104,450	109,896	117,886	105,202
3.5 ♦ Travel	(6)	US$ Mn	73,320	76,949	81,459	85,323	79,222
3.6 ♦ Passenger transport		US$ Mn	26,149	27,501	28,437	32,563	25,980
Expenditure by main purpose of the trip							
3.7 Total		US$ Mn	73,320	76,949	81,459	85,323	79,222
3.8 ♦ Personal		US$ Mn	72,962	76,571	81,057	84,899	78,812
3.9 ♦ Business and professional		US$ Mn	358	378	402	424	410
Indicators							
3.10 Average length of stay		Days	16.40	16.20	17.40	18.00	18.50
3.11 Average expenditure per day		US$	66.2	69.9	68.5	69.7	64.4
4. TOURISM INDUSTRIES							
Data							
Number of establishments							
4.1 Total		Units	..	..	..	..	..
4.2 ♦ Accommodation for visitors		Units	..	..	..	..	..
4.3 * of which, "hotels and similar establishments"	(10)	Units	47,590	47,135	48,062	49,505	50,800
4.4 ♦ Food and beverage serving activities		Units	..	..	..	..	..
4.5 ♦ Passenger transportation		Units	..	..	..	..	..
4.6 ♦ Travel agencies and other reservation services activities		Units	..	..	..	..	..
4.7 ♦ Other tourism industries		Units	..	..	..	..	..
Accommodation for visitors in hotels and similar establishments							
Monetary data							
4.8 ♦ Output	(11)	US$ Mn	123,831.0	132,827.0	142,451.0	148,261.0	125,707.0
4.9 ♦ Intermediate consumption		US$ Mn	..	..	..	..	..
4.10 ♦ Gross value added		US$ Mn	..	..	..	..	..
4.11 ♦ Compensation of employees		US$ Mn	..	..	..	..	..
4.12 ♦ Gross fixed capital formation		US$ Mn	..	..	..	..	..
Non-monetary data	(10)						
4.13 ♦ Number of establishments		Units	47,590	47,135	48,062	49,505	50,800
4.14 ♦ Number of rooms		Units	4,402,466	4,389,443	4,476,191	4,626,348	4,762,095
4.15 ♦ Number of bed-places		Units	..	..	..	..	..
Indicators							
4.16 Occupancy rate / rooms		Percent	..	..	..	..	..
4.17 Occupancy rate / bed-places	(12)	Percent	63.10	63.30	63.10	60.40	55.10
4.18 Average length of stay	(13)	Nights	7.80	7.50	7.90	8.30	8.20
4.19 Available capacity (bed-places per 1000 inhabitants)		Units	..	..	..	..	..
5. EMPLOYMENT							
Data							
Number of employees by tourism industries	(14)						
5.1 Total		('000)	5,766.0	5,847.0	5,909.0	5,907.0	5,649.0
5.2 ♦ Accommodation services for visitors (hotels and similar establishments)	(15)	('000)	1,358.0	1,363.0	1,376.0	1,376.0	1,297.0
5.3 ♦ Other accommodation services		('000)	..	..	..	..	..
5.4 ♦ Food and beverage serving activities	(16)	('000)	1,859.0	1,908.0	1,940.0	1,944.0	1,899.0
5.5 ♦ Passenger transportation	(17)	('000)	452.0	447.0	452.0	454.0	428.0
5.6 ♦ Travel agencies and other reservation services activities		('000)	..	..	..	..	..
5.7 ♦ Other tourism industries	(18)	('000)	2,097.0	2,129.0	2,141.0	2,133.0	2,025.0

UNITED STATES OF AMERICA

Basic data and indicators	Notes	Units	2005	2006	2007	2008	2009
6. COMPLEMENTARY INDICATORS							
Demand							
6.1 Gross travel propensity		Units	..	..	..	..	..
6.2 Carrying capacity (arrivals/population)		Units	0.17	0.17	0.19	0.19	0.18
Macroeconomic indicators related to international tourism							
6.3 Inbound tourism expenditure over GDP		Percent	1.0	1.0	1.0	1.2	1.0
6.4 Outbound tourism expenditure over GDP		Percent	0.8	0.8	0.8	0.8	0.7
6.5 Tourism balance (inbound minus outbound tourism expenditure) over GDP		Percent	0.2	0.2	0.3	0.3	0.3
6.6 Tourism openness (inbound plus outbound tourism expenditure) over GDP		Percent	1.8	1.7	1.8	2.0	1.8
6.7 Tourism coverage (inbound over outbound tourism expenditure)		Percent	123.7	123.5	132.2	141.1	140.3
6.8 Inbound tourism expenditure over exports of goods		Percent	13.5	12.4	12.5	12.7	13.8
6.9 Inbound tourism expenditure over exports of services		Percent	33.4	31.2	30.0	31.4	29.6
6.10 Inbound tourism expenditure over exports of goods and services		Percent	9.6	8.9	8.8	9.0	9.4
6.11 Inbound tourism expenditure over current account credits		Percent	6.7	6.0	5.8	6.3	6.8
6.12 Outbound tourism expenditure over imports of goods		Percent	5.9	5.6	5.5	5.5	6.7
6.13 Outbound tourism expenditure over imports of services		Percent	33.0	31.1	30.0	29.7	28.5
6.14 Outbound tourism expenditure over imports of goods and services		Percent	5.0	4.7	4.7	4.6	5.4
6.15 Outbound tourism expenditure over current account debits		Percent	3.9	3.5	3.4	3.5	4.1

UNITED STATES VIRGIN ISLANDS

Basic data and indicators	Notes	Units	2005	2006	2007	2008	2009
1. INBOUND TOURISM							
Data							
Arrivals							
1.1 Total		('000)	2,602	2,571	2,606	2,435	2,246
1.2 ♦ Overnight visitors (tourists)		('000)	593	570	586	574	562
1.3 ♦ Same-day visitors (excursionists)		('000)	2,009	2,001	2,020	1,861	1,684
1.4 * of which, cruise passengers		('000)	1,913	1,903	1,918	1,757	1,582
Arrivals by region	(1)						
1.5 Total		('000)	617	701	679	740	787
1.6 ♦ Africa		('000)	..	..	..	..	..
1.7 ♦ Americas		('000)	569	649	651	720	767
1.8 ♦ East Asia and the Pacific		('000)	..	..	..	..	..
1.9 ♦ Europe		('000)	19	15	15	16	16
1.10 ♦ Middle East		('000)	..	..	..	..	..
1.11 ♦ South Asia		('000)	..	..	..	..	..
1.12 ♦ Other not classified		('000)	29	37	13	4	4
1.13 * of which, nationals residing abroad		('000)	..	..	..	..	..
Arrivals by mode of transport							
1.19 Total		('000)	2,602	2,570	2,606	2,435	2,246
1.20 ♦ Air	(2)	('000)	689	667	688	678	664
1.21 ♦ Water	(3)	('000)	1,913	1,903	1,918	1,757	1,582
1.22 ♦ Land		('000)	..	..	..	..	..
1.23 * railway		('000)	..	..	..	..	..
1.24 * road		('000)	..	..	..	..	..
1.25 * others		('000)	..	..	..	..	..
Accommodation							
Total							
1.29 ♦ Guests		('000)	..	..	..	..	..
1.30 ♦ Overnights	(4)	('000)	1,094	1,041	1,100	1,074	998
Hotels and similar establishments							
1.31 ♦ Guests		('000)	618	701	680	740	787
1.32 ♦ Overnights		('000)	..	..	..	..	..
Expenditure							
1.33 Total	(5)	US$ Mn	1,432	1,467	1,512	1,520	1,468
1.34 ♦ Travel		US$ Mn	..	..	..	..	..
1.35 ♦ Passenger transport		US$ Mn	..	..	..	..	..
2. DOMESTIC TOURISM							
Data							
Accommodation							
Total							
2.19 ♦ Guests		('000)	..	..	..	..	..
2.20 ♦ Overnights		('000)	..	..	..	..	..
Hotels and similar establishments							
2.21 ♦ Guests		('000)	80	103	82	77	79
2.22 ♦ Overnights		('000)	..	..	..	..	..
4. TOURISM INDUSTRIES							
Data							
Accommodation for visitors in hotels and similar establishments							
Non-monetary data							
4.13 ♦ Number of establishments		Units	47	47	46	47	46
4.14 ♦ Number of rooms	(6)	Units	4,761	4,812	4,757	4,857	4,948
4.15 ♦ Number of bed-places		Units	..	..	..	..	..
Indicators							
4.16 Occupancy rate / rooms	(6)	Percent	63.80	60.10	64.40	60.00	54.90
4.17 Occupancy rate / bed-places		Percent	..	..	..	..	..
4.18 Average length of stay		Nights	4.30	4.30	4.40	4.30	..
4.19 Available capacity (bed-places per 1000 inhabitants)		Units	..	..	..	..	..
6. COMPLEMENTARY INDICATORS							
Demand							
6.1 Gross travel propensity		Units	..	..	..	..	..
6.2 Carrying capacity (arrivals/population)		Units	5.41	5.19	5.34	5.23	5.12

URUGUAY

Basic data and indicators	Notes	Units	2005	2006	2007	2008	2009
1. INBOUND TOURISM							
Data							
Arrivals							
1.1 Total		('000)	1,917	1,824	1,815	2,255	2,304
1.2 ♦ Overnight visitors (tourists)		('000)	1,808	1,749	1,753	1,938	2,056
1.3 ♦ Same-day visitors (excursionists)		('000)	109	75	62	317	248
1.4 * of which, cruise passengers		('000)	..	..	..	257	206
Arrivals by region							
1.5 Total		('000)	1,918	1,824	1,815	1,997	2,098
1.6 ♦ Africa		('000)	..	..	..	..	..
1.7 ♦ Americas		('000)	1,498	1,403	1,407	1,544	1,643
1.8 ♦ East Asia and the Pacific		('000)	12	13	13	14	17
1.9 ♦ Europe		('000)	120	124	133	139	140
1.10 ♦ Middle East		('000)	..	..	..	..	..
1.11 ♦ South Asia		('000)	..	..	..	..	..
1.12 ♦ Other not classified		('000)	288	284	262	300	298
1.13 * of which, nationals residing abroad		('000)	285	281	260	274	297
Arrivals by main purpose							
1.14 Total		('000)	1,917	1,824	1,815	1,998	2,098
1.15 ♦ Personal		('000)	1,780	1,684	1,704	1,869	1,924
1.16 * holidays, leisure and recreation		('000)	1,249	1,180	1,193	1,400	1,304
1.17 * other personal purposes		('000)	531	504	511	469	620
1.18 ♦ Business and professional		('000)	137	140	111	129	174
Arrivals by mode of transport							
1.19 Total		('000)	1,917	1,824	1,812	1,998	2,098
1.20 ♦ Air		('000)	406	419	437	458	468
1.21 ♦ Water		('000)	692	775	897	990	983
1.22 ♦ Land		('000)	819	630	478	550	647
1.23 * railway		('000)	..	6	..	..	..
1.24 * road	(1)	('000)	819	624	478	546	643
1.25 * others		('000)	..	..	..	4	4
Accommodation							
Total							
1.29 ♦ Guests		('000)	649	656	618	818	887
1.30 ♦ Overnights		('000)	2,925	3,020	3,139	4,458	5,042
Hotels and similar establishments							
1.31 ♦ Guests		('000)	608	625	596	760	844
1.32 ♦ Overnights		('000)	2,620	2,791	2,964	4,014	4,619
Expenditure							
1.33 Total		US$ Mn	699	711	928	1,193	1,408
1.34 ♦ Travel		US$ Mn	594	598	809	1,051	1,312
1.35 ♦ Passenger transport		US$ Mn	105	113	119	142	96
Indicators							
1.39 Average size of travel party		Persons	..	..	..	..	..
Average length of stay							
1.40 Total		Days	..	..	..	..	7.20
1.41 ♦ For all commercial accommodation services	(2)	Nights	4.51	4.51	5.08	5.54	5.40
1.42 * of which, "hotels and similar establishments"		Nights	..	..	..	..	..
1.43 ♦ For non commercial accommodation services		Days	..	..	..	..	..
1.44 Average expenditure per day		US$	..	..	..	..	85.9
2. DOMESTIC TOURISM							
Data							
Trips							
2.1 Total		('000)	..	..	..	..	2,438
2.2 ♦ Overnight visitors (tourists)		('000)	..	..	..	..	..
2.3 ♦ Same-day visitors (excursionists)		('000)	..	..	..	..	..
Trips by main purpose							
2.4 Total		('000)	..	..	..	..	2,438
2.5 ♦ Personal		('000)	..	..	..	..	2,400
2.6 * holidays, leisure and recreation		('000)	..	..	..	..	1,222
2.7 * other personal purposes		('000)	..	..	..	..	1,178
2.8 ♦ Business and professional		('000)	..	..	..	..	38

URUGUAY

Basic data and indicators	Notes	Units	2005	2006	2007	2008	2009
Trips by mode of transport							
2.9 Total		('000)	..	..	..	..	2,438
2.10 ◆ Air		('000)	..	..	..	..	2
2.11 ◆ Water		('000)	..	..	..	..	..
2.12 ◆ Land		('000)	..	..	..	..	2,436
2.13 * railway		('000)	..	..	..	..	..
2.14 * road		('000)	..	..	..	..	2,387
2.15 * others		('000)	..	..	..	..	49
Accommodation							
Total							
2.19 ◆ Guests		('000)	..	..	..	..	..
2.20 ◆ Overnights		('000)	..	..	7,472	..	..
Hotels and similar establishments							
2.21 ◆ Guests		('000)	..	..	51	..	310
2.22 ◆ Overnights		('000)	..	..	776	..	..
Indicators							
2.23 Average size of travel party		Persons	..	..	..	..	..
Average length of stay							
2.24 Total		Days	..	..	..	..	..
2.25 ◆ For all commercial accommodation services		Nights	..	..	4.85	..	..
2.26 * of which, "hotels and similar establishments"		Nights	..	..	..	..	..
2.27 ◆ For non commercial accommodation services		Days	..	..	..	..	..
2.28 Average expenditure per day		US$	..	..	..	..	..

3. OUTBOUND TOURISM

	Notes	Units	2005	2006	2007	2008	2009
Data							
Departures							
3.1 Total		('000)	..	..	..	..	..
3.2 ◆ Overnight visitors (tourists)		('000)	658	666	635	734	826
3.3 ◆ Same-day visitors (excursionists)		('000)	..	..	..	..	..
Expenditure							
3.4 Total		US$ Mn	331	305	354	466	436
3.5 ◆ Travel		US$ Mn	252	213	239	358	336
3.6 ◆ Passenger transport		US$ Mn	79	92	115	108	100
Indicators							
3.10 Average length of stay		Days	..	..	..	..	7.30
3.11 Average expenditure per day		US$	..	..	..	..	55.8

4. TOURISM INDUSTRIES

	Notes	Units	2005	2006	2007	2008	2009
Data							
Accommodation for visitors in hotels and similar establishments							
Non-monetary data							
4.13 ◆ Number of establishments		Units	..	..	..	..	..
4.14 ◆ Number of rooms	(3)	Units	14,729	14,350	13,216	18,521	17,613
4.15 ◆ Number of bed-places	(3)	Units	26,222	29,604	30,432	45,285	42,214
Indicators							
4.16 Occupancy rate / rooms		Percent	..	..	..	..	..
4.17 Occupancy rate / bed-places		Percent	..	..	..	..	..
4.18 Average length of stay		Nights	4.31	4.31	5.08	5.54	5.40
4.19 Available capacity (bed-places per 1000 inhabitants)		Units	7.93	8.93	9.16	13.58	12.62

5. EMPLOYMENT

	Notes	Units	2005	2006	2007	2008	2009
Data							
Number of employees by tourism industries							
5.1 Total		('000)	..	..	..	122.0	126.8
5.2 ◆ Accommodation services for visitors (hotels and similar establishments)		('000)	..	..	..	9.0	9.8
5.3 ◆ Other accommodation services	(4)	('000)	..	..	..	6.4	6.3
5.4 ◆ Food and beverage serving activities		('000)	..	..	..	32.1	36.0
5.5 ◆ Passenger transportation		('000)	..	..	..	33.4	33.6
5.6 ◆ Travel agencies and other reservation services activities		('000)	..	..	..	2.1	1.9
5.7 ◆ Other tourism industries		('000)	..	..	..	39.0	39.3

URUGUAY

Basic data and indicators	Notes	Units	2005	2006	2007	2008	2009
6. COMPLEMENTARY INDICATORS							
Demand							
6.1 Gross travel propensity		Units	..	..	..	..	..
6.2 Carrying capacity (arrivals/population)		Units	0.55	0.53	0.53	0.58	0.61
Macroeconomic indicators related to international tourism							
6.3 Inbound tourism expenditure over GDP		Percent	4.0	3.6	3.9	3.8	4.5
6.4 Outbound tourism expenditure over GDP		Percent	1.9	1.5	1.5	1.6	1.4
6.5 Tourism balance (inbound minus outbound tourism expenditure) over GDP		Percent	2.1	2.1	2.4	2.2	3.1
6.6 Tourism openness (inbound plus outbound tourism expenditure) over GDP		Percent	5.9	5.1	5.4	5.3	5.9
6.7 Tourism coverage (inbound over outbound tourism expenditure)		Percent	211.3	233.2	262.5	242.5	325.6
6.8 Inbound tourism expenditure over exports of goods		Percent	18.5	16.2	18.2	16.6	22.2
6.9 Inbound tourism expenditure over exports of services		Percent	53.3	51.2	50.7	53.1	65.7
6.10 Inbound tourism expenditure over exports of goods and services		Percent	13.8	12.3	13.4	12.6	16.6
6.11 Inbound tourism expenditure over current account credits		Percent	12.0	10.6	11.7	11.5	15.4
6.12 Outbound tourism expenditure over imports of goods		Percent	8.8	6.2	6.3	5.6	6.5
6.13 Outbound tourism expenditure over imports of services		Percent	35.2	31.2	31.6	34.4	40.0
6.14 Outbound tourism expenditure over imports of goods and services		Percent	7.1	5.2	5.2	4.8	5.6
6.15 Outbound tourism expenditure over current account debits		Percent	5.7	4.3	4.3	4.2	4.9

UZBEKISTAN

Basic data and indicators	Notes	Units	2005	2006	2007	2008	2009
1. INBOUND TOURISM							
Data							
Arrivals							
1.1 Total		('000)	..	..	..	..	..
1.2 ♦ Overnight visitors (tourists)		('000)	242	560	903	1,069	1,215
1.3 ♦ Same-day visitors (excursionists)		('000)	..	..	..	..	..
1.4 * of which, cruise passengers		('000)	..	..	..	..	..
Arrivals by region							
1.5 Total		('000)	..	560	903	1,069	1,215
1.6 ♦ Africa		('000)	..	2	2	2	..
1.7 ♦ Americas		('000)	..	6	8	8	7
1.8 ♦ East Asia and the Pacific		('000)	..	296	443	579	649
1.9 ♦ Europe		('000)	..	216	370	385	333
1.10 ♦ Middle East		('000)	..	30	50	55	67
1.11 ♦ South Asia		('000)	..	10	30	40	159
1.12 ♦ Other not classified		('000)	..	..	..	..	..
1.13 * of which, nationals residing abroad		('000)	..	..	..	..	..
Arrivals by main purpose							
1.14 Total		('000)	242	560	903	1,070	1,215
1.15 ♦ Personal		('000)	194	480	792	939	1,111
1.16 * holidays, leisure and recreation		('000)	38	53	80	217	196
1.17 * other personal purposes		('000)	156	427	712	722	915
1.18 ♦ Business and professional		('000)	48	80	111	131	104
Arrivals by mode of transport							
1.19 Total		('000)	242	560	903	1,069	1,215
1.20 ♦ Air		('000)	217	523	855	1,001	1,007
1.21 ♦ Water		('000)	..	..	..	..	..
1.22 ♦ Land		('000)	25	37	48	68	208
1.23 * railway		('000)	23	35	45	65	190
1.24 * road		('000)	2	2	3	3	18
1.25 * others		('000)	..	..	..	..	..
Accommodation							
Total							
1.29 ♦ Guests		('000)	..	..	..	..	..
1.30 ♦ Overnights		('000)	840	1,350	1,770	2,636	2,810
Hotels and similar establishments							
1.31 ♦ Guests		('000)	..	..	..	..	..
1.32 ♦ Overnights		('000)	448	1,289	1,659	1,861	1,942
Expenditure	(1)						
1.33 Total		US$ Mn	..	..	..	..	..
1.34 ♦ Travel		US$ Mn	28	43	51	64	99
1.35 ♦ Passenger transport		US$ Mn	..	..	..	..	..
Indicators							
1.39 Average size of travel party		Persons	..	..	..	..	..
Average length of stay							
1.40 Total		Days	..	..	..	..	..
1.41 ♦ For all commercial accommodation services		Nights	2.30	2.40	2.00	2.50	2.90
1.42 * of which, "hotels and similar establishments"		Nights	..	..	..	..	..
1.43 ♦ For non commercial accommodation services		Days	..	..	..	..	..
1.44 Average expenditure per day		US$	..	..	..	..	..
2. DOMESTIC TOURISM							
Data							
Accommodation							
Total							
2.19 ♦ Guests		('000)	..	..	..	..	..
2.20 ♦ Overnights		('000)	1,312	1,337	1,770	2,636	1,942
Hotels and similar establishments							
2.21 ♦ Guests		('000)	..	..	..	..	..
2.22 ♦ Overnights		('000)	321	872	1,046	1,044	1,065
Indicators							
2.23 Average size of travel party		Persons	..	..	..	..	..
Average length of stay							
2.24 Total		Days	..	..	..	..	..
2.25 ♦ For all commercial accommodation services		Nights	..	..	..	..	..
2.26 * of which, "hotels and similar establishments"		Nights	..	..	..	..	1.90
2.27 ♦ For non commercial accommodation services		Days	..	..	..	..	..
2.28 Average expenditure per day		US$	..	..	..	..	..

UZBEKISTAN

Basic data and indicators	Notes	Units	2005	2006	2007	2008	2009
3. OUTBOUND TOURISM							
Data							
Departures							
3.1 Total		('000)	..	..	..	..	..
3.2 ♦ Overnight visitors (tourists)		('000)	572	893	1,248	1,150	1,317
3.3 ♦ Same-day visitors (excursionists)		('000)	..	..	..	..	..
4. TOURISM INDUSTRIES							
Data							
Accommodation for visitors in hotels and similar establishments							
Non-monetary data							
4.13 ♦ Number of establishments		Units	..	..	..	..	..
4.14 ♦ Number of rooms		Units	8,598	9,240	9,537	13,970	19,180
4.15 ♦ Number of bed-places		Units	17,152	16,985	17,545	25,440	52,862
Indicators							
4.16 Occupancy rate / rooms		Percent	..	..	..	..	..
4.17 Occupancy rate / bed-places		Percent	..	36.30	46.10	45.00	54.40
4.18 Average length of stay		Nights	2.30	2.20	2.00	2.30	2.90
4.19 Available capacity (bed-places per 1000 inhabitants)		Units	0.66	0.64	0.65	0.93	1.90
6. COMPLEMENTARY INDICATORS							
Demand							
6.1 Gross travel propensity		Units	..	..	..	..	..
6.2 Carrying capacity (arrivals/population)		Units	0.01	0.02	0.03	0.04	0.04

VANUATU

Basic data and indicators	Notes	Units	2005	2006	2007	2008	2009
1. INBOUND TOURISM							
Data							
Arrivals							
1.1 Total		('000)	126	154	167	197	226
1.2 ♦ Overnight visitors (tourists)	(1)	('000)	62	68	81	91	101
1.3 ♦ Same-day visitors (excursionists)		('000)	64	86	86	106	125
1.4 * of which, cruise passengers		('000)	64	86	86	106	125
Arrivals by region	(1)						
1.5 Total		('000)	62	68	81	91	101
1.6 ♦ Africa		('000)	..	..	..	..	..
1.7 ♦ Americas		('000)	2	2	3	3	3
1.8 ♦ East Asia and the Pacific		('000)	56	61	73	81	91
1.9 ♦ Europe		('000)	3	4	4	5	5
1.10 ♦ Middle East		('000)	..	..	..	..	..
1.11 ♦ South Asia		('000)	..	..	..	..	..
1.12 ♦ Other not classified		('000)	1	1	1	2	2
1.13 * of which, nationals residing abroad		('000)	..	..	..	..	..
Arrivals by main purpose	(1)						
1.14 Total		('000)	62	68	81	91	101
1.15 ♦ Personal		('000)	54	59	70	81	91
1.16 * holidays, leisure and recreation		('000)	48	53	63	70	85
1.17 * other personal purposes		('000)	6	6	7	11	6
1.18 ♦ Business and professional		('000)	8	9	11	10	10
Arrivals by mode of transport							
1.19 Total		('000)	126	154	167	197	226
1.20 ♦ Air	(1)	('000)	62	68	81	91	101
1.21 ♦ Water		('000)	64	86	86	106	125
1.22 ♦ Land		('000)	..	..	..	..	..
1.23 * railway		('000)	..	..	..	..	..
1.24 * road		('000)	..	..	..	..	..
1.25 * others		('000)	..	..	..	..	..
Accommodation							
Total							
1.29 ♦ Guests		('000)	..	..	..	..	..
1.30 ♦ Overnights		('000)	..	..	..	..	..
Hotels and similar establishments							
1.31 ♦ Guests		('000)	..	..	..	..	..
1.32 ♦ Overnights		('000)	..	..	396	..	..
Expenditure							
1.33 Total		US$ Mn	104	109	142	..	..
1.34 ♦ Travel		US$ Mn	85	92	119	..	..
1.35 ♦ Passenger transport		US$ Mn	19	17	23	..	..
Expenditure by main purpose of the trip							
1.36 Total		US$ Mn	85	92	118	..	..
1.37 ♦ Personal		US$ Mn	1	1	1	..	..
1.38 ♦ Business and professional		US$ Mn	84	91	117	..	..
Indicators							
1.39 Average size of travel party		Persons	..	..	..	..	..
Average length of stay							
1.40 Total		Days	..	..	..	..	..
1.41 ♦ For all commercial accommodation services	(2)	Nights	9.70	9.80	9.20	..	..
1.42 * of which, "hotels and similar establishments"		Nights	..	..	..	..	..
1.43 ♦ For non commercial accommodation services		Days	..	..	..	..	..
1.44 Average expenditure per day		US$	..	..	..	..	..

VANUATU

Basic data and indicators	Notes	Units	2005	2006	2007	2008	2009
3. OUTBOUND TOURISM							
Data							
Departures							
3.1 Total		('000)	..	..	..	..	..
3.2 ♦ Overnight visitors (tourists)		('000)	14	15	16	19	..
3.3 ♦ Same-day visitors (excursionists)		('000)	..	..	..	..	..
Expenditure							
3.4 Total		US$ Mn	13	11	13	..	..
3.5 ♦ Travel		US$ Mn	11	9	11	..	..
3.6 ♦ Passenger transport		US$ Mn	2	2	2	..	..
Expenditure by main purpose of the trip							
3.7 Total		US$ Mn	11	8	11	..	..
3.8 ♦ Personal		US$ Mn	2	1	2	..	..
3.9 ♦ Business and professional		US$ Mn	9	7	9	..	..
4. TOURISM INDUSTRIES							
Data							
Accommodation for visitors in hotels and similar establishments							
Non-monetary data							
4.13 ♦ Number of establishments		Units	..	..	..	..	..
4.14 ♦ Number of rooms		Units	886	924	1,219	..	..
4.15 ♦ Number of bed-places		Units	2,382	2,466	2,450	..	..
Indicators							
4.16 Occupancy rate / rooms		Percent	52.30	51.60	57.70	..	..
4.17 Occupancy rate / bed-places		Percent	..	..	..	..	..
4.18 Average length of stay		Nights	9.70	9.80	9.20	..	..
4.19 Available capacity (bed-places per 1000 inhabitants)		Units	11.01	11.10	10.75	..	..
6. COMPLEMENTARY INDICATORS							
Demand							
6.1 Gross travel propensity		Units	..	..	..	..	..
6.2 Carrying capacity (arrivals/population)		Units	0.29	0.31	0.36	0.39	0.42
Macroeconomic indicators related to international tourism							
6.3 Inbound tourism expenditure over GDP		Percent	..	..	..	..	..
6.4 Outbound tourism expenditure over GDP		Percent	..	..	..	..	..
6.5 Tourism balance (inbound minus outbound tourism expenditure) over GDP		Percent	..	..	..	..	..
6.6 Tourism openness (inbound plus outbound tourism expenditure) over GDP		Percent	..	..	..	..	..
6.7 Tourism coverage (inbound over outbound tourism expenditure)		Percent	770.9	1,026.5	1,137.6	..	..
6.8 Inbound tourism expenditure over exports of goods		Percent	273.9	290.3	423.5	..	..
6.9 Inbound tourism expenditure over exports of services		Percent	75.2	75.0	76.4	..	..
6.10 Inbound tourism expenditure over exports of goods and services		Percent	59.0	59.6	64.7	..	..
6.11 Inbound tourism expenditure over current account credits		Percent	45.3	44.6	50.4	..	..
6.12 Outbound tourism expenditure over imports of goods		Percent	10.3	7.2	7.1	..	..
6.13 Outbound tourism expenditure over imports of services		Percent	18.4	15.0	16.5	..	..
6.14 Outbound tourism expenditure over imports of goods and services		Percent	6.6	4.9	5.0	..	..
6.15 Outbound tourism expenditure over current account debits		Percent	5.1	3.9	4.0	..	..

VENEZUELA

Basic data and indicators	Notes	Units	2005	2006	2007	2008	2009
1. INBOUND TOURISM							
Data							
Arrivals							
1.1 Total		('000)	841	911	913	857	695
1.2 ♦ Overnight visitors (tourists)		('000)	706	748	771	745	615
1.3 ♦ Same-day visitors (excursionists)		('000)	135	163	142	112	80
1.4 * of which, cruise passengers		('000)	135	163	142	112	80
Arrivals by region							
1.5 Total		('000)	706	748	770	744	616
1.6 ♦ Africa		('000)	1	1	1	1	1
1.7 ♦ Americas		('000)	374	412	420	408	340
1.8 ♦ East Asia and the Pacific		('000)	17	17	19	19	15
1.9 ♦ Europe		('000)	296	298	316	302	241
1.10 ♦ Middle East		('000)	10	10	10	10	9
1.11 ♦ South Asia		('000)	2	2	1	1	2
1.12 ♦ Other not classified		('000)	6	8	3	3	8
1.13 * of which, nationals residing abroad		('000)	..	..	..	..	..
Arrivals by main purpose							
1.14 Total		('000)	706	748	770	745	615
1.15 ♦ Personal		('000)	433	489	551	550	457
1.16 * holidays, leisure and recreation		('000)	173	169	246	220	190
1.17 * other personal purposes		('000)	260	320	305	330	267
1.18 ♦ Business and professional		('000)	273	259	219	195	158
Arrivals by mode of transport							
1.19 Total		('000)	706	748	771	745	615
1.20 ♦ Air		('000)	704	723	737	698	581
1.21 ♦ Water		('000)	2	2	2	2	7
1.22 ♦ Land		('000)	..	23	32	45	27
1.23 * railway		('000)	..	..	..	..	..
1.24 * road		('000)	..	23	32	45	27
1.25 * others		('000)	..	..	..	..	..
Accommodation							
Total							
1.29 ♦ Guests		('000)	..	..	..	..	..
1.30 ♦ Overnights		('000)	..	..	..	..	..
Hotels and similar establishments							
1.31 ♦ Guests		('000)	435	387	395	344	280
1.32 ♦ Overnights		('000)	..	..	..	..	..
Expenditure							
1.33 Total		US$ Mn	722	843	894	984	853
1.34 ♦ Travel		US$ Mn	650	768	817	917	788
1.35 ♦ Passenger transport		US$ Mn	72	75	77	67	65
Expenditure by main purpose of the trip							
1.36 Total		US$ Mn	650	768	817	917	788
1.37 ♦ Personal		US$ Mn	375	498	559	625	579
1.38 ♦ Business and professional		US$ Mn	275	270	258	292	209
Indicators							
1.39 Average size of travel party		Persons	..	..	..	..	..
Average length of stay							
1.40 Total		Days	..	..	..	..	..
1.41 ♦ For all commercial accommodation services		Nights	16.65	18.13	19.43	20.39	19.70
1.42 * of which, "hotels and similar establishments"		Nights	..	..	..	..	..
1.43 ♦ For non commercial accommodation services		Days	..	..	..	..	..
1.44 Average expenditure per day		US$	..	..	..	..	..
2. DOMESTIC TOURISM							
Data							
Trips							
2.1 Total		('000)	17,839	17,372	17,248	22,085	16,528
2.2 ♦ Overnight visitors (tourists)		('000)	..	10,931	10,720	14,113	12,644
2.3 ♦ Same-day visitors (excursionists)		('000)	..	6,411	6,528	7,972	3,884
Trips by main purpose							
2.4 Total		('000)	..	17,371	17,248	22,085	16,528
2.5 ♦ Personal		('000)	..	16,288	16,221	20,769	15,831
2.6 * holidays, leisure and recreation		('000)	..	6,441	6,528	9,301	6,677
2.7 * other personal purposes		('000)	..	9,847	9,693	11,468	9,154
2.8 ♦ Business and professional		('000)	..	1,083	1,027	1,316	697

VENEZUELA

Basic data and indicators	Notes	Units	2005	2006	2007	2008	2009
Trips by mode of transport							
2.9 Total		('000)	..	17,372	17,248	22,085	16,528
2.10 ♦ Air		('000)	..	182	251	257	270
2.11 ♦ Water		('000)	..	553	547	871	582
2.12 ♦ Land		('000)	..	16,637	16,450	20,957	15,676
2.13 * railway		('000)	..	..	..	..	..
2.14 * road		('000)	..	15,755	16,084	20,684	15,437
2.15 * others		('000)	..	882	366	273	239
Trips by form of organization							
2.16 Total		('000)	..	..	17,248	..	16,528
2.17 ♦ Package tour		('000)	..	..	81	..	142
2.18 ♦ Other forms		('000)	..	..	17,167	..	16,386
Indicators							
2.23 Average size of travel party		Persons	..	..	..	..	..
Average length of stay							
2.24 Total		Days	..	..	..	..	..
2.25 ♦ For all commercial accommodation services		Nights	4.38	4.65	4.66	4.53	5.00
2.26 * of which, "hotels and similar establishments"		Nights	..	..	..	..	..
2.27 ♦ For non commercial accommodation services		Days	..	..	..	..	..
2.28 Average expenditure per day		US$	..	..	..	..	..

3. OUTBOUND TOURISM

Data

	Notes	Units	2005	2006	2007	2008	2009
Departures							
3.1 Total		('000)	..	..	..	..	..
3.2 ♦ Overnight visitors (tourists)		('000)	1,067	1,095	1,410	1,745	1,651
3.3 ♦ Same-day visitors (excursionists)		('000)	..	..	..	..	..
Expenditure							
3.4 Total		US$ Mn	1,843	1,807	2,227	2,566	2,234
3.5 ♦ Travel		US$ Mn	1,276	1,229	1,520	1,784	1,568
3.6 ♦ Passenger transport		US$ Mn	567	578	707	782	666
Expenditure by main purpose of the trip							
3.7 Total		US$ Mn	1,276	1,229	1,520	1,784	1,568
3.8 ♦ Personal		US$ Mn	857	839	1,150	1,389	1,271
3.9 ♦ Business and professional		US$ Mn	419	390	370	395	297

4. TOURISM INDUSTRIES

Data

	Notes	Units	2005	2006	2007	2008	2009
Number of establishments							
4.1 Total		Units	..	..	..	..	..
4.2 ♦ Accommodation for visitors		Units	..	..	..	..	..
4.3 * of which, "hotels and similar establishments"	(1)	Units	1,580	1,824	1,824	2,741	2961
4.4 ♦ Food and beverage serving activities		Units	..	..	..	..	..
4.5 ♦ Passenger transportation		Units	..	..	..	..	..
4.6 ♦ Travel agencies and other reservation services activities		Units	..	..	..	..	..
4.7 ♦ Other tourism industries		Units	..	..	..	..	..
Accommodation for visitors in hotels and similar establishments							
Non-monetary data							
4.13 ♦ Number of establishments	(1)	Units	1,580	1,824	1,824	2,741	2,961
4.14 ♦ Number of rooms	(1)	Units	68,819	74,976	74,976	86,525	67,886
4.15 ♦ Number of bed-places	(1)	Units	157,112	172,433	172,433	202,718	153,386
Indicators							
4.16 Occupancy rate / rooms		Percent	..	..	..	..	..
4.17 Occupancy rate / bed-places		Percent	..	78.93	76.97	75.95	64.64
4.18 Average length of stay		Nights	..	18.13	19.43	18.54	19.70
4.19 Available capacity (bed-places per 1000 inhabitants)		Units	5.91	6.38	6.27	7.26	5.40

VENEZUELA

Basic data and indicators	Notes	Units	2005	2006	2007	2008	2009
6. COMPLEMENTARY INDICATORS							
Demand							
6.1 Gross travel propensity		Units	..	..	..	..	..
6.2 Carrying capacity (arrivals/population)		Units	0.03	0.43	0.42	0.53	0.47
Macroeconomic indicators related to international tourism							
6.3 Inbound tourism expenditure over GDP		Percent	0.5	0.5	0.4	0.3	0.3
6.4 Outbound tourism expenditure over GDP		Percent	1.3	1.0	1.0	0.8	0.7
6.5 Tourism balance (inbound minus outbound tourism expenditure) over GDP		Percent	-0.8	-0.5	-0.6	-0.5	-0.4
6.6 Tourism openness (inbound plus outbound tourism expenditure) over GDP		Percent	1.8	1.4	1.4	1.1	0.9
6.7 Tourism coverage (inbound over outbound tourism expenditure)		Percent	39.2	46.7	40.1	38.3	38.2
6.8 Inbound tourism expenditure over exports of goods		Percent	1.3	1.3	1.3	1.0	1.5
6.9 Inbound tourism expenditure over exports of services		Percent	53.8	54.6	50.6	45.5	42.5
6.10 Inbound tourism expenditure over exports of goods and services		Percent	1.3	1.3	1.3	1.0	1.4
6.11 Inbound tourism expenditure over current account credits		Percent	1.2	1.1	1.1	0.9	1.4
6.12 Outbound tourism expenditure over imports of goods		Percent	7.6	5.4	4.8	5.2	5.8
6.13 Outbound tourism expenditure over imports of services		Percent	34.5	30.3	25.5	24.4	23.2
6.14 Outbound tourism expenditure over imports of goods and services		Percent	6.2	4.6	4.1	4.3	4.6
6.15 Outbound tourism expenditure over current account debits		Percent	5.1	3.7	3.5	3.8	4.2

VIET NAM

Basic data and indicators	Notes	Units	2005	2006	2007	2008	2009
1. INBOUND TOURISM							
Data							
Arrivals							
1.1 Total	(1)	('000)	3,477	3,583	4,229	4,236	3,747
1.2 ♦ Overnight visitors (tourists)		('000)	..	..	..	..	..
1.3 ♦ Same-day visitors (excursionists)		('000)	200	224	225	152	66
1.4 * of which, cruise passengers	(2)	('000)	200	224	225	152	66
Arrivals by region	(1)						
1.5 Total		('000)	3,477	3,583	4,229	4,236	3,747
1.6 ♦ Africa		('000)	..	..	..	..	..
1.7 ♦ Americas		('000)	394	459	498	502	488
1.8 ♦ East Asia and the Pacific		('000)	2,364	2,355	2,728	2,791	2,422
1.9 ♦ Europe		('000)	441	468	620	624	618
1.10 ♦ Middle East		('000)	..	..	..	..	..
1.11 ♦ South Asia		('000)	..	..	..	..	..
1.12 ♦ Other not classified		('000)	278	301	383	319	219
1.13 * of which, nationals residing abroad		('000)	..	..	..	..	..
Arrivals by main purpose	(1)						
1.14 Total		('000)	3,477	3,583	4,229	4,236	3,747
1.15 ♦ Personal		('000)	2,981	3,007	3,555	3,392	3,005
1.16 * holidays, leisure and recreation		('000)	2,038	2,069	2,605	2,613	2,241
1.17 * other personal purposes		('000)	943	938	950	779	764
1.18 ♦ Business and professional		('000)	496	576	674	844	742
Arrivals by mode of transport	(1)						
1.19 Total		('000)	3,477	3,583	4,229	4,236	3,747
1.20 ♦ Air		('000)	2,335	2,702	3,301	3,283	3,025
1.21 ♦ Water	(2)	('000)	200	224	225	152	66
1.22 ♦ Land		('000)	942	657	703	801	656
1.23 * railway		('000)	..	..	..	..	..
1.24 * road		('000)	942	657	703	801	656
1.25 * others		('000)	..	..	..	..	..
Expenditure	(3)						
1.33 Total		US$ Mn	2,300	2,850	3,750	3,930	3,050
1.34 ♦ Travel		US$ Mn	..	..	..	..	..
1.35 ♦ Passenger transport		US$ Mn	..	..	..	..	..
3. OUTBOUND TOURISM							
Data							
Expenditure	(3)						
3.4 Total		US$ Mn	900	1,050	1,220	1,300	1,100
3.5 ♦ Travel		US$ Mn	..	..	..	..	..
3.6 ♦ Passenger transport		US$ Mn	..	..	..	..	..
4. TOURISM INDUSTRIES							
Data							
Accommodation for visitors in hotels and similar establishments							
Non-monetary data							
4.13 ♦ Number of establishments		Units	..	..	..	..	..
4.14 ♦ Number of rooms		Units	130,000	142,585	..	..	..
4.15 ♦ Number of bed-places		Units	..	..	..	..	..
Indicators							
4.16 Occupancy rate / rooms		Percent	..	..	..	..	..
4.17 Occupancy rate / bed-places		Percent	..	51.95	..	..	..
4.18 Average length of stay		Nights	..	..	..	..	..
4.19 Available capacity (bed-places per 1000 inhabitants)		Units	..	..	..	..	..
6. COMPLEMENTARY INDICATORS							
Demand							
6.1 Gross travel propensity		Units	..	..	..	..	..
6.2 Carrying capacity (arrivals/population)		Units	0.04	0.04	0.05	0.05	0.04

YEMEN

Basic data and indicators	Notes	Units	2005	2006	2007	2008	2009
1. INBOUND TOURISM							
Data							
Arrivals							
1.1 Total		('000)	..	..	..	..	..
1.2 ♦ Overnight visitors (tourists)		('000)	336	382	379	404	434
1.3 ♦ Same-day visitors (excursionists)		('000)	..	..	..	..	..
1.4 * of which, cruise passengers		('000)	..	..	..	..	..
Arrivals by region							
1.5 Total		('000)	336	382	379	404	434
1.6 ♦ Africa		('000)	13	21	20	18	24
1.7 ♦ Americas		('000)	18	19	18	18	25
1.8 ♦ East Asia and the Pacific		('000)	24	19	20	20	26
1.9 ♦ Europe		('000)	26	33	33	36	43
1.10 ♦ Middle East		('000)	239	270	268	293	290
1.11 ♦ South Asia		('000)	16	20	20	19	26
1.12 ♦ Other not classified		('000)	..	..	..	..	..
1.13 * of which, nationals residing abroad		('000)	..	..	..	..	..
Arrivals by mode of transport							
1.19 Total		('000)	..	381	380	404	434
1.20 ♦ Air		('000)	..	145	144	143	206
1.21 ♦ Water		('000)	..	4	3	13	6
1.22 ♦ Land		('000)	..	232	233	248	222
1.23 * railway		('000)	..	..	..	..	..
1.24 * road		('000)	..	232	233	248	222
1.25 * others		('000)	..	..	..	..	..
Accommodation							
Total							
1.29 ♦ Guests		('000)	..	..	..	..	..
1.30 ♦ Overnights		('000)	..	..	..	..	..
Hotels and similar establishments							
1.31 ♦ Guests		('000)	..	..	..	..	..
1.32 ♦ Overnights		('000)	2,017	2,294	3,035	3,236	3,471
Expenditure							
1.33 Total		US$ Mn	..	..	..	..	..
1.34 ♦ Travel		US$ Mn	181	181	425	453	496
1.35 ♦ Passenger transport		US$ Mn	..	..	..	..	..
Indicators							
1.39 Average size of travel party		Persons	..	..	..	..	..
Average length of stay							
1.40 Total		Days	..	..	..	..	..
1.41 ♦ For all commercial accommodation services		Nights	6.00	6.00	8.00	8.00	8.00
1.42 * of which, "hotels and similar establishments"		Nights	..	..	..	..	..
1.43 ♦ For non commercial accommodation services		Days	..	..	..	..	..
1.44 Average expenditure per day		US$	..	..	..	..	..
2. DOMESTIC TOURISM							
Data							
Accommodation							
Total							
2.19 ♦ Guests		('000)	..	..	..	..	..
2.20 ♦ Overnights		('000)	..	..	..	..	..
Hotels and similar establishments							
2.21 ♦ Guests		('000)	..	679	569	618	594
2.22 ♦ Overnights		('000)	4,172	4,074	7,962	8,655	8,319
Indicators							
2.23 Average size of travel party		Persons	..	..	..	..	..
Average length of stay							
2.24 Total		Days	..	..	..	..	..
2.25 ♦ For all commercial accommodation services		Nights	..	..	14.00	14.00	14.00
2.26 * of which, "hotels and similar establishments"		Nights	..	..	..	..	..
2.27 ♦ For non commercial accommodation services		Days	..	..	..	..	..
2.28 Average expenditure per day		US$	..	..	..	..	..

YEMEN

Basic data and indicators	Notes	Units	2005	2006	2007	2008	2009
3. **OUTBOUND TOURISM**							
Data							
Expenditure							
3.4 Total		US$ Mn	224	225	247	246	277
3.5 ♦ Travel		US$ Mn	167	162	184	183	214
3.6 ♦ Passenger transport		US$ Mn	57	63	63	63	63
4. **TOURISM INDUSTRIES**							
Data							
Number of establishments							
4.1 Total		Units	..	..	..	..	..
4.2 ♦ Accommodation for visitors		Units	..	..	..	..	..
4.3 * of which, "hotels and similar establishments"		Units	692	1,166	1,163	1,163	1,163
4.4 ♦ Food and beverage serving activities		Units	..	..	..	..	..
4.5 ♦ Passenger transportation		Units	..	..	..	..	..
4.6 ♦ Travel agencies and other reservation services activities		Units	..	..	..	..	..
4.7 ♦ Other tourism industries		Units	..	..	..	..	..
Accommodation for visitors in hotels and similar establishments							
Non-monetary data							
4.13 ♦ Number of establishments		Units	692	1,166	1,163	1,163	1,163
4.14 ♦ Number of rooms		Units	15,265	22,163	23,180	23,180	23,180
4.15 ♦ Number of bed-places		Units	34,844	50,381	52,891	52,891	52,891
Indicators							
4.16 Occupancy rate / rooms		Percent	..	..	..	..	..
4.17 Occupancy rate / bed-places		Percent	..	..	..	..	..
4.18 Average length of stay		Nights	..	..	..	..	..
4.19 Available capacity (bed-places per 1000 inhabitants)		Units	1.66	2.33	2.38	2.31	2.24
6. **COMPLEMENTARY INDICATORS**							
Demand							
6.1 Gross travel propensity		Units	..	..	..		
6.2 Carrying capacity (arrivals/population)		Units	0.02	0.02	0.02	0.02	0.02
Macroeconomic indicators related to international tourism							
6.3 Inbound tourism expenditure over GDP		Percent	1.0	0.9	1.8	3.1	..
6.4 Outbound tourism expenditure over GDP		Percent	1.3	1.1	1.0	0.9	..
6.5 Tourism balance (inbound minus outbound tourism expenditure) over GDP		Percent	-0.2	-0.2	0.8	2.2	..
6.6 Tourism openness (inbound plus outbound tourism expenditure) over GDP		Percent	2.3	1.9	2.8	3.9	..
6.7 Tourism coverage (inbound over outbound tourism expenditure)		Percent	80.6	80.4	172.6	361.3	..
6.8 Inbound tourism expenditure over exports of goods		Percent	2.8	2.5	6.0	9.9	..
6.9 Inbound tourism expenditure over exports of services		Percent	48.6	32.9	58.7	73.5	..
6.10 Inbound tourism expenditure over exports of goods and services		Percent	2.7	2.3	5.5	8.7	..
6.11 Inbound tourism expenditure over current account credits		Percent	2.1	1.9	4.4	7.0	..
6.12 Outbound tourism expenditure over imports of goods		Percent	4.8	3.8	3.3	2.6	..
6.13 Outbound tourism expenditure over imports of services		Percent	18.1	12.1	13.2	10.4	..
6.14 Outbound tourism expenditure over imports of goods and services		Percent	3.8	2.9	2.6	2.1	..
6.15 Outbound tourism expenditure over current account debits		Percent	2.9	2.4	2.2	1.8	..

ZAMBIA

Basic data and indicators	Notes	Units	2005	2006	2007	2008	2009
1. INBOUND TOURISM							
Data							
Arrivals							
1.1 Total		('000)	..	..	..	..	..
1.2 ♦ Overnight visitors (tourists)		('000)	669	757	897	812	710
1.3 ♦ Same-day visitors (excursionists)		('000)	..	..	..	..	..
1.4 * of which, cruise passengers		('000)	..	..	..	..	..
Arrivals by region							
1.5 Total		('000)	670	756	898	812	710
1.6 ♦ Africa		('000)	461	510	661	607	467
1.7 ♦ Americas		('000)	38	52	51	47	63
1.8 ♦ East Asia and the Pacific		('000)	40	38	28	35	39
1.9 ♦ Europe		('000)	122	143	146	109	128
1.10 ♦ Middle East		('000)	..	..	..	..	..
1.11 ♦ South Asia		('000)	9	13	12	14	13
1.12 ♦ Other not classified		('000)	..	..	..	..	..
1.13 * of which, nationals residing abroad		('000)	..	..	..	..	..
Arrivals by main purpose							
1.14 Total		('000)	669	756	897	811	710
1.15 ♦ Personal		('000)	416	466	557	472	451
1.16 * holidays, leisure and recreation		('000)	206	242	204	184	172
1.17 * other personal purposes		('000)	210	224	353	288	279
1.18 ♦ Business and professional		('000)	253	290	340	339	259
Arrivals by mode of transport							
1.19 Total		('000)	668	757	897	812	710
1.20 ♦ Air		('000)	164	227	281	236	191
1.21 ♦ Water		('000)	..	..	..	..	..
1.22 ♦ Land		('000)	504	530	616	576	519
1.23 * railway		('000)	..	..	..	..	35
1.24 * road		('000)	504	530	616	576	484
1.25 * others		('000)	..	..	..	..	..
Expenditure							
1.33 Total		US$ Mn	..	..	..	..	..
1.34 ♦ Travel		US$ Mn	98	110	138	148	98
1.35 ♦ Passenger transport		US$ Mn	..	..	..	..	..
Expenditure by main purpose of the trip							
1.36 Total		US$ Mn	98	110	138	148	98
1.37 ♦ Personal		US$ Mn	65	73	92	99	65
1.38 ♦ Business and professional		US$ Mn	33	37	46	49	33
Indicators							
1.39 Average size of travel party		Persons	..	..	..	..	..
Average length of stay							
1.40 Total		Days	..	..	..	..	..
1.41 ♦ For all commercial accommodation services	(1)	Nights	6.00	6.00	6.00	6.00	7.00
1.42 * of which, "hotels and similar establishments"		Nights	..	..	..	..	..
1.43 ♦ For non commercial accommodation services		Days	..	..	..	..	..
1.44 Average expenditure per day		US$	..	..	..	..	..
2. DOMESTIC TOURISM							
Data							
Accommodation							
Total							
2.19 ♦ Guests		('000)	..	..	..	..	..
2.20 ♦ Overnights		('000)	..	..	..	..	..
Hotels and similar establishments							
2.21 ♦ Guests		('000)	..	..	..	..	..
2.22 ♦ Overnights		('000)	289	310	..	..	..

ZAMBIA

Basic data and indicators	Notes	Units	2005	2006	2007	2008	2009
3. OUTBOUND TOURISM							
Data							
Expenditure							
3.4 Total		US$ Mn	88	97	98	107	83
3.5 ♦ Travel		US$ Mn	58	68	56	64	39
3.6 ♦ Passenger transport		US$ Mn	30	29	42	43	44
Expenditure by main purpose of the trip							
3.7 Total		US$ Mn	58	68	56	..	..
3.8 ♦ Personal		US$ Mn	5	5	5	..	..
3.9 ♦ Business and professional		US$ Mn	53	63	51	..	..
4. TOURISM INDUSTRIES							
Data							
Number of establishments							
4.1 Total		Units	..	..	..	..	..
4.2 ♦ Accommodation for visitors		Units	..	..	..	..	..
4.3 * of which, "hotels and similar establishments"		Units	592	639	687		
4.4 ♦ Food and beverage serving activities		Units	..	..	..	..	..
4.5 ♦ Passenger transportation		Units	..	..	..	..	..
4.6 ♦ Travel agencies and other reservation services activities		Units	..	..	..	..	..
4.7 ♦ Other tourism industries		Units	..	..	..	..	..
Accommodation for visitors in hotels and similar establishments							
Non-monetary data							
4.13 ♦ Number of establishments		Units	592	639	687	..	
4.14 ♦ Number of rooms		Units	5,521	5,667	5,549	5,979	..
4.15 ♦ Number of bed-places		Units	9,417	9,960	9,660	9,894	..
Indicators							
4.16 Occupancy rate / rooms		Percent	57.20	61.00	61.10	63.10	..
4.17 Occupancy rate / bed-places		Percent	..	..	..	..	..
4.18 Average length of stay		Nights	..	..	..	..	..
4.19 Available capacity (bed-places per 1000 inhabitants)		Units	0.80	0.83	0.78	0.78	..
6. COMPLEMENTARY INDICATORS							
Demand							
6.1 Gross travel propensity		Units	..	..	..	..	
6.2 Carrying capacity (arrivals/population)		Units	0.06	0.06	0.07	0.06	0.05
Macroeconomic indicators related to international tourism							
6.3 Inbound tourism expenditure over GDP		Percent	1.4	1.0	1.2	1.0	..
6.4 Outbound tourism expenditure over GDP		Percent	1.2	0.9	0.8	0.7	..
6.5 Tourism balance (inbound minus outbound tourism expenditure) over GDP		Percent	0.1	0.1	0.3	0.3	..
6.6 Tourism openness (inbound plus outbound tourism expenditure) over GDP		Percent	2.6	1.9	2.0	1.7	..
6.7 Tourism coverage (inbound over outbound tourism expenditure)		Percent	111.8	113.3	141.3	136.2	..
6.8 Inbound tourism expenditure over exports of goods		Percent	4.4	2.8	3.1	2.9	..
6.9 Inbound tourism expenditure over exports of services		Percent	36.0	48.2	50.4	49.2	..
6.10 Inbound tourism expenditure over exports of goods and services		Percent	3.9	2.6	2.9	2.8	..
6.11 Inbound tourism expenditure over current account credits		Percent	3.6	2.4	2.5	2.4	..
6.12 Outbound tourism expenditure over imports of goods		Percent	4.1	3.7	2.7	2.4	..
6.13 Outbound tourism expenditure over imports of services		Percent	18.7	16.5	10.7	11.8	..
6.14 Outbound tourism expenditure over imports of goods and services		Percent	3.3	3.0	2.2	2.0	..
6.15 Outbound tourism expenditure over current account debits		Percent	2.7	2.2	1.6	1.5	..

ZIMBABWE

Basic data and indicators	Notes	Units	2005	2006	2007	2008	2009
1. INBOUND TOURISM							
Data							
Arrivals							
1.1 Total		('000)	1,559	2,287	2,506	1,956	2,017
1.2 ♦ Overnight visitors (tourists)		('000)	..	..	..	..	..
1.3 ♦ Same-day visitors (excursionists)		('000)	..	..	..	..	..
1.4 * of which, cruise passengers		('000)	..	..	..	..	..
Arrivals by region							
1.5 Total		('000)	1,559	2,287	2,506	1,955	2,016
1.6 ♦ Africa		('000)	1,356	2,083	2,290	1,732	1,679
1.7 ♦ Americas		('000)	44	45	40	43	58
1.8 ♦ East Asia and the Pacific		('000)	39	54	58	63	104
1.9 ♦ Europe		('000)	113	97	112	111	160
1.10 ♦ Middle East		('000)	2	4	1	1	5
1.11 ♦ South Asia		('000)	5	4	5	5	10
1.12 ♦ Other not classified		('000)	..	..	..	..	..
1.13 * of which, nationals residing abroad		('000)	..	..	..	..	..
Arrivals by main purpose							
1.14 Total		('000)	1,558	2,287	2,506	1,956	2,017
1.15 ♦ Personal		('000)	1,293	1,894	2,128	1,827	1,881
1.16 * holidays, leisure and recreation		('000)	970	1,850	2,116	1,820	1,874
1.17 * other personal purposes		('000)	323	44	12	7	7
1.18 ♦ Business and professional		('000)	265	393	378	129	136
Arrivals by mode of transport							
1.19 Total		('000)	1,558	2,287	2,506	1,955	2,017
1.20 ♦ Air		('000)	327	275	982	429	573
1.21 ♦ Water		('000)	..	..	..	..	..
1.22 ♦ Land		('000)	1,231	2,012	1,524	1,526	1,444
1.23 * railway		('000)	..	..	..	..	..
1.24 * road		('000)	1,231	2,012	1,524	1,526	1,444
1.25 * others		('000)	..	..	..	..	..
Accommodation							
Total							
1.29 ♦ Guests		('000)	..	..	..	..	..
1.30 ♦ Overnights		('000)	210	257	288	324	..
Hotels and similar establishments							
1.31 ♦ Guests		('000)	57	67	70	90	..
1.32 ♦ Overnights		('000)	171	201	210	254	..
Expenditure							
1.33 Total	(1)	US$ Mn	99	338	365	294	314
1.34 ♦ Travel		US$ Mn	..	..	..	..	..
1.35 ♦ Passenger transport		US$ Mn	..	..	..	..	..
Indicators							
1.39 Average size of travel party		Persons	..	..	..	..	..
Average length of stay							
1.40 Total		Days	..	..	..	..	..
1.41 ♦ For all commercial accommodation services		Nights	3.00	3.00	3.00	3.00	3.00
1.42 * of which, "hotels and similar establishments"		Nights	..	..	..	..	..
1.43 ♦ For non commercial accommodation services		Days	..	..	..	..	..
1.44 Average expenditure per day		US$	..	..	..	..	..

ZIMBABWE

Basic data and indicators	Notes	Units	2005	2006	2007	2008	2009
2. DOMESTIC TOURISM							
Data							
Trips							
2.1 Total		('000)	..	..	..	947	1,022
2.2 ♦ Overnight visitors (tourists)		('000)	..	..	..	529	805
2.3 ♦ Same-day visitors (excursionists)	(2)	('000)	..	..	..	418	217
Accommodation							
Total							
2.19 ♦ Guests		('000)	..	..	540	529	588
2.20 ♦ Overnights		('000)	1,505	1,596	2,143	2,204	2,289
Hotels and similar establishments							
2.21 ♦ Guests		('000)	419	412	391	399	443
2.22 ♦ Overnights		('000)	1,256	1,236	1,173	1,197	1,330
Indicators							
2.23 Average size of travel party		Persons	..	..	..	..	..
Average length of stay							
2.24 Total		Days	..	..	..	..	..
2.25 ♦ For all commercial accommodation services		Nights	3.00	3.00	3.00	3.00	3.00
2.26 * of which, "hotels and similar establishments"		Nights	..	..	..	..	..
2.27 ♦ For non commercial accommodation services		Days	..	..	..	..	..
2.28 Average expenditure per day		US$	..	..	..	..	..
3. OUTBOUND TOURISM							
Data							
Departures							
3.1 Total		('000)	..	..	..	..	..
3.2 ♦ Overnight visitors (tourists)	(3)	('000)	474	541	547	593	631
3.3 ♦ Same-day visitors (excursionists)		('000)	..	..	..	..	..
4. TOURISM INDUSTRIES							
Data							
Accommodation for visitors in hotels and similar establishments							
Non-monetary data							
4.13 ♦ Number of establishments		Units	..	..	..	..	..
4.14 ♦ Number of rooms	(4)	Units	5,657	6,022	6,266	6,319	6,319
4.15 ♦ Number of bed-places	(4)	Units	11,282	11,578	11,609	11,855	11,855
Indicators							
4.16 Occupancy rate / rooms		Percent	39.00	38.00	43.00	42.00	46.00
4.17 Occupancy rate / bed-places		Percent	28.00	27.00	31.00	32.00	35.00
4.18 Average length of stay		Nights	3.00	3.00	3.00	3.00	3.00
4.19 Available capacity (bed-places per 1000 inhabitants)		Units	0.90	0.93	0.93	0.95	0.95
6. COMPLEMENTARY INDICATORS							
Demand							
6.1 Gross travel propensity		Units	..	..	..	0.1	0.1
6.2 Carrying capacity (arrivals/population)		Units	0.10	0.20	0.20	0.10	0.10
Macroeconomic indicators related to international tourism	(5)						
6.3 Inbound tourism expenditure over GDP		Percent	..	..	..	6.0	9.0
6.4 Outbound tourism expenditure over GDP		Percent	..	..	..	..	..
6.5 Tourism balance (inbound minus outbound tourism expenditure) over GDP		Percent					
6.6 Tourism openness (inbound plus outbound tourism expenditure) over GDP		Percent	..	..	..	..	..
6.7 Tourism coverage (inbound over outbound tourism expenditure)		Percent					
6.8 Inbound tourism expenditure over exports of goods		Percent	..	..	..	..	..
6.9 Inbound tourism expenditure over exports of services		Percent	..	..	..	..	..
6.10 Inbound tourism expenditure over exports of goods and services	(6)	Percent	13.5	14.9	17.9	16.0	19.7
6.11 Inbound tourism expenditure over current account credits		Percent	..	..	..	..	..
6.12 Outbound tourism expenditure over imports of goods		Percent	..	..	..	..	..
6.13 Outbound tourism expenditure over imports of services		Percent	..	..	..	..	..
6.14 Outbound tourism expenditure over imports of goods and services		Percent	..	..	..	..	..
6.15 Outbound tourism expenditure over current account debits		Percent	..	..	..	..	..

Index of indicators and basic data /

Indice des indicateurs et données de base /

Índice de indicadores y datos básicos

INDEX OF INDICATORS AND BASIC DATA

Basic data and indicators	Notes	Units
1. INBOUND TOURISM		
Data		
Arrivals		
1.1 Total		('000)
1.2 ♦ Overnight visitors (tourists)		('000)
1.3 ♦ Same-day visitors (excursionists)		('000)
1.4 * of which, cruise passengers		('000)
Arrivals by region		
1.5 Total		('000)
1.6 ♦ Africa		('000)
1.7 ♦ Americas		('000)
1.8 ♦ East Asia and the Pacific		('000)
1.9 ♦ Europe		('000)
1.10 ♦ Middle East		('000)
1.11 ♦ South Asia		('000)
1.12 ♦ Other not classified		('000)
1.13 * of which, nationals residing abroad		('000)
Arrivals by main purpose		
1.14 Total		('000)
1.15 ♦ Personal		('000)
1.16 * holidays, leisure and recreation		('000)
1.17 * other personal purposes		('000)
1.18 ♦ Business and professional		('000)
Arrivals by mode of transport		
1.19 Total		('000)
1.20 ♦ Air		('000)
1.21 ♦ Water		('000)
1.22 ♦ Land		('000)
1.23 * railway		('000)
1.24 * road		('000)
1.25 * others		('000)
Arrivals by form of organization of the trip		
1.26 Total		('000)
1.27 ♦ Package tour		('000)
1.28 ♦ Other forms		('000)
Accommodation		
Total		
1.29 ♦ Guests		('000)
1.30 ♦ Overnights		('000)
Hotels and similar establishments		
1.31 ♦ Guests		('000)
1.32 ♦ Overnights		('000)
Expenditure		
1.33 Total		US$ Mn
1.34 ♦ Travel		US$ Mn
1.35 ♦ Passenger transport		US$ Mn
Expenditure by main purpose of the trip		
1.36 Total		US$ Mn
1.37 ♦ Personal		US$ Mn
1.38 ♦ Business and professional		US$ Mn
Indicators		
1.39 Average size of travel party		Persons
Average length of stay		
1.40 Total		Days
1.41 ♦ For all commercial accommodation services		Nights
1.42 * of which, "hotels and similar establishments"		Nights
1.43 ♦ For non commercial accommodation services		Days
1.44 Average expenditure per day		US$

Basic data and indicators	Notes	Units
2. DOMESTIC TOURISM		
Data		
Trips		
2.1 Total		('000)
2.2 ♦ Overnight visitors (tourists)		('000)
2.3 ♦ Same-day visitors (excursionists)		('000)
Trips by main purpose		
2.4 Total		('000)
2.5 ♦ Personal		('000)
2.6 * holidays, leisure and recreation		('000)
2.7 * other personal purposes		('000)
2.8 ♦ Business and professional		('000)
Trips by mode of transport		
2.9 Total		('000)
2.10 ♦ Air		('000)
2.11 ♦ Water		('000)
2.12 ♦ Land		('000)
2.13 * railway		('000)
2.14 * road		('000)
2.15 * others		('000)
Trips by form of organization		
2.16 Total		('000)
2.17 ♦ Package tour		('000)
2.18 ♦ Other forms		('000)
Accommodation		
Total		
2.19 ♦ Guests		('000)
2.20 ♦ Overnights		('000)
Hotels and similar establishments		
2.21 ♦ Guests		('000)
2.22 ♦ Overnights		('000)
Indicators		
2.23 Average size of travel party		Persons
Average length of stay		
2.24 Total		Days
2.25 ♦ For all commercial accommodation services		Nights
2.26 * of which, "hotels and similar establishments"		Nights
2.27 ♦ For non commercial accommodation services		Days
2.28 Average expenditure per day		US$
3. OUTBOUND TOURISM		
Data		
Departures		
3.1 Total		('000)
3.2 ♦ Overnight visitors (tourists)		('000)
3.3 ♦ Same-day visitors (excursionists)		('000)
Expenditure		
3.4 Total		US$ Mn
3.5 ♦ Travel		US$ Mn
3.6 ♦ Passenger transport		US$ Mn
Expenditure by main purpose of the trip		
3.7 Total		US$ Mn
3.8 ♦ Personal		US$ Mn
3.9 ♦ Business and professional		US$ Mn
Indicators		
3.10 Average length of stay		Days
3.11 Average expenditure per day		US$

INDEX OF INDICATORS AND BASIC DATA

Basic data and indicators	Notes	Units
4. TOURISM INDUSTRIES		
Data		
Number of establishments		
4.1 Total		Units
4.2 ♦ Accommodation for visitors		Units
4.3 * of which, "hotels and similar establishments"		Units
4.4 ♦ Food and beverage serving activities		Units
4.5 ♦ Passenger transportation		Units
4.6 ♦ Travel agencies and other reservation services activities		Units
4.7 ♦ Other tourism industries		Units
Accommodation for visitors in hotels and similar establishments		
Monetary data		
4.8 ♦ Output		US$ Mn
4.9 ♦ Intermediate consumption		US$ Mn
4.10 ♦ Gross value added		US$ Mn
4.11 ♦ Compensation of employees		US$ Mn
4.12 ♦ Gross fixed capital formation		US$ Mn
Non-monetary data		
4.13 ♦ Number of establishments		Units
4.14 ♦ Number of rooms		Units
4.15 ♦ Number of bed-places		Units
Indicators		
4.16 Occupancy rate / rooms		Percent
4.17 Occupancy rate / bed-places		Percent
4.18 Average length of stay		Nights
4.19 Available capacity (bed-places per 1000 inhabitants)		Units
Travel agencies and other reservation service activities		
Monetary data		
4.20 ♦ Output		US$ Mn
4.21 ♦ Intermediate consumption		US$ Mn
4.22 ♦ Gross value added		US$ Mn
4.23 ♦ Compensation of employees		US$ Mn
4.24 ♦ Gross fixed capital formation		US$ Mn
Non-monetary data		
♦ Domestic trips		
4.25 * with package tour		Percent
4.26 * without package tour		Percent
♦ Inbound trips		
4.27 * with package tour		Percent
4.28 * without package tour		Percent
♦ Outbound trips		
4.29 * with package tour		Percent
4.30 * without package tour		Percent

Basic data and indicators	Notes	Units
5. EMPLOYMENT		
Data		
Number of employees by tourism industries		
5.1 Total		('000)
5.2 ♦ Accommodation services for visitors (hotels and similar establishments)		('000)
5.3 ♦ Other accommodation services		('000)
5.4 ♦ Food and beverage serving activities		('000)
5.5 ♦ Passenger transportation		('000)
5.6 ♦ Travel agencies and other reservation services activities		('000)
5.7 ♦ Other tourism industries		('000)
Number of jobs by status in employment		
5.8 Total		('000)
5.9 ♦ Employees		('000)
5.10 ♦ Self employed		('000)
Indicators		
Number of full-time equivalent jobs by status in employment		
5.11 Total		('000)
5.12 ♦ Employees		('000)
5.13 * male		('000)
5.14 * female		('000)
5.15 ♦ Self employed		('000)
5.16 * male		('000)
5.17 * female		('000)
6. COMPLEMENTARY INDICATORS		
Demand		
6.1 Gross travel propensity		Units
6.2 Carrying capacity (arrivals/population)		Units
Macroeconomic indicators related to international tourism		
6.3 Inbound tourism expenditure over GDP		Percent
6.4 Outbound tourism expenditure over GDP		Percent
6.5 Tourism balance (inbound minus outbound tourism expenditure) over GDP		Percent
6.6 Tourism openness (inbound plus outbound tourism expenditure) over GDP		Percent
6.7 Tourism coverage (inbound over outbound tourism expenditure)		Percent
6.8 Inbound tourism expenditure over exports of goods		Percent
6.9 Inbound tourism expenditure over exports of services		Percent
6.10 Inbound tourism expenditure over exports of goods and services		Percent
6.11 Inbound tourism expenditure over current account credits		Percent
6.12 Outbound tourism expenditure over imports of goods		Percent
6.13 Outbound tourism expenditure over imports of services		Percent
6.14 Outbound tourism expenditure over imports of goods and services		Percent
6.15 Outbound tourism expenditure over current account debits		Percent

Données de base et indicateurs	Notes	Unités
1. TOURISME RÉCEPTEUR		
Données		
Arrivées		
1.1 Total		('000)
1.2 ♦ Visiteurs qui passent la nuit (touristes)		('000)
1.3 ♦ Visiteurs de la journée (excursionnistes)		('000)
1.4 * dont croisiéristes		('000)
Arrivées par région		
1.5 Total		('000)
1.6 ♦ Afrique		('000)
1.7 ♦ Amériques		('000)
1.8 ♦ Asie de l'Est et Pacifique		('000)
1.9 ♦ Europe		('000)
1.10 ♦ Moyen-Orient		('000)
1.11 ♦ Asie du Sud		('000)
1.12 ♦ Autres, non classés		('000)
1.13 * dont nationaux résidant à l'étranger		('000)
Arrivées, par motif principal		
1.14 Total		('000)
1.15 ♦ Motifs personnels		('000)
1.16 * vacances, loisirs et détente		('000)
1.17 * autres motifs personnels		('000)
1.18 ♦ Affaires et motifs professionnels		('000)
Arrivées, par mode de transport		
1.19 Total		('000)
1.20 ♦ Voie aérienne		('000)
1.21 ♦ Voie fluviale		('000)
1.22 ♦ Voie terrestre		('000)
1.23 * chemin de fer		('000)
1.24 * route		('000)
1.25 * autres		('000)
Arrivées, par mode d'organisation du voyage		
1.26 Total		('000)
1.27 ♦ Voyages à forfait		('000)
1.28 ♦ Autres		('000)
Hébergement		
Total		
1.29 ♦ Clients		('000)
1.30 ♦ Nuitées		('000)
Hôtels et établissements assimilés		
1.31 ♦ Clients		('000)
1.32 ♦ Nuitées		('000)
Dépenses		
1.33 Total		Mn $E.U.
1.34 ♦ Voyages		Mn $E.U.
1.35 ♦ Transport de passagers		Mn $E.U.
Dépenses, par motif principal du voyage		
1.36 Total		Mn $E.U.
1.37 ♦ Motifs personnels		Mn $E.U.
1.38 ♦ Affaires et motifs professionnels		Mn $E.U.
Indicateurs		
1.39 Taille moyenne du groupe de voyageurs		Personnes
Durée moyenne du séjour		
1.40 Total		Journées
1.41 ♦ Pour tous les services d'hébergement commercial		Nuitées
1.42 * dont "hôtels et établissements assimilés"		Nuitées
1.43 ♦ Pour les services d'hébergement non commercial		Journées
1.44 Dépenses moyennes par jour		$E.U.

Données de base et indicateurs	Notes	Unités
2. TOURISME INTERNE		
Données		
Voyages		
2.1 Total		('000)
2.2 ♦ Visiteurs qui passent la nuit (touristes)		('000)
2.3 ♦ Visiteurs à la journée (excursionnistes)		('000)
Voyages, par motif principal		
2.4 Total		('000)
2.5 ♦ Voyages personnels		('000)
2.6 * vacances, loisirs et détente		('000)
2.7 * autres motifs personnels		('000)
2.8 ♦ Affaires et motifs professionnels		('000)
Voyages, par mode de transport		
2.9 Total		('000)
2.10 ♦ Voie aérienne		('000)
2.11 ♦ Voie fluviale		('000)
2.12 ♦ Voie terrestre		('000)
2.13 * chemin de fer		('000)
2.14 * route		('000)
2.15 * autres		('000)
Voyages, par mode d'organisation		
2.16 Total		('000)
2.17 ♦ Voyages à forfait		('000)
2.18 ♦ Autres		('000)
Hébergement		
Total		
2.19 ♦ Clients		('000)
2.20 ♦ Nuitées		('000)
Hôtels et établissements assimilés		
2.21 ♦ Clients		('000)
2.22 ♦ Nuitées		('000)
Indicateurs		
2.23 Taille moyenne du groupe de voyageurs		Personnes
Durée moyenne du séjour		
2.24 Total		Journées
2.25 ♦ Pour tous les services d'hébergement commercial		Nuitées
2.26 * dont "hôtels et établissements assimilés"		Nuitées
2.27 ♦ Pour les services d'hébergement non commercial		Journées
2.28 Dépenses moyennes par jour		$E.U.
3. TOURISME ÉMETTEUR		
Données		
Départs		
3.1 Total		('000)
3.2 ♦ Visiteurs qui passent la nuit (touristes)		('000)
3.3 ♦ Visiteurs à la journée (excursionnistes)		('000)
Dépenses		
3.4 Total		Mn $E.U.
3.5 ♦ Voyages		Mn $E.U.
3.6 ♦ Transport de passagers		Mn $E.U.
Dépenses, par motif principal du voyage		
3.7 Total		Mn $E.U.
3.8 ♦ Motifs personnels		Mn $E.U.
3.9 ♦ Affaires et motifs professionnels		Mn $E.U.
Indicateurs		
3.10 Durée moyenne du séjour		Journées
3.11 Dépenses moyennes par jour		$E.U.

Données de base et indicateurs	Notes	Unités
4. SOUS-SECTEURS TOURISTIQUES		
Données		
Nombre d'établissements		
4.1 Total		Unités
4.2 ♦ Hébergement des visiteurs		Unités
4.3 * dont "hôtels et établissements assimilés"		Unités
4.4 ♦ Restaurants et débits de boissons		Unités
4.5 ♦ Transport de passagers		Unités
4.6 ♦ Agences de voyage et autres activités de services de réservation		Unités
4.7 ♦ Autres sous-secteurs touristiques		Unités
Hébergement des visiteurs dans des hôtels et des établissements assimilés		
Données monétaires		
4.8 ♦ Données de sortie		Mn $E.U.
4.9 ♦ Consommation intermédiaire		Mn $E.U.
4.10 ♦ Valeur ajoutée brute		Mn $E.U.
4.11 ♦ Rémunération des salariés		Mn $E.U.
4.12 ♦ Formation brute de capital fixe		Mn $E.U.
Données non monétaires		
4.13 ♦ Nombre d'établissements		Unités
4.14 ♦ Nombre de chambres		Unités
4.15 ♦ Nombre de places-lit		Unités
Indicateurs		
4.16 Taux d'occupation / chambres		Pour cent
4.17 Taux d'occupation / places-lit		Pour cent
4.18 Durée moyenne du séjour		Nuitées
4.19 Capacité disponible (places-lit pour 1000 habitants)		Unités
Agences de voyage ct autres activités de services de réservation		
Données monétaires		
4.20 ♦ Données de sortie		Mn $E.U.
4.21 ♦ Consommation intermédiaire		Mn $E.U.
4.22 ♦ Valeur ajoutée brute		Mn $E.U.
4.23 ♦ Rémunération des salariés		Mn $E.U.
4.24 ♦ Formation brute de capital fixe		Mn $E.U.
Données non monétaires		
♦ Voyages internes		
4.25 * avec forfait		Pour cent
4.26 * sans forfait		Pour cent
♦ Voyages récepteurs		
4.27 * avec forfait		Pour cent
4.28 * sans forfait		Pour cent
♦ Voyages émetteurs		
4.29 * avec forfait		Pour cent
4.30 * sans forfait		Pour cent

Données de base et indicateurs	Notes	Unités
5. EMPLOI		
Données		
Nombre d'employés par sous-secteur touristique		
5.1 Total		('000)
5.2 ♦ Services d'hébergement pour les visiteurs (hôtels et établissements assimilés)		('000)
5.3 ♦ Autres services d'hébergement		('000)
5.4 ♦ Restaurants et débits de boissons		('000)
5.5 ♦ Transport de passagers		('000)
5.6 ♦ Agences de voyage et autres activités de services de réservation		('000)
5.7 ♦ Autres industries touristiques		('000)
Nombre d'emplois par statut		
5.8 Total		('000)
5.9 ♦ Employés		('000)
5.10 ♦ Travailleurs indépendants		('000)
Indicateurs		
Nombre d'emplois équivalents à temps plein par statut		
5.11 Total		('000)
5.12 ♦ Employés		('000)
5.13 * hommes		('000)
5.14 * femmes		('000)
5.15 ♦ Travailleurs indépendants		('000)
5.16 * hommes		('000)
5.17 * femmes		('000)
6. INDICATEURS COMPLÉMENTAIRES		
Demande		
6.1 Propension brute à voyager		Unités
6.2 Capacité de charge (arrivées/population)		Unités
Indicateurs macroéconomiques liés au tourisme international		
6.3 Rapport dépenses du tourisme récepteur / PIB		Pour cent
6.4 Rapport dépenses du tourisme émetteur / PIB		Pour cent
6.5 Rapport balance du tourisme (dépenses du tourisme récepteur moins dépenses du tourisme émetteur) / PIB		Pour cent
6.6 Ouverture touristique (dépenses du tourisme récepteur + dépenses du tourisme émetteur / PIB)		Pour cent
6.7 Couverture touristique (rapport dépenses du tourisme émetteur / dépenses du tourisme récepteur)		Pour cent
6.8 Rapport dépenses du tourisme récepteur / exportations de biens		Pour cent
6.9 Rapport dépenses du tourisme récepteur / exportations de services		Pour cent
6.10 Rapport dépenses du tourisme récepteur / exportations de biens et de services		Pour cent
6.11 Rapport dépenses du tourisme récepteur / crédits du compte courant		Pour cent
6.12 Rapport dépenses du tourisme émetteur / importations de biens		Pour cent
6.13 Rapport dépenses du tourisme émetteur / importations de services		Pour cent
6.14 Rapport dépenses du tourisme émetteur / importations de biens et de services		Pour cent
6.15 Rapport dépenses du tourisme émetteur / débits du compte courant		Pour cent

Datos básicos e indicadores	Notas	Unidades
1. TURISMO RECEPTOR		
Datos		
Llegadas		
1.1 Total		('000)
1.2 ♦ Visitantes que pernoctan (turistas)		('000)
1.3 ♦ Visitantes del día (excursionistas)		('000)
1.4 * de los cuales, pasajeros en crucero		('000)
Llegadas por región		
1.5 Total		('000)
1.6 ♦ África		('000)
1.7 ♦ Américas		('000)
1.8 ♦ Asia Oriental y el Pacífico		('000)
1.9 ♦ Europa		('000)
1.10 ♦ Oriente Medio		('000)
1.11 ♦ Asia Meridional		('000)
1.12 ♦ Otros no clasificados		('000)
1.13 * de los cuales, nacionales residentes en el extranjero		('000)
Llegadas por motivo principal		
1.14 Total		('000)
1.15 ♦ Motivos personales		('000)
1.16 * vacaciones, recreo y ocio		('000)
1.17 * otros motivos personales		('000)
1.18 ♦ Negocios y motivos profesionales		('000)
Llegadas por medio de transporte		
1.19 Total		('000)
1.20 ♦ Aéreo		('000)
1.21 ♦ Acuático		('000)
1.22 ♦ Terrestre		('000)
1.23 * ferrocarril		('000)
1.24 * carretera		('000)
1.25 * otros		('000)
Llegadas por forma de organización del viaje		
1.26 Total		('000)
1.27 ♦ Paquete turístico		('000)
1.28 ♦ Otras formas		('000)
Alojamiento		
Total		
1.29 ♦ Huéspedes		('000)
1.30 ♦ Pernoctaciones		('000)
Hoteles y establecimientos asimilados		
1.31 ♦ Huéspedes		('000)
1.32 ♦ Pernoctaciones		('000)
Gastos		
1.33 Total		Mill. $EE.UU.
1.34 ♦ Viajes		Mill. $EE.UU.
1.35 ♦ Transporte de pasajeros		Mill. $EE.UU.
Gastos por motivo principal del viaje		
1.36 Total		Mill. $EE.UU.
1.37 ♦ Motivos personales		Mill. $EE.UU.
1.38 ♦ Negocios y motivos profesionales		Mill. $EE.UU.
Indicadores		
1.39 Tamaño medio de los grupos de viaje		Personas
Duración media de la estancia		
1.40 Total		Días
1.41 ♦ Para todos los servicios de alojamiento comercial		Noches
1.42 * de los cuales, "hoteles y establecimientos asimilados"		Noches
1.43 ♦ Para los servicios de alojamiento no comercial		Días
1.44 Gasto medio por día		$EE.UU.

ÍNDICE DE INDICADORES Y DATOS BÁSICOS

Datos básicos e indicadores	Notas	Unidades
2. TURISMO INTERNO		
Datos		
Viajes		
2.1 Total		('000)
2.2 ♦ Visitantes que pernoctan (turistas)		('000)
2.3 ♦ Visitantes del día (excursionistas)		('000)
Viajes por motivo principal		
2.4 Total		('000)
2.5 ♦ Motivos personales		('000)
2.6 * vacaciones, recreo y ocio		('000)
2.7 * otros motivos personales		('000)
2.8 ♦ Negocios y motivos profesionales		('000)
Viajes por medio de transporte		
2.9 Total		('000)
2.10 ♦ Aéreo		('000)
2.11 ♦ Acuático		('000)
2.12 ♦ Terrestre		('000)
2.13 * ferrocarril		('000)
2.14 * carretera		('000)
2.15 * otros		('000)
Viajes por forma de organización		
2.16 Total		('000)
2.17 ♦ Paquete turístico		('000)
2.18 ♦ Otras formas		('000)
Alojamiento		
Total		
2.19 ♦ Huéspedes		('000)
2.20 ♦ Pernoctaciones		('000)
Hoteles y establecimientos asimilados		
2.21 ♦ Huéspedes		('000)
2.22 ♦ Pernoctaciones		('000)
Indicadores		
2.23 Tamaño medio de los grupos de viaje		Personas
Duración media de la estancia		
2.24 Total		Días
2.25 ♦ Para todos los servicios de alojamiento comercial		Noches
2.26 * de los cuales, "hoteles y establecimientos asimilados"		Noches
2.27 ♦ Para los servicios de alojamiento no comercial		Días
2.28 Gasto medio por día		$EE.UU.
3. TURISMO EMISOR		
Datos		
Salidas		
3.1 Total		('000)
3.2 ♦ Visitantes que pernoctan (turistas)		('000)
3.3 ♦ Visitantes del día (excursionistas)		('000)
Gastos		
3.4 Total		Mill. $EE.UU.
3.5 ♦ Viajes		Mill. $EE.UU.
3.6 ♦ Transporte de pasajeros		Mill. $EE.UU.
Gastos por motivo principal del viaje		
3.7 Total		Mill. $EE.UU.
3.8 ♦ Motivos personales		Mill. $EE.UU.
3.9 ♦ Negocios y motivos profesionales		Mill. $EE.UU.
Indicadores		
3.10 Duración media de la estancia		Días
3.11 Gasto medio por día		$EE.UU.

Datos básicos e indicadores	Notas	Unidades
4. INDUSTRIAS TURÍSTICAS		
Datos		
Número de establecimientos		
4.1 Total		Unidades
4.2 ♦ Alojamiento para visitantes		Unidades
4.3 * de los cuales, "hoteles y establecimientos asimilados"		Unidades
4.4 ♦ Actividades de provisión de alimentos y bebidas		Unidades
4.5 ♦ Transporte de pasajeros		Unidades
4.6 ♦ Actividades de agencias de viajes y de otros servicios de reservas		Unidades
4.7 ♦ Otras industrias turísticas		Unidades
Alojamiento para los visitantes en hoteles y establecimientos asimilados		
Datos monetarios		
4.8 ♦ Producción		Mill. $EE.UU.
4.9 ♦ Consumo intermedio		Mill. $EE.UU.
4.10 ♦ Valor añadido bruto		Mill. $EE.UU.
4.11 ♦ Remuneración de los trabajadores asalariados		Mill. $EE.UU.
4.12 ♦ Formación bruta de capital fijo		Mill. $EE.UU.
Datos no monetarios		
4.13 ♦ Número de establecimientos		Unidades
4.14 ♦ Número de habitaciones		Unidades
4.15 ♦ Número de plazas-cama		Unidades
Indicadores		
4.16 Tasa de ocupación / habitaciones		%
4.17 Tasa de ocupación / plazas-cama		%
4.18 Duración media de la estancia		Noches
4.19 Capacidad disponible (plazas-cama por 1000 habitantes)		Unidades
Actividades de agencias de viajes y de otros servicios de reserva		
Datos monetarios		
4.20 ♦ Producción		Mill. $EE.UU.
4.21 ♦ Consumo intermedio		Mill. $EE.UU.
4.22 ♦ Valor añadido bruto		Mill. $EE.UU.
4.23 ♦ Remuneración de los trabajadores asalariados		Mill. $EE.UU.
4.24 ♦ Formación bruta de capital fijo		Mill. $EE.UU.
Datos no monetarios		
♦ Viajes internos		
4.25 * con paquete turístico		%
4.26 * sin paquete turístico		%
♦ Viajes receptores		
4.27 * con paquete turístico		%
4.28 * sin paquete turístico		%
♦ Viajes emisores		
4.29 * con paquete turístico		%
4.30 * sin paquete turístico		%

Datos básicos e indicadores	Notas	Unidades
5. EMPLEO		
Datos		
Número de empleados por industria turística		
5.1 Total		('000)
5.2 ◆ Servicios de alojamiento para visitantes (hoteles y establecimientos asimilados)		('000)
5.3 ◆ Otros servicios de alojamiento		('000)
5.4 ◆ Actividades de provisión de alimentos y bebidas		('000)
5.5 ◆ Transporte de pasajeros		('000)
5.6 ◆ Actividades de agencias de viajes y de otros servicios de reservas		('000)
5.7 ◆ Otras industrias turísticas		('000)
Número de puestos de trabajo según la situación en el empleo		
5.8 Total		('000)
5.9 ◆ Asalariados		('000)
5.10 ◆ Trabajadores autónomos		('000)
Indicadores		
Número de puestos de trabajo equivalentes a tiempo completo según la situación en el empleo		
5.11 Total		('000)
5.12 ◆ Asalariados		('000)
5.13 * hombres		('000)
5.14 * mujeres		('000)
5.15 ◆ Trabajadores autónomos		('000)
5.16 * hombres		('000)
5.17 * mujeres		('000)
6. INDICADORES COMPLEMENTARIOS		
Demanda		
6.1 Propensión bruta a viajar		Unidades
6.2 Capacidad de carga (llegadas/población)		Unidades
Indicadores macroeconómicos relacionados con el turismo internacional		
6.3 Gasto turístico receptor sobre el PIB		%
6.4 Gasto turístico emisor sobre el PIB		%
6.5 Balanza turística (gasto turístico receptor menos gasto turístico emisor) sobre el PIB		%
6.6 Apertura turística (gasto turístico receptor más gasto turístico emisor) sobre el PIB		%
6.7 Cobertura turística (gasto turístico receptor sobre gasto turístico emisor)		%
6.8 Gasto turístico receptor sobre las exportaciones de bienes		%
6.9 Gasto turístico receptor sobre las exportaciones de servicios		%
6.10 Gasto turístico receptor sobre las exportaciones de bienes y de servicios		%
6.11 Gasto turístico receptor sobre los créditos de la cuenta corriente		%
6.12 Gasto turístico emisor sobre las importaciones de bienes		%
6.13 Gasto turístico emisor sobre las importaciones de servicios		%
6.14 Gasto turístico emisor sobre las importaciones de bienes y de servicios		%
6.15 Gasto turístico emisor sobre los débitos de la cuenta corriente		%

Country notes /

Notes des pays /

Notas de los países

IMF notes (available in English only)

COUNTRY NOTES

ALBANIA

(1) Excluding nationals residing abroad; (2) Source: Short Term Survey; (3) The classification used is NACE Rev. 1 (Statistical classification of economic activities); (4) Value added at Basic prices; (5) Total investments; (6) The figures are updated with the Structural Business Survey.
Institute of Statistics – INSTAT - http://www.instat.gov.al/

ALGERIA

(1) Including nationals residing abroad; (2) Excluding nationals residing abroad.
"Ministère de l'Aménagement du Territoire, de l'Environnement et du Tourisme" and "Office National des Statistiques" - http://www.ons.dz/-Tourisme-.html

AMERICAN SAMOA

(1) Including Western Samoa; (2) Visit friends, relatives.
American Samoa Government - Department of Commerce - Statistics Division - http://www.spc.int/prism/country/as/stats/

ANDORRA

(1) Since May 2009, a new methodology has been applied and therefore, the information is not comparable to previous years.
"Ministerio de Turismo y Medio Ambiente" and "Ministerio de Finanzas" - http://www.estadistica.ad/serveiestudis/web/index.asp?lang=2

ANGOLA

(1) Hotels only.
Note 2008: Provisional data.
"Ministério de Hotelaria e Turismo - Gabinete de Estudos, Planeamento e Estatística"

ANGUILLA

(1) Excluding nationals residing abroad; (2) Same-day visitors (excursionists).
Statistical Department - Ministry of Finance - http://www.gov.ai/statistics/cab_external.htm

ANTIGUA AND BARBUDA

(1) Excluding yacht passenger arrivals; (2) Air arrivals; excluding nationals residing abroad; (3) Cruise passengers only.
Ministry of Tourism - http://www.tourismantiguabarbuda.gov.ag/tourism_programs/statistics.php

ARGENTINA

(1) Hotel Occupancy Survey (EOH); (2) Information obtained in the Permanent Household Survey (EPH) making it possible to estimate jobs in tourism characteristic industries. This survey has limited territorial coverage, and thus its estimates are not fully representative of the entire country; (3) This refers to employees, not jobs; (4) The classification includes non-remunerated employers and family-member workers.
"Dirección de Estudios de Mercado y Estadística - Secretaría de Turismo de la Nación" - http://www.turismo.gov.ar/

ARMENIA

Tourism Department - Ministry of Trade and Economic Development - http://www.armstat.am/en/

ARUBA

(1) Arrivals by air; (2) Cruise passengers only.
Aruba Tourism Authority - http://www.cbs.aw/cbs/do/home.html

AUSTRALIA

(1) Excluding nationals residing abroad and crew members; (2) Arrivals by air; (3) Hotels, motels, guests houses and serviced apartments with 5 rooms or more.
Australian Bureau of Statistics - http://www.abs.gov.au/

AUSTRIA

(1) Non-resident tourists staying in all types of accommodation establishments; (2) Only paid accommodation; excluding stays at friends and relatives and second homes; (3) Hotels only; (4) Leisure and business trips abroad with at least one overnight stay; (5) Based on summer season; (6) Tourism Satellite Account (TSA) data; (7) Full-time equivalents.

COUNTRY NOTES

Statistics Austria - http://www.statistik.at/web_en/statistics/tourism/accommodation/index.html

AZERBAIJAN

Ministry of Culture and Tourism and Statistical Committee - http://www.azstat.org/statinfo/consumermarket/en/tur_en.shtml

BAHAMAS

(1) Arrivals in hotels only; (2) Hotels, apartments, cottages and villas - Licensed properties only.
Bahamas Ministry of Tourism - http://www.tourismtoday.com/prelim/statistics/

BAHRAIN

(1) Excluding nationals residing abroad; (2) Arrivals at Bahrain International Airport; (3) Arrivals at Mina Salman Port; (4) Arrivals through King Fahad Causeway; (5) Classified hotels only.
Tourism Sector - Ministry of Culture and Information

BANGLADESH

Bangladesh Parjatan Corporation

BARBADOS

(1) Hotels, apartment hotels, apartments and cottages, guest houses.
Barbados Tourism Authority

BELARUS

(1) Organized tourism.
State Committee of Frontier Troops and Ministry of Statistics and Analysis

BELGIUM

(1) Non-resident tourists staying in all types of accommodation establishments; (2) Hotels only; (3) Hotels and holiday villages.
"Institut National de Statistique"

BELIZE

Belize Tourist Board - http://www.belizetourism.org/content/view/248/295/

BENIN

Note 2005-2009: Estimates.
"Direction du développement touristique - Ministère de la culture, de l'artisanat et du tourisme"

BERMUDA

(1) Excluding nationals residing abroad; (2) Air arrivals; (3) Cruise passengers; (4) Including overnight stays at private houses.
Bermuda Department of Tourism –
http://www.gov.bm/portal/server.pt?space=CommunityPage&control=SetCommunity&CommunityID=227

BHUTAN

Department of Tourism - Royal Government of Bhutan - http://www.nsb.gov.bt/index.php?id=13

BOLIVIA

(1) Estimated data; (2) Information obtained through the specific percentage breakdown in the Survey "expenditure of inbound and outbound tourism – 2007"; (3) Arrivals by lake; (4) The 7.6% of travellers corresponds to organized tourism; (5) Source: Survey "expenditure of inbound and outbound tourism – 2007"; (6) Department capitals only; (7) Average size of travel party for families: 2.8 persons.
Note: The tourism indicators are obtained from the relationship of the results of the survey "expenditure of inbound and outbound tourism – 2007" between/among the statistics of Foreign Trade, Balance of Payments services, National Accounts (GDP), determining the participation of tourism in each of the sectors.
2006-2009: Provisional data.
"Instituto Nacional de Estadística" and "Viceministerio de Turismo - Ministerio de Producción y Microempresa"
http://www.ine.gov.bo/default.aspx

COUNTRY NOTES

BONAIRE

(1) Source: Central Bank of the Netherlands Antilles.
Tourism Corporation of Bonaire (TCB) - http://www.tourismbonaire.com/contact_services/trade_section/statistical_info/

BOSNIA AND HERZEGOVINA

(1) Non-resident tourists staying in all types of accommodation establishments; (2) Less than 500 arrivals; (3) Since 2007 data refer to the whole of Bosnia and Herzegovina.
Agency for Statistics of Bosnia and Herzegovina - http://www.bhas.ba/eng/Publications.asp?Pripadnost=8&mode=dark

BOTSWANA

Note 2008-2009: Estimated figures.
Department of Tourism - Ministry of Environment, Wildlife and Tourism

BRAZIL

(1) Including nationals residing abroad; (2) Including arrivals by river; (3) Source: Ministry of Tourism and Ministry of Labour / Annual Social Information Report (RAIS) – 2009. The information was estimated based on CADASTUR – "Tourism Service Provider Registry System of the Ministry of Tourism and RAIS"; (4) Formal employees: registered in and covered by social security; (5) Informal workers: self-employed workers and unregistered employees; (6) The difference between the total number of workers of the informal sector, by sex (5.15), and the number of workers of the informal sector (5.10) is due to the reference month used for these estimates, September, the month of collection of the National Household Survey, for sex, and December for the extrapolation of the number of workers of the informal sector.
"Ministério do Turismo" - http://www.dadosefatos.turismo.gov.br/dadosefatos/home.html

BRITISH VIRGIN ISLANDS

(1) The expenditure figures are those provided by the country to UNWTO, which do not appear in the International Monetary Fund data used in the preparation of this edition of the Compendium.
The Development Planning Unit - Ministry of Finance –
http://dpu.gov.vg/index.php?option=com_content&view=article&id=58&Itemid=68

BRUNEI DARUSSALAM

(1) (2/2007) Air arrivals.
Brunei Tourism - Ministry of Industry and Primary Resources

BULGARIA

(1) Transit visitors; (2) Sea and inland waterways; (3) Hotels only.
National Statistical Institute - State Agency for Tourism – http://www.nsi.bg/SocialActivities_e/Tourism_e.htm

BURKINA FASO

(1) Non-resident tourists staying in hotels and similar establishments; (2) Including domestic tourism.
"Service de l'analyse statistique et de la Coopération touristique - Ministère de la Culture, des Arts et du Tourisme"
http://www.insd.bf/

BURUNDI

(1) Including nationals residing abroad; (2) Arrivals by lake.
"Office National du Tourisme"

CAMBODIA

(1) Arrivals by all means of transport; (2) Arrivals by boat; (3) Days.
Ministry of Tourism - http://www.mot.gov.kh

CAMEROON

(1) Non-resident tourists staying in hotels and similar establishments.
"Ministère du Tourisme"

COUNTRY NOTES

CANADA

(1) Data based on customs counts and adjusted using questionnaire surveys; (2) Person-trips (one or more nights).
Canadian Tourism Commission and Statistics Canada –
http://en-corporate.canada.travel/Corporate/Flyout.page?id=369&fid=376

CAPE VERDE

(1) Non-resident tourists staying in hotels and similar establishments.
"Instituto Nacional de Estatística" and "Ministério da Economia, Crescimento e Competitividade" –
http://www.ine.cv/indexBDeo.aspx

CAYMAN ISLANDS

(1) Arrivals by air; (2) Cruise passengers only; (3) Hotels and apartments; (4) The expenditure figures are those provided by the country to UNWTO, which do not appear in the International Monetary Fund data used in the preparation of this edition of the Compendium; (5) Including expenditure by cruise passengers; (6) Days.
Cayman Islands Department of Tourism – http://www.caymanislands.ky/statistics/

CENTRAL AFRICAN REPUBLIC

(1) Arrivals by air to Bangui only; (2) Country data.
Note 2006: Estimates.
"Ministère du Développement du Tourisme et de l'Artisanat"

CHAD

(1) Non-resident tourists staying in hotels and similar establishments.
"Direction des Études et de la Programmation - Ministère du Développement Touristique"

CHILE

(1) Including nationals residing abroad; (2) Figures for 2005 are not comparable with those of previous years due to a revision of the National Census of Tourism Accommodation Establishments.
"Servicio Nacional de Turismo - SERNATUR" – http://www.sernatur.cl/institucional/htm_instit/estadisticas.html

CHINA

(1) Including ethnic Chinese arriving from "Hong Kong, China", "Macao, China", "Taiwan, Province of China" and overseas Chinese, of which most same-day visitors are from "Hong Kong, China" and "Macao, China"; (2) Excluding ethnic Chinese arriving from "Hong Kong, China", "Macao, China", "Taiwan, Province of China" and overseas Chinese; (3) Only refer to the star-rated hotels; (4) Including air crew members and other servicemen; (5) Inbound tourism only.
National Tourism Administration – http://en.cnta.gov.cn/

COLOMBIA

(1) Arrivals of foreign travellers at checkpoints of the Administrative Department of Security (DAS); (2) 2005,2006: excluding the foreign travellers arrived at terrestrial frontier points; 2007-2009: including the foreign travellers arrived at terrestrial frontier points; (3) Including cruise passengers; (4) Excluding the foreign travellers arrived at terrestrial frontier points; (5) Excluding cruise passengers; (6) 2009: including the foreign travellers arrived at terrestrial frontier points; (7) From 2005: "Departamento Nacional de Estadística (DANE)".
"Dirección de Extranjería - Departamento Administrativo de Seguridad (DAS)" –
http://www.mincomercio.gov.co/eContent/home.asp

COMOROS

(1) 2007, (2) Air arrivals only; (3) The expenditure figures are those provided by the country to UNWTO, which do not appear in the International Monetary Fund data used in the preparation of this edition of the Compendium.
"Direction Nationale de la Promotion du Tourisme et de l'Hôtellerie - Ministère du Transport, Tourisme, Postes et Télécommunications" and "Banque centrale des Comores"

CONGO

(1) Non-resident tourists staying in hotels and similar establishments.
"Direction Générale du Tourisme et de l'Hôtellerie - Ministère du tourisme et de l'environnement"

COUNTRY NOTES

COOK ISLANDS

(1) Air and sea arrivals; (2) The expenditure figures are those provided by the country to UNWTO, which do not appear in the International Monetary Fund data used in the preparation of this edition of the Compendium; (3) Hotels and motels.
Cook Islands Tourism Corporation and Cook Islands Statistics Office – http://www.stats.gov.ck/Statistics/Tourism/tournav.htm

COSTA RICA

(1) Pleasure trips and visits to relatives; (2) In the central area of the country; (3) "Five category" establishments in San José Metropolitan Area (survey); (4) This corresponds to persons employed in the division "Hotels and Restaurants" according to the International Standard Industrial Classification of All Economic Activities (ISIC Rev.3); (5) Multi-Purpose Household Survey. Excluding non-remunerated jobs; (6) Corresponds to equivalent jobs generated by visible underemployment referring to employed persons who usually work less than 47 hours a week in their main job and secondary job (if any), who wish to work more hours per week and are available to do so. Excluding non-remunerated jobs.
"Instituto Costarricense de Turismo" and "Instituto Nacional de Estadística y Censos" –
http://www.visitcostarica.com/ict/paginas/modEst/estudios_demanda_turistica.asp?ididioma=1

CROATIA

(1) Non-resident tourists staying in all types of accommodation establishments; (2) Including arrivals in ports of nautical tourism; (3) 2008: New methodology; (4) Since 2004 a new methodology and new coverage have been applied and data are not comparable to previous years; (5) Including nights in ports of nautical tourism.
Central Bureau of Statistics – http://www.dzs.hr/default_e.htm – http://www.mint.hr/default.aspx?id=363

CUBA

(1) Air arrivals; (2) Hotels, motels, apart-hotels, camping/caravaning and other; (3) Hotels, motels & apart-hotels; (4) The expenditure figures are those provided by the country to UNWTO, which do not appear in the International Monetary Fund data used in the preparation of this edition of the Compendium; (5) Including only tours authorized by the "Instituto de Turismo".
"Oficina Nacional de Estadísticas" – http://www.one.cu/sitioone2006.asp

CURAÇAO

(1) Arrivals by air; (2) Differences in overall totals due to incompletion of items on the E/D card by visitors; (3) Cruise ship arrivals; (4) Large and small hotels, guest houses, apartments and bungalows; (5) Source: Central Bank of the Netherlands Antilles; (6) Hotels, guest houses, apartments.
Curaçao Tourist Board – http://www.ctb.an/Statistics.aspx

CYPRUS

(1) Including transit & cruise passengers; (2) Including transit passengers; (3) Accommodation data (arrivals, overnight stays and occupancy rates) is collected from the licensed tourist accommodation establishments on a monthly basis and produced by the C.T.O; (4) Average expenditure per day calculated by dividing the relevant total expenditure (item 1.33) with the total number of inbound overnight tourists (item 1.2) and their average length of stay (item 1.40); (5) The data provided results from the implementation of a TSA system by the Statistical Service of the Republic of Cyprus. The implementation of the TSA system was conducted on a pilot basis, covering the period 2003-2007; (6) Average length of stay calculations are based on overnight stays and arrivals at licensed tourist accommodation establishments; (7) As from 1 January 2008, Statistical Service of Cyprus conducts a monthly survey on the expenses of Cypriots travelling abroad (travel debit). Under this survey, the part of expenses of Cypriots travelling abroad that concerns transportation expenses can be isolated. As a result, this amount is included under transportation services; (8) Outbound tourism from 2003 onwards also includes trips for religion and pilgrimage as a purpose of visit; (9) Average expenditure per day calculated by dividing the relevant Total Expenditure (item 3.4) with the total number of outbound overnight tourists (item 3.2) and their average length of stay (item 3.10); (10) Data concerns all paid accommodation services; (11) Data is compiled and produced by the C.T.O., it concerns hotels and similar licensed tourist accommodation establishments and was not used in the TSA estimates shown in the items 4.1-4.12; (12) Average length of stay calculations are based on overnight stays and arrivals at hotels and similar licensed tourist accommodation establishments.
Note for all the data supplied: information on real estate activities with own or leased property and real estate activities on a fee or contract basis is not included.
Statistical Service of Cyprus and Cyprus Tourism Organization –
http://www.mof.gov.cy/mof/cystat/statistics.nsf/index_en/index_en?OpenDocument

CZECH REPUBLIC

(1) Non-resident tourists staying in all types of accommodation establishments; (2) Hotels and restaurants; (3) Net use of beds; (4) Supporting and auxiliary transport activities, activities of tour-operators and travel agencies.
Czech Statistical Office, TSA – http://www.czso.cz/eng/redakce.nsf/i/home

COUNTRY NOTES

DEMOCRATIC REPUBLIC OF THE CONGO

(1) 2007-2009: Arrivals by air only.
"Office National du Tourisme"

DENMARK

(1) Non-resident tourists staying in all types of accommodation establishments; (2) From 2005: including non-commercial tourism; (3) New methodology from 2006; (4) Hotels only; (5) Source: VisitDenmark; (6) Only hotels and holiday dwellings with 40 beds or more.
VisitDenmark – http://www.dst.dk/HomeUK.aspx

DJIBOUTI

(1) Non-resident tourists staying in hotels.
"Office national du tourisme"

DOMINICA

(1) Days.
Discover Dominica Authority – http://tourism.gov.dm/

DOMINICAN REPUBLIC

(1) Including nationals residing abroad; (2) Arrivals by air only; (3) All arrivals by sea; (4) Hotels; (5) 2009: country data.
"Secretaría de Estado de Turismo" – http://www.bancentral.gov.do/estadisticas.asp?a=Sector_Turismo

ECUADOR

(1) Excluding nationals residing abroad.
"Ministerio de Turismo" – http://www.turismo.gov.ec/index.php?option=com_content&task=view&id=459&Itemid=95

EGYPT

(1) Travel for tourism and non-tourism purposes (more than 50% for work purpose).
Ministry of Tourism

EL SALVADOR

(1) New methodology from 2004; (2) Including private accommodation.
"Corporación Salvadoreña de Turismo (CORSATUR) - Ministerio de Turismo" –
http://www.elsalvador.travel/secciones.php?id_seccion=20&lang=sp&portal=2

ERITREA

(1) Including nationals residing abroad; (2) Only hotels and similar establishments in the three major towns: Asmara, Karen and Massawa; (3) The expenditure figures used were the ones provided by the country to UNWTO, as this data series is more complete than that provided by the International Monetary Fund (IMF) for the preparation of this Compendium; (4) 2005/2006: Only hotels and similar establishments in the three major towns: Asmara, Karen and Massawa; (5) 2007-2009: Twelve major towns; (6) All hotels and similar establishments in Eritrea.
Ministry of Tourism

ESTONIA

(1) Calculated on the basis of accommodation statistics and "Foreign Visitor Survey" carried out by the Statistical Office of Estonia; (2) Non-resident tourists staying in all types of accommodation establishments; (3) Source: household survey by "Statistics Estonia"; (4) 2005-2007: all types of accommodation establishments.
Note: Starting from 2004, border statistics are not collected any more.
Estonian Tourist Board / Enterprise Estonia – http://pub.stat.ee/px-web.2001/I_Databas/Economy/databasetree.asp
http://visitestonia.com/en/additional-navigation/press-room/eas-views-on-tourism/estonian-tourism-statistics

ETHIOPIA

(1) Arrivals through all ports of entry; including nationals residing abroad; (2) 2005: Excluding unclassified hotels.
Ministry of Culture and Tourism

COUNTRY NOTES

FIJI

(1) Excluding nationals residing abroad; (2) Days.
Fiji Islands Bureau of Statistics – http://www.spc.int/prism/Country/FJ/stats/Tourism/tourmigstats_index.htm

FINLAND

(1) Border Interview survey; (2) Accommodation statistics; (3) Balance of Payments (BOP); (4) Finnish Travel survey; (5) Including only domestic leisure trips at rented accommodation for visitors; (6) Overnight trips abroad, including cruises abroad with overnight on board only; (7) Statistics on Enterprises in Finland; (8) Years 2005-2007 according to NACE Rev 1.1 classification, years 2008-2009 according to NACE Rev. 2 classification; (9) Tourism Satellite Account (TSA); (10) Labour Force survey (LFS); (11) Including only accommodation services and food and beverage serving activities.
Tourism Statistics - Statistics Finland – http://www.mek.fi/w5/mekfi/index.nsf/(pages)/Tutkimukset_ja_tilastot

FRANCE

(1) Non resident visitor survey (EVE); (2) All personal purposes; (3) Transit and non specify; (4) All types of accommodation; (5) Hotel occupancy survey. Including unclassified hotels. 2006: renewal of the survey, data not comparable with previous years; (6) Source: "Banque de France"; (7) Inbound average length of stay; (8) Survey "Follow-up of tourism demand" (SDT). Resident population aged 15 years and above. Back-extrapolated results since 2005; (9) Personal trips; (10) Break in the series between 2004 and 2005; (11) Data INSEE on the hotel park; (12) Net room occupancy rate.
"INSEE (Institut national de la statistique et des études économiques) – Section statistique du tourisme" – http://www.insee.fr/fr/default.asp

FRENCH GUIANA

(1) 2005 survey at Cayenne-Rochambeau airport on departure; (2) 2007: Including private accommodation; (3) Hotels only.
"Comité du Tourisme de la Guyane" and "INSEE Guyane"

FRENCH POLYNESIA

(1) Air arrivals only; excluding nationals residing abroad; (2) Days; (3) Hotels and guest houses; at 31st December of each year; (4) Rooms in hotels.
"Service du Tourisme" – http://www.ispf.pf/ISPF/Chiffres/Tourisme.aspx – http://www.tourisme.gov.pf/7671-Les-statistiques.html
http://www.tahiti-tourisme.com/Partners/

GABON

"Centre Gabonais de Promotion Touristique (GABONTOUR)"

GAMBIA

(1) Including nationals residing abroad; (2) Charter tourists only.
Gambia Tourism Authority – http://www.visitthegambia.gm/index.php/en/publications

GEORGIA

(1) Arrivals in hotels only; (2) Source: Survey of hotels and similar establishments; (3) Data refers only to investment in fixed capital.
Note 2009: Preliminary data.
Department of Tourism and Resorts - Ministry of Economic Development and State Department for Statistics - Ministry of Economic Development – http://www.dotr.gov.ge/eng/statistics.php

GERMANY

(1) Non-resident tourists staying in all types of accommodation establishments; (2) Inbound tourism in hotels and similar establishments.
"Statistiches Bundesamt" – http://www.destatis.de

GHANA

(1) Including nationals residing abroad.
Ghana Tourist Board and Ministry of Tourism and Modernisation of the Capital City –
http://www.statsghana.gov.gh/Publications.html

COUNTRY NOTES

GREECE

(1) Information based on administrative data; (2) 2005/2006: Including cruise passengers; (3) Source: Hellenic Chamber of Hotels; (4) Structural Business Survey in Tourism Sector.
Hellenic Statistical Authority (EL STAT.) – http://www.statistics.gr/portal/page/portal/ESYE

GRENADA

(1) Hotels, cottages/apartments and guest houses.
Grenada Board of Tourism

GUADELOUPE

(1) Arrivals by air; excluding the north islands (Saint Martin and Saint Barthelemy); (2) 2005: Data based on a survey conducted at Guadeloupe airport; (3) Hotels.
"Comité du Tourisme des Îles de la Guadeloupe"

GUAM

(1) Air and sea arrivals; (2) Civilian air arrivals only; (3) Rooms available.
Guam Visitors Bureau – http://www.bsp.guam.gov/content/view/94/144/
http://www.visitguam.org/Runtime/GVBResearch.aspx#visitorreport

GUATEMALA

(1) The country provides UNWTO with aggregate expenditure figures that differ significantly from the International Monetary Fund data. The country figures are as follows (US$ Million): 2005: 754; 2006: 789; 2007: 844; 2008: 901; 2009: 799; (2) 2006-2009: All the accommodation establishments registered in INGUAT.
"Instituto Guatemalteco de Turismo - INGUAT" – http://estadisticas.almadelatierra.com/

GUINEA

(1) Arrivals by air at Conakry airport; (2) Hotels only.
"Division Observatoire du Tourisme - Ministère du Tourisme, de l'Hôtellerie et de l'Artisanat"

GUINEA BISSAU

(1) Arrivals at "Osvaldo Vieira" Airport.
"Ministério do Turismo e do Ordenamento do Território"

GUYANA

(1) Arrivals to Timehri airport only.
Guyana Tourism Authority

HAITI

(1) Air arrivals; (2) From 2007 including nationals residing abroad.
"Ministère du Tourisme"

HONDURAS

(1) Source: "Cámara Nacional de Turismo de Honduras".
"Instituto Hondureño de Turismo" – http://www.iht.hn/?page_id=27

HONG KONG, CHINA

(1) The expenditure figures used were the ones provided by the country to UNWTO, as this data series is more complete than that provided by the International Monetary Fund (IMF) for the preparation of this Compendium (Source: HKTB Visitors Survey); (2) From 2006, including Hong Kong residents to Macao and Mainland China; (3) Source: Census and Statistics Department; (4) Hotels (high/medium tariffs) and hostels/ guest houses.
Hong Kong Tourism Board – http://partnernet.hktb.com/pnweb/jsp/comm/index.jsp?charset=en
http://www.censtatd.gov.hk/hong_kong_statistics/index.jsp

HUNGARY

(1) New series from 2004; (2) Modification of data. New data: number of foreign visitors in Hungary. Previous data: non-resident tourists staying in all types of accommodation establishments; (3) The observation of the borders with the countries of the

COUNTRY NOTES

Schengen Area ceased from the year 2008. 2008/2009: the air passenger traffic and road are estimates; (4) Departures of non-resident visitors; (5) By river; (6) 2008/2009: excluding lorry drivers; (7) Free accommodation; (8) Excluding the estimates of private accommodation; (9) July-June; (10) 2005-2007: NACE Rev. 1; (11) 2008/2009: NACE Rev. 2; (12) NACE Rev. 2.
Hungarian Central statistical Office – http://portal.ksh.hu/portal/page?_pageid=38,119919&_dad=portal&_schema=PORTAL

ICELAND

(1) Non-resident tourists staying in all types of accommodation establishments; (2) Arrivals of non-resident tourists at the Icelandic borders. Source: Icelandic Tourist Board.
"Hagstofa Íslands Statistics Iceland" – http://www.statice.is/Statistics/Tourism,-transport-and-informati

INDIA

(1) Excluding nationals residing abroad; (2) Including other purposes; (3) Departures of nationals only, irrespective of purpose; (4) In classified hotels.
Ministry of Tourism - Government of India – http://tourism.gov.in/

INDONESIA

(1) Classified hotels only; (2) All forms of commercial accommodation.
Ministry of Culture and Tourism and BPS Statistics Indonesia –
http://dds.bps.go.id/eng/aboutus.php?tabel=1&id_subyek=16
http://www.budpar.go.id/page.php?ic=621&id=180

IRAN, ISLAMIC REPUBLIC OF

(1) Including rail; (2) Source: Central Bank of Islamic Republic of Iran; (3) Hotels only, 21 March-20 March.
Iran Cultural Heritage and Tourism Organization (ICHTO)

IRAQ

Iraqi Tourism Board

IRELAND

(1) Including tourists from North Ireland; (2) Including rail; (3) Excluding hostels; (4) Hotels only.
Fáilte Ireland – http://www.failteireland.ic/Home

ISRAEL

(1) Excluding nationals residing abroad; (2) Including visit friends and relatives and pilgrimage; (3) Including US Navy personnel on courtesy visits; (4) Including tourists' reentry after a visit of up to 7 days in Sinai; (5) Tourist hotels and aparthotels; (6) Including the expenditures of foreign workers in Israel (US$ Million): 2005: 847; 2006: 909; 2007: 894; (7) Bed-occupancy in hotels and similar establishments open; (8) Inbound tourism in tourist hotels.
Ministry of Tourism – http://www1.cbs.gov.il/reader/?MIval=cw_usr_view_SHTML&ID=432

ITALY

(1) Excluding seasonal and border workers; (2) Border survey of the "Banca d'Italia"; (3) Including cruise passengers; (4) Hotels only; (5) Number of resident tourists (overnight visitors) abroad; (6) Excluding the estimates of private accommodation.
"Banca d'Italia" and "Statistiche sul Turismo - Istituto Nazionale di Statistica (ISTAT)"
http://www.bancaditalia.it/statistiche/rapp_estero/altre_stat/turismo-int
http://www.istat.it/dati/dataset/

JAMAICA

(1) Arrivals of non-resident tourists by air; including nationals residing abroad; E/D cards; (2) Cruise passengers only; (3) New series; including nationals residing abroad; (4) Intended length of stay; (5) Expenditure of non-resident tourists by air; excluding nationals residing abroad; (6) Hotel nights only.
Jamaica Tourist Board – http://www.jtbonline.org/statistics/Annual%20Travel/Forms/AllItems.aspx

JAPAN

(1) Excluding nationals residing abroad; (2) Arrivals of non-resident visitors at national borders; including foreign residents in Japan; (3) The calculation method has been changed since January 2006; (4) Government registered and unregistered hotels and "ryokans" (inns); (5) Occupancy rate of major government registered hotels.
Japan National Tourism Organization - http://www.tourism.jp/english/statistics/index.php

COUNTRY NOTES

JORDAN

(1) Including nationals residing abroad; (2) Arrivals of resident and non resident visitors; (3) For organized tours only.
Ministry of Tourism and Antiquities – http://www.tourism.jo/GuestBook/Statistics.asp

KAZAKHSTAN

Agency of Statistics of the Republic of Kazakhstan – http://www.eng.stat.kz/digital/Tourism/Pages/default.aspx

KENYA

(1) Arrivals of non-resident visitors from all border entry points; excluding nationals residing abroad; (2) Days.
Kenya Tourist Board

KIRIBATI

(1) Air arrivals.Tarawa and Christmas Island; (2) 2006: Tarawa only.
Kiribati National Tourism Office, Ministry of Communication, Transport and Tourism Development –
http://www.spc.int/prism/Country/KI/Stats/Tourism/tourism-index.htm

KOREA, REPUBLIC OF

(1) Including nationals residing abroad and crew members; (2) From 2006 including overseas Koreans and crew members; (3) The country provides UNWTO with aggregate expenditure figures that differ significantly from the International Monetary Fund data used in the preparation of this edition of the Compendium (excluding expenses of students studying overseas). The country figures are as follows (US$ Million): 2005: 12,025; 2006: 14,336; 2007: 16,950; 2008: 14,581; 2009: 11,040; (4) Hotels only.
Ministry of Culture and Tourism – http://kto.visitkorea.or.kr/inout.kto?func_name=search

KUWAIT

(1) Non-resident tourists staying in hotels and similar establishments.
Central Statistical Office – http://mopweb4.mop.gov.kw/

KYRGYZSTAN

(1) Data source: Department of Customs Control.
National Statistical Committee

LAO PEOPLE'S DEMOCRATIC REPUBLIC

(1) Days
Lao National Tourism Administration – http://www.nsc.gov.la/Selected_Statistics.htm

LATVIA

(1) Arrivals of non-resident visitors at national border. Data by State Border Guard; (2) Non-resident departures. Survey of persons crossing the state border; (3) Including visit friends and relatives and health treatment; (4) Overnight stays in all collective accommodation establishments; (5) Source: Border survey; (6) Source: Household survey; (7) Data by State Border Guard.
Transport and Tourism Statistics Section - Central Statistical Bureau – http://www.csb.gov.lv/csp/content/?lng=en&cat=355

LEBANON

(1) Excluding Syrian nationals, Palestinians and students.
"Ministère du Tourisme" – http://www.lebanon-tourism.gov.lb/Ministry/Statistics.aspx

LESOTHO

Lesotho Tourism Development Corporation – http://www.ltdc.org.ls/researchArrivalStats.php

LIBYAN ARAB JAMAHIRIYA

(1) Non-resident tourists staying in hotels and similar establishments.
The General Board of Tourism and Traditional Industries – http://www.libyan-tourism.org/List.aspx?ID=73

COUNTRY NOTES

LIECHTENSTEIN

(1) Non-resident tourists staying in hotels and similar establishments.
"Liechtenstein Tourismus" –
http://www.llv.li/amtstellen/llv_avw_statistik/llv_avw_statistik_amtsgeschaefte/llv-avw-statistik-tourismus.htm

LITHUANIA

(1) 2007: Data of the statistical survey on the flow of visitors crossing border posts; (2) 2007: Number of tourists declined due to decreasing flow of tourists from Belarus and Russian Federation; (3) Non-resident tourists staying in all types of accommodation establishments; (4) Hotels and motels; (5) Hotels, motels and restaurants.
Lithuanian State Department of Tourism –
http://www.stat.gov.lt/en/pages/view/?id=1638&PHPSESSID=0522a6cef6b6d204b72ec646d272a81f

LUXEMBOURG

(1) Non-resident tourists staying in all types of accommodation establishments; including youth hostels, tourist private accommodation and others; (2) Including tourist private accommodation and others; (3) Hotels, inns and guest houses.
"Office National du Tourisme" and "STATEC" – http://www.statistiques.public.lu/fr/publications/series/bulletinStatec/index.html

MACAO, CHINA

(1) 2008: According to Statistics and Census Service, the visitor arrivals figures from year 2008 onward will not include other non-residents namely workers, students, etc; (2) Including ethnic Chinese arriving from "Hong Kong, China"; (3) Including entrees by helicopter; (4) Package tours; (5) Hotels and guest houses.
Macau Statistics and Census Service and Macau Government Tourist Office –
http://www.dsec.gov.mo/Statistic/TourismAndServices/VisitorArrivals.aspx
http://industry.macautourism.gov.mo/en/index.php

MADAGASCAR

(1) Arrivals of non-resident tourists by air.
"Ministère des Transports et du Tourisme"

MALAWI

(1) Departures; (2) Source: Reserve Bank of Malawi.
Ministry of Information and Tourism

MALAYSIA

(1) Including Singapore residents crossing the frontier by road through Johore Causeway; (2/2005/2006) (4) Peninsular Malaysia only; (3) 2008: Estimated figures; (5) Domestic tourism survey; (6) Hotels with 10 rooms and above; (7) Hotel survey; (8) Annual Services Survey; (9) Services of travel agencies and tour operators only.
Department of Statistics Malaysia and Tourism Malaysia –
http://www.tourism.gov.my/corporate/research.asp?page=facts_figures

MALDIVES

(1) Air arrivals; (2) Days.
Ministry of Tourism – http://www.tourism.gov.mv/stat.php?statId=3

MALI

(1) Non-resident tourists staying in hotels and similar establishments.
"Office malien du tourisme et de l'hôtellerie (O.MA.T.HO)"

MALTA

(1) (2/2007-2009) Departures by air and by sea; (3/2005/2006) (4) Tourist departures by air.
Malta Tourism Authority and National Statistics Office –
http://www.maltatourismauthority.com/page.aspx?id=105
http://www.nso.gov.mt/site/page.aspx?pageid=27

COUNTRY NOTES

MARSHALL ISLANDS

(1) 2005,2009: Air and sea arrivals; (2) 2006-2008: Air arrivals; (3) The expenditure figures are those provided by the country to UNWTO, which do not appear in the International Monetary Fund data used in the preparation of this edition of the Compendium. Fiscal years (October 1 to September 30).
Marshall Islands Visitors Authority – http://www.spc.int/prism/country/mh/Stats/index.htm

MARTINIQUE

(1) The expenditure figures are those provided by the country to UNWTO, which do not appear in the International Monetary Fund data used in the preparation of this edition of the Compendium; (2) Hotels and holiday villages (Club Méditerranée).
"Comité Martiniquais du Tourisme" – http://www.martiniquetourisme.com/martinique/Le-C.M.T/Les-donnees-sur-le-tourisme

MAURITIUS

(1) Large hotels.
Ministry of Tourism and Leisure –
http://www.gov.mu/portal/site/cso/menuitem.dee225f644ffe2aa338852f8a0208a0c/?content_id=52160fa67278c010VgnVCM100 0000a04a8c0RCRD

MEXICO

(1) Including nationals residing abroad; (2) Including visitors of the US border zone with a length of stay under 24 hours; (3) Japan and Republic of Korea only; (4) Including rail; (5) Hotels only; (6) Selected tourism resorts; (7) Foreign tourism only; (8) The information does not correspond to employment, strictly speaking, but to equivalent remunerated jobs needed for the production of goods and services related with tourism activities.
"Secretaría de Turismo de México (SECTUR)" and "Instituto Nacional de Estadística y Geografía (INEGI)" –
http://www.gob.mx/wb/egobierno/egob_Estadisticas_del_sector_turismo
http://www.inegi.org.mx/prod_serv/contenidos/espanol/biblioteca/Default.asp?accion=1&upc=702825224585

MICRONESIA, FEDERATED STATES OF

(1) Arrivals in the States of Kosrae, Chuuk, Pohnpei and Yap; excluding FSM citizens; (2) The expenditure figures are those provided by the country to UNWTO, which do not appear in the International Monetary Fund data used in the preparation of this edition of the Compendium. Fiscal years (October 1 to September 30).
Department of Economic Affairs – http://www.spc.int/prism/country/fm/stats/index.htm

MONACO

(1) Non-resident tourists staying in hotels and similar establishments.
"Direction du Tourisme et des Congrès" –
http://www.monaco.gouv.mc/devwww/wwwnew.nsf/1909$/b9d7989a41d6c875c1256f820057b766fr?OpenDocument&7Fr

MONGOLIA

(1) Excluding diplomats and foreign residents in Mongolia.
National Tourism Center - Ministry of Nature, Environment and Tourism – http://mongoliatourism.gov.mn/

MONTENEGRO

(1) Non-resident tourists staying in all types of accommodation establishments
Ministry of Sustainable Development and Tourism – http://www.monstat.org/EngMeniGodisnjiPodaci.htm

MONTSERRAT

Statistics Department Montserrat

MOROCCO

(1) Including nationals residing abroad; (2) Classified hotels, holiday villages, tourist residences and Riad; (3) Foreign tourists.
"Ministère du tourisme" – http://www.tourisme.gov.ma/francais/5-Tourisme-chiffres/ArriveeTouristes.htm

MOZAMBIQUE

(1) Note 2008: Change of methodology. Until 2007 the data correspond only to 12 border posts. From 2008, the data of all the border posts of the country are used.
Ministry of Tourism and "Instituto Nacional de Estatística" – http://www.ine.gov.mz/sectorias_dir/turismo/

COUNTRY NOTES

MYANMAR

(1) Including tourist arrivals through border entry points to Yangon; (2) State-run hotels and similar establishments only; (3) State-run hotels and private registered guest houses.
Ministry of Hotels and Tourism

NAMIBIA

Ministry of Environment and Tourism – http://www.namibiatourism.com.na/trade_cat_sub.php?sub_cat_id=32

NEPAL

(1) Including arrivals from India; (2) Days; (3) Hotels in Kathmandu and in the interior of the country; 2006-2008: excluding hotels under construction.
Nepal Tourism Board and Ministry of Culture, Tourism and Civil Aviation – http://www.tourism.gov.np/tourismstatistics.php

NETHERLANDS

(1) Non-resident tourists staying in all types of accommodation establishments; (2) Hotels and boarding houses; (3) Holiday departures of nationals; (4) Hotels; (5) All types of accommodation establishments.
Statistics Netherlands – http://www.cbs.nl/en-GB/menu/themas/vrije-tijd-cultuur/nieuws/default.htm

NEW CALEDONIA

(1) Including nationals residing abroad; (2) Hotels in Noumea only; (3) Returning residents; (4) Rooms in Noumea; (5) Days, hotels in Noumea.
"Institut de la Statistique et des Études Économiques (ISEE)" – http://www.isee.nc/

NEW ZEALAND

(1) International Travel and Migration, SNZ; (2) Accommodation Survey, SNZ; (3) International Visitor Survey, MED; (4) Domestic Travel Survey, MED; (5) Business Statistics, SNZ; (6) Includes hotels, motels and backpackers but excludes holiday parks.
Statistics New Zealand (SNZ) and Ministry of Economic Development (MED) – http://www.stats.govt.nz/

NICARAGUA

(1) Including nationals residing abroad; (2) Total number of establishments in the country; (3) Main accommodation establishments in the country (7); (4) 2006-2009: Preliminary estimates; (5) Hotels and similar establishments classified in higher categories; (6) All types of accommodation establishments, inbound tourism.
"Instituto Nicaragüense de Turismo (INTUR)" – http://www.intur.gob.ni/estadisticas.php

NIGER

(1) Days.
"Ministère du Tourisme et de l'Artisanat"

NIGERIA

Nigerian Tourism Development Corporation

NIUE

(1.2) Including Niueans residing usually in New Zealand.
Statistics Niue – http://www.spc.int/prism/country/nu/stats/Migration/Migration_index.htm

NORTHERN MARIANA ISLANDS

(1) Arrivals by air; (2) Including Guam; (3) Covers 68 per cent of the total hotel room inventory.
Marianas Visitors Authority

NORWAY

(1) Figures are based on "The Guest survey" carried out by "Institute of Transport Economics"; (2) United States only; (3) Japan only; (4) Nights in registered establishments; (5) Figures for hotels and similar establishments relate to establishments with 20 or more beds the whole year; (6) Holiday trips.
Statistics Norway and Institute of Transport Economics – http://www.ssb.no/english/subjects/

COUNTRY NOTES

OMAN

Ministry of National Economy and Ministry of Commerce and Industry and Directorate General of Tourism - Ministry of Tourism
http://www.moneoman.gov.om

PAKISTAN

(1) Days.
Pakistan Tourism Development Corporation - Ministry of Tourism – http://www.pakistantourism.gov.pk/downloads.php

PALAU

(1) Air arrivals (Palau International Airport); (2) The expenditure figures are those provided by the country to UNWTO, which do not appear in the International Monetary Fund data used in the preparation of this edition of the Compendium. Fiscal years.
Office of Planning and Statistics, Bureau of Budget and Planning - Ministry of Finance –
http://www.palaugov.net/stats/PalauStats/Tourism/tourism.htm
http://www.visit-palau.com/publication/index.cfm

PALESTINE

(1) Non-resident tourists staying in hotels; (2) Hotels only; (3) West Bank and Gaza.
Palestinian Central Bureau of Statistics – http://www.pcbs.gov.ps/DesktopDefault.aspx?tabID=3039&lang=en

PANAMA

(1) Arrivals of non-resident visitors, Tocúmen International Airport (TIA), Paso Canoa frontier (PCF) and the ports of Cristóbal and Balboa (PCB); (2) Arrivals of non-resident visitors, TIA; (3) Arrivals of non-resident tourists, TIA; (4) Hotels in Panama City; (5) Rooms/bed-places recorded for international tourism.
"Instituto Panameño de Turismo" –
http://www.atp.gob.pa/index.php?option=com_content&view=category&layout=blog&id=44&Itemid=64

PAPUA NEW GUINEA

Papua New Guinea Tourism Promotion Authority

PARAGUAY

(1) E/D cards in the "Silvio Petirossi" airport and passenger counts at the national border crossings - National Police and SENATUR; (2) Excluding nationals residing abroad and crew members; (3) 2009: Inbound tourism survey, March 2008 - March 2009; (4) River; (5) Permanent household survey 2008.
"Secretaría Nacional de Turismo - SENATUR" – http://www.senatur.gov.py/estadisticas.php?language=1

PERU

(1) Including nationals residing abroad; (2) Overnight cruise passengers; (3) Includes the arrivals by river and lake; (4) The data comes from the "National Travel Survey of Residents 2007-2008".
Note 2005-2009: Preliminary data.
"Dirección General de Migraciones y Naturalización (DIGEMIN)" and "Ministerio de Comercio Exterior y Turismo (MINCETUR)"
http://www.mincetur.gob.pe/newweb/Default.aspx?tabid=141

PHILIPPINES

(1) Including nationals residing abroad; (2) Air arrivals; (3) Nights; (4) Including overseas contract workers; (5) Classified hotels only; (6) Classified hotels in Metro Manila.
Department of Tourism – http://www.tourism.gov.ph/Pages/TourismResearch.aspx

POLAND

(1) 2008 and 2009: Since Poland joined the Schengen area, precise counting of incoming traffic is not possible. Data presented here are based on surveys by the Institute of Tourism. Only approximate results can be given this year; (2) Based on surveys by the Institute of Tourism; (3) Data from Central Statistical Office; (4) Both collective and private accommodation establishments, based on surveys by the Institute of Tourism; (5) Trips for 4 nights and more; (6) Outbound trips registered at frontiers.
Institute of Tourism – http://www.intur.com.pl/itenglish/institute_en.htm

COUNTRY NOTES

PORTUGAL

(1) Due to a change in the methodology, from 2004 the data are not comparable with those of previous years. Including national residing abroad; (2) Monetary data for enterprises; (3) Net occupancy rate; (4) All types of accommodation establishments; (5) Tourism Satellite Account (TSA) data.
"Turismo de Portugal, I.P." – http://www.ine.pt/xportal/xmain?xpid=INE&xpgid=ine_princindic&contexto=pi&selTab=tab0

PUERTO RICO

(1) Arrivals of non-resident tourists by air; (2) United States Virgin Islands and the United States only; (3) Including residents and non-residents; (4) The expenditure figures are those provided by the country to UNWTO, which do not appear in the International Monetary Fund data used in the preparation of this edition of the Compendium; (5) Rooms classified by the "Compañía de Turismo" of Puerto Rico; (6) Including rooms occupied by residents of Puerto Rico.
Data: Fiscal years (July-June).
"Junta de Planificación de Puerto Rico" and "Compañía de Turismo de Puerto Rico" – http://www.jp.gobierno.pr/

QATAR

(1) Hotels only; (2) Source: Qatar Central Bank.
The Planning Council - Statistics Department and Qatar Tourism Authority –
http://www.qsa.gov.qa/Eng/GeneralStatistics.htm
http://www.qcb.gov.qa/English/Publications/ReportsAndStatements/Pages/AnnualReports.aspx

REPUBLIC OF MOLDOVA

(1) Visitors who have benefited from tourism servies provided by the tourism agencies and tour operators (titulars of tourism licences).
Note: Excluding the left side of the river Nistru and the municipality of Bender.
National Bureau of Statistics – http://www.statistica.md/category.php?l=en&idc=293&

REUNION

(1) Arrivals by air only; (2) Source: INSEE: Survey on Tourism Flows; (3) Source: INSEE: Survey on Hotel Occupancy; (4) This corresponds to the total number of overnights in classified hotels. Residents and non-residents; (5) The expenditure figures are those provided by the country to UNWTO, which do not appear in the International Monetary Fund data used in the preparation of this edition of the Compendium; (6) Source: INSEE Clap. This corresponds to the all the establishments under the selected nomenclatures. Without certainty about the actual purpose of the activity (tourism-related or not); (7) This corresponds to all the establishments/ rooms/ beds available per day in classified hotels; (8) Source: INSEE Clap. This corresponds to the all the jobs under the selected nomenclatures. Without certainty about the actual purpose of the activity (tourism-related or not).
"Institut National de la Statistique et des Études Économique - INSEE" and "Comité du Tourisme de la Réunion" –
http://webpro.la-reunion-tourisme.com/connaitre2.php3?id_rubrique=71
http://www.insee.fr/fr/themes/theme.asp?theme=13&nivgeo=24

ROMANIA

(1) Only domestic trips for holidays (including visit friends and relatives VFR) and business purposes; (2) The category "Other personal purposes" refers only to VFR trips; (3) Starting with 2005 the categories "air" and "water" are included in the "others" category; (4) Calculated by dividing number of overnights by number of trips. Source: ACTR, household survey; (5) Only for holidays (including VFR) and business purposes. The figures are compiled by dividing the expenditure by the number of overnights; (6) For whole accommodation sector, current prices; (7) At 31st of July, for licensed establishments only; (8) The indicator is represented by the number of tourists purchasing packages/individual services. Please be aware that the values cumulate both tour-operators and classic travel agencies; (9) The indicator is actually represented by the "average number of employees" and the source is represented by Structural Business Statistics which is carried out annually; (10) Includes also freight transportation; (11) This category is not fully in line with tourism industries categories due to high level of aggregation in the publication. It includes also press agencies activities and library and archive services. Meanwhile it excludes fitness center activities and rental of recreational goods.
National Institute of Statistics – https://statistici.insse.ro/shop/index.jsp?page=tempo2&lang=en&context=63

RUSSIAN FEDERATION

(1) Accommodation in hotels and other tourist establishments.
Russian Federal Agency for Tourism

RWANDA

Rwanda Office of Tourism and National Parks (ORTPN) – http://rwandatourism.com/arrivalstats.htm

COUNTRY NOTES

SABA

(1) Mainly from St. Maarten.
Saba Tourist Bureau, Caribbean Tourism Organization and Central Bank of the Netherlands Antilles
http://www.centralbank.an/tables/tables/main-10-6.htm

SAINT EUSTATIUS

(1) Excluding Netherlands Antillean residents.
Central Bank of the Netherlands Antilles – http://www.centralbank.an/tables/tables/main-10-7.htm

SAINT KITTS AND NEVIS

(1) Arrivals of non-resident tourists by air; (2) Yacht and cruise ship arrivals.
Eastern Caribbean Central Bank – http://www.eccb-centralbank.org/Statistics/index.asp#tourismdata

SAINT LUCIA

(1) Excluding nationals residing abroad; (2) Excluding yacht passenger arrivals.
Saint Lucia Tourist Board – http://www.stlucia.gov.lc/

SAINT MAARTEN

(1) By air; including arrivals to Saint Maarten (the French side of the island); (2) Arrivals at Juliana Airport (including visitors destined to Saint Maarten, French side); (3) Including the estimates for Saba and Saint Eustatius. Source: Central Bank of the Netherlands Antilles.
St. Maarten Tourist Bureau – http://www.centralbank.an/tables/tables/main-10-5.htm

SAINT VINCENT AND THE GRENADINES

(1) Arrivals of non-resident tourists by air; (2) Including cruise ship and yacht passengers; (3) Hotels, apartments, cottages, villas and guest houses.
Ministry of Tourism and Culture – http://www.discoversvg.com/index.php/es/about-svg/tourism-statistics

SAMOA

Samoa Tourism Authority and Statistical Services Division (Ministry of Finance) –
http://www.sbs.gov.ws/
http://www.mof.gov.ws/publish/economicreview.shtml

SAN MARINO

(1) Including Italian visitors; (2) Non-resident tourists staying in hotels and similar establishments; including Italian tourists; (3) Hotels only.
Note: New methodology from 2005.
"Segreteria di Stato per il Turismo, lo Sport, le Telecomunicazioni, i Trasporti e la Cooperazione Economica" –
http://www.statistica.sm/on-line/Home/DatiStatistici/docCat.14000570.1.10.1.html?Categoria=Afflusso turistico

SAO TOME AND PRINCIPE

(1) Days..
"Direcçao do Turismo e Hotelaria" – http://www.smfstp.st/estatisticas

SAUDI ARABIA

(1) Source: International Visitor Survey, MAS Center; (2) Nights; (3) Source: Domestic and Outbound Tourism Survey (DOTS), MAS Center; (4) Recreation service; (5) 2009: estimated by MAS Center.
The Saudi Commission for Tourism and Antiquities (SCTA) – http://www.mas.gov.sa/

SENEGAL

(1) Hotels and holiday villages.
"Ministère du Tourisme et des Transports Aériens"

SERBIA

(1) Non-resident tourists staying in all types of accommodation establishments; (2) 5.2+5.3+5.4.
Statistical Office of the Republic of Serbia – http://webrzs.stat.gov.rs/axd/en/drugastrana.php?Sifra=0008&izbor=tabela

COUNTRY NOTES

SEYCHELLES

(1) Nights based on departures; (2) Hotels and guest houses.
National Statistics Bureau – http://www.nsb.gov.sc/

SIERRA LEONE

(1) Arrivals by air; (2) Hotels only.
National Tourist Board

SINGAPORE

(1) Excluding arrivals of Malaysian citizens by land; (2) Days; (3) Hotels (gazetted and non-gazetted); (4) Classified hotels only.
Singapore Tourism Board – http://www.singstat.gov.sg/stats/themes/economy/tourism.html

SLOVAKIA

(1) Change in the series. From 2003, the number of inbound arrivals is based on a combination of accommodation statistics and border survey statistics (as calculated within the Tourism Satellite Account); (2) Non-resident tourists staying in commercial accommodation only (representing approximately 25% of all tourists (item 1.2)); (3) Source: Urban and Municipal Statistics (MOS – MIS); (4) Source: Business Register; (5) Tourism Satellite Account (TSA); (6) Household survey. Number of domestic and outbound tourism trips over 15 years / number of residents over 15 years.
Tourism Section – Ministry of Transportation, Construction and Regional Development and Statistical Office – www.mindop.sk - www.statistics.sk

SLOVENIA

(1) Source: border survey; including all categories of travellers irrespective of purpose of visit; (2) Source: accommodation survey; (3) Aggregates from accommodation survey, shares from 3 yearly surveys on foreign tourists in Slovenia; (4) Source: 3 yearly surveys on foreign tourists in Slovenia; (5) Source: survey on travels of domestic population (due to different methodology differences between data on monthly accommodation statistics and data gathered with household survey may appear); (6) Only private trips are taken into account; (7) Nights are used for unit; (8) Source: Structural Business Statistics; (9) Private accommodations (rented rooms, dwellings), tourists farms with accommodation, mountain huts, company vacations facilities and facilities for youths are not included; (10) Source: Statistical Register of Employment; (11) Information on number of full-time equivalent jobs is not available. Instead number of jobs is used in this indicator.
Statistical Office - Tourism Statistics, Structual Business Statistics, Statistical register of employment – http://www.stat.si/cng/tema_ekonomsko_turizem.asp

SOLOMON ISLANDS

(1) 2005: without 1st quarter.
Solomon Islands National Statistics Office – http://www.spc.int/prism/country/sb/Stats/Migration%20and%20Tourism/Tour-Index.htm

SOUTH AFRICA

(1) Excluding nationals residing abroad. Including arrivals by purpose of holiday, business, study, work, transit, border traffic and contract workers; (2) Excluding arrivals by work and contract workers; (3) Figures for 2005-2008 are based on the 'Tourist accommodation' survey and are not comparable with the discontinued 'Hotels: Trading statistics' survey figures. Figures for 2005-2007 have been revised due to backcasting based on the 2008 sample for the 'Tourist accommodation' survey; (4) Hotels; (5) Tourism Satellite Account (TSA) data.
Statistics South Africa and South African Tourism – http://www.statssa.gov.za/default.asp

SPAIN

(1) Including nationals residing abroad; (2) Japan only; (3) Hotels, "hostales", camping sites, tourism apartments and rural dwellings; (4) Hotels and "hostales" (accommodation establishments providing limited services); (5) Since 2005 a new methodology has been applied and data are not comparable to previous years.
"Instituto de Estudios Turísticos" and "Instituto Nacional de Estadística" –
http://www.iet.tourspain.es/paginas/home.aspx?idioma=es-ES
http://www.ine.es/inebmenu/mnu_hosteleria.htm

SRI LANKA

(1) Excluding nationals residing abroad; (2) Hotels, motels, inns, guest houses and apart-hotels.
Sri Lanka Tourist Board – http://www.sltda.lk/statistics

COUNTRY NOTES

SUDAN

(1) Including nationals residing abroad; (2) The country provides UNWTO with aggregate expenditure figures that differ significantly from the International Monetary Fund data used in the preparation of this edition of the Compendium. The country figures are as follows (US$ Million): 2005: 316; 2006: 409; 2007: 428; 2008: 548; 2009: 522.
Ministry of Tourism and Wildlife

SURINAME

(1) Arrivals at Zanderij Airport; (2) Arrivals via Nw. Nickerie Harbour.
Suriname Tourism Foundation

SWAZILAND

Swaziland Tourism Authority and Ministry of Tourism, Environment and Communications

SWEDEN

(1) Non-resident tourists staying in all types of accommodation establishments, camping including; (2) Hotels only; (3) Number of full-time equivalent jobs; (4) Total 5.2, 5.3 and 5.4.
Tillväxtverket - The Swedish Agency for Economic and Regional Growth –
http://www.tillvaxtverket.se/english
http://www.scb.se/Pages/Product____11830.aspx

SWITZERLAND

(1) Hotels and health establishments; (2) Establishments surveyed; (3) Rooms surveyed; (4) Bed-places surveyed; (5) Net occupancy rates; (6) Employment in full-time equivalents.
Swiss Federal Statistical Office – http://www.bfs.admin.ch/bfs/portal/fr/index/themen/10.html

SYRIAN ARAB REPUBLIC

(1) Including the nationals residing abroad; (2) Non-resident tourists staying in all typres of accommodation establishments; (3) 2009: Excluding the nationals residing abroad.
Note: The Iraqi nationals are included from 2008 only and they have been excluded in the previous years (from the beginning of 2008, they have to require a visa to enter Syria; if they arrived previously to this date, it is considered that they staid for a period longer than a year, becoming residents).
Ministry of Tourism - Survey of the incoming tourism in 2004, 2006 and 2007

TAIWAN, PROVINCE OF CHINA

(1) Including nationals residing abroad.
Planning Division Tourism Bureau - Ministry of Transportation and Communication –
http://admin.taiwan.net.tw/english/statistics/release.asp?relno=6

TAJIKISTAN

Committee of Youth Affairs, Sports and Tourism under the Government of the Republic of Tajikistan

THAILAND

(1) 2006-2009, (2) Excluding arrivals of nationals residing abroad; (3) Including rail; (4) Days.
Ministry of Tourism and Sports – http://www.tourism.go.th/2009/en/statistic/tourism.php?cid=26

THE FORMER YUGOSLAV REPUBLIC OF MACEDONIA

(1) Non-resident tourists staying in all types of accommodation establishments; (2) 2008: New methodology; (3) Average length of stay in all accommodation establishments.
State Statistical Office – http://www.stat.gov.mk/english/glavna_eng.asp?br=110#Tourism

TIMOR-LESTE

(1) Arrivals by air at Dili Airport; (2) 2007 includes data for only 10 months; (3) Hotels survey (20 or more rooms); (4) Source: BPA - Banking and Payments Authority.
"Direcçao Nacional de Estatística" – http://dne.mof.gov.tl/publications/index.htm

COUNTRY NOTES

TOGO

(1) Non-resident tourists staying in hotels and similar establishments; (2) Since 2009 a new methodology and new coverage have been applied and data are not comparable to previous years.
"Ministère de l'Environnement, du Tourisme et des Ressources Forestières"

TONGA

(1) Arrivals by air.
Tonga Visitors Bureau

TRINIDAD AND TOBAGO

(1) Arrivals by air; (2) Including visit friends and relatives.
Note 2009: estimates.
Central Statistical Office - Ministry of Planning and Development – http://www.tdc.co.tt/stopover_statistics.htm

TUNISIA

(1) Excluding nationals residing abroad; (2) Classified and unclassified hotels, boarding houses and holiday villages.
"Ministère du Tourisme - Office National du Tourisme" and "Institut National de la Statistique" –
http://www.ins.nat.tn/indexfr.php

TURKEY

(1) Sea arrivals (excluding one land border from 1989); (2) Departures of non-resident visitors; Source: Departing Visitors Survey - Turkish Statistical Institute (TURKSTAT); (3) Including cruise passengers; (4) Survey in accommodation establishments licensed by Ministry of Tourism; (5) Including camping sites; (6) Including expenditure of the nationals residing abroad; (7) Classified hotels; excluding camping sites.
Ministry of Culture and Tourism –
http://www.kulturturizm.gov.tr/TR/Genel/BelgeGoster.aspx?F6E10F8892433CFF657B96472CD892038020F3B0746F34B3
http://www.turkstat.gov.tr/PreTablo.do?tb_id=51&ust_id=14

TURKMENISTAN

State Committee for Tourism and Sport

TURKS AND CAICOS ISLANDS

Turks and Caicos Tourist Board

TUVALU

Central Statistics Division - Ministry of Finance, Economic Planning and Industry –
http://www.spc.int/prism/Country/TV/Stats/Tourism_migration/tour_index.htm

UGANDA

Ministry of Tourism, Trade and Industry and Uganda Bureau of Statistics –
http://www.ubos.org/?st=pagerelations2&id=19&p=related%20pages%202:Migration%20and%20Tourism%20Statistics
http://www.mtti.go.ug/index.php?option=com_content&view=article&id=117&Itemid=131

UKRAINE

State Statistics Committee of Ukraine – http://www.ukrstat.gov.ua/operativ/operativ2007/tyr/tyr_e/arh_vig_e.html

UNITED KINGDOM

(1) Tunnel; (2) International Passenger survey; Source: Office for National Statistics; (3) Days; (4) Source: EUROSTAT (New Cronos); (5) England only.
VisitBritain – http://www.visitbritain.org/insightsandstatistics/keystats/index.aspx
http://www.statistics.gov.uk/statbase/Product.asp?vlnk=1905&More=N

UNITED REPUBLIC OF TANZANIA

Tourism Division - Ministry of Natural Resources and Tourism and National Bureau of Statistics –
http://www.mnrt.go.tz/index.php/documents-a-publications/category/8-tourism

COUNTRY NOTES

UNITED STATES OF AMERICA

(1) Including Mexicans staying one or more nights in the US; (2) Only Canada same-day automobiles; (3) Overseas only; excluding Mexico (not available); (4) Preliminary estimates; (5) Including a very small percentage (0.2%) of travelers for whom transportation mode is not known; (6) The country provides expenditure figures that differ significantly from the IMF data; these are (US$ Million) for item 1.34: 2005: 81,799; 2006: 85,789; 2007: 96,896; 2008: 109,976; 2009: 93,917; for item 3.5: 2005: 68,970; 2006: 72,104; 2007: 76,331; 2008: 79,726; 2009: 73,230; (7) Including Americans staying one or more nights in Mexico; (8) Source: OTTI, Statistics Canada, Banco de Mexico; (9) U.S. to Canada only. Source: Statistics Canada; (10) Source: American Hotel & Lodging Association (AHLA) (properties of 15+ rooms); (11) Source: U.S. Department of Commerce / Bureau of Economic Analysis. Travel and Tourism Satellite Account system; (12) Source: Smith Travel Research; (13) Source: OTTI, Survey of International Air Travelers (inbound); (14) BEA, recently re-benchmarked revisions; (15) Traveler accommodations; (16) Food services and drinking places; (17) Air transportation services; (18) Residual.
Office of Travel and Tourism Industries (OTTI) – http://tinet.ita.doc.gov/ - http://www.ahla.com/content.aspx?id=3448

UNITED STATES VIRGIN ISLANDS

(1) Non-resident tourists staying in hotels and similar establishments; (2) Visitor air arrivals; excluding resident arrivals and inter-island traffic but including same-day visitors; (3) Cruise passengers; (4) Including domestic tourist nights (about 40% of total); (5) The expenditure figures are those provided by the country to UNWTO, which do not appear in the International Monetary Fund data used in the preparation of this edition of the Compendium; (6) Hotel units and condominium or villa units.
2009: Provisional data.
Bureau of Economic Research – http://www.usviber.org/publications.htm

URUGUAY

(1) Including rail; (2) Days; (3) 2005-2007: Excluding unclassified hotels; (4) Real state services.
"Ministerio de Turismo y Deporte" - http://www.mintur.gub.uy

UZBEKISTAN

(1) The expenditure figures are those provided by the country to UNWTO, which do not appear in the International Monetary Fund data used in the preparation of this edition of the Compendium.
National Company "Uzbektourism".

VANUATU

(1) From November 2006, including arrivals to Luganville; (2) Days.
Vanuatu National Statistics Office – http://www.spc.int/prism/country/vu/Stats/Tourism/tourism-index.htm

VENEZUELA

(1) 2005-2009: Hotels only.
"Ministerio del Poder Popular para el Turismo" – http://www.mintur.gob.ve/contenido.php?id=215

VIET NAM

(1) Including nationals residing abroad; (2) Including cruise and sea passengers; (3) The expenditure figures are those provided by the country to UNWTO, which do not appear in the International Monetary Fund data used in the preparation of this edition of the Compendium.
Viet Nam National Administration of Tourism and General Statistics Office –
http://www.vietnamtourism.com/e_pages/news/index.asp?loai=1&chucnang=07

YEMEN

Ministry of Tourism and Central Statistical Organization –
http://www.yementourism.com/statistics/
http://www.cso-yemen.org/content.php?lng=english&pcat=131

ZAMBIA

(1) Days.
Ministry of Tourism, Environment and Natural Resources

ZIMBABWE

(1) The expenditure figures are those provided by the country to UNWTO, which do not appear in the International Monetary Fund data used in the preparation of this edition of the Compendium; (2) Based on arrivals at national parks; (3) 2006-2008: Projections; (4) Graded hotels only; (5) Country data; (6) Estimates.
Zimbabwe Tourism Authority – ZTA –
http://www.aitbase.co.zw/zta/index.php?option=com_docman&task=cat_view&gid=105&Itemid=183

NOTES DES PAYS

AFRIQUE DU SUD

(1) À l'exclusion des nationaux résidant à l'étranger. Y compris les arrivées par motif de vacances, affaires, études, travail, transit, trafic frontalier et travailleurs contractuels; (2) À l'exclusion des arrivées par travail et les travailleurs contractuels; (3) Les chiffres de 2005-2008, tirés de cette dernière, ne sont pas comparables avec ceux de l'ancienne enquête sur les statistiques de l'activité hôtelière. Les chiffres de 2005-2007 ont été revus par extrapolation rétrospective sur la base de l'échantillon de 2008 de l'enquête sur l'hébergement touristique; (4) Hôtels; (5) Données du Compte satellite du tourisme (CST).
"Statistics South Africa" et "South African Tourism" – http://www.statssa.gov.za/default.asp

ALBANIE

(1) Á l'exclusion des nationaux résidant à l'étranger; (2) Source: Enquête à court terme; (3) La classification utilisée est NACE Rev. 1 (Nomenclature statistique des activités économiques); (4) Valeur ajoutée aux prix de base; (5) Total des investissements; (6) Les chiffres sont mis à jour avec l'enquête sur la structure des entreprises.
"Institute of Statistics - INSTAT" - http://www.instat.gov.al/

ALGÉRIE

(1) Y compris les nationaux résidant à l'étranger; (2) À l'exclusion des nationaux résidant à l'étranger.
Ministère de l'Aménagement du Territoire, de l'Environnement et du Tourisme et Office National des Statistiques - http://www.ons.dz/-Tourisme-.html

ALLEMAGNE

(1) Touristes non résidents dans tous types d'établissements d'hébergement; (2) Tourisme récepteur, hôtels et établissements assimilés.
"Statistiches Bundesamt" – http://www.destatis.de

ANDORRE

(1) Depuis mai 2009, une nouvelle méthodologie a été aplliquée. L'information n'est donc pas comparable à celle des années précédentes.
"Ministerio de Turismo y Medio Ambiente" et "Ministerio de Finanzas" -
http://www.estadistica.ad/serveiestudis/web/index.asp?lang=2

ANGOLA

(1) Hôtels uniquement.
Note 2008: Données provisoires.
"Ministério de Hotelaria e Turismo - Gabinete de Estudos, Planeamento e Estatística"

ANGUILLA

(1) À l'exclusion des nationaux résidant à l'étranger; (2) Visiteurs de la journée (excursionnistes).
"Statistical Department - Ministry of Finance" - http://www.gov.ai/statistics/cab_external.htm

ANTIGUA-ET-BARBUDA

(1) À l'exclusion des arrivées de passagers en yacht; (2) Arrivées par voie aérienne; á l'exclusion des nationaux résidant à l'étranger; (3) Passagers en croisière uniquement.
"Ministry of Tourism" - http://www.tourismantiguabarbuda.gov.ag/tourism_programs/statistics.php

ARABIE SAOUDITE

(1) Source: Enquête sur les touristes venant de l'étranger, Centre MAS; (2) Nuitées; (3) Source: Enquête sur le tourisme interne et vers l'étranger (DOTS), centre MAS; (4) Services de loisirs; (5) 2009: estimation par le centre MAS.
"The Saudi Commission for Tourism and Antiquities (SCTA)" – http://www.mas.gov.sa/

ARGENTINE

(1) Enquête sur l'occupation hôtelière et para-hôtelière; (2) Information provenant de l'enquête permanente auprès des ménages (EPH selon le sigle en espagnol) qui permet d'estimer les emplois dans les branches caractéristiques du tourisme. Les estimations de cette enquête, dont la portée territoriale est limitée, ne sont pas entièrement représentatives de l'ensemble national; (3) Il s'agit d'employés et non pas d'emplois; (4) La classification inclut les employeurs et les travailleurs familiaux non rémunérés.
"Dirección de Estudios de Mercado y Estadística - Secretaría de Turismo de la Nación" - http://www.turismo.gov.ar/

NOTES DES PAYS

ARMÉNIE

"Tourism Department - Ministry of Trade and Economic Development" - http://www.armstat.am/en/

ARUBA

(1) Arrivées par voie aérienne; (2) Passagers en croisière uniquement.
"Aruba Tourism Authority" - http://www.cbs.aw/cbs/do/home.html

AUSTRALIE

(1) À l'exclusion des nationaux résidant à l'étranger et membres des équipages; (2) Arrivées par voie aérienne; (3) Hôtels, motels, pensions de famille et appartements avec services hôteliers avec 5 chambres ou plus.
"Australian Bureau of Statistics" - http://www.abs.gov.au/

AUTRICHE

(1) Touristes non résidents dans tous types d'établissements d'hébergement; (2) Seulement logement payé; sont exclus les séjours chez des amis et membres de la famille et des résidences secondaires; (3) Hôtels seulement; (4) Voyages à l'étranger pour vacances et affaires avec au moins une nuitée; (5) Sur la base de la saison d'été; (6) Données du Compte satellite du tourisme (CST); (7) Équivalents à temps plein.
"Statistics Austria" - http://www.statistik.at/web_en/statistics/tourism/accommodation/index.html

AZERBAÏDJAN

"Ministry of Culture and Tourism" et "Statistical Committee" - http://www.azstat.org/statinfo/consumermarket/en/tur_en.shtml

BAHAMAS

(1) Arrivées dans les hôtels seulement; (2) Hôtels, appartements, bungalows et villas - Etablissements homologués uniquement.
"Bahamas Ministry of Tourism" - http://www.tourismtoday.com/prelim/statistics/

BAHREÏN

(1) À l'exclusion des nationaux résidant à l'étranger; (2) Arrivées à l'aéroport international de Bahreïn; (3) Arrivées au port Mina Salman; (4) Arrivées à travers le "King Fahad Causeway"; (5) Hôtels homologués seulement.
"Tourism Sector - Ministry of Culture and Information"

BANGLADESH

"Bangladesh Parjatan Corporation"

BARBADE

(1) Hôtels, hôtels-appartements, appartements et bungalows, pensions de famille.
"Barbados Tourism Authority"

BÉLARUS

(1) Tourisme organisé.
"State Committee of Frontier Troops" et "Ministry of Statistics and Analysis"

BELGIQUE

(1) Touristes non résidents dans tous types d'établissements d'hébergement; (2) Hôtels uniquement; (3) Hôtels et villages de vacances.
Institut National de Statistique

BELIZE

"Belize Tourist Board" - http://www.belizetourism.org/content/view/248/295/

BÉNIN

Note 2005-2009: Estimations.
Direction du développement touristique - Ministère de la culture, de l'artisanat et du tourisme

NOTES DES PAYS

BERMUDES

(1) À l'exclusion des nationaux résidant à l'étranger; (2) Arrivées par voie aérienne; (3) Passagers en croisière; (4) Y compris les nuitées dans les résidences particulières.
"Bermuda Department of Tourism" –
http://www.gov.bm/portal/server.pt?space=CommunityPage&control=SetCommunity&CommunityID=227

BHOUTAN

"Department of Tourism - Royal Government of Bhutan" - http://www.nsb.gov.bt/index.php?id=13

BOLIVIE

(1) Données estimées; (2) Information obtenue à partir des valeurs en pourcentage de l'Enquête « dépenses du tourisme récepteur et émetteur – 2007 »; (3) Arrivées par voie lacustre; (4) 7,6% des voyageurs correspondant au tourisme organisé; (5) Source: Enquête « dépenses du tourisme récepteur et émetteur – 2007 »; (6) Capitales de département seulement; (7) Taille moyenne des groupes de touristes pour les familles : 2,8 personnes.
Note: Les indicateurs du tourisme sont tirés de la relation des résultats de l'enquête « dépenses du tourisme récepteur et émetteur – 2007 » entre les statistiques du commerce extérieur, services de la balance des paiements, la comptabilité nationale (PIB), ce qui détermine la part du tourisme dans chacun des secteurs.
2006-2009: Données provisoires.
"Instituto Nacional de Estadística" et "Viceministerio de Turismo - Ministerio de Producción y Microempresa"
http://www.ine.gov.bo/default.aspx

BONAIRE

(1) Source: "Central Bank of the Netherlands Antilles".
"Tourism Corporation of Bonaire (TCB)" - http://www.tourismbonaire.com/contact_services/trade_section/statistical_info/

BOSNIE-HERZÉGOVINE

(1) Touristes non résidents dans tous types d'établissements d'hébergement; (2) Moins de 500 arrivées; (3) Depuis 2007, les données se réfèrent à l'ensemble de la Bosnie-Herzégovine.
"Agency for Statistics of Bosnia and Herzegovina" - http://www.bhas.ba/eng/Publications.asp?Pripadnost=8&mode=dark

BOTSWANA

Note 2008-2009: Chiffres estimés.
"Department of Tourism - Ministry of Environment, Wildlife and Tourism"

BRÉSIL

(1) Y compris les nationaux résidant à l'étranger; (2) Y compris les arrivées par voie fluviale; (3) Source : ministère du Tourisme et ministère du Travail / Recueil annuel d'informations sociales – 2009. L'information a été estimée à partir de CADASTUR – « Sistema de Cadastro de Prestadores de Serviços Turísticos do Ministério do Turismo e RAIS »; (4) Salariés formels: déclarés et couverts par la sécurité sociale; (5) Travailleurs informels : travailleurs indépendants et employés non déclarés; (6) La différence entre le nombre total de travailleurs du secteur informel par sexe (5.15) et le nombre de travailleurs du secteur informel (5.10) provient du mois de référence utilisé pour ces estimations. Il s'agit de septembre pour la collecte de l'Enquête nationale auprès des ménages qui donne le nombre de travailleurs par sexe et de décembre pour l'extrapolation du nombre de travailleurs du secteur informel.
"Ministério do Turismo" - http://www.dadosefatos.turismo.gov.br/dadosefatos/home.html

BRUNÉI DARUSSALAM

(1) (2/2007) Arrivées par voie aérienne.
"Brunei Tourism - Ministry of Industry and Primary Resources"

BULGARIE

(1) Visiteurs en transit; (2) Mer et voies d'eau intérieures; (3) Hôtels uniquement.
"National Statistical Institute - State Agency for Tourism" – http://www.nsi.bg/SocialActivities_e/Tourism_e.htm

BURKINA FASO

(1) Touristes non résidents dans les hôtels et établissements assimilés; (2) Y compris le tourisme interne.
Service de l'analyse statistique et de la Coopération touristique - Ministère de la Culture, des Arts et du Tourisme
http://www.insd.bf/

NOTES DES PAYS

BURUNDI

(1) Y compris les nationaux résidant à l'étranger; (2) Arrivées par voie lacustre.
Office National du Tourisme

CAMBODGE

(1) Arrivées par tous moyens de transport; (2) Arrivées par navire; (3) Jours.
"Ministry of Tourism" - http://www.mot.gov.kh

CAMEROUN

(1) Touristes non résidents dans les hôtels et établissements assimilés.
Ministère du Tourisme

CANADA

(1) Données élaborées à partir des inventaires douaniers et ajustées en fonction des résultats d'enquêtes; (2) Voyages-personnes (une/plusieurs nuits).
"Canadian Tourism Commission" et "Statistics Canada" –
http://en-corporate.canada.travel/Corporate/Flyout.page?id=369&fid=376

CAP-VERT

(1) Touristes non résidents dans les hôtels et établissements assimilés.
"Instituto Nacional de Estatística" et "Ministério da Economia, Crescimento e Competitividade" –
http://www.ine.cv/indexBDeo.aspx

CHILI

(1) Y compris les nationaux résidant à l'étranger; (2) Les chiffres de 2005 ne sont pas comparables à ceux des années précédentes en raison de la mise à jour du recensement national des établissements d'hébergement touristique.
"Servicio Nacional de Turismo - SERNATUR" – http://www.sernatur.cl/institucional/htm_instit/estadisticas.html

CHINE

(1) Y compris les arrivées de personnes d'origine ethnique chinoise en provenance de "Hong-Kong (Chine)", "Macao (Chine)", "Taïwan (Province de Chine)" et chinois de l'étranger, la plupart visiteurs de la journée (excursionnistes) en provenance de "Hong-Kong (Chine)" et de "Macao (Chine)"; (2) À l'exclusion des arrivées de personnes d'origine chinoise de souche en provenance de "Hong-Kong (Chine)", "Macao (Chine)", "Taïwan (Province de Chine)" et chinois de l'étranger; (3) Ne concernent que les hôtels classés par étoiles; (4) Y compris les membres des équipages et autres membres des forces armées; (5) Tourisme récepteur uniquement.
"National Tourism Administration" – http://en.cnta.gov.cn/

CHYPRE

(1) Y compris les passagers en croisière/transit; (2) Y compris les passagers en croisière; (3) Les données sur l'hébergement (arrivées, nuitées et taux d'occupation) ont été collectées tous les mois auprès des établissements hôteliers de tourisme agréés et fournies par l'O.T.C; (4) La dépense quotidienne moyenne est obtenue en divisant le total des dépenses concernées (élément 1.33) par le nombre de touristes entrants et séjournant au moins une nuit (élément 1.2) et la durée moyenne de leur séjour (élément 1.40); (5) Les données fournies résultent de la mise en place d'un système CST par le service des statistiques de la République de Chypre. La mise en place du système CST a été faite sur la base d'un projet pilote et a couvert la période 2003-2007; (6) La durée moyenne d'un séjour est basée sur le nombre d'arrivées et de nuitées dans les établissements hôteliers de tourisme agréés; (7) À partir du 1er Janvier 2008, le Service statistique de Chypre mène une enquête mensuelle sur les dépenses des Chypriotes qui voyagent à l'étranger (voyage - débit). Dans le cadre de cette enquête, la part des dépenses des Chypriotes qui voyagent à l'étranger peut être mesurée séparément. En conséquence, ce montant est inclus dans les services de transport; (8) Le tourisme sortant à partir de 2003 inclut également comme motif de déplacement les voyages d'ordre religieux et les pèlerinages; (9) La dépense quotidienne moyenne est calculée en divisant le total des dépenses concernées (élément 3.4) par le nombre total des touristes partants pour plus d'une nuitée (élément 3.2) et la durée moyenne de leur séjour (élément 3.10); (10) Les données représentent tous les services d'hébergement; (11) Les données sont traitées et fournies par l'Office du tourisme de Chypre et concernent les hôtels et autres établissements agréés similaires d'hébergement pour touristes. Elles n'étaient pas utilisées dans les estimations CST indiquées pour les éléments 4.1 à 4.12; (12) Les calculs de durée moyenne de séjour sont basés sur les nuitées et les arrivées dans les hôtels et autres établissements agréés similaires d'hébergement pour touristes;
Remarque sur l'ensemble des données fournies: sont exclues les informations sur les activités immobilières en bien propre ou en location et les opérations immobilières basées sur une redevance ou un contrat.
"Statistical Service of Cyprus" et "Cyprus Tourism Organization" –
http://www.mof.gov.cy/mof/cystat/statistics.nsf/index_en/index_en?OpenDocument

COLOMBIE

(1) Arrivées de voyageurs étrangers par des points de contrôle du Département Administratif de Sécurité (DAS); (2) 2005,2006: exclus les voyageurs étrangers arrivés par des points frontaliers terrestres; 2007-2009: y compris les voyageurs étrangers arrivés par des points frontaliers terrestres; (3) Y compris les passagers en croisière; (4) Exclus les voyageurs étrangers arrivés par des points frontaliers terrestres; (5) Exclus les passagers en croisière; (6) 2009: y compris les voyageurs étrangers arrivés par des points frontaliers terrestres; (7) Á partir de 2005: "Departamento Nacional de Estadística (DANE)".
"Dirección de Extranjería - Departamento Administrativo de Seguridad (DAS)" –
http://www.mincomercio.gov.co/eContent/home.asp

COMORES

(1) 2007, (2) Arrivées par voie aérienne seulement; (3) Les chiffres de dépense sont ceux que le pays a fourni à l'OMT mais ils ne figurent pas dans les données du Fonds monétaire international qui ont servi à la préparation de la présente édition du Compendium.
Direction Nationale de la Promotion du Tourisme et de l'Hôtellerie - Ministère du Transport, Tourisme, Postes et Télécommunications et Banque centrale des Comores

CONGO

(1) Touristes non résidents dans les hôtels et établissements assimilés.
Direction Générale du Tourisme et de l'Hôtellerie - Ministère du tourisme et de l'environnement

CORÉE (RÉPUBLIQUE DE)

(1) Y compris les nationaux résidant à l'étranger et membres des équipages; (2) Depuis 2006, les nationaux résidant à l'étranger et membres des équipages sont inclus; (3) Pour la dépense, le pays fournit à l'OMT des niveaux d'agrégation qui diffèrent de façon significative des données du Fonds monétaire international utilisées pour la préparation de la présente édition du Compendium (à l'exclusion des dépenses des étudiants qui font des études à l'étranger). Les données du pays sont les suivantes (Mn $E.U.): 2005: 12.025; 2006: 14.336; 2007: 16.950; 2008: 14.581; 2009: 11.040; (4) Hôtels seulement.
"Ministry of Culture and Tourism" – http://kto.visitkorea.or.kr/inout.kto?func_name=search

COSTA RICA

(1) Voyages d'agrément et visites aux parents; (2) Dans la zone centrale du pays; (3) Etablissements de catégorie "5 étoiles" dans la zone métropolitaine de San José (enquête); (4) Il s'agit des personnes occupées dans la branche d'activité « Hôtels et restaurants » selon la Classification industrielle type, par industrie, de toutes les branches d'activités économiques (CITI 3); (5) Enquête à buts multiples auprès des ménages. Les emplois non rémunérés ne sont pas inclus; (6) Il s'agit des équivalents emplois générés par le sous-emploi visible qui concerne les personnes occupées travaillant habituellement moins de 47 heures par semaine dans une occupation principale et dans une occupation secondaire (si elles en ont une), qui souhaitent travailler davantage d'heures par semaine et qui sont disponibles pour ce faire. Les emplois non rémunérés sont exclus.
"Instituto Costarricense de Turismo" et "Instituto Nacional de Estadística y Censos" –
http://www.visitcostarica.com/ict/paginas/modEst/estudios_demanda_turistica.asp?ididioma=1

CROATIE

(1) Touristes non résidents dans tous types d'établissements d'hébergement; (2) Y compris les arrivées dans des ports à tourisme nautique; (3) 2008: Nouvelle méthodologie; (4) Depuis 2004, une nouvelle méthodologie et une nouvelle couverture ont été appliquées. L'information n'est donc pas comparable à celle des années précédentes; (5) Y compris les nuitées dans des ports à tourisme nautique.
"Central Bureau of Statistics" – http://www.dzs.hr/default_e.htm – http://www.mint.hr/default.aspx?id=363

CUBA

(1) Arrivées par voie aérienne; (2) Hôtels, motels, apart-hôtels, terrains de camping/caravaning et autres; (3) Hôtels, motels et apart-hôtels; (4) Les chiffres de dépense sont ceux que le pays a fournis à l'OMT mais ils ne figurent pas dans les données du Fonds monétaire international qui ont servi à la préparation de la présente édition du Compendium; (5) Comprend seulement circuits contrôlés par l'Instituto de Turismo.
"Oficina Nacional de Estadísticas" – http://www.one.cu/sitioone2006.asp

CURAÇAO

(1) Arrivées par voie aérienne; (2) Les différences entre les totaux globaux sont dues au caractère incomplet des cartes d'embarquement et de débarquement remplies par les visiteurs; (3) Arrivées de passagers en croisière; (4) Grands et petits hôtels, pensions de famille, appartements et bungalows; (5) Source: "Central Bank of the Netherlands Antilles"; (6) Hôtels, pensions de famille, appartements.
"Curaçao Tourist Board" – http://www.ctb.an/Statistics.aspx

NOTES DES PAYS

DANEMARK

(1) Touristes non résidents dans tous types d'établissements d'hébergement; (2) Á partir de 2005: y compris le tourisme non commercial; (3) Nouvelle méthodologie à partir de 2006; (4) Hôtels uniquement; (5) Source: "VisitDenmark"; (6) Hôtels et logements pour vacances avec 40 lits et plus seulement.
"VisitDenmark" – http://www.dst.dk/HomeUK.aspx

DJIBOUTI

(1) Touristes non résidents dans les hôtels.
Office national du tourisme

DOMINIQUE

(1) Jours.
"Discover Dominica Authority" – http://tourism.gov.dm/

ÉGYPTE

(1) Voyages à des fins de tourisme et de non-tourisme (plus de 50 % des départs ont lieu pour des motifs de travail).
"Ministry of Tourism"

EL SALVADOR

(1) Nouvelle méthodologie à partir de 2004; (2) Y compris l'hébergement privé.
"Corporación Salvadoreña de Turismo (CORSATUR) - Ministerio de Turismo" –
http://www.elsalvador.travel/secciones.php?id_seccion=20&lang=sp&portal=2

ÉQUATEUR

(1) À l'exclusion des nationaux résidant à l'étranger.
"Ministerio de Turismo" – http://www.turismo.gov.ec/index.php?option=com_content&task=view&id=459&Itemid=95

ÉRYTHRÉE

(1) Y compris les nationaux résidant à l'étranger; (2) Uniquement hôtels et établissements assimilés dans les trois villes principales: Asmara, Karen et Massawa; (3) Les données de dépense sont celles que le pays a fournies à l'OMT car il s'agit d'une série plus complète que celle obtenue du Fonds monétaire International (FMI) pour la préparation de la présente édition du Compendium; (4) 2005/2006: Uniquement hôtels et établissements assimilés dans les trois villes principales: Asmara, Karen et Massawa; (5) 2007-2009: Douze villes principales; (6) Tous les hôtels et établissements assimilés en Erythrée.
"Ministry of Tourism"

ESPAGNE

(1) Y compris les nationaux résidant à l'étranger; (2) Japon seulement; (3) Hôtels, "hostales", terrains de camping, appartements touristiques et logements ruraux; (4) Hôtels et "hostales" (établissements d'hébergement offrant des services limités); (5) Nouvelle méthodoligie à partir de 2005. L'information n'est donc pas comparable à celle des années précédentes.
"Instituto de Estudios Turísticos" et "Instituto Nacional de Estadística" –
http://www.iet.tourspain.es/paginas/home.aspx?idioma=es-ES
http://www.ine.es/inebmenu/mnu_hosteleria.htm

ESTONIE

(1) Calculé sur la base des statistiques d'hébergement et de la "Foreign Visitor Survey" menée par la "Statistical Office of Estonia"; (2) Touristes non résidents dans tous types d'établissements d'hébergement; (3) Source: enquête auprès des ménages par "Statistics Estonia"; (4) 2005-2007: tous les types d'établissements d'hébergement.
Note: À partir de 2004, les statistiques de frontière ne sont plus collectées.
"Estonian Tourist Board / Enterprise Estonia" – http://pub.stat.ee/px-web.2001/I_Databas/Economy/databasetree.asp
http://visitestonia.com/en/additional-navigation/press-room/eas-views-on-tourism/estonian-tourism-statistics

ÉTATS-UNIS D'AMÉRIQUE

(1) Y compris les Mexicains passant une nuit ou plus aux États-Unis; (2) Seulement les voitures du Canada qui entrent/sortent le même jour; (3) Outre-mer uniquement; à l'exclusion du Mexique (les données ne sont pas disponibles); (4) Estimations préliminaires; (5) Y compris un très petit pourcentage (0.2%) de voyageurs dont on ne connaît pas le mode de transport utilisé; (6) Le pays fournit des données qui diffèrent de façon significative des données du FMI. Les données sont (Mn $E.U.) pour 1.34: 2005: 81.799; 2006: 85.789; 2007: 96.896; 2008: 109.976; 2009: 93.917; pour 3.5: 2005: 68.970; 2006: 72.104; 2007: 76.331; 2008: 79.726; 2009: 73.230; (7) Y compris les Américains passant une nuit ou plus au Mexique; (8) Source: "OTTI,

Statistics Canada, Banco de Mexico"; (10) Source "American Hotel & Lodging Association (AHLA)"; (9) É-U vers le Canada seulement. Source: Statistiques du Canada; (10) Demeures comportant au moins 15 pièces et plus; (11) Source: Département du Commerce des É-U. / Bureau des analyses économiques. Système de comptes satellites du tourisme et des voyages; (12) Source: Smith Travel Research; (13) Source: OTTI, Enquête sur les voyageurs internationaux par voie aérienne (arrivant de l'étranger); (14) BEA, révisions récemment ré-étalonnées; (15) Hébergement des voyageurs; (16) Services de restauration et débits de boisson; (17) Services de transports aériens; (18) Résiduel.
"Office of Travel and Tourism Industries (OTTI)" – http://tinet.ita.doc.gov/ - http://www.ahla.com/content.aspx?id=3448

ÉTHIOPIE

(1) Arrivées à travers tous les ports d'entrée; y compris les nationaux résidant à l'étranger; (2) 2005: À l'exclusion des hôtels non-homologués.
"Ministry of Culture and Tourism"

EX-RÉPUBLIQUE YOUGOSLAVE DE MACÉDOINE

(1) Touristes non résidents dans tous types d'établissements d'hébergement; (2) 2008: Nouvelle méthodologie; (3) Durée moyenne du séjour dans tous les établissements d'hébergement.
"State Statistical Office" – http://www.stat.gov.mk/english/glavna_eng.asp?br=110#Tourism

FÉDÉRATION DE RUSSIE

(1) Hébergement dans les hôtels et autres établissements touristiques.
"Russian Federal Agency for Tourism"

FIDJI

(1) À l'exclusion des nationaux résidant à l'étranger; (2) Jours.
"Fiji Islands Bureau of Statistics" – http://www.spc.int/prism/Country/FJ/stats/Tourism/tourmigstats_index.htm

FINLANDE

(1) Enquête basée sur des questionnaires à la frontière; (2) Statistiques d'hébergement; (3) Balance des paiements (BdP); (4) Enquête finlandaise sur les voyages; (5) Ne comprend que les voyages d'agrément intérieurs dans des locations pour les visiteurs; (6) Voyages à l'étranger, croisières avec nuitées à bord comprises; (7) Statistiques sur les entreprises en Finlande; (8) Années 2005-2007 selon la classification NACE Rév. 1.1, années 2008-2009 selon la classification NACE Rév. 2; (9) Données du Compte satellite du tourisme (CST); (10) Étude sur la population active (Labour Force Survey - LFS); (11) Ne comprenant que les services d'hébergement et les services de restauration et de boisson.
"Tourism Statistics - Statistics Finland" – http://www.mek.fi/w5/mekfi/index.nsf/(pages)/Tutkimukset_ja_tilastot

FRANCE

(1) Enquête auprès des visiteurs venant de l'étranger (EVE); (2) Tous motifs personnels; (3) Transit et non spécifiés; (4) Tous modes d'hébergement; (5) Enquête de fréquentation hôtelière. Y compris hôtels non homologués. 2006: rénovation de l'enquête, données non comparables aux années antérieures; (6) Source: Banque de France; (7) Durée moyenne du séjour récepteur; (8) Enquête "Suivi de la demande touristique" (SDT). Population résidente de 15 ans et plus. Résultats rétropolés depuis 2005; (9) Voyages personnels; (10) Rupture de série entre 2004 et 2005; (11) Données INSEE relatives au parc hôtelier; (12) Taux net des chambres.
INSEE (Institut national de la statistique et des études économiques) – Section statistique du tourisme – http://www.insee.fr/fr/default.asp

GABON

Centre Gabonais de Promotion Touristique (GABONTOUR)

GAMBIE

(1) Les nationaux résidant à l'étranger sont inclus; (2) Arrivées en vols à la demande seulement.
"Gambia Tourism Authority" – http://www.visitthegambia.gm/index.php/en/publications

GÉORGIE

(1) Arrivées dans les hôtels seulement; (2) Source: Enquête sur les hôtels et établissements assimilés; (3) Les données se réfèrent uniquement à l'investissement en capital fixe.
Note 2009: Données préliminaires.
"Department of Tourism and Resorts - Ministry of Economic Development" et "State Department for Statistics - Ministry of Economic Development" – http://www.dotr.gov.ge/eng/statistics.php

NOTES DES PAYS

GHANA

(1) Y compris les nationaux résidant à l'étranger.
"Ghana Tourist Board" et "Ministry of Tourism and Modernisation of the Capital City" –
http://www.statsghana.gov.gh/Publications.html

GRÈCE

(1) Information tirée de données administratives; (2) 2005/2006: Y compris les passagers en croisière; (3) Source: "Hellenic Chamber of Hotels"; (4) Enquête sur la structure des entreprises dans le secteur du tourisme.
"Hellenic Statistical Authority (EL STAT.)" – http://www.statistics.gr/portal/page/portal/ESYE

GRENADE

(1) Hôtels, bungalows/ appartements et pensions de famille.
"Grenada Board of Tourism"

GUADELOUPE

(1) Arrivées par voie aérienne; À l'exclusion des îles du nord (Saint Martin et Saint Barthélemy); (2) 2005: Données tirées d'une enquête réalisée à l'aéroport de Guadeloupe; (3) Hôtels.
Comité du Tourisme des Îles de la Guadeloupe

GUAM

(1) Arrivées par voies aérienne et maritime; (2) Uniquement arrivées de civils par voie aérienne; (3) Chambres disponibles.
"Guam Visitors Bureau" – http://www.bsp.guam.gov/content/view/94/144/
http://www.visitguam.org/Runtime/GVBResearch.aspx#visitorreport

GUATEMALA

(1) Pour la dépense, le pays fournit à l'OMT des niveaux d'agrégation qui diffèrent de façon significative des données du Fonds monétaire international. Les données du pays sont les suivantes (Mn $E.U.): 2005: 754; 2006: 789; 2007: 844; 2008: 901; 2009: 799; (2) 2006-2009: Ensemble des établissements d'hébergement inscrits à l'INGUAT.
"Instituto Guatemalteco de Turismo - INGUAT" – http://estadisticas.almadelatierra.com/

GUINÉE

(1) Arrivées par voie aérienne à l'aéroport de Conakry; (2) Hôtels seulement.
Division Observatoire du Tourisme - Ministère du Tourisme, de l'Hôtellerie et de l'Artisanat

GUINÉE-BISSAU

(1) Arrivées à l'aéroport "Osvaldo Vieira".
"Ministério do Turismo e do Ordenamento do Território"

GUYANE

(1) Arrivées à l'aéroport de Timehri seulement.
"Guyana Tourism Authority"

GUYANE FRANÇAISE

(1) Enquête 2005 au départ de l'aéroport de Cayenne-Rochambeau; (2) 2007: Y compris l'hébergement privé; (3) Hôtels uniquement.
Comité du Tourisme de la Guyane et INSEE Guyane

HAÏTI

(1) Arrivées par voie aérienne; (2) Depuis 2007, les nationaux résidant à l'étranger sont inclus.
Ministère du Tourisme

HONDURAS

(1) Source: "Cámara Nacional de Turismo de Honduras".
"Instituto Hondureño de Turismo" – http://www.iht.hn/?page_id=27

NOTES DES PAYS

HONG-KONG (CHINE)

(1) Les données de dépense sont celles que le pays a fournies à l'OMT car il s'agit d'une série plus complète que celle obtenue du Fonds monétaire international (FMI) pour la préparation de la présente édition du Compendium. (Source: "HKTB Visitors Survey"); (2) À partir de 2006, les résidents de Hong-Kong voyageant à Macao et Chine sont inclus; (3) Source: "Census and Statistics Department"; (4) Hôtels (tarifs élevés/moyens) et auberges/ pensions de famille.
"Hong Kong Tourism Board" – http://partnernet.hktb.com/pnweb/jsp/comm/index.jsp?charset=en
http://www.censtatd.gov.hk/hong_kong_statistics/index.jsp

HONGRIE

(1) Nouvelle série à partir de 2004; (2) Modification des données. Nouvelles données: nombre de visiteurs étrangers en Hongrie. Données antérieures: touristes non résidents dans tous types d'établissements d'hébergement; (3) L'observation des frontières avec les pays de l'espace de Schengen a cessé à partir de l'an 2008. 2008/2009: le trafic aérien de passagers et de la route sont des estimations; (4) Départs de visiteurs non résidents; (5) Voie fluviale; (6) Á l'exclusion des chauffeurs de camion; (7) Hébergement gratuit; (8) Non compris les estimations des logements privés; (9) Juillet-juin; (10) 2005-2007: NACE Rév. 1; (11) 2008/2009: NACE Rév. 2; (12) NACE Rév. 2.
"Hungarian Central statistical Office" – http://portal.ksh.hu/portal/page?_pageid=38,119919&_dad=portal&_schema=PORTAL

ÎLES CAÏMANES

(1) Arrivées par voie aérienne; (2) Passagers en croisière uniquement; (3) Hôtels et appartements; (4) Les chiffres de dépense sont ceux que le pays a fournis à l'OMT mais ils ne figurent pas dans les données du Fonds monétaire international qui ont servi à la préparation de la présente édition du Compendium; (5) Y compris les dépenses des passagers en croisière; (6) Jours.
"Cayman Islands Department of Tourism" – http://www.caymanislands.ky/statistics/

ÎLES COOK

(1) Arrivées par voies aérienne et maritime; (2) Les chiffres de dépense sont ceux que le pays a fournis à l'OMT mais ils ne figurent pas dans les données du Fonds monétaire international qui ont servi à la préparation de la présente édition du Compendium; (3) Hôtels et motels.
"Cook Islands Tourism Corporation" et "Cook Islands Statistics Office" – http://www.stats.gov.ck/Statistics/Tourism/tournav.htm

ÎLES MARIANNES SEPTENTRIONALES

(1) Arrivées par voie aérienne; (2) Y compris Guam; (3) Couvre 68 pour cent du nombre total de chambres recensées.
"Marianas Visitors Authority"

ÎLES MARSHALL

(1) 2005,2009: Arrivées par voies aérienne et maritime; (2) 2006-2008: Arrivées par voie aérienne; (3) Les chiffres de dépense sont ceux que le pays a fournis à l'OMT mais ils ne figurent pas dans les données du Fonds monétaire international qui ont servi à la préparation de la présente édition du Compendium. Années fiscales (1 octobre - 30 septembre).
"Marshall Islands Visitors Authority" – http://www.spc.int/prism/country/mh/Stats/index.htm

ÎLES SALOMON

(1) 2005: à l'exclusion du 1er trimestre.
"Solomon Islands National Statistics Office" –
http://www.spc.int/prism/country/sb/Stats/Migration%20and%20Tourism/Tour-Index.htm

ÎLES TURQUES ET CAÏQUES

"Turks and Caicos Tourist Board"

ÎLES VIERGES AMÉRICAINES

(1) Touristes non résidents dans les hôtels et établissements assimilés; (2) Arrivées de visiteurs par voie aérienne; à l'exclusion des arrivées de résidents et le trafic entre les îles, mais compris les visiteurs de la journée (excursionnistes); (3) Passagers en croisière; (4) Y compris celles de touristes nationaux (environ 40 pour cent de l'ensemble); (5) Les chiffres de dépense sont ceux que le pays a fournis à l'OMT mais ils ne figurent pas dans les données du Fonds monétaire international qui ont servi à la préparation de la présente édition du Compendium; (6) Hôtels et condominiums ou villas.
2009: Données provisoires.
"Bureau of Economic Research" – http://www.usviber.org/publications.htm

NOTES DES PAYS

ÎLES VIERGES BRITANNIQUES

(1) Les chiffres de dépense sont ceux que le pays a fournis à l'OMT mais ils ne figurent pas dans les données du Fonds monétaire international qui ont servi à la préparation de la présente édition du Compendium.
"The Development Planning Unit - Ministry of Finance" –
http://dpu.gov.vg/index.php?option=com_content&view=article&id=58&Itemid=68

INDE

(1) À l'exclusion des nationaux résidant à l'étranger; (2) Y compris autres motifs; (3) Départs de nationaux seulement, pour tous motifs de visite; (4) Hôtels homologués.
"Ministry of Tourism - Government of India" – http://tourism.gov.in/

INDONÉSIE

(1) Hôtels homologués seulement; (2) Toutes formes d'hébergement commercial.
"Ministry of Culture and Tourism" et "BPS Statistics Indonesia" –
http://dds.bps.go.id/eng/aboutus.php?tabel=1&id_subyek=16
http://www.budpar.go.id/page.php?ic=621&id=180

IRAN (RÉPUBLIQUE ISLAMIQUE D')

(1) Y compris chemin de fer; (2) Source: "Central Bank of Islamic Republic of Iran"; (3) Hôtels seulement, 21 mars - 20 mars.
"Iran Cultural Heritage and Tourism Organization (ICHTO)"

IRAQ

"Iraqi Tourism Board"

IRLANDE

(1) Y compris les touristes en provenance de l'Irlande du Nord; (2) Y compris chemin de fer; (3) À l'exclusion des hôtelleries; (4) Hôtels seulement.
"Fáilte Ireland" – http://www.failteireland.ie/Home

ISLANDE

(1) Touristes non résidents dans tous types d'établissements d'hébergement; (2) Arrivées de touristes non résidents aux postes-frontières islandais. Source: "Icelandic Tourist Board".
"Hagstofa Íslands Statistics Iceland" – http://www.statice.is/Statistics/Tourism,-transport-and-informati

ISRAËL

(1) À l'exclusion des nationaux résidant à l'étranger; (2) Y compris visites à des parents et amis et pèlerinages; (3) Y compris les membres de la marine des États-Unis en visite de courtoisie; (4) Y compris nouvelles entrées de touristes après une visite au Sinaï d'un maximum de 7 jours; (5) Hôtels de touristes et aparthôtels; (6) Y compris les dépenses des travailleurs étrangers en Israël (Mn $E.U.): 2005: 847; 2006: 909; 2007: 894; (7) Taux d'occupation/lits dans hôtels et établissements assimilés ouverts; (8) Tourisme récepteur dans hôtels touristiques.
"Ministry of Tourism" – http://www1.cbs.gov.il/reader/?MIval=cw_usr_view_SHTML&ID=432

ITALIE

(1) À l'exclusion des travailleurs saisonniers et frontaliers; (2) Enquête aux frontières de la "'Banca d'Italia"; (3) Y compris les passagers en croisière; (4) Hôtels seulement; (5) Nombre de touristes résidents (visiteurs qui passent la nuit) voyageant à l'étranger; (6) Non compris les estimations des logements privés.
"Banca d'Italia" et "Statistiche sul Turismo - Istituto Nazionale di Statistica (ISTAT)"
http://www.bancaditalia.it/statistiche/rapp_estero/altre_stat/turismo-int
http://www.istat.it/dati/dataset/

JAMAHIRIYA ARABE LIBYENNE

(1) Touristes non résidents dans les hôtels et établissements assimilés.
"The General Board of Tourism and Traditional Industries" – http://www.libyan-tourism.org/List.aspx?ID=73

NOTES DES PAYS

JAMAÏQUE

(1) Arrivées de touristes non résidents par voie aérienne; y compris les nationaux résidant à l'étranger; cartes E/D; (2) Passagers en croisière uniquement; (3) Nouvelle série; y compris les nationaux résidant à l'étranger; (4) Durée de séjour prévue; (5) Dépense des touristes non-résidents par voie aérienne; à l'exclusion des nationaux résidant à l'étranger; (6) Nuitées dans les hôtels seulement.
"Jamaica Tourist Board" – http://www.jtbonline.org/statistics/Annual%20Travel/Forms/AllItems.aspx

JAPON

(1) À l'exclusion des nationaux résidant à l'étranger; (2) Arrivées de visiteurs non résidents aux frontières nationales; y compris les résidents étrangers au Japon; (3) La méthode de calcul a changé depuis janvier 2006; (4) Hôtels homologués et non homologués, ainsi que "ryokans" (auberges); (5) Taux d'occupation des principaux hôtels gouvernementaux homologués.
"Japan National Tourism Organization" - http://www.tourism.jp/english/statistics/index.php

JORDANIE

(1) Y compris les nationaux résidant à l'étranger; (2) Arrivées de visiteurs résidents et non résidents; (3) Circuits organisés seulement.
"Ministry of Tourism and Antiquities" – http://www.tourism.jo/GuestBook/Statistics.asp

KAZAKHSTAN

"Agency of Statistics of the Republic of Kazakhstan" – http://www.eng.stat.kz/digital/Tourism/Pages/default.aspx

KENYA

(1) Arrivées de visiteurs non résidents à travers tous les postes frontière; à l'exclusion des nationaux résidant à l'étranger; (2) Jours.
"Kenya Tourist Board"

KIRGHIZISTAN

(1) Source d'information: Département du Contrôle douanier.
"National Statistical Committee"

KIRIBATI

(1) Arrivées par voie aérienne. Tarawa et Ile Christmas; (2) 2006: Tarawa uniquement.
"Kiribati National Tourism Office, Ministry of Communication, Transport and Tourism Development" –
http://www.spc.int/prism/Country/KI/Stats/Tourism/tourism-index.htm

KOWEÏT

(1) Touristes non résidents dans les hôtels et établissements assimilés.
"Central Statistical Office" – http://mopweb4.mop.gov.kw/

LESOTHO

"Lesotho Tourism Development Corporation" – http://www.ltdc.org.ls/researchArrivalStats.php

LETTONIE

(1) Arrivées de visiteurs non résidents aux frontières nationales. Données provenant de la Police d'Etat aux frontières; (2) Départs des non-résidents. Enquête auprès des personnes qui traversent les frontières du pays; (3) Y compris les visites à des parents et amis et traitement médical; (4) Nuitées dans tous les établissements d'hébergement collectif; (5) Source: enquête aux frontières; (6) Source: enquête auprès des ménages; (7) Données provenant de la Police d'Etat aux frontières.
"Transport and Tourism Statistics Section - Central Statistical Bureau" – http://www.csb.gov.lv/csp/content/?lng=en&cat=355

LIBAN

(1) À l'exclusion des ressortissants syriens, palestiniens et sous-études.
Ministère du Tourisme – http://www.lebanon-tourism.gov.lb/Ministry/Statistics.aspx

LIECHTENSTEIN

(1) Touristes non résidents dans les hôtels et établissements assimilés.
"Liechtenstein Tourismus" –
http://www.llv.li/amtstellen/llv_avw_statistik/llv_avw_statistik_amtsgeschaefte/llv-avw-statistik-tourismus.htm

NOTES DES PAYS

LITUANIE

(1) 2007: Données de l'enquête statistique sur les flux de visiteurs franchissant les postes-frontières; (2) 2007: La baisse dans le nombre de touristes est due à la diminution du flux de touristes depuis le Bélarus et la Fédération de Russie; (3) Touristes non résidents dans tous types d'établissements d'hébergement; (4) Hôtels et motels; (5) Hôtels, motels et restaurants.
"Lithuanian State Department of Tourism" –
http://www.stat.gov.lt/en/pages/view/?id=1638&PHPSESSID=0522a6cef6b6d204b72ec646d272a81f

LUXEMBOURG

(1) Touristes non résidents dans tous types d'établissements d'hébergement; y compris auberges de jeunesse, hébergement touristique privé et autres; (2) Y compris l'hébergement touristique privé et autres; (3) Hôtels, auberges et pensions de famille.
Office National du Tourisme et STATEC – http://www.statistiques.public.lu/fr/publications/series/bulletinStatec/index.html

MACAO (CHINE)

(1) 2008: Selon le Service de Statistique et Recensement, à partir de 2008, les figures d'arrivées de visiteurs n'incluront pas les autres non-résidents, à savoir travailleurs, étudiants, etc; (2) Y compris chinois de souche provenant de "Hong-Kong, Chine"; (3) Y compris les arrivées en hélicoptère; (4) Circuits organisés; (5) Hôtels et pensions de famille.
"Macau Statistics and Census Service" et "Macau Government Tourist Office" –
http://www.dsec.gov.mo/Statistic/TourismAndServices/VisitorArrivals.aspx
http://industry.macautourism.gov.mo/en/index.php

MADAGASCAR

(1) Arrivées de touristes non résidents par voie aérienne.
Ministère des Transports et du Tourisme

MALAISIE

(1) Y compris les résidents de Singapour qui traversent la frontière par le Johore Causeway; (2/2005/2006) (4) Péninsule de Malaisie seulement; (3) 2008: Chiffres estimés; (5) Enquête sur le tourisme interne; (6) Hôtels avec 10 chambres et plus; (7) Enquête dans les hôtels; (8) Enquête annuelle sur les services; (9) Services d'agences de voyages et tour-opérateurs seulement.
"Department of Statistics Malaysia" et "Tourism Malaysia" –
http://www.tourism.gov.my/corporate/research.asp?page=facts_figures

MALAWI

(1) Départs; (2) Source: "Reserve Bank of Malawi".
"Ministry of Information and Tourism"

MALDIVES

(1) Arrivées par voie aérienne; (2) Jours.
"Ministry of Tourism" – http://www.tourism.gov.mv/stat.php?statId=3

MALI

(1) Touristes non résidents dans les hôtels et établissements assimilés.
Office malien du tourisme et de l'hôtellerie (O.MA.T.HO)

MALTE

(1) (2/2007-2009) Départs par voies aérienne et maritime; (3/2005/2006) Départs de touristes par voie aérienne.
"Malta Tourism Authority" et "National Statistics Office" –
http://www.maltatourismauthority.com/page.aspx?id=105
http://www.nso.gov.mt/site/page.aspx?pageid=27

MAROC

(1) Y compris les nationaux résidant à l'étranger; (2) Hôtels homologués, villages de vacances, résidences touristiques et Riad; (3) Touristes étrangers.
Ministère du tourisme – http://www.tourisme.gov.ma/francais/5-Tourisme-chiffres/ArriveeTouristes.htm

NOTES DES PAYS

MARTINIQUE

(1) Les chiffres de dépense sont ceux que le pays a fournis à l'OMT mais ils ne figurent pas dans les données du Fonds monétaire international qui ont servi à la préparation de la présente édition du Compendium; (2) Hôtels et villages de vacances (Club Méditerranée).
Comité Martiniquais du Tourisme – http://www.martiniquetourisme.com/martinique/Le-C.M.T/Les-donnees-sur-le-tourisme

MAURICE

(1) Grands hôtels.
"Ministry of Tourism and Leisure" –
http://www.gov.mu/portal/site/cso/menuitem.dee225f644ffe2aa338852f8a0208a0c/?content_id=52160fa67278c010VgnVCM100 0000a04a8c0RCRD

MEXIQUE

(1) Y compris les nationaux résidant à l'étranger; (2) Y compris les visiteurs de la frange frontalière avec les États-Unis avec séjour inférieur à 24h; (3) Japon et République de Corée uniquement; (4) Y compris chemin de fer; (5) Hôtels seulement; (6) Sélection de centres touristiques; (7) Tourisme étranger seulement; (8) L'information ne se réfère pas exactement à l'emploi mais aux équivalents emplois rémunérés nécessaires pour produire les biens et les services liés aux activités touristiques.
"Secretaría de Turismo de México (SECTUR)" et "Instituto Nacional de Estadística y Geografía (INEGI)" –
http://www.gob.mx/wb/egobierno/egob_Estadisticas_del_sector_turismo
http://www.inegi.org.mx/prod_serv/contenidos/espanol/biblioteca/Default.asp?accion=1&upc=702825224585

MICRONÉSIE (ÉTATS FÉDÉRÉS DE)

(1) Arrivées dans les États de Kosrae, Chuuk, Pohnpei et Yap; à l'exclusion des citoyens de EFM; (2) Les chiffres de dépense sont ceux que le pays a fournis à l'OMT mais ils ne figurent pas dans les données du Fonds monétaire international qui ont servi à la préparation de la présente édition du Compendium. Années fiscales (1 octobre - 30 septembre).
"Department of Economic Affairs" – http://www.spc.int/prism/country/fm/stats/index.htm

MONACO

(1) Touristes non résidents dans les hôtels et établissements assimilés.
Direction du Tourisme et des Congrès –
http://www.monaco.gouv.mc/devwww/wwwnew.nsf/1909$/b9d7989a41d6c875c1256f820057b766fr?OpenDocument&7Fr

MONGOLIE

(1) Sont exclus les diplomates et les étrangers qui résident en Mongolie.
"National Tourism Center - Ministry of Nature, Environment and Tourism" – http://mongoliatourism.gov.mn/

MONTÉNÉGRO

(1) Touristes non résidents dans tous types d'établissements d'hébergement.
"Ministry of Sustainable Development and Tourism" – http://www.monstat.org/EngMeniGodisnjiPodaci.htm

MONTSERRAT

"Statistics Department Montserrat"

MOZAMBIQUE

(1) Note 2008: Changement de méthodologie. Jusqu'en 2007, les données correspondent seulement à 12 postes frontaliers. A partir de 2008, les données de tous les postes frontaliers du pays sont utilisées.
"Ministry of Tourism" et "Instituto Nacional de Estatística" – http://www.ine.gov.mz/sectorias_dir/turismo/

MYANMAR

(1) Comprenant les arrivées de touristes aux postes-frontières de Yangon; (2) Hôtels et établissements assimilés gérés uniquement par l'État; (3) Hôtels gérés par l'État et pensions de famille privées homologuées.
"Ministry of Hotels and Tourism"

NAMIBIE

"Ministry of Environment and Tourism" – http://www.namibiatourism.com.na/trade_cat_sub.php?sub_cat_id=32

NOTES DES PAYS

NÉPAL

(1) Y compris les arrivées en provenance de l'Inde; (2) Jours; (3) Hôtels à Katmandou et à l'intérieur du pays; 2006-2008: à l'exclusion des hôtels en cours de construction.
"Nepal Tourism Board" et "Ministry of Culture, Tourism and Civil Aviation" – http://www.tourism.gov.np/tourismstatistics.php

NICARAGUA

(1) Nationaux résidant à l'étranger compris; (2) Total de établissements dans l'ensemble du pays; (3) Principaux établissements d'hébergement dans l'ensemble du pays (7); (4) 2006-2009: Estimations préliminaires; (5) Hôtels et établissements assimilés classés en catégories supérieures; (6) Tous types d'établissements d'hébergement, tourisme récepteur.
"Instituto Nicaragüense de Turismo (INTUR)" – http://www.intur.gob.ni/estadisticas.php

NIGER

(1) Jours.
Ministère du Tourisme et de l'Artisanat

NIGÉRIA

"Nigerian Tourism Development Corporation"

NIOUÉ

(1) Y compris les nationaux résidant normalement en Nouvelle-Zélande.
"Statistics Niue" – http://www.spc.int/prism/country/nu/stats/Migration/Migration_index.htm

NORVÈGE

(1) Les chiffres se fondent sur "l'enquête auprès de la clientèle" de l'Institut d'économie des transports; (2) États-Unis seulement; (3) Japon seulement; (4) Nuitées dans les établissements classés; (5) Les chiffres des hôtels et établissements assimilés se réfèrent aux établissements de 20 places-lit et plus tout au long de l'année; (6) Voyages pour vacances.
"Statistics Norway" et "Institute of Transport Economics" – http://www.ssb.no/english/subjects/

NOUVELLE-CALÉDONIE

(1) Y compris les nationaux résidant à l'étranger; (2) Hôtels de Nouméa uniquement; (3) Retours des résidents; (4) Chambres à Nouméa; (5) Jours, hôtels de Nouméa.
Institut de la Statistique et des Études Économiques (ISEE) – http://www.isee.nc/

NOUVELLE-ZÉLANDE

(1) Voyages internationaux et migration, SNZ; (2) Enquête sur l'hébergement, SNZ; (3) Enquête auprès des visiteurs internationaux, MED; (4) Enquête voyages intérieurs, MED; (5) Enquête d'affaires, SNZ; (6) Comprend les hôtels, motels et les routards, mais exclut les parcs de vacances.
"Statistics New Zealand (SNZ)" et "Ministry of Economic Development (MED)" – http://www.stats.govt.nz/

OMAN

"Ministry of National Economy and Ministry of Commerce and Industry" et "Directorate General of Tourism - Ministry of Tourism"
http://www.moneoman.gov.om

OUGANDA

"Ministry of Tourism, Trade and Industry" et "Uganda Bureau of Statistics" –
http://www.ubos.org/?st=pagerelations2&id=19&p=related%20pages%202:Migration%20and%20Tourism%20Statistics
http://www.mtti.go.ug/index.php?option=com_content&view=article&id=117&Itemid=131

OUZBÉKISTAN

(1) Les chiffres de dépense sont ceux que le pays a fournis à l'OMT mais ils ne figurent pas dans les données du Fonds monétaire international qui ont servi à la préparation de la présente édition du Compendium.
"National Company "Uzbektourism".

PAKISTAN

(1) Jours.
"Pakistan Tourism Development Corporation - Ministry of Tourism" – http://www.pakistantourism.gov.pk/downloads.php

NOTES DES PAYS

PALAOS

(1) Arrivées par voie aérienne (aéroport international de Palau); (2) Les chiffres de dépense sont ceux que le pays a fournis à l'OMT mais ils ne figurent pas dans les données du Fonds monétaire international qui ont servi à la préparation de la présente édition du Compendium. Années fiscales.
"Office of Planning and Statistics, Bureau of Budget and Planning - Ministry of Finance" –
http://www.palaugov.net/stats/PalauStats/Tourism/tourism.htm
http://www.visit-palau.com/publication/index.cfm

PALESTINE

(1) Touristes non résidents dans les hôtels; (2) Hôtels seulement; (3) Cisjordanie et Gaza.
"Palestinian Central Bureau of Statistics" – http://www.pcbs.gov.ps/DesktopDefault.aspx?tabID=3039&lang=en

PANAMA

(1) Arrivées de visiteurs non résidents, aéroport international de Tocúmen (AIT), frontière de Paso Canoa (FPC) et ports de Cristóbal et Balboa (PCB); (2) Arrivées de visiteurs non résidents, AIT; (3) Arrivées de touristes non résidents, AIT; (4) Hôtels de Panama-City; (5) Chambres/places-lit recensées pour le tourisme international.
"Instituto Panameño de Turismo" –
http://www.atp.gob.pa/index.php?option=com_content&view=category&layout=blog&id=44&Itemid=64

PAPOUASIE-NOUVELLE-GUINÉE

"Papua New Guinea Tourism Promotion Authority"

PARAGUAY

(1) Cartes d'embarquement et de débarquement à l'aéroport Silvio Petirossi et comptages des passagers lors du franchissement des frontières nationales – Police nationale et SENATUR; (2) À l'exclusion des nationaux résidant à l'étranger et membres des équipages; (3) 2009: Enquête du tourisme récepteur, mars 2008 - mars 2009; (4) Voie fluviale; (5) Enquête permanente auprès des ménages 2008.
"Secretaría Nacional de Turismo - SENATUR" – http://www.senatur.gov.py/estadisticas.php?language=1

PAYS-BAS

(1) Touristes non résidents dans tous types d'établissements d'hébergement; (2) Hôtels et pensions; (3) Départs en vacances des ressortissants nationaux; (4) Hôtels; (5) Tous types d'établissements d'hébergement.
"Statistics Netherlands" – http://www.cbs.nl/en-GB/menu/themas/vrije-tijd-cultuur/nieuws/default.htm

PÉROU

(1) Y compris les nationaux résidant à l'étranger; (2) Passagers en croisière qui passent la nuit; (3) Comprend les arrivées par voie fluviale et lacustre; (4) Les données proviennent de l'"Enquête nationale sur les voyages des résidents 2007-2008".
Note 2005-2009: Données préliminaires.
"Dirección General de Migraciones y Naturalización (DIGEMIN)" et "Ministerio de Comercio Exterior y Turismo (MINCETUR)"
http://www.mincetur.gob.pe/newweb/Default.aspx?tabid=141

PHILIPPINES

(1) Y compris les nationaux résidant à l'étranger; (2) Arrivées par voie aérienne; (3) Nuitées; (4) Y compris les travailleurs sous contrat en provenance d'outre-mer; (5) Hôtels homologués seulement; (6) Hôtels homologués dans la région de Manille seulement.
"Department of Tourism" – http://www.tourism.gov.ph/Pages/TourismResearch.aspx

POLOGNE

(1) 2008 et 2009: Depuis que la Pologne est entrée dans l'espace Schengen, le comptage précis du trafic entrant n'est pas possible. Les données présentées ici sont basées sur les enquêtes de l'Institut du Tourisme. Seuls des résultats approximatifs peuvent être fournis cette année; (2) D'après les enquêtes de l'Institut du tourisme; (3) Données du Bureau central des statistiques; (4) Établissements d'hébergement collectif et privé, d'après les enquêtes de l'Institut du tourisme; (5) Voyages de 4 nuits et plus; (6) Voyages du tourisme émetteur enregistrés aux frontières.
"Institute of Tourism" – http://www.intur.com.pl/itenglish/institute_en.htm

NOTES DES PAYS

POLYNÉSIE FRANÇAISE

(1) Arrivées par voie aérienne uniquement; à l'exclusion des nationaux résidant à l'étranger; (2) Jours; (3) Hôtels et pensions de famille; au 31 décembre de chaque année; (4) Chambres dans hôtels.
Service du Tourisme – http://www.ispf.pf/ISPF/Chiffres/Tourisme.aspx – http://www.tourisme.gov.pf/7671-Les-statistiques.html
http://www.tahiti-tourisme.com/Partners/

PORTO RICO

(1) Arrivées de touristes non résidents par voie aérienne; (2) Îles Vierges Américaines et États-Unis seulement; (3) Y compris résidents et non résidents; (4) Les chiffres de dépense sont ceux que le pays a fournis à l'OMT mais ils ne figurent pas dans les données du Fonds monétaire international qui ont servi à la préparation de la présente édition du Compendium; (5) Chambres classées par la "Compañía de Turismo" de Porto Rico; (6) Y compris les chambres occupées par des résidents de Porto Rico.
Données: Années fiscales (juillet-juin).
"Junta de Planificación de Puerto Rico" et "Compañía de Turismo de Puerto Rico" – http://www.jp.gobierno.pr/

PORTUGAL

(1) La méthodologie a été modifiée et pour cela, à partir de 2004 les données ne sont pas comparables avec celles des années précédentes. Y compris les nationaux résidant à l'étranger; (2) Données monétaires des sociétés; (3) Taux d'occupation net; (4) Tous types d'établissements d'hébergement; (5) Données du Compte satellite du tourisme (CST).
"Turismo de Portugal, I.P." – http://www.ine.pt/xportal/xmain?xpid=INE&xpgid=ine_princindic&contexto=pi&selTab=tab0

QATAR

(1) Hôtels seulement; (2) Source: "Qatar Central Bank".
"The Planning Council - Statistics Department" et "Qatar Tourism Authority" –
http://www.qsa.gov.qa/Eng/GeneralStatistics.htm
http://www.qcb.gov.qa/English/Publications/ReportsAndStatements/Pages/AnnualReports.aspx

RÉPUBLIQUE ARABE SYRIENNE

(1) Y compris les nationaux résidant à l'étranger; (2) Touristes non résidents dans tous types d'établissements d'hébergement; (3) 2009: À l'exclusion des nationaux résidant à l'étranger.
Note: Les citoyens de l'Iraq sont inclus uniquement à partir de 2008 et ont été exclus des années précédentes (depuis le début de l'année 2008, ils doivent demander un visa pour entrer en Syrie ; s'ils sont entrés avant 2008, il est considéré que leur séjour est maintenant supérieur à un an et qu'ils sont de ce fait devenus des résidents).
"Ministry of Tourism" - Enquête du tourisme récepteur en 2004, 2006 et 2007

RÉPUBLIQUE CENTRAFRICAINE

(1) Arrivées par voie aérienne à Bangui uniquement; (2) Données du pays.
Note 2006: Estimations.
Ministère du Développement du Tourisme et de l'Artisanat

RÉPUBLIQUE DE MOLDOVA

(1) Visiteurs qui ont bénéficié des services touristiques des agences de tourisme et des voyagistes (titulaires d'une licence touristique).
Note: À l'exception de la rive gauche de la rivière Nistru et de la municipalité de Bender.
"National Bureau of Statistics" – http://www.statistica.md/category.php?l=en&idc=293&

RÉPUBLIQUE DÉMOCRATIQUE DU CONGO

(1) 2007-2009: Arrivées par voie aérienne uniquement.
Office National du Tourisme

RÉPUBIQUE DÉMOCRATIQUE POPULAIRE LAO

(1) Jours.
"Lao National Tourism Administration" – http://www.nsc.gov.la/Selected_Statistics.htm

RÉPUBLIQUE DOMINICAINE

(1) Y compris les nationaux résidant à l'étranger; (2) Arrivées par voie aérienne uniquement; (3) Toutes les arrivées par voie maritime; (4) Hôtels; (5) 2009: données du pays.
"Secretaría de Estado de Turismo" – http://www.bancentral.gov.do/estadisticas.asp?a=Sector_Turismo

NOTES DES PAYS

RÉPUBLIQUE TCHÈQUE

(1) Touristes non résidents dans tous types d'établissements d'hébergement; (2) Hôtels et restaurants; (3) Utilisation nette de lits; (4) Les activités de soutien et de transport annexe, les activités des tours opérateurs et des agences de voyage.
"Czech Statistical Office, TSA" – http://www.czso.cz/eng/redakce.nsf/i/home

RÉPUBLIQUE-UNIE DE TANZANIE

"Tourism Division - Ministry of Natural Resources and Tourism" et "National Bureau of Statistics" –
http://www.mnrt.go.tz/index.php/documents-a-publications/category/8-tourism

RÉUNION

(1) Arrivés par voie aérienne uniquement ; (2) Source : INSEE : Enquête flux touristiques ; (3) Source : INSEE : Enquête de fréquentation hôtelière ; (4) Il s'agit de l'ensemble des nuitées passées dans les hôtels classés. Résidents et non résidents ; (5) Les chiffres de dépense sont ceux que le pays a fournis à l'OMT mais ils ne figurent pas dans les données du Fonds monétaire international qui ont servi à la préparation de la présente édition du Compendium ; (6) Source : INSEE Clap. Il s'agit de l'ensemble des établissements des nomenclatures sélectionnées. Sans certitude sur la destination réelle de l'activité (touristique ou non) ; (7) Il s'agit de l'ensemble des établissements/chambres/lits disponibles par jour dans les hôtels classés ; (8) Source : INSEE Clap. Il s'agit de l'ensemble des emplois des nomenclatures sélectionnées. Sans certitude sur la destination réelle de l'activité (touristique ou non).
Institut National de la Statistique et des Études Économique - INSEE et Comité du Tourisme de la Réunion –
http://webpro.la-reunion-tourisme.com/connaitre2.php3?id_rubrique=71
http://www.insee.fr/fr/themes/theme.asp?theme=13&nivgeo=24

ROUMANIE

(1) Seulement les voyages intérieurs pour les vacances (y compris les visites aux amis et à la famille VAF) et pour raisons professionnelles ; (2) La catégorie "Autres raisons personnelles" ne fait référence qu'aux voyages VAF ; (3) A partir de 2005, les catégories " voie aérienne" et "voie fluviale" sont incluses dans les catégories "autres" ; (4) Calculé en divisant le nombre de nuitées par le nombre de voyages. Source : ACTR, Enquête sur les foyers ; (5) Seulement pour les vacances (y compris les VAF) et pour raisons professionnelles. Les chiffres sont obtenus en divisant la dépense par le nombre de nuitées ; (6) Pour tout le secteur d'hébergement, à prix courants ; (7) Au 31 juillet, pour les établissements agréés seulement ; (8) L'indicateur est représenté par le nombre de touristes qui achètent des services à forfait/individuels. Il est à noter que les chiffres cumulent les tours-opérateurs et les agences de voyage classiques ; (9) L'indicateur est représenté réellement par "le nombre moyen d'employés" et la source est représentée par les statistiques structurelles sur les entreprises qui sont établies annuellement ; (10) Inclus aussi le transport du fret ; (11) Cette catégorie ne correspond pas parfaitement aux catégories de l'industrie du tourisme car elle est publiée avec un niveau de consolidation plus élevé. Elle comprend aussi les activités des points de distribution de la presse, les bibliothèques et les services d'archive. Cependant, elle n'inclut pas les activités des centres de mise en forme et la location d'équipements pour les loisirs.
"National Institute of Statistics" – https://statistici.insse.ro/shop/index.jsp?page=tempo2&lang=en&context=63

ROYAUME-UNI

(1) Tunnel; (2) Enquête sur les passagers internationaux; Source: "Office for National Statistics"; (3) Jours; (4) Source: "EUROSTAT (New Cronos)"; (5) Angleterre seulement.
"VisitBritain" – http://www.visitbritain.org/insightsandstatistics/keystats/index.aspx
http://www.statistics.gov.uk/statbase/Product.asp?vlnk=1905&More=N

RWANDA

Office rwandais du tourisme et des parcs nationaux (ORTPN) – http://rwandatourism.com/arrivalstats.htm

SABA

(1) Principalement de St. Martin.
"Saba Tourist Bureau", "Caribbean Tourism Organization" et "Central Bank of the Netherlands Antilles"
http://www.centralbank.an/tables/tables/main-10-6.htm

SAINT-EUSTACHE

(1) À l'exclusion des résidents des Antilles Néerlandaises.
"Central Bank of the Netherlands Antilles" – http://www.centralbank.an/tables/tables/main-10-7.htm

SAINT-KITTS-ET- NEVIS

(1) Arrivées de touristes non résidents par voie aérienne; (2) Arrivées en yacht et en bateau de croisière.
"Eastern Caribbean Central Bank" – http://www.eccb-centralbank.org/Statistics/index.asp#tourismdata

NOTES DES PAYS

SAINT- MARIN

(1) Y compris les visiteurs Italiens; (2) Touristes non résidents dans les hôtels et établissements assimilés; y compris les touristes Italiens; (3) Hôtels seulement.
Note: Nouvelle méthodologie à partir de 2005.
"Segreteria di Stato per il Turismo, lo Sport, le Telecomunicazioni, i Trasporti e la Cooperazione Economica" – http://www.statistica.sm/on-line/Home/DatiStatistici/docCat.14000570.1.10.1.html?Categoria=Afflusso turistico

SAINT-MARTIN

(1) Par voie aérienne; y compris les arrivées à Saint-Martin (côté français de l'île); (2) Arrivées à l'aéroport "Juliana" (y compris les visiteurs à destination de Saint-Martin (côté français); (3) Y compris estimations pour Saba et Saint-Eustache. Source: "Central Bank of the Netherlands Antilles".
"St. Maarten Tourist Bureau" – http://www.centralbank.an/tables/tables/main-10-5.htm

SAINT-VINCENT-ET-LES-GRENADINES

(1) Arrivées de touristes non résidents par voie aérienne; (2) Y compris les passagers en croisière et en yacht; (3) Hôtels, appartements, bungalows, villas et pensions de famille.
"Ministry of Tourism and Culture" – http://www.discoversvg.com/index.php/es/about-svg/tourism-statistics

SAINTE-LUCIE

(1) À l'exclusion des nationaux résidant à l'étranger; (2) À l'exclusion des arrivées de passagers en yacht.
"Saint Lucia Tourist Board" – http://www.stlucia.gov.lc/

SAMOA

"Samoa Tourism Authority" et "Statistical Services Division (Ministry of Finance)" –
http://www.sbs.gov.ws/
http://www.mof.gov.ws/publish/economicreview.shtml

SAMOA AMÉRICAINES

(1) Y compris le Samoa occidental; (2) Visites à des parents, amis.
"American Samoa Government - Department of Commerce - Statistics Division" - http://www.spc.int/prism/country/as/stats/

SAO TOMÉ-ET-PRINCIPE

(1) Jours.
"Direcçao do Turismo e Hotelaria" – http://www.smfstp.st/estatisticas

SÉNÉGAL

(1) Hôtels et villages de vacances.
Ministère du Tourisme et des Transports Aériens

SERBIE

(1) Touristes non résidents dans tous types d'établissements d'hébergement; (2) 5.2+5.3+5.4.
"Statistical Office of the Republic of Serbia" – http://webrzs.stat.gov.rs/axd/en/drugastrana.php?Sifra=0008&izbor=tabela

SEYCHELLES

(1) Chiffres des nuitées élaborés à partir des départs; (2) Hôtels et pensions de famille.
"National Statistics Bureau" – http://www.nsb.gov.sc/

SIERRA LEONE

(1) Arrivées par voie aérienne; (2) Hôtels seulement.
"National Tourist Board"

SINGAPOUR

(1) À l'exclusion des arrivées de Malaisiens par voie terrestre; (2) Jours; (3) Hôtels (homologués et non-homologués); (4) Hôtels homologués seulement.
"Singapore Tourism Board" – http://www.singstat.gov.sg/stats/themes/economy/tourism.html

NOTES DES PAYS

SLOVAQUIE

(1) Modification des séries. À partir de 2003, le nombre d'arrivées du tourisme récepteur est basée sur une combinaison de statistiques du logement et statistiques de l'enquête aux frontières (tel que calculé par le Compte satellite du tourisme); (2) Touristes non résidants hébergés dans des établissements commerciaux seulement (représentant environ 25 % de l'ensemble des touristes (élément 1.2)); (3) Source: Statistiques urbaines et municipales (MOS – MIS); (4) Source : Répertoire des entreprises; (5) Compte satellite du tourisme (CST); (6) Enquête sur les foyers. Nombre de voyages touristiques intérieurs ou vers l'étranger pendant une période de 15 ans / nombre de résidants pendant la période de 15 ans.
"Tourism Section – Ministry of Transportation, Construction and Regional Development" et "Statistical Office" –
www.mindop.sk - www.statistics.sk

SLOVÉNIE

(1) Source : Enquête à la frontière ; comprenant toutes les catégories de voyageurs quelle que soit le motif de leur déplacement ; (2) Source : Enquête sur l'hébergement ; (3) Agrégats issus d'une enquête sur le logement, pourcentages issus de 3 enquêtes annuelles sur les touristes étrangers en Slovénie ; (4) Source : 3 enquêtes annuelles sur les touristes étrangers en Slovénie ; (5) Source : Enquête sur les voyages de la population nationale (comme les méthodologies sont différentes, des différences peuvent apparaître entre les statistiques sur les nuitées mensuelles et les données issues de l'enquête sur les ménages) ; (6) Seuls les voyages d'ordre privé sont pris en compte ; (7) L'unité de mesure est la nuitée ; (8) Source : statistiques structurelles sur les entreprises ; (9) L'hébergement du secteur privé (chambres à louer, résidences), les fermes d'hôtes, les refuges de montagne, les centres de vacances d'entreprise et les centres pour la jeunesse sont exclues ; (10) Source : Registre statistique de l'emploi ; (11) Les données sur le nombre de postes équivalents plein temps ne sont pas disponibles. En remplacement, l'indicateur est basé sur le nombre d'emplois.
"Statistical Office - Tourism Statistics, Structual Business Statistics, Statistical register of employment" –
http://www.stat.si/eng/tema_ekonomsko_turizem.asp

SOUDAN

(1) Y compris les nationaux résidant à l'étranger; (2) Pour la dépense, le pays fournit à l'OMT des niveaux d'agrégation qui diffèrent de façon significative des données du Fonds monétaire international utilisées pour la préparation de la présente édition du Compendium. Les données du pays sont les suivantes (Mn $E.U.): 2005: 316; 2006: 409; 2007: 428; 2008: 548; 2009: 522.
"Ministry of Tourism and Wildlife"

SRI LANKA

(1) À l'exclusion des nationaux résidant à l'étranger; (2) Hôtels, motels, auberges, pensions de famille et apart-hôtels.
"Sri Lanka Tourist Board" – http://www.sltda.lk/statistics

SUÈDE

(1) Touristes non résidents dans tous types d'établissements d'hébergement; y compris camping; (2) Hôtels seulement; (3) Nombre d'emplois équivalents à temps plein; (4) Total 5.2, 5.3 et 5.4.
"Tillväxtverket - The Swedish Agency for Economic and Regional Growth" –
http://www.tillvaxtverket.se/english
http://www.scb.se/Pages/Product____11830.aspx

SUISSE

(1) Hôtels et établissements de cure; (2) Établissements enquêtés; (3) Chambres enquêtées; (4) Places-lit enquêtées; (5) Taux d'occupation nets; (6) Emplois équivalents à temps plein.
"Swiss Federal Statistical Office" – http://www.bfs.admin.ch/bfs/portal/fr/index/themen/10.html

SURINAME

(1) Arrivées à l'aéroport de Zanderij; (2) Arrivées au port Nw. Nickerie.
"Suriname Tourism Foundation"

SWAZILAND

"Swaziland Tourism Authority" et "Ministry of Tourism, Environment and Communications"

TADJIKISTAN

"Committee of Youth Affairs, Sports and Tourism under the Government of the Republic of Tajikistan"

NOTES DES PAYS

TAÏWAN (PROVINCE DE CHINE)

(1) Y compris les nationaux résidant à l'étranger.
"Planning Division Tourism Bureau - Ministry of Transportation and Communication" –
http://admin.taiwan.net.tw/english/statistics/release.asp?relno=6

TCHAD

(1) Touristes non résidents dans les hôtels et établissements assimilés.
Direction des Études et de la Programmation - Ministère du Développement Touristique

THAÏLANDE

(1) 2006-2009, (2) À l'exclusion des arrivées des nationaux résidant à l'étranger; (3) Y compris chemin de fer; (4) Jours.
"Ministry of Tourism and Sports" – http://www.tourism.go.th/2009/en/statistic/tourism.php?cid=26

TIMOR-LESTE

(1) Arrivées par voie aérienne à l'aéroport de Dili; (2) 2007 comprend uniquement des données pour 10 mois; (3) Enquête dans les hôtels (20 chambres ou plus); (4) Source: BPA - L'autorité bancaire et des paiements.
"Direcçao Nacional de Estatística" – http://dne.mof.gov.tl/publications/index.htm

TOGO

(1) Touristes non résidents dans les hôtels et établissements assimilés; (2) Depuis 2009, une nouvelle méthodologie et une nouvelle couverture ont été appliquées. L'information n'est donc pas comparable à celle des années précédentes.
Ministère de l'Environnement, du Tourisme et des Ressources Forestières

TONGA

(1) Arrivées par voie aérienne.
"Tonga Visitors Bureau"

TRINITÉ-ET-TOBAGO

(1) Arrivées par voie aérienne; (2) Y compris les visites à des parents et amis.
Note 2009: estimations.
"Central Statistical Office - Ministry of Planning and Development" – http://www.tdc.co.tt/stopover_statistics.htm

TUNISIE

(1) À l'exclusion des nationaux résidant à l'étranger; (2) Hôtels homologués et non-homologués, pensions et villages de vacances.
Ministère du Tourisme - Office National du Tourisme et Institut National de la Statistique –
http://www.ins.nat.tn/indexfr.php

TURKMÉNISTAN

"State Committee for Tourism and Sport"

TURQUIE

(1) Arrivées par mer (à l'exclusion d'une frontière terrestre depuis 1989); (2) Départs de visiteurs non résidents; Source: "Departing Visitors Survey - Turkish Statistical Institute (TURKSTAT)"; (3) Y compris les passagers en croisière; (4) Enquête auprès des établissements d'hébergement homologués par le Ministère du Tourisme; (5) Y compris les terrains de camping; (6) Y compris les dépenses des nationaux résidant à l'étranger; (7) Hôtels homologués; à l'exclusion des terrains de camping.
"Ministry of Culture and Tourism" –
http://www.kulturturizm.gov.tr/TR/Genel/BelgeGoster.aspx?F6E10F8892433CFF657B96472CD892038020F3B0746F34B3
http://www.turkstat.gov.tr/PreTablo.do?tb_id=51&ust_id=14

TUVALU

"Central Statistics Division - Ministry of Finance, Economic Planning and Industry" –
http://www.spc.int/prism/Country/TV/Stats/Tourism_migration/tour_index.htm

UKRAINE

"State Statistics Committee of Ukraine" – http://www.ukrstat.gov.ua/operativ/operativ2007/tyr/tyr_e/arh_vig_e.html

NOTES DES PAYS

URUGUAY

(1) Y compris chemin de fer; (2) Jours; (3) 2005-2007: À l'exclusion des hôtels non-homologués; (4) Services immobiliers.
"Ministerio de Turismo y Deporte" - http://www.mintur.gub.uy

VANUATU

(1) À partir de novembre 2006, les arrivées à Luganville sont inclues; (2) Jours.
"Vanuatu National Statistics Office" – http://www.spc.int/prism/country/vu/Stats/Tourism/tourism-index.htm

VENEZUELA

(1) 2005-2009: Hôtels uniquement.
"Ministerio del Poder Popular para el Turismo" – http://www.mintur.gob.ve/contenido.php?id=215

VIET NAM

(1) Y compris les nationaux résidant à l'étranger; (2) Y compris les arrivées de passagers en croisière et par voie maritime; (3) Les chiffres de dépense sont ceux que le pays a fournis à l'OMT mais ils ne figurent pas dans les données du Fonds monétaire international qui ont servi à la préparation de la présente édition du Compendium.
"Viet Nam National Administration of Tourism" et "General Statistics Office" – http://www.vietnamtourism.com/e_pages/news/index.asp?loai=1&chucnang=07

YÉMEN

"Ministry of Tourism" et "Central Statistical Organization" – http://www.yementourism.com/statistics/
http://www.cso-yemen.org/content.php?lng=english&pcat=131

ZAMBIE

(1) Jours.
"Ministry of Tourism, Environment and Natural Resources"

ZIMBABWE

(1) Les chiffres de dépense sont ceux que le pays a fournis à l'OMT mais ils ne figurent pas dans les données du Fonds monétaire international qui ont servi à la préparation de la présente édition du Compendium; (2) Sur la base des arrivées dans les parcs nationaux; (3) 2006-2008: Projections; (4) Hôtels classés uniquement; (5) Données du pays; (6) Estimations.
"Zimbabwe Tourism Authority – ZTA" – http://www.aitbase.co.zw/zta/index.php?option=com_docman&task=cat_view&gid=105&Itemid=183

NOTAS DE LOS PAÍSES

ALBANIA

(1) Excluidos los nacionales residentes en el extranjero; (2) Fuente: Encuesta a corto plazo; (3) La clasificación utilizada es NACE Rev. 1 (Nomenclatura estadística de actividades económicas); (4) Valor añadido a precios básicos; (5) Total de inversiones; (6) Las cifras son actualizadas con la encuesta sobre la estructura de negocios.
"Institute of Statistics - INSTAT" - http://www.instat.gov.al/

ALEMANIA

(1) Turistas no residentes alojados en todo tipo de establecimientos de alojamiento; (2) Turismo receptor, hoteles y establecimientos asimilados.
"Statistiches Bundesamt" – http://www.destatis.de

ANDORRA

(1) Desde mayo de 2009 se aplicó una nueva metodología y por lo tanto la información no es comparable con años anteriores.
Ministerio de Turismo y Medio Ambiente y Ministerio de Finanzas -
http://www.estadistica.ad/serveiestudis/web/index.asp?lang=2

ANGOLA

(1) Hoteles únicamente.
Nota 2008: Datos provisionales.
"Ministério de Hotelaria e Turismo - Gabinete de Estudos, Planeamento e Estatística"

ANGUILA

(1) Excluidos los nacionales residentes en el extranjero; (2) Visitantes del día (excursionistas).
"Statistical Department - Ministry of Finance" - http://www.gov.ai/statistics/cab_external.htm

ANTIGUA Y BARBUDA

(1) Excluidas las llegadas de pasajeros en yate; (2) Llegadas por vía aérea; excluidos los nacionales residentes en el extranjero; (3) Pasajeros en crucero únicamente.
"Ministry of Tourism" - http://www.tourismantiguabarbuda.gov.ag/tourism_programs/statistics.php

ARABIA SAUDITA

(1) Fuente: Encuesta internacional de visitantes, MAS Center; (2) Noches; (3) Fuente: Encuesta de turismo interno y emisor, MAS Center; (4) Servicio de esparcimiento; (5) 2009: estimado por el MAS Center.
"The Saudi Commission for Tourism and Antiquities (SCTA)" – http://www.mas.gov.sa/

ARGELIA

(1) Incluidos los nacionales residentes en el extranjero; (2) Excluidos los nacionales residentes en el extranjero.
"Ministère de l'Aménagement du Territoire, de l'Environnement et du Tourisme" y "Office National des Statistiques" - http://www.ons.dz/-Tourisme-.html

ARGENTINA

(1) Encuesta de ocupación hotelera (EOH); (2) Información obtenida en la encuesta permanente de hogares (EPH) que permite estimar los empleos en las ramas características del turismo. Dicha encuesta tiene una cobertura territorial limitada, lo que explica que sus estimaciones no sean totalmente representativas del conjunto nacional; (3) Corresponde a empleados, no puestos de trabajo; (4) La clasificación incluye patrones y trabajadores familiares sin remuneración.
Dirección de Estudios de Mercado y Estadística - Secretaría de Turismo de la Nación - http://www.turismo.gov.ar/

ARMENIA

"Tourism Department - Ministry of Trade and Economic Development" - http://www.armstat.am/en/

ARUBA

(1) Llegadas por vía aérea; (2) Pasajeros en crucero únicamente.
"Aruba Tourism Authority" - http://www.cbs.aw/cbs/do/home.html

NOTAS DE LOS PAÍSES

AUSTRALIA

(1) Excluidos los nacionales residentes en el extranjero y miembros de tripulaciones; (2) Llegadas por vía aérea; (3) Hoteles, moteles, casas de huéspedes y apartamentos de servicio hotelero con 5 habitaciones o más.
"Australian Bureau of Statistics" - http://www.abs.gov.au/

AUSTRIA

(1) Turistas no residentes alojados en todo tipo de establecimientos de alojamiento; (2) Únicamente alojamiento de pago; excluidas las estancias con amigos y familiares y las viviendas secundarias; (3) Hoteles únicamente; (4) Viajes al extranjero por vacaciones y negocios con al menos una pernoctación; (5) Basado en la temporada de verano; (6) Datos de la Cuenta Satélite de Turismo (CST); (7) Equivalentes a tiempo completo.
"Statistics Austria" - http://www.statistik.at/web_en/statistics/tourism/accommodation/index.html

AZERBAIYÁN

"Ministry of Culture and Tourism" y "Statistical Committee" - http://www.azstat.org/statinfo/consumermarket/en/tur_en.shtml

BAHAMAS

(1) Llegadas en hoteles únicamente; (2) Hoteles, apartamentos, bungalows y villas - Establecimientos homologados únicamente.
"Bahamas Ministry of Tourism" - http://www.tourismtoday.com/prelim/statistics/

BAHREIN

(1) Excluidos los nacionales residentes en el extranjero; (2) Llegadas al aeropuerto internacional de Bahrein; (3) Llegadas al puerto Mina Salman; (4) Llegadas a través del "King Fahad Causeway"; (5) Únicamente hoteles clasificados.
"Tourism Sector - Ministry of Culture and Information"

BANGLADESH

"Bangladesh Parjatan Corporation"

BARBADOS

(1) Hoteles, hoteles-apartamento, apartamentos y bungalows, casas de huéspedes.
"Barbados Tourism Authority"

BÉLARÚS

(1) Turismo organizado.
"State Committee of Frontier Troops" y "Ministry of Statistics and Analysis"

BÉLGICA

(1) Turistas no residentes alojados en todo tipo de establecimientos de alojamiento; (2) Hoteles únicamente; (3) Hoteles y poblados de vacaciones.
"Institut National de Statistique"

BELICE

"Belize Tourist Board" - http://www.belizetourism.org/content/view/248/295/

BENIN

Nota 2005-2009: Estimaciones.
"Direction du développement touristiques - Ministère de la culture, de l'artisanat et du tourisme"

BERMUDA

(1) Excluidos los nacionales residentes en el extranjero; (2) Llegadas por vía aérea; (3) Pasajeros en crucero; (4) Incluidas las pernoctaciones en casas particulares.
"Bermuda Department of Tourism" –
http://www.gov.bm/portal/server.pt?space=CommunityPage&control=SetCommunity&CommunityID=227

NOTAS DE LOS PAÍSES

BHUTÁN

"Department of Tourism - Royal Government of Bhutan" - http://www.nsb.gov.bt/index.php?id=13

BOLIVIA

(1) Datos estimados; (2) Información obtenida a través de la estructura porcentual determinada en la Encuesta "Gasto del Turismo Receptor y Emisor – 2007"; (3) Llegadas por vía lacustre; (4) El 7,6% de los viajeros corresponde a turismo organizado; (5) Fuente: Encuesta "Gasto del Turismo Receptor y Emisor – 2007"; (6) Capitales de departamento únicamente; (7) Tamaño promedio grupos de viaje en familia: 2,8 personas.
Nota: Los indicadores de turismo son obtenidos a partir de la relación de los resultados de la encuesta "Gasto del Turismo Receptor y Emisor – 2007" entre las estadísticas de Comercio Exterior, Servicios de la Balanza de Pagos, Cuentas Nacionales (PIB), determinando la participación del turismo en cada uno de los sectores.
2006-2009: Datos preliminares.
Instituto Nacional de Estadística y Viceministerio de Turismo - Ministerio de Producción y Microempresa
http://www.ine.gov.bo/default.aspx

BONAIRE

(1) Fuente: "Central Bank of the Netherlands Antilles".
"Tourism Corporation of Bonaire (TCB)" - http://www.tourismbonaire.com/contact_services/trade_section/statistical_info/

BOSNIA Y HERZEGOVINA

(1) Turistas no residentes alojados en todo tipo de establecimientos de alojamiento; (2) Menos de 500 llegadas; (3) Desde 2007 los datos se refieren al conjunto de Bosnia y Herzegovina.
"Agency for Statistics of Bosnia and Herzegovina" - http://www.bhas.ba/eng/Publications.asp?Pripadnost=8&mode=dark

BOTSWANA

Nota 2008-2009: Cifras estimadas.
"Department of Tourism - Ministry of Environment, Wildlife and Tourism"

BRASIL

(1) Incluidos los nacionales residentes en el extranjero; (2) Incluidas las llegadas por vía fluvial; (3) Fuente: Ministerio de Turismo y Ministerio de Trabajo / Relación Anual de Informaciones Sociales – 2009. La información se estimó a partir de CADASTUR – "Sistema de Cadastro de Prestadores de Serviços Turísticos do Ministério do Turismo e RAIS"; (4) Asalariados formales: registrados y cubiertos por la seguridad social; (5) Trabajadores informales: trabajadores autónomos y empleados sin registro; (6) La diferencia entre el número total de trabajadores del sector informal, por sexo (5.15) y el número de trabajadores del sector informal (5.10) se debe al mes de referencia utilizado para estas estimaciones, septiembre, mes de la recogida de la Encuesta Nacional de Hogares, para el sexo y diciembre, para extrapolar el número de trabajadores del sector informal.
"Ministério do Turismo" - http://www.dadosefatos.turismo.gov.br/dadosefatos/home.html

BRUNEI DARUSSALAM

(1) (2/2007) Llegadas por vía aérea.
"Brunei Tourism - Ministry of Industry and Primary Resources"

BULGARIA

(1) Visitantes en tránsito; (2) Mar y ríos del interior del país; (3) Hoteles únicamente.
"National Statistical Institute - State Agency for Tourism" – http://www.nsi.bg/SocialActivities_e/Tourism_e.htm

BURKINA FASO

(1) Turistas no residentes alojados en hoteles y establecimientos asimilados; (2) Incluido el turismo interno.
"Service de l'analyse statistique et de la Coopération touristique - Ministère de la Culture, des Arts et du Tourisme" – http://www.insd.bf/

BURUNDI

(1) Incluidos los nacionales residentes en el extranjero; (2) Llegadas por vía lacustre.
"Office National du Tourisme"

NOTAS DE LOS PAÍSES

CABO VERDE

(1) Turistas no residentes alojados en hoteles y establecimientos asimilados.
"Instituto Nacional de Estatística" y "Ministério da Economia, Crescimento e Competitividade" –
http://www.ine.cv/indexBDeo.aspx

CAMBOYA

(1) Llegadas por todo el conjunto de medios de transporte; (2) Llegadas por barco; (3) Días.
"Ministry of Tourism" - http://www.mot.gov.kh

CAMERÚN

(1) Turistas no residentes alojados en hoteles y establecimientos asimilados.
"Ministère du Tourisme"

CANADÁ

(1) Datos basados en la contabilidad aduanera, ajustándola en función de los resultados de las encuestas; (2) Viajes-persona (una/varias noches).
"Canadian Tourism Commission" y "Statistics Canada" –
http://en-corporate.canada.travel/Corporate/Flyout.page?id=369&fid=376

CHAD

(1) Turistas no residentes alojados en hoteles y establecimientos asimilados.
"Direction des Études et de la Programmation - Ministère du Développement Touristique"

CHILE

(1) Incluidos los nacionales residentes en el extranjero; (2) Las cifras de 2005 no son comparables con años anteriores debido a una actualización del Censo con cobertura nacional de Establecimientos de Alojamiento Turístico.
Servicio Nacional de Turismo - SERNATUR – http://www.sernatur.cl/institucional/htm_instit/estadisticas.html

CHINA

(1) Incluidas las llegadas de personas de origen étnico chino procedentes de "Hong Kong (China)", "Macao (China)", "Taiwán (Provincia de China)" y de ultramar, la mayor parte de excursionistas proceden de "Hong Kong (China)" y "Macao (China)"; (2) Excluidas las llegadas de turistas de origen étnico chino procedentes de "Hong Kong (China)", "Macao (China)", "Taiwán (Provincia de China)" y de ultramar; (3) Referido sólo a los hoteles clasificados con estrellas; (4) Incluidos los miembros de las tripulaciones y otros miembros de las fuerzas armadas; (5) Turismo receptor.
"National Tourism Administration" – http://en.cnta.gov.cn/

CHIPRE

(1) Incluidos los pasajeros en crucero y en tránsito; (2) Incluidos los pasajeros en crucero; (3) Los datos sobre alojamiento (llegadas, pernoctaciones y tasas de ocupación) los recopila mensualmente entre los establecimientos de alojamiento turístico autorizados y los produce la C.T.O.; (4) Gasto medio diario calculado dividiendo el gasto total (punto 1.33) por el número total de turistas recibidos que pernoctan (punto 1.2) y la duración media de su estancia (punto 1.40); (5) Los datos facilitados son resultado de la implantación de un sistema de CST por parte del Servicio de Estadística de la República de Chipre. La implantación del sistema de la CST se efectuó con carácter experimental para el periodo 2003-2007; (6) Los cálculos de la duración media de la estancia se basan en las pernoctaciones y las llegadas registradas en establecimientos de alojamiento turístico autorizados; (7) A partir del 1 de enero de 2008, el Servicio de Estadística de Chipre realiza mensualmente una encuesta sobre los gastos de los chipriotas que viajan al extranjero (viajes - débito). En virtud de este estudio, la parte de los gastos de los chipriotas que viajan al extranjero que se refiere a gastos de transporte puede ser medida por separado. Como resultado de ello, esta cantidad se incluye en los servicios de transporte; (8) El turismo emisor a partir de 2003 incluye también los viajes por motivos religiosos o de peregrinación; (9) Gasto medio diario calculado dividiendo el gasto total (punto 3.4) por el número total de turistas recibidos que pernoctan (punto 3.2) y la duración media de su estancia (punto 3.10); (10) Los datos se refieren a todos los servicios de alojamiento de pago; (11) Los datos los compila y produce la C.T.O. Se refieren a hoteles y establecimientos de alojamiento turístico autorizado y no se han utilizado en las estimaciones de la CST que muestran los puntos que van del 4.1 al 4.12; (12) Los cálculos de la duración media de la estancia se basan en las pernoctaciones y las llegadas registradas en hoteles y en establecimientos de alojamiento turístico similares autorizados.
Nota para todos los datos suministrados: No está incluida la información sobre las actividades inmobiliarias realizadas con bienes propios o arrendados y las actividades inmobiliarias realizadas a cambio de una retribución o por contrata.
"Statistical Service of Cyprus" y "Cyprus Tourism Organization" –
http://www.mof.gov.cy/mof/cystat/statistics.nsf/index_en/index_en?OpenDocument

NOTAS DE LOS PAÍSES

COLOMBIA

(1) Llegadas de viajeros extranjeros por puntos de control del Departamento Administrativo de Seguridad (DAS); (2) 2005,2006: excluidos los viajeros extranjeros llegados por puntos fronterizos terrestres; 2007-2009: incluidos los viajeros extranjeros llegados por puntos fronterizos terrestres; (3) Incluidos los pasajeros en crucero; (4) Excluidos los viajeros extranjeros llegados por puntos fronterizos terrestres; (5) Excluidos los pasajeros en crucero; (6) 2009: incluidos los viajeros extranjeros llegados por puntos fronterizos terrestres; (7) Fuente a partir de 2005: Departamento Nacional de Estadística (DANE).
Dirección de Extranjería - Departamento Administrativo de Seguridad (DAS) –
http://www.mincomercio.gov.co/eContent/home.asp

COMORAS

(1) 2007, (2) Llegadas por via aérea únicamente; (3) Las cifras de gasto corresponden a las facilitadas por el país a la OMT y que, sin embargo, no figuran en los datos del Fondo Monetario Internacional utilizados para la preparación de esta edición del Compendio.
"Direction Nationale de la Promotion du Tourisme et de l'Hôtellerie - Ministère du Transport, Tourisme, Postes et Télécommunications" y "Banque centrale des Comores"

CONGO

(1) Turistas no residentes alojados en hoteles y establecimientos asimilados.
"Direction Générale du Tourisme et de l'Hôtellerie - Ministère du tourisme et de l'environnement"

COREA (REPÚBLICA DE)

(1) Incluidos los nacionales residentes en el extranjero y miembros de las tripulaciones; (2) A partir de 2006, excluidos los nacionales residentes en el extranjero y los miembros de las tripulaciones; (3) El país facilita a la OMT niveles agregados de gasto que son significativamente diferentes a los datos del Fondo Monetario Internacional utilizados para la preparación de esta edición del Compendio (excluidos los gastos de los estudiantes que realizan sus estudios fuera del país). Los datos del país son (Mill. $EE.UU.): 2005: 12.025; 2006: 14.336; 2007: 16.950; 2008: 14.581; 2009: 11.040; (4) Hoteles únicamente.
"Ministry of Culture and Tourism" – http://kto.visitkorea.or.kr/inout.kto?func_name=search

COSTA RICA

(1) Viajes de placer y visita a familiares; (2) En la zona central del país; (3) En establecimientos de "cinco categorías" en el Gran Área Metropolitana de San José (estudio por muestreo); (4) Corresponde a las personas ocupadas en la rama de actividad "Hoteles y restaurantes" según la Clasificación Industrial Internacional Uniforme (CIIU 3); (5) Encuesta de Hogares de Propósitos Múltiples. Excluidos los puestos de trabajo no remunerados; (6) Corresponde a los puestos equivalentes generados por el subempleo visible que se refiere a las personas ocupadas que trabajan habitualmente menos de 47 horas por semana en su ocupación principal y en su ocupación secundaria (si la tienen), que desean trabajar más horas por semana y están disponibles para hacerlo. Excluidos los puestos de trabajo no remunerados.
Instituto Costarricense de Turismo e Instituto Nacional de Estadística y Censos –
http://www.visitcostarica.com/ict/paginas/modEst/estudios_demanda_turistica.asp?ididioma=1

CROACIA

(1) Turistas no residentes alojados en todo tipo de establecimientos de alojamiento; (2) Incluidas las llegadas a los puertos de turismo náutico; (3) 2008: Nueva metodología; (4) Desde 2004 se aplicó una nueva metodología y cobertura y por lo tanto la información no es comparable con años anteriores; (5) Incluidas las pernoctaciones en puertos de turismo náutico.
"Central Bureau of Statistics" – http://www.dzs.hr/default_e.htm – http://www.mint.hr/default.aspx?id=363

CUBA

(1) Llegadas por vía aérea; (2) Hoteles, moteles, aparthoteles, terrenos de camping/caravaning y otros; (3) Hoteles, moteles y aparthoteles; (4) Las cifras de gasto corresponden a las facilitadas por el país a la OMT y que, sin embargo, no figuran en los datos del Fondo Monetario Internacional utilizados para la preparación de esta edición del Compendio; (5) Comprende sólo giras controladas por el Instituto del Turismo.
Oficina Nacional de Estadísticas – http://www.one.cu/sitioone2006.asp

CURAÇAO

(1) Llegadas por vía aérea; (2) Diferencias en los totales globales debido a la falta de datos completos en las tarjetas de embarque y desembarque de los visitantes; (3) Llegadas de pasajeros en crucero; (4) Grandes y pequeños hoteles, casas de huéspedes, apartamentos y bungalows; (5) Fuente: "Central Bank of the Netherlands Antilles"; (6) Hoteles, casas de huéspedes y apartamentos.
"Curaçao Tourist Board" – http://www.ctb.an/Statistics.aspx

NOTAS DE LOS PAÍSES

DINAMARCA

(1) Turistas no residentes alojados en todo tipo de establecimientos de alojamiento; (2) A partir de 2005: incluye el turismo no comercial; (3) Nueva metodología a partir de 2006; (4) Hoteles únicamente; (5) Fuente: "VisitDenmark"; (6) Únicamente hoteles y alojamientos de vacaciones con 40 camas o más.
"VisitDenmark" – http://www.dst.dk/HomeUK.aspx

DJIBOUTI

(1) Turistas no residentes alojados en hoteles.
"Office national du tourisme"

DOMINICA

(1) Días.
"Discover Dominica Authority" – http://tourism.gov.dm/

ECUADOR

(1) Excluidos los nacionales residentes en el extranjero.
Ministerio de Turismo – http://www.turismo.gov.ec/index.php?option=com_content&task=view&id=459&Itemid=95

EGIPTO

(1) Viajes por turismo y no-turismo (más del 50% por motivo de trabajo).
"Ministry of Tourism"

EL SALVADOR

(1) Nueva metodología a partir de 2004; (2) Incluido el alojamiento privado.
Corporación Salvadoreña de Turismo (CORSATUR) - Ministerio de Turismo –
http://www.elsalvador.travel/secciones.php?id_seccion=20&lang=sp&portal=2

ERITREA

(1) Incluidos los nacionales residentes en el extranjero; (2) Únicamente hoteles y establecimientos asimilados en las tres principales ciudades: Asmara, Karen y Massawa; (3) Los datos de gastos corresponden a los facilitados por el país a la OMT, por tratarse de una serie más completa que la facilitada por el Fondo Monetario Internacional (FMI) para la preparación de esta edición del Compendio; (4) 2005/2006: Únicamente hoteles y establecimientos asimilados en las tres principales ciudades: Asmara, Karen y Massawa; (5) 2007-2009: Doce principales ciudades; (6) Todos los hoteles y establecimientos asimilados en Eritrea.
"Ministry of Tourism"

ESLOVAQUIA

(1) Cambio en la serie. A partir de 2003, el número de llegadas del turismo receptor se basa en una combinación de las estadísticas de alojamiento y las estadísticas de encuestas en fronteras (según los cálculos de la Cuenta satélite de turismo); (2) Solo los turistas no residentes que se alojan en establecimientos comerciales (y que representan aproximadamente el 25% del total de turistas [punto 1.2]); (3) Fuente: Estadísticas urbanas y municipales; (4) Fuente: Registro mercantil; (5) Cuenta satélite de turismo (CST); (6) Encuesta de hogares. Número de viajes de turismo interno y emisor durante 15 años / número de residentes durante 15 años.
"Tourism Section – Ministry of Transportation, Construction and Regional Development" y "Statistical Office" –
www.mindop.sk - www.statistics.sk

ESLOVENIA

(1) Fuente: encuesta de fronteras, incluidas todas las categorías de viajeros independientemente del motivo de la visita; (2) Fuente: encuesta de alojamiento; (3) Agregados de la encuesta de alojamiento, parte de las encuestas trienales sobre turistas extranjeros en Eslovenia; (4) Fuente: encuestas trienales sobre turistas extranjeros en Eslovenia; (5) Fuente: encuesta sobre viajes de población nacional (debido a la aplicación de diferentes metodologías, pueden surgir diferencias entre los datos de las estadísticas mensuales de alojamiento y los datos extraídos de las encuestas de hogares); (6) Solo se tienen en cuenta los viajes privados; (7) Las noches se utilizan como unidad; (8) Fuente: estadísticas estructurales de las empresas; (9) No se incluye el alojamiento privado (habitaciones alquiladas, viviendas), las casas de campo turísticas que ofrecen alojamiento, las cabañas de montaña, las instalaciones vacacionales de las empresas y las instalaciones para jóvenes; (10) Fuente: Registro estadístico de empleo; (11) No se dispone de información sobre el número de puestos de trabajo equivalentes a puestos de jornada completa. En su lugar, en este indicador se usa el número de puestos de trabajo.
"Statistical Office - Tourism Statistics, Structual Business Statistics, Statistical register of employment" –
http://www.stat.si/eng/tema_ekonomsko_turizem.asp

NOTAS DE LOS PAÍSES

ESPAÑA

(1) Incluidos los nacionales residentes en el extranjero; (2) Japón únicamente; (3) Hoteles, hostales, terrenos de camping, apartamentos turísticos y alojamientos/casas rurales; (4) Hoteles y hostales; (5) Desde 2005 se aplicó una nueva metodología y por lo tanto la información no es comparable con años anteriores.
Instituto de Estudios Turísticos e Instituto Nacional de Estadística –
http://www.iet.tourspain.es/paginas/home.aspx?idioma=es-ES
http://www.ine.es/inebmenu/mnu_hosteleria.htm

ESTADOS UNIDOS DE AMÉRICA

(1) Incluidos los mexicanos que pasan una noche o más en EE.UU.; (2) Solo automóviles de Canadá en visitas del día; (3) Ultramar únicamente; excluido México (no disponible); (4) Estimaciones preliminares; (5) Incluye un muy pequeño porcentaje (0.2%) de viajeros cuyo modo de transporte no se conoce; (6) El país facilita datos de gasto que son significativamente diferentes a los del FMI. Los datos son (Mill. $EE.UU.) para 1.34: 2005: 81.799; 2006: 85.789; 2007: 96.896; 2008: 109.976; 2009: 93.917; para 3.5: 2005: 68.970; 2006: 72.104; 2007: 76.331; 2008: 79.726; 2009: 73.230; (7) Incluidos los americanos que pasan una o varias noches en México; (8) Fuente: "OTTI, Statistics Canada, Banco de Mexico"; (10) Fuente: "American Hotel & Lodging Association (AHLA)"; (9) Solo de Estados Unidos a Canadá. Fuente: Statistics Canada; (10) Propiedades de más de 15 habitaciones; (11) Fuente: Departamento de Comercio de los Estados Unidos / Oficina de Análisis Económico. Sistema de cuenta satélite de viajes y turismo; (12) Fuente: Smith Travel Research; (13) Fuente: OTTI, encuesta de viajeros aéreos internacionales (recibidos); (14) BEA; las revisiones se han vuelto a referenciar recientemente; (15) Alojamientos para viajeros; (16) Servicios de alimentación y lugares donde se sirven bebidas; (17) Servicios de transporte aéreo; (18) Residual.
"Office of Travel and Tourism Industries (OTTI)" – http://tinet.ita.doc.gov/ - http://www.ahla.com/content.aspx?id=3448

ESTONIA

(1) Calculado en base a las estadísticas de alojamiento y a la "Foreign Visitor Survey" realizada por la "Statistical Office of Estonia"; (2) Turistas no residentes alojados en todo tipo de establecimientos de alojamiento; (3) Fuente: encuesta de hogares por "Statistics Estonia"; (4) 2005-2007: todo tipo de establecimientos de alojamiento.
Nota: A partir de 2004 no se recopilan las estadísticas de fronteras.
"Estonian Tourist Board / Enterprise Estonia" – http://pub.stat.ee/px-web.2001/I_Databas/Economy/databasetree.asp
http://visitestonia.com/en/additional-navigation/press-room/eas-views-on-tourism/estonian-tourism-statistics

ETIOPÍA

(1) Llegadas a todos los puestos fronterizos; incluidos los nacionales residentes en el extranjero; (2) 2005: Excluidos los hoteles sin homologar.
"Ministry of Culture and Tourism"

EX REPÚBLICA YUGOSLAVA DE MACEDONIA

(1) Turistas no residentes alojados en todo tipo de establecimientos de alojamiento; (2) 2008: Nueva metodología; (3) Duración media de la estancia en todos los establecimientos de alojamiento.
"State Statistical Office" – http://www.stat.gov.mk/english/glavna_eng.asp?br=110#Tourism

FEDERACIÓN DE RUSIA

(1) Alojamiento en hoteles y en otros establecimientos de carácter turístico.
"Russian Federal Agency for Tourism"

FIJI

(1) Excluidos los nacionales residentes en el extranjero; (2) Días.
"Fiji Islands Bureau of Statistics" – http://www.spc.int/prism/Country/FJ/stats/Tourism/tourmigstats_index.htm

FILIPINAS

(1) Incluidos los nacionales residentes en el extranjero; (2) Llegadas por vía aérea; (3) Noches; (4) Incluidos los trabajadores con contrato procedentes de ultramar; (5) Hoteles homologados únicamente; (6) Hoteles homologados en Metro Manila.
"Department of Tourism" – http://www.tourism.gov.ph/Pages/TourismResearch.aspx

FINLANDIA

(1) Encuesta de entrevistas de fronteras; (2) Estadísticas de alojamiento; (3) Balanza de pagos (BdP); (4) Encuesta de viajes finlandesa; (5) Incluidos únicamente los viajes internos de ocio en alojamientos para visitantes alquilados; (6) Viajes al extranjero, incluidos los cruceros con pernoctaciones a bordo; (7) Estadísticas sobre empresas radicadas en Finlandia; (8) Años 2005-2007 según la clasificación de la NACE Rev 1.1, años 2008-2009 según la clasificación de la NACE Rev. 2; (9) Datos de la Cuenta Satélite de Turismo (CST); (10) Encuesta sobre fuerza laboral; (11) Solo se incluyen los servicios de alojamiento y las actividades de provisión de alimentos y bebidas.

NOTAS DE LOS PAÍSES

"Tourism Statistics - Statistics Finland" – http://www.mek.fi/w5/mekfi/index.nsf/(pages)/Tutkimukset_ja_tilastot

FRANCIA

(1) Encuesta a los visitantes que vienen del extranjero (EVE); (2) Todos los motivos personales; (3) Tránsito y sin especificar; (4) Todo tipo de alojamiento; (5) Encuesta de ocupación hotelera. Incluidos los hoteles sin clasificar. 2006: renovación de la encuesta, datos no comparables con años anteriores; (6) Fuente: "Banque de France"; (7) Duración media de la estancia del turismo receptor; (8) Encuesta "Seguimiento de la demanda turística" (SDT). Población residente de 15 años o más. Resultados extrapolados retroactivamente desde 2005; (9) Viajes por motivos personales; (10) Ruptura de serie entre 2004 y 2005; (11) Datos INSEE relativos al parque hotelero; (12) Tasa neta de ocupación de las habitaciones.
"INSEE (Institut national de la statistique et des études économiques) – Section statistique du tourisme" – http://www.insee.fr/fr/default.asp

GABÓN

"Centre Gabonais de Promotion Touristique (GABONTOUR)"

GAMBIA

(1) Incluidos los nacionales residentes en el extranjero; (2) Llegadas en vuelos fletados únicamente.
"Gambia Tourism Authority" – http://www.visitthegambia.gm/index.php/en/publications

GEORGIA

(1) Llegadas en hoteles únicamente; (2) Fuente: Encuesta de hoteles y establecimientos asimilados; (3) Los datos se refieren únicamente a la inversión en capital fijo.
Nota 2009: Datos preliminares.
"Department of Tourism and Resorts - Ministry of Economic Development" y "State Department for Statistics - Ministry of Economic Development" – http://www.dotr.gov.ge/eng/statistics.php

GHANA

(1) Incluidos los nacionales residentes en el extranjero.
"Ghana Tourist Board" y "Ministry of Tourism and Modernisation of the Capital City" – http://www.statsghana.gov.gh/Publications.html

GRANADA

(1) Hoteles, bungalows/ apartamentos y casas de huéspedes.
"Grenada Board of Tourism"

GRECIA

(1) Información procedente de datos administrativos; (2) 2005/2006: Incluidos los pasajeros en crucero; (3) Fuente: "Hellenic Chamber of Hotels"; (4) Encuesta sobre la estructura de negocios en el sector del turismo.
"Hellenic Statistical Authority (EL STAT.)" – http://www.statistics.gr/portal/page/portal/ESYE

GUADALUPE

(1) Llegadas por vía aérea; excluidas las islas del norte (San Martín y San Barthelemy); (2) 2005: Datos obtenidos en una encuesta realizada en el aeropuerto de Guadalupe; (3) Hoteles.
"Comité du Tourisme des Îles de la Guadeloupe"

GUAM

(1) Llegadas por vías aérea y marítima; (2) Llegadas de civiles por vía aérea únicamente; (3) Habitaciones disponibles.
"Guam Visitors Bureau" – http://www.bsp.guam.gov/content/view/94/144/
http://www.visitguam.org/Runtime/GVBResearch.aspx#visitorreport

GUATEMALA

(1) El país facilita a la OMT niveles agregados de gasto que son significativamente diferentes a los datos del Fondo Monetario Internacional. Los datos del país son (Mill. $EE.UU.): 2005: 754; 2006: 789; 2007: 844; 2008: 901; 2009: 799; (2) 2006-2009: Todos los establecimientos de hospedaje inscritos en INGUAT.
Instituto Guatemalteco de Turismo - INGUAT – http://estadisticas.almadelatierra.com/

NOTAS DE LOS PAÍSES

GUINEA

(1) Llegadas por vía aérea al aeropuerto de Conakry; (2) Hoteles únicamente
"Division Observatoire du Tourisme - Ministère du Tourisme, de l'Hôtellerie et de l'Artisanat"

GUINEA-BISSAU

(1) Llegadas al aeropuerto "Osvaldo Vieira".
"Ministério do Turismo e do Ordenamento do Território"

GUYANA

(1) Llegadas al aeropuerto de Timehri únicamente.
"Guyana Tourism Authority"

GUYANA FRANCESA

(1) Encuesta 2005 en el aeropuerto de Cayenne-Rochambeau a la salida; (2) 2007: Incluido el alojamiento privado; (3) Hoteles únicamente.
"Comité du Tourisme de la Guyane" y "INSEE Guyane"

HAITÍ

(1) Llegadas por vía aérea; (2) A partir de 2007 se incluye a los nacionales residentes en el extranjero.
"Ministère du Tourisme"

HONDURAS

(1) Fuente: Cámara Nacional de Turismo de Honduras.
Instituto Hondureño de Turismo – http://www.iht.hn/?page_id=27

HONG KONG (CHINA)

(1) Las datos de gastos corresponden a los facilitados por el país a la OMT, por tratarse de una serie más completa que la facilitada por el Fondo Monetario Internacional (FMI) para la preparación de esta edición del Compendio. (Fuente: "HKTB Visitors Survey"); (2) A partir de 2006 se incluyen los residentes de Hong Kong viajando a Macao y China; (3) Fuente: "Census and Statistics Department"; (4) Hoteles (tarifas altas/medias) y albergues/ casas huéspedes.
"Hong Kong Tourism Board" – http://partnernet.hktb.com/pnweb/jsp/comm/index.jsp?charset=en
http://www.censtatd.gov.hk/hong_kong_statistics/index.jsp

HUNGRÍA

(1) Nueva serie a partir de 2004; (2) Modificación de los datos. Nuevos datos: número de visitantes extranjeros en Hungría. Datos anteriores: turistas no residentes alojados en todo tipo de establecimientos de alojamiento; (3) La observación de las fronteras con los países del espacio de Schengen cesó a partir del año 2008. 2008/2009: el tráfico aéreo de pasajeros y carretera son estimaciones; (4) Salidas de visitantes no residentes; (5) Por vía fluvial; (6) Se excluyen los conductores de camiones; (7) Alojamiento gratuito; (8) Excluidas las estimaciones sobre alojamiento privado; (9) Julio-junio; (10) 2005-2007: NACE Rev. 1; (11) 2008/2009: NACE Rev. 2; (12) NACE Rev. 2.
"Hungarian Central statistical Office" – http://portal.ksh.hu/portal/page?_pageid=38,119919&_dad=portal&_schema=PORTAL

INDIA

(1) Excluidos los nacionales residentes en el extranjero; (2) Incluye otros motivos; (3) Salidas de nacionales del país únicamente, por cualquier motivo de visita; (4) En hoteles homologados.
"Ministry of Tourism - Government of India" – http://tourism.gov.in/

INDONESIA

(1) Únicamente hoteles clasificados; (2) Conjunto de los medios comerciales de alojamiento.
"Ministry of Culture and Tourism" y "BPS Statistics Indonesia" –
http://dds.bps.go.id/eng/aboutus.php?tabel=1&id_subyek=16
http://www.budpar.go.id/page.php?ic=621&id=180

IRÁN (REPÚBLICA ISLÁMICA DEL)

(1) Incluye ferrocarril; (2) Fuente "Central Bank of Islamic Republic of Iran"; (3) Hoteles únicamente, 21 de Marzo-20 de Marzo.
"Iran Cultural Heritage and Tourism Organization (ICHTO)"

NOTAS DE LOS PAÍSES

IRAQ

"Iraqi Tourism Board"

IRLANDA

(1) Incluidos los turistas procedentes de Irlanda del Norte; (2) Incluye ferrocarril; (3) Excluidos los hostales; (4) Hoteles únicamente.
"Fáilte Ireland" – http://www.failteireland.ie/Home

ISLANDIA

(1) Turistas no residentes alojados en todo tipo de establecimientos de alojamiento; (2) Llegadas de turistas no residentes a las fronteras islandesas. Fuente: "Icelandic Tourist Board".
"Hagstofa Íslands Statistics Iceland" – http://www.statice.is/Statistics/Tourism,-transport-and-informati

ISLAS CAIMÁN

(1) Llegadas por vía aérea; (2) Pasajeros en crucero únicamente; (3) Hoteles y apartamentos; (4) Las cifras de gasto corresponden a las facilitadas por el país a la OMT y que, sin embargo, no figuran en los datos del Fondo Monetario Internacional utilizados para la preparación de esta edición del Compendio; (5) Incluidos los gastos de los pasajeros en crucero; (6) Días.
"Cayman Islands Department of Tourism" – http://www.caymanislands.ky/statistics/

ISLAS COOK

(1) Llegadas por vías aérea y marítima; (2) Las cifras de gasto corresponden a las facilitadas por el país a la OMT y que, sin embargo, no figuran en los datos del Fondo Monetario Internacional utilizados para la preparación de esta edición del Compendio; (3) Hoteles y moteles.
"Cook Islands Tourism Corporation" y "Cook Islands Statistics Office" – http://www.stats.gov.ck/Statistics/Tourism/tournav.htm

ISLAS MARIANAS SEPTENTRIONALES

(1) Llegadas por vía aérea; (2) Incluye Guam; (3) Cubre el 68 por ciento del total de habitaciones censadas.
"Marianas Visitors Authority"

ISLAS MARSHALL

(1) 2005,2009: Llegadas por vías aérea y marítima; (2) 2006-2008: Llegadas por vía aérea; (3) Las cifras de gasto corresponden a las facilitadas por el país a la OMT y que, sin embargo, no figuran en los datos del Fondo Monetario Internacional utilizados para la preparación de esta edición del Compendio. Años fiscales (1 octubre - 30 septiembre).
"Marshall Islands Visitors Authority" – http://www.spc.int/prism/country/mh/Stats/index.htm

ISLAS SALOMÓN

(1) 2005: excluido el 1er trimestre.
"Solomon Islands National Statistics Office" –
http://www.spc.int/prism/country/sb/Stats/Migration%20and%20Tourism/Tour-Index.htm

ISLAS TURCAS Y CAICOS

"Turks and Caicos Tourist Board"

ISLAS VÍRGENES AMERICANAS

(1) Turistas no residentes alojados en hoteles y establecimientos asimilados; (2) Llegadas de visitantes por vía aérea; excluidas las llegadas de residentes y el tráfico entre las islas pero incluidos los excursionistas; (3) Pasajeros en crucero; (4) Incluido el turismo interno (cerca del 40% del total); (5) Las cifras de gasto corresponden a las facilitadas por el país a la OMT y que, sin embargo, no figuran en los datos del Fondo Monetario Internacional utilizados para la preparación de esta edición del Compendio; (6) Hoteles y condominios o villas.
2009: Datos provisionales.
"Bureau of Economic Research" – http://www.usviber.org/publications.htm

NOTAS DE LOS PAÍSES

ISLAS VÍRGENES BRITÁNICAS

(1) Las cifras de gasto corresponden a las facilitadas por el país a la OMT y que, sin embargo, no figuran en los datos del Fondo Monetario Internacional utilizados para la preparación de esta edición del Compendio.
"The Development Planning Unit - Ministry of Finance" –
http://dpu.gov.vg/index.php?option=com_content&view=article&id=58&Itemid=68

ISRAEL

(1) Excluidos los nacionales residentes en el extranjero; (2) Incluidas las visitas a familiares y amigos y peregrinaciones; (3) Incluido el personal de la flota de EE.UU. en visita de cortesía; (4) Incluidas las nuevas entradas tras una visita de hasta 7 días en el Sinaí; (5) Hoteles turísticos y apart-hoteles; (6) Incluidos los gastos de los trabajadores extranjeros en Israel (Millones de $EE.UU.): 2005: 847; 2006: 909; 2007: 894; (7) Tasa de ocupación/camas en hoteles y establecimientos asimilados abiertos; (8) Turismo receptor en hoteles turísticos.
"Ministry of Tourism" – http://www1.cbs.gov.il/reader/?MIval=cw_usr_view_SHTML&ID=432

ITALIA

(1) Excluidos los trabajadores estacionales o fronterizos; (2) Encuesta en fronteras de la "Banca d'Italia"; (3) Incluidos los pasajeros en crucero; (4) Hoteles únicamente; (5) Número de turistas residentes (visitantes que pernoctan) que viajan al extranjero; (6) Excluidas las estimaciones sobre alojamiento privado.
"Banca d'Italia" y "Statistiche sul Turismo - Istituto Nazionale di Statistica (ISTAT)"
http://www.bancaditalia.it/statistiche/rapp_estero/altre_stat/turismo-int
http://www.istat.it/dati/dataset/

JAMAHIRIYA ÁRABE LIBIA

(1) Turistas no residentes alojados en hoteles y establecimientos asimilados.
"The General Board of Tourism and Traditional Industries" – http://www.libyan-tourism.org/List.aspx?ID=73

JAMAICA

(1) Llegadas por vía aérea de turistas no residentes; incluidos los nacionales residentes en el extranjero; tarjetas E/D; (2) Pasajeros en crucero únicamente; (3) Nueva seri; incluidos los nacionales residentes en el extranjero; (4) Duración de estancia prevista; (5) Gasto de turistas no residentes por vía aérea; excluidos los nacionales residentes en el extranjero; (6) Pernoctaciones en los hoteles únicamente.
"Jamaica Tourist Board" – http://www.jtbonline.org/statistics/Annual%20Travel/Forms/AllItems.aspx

JAPÓN

(1) Excluidos los nacionales residentes en el extranjero; (2) Llegadas de visitantes no residentes en las fronteras nacionales; incluidos los residentes extranjeros en Japón; (3) El método de cálculo ha sido cambiado desde enero de 2006; (4) Hoteles homologados y no homologados así como "ryokans" (posadas); (5) Tasa de ocupación de los principales hoteles gubernamentales homologados.
"Japan National Tourism Organization" - http://www.tourism.jp/english/statistics/index.php

JORDANIA

(1) Incluidos los nacionales residentes en el extranjero; (2) Llegadas de visitantes residentes y no residentes; (3) Para visitas organizadas únicamente.
"Ministry of Tourism and Antiquities" – http://www.tourism.jo/GuestBook/Statistics.asp

KAZAJSTÁN

"Agency of Statistics of the Republic of Kazakhstan" – http://www.eng.stat.kz/digital/Tourism/Pages/default.aspx

KENYA

(1) Llegadas de visitantes no residentes a través de todos los puestos fronterizos; excluidos los nacionales residentes en el extranjero; (2) Días.
"Kenya Tourist Board"

KIRGUISTÁN

(1) Fuente de información: Departamento de Control Aduanero.
"National Statistical Committee"

NOTAS DE LOS PAÍSES

KIRIBATI

(1) Llegadas por vía aérea. Tarawa e Isla Christmas; (2) 2006: Tarawa únicamente.
"Kiribati National Tourism Office, Ministry of Communication, Transport and Tourism Development" –
http://www.spc.int/prism/Country/KI/Stats/Tourism/tourism-index.htm

KUWAIT

(1) Turistas no residentes alojados en hoteles y establecimientos asimilados.
"Central Statistical Office" – http://mopweb4.mop.gov.kw/

LESOTHO

"Lesotho Tourism Development Corporation" – http://www.ltdc.org.ls/researchArrivalStats.php

LETONIA

(1) Llegadas de visitantes no residentes en las fronteras nacionales. Datos procedentes de la Policía Estatal de Fronteras; (2) Salidas de no residentes. Encuesta realizada en los puestos fronterizos del país; (3) Incluidas las visitas a parientes y amigos y tratamientos de salud; (4) Pernoctaciones en todos los establecimientos de alojamiento colectivo; (5) Fuente: encuesta en las fronteras; (6) Fuente: encuesta de hogares; (7) Datos procedentes de la Policía Estatal de Fronteras.
"Transport and Tourism Statistics Section - Central Statistical Bureau" – http://www.csb.gov.lv/csp/content/?lng=en&cat=355

LÍBANO

(1) Excluidos nacionales de Siria, Palestina y estudiantes.
"Ministère du Tourisme" – http://www.lebanon-tourism.gov.lb/Ministry/Statistics.aspx

LIECHTENSTEIN

(1) Turistas no residentes alojados en hoteles y establecimientos asimilados.
"Liechtenstein Tourismus" –
http://www.llv.li/amtstellen/llv_avw_statistik/llv_avw_statistik_amtsgeschaefte/llv-avw-statistik-tourismus.htm

LITUANIA

(1) 2007: Datos de la encuesta estadística sobre la afluencia de visitantes que cruzaron puestos fronterizos; (2) 2007: La bajada en el número de turistas se debe a la disminución del flujo de turistas desde Belarús y la Federación de Rusia; (3) Turistas no residentes alojados en todo tipo de establecimientos de alojamiento; (4) Hoteles y moteles; (5) Hoteles, moteles y restaurantes.
"Lithuanian State Department of Tourism" –
http://www.stat.gov.lt/en/pages/view/?id=1638&PHPSESSID=0522a6cef6b6d204b72ec646d272a81f

LUXEMBURGO

(1) Turistas no residentes alojados en todo tipo de establecimientos de alojamiento; incluye albergues de juventud, alojamientos turísticos privados y otros; (2) Incluidos los alojamientos turísticos privados y otros; (3) Hoteles, albergues y casas de huéspedes.
"Office National du Tourisme" y "STATEC" – http://www.statistiques.public.lu/fr/publications/series/bulletinStatec/index.html

MACAO (CHINA)

(1) 2008: Según el Servicio de Estadísticas y Censos, a partir de 2008, las cifras de llegadas de visitantes no incluirán "otros no residentes" como trabajadores, estudiantes, etc; (2) Incluidas las personas de origen étnico chino procedentes de "Hong Kong, China"; (3) Incluidas las llegadas en helicóptero; (4) Viajes organizados; (5) Hoteles y casas de huéspedes.
"Macau Statistics and Census Service" y "Macau Government Tourist Office" –
http://www.dsec.gov.mo/Statistic/TourismAndServices/VisitorArrivals.aspx
http://industry.macautourism.gov.mo/en/index.php

MADAGASCAR

(1) Llegadas de turistas no residentes por vía aérea.
"Ministère des Transports et du Tourisme"

NOTAS DE LOS PAÍSES

MALASIA

(1) Incluidos los residentes de Singapur que cruzan la frontera por la Johore Causeway; (2/2005/2006) (4) Península de Malasia únicamente; (3) 2008: Cifras estimadas; (5) Encuesta de turismo interno; (6) Hoteles con 10 habitaciones y más; (7) Encuesta en hoteles; (8) Encuesta anual de servicios; (9) Servicios de agencias de viajes y operadores turísticos únicamente.
"Department of Statistics Malaysia" y "Tourism Malaysia" –
http://www.tourism.gov.my/corporate/research.asp?page=facts_figures

MALAWI

(1) Salidas; (2) Fuente: "Reserve Bank of Malawi".
"Ministry of Information and Tourism"

MALDIVAS

(1) Llegadas por vía aérea; (2) Días.
"Ministry of Tourism" – http://www.tourism.gov.mv/stat.php?statId=3

MALÍ

(1) Turistas no residentes alojados en hoteles y establecimientos asimilados.
"Office malien du tourisme et de l'hôtellerie (O.MA.T.HO)"

MALTA

(1) (2/2007-2009) Salidas de turistas por vías aérea y marítima; (3/2005/2006) Salidas de turistas por vía aérea.
"Malta Tourism Authority" y "National Statistics Office" –
http://www.maltatourismauthority.com/page.aspx?id=105
http://www.nso.gov.mt/site/page.aspx?pageid=27

MARRUECOS

(1) Incluidos los nacionales residentes en el extranjero; (2) Hoteles homologados, ciudades de vacaciones, residencias turísticas y Riad; (3) Turistas extranjeros.
"Ministère du tourisme" – http://www.tourisme.gov.ma/francais/5-Tourisme-chiffres/ArriveeTouristes.htm

MARTINICA

(1) Las cifras de gasto corresponden a las facilitadas por el país a la OMT y que, sin embargo, no figuran en los datos del Fondo Monetario Internacional utilizados para la preparación de esta edición del Compendio; (2) Hoteles y ciudades de vacaciones ("Club Méditerranée").
"Comité Martiniquais du Tourisme" – http://www.martiniquetourisme.com/martinique/Le-C.M.T/Les-donnees-sur-le-tourisme

MAURICIO

(1) Grandes hoteles.
"Ministry of Tourism and Leisure" –
http://www.gov.mu/portal/site/cso/menuitem.dee225f644ffe2aa338852f8a0208a0c/?content_id=52160fa67278c010VgnVCM100
0000a04a8c0RCRD

MÉXICO

(1) Incluidos los nacionales residentes en el extranjero; (2) Incluidos los visitantes de la franja fronteriza con los Estados Unidos y estancia inferior a 24h; (3) Japón y República de Corea únicamente; (4) Incluye ferrocarril; (5) Hoteles únicamente; (6) Centros turísticos seleccionados; (7) Turismo extranjero únicamente; (8) La informacón no corresponde propiamente a empleo sino a puestos de trabajo equivalentes remunerados necesarios para realizar la producción de los bienes y servicios relacionados con actividades turísticas.
Secretaría de Turismo de México (SECTUR) e Instituto Nacional de Estadística y Geografía (INEGI) –
http://www.gob.mx/wb/egobierno/egob_Estadisticas_del_sector_turismo
http://www.inegi.org.mx/prod_serv/contenidos/espanol/biblioteca/Default.asp?accion=1&upc=702825224585

MICRONESIA (ESTADOS FEDERADOS DE)

(1) Llegadas en los Estados de Kosrae, Chuuk, Pohnpei y Yap; excluidos los ciudadanos de EFM; (2) Las cifras de gasto corresponden a las facilitadas por el país a la OMT y que, sin embargo, no figuran en los datos del Fondo Monetario Internacional utilizados para la preparación de esta edición del Compendio. Años fiscales (1 octubre - 30 septiembre).
"Department of Economic Affairs" – http://www.spc.int/prism/country/fm/stats/index.htm

NOTAS DE LOS PAÍSES

MÓNACO

(1) Turistas no residentes alojados en hoteles y establecimientos asimilados.
"Direction du Tourisme et des Congrès" –
http://www.monaco.gouv.mc/devwww/wwwnew.nsf/1909$/b9d7989a41d6c875c1256f820057b766fr?OpenDocument&7Fr

MONGOLIA

(1) Excluidos los diplomáticos y extranjeros residentes en Mongolia.
"National Tourism Center - Ministry of Nature, Environment and Tourism" – http://mongoliatourism.gov.mn/

MONTENEGRO

(1) Turistas no residentes alojados en todo tipo de establecimientos de alojamiento.
"Ministry of Sustainable Development and Tourism" – http://www.monstat.org/EngMeniGodisnjiPodaci.htm

MONTSERRAT

"Statistics Department Montserrat"

MOZAMBIQUE

(1) Nota 2008: Cambio de metodología. Hasta 2007 los datos corresponden únicamente a 12 puestos fronterizos. A partir de 2008 se utilizan los datos de todos los puestos fronterizos del país.
"Ministry of Tourism" y "Instituto Nacional de Estatística" – http://www.ine.gov.mz/sectorias_dir/turismo/

MYANMAR

(1) Incluidas las llegadas de turistas a través de los puntos de entrada fronterizos a Yangon; (2) Hoteles y establecimientos asimilados administrados por el Estado únicamente; (3) Hoteles administrados por el Estado y casas de huéspedes privadas homologadas.
"Ministry of Hotels and Tourism"

NAMIBIA

"Ministry of Environment and Tourism" – http://www.namibiatourism.com.na/trade_cat_sub.php?sub_cat_id=32

NEPAL

(1) Incluidas las llegadas procedentes de la India; (2) Días; (3) Hoteles en Katmandú y en el interior del país; 2006-2008: excluidos los hoteles en proceso de construcción.
"Nepal Tourism Board" y "Ministry of Culture, Tourism and Civil Aviation" – http://www.tourism.gov.np/tourismstatistics.php

NICARAGUA

(1) Incluidos los nacionales residentes en el extranjero; (2) Total de establecimientos del país; (3) Principales establecimientos de alojamiento del país (7); (4) 2006-2009: Estimaciones preliminares; (5) Hoteles y establecimientos asimilados ubicados en categorías superiores; (6) Todo tipo de establecimientos de alojamiento, turismo receptor.
Instituto Nicaragüense de Turismo (INTUR) – http://www.intur.gob.ni/estadisticas.php

NÍGER

(1) Días.
"Ministère du Tourisme et de l'Artisanat"

NIGERIA

"Nigerian Tourism Development Corporation"

NIUE

(1) Incluidos los nacionales de Niue que residen normalmente en Nueva Zelandia.
"Statistics Niue" – http://www.spc.int/prism/country/nu/stats/Migration/Migration_index.htm

NOTAS DE LOS PAÍSES

NORUEGA

(1) Las cifras se basan en "The Guest Survey", un estudio realizado por el "Institute of Transport Economics"; (2) Estados Unidos únicamente; (3) Japón únicamente; (4) Pernoctaciones en establecimientos homologados; (5) Las cifras para hoteles y establecimientos asimilados se refieren a establecimientos con 20 camas o más durante todo el año; (6) Viajes por vacaciones.
"Statistics Norway" y "Institute of Transport Economics" – http://www.ssb.no/english/subjects/

NUEVA CALEDONIA

(1) Incluidos los nacionales residentes en el extranjero; (2) Hoteles en Noumea únicamente; (3) Residentes que regresan; (4) Habitaciones en Noumea; (5) Días, hoteles en Noumea.
"Institut de la Statistique et des Études Économiques (ISEE)" – http://www.isee.nc/

NUEVA ZELANDIA

(1) Viajes internacionales y Migración, SNZ; (2) Encuesta de alojamiento, SNZ; (3) Encuesta de visitantes internacionales; MED; (4) Encuesta de viajes nacionales, MED; (5) Estadística de negocios, SNZ; (6) Incluye hoteles, moteles y mochileros, pero excluye los parques de vacaciones.
"Statistics New Zealand (SNZ)" y "Ministry of Economic Development (MED)" – http://www.stats.govt.nz/

OMÁN

"Ministry of National Economy and Ministry of Commerce and Industry" y "Directorate General of Tourism - Ministry of Tourism"
http://www.moneoman.gov.om

PAÍSES BAJOS

(1) Turistas no residentes alojados en todo tipo de establecimientos de alojamiento; (2) Hoteles y pensiones; (3) Salidas de nacionales por vacaciones; (4) Hoteles; (5) Todo tipo de establecimientos de alojamiento.
"Statistics Netherlands" – http://www.cbs.nl/en-GB/menu/themas/vrije-tijd-cultuur/nieuws/default.htm

PAKISTÁN

(1) Días.
"Pakistan Tourism Development Corporation - Ministry of Tourism" – http://www.pakistantourism.gov.pk/downloads.php

PALAU

(1) Llegadas por vía aérea (aeropuerto internacional de Palau); (2) Las cifras de gasto corresponden a las facilitadas por el país a la OMT y que, sin embargo, no figuran en los datos del Fondo Monetario Internacional utilizados para la preparación de esta edición del Compendio. Años fiscales.
"Office of Planning and Statistics, Bureau of Budget and Planning - Ministry of Finance" –
http://www.palaugov.net/stats/PalauStats/Tourism/tourism.htm
http://www.visit-palau.com/publication/index.cfm

PALESTINA

(1) Turistas no residentes alojados en hotels; (2) Hoteles únicamente; (3) Cisjordania y Gaza.
"Palestinian Central Bureau of Statistics" – http://www.pcbs.gov.ps/DesktopDefault.aspx?tabID=3039&lang=en

PANAMÁ

(1) Llegadas de visitantes no residentes: Aeropuerto Internacional Tocúmen (AIT), frontera de Paso Canoa (FPC) y puertos de Cristóbal y Balboa (PCB); (2) Llegadas de visitantes no residentes, AIT; (3) Llegadas de turistas no residentes, AIT; (4) Hoteles de la Ciudad de Panamá; (5) Habitaciones/ plazas cama inventariadas para turismo internacional.
Instituto Panameño de Turismo –
http://www.atp.gob.pa/index.php?option=com_content&view=category&layout=blog&id=44&Itemid=64

PAPUA NUEVA GUINEA

"Papua New Guinea Tourism Promotion Authority"

PARAGUAY

(1) Tarjetas E/D en el aeropuerto Silvio Petirossi y planillas de pasajeros en los puestos terrestres - Policía Nacional y SENATUR; (2) Excluidos los nacionales residentes en el extranjero y miembros de tripulación; (3) 2009: Encuesta de turismo receptor marzo, 2008 - marzo 2009; (4) Vía fluvial; (5) Encuesta permanente de hogares 2008.
Secretaría Nacional de Turismo - SENATUR – http://www.senatur.gov.py/estadisticas.php?language=1

NOTAS DE LOS PAÍSES

PERÚ

(1) Incluidos los nacionales residentes en el extranjero; (2) Pasajeros en crucero que pernoctan; (3) Incluye las llegadas por vía fluvial y lacustre; (4) Los datos proceden de la "Encuesta Nacional de Viajes de los Residentes 2007-2008".
Nota 2005-2009: Datos preliminares.
Dirección General de Migraciones y Naturalización (DIGEMIN) y Ministerio de Comercio Exterior y Turismo (MINCETUR)
http://www.mincetur.gob.pe/newweb/Default.aspx?tabid=141

POLINESIA FRANCESA

(1) Llegadas por vía aérea únicamente; excluidos los nacionales residentes en el extranjero; (2) Días; (3) Hoteles y casas de huéspedes; al 31 de diciembre de cada año; (4) Habitaciones en hoteles.
"Service du Tourisme" – http://www.ispf.pf/ISPF/Chiffres/Tourisme.aspx – http://www.tourisme.gov.pf/7671-Les-statistiques.html
http://www.tahiti-tourisme.com/Partners/

POLONIA

(1) 2008 y 2009: Dado que Polonia se unió al espacio Schengen, el recuento preciso de tráfico entrante no es posible. Los datos presentados aquí se basan en encuestas realizadas por el Instituto de Turismo. Para este año únicamente se pueden dar resultados aproximados; (2) Según encuestas del Instituto de Turismo; (3) Datos de la Oficina central de estadística; (4) Establecimientos de alojamiento colectivo y privado, según encuestas del Instituto de Turismo; (5) Viajes de 4 noches y más; (6) Viajes de turismo emisor registrados en las fronteras.
"Institute of Tourism" – http://www.intur.com.pl/itenglish/institute_en.htm

PORTUGAL

(1) Debido a un cambio de metodología, a partir de 2004 los datos no son comparables con los años anteriores. Incluidos los nacionales residentes en el extranjero; (2) Datos monetarios de empresas; (3) Tasa de ocupación neta; (4) Todo tipo de establecimientos de alojamiento; (5) Datos de la Cuenta Satélite de Turismo (CST).
"Turismo de Portugal, I.P." – http://www.ine.pt/xportal/xmain?xpid=INE&xpgid=ine_princindic&contexto=pi&selTab=tab0

PUERTO RICO

(1) Llegadas de turistas no residentes por vía aérea; (2) Únicamente Islas Vírgenes Americanas y Estados Unidos; (3) Incluye residentes y no residentes; (4) Las cifras de gasto corresponden a las facilitadas por el país a la OMT y que, sin embargo, no figuran en los datos del Fondo Monetario Internacional utilizados para la preparación de esta edición del Compendio; (5) Habitaciones endosadas por la Compañía de Turismo de Puerto Rico; (6) Incluidas las habitaciones ocupadas por residentes de Puerto Rico.
Datos: Años fiscales (julio-junio).
Junta de Planificación de Puerto Rico y Compañía de Turismo de Puerto Rico – http://www.jp.gobierno.pr/

QATAR

(1) Hoteles únicamente; (2) Fuente: "Qatar Central Bank".
"The Planning Council - Statistics Department" y "Qatar Tourism Authority" –
http://www.qsa.gov.qa/Eng/GeneralStatistics.htm
http://www.qcb.gov.qa/English/Publications/ReportsAndStatements/Pages/AnnualReports.aspx

REINO UNIDO

(1) Túnel; (2) Encuesta internacional de pasajeros; Fuente: "Office for National Statistics"; (3) Días; (4) Fuente: "EUROSTAT (New Cronos)"; (5) Inglaterra únicamente.
"VisitBritain" – http://www.visitbritain.org/insightsandstatistics/keystats/index.aspx
http://www.statistics.gov.uk/statbase/Product.asp?vlnk=1905&More=N

REPÚBLICA ÁRABE SIRIA

(1) Incluidos los nacionales residentes en el extranjero; (2) Turistas no residentes alojados en todo tipo de establecimientos de alojamiento; (3) 2009: Excluidos los nacionales residentes en el extranjero.
Nota: Los nacionales de Iraq se incluyen únicamente a partir de 2008 y se han excluido en los años anteriores (desde principios de 2008, tienen que pedir un visado para entrar en Siria; si entraron anteriormente a esa fecha, se considera que han permanecido por un periodo superior a un año, convirtiéndose en residentes).
"Ministry of Tourism" - Encuesta del turismo receptor en 2004, 2006 y 2007

REPÚBLICA CENTROAFRICANA

(1) Llegadas por vía aérea a Bangui únicamente; (2) Datos del país.
Nota 2006: Estimaciones.
"Ministère du Développement du Tourisme et de l'Artisanat"

NOTAS DE LOS PAÍSES

REPÚBLICA CHECA

(1) Turistas no residentes alojados en todo tipo de establecimientos de alojamiento; (2) Hoteles y restaurantes; (3) Utilización neta de camas; (4) Actividades de apoyo y transporte auxiliar, actividades de agencias de viajes y operadores turísticos.
"Czech Statistical Office, TSA" – http://www.czso.cz/eng/redakce.nsf/i/home

REPÚBLICA DE MOLDOVA

(1) Visitantes que se beneficiaron de los servicios turísticos de las agencias de turismo y operadores turísticos (titulares de licencias turísticas).
Nota: Excluido el margen izquierdo del río Nistru y la municipalidad de Bender.
"National Bureau of Statistics" – http://www.statistica.md/category.php?l=en&idc=293&

REPÚBLICA DEMOCRÁTICA DEL CONGO

(1) 2007-2009: Llegadas por vía aérea únicamente.
"Office National du Tourisme"

REPÚBLICA DEMOCRÁTICA POPULAR LAO

(1) Días.
"Lao National Tourism Administration" – http://www.nsc.gov.la/Selected_Statistics.htm

REPÚBLICA DOMINICANA

(1) Incluidos los nacionales residentes en el extranjero; (2) Llegadas por vía aérea únicamente; (3) Todas las llegadas por mar; (4) Hoteles; (5) 2009: datos del país.
Secretaría de Estado de Turismo – http://www.bancentral.gov.do/estadisticas.asp?a=Sector_Turismo

REPÚBLICA UNIDA DE TANZANÍA

"Tourism Division - Ministry of Natural Resources and Tourism" y "National Bureau of Statistics" – http://www.mnrt.go.tz/index.php/documents-a-publications/category/8-tourism

REUNIÓN

(1) Llegadas por vía aérea únicamente; (2) Fuente: INSEE, encuesta de flujos turísticos; (3) Fuente: INSEE, encuesta de ocupación hotelera; (4) Se trata del conjunto de pernoctaciones en los hoteles clasificados. Residentes y no residentes; (5) Las cifras de gasto corresponden a las facilitadas por el país a la OMT y que, sin embargo, no figuran en los datos del Fondo Monetario Internacional utilizados para la preparación de esta edición del Compendio; (6) Fuente: INSEE Clap. Se trata del conjunto de establecimientos de las nomenclaturas seleccionadas. No se conoce con certeza el destino real de la actividad (turístico o no); (7) Se trata del conjunto de establecimientos/ habitaciones/ camas disponibles diariamente en los hoteles clasificados; (8) Fuente: INSEE Clap. Se trata del conjunto de empleos de las nomenclaturas seleccionadas. No se conoce con certeza el destino real de la actividad (turístico o no).
"Institut National de la Statistique et des Études Économique - INSEE" y "Comité du Tourisme de la Réunion" – http://webpro.la-reunion-tourisme.com/connaitre2.php3?id_rubrique=71
http://www.insee.fr/fr/themes/theme.asp?theme=13&nivgeo=24

RUMANÍA

(1) Solo los viajes internos por motivo de vacaciones (incluidas las visitas a amigos y familiares) y de negocios; (2) La categoría «otro motivo personal» se refiere solo a los viajes para visitar a amigos y familiares; (3) A partir de 2005, las categorías «aire» y «vías de navegación» se incluyen en la categoría «otros»; (4) Calculado dividiendo el número de pernoctaciones por el número de viajes. Fuente: ACTR, encuesta de hogares; (5) Solo por motivo de vacaciones (incluidas visitas a amigos y familiares) y de negocios. Las cifras se compilan dividiendo el gasto por el número de pernoctaciones; (6) Para el conjunto del sector del alojamiento, precios corrientes; (7) A 31 de julio, solo para establecimientos autorizados; (8) El indicador consiste en el número de turistas que compran servicios combinados/ individuales. Debe tenerse en cuenta que los valores incluyen tanto a operadores turísticos como a las clásicas agencias de viajes; (9) El indicador está representado en realidad por el «número medio de asalariados » y la fuente consiste en las estadísticas estructurales de las empresas que se compilan cada año; (10) Incluye también el transporte de carga; (11) Esta categoría no concuerda exactamente con las categorías de las industrias turísticas debido al alto nivel de agregación de la publicación. Incluye también actividades de agencias de prensa y servicios de bibliotecas y archivos. En cambio, excluye las actividades de los gimnasios y el alquiler de bienes recreativos.
"National Institute of Statistics" – https://statistici.insse.ro/shop/index.jsp?page=tempo2&lang=en&context=63

RWANDA

"Office rwandais du tourisme et des parcs nationaux (ORTPN)" – http://rwandatourism.com/arrivalstats.htm

NOTAS DE LOS PAÍSES

SABA

(1) Principalmente desde San Martín.
"Saba Tourist Bureau", "Caribbean Tourism Organization" y "Central Bank of the Netherlands Antilles" –
http://www.centralbank.an/tables/tables/main-10-6.htm

SAINT KITTS Y NEVIS

(1) Llegadas de turistas no residentes por vía aérea; (2) Llegadas en yates y cruceros.
"Eastern Caribbean Central Bank" – http://www.eccb-centralbank.org/Statistics/index.asp#tourismdata

SAMOA

"Samoa Tourism Authority" y "Statistical Services Division (Ministry of Finance)" –
http://www.sbs.gov.ws/
http://www.mof.gov.ws/publish/economicreview.shtml

SAMOA AMERICANA

(1) Incluye Samoa Occidental; (2) Visitas a parientes, amigos.
"American Samoa Government - Department of Commerce - Statistics Division" - http://www.spc.int/prism/country/as/stats/

SAN EUSTAQUIO

(1) Excluidos los residentes de las Antillas Neerlandesas.
"Central Bank of the Netherlands Antilles" – http://www.centralbank.an/tables/tables/main-10-7.htm

SAN MARINO

(1) Incluidos los visitantes italianos; (2) Turistas no residentes alojados en hoteles y establecimientos asimilados; incluidos los turistas italianos; (3) Hoteles únicamente.
Nota: Nueva metodología a partir de 2005.
"Segreteria di Stato per il Turismo, lo Sport, le Telecomunicazioni, i Trasporti e la Cooperazione Economica" –
http://www.statistica.sm/on-line/Home/DatiStatistici/docCat.14000570.1.10.1.html?Categoria=Afflusso turistico

SAN MARTÍN

(1) Por vía aérea; incluidas las llegadas a San Martín (parte francesa de la isla); (2) Llegadas al aeropuerto "Juliana" (incluidos los visitantes con destino a San Martín (parte francesa); (3) Incluidas las estimaciones para Saba y San Eustaquio. Fuente: "Central Bank of the Netherlands Antilles".
"St. Maarten Tourist Bureau" – http://www.centralbank.an/tables/tables/main-10-5.htm

SAN VICENTE Y LAS GRANADINAS

(1) Llegadas de turistas no residentes por vía aérea; (2) Incluidos los pasajeros en crucero y en yate; (3) Hoteles, apartamentos, bungalows, villas y casas de huéspedes.
"Ministry of Tourism and Culture" – http://www.discoversvg.com/index.php/es/about-svg/tourism-statistics

SANTA LUCÍA

(1) Excluidos los nacionales residentes en el extranjero; (2) Excluidas las llegadas de pasajeros en yate.
"Saint Lucia Tourist Board" – http://www.stlucia.gov.lc/

SANTO TOMÉ Y PRÍNCIPE

(1) Días.
"Direcçao do Turismo e Hotelaria" – http://www.smfstp.st/estatisticas

SENEGAL

(1) Hoteles y ciudades de vacaciones.
"Ministère du Tourisme et des Transports Aériens"

SERBIA

(1) Turistas no residentes alojados en todo tipo de establecimientos de alojamiento; (2) 5.2+5.3+5.4.
"Statistical Office of the Republic of Serbia" – http://webrzs.stat.gov.rs/axd/en/drugastrana.php?Sifra=0008&izbor=tabela

NOTAS DE LOS PAÍSES

SEYCHELLES

(1) Pernoctaciones basadas en las salidas; (2) Hoteles y casas de huéspedes.
"National Statistics Bureau" – http://www.nsb.gov.sc/

SIERRA LEONA

(1) Llegadas por vía aérea; (2) Hoteles únicamente.
"National Tourist Board"

SINGAPUR

(1) Excluidas las llegadas de ciudadanos malasios por vía terrestre; (2) Días; (3) Hoteles (homologados y no homologados); (4) Hoteles homologados únicamente.
"Singapore Tourism Board" – http://www.singstat.gov.sg/stats/themes/economy/tourism.html

SRI LANKA

(1) Excluidos los nacionales residentes en el extranjero; (2) Hoteles, moteles, albergues, casas de huéspedes y aparthoteles.
"Sri Lanka Tourist Board" – http://www.sltda.lk/statistics

SUDÁFRICA

(1) Excluidos los nacionales residentes en el extranjero. Incluidas las llegadas por motivo de vacaciones, negocios, estudios, trabajo, tránsito, tráfico fronterizo y trabajadores con contrato; (2) Excluidas las llegadas por trabajo y los trabajadores con contrato; (3) Las cifras de 2005-2008 se basan en la encuesta de "Alojamiento turístico" y no son comparables con las cifras de la encuesta sobre "Hoteles: estadísticas comerciales". Las cifras de 2005-2007 se han revisado debido al cálculo retrospectivo basado en la muestra de 2008 para la encuesta de "Alojamiento turístico"; (4) Hoteles; (5) Datos de la Cuenta Satélite de Turismo (CST).
"Statistics South Africa" y "South African Tourism" – http://www.statssa.gov.za/default.asp

SUDÁN

(1) Incluidos los nacionales residentes en el extranjero; (2) El país facilita a la OMT niveles agregados de gasto que son significativamente diferentes a los datos del Fondo Monetario Internacional utilizados para la preparación de esta edición del Compendio. Los datos del país son (Mill. $EE.UU.): 2005: 316; 2006: 409; 2007: 428; 2008: 548; 2009: 522.
"Ministry of Tourism and Wildlife"

SUECIA

(1) Turistas no residentes alojados en todo tipo de establecimientos de alojamiento; incluido camping; (2) Hoteles únicamente; (3) Número de puestos de trabajo equivalentes a tiempo completo; (4) Total 5.2, 5.3 y 5.4.
"Tillväxtverket - The Swedish Agency for Economic and Regional Growth" –
http://www.tillvaxtverket.se/english
http://www.scb.se/Pages/Product_____11830.aspx

SUIZA

(1) Hoteles y establecimientos de cura; (2) Establecimientos encuestados; (3) Habitaciones encuestadas; (4) Plazas-cama encuestadas; (5) Tasa neta de ocupación; (6) Empleos equivalentes a tiempo completo.
"Swiss Federal Statistical Office" – http://www.bfs.admin.ch/bfs/portal/fr/index/themen/10.html

SURINAME

(1) Llegadas al aeropuerto de Zanderij; (2) Llegadas al puerto Nw. Nickerie.
"Suriname Tourism Foundation"

SWAZILANDIA

"Swaziland Tourism Authority" y "Ministry of Tourism, Environment and Communications"

TAILANDIA

(1) 2006-2009, (2) Excluidas las llegadas de nacionales residentes en el extranjero; (3) Incluye ferrocarril; (4) Días.
"Ministry of Tourism and Sports" – http://www.tourism.go.th/2009/en/statistic/tourism.php?cid=26

NOTAS DE LOS PAÍSES

TAIWÁN (PROVINCIA DE CHINA)

(1) Incluidos los nacionales residentes en el extranjero.
"Planning Division Tourism Bureau - Ministry of Transportation and Communication" –
http://admin.taiwan.net.tw/english/statistics/release.asp?relno=6

TAYIKISTÁN

"Committee of Youth Affairs, Sports and Tourism under the Government of the Republic of Tajikistan"

TIMOR-LESTE

(1) Llegadas por vía aérea al Aeropuerto de Dili; (2) 2007 incluye únicamente los datos de 10 meses; (3) Encuesta en hoteles (20 habitaciones o más); (4) Fuente: BPA - Autoridad bancaria y de pagos.
"Direcçao Nacional de Estatística" – http://dne.mof.gov.tl/publications/index.htm

TOGO

(1) Turistas no residentes alojados en hoteles y establecimientos asimilados; (2) Desde 2009 se aplicó una nueva metodología y cobertura y por lo tanto la información no es comparable con años anteriores.
"Ministère de l'Environnement, du Tourisme et des Ressources Forestières"

TONGA

(1) Llegadas por vía aérea.
"Tonga Visitors Bureau"

TRINIDAD Y TABAGO

(1) Llegadas por vía aérea; (2) Incluidas las visitas a familiares y amigos.
Nota 2009: estimaciones.
"Central Statistical Office - Ministry of Planning and Development" – http://www.tdc.co.tt/stopover_statistics.htm

TÚNEZ

(1) Excluidos los nacionales residentes en el extranjero; (2) Hoteles homologados y no homologados, pensiones y ciudades de vacaciones.
"Ministère du Tourisme - Office National du Tourisme" y "Institut National de la Statistique" –
http://www.ins.nat.tn/indexfr.php

TURKMENISTÁN

"State Committee for Tourism and Sport"

TURQUÍA

(1) Llegadas por mar (excluida una frontera terrestre desde 1989); (2) Salidas de visitantes no residentes; Fuente: "Departing Visitors Survey - Turkish Statistical Institute (TURKSTAT)"; (3) Incluidos los pasajeros en crucero; (4) Encuesta en establecimientos de alojamiento homologados por el Ministerio de Turismo; (5) Incluidos los terrenos de camping; (6) Incluidos los gastos de los nacionales residentes en el extranjero; (7) Hoteles homologados, excluidos los terrenos de camping.
"Ministry of Culture and Tourism" –
http://www.kulturturizm.gov.tr/TR/Genel/BelgeGoster.aspx?F6E10F8892433CFF657B96472CD892038020F3B0746F34B3
http://www.turkstat.gov.tr/PreTablo.do?tb_id=51&ust_id=14

TUVALU

"Central Statistics Division - Ministry of Finance, Economic Planning and Industry" –
http://www.spc.int/prism/Country/TV/Stats/Tourism_migration/tour_index.htm

UCRANIA

"State Statistics Committee of Ukraine" – http://www.ukrstat.gov.ua/operativ/operativ2007/tyr/tyr_e/arh_vig_e.html

UGANDA

"Ministry of Tourism, Trade and Industry" y "Uganda Bureau of Statistics" –
http://www.ubos.org/?st=pagerelations2&id=19&p=related%20pages%202:Migration%20and%20Tourism%20Statistics
http://www.mtti.go.ug/index.php?option=com_content&view=article&id=117&Itemid=131

NOTAS DE LOS PAÍSES

URUGUAY

(1) Incluye ferrocarril; (2) Días; (3) 2005-2007: Excluidos los hoteles sin homologar; (4) Servicios inmobiliarios.
Ministerio de Turismo y Deporte - http://www.mintur.gub.uy

UZBEKISTÁN

(1) Las cifras de gasto corresponden a las facilitadas por el país a la OMT y que, sin embargo, no figuran en los datos del Fondo Monetario Internacional utilizados para la preparación de esta edición del Compendio.
"National Company "Uzbektourism".

VANUATU

(1) A partir de Noviembre de 2006, se incluyen las llegadas a Luganville; (2) Días.
"Vanuatu National Statistics Office" – http://www.spc.int/prism/country/vu/Stats/Tourism/tourism-index.htm

VENEZUELA

(1) 2005-2009: Hoteles únicamente.
Ministerio del Poder Popular para el Turismo – http://www.mintur.gob.ve/contenido.php?id=215

VIET NAM

(1) Incluidos los nacionales residentes en el extranjero; (2) Incluidas las llegadas de pasajeros en crucero y por vía marítima; (3) Las cifras de gasto corresponden a las facilitadas por el país a la OMT y que, sin embargo, no figuran en los datos del Fondo Monetario Internacional utilizados para la preparación de esta edición del Compendio.
"Viet Nam National Administration of Tourism" y "General Statistics Office" –
http://www.vietnamtourism.com/e_pages/news/index.asp?loai=1&chucnang=07

YEMEN

"Ministry of Tourism" y "Central Statistical Organization" –
http://www.yementourism.com/statistics/
http://www.cso-yemen.org/content.php?lng=english&pcat=131

ZAMBIA

(1) Días.
"Ministry of Tourism, Environment and Natural Resources"

ZIMBABWE

(1) Las cifras de gasto corresponden a las facilitadas por el país a la OMT y que, sin embargo, no figuran en los datos del Fondo Monetario Internacional utilizados para la preparación de esta edición del Compendio; (2) Sobre la base de las llegadas en los parques nacionales; (3) 2006-2008: Proyecciones; (4) Sólo hoteles clasificados; (5) Datos del país; (6) Estimaciones.
"Zimbabwe Tourism Authority – ZTA" –
http://www.aitbase.co.zw/zta/index.php?option=com_docman&task=cat_view&gid=105&Itemid=183

ALBANIA

Transportation

Passenger. To obtain data for sea, air, and other kinds of transport, the BOA uses bank reports.

Travel

The main travel category is business and personal, and the subcategories are expenditure by seasonal and border workers, other business; health-related, education-related, and other personal-related expenditure. The BOA compiles credits and debits for this category by combining results from the travel survey (conducted by the BOA and the Institute of Statistics four times a year) with data from the Ministry of Interior on arrivals and departures of Albanians and foreign travelers. The BOA uses the travel survey for estimating the average duration of stay and the average daily expenditures per traveler and by ports. Since the second quarter of 2006, the authorities from the Ministry of Interior have expanded the coverage of border crossing. In addition to the travel survey, the BOA has conducted an ad hoc survey (twice a year) on minor border crossing.

ANGOLA

Services

This category covers the following components: transportation, travel, construction, insurance, royalties and license fees, other business services, and government services not included elsewhere. The information is obtained through the surveys of oil and diamond companies, from various companies rendering services; and also from BNA on the use of budgetary resources and treasury draft orders.

ANGUILLA

See Eastern Caribbean Currency Union.

ANTIGUA AND BARBUDA

See Eastern Caribbean Currency Union.

ARGENTINA

Transportation

INDEC compiles statistics on transportation. For passenger fares, on-board services, and excess baggage charges, it obtains data from surveys of the sea, air, and road passenger transport companies operating in Argentina. Data include both the international operations of resident carriers (credit) and the domestic operations of nonresident carriers (debit).

For passenger road transport, the estimates are based on the number of international trips provided by the companies and on the cost of the tickets. They are also based on surveys conducted monthly of departing and incoming buses to ascertain information on the average occupancy rate of the vehicles and the percentage of resident and nonresident passengers.

Travel

This item is calculated on the basis of the estimated number of passengers entering and departing Argentina, the number of days they stay, and the estimated average expenditure per person. The data are based on the number of people crossing borders provided by Dirección Nacional de Migraciones and a survey conducted at main border crossings.

ARMENIA

Transportation

In addition to the estimates made for the transportation of imported goods referred to above, the BPD gathers additional data from other sources, such as surveys of transportation companies. These surveys collect information on both freight and passenger fares. The BPD derives the estimates from the statistical survey on services conducted in 1999.

Travel

For travel, the BPD collects data from surveys carried out by the NSS.

To estimate the total amount of receipts and payments related to travel, the BPD collects data on the number of foreign arrivals and resident departures, the countries of origin and destination, length of stays, and cost of transportation, hotel, meals, and incidental costs. These estimates include expenditures in Armenia by nonresidents and by Armenians in foreign countries on short-term work assignments (that is, for periods of less than one year). The BPD derives the estimates from the statistical survey on services conducted in 2006–2007. Government ministries and agencies also provide data on expenditures on business trips abroad.

INTERNATIONAL MONETARY FUND (IMF) NOTES

ARUBA

Transportation

The item comprises harbor dues and fees, freight, and passenger fares.

Travel

This item includes receipts from transactions in foreign currency, traveler's checks, and credit cards, as well as goods carried out of Aruba by tourists and paid for in foreign currency, traveler's checks, or credit cards. However, because of the difficulty of obtaining a breakdown of the expenses of resident credit-card holders, the local expenses of these credit-card holders are also included in this item. Steps have been taken to adjust the data on travel for these expenses. In this regard, the CBA is now conducting a factual update of the reported credit-card transactions. The item also includes payments related to medical treatments and expenditures of students abroad.

AUSTRALIA

Transportation

Passenger. Data cover passenger services provided by sea and air. The main source of data is the quarterly ABS Survey of International Trade in Services (SITS). From the September quarter 1993 onward, for confidentiality reasons, the credit series also includes the air transport component of other transportation services, which relates to agency fees and commission receipts. For confidentiality reasons, before the September quarter 1997, the debit series includes cruise fares. From the September quarter 1997 onward, these cruise fares are included in travel debits.

Travel

ABS derives travel credits largely from data collected in the International Visitor Survey conducted by Tourism Research Australia. ABS uses these data in conjunction with results from its monthly overseas arrivals and departures statistics, which it compiles from information collected by the Department of Immigration and Citizenship from arriving and departing international travelers.

Travel credits also include the receipts by domestic airlines from international airlines for the on-carriage, in Australia, of foreign visitors who have purchased tickets abroad. The source is the ABS SITS. Also included is the estimated expenditure of foreign military personnel on rest and recreation in Australia.

ABS compiles information on students' expenditure in Australia from student numbers, provided by the Department of Immigration and Citizenship, and their associated fees and estimated average expenditure on other goods and services sourced from the Survey of International Student Spending, provided by the Department of Employment, Education, and Workplace Relations.

From the September quarter 1995, the ABS has derived travel debits largely from data collected in the National Visitor Survey conducted by Tourism Research Australia. ABS uses these data in conjunction with its monthly overseas arrivals and departures statistics, which are compiled from information collected by the Department of Immigration and Citizenship from arriving and departing international travelers. Prior to the September quarter 1995, benchmark estimates for travel debits were compiled from a periodic household survey of returning Australian travelers. The survey provided a dissection of the average expenditure per travelers by purpose of travel (business and personal), and by income earned abroad and cash taken abroad. Between these surveys, the bureau compiled estimates using data from the SITS, which covered businesses providing travel finance and outbound travel and collected data on prepaid tours, credit card usage, and traveler's checks issued.

AUSTRIA

Transportation

This item covers freight revenues and expenditures, as well as international passenger transport and auxiliary services.

Travel

Travel excludes international passenger transport. One of the most important sources for the credit side of travel is the official statistics on overnight stays and arrivals of nonresident visitors, which is the key indicator of the volume of overnight nonresident visitors to Austria.

Furthermore, studies and sources provided by other institutions are used, e.g., the new Austrian Guest Inquiry "T-Mona," which is an instrument that measures the average daily expenditure of foreign tourists in Austria.

The main source for measuring the expenditure of Austrians abroad is a quarterly household survey operated by Statistics Austria.

Credit card data are mainly used for plausibility checks on the data from the above-mentioned sources and for compiling the geographical breakdowns on a detailed country level.

Various supplementary data sources are used in the compilation process to provide the necessary data that cannot be obtained from the main sources. These sources are used to measure directly specific variables; for example, direct imports of cars by households are taken from the car registration statistics. The expenditure of "fuel tourists" contributing to the credit side of the travel item is relatively high; a model is therefore used to measure it.

Concerning the debit side of the travel item, expenditure on health services abroad—in particular related to "dental tourism"—is significant. As this kind of travel is not or only partly covered by the household survey, an estimation model is employed, which takes into account the supply structure of dentists near the Austrian border (in particular, the border with Hungary).

Supplementary data sources are also used to corroborate the reliability of outcomes of highly important variables that depend on weaker data sources. Examples of supplementary sources are data provided by other countries or institutions such as Eurostat or the World Tourism Organization (UNWTO), data from private institutions, or other macroeconomic indicators, such as GDP, the consumer price index, and statistics on wages studies on the mobility of students.

AZERBAIJAN

Transportation

This category covers freight and passenger transportation and port services for all modes of transport. Data on passenger fares and port service charges are based mainly on information the SSC collects from marine shipping, airline, railway, and road transport companies.

Travel

Data for the travel component are estimated by combining the SCC data on the number of foreign visitors entering Azerbaijan and Azerbaijan residents traveling abroad with data collected from the commercial banks on the average per capita expenditures of travelers.

BAHAMAS

Transportation

The data on freight and passenger services cover all modes of transport and port services. CBOB obtains entries for transportation services from surveys of both foreign and resident shipping and airline companies.

Travel

Regarding travel credit, CBOB compiles entries using the Ministry of Tourism's tourist expenditure estimates, which are in turn based on exit surveys of foreign visitors (cruise and stopovers) conducted by the Ministry of Tourism. Estimates are compiled by taking the product of the number of foreign visitors and an estimate of an average expenditure per visit.

Regarding travel debit, CBOB compiles entries using exchange control records.

BAHRAIN

Transportation

For transportation service credits, FSD derives entries from information provided by Gulf Air for tickets sold by its offices outside Bahrain and payments received by port and airport authorities against services provided to foreign ships and airlines.

Travel

Credits. Tourists and business travelers coming via air and sea and 10 percent of Saudi tourists coming to Bahrain via the causeway are assumed to stay in hotels and other apartments. FSD obtains data from MOF on gross output (revenue) of hotels (covering room rent and other revenue) and restaurants (sales). All rental revenue of hotels is assumed to be earned from nonresidents, while assumptions are made on the proportion of other revenue of hotels and sales of restaurants ascribable to nonresidents.

Using these estimates and data on the number of persons staying in hotels, obtained from the Tourism Directorate, FSD derives estimates of per capita expenditure. A lower estimate of per capita expenditure is applied to the number of tourists not staying in hotels. In addition, FSD makes an allowance for miscellaneous expenditures (e.g., taxi fares, purchases of souvenirs, etc.). Ninety percent of Saudis arriving via the causeway are considered day travelers and assumed to spend about BD 40 per person.

Debits. Bahrainis crossing the causeway are assumed to spend, on average, BD 30 per person. In addition, FSD makes an allowance for the overseas training costs of Bahraini officials. The directorate also uses survey reports on bank transactions, covering records on foreign currency notes and traveler's checks sold to residents (e.g., tourists, businessmen, students studying abroad).

BANGLADESH

Transportation

Transportation covers those services performed by residents in one economy for those of another, by all modes of transportation that are involved with the carriage of passengers, movement of goods (freight), charter of carriers with crew, and other related supporting and auxiliary services.

Travel

The Statistics Department collects data on travel transactions through the banks. It records as credits the receipts from foreign visitors, and as debits the expenditures abroad of residents.

BARBADOS

Transportation

For passenger service debits, which represent sea and air fares paid by Barbadians to nonresident carriers, the CBB estimates the entries from survey forms returned by nonresident carriers. The credit entries cover receipts of domestic carriers for similar services.

The port and airport authorities provide data on other transport services.

Travel

The CBB obtains these estimates from CTO estimates. The CTO obtains values representing travelers' expenditures from information derived from exit surveys of travelers on the length of stay and type of accommodation. For the credit entries, the compilers apply estimated average daily expenditures to the number of visitors recorded. For the debit entries, the CBB supplements the CBB's survey data with exchange record information.

In the case of business travel, the credit entries include expenditures by foreign seasonal workers in Barbados, and the debit entries include expenditures abroad by resident seasonal workers. The Ministry of Labor provides these data.

In the case of personal travel, compilers classify the data by purpose of travel into health, education, and other. Compilers base credit estimates for students and health-related travelers on a survey of colleges and hospitals; they base debit entries on exchange record data.

BELARUS

Transportation

This category covers freight and passenger services by all modes of transport and port services. The main source of information for the transportation services is the Belstat surveys of transport companies.

Travel

Travel data are estimated by the NBB. Compilers estimate travel services via a model, using data on the number of border crossings classified by purpose of travel, average time of stay, and average expenditure per trip. The main sources of data for estimation are (1) the Belstat surveys of hotels and tourist companies, (2) information on the number of foreign visitors and residents of the Republic of Belarus who enter and leave the country, and (3) other official sources of information, such as reports from the MF and SCC.

Belstat provides data on the number of travelers, country of origin (for inward travelers), country of destination (for outward travelers), and types of travel (private, business, tourism, transit, etc.). In addition, the NBB uses partner country data (primarily the Russian Federation).

BELGIUM

Services

The main features of the collection system for services can be described as follows:

(i) cross-border transactions are obtained directly from residents;

(ii) the system is based partly on exhaustiveness (for the financial sector) and partly on a sample survey method (for the nonfinancial sector);

(iii) the nonfinancial sector is divided into several populations in relation to the activities to be measured. Each population has its own questionnaire where the details (e.g., the economic nature) of the transactions are specific to each one (note that some transactions are aggregated); and

(iv) there is a combination of several reporting periodicities.

Purchases of services by individuals are not covered by the data collection system and estimates should be made.

The definition of services in the different surveys complies with the *BPM5*.

BELIZE

Transportation

Since Belize has no international shipping lines or international airline, credit entries contain only revenues collected from foreign carriers. The CBB collects these data from annual surveys of the International Airport and Port Authorities. It calculates the freight debit as 8 percent (derived from the survey of customs declaration forms) of the c.i.f. value of merchandise imports as reported by the SIB. It subtracts the value of banana and papaya boxes from the import numbers before the calculation of freight charges. No attempt is made to disaggregate freight services by air and land from sea shipping since the use of these types of air and land transportation for imports is minimal.

The credit information represents revenues from foreign shipping companies to the port for services and to domestic agents for commission payments and other services rendered. The CBB deducts from these inflows and outflows the money sent to the shipping agencies to pay the nonresident crew of foreign vessels.

The debit entry for air transport–passenger consists only of payments for air tickets sold by airline agents. The ticket sales from branch offices of foreign airlines in Belize are not recorded here, since the branch offices are treated as resident companies, so remittances abroad are recorded under profits in income.

Travel

For travel credits, the CBB derives information by estimating expenditures of five main categories of nonresidents—seasonal and border workers, business, students, cruise ship passengers, and stay-over tourists. It estimates expenditures by seasonal and border workers in the country at 69 percent of the income earned by border and seasonal workers. This percentage was derived from a 2004 survey of nonresident workers. No information is collected on residents working temporarily abroad.

Expenditure by business and official visitors is obtained by taking the number of business and official visitor arrivals from the Immigration Department numbers and multiplying this by the average length of stay and average daily expenditure per person for business visitors obtained from the 2009 Visitor Expenditure and Motivation Survey (VEMS). The debit reflects expenditure on business travel by the public service (as recorded in the Overseas Expenditure of the Public Service database) and the public (as recorded in the database of all outflows of foreign currency from the banking system).

For expenditures by foreign students, the CBB obtains the data from the annual balance of payments survey of educational establishments and the commercial banks' reported inflows to educational institutions not covered by the annual balance of payments survey. The total obtained is assumed to represent 90 percent of foreign student coverage, so the number is adjusted accordingly.

The CBB obtains its estimate of national tourism expenditures using stay-over tourist arrival numbers from the Immigration Department, cruise ship arrival numbers from the Belize Tourism Board, and estimates of average daily expenditure and average length of stay derived from the 2009 VEMS.

Owing to the large numbers of people who move daily between Belize and Guatemala and between Belize and Mexico, it is necessary to adjust downward the number of arrivals through these two land borders. Certain ratios, developed during the expenditure surveys, are used to estimate the actual numbers of stay-over visitors. These ratios removed people traveling in-transit, adjusted for tourists who traveled for a short day trip to a neighboring country and were recorded as entering the country twice (called multiple-entry tourists), and removed seasonal/border workers and students who are accounted for elsewhere. At the international airport, citizens who reside abroad but travel to Belize using their Belizean passports are added, while in-transit visitors are excluded.

Travel debits consist of the total number of residents traveling through the international airport and multiplying this number by an average expenditure of BZ$1,877.49 per person. This number is checked by comparing the outflows on vacation travel and outbound credit card payments recorded by the commercial banks. Only part of the credit card outflows is attributed to travel, since businesses use credit cards to pay for imports.

INTERNATIONAL MONETARY FUND (IMF) NOTES

BENIN

Transportation

This item covers freight and insurance relating to international shipping, other passenger transportation services (regardless of the mode of transport used), and port services. BCEAO estimates transportation services based on data gathered from the Joint Benin-Niger Railways and Transportation Organization, port authorities, ship owners and shipping agents, foreign airlines, and the Air Navigation Safety Agency.

Travel

BCEAO derives credit entries from hotel and travel-agency surveys conducted by the Tourism and Hotel Business Directorate. Estimates are calculated based on the number of visitors, number of overnight stays, and estimated average expenditure by tourists.

Debit entries are drawn from (1) pilgrimage data provided by the Islamic Union of Benin, (2) government official-mission expenditure data provided by the General Directorate of the Budget and Equipment, and (3) an estimate of the holiday expenditures of technical assistants and other nonresidents.

These credit and debit entries are supplemented with the amounts obtained from the breakdown, by economic type, of exchanges of BCEAO banknotes between West African Economic and Monetary Union (WAEMU) member countries.

BERMUDA

Transportation

Estimates are compiled directly from the quarterly survey data and grossed up to derive population estimates.

Travel

Business travel debit. This is calculated by multiplying the number of resident business trips abroad by the average spent per trip. The average spent per trip is calculated by taking the 2004 expenditure from the Household Expenditure Survey (HES), allocating it quarterly, and then advancing the number by the average increases in the quarterly All Items consumer price index (CPI) for the United States.

Medical travel debit. This is calculated by first taking the annual estimated expenditure of Bermuda residents on health expenditure overseas as obtained from the Bermuda Health Systems and Services Profile report for 2006. This expenditure is allocated quarterly, and then advanced by the average increases in the quarterly CPI for medical care for the United States.

Personal travel debit. This is calculated as the sum of:

(a) spending abroad by residents while on vacation. The value of this spending is obtained from the 2004 HES and allocated quarterly for that year. The number is advanced by first multiplying the change in the number of resident trips abroad and then by the average increases in the quarterly All Items CPI for the United States.

(b) resident purchases abroad as declared at the Bermuda Airport.

(c) unreported resident purchases abroad (estimated as 30 percent of resident purchases abroad as declared at the Bermuda Airport).

Education travel debit. Expenditure on education recorded in the 2004 HES is split into two groups: studies requiring travel overseas, and distance/correspondence (on-island) courses. The total on-island courses amount is divided by four and blown up by the year-on-year percentage change in the Canadian tuition CPI. This amount is then blown up by the year-on-year percentage change in the U.S./Canadian exchange rate. This produces the amount spent each quarter on distance/correspondence courses. The total amount for physical overseas education is multiplied by the percentage of students traveling overseas for study (based on the annual number) in the quarter. It is then multiplied by the year-on-year percentage change in the U.S./Canadian exchange rate. It is then multiplied by the year-on-year percentage change in the Canadian CPI for tuition fees and the year-on-year percentage change in the Canadian CPI for all items. These two price indices are weighted by the 59.9 percent students would spend (on average) for their tuition to be applied to the tuition fee CPI and 40.1 percent applied to the all-items CPI.

BHUTAN

Transportation

Data are collected from the RMA and the Druk Air Corporation Limited. Credit entries are the Indian rupee and foreign exchange earnings of Druk Air on passenger services. Major debit entries are payments related to freight services for shipment of aircraft parts and passenger-service costs borne by Bhutanese residents using nonresident carriers.

Travel

Data are collected from the Tourism Council of Bhutan and the RMA. Major credit entries include foreign exchange earnings from tourism, the monthly records of which are maintained by the Tourism Council of Bhutan. Visitors from Bangladesh, Maldives, and India do not require visas to enter Bhutan, and no records are currently kept on visitors from these countries. However, based on 2004 estimates of Indian visitors by the Association of Bhutanese Tour Operators, the RMA estimates travel expenditures by Indian tourists in Bhutan. On the debit side, residents traveling to COTI require RMA's authorization for access to foreign exchange, and, therefore, data for travel debits, mainly education-related and official/business travel, are sourced from the RMA's Foreign Exchange and Reserve Management Department. Travel debits for balance of payments with India, mainly private-education related travel, are estimated by the RMA.

BOLIVIA

Transportation

This account covers freight and passenger services for all modes of transport. The BCB obtains transportation services data from surveys it conducts for this purpose.

Travel

Since 2000, this information is obtained through an annual survey conducted by the INE. This is in accordance with an agreement signed by the BCB, the Vice Ministry of Tourism, the National Service of Migration, and the INE. Travel transactions are broken down between business and personal travel.

BOSNIA AND HERZEGOVINA

Transportation

Transportation services comprise transport of goods and passengers and other income and costs linked to transportation services that residents provide to nonresidents, and vice versa. Source data are collected through a direct survey, conducted by the CBBH, on transport companies and commercial banks in BH.

In 2008, the CBBH initiated a survey on transportation services of BH residents to nonresidents for 2007. This survey consists of BH companies registered for providing services in international road transport, railroad transport, and air transport.

The value of services of transportation of goods is calculated on the basis of the estimated difference between the value of imported goods at c.i.f. and f.o.b. values. Out of this amount, a part related to the transport services of nonresident carriers is estimated.

Services of passenger transport include the data of Sarajevo airport statistics on air traffic of local and foreign carriers. In addition, the CBBH surveys bus transport of nonresidents by resident carriers and residents in international traffic by nonresident carriers.

Travel

Travel services cover inflow/outflow of goods and services provided to nonresidents in BH and services to residents for their travel abroad for the duration of less than one year.

Tourist consumption is divided into business travel and private travel and consists of tourism, education, and medical care.

Business travel is estimated according to the CBBH research on the proportion of business in total (business and private) travel, which is conducted for neighboring countries.

For private travel, data used are provided by statistical institutes in BH on the stay of foreign tourists, and statistical data of other countries on BH tourists in these countries. The CBBH estimates the data for unregistered tourists, the staying expenses of foreign staff in BH, and cross-border daily shopping.

BOTSWANA

Transportation

Transportation services cover air, road, and rail transport for freight, passenger, and courier services. Annual surveys of transport companies (both private and parastatals) provided some of these data in the past, but owing to low response rates the surveys have been discontinued. As a result, freight data are estimated using data from customs.

Travel

In the past, travel estimates were based on amounts reported on Forms A and S in a bank's exchange reporting system. These estimates were considered likely to be understated, particularly on the credit side, because of the incidence of prepaid travel settled offshore and the likelihood that expenditure by nonresident visitors while in Botswana will not be classified to the travel item.

To improve the estimates on the credit side, a methodology was established using arrival statistics and the results of a Department of Tourism Visitor Survey. The TSU compiles arrival statistics from migration cards, which classify noncitizen visitors according to their reasons for entering Botswana, based on the Visitor Survey. The survey was first conducted for 1998 and is now being repeated approximately every two years. It also provides useful measures of lengths of stay and average expenditure in various categories of visitors. Estimates are made using information on the average length of stay and expenditure data for each category of visitor applied to the appropriate arrivals data.

The BOB derives data on travel by Botswana government officials from the MFDP's Cash Flow Unit.

On the debit side, the coverage of the item has been improved by the addition of a number of categories of expenditure that were not previously measured. These include:

- Student expenditure abroad (derived from Ministry of Education disbursements);

- Expenditure abroad by resident air travelers (estimated from air departures and assumptions about length of stay and average expenditure); and

- Similar expenditure abroad by resident land travelers (estimated from purchases of foreign exchange for travel reported on Form A, less the amount estimated for air travelers).

BRAZIL

Transportation

For transportation of goods, the BCB uses data provided directly by Brazilian seagoing shipping companies, the International Air Transportation Agency (ANAC), and the National Waterways Transportation Agency (ANTAQ), supplemented by ITRS data. The staff monitors separately the operations involving air, sea, and other (river/land) modes of transportation.

The source of data on passenger transport is the ITRS, cross-checked with ANAC data. For charters, the BCB uses data from the ITRS and data provided by ANTAQ, which along with companies also supplies data on freight and cross-trade. Data on other transportation services are either reported by companies or based on the ITRS.

Travel

To compile the travel account, the BCB uses ITRS data. The data cover revenues and expenditures regarding sales and purchases by means such as international credit cards, currency transactions between travelers and authorized exchange operators, and receipts and payments between domestic and foreign travel operators.

BULGARIA

Transportation

Passenger. Credit and debit entries are based on BNB estimates.

Travel

The BNB compiles estimates using a data model that combines data on the number of travelers to and from Bulgaria with estimates of per capita expenditure to calculate the total credit and debit entries.

Until 2006, the data on travel were obtained from the Ministry of Internal Affairs' data on the number of travelers crossing the borders and on estimates of per capita expenditures, which were based on the methodology for estimation of the receipts and expenditures from travel services – "Methodology For Estimation of the Receipts and Expenditures from Travel in the Bulgarian Balance of Payments" (Bulgarian National Bank, Ministry of Trade and Tourism, November 18, 1999).

As of the beginning of 2007, data for the number and the structure of foreigners who visited the country are based on information from the border police and the NSI estimates. With the January 2010 data, the BNB applies new methodology for estimation of the receipts and expenditures for travel and passenger transportation. The estimation model for the travel item is based on the product of the number of travelers and the expenditure related to the type or purpose of the travel. The estimates of the expenditures (receipts) by purpose of the travel are based on the data collected during the Border Survey among Traveling Bulgarians and Foreigners, conducted by the BNB during the period July 2007 – August 2008. The new methodology was applied for the first time with the data for January 2010. Monthly data for the years 2007, 2008, and 2009 were revised.

BURUNDI

Transportation

For passenger services, the BRB compiles data on the basis of a survey of air carriers conducted by BRB's Financial Operations Department. The data are drawn exclusively from receipts from these companies and are recorded in the settlement statement.

Travel

The BRB derives the entries for travel from a survey of hotels, foreign tourist spending in Burundi, and spending abroad by residents (BRB statement of exchange transactions).

CAMBODIA

Transportation

Separate estimates are made for air and sea transportation services.

For *air* transportation services, freight on imports carried by nonresident airlines is estimated by applying an average freight rate per ton to the quantity of imports. The same methodology is used to estimate details of freight on exports carried by the resident airline.

Passenger fares paid by residents to nonresident airlines are estimated by combining information on the number of passengers collected from the Ministry of the Interior on the numbers of resident and nonresident arrivals and departures, an average weighted airfare, and passenger loadings by the different airlines serving Phnom Penh. Passenger fares paid by nonresidents to the resident airline are estimated in the same manner.

Other air transportation services are estimated from information provided by the resident airline for expenditure in foreign ports and from information provided by the Civil Aviation Authority for expenditure in Cambodia by nonresident airlines.

For *sea* transport, freight on imports carried by nonresident carriers is estimated by deducting freight on air imports from the estimate of freight on total imports and applying to the result the share of nonresident shipping. Freight on exports carried by resident carriers is by multiplying an average freight rate for exported goods by the proportion of the tonnage of exports estimated to be carried by residents. ITRS data are used to estimate passenger fares for sea transport.

Other sea transportation services are estimated from information provided by resident shipping agents and port authorities.

For 2003 onward, ITRS data are used to estimate other transport: freight, passenger fares, and other transportation services.

Travel

For travel credits, separate estimates are made for expenditures by gamblers, tourists, business travelers, and diplomats and official travelers. For example, for tourists and business travelers, data on the number of arrivals are combined with data on the length of stay and the average pattern of expenditure collected from the NBC International Visitors Survey conducted in 2005 and 2006, Ministry of Tourism, and travel agents. For short-term employees of international organizations in Cambodia and employees of aid agencies, estimates are based on the number of such staff and the pattern of expenditure.

Travel debits include estimates based on numbers of departures of residents obtained from Ministry of Interior and Ministry of Tourism data, and their estimated length of stay abroad, and their pattern of expenditure from the NBC Returned Cambodian Travelers' Survey conducted in 2005 and 2006. The distinction between business and personal travel is not disseminated.

CAMEROON

Services

The balance of payments staff prepare the data on the various types of services using the settlement balance obtained from bank forms—reports prepared by commercial banks concerning the transactions of their customers.

To supplement the information in the settlement balance, staff use the data obtained, on the one hand, from questionnaires sent to consignees and to airline and insurance companies and, on the other hand, from the annual reports of reporting entities.

CANADA

Transportation

For *passenger* transport, BOPD relies on monthly administrative data, combined with estimates of average passenger fares from a quarterly sample survey of expenditure characteristics by the Culture, Tourism, and Center for Education Statistics

Division (CTCES) of Statistics Canada. Included with passenger transport is coverage of cruise fares, which international standards define as travel.

Travel

The CTCES Division compiles the basic Canadian travel statistics. CTCES derives these statistics from a combination of census data and sample counts of travelers crossing the border, coupled with sample surveys used to collect specific information from travelers, including their expenditures and main purpose of visit. Beginning with the reference year 2000, a new air exit survey introduced on-site interviews for foreign travelers at eight key Canadian airports.

Travel is subdivided into travel for business reasons and travel for personal reasons: *Business* travel covers expenditures by cross-border workers, but insufficient data bar their identification as such in the Canadian statistics. Also, as a result of data limitations, cruise fares as noted above are recorded under transportation services rather than travel. As part of the business travel item, the CTCES calculates estimates of spending by crews (of airplanes, ships, boats, trains, and trucks).

For *personal* travel, data for health-related travel consist of foreign spending for hospital services in Canada. CTCES records these data from the annual hospital survey of the Canadian Institute for Health Information, projecting data for recent years where survey results are not yet available. With the 1995 reference year, CTCES introduced estimates for physician services linked to U.S. data on the payments side. Also starting in 1995, access to U.S. sources has enabled a fuller estimate covering payments, beyond provincial health plans, at major medical centers and university hospitals located in the United States.

On the receipt side of the education series, CTCES produces the estimates by combining the time series on the number of students with average tuition rates and adding estimates of other expenditure. For expenditures of Canadian students in the United States, the data have been supplied by the U.S. BEA from 1981 onward and were linked with balance of payments data for prior years. CTCES updates the data on student expenditures overseas to incorporate volume and expenditure estimates.

CAPE VERDE

Transportation

The DEE obtains information on freight from the exchange record and from customs data on goods entering the country on a c.i.f. basis. Staff derive the data on passenger and other transportation services from the exchange record and surveys of the national airline, fuel suppliers, and port and airport authorities.

Travel

Entries in the travel category include tourism, business travel, students, civil servants, and other travelers. Staff collect data from the exchange record.

CHILE

Transportation

Passenger. Credit and debit entries for passenger services are estimated on the basis of information obtained from quarterly forms provided by resident carriers (i.e., shipping companies and airlines) and by representatives of nonresident transport companies. The CBC supplements the data with information from a benchmark survey of other carriers, and data on vehicles crossing the border. Before complete information is obtained from the forms and surveys, preliminary estimates are made.

Travel

Both credit and debit entries are estimated by combining monthly data provided by immigration authorities on the number of foreign visitors and Chilean travelers who enter and exit the country, with data on average expenditures and length of stay obtained from surveys, which cover tourism by both incoming and outgoing travelers. The surveys are undertaken in accordance with an agreement between the CBC and the National Tourism Service, a government agency.

CHINA

Transportation

Until 1995, the SAFE obtained credit entries for transportation (shipment) and port services from the Ministry of Communications and the Ministry of Railways, among other sources. Beginning in 1996, the SAFE derives credit entries from the ITRS. Debit entries are drawn from import statistics compiled by Customs and from information derived from the ITRS.

Travel

The compilers obtain data on travel credits from the National Tourism Administration (NTA). The NTA collects the data through sample surveys conducted by the National Bureau of Statistics. Travel debits are calculated using data from the Immigration Administration Department of the Ministry of Public Security and relevant receipts of main international travel destinations (countries or areas) outside China.

COLOMBIA

Transportation

Regarding passenger services and other transportation, BR compiles credit and debit entries on the basis of data supplied by national and foreign airlines.

Travel

The travel component measures nonborder travel (via airports) and cross-border travel (through land-border crossing points). The data for nonborder travel are estimated on the basis of information on international passenger movements provided by the Civil Aviation authorities, the Administrative Department of Security, and the travel expenses reported in the "Boleta de Viajeros" applied by DIAN and the BR. Regarding cross-border travel, BR derives data from quarterly surveys conducted at five land-border crossing points.

CONGO

Transportation

BEAC values shipping costs either directly, based on the reports of enterprises, the postal administration, and banks, or, if this is not available, by assuming that shipping costs are 18 percent of the c.i.f. value of imports.

Other transportation entries include services rendered by carriers, mainly for the international transportation of passengers, and goods and services purchased by carriers and consumed in the course of their business.

Travel

Credit entries include expenditure in the Republic of Congo by foreign travelers, and debit entries include current expenditure by residents traveling abroad, regardless of the nature of the travel. The postal administration (SOPECO) and banks report the amounts for both types of entries; the banks report transactions in foreign banknotes, traveler's checks, transfers of travel agencies, tourists transiting the Republic of Congo, etc.

BEAC also collects the information by means of questionnaires sent to the United Nations and its affiliated agencies, the Congolese Public Treasury, and embassies (for scholarships paid directly abroad). It supplements these figures by an estimate of flows of BEAC and franc zone currency notes and an estimate of expenditure by technical assistants during their leave abroad.

COSTA RICA

Transportation

The CBCR obtains data on freight, passenger, and other transportation services, as well as on other international transactions by air, land, and sea transportation companies, from information reported in the questionnaires it sends to such companies, as well as from the customs records.

Travel

The CBCR bases estimates on data the ICT reports on the number of foreigners visiting Costa Rica and residents traveling abroad. It also uses data from ICT sample surveys on per capita spending and average length of stay. The Directorate General of Migration and Foreign Travel provides the ICT with monthly data on the number of nonresident travelers entering Costa Rica and the number of residents leaving the country. The ICT undertakes surveys quarterly to derive the average amount spent and the average stay.

CÔTE D'IVOIRE

Transportation

For passenger services, the data are collected from the national airline, Air Ivoire, and the offices of nonresident airlines.

Travel

Credit entries are obtained primarily from statistics on arrivals of foreign tourists and hotel occupancy, provided by the Ministry of Tourism and Crafts (formerly High Commission for Tourism). A direct survey of hotels is also conducted.

Debit entries are based on estimates and mainly cover expenditure of non-Ivoirien residents while out of the country. These figures are derived from the income of nonnationals working in the private sector, the wages of technical assistants and non-Ivoirien staff of international organizations with offices in Côte d'Ivoire, and the length of the leave of such persons.

Figures on government missions are obtained from the Payroll Directorate.

The expenditure of Ivoirien students abroad is primarily taken from surveys of donors for foreign scholarships and of the Ministry of Higher Education for scholarships granted by the Ivoirien government.

CROATIA

Transportation

This category covers the international transportation of passengers, goods, and other transportation services.

From 1993 to 1998, the data sources were the ITRS and questionnaires that the CNB received from enterprises engaged in the international transportation of goods and passengers. Expenditures on transportation services also included (1) part of the differences between c.i.f. and f.o.b. imports, pertaining to services provided by nonresidents; and (2) estimates of the operating costs of Croatian transportation companies in international transportation.

As of the first quarter 1999, the CNB compiles revenues and expenditures from transportation services on the basis of data from the new CNB survey on international transportation services, with two exceptions: First, revenues and expenditures from road transport are still compiled from ITRS data, and second, data on c.i.f./f.o.b. adjustments for nonresident carriers are obtained from the questionnaires on transportation costs related to imports of goods, classified by modes of transportation and residency. From the first quarter of 1999, a breakdown by mode of transportation is available.

Travel

The travel component shows income from services rendered to foreign travelers and tourists, as well as expenditures incurred by domestic travelers and tourists abroad. Beginning with the second half of 1998, the CNB has conducted a survey of consumption by foreign travelers in Croatia and domestic travelers abroad. Since early 1999, the CNB data compilers have combined the results of this survey (stratified sample) with the Ministry of the Interior data on the total number of foreign and domestic travelers, along with the data on distribution of foreign travelers by countries contained in the CBS report on tourism for compiling the travel component.

CYPRUS

Transportation

This category covers freight and passenger services provided by sea and air transport operators. The CBC derives debit entries for freight services from the estimates made to convert imports from a c.i.f. to an f.o.b. basis (i.e., freight and insurance are assumed to equal 8 percent of imports c.i.f.).

Concerning passenger transport, banks report the data through the settlements system. With respect to credits, the CBC cross-checks the figures with data obtained from an annual survey of major resident passenger transport operators. The staff supplement settlement data for supporting, auxiliary, and other transport services with data from the financial statements or reports of international business companies engaged in such activities.

Travel

For travel credits for tourism, the CBC obtains data from CYSTAT, which conducts a monthly frontier survey on tourist expenditure in Cyprus. To obtain geographical allocation for travel credits, the CBC combines per person expenditure derived from the survey with the number of tourist arrivals, as given by the frontier survey of incoming travelers, which CYSTAT also conducts.

With regard to education-related revenue, the CBC conducts an annual survey among those colleges and universities that provide educational services to nonresidents and compares the survey results with data reported by banks under the settlements system.

In 2004, CYSTAT launched a new survey to measure the expenditures of nonresidents in their residential properties in Cyprus. The results of the survey are included in the "travel" item.

For travel debits, the CBC also obtains the value from the monthly frontier survey conducted by CYSTAT. Reported data are cross-checked with those reported under the settlements system as well as foreign exchange outflows through credit or debit cards.

CZECH REPUBLIC

Transportation

Until 2003, the CNB collected data on air transport of goods and passengers directly from transportation companies. For other kinds of transport, the data were based on the commercial banks' records. Additional data were required from companies involved with transporting natural gas through the territory of the Czech Republic to Western Europe (credit) and transporting gas and oil through the Slovak Republic to the Czech Republic (debit).

A new CZSO system for collecting data on transport services has been used from the first quarter of 2007. Data from a CZSO pilot survey-based project have been used for a 2004–06 revision. The new data collection system is based on direct data reporting of the representative sample of respondents according to the EBOPS classification.

Travel

From 1999 to 2007, the main sources for compiling the travel item were banking statistics, information on credit card transactions from their bank and nonbank issuers, and information from nonbank exchange offices. These sources were complemented by partner country data and the CZSO survey of travelers at accommodation establishments (by country) and household surveys. The travel data were also supplemented with data on personal expenditures on goods and services by seasonal and border workers (published by the CZSO). Information from the Ministry of Education, Youth and Sports, the Ministry of Health, and health insurance companies was important for compiling education and health items. Additional information was obtained from tourist providers and from a special agency (funded by the Ministry for Regional Development) engaged in travel studies.

Starting from 2008, the CNB has adopted a modified system for collecting travel data. Collection of data through banking statistics was abandoned, and quarterly information on credit card transactions from the Bank Card Association has become the dominant source for the travel item. All other information sources continue to be used.

From 2001 onward, the CNB produces data showing the split between business and personal travel.

DENMARK

Services

Statistics Denmark conducts a combined monthly (covering approximately 400 enterprises) and quarterly (covering approximately 1,200 enterprises) sample survey on trade in services and transfers. The sample has been drawn on the basis of the settlement system, partly using a cut-off method (for monthly reporters) and partly a stratified sample method (for quarterly reporters).

The sample is considered fixed, but will be summarily updated each year to ensure representativeness by excluding certain enterprises and including others. A new major initiative in updating the sample is being prepared.

The survey allows a full breakdown by country.

The import of travel is primarily based on a separate survey on holiday and business journeys. The export of travel is partly based on accommodation statistics combined with a survey on overnight travelers' spending in Denmark and partly on different border surveys covering travelers on same-day visits. The rest of the travel item is based on the general survey of trade in services.

Monthly data on services are estimated by grossing up figures from the monthly reporters using monthly extrapolations for the quarterly reporters to the survey of trade in services and adding estimates for the travel item.

DJIBOUTI

Transportation

This item includes freight and passenger services, regardless of the mode of transportation used. Data on transportation services are obtained from surveys of air, sea, and rail transport companies. Data on the auxiliary transport services are collected from harbor authorities and various private operators (primarily shipping agents, transit agents).

Travel

Credit entries for travel are obtained from statements of the exchanges offices, hotels, and restaurants. Debit entries are based on Treasury statements on scholarships and missions and on private company statements for business travel.

DOMINICA

See Eastern Caribbean Currency Union.

DOMINICAN REPUBLIC

Transportation

The BCRD's International Department compiles and classifies credit and debit entries by mode of transportation (sea, air, and land) and category of transportation (freight, passenger, and other transportation services). Dominican residents' freight services are obtained by importers based on the customs declarations. Freight services of nonresidents are derived from freight services provided by residents. For passenger transportation, data are based on the quarterly surveys of resident shipping and airline companies. Data are also collected on port services from the port authorities.

Travel

The International Department staff derive data on the revenues from tourism based on estimated average stay of nonresident travelers and on expenditure of nonresident and resident travelers. The department obtains the number of travelers from the BCRD's daily records of arrivals and departures at national airports. The staff cross-check the data with data from the National Statistics Office and the Ministry of Tourism. Data from the National Migration Office are not used because of the delay in their availability. Staff obtain average stay and expenditure estimates from quarterly surveys undertaken by the BCRD's National Accounts Department.

EASTERN CARIBBEAN CURRENCY UNION

Transportation

The estimates for passenger services cover receipts and payments for the transportation of passengers. The ECCB obtains the data from an annual balance of payments survey of airline companies and agencies.

Travel

On the credit side, this item covers total expenditures by visitors to the member countries. The ECCB derives the figures by combining data on the number of visitors and their average length of stay (obtained from the immigration departments of member countries), with an estimate of the average daily expenditure per category of visitor. The latter component is obtained through benchmark surveys of visitor expenditures, conducted periodically and adjusted annually for inflation.

Estimates of travel debits are obtained from commercial banking statistics on sales of foreign exchange for travel purposes, as well as official sources providing data on student maintenance overseas and on travel to attend international conferences.

ECUADOR

Transportation

For credits and debits on sea transport, the CBE uses its quarterly and annual surveys of shipping companies operating in Ecuador. To supplement that data, it uses information on passengers and cargo from the Merchant Marine and Coastal Administration (Dirección de la Marina Mercante y del Litoral, DIMERC)—the government regulatory authority for maritime traffic in Ecuador.

For air transport, the CBE uses information supplied by the Civil Aviation Administration (Dirección General de Aviación Civil, DAC). The CBE also obtains data from its merchandise trade database, containing information about f.o.b. and c.i.f. goods imports.

Travel

The National Migration and Aliens Office (Dirección Nacional de Migración y Extranjería) supplies data on inbound and outbound tourism, obtained through nationwide surveys based on type of visa and place of entry/exit (ports and airports). Only nonimmigrant visas are considered for balance of payments purposes. These sources are supplemented by surveys of hotels, travel agencies, etc., to be carried out by the Ministry of Tourism.

For travel expenditures, the CBE estimates data from information derived from surveys on travelers and hotels on the length of stay and type of accommodation. The CBE applies the estimated average daily expenditure to the number of visitors recorded.

EGYPT

Transportation

The credit entries for transportation cover amounts received by Egyptian shipping and airline companies for freight and passenger services. Other transportation covers receipts of Suez Canal dues and receipts of the Suez Mediterranean oil pipeline for transporting foreign companies' oil through pipeline services.

The debit entries for transportation cover amounts transferred to foreign shipping and airline companies for freight and passenger services, as well as payments for freight on imports estimated from the c.i.f. value of imports (10 percent). The entries also include payments made for maintenance and repair of Egyptian ships and aircraft at foreign ports and airports.

Travel

For travel credit, compilers base the entries on the number of nights spent by tourists in Egypt (data from the Ministry of Tourism) and the average expenditure per night (CBE estimates based on a survey conducted by the Ministry of Tourism). Separate details are not available for business and personal travel.

The debit entries for travel cover expenditures of government officials and private employees traveling abroad, pilgrimage, expenditures of students studying abroad, training, technical and educational missions, and expenditures abroad for medical care.

EL SALVADOR

Transportation

The item includes freight and all modes of passenger transportation, including rental of transportation equipment with crew.

For freight transportation, CRB derives the credit data from surveys of enterprises operating in this field. It obtains debit data from customs forms, after deducting freight transportation carried out by resident enterprises.

For other forms of transportation, the credit data correspond to expenditure in the country by nonresident carriers. CRB obtains these data by means of surveys of these enterprises, supplemented with information from the Autonomous Executive Port Commission (CEPA). The debit data record expenditure abroad by resident enterprises.

For land and air transportation, CRB obtains the data from various resident and nonresident enterprises surveyed.

Travel

Credit and debt entries are based on travel surveys, conducted by a private enterprise. In turn, the data are based on total expenditures estimated through the travel survey (Profile of the International Visitor) from the Ministry of Tourism.

ESTONIA

Transportation

The transportation services item is compiled mainly on the basis of the transportation companies' surveys and supplemented by data from the ITRS. The BOPD conducts the transportation survey each quarter with nearly 500 local transport companies that provide international freight and passenger services. The surveys include services broken down by the mode of transport and by the passenger, freight, and other forms of transportation. The geographical breakdown for those data is available.

Information on resident passenger services rendered by nonresident companies is obtained mainly from the SE. Most of these companies are involved in road transport, followed in importance by sea, air, and rail transport.

Travel

The main sources of information for travel services are (1) the travel border sample survey on *per capita* expenditures conducted by the SE and (2) the monthly data based on mobile positioning services, giving the number of nonresidents' visits in Estonia and residents' visits abroad by countries, conducted by OÜ Positium LBS, a spinoff company of University of Tartu scientists. Supplementary data sources are accommodation statistics of the SE and border statistics on the Estonian-Russian border, provided by the Board of Border Guard.

Relying on results of sample surveys, the BOPD compiles expenditures-per-trip estimates of such visits. If actual data of sample surveys are missing, the data for previous year are used. Different models are used for calculating expenditures of one-day and overnight visitors. The total amount of travel receipts and payments is calculated by multiplying expenditures-by-trip by number-of-visits using available geographical breakdown.

The credit and debit entry for travel also includes approximately 50 percent of the net wages and salaries earned by nonresidents who have worked in Estonia and residents who have worked abroad for less than one year. Health-related and educational expenditures made by medical patients and students are treated as travel services.

Regular bilateral comparison is carried out every year and corrected if needed.

ETHIOPIA

Transportation

The NBE obtains data from transportation companies. A survey form prepared by the NBE's External Economic Analysis and International Relations Directorate is sent to these companies and compiled quarterly by the staff of the Directorate.

Travel

The SDPA provides data on travel receipts, while travel payment data reflecting payments made by residents to nonresident transport companies are obtained both from SDPA and the Ethiopian Airlines (EAL).

INTERNATIONAL MONETARY FUND (IMF) NOTES

FIJI

Transportation

FIBOS derives the data largely from its balance of payments survey covering resident and nonresident airlines, ports, and airports. Fiji's resident airlines, Air Pacific operating on international routes, report their passenger fare earnings from nonresidents. Ports and airport agencies provide aviation fees and charges, port dues, pilotage, and stevedoring. Foreign airlines provide figures on passenger fares earned from residents.

Travel

FIBOS derives travel credit entries from estimates of tourist expenditures and the per diem information, obtained from the International Visitor Survey (IVS), conducted by the MOT. Until the IVS results become available, FIBOS derives estimates of tourist expenditure per diem for the current reference period by inflating the per diem derived from the last IVS results by an index (referred to as the tourism expenditure index [TEI]). This index is calculated from the results of a FIBOS quarterly survey of hotels (TEI survey).

Travel debits are sourced entirely from the OET system.

FINLAND

Transportation

This category covers freight and passenger services by all modes of transport and port services. For sea transport, the BOF derives data from a quarterly survey of shipping companies; the survey seeks information on freight earnings from foreign traffic, passenger transport, and port expenditures abroad. For the estimates of freight that are deducted from imports in the trade statistics on the debit side (the c.i.f./f.o.b. adjustment), the BOF derives the data from a survey conducted by the Board of Customs.

For air transport, the BOF obtains data from Finnair and the National Board of Aviation; for railway transport, from the state railways.

Travel

From 1999 onward, the data are based on border interviews and other tourism statistics conducted and compiled by Statistics Finland. Until 1998, data were derived from settlements reported by domestic banks; they included purchases of foreign currency by residents at home and abroad and sales of Finnish markkas to nonresidents in Finland and abroad. In addition, an estimate of foreign exchange transactions by Finnish residents abroad was added to travel income and expenditure. Other sources of information on travel included the use of travelers' checks and credit cards.

FRANCE

Transportation

The data are broken down by sea, air, and other transport, and, when significant, passenger and merchandise transportation services. The latter comprise an estimate of the portion of costs of transportation included in merchandise payments (c.i.f./f.o.b. correction).

Travel

Data on travel are based mainly on three surveys on inward and outward travel. Since 2003, a distinction is made between business and other travel.

GABON

Transportation

For passenger services, the entries cover earnings of air, sea, and land carriers.

Travel

Entries cover expenditures in Gabon by foreign travelers (credit) and expenditures of Gabonese residents traveling abroad (debit) for all purposes (tourism, business, study, holiday, medical care, official missions, etc.) and by any means of payment (banknotes, checks, credit transfers, money orders, etc.).

INTERNATIONAL MONETARY FUND (IMF) NOTES

GAMBIA

Transportation

Data for transportation services are derived from returns provided by the Gambia ports authority and Civil Aviation Authority. Credit entries comprise services provided to nonresidents through the Trans-Gambia and the Banjul-Barra ferries, airport fees, landing and parking fees, and port services. Debit entries cover freight services acquired by importers estimated to be 12.4 percent of the value of imports c.i.f., remittances for airline tickets and port services, and foreign expenditure of the above-mentioned enterprises.

Travel

In calculating travel credit, a model-based approach is used. The CBG's Economic Research Department uses data provided by the Gambia Tourism Authority (GTA). The estimated average out-of-pocket expenditure is multiplied by tourist arrivals to obtain total tourist expenditure. This is added to income from hotel beds and arrival and departure fees. Travel debits are derived from data supplied by parastatals and government departments on staff travel and education-related expenditures.

GEORGIA

Transportation

The main data sources are information from the Georgian Railways Limited and from the Georgian ports and airports. The BPD estimates additional data based on information from the Department of Border Defense regarding the means of transport and number of individuals entering and leaving the country. The pipeline transportation services are estimated based on information received from British Petroleum. The data are recalculated to market prices according to the IMF methodology.

Travel

The BPD compiles travel data on the basis of information from the regular household survey. It collects information on business travel from governmental institutions (ministries, departments, the NBG, etc.), as well as from the banking sector.

The BPD also uses, as data sources, the indirect estimates based on (1) information from the Department of Border Defense regarding the number of individuals entering and leaving the country, (2) expenses abroad of those individuals engaged in export-import operations in goods, and (3) expenses of those working abroad for less than one year.

GERMANY

Transportation

The reporting system provides data on passenger services and some basic information on freight services, broken down by modes of transport.

Travel

For travel expenditures, a household sample survey was introduced in 2001 to cover for the loss of information on banknote transactions resulting from the introduction of the euro. This sample survey is conducted by a private institute on behalf of the Deutsche Bundesbank on a continuous basis. Since the data from this survey are only available with a time lag of five to six months after the reference quarter, preliminary figures are estimated (ARIMA model). The credit side of the travel account is compiled on the basis of ITRS reports (special reporting requirements of MFIs), supplemented by partner country data and additional, secondary data sources, like the accommodation statistics that are available at the FSO. The purchase and sale of goods by border workers are included under travel. A breakdown between business travel and personal travel is available for the debit side.

GHANA

Transportation

This category covers freight and passenger services by air, land, and sea transport, as well as services rendered and acquired at the ports. The BOG's Balance of Payments Office therefore estimates entries for transportation services from information provided by the port authorities, airlines, and shipping companies, both local and foreign.

Travel

Since 2005, the Ghana Tourist Board (the regulatory and monitoring governmental agency for tourism) has reported data on estimates of expenditures incurred abroad by returning Ghanaian residents and anticipated expenditures of nonresidents in Ghana.

GREECE

Transportation

The BoG compiles the transportation items on the basis of settlements, supplemented with estimates derived from the conversion of imports from c.i.f. to f.o.b. Data are broken down by means of transport (sea, air, rail, and other means) as well as by transportation category (freight and passengers). The main category is sea transport–cross-trading activity.

Travel

Prior to 2002, the BoG compiled travel data on the basis of settlements. The introduction of the euro called for methodological changes in the compilation of travel data for balance of payments purposes. On a pilot basis in May 2002, the BoG started a monthly frontier travel survey aimed at estimating travel expenditure and, since January 2003, has conducted the survey on a permanent basis.

GRENADA

See Eastern Caribbean Currency Union.

GUATEMALA

Transportation

For passenger services and other transportation services, the data are collected from port authorities and entrepreneurial surveys.

Travel

For credits and debits, the BOG compiles the entries by combining the data on tourists arrivals and departures (provided by the Migration Directorate) with the estimates of their average daily expenditures and their average length of stay (provided by the Guatemalan Institute of Tourism, for credits) and the estimation on the amounts carried by Guatemalan travelers outside the country (from the foreign exchange statistics, and the Guatemalan Institute of Tourism, for debits). These estimations are based on the most recent survey of tourism carried out by the Guatemalan Tourism Institute.

GUINEA

Transportation

The central bank asks banks and mining companies to perform their own surveys to estimate freight and insurance for imports they have reported on a c.i.f. or cost and freight basis. Otherwise, the central bank makes the estimates.

Travel

The central bank's sources for data are from over-the-counter exchange transactions conducted through the banking system and via travel agencies, as well as mission expenses of civil servants and staff of the semipublic mining companies. When the travel purpose is not clear, compilers list the amounts under *personal travel.*

GUINEA-BISSAU

Transportation

This category covers freight and passenger services on all modes of transport, as well as port services. Debit entries are estimated on the basis of freight and insurance data obtained from the pre-import registration slip. Transportation costs are not usually declared on this slip. When necessary, expenditure on freight and insurance is estimated at 17.5 percent of c.i.f. imports.

Travel

For credit, compilers derive entries from surveys of commercial banks and hotels concerning the expenditure of foreign visitors. For debit, they derive entries from the records of banks and ministries.

GUYANA

Transportation

This category covers freight and passenger services for sea and air transport. Surveys are conducted to obtain these data.

INTERNATIONAL MONETARY FUND (IMF) NOTES

Travel

Credit entries include all receipts from transactions in foreign currency at bank and nonbank "cambios" and traveler's checks encashed. Debit entries comprise purchases of traveler's checks and foreign currency sold at cambios.

HAITI

Transportation

Data on transportation services are estimated on the basis of information provided by the port and airport authorities and on the basis of annual surveys carried out at Haitian and foreign airlines and at shipping agencies.

Travel

The Secretariat of State for Tourism gathers monthly statistics on the number of tourists in Haiti. Estimated income from travel is distributed under separate headings for tourists arriving by air, ship, and road, respectively. For those arriving by air, the number of tourists recorded during the period in question is multiplied by the average duration of their stay and by their estimated daily expenditures. Data coming from the airport authority related to the number of travelers are also used by the IED.

For those arriving by ship and spending a maximum of 24 hours in Haiti (excursionists), the number is multiplied by an estimate of the sum spent on the day in question. The number of tourists crossing the border is obtained from data of the central bank's Tax Operations Division on tolls paid at counters.

Travel debits are estimated based on the number of Haitians leaving the country.

HONDURAS

Transportation

Data on passenger transportation are obtained by periodic surveys and administrative records provided by the ENP, the Airports Commission, and other institutions.

Travel

Credit and debit entries for travel are based on information provided by the IHT and the DGPM.

HONG KONG, CHINA

Services

The C&SD collects data on trade in services primarily from the *Annual Survey of Imports and Exports of Services (ASIES)*, supplemented by results from other annual or quarterly surveys and administrative data sources. Data from administrative sources include those from the Hong Kong Tourism Board, the Immigration Department, and the Treasury. The value of financial intermediation services is indirectly measured using the "reference rate" method. Services data for 2009 presented in this *Yearbook* contain only the net balance and total credits and debits. A full breakdown of 11 service items will be compiled when the *ASIES* results for 2009 become available.

HUNGARY

Transportation

Up to 2004, the MNB compiled the data. The primary ITRS data source (reports of monetary institutions) provided a breakdown by transportation category (passenger, freight, and other) but did not distinguish the means of transportation (sea, air, or other).

Since 2005, the HCSO has compiled the data. The main source is the direct reporting of companies. Additionally, administrative data are used.

In addition to the primary information source, which records transportation services on separate accounts, an adjustment (related to the change in the terms of delivery of goods) relies on the data derived from the external trade statistics. Transportation services are adjusted with a value equal to the adjustment in the terms of delivery of goods, but with the opposite sign. The estimation of the terms of delivery correction and its allocation between debits and credits for transportation services are based on bills of clearance. The HCSO carries out the estimation and allocation, and the MNB uses the data obtained.

Travel

Since 2004, the travel item (both inbound and outbound) of balance of payments is compiled from results of border surveys. In the course of these surveys, Hungarians returning from abroad and foreigners leaving Hungary are asked about their travel-related expenses. Data include part of international transport fares and some other package tour elements (commission). Based on the survey results, the ITRS-based time series on travel have been revised going back to 2000.

Up to 2003, settlement data (reports by the MNB, commercial banks, exchange offices, and companies holding accounts abroad) were used for compiling travel services. Travel-related flows reported by banks and exchange offices were corrected with the following:

- The balance of cash transactions affecting households' foreign exchange accounts held at resident banks, as well as the balance of forint/foreign currency exchange transactions carried out at banks, were recorded under travel. As of 2003, relying on a direct survey of account holders (2000) and natural indicators, the MNB estimated separately the breakdown by various components (travel, income, current transfers, real estate investment) of the credit and debit entries for these cash transactions. It recorded the transaction values obtained under the appropriate items in the balance of payments. Simultaneously with the methodological switch, it had revised the time series going back to 1995.

- The MNB primarily classified as travel the foreign exchange bought by exchange offices from residents. Therefore, as of 1998, travel receipts included the excess of foreign currency purchased by exchange offices from residents over a benchmark value (of a similar item in 1997 for the period between 1998 and 2000, and from 2001, an amount equaling 5 percent of travel expenditures in the previous month). Before 1998, the MNB treated these transactions as reexchange of foreign exchange previously bought for travel purposes by residents. It recorded them as correction entries to travel debit.

ICELAND

Services

SI reports quarterly on the external trade in services; basing its compilation on surveying. Quarterly, it surveys all companies defined as large enterprises in the sampling frame (about 100) about their trade in services to and from abroad in the current year.

From the population of about 4,500 small- and medium-sized enterprises, SI takes a sample of about 700 small- and medium-sized enterprises, surveying them about the external trade in services to and from abroad during last year and using the information to estimate their activities in the current year. More detailed metadata can be obtained from the SI website http://www.statice.is

INDIA

Transportation

This category covers all modes of transport and port services; the data are based mainly on the receipts and payments reported by the banks in respect of transportation items. In addition to the foreign exchange transactions records, the survey of unclassified receipts is also used as a source. These sources are supplemented by information collected from major airline and shipping companies in respect of payments from foreign accounts. A benchmark Survey of Freight and Insurance on Exports is also used to estimate freight receipts on account of exports.

Travel

Travel data are obtained from foreign exchange transactions records, supplemented by information from the surveys of unclassified receipts. The estimates of travel receipts also use the information on foreign tourist arrivals and expenditure, received from the Ministry of Tourism as a cross-check of the foreign exchange transactions and survey data.

INDONESIA

Transportation

This category covers freight, passenger, and other by all modes of transport. Entries for the value of freight debits are mainly estimated on the basis of information on freight furnished in customs declaration forms.

For passenger and freight credits, the BI collects data from the ITRS. Data on passenger transportation debits are estimated based on a survey of travelers and average air fares derived from a survey of travel agencies.

Travel

For travel credits and debits, the BI derives entries from censuses and surveys conducted by the Ministry of Tourism and the Central Bureau of Statistics. Estimates are made by combining the number of foreign visitors and the number of Indonesian travelers abroad with estimation of their average expenditures. It should be noted that part of the travel debit item is accounted for by *hajj* pilgrimages.

IRAN, ISLAMIC REPUBLIC OF

Services

The entries for transactions in services cover passenger services, freight and insurance, travel, and other public and private services—most of which are derived from the foreign exchange records of the banking system and from reports on receipts and payments provided by banks. The largest debit items are freight, other business services, and insurance, whereas the largest credit items are government and other business services.

Freight and insurance services are estimated based on the information on transportation undertaken by residents, which the central bank obtains from the foreign exchange records of the banking system. To compare and adjust this figure, the CBI uses reports from the major land transportation companies. It also includes an adjustment on the basis of statistics supplied by maritime transportation companies.

For other services items, the central bank obtains data from the foreign exchange records of the banking system, which are recorded on a cash basis. Other services items include travel (university students and patients), other transport services (transportation companies), public services (including membership fees paid to international organizations), commissions, financial services, and cultural services (purchase of books and articles from abroad).

To derive the travel entreis, the CBI uses statistics released by the Iran Touring and Tourism Organization (prepared for the World Tourism Organization) and a household budget questionnaire.

IRAQ

Transportation

This category covers various modes of transport and port services. Data on passenger fares for travel by official travelers are based on estimates from the grants received, and on information provided by the MOPDC and other governmental agencies.

Travel

Data on travel are estimated on the basis of average expenditures, number of residents traveling abroad and nonresidents traveling in Iraq, and the duration of their stay. The major data sources are (1) statistics provided by the Residency and Nationality Department of the government, (2) statistics from different ministries and banks of persons sent abroad on official missions, (3) data on numbers of Iraqi pilgrims from the Nationality and Passport Affairs Department, (4) data from the MOF for Iraqis on study leave, and (5) estimates of grants used for foreign missions and training purposes.

IRELAND

Transportation

Passenger fares paid by residents of Ireland to foreign transport companies generally cannot be distinguished and are instead included in the travel (debit) item. Disbursements in Irish ports and airports by foreign carriers, time charters, and other receipts from abroad by Irish carriers are included in the air and sea transport items. These data are collected from administrative sources.

Travel

Data are based on estimates of the number of travelers and their per capita expenditures, provided internally by the CSO's Tourism and Travel Section. These estimates of the number of travelers cover those traveling by public carriers (based on information supplied by sea, air, and land transport companies operating in international traffic) and those traveling privately by road across the Northern Ireland border.

Expenditures by Irish residents abroad and by foreign visitors to Ireland are estimated from information from the large sample survey of travelers (i.e., the *Passenger Card Inquiry*) conducted by the CSO, as well as information from CSO's *Household Travel Survey*. See also information under "Transportation" above.

ISRAEL

Transportation

The major sources for freight and transportation are Israeli companies that operate ships and aircraft on international routes, foreign shipping and aviation companies that operate in Israel, the Ports Authority in Israel, ship and aircraft repair companies, companies that supply food and bunker oil to ships and aircraft, and the Civil Aviation Service of the Ministry of Transport.

Transactions include receipts resulting from the transport of cargo by foreign carriers temporarily leased by Israeli companies. The data also include receipts and payments by ships owned by Israeli subsidiaries under a foreign flag (convenience flag), operated by Israeli agents only.

Some reports of Israeli shipping and aviation companies include a detailed breakdown of expenditures according to type of currency and not according to the location of the expenditures—in Israel or abroad. Compilers correct or adjust the item *other expenditures* in these reports (which includes information from other sources), such as the purchase of tickets for travel abroad by Israelis in foreign currency or the purchase in Israel of bunker oil in foreign currency.

Beginning in 1971, repairs of Israeli ships and aircraft performed abroad by foreign insurance agents have been included in expenditures of Israeli shipping and aviation companies. At the same time, these expenditures have been recorded as income from insurance claims in the insurance item. Until 1971, this listing, as well as that included in the insurance item, was a net figure.

Travel

For estimation of credit entries, compilers use a semiannual survey of foreign tourists, conducted by the Ministry of Tourism and under the supervision of the Central Bureau of Statistics (CBS). The survey provides the average expenditure per tourist during each half year, while the total expenditure of foreign tourists is estimated according to the average expenditure and the total number of tourists leaving Israel each quarter. (This latter figure is obtained from the statistics of the CBS Demography Department.)

Debits are estimated on the basis of a quarterly updated survey conducted by the CBS for 1997, regarding the average expenditure per tourist, and on current data on departures abroad of Israel residents, published by the CBS.

ITALY

Transportation

Passenger transport items were estimated on the basis of the sample survey of transport enterprises and the sample survey of international tourism (for data on the number of passengers). Starting from 2002, BI derives both passengers' transport costs and number of passengers from its survey on international tourism.

Travel

Up to 1989, BI compiled the data from transfers related to international trips for tourism, business, health, and education purposes and from credit card transactions. A monthly sample survey of travelers, introduced in 1996 and covering about 60 border points, has now become the main source of data for travel services. The survey provides a detailed breakdown by purpose of the travel, according to the supplementary items indicated in *BPM5*. Historical data for 1990–95 have been revised and adjusted in a linear manner with the results of the survey.

JAMAICA

Transportation

This category covers freight and passenger services by all types of transportation. The Port and Airport Authorities of Jamaica provide data for port services. The BOJ also derives data from annual surveys of the national airlines, foreign airlines, and shipping companies. It obtains information on passenger services from surveys of national airlines and foreign airlines.

Travel

Compilers derive travel credits from expenditure surveys carried out by the Jamaica Tourist Board. Credit data also come from immigration statistics on the number of visitors and their average length of stay. Travel debits are compiled from banking records and from data supplied by the Ministry of Labor.

JAPAN

Transportation

The data are obtained from the reports on revenue and expenditure of airline and ship operators and the Payments Reports. This item includes the value of freight, deducted from the value of imports in the trade statistics. Distinctions between subitems, such as *sea transport* and *air transport*, depend on mode of transport.

Travel

Travel estimates are prepared by combining data on numbers of travelers (the statistics on tourists), with data on estimates of average expenditures on goods and services.

INTERNATIONAL MONETARY FUND (IMF) NOTES

Estimates of other expenditures, not covered by the above-mentioned estimates, are prepared by using other data sources. The expenditures of long-term international students are estimated by using data published by government agencies. Data on large amounts of medical expenses are obtained from the Payments Reports.

JORDAN

Transportation

For credit and debit entries for transportation services (freight and passenger), CBJ derives data from information provided by Aqaba Port Authority and by airline shipping and land companies, respectively. CBJ records entries for freight credits on the basis of data on freight and other transportation extracted from ITRS forms.

The breakdown between "passengers" and "other transportation" is estimated based on available information and indicators from the main transportation companies. Entries for freight debits are estimated at 9 percent of c.i.f. imports.

Travel

For travel, CBJ bases entries on the number of departures and arrivals, provided by the Ministry of Tourism and Antiquities in cooperation with the Ministry of Interior, and on the results of tourism surveys, conducted by DOS. These surveys provide information on the average expenditure of foreign tourists coming into Jordan and resident tourists traveling abroad, and on the average duration of stay.

Compilers use data on the number of Jordanians studying abroad—sourced from the Ministry of Higher Education—to estimate education expenditures abroad; these estimates are included in the travel debits.

KAZAKHSTAN

Transportation

This category covers all modes of transport and port services. The NBK bases the data for passenger fares and port charges mainly on reports it collects from marine shipping, airline, railway, and road companies.

Travel

The NBK estimates data on travel on the basis of estimated average expenditures, number of residents traveling abroad and nonresidents traveling in Kazakhstan, and the estimated duration of their stay. Information on travelers by country of origin or destination and type of travel is also available. Beginning with data for 2007, payments by resident households for health and education services acquired abroad are also included. The data are sourced from the reports of commercial banks, in accordance with the Unified Payment Purpose Classifier (UPPC).

KENYA

Transportation

This category covers passenger fares, freight services by all modes of transport, and port services. The credit entries are derived from information obtained from Kenya Railways, sea transport, air road, inland waterway (Lake Victoria), and pipeline transport firms. Data on passenger fares, port services, and leases are obtained from Kenya Airways (KA), the Kenya Airport Authority (KAA), Nairobi Airport Services, bus companies, and Kenya Ports Authority. Port services include services to shipping lines.

Travel

Data are obtained from CBK returns on foreign exchange statistics from commercial banks. The data are adjusted using the ratios obtained from inbound and outbound surveys.

KOREA, REPUBLIC OF

Transportation

For transportation services, the BOK derives entries from the KFX and surveys of resident airlines and shipping companies. The KFX data provide a breakdown by transportation category (i.e., passenger transportation, freight, or other transportation).

Travel

The KFX data include both nonresidents' sales of foreign currency in Korea and residents' purchases of foreign currency in Korea. The KFX also covers the use of traveler's checks and credit cards. Business and personal travel has been distinguished since 2006.

KUWAIT

Transportation

Since 2007, the International Air Transport Association (IATA) has been providing information on passenger ticket sales to residents by foreign airlines. The CBK estimates the freight component as a percentage of imports (14 percent of c.i.f. imports). The CBK allocates 95 percent of the estimated freight services to shipping services for imports and 80 percent of the estimated insurance services to foreign carriers and providers. For credit entries, the KAC provides information on passenger ticket sales abroad. The CBK compiles estimates for transportation services provided to nonresidents from reports provided by the KOTC and other shipping companies.

For the *other transportation* item, the CBK compiles estimates of expenses abroad on the basis of data provided by the KAC and Kuwaiti shipping companies. On the credit side, the CBK compiles estimates from questionnaires and reports provided by the KAC, Kuwaiti shipping companies, the Kuwait Ports Authority (for port dues), and the General Directorate of Civil Aviation (for airport dues). These estimates include transport and storage services provided to the international coalition forces stationed in Kuwait and Iraq from 2003 onward.

Travel

For travel debit entries, the CBK compiles estimates on the basis of surveys implemented by the CBK and reports submitted by government agencies on expenses paid for education, conferences, training, medical treatment, and official missions abroad. For credit entries, the CBK estimates are based on the number of nonresident visitors to Kuwait and their average expenditures. The Immigration Department provides data on the number of nonresident visitors.

KYRGYZSTAN

Transportation

The NSC collects data from domestic airlines, railway, and road transportation companies. The NBKR supplements these data with information it collects from enterprises and the ITRS. Up to 2007, the NBKR derived freight on imports provided by nonresidents from the estimated freight included in the c.i.f. value of imports and adjusted to exclude transportation provided by resident carriers. Since 2007, the NSC has introduced its own methodology to calculate freight services.

Travel

The NSC assesses travel services on the basis of the estimated average per diem expenditures, number of residents traveling abroad and nonresidents traveling in the Kyrgyz Republic, and the estimated duration of their stay. The SCI provides data on the number of travelers, country of origin (for foreign travelers), country of destination (for domestic travelers), and types of travel (private, business, etc.).

LAO PEOPLE'S DEMOCRATIC REPUBLIC

Transportation

This item covers freight, passenger transportation by overflights, and other types of transportation. The BOL's Operation Department provides data on overflights, and the remaining elements are based on BOL staff estimates.

Travel

Credit entries are derived from information in surveys conducted by the National Tourism Authority of Lao P.D.R., including the number of visitors arriving in the country, the number of overnight stays, and the estimated average expenditure.

Debit entries are derived from data from the Receipts and Payments reporting system provided by the commercial banks, and some data are estimated by BOP staff.

LATVIA

Transportation

Compilers obtain data from the quarterly survey of transportation and intermediary services and the statistics on nonbanks' external payments (ITRS). Data cover transportation services rendered/received by mode of transport. In addition, staff use foreign trade statistics to obtain, in accordance with the calculation methodology described in the section *Goods*, the difference between c.i.f. and f.o.b. values of imported goods. The share of transportation services carried out by nonresidents is set apart from the obtained figure and included under transportation in the balance of payments.

For credit entries for passenger transportation by air, reporting agents declare total amounts received for the international carriage of passengers in the quarterly survey on transportation and intermediary services. The compilers use the data on the monthly number of residents and nonresidents crossing the state border, broken down by mode of transportation, for calculating the proportion of nonresidents in total border crossings. They use this ratio to determine the nonresident part of the international carriage of passengers broken down by mode of transportation.

Debit entries are obtained by calculation, using (1) data on the number of departing passengers by airlines, submitted by the Riga international airport; (2) CSB data on the monthly number of residents and nonresidents crossing the state border by air; and (3) information on the average prices of airline tickets.

Travel

Compilers derive the data on travel from the CSB aggregated data on persons entering and leaving the country. Travelers are polled at border control points four times a year to obtain information about nonresident spending in Latvia and resident spending abroad. Using mathematical methods, the compilers calculate the average spending of a traveler and, thereafter, obtain travelers' total spending. The number of travelers is available from the State Border Guard of the Republic of Latvia, which registers persons entering and leaving the country.

For personal travel credit entries, compilers estimate expenditures of students, using the number of foreign students in Latvia, submitted by the Ministry of Education and universities. For debit entries, compilers use the information submitted by foreign embassies in Latvia on the number of Latvian students and average expenditures by country.

LEBANON

Transportation

Only public sector operations were recorded before 2003. Using the information obtained from the ITRS, as of 2003, the ESS also includes data on private sector transactions (banks; the nonbank financial sector; and the private sector, comprising households and private companies). This section also comprises freight transactions, estimated by applying a 7.5 percent average rate on the value of imports c.i.f. The obtained figure is subdivided among the sea, air, and other transport sections according to the weights obtained from the records of goods by the different ports of entry.

Travel

The ESS bases estimates on the General Directorate of General Security data on arriving and departing travelers through all borders and on an evaluation of the average spending per individual. It also derives statistics from basic circular #1564 (decision #6754), dated October 3, 1997, related to automated teller machines [ATMs] and credit cards. (This circular has been amended twice: (1) in June 10, 1999, by circular #63, decision #7299, and (2) in August 26, 2002, by circular #24, decision #8216.) The ESS adds these statistics to the data with the aim of improving the estimate of tourist expenditures and revenues. This circular covers all transactions done via ATMs, as well as debit and credit cards, to keep track of nonresident expenditures in Lebanon and resident expenditures abroad. As of 2003, data from the ITRS have been added, giving this item a wider statistical coverage.

LESOTHO

Transportation

Data on passenger services/air travel are obtained through a continuous quarterly survey covering travel agencies in Lesotho.

Travel

Data on expenditure by foreign visitors to Lesotho are obtained from the Lesotho Tourism Development Corporation, which phased out the old Lesotho Tourist Board. Data on expenditure by Lesotho residents on official trips abroad are obtained from the Ministry of Finance and Development Planning.

Data on expenditure by government-funded Basotho students studying abroad are obtained from the National Manpower Development Secretariat. Data on expenditure by privately funded Basotho students studying abroad are obtained from the CBL's Policy and Exchange Control Division (PECD). The National University of Lesotho, Center for Accounting Studies, Lesotho Agricultural College, and Lesotho College of Education (formerly known as the National Teachers Training College) provide information on fees and living expenditures by foreign students studying in Lesotho, although the figures are small.

LIBERIA

Transportation

Passenger travel represents fares paid by residents to nonresident airlines (debit), and is derived from a data model that uses interview-based information from foreign airlines in Liberia.

Travel

The credit entry of business travel covers purchases by nonresidents of goods and services in Liberia, including diplomatic staff and expatriates treated as nonresidents, the military contingent of UNMIL, and other visitors, mainly business travelers. The category of expatriates covers international staff of UNMIL and other donor projects, such as foreign governments, the European Union, UNOs, and other international organizations.

The expenditures on local purchases by expatriates are derived from a comprehensive *Compilation Framework on Foreign Assistance (FACF)*, which uses (1) actual detailed data on UNMIL expenditure and (2) the data on donor projects, disbursements, and commitments, as available. The latter are collected from the Aid Management Unit of the Ministry of Finance of Liberia (MOF) by donor projects, such as expenditures by donors broken down by four Poverty Reduction Strategy (PRS) Development Pillars. In addition, the model also incorporates the results of the Pilot Survey of Hotels in Monrovia.

The debit entry of business travel covers state budget expenditure on official travel derived from the MOF.

Expenditures on medical travel and *expenditures of residents traveling abroad* are both model-based data estimates employing ad hoc information on the number of travelers abroad obtained from airline carriers and the assumption of the average expenditure abroad by resident travelers.

LIBYAN ARAB REPUBLIC

Transportation

The item includes passenger and freight services. The CBL derives the data mainly from commercial bank records and reporting by transportation companies.

Travel

The CBL obtains data on travel (for tourism, education, and medical expense) credits and debits from its records and commercial banks.

LITHUANIA

Transportation

Transport services of passengers cover all services provided in international transportation. They also include transportation of passenger baggage and other items that may be carried at no extra cost, and rental services of all passenger vehicles with an operator.

Travel

Covers primarily goods and services acquired from an economy by travelers during visits of less than one year to that economy. Goods and services are purchased by, or on behalf of, travelers or provided, without a quid pro quo (that is, are provided as a gift), for travelers to use or give away. This item excludes transportation expenses of travelers within the economies they are visiting (where such transportation is provided by carriers not resident in a particular economy being visited), as well as the international carriage of travelers, both of which are covered in passenger services under transportation. This item also excludes travelers' goods purchased for resale in the traveler's own economy or in any other economy. Travel is divided into two subcomponents: business and personal.

Data on travel services use various sources: monthly data on arrivals from non-EU countries into and resident departures from Lithuania, as provided by the State Border Guard Service at the Ministry of the Interior. Data also come from Statistics Lithuania research on Lithuanian travelers and their average expenditure and length of stay abroad and from quarterly surveys of enterprises providing accommodation services (hotels, health spas, etc.) and enterprises involved in sales of tour packages.

LUXEMBOURG

Travel

The main sources are surveys, other statistics, and administrative data. Compilers record under business travel the personal expenditures on goods and services by nonresident cross-border workers.

MACAO, CHINA

Transportation

The data on passenger, freight, and other transportation are obtained from statistics of various activity surveys and national accounts. Because the current survey system does not differentiate the value of this service among different modes of transportation, no breakdown on the type of transportation is available.

INTERNATIONAL MONETARY FUND (IMF) NOTES

Travel

Credit entries for travel are mainly derived from national account statistics that include travelers' expenditures on gaming, accommodation, and other expenses, utilizing data of the Visitor Expenditure Survey, Hotel Survey, and administrative records on hotel and gaming receipts. Gaming expenditures of nonresidents are estimated based on an appropriate method and proportion applied to the gross gaming receipts on administrative records.

Travelers' expenditures on accommodation are estimated from the number of room nights sold and the average room rates, whereas expenditures on other areas are estimated by using the number of visitor arrivals, per capita spending of visitors, and other tourism data. The split between business and personal travel is based on purpose of visit reported by interviewed visitors.

Entries for business travel (debit) are mainly derived from the enterprise surveys and activity surveys, whereas those for personal travel (debit) are principally extracted from national account statistics that are mainly estimated from the Household Budget Survey and other statistics.

MALAWI

Transportation

The main subcomponents of transport are passenger, freight, and landing fees. Credits on passenger and freight transportation relate mostly to air transport, collected from the sole domestic airline operator, Air Malawi.

Travel

Data on travel debits are obtained from the exchange control records through forms that are completed for purchases and sales of foreign currency from authorized dealers. Credits are compiled on the basis of exit cards completed by tourists returning abroad to their original economies. The data tend to underestimate credits on travel.

MALAYSIA

Transportation

This category covers freight and passenger services by all modes of transport and port services. For transportation services, the source is the Quarterly Survey of International Trade in Services (ITS). The survey canvasses companies that provide transport services, particularly airline and shipping companies, airports and seaport authorities. Debit entries for freight and insurance are estimated between 5 to 8 percent of the value of imports c.i.f. Freight and insurance estimates are further supplemented with information derived from other agencies.

Travel

For travel credits, DoSM compiles data from expenditure surveys of foreign visitors carried out by Tourism Malaysia. DoSM compiles estimates by combining the number of foreign visitors with estimates of average expenditures.

For travel debits, DoSM compiles entries from the BNM records, supplemented with information provided by the Pilgrimage Fund Board and other ministries and agencies.

MALDIVES

Transportation

This category covers transportation of passengers, freight, and other items. The MPRD obtains data on passenger services and port services from MACL and estimates based on data obtained a few years back from Maldives Ports Limited and Maldives National Shipping Limited (MNSL).

Travel

Travel credits (receipts) are the MMA estimates based on data obtained from the MOTAC regarding tourist arrivals, tourist bed nights, and expected change in room rates in resorts and hotels. Estimates are adjusted for seasonality.

The MMA calculates travel receipts from three items: receipts by tour operators, purchases at resorts, and expenditure outside of resorts. The first item, receipts by tour operators, is calculated by multiplying bed nights by an estimated average daily expenditure. The other two items are aimed at covering the cost of incidentals, souvenirs, and similar—that is, any expenditure other than what is spent on the tour package. The MMA calculates purchases at resorts on the basis of a per diem estimate, while it bases estimates of expenditure outside of resorts on numbers of arrivals.

For travel debits, the MMA obtains estimates from various sources. The business travel and health-related expenditure component under Personal Travel covers expenditures relating to government travel and government-sponsored medical treatment abroad, based on data obtained from the foreign exchange records maintained by the MMA.

For expenditure on education-related travel, the MMA used to obtain estimates from the Ministry of Human Resources, Youth, and Sports (MHRYS), which provided information on expenses associated with scholarships under the Education and Training project. However, because these estimates have not been reported in the past few years, the earlier estimates have been used as a base for the recent estimates.

The above-mentioned travel debits would not include overseas education or health-related travel financed by private individuals or sponsored by nongovernment entities, which would be recorded under other travel as a residual.

For other travel, estimates are derived as the sum of total expenditure on hajj travel (obtained from hajj tour organizers and relevant government authorities) and the residual between the estimate of total expenditures by Maldivian travelers and travel under the other categories.

MALI

Transportation

Data on passenger services are collected from national and foreign airlines.

Travel

The amounts posted as credits to this account are determined from the results of surveys of the Tourism Commissioner's Office and of hotels concerning arrivals of foreign tourists and hotel occupancy.

The debits posted are mainly expenditures by non-Malian residents on leave. This expenditure is estimated on the basis of the income of expatriates working in the private sector, compensation of technical assistance personnel and non-Malian permanent staff in international organizations, as well as the length of leave of these groups of persons.

However, the figures pertaining to government missions are sourced from the National Directorate of the Treasury and Public Accounting.

Expenditure by Malian students abroad is estimated from scholarships. Data on these scholarships, whether foreign or granted by the Malian government, are basically collected from the Ministry of Higher Secondary Education and Scientific Research.

MALTA

Transportation

The source for passenger transportation, separated by mode of transport, is the monthly survey of airline and shipping companies.

Travel

Regarding travel, NSO derives gross earnings from tourism from its frontier surveys—TOURSTAT and CRUISTAT. Data have been revised back to 1995 for comparability.

Gross expenditure by residents traveling abroad is derived from information provided by the Tourism unit within the NSO. These data are replacing the previous source, emanating from foreign currency transactions that banking institutions and other authorized dealers reported to the CBM on a monthly basis.

MAURITIUS

Transportation

The main data sources are the survey of airline and shipping companies (quarterly since 1999; half-yearly prior to then) and the CSO. Transportation credits measure receipts by domestic carriers from passenger fares, freight on exports and shipments between other countries, and other port disbursements. Transportation debits measure payments made to nonresident carriers for passenger fares, freight on imports, and other port disbursements.

Travel

Travel credits are derived from purchases by banks of foreign exchange from tourists, business travelers, hotels, cash dealers, and traders. Travel debit estimates are derived from the banking records of banks.

MEXICO

Transportation

For passenger fares, BM estimates the entries from information provided by the resident airlines on their total earnings on international transportation. It supplements these estimates with information from migration statistics on the number of residents and nonresidents traveling by air and from travel surveys on expenditures on ticket purchases by travelers.

Travel

BM bases credit entries on immigration authorities' reports on the number of nonresidents visiting Mexico and on its own sample surveys on travelers' average expenditure. It obtains the debit entries using a similar procedure.

Travel is broken down into tourists and excursionists (one-day visitors). Tourists are defined as those who have spent at least one night in the host country and as those who, having not spent at least one night in the host country, have visited it beyond the border area; excursionists are defined as those who have not spent the night in the host country. No distinction is made between business and personal travel.

MONGOLIA

Transportation

The Mongolian Railways and Mongolian Airlines (MIAT) report information for the credit and debit entries for passenger fares and other distributive and auxiliary services.

Travel

Up to 1996, the IED derived credit and debit entries for travel from the foreign exchange record. From 1997 onward, travel is estimated on the basis of information on the number of travelers combined with an estimate of the average duration of stay and an estimate of the per capita expenditures. The General Authority for Border Protection of Mongolia compiles the data on the number of travelers, while the National Tourism Agency of the Ministry of Roads, Transportation, and Tourism estimates and provides the average number of nights per visit and the average daily expenditure.

MONTENEGRO

Transportation

The transportation services item is classified according to the type of transport (sea, air, railway, and other) and on the basis of the category of services (freight, passengers, and other). Passenger services cover all services provided in the international transport of nonresidents by resident carriers (credit) and that of residents by nonresident carriers (debit). Freight services refer to transportation regarding merchandise trade and can be provided to or acquired from abroad either by resident or nonresident carriers. The main source for recording transportation services is the ITRS.

Travel

Travel revenues are calculated on a basis of estimations and the ITRS. The estimation is based on the results of the survey conducted by the CBM to determine the average daily expenditure by foreign visitors in Montenegro as well as Monstat data on overnight stays. The data on travel revenues, besides estimates, includes data derived from the ITRS on expenditures by those traveling for health and educational purposes. The travel expenditures abroad by Montenegrin residents are estimated based on the data compiled from the ITRS.

MONTSERRAT

See Eastern Caribbean Currency Union.

MOROCCO

Transportation

This item records, on both the credit and debit sides, payments relating to the transportation of goods and passengers, broken down by means of transportation: sea, air, and other.

Travel

Travel credits correspond to receipts from (1) abroad received by tourism sector operators (travel agencies, hotels, clubs, tourist transportation, etc.), (2) encashment of traveler's checks and international credit card payments, as well as foreign currency banknotes exchanged via the banking system or exchange bureaus by tourists during their stay in Morocco, and (3) part of the foreign currency banknotes exchanged by Moroccans residing abroad that are used to cover their board and lodging in Morocco.

Debit entries cover the various allocations of foreign banknotes to residents when they travel for purposes of tourism, business, education, medical care, training and missions, or pilgrimages. Debits also cover bank or postal transfers made to cover expenses incurred during their travel.

MOZAMBIQUE

Transportation

The BM compiles data on transportation services from reports presented by the authorized foreign exchange banks and from balance of payments surveys. Since 1995, it has introduced specific surveys of selected transportation companies (railways, national airlines, and shipping). Very recently, owing to the process of improving the collection of transportation data by the BM's Balance of Payments Unit, the response rate of the surveys has improved substantively.

Travel

Data on travel credits and debits are based on reports presented by the authorized foreign exchange banks, exchange bureaus, central bank, and the National Tourism Authority. A specific survey has been introduced in various hotels in the country.

MYANMAR

Transportation

This item includes freight and passenger services for all modes of transport and port services. The source is the ITRS.

Travel

In compiling the travel item, the CBM uses the ITRS source, supplemented with estimates derived from data from the Immigration and Population Department for the number of tourists and from the Ministry of Hotels and Tourism for total travel expenditure.

NAMIBIA

Transportation

This component is estimated from the external trade data and data from a survey of airlines. In 1995, a specific survey was instituted, but the response rate was very low, owing to a lack of cooperation from the reporting units (i.e., the national airlines, railways, and road transport operators) and the lack of awareness of the importance of balance of payments statistics among the respondents. However, the RD is now able to obtain a reasonable response rate from the main airlines.

Travel

Data on travel credits and debits are estimated on the basis of the Exit Survey 2002 contracted by the Ministry of Environment and Tourism because of the absence of comprehensive data. Estimates of data on travelers arriving in and departing from Namibia are made on the basis of information from a variety of sources, including the Ministry of Home Affairs, national airlines, and various hotels in the country.

NEPAL

Transportation

The data are collected from commercial banks, the NRB, Indian airlines having offices in Nepal, and domestic airlines for three main categories—freight, passenger services, and other transportation. The main credit items are the foreign exchange earnings of local airlines on passenger services and enterprises engaged in land transport. Debits reflect mainly freight charges, passenger services, and payments made to the foreign transport companies.

Travel

Data on travel are collected from the ITRS and the NRB's Foreign Exchange Management Department. This item includes, as credits, the receipts from foreign visitors in the form of cash, traveler's checks, drafts, etc., and the foreign exchange earnings from nonresidents of local hotels, travel agencies, and certain service agencies.

The item includes, as debits, the residents' expenditures abroad for business and personal travel, education expenses, medical treatment, and passport facilities (foreign exchange facilities provided to Nepalese passport holders going abroad).

NETHERLANDS

Services

As of the second quarter of 2003, Statistics Netherlands also provides quarterly data on international trade in services. To that end, it adopted a new quarterly survey. In 2007, the reporting population for this survey comprised a sample of 5,350 reporting agents. A small number (350) of large entities reports extensive services data. In addition, Statistics Netherlands surveys a larger number (5,000) of small and medium enterprises with less detail. The results are grossed up to a national level.

NETHERLANDS ANTILLES

Transportation

The BNA derives transportation entries from surveys, the ITRS data, and the estimates of the freight costs on imports (calculated as 2.5 percent of the import value).

Travel

For average expenditures of foreign tourists, the BNA derives data from exit surveys of foreign visitors (cruise and stayover), conducted by the tourism organizations of the islands forming the Netherlands Antilles. Thereafter, compilers calculate credit entries by multiplying the average expenditures with the average length of stay and the number of foreign tourists.

The debit entries are derived from the ITRS.

NEW ZEALAND

Transportation

The main types of transportation services data collected are for the carriage of goods (freight) and passengers. Also included under transportation services are charters of carriers, tugboat services, airport and harbor fees, and goods consumed by carriers in the course of their operations, including bunkering and provisioning. These data are provided from quarterly and annual surveys of resident airlines and shipping companies, nonresident airlines (through their New Zealand offices), and New Zealand agents acting for nonresident ship operators.

Travel

Data on the expenditure of overseas tourists in New Zealand are derived from the International Visitors' Survey (IVS), conducted by Covec Ltd, an economic consulting company, for the New Zealand Ministry of Tourism. In January 2003, the sampling in the IVS was changed to a "flight-based" basis. Flight-based sampling is a nonrandom method of sampling, allowing the specific targeting of passengers with certain characteristics that are to be represented in the sample of international visitors. Departure cards of passengers generate data on the passenger characteristics. The sample is selected from departing visitors at New Zealand's three largest international airports—Auckland, Wellington, and Christchurch.

Separate estimates are also made for expenditure on education- and health-related travel by nonresidents. The estimates for education-related travel are derived from New Zealand Ministry of Education data on international student numbers and tuition fees. Living costs are estimated relative to tuition fees and added to derive total student expenditure. Health expenditure is derived from Crown Health Entity data.

Information on the expenditure of New Zealand residents traveling overseas is derived from a model that uses information obtained from a benchmark survey of returned New Zealand travelers.

NICARAGUA

Transportation

Credit entries for freight are estimated on the basis of information provided by Customs. For freight services obtained by importers, BCN uses data recorded in the customs declarations. For air passenger services, it bases the data on an annual enterprise survey. Data on other transport include services reported by the National Ports Enterprise.

Travel

To estimate credit and debit entries, BCN combines information provided by the Directorate General of Migration and Aliens (on the number of nonresident and resident travelers) with information derived from the monthly survey elaborated by the Central Bank of Nicaragua (on the travelers' expenditures and average stay) plus the External Programming Department's estimates.

NIGER

Transportation

Transportation includes the movement of goods (freight), transportation of passengers, and other types of transportation services.

Travel

The credit side of travel is estimated on the basis of questionnaires completed by hotels and data reported by the Ministry of Tourism. The debit side is estimated from questionnaires completed by companies, which declare the cost of missions abroad, and by the national scholarship agency (ANAB), pilgrimage agencies, and the Budget Directorate for expenditure by residents abroad for education, pilgrimages to Mecca, medical care, and travel by government officials. These data are reconciled with data from currency-changing services and the repatriation of banknotes between BCEAO agencies.

NIGERIA

Services

In respect of payments and receipts for all categories of services, the BOPSO explores data available in the cash flow statement that RED compiles for the public sector components, while the private sector counterparts are obtained from specialized returns of the DMBs to the CBN, such as sectoral utilization of foreign exchange (valid and not valid), domiciliary and external accounts inflows, etc. In January 2008, TED incorporated the World Trade Organization (WTO) format for reporting data on invisible transactions in the e-FASS. This has ensured the availability of more details on trade in services. As a result of this effort, the BOPSO is now able to produce data on all eleven major categories of trade in services as stipulated by the IMF's *BPM5*.

NORWAY

Transportation

The estimation of receipts from the provision of maritime freight and passenger services of nonresidents is based on the ocean transport survey compiled by SN. Compiled on both an annual and quarterly basis, the ocean transport survey is based on reports from shipping companies on both operating income and expenditures broken down by type of transportation.

Travel

Through 2004, entries for travel were based almost entirely upon data supplied by NCB on the sale of local currency in exchange for foreign currency, supplemented with data from credit card companies. From 2005 onward, the sources have been changed toward tourist statistics (i.e., accommodation statistics, passenger transport statistics) and travel surveys.

OMAN

Transportation

Data on transportation credits reflect the value of services provided to nonresidents at Omani ports. The CBO takes these data, representing payments of port dues, stevedoring, and demurrage charges, from the annual statements of the Port Services Corporation Ltd. Debit entries include estimated freight values on imports.

Travel

Travel credit estimates are based on the number of foreign tourist arrivals as provided by the immigration authorities, multiplied by the average expenditure per tourist as estimated through a comprehensive survey. Data on travel payments have been revised based on findings in the third tourism satellite project of the Ministry of Tourism.

Travel debits represent the estimated expenditure of students studying abroad, Omani pilgrims abroad, and health treatment received by Omani nationals abroad. Debits include estimates of expenditure by Omani residents abroad.

In 2003, a change in the methodology to compile statistics on travel data took into account the findings of a new tourism survey.

PAKISTAN

Transportation

This component covers all modes of transport and port services. Surveys of foreign shipping companies and airlines and the reporting of Pakistani shipping companies and airlines provide data for the freight, passenger, and other services components.

Travel

Data for both business and personal travel are collected through receipts and payments of the banking sector, plus the inward and outward remittances on travel through exchange companies operating in Pakistan.

Further, the travel expenses of crews of foreign shipping companies and airlines while staying in Pakistan and the travel expenses of crews of local shipping companies and airlines while staying abroad are collected through surveys of the respective companies/airlines.

PALESTINE (WEST BANK AND GAZA)

Transportation

This item consists of the transportation costs of passengers and goods, as well as auxiliary services, such as storage, cargo handling, etc. The data are obtained from economic surveys conducted by the PCBS.

Travel

The main sources used to compile the data on travel credits and debits are economic surveys, a hotel survey, the balance of payments annex to the labor force survey, the labor force survey, and data from the Ministry of Islamic Affairs, the Ministry of Health, and the Ministry of High Education.

For the debit data, these surveys and administrative records cover all travel transactions of residents abroad, such as students abroad, medication costs abroad, part of the wages of Palestinian border workers in Israel, and the expenditure of pilgrims (visitors to Mecca, the holy city of Muslims).

The credit data cover nonresidents coming to the Palestinian Territories, such as tourists, foreign employees of foreign consulates, representatives, international organizations, those visiting relatives, etc.

PANAMA

Transportation

INEC derives information on freight on imports from customs declarations. It obtains data on passenger services from surveys of national airlines and agents of foreign airlines. For port services, it obtains data from agents of foreign air and shipping lines, national airlines, container terminals ports, and the Panama Canal Authority (for tolls and other services to Canal users).

Travel

INEC bases data on sample surveys it conducts in conjunction with the Panamanian Tourism Institute, on the expenditures of foreign visitors in Panama and of Panamanian residents on their trips abroad, and on information derived from migration statistics on the number of travelers.

PAPUA NEW GUINEA

Transportation

Transportation services include receipts and payments from freight, port handling, or other transportation-related services on traded goods.

Travel

Travel data cover passenger services by all modes of transport and port services related to the transportation of passengers. The data include tickets, hotel rooms, airport taxes, and other travel expenses and receipts. A separate component of travel shows education-related expenditures, including all tutorial fees and remittances or receipts associated with education at all levels.

PARAGUAY

Transportation

The CBP obtains data to compile passenger services from the Capital Police, which reports the number of passengers entering and leaving the country using different carriers (air or land), multiplied by the ticket prices collected in surveys of local tourism operators.

Travel

Concerning inward tourism, the CBP obtains data monthly from the Directorate General of Tourism on the number of excursionists (mainly related to cross-border shopping) and tourists (who stay in the country for more than 24 hours). The central bank multiplies these data by an estimated daily expenditure based on UN estimates.

For outward tourism, the Capital Police provide data on the number of Paraguayan nationals leaving the country and, for air travel, their points of departure and destination. To calculate expenditure, the CBP uses a UN schedule of expenditure together with estimates based on interviews with tourism agents on cross-border shopping.

PERU

Transportation

The CRBP bases the credit and debit entries on its quarterly survey of international transport companies and agents. It surveys all national companies and foreign airlines. Transactions of foreign shipping companies are reported by their agents or representatives in Peru.

The survey provides data on freight charges, sale of passenger fares, and supporting and auxiliary services by mode of transport (air, sea, and other transport). Compilers also use the import freight charges recorded in customs declaration forms after they adjust the data to subtract freight services provided by resident enterprises.

Travel

Data are estimated on the basis of tourism surveys (inward and outward) that the CRBP and PROMPERU conduct at the Jorge Chavez International Airport, the Santa Rosa post on the Chilean border, and the Yunguyo post on the Bolivian border. These surveys provide estimates on the average expenditure of nonresident travelers in Peru and resident travelers abroad.

The number of international travelers is provided by the Directorate General of Migration and Naturalization, an agency of the Ministry of the Interior. Data include travelers that cross the border and spend more than a night abroad and same-day visitors abroad (outward tourism) or in Peru (inward tourism). Debit entries also include the contra-entry of scholarships recorded as current transfers.

PHILIPPINES

Transportation

Transportation refers largely to data on merchandise freight, sourced mainly from the foreign trade statistics. Other components of transportation services are provided by the ITRS and the CAB administrative data.

Travel

For travel receipts, the DES estimates data based on the Visitors Sample Survey (VSS) conducted by the DOT. The VSS provides information on the average expenditure of foreign tourists and their average length of stay in the Philippines. For tourist-related travel expenditures abroad by residents, data are derived from the ITRS and CBTS.

Beginning with the 1999 report, travel credits include nonresident OFs' expenditures in the Philippines during home visits. Travel debits cover expenditures of resident OFs in the host countries where they are deployed.

POLAND

Transportation

Data provided by the banking system on payments and by the surveys on enterprises for transportation services include services broken down by type (sea, air, railway, and other). These data are broken down by passenger transportation, freight, and other forms. Data received from the c.i.f./f.o.b. adjustment of the goods item are also included in freight transportation services. The value of these services is compiled as a fixed rate of the value of goods imports in the foreign trade statistics.

Travel

The travel item is compiled using data of the Institute of Tourism, which come from border surveys. The NBP receives data on travelers' expenditures: foreigners in Poland and Poles abroad.

PORTUGAL

Transportation

Transportation data are based on settlement data, supplemented with the estimates (see above) used to convert c.i.f. to f.o.b.-valued goods. Data distinguish the means of transportation (sea, air, rail, or other transport) and provide a breakdown by transportation category (passenger, freight, or other transportation).

Travel

Travel data are based on settlements (e.g., bank transfers, cash, traveler's checks, debit and credit cards, and other means of settlement), on information provided by travel agencies, and, on the credit side, on estimates produced by the BdP based on real indicators and prices of tourist activity (tourism statistics provided by the INE). Periodic border surveys are used to check the monthly figures and to estimate the split between business and personal travel.

REPUBLIC OF MOLDOVA

Transportation

Besides the estimates made for transportation payments related to imported goods, referred to above, additional data are obtained from other sources. The main sources are the ITRS and the NBS' data on transportation services, which are collected from companies that provide transport services, as well as the data on fees resulting from the pipeline transportation through Moldova. Disaggregating is done by type of transportation (air, sea, rail, road, and pipeline) and by category of services (freight, passenger, and other).

Travel

Data on travel are compiled using information provided by the NBS, the banking system, institutions that provide travel, and accommodation services. Estimates of expenditures made abroad by persons engaged in the export/import of goods, by business travelers, and by workers residing abroad for less than one year are also calculated. Estimates of students' travel expenditures are made from data provided by the Ministry of Education.

ROMANIA

Transportation

Banking records are the main source for compilation of export freight services. The credit side of the transportation balance is recorded on the basis of banks' customers' declarations.

Travel

Data are based on information obtained from the banks, on an individual basis (transaction-by-transaction data collected from bank customers), as well as aggregated data on credit and debit card cross-border payments, supplemented by additional data based on the transactions of the exchange offices, compiled by the SD.

Estimates are made of the amounts of foreign exchange used by residents traveling abroad. The foreign exchange transactions of nonresidents made through bureaus of exchange (credits) are derived as the difference between the amounts of foreign exchange sold and purchased by nonresidents in the reporting period.

RUSSIAN FEDERATION

Services

The BR derives the data on transportation, royalties and license fees, and operational leases from enterprise surveys conducted by Rosstat.

Compilers estimate travel services via a model, using data on the number of border crossings classified by purpose of travel, average time of stay, and average expenditure per trip. The model uses data obtained from Rosstat surveys, the Federal Frontier Service of Russia, the Minfin of Russia, the Federal Migration Service of the Ministry of Internal Affairs, and specialized databases on services related to travel. Also used are partner country and mass media data. In addition, the BR estimates the number of cars imported for personal use—the costs of such cars being recorded under the travel debit item.

The BR obtains the data on all other services mainly from the ITRS. BR also uses, supplementary to ITRS, the information from the Minfin of Russia, local governments, and international organizations for calculating financial services. It also uses data from the Minfin of Russia and other ministries for compiling government services.

RWANDA

Transportation

Passenger. Transportation services include the (1) transportation of nonresident passengers by the national airlines and road-transport companies and (2) transportation of resident passengers by foreign airlines.

Travel

The NBR derives credit entries from surveys conducted at hotels, guesthouses, and the Rwanda Office of Tourism and National Parks and from the exchange records. The amounts entered as debits are also drawn from the exchange records, supplemented with information from the ministries of National Education and Foreign Affairs and Cooperation, the Interior's Immigration and Emigration Service, and the Students Financing Agency for Rwanda.

These data were not gathered for 1994–2000, and the balance of payments for those years was compiled on the basis of estimates. Since 2001 survey data have been used to compile this item.

SAINT KITTS AND NEVIS

See Eastern Caribbean Currency Union.

SAINT LUCIA

See Eastern Caribbean Currency Union.

SAINT VINCENT AND THE GRENADINES

See Eastern Caribbean Currency Union.

SAMOA

Transportation

Entries for transportation services are derived from the ticket system (mainly for data on services transactions of foreign shipping companies, the local shipping company, and the local airline) and from a monthly survey of one foreign airline. Because imports are valued f.o.b., freight and insurance debits are included in the services account, while there is a proposed transportation survey for foreign shipping agents, as well as the adding of a new airline to the airline survey.

Travel

Monthly entries for travel credits are estimated on the basis of tourist arrivals and the average tourist expenditure derived from the Samoa Visitor Survey conducted in 2002 and subsequently adjusted for price changes using the tourism price index. (Travel credits captured in the ticket system are replaced by the above entries.) Travel debits are taken from the ITRS data.

SAO TOME AND PRINCIPE

Services

Exports

Travel and tourism. Based on the information provided by the immigration and customs services, and taking the years 2001–03 as a baseline, it was inferred, by evaluating rates of change, that the proportions of business travel and personal travel were 40 percent and 60 percent, respectively.

SAUDI ARABIA

Transportation

This item covers all air, marine, and land transport services and includes passenger, freight, and other services. Data on air, marine, and land transport are obtained from the airlines operating in Saudi Arabia, the General Authority of Civil Aviation, the General Ports Authority, and the Saudi Land Transportation Company. Data on freight are estimated.

Travel

Foreign visitors are mainly pilgrims and Umrah performers year-round—especially those who visit Saudi Arabia around the months of Dhul-Hijjah and Ramadan each year. Expenditures are estimated on the basis of data received from the Ministry of Interior on actual numbers of pilgrims and other visitors. Data on travel by residents of Saudi Arabia abroad are obtained from the commercial banks, which record the purpose for sales of foreign exchange.

SENEGAL

Transportation

This item covers freight, passenger services, and port services. Freight costs are estimated at 10 percent of c.i.f. imports, after adjustments. Passenger transportation information is obtained from airline companies. Port services data are obtained from surveys of port and airport authorities and from the consignees of shipping companies.

Transportation receipts consist essentially of National Railroad Company receipts (Société Nationale des Chemins de Fer du Sénégal) from merchandise in transit to neighboring countries.

Travel

Credit entries are taken from surveys of hotels, tourist sites, etc., by the Ministry of Tourism. Estimates are based on the number of foreign visitors, their estimated average expenditure, and their average length of stay.

Debit entries are obtained from statements of tourist allocations (including pilgrimage operations) granted by banks, plus data collected from airport authorities and travel agencies.

SERBIA

Transportation

This category covers international transportation of passengers, goods, and other transportation services in detail. Expenditures on transportation services also include part of the differences between c.i.f. and f.o.b. import values, pertaining to services provided by nonresidents.

Travel

Travel services are estimated on the basis of data obtained from various reporting codes of the ITRS. The ITRS provides data on international account-to-account transactions coded as travel, receipts by Serbian hotels, and transactions of foreign-issued credit and debit cards in Serbia, as well as Serbian-issued cards abroad. The estimate for business travel receipts is based on data obtained from payments to hotels and payments using credit cards and bank transactions, while cash transactions are included in estimates of tourist (personal) travel receipts. The cash component of tourists' travel expenditure is estimated to account for approximately EUR 50 per tourist per day, based on reference data obtained from the tourism office in Belgrade. The number of travelers visiting Serbia is obtained from the SORS, based on immigration records. Travel debits are entirely based on ITRS records, including an estimate of foreign currency purchased by individuals for spending abroad.

SEYCHELLES

Transportation

This item consists mainly of revenue from passenger services, port services, and freight. Passenger services mainly represent air transportation; data are obtained from Air Seychelles and agents of foreign airlines based in Seychelles. Port revenue includes data on general marine and port charges and agency service income, obtained from shipping agents. Air Seychelles provides data on airport handling fees. The Seychelles Civil Aviation Authority provides data on aircraft landing fees in Seychelles, and Air Seychelles provides data on landing fees abroad.

Travel

Until 1991, revenue from travel was based on commercial bank records and a tourism expenditure survey carried out by the NSB. From 1992 to 1995, the emergence of a parallel market for foreign exchange reduced the coverage of commercial bank records, and total revenues from 1992 to 1995 are based on the NSB survey, although commercial bank receipts are also shown as part of overall revenue. From 1996 to 2008, revenue includes commercial bank receipts and an estimate of inflows outside the official banking system. In 2009, revenue was obtained from an enterprise survey. For foreign travel, bank records remain the source of data.

SIERRA LEONE

Transportation

This category covers freight and passenger services for all modes of transport and port services. BSL derives data for transport services from an annual survey of airline and shipping companies that operate in Sierra Leone. It draws data on seaport charges and airport fees from information provided by the seaports and airport authorities.

Travel

BSL compiles estimates of travel credits by combining data on tourist arrivals with estimates of their average expenditures—both of which are provided by the Sierra Leone Tourist Board.

Regarding government travel, banking records provide information.

SINGAPORE

Transportation

Transportation covers freight, passenger, and port services. The credit entries for freight cover freight earnings of local shipping lines and airlines. Data are obtained from the TIS. The debit entries cover payments to nonresidents for freight services provided. The total cost of freight on imports is estimated by applying freight factors to the value of imports (c.i.f.). These factors come from a survey of importers. Data on passenger and port services are obtained from the TIS and accounts of harbor and airport authorities.

Travel

The main source of information on expenditure by visitors who come in by air and sea is the Survey of Overseas Visitors to Singapore conducted by the Singapore Tourism Board. Estimates are also made for the expenditure of visitors coming to Singapore by road and rail. Entries for travel debits are derived from the number of returning Singapore residents and the estimated average expenditure per person.

SLOVAKIA

Transportation

This category covers all modes of transportation, including transit and passenger services. The NBS generally obtains the transportation data from the monthly report on foreign exchange income and payments and the monthly report on receipts and payments for the account of nonresidents. Individual respondents (such as pipeline operators) also directly report several items, including pipeline transit.

Travel

Data for travel are obtained from the monthly report on foreign exchange income and payments and the monthly report on receipts and payments for the account of nonresidents. The collection system covers purchases and sales of foreign exchange and cashless payments (i.e., transfers from one account to another), credit card data for travel credits and debits from commercial banks, border surveys produced by the Institute of Tourism and statistical information on travel from the SOSR, surveys of tourist intermediaries (e.g., travel agencies), and surveys of travelers at accommodation establishments.

SLOVENIA

Transportation

Transportation services are broken down by categories of transport (sea, air, road, rail, other transport) and services (passenger, freight, other). The main source for recording transportation services was the ITRS until 2007 and BST reports from 2008 onward.

Travel

Methodology until 2004: The ITRS sources used in compiling the incoming travel category included (1) health- and education-related services, (2) payments made by nonresidents to Slovenian tourist agencies, (3) net withdrawals in tolars from nonresident accounts, (4) money spent in casinos by nonresidents, (5) data on sales of goods to nonresidents in duty-free shops and consignment warehouses, (6) payments with credit cards, and (7) sales of tolars to nonresidents abroad.

Regarding sales of tolars to nonresidents in Slovenia, the Bank of Slovenia estimates the data based on the number of border crossings of foreign travelers and on the number of nights spent in the country by foreign tourists.

Data for expenditure on travel came from the ITRS and estimations.

Methodology from 2005 onward: Main data sources to estimate the export of travel are the following surveys and researches conducted by Statistical Office of the Republic of Slovenia (SURS): (1) triennial survey (last conducted in 2006) on foreign tourists in summer season, used to define the structure of foreign tourists according to their primary aim of travel (business travel, health care, education, other) and expenditures of each type of foreign tourists; (2) survey on foreign travelers (to define the structure of travelers broken down by same-day travelers and transit travelers and their respective expenditures); (3) monthly survey of arrivals and overnight stays of foreign tourists, broken down by countries of their residency; and (4) number of border crossings (to define the population of foreigners entering Slovenia).

The main data source to estimate the import of travel is SURS's survey TU_ČAP (quarterly survey on travel of domestic citizens). The survey provides the value of expenditures of domestic population traveling abroad (same-day trips and longer trips) and the amount spent for transportation to and from the foreign destination, which is then subtracted from total expenditures to avoid double counting (since it is already included in transport services).

SOLOMON ISLANDS

Transportation

Included here are passenger and freight services. Data are mainly derived from the survey of airport and seaport authorities.

Travel

Data on travel credits and debits are compiled from a travel model derived from NSO travel data and international visitor survey results, adjusted for inflation.

SOUTH AFRICA

Transportation

This category covers freight and passenger services; information is obtained from the SARS, transport operators, and other organizations involved in these transactions.

Travel

Estimates are based on statistics compiled by the Statistics South Africa regarding the number of foreign tourists visiting South Africa and the number of South African tourists traveling abroad. Data (per capita spending) are taken from periodic surveys conducted by South African Tourism and from questionnaires completed during buying and selling of foreign exchange.

SPAIN

Travel

For travel credits, since 2002, owing to the introduction of euro banknotes, ITRS data are complemented with tourism indicators, some of them provided by the NSO and some by the Instituto de Estudios Turísticos (IET – the Spanish Tourism Research Institute, TRI). In 2006, the border spending survey, EGATUR, was implemented as the only information source for the estimation of the credits. Since 2007, and for data from January 2005 onward, a statistical factor model has been implemented for the estimation of the travel credits. The model combines the historical information on travel credits and a set of relevant credit tourism indicators, including the border spending survey and nonresident visitors, among others. The weights of the indicators in the estimation method take into account the dynamic correlation between the indicators and the travel credits. For the time being, only evolution rates have been incorporated. The geographical breakdown, in the case of the credits, is based on EGATUR results.

For travel debits, estimates are based on information available from the ITRS, complemented with data on transactions settled through credit cards, provided by the BdE Payment Systems Department. Results are periodically checked with counterpart country data. In the case of the debits, the geographical distribution relies on ITRS data.

SRI LANKA

Transportation

This category covers all modes of transport and port services, divided into subcategories of passenger fares, freight, other (port and other) earnings and expenditure, and other related transactions.

The main source of data is the international transactions reporting system (ITRS) of commercial banks, which records values of transactions by purpose and currency of each transaction. In addition, for port-related services and passenger fares, the CBSL obtains data from relevant institutions, using a sample survey to check the consistency of data recorded by the ITRS.

Travel

This category includes receipts and payments on official, business, medical, and educational travel. The ITRS is the main source of data. The CBSL makes the necessary adjustments to receipts on travel, based on SLTDA data on the number of tourist arrivals, their average duration of stay, and their average daily expenditure.

SUDAN

Transportation

Freight and passenger services. This category covers all modes of transport and port services. The CBOS, the Ministry of Energy and Mining, commercial banks, and Sudan Customs are the main sources of data for freight and passenger services.

Travel

Sources are the reports of the commercial banks, hotels, and the foreign exchange bureaus; the reports include purchases of foreign currencies by residents at home and abroad and sales of Sudanese gineh to nonresidents in Sudan and abroad. The use of traveler's checks and credit cards is another source of information on travel.

SURINAME

Transportation

For the transportation component, CBS derives information from the ITRS, which provides a breakdown (i.e., sea transport, air transport, and other transportation). Adjustments are made with data received from the national airline company.

Travel

For the travel component, CBS derives data from the ITRS. Adjustments are made to include data provided by the national carrier.

SWAZILAND

Transportation

Data for transportation services are derived from the surveys of transport companies and their agencies and are supplemented by the ITRS. Individual companies that are not part of the transport industry but pay for transportation services also supply data under this item.

Travel

These data are compiled from surveys of hotels, curio/gift shops, car hire services, travel agents, and educational institutions, collected by the Balance of Payments Unit, in conjunction with the DEO. The ITRS provides a substantial supplement to this set of statistics.

SWEDEN

Transportation

Transportation data are based on a survey compiled by Statistics Sweden and supplemented by estimations for some sectors, such as sea transport.

Travel

For the travel component, Statistics Sweden uses three sources: (1) reports from banks and currency dealers on sales and purchases to/from the public of banknotes and travelers' checks, as well as banks' sales and purchases of Swedish banknotes vis-à-vis foreign banks; (2) reports on transactions made with credit cards, and (3) quarterly surveys covering, for example, travel agencies and other travel-related services such as health and educational services. A recurrent supplementary household survey serves as a basis for estimation of a split between tourism and business travel; it also supplies information for geographical breakdown estimates.

SWITZERLAND

Transportation

The data cover passenger transportation and transport services for goods exported and imported, for goods traffic through Switzerland on behalf of nonresidents, and for supporting services provided in connection with air and rail travel. The modes of transport include rail, air, sea, and transport by the Rhine fleet. The data sources are the annual and quarterly surveys carried out by the SNB.

INTERNATIONAL MONETARY FUND (IMF) NOTES

Travel

The data cover business and personal travel, stays at health resorts and hospitals, travel related to studies, same-day travel, and transit travel, as well as adjustments for small volumes in cross-border traffic, duty-free shops, and consumption expenditure by cross-border commuters and holders of short-term residence permits. The data sources are surveys carried out by the Federal Statistical Office (FSO) and the SNB.

SYRIAN ARAB REPUBLIC

Transportation

Passenger services: For air transport, the CBS derives the data from information provided by the Syrian airline company (credit) and foreign airlines (debit). For sea transport, the CBS obtains the data from the Syrian institution for navigation and maritime transport. Regarding other transport, the CBS obtains this data from the Syrian Public Institution for Railways.

CBS cross-checks these data (air, sea, and other passenger transport) with information obtained from the ITRS.

Travel

For travel credits, the CBS obtains data from the tourism survey conducted by the Ministry of Tourism (MOT) in coordination with CBStat. For travel debits, the CBS uses a survey conducted by MOT, determining the number of Syrian residents traveling abroad according to destination. CBS uses estimates of the travelers' expenditure depending on their destination. It also includes goods purchased abroad by Syrian travelers and recorded by Customs.

THAILAND

Transportation

For passenger services, the BOT derives estimates from the ITRS and reports from airline companies. For other transportation, entries are derived from the ITRS.

Travel

For travel credits, the BOT compiles entries by combining the number of foreign visitors and their average length of stay, obtained from the Tourism Authority of Thailand (TAT), with adjusted estimates of average expenditures per person per day. The estimates were adjusted annually before 1999, and quarterly since, and the average expenditures per capita are based on expenditure surveys of foreign visitors carried out by the TAT.

Since 1992, travel receipts have been adjusted upward by approximately 5 percent from the TAT baseline figures. This is to reflect the difference in the coverage and concepts used by the two institutions (i.e., the TAT defines the length of stay as between one and ninety days, whereas the BOT's definition is up to one year to conform with *BPM5*).

Travel debit entries are derived from foreign exchange records and quarterly surveys of Thai travelers carried out by the TAT.

THE FORMER YUGOSLAV REPUBLIC OF MACEDONIA

Transportation

Data on transportation are sourced from the ITRS and monthly reports. Data are broken down by type of transport (air, sea, railway, and road) and on the basis of the category of services (freight, passengers, and other). An adjustment is made for the outflow of transportation services (transport of goods) regarding the c.i.f./f.o.b. coefficient for the costs of transport of goods provided by nonresidents.

Travel

Data originate from the ITRS and monthly reports.

TOGO

Transportation

Data relate to port services and passenger services, excluding freight. Staff make entries on the basis of questionnaires sent to the port, airlines and shipping companies, domestic carriers, transit and consignment companies, etc. The data also include ticket issues, leased transportation, fueling, etc.

Travel

This component covers tourism transactions and expenditure on business travel and pilgrimages. It also covers the expenditure of Togolese students abroad. The sources of these data are the hotels, Ministry of Tourism, Directorates of Finance and of Scholarships and Training Courses, organizations dealing with pilgrimages to the holy places, university and regional schools, etc.

TONGA

Transportation

The SD derives transportation data from OET statistics, with adjustments made for freight and insurance on imports. Ports and airports provide additional data on wharfage, aviation fees, and other charges.

Travel

The SD derives travel credit estimates from civil aviation data and OET. Travel debit estimates are derived from OET and the MOF. The MOF provides data on expenditure abroad for medical expenses and scholarships financed by the Tongan government. These data are used to adjust OET expenditures to provide estimates of medical travel and educational travel.

TRINIDAD AND TOBAGO

Transportation

Subsumed under this category are passenger services, port services, and the provision of freight services by the national airline. Passenger fares (credit) relate to the passenger fares and excess baggage receipts accruing from nonresidents. Passenger fares (debit) pertain to similar payments by residents to foreign-owned carriers, as reported in the airline surveys. The national airline also supplies information on the value of freight services it provides to nonresidents (credit).

Travel

Compilers derive the estimates of travel credits from expenditure surveys conducted by the Central Statistical Office and from tourist arrival and departure information from the same source. Also included are estimates of expenditures by foreign students enrolled at the University of the West Indies. For travel debits, the compilers source the data from banking records.

TUNISIA

Transportation

In collecting the data, DBPEPC uses periodic surveys of airlines and shipping lines operating in Tunisia, in addition to the bank settlement statements.

Travel

For operations not subject to a settlement in connection with studies and internships, DBPEPC obtains data from surveys of the pertinent government agencies and organizations.

TURKEY

Transportation

TURKSTAT provides freight and insurance expenses, decomposed by the residency of operations and modes of transportation. Since freight and insurance income data become available with a one-year lag, these data are estimated based on the previous years' ratios.

Regarding air transportation, the CBRT obtains data from the domestic airline operators and agencies of foreign airline operators.

Travel

For travel, the CBRT bases data on sample surveys conducted by TURKSTAT in cooperation with the Ministry of Culture and Tourism and the CBRT. These surveys cover the expenditure per capita of foreign visitors and citizens living abroad and of residents on their trips abroad.

Estimates are then computed by multiplying the number of foreign visitors, citizens living abroad, and residents traveling abroad by the related average expenditure, obtained from surveys. In the surveys, business and personal travel are identified separately.

TURKMENISTAN

Transportation

For transportation services, CBT sources data from bank payment documents, as well as from information supplied by transport companies and other sources. Data on freight on imports are not separately available; they are estimated at 9 percent of the c.i.f. value to bring them to an f.o.b. price.

Travel

Data come from the banking system on settlements between national and foreign travel agencies for group and individual travel, payments made by credit cards, and expenses for business, training, and health trip costs.

The CBT survey also includes data obtained from hotels and tourist agencies and from the National Institute of Statistics and Information of Turkmenistan.

UGANDA

Transportation

This category is intended to cover all modes of transport. Passenger transportation is reported for air and road. Air passenger debits are reported with effect from January 2006 and are derived as the product of the monthly number of resident travelers departing from Entebbe Airport by destination (provided by the UBOS) and the average return airfare for respective destinations. The average airfare is computed as the average for all airlines that fly out of Entebbe to the respective destinations. No credits are reported since there is no operational resident-owned airline. Road passenger credits and debits have been revised back based on a similar methodology. In the past, growth has been estimated by a survey estimate obtained in 1995 using GDP growth. However, these data have been revised backward for credits by multiplying the number of nonresident travelers (both arrivals and departures) through Malaba, Busia, and other border posts by the average transport fare quoted by different bus companies and the share of resident buses to the total number of buses that ply the respective routes. In the case of debits for transportation by road, passenger debits have been obtained by multiplying the number of resident travelers (both arrivals and departures) through Malaba, Busia, and other border posts by the average transport fare quoted by different bus companies and the share of nonresident-owned buses to the total number of buses that ply the respective routes. The average route fare is computed as the average for all buses plying the respective destinations. Debit entries are also compiled for freight and auxiliary service amounts obtained after adjusting imports from c.i.f. values to f.o.b. values.

Travel

Travel (credit) estimates are projected forward from results of a survey conducted in 1993–94 for the years up to 1999. These travel estimates were derived from data on the number of travelers (recorded in immigration forms) with estimates for the average length of stay and the daily expenditures of foreign travelers. Figures for 1999, 2000, 2001, and 2002 are based on results from a survey conducted by the Ministry of Trade, Tourism, and Industry (MTTI) in 2001, while figures for 2003 are based on results from another survey conducted by the MTTI in 2003 and data on travel (arrivals of nonresidents) provided by the UBOS compiled from data provided by the Immigration Department. From 2004 onward, travel credits are based on surveys conducted by the BOU for weighted average expenditures of nonresidents in Uganda and the UBOS for nonresident arrivals data. Total travel credits are then computed as a product of the weighted average expenditure by the inward travelers .The total expenditure figures are grossed up to account for expenditures by travelers who arrive through other border posts not considered by the UBOS. There are currently no travel debits up to 2003, but estimates for 2004 onward are obtained from the product of average expenditure of Ugandan residents returning from abroad obtained through surveys conducted by the BOU and data from the UBOS on the number of travelers. In addition, a distinction is made between official and personal travel, based on the immigration statistics provided by the UBOS. In the case of travel credits, a further breakdown of personal travel into education and other personal reasons is estimated from 2003 onward based on surveys of nonresident students in Ugandan education institutions. The survey, however, covers a sample of secondary and tertiary institutions and omits primary education institutions, many of which provide free education under the government's policy of universal primary education for residents.

UKRAINE

Transportation

For freight and passenger services, the main sources of data are banking reports and the SSC survey of transportation companies. However, coverage is incomplete, and it is necessary to estimate missing information, especially for the debit entries. These estimates for freight are used in the conversion of data on c.i.f. imports from Customs to an f.o.b. basis.

Travel

Up to 2004, entries for this item were obtained by combining information derived from an SCSU quarterly survey on the basis of reports supplied by hotels and tour companies, and banks' reports on the purchase/sale of foreign currency and travelers' checks. Starting from 2004, the estimation of exports/imports of travel services is based on quarterly data on the number of nonresidents and Ukrainians crossing the border (classified by country and purpose of travel), average length of stay, and average expenditure per trip.

Data on the number of travelers are obtained from Ukraine's State Border Administration. Sources of data for estimating average length of stay and average expenditure per trip are the Cabinet of Ministers' regulations on the reimbursement of expenditures on business trips, SCSU survey data, data from the State Service on Tourism and Resorts of Ukraine's Ministry of Culture and Tourism, the Internet, and the mass media.

UNITED KINGDOM

Transportation

For passenger fares paid to nonresident operators, ONS derives estimates from its IPS.

Travel

This item covers goods and services provided to U.K. residents during trips of less than one year in foreign countries (and provided to nonresidents during similar trips to the U.K.), net of any purchases made with money earned or provided locally.

ONS bases the estimates primarily on the IPS, which seeks information on expenditure from samples of foreign visitors leaving the U.K. and of U.K. residents returning from abroad. The survey distinguishes several purposes of visits, which are then aggregated as either business or personal.

For package tourists, ONS deducts estimates of the transport elements from the reported total package costs. For expenditure by U.K. residents on personal imports of cars, ONS derives estimates from the data received by HMRC.

UNITED REPUBLIC OF TANZANIA

Transportation

The main entry under transportation relates to freight transactions. Statistics on freight and insurance imports are computed using the ratios of total imports. The ratios are derived from detailed data on imports obtained from the Pre-Inspection Company. Currently, the ratio of 9 percent of total imports covers payments of both freight and insurance services: freight accounts for about 97 percent of the ratio and insurance for the remaining 3 percent.

Travel

For travel debits, compilers obtain data from commercial banks' exchange records and from bureaus of exchange.

For travel credits, the Ministry of Tourism and Natural Resources, in collaboration with the BoT, the National Bureau of Statistics (NBS), the Immigration Department, and the Zanzibar Commission for Tourism, conducts a Tourism Visitors' Exit Survey to obtain data on tourism earnings.

UNITED STATES OF AMERICA

Transportation

For passenger services, BEA bases estimates on data on numbers of travelers (provided by the Department of Homeland Security) and estimates of average passenger fares (developed from a travel survey administered by the U.S. Department of Commerce).

Travel

BEA prepares travel estimates (except for transactions with Canada and Mexico) by combining data on numbers of travelers, provided by the U.S. Department of Homeland Security, with estimates of average expenditures, obtained from a travel survey administered by the U.S. Department of Commerce. BEA derives estimates of travel transactions between the United States and Canada and between the United States and Mexico from data prepared by Statistics Canada and the Bank of Mexico.

URUGUAY

Transportation

The DSE derives data for passenger fares from the annual survey of resident land, sea, and air transport companies and agents of foreign companies. It also conducts a survey of the main carriers on a quarterly basis.

Travel

For both travel credits and debits, the Ministry of Tourism compiles estimates on the basis of sample surveys of both inward and outward tourism, supplemented with data the National Migration Directorate provides on the number of travelers.

VANUATU

Transportation

The category covers freight and passenger services by all modes of transport (i.e., sea and air) and port services. For transportation services, RBV derives entries from information provided by airport and seaport authorities, Air Vanuatu, other airlines, and stevedoring companies.

Travel

For travel credits, the RBV derives the entries from information on the number of foreign visitors, their average daily expenditures, and their average length of stay. The expenditure estimates are based on the 2005 Visitor's Survey, conducted by the National Statistics Office in collaboration with the RBV, the National Tourism Office, and the Tourism Council of the South Pacific, and are rated forward, using CPI movements. On the number of visitors, the RBV obtains data quarterly from migration statistics published by the National Statistics Office. The movement of the major tourist origin exchange rate (AUS and ANZ) is now incorporated into the model.

For travel debits, the RBV derives entries from an average expenditure figure provided by the Department of Finance and the residents' departure numbers from the National Statistics Office. The item also includes 70 percent of the value of training scholarships. (The contra-entry is included in current transfers, general government). There has been a lot of work on the revision of these data to conform to the *BPM6* requirement.

VENEZUELA

Transportation

This item includes the national oil industry's income and the private air companies' freight services and sale of tickets for international flights. The CBV uses surveys to gather both sets of data. The item also includes income from ports, airports, and navigation routes received by the national oil industry, the National Institute of Canals, and the principal ports and airports of the country. The CBV obtains these data through questionnaires and administrative registries.

Debit entries are registered for freight, estimated through a coefficient applied to total imports of goods f.o.b., according to the nandina (Andean Community customs tariff), modality of transportation, region, etc. The item also includes payments for passenger transport on nonresident airlines and payments for port and airport services that the public oil industry and private airline companies make, estimated through surveys and indicators of volume of aircraft that the principal airport of the country reports.

Travel

For travel, the CBV measures credits and debits through a sample survey the INE and CBV carry out every quarter in the principal airport of the country. Compilers obtain data on average daily spending in U.S. dollars by category of traveler and reason for visit, average number of nights spent, and other indicators that allow an evaluation of the general profile of the traveler. These sample data are extrapolated by the total number of foreign visitors reported by the airports.

In addition, the category includes expenses for scholarships and missions that the public petroleum sector and nonpetroleum public sector incur abroad. The CBV validates the estimate through indicators of the activity, interviews for opinions in the principal hotels and travel agencies of the country, and reports and specialized journals.

VIET NAM

Transportation

This category covers freight and passenger services for air and sea transport. The GSO uses information collected directly from Vietnam Airlines Corporation and Vietnam National Shipping Lines Corporation.

Travel

The SBV compiles estimates of the travel component by combining data on tourist arrivals with estimates of their average expenditures based on the result of the GSO survey on expenditures of foreign tourists visiting Vietnam. The survey is conducted every two years.

YEMEN

Transportation

Data on debit entries for freight are estimated at 10 percent of the c.i.f. value of imports. BOPD records the data it collects from airport authorities as credit entries under other air transportation, while it records data it collects from seaport authorities as credit entries under other sea transportation.

Travel

The Ministry of Tourism collects data from the immigration authorities on the number of foreign tourist arrivals. Number of tourist nights is estimated through a comprehensive survey to estimate the travel receipts. The BOPD reflects the data obtained from the Ministry of Tourism in the balance of payments statistics.

Travel debits are estimated from the CBY records and the monthly international transactions reporting survey (ITRS) of commercial banks for students studying abroad, Yemeni pilgrims, and health treatments of Yemeni nationals abroad.

ZAMBIA

Transportation

Credit data comprise freight services only, estimated as 5.5 percent of the c.i.f. value of nontraditional exports, plus data on inland freight reported by the mining companies on their metal exports, calculated as average cost per ton of copper multiplied by total volume of copper exported.

Debits comprise estimates for freight, passenger, and other transport services. Freight debits are estimated as 10 percent of the c.i.f. value of imports. Data on passenger transport and other transport services are estimated based on historical data. The BoZ plans to launch two enterprise surveys that would form the basis of compiling estimates of passenger and other transport services. These would consist of a quarterly survey of resident transportation companies and a survey of agents of nonresident airlines, primarily designed to capture data on passenger transportation.

Travel

Prior to June 1999, the BoZ compiled data on travel credits from reports the Zambia National Tourist Board (ZNTB) submitted. In June 1999 the MTENR took over from ZNTB the task of conducting surveys of enterprises involved in providing travel services. The BoZ, collaborating with the MTENR, has designed quarterly survey forms to capture, primarily, tourism revenues from hotels and companies involved in tours, car hires, and air charters. The first survey was launched in October of 2000 but has not been undertaken consistently, owing to a lack of funding and staff shortages.

Travel debits are estimated based on data on government employees' travel allowances and on government and quasi-government employees studying abroad. However, the BoZ is establishing reporting arrangements with the Ministry of Finance, the Ministry of Education, and the Cabinet Office for data on official expenditure on travel for purposes of education, medicine, and training.

In the past, this information was captured from the banks and the exchange bureau reporting system on purchases and sale of foreign exchange. However, the liberalization of the foreign exchange market in Zambia resulted in incomplete coverage. That is, banks are no longer obliged to report all their foreign exchange transactions, and ordinary customers are not legally required to declare the purpose of the foreign currency that they purchase from banks and bureaus of exchange.

Conceptual references and technical notes /

- Annex 1. National System of Tourism Statistics and international comparability
- Annex 2. Understanding tourism: basic glossary
- Annex 3. Finding tourism in International Standard Classifications
- Annex 4. List of tourism industries and grouping by main categories according to ISIC Rev. 4

Références conceptuelles et notes techniques /

- Annexe 1. Système national de statistiques du tourisme et comparabilité internationale
- Annexe 2. Comprendre le tourisme: glossaire de base
- Annexe 3. Trouver le tourisme dans les classifications internationales types
- Annexe 4. Liste des industries touristiques regroupées par principales catégories conformément à la CITI Rev. 4

Referencias conceptuales y notas técnicas

- Anexo 1. Sistema nacional de estadísticas de turismo y comparabilidad internacional
- Anexo 2. Comprender el turismo: glosario básico
- Anexo 3. Cómo encontrar el turismo en las clasificaciones internacionales uniformes
- Anexo 4. Lista de industrias turísticas y agrupadas por categorías principales según la CIIU, Rev. 4

CONCEPTUAL REFERENCES and TECHNICAL NOTES *

1. INBOUND TOURISM

Inbound tourism comprises the activities of a non-resident visitor within the country of reference on an inbound tourism trip. The corresponding expenditure of such a visitor is identified as inbound tourism expenditure.

Data

Arrivals

Arrivals data measure the flows of international visitors to the country of reference: each arrival corresponds to one inbound tourism trip. If a person visits several countries during the course of a single trip, his/her arrival in each country is recorded separately. In an accounting period, arrivals are not necessarily equal to the number of persons travelling (when a person visits the same country several times a year, each trip by the same person is counted as a separate arrival).

Arrivals data should correspond to *inbound visitors* by including both tourists and same-day non-resident visitors. All other types of travellers (such as border, seasonal and other short-term workers, long-term students and others) should be excluded, as they do not qualify as visitors.

Data are obtained from different sources: administrative records (immigration, traffic counts, and other possible types of controls), border surveys or a mix of them. If data are obtained from accommodation surveys, the number of guests is used as estimate of arrival figures; consequently, in this case, breakdowns by regions, main purpose of the trip, modes of transport used or forms of organization of the trip are based on complementary visitor surveys.

Arrivals are broken down by five characteristics; two of them deserve some comments:
- Type of visitors (<u>Compendium</u> items 1.1 to 1.4). If a country cannot distinguish between overnight visitors and same-day visitors, no breakdown is provided.
- Regions (<u>Compendium</u> items 1.5 to 1.13). The basic concept behind is that the country associated to the arrival should be the country of residence. Some countries do not accept UNWTO recommendations and classify nationals residing abroad instead of as residents in such countries as a separate category (<u>Compendium</u> item 1.13).

The *main purpose* of a trip is defined as the purpose in the absence of which the trip would not have taken place. The following classification applies:

1. Personal
    1.1. Holidays, leisure and recreation
    1.2. Visiting friends and relatives
    1.3. Education and training
    1.4. Health and medical care
    1.5. Religion/pilgrimages
    1.6. Shopping
    1.7. Transit
    1.8. Other
2. Business and professional

Complementary information is provided in the UNWTO Yearbook of Tourism Statistics that contains arrivals with a breakdown by country of origin:

- Table 1. Arrivals of non-resident overnight visitors (tourists) at national borders
- Table 2. Arrivals of non-resident visitors (overnight visitors – tourists – and same-day visitors – excursionists –) at national borders

---

- This document also includes four annexes:
    Annex 1. National System of Tourism Statistics and international comparability
    Annex 2. Understanding tourism: basic glossary
    Annex 3. Finding tourism in International Standard Classifications
    Annex 4. List of tourism industries and grouping by main categories according to ISIC Rev. 4

For additional references, visit
http://www.unwto.org/statistics/
http://unstats.un.org/unsd/tradeserv/tourism/08-40120%20IRTS%202008_WEB_final%20version%20_22%20February%202010.pdf

CONCEPTUAL REFERENCES and TECHNICAL NOTES

Accommodation

The term "accommodation" refers to services provided by commercial establishments to visitors. Of these, the most important post is usually "hotels and similar establishments", identified in ISIC, Rev.4 as 5510 "Short term accommodation activities".

Overnights (or "guest nights") refers to the number of nights spent by non-resident guests (inbound tourists).

Complementary information is provided in the UNWTO Yearbook of Tourism Statistics that contains data on guests with a breakdown by country of origin*:

- Table 3. Arrivals of non-resident overnight visitors (tourists) in "hotels and similar establishments"
- Table 4. Arrivals of non-resident overnight visitors (tourists) in all types of establishments providing accommodation services for visitors
- Table 5. Overnight stays of non-resident overnight visitors (tourists) in "hotels and similar establishments"
- Table 6. Overnight stays of non-resident overnight visitors (tourists) in all types of establishments providing accommodation services for visitors

Expenditure

Expenditure associated with the activity of international visitors has been traditionally identified with the travel item of the Balance of Payments (BOP): in the case of inbound tourism, those expenditures associated with inbound visitors are registered as "credits" in the BOP and refers to "travel receipts".

The *2008 International Recommendations for Tourism Statistics* consider that "tourism industries and products" includes transport of passengers. Consequently, a better estimate of tourism-related expenditure by inbound and outbound visitors in an international scenario would be, in terms of the BOP, the value of the travel item plus that of the passenger transport item.

Nevertheless, users should be aware that BOP estimates include, in addition to expenditures associated to visitors, those related to other types of travellers (these might be substantial in some countries; for instance, long-term students or patients, border and seasonal workers, etc).

Also data on expenditure by *main purpose of the trip* are BOP data.

The data published correspond to those published by the International Monetary Fund (IMF) (and provided by the Central Banks); in the case of a significant difference with data provided to UNWTO by National Tourism Administrations (NTAs) for the preparation of this <u>Compendium</u>, the NTA data will be given separately in the "Country notes".

Indicators

Average size of travel party

A travel party is defined as visitors travelling together on a trip and whose expenditures are pooled. The average size of travel parties allows for an estimate of the total number of trips by international visitors, which is useful for marketing and policy design purposes.

Average length of stay

All these indicators refer to the duration of inbound tourism trips by international visitors (expressed as number of days or nights).

Total average length of stay refers to both commercial and non commercial accommodation services provided to visitors, as well as to other types of stays.

Since a non-resident visitor might use different accommodation facilities during his / her stay, such total figures can only be estimated using border survey information or by checking dates from official arrival/departure cards for a sample (or the totality) of visitors.

- The Yearbook of Tourism Statistics will be revised and the present wording will be updated in accordance to IRTS 2008.

CONCEPTUAL REFERENCES and TECHNICAL NOTES

Average expenditure per day

This indicator refers to total expenditure of overall visitors divided by the total number of days spent, estimated using visitors' survey.

2. DOMESTIC TOURISM

Domestic tourism comprises the activities of a resident visitor within the country of reference (either as part of a domestic tourism trip or part of an outbound tourism trip).

The corresponding expenditure in the economy of reference of such a visitor is identified as domestic tourism expenditure. Also, the expenditure of outbound visitors on products received from resident businesses is included in domestic expenditure.

Data

Trips taken by visitors are tourism trips. A domestic tourism trip refers to the travel of a visitor from the time of leaving his/her usual residence until he/she returns: it refers to a roundtrip.

The term "accommodation" refers to services provided by commercial establishments to visitors. Of these, the most important post is usually "hotels and similar establishments", identified in ISIC, Rev.4 as 5510 "Short term accommodation activities".

Overnights (or "guest nights") refer to the number of nights spent by resident guests (domestic tourists). Accommodation surveys (addressed to establishments) should be the preferred source of data.

Indicators

Average length of stay

Total average length of stay refers to both commercial and non commercial accommodation services provided to visitors, as well as to other types of stays.

Total data can only be estimated using household surveys.

Average expenditure per day

This indicator refers to total expenditure divided by the total number of days spent, estimated using visitors' survey.

3. OUTBOUND TOURISM

Outbound tourism comprises the activities of a resident visitor outside the country of reference (either as part of an outbound tourism trip or as part of a domestic tourism trip). The corresponding expenditure of such a visitor is identified as outbound tourism expenditure.

Data

Departures data measure the flows of resident visitors leaving the country of reference. Departures are not necessarily equal to the number of arrivals reported by international destinations for the country of reference.

Expenditure associated with the activity of visitors has been traditionally identified with the travel item of the Balance of Payments (BOP): in the case of outbound tourism, those expenditures associated with resident visitors are registered as "debits" in the BOP and refers to "travel expenditure". As in the case of *inbound tourism*, BOP data are used.

The 2008 International Recommendations for Tourism Statistics consider that "tourism industries and products" includes transport of passengers. Consequently, a better estimate of tourism-related expenditures data by resident and non-resident visitors in an international scenario would be, in terms of the BOP, the value of the travel item plus that of the passenger transport item.

Nevertheless, users should be aware that BOP estimates include, in addition to expenditures associated with visitors, those related to other types of travellers.

Likewise, data on expenditure by *main purpose* of the trip are BOP data.

CONCEPTUAL REFERENCES and TECHNICAL NOTES

The data published correspond to those published by the International Monetary Fund (IMF) (and provided by the Central Banks); in the case of a significant difference with data provided to UNWTO by National Tourism Administrations (NTAs) for the preparation of this Compendium, the NTA data will be given separately in the "Country notes".

Complementary information on "trips abroad by resident visitors to countries of destination" can be obtained through the website http://www.e-unwto.org/home/main.mpx. It is important to point out that the information presented is obtained on the basis of data supplied by each of the destination countries and therefore corresponds to arrivals in these countries.

Indicators

Average length of stay

This indicator refers to the duration of trips abroad by outbound visitors (expressed as number of days) and reflects the total average using border surveys and/or household information.

Average expenditure per day

This indicator refers to total expenditure divided by total days spent using border surveys and/or household information.

4. TOURISM INDUSTRIES

The term *tourism industries* includes those industries that typically produce tourism characteristic products; it is equivalent to the more colloquial term "tourism sector". The following list identifies such industries:

1. Accommodation for visitors
2. Food and beverage serving activities
3. Railway passenger transport
4. Road passenger transport
5. Water passenger transport
6. Air passenger transport
7. Transport equipment rental
8. Travel agencies and other reservation services activities
9. Cultural activities
10. Sports and recreational activities
11. Retail trade of country-specific tourism characteristic goods
12. Other country-specific tourism characteristic activities

The following explanatory notes refer to *Accommodation for visitors* and *Travel agencies and other reservation services activities* being the only two industries for which monetary and non-monetary data are published in this Compendium.

These notes can be consulted in Annex 4; they have been extracted from *International Standard Industrial Classification of All Economic Activities (ISIC), Rev. 4.* Statistical papers (Series M No. 4/Rev.4), United Nations. New York, 2008.

Accommodation for visitors

The number of establishments in the *Accommodation for visitors* industry (Compendium item 4.2) refers to all type of establishments providing accommodation services to visitors on a commercial (market) basis; that is, as a paid service. Consequently, data should include all the following ISIC classes:

5510 Short term accommodation activities

This class is labelled in the Compendium section 4 as "*Accommodation for visitors in hotels and similar establishments*" and includes the provision of accommodation, typically on a daily or weekly basis, principally for short stay by visitors. This includes the provision of furnished accommodation in guest rooms and suites or complete self-contained units with kitchens, with or without daily or other regular housekeeping services, and may often include a range of additional services such as food and beverage services, parking, laundry services, swimming pools and exercise rooms, recreational facilities and conference and convention facilities.

This class includes the provision of short-term accommodation provided by:
- hotels
- resort hotels
- suite / apartment hotels
- motels
- motor hotels
- guesthouses
- pensions
- bed and breakfast units
- visitor flats and bungalows
- time-share units
- holiday homes
- chalets, housekeeping cottages and cabins
- youth hostels and mountain refuges

This class excludes:
- provision of homes and furnished or unfurnished flats or apartments for more permanent use, typically on a monthly or annual basis, see division 68

5520 Camping grounds, recreational vehicle parks and trailer parks

This class includes:
- provision of accommodation in campgrounds, trailer parks, recreational camps and fishing and hunting camps for short stay visitors
- provision of space and facilities for recreational vehicles

This class also includes accommodation provided by:
- protective shelters or plain bivouac facilities for placing tents and/or sleeping bags

5590 Other accommodation

This class includes the provision of temporary or longer-term accommodation in single or shared rooms or dormitories for students, migrant (seasonal) workers and other individuals.

This class includes accommodation provided by:
- student residences
- school dormitories
- workers hostels
- rooming and boarding houses
- railway sleeping cars

6810 Real estate activities with own or leased property

This class includes:
- buying, selling, renting and operating of self-owned or leased real estate, such as:
  - apartment buildings and dwellings
  - non-residential buildings, including exhibition halls, self-storage facilities, malls and shopping centers
  - land
- provision of homes and furnished or unfurnished flats or apartments for more permanent
- use, typically on a monthly or annual basis

This class also includes:
- development of building projects for own operation, i.e. for renting of space in these buildings
- subdividing real estate into lots, without land improvement
- operation of residential mobile home sites

This class excludes:
- development of building projects for sale, see 4100
- subdividing and improving of land, see 4290
- operation of hotels, suite hotels and similar accommodation, see 5510
- operation of campgrounds, trailer parks and similar accommodation, see 5520
- operation of workers hostels, rooming houses and similar accommodation, see 5590

6820 Real estate activities on a fee or contract basis

This class includes the provision of real estate activities on a fee or contract basis including real estate related services.

This class includes:
- activities of real estate agents and brokers
- intermediation in buying, selling and renting of real estate on a fee or contract basis
- management of real estate on a fee or contract basis
- appraisal services for real estate
- activities of real estate escrow agents

This class excludes:
- legal activities, see 6910
- facilities support services, see 8110
- management of facilities, such as military bases, prisons and other facilities (except computer facilities management), see 8110

Travel agencies and other reservation service activities

7911 Travel agency activities

This class includes:
- activities of agencies primarily engaged in selling travel, tour, transportation and accommodation services to the general public and commercial clients

7912 Tour operator activities

This class includes:
- arranging and assembling tours that are sold through travel agencies or directly by tour operators. The tours may include any or all of the following:
  - transportation
  - accommodation
  - food
  - visits to museums, historical or cultural sites, theatrical, musical or sporting events

7990 Other reservation service and related activities

This class includes:
- provision of other travel-related reservation services:
  - reservations for transportation, hotels, restaurants, car rentals, entertainment and sport etc.
- provision of time-share exchange services
- ticket sales activities for theatrical, sports and other amusement and entertainment events
- provision of visitor assistance services:
  - provision of travel information to visitors
  - activities of tourist guides
- tourism promotion activities

This class excludes:
- activities of travel agencies and tour operators, see 7911, 7912
- organization and management of events such as meetings, conventions and conferences, see 8230

Data

Regarding the *number of establishments*, (Compendium item 4.3) includes establishments associated with classes 5520, 5590, 6810 and 6820 (see above explanatory notes for accommodation for visitors).

The number of *rooms* and *bed-places* refers to the capacity in "hotels and similar establishments" for providing temporary accommodation to visitors.

Indicators

All of the first three indicators are based on the overall number of overnights of both resident and non-residents tourists in hotels and similar establishments.

CONCEPTUAL REFERENCES and TECHNICAL NOTES

Occupancy rates refer to the relationship between existing capacity to provide accommodation services to visitors and the extent to which it is used. This rate may refer to the use of rooms or of bed-places.

Available capacity refers to the number of bed-places in hotels and similar establishments per 1000 inhabitants of the permanent resident population of the country of reference. Data are assigned by UNWTO if not provided by the country.

5. EMPLOYMENT

The category of persons employed in the tourism industries can be either *employees* (persons who work for an enterprise in return for remuneration in cash or in kind as agreed) or *self-employed* (own-account workers who hold the type of job defined as "self-employment job" and have not engaged on a continuous basis any "employees" during the reference period).
Some employed persons may have more than one job; consequently, the number of jobs (demand side) and the number of persons employed (supply side) are dissimilar categories and therefore usually do not match.

The intensity of work may vary from job to job, industry to industry and from period to period. Jobs may differ by working time of persons employed and therefore be expressed in terms of full- or part-time jobs. For this reason, it is not sufficient to have data on the number of jobs or persons employed in order to obtain information on the volume of labour performed during a specified period of time (for example, a month or a year). Data on the total number of working hours will be required. Finally, if all jobs are converted into full-time equivalent employment or annual total hours worked, the total volume of labour of a given tourism industry for a given period can be obtained.

Figures on "Number of jobs by status in employment" and "Number of full time equivalent jobs by status in employment" should refer to tourism industries.

6. COMPLEMENTARY INDICATORS

These indicators are derived from the Balance of Payments, National Accounts and tourism statistics.

Demand

Gross travel propensity measures the number of outbound and domestic tourism trips in terms of total permanent resident population of the country of reference. Bigger values of the indicator mean greater frequency of such trips, indicating the present mobility of the population travelling abroad.

Carrying capacity measures total arrivals (both domestic and inbound) in relation to the total permanent resident population and provides an estimate of tourism potential in the country of reference.

Macroeconomic International Tourism Related Indicators

Data are based on the International Monetary Fund's *Balance of Payments Statistics* and *International Financial Statistics* and compiled by UN Economic Commission for Latin America and the Caribbean (ECLAC) for the World Tourism Organization (UNWTO). The dataset used for the Compendium of Tourism Statistics 2011 refer to March 2011.

These and other complementary indicators represent a preliminary and very basic evaluation of tourism's economic contribution to the national economy, valuable because they are largely available for most countries, internationally comparable, and comparable to other economic indicators.

It must be noted that the term 'expenditure' is used similarly for inbound as well as for outbound tourism to indicate "the amount paid for the acquisition of consumption goods and services, as well as valuables, for own use or to give away, for and during tourism trips". Foreign visitors in the reference country generate inbound tourism expenditure (credits in the Balance of Payments), while resident visitors in foreign countries generate outbound tourism expenditure (debits in the Balance of Payments).

Inbound tourism expenditure over GDP
Reflects the weight of expenditure by inbound visitors as a part of the total value of economic activity in the economy of reference. From the perspective of international trade, this indicator captures the economic importance of foreign revenue inflow associated to expenditures by such visitors.

CONCEPTUAL REFERENCES and TECHNICAL NOTES

Outbound tourism expenditure over GDP
Reflects the importance of the spending abroad by outbound visitors, expressed in terms of the national economy. From the perspective of international trade, this indicator captures the economic importance of domestic revenue outflow by means of such visitors.

Tourism balance over GDP
Reflects the economic importance of net tourism (inbound minus outbound) expenditures relative to the economy of reference. A significant surplus or deficit affects the country's balance of trade, and thus its GDP.

Tourism openness
Reflects how important the sum of cross-border tourism expenditures (i.e. international tourism, the sum of inbound and outbound tourism expenditure) are relative to the economy of reference. It could be used as a measure of the free flow of tourism between the country of reference and the rest of the world.

Tourism coverage
Reflects the proportion between inbound tourism expenditure and outbound tourism expenditure to show in what degree foreign revenue inflow cover for domestic revenue outflow. A value higher than 100 % means that inbound tourism indirectly finances more than all the expenditure of outbound visitors; a value lower than 100 % means that inbound tourism does not cover the expenditure of such visitors abroad.

Inbound tourism expenditure over exports of goods,
Inbound tourism expenditure over exports of services, and
Inbound tourism expenditure over exports of goods and services
These three measures reflect the importance of tourism as an internationally traded service relative to other categories of exports. At the same time, such measures reveal the degree of tourism specialization in a country's export structure and the relative capability of tourism in generating foreign revenues.

Inbound tourism expenditure over current account credits
The current account credits of the Balance of Payments refer to all inflow of goods, services, income and current transfers into an economy. The larger the share of tourism in this aggregate, the larger is the importance of tourism activity in generating foreign revenue inflows.

Outbound tourism expenditure over imports of goods,
Outbound tourism expenditure over imports of services, and
Outbound tourism expenditure over imports of goods and services
These three measures reflect the importance of tourism as an internationally traded service relative to other categories of imports. At the same time, such measures reveal the predilection for tourism in a country's import structure and the relative degree of an economy's domestic revenue outflows due to international tourism.

Outbound tourism expenditure over current account debits
The current account debits of the Balance of Payments refer to all outflows of goods, services, income and current transfers from an economy to the rest of the world. The larger the share of tourism in this aggregate, the larger is the importance of tourism activity in the leakage of domestic revenue.

Annex 1. National System of Tourism Statistics and international comparability

The structure of the <u>Compendium of Tourism Statistics</u> is based on the following scheme referred to the basic information framework of national Systems of Tourism Statistics for international comparability purposes[1].

The conceptual background for such a basic core of data and indicators is the *International Recommendations for Tourism Statistics 2008* (IRTS 2008).

International comparability and tourism statistics: the basic information framework

I.   Conceptual framework

Concepts	Observation units	Main related characteristics
Visitor	Visitor	Classes (Overnight visitor-tourist-/same-day visitor-excursionist)
		Country of residence / regions
	Travel party	Size
Trip	Tourism trip	Main purpose
		Duration
		Main destination
		Modes of transport
		Types of accommodation used
		Organization
		Expenditure
Tourism industries	Establishment	<u>Monetary</u>
		Output
		Intermediate consumption
		Gross value added
		Compensation of employees
		Gross Fixed Capital Formation
		<u>Non-monetary</u>
		Non-monetary characteristics specific to each tourism industry
Employment	Establishment (in the tourism industries)	Persons
		Size
		Status in employment
		Jobs
	Households	Duration of work
		Full-time equivalent jobs

II.   Classifications

    1.   Forms of tourism
    2.   Classification of consumption products acquired by visitors
    3.   Classification of productive activities serving visitors
    4.   Other classifications

III. Tables of results

    1.   Inbound tourism
    2.   Domestic tourism
    3.   Outbound tourism
    4.   Tourism industries
    5.   Employment
    6.   Complementary indicators

---

1 <u>http://www.unwto.org/statistics/sts/description/sts_text.pdf</u>

Annex 2. Understanding tourism: basic glossary *

Domestic tourism	Comprises the activities of a resident *visitor* within the country of reference, either as part of a *domestic tourism trip* or part of an *outbound tourism trip*.
Domestic visitor	As a *visitor travels* within his/her country of residence, he/she is a *domestic visitor* and his/her activities are part of *domestic tourism*.
Employment in tourism industries	*Employment in tourism industries* may be measured as a count of the persons employed in *tourism industries* in any of their jobs, as a count of the persons employed in *tourism industries* in their main job, or as a count of the jobs in *tourism industries*.
Inbound tourism	Comprises the *activities* of a non-resident *visitor* within the country of reference on an *inbound tourism trip*.
Outbound tourism	Comprises the *activities* of a resident *visitor* outside the country of reference, either as an *outbound tourism trip* or as part of a *domestic tourism trip*.
Place of usual residence	The *place of usual residence* is the geographical place where the visitor usually resides, and is defined by the location of his/her principal dwelling (Principles and recommendations for population and housing censuses of the United Nations).
Purpose of a tourism trip (main)	The *main purpose* of a *tourism trip* is defined as the purpose in the absence of which the trip would not have taken place. Classification of *tourism trips* according to the *main purpose* refers to nine categories: this typology allows the identification of different subsets of *visitors* (business visitors, transit visitors, etc).
Tourism characteristic activities / products	*Tourism characteristic activities* are the activities that typically produce *tourism characteristic products*. *Tourism characteristic products* are those that satisfy one or both of the following criteria: (a) *Tourism expenditure* on the product (either good or service) should represent a significant share of total *tourism expenditure* (share-of-expenditure/demand condition); (b) *Tourism expenditure* on the product should represent a significant share of the supply of the product in the economy (share-of-supply condition). This criterion implies that the supply of a *tourism characteristic product* would cease to exist in meaningful quantity in the absence of visitors.
Tourism expenditure	*Tourism expenditure refers to the amount paid for the acquisition of consumption goods and services, as well as valuables, for own use or to give away, for and during tourism trips.*
Tourism industries	*The tourism industries comprise all establishments for which the principal activity is a tourism characteristic activity.*
Tourist (or overnight visitor) and Excursionist (or day visitor)	*A visitor (domestic, inbound or outbound) is classified as a tourist (or overnight visitor) if his/her trip includes an overnight stay, or as a same-day visitor (or excursionist) otherwise.*
Travel / tourism	*Travel refers to the activities of travellers. A traveller is someone who moves between different geographic locations, for any purpose and any duration. The visitor is a particular type of traveller and consequently tourism is a subset of travel*
Travel party	*A travel party is defined as visitors travelling together on a trip and whose expenditures are pooled.*
Trip	*A trip refers to the travel by a person from the time of departure from his/her usual residence until he/she returns: it thus refers to a round trip. Trips taken by visitors are tourism trips.*
Usual environment	*The usual environment of an individual, a key concept in tourism, is defined as the geographical area (though not necessarily a contiguous one) within which an individual conducts his/her regular life routines.*
Vacation home	*A vacation home (sometimes also designated as a holiday home) is a secondary dwelling that is visited by the members of the household mostly for purposes of recreation, vacation or any other form of leisure.*
Visit	*A trip is made up of visits to different places. The term "tourism visit" refers to a stay in a place visited during a tourism trip.*
Visitor	*A visitor is a traveller taking a trip to a destination outside his/her usual environment, for less than a year, for any purpose (business, leisure or other personal purpose) other than to be employed by a resident entity in the country or place visited.*

(*) This Annex includes some key concepts and the corresponding definitions as in the *IRTS 2008*. http://unstats.un.org/unsd/tradeserv/tourism/08-40120%20IRTS%202008_WEB_final%20version%20_22%20February%202010.pdf

Annex 3.   Finding tourism in International Standard Classifications

The importance of Tourism and the need to define and measure its significance as a part of the UN System of Statistics was recognized by the United Nations Statistical Commission with the approval in 1993 of "Recommendations on Tourism Statistics". The revised version of these recommendations was approved by the UN Statistical Commission in 2008 as *International Recommendations for Tourism Statistics 2008* (IRTS 2008).

To study the economic contribution of Tourism to the national economy, there was a need to integrate the economic analysis of Tourism into the reference framework of the System of National Accounts (SNA '93), leading to the approval by the United Nations Statistical Commission in 2000 of the "Tourism Satellite Account: Recommended Methodological Framework". This framework has been updated as *Tourism Satellite Account: Recommended Methodological Framework 2008* (TSA:RMF 2008).

The concepts, definitions and classifications in IRTS 2008 have been made consistent with TSA:RMF 2008 which in turn has been harmonized with the 2008 System of National Accounts, Balance of Payments and International Trade in Services.

For Tourism, there is an interest in identifying the products purchased by visitors, directly and indirectly, and the activities that produce them. The classifications used for the detailed activities and products required in the study of Tourism are drawn directly from and related to the United Nations reference classifications, ISIC and the CPC.

The focus of interest for Tourism analysis is the visitor. Initially, it is of interest to measure visitor expenditure and to identify the products, both goods and services, purchased by visitors, as well as the activities that produce those products. In a macroeconomic framework, such as the TSA, the concept of Tourism comprises both a demand perspective consisting of visitor consumption, tourism collective consumption, and tourism gross fixed capital formation and a supply perspective of tourism activities (a special issue being the share of their production that is purchased by visitors). Tourism, as such, is not identified in SNA 93 or in ISIC. For purposes of Tourism, activities from across the spectrum of ISIC, that produce goods and services that satisfy tourism demand are brought together and grouped as tourism activities.

The approach being from the demand side, the visitor is the basic unit of observation and analysis, and visitor expenditure is observed in terms of products (primarily services). On the supply side, related as it is to the System of National Accounts, Tourism statistics uses the "establishment" as the basic statistical unit as defined in the SNA, and uses "industry" as the unit of presentation and analysis, industry being defined as "groups of establishments engaged in the same kind of productive activities".

In the first instance it is necessary to identify the products purchased by visitors. For purposes of data collection from a demand perspective, products are grouped into broad categories by purpose; however, Tourism requires the simultaneous analysis of consumption and production hence the classification used for defining products is the Central Product Classification (CPC v 2.). The products purchased by visitors can be classified within the detailed classes of the CPC and the activities that produce them can be identified in terms of the detailed classes of ISIC.

Tourism defines certain of those products purchased by visitors and the activities that produce them, as Tourism characteristic products (those that satisfy certain criteria) and Tourism characteristic activities (those that typically produce tourism characteristic products). The IRTS 2008 explains in great detail the underlying concepts, definitions and classifications to be used in compiling Tourism statistics and the identification of Tourism characteristic products and activities. To facilitate international comparison, lists of these characteristic products and activities have been compiled. Annex 3 of the document provides a List of Tourism characteristic activities (tourism industries) grouped into main categories according to ISIC rev 4. Annex 4 provides a list of Tourism characteristic products grouped by main categories according to CPC ver 2. Even though the actual product purchased by the visitor may constitute only a portion of the CPC class or the activity producing it may constitute only a portion of the 4 digit ISIC class, by being expressed in terms of CPC classes and aggregations of ISIC classes, the lists provide a defined class within which each product or activity can be placed. Countries are advised to create more detailed classes below the lowest level of the CPC and ISIC for their own analytical purposes, if required.

The scope for analysis of Tourism statistics is widened when they are placed within the framework of the Tourism Satellite Account. Again in the core accounting framework, products and activities are expressed in terms of CPC v 2 and ISIC rev 4, including the products and activities associated with Tourism. The international product and activity classifications used to compile data for the TSA:RMF 2008 which in turn, establishes structural links with the System of National Accounts, make possible a deeper appreciation of tourism's linkages to other economic areas.

Annex 4. List of tourism industries and grouping by main categories according to ISIC Rev. 4

	List of tourism industries (characteristic activities) and grouping by main categories according to ISIC Rev. 4		
	Tourism industries	**ISIC Rev. 4**	**Description**
1.	Accommodation for visitors		
		5510	Short term accommodation activities
		5520	Camping grounds, recreational vehicle parks and trailer parks
		5590	Other accommodation
		6810	Real estate activities with own or leased property*
		6820	Real estate activities on a fee or contract basis*
2.	Food and beverage serving activities		
		5610	Restaurants and mobile food service activities
		5629	Other food service activities
		5630	Beverage serving activities
3.	Railway passenger transport		
		4911	Passenger rail transport, interurban
4.	Road passenger transport		
		4922	Other passenger land transport
5.	Water passenger transport		
		5011	Sea and coastal passenger water transport
		5021	Inland passenger water transport
6.	Air passenger transport		
		5110	Passenger air transport
7.	Transport equipment rental		
		7710	Renting and leasing of motor vehicles
8.	Travel agencies and other reservation service activities		
		7911	Travel agency activities
		7912	Tour operator activities
		7990	Other reservation service and related activities
9.	Cultural activities		
		9000	Creative, arts and entertainment activities
		9102	Museums activities and operation of historical sites and buildings
		9103	Botanical and zoological gardens and nature reserves activities
10.	Sports and Recreational activities		
		7721	Renting and leasing of recreational and sports goods
		9200	Gambling and betting activities
		9311	Operation of sports facilities
		9319	Other sports activities
		9321	Activities of amusement parks and theme parks
		9329	Other amusement and recreation activities n.e.c.
11.	Retail trade of country-specific tourism characteristic goods		
			Duty free shops**
			Specialized retail trade of souvernirs**
			Specialized retail trade of handicrafts**
			Other specialized retail trade of tourism characteristic goods**
12.	Other country-specific tourism characteristic activities		

* Part related to second homes and timeshare properties
** Not a 4 digit ISIC

Explanatory notes

These explanatory notes refer exclusively to internationally comparable tourism characteristic activities and follow the same order as in Annex 4 above.

They have been extracted from *International Standard Industrial Classification of All Economic Activities (ISIC), Rev. 4.* Statistical papers (Series M No. 4/Rev.4), United Nations. New York, 2008.

The complete document can be consulted in http://unstats.un.org/unsd/cr/registry/regdntransfer.asp?f=135

Accommodation for visitors

5510 Short term accommodation activities

This class includes the provision of accommodation, typically on a daily or weekly basis, principally for short stay by visitors. This includes the provision of furnished accommodation in guest rooms and suites or complete self-contained units with kitchens, with or without daily or other regular housekeeping services, and may often include a range of additional services such as food and beverage services, parking, laundry services, swimming pools and exercise rooms, recreational facilities and conference and convention facilities.

This class includes the provision of short-term accommodation provided by:
- hotels
- resort hotels

- suite / apartment hotels
- motels
- motor hotels
- guesthouses
- pensions
- bed and breakfast units
- visitor flats and bungalows
- time-share units
- holiday homes
- chalets, housekeeping cottages and cabins
- youth hostels and mountain refuges

This class excludes:
- provision of homes and furnished or unfurnished flats or apartments for more permanent use, typically on a monthly or annual basis, see division 68

5520 Camping grounds, recreational vehicle parks and trailer parks

This class includes:
-provision of accommodation in campgrounds, trailer parks, recreational camps and fishing and hunting camps for short stay visitors
-provision of space and facilities for recreational vehicles

This class also includes accommodation provided by:
-protective shelters or plain bivouac facilities for placing tents and/or sleeping bags

5590 Other accommodation

This class includes the provision of temporary or longer-term accommodation in single or shared rooms or dormitories for students, migrant (seasonal) workers and other individuals.

This class includes accommodation provided by:
- student residences
- school dormitories
- workers hostels
- rooming and boarding houses
- railway sleeping cars

6810 Real estate activities with own or leased property

This class includes:
- buying, selling, renting and operating of self-owned or leased real estate, such as:
  - apartment buildings and dwellings
  - non-residential buildings, including exhibition halls, self-storage facilities, malls and shopping centers
  - land
- provision of homes and furnished or unfurnished flats or apartments for more permanent
- use, typically on a monthly or annual basis

This class also includes:
- development of building projects for own operation, i.e. for renting of space in these buildings
- subdividing real estate into lots, without land improvement
- operation of residential mobile home sites

This class excludes:
- development of building projects for sale, see 4100
- subdividing and improving of land, see 4290
- operation of hotels, suite hotels and similar accommodation, see 5510
- operation of campgrounds, trailer parks and similar accommodation, see 5520
- operation of workers hostels, rooming houses and similar accommodation, see 5590

6820 Real estate activities on a fee or contract basis

This class includes the provision of real estate activities on a fee or contract basis including real estate related services.

This class includes:
- activities of real estate agents and brokers
- intermediation in buying, selling and renting of real estate on a fee or contract basis
- management of real estate on a fee or contract basis
- appraisal services for real estate
- activities of real estate escrow agents

This class excludes:
- legal activities, see 6910
- facilities support services, see 8110
- management of facilities, such as military bases, prisons and other facilities (except computer facilities management), see 8110

Food and beverage serving activities

5610 Restaurants and mobile food service activities

This class includes the provision of food services to customers, whether they are served while seated or serve themselves from a display of items, whether they eat the prepared meals on the premises, take them out or have them delivered. This includes the preparation and serving of meals for immediate consumption from motorized vehicles or nonmotorized carts.

This class includes activities of:
- restaurants
- cafeterias
- fast-food restaurants
- pizza delivery
- take-out eating places
- ice cream truck vendors
- mobile food carts
- food preparation in market stalls

This class also includes:
- restaurant and bar activities connected to transportation, when carried out by separate units

This class excludes:
- concession operation of eating facilities, see 5629

5629 Other food service activities

This class includes industrial catering, i.e. the provision of food services based on contractual arrangements with the customer, for a specific period of time.

Also included is the operation of food concessions at sports and similar facilities. The food is often prepared in a central unit.

This class includes:
- activities of food service contractors (e.g. for transportation companies)
- operation of food concessions at sports and similar facilities
- operation of canteens or cafeterias (e.g. for factories, offices, hospitals or schools) on a concession basis

This class excludes:
- manufacture of perishable food items for resale, see 1079
- retail sale of perishable food items, see division 47

5630 Beverage serving activities

This class includes the preparation and serving of beverages for immediate consumption on the premises.

This class includes activities of:
- bars
- taverns
- cocktail lounges
- discotheques (with beverage serving predominant)

- beer parlors and pubs
- coffee shops
- fruit juice bars
- mobile beverage vendors

This class excludes:
- reselling packaged/prepared beverages, see 4711, 4722, 4781, 4799
- operation of discotheques and dance floors without beverage serving, see 9329

Railway passenger transport

4911 Passenger rail transport, interurban

This class includes:
- passenger transport by inter-urban railways
- operation of sleeping cars or dining cars as an integrated operation of railway companies

This class excludes:
- passenger transport by urban and suburban transit systems, see 4921
- passenger terminal activities, see 5221
- operation of sleeping cars or dining cars when operated by separate units, see 5590, 5610

Road passenger transport

4922 Other passenger land transport

This class includes:
- other passenger road transport:
  - scheduled long-distance bus services
  - charters, excursions and other occasional coach services
  - taxi operation
  - airport shuttles
- operation of telfers (téléphériques), funiculars, ski and cable lifts if not part of urban or suburban transit systems

This class also includes:
- other renting of private cars with driver
- operation of school buses and buses for transport of employees
- passenger transport by man- or animal-drawn vehicles

This class excludes:
- ambulance transport, see 8690

Water passenger transport

5011 Sea and coastal passenger water transport

This class includes:
- transport of passengers over seas and coastal waters, whether scheduled or not:
  - operation of excursion, cruise or sightseeing boats
  - operation of ferries, water taxis etc.

This class also includes:
- renting of pleasure boats with crew for sea and coastal water transport (e.g. for fishing cruises)

This class excludes:
- restaurant and bar activities on board ships, when provided by separate units, see 5610, 5630
- operation of "floating casinos", see 9200

5021 Inland passenger water transport

This class includes:
- transport of passenger via rivers, canals, lakes and other inland waterways, including inside harbours and ports

This class also includes:
- renting of pleasure boats with crew for inland water transport

Air passenger transport

5110 Passenger air transport

This class includes:
- transport of passengers by air over regular routes and on regular schedules
- charter flights for passengers
- scenic and sightseeing flights

This class also includes:
- renting of air-transport equipment with operator for the purpose of passenger transportation
- general aviation activities, such as:
  - transport of passengers by aero clubs for instruction or pleasure

Transport equipment rental

7710 Renting and leasing of motor vehicles

This class includes:
- renting and operational leasing of the following types of vehicles:
  - passenger cars (without drivers)
  - trucks, utility trailers and recreational vehicles

This class excludes:
- renting or leasing of vehicles or trucks with driver, see 4922, 4923
- financial leasing, see 6491

Travel agencies and other reservation service activities

7911 Travel agency activities

This class includes:
- activities of agencies primarily engaged in selling travel, tour, transportation and accommodation services to the general public and commercial clients

7912 Tour operator activities

This class includes:
- arranging and assembling tours that are sold through travel agencies or directly by tour operators. The tours may include any or all of the following:
  - transportation
  - accommodation
  - food
  - visits to museums, historical or cultural sites, theatrical, musical or sporting events

7990 Other reservation service and related activities

This class includes:
- provision of other travel-related reservation services:
  - reservations for transportation, hotels, restaurants, car rentals, entertainment and sport etc.
- provision of time-share exchange services
- ticket sales activities for theatrical, sports and other amusement and entertainment events
- provision of visitor assistance services:
  - provision of travel information to visitors
  - activities of tourist guides

- tourism promotion activities

This class excludes:
- activities of travel agencies and tour operators, see 7911, 7912
- organization and management of events such as meetings, conventions and conferences, see 8230

Cultural activities

9000 Creative, arts and entertainment activities

This class includes the operation of facilities and provision of services to meet the cultural and entertainment interests of their customers. This includes the production and promotion of, and participation in, live performances, events or exhibits intended for public viewing; the provision of artistic, creative or technical skills for the production of artistic products and live performances.

This class includes:
- production of live theatrical presentations, concerts and opera or dance productions and other stage productions:
  - activities of groups, circuses or companies, orchestras or bands
  - activities of individual artists such as authors, actors, directors, musicians, lecturers or speakers, stage-set designers and builders etc.
- operation of concert and theatre halls and other arts facilities
- activities of sculptors, painters, cartoonists, engravers, etchers etc.
- activities of individual writers, for all subjects including fictional writing, technical writing etc.
- activities of independent journalists
- restoring of works of art such as paintings etc.

This class also includes:
- activities of producers or entrepreneurs of arts live events, with or without facilities

This class excludes:
- restoring of stained glass windows, see 2310
- manufacture of statues, other than artistic originals, see 2396
- restoring of organs and other historical musical instruments, see 3319
- restoring of historical sites and buildings, see 4100
- motion picture and video production, see 5911, 5912
- operation of cinemas, see 5914
- activities of personal theatrical or artistic agents or agencies, see 7490
- casting activities, see 7810
- activities of ticket agencies, see 7990
- operation of museums of all kinds, see 9102
- sports and amusement and recreation activities, see division 93
- restoring of furniture (except museum type restoration), see 9524

9102 Museums activities and operation of historical sites and buildings

This class includes:
- operation of museums of all kinds:
  - art museums, museums of jewellery, furniture, costumes, ceramics, silverware
  - natural history, science and technological museums, historical museums, including military museums
  - other specialized museums
  - open-air museums
- operation of historical sites and buildings

This class excludes:
- renovation and restoration of historical sites and buildings, see section F
- restoration of works of art and museum collection objects, see 9000
- activities of libraries and archives, see 9101

9103 Botanical and zoological gardens and nature reserves activities

This class includes:
- operation of botanical and zoological gardens, including children's zoos
- operation of nature reserves, including wildlife preservation, etc.

This class excludes:
- landscape and gardening services, see 8130
- operation of sport fishing and hunting preserves, see 9319

Sports and recreational activities

7721 Renting and leasing of recreational and sports goods

This class includes:
- renting of recreational and sports equipment:
  - pleasure boats, canoes, sailboats,
  - bicycles
  - beach chairs and umbrellas
  - other sports equipment
  - skis

This class excludes:
- renting of video tapes and disks, see 7722
- renting of other personal and household goods n.e.c., see 7729
- renting of leisure and pleasure equipment as an integral part of recreational facilities, see 9329

9200 Gambling and betting activities

This class includes:
- bookmaking and other betting operations
- off-track betting
- operation of casinos, including "floating casinos"
- sale of lottery tickets
- operation (exploitation) of coin-operated gambling machines
- operation of virtual gambling web sites

This class excludes:
- operation (exploitation) of coin-operated games, see 9329

9311 Operation of sports facilities

This class includes:
- operation of facilities for indoor or outdoor sports events (open, closed or covered, with or without spectator seating):
  - football, hockey, cricket, baseball, jai-alai stadiums
  - racetracks for auto, dog, horse races
  - swimming pools and stadiums
  - track and field stadiums
  - winter sports arenas and stadiums
  - ice-hockey arenas
  - boxing arenas
  - golf courses
  - bowling lanes
  - fitness centers
- organization and operation of outdoor or indoor sports events for professionals or amateurs by organizations with own facilities

This class includes managing and providing the staff to operate these facilities.

This class excludes:
- renting of recreation and sports equipment, see 7721
- operation of ski hills, see 9329
- park and beach activities, see 9329

9319Other sports activities

This class includes:
- activities of producers or promoters of sports events, with or without facilities
- activities of individual own-account sportsmen and athletes, referees, judges, timekeepers etc.
- activities of sports leagues and regulating bodies
- activities related to promotion of sporting events
- activities of racing stables, kennels and garages
- operation of sport fishing and hunting preserves
- activities of mountain guides
- support activities for sport or recreational hunting and fishing

This class excludes:
- breeding of racing horses, see 0142
- renting of sports equipment, see 7721
- activities of sport and game schools, see 8541
- activities of sports instructors, teachers, coaches, see 8541
- organization and operation of outdoor or indoor sports events for professionals or amateurs by sports clubs with/without own facilities, see 9311, 9312
- park and beach activities, see 9329

9321Activities of amusement parks and theme parks

This class includes:
- activities of amusement parks or theme parks, including the operation of a variety of attractions, such as mechanical rides, water rides, games, shows, theme exhibits and picnic grounds

9329Other amusement and recreation activities n.e.c.

This class includes:
- activities of recreation parks, beaches, including renting of facilities such as bathhouses, lockers, chairs etc.
- operation of recreational transport facilities, e.g. marinas
- operation of ski hills
- renting of leisure and pleasure equipment as an integral part of recreational facilities
- operation of fairs and shows of a recreational nature
- operation of discotheques and dance floors
- operation (exploitation) of coin-operated games
- other amusement and recreation activities (except amusement parks and theme parks) not elsewhere classified

This class also includes:
- activities of producers or entrepreneurs of live events other than arts or sports events, with or without facilities

This class excludes:
- fishing cruises, see 5011, 5021
- provision of space and facilities for short stay by visitors in recreational parks and forests and campgrounds, see 5520
- beverage serving activities of discotheques, see 5630
- trailer parks, campgrounds, recreational camps, hunting and fishing camps, campsites and campgrounds, see 5520
- separate renting of leisure and pleasure equipment, see 7721
- operation (exploitation) of coin-operated gambling machines, see 9200
- activities of amusement parks and theme parks, see 9321

RÉFÉRENCES CONCEPTUELLES et NOTES TECHNIQUES *

1. TOURISME RÉCEPTEUR

Le tourisme récepteur comprend les activités d'un visiteur non résident dans les limites du pays de référence, dans le cadre d'un voyage de tourisme récepteur. Les dépenses correspondantes sont recensées comme dépenses du tourisme récepteur.

Données

Arrivées

Les données concernant les *arrivées* mesurent les flux de visiteurs internationaux dans le pays de référence : chaque arrivée correspond à un voyage du tourisme récepteur. Si une personne se rend dans plusieurs pays à l'occasion d'un seul voyage, chaque arrivée dans un pays est comptabilisée séparément. Sur une période comptable, le nombre d'arrivées n'est pas forcément égal au nombre de personnes qui voyagent (quand une personne se rend dans un même pays plusieurs fois par an, chacun de ses voyages est comptabilisé comme une arrivée).

Les données concernant les *arrivées* doivent correspondre aux *visiteurs du tourisme récepteur* et inclure aussi bien les touristes que les visiteurs de la journée non résidents. Tous les autres types de voyageurs (comme les travailleurs frontaliers, les saisonniers et les autres personnes ayant un contrat de travail à court terme, les étudiants à long terme, etc.) doivent être exclus étant donné qu'ils n'entrent pas dans la catégorie des visiteurs.

Les données proviennent de différentes sources : dossiers administratifs (immigration, comptage de la circulation et autres types de contrôles), enquêtes aux frontières, ou une combinaison de tout cela. Si l'on dispose de données provenant d'enquêtes sur l'hébergement, le nombre de clients est utilisé pour estimer le nombre d'arrivées ; dans ce cas, la ventilation par région, motif principal du voyage, moyens de transport utilisés ou modes d'organisation du voyage se base sur des enquêtes complémentaires auprès des visiteurs.

Les arrivées sont ventilées en fonction de cinq caractéristiques dont deux appellent des commentaires :
- Type de visiteurs (points 1.1 à 1.4 du Compendium). Les données ne sont pas ventilées lorsqu'un pays ne peut distinguer un touriste d'un excursionniste.
- Régions (points 1.5 à 1.13 du Compendium). Le concept sous-jacent de base est que le pays associé à l'arrivée doit être le pays de résidence. Certains pays n'acceptent pas les recommandations de l'OMT et classent leurs ressortissants qui résident à l'étranger dans une catégorie distincte au lieu de les considérer comme résidents des pays en question (point 1.13 du Compendium).

Le *motif principal* d'un voyage se définit comme le motif en l'absence duquel le voyage n'aurait pas eu lieu. On applique la classification suivante :
  1. Motifs personnels
      1.1. Vacances, loisirs et détente
      1.2. Visites aux amis et à la famille
      1.3. Éducation et formation
      1.4. Santé et soins médicaux
      1.5. Religion/pèlerinages
      1.6. Achats
      1.7. Transit
      1.8. Autres
  2. Affaires et motifs professionnels

- Le présent document comprend aussi quatre annexes :
    Annexe 1. Système national de statistiques du tourisme et comparabilité internationale
    Annexe 2. Comprendre le tourisme : glossaire de base
    Annexe 3. Trouver le tourisme dans les classifications internationales types
    Annexe 4. Liste des industries touristiques regroupées par principales catégories conformément à la CITI Rev. 4

Pour des références complémentaires, voir
http://wwww.unwto.org/statistics/
http://unstats.un.org/unsd/tradeserv/tourism/08-40120%20IRTS%202008_WEB_final%20version%20_22%20February%202010.pdf

RÉFÉRENCES CONCEPTUELLES et NOTES TECHNIQUES

L'Annuaire des statistiques du tourisme de l'OMT contient des informations complémentaires et précise la répartition des arrivées par pays d'origine :

- Tableau 1. Arrivées aux frontières nationales de visiteurs non résidents qui passent la nuit (touristes)
- Tableau 2. Arrivées aux frontières nationales de visiteurs non résidents (visiteurs qui passent la nuit [touristes] et visiteurs de la journée [excursionnistes])

Hébergement

Le terme « hébergement » renvoie à des services fournis aux visiteurs par des établissements commerciaux. La catégorie la plus importante est généralement celle des « hôtels et établissements assimilés » recensée dans les CITI, Rev. 4, à la classe 5510 : « Activités d'hébergement temporaire ».

Les nuitées renvoient au nombre de nuits passées par les visiteurs non résidents (voyageurs du tourisme récepteur).

L'Annuaire des statistiques du tourisme de l'OMT contient des informations complémentaires et précise la répartition des arrivées et des nuitées par pays d'origine*:

- Tableau 3. Arrivées de visiteurs non résidents qui passent la nuit (touristes) dans des « hôtels et établissements assimilés »
- Tableau 4. Arrivées de visiteurs non résidents qui passent la nuit (touristes) dans tous les types d'établissements offrant des services d'hébergement pour les visiteurs
- Tableau 5. Nuitées de visiteurs non résidents (touristes) dans des « hôtels et établissements assimilés »
- Tableau 6. Nuitées de visiteurs non résidents (touristes) dans tous les types d'établissements offrant des services d'hébergement pour les visiteurs

Dépenses

Les *dépenses* associées à l'activité des visiteurs internationaux ont jusqu'à présent été tirées du poste voyages de la balance des paiements : pour le tourisme récepteur, les dépenses associées aux visiteurs du tourisme récepteur sont enregistrées comme « crédits » dans la balance des paiements et renvoient aux « recettes des voyages ».

Selon les *Recommandations internationales 2008 sur les statistiques du tourisme*, les « industries et produits touristiques » incluent le transport de passagers. Dans la balance des paiements, il faudrait donc, pour obtenir une estimation plus exacte des dépenses touristiques faites par les visiteurs du tourisme récepteur et du tourisme émetteur au niveau international, ajouter à la valeur du poste voyages celle du poste transport de passagers.

Toutefois, les utilisateurs devraient savoir que les estimations de la balance des paiements incluent, outre les dépenses associées aux visiteurs, celles liées à d'autres types de voyageurs (qui peuvent être importantes dans certains pays, par exemple dans ceux accueillant de nombreux étudiants ou patients de longue durée, travailleurs frontaliers ou saisonniers, etc.).

Les données relatives aux dépenses selon le *motif principal du voyage* sont également des données de la balance des paiements.

Les données publiées correspondent à celles diffusées par le Fonds monétaire international (FMI) (et fournies par les banques centrales) ; en cas de divergence importante avec les données fournies à l'OMT par les administrations nationales du tourisme (ANT) pour la préparation du présent <u>Compendium</u>, les données des ANT figurent séparément dans les « notes du pays ».

Indicateurs

Taille moyenne du groupe de voyageurs

Un groupe de voyageurs se définit comme un ensemble de visiteurs qui réalisent ensemble un voyage et dont les dépenses sont mises en commun. La taille moyenne des groupes de voyageurs permet de procéder à une estimation du nombre total de voyages des visiteurs internationaux, estimation utile pour le marketing et la formulation de politiques.

- L'Annuaire des statistiques du tourisme sera révisé et la rédaction actuelle sera mise à jour conformément aux RIST 2008.

RÉFÉRENCES CONCEPTUELLES et NOTES TECHNIQUES

Durée moyenne du séjour

Tous ces indicateurs renvoient à la durée des voyages à l'étranger des visiteurs internationaux (exprimés en nombre de jours ou de nuits).

La durée moyenne totale du séjour renvoie aux services d'hébergement commerciaux et non commerciaux fournis aux visiteurs, ainsi qu'à d'autres types de séjours.

Attendu qu'un visiteur non résident peut utiliser plusieurs installations d'hébergement pendant son séjour, le total ne peut être estimé qu'en utilisant les informations recueillies dans le cadre des enquêtes aux frontières ou en vérifiant les dates des cartes d'arrivée et de départ d'un échantillon (ou de l'ensemble) de visiteurs.

Dépenses moyennes par jour

Cet indicateur se réfère aux dépenses totales de l'ensemble des visiteurs divisées par le nombre total de jours passés, calculées sur la base d'enquêtes menées auprès des visiteurs.

2. TOURISME INTERNE

Le tourisme interne comprend les activités d'un visiteur résident dans les limites du pays de référence (dans le cadre d'un voyage de tourisme interne ou d'un voyage de tourisme émetteur).

Les dépenses correspondantes de ce visiteur dans l'économie de référence sont recensées comme dépenses de tourisme interne. En outre, les dépenses des visiteurs du tourisme émetteur relatives aux produits fournis par des entreprises résidentes sont inclues dans les dépenses internes.

Données

Les voyages effectués par les visiteurs sont des voyages touristiques. Un voyage de tourisme interne désigne le voyage d'un visiteur à partir du moment où il quitte son lieu de résidence habituelle jusqu'à son retour : il s'agit d'un voyage aller-retour.

Le terme « hébergement » renvoie à des services fournis aux visiteurs par des établissements commerciaux. La catégorie la plus importante est généralement celle des « hôtels et établissements assimilés » recensée dans les CITI, Rev. 4, à la classe 5510 : « Activités d'hébergement temporaire ».

Les nuitées renvoient au nombre de nuits passées par les visiteurs résidents (voyageurs du tourisme interne). Il y a lieu de privilégier, comme source de données, les enquêtes sur l'hébergement (adressées aux établissements).

Indicateurs

Durée moyenne du séjour

La durée moyenne totale du séjour renvoie aux services d'hébergement commerciaux et non commerciaux fournis aux visiteurs, ainsi qu'à d'autres types de séjours.

Les données totales ne peuvent être estimées que grâce à des enquêtes menées auprès des ménages.

Dépenses moyennes par jour

Cet indicateur se réfère aux dépenses totales divisées par le nombre total de jours passés, calculées sur la base d'enquêtes menées auprès des visiteurs.

3. TOURISME ÉMETTEUR

Le tourisme émetteur désigne les activités d'un visiteur résident hors du pays de référence (dans le cadre d'un voyage du tourisme émetteur ou d'un voyage de tourisme interne). Les dépenses correspondantes sont recensées comme dépenses du tourisme émetteur.

Données

Les données concernant les *départs* mesurent les flux de visiteurs résidents qui quittent le pays de référence. Le nombre de départs n'est pas forcément égal au nombre d'arrivées déclarées par les destinations internationales pour le pays de référence.

RÉFÉRENCES CONCEPTUELLES et NOTES TECHNIQUES

Les *dépenses* associées à l'activité des visiteurs ont jusqu'à présent été tirées du poste voyages de la balance des paiements : pour le tourisme émetteur, les dépenses associées aux visiteurs résidents sont enregistrées comme « débits » dans la balance des paiements et renvoient aux « dépenses de voyages ». Comme dans le cas du *tourisme récepteur*, on utilise les données de la balance des paiements.

Selon les *Recommandations internationales 2008 sur les statistiques du tourisme*, les « industries et produits touristiques » incluent le transport de passagers. Dans la balance des paiements, il faudrait donc, pour obtenir une estimation plus exacte des dépenses touristiques faites par les visiteurs résidents et non résidents au niveau international, ajouter à la valeur du poste voyages celle du poste transport de passagers.

Toutefois, les utilisateurs devraient savoir que les estimations de la balance des paiements incluent, outre les dépenses associées aux visiteurs, celles liées à d'autres types de voyageurs.

Les données relatives aux dépenses selon le *motif principal* du voyage sont également des données de la balance des paiements.

Les données publiées correspondent à celles diffusées par le Fonds monétaire international (FMI) (et fournies par les banques centrales) ; en cas de divergence importante avec les données fournies à l'OMT par les administrations nationales du tourisme (ANT) pour la préparation du présent <u>Compendium</u>, les données des ANT seront données séparément dans les « notes du pays ».

Des informations complémentaires sur « les voyages à l'étranger des visiteurs résidents vers les pays de destination » sont disponibles à l'adresse suivante : http://www.e-unwto.org/home/main.mpx. Il y a lieu de préciser que les informations données dans les tableaux sont basées sur les données fournies par chaque pays de destination et qu'elles correspondent donc aux arrivées dans ces pays.

Indicateurs

Durée moyenne du séjour

Cet indicateur renvoie à la durée des voyages à l'étranger des visiteurs du tourisme émetteur (exprimée en nombre de jours) et reflète la moyenne totale, établie sur la base d'enquêtes aux frontières et/ou d'informations fournies par les ménages.

Dépenses moyennes par jour

Cet indicateur se réfère aux dépenses totales divisées par le nombre total de jours passés, calculées sur la base d'enquêtes aux frontières et/ou d'informations fournies par les ménages.

4. INDUSTRIES TOURISTIQUES

L'expression *industries touristiques* désigne les industries qui produisent généralement des produits caractéristiques du tourisme ; elle équivaut à l'expression plus courante de « secteur touristique ». Ces industries sont recensées ci-dessous :

1. Hébergement des visiteurs
2. Activités de services de restauration et de consommation de boissons
3. Transport de voyageurs par chemin de fer
4. Transport routier de voyageurs
5. Transport de voyageurs par voies navigables
6. Transport de voyageurs par voie aérienne
7. Location de matériels de transport
8. Activités des agences de voyages et autres activités de services de réservation
9. Activités culturelles
10. Activités sportives et récréatives
11. Commerce de détail de biens caractéristiques du tourisme, propres à chaque pays
12. Autres activités caractéristiques du tourisme, propres à chaque pays

Les notes explicatives suivantes se réfèrent aux industries *Hébergement des visiteurs* et *Activités des agences de voyages et autres activités de services de réservation*, qui sont les deux seules industries pour lesquelles des données monétaires et non monétaires sont publiées dans le présent <u>Compendium</u>.

Ces notes, qui peuvent être consultées à l'annexe 4, sont tirées de la *Classification internationale type, par industrie, de toutes les branches d'activité économique (CITI), Rev. 4.* Études statistiques (Série M, N° 4/Rev.4), Nations Unies. New York, 2008.

Hébergement des visiteurs

Le nombre d'établissements de l'industrie d'*Hébergement des visiteurs* (point 4.2. du Compendium) renvoie à tous les types d'établissements qui offrent des services d'hébergement aux visiteurs sur une base commerciale (de marché), c'est-à-dire moyennant rémunération. Par conséquent, les données doivent comprendre toutes les classes suivantes de l'ISIC :

5510 Activités d'hébergement temporaire

Cette classe figure dans la section 4 du Compendium sous le titre « Hébergement des visiteurs dans des hôtels et des établissements assimilés » et couvre les activités d'hébergement, généralement assuré à la journée ou à la semaine, essentiellement à l'intention de visiteurs pour des séjours temporaires. Il s'agit d'hébergement dans des chambres d'hôtes meublées, ou de plusieurs pièces attenantes ou encore d'appartements avec cuisine, avec ou sans services quotidiens de ménage, et pouvant souvent comprendre une gamme de services complémentaires tels que des services de repas et de boissons, de garage, de lessive, de piscines et de gymnastique, ainsi que installations récréatives et des salles de réunions et de conférences.

Cette classe comprend la fourniture d'hébergement temporaire assuré par les établissements suivants :
- hôtels
- centres de villégiature
- hôtels offrant des suites/appartements
- motels
- hôtels pour automobilistes
- chambres d'hôtes
- pensions
- foyers assurant gîte et couvert
- appartements et bungalows
- établissements d'hébergement en multipropriété
- maisons de vacances
- chalets, cottages et maisonnettes
- auberges de jeunesse et refuges de montagne

Exclusions :
- fourniture de maisons ou d'appartements meublés ou non meublés pour de plus longues durées, généralement sur une base mensuelle ou annuelle, voir division 68

5520 Terrains de camping, parcs pour véhicules de loisirs et caravanes

Cette classe comprend les activités suivantes :
- fourniture d'installations d'hébergement telles que terrains de camping, terrains de caravanage, parcs de loisirs, d'espaces de chasse et de pêche à l'intention de visiteurs temporaires
- fourniture d'espaces et d'installations pour les véhicules de loisirs.

Cette classe couvre en outre des lieux d'hébergement tels que :
- abris protecteurs ou aires de campement pour dresser des tentes et/ou installer des sacs de couchage

5590 Autres activités d'hébergement

Cette classe comprend la fourniture d'hébergement temporaire ou à plus long terme dans une seule pièce ou en salles communes ou dortoirs pour étudiants, travailleurs migrants (saisonniers) et autres personnes.

Cette classe comprend la fourniture de logement assurée par les entités suivantes :
- résidences d'étudiants
- dortoirs de pensionnats
- foyers pour travailleurs
- pensions
- voitures-lits de chemins de fer

6810 Activités immobilières sur biens propres ou loués

Cette classe comprend les activités suivantes :
- achat, vente, location et exploitation de biens immobiliers propres ou loués :
  - immeubles résidentiels et habitations
  - bâtiments non résidentiels, y compris les halls d'exposition, les installations d'entreposage pour particuliers, les galeries marchandes et les centres commerciaux
  - terrains
- fourniture de maisons individuelles et d'appartements meublés et non meublés pour une utilisation plus permanente généralement sur une base mensuelle ou annuelle

Cette classe comprend en outre les activités suivantes :
- mise en œuvre de projets de construction immobilière pour compte propre en vue, par exemple, de locations dans ces immeubles
- subdivision de biens immobiliers en lotissements, sans viabilisation de terrains
- exploitation d'emplacements pour caravanes

Exclusions :
- mise en œuvre de projets de construction immobilière dans un but de vente, voir 4100
- subdivision et viabilisation de terrains, voir 4290
- exploitation d'hôtels, appartements en hôtel et lieux d'hébergement analogues, voir 5510
- exploitation de terrains de camping, de parcs pour caravanes et autres lieux d'hébergement, voir 5520
- exploitation de foyers de travailleurs, de maisons meublées et autres lieux d'hébergement, voir 5590

6820 Activités immobilières à forfait ou sous contrat

Cette classe couvre la prestation d'activités dans le domaine de l'immobilier, à forfait ou sous contrat, y compris les services connexes

Cette classe comprend les activités suivantes :
- activités des agents et courtiers immobiliers
- intermédiation en matière d'achat, vente et location immobilière à forfait ou sous contrat
- gestion de biens immobiliers à forfait ou sous contrat
- services d'évaluation pour l'immobilier
- activités des dépositaires légaux en matière immobilière

Exclusions :
- activités juridiques, voir 6910
- services d'appui aux installations, voir 8110
- gestion d'installations, par exemple les bases militaires, les prisons, etc. (sauf la gestion d'installations informatiques), voir 8110

Activités des agences de voyages et autres activités de services de réservation

7911 Activités des agences de voyages

Cette classe comprend les activités suivantes :
- activités d'agences dont le rôle principal est de vendre des voyages, des excursions, des services de transport et d'hébergement au grand public et à des clients commerciaux.

7912 Activités des voyagistes

Cette classe comprend les activités suivantes :
- organisation et groupement d'excursions vendues par l'intermédiaire d'agences de voyage ou directement par des voyagistes. Les excursions peuvent inclure toutes ou partie des activités suivantes :
  - transport
  - hébergement
  - restauration
  - visites de musées, de sites historiques ou culturels, théâtre, événements musicaux ou sportifs

7990 Autres activités de services de réservation et activités connexes

Cette classe comprend les activités suivantes :
- fourniture d'autres services de réservation relatifs aux voyages :
  - réservations dans les moyens de transport, les hôtels, les restaurants, location de voitures, spectacles et événements sportifs, etc.
- fourniture de services en multipropriété
- vente de billets pour le théâtre, les événements sportifs et spectacles divers
- fourniture de services d'assistance aux visiteurs :
  - fourniture de renseignements concernant les voyages
  - activités de guides touristiques
- activités de promotion du tourisme

Exclusions :
- activités d'agences de voyage et de voyagistes, voir 7911, 7912
- organisation et gestion d'événements tels que réunions, congrès et conférences, voir 8230

Données

Concernant le *nombre d'établissements*, le point 4.3 du <u>Compendium</u> inclut les établissements associés aux classes 5520, 5590, 6810 et 6820 (voir plus haut les notes explicatives pour l'hébergement des visiteurs).

Le nombre de *chambres* et de *places-lits* se réfère à la capacité des « hôtels et établissements assimilés » de fournir un hébergement temporaire aux visiteurs.

Indicateurs

Les trois premiers indicateurs se basent sur le nombre total de nuitées des touristes résidents et non résidents dans des hôtels et établissements assimilés.

Le *taux d'occupation* se réfère au rapport entre la capacité existante de fournir des services d'hébergement aux visiteurs et le degré d'utilisation de ces services. Ce taux peut se référer à l'utilisation soit des chambres soit des places-lits.

La *capacité disponible* renvoie au nombre de places-lits dans les hôtels et établissements similaires pour 1 000 habitants de la population résidente permanente du pays de référence. Les données sont attribuées par l'OMT lorsqu'elles ne sont pas fournies par le pays.

5. EMPLOI

Les personnes qui travaillent dans les industries touristiques peuvent être des *employés* (personnes qui travaillent pour une entreprise moyennant une rémunération en espèces ou en nature, selon ce qui a été convenu) ou des *travailleurs indépendants* (personnes qui travaillent à leur compte, ont un « travail indépendant » et n'ont engagé de manière continue aucun « employé » durant la période de référence).

Certains employés peuvent avoir plusieurs postes de travail ; par conséquent, le nombre de postes de travail (du côté de la demande) et le nombre de personnes employées (du côté de l'offre) ne sont pas des catégories similaires et en général elles ne coïncident pas.

L'intensité du travail peut varier selon le poste, l'industrie ou la période. Les postes de travail peuvent être différents selon le temps de travail des personnes employées et donc être exprimés en termes d'emplois à temps plein ou à temps partiel. C'est pourquoi il ne suffit pas de disposer de données sur le nombre de postes de travail ou de personnes employées pour avoir des informations sur le volume du travail accompli durant une période déterminée (par exemple, un mois ou un an). Des données sur le nombre total d'heures de travail seront nécessaires. Enfin, si l'on convertit tous les postes de travail en emploi à plein temps équivalent ou en nombre total d'heures travaillées par an, on pourra obtenir le volume total du travail d'une industrie touristique donnée pour une période donnée.

Les chiffres concernant le « Nombre d'emplois par situation dans la profession » et le « Nombre d'emplois équivalents plein temps par situation dans la profession » doivent renvoyer aux industries touristiques.

6. INDICATEURS COMPLÉMENTAIRES

Ces indicateurs proviennent de la balance des paiements, des comptes nationaux et des statistiques du tourisme.

RÉFÉRENCES CONCEPTUELLES et NOTES TECHNIQUES

Demande

La propension brute à voyager mesure le nombre de voyages du tourisme émetteur et du tourisme interne au regard du total de la population résidente permanente du pays de référence. Des valeurs élevées de cet indicateur indiquent une grande fréquence des voyages et traduisent la mobilité actuelle de la population voyageant à l'étranger.

La capacité de charge mesure le nombre total d'arrivées (du tourisme interne et du tourisme récepteur) par rapport au total de la population résidente permanente et donne une estimation du potentiel touristique du pays de référence.

Indicateurs macroéconomiques liés au tourisme international

Les données se fondent sur les *Statistiques de la balance des paiements* et les *Statistiques financières internationales* du Fonds monétaire international, telles que compilées par la Commission économique pour l'Amérique latine et les Caraïbes (CEPALC) des Nations Unies pour l'Organisation mondiale du tourisme (OMT). L'ensemble de données utilisé pour le <u>Compendium des statistiques du tourisme</u> 2011 se réfère à mars 2011.

Ces indicateurs, et d'autres indicateurs complémentaires, constituent un système préliminaire très simple d'évaluation de la contribution économique du tourisme à l'économie nationale. Ils sont précieux du fait qu'ils sont généralement disponibles dans la plupart des pays, que l'on peut les comparer sur le plan international et les rapprocher d'autres indicateurs économiques.

Il y a lieu de remarquer que le terme « dépenses » est utilisé de la même manière dans le tourisme récepteur et le tourisme émetteur pour indiquer la somme payée pour l'acquisition de biens et de services de consommation, mais aussi de biens de valeur, en vue de leur usage personnel ou pour les offrir, pour et durant des voyages touristiques. Les visiteurs étrangers dans le pays de référence réalisent des dépenses de tourisme récepteur (crédits dans la balance des paiements), tandis que les visiteurs résidents présents dans des pays étrangers réalisent des dépenses du tourisme émetteur (débits dans la balance des paiements).

Dépenses du tourisme récepteur sur PIB
Elles reflètent le poids des dépenses des visiteurs du tourisme récepteur en tant qu'élément de la valeur totale de l'activité économique dans l'économie de référence. Du point de vue du commerce international, cet indicateur rend compte de l'importance économique des rentrées de devises associées aux dépenses de ces visiteurs.

Dépenses du tourisme émetteur sur PIB
Elles reflètent l'importance des dépenses à l'étranger des visiteurs du tourisme émetteur au regard de l'économie nationale. Du point de vue du commerce international, cet indicateur rend compte de l'importance économique des sorties de revenus nationaux attribuables à ces visiteurs.

Balance des paiements du tourisme sur PIB
Elle rend compte de l'importance économique des dépenses nettes du tourisme (récepteur moins émetteur) pour l'économie de référence. Un excédent ou un déficit important affecte la balance commerciale du pays, et par conséquent son PIB.

Ouverture touristique
Elle montre l'importance de la somme des dépenses touristiques transfrontalières (c'est-à-dire du tourisme international, la somme des dépenses du tourisme récepteur et émetteur) pour l'économie de référence. Cet indicateur pourrait également être utilisé pour mesurer le flux libre de tourisme entre le pays de référence et le reste du monde.

Couverture touristique
Elle rend compte de la proportion entre les dépenses du tourisme récepteur et les dépenses du tourisme émetteur pour montrer dans quelle mesure les influx de revenus étrangers couvrent les sorties de revenus nationaux. Une valeur supérieure à 100 signifie que le tourisme récepteur finance indirectement plus que toutes les dépenses des visiteurs du tourisme émetteur, tandis qu'une valeur inférieure à 100 signifie que le tourisme récepteur ne couvre pas les dépenses que font les visiteurs résidents à l'étranger.

RÉFÉRENCES CONCEPTUELLES et NOTES TECHNIQUES

Dépenses du tourisme récepteur sur exportations de biens
Dépenses du tourisme récepteur sur exportations de services
Dépenses du tourisme récepteur sur exportations de biens et de services
Ces trois indicateurs reflètent l'importance du tourisme en tant que service dont le commerce s'effectue à l'échelle internationale par rapport à d'autres catégories d'exportations. En même temps, ils révèlent le degré de spécialisation touristique de la structure des exportations d'un pays, et la capacité relative du tourisme de générer des devises.

Dépenses du tourisme récepteur sur crédits du compte courant
Les crédits du compte courant de la balance des paiements se réfèrent à tous les afflux de biens et de services, de revenus et de transferts courants dans une économie. Plus la part occupée par le tourisme dans cet ensemble est grande, plus l'activité touristique est importante en tant que génératrice d'afflux de devises.

Dépenses du tourisme émetteur sur importations de biens
Dépenses du tourisme émetteur sur importations de services
Dépenses du tourisme émetteur sur importations de biens et de services

Ces trois indicateurs reflètent l'importance du tourisme en tant que service dont le commerce s'effectue à l'échelle internationale par rapport à d'autres catégories d'importations. En même temps, ils montrent la prédilection pour le tourisme de la structure des importations d'un pays et le degré relatif de sorties de revenus nationaux d'une économie résultant du tourisme international.

Dépenses du tourisme émetteur sur débits des comptes courants
Les débits du compte courant de la balance des paiements se réfèrent à toutes les sorties de biens, de services, de revenus et de transferts courants d'un pays vers le reste du monde. Plus la part du tourisme dans cet ensemble est grande, plus l'activité touristique occupe une place importante dans la fuite de revenus nationaux.

Annexe 1. Système national de statistiques du tourisme et comparabilité internationale

La structure du <u>Compendium des statistiques du tourisme</u> se fonde sur le système suivant qui renvoie au cadre d'informations de base des systèmes nationaux de statistiques du tourisme à des fins de comparabilité internationale[1].

Les *Recommandations internationales 2008 sur les statistiques du tourisme* (RIST 2008) constituent le cadre conceptuel de ce noyau essentiel de données et d'indicateurs.

Comparabilité internationale et statistiques du tourisme : le cadre d'informations de base

I.   Cadre conceptuel

Concepts	Unités d'observation	Principales caractéristiques connexes
Visiteur	Visiteur	Classes : Visiteur qui passe la nuit (touriste), visiteur de la journée (excursionniste) Pays de résidence/régions
	Groupe de voyageurs	Taille
Voyage	Voyage touristique	Motif principal Durée Destination principale Modes de transport Types d'hébergement utilisés Organisation Dépenses

Industries touristiques	Établissement	<u>Monétaires</u>
		   Production
		   Consommation intermédiaire
		   Valeur ajoutée brute
		   Rémunération des employés
		   Formation brute de capital fixe
		<u>Non monétaires</u>
		   Caractéristiques non monétaires propres à chaque industrie touristique

Emploi	Établissement (dans les industries touristiques)	Personnes Taille Statut Postes de travail Durée du travail Postes de travail équivalents à temps plein

II.   Classifications

    1.   Formes de tourisme
    2.   Classification des produits de consommation achetés par les visiteurs
    3.   Classification des activités productives au service des visiteurs
    4.   Autres classifications

III. Tableaux de résultats

    1.   Tourisme récepteur
    2.   Tourisme interne
    3.   Tourisme émetteur
    4.   Industries touristiques
    5.   Emploi
    6.   Indicateurs complémentaires

---

1 <u>http://www.unwto.org/statistics/sts/description/sts_text.pdf</u>

Annexe 2. Comprendre le tourisme : glossaire de base *

Activités/produits caractéristiques du tourisme

Les activités caractéristiques du tourisme désignent les activités productives dont la production principale est caractéristique du tourisme.

Les produits caractéristiques du tourisme sont ceux qui remplissent au moins une des deux conditions suivantes :

a. Les dépenses touristiques concernant le produit (bien ou service) doivent représenter une part importante des dépenses touristiques totales (condition relative à la part correspondant aux dépenses/demande) ;

b. Les dépenses touristiques concernant le produit doivent représenter une part importante de l'offre du produit dans l'économie (condition relative à la part correspondant à l'offre). Cette condition suppose que la fourniture d'un produit caractéristique du tourisme serait susceptible de cesser d'exister en quantité significative en cas d'absence de visiteurs.

Dépenses touristiques

Les dépenses touristiques renvoient à la somme payée pour l'acquisition de biens et de services de consommation, mais aussi de biens de valeur, en vue de leur usage personnel ou pour les offrir, pour et durant des voyages touristiques.

Emploi dans les industries touristiques

L'emploi dans les industries touristiques peut être mesuré en effectuant le dénombrement des personnes employées dans les industries touristiques, quel que soit leur poste de travail, le dénombrement des personnes ayant leur emploi principal dans les industries touristiques, ou le dénombrement des postes de travail dans les industries touristiques.

Environnement habituel

L'environnement habituel d'une personne, concept clé du tourisme, se définit comme la zone géographique (pas forcément contiguë) à l'intérieur de laquelle une personne mène ses activités quotidiennes habituelles.

Groupe de voyageurs

Un groupe de voyageurs se définit comme un ensemble de visiteurs qui réalisent ensemble un voyage et dont les dépenses sont mises en commun.

Industries touristiques

Les industries touristiques désignent tous les établissements dont l'activité productive principale est une activité caractéristique du tourisme.

Lieu de résidence habituelle

Le lieu de résidence habituelle est le lieu géographique où le visiteur réside habituellement, et se définit par l'endroit de son lieu d'habitation principal (Principes et recommandations pour les recensements de la population et de l'habitation, Nations Unies).

Maison de vacances

Une maison de vacances est une habitation secondaire où se rendent les membres du ménage essentiellement à des fins récréatives, pour des vacances ou toute autre forme de loisir.

Motif (principal) d'un voyage touristique

Le motif principal d'un voyage touristique se définit comme le motif en l'absence duquel le voyage n'aurait pas eu lieu. La classification des voyages touristiques en fonction du motif principal du voyage se réfère à neuf catégories : cette typologie permet d'identifier différents sous-ensembles de visiteurs (visiteurs en voyages d'affaires, visiteurs en transit, etc.).

Tourisme émetteur

Comprend les activités d'un visiteur résident hors du pays de référence, dans le cadre d'un voyage du tourisme émetteur ou d'un voyage de tourisme interne.

Tourisme interne

Comprend les activités d'un visiteur résident dans les limites du pays de référence, dans le cadre d'un voyage de tourisme interne ou d'un voyage du tourisme émetteur.

Tourisme récepteur

Comprend les activités d'un visiteur non résident dans les limites du pays de référence, dans le cadre d'un voyage du tourisme récepteur.

Touriste (ou visiteur qui passe la nuit) et excursionniste (visiteur de la journée)

Un visiteur (du tourisme interne, récepteur ou émetteur) est qualifié de touriste (ou visiteur qui passe la nuit) s'il passe une nuit sur place, et de touriste de la journée (ou excursionniste) dans le cas contraire.

(*) Cette annexe reprend certains concepts clés qu'elle définit conformément aux nouvelles RIST 2008. http://unstats.un.org/unsd/tradeserv/tourism/08-40120%20IRTS%202008_WEB_final%20version%20_22%20February%202010.pdf

Visite	Un voyage se compose de visites effectuées à différents endroits. L'expression « visite touristique » fait référence à un séjour dans un endroit visité durant un voyage touristique.
Visiteur	Un visiteur est une personne qui se déplace vers une destination située en dehors de son environnement habituel, pour une durée inférieure à un an, et dont le motif de la visite (affaires, loisirs ou autre motif personnel) est autre que celui d'exercer une activité rémunérée dans le pays ou le lieu visité.
Visiteur interne	Une personne qui se rend dans un lieu situé dans son pays de résidence est un visiteur interne et ses activités s'inscrivent dans le cadre du tourisme interne.
Voyage	Un voyage désigne le déplacement d'une personne depuis le moment où elle quitte son lieu de résidence habituelle jusqu'à son retour : il s'agit donc d'un voyage aller-retour. Les voyages des visiteurs sont des voyages touristiques.
Voyage/Tourisme	Le terme « voyage » désigne les activités des voyageurs. Un voyageur est une personne qui se déplace entre différents lieux géographiques pour quelque motif et durée que ce soit. Le visiteur est un type particulier de voyageur, de sorte que le tourisme est un sous-ensemble des voyages.

Annexe 3. Trouver le tourisme dans les classifications internationales types

L'importance du tourisme et la nécessité de définir et de mesurer son importance au sein du système de statistique des Nations Unies a été reconnue par la Commission de statistique de l'ONU avec l'approbation en 1993 des Recommandations sur les statistiques du tourisme. Ladite Commission a approuvé en 2008 la version révisée de ces recommandations, intitulée *Recommandations internationales 2008 sur les statistiques du tourisme* (RIST 2008).

Pour étudier la contribution économique du tourisme à l'économie nationale, il était nécessaire d'intégrer l'analyse économique du tourisme dans le cadre de référence du Système de comptabilité nationale (le SCN 1993). Cela a conduit à l'approbation, en 2000, par la Commission de statistique de l'ONU du « Compte satellite du tourisme : Recommandations concernant le cadre conceptuel », qui a été actualisé par la suite en tant que « Compte satellite du tourisme : Recommandations concernant le cadre conceptuel 2008 » (CST : RCC 2008).

Les concepts, définitions et classifications contenus dans les RIST 2008 ont été harmonisés avec le CST:RCC 2008, lequel a été harmonisé à son tour avec le Système de comptabilité nationale de 2008, la balance des paiements et le commerce international de services.

Pour le tourisme, il est intéressant de recenser les produits achetés par les visiteurs, directement et indirectement, et les activités qui en sont à l'origine. Les classifications utilisées pour les activités et les produits détaillés requis dans l'étude du tourisme sont tirées directement des classifications de référence des Nations Unies, et y sont liées : CITI et CPC.

L'analyse du tourisme est axée sur le visiteur. Dans un premier temps, il est intéressant de mesurer les dépenses des visiteurs et de recenser les produits, tant les biens que les services, achetés par les visiteurs, ainsi que les activités qui sont à l'origine de ces produits. Dans un cadre macroéconomique, comme celui du CST, le concept de tourisme englobe aussi bien la perspective de la demande, qui consiste en la consommation du visiteur, la consommation touristique collective et la formation brute de capital fixe du tourisme, que la perspective de l'offre d'activités touristiques (en s'intéressant en particulier à la part de leur production achetée par les visiteurs). Le tourisme en tant que tel n'est pas mentionné dans le SCN 1993 ni dans la CITI. S'agissant du tourisme, les activités couvertes par la CITI qui produisent des biens et des services satisfaisant la demande touristique sont réunies et regroupées en tant qu'activités touristiques.

Si l'on se place du point de vue de la demande, le visiteur est l'unité basique d'observation et d'analyse, et les dépenses des visiteurs sont observées en termes de produits (essentiellement des services). Du point de vue de l'offre, vu leur relation avec le système de comptabilité nationale, les statistiques du tourisme utilisent « l'établissement » comme unité statistique de base, ainsi qu'il est défini dans le SCN, et « l'industrie » comme unité de présentation et d'analyse, l'industrie étant définie comme un « groupe d'établissements exerçant le même type d'activités de production ».

Au premier chef, il y a lieu de recenser les produits achetés par les visiteurs. Pour la compilation des données du point de vue de la demande, les produits sont regroupés en grandes catégories en fonction du motif ; cependant, le tourisme exige une analyse simultanée de la consommation et de la production, d'où la classification utilisée pour définir les produits dans la Classification centrale de produits (CPC ver. 2.). Les produits achetés par les visiteurs peuvent être regroupés dans les classes détaillées de la CPC et les activités qui en sont à l'origine recensées sur la base des classes détaillées de la CITI.

Le tourisme définit certains des produits achetés par les visiteurs et les activités qui en sont à l'origine comme des « produits caractéristiques du tourisme » (ceux qui réunissent certaines conditions) et des « activités caractéristiques du tourisme » (celles qui produisent normalement des produits caractéristiques du tourisme). Les RIST 2008 expliquent de manière détaillée les concepts sous-jacents, les définitions et les classifications qui doivent être utilisés pour compiler les statistiques du tourisme et recenser les produits et activités caractéristiques du tourisme. Pour faciliter la comparaison au niveau international, des listes de ces produits et activités caractéristiques ont été dressées. L'annexe 3 du présent document fournit une liste des activités caractéristiques du tourisme (industries touristiques) regroupées en grandes catégories d'après la CITI rev. 4. L'annexe 4 quant à elle fournit une liste des produits caractéristiques du tourisme regroupés par grandes catégories d'après la CPC ver. 2. Même dans le cas où le produit acheté par le visiteur ne constitue qu'une partie de la classe de la CPC ou lorsque l'activité qui en est à l'origine ne constitue qu'une partie d'une classe à quatre chiffres de la CITI, les listes étant exprimées en termes de classes de la CPC et d'agrégats des classes de la CITI, elles fournissent une classe définie dans laquelle chaque produit ou activité peut être placé. Il est recommandé aux pays qui en auraient besoin pour leur propre analyse de créer des classes plus détaillées en dessous du niveau le plus bas de la CPC et de la CITI.

La portée de l'analyse des statistiques du tourisme est plus large quand on place celles-ci dans le cadre du compte satellite du tourisme. Dans le cadre de la comptabilité, les produits et les activités sont exprimés au regard de la CPC ver. 2 et de la CITI rev. 4, notamment ceux et celles associés au tourisme. Les classifications internationales de produits et d'activités utilisées pour compiler les données pour le CST:RCC 2008, lequel établit des liens structurels avec le système de comptabilité nationale, permettent une meilleure appréciation des liens qui unissent le tourisme à d'autres secteurs économiques.

Annexe 4. Liste des industries touristiques regroupées par principales catégories conformément à la CITI Rev. 4

	Liste des industries touristiques (activités caractéristiques) regroupées par principales catégories, conformément à la CITI Rev. 4		
	Industries touristiques	**CITI Rev.4**	**Description**
1.	Hébergement des visiteurs	5510	Activités d'hébergement temporaire
		5520	Terrains de camping, parcs pour véhicules de loisirs et caravanes
		5590	Autres activités d'hébergement
		6810	Activités immobilières sur biens propres ou loués*
		6820	Activités immobilières à forfait ou sous contrat*
2.	Activités de services de restauration et de consommation de boissons	5610	Activités de restaurants et de services de restauration mobiles
		5629	Autres activités de services de restauration
		5630	Activités de consommation de boissons
3.	Transport de voyageurs par chemin de fer	4911	Transport de voyageurs par chemin de fer interurbain
4.	Transport routier de voyageurs	4922	Autres transports terrestres de voyageurs
5.	Transport de voyageurs par voies navigables	5011	Transports maritimes et côtiers de voyageurs
		5021	Transport de voyageurs par voies navigables intérieures
6.	Transport de voyageurs par voie aérienne	5110	Transport aérien de voyageurs
7.	Location de matériels de transport	7710	Location de véhicules automobiles
8.	Activités des agences de voyages et autres activités de services de réservation	7911	Activités des agences de voyages
		7912	Activités des voyagistes
		7990	Autres activités de services de réservation et activités connexes
9.	Activités culturelles	9000	Activités créatives, arts et spectacles
		9102	Activités des musées et exploitation des sites et monuments historiques
		9103	Activités des jardins botaniques et zoologiques et des réserves naturelles
10.	Activités sportives et récréatives	7721	Location d'articles pour le sport et les loisirs
		9200	Activités de jeux de hasard et de pari
		9311	Exploitation d'installations sportives
		9319	Autres activités sportives
		9321	Activités des parcs d'attraction et à thèmes
		9329	Autres activités récréatives et de loisirs, n.c.a.
11.	Commerce de détail de biens caractéristiques du tourisme, propres à chaque pays		Boutiques hors taxes** Commerce de détail de souvenirs dans des établissements spécialisés** Commerce de détail d'artisanat dans des établissements spécialisés** Autre commerce de détail de biens caractéristiques du tourisme dans des établissements spécialisés**
12.	Autres activités caractéristiques du tourisme, propres à chaque pays		

* partie relative aux résidences secondaires et multipropriétés
** pas d'indice CITI à quatre chiffres

Notes explicatives

Ces notes explicatives font référence uniquement à des activités caractéristiques du tourisme comparables au plan international et suivent l'ordre donné ci-dessus à l'annexe 4.

Elles sont tirées de la *Classification internationale type, par industrie, de toutes les branches d'activité économique (CITI), Rev. 4*. Études statistiques (Série M, N° 4/Rev.4), Nations Unies, New York, 2008.

Le document complet est disponible à l'adresse suivante :
http://unstats.un.org/unsd/cr/registry/regdntransfer.asp?f=135

Hébergement des visiteurs

5510 Activités d'hébergement temporaire

Cette classe couvre les activités d'hébergement, généralement assuré à la journée ou à la semaine, essentiellement à l'intention de visiteurs pour des séjours temporaires. Il s'agit d'hébergement dans des chambres d'hôtes meublées, ou de plusieurs pièces attenantes ou encore d'appartements avec cuisine, avec ou sans services quotidiens de ménage, et pouvant souvent comprendre une gamme de services complémentaires tels que des services de repas et de boissons, de garage, de lessive, de piscines et de gymnastique, ainsi que des salles de réunions et de conférences et des installations récréatives.

Cette classe comprend la fourniture d'hébergement temporaire assuré par les établissements suivants :
- hôtels
- centres de villégiature
- hôtels offrant des suites/appartements
- motels
- hôtels pour automobilistes
- chambres d'hôtes
- pensions
- foyers assurant gîte et couvert
- appartements et bungalows
- établissements d'hébergement en multipropriété
- maisons de vacances
- chalets, cottages et maisonnettes
- auberges de jeunesse et refuges de montagne

Exclusions :
- fourniture de maisons ou d'appartements meublés ou non meublés pour de plus longues durées, généralement sur une base mensuelle ou annuelle, voir division 68

5520 Terrains de camping, parcs pour véhicules de loisirs et caravanes

Cette classe comprend les activités suivantes :
- fourniture d'installations d'hébergement telles que terrains de camping, terrains de caravanage, parcs de loisirs, d'espaces de chasse et de pêche à l'intention de visiteurs temporaires
- fourniture d'espaces et d'installations pour les véhicules de loisirs.

Cette classe couvre en outre des lieux d'hébergement tels que :
- abris protecteurs ou aires de campement pour dresser des tentes et/ou installer des sacs de couchage

5590 Autres activités d'hébergement

Cette classe comprend la fourniture d'hébergement temporaire ou à plus long terme dans une seule pièce ou en salles communes ou dortoirs pour étudiants, travailleurs migrants (saisonniers) et autres personnes.

Cette classe comprend la fourniture de logement assurée par les entités suivantes :
- résidences d'étudiants
- dortoirs de pensionnats
- foyers pour travailleurs
- pensions
- voitures-lits de chemins de fer

6810 Activités immobilières sur biens propres ou loués

Cette classe comprend les activités suivantes :
- achat, vente, location et exploitation de biens immobiliers propres ou loués :
  - immeubles résidentiels et habitations
  - bâtiments non résidentiels, y compris les halls d'exposition, les installations d'entreposage pour particuliers, les galeries marchandes et les centres commerciaux
  - terrains
- fourniture de maisons individuelles et d'appartements meublés et non meublés pour une utilisation plus permanente généralement sur une base mensuelle ou annuelle

Cette classe comprend en outre les activités suivantes :
- mise en œuvre de projets de construction immobilière pour compte propre en vue, par exemple, de locations dans ces immeubles
- subdivision de biens immobiliers en lotissements, sans viabilisation de terrains
- exploitation d'emplacements pour caravanes

Exclusions :
- mise en œuvre de projets de construction immobilière dans un but de vente, voir 4100
- subdivision et viabilisation de terrains, voir 4290
- exploitation d'hôtels, appartements en hôtel et lieux d'hébergement analogues, voir 5510
- exploitation de terrains de camping, de parcs pour caravanes et autres lieux d'hébergement, voir 5520
- exploitation de foyers de travailleurs, de maisons meublées, etc., voir 5590

6820 Activités immobilières à forfait ou sous contrat

Cette classe couvre la prestation d'activités dans le domaine de l'immobilier, à forfait ou sous contrat, y compris les services connexes.

Cette classe comprend les activités suivantes :
- activités des agents et courtiers immobiliers
- intermédiation en matière d'achat, vente et location immobilière à forfait ou sous contrat
- gestion de biens immobiliers à forfait ou sous contrat
- services d'évaluation pour l'immobilier
- activités des dépositaires légaux en matière immobilière

Exclusions :
- activités juridiques, voir 6910
- services d'appui aux installations, voir 8110
- gestion d'installations, par exemple les bases militaires, les prisons, etc. (sauf la gestion d'installations informatiques), voir 8110

Activités de services de restauration et de consommation de boissons

5610 Activités de restaurants et de services de restauration mobiles

Cette classe couvre la fourniture de services de restauration à des clients, que ces derniers soient servis à table ou se servent eux-mêmes, choisissant parmi un assortiment de plats qu'ils peuvent manger sur place, ou emporter ou se faire livrer. Est également comprise dans cette classe la préparation et le service de repas destinés à une consommation immédiate, vendus à bord de véhicules automobiles ou non.

Cette classe comprend les activités des entités suivantes :
- restaurants
- cafétérias
- établissements de restauration rapide
- pizzerias
- restaurants servant des plats à emporter
- marchands ambulants (motorisés) de crème glacée
- marchands ambulants de produits alimentaires
- préparation d'aliments sur des éventaires de marché

Cette classe comprend également :
- les activités des restaurants et bars liés aux transports lorsqu'ils sont exploités par des unités distinctes

Exclusions :
- exploitation de concessions de restauration dans diverses installations, voir 5629

5629 Autres activités de services de restauration

Cette classe couvre les activités des restaurants d'entreprises, à savoir la fourniture de services de restauration sur la base d'arrangements contractuels passés avec le client pour une période déterminée.

Elle porte également sur les concessions de restauration dans les installations sportives ou installations similaires. Les plats sont souvent confectionnés dans une unité de préparation centrale.

Cette classe comprend les activités suivantes :
- activités de sous-traitants en restauration (par exemple pour les compagnies de transports)
- exploitation de concessions de restauration dans les installations sportives et installations similaires
- exploitation de cantines ou de cafétérias (par exemple dans les usines, bureaux, hôpitaux ou écoles) au titre d'une concession.

Exclusions :
- fabrication de produits alimentaires périssables destinés à la revente, voir 1079
- commerce de détail de denrées périssables, voir division 47

5630 Activités de consommation de boissons

Cette classe comprend la préparation et le service de boissons à consommer sur place immédiatement.

Cette classe comprend les activités des établissements suivants :
- bars
- cafés
- salons pour apéritifs
- discothèques (où prédomine le service de boissons)
- brasseries, bars à bière
- cafétérias
- bars à jus de fruits
- distributeurs mobiles de boissons

Exclusions :
- revente de boissons sous emballage/préparées, voir 4711, 4722, 4781, 4799
- exploitation de discothèques et de pistes de danse, sans service de boissons, voir 9329

Transport de voyageurs par chemin de fer

4911 Transport de voyageurs par chemin de fer interurbain

Cette classe comprend les activités suivantes :
- transport de voyageurs par chemin de fer interurbain
- exploitation de voitures-lits et de voitures-restaurants en tant qu'exploitation intégrée des compagnies de chemin de fer

Exclusions :
- transport de voyageurs par des réseaux de transport urbain et suburbain, voir 4921
- exploitation de gares de voyageurs, voir 5221
- exploitation de voitures-lits et de voitures-restaurants par des unités distinctes, voir 5590, 5610

Transport routier de voyageurs

4922 Autres transports terrestres de voyageurs

Cette classe comprend les activités suivantes :
- autres transports routiers de voyageurs :
  - services réguliers d'autocars sur de longues distances
  - transports à demande, excursions et autres services occasionnels de transports par autocar
  - exploitation de taxis
  - navettes desservant les aéroports
- exploitation de téléphériques, de funiculaires, de télésièges et remonte-pentes s'ils ne font pas partie des réseaux suburbains de transit

Cette classe comprend en outre les activités suivantes :
- autres locations de voitures particulières avec chauffeur
- exploitation d'autocars scolaires et d'autobus pour le transport d'employés
- transport de personnes par véhicules à traction humaine ou animale

Exclusions :
- transport par ambulance, voir 8690

Transport maritime de voyageurs

5011 Transports maritimes et côtiers de voyageurs

Cette classe comprend les activités suivantes :
- transports maritimes et côtiers de voyageurs, même réguliers :
  • exploitation de bateaux d'excursion, de croisière et de tourisme
  • exploitation de bacs, bateaux-taxis, etc.

Cette classe comporte aussi les activités suivantes :
- location de bateaux de plaisance avec équipage pour le transport maritime et côtier de voyageurs (par exemple : pour des croisières de pêche)

Exclusions :
- activités de restauration et de bar à bord de bateaux lorsqu'elles sont fournies par des unités séparées, voir 5610, 5630
- exploitation de « casinos flottants », voir 9200

5021 Transport de voyageurs par voies navigables intérieures

Cette classe comprend les activités suivantes :
- transport de voyageurs sur les cours d'eau, les canaux, lacs et autres voies d'eau intérieures, y compris les zones portuaires

Cette classe comporte en outre les activités suivantes :
- location de bateaux de plaisance avec équipage pour le transport sur les voies navigables intérieures

Transport aérien de voyageurs

5110 Transport aérien de voyageurs

Cette classe comprend les activités suivantes :
- transport aérien de voyageurs sur des lignes régulières avec des horaires réguliers
- vols affrétés pour voyageurs
- vols d'excursion

Cette classe comporte également les activités suivantes :
- location d'équipements de transport aérien avec pilote en vue de transporter des voyageurs
- activités générales d'aviation, par exemple :
  • transport de voyageurs par des aéroclubs pour apprendre à piloter ou pour le plaisir

Location de matériels de transport

7710 Location de véhicules automobiles

Cette classe comprend les activités suivantes :
- location et location-exploitation des types suivants de véhicules :
  • voitures particulières (sans chauffeur)
  • camions, remorques utilitaires et véhicules de loisirs

Exclusions :
- location de véhicules avec chauffeur, voir 4922, 4923
- crédit-bail, voir 6491

Activités des agences de voyages et autres activités de services de réservation

7911 Activités des agences de voyages

Cette classe comprend les activités suivantes :
- activités d'agences dont le rôle principal est de vendre des voyages, des excursions, des services de transport et d'hébergement au grand public et à des clients commerciaux.

7912 Activités des voyagistes

Cette classe comprend les activités suivantes :
- organisation et groupement d'excursions vendues par l'intermédiaire d'agences de voyage ou directement par des voyagistes. Les excursions peuvent inclure toutes ou partie des activités suivantes :
  - transport
  - hébergement
  - restauration
  - visites de musées, de sites historiques ou culturels, théâtre, événements musicaux ou sportifs

7990 Autres activités de services de réservation et activités connexes

Cette classe comprend les activités suivantes :
- fourniture d'autres services de réservation relatifs aux voyages :
  - réservations dans les moyens de transport, les hôtels, les restaurants ; location de voitures, spectacles et événements sportifs, etc.
- fourniture de services en multipropriété
- vente de billets pour le théâtre, les événements sportifs et spectacles divers
- fourniture de services d'assistance aux touristes :
  - fourniture de renseignements concernant les voyages
  - activités de guides touristiques
- activités de promotion du tourisme

Exclusions :
- activités d'agences de voyage et de voyagistes, voir 7911, 7912
- organisation et gestion d'événements tels que réunions, congrès et conférences, voir 8230

Activités culturelles

9000 Activités créatives, arts et spectacles

Cette classe couvre l'exploitation d'installations et la fourniture de services pour répondre aux besoins des clients dans les domaines de la culture et des spectacles. Ces activités comprennent la production et la promotion de spectacles en direct, d'événements et d'expositions pour le public, et la participation de celui-ci à ces activités ; la promotion de talents artistiques, de compétences créatrices ou techniques pour la production d'œuvres artistiques et de spectacles en direct.

Cette classe comprend les activités suivantes :
- production de représentations théâtrales, de concerts et d'opéras ou de ballets et autres productions de scène :
  - activités de groupes, de compagnies de cirque, d'orchestres symphoniques ou autres formations musicales
  - activités individuelles d'artistes, tels que les auteurs, acteurs, metteurs en scène, musiciens, conférenciers ou orateurs, décorateurs de théâtre, etc.
- exploitation de salle de théâtre et de concerts et d'autres installations pour la production de spectacles
- activités des sculpteurs, peintres, caricaturistes, graveurs d'art au burin et à l'eau forte, etc.
- activités d'écrivains sur tous les sujets, y compris les ouvrages de fiction, les ouvrages techniques, etc.
- activités de journalistes indépendants
- restauration d'œuvres d'art telles que les tableaux, etc.

Cette classe comporte aussi les activités suivantes :
- réalisations de producteurs ou d'organisateurs de manifestations artistiques en direct avec ou sans installations

Exclusions :
- restauration de vitraux, voir 2310
- fabrication de statues autres que les originaux d'artistes, voir 2396
- restauration d'orgues et autres instruments de musiques historiques, voir 3319
- restauration de sites et monuments historiques, voir 4100
- production de films cinématographiques et vidéo, voir 5911, 5912
- exploitation de salles de cinéma, voir 5914
- activités des agences de professionnels du théâtre et d'artistes, voir 7490
- activités de distribution des rôles, voir 7810
- activités des billetteries, voir 7990
- exploitation de musées de types divers, voir 9102
- activités de sports et de loisirs et activités récréatives, voir division 93
- restauration de meubles (à l'exception des meubles de musées), voir 9524

9102 Activités des musées et exploitation des sites et monuments historiques

Cette classe comprend les activités suivantes :
- exploitation de tous types de musées :
  - musées d'art, d'orfèvrerie, de meubles, de costumes, de céramique, d'argenterie
  - musées d'histoire naturelle, des sciences et des techniques, musées d'histoire, y compris les musées militaires
  - autres musées spécialisés
  - musées en plein air
- gestion et préservation de sites et monuments historiques

Exclusions :
- rénovation et restauration de sites et monuments historiques, voir section F
- restauration d'œuvres d'art et d'objets appartenant à des collections de musées, voir 9000
- activités des bibliothèques et des archives, voir 9101

9103 Activités des jardins botaniques et zoologiques et des réserves naturelles

Cette classe couvre les activités suivantes :
- administration des jardins botaniques et zoologiques, y compris les zoos pour enfants
- administration de réserves naturelles, y compris la protection de la flore et de la faune sauvages, etc.

Exclusions :
- services d'entretien des espaces verts, voir 8130
- exploitation des réserves consacrées à la chasse et à la pêche sportives, voir 9319

Activités sportives et récréatives

7721 Location d'articles pour le sport et les loisirs

Cette classe couvre les activités suivantes :
- location d'articles pour le sport et les loisirs :
  - bateaux de plaisance, canoës, bateaux à voile
  - bicyclettes
  - chaises de plage et parasols
  - autres articles de sport
  - skis

Exclusions :
- location de vidéocassettes et de vidéodisques, voir 7722
- location d'articles personnels et ménagers, n.c.a., voir 7729
- locations d'articles pour les activités récréatives et les loisirs en tant que parties intégrantes des installations récréatives, voir 9329

9200 Activités de jeux de hasard et de pari

Cette classe couvre les activités suivantes :
- activités de bookmakers et autres opérations de pari
- pari sur les courses de chevaux
- activités des casinos, y compris les casinos à bord de navires de croisière
- vente de billets de loterie
- exploitation de machines de jeu automatiques (à pièces de monnaie)
- exploitation de sites Web de jeux virtuels

Exclusions :
- exploitation de machines à sous, voir 9329

9311 Exploitation d'installations sportives

Cette classe comprend les activités suivantes :
- exploitation d'installations pour les activités sportives en plein air ou en salle (ouverte, fermée ou couverte avec ou sans places assises) :
  - terrains de football, de hockey, de cricket, de baseball, de jai alai
  - champs de courses pour les courses d'automobiles, de chiens, de chevaux, etc.
  - piscines et stades
  - stades d'athlétisme
  - arènes et stades de sports d'hiver
  - arènes de hockey sur glace
  - arènes de boxe
  - terrains de golfe
  - pistes de quilles
  - centres de mise en forme physique
- Mise en place et exploitation de manifestations sportives en plein air ou en salle pour les sportifs professionnels ou amateurs par des organisations dotées de leurs propres installations.

Les activités rangées dans cette classe comprennent la gestion et la fourniture du personnel chargé du fonctionnement de ces installations.

Exclusions :
- location de matériel de sport et de loisirs, voir 7721
- exploitation de pistes de ski, voir 9329
- activités de parcs et de plages, voir 9329

9319 Autres activités sportives

Cette classe comprend les activités suivantes :
- activités des producteurs ou promoteurs de manifestations sportives même sans installations
- activités des sportifs individuels pour compte propre et des athlètes, arbitres, juges, chronométreurs, etc.
- activités des ligues sportives et d'organismes régulateurs
- activités relatives à la promotion de manifestations sportives
- activités des écuries de course, des chenils et des garages
- exploitation des réserves de pêche et de chasse sportives
- activités des guides de montagne
- activités d'appui à la chasse ou à la pêche sportive ou de loisir

Exclusions :
- élevage de chevaux de courses, voir 0142
- location de matériel de sport, voir 7721
- activités des écoles de sport ou de jeu, voir 8541
- activités des moniteurs, instructeurs, entraîneurs, voir 8541
- organisation et réalisation de manifestations sportives en plein air ou en salle pour professionnels ou amateurs par des clubs sportifs dotés ou non de leurs propres installations, voir 9311, 9312
- activités de parcs et de plages, voir 9329

9321 Activités des parcs d'attractions et à thèmes

Cette classe comprend les activités suivantes :
- activités de parcs d'attractions ou de parcs à thèmes, y compris l'exploitation d'attractions foraines, manèges, tours aquatiques, jeux, spectacles, expositions à thèmes et terrains de pique-nique.

9329 Autres activités récréatives et de loisirs, n.c.a.

Cette classe comprend :
- activités de parcs d'attraction et de plages, y compris la location d'installations telles que les cabines de bain, de vestiaires, de sièges, etc.
- exploitation d'installations de transport à des fins récréatives, par exemple les marinas

- exploitation des pistes de ski

- location de matériel pour l'amusement et le divertissement en tant que partie intégrante d'équipements récréatifs
- organisation de foires et expositions à des fins récréatives
- exploitation de discothèques et de salles de bal
- exploitation de jeux électroniques payants
- autres activités d'amusement et de divertissement (sauf les parcs d'attractions et les parcs à thèmes), n.c.a.

Exclusions :
- activités de producteurs et d'organisateurs de manifestations en direct autres que des manifestations relatives aux arts ou aux sports même sans installations.

Exclusions :
- croisières de pêche, voir 5011, 5021
- fourniture d'espace et d'installations pour de courts séjours de visiteurs dans des parcs et forêts de loisirs et les terrains de camping, voir 5520
- services de boissons dans les discothèques, voir 5630
- parcs de stationnement de caravanes, terrains de camping, camps de loisirs, réserves de chasse et de pêche, campings, campements, voir 5520
- location séparée de matériel pour les activités de divertissement et de loisirs, voir 7721
- exploitation de machines de jeu automatiques à pièces de monnaie, voir 9200
- activités des parcs d'attraction et à thèmes, voir 9321

REFERENCIAS CONCEPTUALES y NOTAS TÉCNICAS *

1. TURISMO RECEPTOR

El turismo receptor comprende las actividades de un visitante no residente dentro del país de referencia en un viaje de turismo receptor. El gasto de ese visitante se identifica como gasto del turismo receptor.

Datos

Llegadas

Los datos de *llegadas* miden la afluencia de visitantes internacionales al país de referencia: cada llegada corresponde a un viaje de turismo receptor. Si una persona visita varios países en el transcurso de un solo viaje, cada llegada a un país se registra separadamente. En un ejercicio contable, la cifra de llegadas no es necesariamente igual a la del número de personas que viajan (cuando una persona visita el mismo país varias veces al año, cada viaje de esa misma persona se contabiliza como una llegada distinta).

Los datos de *llegadas* deben corresponder a los *visitantes recibidos* (no residentes en el país visitado) incluidos tanto los turistas como los visitantes del día no residentes. Deben excluirse todos los demás tipos de viajeros (trabajadores fronterizos, estacionales y con contratos de corta duración, estudiantes por periodos largos, etc.), ya que no pueden calificarse de visitantes.

Los datos se obtienen de diversas fuentes: registros administrativos (inmigración, censos de tránsito y otros posibles tipos de control), encuestas de fronteras o una combinación de todos ellos. Si se obtienen datos de encuestas sobre alojamiento, el número de huéspedes sirve para estimar las cifras de llegadas; por consiguiente, en este caso, los desgloses por regiones, motivo principal del viaje, medio de transporte utilizado o formas de organización del viaje se basan en encuestas de visitantes complementarias.

Las llegadas se dividen en función de cinco características, de las cuales dos merecen algunos comentarios:
- Tipo de visitantes (del punto 1.1 al 1.4 del Compendio). Por consiguiente, si un país no puede distinguir entre visitantes que pernoctan y visitantes del día, no se proporciona ningún desglose.
- Regiones (del punto 1.5 al 1.13 del Compendio). El concepto básico subyacente es que el país asociado a la llegada debe ser el país de residencia. Algunos países no aceptan las recomendaciones de la OMT y clasifican a los nacionales del país residentes en el extranjero en lugar de como residentes en esos países como una categoría separada (punto 1.13 del Compendio).

El *motivo principal* de un viaje se define como el motivo en ausencia del cual el viaje no habría tenido lugar. La clasificación aplicada es la siguiente:

1. Motivos personales
    1.1. Vacaciones, recreo y ocio
    1.2. Visitas a familiares y amigos
    1.3. Educación y formación
    1.4. Salud y atención médica
    1.5. Religión/peregrinaciones
    1.6. Compras
    1.7. Tránsito
    1.8. Otros motivos
2. Negocios y motivos profesionales

- Este documento contiene además cuatro anexos:
    Anexo 1. Sistema nacional de estadísticas de turismo y comparabilidad internacional
    Anexo 2. Comprender el turismo: glosario básico
    Anexo 3. Cómo encontrar el turismo en las clasificaciones internacionales uniformes.
    Anexo 4. Lista de industrias turísticas y agrupadas por categorías principales según la CIIU, Rev. 4

Para consultar referencias adicionales, visite:
http://www.unwto.org/statistics/
http://unstats.un.org/unsd/tradeserv/tourism/08-
40120%20IRTS%202008_WEB_final%20version%20_22%20February%202010.pdf

REFERENCIAS CONCEPTUALES y NOTAS TÉCNICAS

En el Anuario de estadísticas de turismo de la OMT se incluye información complementaria sobre llegadas, desglosadas por país de origen*.

- Cuadro 1.   Llegadas a las fronteras nacionales de visitantes no residentes que pernoctan (turistas).
- Cuadro 2.   Llegadas a las fronteras nacionales de visitantes no residentes (que pernoctan – turistas– y visitantes del día –excursionistas–).

Alojamiento

El término «alojamiento» se refiere a los servicios prestados por establecimientos comerciales a los visitantes, siendo normalmente la categoría más importante la de «hoteles y establecimientos asimilados», identificada en la CIIU, Rev.4 como 5510 «Actividades de alojamiento para estancias cortas».

Las *pernoctaciones* (o «noches de huéspedes») se refieren al número de noches que pasan los huéspedes no residentes (turistas recibidos).

En el Anuario de estadísticas de turismo de la OMT se incluye información complementaria sobre los huéspedes, desglosada por país de origen*.

- Cuadro 3.   Llegadas de visitantes no residentes que pernoctan (turistas) a «hoteles y establecimientos asimilados»
- Cuadro 4.   Llegadas de visitantes no residentes que pernoctan (turistas) a todo tipo de establecimientos que ofrezcan servicios de alojamiento para visitantes.
- Cuadro 5.   Pernoctaciones de visitantes no residentes (turistas) a «hoteles y establecimientos asimilados»
- Cuadro 6.   Pernoctaciones de visitantes no residentes (turistas) a todo tipo de establecimientos que ofrezcan servicios de alojamiento para visitantes.

Gasto

El *gasto* asociado con la actividad de los visitantes internacionales se ha identificado tradicionalmente con la partida de viajes en la balanza de pagos: en el caso del turismo receptor, estos gastos asociados con los visitantes recibidos se registran como «crédito» en la balanza de pagos y se denominan «ingresos por viajes».

Las *Recomendaciones internacionales para estadísticas de turismo de 2008* consideran que en las «industrias y productos turísticos» se incluye el transporte de pasajeros. Por lo tanto, en términos de balanza de pagos, sería mejor para la estimación de los datos de gastos relacionados con el turismo, efectuados por los visitantes recibidos y emitidos en un contexto internacional, contar el valor de la partida de viajes más el de la partida de transporte de pasajeros.

No obstante, los usuarios deberían ser conscientes de que las estimaciones de la balanza de pagos incluyen, además de los gastos asociados a los visitantes, los relativos a otros tipos de viajeros (que pueden ser sustanciales en algunos países, por ejemplo, estudiantes o pacientes por periodos largos, trabajadores fronterizos y estacionales, etc.).

También los datos de gastos por *motivo principal del viaje* son datos de la balanza de pagos.

Los datos publicados corresponden a los que publica el Fondo Monetario Internacional (FMI) (y que proporcionan los bancos centrales); en el caso de detectarse una diferencia significativa con los datos suministrados a la OMT por las administraciones nacionales de turismo (ANT) para la preparación del Compendio, los datos de las ANT se facilitarán separadamente en las «notas de los países».

Indicadores

Tamaño medio del grupo de viaje

Un grupo de viaje se define como un conjunto de visitantes que realizan juntos un viaje y comparten los gastos. El tamaño medio de los grupos de viaje permite la estimación del número total de viajes de visitantes internacionales, una estimación útil para labores de marketing y formulación de políticas.

- El Anuario de estadísticas de turismo va a revisarse para ajustar su actual redacción a las RIET 2008.

REFERENCIAS CONCEPTUALES y NOTAS TÉCNICAS

Duración media de la estancia

Todos estos indicadores se refieren a la duración de los viajes de turismo receptor realizados por visitantes internacionales (expresados como número de días o de noches).

La duración media de la estancia se refiere a los servicios de alojamiento tanto comerciales como no comerciales suministrados a los visitantes, así como a otros tipos de estancias.

Puesto que un visitante no residente podría alojarse en diferentes instalaciones durante su estancia, esas cifras totales solo pueden estimarse utilizando la información de las encuestas de fronteras o comprobando las fechas en las tarjetas oficiales de llegada/partida para una muestra de visitantes (o para todos ellos).

Gasto medio por día

Este indicador se refiere al gasto total de los visitantes en general, dividido por el número total de días empleados, estimado mediante la encuesta de visitantes.

2. TURISMO INTERNO

El turismo interno comprende las actividades de un visitante residente dentro del país de referencia (como parte de un viaje de turismo interno o como parte de un viaje de turismo emisor).

El gasto correspondiente de ese visitante en la economía de referencia se identifica como gasto turístico interno. Además, el gasto de los visitantes emitidos en productos recibidos de empresas residentes se incluye en el gasto interno.

Datos

Los *viajes* de los visitantes son viajes turísticos. Un viaje de turismo Interno se refiere al viaje de un visitante desde el momento de dejar su residencia habitual hasta que regresa; se refiere a un viaje de ida y vuelta.

El término «alojamiento» se refiere a los servicios prestados por establecimientos comerciales a los visitantes, siendo normalmente la categoría más importante la de «hoteles y establecimientos asimilados», identificada en la CIIU, Rev.4 como 5510 «Actividades de alojamiento para estancias cortas».

Las *pernoctaciones* (o «noches de huéspedes») se refieren al número de noches que pasan los huéspedes residentes (turistas internos). Las encuestas sobre alojamiento (dirigidas a los establecimientos) deberían ser la fuente de datos preferida.

Indicadores

Duración media de la estancia

La duración media de la estancia se refiere a los servicios de alojamiento tanto comerciales como no comerciales suministrados a los visitantes, así como a otros tipos de estancias.

Los datos totales solo pueden estimarse utilizando las encuestas de hogares.

Gasto medio por día

Este indicador se refiere al gasto total, dividido por el número total de días empleados, estimado mediante la encuesta de visitantes.

3. TURISMO EMISOR

El turismo emisor comprende las actividades de un visitante residente fuera del país de referencia (como parte de un viaje de turismo emisor o como parte de un viaje de turismo interno). El gasto correspondiente de ese visitante se identifica como gasto del turismo emisor.

REFERENCIAS CONCEPTUALES y NOTAS TÉCNICAS

Datos

Los datos de *salidas* miden el flujo de visitantes residentes que salen del país de referencia. Las salidas no coinciden necesariamente con el número de llegadas notificadas por los destinos internacionales para el país de referencia.

El *gasto* asociado con la actividad de los visitantes se ha identificado tradicionalmente con la partida de viajes en la balanza de pagos: en el caso del turismo emisor, estos gastos asociados con los visitantes no residentes se registran como «débito» en la balanza de pagos y se denominan «gastos por viajes». Como en el caso del *turismo receptor*, se utilizan los datos de la balanza de pagos.

Las Recomendaciones internacionales para estadísticas de turismo de 2008 consideran que en las «industrias y productos turísticos» se incluye el transporte de pasajeros. Por lo tanto, en términos de balanza de pagos, sería mejor para la estimación de los datos de gastos relacionados con el turismo, efectuados por los visitantes residentes y no residentes en un contexto internacional, contar el valor de la partida de viajes más el de la partida de transporte de pasajeros.

No obstante, los usuarios deberían ser conscientes de que las estimaciones de la balanza de pagos incluyen, además de los gastos asociados a los visitantes, los relativos a otros tipos de viajeros.

De igual forma, los datos de gastos por *motivo principal* del viaje son datos de la balanza de pagos.
Los datos publicados corresponden a los que publica el Fondo Monetario Internacional (FMI) (y que proporcionan los bancos centrales); en el caso de detectarse una diferencia significativa con los datos suministrados a la OMT por las administraciones nacionales de turismo (ANT) para la preparación del Compendio, los datos de las ANT se facilitarán separadamente en las «notas de los países».

Puede obtenerse información complementaria sobre «viajes al extranjero de visitantes residentes a países de destino» en la página web: http://www.e-unwto.org/home/main.mpx. Es importante indicar que la información presentada se basa en los datos suministrados por cada país de destino y corresponde por lo tanto a las llegadas a esos países.

Indicadores

Duración media de la estancia

Este indicador se refiere a la duración de los viajes de visitantes emitidos (expresada en número de días) y refleja la media total utilizando las encuestas de fronteras o la información de los hogares.

Gasto medio por día

Este indicador se refiere al gasto total dividido por el número total de días empleados, calculado a partir de las encuestas de fronteras o la información de los hogares.

4. INDUSTRIAS TURÍSTICAS

El término *industrias turísticas* incluye aquellas industrias que producen normalmente productos característicos del turismo; equivale al más coloquial de «sector turístico». En la siguiente lista se especifican esas industrias:

1. Alojamiento para visitantes
2. Actividades de provisión de alimentos y bebidas
3. Transporte de pasajeros por ferrocarril
4. Transporte de pasajeros por carretera
5. Transporte de pasajeros por agua
6. Transporte aéreo de pasajeros
7. Alquiler de equipos de transporte
8. Actividades de agencias de viajes y de otros servicios de reservas
9. Actividades culturales
10. Actividades deportivas y recreativas
11. Comercio al por menor de bienes característicos del turismo, específicos de cada país
12. Otras actividades características del turismo, específicas de cada país

Las siguientes notas explicativas se refieren al *alojamiento para visitantes* y a *agencias de viajes y otros servicios de reservas*, que son las dos únicas industrias para las que se publican datos monetarios y no monetarios en este Compendio.

REFERENCIAS CONCEPTUALES y NOTAS TÉCNICAS

Estas notas pueden consultarse en el Anexo 4: Se han extraído del documento *Clasificación Industrial Internacional Uniforme de todas las actividades económicas (CIIU), Rev.4*. Informes estadísticos (serie M, No. 4/Rev.4), Naciones Unidas. Nueva York, 2008.

Alojamiento para visitantes

El número de establecimientos en la industria de *Alojamiento para visitantes* (punto 4.2 del Compendio se refiere a todos los tipos de establecimientos que ofrecen servicios de alojamiento a los visitantes con carácter comercial (de mercado), es decir, mediante pago. Por consiguiente, los datos deberían incluir las siguientes clases de la CIIU:

5510 Actividades de alojamiento para estancias cortas

Esta clase figura en la sección 4 del Compendio como «*alojamiento para visitantes en hoteles y establecimientos asimilados*» e incluye el suministro de alojamiento, normalmente por días o semanas, sobre todo para estancias cortas de visitantes. Abarca el suministro de alojamiento amueblado en habitaciones y apartamentos o unidades totalmente independientes con cocina, con o sin servicio diario o regular de limpieza, y que incluyen a menudo diversos servicios adicionales, como los de comidas y bebidas, aparcamiento, lavandería, piscina y gimnasio, instalaciones de recreo e instalaciones para conferencias y convenciones.

Esta clase comprende el suministro de alojamiento por estancias cortas en:
- hoteles
- centros vacacionales
- hoteles de suites/apartamentos
- moteles
- hoteles para automovilistas
- casas de huéspedes
- pensiones
- unidades de alojamiento y desayuno
- pisos y bungalows
- unidades utilizadas en régimen de tiempo compartido
- casas de vacaciones
- chalets y cabañas con servicio de mantenimiento y limpieza
- albergues juveniles y refuglos de montaña

No se incluyen las siguientes actividades:
- suministro de viviendas y de pisos o apartamentos amueblados o sin amueblar para períodos más largos, en general por meses o por años; véase la división 68

5520 Actividades de campamentos, parques de vehículos de recreo y parques de caravanas

Esta clase comprende las siguientes actividades:
- suministro de alojamiento en campamentos, parques para caravanas, campamentos recreativos y campamentos de caza y de pesca para estancias cortas
- suministro de espacio e instalaciones para vehículos de recreo

Se incluyen también los servicios de alojamiento de:
- refugios o simples instalaciones de acampada para plantar tiendas o pernoctar en sacos de dormir

5590 Otras actividades de alojamiento

Esta clase comprende el suministro de alojamiento temporal o a largo plazo en habitaciones individuales o compartidas o dormitorios para estudiantes, trabajadores migrantes (estacionales) y otras categorías de personas.

Se incluyen los servicios de alojamiento proporcionados por:
- residencias de estudiantes
- dormitorios escolares
- albergues para trabajadores
- casas de huéspedes e internados
- coches cama ferroviarios

6810 Actividades inmobiliarias realizadas con bienes propios o arrendados

Esta clase comprende las siguientes actividades:
- compra, venta, alquiler y explotación de bienes inmuebles propios o arrendados, como:
  - edificios de apartamentos y viviendas
  - edificios no residenciales, incluso salas de exposiciones, instalaciones de autoalmacenamiento y centros comerciales
  - terrenos
- alquiler de casas y pisos o apartamentos amueblados o sin amueblar por períodos largos, en general por meses o por años

Se incluyen también las siguientes actividades:
- promoción de proyectos de construcción para su posterior explotación, es decir, para alquilar espacio en esos edificios
- subdivisión de propiedades inmobiliarias en lotes, sin mejora de los terrenos
- explotación de campamentos residenciales para casas móviles

No se incluyen las siguientes actividades:
- promoción de proyectos de construcción para la venta; véase la clase 4100
- subdivisión y mejora de terrenos; véase la clase 4290
- explotación de hoteles, hoteles de apartamentos e instalaciones de alojamiento similares; véase la clase 5510
- explotación de campamentos, parques de caravanas e instalaciones de alojamiento similares; véase la clase 5520
- explotación de albergues para trabajadores, casas de huéspedes e instalaciones de alojamiento similares; véase la clase 5590

6820 Actividades inmobiliarias realizadas a cambio de una retribución o por contrata

Esta clase comprende las actividades inmobiliarias que se realizan a cambio de una retribución o por contrata, incluidos los servicios inmobiliarios.

Esta clase comprende las siguientes actividades:
- actividades de agentes y corredores inmobiliarios
- intermediación en la compra, la venta y el alquiler de bienes inmuebles a cambio de una retribución o por contrata
- administración de bienes inmuebles a cambio de una retribución o por contrata
- servicios de tasación inmobiliaria
- actividades de agentes depositarios de plicas inmobiliarias

No se incluyen las siguientes actividades:
- actividades jurídicas; véase la clase 6910
- servicios de apoyo a instalaciones; véase la clase 8110
- administración de instalaciones, como bases militares, prisiones y otras instalaciones (excepto administración de instalaciones informáticas); véase la clase 8110

Actividades de agencias de viajes y de otros servicios de reservas

7911 Actividades de agencias de viajes

Esta clase comprende las siguientes actividades:
- actividades de agencias dedicadas principalmente a vender servicios de viajes, de viajes organizados, de transporte y de alojamiento al público en general y a clientes comerciales

7912 Actividades de operadores turísticos

Esta clase comprende las siguientes actividades:
- organización de paquetes de servicios de viajes para su venta a través de agencias de viajes o por los propios operadores turísticos. Esos viajes organizados pueden incluir uno o varios de los elementos siguientes:
  - transporte
  - alojamiento
  - comidas
  - visitas a museos, lugares históricos o culturales y asistencia a espectáculos teatrales, musicales o deportivos

7990 Otros servicios de reservas y actividades conexas

Esta clase comprende las siguientes actividades:
- prestación de otros servicios de reservas relacionados con los viajes:
  • reservas de transporte, hoteles, restaurantes, alquiler de automóviles, entretenimiento y deporte, etcétera
- prestación de servicios de intercambio en régimen de tiempo compartido o multipropiedad
- actividades de venta de billetes para obras de teatro, competiciones deportivas y otras actividades de diversión y entretenimiento
- prestación de servicios de asistencia a los visitantes:
  • suministro a los clientes de información sobre los viajes
  • actividades de guías de turismo
- actividades de promoción turística

No se incluyen las siguientes actividades:
- actividades de agencias de viajes y operadores turísticos, véanse las clases 7911 y 7912
- organización y gestión de reuniones, convenciones, conferencias y acontecimientos similares; véase la clase 8230

Datos

Respecto al *número de establecimientos* (punto 4.3 del Compendio) incluye los establecimientos asimilados a las clases 5520, 5590, 6810 y 6820 (véanse las notas explicativas anteriores sobre alojamiento para visitantes).

El número de *habitaciones* y *plazas-cama* se refiere a la capacidad de «hoteles y establecimientos asimilados» de proporcionar alojamiento temporal a los visitantes.

Indicadores

Los tres primeros indicadores se basan en el número global de pernoctaciones de turistas residentes y no residentes en hoteles y establecimientos asimilados.

Las *tasas de ocupación* se refieren a la relación entre la capacidad existente de prestar servicios de alojamiento a los visitantes y la medida en que se utilizan. Esta tasa puede referirse al uso de habitaciones o de plazas-cama.

La *capacidad disponible* se refiere al número de plazas-cama en hoteles y establecimientos asimilados por cada 1000 habitantes de la población residente permanente del país de referencia. Cuando el país no aporta los datos, lo hace la OMT.

5. EMPLEO

La categoría de personas empleadas en las industrias turísticas puede ser de *asalariados* (personas que trabajan para una empresa a cambio de una remuneración en efectivo o en especie según lo convenido) o de *autoempleados* (trabajadores por cuenta propia que tienen el tipo de trabajo definido como «empleo independiente» y no han contratado de manera continua a ningún «asalariado» durante el periodo de referencia).

Algunas personas empleadas pueden tener más de un puesto de trabajo; por consiguiente el número de puestos de trabajo (por el lado de la demanda) y el número de personas empleadas (por el lado de la oferta) son categorías diferentes y por lo general no suelen coincidir.

La intensidad del trabajo puede variar de un puesto a otro, de una industria a otra y de un periodo a otro. Los puestos de trabajo pueden diferir en el horario laboral de las personas empleadas y, por lo tanto, pueden expresarse en términos de empleos a tiempo completo o a tiempo parcial. Por esta razón, no es suficiente con tener datos sobre el número de puestos de trabajo o personas empleadas para obtener información sobre el volumen del trabajo efectuado durante un determinado periodo de tiempo (por ejemplo, un mes o un año). Harán falta datos sobre el número total de horas de trabajo. Finalmente, si todos los puestos de trabajo se convierten en empleo equivalente a tiempo completo o total de horas trabajadas al año, podrá obtenerse el volumen total del trabajo de una determinada industria por un periodo determinado.

Las cifras sobre «número de puestos de trabajo por situación en el empleo» y «número de puestos de trabajo equivalentes a empleos de jornada completa por situación en el empleo» deben referirse a las industrias turísticas.

6. INDICADORES COMPLEMENTARIOS

Estos indicadores se derivan de la balanza de pagos, las cuentas nacionales y las estadísticas de turismo.

Demanda

La *propensión bruta a viajar* mide el número de viajes de turismo emisor e interno en términos de población residente permanente total del país de referencia. Los valores más altos del indicador implican la mayor frecuencia de estos viajes e indican la movilidad presente de la población que viaja al extranjero.

La *capacidad de acogida* mide el total de llegadas (tanto internas como recibidas) en relación con el total de población residente permanente y ofrece una estimación del potencial turístico del país de referencia.

Indicadores macroeconómicos relacionados con el turismo internacional

Los datos se basan en las *estadísticas de balanza de pagos* y las *estadísticas financieras internacionales* del Fondo Monetario Internacional y han sido compilados por la Comisión Económica de las Naciones Unidas para América Latina y el Caribe (CEPAL) para la Organización Mundial del Turismo (OMT). El conjunto de datos utilizado para el <u>Compendio de estadísticas de turismo</u> de 2011 se refiere a marzo de 2011.

Estos y otros indicadores complementarios representan un sistema preliminar muy básico de evaluación de la contribución económica del turismo a la economía nacional, y son valiosos porque disponen de ellos la mayoría de los países, son comparables internacionalmente y pueden compararse también con otros indicadores económicos.

Cabe observar que el término «gasto» se utiliza del mismo modo para el turismo receptor que para el emisor a fin de indicar «el importe pagado para la adquisición de bienes de consumo y servicios, así como de objetos de valor, para uso propio o para regalo, para y durante los viajes turísticos». Los visitantes extranjeros en el país de referencia generan un gasto de turismo receptor (crédito en la balanza de pagos), mientras que los visitantes residentes que se encuentran en países extranjeros generan un gasto de turismo emisor (débito en la balanza de pagos).

Gasto turístico receptor sobre el PIB
Refleja el peso del gasto de los visitantes recibidos como parte del valor total de la actividad económica en la economía de referencia. Desde la perspectiva del comercio internacional, este indicador capta la importancia económica de la afluencia de ingresos procedentes del extranjero asociada al gasto de estos visitantes.

Gasto turístico emisor sobre el PIB
Refleja la importancia del gasto en el extranjero de los visitantes emitidos, expresada en términos de la economía nacional. Desde la perspectiva del comercio internacional, este indicador capta la importancia económica de la salida de ingresos nacionales a través de estos visitantes.

Balanza turística sobre el PIB
Refleja la importancia económica del gasto turístico neto (turismo receptor menos turismo emisor) en relación con la economía de referencia. Un superávit o un déficit significativo afecta a la balanza comercial del país y, por lo tanto, a su PIB.

Apertura turística
Refleja la importancia de la suma del gasto del turismo transfronterizo (es decir, el turismo internacional, la suma del gasto del turismo receptor y el emisor) en relación con la economía de referencia. También podría utilizarse como medida del flujo libre de turismo bilateral entre el país de referencia y el resto del mundo.

Cobertura turística
Refleja la proporción entre el gasto del turismo receptor y el gasto del turismo emisor para mostrar en qué grado la afluencia de ingresos procedentes del extranjero cubre la salida de ingresos nacionales. Un valor superior al 100% significa que el turismo receptor financia indirecta y sobradamente el gasto de los visitantes emitidos; un valor inferior al 100% significa que el turismo receptor no cubre el gasto de estos visitantes en el extranjero.

Gasto turístico receptor sobre las exportaciones de bienes
Gasto turístico receptor sobre las exportaciones de servicios
Gasto turístico receptor sobre las exportaciones de bienes y servicios
Estas tres medidas reflejan la importancia del turismo como servicio con el que se comercia internacionalmente en relación con otras categorías de exportaciones. Al mismo tiempo, estas medidas revelan el grado de especialización turística de la estructura exportadora de un país y la capacidad relativa del turismo de generar ingresos procedentes del extranjero.

Gasto turístico receptor sobre los créditos de la cuenta corriente
Los créditos de la cuenta corriente de la balanza de pagos se refieren a toda la afluencia de bienes, servicios, ingresos y transferencias corrientes a la economía. Cuanto mayor es la cuota del turismo en este agregado, mayor es la importancia de la actividad turística en la generación de una afluencia de ingresos procedentes del extranjero.

Gasto turístico emisor sobre las importaciones de bienes
Gasto turístico emisor sobre las importaciones de servicios
Gasto turístico emisor sobre las importaciones de bienes y servicios
Estas tres medidas reflejan la importancia del turismo como servicio con el que se comercia internacionalmente en relación con otras categorías de importaciones. Al mismo tiempo, estas medidas revelan la predilección por el turismo de la estructura importadora de un país y el grado relativo de salida de ingresos nacionales de una economía a causa del turismo internacional.

Gasto turístico emisor sobre los débitos de la cuenta corriente
Los débitos de la cuenta corriente de la balanza de pagos se refieren a toda la salida de bienes, servicios, ingresos y transferencias corrientes de una economía al resto del mundo. Cuanto mayor es la cuota del turismo en este agregado, mayor es la importancia de la actividad turística en la fuga de ingresos nacionales.

Anexo 1. Sistema nacional de estadísticas de turismo y comparabilidad internacional

La estructura del Compendio de estadísticas de turismo se basa en el siguiente esquema, referido al marco de información básico de los sistemas nacionales de estadísticas de turismo con fines de comparabilidad internacional[1].

El marco conceptual para este núcleo básico de datos e indicadores está constituido por las *Recomendaciones internacionales para estadísticas de turismo 2008* (RIET 2008).

Comparabilidad internacional y estadísticas de turismo: el marco de información básico

I.   Marco conceptual

Conceptos	Unidades de observación	Principales características relacionadas
Visitante	Visitante	Clases: visitante que pernocta (turista), visitante del día (excursionista)
		País de residencia / regiones
	Grupo de viaje	Tamaño
Viaje	Viaje por turismo	Motivo principal
		Duración
		Destino principal
		Medio de transporte
		Tipos de alojamiento utilizado
		Organización
		Gasto
Industrias turísticas	Establecimiento	Monetarios
		Producción
		Consumo intermedio
		Valor añadido bruto
		Remuneración de los trabajadores asalariados
		Formación bruta de capital fijo
		No-monetarios
		Características específicas no monetarias para cada industria turística
Empleo	Establecimiento (en las industrias turísticas)	Personas
		Tamaño
		Situación en el empleo
		Puestos de trabajo
		Duración del trabajo
		Puestos de trabajo equivalentes a tiempo completo

II.   Clasificaciones

    1.   Formas de turismo
    2.   Clasificación de los productos de consumo adquiridos por los visitantes
    3.   Clasificación de las actividades productivas que dan servicio a los visitantes
    4.   Otras clasificaciones

III. Tablas de resultados

    1.   Turismo receptor
    2.   Turismo interno
    3.   Turismo emisor
    4.   Industrias turísticas
    5.   Empleo
    6.   Indicadores complementarios

---

1 http://www.unwto.org/statistics/sts/description/sts_text.pdf

Anexo 2. Comprender el turismo: glosario básico *

Actividades / productos característicos del turismo	Las *actividades características del turismo* son aquellas que generan principalmente *productos característicos del turismo*. Los *productos característicos del turismo* son aquellos que cumplen uno o ambos de los siguientes criterios: (a) El *gasto turístico* en el producto debería representar una parte importante del *gasto total turístico* (condición de la proporción que corresponde al gasto/demanda). (b) El *gasto turístico* en el producto debería representar una parte importante de la oferta del producto en la economía (condición de la proporción que corresponde a la oferta). Este criterio supone que la oferta de un *producto característico del turismo* se reduciría considerablemente si no hubiera visitantes.
Empleo en las industrias turísticas	El *empleo en las industrias turísticas* puede medirse como un recuento de las personas empleadas en las *industrias turísticas*, en cualquiera de sus empleos, como un recuento de las personas que desempeñan su empleo principal en las *industrias turísticas*, o como un recuento de los empleos en las *industrias turísticas*.
Entorno habitual	*El entorno habitual de una persona, concepto clave en turismo, se define como la zona geográfica (aunque no necesariamente contigua) en la que una persona realiza sus actividades cotidianas habituales.*
Gasto turístico	*El gasto turístico hace referencia a la suma pagada por la adquisición de bienes y servicios de consumo, y de objetos valiosos, para uso propio o para regalar, durante los viajes turísticos y para los mismos.*
Grupo de viaje	*Un grupo de viaje se define como visitantes que realizan juntos un viaje y comparten los gastos vinculados con el mismo.*
Industrias turísticas	*Las industrias turísticas incluyen todos los establecimientos en los cuales la actividad principal es una actividad característica del turismo.*
Lugar de residencia habitual	El *lugar de residencia habitual* es el lugar geográfico en que el visitante reside habitualmente, y se define por la ubicación de su vivienda principal (Principios y recomendaciones para los censos de población y habitación de las Naciones Unidas).
Motivo (principal) de un viaje turístico	El *motivo principal* de un *viaje turístico* se define como el motivo sin el cual el *viaje* no habría tenido lugar. La clasificación de los *viajes turísticos* con arreglo al *motivo principal* hace referencia a nueve categorías: esta tipología permite identificar diferentes subconjuntos de *visitantes* (visitantes de negocios, visitantes en tránsito, etc.).
Turismo emisor	El *turismo emisor* abarca las *actividades* realizadas por un *visitante* residente fuera del país de referencia, como parte de un *viaje turístico emisor* o de un *viaje turístico interno*.
Turismo interno	El *turismo interno* incluye las actividades realizadas por un *visitante residente* en el *país de referencia*, como parte de *un viaje turístico interno* o de un *viaje turístico emisor*.
Turismo receptor	Engloba las *actividades* realizadas por un *visitante* no residente en el *país de referencia*, como parte de un *viaje turístico receptor*.
Turista (o visitante que pernocta) y excursionista (o visitante del día)	*Un visitante (interno, receptor o emisor) se clasifica como turista (o visitante que pernocta), si su viaje incluye una pernoctación, o como visitante del día (o excursionista) en caso contrario.*
Viaje / turismo	*El termino viaje designa la actividad de los viajeros. Un viajero es toda persona que se desplaza entre dos lugares geográficos distintos por cualquier motivo y duración. El visitante es un tipo particular de viajero y, por lo tanto, el turismo es un subconjunto de viaje.*
Viaje turístico	*El término viaje turístico designa todo desplazamiento de una persona a un lugar fuera de su lugar de residencia habitual, desde el momento de su salida hasta su regreso. Por lo tanto, se refiere a un viaje de ida y vuelta. Los viajes de los visitantes son viajes turísticos.*
Visita	*Un viaje se compone de visitas a diferentes lugares. El término «visita turística» hace referencia a una estancia en un lugar visitado durante un viaje turístico.*

(*) En este Anexo se incluyen algunos conceptos fundamentales y las definiciones correspondientes según las *RIET 2008*.
http://unstats.un.org/unsd/tradeserv/tourism/08-40120%20IRTS%202008_WEB_final%20version%20_22%20February%202010.pdf

Visitante

Un visitante es una persona que viaja a un destino principal distinto al de su entorno habitual, por una duración inferior a un año, con cualquier finalidad principal (ocio, negocios u otro motivo personal) que no sea la de ser empleado por una entidad residente en el país o lugar visitados.

Visitante interno

Cuando un visitante viaja dentro de su propio país de residencia, se trata de un visitante interno y sus actividades forman parte del turismo interno.

Vivienda de vacaciones

Una vivienda de vacaciones (también conocida como casa u hogar de vacaciones) es una vivienda secundaria visitada por los miembros del hogar, fundamentalmente con fines de ocio, vacaciones o cualquier otra forma de esparcimiento.

Anexo 3.   Cómo encontrar el turismo en las clasificaciones internacionales uniformes.

La importancia del turismo y la necesidad de definir y medir su significación dentro del sistema de estadísticas de las Naciones Unidas fueron reconocidas por la Comisión de Estadística de las Naciones Unidas con la aprobación en 1993 de las *Recomendaciones sobre estadísticas del turismo*. La versión revisada de estas recomendaciones fue aprobada por la Comisión de Estadística de las Naciones Unidas en 2008 bajo el título de *Recomendaciones internacionales para estadísticas de turismo 2008* (RIET 2008).

Para estudiar la contribución del turismo a la economía nacional, era necesario integrar el análisis económico del turismo en el marco de referencia del Sistema de Cuentas Nacionales (SCN 93), lo cual condujo a la aprobación por parte de la Comisión de Estadística de las Naciones Unidas en 2000 de *Cuenta satélite de turismo: Recomendaciones sobre el marco conceptual*. Este marco se actualizó posteriormente como *Cuenta satélite de turismo: Recomendaciones sobre el marco conceptual 2008* (CST:RMC 2008).

Los conceptos, las definiciones y las clasificaciones de las RIET 2008 son coherentes con los de CST:RMC 2008, que a su vez se habían armonizado con el Sistema de Cuentas Nacionales de 2008, la balanza de pagos y el comercio internacional de servicios.

Para el turismo, es interesante identificar los productos que compran los visitantes, directa e indirectamente, y las actividades que los producen. Las clasificaciones utilizadas para las actividades y los productos detallados que se piden en el estudio del turismo se extraen directamente y se relacionan con las clasificaciones de referencia de las Naciones Unidas: la CIIU y la CCP.

El foco de interés para el análisis del turismo es el visitante. En un principio, resulta interesante medir el gasto de los visitantes y localizar los productos, tanto bienes como servicios, que compran los visitantes, así como las actividades que producen estos productos. En un marco macroeconómico, como el de la CST, el concepto de turismo engloba tanto la perspectiva de la demanda, consistente en el consumo de los visitantes, el consumo colectivo turístico y la formación bruta de capital fijo del turismo, como la perspectiva de la oferta de las actividades turísticas (siendo un punto especial la cuota de su producción que es adquirida por los visitantes). El turismo, como tal, no se identifica en la SCN 93 o en la CIIU. A efectos de turismo, las actividades de todo el espectro de la CIIU que producen bienes y servicios que satisfacen la demanda turística se reúnen y agrupan como actividades turísticas.

Si se adopta el enfoque de la demanda, el visitante es la unidad básica de observación y análisis y el gasto de los visitantes se estudia en términos de productos (primordialmente servicios). Desde el punto de vista de la oferta, teniendo en cuenta su relación con el Sistema de Cuentas Nacionales, las estadísticas de turismo utilizan el «establecimiento» como unidad estadística básica, tal como se define en el SCN y utilizan «industria» como la unidad de presentación y análisis, definida como «grupos de establecimientos dedicados a la misma clase de actividad productiva».

En primera instancia, es preciso reconocer qué productos compran los visitantes. A efectos de recopilación de datos desde la perspectiva de la demanda, los productos se agrupan en categorías amplias en función del motivo; no obstante, el turismo requiere el análisis simultáneo del consumo y de la producción y, por tanto, la clasificación utilizada para definir los productos es la Clasificación Central de Productos (CCP ver. 2.). Los productos adquiridos por los visitantes pueden agruparse en clases detalladas de la CCP y las actividades que los producen pueden identificarse en los términos de las clases detalladas en la CIIU.

El turismo define algunos de los productos que compran los visitantes y las actividades que los producen como «productos característicos del turismo» (los que satisfacen ciertos criterios) y «actividades características del turismo» (las que normalmente producen productos característicos del turismo). Las RIET 2008 explican en todo detalle los conceptos subyacentes, las definiciones y las clasificaciones que deben utilizarse para compilar estadísticas de turismo e identificar los productos y actividades característicos del turismo. A fin de facilitar la comparación internacional, se han preparado listas de estos productos y actividades característicos. En el anexo 3 de este documento figura la lista de las actividades características del turismo (industrias turísticas) agrupadas en categorías principales según la CIIU rev 4. El anexo 4 muestra una lista de productos característicos del turismo agrupados por categorías principales según la CCP ver 2. Aun cuando el verdadero producto adquirido por el visitante pueda constituir solo una porción de la clase de la CCP o la actividad productora pueda ser solo una parte de la clase de cuatro dígitos de la CIIU, al expresarse en términos de clases de la CCP y agregados de clases de la CIIU, las listas ofrecen una clase definida en la que es posible incluir cada uno de los productos o actividades. Se aconseja a los países que, en caso de que lo requieran para sus propios análisis, creen clases más detalladas por debajo del nivel inferior de la CCP y la CIIU.

El alcance del análisis de las estadísticas de turismo se amplía cuando se sitúan en el marco de la cuenta satélite de turismo. De nuevo, en el marco esencial de contabilidad, los productos y las actividades se expresan en los términos de la CCP ver. 2 y la CIIU ver. 4, incluyendo los productos y las actividades asociados con el turismo. Las clasificaciones internacionales de productos y actividades empleadas para compilar los datos para CST:RMC 2008 que, a su vez, establecen vínculos estructurales con el Sistema de Cuentas Nacionales, hacen posible una apreciación más profunda de los vínculos del turismo con otros ámbitos económicos.

Anexo 4. Lista de industrias turísticas y agrupadas por categorías principales según la CIIU, Rev. 4

<table>
<tr><th colspan="3">Lista de industrias turísticas (actividades características) y agrupadas por categorías principales según la CIIU, rev.4</th></tr>
<tr><th colspan="2">Industrias turísticas</th><th>CIIU Rev. 4</th><th>Descripción</th></tr>
<tr>
<td>1.</td><td>Alojamiento para visitantes</td>
<td>5510
5520
5590
6810
6820</td>
<td>Actividades de alojamiento para estancias cortas
Actividades de campamentos, parques de vehículos recreativos y parques de caravanas
Otras actividades de alojamiento
Actividades inmobiliarias realizadas con bienes propios o arrendados*
Actividades inmobiliarias realizadas a cambio de una retribución o por contrata*</td>
</tr>
<tr>
<td>2.</td><td>Actividades de provisión de alimentos y bebidas</td>
<td>5610
5629
5630</td>
<td>Actividades de restaurantes y de servicio móvil de comidas
Otras actividades de servicio de comidas
Actividades de servicio de bebidas</td>
</tr>
<tr>
<td>3.</td><td>Transporte de pasajeros por ferrocarril</td>
<td>4911</td>
<td>Transporte interurbano de pasajeros por ferrocarril</td>
</tr>
<tr>
<td>4.</td><td>Transporte de pasajeros por carretera</td>
<td>4922</td>
<td>Otras actividades de transporte por vía terrestre</td>
</tr>
<tr>
<td>5.</td><td>Transporte de pasajeros por agua</td>
<td>5011
5021</td>
<td>Transporte de pasajeros marítimo y de cabotaje
Transporte de pasajeros por vías de navegación interiores</td>
</tr>
<tr>
<td>6.</td><td>Transporte aéreo de pasajeros</td>
<td>5110</td>
<td>Transporte de pasajeros por vía aérea</td>
</tr>
<tr>
<td>7.</td><td>Alquiler de equipos de transporte</td>
<td>7710</td>
<td>Alquiler y arrendamiento de vehículos automotores</td>
</tr>
<tr>
<td>8.</td><td>Actividades de agencias de viajes y de otros servicios de reservas</td>
<td>7911
7912
7990</td>
<td>Actividades de agencias de viajes
Actividades de operadores turísticos
Otros servicios de reservas y actividades conexas</td>
</tr>
<tr>
<td>9.</td><td>Actividades culturales</td>
<td>9000
9102
9103</td>
<td>Actividades creativas, artísticas y de entretenimiento
Actividades de museos y conservación de lugares y edificios históricos
Actividades de jardines botánicos y zoológicos y de reservas naturales</td>
</tr>
<tr>
<td>10.</td><td>Actividades deportivas y recreativas</td>
<td>7721
9200
9311
9319
9321
9329</td>
<td>Alquiler y arrendamiento de equipo recreativo y deportivo
Actividades de juegos de azar y apuestas
Gestión de instalaciones deportivas
Otras actividades deportivas
Actividades de parques de atracciones y parques temáticos
Otras actividades de esparcimiento y recreativas n.c.p.</td>
</tr>
<tr>
<td>11.</td><td>Comercio al por menor de bienes característicos del turismo, específicos de cada país</td>
<td></td>
<td>Comercios libres de impuestos**
Comercio al por menor de recuerdos en establecimientos especializados**
Comercio al por menor de artesanía en establecimientos especializados**
Otro comercio al por menor de bienes característicos del turismo en establecimientos especializados**</td>
</tr>
<tr>
<td>12.</td><td>Otras actividades características del turismo, específicas de cada país</td>
<td></td>
<td></td>
</tr>
</table>

* Parte relacionada con segundos hogares y multipropiedades
** No es una categoría de cuatro cifras de la CIIU

Notas explicativas

Estas notas explicativas hacen referencia exclusivamente a actividades características del turismo internacionalmente comparables, y siguen el mismo orden que en el anexo 4 que figura más arriba.

Se han extraído del documento *Clasificación Industrial Internacional Uniforme de todas las actividades económicas (CIIU), Rev.4.* Informes estadísticos (serie M, No. 4/Rev.4), Naciones Unidas. Nueva York, 2008.

El documento completo puede consultarse en el sitio Web:
http://unstats.un.org/unsd/cr/registry/regdntransfer.asp?f=135

Alojamiento para visitantes

5510 Actividades de alojamiento para estancias cortas

Esta clase comprende el suministro de alojamiento, en general por días o por semanas, principalmente para estancias cortas de los visitantes. Abarca el suministro de alojamiento amueblado en habitaciones y apartamentos o unidades totalmente independientes con cocina, con o sin servicio diario o regular de limpieza, y que incluyen a menudo diversos servicios adicionales, como los de comidas y bebidas, aparcamiento, lavandería, piscina y gimnasio, instalaciones de recreo e instalaciones para conferencias y convenciones.

Esta clase comprende el suministro de alojamiento por estancias cortas en:
- hoteles
- centros vacacionales
- hoteles de suites/apartamentos
- moteles
- hoteles para automovilistas
- casas de huéspedes
- pensiones
- unidades de alojamiento y desayuno
- pisos y bungalows
- unidades utilizadas en régimen de tiempo compartido
- casas de vacaciones
- chalets y cabañas con servicio de mantenimiento y limpieza
- albergues juveniles y refugios de montaña

No se incluyen las siguientes actividades:
- suministro de viviendas y de pisos o apartamentos amueblados o sin amueblar para períodos más largos, en general por meses o por años; véase la división 6868

5520 Actividades de campamentos, parques de vehículos de recreo y parques de caravanas

Esta clase comprende las siguientes actividades:
- suministro de alojamiento en campamentos, parques para caravanas, campamentos recreativos y campamentos de caza y de pesca para estancias cortas
- suministro de espacio e instalaciones para vehículos de recreo

Se incluyen también los servicios de alojamiento de:
- refugios o simples instalaciones de acampada para plantar tiendas o pernoctar en sacos de dormir

5590 Otras actividades de alojamiento

Esta clase comprende el suministro de alojamiento temporal o a largo plazo en habitaciones individuales o compartidas o dormitorios para estudiantes, trabajadores migrantes (estacionales) y otras categorías de personas.

Se incluyen los servicios de alojamiento proporcionados por:
- residencias de estudiantes
- dormitorios escolares
- albergues para trabajadores
- casas de huéspedes e internados
- coches cama ferroviarios

6810 Actividades inmobiliarias realizadas con bienes propios o arrendados

Esta clase comprende las siguientes actividades:
- compra, venta, alquiler y explotación de bienes inmuebles propios o arrendados, como:
  • edificios de apartamentos y viviendas
  • edificios no residenciales, incluso salas de exposiciones, instalaciones de autoalmacenamiento y centros comerciales
  • terrenos
- alquiler de casas y pisos o apartamentos amueblados o sin amueblar por
- períodos largos, en general por meses o por años

Se incluyen también las siguientes actividades:
- promoción de proyectos de construcción para su posterior explotación, es decir, para alquilar espacio en esos edificios

- subdivisión de propiedades inmobiliarias en lotes, sin mejora de los terrenos
- explotación de campamentos residenciales para casas móviles

No se incluyen las siguientes actividades:
- promoción de proyectos de construcción para la venta; véase la clase 4100
- subdivisión y mejora de terrenos; véase la clase 4290
- explotación de hoteles, hoteles de apartamentos e instalaciones de alojamiento similares; véase la clase 5510
- explotación de campamentos, parques de caravanas e instalaciones de alojamiento similares; véase la clase 5520
- explotación de albergues para trabajadores, casas de huéspedes e instalaciones de alojamiento similares; véase la clase 5590

6820 Actividades inmobiliarias realizadas a cambio de una retribución o por contrata

Esta clase comprende las actividades inmobiliarias que se realizan a cambio de una retribución o por contrata, incluidos los servicios inmobiliarios.

Esta clase comprende las siguientes actividades:
- actividades de agentes y corredores inmobiliarios
- intermediación en la compra, la venta y el alquiler de bienes inmuebles a cambio de una retribución o por contrata
- administración de bienes inmuebles a cambio de una retribución o por contrata
- servicios de tasación inmobiliaria
- actividades de agentes depositarios de plicas inmobiliarias

No se incluyen las siguientes actividades:
- actividades jurídicas; véase la clase 6910
- servicios de apoyo a instalaciones; véase la clase 8110
- administración de instalaciones, como bases militares, prisiones y otras instalaciones (excepto administración de instalaciones informáticas); véase la clase 8110

Actividades de provisión de alimentos y bebidas

5610 Actividades de restaurantes y de servicio móvil de comidas

Esta clase comprende el servicio de comidas a los clientes, ya se les sirvan en mesas o se sirvan ellos mismos de un surtido de platos expuestos, y ya se trate de comida para consumir en el local, para llevar o para entrega a domicilio. Abarca la preparación y el servicio de comidas para su consumo inmediato desde vehículos, sean o no motorizados

Esta clase comprende las actividades de:
- restaurantes
- cafeterías
- restaurantes de comida rápida
- reparto de pizza a domicilio
- restaurantes de comida para llevar
- vendedores ambulantes de helados
- puestos ambulantes de comida
- preparación de alimentos en puestos de mercado

Se incluyen también las siguientes actividades:
- actividades de restaurantes y bares vinculadas a actividades de transporte, si las realizan unidades separadas

No se incluyen las siguientes actividades:
- explotación de instalaciones de comedor en régimen de concesión; véase la clase 56290

5629 Otras actividades de servicio de comidas

Esta clase comprende el suministro industrial de comidas por encargo, es decir, el suministro de comidas basado en acuerdos contractuales con los clientes, durante un período convenido.

Abarca también la explotación de concesiones de servicio de comida en instalaciones deportivas e instalaciones similares. La comida se prepara a menudo en una unidad central.

Esta clase comprende las siguientes actividades:
- actividades de contratistas de servicio de comidas (p. ej., para compañías de transporte)
- explotación de concesiones de servicio de comidas en instalaciones deportivas e instalaciones similares
- explotación de cantinas o cafeterías (p. ej., para fábricas, oficinas, hospitales o escuelas) en régimen de concesión

No se incluyen las siguientes actividades:
- elaboración de productos alimenticios perecederos para su reventa; véase la clase 1079
- venta al por menor de productos alimenticios perecederos; véase la división 47

5630 Actividades de servicio de bebidas

Esta clase comprende la preparación y el servicio de bebidas para su consumo inmediato en el local.

Esta clase comprende las actividades de:
- bares
- tabernas
- coctelerías
- discotecas (con predominio del servicio de bebidas)
- cervecerías y pubs
- cafeterías
- tiendas de jugos de frutas
- vendedores ambulantes de bebidas

No se incluyen las siguientes actividades:
- reventa de bebidas envasadas o preparadas; véanse las clases 4711, 4722, 4781 y 4799
- explotación de discotecas y salas de baile sin servicio de bebidas; véase la clase 9329

Transporte de pasajeros por ferrocarril

4911 Transporte interurbano de pasajeros por ferrocarril

Esta clase comprende las siguientes actividades:
- transporte de pasajeros por ferrocarriles interurbanos
- servicios de coches cama y coches restaurante integrados en los servicios de las compañías de ferrocarril

No se incluyen las siguientes actividades:
- transporte de pasajeros por los sistemas de transporte urbano y suburbano; véase la clase 4921
- actividades de terminales de pasajeros; véase la clase 5221
- servicios de coches cama y coches restaurante cuando los suministran unidades separadas, véanse las clases 5590 y 5610

Transporte de pasajeros por carretera

4922 Otras actividades de transporte de pasajeros por vía terrestre

Esta clase comprende las siguientes actividades:
- otras actividades de transporte de pasajeros por carretera:
  - servicios regulares de autobuses de larga distancia
  - servicios de viajes contratados, excursiones y otros servicios ocasionales de transporte en autobús
  - servicios de taxis
  - servicios de enlace con aeropuertos
- servicios de teleféricos, funiculares, telesillas y telecabinas, si no forman parte de sistemas de transporte urbano o suburbano

Se incluyen también las siguientes actividades:
- otras actividades de alquiler de automóviles privados con conductor
- servicios de autobuses escolares y autobuses para el transporte de empleados
- transporte de pasajeros en vehículos de tracción humana o animal

No se incluyen las siguientes actividades:

- transporte en ambulancia; véase la clase 8690

Transporte de pasajeros por agua

5011Transporte de pasajeros marítimo y de cabotaje

Esta clase comprende las siguientes actividades:
- transporte marítimo y de cabotaje, regular y no regular, de pasajeros y carga:
  • explotación de embarcaciones de excursión, de crucero o de turismo
  • explotación de transbordadores, taxis acuáticos, etcétera

Se incluyen también las siguientes actividades:
- alquiler de embarcaciones de placer con tripulación para el transporte marítimo y de cabotaje (p. ej., cruceros de pesca)

No se incluyen las siguientes actividades:
- actividades de servicios de bar y de restaurante a bordo de embarcaciones, si las realizan unidades separadas; véanse las clases 5610 y 5630
- explotación de «casinos flotantes»; véase la clase 9200

5021Transporte de pasajeros por vías de navegación interiores

Esta clase comprende las siguientes actividades:
- transporte de pasajeros por ríos, canales, lagos y otras vías de navegación interiores, incluidos puertos interiores

Se incluyen también las siguientes actividades:
- alquiler de embarcaciones de placer con tripulación para el transporte por vías de navegación interiores

Transporte aéreo de pasajeros

5110Transporte de pasajeros por vía aérea

Esta clase comprende las siguientes actividades:
- transporte aéreo de pasajeros con itinerarios y horarios establecidos
- vuelos contratados (charter) para pasajeros
- vuelos panorámicos y turísticos

Se incluyen también las siguientes actividades:
- alquiler de equipo de transporte aéreo con operadores para el transporte de pasajeros
- actividades generales de aviación, como:
  • transporte de pasajeros por clubes aéreos con fines de instrucción o de recreo

Alquiler de equipos de transporte

7710Alquiler y arrendamiento de vehículos automotores

Esta clase comprende las siguientes actividades:
- alquiler y arrendamiento con fines operativos de los siguientes tipos de vehículos:
  • automóviles de pasajeros (sin conductor)
  • camiones, remolques y vehículos de recreo

No se incluyen las siguientes actividades:
- alquiler o arrendamiento de vehículos o camiones con conductor; véanse las clases 4922 y 4923
- arrendamiento financiero; véase la clase 6491

Actividades de agencias de viajes y de otros servicios de reservas

7911 Actividades de agencias de viajes

Esta clase comprende las siguientes actividades:
- actividades de agencias dedicadas principalmente a vender servicios de viajes, de viajes organizados, de transporte y de alojamiento al público en general y a clientes comerciales

7912 Actividades de operadores turísticos

Esta clase comprende las siguientes actividades:
- organización de paquetes de servicios de viajes para su venta a través de agencias de viajes o por los propios operadores turísticos. Esos viajes organizados pueden incluir uno o varios de los elementos siguientes:
  - transporte
  - alojamiento
  - comidas
  - visitas a museos, lugares históricos o culturales y asistencia a espectáculos teatrales, musicales o deportivos

7990 Otros servicios de reservas y actividades conexas

Esta clase comprende las siguientes actividades:
- prestación de otros servicios de reservas relacionados con los viajes:
  - reservas de transporte, hoteles, restaurantes, alquiler de automóviles, entretenimiento y deporte, etcétera
- prestación de servicios de intercambio en régimen de tiempo compartido o multipropiedad
- actividades de venta de billetes para obras de teatro, competiciones deportivas y otras actividades de diversión y entretenimiento
- prestación de servicios de asistencia a los visitantes:
  - suministro a los clientes de información sobre los viajes
  - actividades de guías de turismo
- actividades de promoción turística

No se incluyen las siguientes actividades:
- actividades de agencias de viajes y operadores turísticos, véanse las clases 7911 y 7912
- organización y gestión de reuniones, convenciones, conferencias y acontecimientos similares; véase la clase 8230

Actividades culturales

9000 Actividades creativas, artísticas y de entretenimiento

Esta clase comprende la explotación de instalaciones y la prestación de servicios para atender a los intereses culturales y de entretenimiento de los clientes. Abarca la producción y promoción de espectáculos, actos o exposiciones destinados al público, y la participación en ellos; y la aportación de conocimientos y aptitudes artísticos, creativos o técnicos para la creación de productos artísticos y espectáculos.

Esta clase comprende las siguientes actividades:
- producción de obras de teatro, conciertos, espectáculos operísticos o de danza y otras producciones escénicas:
  - actividades de grupos, circos o compañías, orquestas o bandas
  - actividades de artistas individuales, como escritores, directores, músicos, conferenciantes, escenógrafos y constructores de decorados, etcétera
- gestión de salas de conciertos, teatros y otras instalaciones similares
- actividades de escultores, pintores, dibujantes, grabadores, etcétera
- actividades de escritores de todo tipo; por ejemplo, de obras de ficción, de obras técnicas, etcétera
- actividades de periodistas independientes
- restauración de obras de arte, como cuadros, etcétera

Se incluyen también las siguientes actividades:
- actividades de productores o empresarios de espectáculos artísticos en vivo, aporten o no ellos mismos las instalaciones correspondientes

No se incluyen las siguientes actividades:

- restauración de vidrieras de colores; véase la clase 2310
- fabricación de estatuas, excepto originales artísticos; véase la clase 2396
- restauración de órganos y otros instrumentos musicales históricos; véase la clase 3319
- restauración de lugares y edificios históricos; véase la clase 4100
- producción de películas cinematográficas y vídeos; véanse las clases 5911 y 5912
- explotación de cines; véase la clase 5914
- actividades de agentes o agencias de actores y artistas; véase la clase 7490
- actividades de selección de actores; véase la clase 7810
- actividades de venta de entradas; véase la clase 7990
- gestión de museos de todo tipo; véase la clase 9102
- actividades deportivas, de esparcimiento y recreativas; véase la división 93
- restauración de muebles (excepto la del tipo realizado en museos); véase la clase 9524

9102 Actividades de museos y gestión de lugares y edificios históricos

Esta clase comprende las siguientes actividades:
- actividades de todo tipo de museos:
  - museos de arte, orfebrería, muebles, trajes, cerámica, platería
  - museos de historia natural y de ciencias, museos tecnológicos y museos históricos, incluidos los museos militares
  - otros museos especializados
  - museos al aire libre
- gestión de lugares y edificios históricos

No se incluyen las siguientes actividades:
- renovación y restauración de lugares y edificios históricos; véase la sección F
- restauración de obras de arte y piezas de museo; véase la clase 9000
- actividades de bibliotecas y archivos; véase la clase 9101

9103 Actividades de jardines botánicos y zoológicos y reservas naturales

Esta clase comprende las siguientes actividades:
- gestión de jardines botánicos y zoológicos, incluidos zoológicos infantiles
- gestión de reservas naturales, incluidas las actividades de preservación de la flora y la fauna silvestres, etcétera

No se incluyen las siguientes actividades:
- servicios de paisajismo y jardinería; véase la clase 8130
- explotación de reservas de pesca y de caza deportivas; véase la clase 9319

Actividades deportivas y recreativas

7721 Alquiler y arrendamiento de equipo recreativo y deportivo

Esta clase comprende las siguientes actividades:
- alquiler de equipo recreativo y deportivo:
  - embarcaciones de recreo, canoas, veleros
  - bicicletas
  - hamacas de playa y sombrillas
  - otros tipos de equipo de deporte
  - esquíes

No se incluyen las siguientes actividades:
- alquiler de cintas de vídeo y discos; véase la clase 7722
- alquiler de otros efectos personales y enseres domésticos n.c.p.; véase la clase 7729
- alquiler de equipo de esparcimiento y recreo como parte integral de servicios de esparcimiento; véase la clase 9329

9200 Actividades de juegos de azar y apuestas

Esta clase comprende las siguientes actividades:
- apuestas sobre carreras de caballos en el propio hipódromo y otros servicios de apuestas
- apuestas sobre carreras de caballos fuera del hipódromo
- explotación de casinos, incluidos «casinos flotantes»
- venta de boletos de lotería
- gestión (explotación) de máquinas de juegos de azar accionadas con monedas
- gestión de sitios web de juegos de azar virtuales

No se incluyen las siguientes actividades:
- gestión (explotación) de juegos accionados con monedas; véase la clase 9329

9311Gestión de instalaciones deportivas

Esta clase comprende las siguientes actividades:
- gestión de instalaciones para actividades deportivas bajo techo o al aire libre (abiertas, cerradas o techadas, con o sin asientos para espectadores):
  - campos y estadios de fútbol, hockey, cricket, béisbol, canchas de frontón
  - circuitos de carreras de automóviles, canódromos, hipódromos
  - piscinas y estadios
  - estadios de atletismo
  - pistas y estadios para deportes de invierno
  - pistas de hockey sobre hielo
  - pabellones de boxeo
  - campos de golf
  - boleras
  - gimnasios
- organización y gestión de competiciones deportivas al aire libre o bajo techo, con participación de deportistas profesionales o aficionados, por parte de organizaciones con instalaciones propias

Se incluyen la gestión de esas instalaciones y la dotación del personal necesario para su funcionamiento.

No se incluyen las siguientes actividades:
- alquiler de equipo recreativo y deportivo; véase la clase 7721
- gestión de estaciones de esquí; véase la clase 9329
- actividades realizadas en parques y playas; véase la clase 9329

9319Otras actividades deportivas

Esta clase comprende las siguientes actividades:
- actividades de productores o promotores de competiciones deportivas, con o sin instalaciones
- actividades por cuenta propia de deportistas y atletas, árbitros, jueces, cronometradores, etcétera
- actividades de ligas y órganos reguladores
- actividades relacionadas con la promoción de competiciones deportivas
- actividades relacionadas con carreras de caballos, galgos y automóviles
- gestión de reservas de pesca y caza deportivas
- actividades de guías de montaña
- actividades de apoyo para la caza y la pesca deportivas o recreativas

No se incluyen las siguientes actividades:
- cría de caballos de carreras; véase la clase 0142
- alquiler de equipo de deporte; véase la clase 7721
- actividades de escuelas de deportes y de juegos; véase la clase 8541
- actividades de instructores, profesores y entrenadores; véase la clase 8541
- organización y explotación de competiciones deportivas al aire libre o bajo techo, con participación de deportistas profesionales o aficionados, por parte de clubes deportivos con o sin instalaciones propias, véanse las clases 9311 y 9312
- actividades realizadas en parques y playas; véase la clase 9329

9321Actividades de parques de atracciones y parques temáticos

Esta clase comprende las siguientes actividades:
- actividades de parques de atracciones y parques temáticos, incluida la explotación de diversas atracciones mecánicas y acuáticas, juegos, espectáculos, exposiciones temáticas y lugares para picnics

9329Otras actividades de esparcimiento y recreativas n.c.p.

Esta clase comprende las siguientes actividades:
- actividades de parques recreativos y playas, incluido el alquiler de casetas, taquillas, hamacas, etcétera
- gestión de instalaciones de transporte recreativo;
- gestión de estaciones de esquí

- alquiler de equipo de esparcimiento y recreo como parte integral de servicios de esparcimiento
- explotación de ferias y exposiciones de carácter recreativo
- explotación de discotecas y pistas de baile
- operación (explotación) de juegos accionados por monedas
- otras actividades de esparcimiento y recreativas (excepto las de parques de atracciones y parques temáticos) no clasificadas en otra parte

Se incluyen también las siguientes actividades:
- actividades de productores o empresarios de espectáculos en vivo, que no sean ni artísticos ni deportivos, aporten o no ellos mismos las instalaciones correspondientes

No se incluyen las siguientes actividades:
- cruceros de pesca, véanse las clases 5011 y 5021
- suministro de espacio e instalaciones para estancias cortas en parques recreativos, parques forestales y campamentos; véase la clase 5520
- actividades de servicio de bebidas en discotecas; véase la clase 5630
- parques de caravanas, campamentos, campamentos recreativos, campamentos de caza y de pesca; véase la clase 5520
- alquiler por separado de equipo recreativo; véase la clase 7721
- gestión (explotación) de máquinas de juegos accionadas con monedas; véase la clase 9200
- actividades de parques de atracciones y parques temáticos; véase la clase 9321